A History of the World

AKIRA IRIYE AND JÜRGEN OSTERHAMMEL, GENERAL EDITORS

A World Connecting

1870–1945

Edited by

Emily S. Rosenberg

The Belknap Press of Harvard University Press
CAMBRIDGE, MASSACHUSETTS
LONDON, ENGLAND
2012

This volume is a joint publication of Harvard University Press and C. H. Beck Verlag.

German language edition © 2012 by C. H. Beck Verlag.

Maps by Isabelle Lewis

Series design by Dean Bornstein

Library of Congress Cataloging-in-Publication Data

A world connecting, 1870–1945 / edited by Emily S. Rosenberg.
    p.   cm. — (A history of the world)
  Includes bibliographical references and index.
  ISBN 978-0-674-04721-1 (alk. paper)
  1. History, Modern—19th century.   2. History, Modern—20th century.
3. Nation-state—History—19th century.   4. Nation-state—History—20th century.
5. Imperialism—History—19th century.   6. Imperialism—History—20th century.
7. Emigration and immigration—History—19th century.   8. Emigration and
immigration—History—20th century.   9. International trade—History—19th century.
10. International trade—History—20th century.   11. Cultural relations—History—19th
century.   12. Cultural relations—History—20th century.   I. Rosenberg, Emily S., 1944–
    D359.7.W67   2012
    909.82′1—dc23   2012015775

Contents

INTRODUCTION · 3
Emily S. Rosenberg

ONE

Leviathan 2.0: Inventing Modern Statehood
Charles S. Maier

Introduction		29
1.	The World Is Weary of the Past	40
2.	Reconstruction on a World Scale	93
3.	The Human Zoo	153
4.	States of Exception	196

TWO

Empires and the Reach of the Global
Tony Ballantyne and Antoinette Burton

Introduction		285
1.	Reterritorializing Empires	306
2.	Remaking the World	348
3.	Global Empires, Transnational Connections	390

THREE

Migrations and Belongings
Dirk Hoerder

Introduction		435
1.	A *Longue-Durée* Perspective	444
2.	The Global and the Local	468

3. Migrations, Free and Bound 491

4. Migrations during War and Depression 548

5. The Aftermath of War and Decolonization 579

FOUR

Commodity Chains in a Global Economy
Steven C. Topik and Allen Wells

Introduction 593

1. Transformations 600

2. The Sinews of Trade 628

3. Commodity Chains 685

FIVE

Transnational Currents in a Shrinking World
Emily S. Rosenberg

Introduction 815

1. Currents of Internationalism 823

2. Social Networking and Entangled Attachments 849

3. Exhibitionary Nodes 886

4. Circuits of Expertise 919

5. Spectacular Flows 960

Notes 999

Selected Bibliography 1097

Contributors 1137

Index 1139

Introduction

Emily S. Rosenberg

OVER the period from 1870 to 1945 the world became both a more familiar and a stranger place. Fast ships, railroads, telegraph lines, inexpensive publications, and film all reached into hinterlands and erased distance. The exchange of people and products accelerated, while the fascination with traveling around and describing foreign areas—long evident in human history—reached new heights. Jules Verne's famous 1873 book *Le tour du monde en quatre-vingts jours (Around the World in Eighty Days)* imagined the new age, and many others tried their hand. The Chinese official Li Gui described his trip around the world in 1876; in the early 1880s King Kalakaua of Hawai'i claimed distinction as the first ruling monarch to accomplish a global tour; American journalist Elizabeth Cochrane Seaman ("Nellie Bly") scored a speed record for circling the globe in 1889; and Bengali poet Rabindranath Tagore set a more deliberative pace in visitations that took him across the Pacific in 1916 and the Atlantic in the early 1920s. As the numbers of travelers grew exponentially in the first half of the twentieth century, accounts and images of distant places multiplied and became accessible to all but the most remote of the world's inhabitants. Yet the very possibility of familiarity also bred strangeness. New connections highlighted all kinds of regional differences, and the awareness of difference could promote suspicion and repulsion perhaps even more easily than it facilitated understanding and communication.

This volume focuses on an era in world history marked by ever greater global interconnectedness—and by the excitement and anxiety, hope and violence that accompanied the complex mix often called modernity. Drawing on interpretations and approaches of the past few decades of historical scholarship, it provides both general readers and specialists with a thematic overview. Its five chapters each highlight a particular theme: modern state building, imperial encounters, flows of migration, commodity chains, and transnational social and cultural networks. Together, these themes collectively explore the tensions between the intensifying global interconnectedness and the attempts to stabilize, control, or shape the effects of sweeping change. The new age brought flux and attempts to ward off its consequences; it brought disintegration of old orders and efforts to create and rationalize new ones.

There are, of course, many ways to present overarching patterns in world history. Some histories unfold chronologically around large events such as global wars and economic depressions. Others slice the world into geographical areas such as Europe, Africa, Asia, the Middle East, and Latin America. While not neglecting chronology and geography, the chapters in this book are focused around themes that extend over both time and place and play out often unpredictably according to historically grounded circumstances. Breaking away from a common chronological spine or an area-by-area approach can help reveal the overall dynamic between outreach and containment—between flux and attempts to stabilize—that characterized and gave variability to world history in this era.

Specifically, our chapters highlight both the diverse and interactive regional and global networks of the era and the simultaneous efforts to define territorial borders. Chapter 1, on the emergence of modern statehood, and Chapter 2, on efforts to build and to resist empires, emphasize the problematic of formulating and policing geographical boundedness. How and with what consequences did modern states and empires give shape to this period? Chapters 3–5 explore the transnational flows of people, products, capital, technologies, and affiliations that cut across bounded spaces. In a world in which these flows increasingly touched and changed people's lives, things fell apart and also came together differently. The organization of the topics in this volume, then, emphasizes an ever-changing dyad of enclosure and permeability. Presenting the multiple processes of disintegration and reintegration that lie at the center of histories of national states, empires, demographic patterns, economic connections, and cultural affinities provides the major contribution of this volume.

In dealing with the dynamic tensions in this period, the volume avoids claims about some single motive-force of history. There is no presumption, for example, that states are the fundamental organizing blocks of world history, that economic motives are primary in ordering the world, or that Europe provides the driving center of historical change. Questions of cause and effect and explanations of change over time surface in many of these chapters, but the volume as a whole proposes no metatheory of history. Instead, it follows recent scholarship in em-

phasizing change as processual and uneven, forged within exchange and relation-
ality rather than by one-way, overarching forces. The chapters seek to be attentive
to the interchange among different scales of local, regional, and global networks
and the irregularities that may arise from different positionalities conditioned by
race, ethnicity, nationality, region, geography and environment, class, gender, and
religion.

Periodization

The case for segmenting out any particular slice of historical time generally raises
as many objections as justifications. This volume, therefore, presents the years
from 1870 to 1945 as a distinct period while, at the same time, it gives our chapters
the flexibility to challenge the points of beginning and end and significant turns.
Chapter 1, by Charles Maier, thus looks back several decades, indeed a century,
before 1870 in order to chart what Maier sees as the arc of modern statehood
that reached an apogee in our period. Chapter 3, by Dirk Hoerder, similarly
opens with an extensive prologue on the substantial demographic trends and
shifts in definitions of belonging that preceded 1870 and presaged the great
migrations that accelerated during the last three decades of the nineteenth century. Similarly, in Chapter 4, by Steven C. Topik and Allen Wells, the Second
Industrial Revolution is understood as being shaped and conditioned by the
First Industrial Revolution. Each of our particular thematic emphases suggests
its appropriate chronological trajectory.

   Moreover, individual chapters present their themes within different conceptions of periodization, as specific chronological milestones and trends will be
either more or less relevant for any particular thematic trajectory. In Chapter 3,
for example, Hoerder sees World War II marking a general shift in immigration
patterns from the huge labor-related migrations of the late nineteenth and early
twentieth centuries to the war-refugee migrations associated with the almost
unfathomable disruptions of that global conflict. Chapter 2, by Tony Ballantyne
and Antoinette Burton, on a different theme, works against the usual portrayal of
World War II as a dividing line between an "imperial" and an "anti-imperial" age.
Rather, the authors argue that the post–World War II anti-imperialism, expressed, for example, at the Bandung Conference of 1955, should be understood

against a previous history in which imperial policies and anti-imperial networks took shape in tandem with each other, even if with asymmetrical power. Chapter 5, my own contribution, endorses the familiar argument that World War I shattered the visions of some late nineteenth-century internationalists, as old empires fell apart and communism and fascism emerged to challenge the spread of liberal republics. It also shows, however, that the extension of transnational networks in science, health, entertainment, and a variety of other specific affiliations accelerated after World War I. In many realms, the Great War did not serve as a pivot marking a decisive retreat from transnational network building. In Chapter 4, Topik and Wells present wars and economic events as sometimes altering the flows of commodities. New inventions, seed importations, and climate effects, however, could all produce equally dramatic changes. Chronological frames for one theme, in short, may need to be shifted for others.

At first glance it might appear that our thematic organization underplays key events of global significance within the traditional periodization of this era. There are no chapter headings, for example, called "The Russo-Japanese War," "World War I," "The Great Depression," or "World War II." The careful reader of these chapters, though, will certainly find significant guideposts, such as global wars and economic depressions, but will see them articulated in terms of their relevance to our five broad themes. The overall history of the era from 1870 to 1945 emerges the richer and the more complex for the multiple contexts in which such traditional guideposts appear. No periodization or organizational scheme can capture the past in its entirety. History is representational, not replicative, and the necessity of selectivity means that every framework inescapably illuminates some elements and relegates others to the shadows. For the era from 1870 to 1945, a topical organization provides the flexibility to advance multiple frames and, thus, to take maximum advantage of the diverse recent scholarship and methodologies in world history.

Unifying Characteristics

While emphasizing the dynamic between flux and stabilization and malleable chronological parameters, these chapters collectively delineate several characteristics that unify the period from 1870 to 1945. These include the dramatic shrinking of time and space as a result of the revolution in communications and transportation; the accompanying acceleration in mobility of people, goods, and ideas, as global networks of various kinds thicken; the hegemonic power of the West under systems of modern statehood and imperialism; the intersections and mutual constructions of global and local; the increasing prominence of global cities; the proliferation of technologies of mass production and consumption; the power of (and challenges to) nationalism and racialist ideologies; and the unparalleled violence that new authoritarian forms and more efficient means of killing brought to almost every continent. These and other characteristics, which lace through the chapters, are amplified as they are refracted through our disparate thematic lenses.

During our period, the global flows of migrants, commodities, and ideas surged through circuitry that, generally, became denser—but at different speeds and with various effects. All of these chapters stress the compression of time and space that brought more and more people into personal, or at least virtual, contact with others far away. All thus emphasize the interaction between their distinct historical themes and the rationalization of systems of time and of the revolutions in ocean travel, railroads, telegraphy, and radio. Time and space, never fixed and always contingent in history, shrank dramatically for many, although the accompanying transformations reached more-isolated or self-contained populations in very uneven ways. The gap between relatively connected worlds and relatively disconnected ones consequently widened, with significant consequences for an array of economic, cultural, and political patterns.

Were these flows and networks under control of "the West"? The rising power of the West used to be almost synonymous with "world history." William H. McNeill's *Rise of the West* (1963), for instance, provided a widely used text for a generation. In a more critical and materialist vein, Immanuel Wallerstein's influential analysis of the modern "world system" still placed Europe at the center of a reactive "periphery." Works such as these helped to construct the field of world history, but they often normalized the West's own version of its own centrality. Recent scholarship, including rethinkings by both McNeill and Wallerstein, has challenged the idea of a single, foreordained geographic center.[1]

The importance of Europe, especially shaped through formal and informal imperial systems, clearly remains an important theme in the era from 1870 to

1945. Kenneth Pomeranz's pathbreaking work has illustrated, for example, the "great divergence" between Asia and Europe, one that widened dramatically in the nineteenth century as coal, steam, and access to the resources in the New World accelerated industrialization in Western Europe. A "settler revolution," especially strong in Anglophone polities, accentuated this divergence. In the regions that Anglophone settlers came to dominate, immigration, urbanization, and infrastructure building helped spark agricultural revolutions, which then spilled their abundance into global markets. As this Anglo-world boomed, new forms of banking, incorporation, credit, and property protection facilitated international investment, even as liberal ideologies helped pry open new opportunities. The Great Depression of the 1930s, of course, hit the capitalist centers of Europe, rippled into past and present colonies, and strengthened the challengers to Euro-American liberalism. But neither World War II nor the emerging anticolonial movements throughout the globe reversed the general pattern of divergence.

Recently scholars examining the connections between liberalism and European imperialism have explored the many ways in which virtue and self-interest were reconciled within a discourse of progress. Jürgen Osterhammel and Michael Adas, among many others, have emphasized this period as one in which the West's "civilizing mission" became hegemonic by coercion and consent. Civilizing missions—that is, attempts to universalize one's own cultural position—go back for centuries, of course, but Europeans became particularly confident of their mission over most of this period. Osterhammel has written that in the eighteenth century, Europe often compared itself to Asia; in the nineteenth century, Europe considered itself incomparable. Our chapters take into account how this scholarship has reconceptualized the growing economic, political, and cultural ascendancy of Europe.[2]

As elites in the West came to dominate certain networks by scooping up new resources, elaborating mechanisms to leverage capital, and proclaiming a predetermined civilizational mission, however, they did so within interactive relationships. The chapters in this volume follow recent scholarship by conceiving of the terrain of the world as radiating from no single region but as best understood through the variety of social, cultural, political, and economic exchanges and networks that linked (or failed to link) people. Indeed, this book joins those who see the very idea of world history as working against any kind of static geography of place in favor of a geography of linkages. As C. A. Bayly's influential *The Birth of the Modern World* argues, the world during this era may be seen "as a complex of overlapping networks of global reach, while at the same time acknowledging the vast differentials of power which inhered in them." Europeans could often bend existing networks to their will, yet "it was the parasitic and 'networked' nature of Western domination and power which gave it such strength, binding together, and tapping into, a vast range of viable networks and aspirations." The growing importance of the West in this period seems, in short, best understood in the context of a variety of interactive networks in which both global uniformities and local diversities took shape.[3] Chapter 2 elaborates this view by theorizing the condition of "imperial globality."

Global interactions in this period may have strengthened the West, but they were certainly not all generated there, and the effects of global interconnectedness brought both homogeneity and differentiation. As A. G. Hopkins has emphasized, the global and the local—the self-styled universal and the particular—often created each other and coexisted in mixes that depended on time, place, and circumstance.[4]

Over the past few decades, several theoretical discussions have been particularly influential in moving historical scholarship away from a Eurocentric to a multicentric, networked perspective. Postcolonial theory, gender studies, and subaltern studies, for example, have raised important questions about silences and subjectivities in history and have sought to render visible and active those areas and peoples that earlier scholarship tended to present as peripheral and reactive. In addition, the so-called cultural turn has suggested methodologies for dealing with the discursive creation of reality, with positionality, and with multiplicity of meanings. Close attention to language and symbols, in particular, has encouraged historians to interrogate more carefully words such as *progress* and *reform* as well as the processes by which categories related to nation, gender, race, ethnicity, religion, and others become constituted. Finally, anthropologists such as James Clifford and Arjun Appadurai have encouraged historians to see culture as relational rather than located, coherent, or enclosed. Their work has emphasized process rather than essence and presented the connectivities of modernity as simultaneously producing both homogeneity and difference. Although in the interests of accessibility our chapters have kept in the background any extensive consideration of the theoretical turns of recent decades, they draw on recent scholarship shaped by such currents.

Other significant characteristics of the period 1870 to 1945 relate to the spread of global urbanism and to the emergence of different conceptions of modernity. Cities on every continent began to boast electrification, sanitary systems, modernized ports and transit systems, movie houses, and other attributes of mass consumer culture.[5] Modern states mobilized behind these transformations and asserted their role in helping to implement and rationalize the vast changes that accompanied mechanization and mediazation. International standards of time and measurement spread, along with hopes (and fears) about the emergence of universalized international laws and values. As Chapter 5 especially emphasizes, styles, tastes, traded (often branded) goods, and scientific and technical expertise of all kinds developed superficial similarities even across vast distances. Despite the appearances of urban modernity and the theories of convergence that frequently accompanied such visible material attributes, however, historians have increasingly understood how practices of modernity developed culturally specific forms within their global circulation.

Our chapters show how a variety of visions that promoted ways of organizing states, empires, or global orders arose in different historical and geographical settings. Often worldviews competed with each other, sometimes on vastly unequal turf. In other cases, aspirations for modernity fed off of each other but also sparked clashes over which groups, exactly, would dominate. Moreover, the majority of the world's people still lived rural lives that were affected to varying degrees by the interconnectedness that showed so visibly in cosmopolitan cities. The commercial revolutions that reached ever more extensively into the countryside, as almost all of the chapters emphasize, had far-reaching effects on state making, empire building, migration, and exchange of goods. Yet the technological modernity and state building that seemed to be hallmarks of this age proved culturally varied and dramatically uneven in their transformative effects. One response, as James C. Scott's work has underscored, could be to retreat to the "hills" or other non-state spaces, thus honing an "art of not being governed" by encroaching politics or markets.[6]

The chapters that follow also highlight ways in which universalistic ideas of a coming global order of modernity accompanied highly particularist ideologies of ethno-nationalism and cultural essentialism. The period's virulent nationalist ideologies complemented institutional state-building processes that included all kinds of inclusions and exclusions, from legal restrictions governing citizenship, to professorial historical practices that focused on—and glorified—certain state actors, to programs of ethnic cleansing. In Chapter 1, Maier sets the constructions of various forms of modern states against the backdrop of the disruptive forces that were commodifying the countryside and shows how competing versions of modern nationalisms helped propel the high imperialism of the age and the rivalries that erupted in dozens of regional and local conflicts and in two great world wars. State building, empire, and armed conflict, in turn, reinforced ideologies of cultural boundedness. In addition, the more that flows of commerce, migration, and imperial outreach brought different peoples of the world together, the more distinctions labeled "racial" stood out. In what Sebastian Conrad has called the "globalization of the national," by the turn of the century many states, and not just in Europe, began to image themselves as cultural units. Both colonial and anticolonial movements often embraced discourses of monoculturalism. It was thus the very connectedness of the age, not so oddly perhaps, that spread ideologies of national separateness. Nationalisms, as C. A. Bayly and Sebastian Conrad have both illustrated, are produced transnationally.[7]

As new forms of contact among the world's peoples highlighted difference, and as the interplay of nationalistic and imperial visions sparked clashes, our period became darkened by unparalleled paroxysms of violence. War making provides another theme that cuts across our chapters, as the technological revolutions of the age proved perhaps better at killing than connecting. Science and engineering, which their apostles had once hailed as politically neutral realms, could turn deadly when imperial might, national pride, and potential profits seemed at stake.

Before the world wars of the first half of the twentieth century, nationalism and empire building sparked numerous regional conflicts and violence on many of the world's peripheries, frontiers, and colonies. These conflicts constituted prologues to the violence of the twentieth-century wars. The Franco-Prussian War of 1870–1871, the Anglo-Zulu War of 1879, the Sino-Japanese War of 1894–1895, the South African War (Second Boer War) of 1899–1902, the Russo-Japanese War of 1904–1905 were named conflicts, but violence was much more widespread than a list of discrete "wars" would suggest. In the American West, Australia,

Argentina, German South West Africa, and other places, European settlers systematically removed, through killing and deprivation, native peoples from coveted lands. Resource-rich territories suffered the most coercion and death. Perhaps ten million people perished in King Leopold's Congo in the late nineteenth and early twentieth centuries. The German repression of uprisings by the Nama and Herero peoples in their South West African colony used genocidal methods. US troops in the Philippine-American War of 1899–1903 decimated Filipino resistance fighters, concentrated civilians into camps, and adopted even harsher tactics in the Moro War, waged until 1913 against resistance from the Muslim-dominated island of Mindanao. Anglo-Egyptian troops used superior firepower to inflict tens of thousands of casualties and bring down the Mahdist regime in Sudan in 1898. As these examples suggest, colonial areas often served as proving grounds for military forces; every principal belligerent in the world wars had warmed up in colonial or regional engagements. Indeed, Maier shows how war making became a vital center of state making.

These forces of nationalism and empire building led to ever greater levels of bloodshed once major national states turned on each other. The Great War in Europe became a world war precisely because of the global connections that had been forged in previous decades. Support for England and France broadened to include most of the Americas, Australia, New Zealand, and Japan. German power extended its outreach into Islamic areas and proved successful in leading East African colonial troops against British, South African, French, Belgian, and Portuguese allies in sub-Saharan Africa. World War I killed almost ten million, left twenty-one million wounded, and broke up the Russian, Habsburg, German, and Ottoman empires.

Even as World War I temporarily disrupted networks of trade, finance, and personal bonds, it highlighted the world's accelerating connectedness. All nations, for example, grew more keenly aware of their need for access to strategic raw materials and control over communication networks. Moreover, millions of soldiers left their localities and traveled to distant battlefields. Those who survived often returned home changed—some broken and some broadened. (A popular postwar American song, embraced especially by African-American jazz orchestras, asked "How ya gonna keep 'em down on the farm after they've seen Paree?") Toward the end of the war, the devastating influenza pandemic confirmed the flimsiness of political borders and the deadly nature of globalized warfare.

As the war and its end brought economic dislocation, spreading disease and the specter of famine to Europe, a struggle emerged among rival ideologies—communism, liberal republicanism, and fascism. Each of these vied to lead a new order for the world, and their rivalries dominated world history from the 1920s to the 1940s and beyond. Although each of these competing forms became exemplified within particular national states and infused with particular nationalisms, each also found adherents across transnational networks. Thus, not only did World War I sap the old European order, but its aftermath provided a context for the growing power of anticolonial movements and for the ideological and geopolitical rivalries that would erupt in the much larger world war to come.

Under the strains of the 1920s and the economic implosion of the 1930s, polities in many countries fragmented into camps that both figuratively and literally warred against each other while building networks of allies and enemies both within and without. The metastasizing Great Depression—the spread of banking crises, currency devaluations, unemployment, and shrinking trade—confirmed the globalized nature of the world's economic system and provoked sharp reactions against it. In most countries and imperial zones, calls mounted for abandonment of gold, greater protectionism, and creation of regional trading blocs—all nationalistic challenges to the liberal ideal of economic globalization. The Soviet Union, which had kept itself aloof and off of the gold standard, remained somewhat shielded from the downturn. Soviet leaders celebrated the apparent bankruptcy of capitalism and proclaimed the superiority of state-run centralized planning. At the same time, the imperial dreams of the expansionist regimes in Germany and Japan held out a very different vision of what a newly conceived globalization, under their rule, might look like.

The United States, the world's most powerful economy, turned inward in face of the mounting global depression of the early 1930s and failed to play the role of economic stabilizer, while the interwar gold standard worked against countercyclical interventions by national states. As the institutions of liberal democracy weakened, the appeal of fascist and communist leaders grew, as did their antagonism toward each other. The continent that, in the late nineteenth century, had confidently proclaimed its enlightened mission entered what Eric Hobsbawm

called an "age of extremes," in which authoritarian rule flourished and liberal democracy seemed on the defensive, at least until after World War II.[8]

Over our period, with each exercise of military power, the intensity of killing
mounted as the technologies of firepower grew more lethal. Aerial bombardment, for example, became ever more sophisticated and thus ever more deadly
for both military and civilian populations. Less than two decades separated the
small aircraft that strafed insurgents in the colonial wars of the 1920s, such as
those waged by the United States in Nicaragua and by the British in Iraq, from
the strategic bombers and the atomic-bomb-carrying *Enola Gay* of World War
II. And mass killings came in waves and with ever greater efficiency: Armenians
sent into the desert to die during and after World War I; Joseph Stalin's deadly
famine in Ukraine and his executions during the purges of the 1930s, which may
have resulted in fifteen to twenty million deaths; the Third Reich's industrial-
style genocides.[9]

As extremes fostered even greater extremes, brutality could become normal.
In areas that Timothy Snyder has called "the bloodlands," where Stalin's and
Hitler's competition for empire was fiercest, some fourteen million Jews, Roma,
and Eastern Europeans perished. Both Nazi and Japanese militarists, whose expansionism triggered World War II, wedded dreams of landed empires—in
Eastern Europe and Manchuria, respectively—to ideologies that justified elimination of "inferiors" who might be in the way. World War II revealed the darkest
and most brutal impulses of the era and became the greatest global bloodletting
in human history. The death toll, which reached some forty to fifty million
people, perhaps half of them civilians, dwarfed the casualties of World War I,
not to mention those of earlier regional struggles.[10]

New technologies had connected people together, but what arose from contact
could turn into hatred and horror. The exponential rise in the capacity to destroy
life—of civilians as well as military personnel—was not antithetical to the connectivity of the age; it was its accompaniment. All of our chapters, in different
ways, develop the dynamic between the new era of globalization and the mounting
instabilities—wars and revolutions—that picked up pace after about 1895.

As the "dark continent" of Europe spread its killing technologies during our
period, the consequences of mechanization also fell on the natural environment,
as Topik and Wells note in Chapter 4. Indeed, the late nineteenth and early

twentieth centuries saw a massive acceleration of another kind of war, one waged against species and natural systems. Not that those who often boasted about the spread of civilization usually *intended* to ravage the diverse plant and animal life that inhabited the planet, but intentions are not a good measure of outcomes. Systematic destruction was sometimes deliberate: land-hungry Americans, for example, slaughtered millions of buffalo on the Great Plains, partly for fun and profit and partly as a measure to deprive natives of the capacity to resist white expansion. But more often, environmental damage came from ignorance about natural balances or from assumptions that natural bounty was inexhaustible. The great flocks of migrating birds that still darkened the skies in 1850 quickly dwindled; the huge herds of animals on the African continent fell victim to animal traders and other kinds of profit seekers. Acclimatizers imagined that the accelerating horticultural trade would enhance diversity through hybridization and adaptation, but plant seekers who penetrated into almost every untracked region brought destruction as often as recognition for exotic varieties. Moreover, the rapid spread of plantations exchanged profitable monocultures for nature's rich diversity. Railroads, ports, dams, and other engineered transformations altered natural systems in often unpredictable and dangerous ways. "Reclamation" of land, with its discourse of uplift and efficiency, could ruthlessly target communities of current dwellers.[11] Disruptions to natural systems, like the clash of cultures, made the new connectedness of the age both promising and perilous.

The Chapters

These chapters, again, present the world that took shape in the years 1870–1945 within five major themes: the arc of modern state building; the globality of imperial connections and of anti-imperialism; the global and regional migrations of peoples; the extension, thickening, and volubility of commodity chains; and the currents of social and cultural attachment and entanglement. Within these themes, the chapters highlight the reciprocal relationships between impulses of flux and of stabilization and foreground both the commonalities and the differentiations that emerged in the period. None of the chapters claim to "cover" the world's diverse regions and peoples in an all-inclusive way; they have sought to be more illustrative of historical processes than globally comprehensive. A short preview of each chapter will help suggest the contribution that each makes toward shaping a history of the world in this era.

In Chapter 1, Charles Maier sets a framework for the book by going beyond the borders of our time period to place in broad context what he calls the rise of Leviathan 2.0—the "modern statehood" that arose between the mid-nineteenth and mid-twentieth centuries. He first looks back to the previous century's instabilities—the clash produced when onrushing markets, imperial expansion, liberal ideas, and republican discourses of "rights" met backlashes that emerged from threatened traditional elites, marginalized sectors, religious bureaucracies and renewal movements, utopianism, and other resisters of globalizing impulses. In a survey of a century of political developments throughout the globe, he explains how this tumultuous disintegration of an older order provided the backdrop against which modern statehood emerged.

Territorial states were torn apart and reconstituted in midcentury "wars of national reconstitution" from roughly 1845 to 1880. On a global scale the political jurisdictions and the social origins and aspirations of leaders changed. The Western Hemisphere saw a reconstituted United States, a reorganized Canadian federation, the Mexican defeat of a French invasion followed by consolidation, and Argentina's rejection of dictatorship. In Europe, leaders of Italy, Germany, Austria-Hungary, Spain, the Ottoman Empire, and the Russian Empire all sought to patch together modern states. In East Asia, Japanese administrators and Chinese officials tried to mitigate foreign incursions through state-building measures. In many regions, new programs of modernization and rationalization signaled the "last stand" for indigenous political autonomy. "Why," at this moment, Maier asks, "does history become global?" The process of state construction, he shows, "was infectious," as states became reshaped not only in a competitive global universe but also in response to specific internal dynamics in which everyone, even the lowly, felt the winds of change.

Deploying new systems of communications, record keeping, land use and ownership, taxation, technology, weapons, bureaucratic agencies, law, and racial justifications, the leaders of these new and refreshened states after about 1880 signaled their interest in methods of governmentality. Seeking to define the relationships between the state and the "social," they turned attention to labor, education, health and sanitation, and cultural uplift, and often to related imperial missions as well as to the technological improvements that would confirm their economic and war-making powers. Various strains of cultural nationalism came together to constitute and animate loyalties. The interest in modernized statehood brought a global wave of revolution at the turn of the century: in China, Russia, Iran, Ottoman Turkey, and Mexico. Although separated geographically, each with its own variation, all were revolutions against authorities seen as "complicit in national dependency and even humiliation." All tried to erect some kind of parliamentary governance and articulated a positive role for the state. As states in this period embraced modernization, even monarchies, such as those in Thailand and Ethiopia, followed suit. Maier cautions, however, against overstating state power. Before World War I, tax revenues were light and real administrative powers, both in empires and in the countryside, were exercised by or in cooperation with local notables or private authorities.

Ethnic, racial, class, and gender divisions made the problem of representation in the modern state particularly complicated. Who should be included and on what terms? What should be the relationship between state and society? Economic growth often accentuated rather than diminished the dilemmas of representation. And the rise of nationalism in colonies and the weakening of colonial empires also brought new tensions: who had the right (or the power) to constitute a national or imperial body? The bonds of public discipline in the modern states and empires could seem liberatory to some but exclusionary and crushing to others.

The additional turmoil of World War I and the economic collapse that deepened throughout the 1930s proved fertile soil for new authoritarian forms of statehood—Bolshevism and fascism. The Soviet Union instituted a one-party state justified as embodying internationalism and proletarian collectivism but based on terror. Fascism, first in Italy but far more virulently in Germany, presented authoritarianism in terms of the social value of war to renew manhood. Nazism fused war-making with its visions of an ethnoracially defined state. The centralized power in these exceptional hyperstates rested not on individuals with inalienable rights but on special police forces that imposed obligations and brutally enforced lines of national inclusion and exclusion. By the late 1930s, with liberal capitalism in crisis everywhere, it seemed that the momentum of history pointed toward such "disciplined collectives" that glorified war and murdered dissenters.

At the end of World War II, several variants of the modern state remained: the "welfare state," which embraced some degree of state planning on behalf of social welfare and economic growth; single-party state socialist governments that adapted attributes of the Soviet model; and governments dominated by modernizing military institutions, which became prevalent in some countries of Latin America, Asia, and the Middle East. After the 1970s all of these forms of modern statehood stood in growing tension with the transformative influences of "globalization," especially the mobilities of capital and the justifications for reconfigured forms of transnational economic power. The future contours of modern statehood seemed increasingly uncertain.

"Between the mid-nineteenth and mid-twentieth centuries," Maier concludes, "states had recreated themselves in many ways: they had fought for territorial cohesion; enlisted the middle classes, consolidated territory, subjugated 'nomadic' or tribal peoples, and turned on each other in unparalleled wars. They had experimented with revolutionary parties whose members were intoxicated by visions of transformation through violence and had virtually worshiped the most brutal of leaders. And finally they had sought normalcy and a precarious equilibrium with the ever more powerful forces of the economy."

The modern states that worked to consolidate boundaries and to develop modes of governance also participated in a competition of empire building. In Chapter 2, Tony Ballantyne and Antoinette Burton look more deeply into imperial encounters, analyzing both the supports for and the resistances to empire. Building on the many studies now often associated with what has been called the new imperial history, they stress that empire was not a thing made in European capitals and implemented "out there." Rather, imperial systems, with their many racial, gendered, and economic forms, affected empires in all of their parts. Their chapter, therefore, deals with "imperial globality"—the multiple territorializing regimes that established colonies throughout the globe while also competing with each other for extractable resources and control over labor forces.

Their chapter emphasizes that the "imperial global" was hardly a coherent or all-encompassing juggernaut but instead a highly uneven "set of intermittently integrative processes that shared no single common motor, processes that reflected the vagaries of conjuncture and divergence, of appetite and indifference, of intentionality and inertia." While sensitive to the role of imperial power in making the global, therefore, they also emphasize the limits, anxieties, and vulnerabilities associated with imperial authority and view empires not mainly from their centers but from a variety of angles, spaces, and microlevels.

Ballantyne and Burton begin Chapter 2 by examining the spatial logics and cultural forms of modern empires. Seeing empires as "place-making regimes" that both deterritorialize and reterritorialize geographic space, and drawing examples from many imperial systems, they analyze key institutions of imperial interaction—militaries, missionaries, workplaces, and households. In all of these domains, imperial officials sought to manage indigenous populations but had to reckon with existing local practices. Conflicts arising over the organization and use of space often became evident in moments of political imperial crisis. In taking up the challenge of trying to understand what role these social cartographies of empire played in shaping the character of imperial power, the authors look not only to "the contact and contest born out of empires, but equally [to] the continued viability of native lifeways in both the autonomous and segregated spaces that were a consequential effect of imperial authority." They give special and sustained attention to issues of culture, work, and social position involving race, gender, and sexuality. "Questions of gender and sexuality, race and ethnicity, class and status," they write, "were utterly instrumental to how empires unfolded."

The chapter then looks at the worldwide changes in communication, transportation, and economic patterns that were instrumental to empire building. Focusing on three very different empires as examples—the British, the Japanese, and the Ottoman—the authors examine the patterns of connections among technology, industry, and imperial organization. Diverse imperial connections, they demonstrate, contributed to the shrinkage of time and space, if unevenly. Growing interconnectedness also held often-unexpected consequences for other realms—from the living and working patterns in port cities, to the reach of various religious practices, to the spread of disease, to the impacts of print culture.

Finally, Ballantyne and Burton analyze, through a variety of examples, how imperial encroachments often provoked opposition. There was no single pattern to such imperial/anti-imperial conflicts, which mostly played out in fields, factories, schools, and prisons—the locations of everyday lives. At times, subject peoples engaged imperial power directly, but often challengers were careful and guarded. Gradually, however, transnational networks of anti-imperialists emerged. "Global spaces were breeding grounds for organized forms of anticolonial sentiment at the end of the nineteenth century, even if the majority of full-fledged nationalist movements did not achieve their ends until the interwar period." Through this discussion, which continues to stress the importance of using lenses of race and gender to complicate imperial/anti-imperial impulses, Chapter 2 illuminates how the imperial world order was both made and unmade in this era. "Anticolonial nationalists in this period may not have all communicated or known each other, but the parallels between movements are as striking as the resemblances between and among imperial orders themselves." The chapter thus directs attention to the formal mechanisms of empire without overstating their reach and power. Significant anti-imperialist movements generally emerged in the 1890s, found a fertile milieu during and after World War I, and grew ever more influential in the interwar period.

Chapters 3–5 deal with currents and networks that often crosscut the kinds of boundaries that states and empires sought to stabilize. By focusing on migrations of people, on shifting chains of commodities, and on circulations of diverse ideas and affiliations, these chapters portray a world in motion.

In Chapter 3, Dirk Hoerder examines the flows of people that shaped the mass migrations of this period. He opens with a global sweep through African, South Asian, European, and Russian migrations, explaining the context of mobilities—and immobilities—that gave rise to each. From this perspective, he decenters Europe in the story of migrations in our period and instead examines all of the macroregions that saw massive transfers of population from the 1870s to the 1910s or, in some places, to the 1930s. Hoerder traces how the new railroad lines, port cities, steamships, and large population growth from the 1870s onward increased the speed and volume of travel generally. A large outbound "proletarian mass migration" accelerated from Europe (even with many returns home), while regimes of temporary bondage spurred huge migrations of men and women from areas around the Indian Ocean and, somewhat later, East Asia into the world's various plantation belts and mining nodes. After African slavery had mostly ended in the Americas (by the 1880s), European colonizer states and investors generally came to control the mobility of African peoples. Huge internal migrations occurred in China, India, Europe, North America, European Russia, and some parts of Latin America and colonized Africa, as men and women left areas with labor surpluses and swelled regions of urban, mining, and industrial growth.

Hoerder emphasizes how population flows were shaped by colonialism, changing economic interconnections, and the aspirations of people who were often caught in highly restricted circumstances. Migrations within and among regions and empires, he shows, produced both population mixing and also new categories and methods of stratification. He is closely attentive to the ways in which the choices and experiences of migration (and, indeed, of those who remained in place) were highly gendered and contingent on income, racial designation, and ethnicity.

Chapter 3 also describes the refugee migrations arising from the depression of the 1930s and the two world wars. This discussion considers the intellectual migrations that fed a global critique of colonialism and racism, and it thus foreshadows some of the displacements and migrations that would extend into future decades.

Migration history, Hoerder emphasizes, cannot be captured within descriptions of a few exemplary experiences. Rather, stories about migration are highly multiple and contingent. Within his global, historicized overview of our period, he elaborates an analytical frame of concepts and categories within which the mobilities and constraints that shaped individual lives may be understood. He rejects often-used but too-rigid categories such as "free" and "unfree" and words such as "identity" and "assimilation." Instead, his interpretation highlights the "processual structures" within which both men and women lived their lives, and stresses the complex variables involved in acculturation and the processes by which "belonging" takes shape—how it is offered, withheld, and adapted. Migrants negotiated and struck compromises with new environments, trying to assert things they valued from their past while trying to abandon what they may have wished to leave behind. Migrations, in this view, question the "container" view of states or cultures, because people who move "acquire familiarity with more than one way of life." Hoerder's chapter thus makes a major contribution to understanding the movement of people in this period by employing a "systems approach" that considers the variable conditions of departure, transit, and arrival.

In Chapter 4, Steven C. Topik and Allen Wells focus on commodities on the move. As world commerce and finance knit parts of the world together, commodity chains linked producers to processors to transporters to buyers. Following these chains provides innovative ways of understanding the wide variability in markets and of charting the rise and fall in the fortunes of various regions in the linked-together world. Topik and Wells rightly place the huge agricultural revolutions of this era near the center of the story of commodity chains. Agricultural production made up the bulk of global trade and therefore provides a window into myriad economic and social transformations throughout the world.

Focusing on the global flows of some of the world's most valuable traded commodities highlights how technological innovations of the age simultaneously transformed both agricultural and industrial production. Extraordinary increases in food supplies, shipped by more efficient transportation systems, provided sustenance to growing cities and their urban workforces. Similarly, urban industrial life brought an ever-escalating demand for affordable agricultural products from fields both near and far.

Chapter 4 illustrates the sweep of material change: How revolutions in transportation and finance, together with new corporate forms and oligopolies, accompanied the expansion of certain industrial and agricultural sectors. How the railroad and then auto industries propelled backward linkages that boosted production of fuels such as coal and petroleum and newly important commodities such as steel, aluminum, and rubber. How the gigantic trade in wheat became linked to the development of futures markets, managerial capitalism, railroad building, agricultural mechanization, advertising—all innovations that spilled into every other area of economic life as well. How the packaging of grains stimulated the growing of jute in India, manila in the Philippines, henequen in Yucatán. How commodity flows, interlacing with the contesting logics of empire and conglomerate building, both contributed to and were shaped by warfare. How accelerating commodification changed natural systems, even as forces of nature also altered commodity chains. And how advertising and branding helped transform all kinds of commodities into new products such as crackers, soda pop, and instant coffee.

There was no simple pattern to this era's commodity chains. Some commodities, like sugar, were grown throughout the globe and in vastly different circumstances and with varying effects. Others, like coffee, became more predominant in a single place (such as the large semitropical tracts of Brazil). Some, such as tea in this period, followed lines of formal or informal empire; others, such as coffee, followed no imperial boundaries and in fact found advantage by being outside of them. For most commodities, the people and places who dominated pricing and market share changed over time. On the opposing ends of commodity chains, as Topik and Wells show, were workers and consumers—each group hardly visible to the other. And both were separated by many different moneymaking links that were often equally invisible to either group. The independent rubber tappers in Brazil or the coerced rubber workers elsewhere, for example, hardly knew the world inhabited by the automobile consumers whose new "necessities" skyrocketed the demand for rubber, and neither group understood much about the layers of intermediaries—middlemen, transporters, manufacturers, advertisers, and retailers—who became so economically and socially vital in this period.

As links in the commodity chains stretched out globally, more and more goods ended up as financed and branded commodities that could bring growing profits to the industrialized countries, which leaped ahead in the world economy of this period. As the volume in global trade and marketing rose sharply and brought prosperity to certain favored regions, the economies of Europe and the neo-Europes benefited the most. Controlling the infrastructure of the world economy—the transportation, communication, and finance that could mobilize more and more resources—brought huge profits to those who owned and managed the systems, and accelerated the growing gap between different regions of the world and different classes of people.

Chapter 4 demonstrates the value of using commodity chains to illustrate the interactive transformations of this era. Topik and Wells highlight how global circulations of agricultural and industrial goods accelerated in this period and variably shaped and reshaped production and consumption.

In Chapter 5, I highlight the variety of transnational social-cultural currents—ideas, affiliations, and images—that circulated in the networked world of the era from 1870 to 1945. I emphasize that these currents did not stand apart from nations or empires, nor did they represent some unified globalizing project or the beginnings of some evolutionary phase beyond nation and empire. Rather, these currents worked in tandem with the themes of the other chapters: they both bolstered and undermined national and imperial structures; they grew out of and also helped produce the migrations of people and commodities.

Employing the term *differentiated commonalities,* Chapter 5 emphasizes both the universalizing and the differentiating aspects of transnational social and cultural currents. The idea of currents, indeed, provides a central metaphor. It suggests crisscrossing flows of power and an interactive, though often asymmetrical, dynamic. This chapter provides a tentative map for some of the global connectivities that have been highlighted in recent work in transnational history and examines currents within five areas—international rule-setting institutions; transnational social networks and attachments; exhibitionary centers such as world fairs, museums, and gardens; epistemic affiliations based on expertise; and the spectacular flows of mass-marketed adventure, media, and consumerism. The cultural circulations produced within such currents, I suggest, coexisted with the violence that accompanied clashing national ideologies and the forging of formal and informal empires.

In Chapter 5 I also stress the distinctive ways in which the technological innovations of "modernity" wedded together science and spectacle. From the 1870s, globe-spanning technologies (telegraph cables, railroads and faster ships, radio, cameras, airplanes, and others) extended their reach and brought rapid and dramatic change. Many of technology's innovations created a secular realm of the miraculous. In this new world, suddenly ablaze with electric lights and motion pictures, images dazzled; speed amazed; illumination seemed to promise to sweep away darkness, both physically and metaphorically. Possibilities beckoned—the possibility of an abundance that industrial technologies and trade seemed to forecast, the possibility of creating strong bodies and strong nations, the possibility of being "modern," whatever that meant to whomever used the term; the possibility of ultimate weapons and victories in war.

People in diverse situations throughout the world were situated differently with respect to the spectacular science and technology of the modern age, but few could escape its fascinations and its rippling effects. The spectacles embedded in the narratives of mechanical and scientific transformation captivated people on every continent and hailed many to embrace some version of the progress that was not just a Western imposition but a global phenomenon generated in differentiated localities. At the same time, the technologies and spectacles of modernity might also quite literally *captivate* people by hardening regimes of racial and geographical inequalities. The sirens of modernity could lure with songs of freedom and self-fashioning while obscuring the rocky hierarchies of power.

Chapter 5 underscores how "homogenization and differentiation, the global and the local, trans- or internationalism and nationalism, reason and spectacle" are all sets, not of opposites, but of complements that operate in creative tension with each other in this era of transnational networks. Seemingly binary poles emerge as coproductive counterparts that make up the landscape of modernity.

This volume, in sum, deals with the transitions and networked connections of the changing industrial-commercial-imperial age between about 1870 and 1945. It tries to attend to both the commonalities and differences that emerged over this era; it encompasses the promises of interconnectedness and the destructive hatreds generated within the currents of a shrinking world. Greatly indebted to recent scholarship, the topical arrangement of these chapters emphasizes process over place and presents attributes of time and periodization as framework-contingent. Together, the five chapters foreground the state-building and imperial projects of the era while contextualizing them within other themes organized around flows, encounters, and networking. Flux and heterogeneity, with their flip side of stabilization and containment, marked the onrushing modernity of the age.

·[ONE]·

Leviathan 2.0:
Inventing Modern Statehood

Charles S. Maier

Introduction

START perhaps in the foothills of southern Montana on a summer day almost a century and a half ago—not a long time really, indeed in the very year that my grandfather was born in a densely settled neighborhood of Central Europe five thousand miles to the East. The United States Army has deployed about seven hundred cavalry against an alliance of Lakota, Arapaho, and Cheyenne communities concluded the year before under the leadership of Chief Sitting Bull, after white miners, beckoned by reports of gold discoveries in the Black Hills of South Dakota, had streamed into lands allocated to the Indians by treaty in 1868. There have been clashes through the spring of 1876, and Washington has sent three columns of troops into the Montana territory to engage the Indian warriors and press them back westward. On this day, June 25, the soldiers of the southern column, comprising the 7th Cavalry, are attacking an Indian settlement in the valley of the Little Bighorn River and realize belatedly that they face more enemies than they had anticipated.

Were these endangered soldiers really confident that these hills and river valleys were their country's own? What might such an assertion signify? What status did it portend for the Lakota people, whose own grandparents had welcomed the explorers Lewis and Clark three-quarters of a century earlier but now faced a continuous incursion of miners, ranchers, and homesteaders? The Native Americans have their own economic relationship to these lands that includes hunting and seasonal migration as well as cultivation, confirmed by custom, but apparently unrecognized by the new settlers who keep arriving to mine, farm, and graze. Perhaps neither side really comprehends why the other must claim such a vast landscape. Under pressure the Indians have signed many agreements they believed would preserve diminished but guaranteed territory; but they have watched as these pacts have been unilaterally amended and their lands reduced. On this day, at least, they will give pause to their pursuers. Finally aware that he has imperiled his forces, General George A. Custer will divide his men in the river valley into three detachments. Two of them will hold off their attackers after costly retreat, but the 210 men under his command, forced against the crest of the bordering hills, will be overwhelmed within an hour. By the end of the day they will all be dead, their equipment stripped, most of them with heads scraped of flesh and hair.[1]

In the long run, however, the victors of that day will be the losers. Their reservation will be diminished again. More cavalry will come, the railroads will bring new settlers, and the tribes will be continuously pressed into the inhospitable highlands over the years to come, until one of their leaders makes a final capitulation a generation later. The victorious chief of the summer of 1876 will be killed on the allotment his people were granted, an old man, in 1913. Still, let us start with them, with those who across the world resisted the encroachments of the modern state, with its aspirations for territorial expansion, its exploitation of steam and steel, and its highly developed organization of government. Let us give the communities who faced these instruments of domination (for so they encountered them) a last chance to preserve their homelands under their own control. The tableau they offer is a familiar one captured in nineteenth-century novels, paintings, and the engravings commissioned for weekly newsmagazines, and later, after the administration of final defeat, by the haunting melancholy of silver halide photographs of "noble" warriors or disconsolate families confronting the unrelenting pressure of settlers and explorers and soldiers.

Communities we used to label casually as nomadic or tribal—whether (to cite only a few generic cases) of desert Bedouins on the fringes of the Ottoman Empire, the villagers of the Caucasus or the highlands of Central Asia facing the tsar's administrators, the Indians of the North American arid lands, and the peoples of the African savannas—were slowly but inexorably subjugated. Their long and difficult retreat, of course, had started well before the late nineteenth century: when Europeans reached the Americas, the Portuguese and Dutch pressed inland from the coasts of southern Africa, the French and British sought to control the North American Great Lakes, or the Qing and Romanov dynasties established adjacent imperial control over Xinjiang and Mongolia. By the twentieth century they survived as depleted units, allowed legalized or de facto tribal habitations, sometimes even subsidiary states within the empires, but their earlier confederations and international roles were just a memory—often neglected by the later anthropologists who studied their local customs and family structures but not their politics, or ignored by the historians who were encouraged by all the resources of the victorious states to focus on their nations' success stories.

But just occasionally, the indigenous defenders of these sprawling regions gave pause to the steamroller of "civilization." This is what happened on June 25, 1876, at the Little Bighorn. So, too, three years later, when Zulu soldiers destroyed an encroaching British encampment at the Battle of Isandlwana. Between 1881 and 1898, the extensive Mahdist uprising in the Sudan, waged in the name of a purified Islam, inflicted costly defeats on the Turco-Egyptian governors in Cairo and the British commanders who led their makeshift armies. In 1893 the Rif tribesmen, in theory subjects of the king of Morocco, besieged and defeated Spanish troops at Melilla. Ethiopian soldiers wiped out Italian detachments at Dogali in 1891 and even more catastrophically at Adwa in 1896. Ethiopia, of course, was no mere tribal region, but one of the globe's oldest kingdoms. The Europeans, set back for a decade or two—until 1935–1936 in the case of Italy's assault on Ethiopia—hardly took account of the complex political and religious polities that managed to slow their conquest. They beheld a series of savage last stands on the part of nomads and tribes.

In fact, the common word *tribes* does not adequately summarize any of these regional peoples' political existence, for they too had states or quasi states.[2] Tribes refers to communities who believe themselves organized by descent from early founders or chiefs, which, after all, was also the theoretical claim of the Ottoman Turks and of the Qing Dynasty, which had ruled China since 1644. But tribes were also political units, sometimes taking decisions of war and peace in confederal assemblies, although usually without the population density and the differentiated offices that marked the European states. The Spanish had conquered two elaborately organized tribal empires in central Mexico and Peru in the sixteenth century. The early United States repeatedly signed (and then unilaterally revised) treaties with the Indian nations of North America that recognized aspects of tribal statehood, including control of territory, as well as degrees of incorporation within the international boundaries of the North American republic. The Creek and Seminole, and Cherokee, Iroquois, Comanche, Sioux, and Apache, occupied extensive territories, sometimes exclusively, sometimes in symbiotic exploitation of rival peoples. Under their charismatic and ruthless leader

Shaka, the Zulu had created a robust nineteenth-century polity that dealt with neighboring Boer republics and British intruders. Some tribes might find it advantageous to move their abodes in a yearly or periodic pattern, whether to take advantage of animal hunts, as on the Great Plains, or of different elevations and their seasonal climates for animal husbandry. But many others had become sedentary and agricultural. Along the steppe lands of Russia, dozens of tribal confederations and hundreds of subunits recognized only the wispy remote claims of a Russian power thousands of miles away, as did the communities on the southern sides of the Himalayas and Afghan frontiers who dealt with Queen Victoria's local agents. As in the American West or Zulu South Africa, the Islamic khanates of the Turkestan region were subjugated as political units only in the 1870s and 1880s, as were the Kurdish tribes of southeastern Anatolia and northern Iraq at the hand of Ottoman military forces throughout the 1880s and 1890s.[3]

These decades signaled the last stand for indigenous political autonomy, for many reasons that will be explored below. Despite the lethal capacity of spears and bows and tomahawks, tribes recognized the advantage of firepower and had acquired rifles. But they depended on the horse (or camel), and had not developed the more recent railroad, which limited the size of their military mobilizations. They might claim large areas of terrain as their own but imposed no fixed boundaries and moved about without efforts at permanent settlement throughout. Although their statesmen might negotiate compacts and alliances, tribes also fought each other over decades, often in ritualized and savage warfare. And, fatal for their own collective survival, they had often solicited the European peoples encroaching on their lands to help tilt the balance in their own intertribal warfare. Still, for all its momentum the state did not penetrate everywhere. Large regions of upland or deep forest remained refuges for smaller peoples stubbornly seeking not to be governed, in the phrase of James C. Scott, who has celebrated their refractory evasiveness, which in part can be attributed to the inaccessible terrains they inhabited.[4]

The winners were the well-organized representatives of Europeans and their American or African or Asian descendants organized into the most efficient engine of expansion and governance that the world had seen for centuries: the modern nation-state. This was a large-scale unit organized to permeate and master territory, to pursue sedentary agriculture and industrial technology, possessing complex legal systems that allowed the preservation and transmission of family and individual property, the salaried employment of large-scale private and public workforces, the rapid communication of commercial and policy decisions by electrical telegraph, the ministerial archives and records that ensured institutional memory, and ideologies of rivalry and group purpose that generated intense loyalties.

Looking at the forces that drove the historical development of the modern state over two centuries, I would emphasize three. Critical thinking was crucial in undermining the old regimes; formal ideas but also the dramaturgies of discontent and protest played a major role in the constant questioning of existing institutions and the imagining of new ones that operated so powerfully after 1750. Technological inventiveness—that is, a different range of ideas, thinking applied to the material world—was crucial to the transformations of the mid-nineteenth century. The inventions that overcame the constraints of distance and time allowed the global restructuring of territory that transformed the states of the mid-nineteenth century. At the same time they introduced new forms of social stratification that renewed intellectual discontent, no longer just with a timeworn status quo but impatience with the new results of economic and political transformation. For the eighteenth and nineteenth century these impulses tended to originate in Europe and its New World offshoots and radiated outward, compelling the massive societies of Asia to take up the same processes by the twentieth century. The third major force was more a condition of global territorial organization and less an active agent. It was the fact that states have always existed in the plural—in continuing competition, if not open warfare. Any history of the state, like it or not, must follow an institution whose organization and social divisions have been premised on insecurity. The fact that this circumstance has continually contributed to the maintenance of internal hierarchies, even in modern societies, does not make it less real.

. . .

State is a heavy word, not so easy to define. It refers to the institution to which human communities have entrusted the coercive power they find necessary for the legal regulation of collective life.[5] How much power, with what limits, for what ends remain issues contested in the West since at least the ancient Greeks. Much of the history of the world's peoples has been told in terms of the rise and fall of their states. States, of course, are ancient structures, hierarchies of political and administrative decision-making designed to ensure ongoing control for elites and continuing security for those who accept their claims to rule. States are abstractions. While they have often been represented in the person of their rulers, they usually generate an ideology of existence as communities in their own right. States claim to operate according to general laws or norms (although they may legislate different levels of privilege and entitlement for different groups within their jurisdiction), and these rules are the basis for their claims to legitimacy— that is, to their meriting loyalty from citizens and recognition from foreigners on grounds that go beyond the mere exercise of coercive power.

The fact that states have remained stubbornly plural throughout history means they each have claimed a degree of supreme authority (usually defined in terms of geographical reach or territory), which theoretically excludes the writ of other states—a condition called sovereignty. Although political theorists have often insisted that sovereignty is absolute, in practice it has often been partial or nested within imperial or associative structures. States have sometimes accepted some overarching claims against their freedom of action, whether as protectorates or tributary units, and often even large states have had to grant privileged legal enclaves or functions to other powers. Increasingly states have agreed to cede functions and authority, whether over their economies or their military or even their frontiers, to common authorities such as today's European Union. Sovereignty has never excluded the prerogative of making self-limiting treaties.

Because states are always interacting, sometimes peacefully through trade, migration, or diplomacy, sometimes through warfare, it is natural enough that they often reform themselves as a group and not just one by one. Renovation therefore has come in waves. From time to time states are reorganized, reconstituted on new principles, endowed with new goals, and claim new capacities. This does not mean that all states successfully renovated themselves. Some, especially the old imperial structures such as China or the Ottoman Empire, made important efforts but could not sustain their territorial integrity or capacity to ensure internal "order." Still, a global perspective suggests that a "long century of modern statehood," proposed here as a meaningful description for political modernity, extended from about 1850 to the 1970s. This is a history of how it arose, what innovations it brought, and why it seems to have ended.

The modern Western language of statehood is generally regarded as assuming its modern form in the sixteenth and seventeenth centuries to differentiate claims to govern from the powerful religious claims asserted and contested at the time. By the end of the sixteenth century, so Quentin Skinner explains, the concept of the state had become "the most important object of analysis in European political thought" as the "form of public power separate from both the ruler and the ruled, and constituting the supreme political authority within a certain defined territory."⁶ This European-wide discourse reflected the vast transnational splintering of post-Reformation Christian authority, the intensive communication of ideas in an era of print culture, and the painful search for alternative nonreligious principles of legitimacy. Late sixteenth- and seventeenth-century writers (such as Jean Bodin in the 1570s and Thomas Hobbes in the 1640s and 1650s) focused on the absolute authority that such sovereignty required. Without a powerful ruler, so Hobbes argued in *Leviathan* (1651), individuals within territories must live in the same insecure and violence-prone "state of nature" as nations did in the international realm.

The international properties of statehood and sovereignty are usually deemed to have been defined most decisively with the end of the Thirty Years War and the Treaties of Westphalia (Münster and Osnabrück) in 1648 that finally closed that long and complex struggle in Central Europe. The idea of sovereignty thus emerged with a dual thrust. Looking "inward," sovereignty was defined as the prince's governmental supremacy within the territorial unit—supremacy especially above any rival claims of religious authority. Looking "outward" to the collection of states as a whole, sovereignty was defined as the international independence sanctioned by the Treaties of Westphalia or recognition by other states more generally. Precisely because these properties of statehood—a supreme legal power within a home territory and full rights vis-à-vis other states—continued to be highly theorized after 1648, we tend to refer today to the "Westphalian" order.⁷

We should not overgeneralize. Such a vision of state sovereignty, absolute and integral, was foreign to large areas of the world with respect to both external relations and internal authority. Within South Asia, for example, the Mughal Empire and its successor, the British Raj, recognized partial sovereignty for hundreds of princes or rajas or sultans, and claimed only what medieval European law often defined as suzerainty. In East Asia, where the massive and venerable Chinese Empire dominated the mainland, the Westphalian paradigm of state equality would have seemed unnatural. The communities around the rim of that megastate recognized its primacy although expected no real interference in their domestic affairs.[8]

Just as fundamental, the inner coherence of the Chinese state seemed to rest on a particular relationship with the realm of the sacred. Whereas in Christian realms, religion was invoked to support the state and its leaders, the religious sphere still remained distinguishable from what the state had come to be about. At least since the Investiture Conflict of the eleventh century, popes and emperors alike insisted on distinguishable, if sometimes overlapping, missions. That dualism was reaffirmed implicitly even as the seventeenth-century construction of Leviathan 1.0 subordinated the political claims of religious officials to secular rulers. To be sure, wherever an anointed monarch reigned, the separation was hardly absolute. Religious officials still often claimed the authority of an autonomous normative order, and it was the task of the monarch to protect their claims. Roman Catholic Church officials served as the political rulers of various territories within the Holy Roman Empire until 1803 and in Italy until 1870. In Islamic regions, the relationship was fully as complex. Although Islam originally envisaged a political domain coterminous with the community of believers, a succession of rival imperial units had come to contest the vast territories where Muslim affiliations prevailed. Ottomans, Persians, and Mughal rulers in India usually made allowance for alternative worship but in so doing often conceded the preeminent role of Islamic religious authorities and law. The Ottomans, moreover, sought to claim the earlier extensive idea of Islamic political rule and the function of the caliphate until the Turks abolished the office and the empire in 1922. In East Asia the claims were different still. The Japanese emperor, no matter how weak over the centuries, retained an aura of divine origin that was celebrated through special rites; and until 1945 modern nationalists sought to strengthen his divine status. The Confucian legacy perhaps overcame to the greatest degree the dualism of sacred and political authority that persisted elsewhere at least until recent decades. Somewhat as in the earlier Mesoamerican polities destroyed by the Spanish, the Chinese emperor, deep into the nineteenth century, was to ensure the good order of a society by ritual practice in a cosmos that extended from the family to the heavens. Any tourist who follows his and his servants' processions to ensure the year's crops through the precincts of the Temple of Heaven in Beijing can sense that the world's largest state had an aura of its own.[9]

Not that Chinese imperial functions and structure cannot be compared with Western institutions—they certainly can—but the language developed in the West, and taken for reasons of familiarity as a discursive base for this history, does not capture the vibrations that filled other realms. The Westphalian concepts were thus restricted in scope, but as European influence spread through trade, diplomacy, and conquest, the more absolute categories of state and nation also diffused. By the late nineteenth century, states possessed a degree of dedication to governance, of bureaucratic functionality, of at-oneness with fixed territorial space, of belief in their own competitive mission, that was unprecedented.

Nonetheless, that climax was also a renewal and partial transformation. New technologies of communication and transportation allowed a decisive intensification of state ambition and governmental power in the second half of the nineteenth and first half of the twentieth century, sufficient to justify the numerical suffix used for computer software: Leviathan 2.0. The fundamental properties of the state—the supremacy of its legal norms at home and its reliance on a territorial base—remained the same. But territorial ambitions became vastly greater in an age of renewed imperialism, no longer content with trading rights and enclaves, but pursuing enclosure of vast territories abroad.

Moreover, the older ideals of an autonomous and supreme legal order, of government by law, whether bureaucratic and monarchical or based on popular sovereignty, also changed. Leviathan 2.0 seemed to accept that its own supposedly transcendent legal norms become entangled with economic interest groups and political caucuses. To be sure, the Anglo-Scottish (and later North American) interpretation of a legal order never separated the law so formally from the world of commerce and association as did continental legal theory. With the struggle against supposed Stuart absolutism behind them by the eighteenth century, British Whig, if not Tory, publicists measured human progress less by the unsullied transcendence of law than by economic progress and the development of civility. Continental liberal thinkers, struggling until the mid-nineteenth century to limit monarchical authority, still retained a more transcendent concept of law as "above" interests, just as it was above personal rule. Still, by the early twentieth century the ideal of a pristine state was difficult to maintain. It was hard to disentangle from the web of corporate interests, labor unions, and political parties that claimed the right to govern, whether in a competitive system or exclusively and without tolerating rivals. Only a century or so after the idea of a government of laws had slowly disengaged itself as the ideology of Enlightenment politics, the state seemed about to be reabsorbed as just a regime of party or of interests.[10]

How far any of those trends might be pursued without undermining the state as such remained a question for political actors and—in retrospect—for scholars. Looking ahead to the late twentieth century, we can grasp that the abuses of single-party and military regimes became so terrifying that political activists wanted to revive the theory and the practices of liberal government. But the old idea of a transcendent state and legal order no longer promised a realistic liberal refuge. Instead theorists and practitioners accepted, and sometimes celebrated, the entanglement of the public legal order in the welter of associative interests, churches, unions, economic enterprises, and the media. These entanglements might seem menacing or beneficial. When economic difficulties threatened, as in the 1970s, many analysts envisaged a recourse to private–public bargaining they labeled neo-corporatism. When authoritarian rule crumbled, as in the later 1980s and 1990s, they celebrated the benevolent forces of civil society that had resisted dictatorship. In either case state and society seemed hard to disengage. Not, however, that those forms seem inscribed for permanence. By the late twentieth century many commentators were theorizing the state as a regime of discursive expertise, hopefully protected from untutored populist pressures—perhaps to be designated by some future historian as Leviathan 3.0.

. . .

To return to the 1870s, arrayed against the encroaching machinelike national communities, the momentary tribal victors of the Little Bighorn or southern Africa did not really have a chance. The states had superior weaponry, particularly the rapid-firing guns, railroads, and river gunboats decisively improved in the late nineteenth century. The states had the agencies to persist in policy and to replace those boastful military leaders who so often courted defeat. States came back—they wore down the tribes, reduced them by disease and, from time to time if resistance persisted, by genocidal repression and driving them into the deserts, where they could be left to die of thirst, hunger, and exposure. Still, many of these tribal communities survived to bear witness. Some clung to highland areas whose arduous climate did not encourage dense settlement. Some continued on the steppe, driving their animals in yearly patterns from summer pasturages to more sheltered winter terrain. Some emerged as the components of the states created in the wake of decolonization after 1945. The desert Bedouins benefited from the inhospitable margins of a weak empire. The American Indians were settled in hardscrabble reservations, continually diminished in size, where the price they often paid for the continuity of their tribal life was economic stagnation and alcoholism, or chose assimilation and intermarriage, retaining only the memory of their collective past and perhaps nurturing revivalist myths and folklore.

"Bury my heart at Wounded Knee," or at Kokand in Turkestan, or Melilla in Morocco, or Omdurman in the Sudan—battles occasionally won by those resisting, usually lost, in any case episodes in the global triumph of the modern state and the marginalization of a nomadic alternative. In some locations, as in Central Asia, the tribes might continue traditional modes of life, wandering across new and weakly established frontiers. In the Americas they gave up their collective property rights, and access to land, and the rights to mineral wealth they might have developed. Where the Europeans came from afar, as in Africa, the tribes faced harsh regimentation, reinforced by doctrines of racial hierarchy. The states won, expanded, and then turned with murderous single-mindedness on each other and sometimes on their own citizens.

The rest of this chapter examines the ascent and transformations of the modern state. From the 1860s to the 1970s these units of territorial organization prevailed without any real alternative institutions to contest their triumph. Then they entered a period we still live in, one that seems to have imposed some important limitations on their freedom of action and even perhaps on the loyalties they compel. In the course of their trajectory, the violence they inflicted on each other dwarfed in scale the casualties they took at their tribal margins.

1. The World Is Weary of the Past

THE LINE is from Shelley, the twenty-nine-year-old British poet living in Italy and intoxicated by the opening of the Greek rebellion against the Turks:

> The world's great age begins anew,
> The golden years return,
> The earth doth like a snake renew
> Her wintry weeds outworn . . .
> The world is weary of the past,
> Oh might it die or rest at last!

When did the past die at last? Sadly, the impatient Shelley went first, drowning a year after he wrote his ode "Hellas" in 1821. This history proposes that insofar as statehood and public institutions were concerned, the past died in the mid-nineteenth century. As the poet suggested, the end of an old order and the birth (or rebirth) of a new are part of the same process. Still, rather than presenting the revolutionary era of 1776 to 1830 or even to 1848 as the seedtime of a global future, I argue that we better understand the entire century from 1750 to 1850 as one of institutional meltdown. Assuming that the ideas and practices of the early modern state—call it, after Thomas Hobbes's tough-minded treatise of 1651, "Leviathan 1.0"—arose in the seventeenth century, then fell into difficulty in the later eighteenth century, they were reconstituted after 1850 as "Leviathan 2.0." That process of reconstruction lasted, I will suggest, through the 1960s and 1970s, since which time the edifices of modern statehood have begun to decompose in their turn.

To propose the importance of two roughly hundred-year epochs divided at 1850 raises a labeling problem, as they straddle the more familiar divisions of the eighteenth, nineteenth, and twentieth centuries.[11] Neither do they coincide with such conventionally inscribed periods as the Enlightenment, "the age of revolution," or "the era of world wars." In particular, most historians have seen the decades around the French Revolution as so fundamental a rupture (at least for Europe) that they have tended to divide the prerevolutionary era from that which followed. For modern Middle Eastern history, they pivoted "before" and "after" around 1798, the year of Napoleon's invasion of Egypt. For China, until recently historians regarded the Opium War of 1842 as a crucial rupture. Similarly, many have accepted the notion of a short twentieth century, an epoch of ideological and military conflict beginning with the outbreak of World War I and ending with the fall of the communist system in Russia and Eastern Europe between 1989 and 1991. Without denying that such dramatic moments structure what I have called our moral narratives, I am urging that we need to keep a different tempo and follow long-term processes.[12]

Still, the argument here is not simply that institutions fell apart from 1750 to 1850, whereas in the subsequent long century strong leaders reasserted the capacity to rule. Revolutionary crises in the first epoch simultaneously reshaped institutions. New principles of political recruitment, new concepts of rights, a redefined sphere for religious authority, administrative rationalization, geographical reconstruction, and legal codification mark the history of the American territories and of French-dominated Europe from the 1760s on. Conversely, widespread and protracted upheavals in Asia and Latin America as well as political violence in Europe punctuated the long century of state formation after 1850. Within that second extended century we have also lived through an extensive era of crisis, which brought a world war, widespread revolution, massive unemployment, and a second global conflict and the replacement of colonial empires with the Soviet and American spheres of influence. Both century-long spans were periods of transformation; both constituted long episodes in the creation of what historians think of as modernity. This section examines the era from 1750 to about 1850; the remaining sections discuss what has followed. The conclusion attempts to take stock of what trends have intervened since 1970—that is, the world in formation. Older readers of this book have been imprinted with experiences and mentalities shaped by the long century of modern statehood that began in 1850. Younger readers have come of age since 1970 in the flux of newer currents and rapidly evolving institutions. Hopefully what follows makes sense of both.

Contagious Ideas

Return for now to the years after 1850 and generalize extravagantly, as must any history on a global scale. In the decades receding into the past as of the mid-nineteenth century—remain for the moment in the domain of Western culture and sensibility—youthful, enthusiastic, sometimes utopian and even violent yearnings marked advocates of change. Conservative opponents summoned up visions of allegedly organic communities that would be arbitrarily destroyed. In the decades ahead, harsher and more realistic calculations will govern group behavior. There will be no less a recourse to violence, but it will be governed more by the alleged requirements of ethnic and national necessity, and less frequently by utopian hopes. Already dissipating as of 1850 is a fervor for revolution, although such exiles in Paris as Richard Wagner or Alexander Herzen echo accents of a generation earlier (again we choose that Romantic radical, Shelley):

> To defy Power, which seems omnipotent . . .
> Neither to change, nor falter, nor repent:
> This, like thy glory, Titan, is to be . . . free;
> This is alone Life, Joy, Empire, and Victory.[13]

By midcentury such a sentiment seems more bombast than enthusiasm. Dated, too, is the fervor for "young" national societies (Young Italy, Young America), for utopian communities, for socialist equality among radicals, or for enchanted estatist hierarchies for conservatives. Instead, for those who followed after 1850, a different spirit will dominate: a utilitarian commitment to "order and progress," the Comtean motto that foreswore revolutionary juvenilia and came to terms with power—the power of soldiers, of machines, of artillery and repeating rifles, of finance, of electricity. Summoned to serious work, the post-1850s generation will grow the heavy white beards of mature citizens. They will take precautions against the rebellious potential of the threatening street, become attuned to Darwin's "survival of the fittest" (misinterpreting it to mean survival of the strongest) and the apparently inexorable laws of social development. In fact, the generation that straddled that mid-1800s line will make the conversion in their own lifetime, passing from romantic fervor to convinced sobriety—as over a century later, the protesting youth of the 1960s will buckle down as middle-aged adults to programs of realistic reform or even repentant reaction.

The currents of ideas—first romantic, then realistic—coursed through Europe and the societies settled by Europeans in North and South America or dominated by their colonial administrators in Bengal, Batavia, and elsewhere. In the first half of the nineteenth century they were already exerting a powerful and unsettling impact in the Ottoman Empire, whose administrators and intellectuals had confronted Europeans across their borders and in the Mediterranean for centuries. The Ottomans had fallen under increasing pressure in military encounters—having had to cede territory on the north shore of the Black Sea to Russia and in 1798 having experienced a disastrous French military invasion, which only the British fleet and not their own soldiers had compelled to withdraw, and then in the first decades of the nineteenth century facing open rebellion in Greece and then Serbia.

Traditional Islam, represented by a conservative establishment of judges and scholars, collectively known throughout the Middle East as the 'ulama', and ethnic Turkish loyalty to the house of Osman no longer seemed to provide the legitimacy for this large domain to stand up to more universal concepts of citizenship that had come with the French armies and books. Its organizational principles—based on the management of religious and ethnic diversity by drafting talented Albanians, Greeks, and others to high office, allowing non-Muslims their own communal authorities (the *millets*), and relying on extensive clientelist networks with regional notables—had served a vigorous expansionist empire well. But in an era of unrelenting pressure and the fashionable emerging European notions of homogeneous nationhood, they appeared creaky and backward.[14] East and south of the Ottoman Empire, throughout the great arc of South Asia, a great ferment of Islamic revivalist ideas challenged rulers in Persia, in the Central Asian khanates, and in the decrepit Mughal Empire. Emerging in religious schools and focusing on nonpolitical moral renewal, Islamic revivalism tended to undermine the regimes in which their doctrines took hold, whereas the Western currents were increasingly oriented toward enhancing political structures.

European missionaries had arrived in China and Japan by the sixteenth century. Once the Tokugawa leaders secured decisive control of their realm, they moved to reverse Christian inroads and extirpate the converts by the 1620s.

Jesuits and Franciscans would vie for influence at the Ming court, but the Chinese seemed interested primarily in assimilating the Westerners' ideas to their own Confucian principles. Insofar as Chinese policy intellectuals later tuned into the ferment in the West, they latched on to practical writings of the Victorians, such as Samuel Smiles's tract on self-help. The Japanese listened more closely, and a few of the quasi-autonomous feudal domains into which the Tokugawa rulers had divided the islands sought Western learning, but the age of intellectual infatuation and importation would come after the mid-1800s. Still, contemplating the diverse global currents of intellectual ferment, any observer from outside the planet would have had to admit that the clash of ideas in the West was claiming increasing attention. Emanating from the West were notions of citizenship, that is, the idea that ordinary male adults, at least those with some property of their own, could claim a voice in constituting a nation and judging its policies; concepts of inherent rights; appeals to a literate and propertied middle class as a key political actor; and the appropriateness of becoming wealthy.

We shall have to examine more closely the physical milieu and built environments in which this remarkable moral trajectory took place. The technological transformation was leaving obvious tracks across on the landscape. The Industrial Revolution is usually dated from the accumulation of mid-eighteenth-century innovations in British textile production and the breakthroughs in harnessing steam power. Its effects increased exponentially after the Napoleonic wars. Textile factories brought new urbanization: the metropolises of 1800 had been administrative and court centers or commercial ports: London, Paris, Madrid, Dublin, Naples, St. Petersburg, Constantinople, Edo/Tokyo, Guangzhou (Canton), Calcutta (Kolkata). Alongside these cities after midcentury would emerge the industrial suburbs and conurbations of the Midlands, the Ruhr, eventually New York, Chicago, and so on. Steam power, and the capacity to smelt iron and then steel, meant the feasibility of railroads and new migration and production for distant markets. The telegraph meant that empires and large nations could be run in real time. Midcentury wars—the large, brutal combats that severed the first half of the century from the second: Crimea, the American Civil War, the German wars of unification—accelerated the technology and the movement of individuals.

Everyone could see the impact of these changes and write, as did William Cobbett early in the century, about their effect on the landscape or their creation of an impoverished urban laboring mass—sometimes in factories, often in small workshops or performing casual physical labor—that nineteenth-century social commentators a generation later, following the German historian of French social movements, Lorenz von Stein, would now define as a proletariat. Nonetheless, the gradual transformation of life on the land acted as profoundly on world populations even if unattended by such obvious visible signs. These were the changes, after all, that affected the overwhelming mass of global population, involving the transition from agriculture as a communal, subsistence-oriented activity, with prescribed routines set in village structures, to a market-oriented enterprise, where land could be bought and sold and peasants could depart for the city or across oceans to new continents, or, if less fortunate, lose their inherited protected status and become wage laborers or bound to their plots as indebted tenants. Market relationships, long established in Britain, and to a degree wherever peasants had to supply cities, were intruding into all the settled ways of rural life.

What was new was the growing liberalization of markets for land and labor. Until the nineteenth century, land and labor had been mutually shielded from market relations in a web of status restrictions and customs. Now in the most fundamental transformation of those under way, they lost their fixity.[15] Peasant emancipation, the vendibility of land, and market insecurities came as a piece, and provided the underlying seismic shifts that helped generate rural uprisings in the seventy-five years before 1850 and then again new revolutions at the threshold of the twentieth century.

These cumulative interacting transformations—in the constitution of the countryside, the application of an energy technology with radical consequences for moving goods and peoples, the altered mentalities—divided the conventionally demarcated nineteenth century into two epochs. Between them lay the mid-1800s watershed: a generation-long set of shocks that inaugurated the era of the modern. Not that what went into that transition was all of a piece culturally, religiously, or in terms of politics and economics. Nor that what emerged would be all of a piece, although the diverse cultures of the second half of the nineteenth century would be far more interconnected than they had been before 1850. But across the world each great geographical or cultural region would be recast and reshaped across that long caesura. And the states and nations that organized political life on the global surface would likewise reemerge transformed.

Interactive Geographies

States are authorities generally based on the control of territory and its inhabitants. Most states have claimed to control the behavior, the loyalty, and often the beliefs of those who resided within their boundaries. Land and sea gave states their most fundamental opportunities and set them basic challenges. High-density settlement required a settled and productive agriculture, whether based on rice, wheat grains, maize (corn), or root crops, such as manioc and potatoes. It usually entailed an ecology in which some of these grains supported animal husbandry, whether for meat, milk, or textiles. Animals in turn provided fertilizer that helped in grain production. High population densities existed in much of Europe, the Valley of Mexico (before devastating European diseases depopulated many of their settlements in the sixteenth century), South Asia, and East Asia. Societies that allocated large expanses of land for animals or left areas forested usually supported a lower density. Sparsely settled areas where hunter-gatherer populations still existed had the lowest density of all, excluding the great deserts and the arctic zones.

Historical transformation often involved an imperial dynamic between "crowded" and "empty" lands, sometimes within already existing empires, sometimes newly joined in imperial units. Earlier epochs had seen nomadic inhabitants of low-density areas (who probably felt the spurs of shortages more immediately than those in regions of settled agriculture and food distribution) conquering contiguous high-density regions. Peoples from the Asian highlands contested Han state expansion (the dynasty ended in 220 CE) and perhaps impelled confederations in western Eurasia against the Roman Empire (third to fifth centuries CE). Islamic Arabs surged across the Byzantine and Persian Middle East, North Africa, and Spain in the seventh century; again when the Mongols of Central Asia conquered the same territories and China itself in the eleventh century; the Turkic Timurids (the term derived from the name of their feared ruler, Timur or Tamerlane) subjugated Asia to the borders of China in the sixteenth while the Ottomans took Anatolia, the Balkans, Syria, Egypt, and Mesopotamia. These conquests were facilitated by the fact that the areas were all part of one land mass with grasslands enough to support horses.

By the end of the fifteenth century, high-density European populations were sending first soldier-adventurers and then settlers into remote territories. Sometimes these might appear as relatively empty lands. Muscovy reversed the Tatar invasions and expanded into the steppe lands of the Urals and farther east. In the New World the population dynamics changed as the Europeans arrived. The Spanish conquerors of Mesoamerica and the Andes quickly subjugated populations themselves precariously organized as recent imperial federations and soon depleted by European-borne diseases. The "discovery" and conquest of the Americas ultimately provided the Spanish, French, and British with vast territories of low population density. For the next two centuries, European conquerors sent enough soldier-adventurers, church organizers, and eventually settlers to exploit their acquisitions for their home states. But high-density populations did not simply flow out in some hydraulic surge to low-density areas. As Alfred Crosby famously described the Columbian exchange, the Europeans exported lethal pathogens that decimated native populations and imported New World crops—corn and later the potato—that allowed population growth at home. Kenneth Pomeranz has relatedly attributed the dynamism of the late eighteenth-century British economy vis-à-vis Chinese stagnation to the "shadow acreage" that British settlers overseas could occupy. North America became a British plantation, producing over time its great cash crop, sugar, then the cotton that was the basis of industrial development, and the grain that allowed it to shift its own growing labor force into commercial and later industrial activities.[16]

The dynamics of population growth changed the land itself. China's population had doubled from two hundred million to over four hundred million, and had pushed toward the north and west, although the Qing expansion into Mongolia or Xinjiang expanded the territory even beyond the newly settled regions. Western Europe's population surged ahead from the mid-eighteenth century on. In part this reflected the fluctuation in climate that ended the relatively cold interval sometimes called the little ice age of the seventeenth century and brought milder temperatures. There were fewer crop failures, fewer famines, more children reaching the age when they could themselves have children, whether in

CHARLES S. MAIER

households solemnized by marriage or not. In China yams, maize, and soybeans, intensively cultivated in the North, provided the expanded carbohydrate base for population growth, with the destabilizing ramifications discussed below. The innovations we associate with the agricultural revolution—new crops, legume rotations that restored the nitrogen content of the soil, ditching, fencing, enclosure—meant higher yields in Europe. Advocates of potato culture helped the crop's spread in Ireland, northern France, and the Low Countries, such that the caloric yield per acre soared. The advent of cotton and more textiles meant the spread of proto-industrialization—multiple households taking on spinning or weaving under the organization of district entrepreneurs—conducive again to families raising more children who in turn founded their own families at an earlier age, and favorable, too, to higher consumption of tea and sugar and thus a surge in colonial settlement and wealth.

These trends, however, meant a pressure on world forest reserves. Britain could live with depleted woodland as it turned toward coal for fuel and got its naval timber from New England and Scandinavia. Japan, which did not pursue the coal option, worked to reverse deforestation. China suffered vast depletion—as a consequence not of industrialization but of the population growth of the eighteenth and nineteenth centuries. The forests were "largely gone by 1820, almost wholly by 1860, but mainly as a result of peasant subsistence cutting, clearing for agriculture and for local sale as both wood and charcoal."[17] Mark Elvin, historian of Chinese ecology, suggests three waves of deforestation: the impact on northern woodlands in the five centuries BCE, a second transition of a millennium ago in the lower Yangzi and the west, and the severe deforestation since about 1700 with commercial timber operations and widespread theft of wood. Deforestation meant not only a shortage of timber but erosion of vast areas and silting of the rivers, including the Yellow River, whose course shifted drastically in the 1850s. The silting had already produced a major crisis in the early 1820s, for where the Yellow River crossed the Grand Canal, the erosion blocked the Canal and with it the provision of rice from the south for the capital. Woodland penury continued in many locations. "We have reached a moment in time when the mountains have been ruined. . . . Our locality is in a state of decomposition and decline," announced a stele of 1851 in the south of Hunan, ordaining that no more cutting could take place.[18] The Brazilian Atlantic rain forest was stripped by different dynamics. It fell prey first to the rapid expansion of coffee cultivation for export and later to the pressure of the immigrant population brought to man the industry. "There is no tool readier to hand than the matchbox for establishing a coffee plantation," has written the historian of the long assault on Brazil's ecology.[19]

The zones of contact where those pushing outward from crowded land met the sparser residents of "empty" land, the Anglo-Americans called the frontier. This frontier was different from what in Europe was called frontier, the borders between settled states. The frontier bred a characteristic "type"—the independent, sometimes quarrelsome and violent leader, who felt that the state on whose borders he settled should protect his acquisitive impulses but otherwise not interfere with his ambitions. This populist roughneck became a character type basic to national self-images: the gaucho or the cowboy or the self-made soldier-politician. Andrew Jackson, the truculent soldier of the southern frontier, anti-elitist American president, domineering over the American Indians, suspicious of the northeastern banking cliques, was one personification. The Argentine dictator Juan Manuel de Rosas, depicted by the Argentine statesman and writer Domingo Faustino Sarmiento, was another. For Sarmiento, the contest between the cultivated elite of the great port of Buenos Aires and the gauchos of the neighboring pampas was that between civilization and barbarism.[20] The cultivated residents of the Roman Rhine frontier and the court poets of Isfahan who had to deal with Mongols in the eleventh century and with Turkic Timurids two hundred years later must have felt the same way. The cinematic depiction of the frontier type continued through the twentieth century in countless Westerns, one of the major genres of popular narrative.

In the crowded lands, population increase and the division of labor that overseas commerce stimulated meant wealth and sometimes development. They were not the same. No traveler to Iberia or to the former Spanish and Portuguese colonies today can fail to note the incredible architecture that colonial wealth and commerce could bestow even on societies that did not generate self-sustained economic growth. Travel out of Oaxaca to the Mixtecan highlands north of the city and marvel at the monasteries and churches—alas, some now damaged by repeated earthquakes—built by the combined effort of Indian and Spanish artisans, that rise from the sparsely populated arid lands; or admire the richly adorned cathedral fronts, whether in the metropole or in the former colonies. Take note of the size and scale of public buildings and grand houses that crowded lands could indulge in. But recall, too, the immense social distance between the masses of population that toiled near subsistence and the grandees or corporations that enjoyed these possessions. Much of that wealth—whether in Europe, or Mughal India, or China—rested on accumulation at home, and the steady improvements of cultivation and willingness to reinvest that constituted what has been termed the "industrious revolution."[21] The surpluses that created modern armies, monuments, music, and art did not require colonies. Nonetheless, the juxtaposition of empty and crowded land created new opportunities for subjugation, on the one hand, and enrichment, on the other.

Imperial Tandems

Major geopolitical patterns were emerging from the juxtaposition of crowded and empty land and would dominate international politics and rivalry throughout the whole era of modern statehood. Empires constituted the state structures that optimally united the flows of commodities, labor, and cultural values between crowded and sparsely settled regions. Economists would say that these assemblages lowered the transaction costs of territorial governance that separate sovereign units would have entailed. This is not to claim that empires were founded for such a sophisticated motive—although Western mercantilist theory by the seventeenth and eighteenth century implicitly posited this premise—only that its logic made imperial expansion "rational," within limits. If we judge by outcomes, the logic of imperial power worked itself out best not by single empires in constant contention but by imperial combinations or tandems. Certainly it remains instructive to compare the particular institutions created by national empires for their own internal organization, such as the colonial assemblies encouraged by the British in North America versus the *audiencias* or royal investigative commissions that reviewed the administration of New Spain and Mexico.[22] But from the viewpoint of global rivalry, what proved decisive were ambitious coalitions for empire negotiated by a cosmopolitan elite across state lines on the basis of dynastic and cultural affinities and common adversaries. Such partnerships constituted in effect three or four imperial enterprises at any time. As of 1800 some had a past, others a future.

After the War of the Spanish Succession and the advent of the Bourbon dynastic line in Spain, French and Spanish interests tended to converge in opposition to British ambitions. In effect a Bourbon colonial realm and agenda emerged involving defense of French and Spanish overseas possessions against British sea power. But between the Treaty of Utrecht in 1714 and the revolts in Latin America a century later, the Bourbon New World empire collapsed in fits and starts. The so-called Bourbon family pact, based on the shared royal-family cousinage and the renewal of conflict in 1739, as the British Whig leader Robert Walpole lost his influence, led to a series of major contests in and for the far-flung peripheries outside Europe—Canada, Hispanic America and the Caribbean, and Bengal. In the mid-eighteenth century, the Franco-Spanish colonial coalition had lost the Canadian coast and Saint Lawrence Valley, but it still played a major role dominating the Great Lakes and the length of the Mississippi Valley, thence west to the California coast and south to Mexico, Central and South America, and half the Caribbean. This was a vast juxtaposition of imperial and European interests, potentially as formidable as the Anglo-American association. Later in the nineteenth century, Southern US slaveholders would from time to time be attracted as possible co-participants, but their bid for secession from the American union came fifty years too late, for by then the French had sacrificed their assets in the Mississippi Valley (as they had earlier in India and Canada), and the Spanish had lost their possessions to the Creoles of Latin America and did not have the means to recover them. Even Napoleon's effort to reconquer the half island of Haiti on behalf of French slave owners was defeated by yellow fever and inspired, if brutal, resistance by the communities of African descent. Bonaparte calculated, probably correctly, that in the long run the French could not retain the Mississippi and New Orleans against the United States' westward expansion, and by 1803 he sold the vast French colonial domain on the lower Mississippi to the American republic. What is more, his very effort to integrate Spain into his continental blockade of British trade by putting his own family candidates on the Spanish throne severed the remaining loyalties that the Spanish Creole elites (the colonists of European family descent but born in the New World) felt toward either the Bonapartist regime in Spain or the restored Bourbons after 1815. French and Spanish dreams of regaining their lost colonies after 1815 were preempted by implicit American and British agreement to prohibit any such moves—what Washington termed the Monroe Doctrine. A later French effort at Mexican conquest, taken while the United States was involved in civil war, also collapsed.[23]

Whereas the Franco-Spanish condominium of the New World was doomed, the Anglo-American co-imperial sphere was soon ascendant. Essentially a large English-speaking Anglo-American association of cotton and wheat growers on the trans-Appalachian as well as coastal lands of the former colonies was increasingly interlocked with the banking, investment, and industrial communities of the British islands. From the beginning of the American republic, both North American ruling groups shared a common language and a Protestant commitment (which more than matched the Bourbons' loyalty to the Roman Catholic Church). Both cooperated in prohibiting any Bourbon reconquest of Hispanic America. After American forces failed to conquer Canada, first in the American Revolution and then later in the War of 1812, Britain and the United States would reach a de facto compromise over Canada. The British would grant it autonomy, the United States would renounce annexation, and the Canadians would finally (by the 1850s) resolve to thrust toward the west and not link up with the country to their south. Such an implicit settlement meant that Anglo-American elites might overcome disputes to claim shared leadership in global politics—an emerging trend confirmed at several junctures before 1850 and then in the century after. By the 1890s the bonding of Anglo-American elites was being cemented in social as well as policy spheres, and this despite the mass of US immigrants who remained outside its charmed circle. Both powers would resist any German efforts to wrest economic influence in Latin America. Finally, from the early twentieth century on, both would effectively cooperate across the Pacific in trying to defend a faltering Chinese state against Japanese efforts to dominate East Asia. The Americans desisted on making any claims in the Indian Ocean area until 1945, while the British refrained from hindering the US claims in Oceania and accepted the US Open Door doctrine with respect to China's future. The Japanese, in fact, remained the most isolated of the imperial contenders in the Pacific, colliding as they did with Russians, Chinese, and eventually British and

Americans. Despite the energy of their efforts to develop the extensive colonies they did acquire—Taiwan and Korea and a growing presence in Manchuria even before its formal takeover in 1932—they never kept a tandem partner. Their later effort in the 1940s to lead an Asian movement against European colonizers recruited some collaborators but ultimately could not prevail against Anglo-American and Anglo-American-Russian resistance.

Anglo-American imperial cooperation rested on maritime strategy. There were potential alternative combinations based on landed domination—above all a possible German-Russian condominium resting on gradually winding down Austrian and Turkish possessions while precluding the reemergence of a Polish nation. German-Russian imperial association promised domination of Eurasia, as the professors of geopolitics during the second half of the nineteenth century would recognize. Dynastic interconnections, the large number of German bureaucrats that the Russian monarchs employed, the common interest in suppressing the independence of Eastern European Slavs, and the growing economic exchanges of the late nineteenth century would all bode well for this coalition between 1850 and 1890. But German politics was too fitful (and in fact too liberal, for all its military trappings) to follow this strategy consistently. Efforts at cooperation could not overcome the tendencies toward mutual suspicion, which would culminate in the two world wars of the twentieth century. The alternative for Germany of keeping the Austrian Empire viable while working with the Ottomans to dominate the Middle East would have rested on partners inherently too weakened by their nationalities problem. The Portuguese, the Dutch by the nineteenth century, and later the Belgians exploited their rich colonial holdings but claimed no larger role of global order, as had the Bourbons earlier and as did the Anglo-Americans or Germans.

No stable combination of Russo-German, Russo-Japanese, or German-Japanese imperium in Asia was easily envisaged. Even when Germans and Japanese shared much common ambition in the Second World War, they could not make their association, the so-called Axis, function in any more than a nominal sense. Between them lay Russia and China, empires too extensive to conquer despite the huge efforts that would be made between 1937 and 1945. There was, however, the potential for a Russo-Chinese combination of interests, which did in fact emerge to dominate inner Asia in the eighteenth century. By the mid-nineteenth century, China, like the Ottoman realms, would be simultaneously the protagonist of an old empire and the object of other empires' piece-by-piece (and function-by-function) colonization. But this had not been the case for the great Qing imperial structure of the late seventeenth and early eighteenth centuries—itself an imperial assemblage of diverse peoples run by a non-Chinese dynasty. From the close of the seventeenth century the Qing negotiated with Russia a frontier settlement that allowed them in effect to constitute an imperial tandem to finally suppress the Zunghar nomadic state in Mongolia and decimate its population by the late 1750s. The subsequent expansionist campaign west to secure the "new dominion" of Xinjiang added a huge territory, but one that remained beset by continuing ethnic and religious resistance to Beijing. The Russians would suppress their "nomads" a century later but face continuing resistance in the Caucasus territories that abutted the weaker Persian and Ottoman states.[24] Empires the world over proved most successful when they could operate as dyads.

Commodification of the Countryside

The immense turbulence of the first half of the nineteenth century did not require the impact of the Industrial Revolution. That development played a large role in some societies. But concentrations of factory labor were still rare outside zones of Western Europe and the northern United States before 1850. The larger reservoirs of unrest lay on the land. Perhaps 75 percent of the world's active population worked the land or rendered services that supported those who farmed directly. The share went from about a third of the population in the England of 1800 to perhaps 70 percent in eastern and southern Europe and probably higher in Asia and Africa.[25] It is customary to think of agricultural communities as traditionalist and quiescent. But the burden of taxes and rents and labor services had ignited frequent protests, most confined to one village or another, but sometimes sweeping up large areas in frightening rebellions. The century or so after 1750 or 1760 was to add a further cause for unrest as market relationships invaded the countryside. Land and labor, fundamental factors of world production, hitherto locked into customary or legally stipulated relations, would become far freer to be bought and sold as ordinary commodities. Peasants who had been bound to a village or a landlord could depart for other villages or towns. Rural estates, controlled for generations by a given family or religious foundation, might be seized by state authorities and auctioned off to a new owner. They were to be swept into the flux of the market, and in the process would shake up state and society.

Market relationships were not, of course, the only transformative agent in play. But they were the newest (and for the moment, at least, perhaps the strongest) among three basic forces that together undermined the structures of the premodern world and prepared for the new regime of modern statehood. Warfare and its inexorable appetite for higher taxes and military modernization continued to exert the pressure it had since the seventeenth century when Jean Bodin had called money the sinews of war. And as a countervailing pressure, religious revivalism sometimes emerged as a manifestation of communal resistance to change, what E. P. Thompson called the "chiliasm of despair."²⁶ Perhaps it is more accurate to say that new religious movements represented an alternative impulse to change—one that radically denied fulfillment through the market, although in some cases, such as the American Latter-day Saints, market skills were annexed to communal and not individualist ends. Commodification of the countryside, the state's search for greater penetration of society to meet the demands of modern war, and religious evangelization would interact in the transition to modern state politics.

Such processes played themselves out within a triangular framework constituted by laboring families on one side, by landlords and their agents on another, and by representatives of the state on the third. The state varied in its role. Peasants might encounter its agents as oppressive tax collectors or dreaded army recruiters. But the state also had an interest in defending hard-pressed peasants against rapacious landlords. The rights of the landlords themselves emanated from different principles, and the revenues they collected were based on different sorts of claims. As "owners" or as stable leaseholders, landlords could collect rents from peasants to whom they let out the land, whether on an individual basis or as residents of a village community. As members of a privileged, legally defined "estate" *(état, Stand)*—that is, a legally defined social stratum with defined tax privileges and conveying in some cases an aristocratic title, and the right to representation in local or national assemblies consulted by the monarch—landholders could claim payments and services by virtue of their inscribed legal status as well as rents from the tenants on their land: an arrangement that Western lawyers often termed feudal. Sometimes these landlords—or recognized local headmen, even if not proprietors—were given the right to collect payments on behalf of the state as well. They became local tax collectors (*zamindars* in Indian agriculture), or even regional tax "farmers" for large areas, being assigned a quota they had to pass on to the state but allowed to collect whatever the market or custom might bear. In some societies, including Britain and Prussia, landlords retained the right to act as local judges in civil and minor criminal cases until the 1870s. In some cases they had the duty of conscripting peasants for military levies, as the Prussian state imposed until 1815. With each layer of duty came new honorific status and "offices" and claims for financial compensation. Over the centuries, "deference" of tenants toward landlords, expressed by gestures of submission, had also become integral to the texture of rural life. In times of hardship or under the influence of charismatic concepts of equality, agrarian subjects might abandon deference for direct efforts to destroy hierarchies they had earlier lived with. Such rebellions, elemental and violent, meant frightening times, and when they were finally suppressed, those in charge usually administered the dismemberment, torture, and executions needed to "teach a lesson."

Mass rebellion seemed infrequent enough and the privileges of aristocratic office sufficiently desirable to attract the wealthy and ambitious. A major attraction was that they often brought the right to be transmitted by inheritance to one or more children. Crucial to the system was the long-term embeddedness of many public functions in the land, specifically in the role of landlords. Thus the laboring peasantry, the class or estate of landowners—who had pretensions to grander living in imposing houses with servants—and the agents of the state, which needed taxes for military expenses, interest payments, display, and public projects, all vied for a share of the earth's yield in a triangular contest. But there were often religious functionaries who also had the right, as officers of great or small churches or monastic communities, to claim a share of rents as landed proprietors along with state-sanctioned taxes (tithes). Monastic organizations were numerous and strong in Roman Catholic countries, in the Orthodox church of Russia, and among Buddhist communities in Southeast Asia, Japan, and China. In the Islamic lands of the Ottoman Empire, there were some rural monastic communities, but also urban religious communities supported by generations of pious gifts as "endowments" or *waqfs*.

There were innumerable variants and complications even in small areas. No automatic correlation made village communities or those benefiting from commercial and market relations in the countryside into revolutionaries. Explanations that serve for one episode sometimes fail for others. Many studies have sought to account for the divergent political choices of adjacent regions in France. William Taylor has found that in the Mexican war of independence Oaxacan Indians engaged in numerous village protests and uprisings but generated no overall revolutionary movement until the southwestern peasant war of the early 1840s—a protest against commercial agriculture exploited by rival elite leaders. To the north, however, Jalisco peasants, whose village bonds were more frayed and their clergy new arrivals, joined in the early war for independence.[27]

Still, we can attempt to sort out the major patterns of agricultural life and labor. Especially in upland communities or frontier zones where population was sparser, or among tribal confederations, the supervisory community remained weak or perhaps nonexistent and freehold farmers produced for their own subsistence and/or brought their goods directly to market and retained the proceeds. This situation pertained in parts of western and northern Europe and North America. The families involved retained legal independence although they might live in grinding poverty and sometimes indebtedness. At the opposite end of the legal structure, usually in areas of dense lowland population, landlords dealt with peasant labor, sometimes as tenants but also as hired labor (or even legally coerced labor) who lived in cottages grouped apart from fields (though they might retain small garden and livestock plots). This sort of agrarian enterprise was often described as a *latifundia* (a term inherited from Roman antiquity); and in North America it tended to become known as plantations. Plantations specialized in crops that benefited from "gang" labor—whether the arduous cultivation of sugar cane in Brazil and the Caribbean or cotton and tobacco in the mainland of the American South. Mediterranean agriculture retained such factory-like agricultural enterprises, which would become more important in the late nineteenth century as land reclamation projects and commercial agriculture increased in significance. The Dutch and the French organized such enterprises for the cultivation of Javanese sugar and Vietnamese rubber.

Such plantation laborers were usually deemed the lowest in status, especially when they were racially segregated, as in the case of black slavery. For about two centuries slaves had been captured in the interior of Africa, herded to the coasts, then forcibly transported in overcrowded, sweltering ships from Africa to the Americas. By the mid-nineteenth century, perhaps ten to twelve million Africans had been transported and reproduced and formed an absolutely basic constituent of the economic interchange between Europe, the Americas, and Africa. The transoceanic slave trade was suppressed in 1808 in the United States by the terms of a compromise at the time of the Constitutional Convention. The French Jacobins abolished slavery in French colonies in 1794, although Napoleon reinstated it. The British abolished the trade throughout their domains in 1807, and the condition of slavery itself in 1832–1833. Still, for slaves "bred" in captivity, the status continued until 1863–1865 in the United States, 1887 in Cuba, and 1889 in Brazil. The Mexican government sold some captured Mayan rebels into Cuban slavery as late as the 1860s; slavelike labor conditions persisted in the mines of the Belgian Congo and elsewhere in Africa, and in the nitrate and copper mines of the Andes, long after formal abolition. Slaves had no legal rights against their owners in court (although a slave supposedly could not be put to death if he did not take up arms or commit ordinary crimes). Slaves could be beaten (as could Eastern European serfs), often at will, their marriages were not given legal status, and, most disabling, the status was deemed hereditary, to be removed only by legal manumission. The fact that the slaves of the New World were defined as distinct according to racial features rendered them particularly tainted, and the racial disabilities were legally enshrined in the United States and South Africa (as were de facto systems for preserving subjection) long after inherited legal bondage formally ended.

Most agrarian laboring families occupied an intermediate status between freehold independence and outright slavery. In areas where slavery had not been sanctioned (as in most of colonial Mexico, where the Spanish had granted *encomiendas* or tracts of land together with their Indian population) or later abolished (as in the United States), peasants could slip into such total dependence on landlords for their seeds and housing that they became bound de facto by their recycled debts. In Europe east of the Elbe River and in Russia, peasants had been reduced to serfdom in the sixteenth and seventeenth centuries; this condition of legal inherited bondage was not alleviated or dissolved until varying points between the 1770s and 1860s. Serfs needed landlords' permission to leave their villages or to marry, and often had to work a varying number of days per week on the lands that their lords farmed directly. Serfs in some locations in Slavic Europe, in particular, could be transferred from one owner to another, whether for purchase or to settle debts, although in the German areas they were usually seen as an appurtenance of the estate to be transferred along with the land. In contrast to slaves, serfs retained higher legal status, including recognition of marriage; their families could not be broken up by landlords. Through the course of the first half of the nineteenth century (and in some areas after 1850), both slavery and serfdom would be eliminated. Traditionalist landlords fought bitterly against the waves of emancipation, but in fact would find that market pressures and control of credit provided most of the enforcement mechanisms they required to retain a compliant labor force.[28]

Crucial to this "old regime" was not just the superiority of the landlords, but the village structure and the claims on the land itself. Emancipation did not usually bring a transfer of ownership to the former slaves or serfs. The idea of endowing each ex-slave family head in the American South with "forty acres and a mule" was never enacted; in Prussia emancipated peasants could claim land only if their assets fell above a certain threshold, and within a generation or two many had fallen into the status of hired hands. In Russia, former serfs would be taxed to redeem the bonds given to landlords for compensation, while the village communes retained control of the land. For better or worse, the village provided a corporate existence: its elders could periodically redivide the farmland among different families, and it retained control of a common pasturage or woodland. We have learned that like a modern trade union, the village could confront a landlord with enough collective strength to keep rents and services tolerable.[29] Elsewhere, including Japan and China, it provided a structure that was often more disciplinary than protective. It stood as an enforcement mechanism in a hierarchy of duties and expectations. Villages could control land, allocate labor, enforce obedience—but they did not own land.

Outright ownership, as envisaged under ancient Roman law or British "freehold" or today's American home ownership, thus remained an alien idea across much of the globe. Land went with people—whether organized in families or villages—and people with land. In Russia estates were graded by the number of attached peasants or "souls." In some societies, especially where a conquering or formally invested sovereign claimed supreme power, ownership was theoretically retained by the conquering sovereign, as in the Ottoman Empire, and rights of "use" (usufruct or the old feudal notion of *dominium utile*) alone were ceded. In fact, after a generation or two it would become almost impossible to reclaim effective control, although programs of national "restoration" might try to reinstitute this claim.

Land ceded by sovereigns or pious donors to monasteries passed to an institution from which it could not easily be reclaimed—until the governments of the sixteenth century in Britain, or the eighteenth and nineteenth centuries in Roman Catholic states. Governments, it was understood, could confiscate, or at least compel sale to the state. Possession of land by charter conferred status rights, but also restricted sale, often to owners who possessed the same "noble" qualifications. This made it hard to hypothecate, or use as collateral for a mortgage loan, and was thus seen as a disadvantage. Such restrictions on marketability or hypothecation were termed entail, and they became less a protection for magnates than a burden. Still, the privileges over control of land that were inherited from feudalism determined the horizontal layering of estatist society and what in Europe was termed the Old Regime.

In some tribal societies, the concept of ownership as Europeans conceived it did not really exist. Land was plentiful, its cultivators—who used it for pasturage and hunting as well as agriculture—scarce, and the idea of exclusive possession (with its rights to sell or bequeath) played no role because use seemed guaranteed. One must be cautious about ascribing such a pastoral or collective mentality: many traditional societies constructed institutional equivalents to family ownership and certainly to tribal custody. White colonizers moved to purchase these residual rights for insignificant sums and sometimes, as in Australia, to claim that the land was *terra nullius* (unclaimed) and theirs for the taking or by right of conquest—modes of expropriation that would exert a devastating impact in the American, Australian, African, and Indonesian settlements. Those who spoke for taking possession pointed to the poverty of collectivist societies. "Several nations of the Americas," John Locke had written, "are rich in Land, and poor in all the Comforts of Life . . . for want of improving [the materials of Plenty] by labour, have not one hundredth part of the Conveniences we enjoy: And a King of a large fruitful Territory there feeds, lodges, and is clad worse than a day Labourer in England."[30] Thus possession, vendibility, tax burdens, and labor claims were all woven together in a complex tapestry of honorific, economic, and political claims. Untwisting the fabric was the work of modernization—the great process of legal and economic change from traditional societies across the globe to their modern successors. Even in China, where family claims on land remained strong, the eighteenth century strengthened the idea of definitive sales and contracts retained importance.[31]

This process added immensely to the unrest that already was inherent in the countryside's economy of scarcity. Peasants and magnates, and indirectly rulers and city dwellers, all depended on the physical extraction of food from the countryside. It was natural enough that the pressures of population increase, the vicissitudes of weather and harvest, and the ravages of disease would produce conflict. Villages living on the margins of subsistence could be provoked by rigorous tax collection and bad harvests, and their discontents could be rendered ideological by popular millenarian religious doctrines. Prosperous peasants might be angered by efforts to tighten up rules that had grown softer over time. Rising prices worked to the advantage of the party that marketed the harvest. If the peasant paid relatively fixed money rents but could bring grain or rice to market on his own, then the landlord and the state would be squeezed in an era of inflation. If the landlord collected his rents in kind, then he benefited from inflationary trends. Peasant revolts, usually localized but occasionally coalescing into broad protest movements, were a frequent seasoning of rural life.

But add to these latent tensions in the years from 1750 to 1860 a new transnational impulse: the penetration of rural land and labor relations by market forces, that is, the commodification of the countryside. Much of the globe's arable land had been farmed in one or another fabric of collective relationships or at least under arrangements that guaranteed tenure and fixed terms of labor and deference. Public authorities had a role: they protected landlords against major protest, raked off shares of harvest proceeds, might call on manpower for military uses. But states needed money. Eighteenth-century war was expensive and endemic. Current ideas among reformist European philosophers and statesmen— above all those who deemed themselves Physiocrats—envisaged that dissolving all the restrictions on the market for land and its crops could significantly increase national wealth. The fruitfulness of land, claimed the Physiocrats, was the ultimate source of society's wealth or surplus. One of their major theoreticians, François Quesnay, had devised a table that showed the cycle of production. Agriculture brought to market yielded more than was spent by the peasants and middlemen who dealt with it. On the basis of that surplus landlords received their rents and the urban sector its payments for its goods and services. From these continuing dividends created by agriculture would be built the roads, harbors, palaces, all the nonagricultural products that a society consumed. Agriculture paid for government and the military and private incomes.

The key to the process was encouraging those who owned land and sowed it to expand their production. That meant creating a broader class of owner-entrepreneurs who would respond to market incentives. It also suggested, in contrast to centuries of efforts to keep grain prices down for fear of public unrest, that the traditional price controls be suspended so that higher prices would entice producers into producing more. Of course, in the eighteenth century, where crops could fail and the harvest might be precarious, higher prices could mean shortages, inflation, urban riots, and unrest. This had been the result of the freeing of grain prices in France and Spain in 1764–1765, and the monarchs retreated. Still the basic insight was amazingly influential.

Americans think of Physiocracy as a curious adulation of the soil held by intellectuals who had visions of agrarian republics. But in fact the underlying insights were broadly influential. The British governor of Bengal, the monarchs of the Iberian states and their Latin American colonies, the reform-minded ministers of the Italian states, whether Austrian-governed Lombardy in the north or prosperous Tuscany or Bourbon Naples and Sicily, all agreed on the major outlines of reform. Transform peasants from downtrodden ignorant workers in thrall to landlords, priests, and religious foundations into an agricultural middle class. Remove the personal restrictions that bound peasants to their village and their owners: let them marry and migrate and contract at will; remove the inherited stigmata of serfdom and slavery, and they would become a class of sturdy yeomen producers. Increase the output of grain, of olives, of wine, of forests, or rice and silk in Japan, tea in India. Invest in agrarian infrastructure—canals, roads, harbors—and in improved techniques of cultivation. Consolidate the patchwork of taxes and spread the burden to the landlords or nobility, who were often exempt, so that it might be lowered overall. Free grain prices to encourage higher production. Remove the impediments to free purchase, sale, and mortgaging of land, and wrest land from churches and abbeys and village communes.

But the concept did not work out so easily. In the late 1760s, following decades of criticism of Roman Catholic institutions, the monarchs of Spain and Portugal decided that they could expropriate the extensive lands of the Jesuit order held in Iberia and in Latin America. As in most such auction procedures, the beneficiaries were not poor peasants but substantial proprietors who could participate in the market. The French revolutionary peasants who freed their holdings from the remaining rents, *corvées,* and occasional labor exactions that still persisted (what French lawyers called feudalism) perhaps fared the best. In most places—whether Central Europe, Ireland, Iberia, and Italy, eventually the American South—the new peasant proprietors fell into the snare of growing indebtedness. The British may have dreamed of awakening the torpid villages of Bengal and making the agrarian middle classes into gentry-like farmers and agents of indirect rule. Their governors thus proposed a "permanent settlement," or freezing of the taxes on agriculture that would supposedly benefit farmers who could turn toward commercial agriculture without fearing tax hikes. They ended up, however, tending to reinforce the power of the tax farmers *(zamindars)* and the reduction of the peasants *(ryots)* from whom they collected rents and taxes into further dependency and poverty.

Physiocracy was only the most formalized version of the underlying trend, which saw the growing commodification of land and the labor that worked it. All the traditional restraints on a pervasive market mentality, whether religious teachings, feudal privileges, the inscribed status of nobles or churches, or the customary village control of common lands, were under pressure. Population growth, the cost of military and colonial competition, and the burdens of alleviating poverty ratcheted up the demands for extracting resources and money from the countryside. Economic development, not yet labeled as such, became a major preoccupation in China, the reform-minded semiautonomous feudal domains or *han* of Japan (such as Tosa), the lands of the East India Company (EIC), the Ottoman Empire, as well as the reformist monarchies of Maria Theresa's Austria and Archduke Leopold's Tuscany, Frederick the Great's Prussia, the Spain of

Charles III, Turgot's France, and throughout the global state system. But the result was agrarian unrest, and there was a cluster of major rural revolts in the 1770s and 1780s: the great Pugachev rebellion in Russia in 1773–1775, the Bohemian revolts in the same period, the French upheaval of 1789 once it spread to the countryside—and outside Europe, the 1780 Inca uprising led by Túpac Amaru II in the viceroyalty of Spanish Peru, and from 1796 the White Lotus rebellion in China.[32]

These diverse upheavals cannot be ascribed solely to commodification or inflationary pressures, although population and markets increased. A great deal depended upon the state of harvests from year to year and the state's pressure to collect taxes and ultimately the tactics it used to assuage grievances or to repress disorder. It would certainly be too simple to ascribe the two great Western political transformations of the late eighteenth century—the American independence movement and formation of a constitutional republic (1775–1787), and the French Revolutions of 1789–1799—to rural turbulence. For even as the idea of a liberal market percolated in the countryside, the accompanying concepts of human rights and participation in government undermined aristocratic and monarchical political claims. Despite such voices for conciliation of the North American colonies as Edmund Burke, George III and his ministers insisted on preserving the decisive rights to raise money and limit colonial voices in government, and the resulting demonstrations and efforts at repression escalated into forcible resistance, thereby provoking claims for the colonies' assumption of independent statehood. As a struggle for independent statehood in a society of middling incomes, class division was not a major theme. Modest family farmers in the interior of the respective colonies often felt resentments at wealthier coastal planters or urban merchants, and in the inland South might align with British forces. Urban concentrations, however, were relatively small, and local opinion leaders, including slaveholders, seized the leadership of the movement and inscribed its claims in traditional terms of English constitutionalism. British efforts to raise slave uprisings limited American slavery opponents from acting more decisively.

French-speaking societies were not so immunized. The sequence of late eighteenth-century fiscal crises and constitutional conflicts led in the late 1780s and 1790s to the astonishing collapse of the French monarchy, and as the European states became involved in this great upheaval, the *gens de couleur* in Haiti and the Creole elites of Mexico and Spanish America decided to follow the same path. Given the great social inequalities in French society, the tax immunities enjoyed by its class of hereditary nobility, and the claims of the French church in the countryside, a political upheaval in that populous country (twenty-five million versus the Americans' four million) was bound to target the privileges accruing to land in the estatist structure of the Old Regime.

Great revolutions and sometimes minor ones as well become vortices that suck in outside rival powers even as they radiate principles of upheaval abroad; and this was true of the American and the French. The French armies (Republican after 1792) who sought to establish an international coalition of like-minded revolutionaries abroad in the Austrian Netherlands (Belgium), the Rhineland territories of the Holy Roman Empire, Switzerland, and the Italian kingdoms, ended up playing on all the tensions that were built into the estatist societies of the late eighteenth century. The French armies took advantage of these tensions, and forced victories that brought their ideological allies to power in the late 1790s. But in some of the societies the new revolutionaries faced opposition not only from the old rulers allied with the anti-French coalition (British, Austrian, Prussian, and fitfully the Russians), but peasant masses who were the uneasy victims of the Physiocratic transformations described above. They helped sweep away the early collaborationist republics in Italy and, during the Bonapartist phase of French expansion a decade later, often joined the indigenous forces opposing the French occupation of Spain. The reimplantation of the revolution abroad step by step after 1801—no longer under the hodgepodge of local Jacobin radicals, but by middle-class or aristocratic reformers working under Napoleon's rationalization of fragmented German and Italian territories—had more enduring effects. The recruits to this cause were often reformers, who wanted to rationalize fiscal burdens, mobilize clerical wealth, modernize law codes, and use French patronage to reorganize their own territories by absorbing all the manifold subordinate jurisdictions—a program that the emperor of the French pushed through from 1803 to 1806, largely at the cost of the Habsburg traditionalist claims. When Prussia resisted and was disastrously defeated in 1806, its aristocratic bureaucrats decided to emulate similar reforms such as formal abolition of serfdom and thereafter military conscription.

. . .

Thus by 1810, the historian can discern throughout Europe and the Americas the outlines of the next generation's transnational alignment of social forces and political programs. They included, first, a conservative cohort of dispossessed or threatened aristocrats aligned with landed church officials—still dominant in Britain, Austria, and among the French exiles—who would recover partial and temporary power after 1815; and, second, a reformist phalanx of leaders who sympathized with the French reforms and were willing to administer Napoleon's European satellites and would establish themselves after 1815 as a more liberal alternative to the Restoration governments. Many of these benefited from the sale of church properties that the French secularized and auctioned off—more to commercially minded bourgeois who formed corporations to buy them than to aspiring peasants.[33] Similar acquisitions, which purchasers could finance by government loans, became available to the Mexican men of property as the revolutionary and then successive governments sold off monastic and Holy Office properties.[34] On the far left the small groups of republican revolutionaries who had supported the Jacobin republic remained in the political wilderness. They comprised preeminently literary intellectuals and political amateurs throughout Western Europe (including some in Britain) and the Americas.

Finally, there were masses of peasants who felt threatened by rural capitalism and resented the attacks on the Catholic Church in the countryside. The Church, after all, at least as represented in the parishes and monastic settlements, was the institution par excellence that resisted the market, baptized their children, knit together their families in marriage, and offered hope as they buried their parents and, alas too often, children. Those peasants who remained religiously loyal (many did not, of course) sustained the anti-French guerrilla forces in occupied Spain and southern Italy and remained pro-Bourbon and pro-clerical and hostile to any whiffs of French-inspired elite reform. After the restoration of the Spanish Bourbons, the aging painter Goya would depict them as superstitious, brooding, ignorant Catholic masses. The proponents of agrarian reforms and the emancipation of landed society from its traditional hierarchies ignored this rural populism at their peril. The Church remained a major strand of peasant protest and revolution deep into the twentieth century, sustaining Catholic guerrillas in Spain and Mexico and peasant mobilization in Russia, China, and Japan.[35]

How these groups might combine or quarrel, and which might prevail, often depended upon the military outcomes—although these in turn reflected the forces that revolutionary principles awakened. Where the French armies conquered, political reorganization usually followed. Russia and Britain remained outside the reach of French armies and thus under traditional rule, which in the latter country meant the government of an oligarchical parliament—a regime that the British sought to institute in Sicily, which they occupied while Napoleonic forces held mainland Italy. As of 1815, when the twenty-five-year-long warfare and economic turmoil provoked by revolutionary France and its contagious principles were finally extinguished, revolutionary claims appeared defeated, but like some dormant volcano they still rumbled under the surface of the Restoration. Certainly they did not triumph. The Bourbon monarchs returned to France (to be succeeded by their Orleanist cousins from 1830 to 1848), but in both cases under regimes that gave a role to an elite drawn from finance, industry, engineering, and the educational establishment. These new forces counted for more than they ever had before, as technological change began visibly to transform the economies and mentalities of the literate classes in France, Belgium, the German states, and Lombardy by the 1830s and 1840s. The political question in the West was whether the traditions of the countryside and its rural hierarchies could keep these new forces in check.

The upshot was more complex, in that rural hierarchies were themselves not just barriers to change but its very agents. As a recent revisionist study of Prussian rural life suggests, "over the centuries the two parties, manor and village, approached one another as combatants, probing for weaknesses and opportunities for gain, now accepting truces, now breaking them to pursue strategic advantages with the court bailiff's lash, at the strike front, or on the judicial battlefield." Nonetheless, in all their contention they acted together as agents of change. "Estate owners and landed villagers need rethinking as market producers open to the nineteenth and early twentieth centuries' technological, material, and political opportunities."[36] However, they also were undermining the old rural order. The stability that had rested on legal estates and patterns of deference and the teachings of religion would have to be reestablished, if at all, by the ligaments of rural capitalism—the pressure of rents and debts and credits. It helped that aristocrats would be flanked by new ambitious peasant proprietors with a stake in rural order.

Historians recognize the Congress of Vienna, which concluded peace after the Napoleonic wars, as a fundamental settlement among nations. The statesmen at Vienna, however, also believed that an enduring peace required a settlement *within* each country that precluded a rekindling of revolutionary energy. Just as Woodrow Wilson would later insist that peace rested on liberal democratic regimes, the Vienna leaders took for granted that it required a conservative social base. They were willing to accept monarchs whom Napoleon had put in place in Sweden and initially in Naples but wanted to reinforce the rural hierarchies of the old regime and guarantee the stability of the countryside. They left behind a structure of periodic consultations that could coordinate transnational counterrevolutionary intervention as well as curb threats to peace, the so-called Congress System. For the restored French Bourbons the Vienna settlement meant accepting a constitution and recognizing that the distribution of land by the intervening revolutionary regime would not be reversed. However, even the moderate Vienna program was soon in shambles. The domestic restoration was breaking down by the 1830s and 1840s. International arrangements collapsed in the 1850s and 1860s. Rick burning in Britain; peasant organization in Ireland; agricultural protest on the continent; that harbinger of discontent, anti-Semitic agitation in Germany; and, outside Europe, creole revolutions throughout Latin America, peasant protests in Japan, and a huge insurrection in China, would characterize the stormy decades from the 1820s into the 1850s. The rhetoric of change could be that of liberal rights and equality; it also could be millenarian, the expression of religious protest. Each society played out these conflicts with different ideological traditions and hierarchical structures, but giving impetus to all of them was the great tension produced by the advent of market transactions for land and of the labor on the land.

The implications were contradictory: yes, expand the market energies of the countryside, mobilize the capacity for wealth; but stifle the unrest that was likely to occur. This is why the early nineteenth century was so punctuated by agricultural unrest. On the one hand, the encroaching market principles undermined the old claims of aristocratic supremacy and the sacramental legitimacy of church and religion. On the other, the actual economic results seemed to bring hard times to the countryside as well as the emerging industrial cities. In the long run the Physiocratic mechanisms might encourage surplus and wealth, but a painful transition of several decades lay in between. Faced with the turmoil, the elite faced a stark alternative. Either they might rule by repression and force (this was the stance that English Tories, frightened by the French Revolution, sought to impose from the trials of alleged "Jacobins" in the 1790s through the "Peterloo massacre" of 1819, when soldiers fired on a crowd of demonstrators in Manchester); or, alternatively, they might seek to hasten the triumph of the market and commodification. This latter course constituted the Liberal program that prevailed after the elections of 1830 and 1832, after the narrow British political class absorbed the lesson of the 1830 revolution across the English Channel and passed the Reform Act of 1832, which expanded the suffrage to the substantial middle classes and redistricted Parliament to accommodate new industrial cities.

Markets, Reforms, Resistance

The rise of British liberalism meant far more than a political transition in an island of twelve million. Perhaps to an even greater degree than the principles and armies of revolutionary France, its ramifications were to be felt worldwide. No friends of revolution, the Tory ministries of the 1820s were still resolved to block any Franco-Spanish reconquest of their rebellious colonies in the Caribbean. In 1807 Britain abolished the transport of slaves on its own ships and after the end of the Napoleonic Wars patrolled West African waters to intercept slave traders. Abolition of slavery itself in British colonies followed in 1833, although the voracious demand of English cotton mills kept the institution continuously profitable in the southern United States. British intervention required a global naval presence, although its financial capacity for underwriting foreign loans would also serve as a continuing asset. Britain's long-serving Whig foreign secretary and later prime minister Lord Palmerston (Henry John Temple), vigorous spokesman for his nation's liberalism, helped midwife a peaceful secession of Belgium from Holland, and indirectly encouraged the Turkish reforms of the mid-nineteenth century. The British adherence to market principles—that is, its insistence on the right of the EIC to sell opium in China and to protect the legal rights of brawling sailors—undermined the Confucian order, as China's resistance resulted in a clamorous military defeat in 1842.

By 1846 the political mobilization that led to abolition of the protective tariff on grain confirmed the country's commitment to industry, international finance, and free trade. This so-called repeal of the Corn Laws was among the most decisive legal affirmations of early nineteenth-century social change. It confirmed Britain's industrial vocation—the calculation of the Whigs that by letting wheat prices sink for a hungry working class (and indirectly the wages that workers needed to pay their food budgets), they would do better than putting tariffs on textile competitors and keeping the prices of industry high. Simply put, there were no major competitors for British or third-country markets. The industrial cities grew; paradoxically the sentimental affection for a rural Britain of pastoral villages also increased.

British loans would support the first generation of independent state leaders in Latin America after the Napoleonic wars and the wars for independence from 1810 to 1825 threw the finances of New Spain, including Mexico, into disarray. The breakdown of Bourbon fiscal systems (which remained efficient in the late eighteenth century far longer than often maintained) and the recourse to local finances advanced the federalist options supported by Latin American liberals but sparked endemic conflicts as well. The new republics and the empire of Brazil depended on British loans and investments. Until the 1850s the relative weakness of the international economy weakened the new states and aggravated the conflicts within them and between them. New loans, taxes, discounted state salaries, and the tendency to localize fiscal systems characterized the threshold of independence.[37] We can construe the financial and market connections between Europe and the Americas and Asia as an early form of what 1970s commentators would call interdependence—what today's analysts call globalization. Perhaps most important, if indirect, was the impact of these early financial and commercial currents on the Ottoman Empire, India, and China. These huge, conglomerate societies already faced deep internal crises, which the interventions of foreign powers only magnified. Whereas French concepts of citizenship backed by military interventions from 1792 to 1815 had forced the harsh choice of resistance or subservience, the British connections after 1815 were weaving a fabric of markets and credits that compelled local elites either to develop liberal reform or to resist at the price of disabling backwardness.

In the Middle East the Ottoman Empire descended into intensified crisis. Ottoman state and society had certain traits that emerged both from its multinational imperial legacy—its responsibility for the European Balkans in the north and west, Arab communities in the southeast, Anatolian Turkish populations threatened by Russian expansion, and religious and ethnic minorities organized into partially self-governing communities in the major cities and the coastal regions—and from its ambitions as an encompassing Muslim state. In the outlying regions of the empire the strength of local notables and their clienteles generated long-term feuds that were impossible to discipline. The practice of administration amounted to divide and rule (and protect) the multifarious identities within the realm. The state had no secure monopoly of violence, often resorting to irregular troops and private forces to keep order.[38] The eighteenth century had brought almost continual warfare and net renunciation of territories, against Habsburgs and Venetians in the west, Persians to the east, Russians to the north.

Selim III, who ruled from 1789 until deposed and executed in 1807/1808, understood the need for reforms as he confronted Russian military threats and watched Europe plunged into new, seemingly total warfare. In theory the army with its two branches—the cavalry of the frontier whose officers were supported by landed fiefs and the garrisoned army of the capital, the Janissaries, who were the sultan's personal force—was totally at odds with the idea of a citizen army that the French Revolution had made so central. What united army and society were the tax obligations of the subjects, which in turn rested upon their well-being within a framework of justice and Islamic law (shari'a) that the sultan had also to guarantee. Over the centuries the societal framework had calcified into a collection of privileged groups defending their privileges, whether urban guilds, local notables, or waqfs. Selim planned a "New Order" based on a new army, including Western uniforms, and a more efficient tax system, but the reforms threatened, on the one hand, the quasi-feudal notables *(ayan)* who during the previous centuries had entrenched themselves as de facto rulers of the countryside and, on the other hand, the privileged Janissaries of the capital, who originally, centuries earlier, had been recruited from conscripting dragnets among the Balkan Christian populations.[39]

Supported by the conservative Muslim judiciary and fomenting rioting in Constantinople, the Janissaries deposed and executed the sultan and those identified with the New Order. In turn they provoked the Balkan *ayan* to march on the capital, kill about a thousand of the opposition, and install a new sultan, Mahmud II, who was compelled to sign a covenant of union that limited his power and that of the viziers. The compromise did not last long. The sultan turned to limit *ayan* ascendancy, then finally moved against the obstreperous Janissaries in 1826, murdering them en masse and burning their barracks. But his regime faced a Greek revolt supported by Western public opinion, then the Russian destruction of the sultan's Black Sea fleet in 1827 and a confrontation with the ambitious reform pasha of Egypt, Muhammad Ali, in the next decade.

Born in what is today Greek territory as the son of an Albanian in the service of the Ottomans, Muhammad Ali would attempt to bring Egypt into the nineteenth century, destroying the Mamluk military caste, expanding irrigation canals, establishing it as a major cotton-growing territory, and reforming its fiscal system and military. He was commissioned by the sultan to quell the advance of the Arabian Ibn Saud dynasty, adherents of the austere Islamic movement, Wahhabism, that had taken hold in the Arabian hinterland. After the Saudis had taken the Holy Cities and interrupted the Hajj or annual pilgrimage routes from Damascus in 1803, Constantinople enlisted its dynamic Egyptian governor to push them back. Although Muhammad Ali retained too great a sense of Ottoman loyalty to challenge the empire or even seize the throne, Constantinople was naturally leery of his power and freedom of action even as they called on him to help suppress the Greek rebellion and added Crete to his territory. Muhammad Ali and his son conquered Syria and Mt. Lebanon (the Beirut region with a significant Christian population) and defeated the sultan's army on the Anatolian frontier, until the British routed them from these territories. For London, a fragile Ottoman state was a useful, if vulnerable, barrier to Russian expansion.[40]

But propping up the Ottoman imperial structure hardly restored its vitality or overcame the multiple challenges that afflicted it. European support for the Greek revolution in the Balkans, continuing Russian pressure in the Black Sea,

French efforts to protect Christians in Lebanon, Islamic religious radicalism in the Arab interior, and an ambitious Egyptian modernization effort meant that Constantinople faced crises on almost every front. The question was whether a vast and creaky empire that for the last few centuries had been governed increasingly through pervasive clientelism and had continually to contend with powerful veto groups—if no longer a corporatized army dominating the capital city, certainly a conservative Muslim establishment claiming to legitimize the monarchy—could change the basis of government.

Emerging from the violence and setbacks of the 1820s, a group of reform-minded bureaucrat-diplomats with particular sensitivity to the dangers from abroad embarked on a modernization of the state in the 1830s and a series of reforms from 1839 into the mid-1870s that would be known as the Tanzimat. They established government departments, a prime minister, public taxation to replace tax farming, and a reform council whose proposals the sultan pledged to institute. The reforms were originally justified as aiming at the regeneration of the role of Islam, and the adherents of civic and political reform could be allies of a vast intercontinental movement for Islamic reform that was culminating in the 1830s.[41] Part of the motive was to appeal to the British Whigs, who would have to provide the backup for the empire against the Egyptian and Russian dangers. All very well, but the more that the Ottoman state moved toward importing principles of citizenship and general law, the more it undermined its traditional cultivation of privileged groups. Could the six-centuries-old empire make the transition from subjects to citizens without disintegrating?

Chinese state and society were also under increasing pressure—even before the Anglo-Chinese Opium War of 1839–1842, which an earlier generation of historians, at least, took as the opening of a national crisis that only deepened in the course of the nineteenth century. Contemporary interpretation has tended to examine the strains arising within the Qing order from its very dynamic growth in the eighteenth century. Population was increasing dramatically—from 300 million in 1700 to perhaps 450 million by 1850—as New World crops, sweet potatoes, maize, and peanuts allowed the relaxation of Malthusian constraints.[42] This brought with it population pressure in the south and the expansion of Han Chinese into the northern provinces that were supposedly the homeland of the Manchu people and its Qing Dynasty that had displaced the Ming in 1644. It put pressure on the earlier Manchu effort to preserve domination of public office as Han officials played an increasingly larger role. The Chinese elite differed from that in Europe: it comprised the provincial and national "gentry," a class that had to pass continuing examinations based on Confucian classics, but then enjoyed office holding and exemptions from state service and corporal punishment. Meritocracy, however, is hard to divorce from class privilege. As population increased, the spread of clientelism, bribes, and the resort to exam schools to gain access to the gentry revealed the strains on the ancient system.

Over the course of the eighteenth century, the Manchu state, under the leadership of two remarkable long-lived monarchs, the Kangxi emperor and his grandson, the Qianlong emperor, had devoted major military efforts to expand into the Mongolian west and had vastly increased the effective territory of the state. But the dense habitations of the southern and central provinces and the two great southern river systems (the Pearl estuaries with Guangzhou, and the Yangzi winding eastward from Sichuan to Shanghai and the coastal cities) proved as major a challenge to effective government. The commercially active populations despised immigrants from other provinces, and the networks of bandits, smugglers, and mafia-like "triads" who exploited the wealth and the conflicts among the "immigrants" challenged the precepts of a Confucian moral order. Outside the channels of social mobility and well-ordered commerce and farming, messianic religious doctrines known as White Lotus Buddhism flourished. Government efforts to suppress the congregations led to massive rebellion in 1796 in the provinces of Taiwan, Sichuan, Guangxi, Hunan, and Guizhou, which would require almost a decade to overpower.[43]

Still, as late as 1800 China could be counted as a wealthy society. The question of how it compared with the West has produced a cottage industry of recent scholarship. In his 1776 *Wealth of Nations,* Adam Smith explained that to account for the prosperity of labor, the critical issue was less the degree of wealth than the comparative rate of growth: a stagnant rich nation was in greater trouble than a poorer but dynamic one: "The poverty of the lower ranks of people in China far surpasses that of the most beggarly nations in Europe."[44] There was trade in land; feudal tenures had been eliminated, although debt relationships kept many in dependency; great estates rarely exceeded 250 acres. Probably a third of agricultural production went into trade, some of it over great distances. Proto-industrial organization produced a great deal of cotton cloth and silk, some of which was processed by owners of several hundred looms. Letters of credit issued by emerging banking houses were replacing shipment of silver bullion. Luxury items such as porcelain and furniture were prized in the West.

Difficulties recurred and increased in the early 1800s. If outright rebellion was stanched, the inner bleeding of the state continued. The grain tribute administration, which had charge of ferrying the major taxes in rice eight hundred miles northward along the Grand Canal from Hangzhou on the Yangzi to Beijing, was undermined by corruption, overhiring, a tripling of boat fees, and growing commercialization of the grain tribute as local officials had to purchase rice from private traders to meet their quotas. If bureaucratic friction, corruption, and monopolistic labor practices were not enough, Yellow River silting blocked the major crossing of the Grand Canal in 1824–1825, even as the vested interests of the river merchants vetoed the alternative of shipment along the coast. The canal route would be restored by borrowing water from the Yellow River to augment the canal, but the sea route had to be adopted by 1845, and by 1853 the advance of the Taiping rebels and the Yellow River's change of course (itself attended by catastrophic flooding and environmental challenges) ended the canal route. The price inflation of the eighteenth century brought a trebling of grain prices. Because taxes on commodities were fixed in quantities of silver, peasants could initially keep up their income as the tax rates increased, but by the 1830s the rapidly expanding opium imports began to drain silver from the country and increased the tax burden in real terms. "Not a year has passed without fears of Yellow River floods, not a year without having to raise funds for river control," lamented the leading intellectual of the era, Wei Yuan, before the Opium War. "This is something unknown in previous ages. Foreign opium has spread throughout the country, and silver flows overseas. Because of this the grain tribute tax and salt monopoly develop ever more evils, the officials and people are ever deeper in trouble.... Standing in the present and surveying the past, the difference is as between black and white."[45] Within the constraints that continuing interpretation of ancient Confucian texts mandated for the elite, he reinterpreted the almost twenty-five-hundred-year-old Book of Odes as a summons for a renewal of literati activism in the public interest and for the court to use the lettered elite to break the bureaucratic blockages the country faced. In a British context one might label such an approach Tory reform, certainly better than no reform but rarely sufficient to master the tides of nineteenth-century economic and demographic change. In the United States its functional equivalent perhaps was the belief, expressed by the Virginian Democratic Republicans of the 1790s, that a "natural aristocracy" could pursue the disinterested public interest—a vision soon submerged under the pressures of commercial development and electoral democracy.

The Daoguang emperor from 1840 did allow a reinvigoration of intellectual life and the cautious application of traditional learning to practical problems such as defense and management of the coasts and frontiers.[46] Pressure from the avid world of commerce abroad, however, came too soon and too rapidly for any gradualist or traditionalist coping. The opium boom, of course, involved China in a disastrous military defeat. Opium had been prohibited by the Chinese in 1821, but traded nonetheless. Addiction grew above all for the smoked leaf. It was an Indian product and the EIC had charge of the trade with China. Growers in Indian territories outside EIC control sought to break into the trade, and rather than cede control, the EIC decided to buy and export greater quantities, although it consigned these exports to Chinese merchants. Because the British sold no other products to China, opium sales also promised a way to balance growing their imports of silk and tea. Moreover, as the EIC also explained at home, even the purchases from the independent Indian producers would let the Indian population buy more British cottons and manufactures.

Chinese merchants and smugglers and even foreign trade officials might connive in the imports, but concern grew that London was insisting on the principled defense of free trade to profit from the addiction of the Chinese population. By the mid-1830s the EIC no longer had a legal trading status, but British representatives spoke for the English merchants based in the official entrepôt of Guangzhou. Chinese officials also believed the trade was responsible for the rise in silver prices and thus the tightening of monetary conditions, although three-quarters of British proceeds flowed back into the country for purchases of tea and silk. The British expected the Chinese to legalize imports, but after a vigorous debate Beijing reaffirmed the ban in 1836. The Beijing court entrusted its policy response to an official, Commissioner Lin Zexu, whose war against drugs led him to confine the British merchants at Guangzhou to their factories until supplies of opium were surrendered. The conflict escalated over the rights of merchants and British citizens, in particular the immunities of British sailors from Chinese law. Still, British authorities and the Chinese court debated policies of concession and resistance, and full-scale warfare followed only after a series of British attacks and withdrawals. At that point British progress upriver toward Nanjing with successive Chinese defeats finally led to Beijing's military humiliation, which compelled the state to cede Hong Kong and extraterritorial rights.[47]

On the face of it Japan was as vulnerable as China. But the unrest provoked by the rise of commercial pressures mobilized not rebels against a nominally unified empire but the ambitious leaders of autonomous feudal domains. Attendance of these *daimyō* at the emperor's court involved a large percentage of their public expenses. Although public order seemed under far better control than in China, the pressures of market forces had an effect in Japan as well. The early Tokugawa after 1600 had thought to escape from decades of anarchic civil strife and to fix a stable order on Japan, to freeze it into a pyramid of isolated and hierarchical Confucian peace and order. The Christianity that had begun to make inroads was violently suppressed between 1600 and 1620; foreign contacts were prohibited by 1630. But over the next two centuries, population rose, a money economy made inroads with all the inflation and debt that entailed; some peasants went into market farming for the cities or specialized in crops such as rapeseed oil or silk worms; merchants and artisans proliferated; new self-made men bought office and title, the samurai lost their military virtues, and the administrative offices within the *han* and at the center proliferated. Peasants began to produce for the markets and became more disputatious as they entered market relations. Retainers, lords, and the shogunate itself fell further into debt—some of the domains owed up to a couple of years of expected revenues—the currency was periodically debased, samurai debts had to be periodically canceled, while after 1800 occasional crop failures, tax gouging, and corruption produced unrest and frequent, if small, rebellions. Administrators in the *daimyō* oscillated between imposing forced loans and writing down interest rates on loans. Some administrators, often samurai of humble origins, attempted heroic reforms in the decades before 1850, whether for the national or the domainal governments.

Occasionally they resorted to setting up state monopolies for commodities. But reformers, whether in Edo or in the domains, could also be forced out by conservative samurai opposition.

Even before Commodore Matthew Perry arrived with his black ships in 1853, the Japanese old regime faced fiscal difficulties and social unrest, although without foreign wars as a source of crisis, which suggested that indigenous development in its own right destabilized societies of legal privilege and rank. Incidents of tax protest rose in the market-oriented domains, where new crops, especially the cultivation of silkworms, were increasing, while Samurai control remained stronger in the less commercially developed *han;* and the divergence characterized the choice of sides in the civil war at the end of the Tokugawa order in the 1860s.[48]

Pause for a moment of skeptical interrogation. Was the world from 1810 through the 1840s really in an epoch of coordinated transition? This historical account argues that world civilizations had arrived at some parallel rhythms of development as they interacted more intensely and systemically. Still, the wary reader and the cautious researcher should distrust any effort just to select convenient parallels. States and cultures do present a persisting individuality, as does any community that can be identified for study, whether at the grandest level of empires, on a middle scale of nations and regions, or at the local level between counties and villages, often between enterprises, parishes, and families. The world the historian investigates is differentiated, so to speak, "all the way down." But it is also fractal, in that at each scale similar pressures and similar rifts can be detected. The historian has to decide the relative importance of what is similar and what is different; these are not measures inscribed in the societies themselves. But he or she must make a persuasive public case for these judgments, which ultimately have to be validated by the critical reader.

We have made the case so far on the basis of fundamental and encompassing transitions: the century-long dissolution of hereditary and ascribed relations in the countryside; the growth of sufficient wealth to reward the growth of commercial agriculture as long-distance markets thrived for wheat and rice, for tea, coffee, naval supplies (timber, hemp, resins), and opium; the accumulating technologies that allowed coal and steam to magnify the energy at the disposal of labor; the denser networks of trust that let payment for investment and trade be postponed and reassigned to distant sources of savings—and the progressive casting of land itself into the maelstrom of the market. The case for the global history rests further on the ever-widening pressure from the West, whether through the unsettling presence of Enlightenment ideas or the capacity to draw on and transfer capital, and to move effective military units to far-flung shores. Europeans and North Americans pressed their demands no longer just on tribal societies (although this pressure continued remorselessly), but on the ancient states of Africa and Asia. Whether demanding that the rulers of East Asia open their realms to trade, or calling on the Islamic territories around the Mediterranean to protect their Christian subjects, continuing to intervene militarily in the republics of the New World or moving to control wider provinces of South Asia, Europeans encroached to an ever greater extent. Where they did not directly take over new territories (as the French did in Algeria in 1830), they pressed capitulary treaties on Asian and African rulers, insisting that their own nationals face trial only in their own courts and that Christian subjects enjoy protected status.

But finally, there was a worldwide blowback that constituted a global response—the mobilization of religious loyalties throughout the globe in large part as a reaction to the tendencies described above. Precisely as the traditional structures of the global old regime became unhinged, religious impulses emerged to offer a compensatory vision. As the West encroached, and traditional rulers seemed powerless to resist or even wished to emulate the new techniques and ideas, prophets and saints emerged to resist. This is not to say religious beliefs were ideological responses to social unrest. They were genuine and sprang from deep convictions. But they erupted as powerful organizing and missionary forces as long-term expectations of economic and political stability melted around newly exposed communities. Caught in the currents, conservative elites would deploy the traditional authorities and congregations to keep control, while the marginal elements of society more vulnerable to social dislocation or wedded to territorial autonomy would flock to doctrines of direct inspiration and leaders who demonstrated it. And subsequently, as states were reconstructed, women would assert their own historical role by establishing a presence in significant sectors of religious and charitable activity.

In their implicit claim to reintegrate emotional wholeness that imperial religious bureaucracies had deadened or market society corroded, all sorts of religious congregations arose to contest the new trends and sort alternative values. Thus, religious activism played a role in the great uncongealing of global society that was occurring. One consequence of the turbulence in the country-side was the generation of new messianic cults. But commodification was not the only incitement. The stirrings of imperialist pressure also contributed. Religions arose from the margins of settlement: whether Wahhabism in eighteenth-century Arabia or Mormonism in the "burnt-over district" of eastern New York state. Similar movements were created every few generations in movements character-ized in the American colonies as Great Awakenings, more generally as revivalist: new revelations, new and unlikely prophets, often women or erotically charis-matic male preachers. These would develop as faiths that tapped an outpouring of emotional energy, whether cathecting on other members of the community or on the deity.

It is not making any judgment on the doctrinal content of religion to analyze its this-worldly functions. Certainly these varied, as did political programs. Most religions could accommodate those who lived in compliance with the secular order and whose values of orderliness, family transmission, and ritual served to strengthen it. As in other epochs, religion could serve as a buttress for social hi-erarchy as it existed. In particular those sects or faiths tied to secular authorities served programs to reestablish authority. Whether the 'ulama' of the Ottoman Empire, the appeals to Neo-Confucianism by conservative Chinese political leaders seeking to restore the empire's defensive capacity against the West and domestic rebels, or the so-called union of throne and altar and the reactionary appeals of the Holy Alliance among the European courts, political programs of monarchical restoration and imperial strengthening found support among the upholders of orthodox religious establishments or rites.

But at the same time the sects of the periphery, or those of the popular classes, fused faith and collective appeals. Their rites seemed destabilizing and subverted hierarchic authority even as they sometimes promised to reenergize outworn creeds. Their prophets, whether Christian or Hasidic, or Muslim Sufi holy men, preached austerity and inwardness or communal love, sometimes intense rigor, sometimes the emancipation from tiresome rules and structures, in either case a return from encrusted formalism. Their adherents sang hymns, danced, flocked to shrines, sometimes enlisted in the armies of prophets and used the inner convictions of the faith to conceive a world of far greater emotional energy and equality. Everywhere they offered an alternative collective vision of individual as well as communal fulfillment. The city of God might become manifest only later, but meanwhile the villages of God enlisted tremendous nineteenth-century energy.

Religious rededication, however, was not just a response of the dispossessed. Older elites and communities turned toward renewed faiths—responding not with Pentecostal zeal, but a puritanical and intellectual rigor or quiet mysticism. Islam in particular—its faithful spread from Nigeria north and east in Africa, to the Balkans and the Middle East, thence via Central Asia and the remembered domains of the Mughal Empire to the sultanates of Malaya and Borneo—was a faith in ferment. The difficulties of the Ottoman provinces of the Middle East were a revealing crossroads. As Constantinople's bureaucrats pressed forward with their secularizing and reformist Tanzimat edicts, the old elites of the outlying empire who had earlier been the agents of administration took contradictory paths. Some benefited from the new commercial activity tied in with European trading and became the local notables of the modernizing empire. Others resented the displacement of the traditional 'ulama' and found new doctrines congealing that called for a purification of Islam. Whether Wahhabi currents from the Arabian interior, or the influence of Algerian exiles who had resisted the French conquest and penetration of the 1830s and 1840s, or old scholars, Islamic reformers called for a return to Quranic doctrine and the removal of centuries-old accreted practices—veneration of Muslim saints and tombs, the use of amulets, and such. The reform movement of Salafism took hold among the educated of Damascus, somewhat as Calvinism had galvanized Swiss and French urban congregations three centuries earlier. Salafism might tap energies similar to those that sparked the Wahhabi revival of the Saudi state in the Arabian Hejaz, but could also argue that Islam had called for tolerance and mutual learning from Christians, whereas the Wahhabi advocated religious war and the slaying of corrupt Muslims.[49] The contemporary reader, who reads about the recruiting by militant Islam in Pakistani madrassas or Asian immigrants in Hamburg or Birmingham, will be more familiar with this phenomenon in the early twenty-first century than one would have been fifty years ago. In the early 1800s no faith was untouched by the resources of radical communal fervor. The religion of the early nineteenth century could serve as a volcanic force.

Moreover, just as state rivalries kindled emerging nationalism, so the new religious energies stimulated and provoked responses from the other faiths contending for the loyalties of spiritual communities: British Protestants carried their message to the new domains being encroached on in South Asia; American Protestants followed the China trade with great energy. And as the imperial courts of East Asia sought to revive their fortunes later in the nineteenth century, successfully in Japan, less so in China, they tried to strengthen supposed national orthodoxies, Shintō and Neo-Confucianism. These religious energies were two-edged swords, however. Imperial rulers—including too the Ottoman sultans and the British in India—might sponsor religious academies and patronize spiritual authorities in the search for reliable intermediaries and propagators of their own legitimacy. But the energies they tapped into had their own crusading vigor and were not always to be contained within a pro-state program. Sufi prophets of spiritual renewal within Islam, for instance, organized their own quasi states in the peripheries of empire, whether the upper Nile or northern Nigeria.[50] As we reflect on the vigorous revival of Islamic practices today (or Christian, too) in the wake of what seemed like an unparalleled US extension of influence after 1989, we should remember that the extension of national and imperial authority across the globe in the later nineteenth century provoked some similar push-back from Islam and other religions. Those who render unto Caesar will awaken those who want to render unto God—sometimes by organizing their own purified state authorities.

Quasi-religious impulses flowed into secular doctrines as well. The transformations of global society could not take place without the most exciting of visions opening up to participants, both those who were enthused and those who were uneasy. Even as some social critics feared that trade, commerce, and the rise of industry and new technologies were debasing community life, others saw the possibility of new concepts of emancipation and fraternity. Socialist theorists and "utopian" projects marked the decades after the French wars. The Scottish industrialist Robert Owen preached the value of collectivist communities, and his disciples organized a few in North America as well as New Lanark in Scotland. The French writer Claude Henri de Rouvroy, count of Saint-Simon, who argued that factory owners and investors constituted a new elite that was far more important than the old upper crust of dukes and archbishops, inspired a movement that preached his doctrines. Remove the decorative nobility and no adverse consequence would follow; remove the productive elite (he termed them *industriels*) and society must stagnate. He was farsighted: it was the new fusion of commercial leaders, educated civil servants, and reformist landlords who would coalesce in midcentury—not only in France but throughout the world— and create the institutions and states that were understood to be modern.

Saint-Simon and his followers were sometimes termed utopian socialists. In a European world where a new urban working class crowded into flimsy tenements, drank hard, often contracted the scourges of microbe-infected air and water, tuberculosis and cholera or typhoid, the "social question" was to become anguishing. The workers of Paris and London at this point were hardly disciplined trade unionists seeking respectability, but migrants from the country seeking work, often casual labor, sometimes reduced to crime and prostitution. Anarchic private development augmented the problem; did not the solution lie in a far greater effort at collective organization, whether by reformist entrepreneurs (as Robert Owen thought), or through workers' cooperatives themselves (as Pierre-Joseph Proudhon insisted), and finally by an encompassing working-class international (as Marx would argue)? Charles Fourier argued for reorienting family and social functions within the boundaries of "phalansteries." As these small but energetic movements recruited followers, they built on otherwise suppressed claims of erotic fulfillment (and in the case of some movements, erotic repression). Others were more strictly based on reorganizing capitalism.

Elusive Revolution

Rebellion is sometimes used as a synonym for *revolution,* but there are shades of difference. A revolution is a rebellion that succeeds in removing a given regime (or escaping from its jurisdiction) and installing another, even if the results are later reversed. Revolutions are supposedly carried out in the cause of an articulated program for government. *Rebellion* refers more to revolts, against rulers domestic or foreign, that ultimately fail to sustain their objectives even if they enjoy interim success. Rebellions can seek to institute radical and even utopian programs of equality, or they can seek to restore economic, political, and social orders that participants recall as less exploitative. Modern history in general has witnessed revolutions and rebellions great and small. In Europe and the Americas, the century after 1750 was an era motivated by a newly discovered discourse of rights and happiness. Its philosophers preached self-realization. Its Romantic sensibility glorified man's revolt against tyranny. All of this culminated in the 1840s and carried over into the 1850s, even as a new phase of state reconstruction got under way.

The era between the 1760s and 1860s concluded with two major revolutionary efforts, one in Europe, the other in China—and a third if the so-called Indian Mutiny of 1856–1857 is also counted. The uprisings of 1848–1849 in the West erupted after several years of difficult economic conditions, including rural immiseration and urban overcrowding, and growing impatience with the status quo on the part of frustrated elites who wanted greater political representation. It was not that reform would not have ensued: in Britain the tariff had been repealed; in Prussia a national parliament, or United Landtag, was finally being summoned; in Rome a new young pope seemed sympathetic to reforms even as nationalist secret societies, the so-called *carbonari,* called for unification of the peninsula. Partial progress only led to more impatient demands and agitation. A frightening peasant revolt against Polish aristocrats in Austrian Poland had taken place in 1846, and Protestant and Catholic Swiss cantons had come to the edge of warfare the year before. The Chartist movement in Britain managed a last active surge as it collected signatures for universal male suffrage annual elections and secret ballots. French leftists, in opposition to the complacent Orleanist regime, were organizing a campaign of political banquets. Revolution happened to be ignited in a state that was one of the weakest but had a reactionary ruler: the restored Bourbon monarchs of the Kingdom of the Two Sicilies or Naples. The parliament of Sicily, renewed during British occupation of the island in 1812, was not a popularly elected legislature, but an assembly of hereditary magnates. On January 12, 1848, they declared themselves in revolt against the monarch across the straits in mainland Naples. Revolution soon spread in the Italian states, and then to France and the Germanies with extraordinary speed. Monarchs quickly abdicated, or at least conceded constitutions and summoned liberal ministers to office, as if the governing powers realized how illegitimate they were held to be. These spring months of easy triumph were precarious in turn, however. They rested on a coalition between democrats infused with ideals of Romantic populism and the reform-minded among the civil servants and new bourgeois who had acceded to influence since 1815. The Romantic intellectuals provided the gestures and the rhetoric; the more solid men sought to build new institutions. But 1848 also saw the emergence of an urban proletariat whose demands and recurrent street demonstrations were frightening enough to alienate the liberals whom they had helped bring to power, and the coalition fell apart. Three days of street fighting in Paris, not in February when the monarchy fell, but in June when the working class threw up barricades, undermined the revolution. In the presidential elections scheduled for December 1848, Louis Napoleon, the nephew of Bonaparte, gathered many of the votes of the urban middle classes frightened by radicalism, and of the peasants who likewise wanted an end to months of demonstrations and liked the name of the emperor, whose reputation for victories and national pride was still powerful.

Elsewhere the process of rolling up the revolution took even less time. Military and tough-minded civilian advisers counseled the king of Prussia and the new young emperor of Austria to reassert their authority. Moreover, the moderates' national agenda failed. Whether in Italy, northern Germany, or the Austrian crown lands, middle-class moderates could realize their objective only by defeating Austria. This they failed to do. They remained concerned preeminently with defending their own cities, but not assisting their fellow rebels in other centers of revolution, thus could be successively defeated by Habsburg generals in their would-be national capitals: Milan, Prague, eventually Venice and Budapest. The German liberals had also sought to summon an all-German legislature in Frankfurt, but did not know how to solve the conflicts that existed among ethnic claims. The Habsburgs, who under the energetic minister-president Felix zu Schwarzenberg and a new, young emperor, Franz Joseph, recovered their nerve and authority by the autumn of 1848, responded to the Frankfurt liberals that if the Austrian Empire was to form part of a new German national federation, the monarchy must enter as an integral unit with its non-German nationalities, Bohemians and Hungarians. The Prussians did not wish to leave out their Polish subjects. The Frankfurt assembly would be suppressed before a "small

German" alternative without the Habsburgs might be launched. Frustrated radicals revolted again in the spring of 1849, most seriously the Hungarians whose national militia defeated the Austrians. Now the Russians decided that the agitation must be calmed and, with Vienna's approval, intervened. The Austrians themselves extinguished the revived Italian national aspirations led by the king of Sardinia (whose kingdom, despite its official name, was based in Piedmont or Savoy) and Venice's own republic, while Louis Napoleon, newly elected as president of the French Republic, wooed French Catholics by sending troops to wipe out the Roman republic that had wrested power from the pope. A detachment of Prussian troops vacated the Frankfurt parliament and restored dynastic authority in Dresden and Baden. Richard Wagner, the composer, and his friend Gottfried Semper—later to design the grandiose Dresden opera house—fled from the Saxon barricades. The Austrian and Neapolitan dynasties were not charitable toward defeated revolutionaries, and their firing squads worked overtime.

What was snuffed out in 1849 was not the entire program, but the romantic elements—the belief that each national group might discover and build a state on its own *Volksgeist,* the genius of its people. Likewise the claims that personal liberty might motivate state building. Some parliaments survived the repression. The Savoy or Piedmontese "statute" and parliament conceded by King Carlo Alberto in the spring of 1848 would become the constitution and parliament of the Kingdom of Italy in 1860–1861. The Prussian parliament summoned in 1847 remained in being, although the suffrage would be restricted and skewed in favor of the wealthy. The last measures of formal serfdom remained abolished in the Austrian Empire. France would never again become a monarchy under its traditional dynastic families. Governments would recognize the force of public opinion as represented in assemblies and the press. The "winners" would continue the program of bringing the market to the countryside—the Piedmontese liberals would embark on extensive secularization in the 1860s, as would the Mexican liberals, who passed the Lerdo Law, dissolving not only church holdings but Indian village communes as well.

There were some exceptions to the revolutionary ferment. Where representative institutions were already in place and public debate remained untrammeled, young, frustrated middle-class crowds did not tend to rush into the streets. The

Americas were liberal enough that no revolutionary upheavals took place. The United States was busy absorbing its recent conquests from Mexico. The slavery issue precluded any coalition of radicals. Britain's institutions were sufficiently liberal—if its suffrage hardly democratic—that it could escape unscathed except for massive outdoor gatherings on behalf of the People's Charter. At the other extreme, Russia was still able to resist and repress any liberal assault before it went beyond salon chatter. Still, elsewhere in the West, the age of positivism, of realism, of solid moneymaking and middle-class aspirations was to begin—and the geographic boundaries of states would soon be transformed.

In Asia, though, the huge convulsions lay elsewhere. China was weakened by the outcome of 1842, and then the vast upheaval of the Taiping, which would cost twenty to thirty million lives. This was hardly a liberal revolution, but in fact a civil war that originated in the ethnic clashes, new endemic banditry, and eschatological protest. The fragmented gentry's capacity for ensuring the stability of the Yangzi region and the tradition of self-policing communities were badly frayed. The dynasty and its administrators faced multiple challenges—the continuing and humiliating pressure from Europeans for economic and legal privileges, the erosion of a precarious economic order among poor and crowded settlements, and the addition of messianic Christian ideas to the repertory of redemptive hopes that frequently inspired protests. The Yangzi region, as during the earlier White Lotus rebellion, was roiled by conflicts among new migrants, Han Chinese, and communities of non-Han peoples, by grievances at the Manchu leadership that had been humiliated in 1842, and by the pressure of taxes in increasingly scarce silver currency. Christian missionaries proposed a gospel that might fuse or confuse radical social ideas with promises of ultimate salvation. A leader emerged in Hong Xiuquan, born to immigrant peasant proprietors in 1814, studious but failing to pass the all-important civil service exams, and then converted to a millenarian Christianity by a Chinese missionary convert with a jumbled but austere doctrine of Chinese degradation and the need for redemption. The "Good Words to Exhort the Age" foresaw Chinese tribulations, such as also usually portended dynastic collapse, and left the concept of heavenly kingdom—imperial or supernatural—ambiguous. For Hong the "Good Words" were combined with denunciations of the Manchus and Confucian appeals to rectitude and good order and his own personal vision of having been transformed physically as well as spiritually by God during a serious illness after his third examination failure. With his own first converts he migrated inland from the Canton coast to preach in the hilly southwest of Guangxi and found a receptive hearing among the fellow Hakka, or northern Chinese migrants in the south. Over the next years branches of the God Worshipping Society metastasized in the province and brought forth new leaders, including a gifted military commander, Yang Xiuqing. Conflicts with locals and bandits under famine conditions during 1849–1850 led to the assembling of an army thousands strong and the proclamation of the Heavenly Kingdom of Great Peace in January 1851. A Manchu force sent to disperse them was defeated and its general decapitated.

Thereafter the Taiping army moved up the Yangzi, growing in size to a horde of over three hundred thousand, taking Wuchang, Anqing, then Nanjing in March 1853, killing all the Manchu inhabitants. Four kings were appointed alongside Hong, who claimed the titles "king of heaven," *Tianwang,* and "second son of God," and allowed Yang Xiuqing to assert his claim as third son, filled with the Holy Spirit. The Land Regulation of the Heavenly Dynasty decreed from Nanjing envisaged that the countryside would be divided into units of twenty-five families each. Wine, opium, and tobacco were prohibited, as were nonmarital sexual relations, which, as might be expected from earlier such utopian foundings, did not preclude exemptions and privileges among the hierarchy. From Nanjing the Taiping divided their forces to attack north and west. But the expedition to Beijing failed at Tianjin, and its remnants were wiped out in the spring of 1855.

The forces of order who organized to resist this wave of what they perceived as Christian radical barbarism were local gentry commanders who had raised ethnic militias since the White Lotus rebellion, the talented Zeng Guofan in the lead. They defended an ideology of puritan Confucianism, which stressed the traditional precepts of a well-ordered social hierarchy under the emperor but combined with a mastery of new military technology, a reorganized Chinese (and not Manchu) army, and a less oppressive tax system. They did not immediately prevail, however. The Taiping held a three-hundred-mile stretch of the Yangzi from Wuchang to Zhenjiang and scored important victories in 1855–1856. Nonetheless, conflicting ambitions and ruthless mutual jealousies were dividing the rival Taiping "kings," who murdered each other successively along with their families and thousands of adherents. Despite the bloodbaths, the Taiping reorganized and found a new gifted military commander and civilian administrator in Hong Ren'gan, who was a cousin of Hong Xiuquan and moved to turn toward a more orthodox Christianity and connections with the mercantile elements downriver in Shanghai. Still, the process of attrition became stronger even though the Beijing court distrusted Zeng's local initiatives and strength. The imperial forces moved to control the Yangzi above the Taiping and scored victories below them. The rebels failed to take the Wuhan cities to their west. Hong Ren'gan sought to assure the British in Shanghai that he would form a more orderly administration than the Manchu court, who had just lost another war against the British. But the British minister in China, Frederick Bruce, was convinced that the Taiping of any stripe were radical, unreliable, and inimical to the interests of commercial order. With French assistance the British helped ferry imperial troops upriver. In July 1864, Hong died, perhaps, so it was rumored, poisoned, and Zeng Guoquan, the brother of Zeng Guofan, conquered Nanjing, massacred its inhabitants, and burned the city.

The civil war had raged over an area equivalent to France and Germany for almost a decade and a half and had involved a million insurgents in military campaigns. Another vast civil war half a world away in the United States was grinding its rebel armies to defeat in the same months. Could the Taiping have prevailed and toppled the Manchu dynasty? They had engendered tremendous loyalties on the basis of an eschatological program. Nonetheless, their communities also remained outside the traditional society of the countryside. In this they differed from some of the other forces for endemic disorder in China, whether the ethnic uprisings of the Miao aborigines in the 1830s or the simultaneous rebellion of the Nian further north, who like the White Lotus and Triads in effect permeated peasant life. Anti-Manchu the Taiping might be, but they also remained outsiders among the Han Chinese majority. The local elites of the Yangzi region, moreover, were not prepared to see a Manchu dynasty toppled at the cost of unrest. In this, as we shall see, they resembled the forces of order, who would build new regimes conducive to reform from above throughout Europe, the Americas, Japan, and the Ottoman Empire.[51]

It was not surprising that the British had decided to join in the suppression of this persistent rebellion. Seven years earlier they had faced their own frightening uprising, the so-called Indian Mutiny of 1857, which in fact had threatened to develop as a major revolt against their thin presence in India. Ostensibly it had started as a revolt among the Muslim soldiers whom the English had recruited to police their growing acquisitions in northern and central India as they wove one native principality after another into their dominion, whether by displacing its ruler or having him recognize London's authority. But, as C. A. Bayly emphasizes, there was a long history of forcible resistance to Mughal taxation and then to the takeover of territory and financial rights by the EIC in the previous decades. "Revolt was inevitable in areas where more fluid, segmented forms of polities had been preserved by climate or terrain from the weaker pressures of Mughal centralisation."[52] The British presence meant new pressure to support the EIC's army and to extract crops for export. It was easier for the English to co-opt urban Indian elites than the diffuse forces of the countryside, which often were galvanized by religious reform movements. But no consistent socioeconomic background seems to have united the revolutionary forces; in some places they were hard-pressed villages squeezed by new taxes; in others, new peasant proprietors that the British had counted on as the basis for a new loyal class. Rural class divisions increased in the decades after 1857, not before. Those magnates who had done well in the preceding half century as the British moved in hesitated to throw in their lot with the rebels, as did civil servants and Indians in commerce.

Still, because the British were a numerically small presence in a massive terrain, the uprisings had the potential to destroy their position throughout the subcontinent. The revolt broke out when the British commander of a local garrison punished soldiers who refused to distribute new rifle cartridges greased with animal fat. The colonizers soon confronted frightening and widespread uprisings, which they believed were encouraged by the shadowy and hardly substantive authority of the Mughal dynasty in Delhi. The rebels held Delhi from May to September 1857 and besieged Lucknow until November. But the British never lost control of the Ganges valley and the trunk road between Delhi and Calcutta, nor of their base in Bengal. They retained the loyalty of the Sikh units in the Punjab and could march east on beleaguered Delhi. Once the British overcame the emergency, they would force the formal end of the Mughals and take over their position, transferring formal power from the EIC to their own officials.

In China they finally threw their lot in on the side of the dynasty, recognizing a fundamentally different structure. The Chinese dynasty was weak, but the country was not built on a substructure of principalities that might be subordinated to London's governance. China remained a still-massive cultural and political entity whose government could grant them the concessions they needed. Between 1856 and 1860, the British gained additional territory for Hong Kong and further commercial connections in the so-called Second Opium (or Arrow) War, triggered by the Guangzhou police's effort to arrest Chinese crew members on an opium vessel, the *Arrow,* formerly—but no longer—under British registry. The move provoked the British admiral to bombard Guangzhou; the Whigs in parliament challenged Prime Minister Palmerston over the bellicose response, but were set back in new elections. Responding to the murder of a French missionary, Napoleon III threw in his forces alongside London's. The British and French attacked Chinese forts up the coast in Tianjin, forced an armistice that opened new treaty ports along the northern coast, allowed missionaries the right to travel, imposed reparations, and finally compelled the Chinese to legalize the domestic sale of opium, a move they had managed to resist after 1842. The right to exploit the opium commerce had been the longer-term objective of the London government. When the newly gained acquisitions proved difficult to enforce, the British commander, Lord Elgin, the son of the Elgin who had carted home the Parthenon's frieze, attacked Beijing, torched the summer palace (partly designed in French rococo style), extracted higher reparations, acquired the Kowloon territory around Hong Kong, and added Tianjin to the treaty ports. It was this debacle coupled with the evident weakness of the rulers that would finally compel reorganization of the empire—increasingly as a Chinese national state and less as a Manchu dynastic enterprise. Having secured the compliance of Beijing, the British decided that propping up their official source of their semicolonized regime was preferable to watching it succumb to xenophobic and unrestrained radicals.[53]

In any case, the end of the Taipings—like the extirpation of the Indian Mutiny seven years earlier, like the defeat of Polish rebels a year earlier in 1863, like the collapse and surrender of the Confederate States of America a year later, and the failure of the feudal Tokugawa forces in 1868 Japan—suggested that rebellion was a forlorn option. The long century of modern statehood would be built on the ashes of revolution, the reform of institutions not from "below"—not by the effort by peasant or national populists to bring about the millennium—but by programs of modernization and rationalization carried out both by farseeing conservative statesmen and middle classes, enthusiasts of the 1840s who had become the sagacious statesmen of the 1850s and 1860s. Their achievement, too, would require violence, but the measured and directed violence of warfare and repression, not rebellion.

2. *Reconstruction on a World Scale*

DEVELOPMENTS from 1850 to 1880 wrought major transformations in the organization of states across the globe. They constitute a genuine "moment" of world history. Political jurisdictions changed as territorial states were torn apart from within and then reconstituted on a more cohesive basis. Local leaders found that more distant authorities had greater say over their power and their finances. The social origins of men claiming public office and influence became more diverse. Whether by virtue of their professional education, or industrial and financial wealth, newcomers who came from outside the ranks of landowning elites, old families, or military office achieved a far greater voice over public affairs. They hardly replaced the former ruling groups; usually they were recruited to serve alongside them in moments when their exclusion threatened state survival or stability.

Long-distance communication, movement of peoples, and shipment of goods became more rapid and dense. Global space seemed more of a continuum, suffused no longer by divine transcendence but by vibrations of unseen energy. Paradoxically, for all the awareness of rapid communication, intellectual systems rarely became more cosmopolitan or tolerant. Ideas of pervasive rivalry and conflict often replaced dreams of fraternity. War "fulfills its cruel but indispensable role in the progress of the human spirit," wrote Italian observers of the Prussian triumph over France in December 1870.[54] The appeal to brotherhood tended to relocate from patriots and poets to proletarians greeting their supposed class brothers.

These developments pose two fundamental puzzles. The first is why so many decisive changes seemed to occur concurrently with such suddenness. The tempo of change is mysterious in many large-scale phenomena—"tipping points" can be modeled for many fields, but why they come when they do remains to challenge natural scientists and historians alike. The second riddle is why so many states and societies worldwide underwent analogous transformations at the same time.

Compression in time and extension across space remain to challenge explanation. Why does history become global? The reconstruction of states became an imperative in the Western Hemisphere, whether in the divided and then reconstituted United States, a reorganized Canadian federation, a Mexico that lost vast territories to its northern neighbor but then went on to defeat a French invader, or an Argentina that threw off dictatorship. Europe, too, was reassembled at its center and at the edges. Italian and German nationalists achieved unification, Austria-Hungary renegotiated its ethnic balance of power; the Spanish monarchy was abolished, briefly pulverized, and then patched together, the Ottoman state redefined its constituent principles; while the military and bureaucrats of the Russian Empire sought to overcome what they recognized as the besetting impediments of serfdom. In East Asia ambitious Japanese samurai administrators determined to create an effective modern state that would challenge the ingrown shogunate; and frustrated Chinese officials endeavored to mobilize Confucian principles to reverse their polity's catastrophic experience of rebellion, floods, and foreign incursion.

No doubt the process was infectious. States exist in an implicitly competitive universe. Major initiatives in one must impact on others. But not just diffusion or contagion was at stake. Pressures for transformation arose from within many societies simultaneously. We can't rerun the course of history to test whether or not regimes in isolation would or would not have reconstructed their institutions. Before 1850 the Japanese state had been the large polity most insulated perhaps from foreign impact. It went into a fifteen-year crisis and transformation only after the outer world seemed finally to press determinedly at its gates, but there were certainly many pressures emanating from its own stratified society that were likely to compel far-reaching adjustment, and we cannot know how much change they would have compelled on their own. Did change, moreover, always emanate from "below"? Marx famously distinguished the "forces of production"—the levels of technology, and the social classes they brought to the fore—from the "relations of production" inscribed in legal and political institutions. He saw the pressures of the former leading to crises and revolutionary adjustments in the latter. Yet most historians are likely to describe a recursive process with many feedbacks, just as they envisage a recursive relationship between the realm of ideas and that of economic progress.

Many aspects of ordinary life, moreover, did not change qualitatively in the period, or changed at a less disrupting pace. This particular history follows the world of political transactions, not household existence and not the bonds of intimate loyalties. For masses of people the events recorded here did not seem to impact on their daily routines. The worker enclosed from sunup to sundown in a noisy textile mill, the domestic servant cleaning and cooking, the young man single-mindedly smitten by the young woman he passed daily on the street, the child savagely cuffed by a stepparent, the rural family facing hunger from drought and erosion, may not have sensed their lives were being transformed by a common sovereign for Naples and Florence, or a new German civil code, a new definition of Ottoman citizenship, or the burning of the Chinese emperor's summer palace by French and British soldiers. The chance to vote for a delegate to a national parliament hardly allowed the abused child to strike back, or the domestic servant to be impertinent, or, in many areas of the world, the young woman to follow her own inclinations in matters of the heart. Nonetheless, states would irrevocably touch even humble lives. They could expand educational opportunities, facilitate employment, encourage (or impede) inward and outward migration, insist on the ending of inherited personal bondage—if only to send the formerly bonded into the constraints of hard agricultural labor or long factory disciplines. States sometimes expanded and probably sometimes constrained the possibilities of personal fulfillment and household life. But then the pressures within millions of households had sent states careening as well.

The state was to be strengthened, but largely to remain viable in a world of state competitiveness, and only indirectly to cope with issues of poverty and income maintenance, except that order had to be maintained. Commentators tended to analyze the social costs of economic transition as a problem of individual or family difficulty, sometimes based on poverty, sometimes on moral failures. They organized charities, benevolent associations, educational reform, and later on, crusades for temperance and against sexual trafficking. Above all, serious-minded middle-class women, who could not go into politics, could devote their energy to these efforts on behalf of respectability and sobriety.[55] In the West, these reformist if sometimes patronizing attitudes had begun to emerge a decade or two before midcentury. The formation of reform associations, which took off in Britain and the United States in the 1830s, but marked the continent in subsequent decades, whether through the St. Vincent de Paul societies in France, or the Lutheran Church Diet in Germany, were part of the tremendous organizational effort that nineteenth-century society generated. Similar earnestness marked those in non-Western societies who responded to the Western challenge. Both Christian and Muslim intellectuals throughout the Levant and Egypt argued for the need to strengthen Eastern societies through urging them to learn about the scientific progress and discoveries recently made in Europe, and infusing them with a stronger sense of unity among "Easterners."[56] The extraordinary influence of the didactic tract *Self-Help* by the British author Samuel Smiles testified to the search for self-strengthening measures. The Scottish author began as a political reformer and a critic of laissez-faire, not the smug justifier of success or wealth. An Arabic translation was published in Cairo and Beirut in several editions as early as 1886, followed over the years by editions in Chinese, Punjabi, and Japanese, which sold a million copies.[57]

The poet Henry Wadsworth Longfellow, supremely talented in giving sentimental voice to middle-class pieties, wrote, "Life is real, life is earnest, and the grave is not its goal." Above all the midcentury world was earnest. Institution building reflected the earnestness. The personalist regimes of the 1820s and 1830s—led by such brilliant, reformist, but often autocratic generals as Simón Bolívar, "the Liberator" in Colombia and Venezuela, Mehmet Ali in Egypt and the Middle East, and, in some respects though under constitutional restraints, Andrew Jackson—seemed less suitable for the midcentury decades. Witness the repeated disasters incurred by the vainglorious Mexican general Antonio López de Santa Anna. Giuseppe Garibaldi, whose small expeditionary force ignited Sicily and southern Italy in 1860, was the closest to the Latin American model, but when he got to the midpoint of the peninsula he turned his forces over to the organizers of Italian unification from the north. The leaders who set their stamp on state building were serious and conservative, personifications of gravitas and patience—whether Abraham Lincoln, Benito Juárez, Otto von Bismarck, Itō Hirobumi, who was active in Meiji politics into the twentieth century, or the remarkable Zeng Guofan, the organizer of victory against the Taiping and continual advocate of Chinese technology and modernization. Chinese conditions, however, did not let such clear-sighted recommendations prevail.

The world of states that emerged by 1880 was a different one from that of a generation earlier—in Asia as well as the West. By then, despite the reluctance of some of its organizers, the state would have to engage with serious social issues—whether farm distress in Central Europe and western North America, factory regulation and even old age in Germany, or opium addiction and military backwardness in China. It was a world of projects and work—the labor of organizing enterprises, of reforming education, of writing huge novels and large symphonies, pressing forward with ambitious political programs, uplifting darker-skinned peoples as well as working them hard for low wages, wagering on warfare.

Iron and Blood

Technological transformation was a critical input to the reorganization of states. Bismarck told the Prussian parliament in 1862 that the great questions of the day were being decided not by high ideals and lofty speeches, but by "blood and iron." He was correct. But the role of iron was newer than the role of blood. The British had achieved commercial supremacy, and built the financial leadership that came with it, originally on mechanized cotton and textile production (and indirectly slave and proletarian labor). The cotton mills erected in new industrial towns such as Manchester or soon thereafter in Lille, France, or Pawtucket, Rhode Island, were large sheds that grouped ingenious but relatively light machines powered by water or steam to spin and weave unprecedented quantities of fiber into textiles. So far as the organization of society was concerned, their epoch-making innovation was to induce a workforce to assemble together under a time discipline set by the proprietors as the condition for tapping hitherto undreamed of quantities of nonanimate power to apply to their labor. Textile factories and later iron-smelting furnaces brought new urbanization, as suggested by the sample of city populations in Table 1.1.

Hard upon this transformed productive process arrived a wave of innovation in transportation of people and goods, based on self-propelled steam engines that ran on parallel rails or were mounted on ships. James Watt had developed the decisive improvements that made the modern steam engine possible as early as the 1730s. His design condensed the spent steam in a cooling compartment

TABLE 1.1

Selected urban populations

	1800	1850	1890
London	959,000	2,362,000	4,212,000
Paris	547,000	1,053,000	2,448,000
Naples	400,000 (est.)	415,000	463,000
New York	63,000	661,000	2,741,000
Chicago	—	30,000	1,100,000
Manchester/Salford	90,000	389,000	704,000
St. Petersburg	270,000	490,000	1,003,000

Source: Adna Ferrin Weber, *The Growth of Cities in the Nineteenth Century* (Ithaca, NY: Cornell University Press, 1967), p. 450, table 163.

separate from the chamber in which the heated steam drove the piston, thus avoiding having to cool the engine between strokes. Watt had also devised the off-center fastening of the connecting rod that could convert the reciprocal action of the piston into the smooth rotary motion of a wheel. From 1803, the innovations were fitted to the paddlewheel boat that could travel upstream and propel a vessel no longer dependent on wind direction. By the 1830s steamboats were traveling intercontinentally. They did not displace sailing vessels right away but in fact led sailing ship designers to perfect the rapid clippers that expanded the China trade. As early as 1804 the steam engine was fitted to a vehicle that could run on parallel rails to haul iron, and a passenger steam train was installed in Wales in 1807. The first routes that had more than curiosity value were opened in 1830 in Britain and the United States—Manchester to Liverpool, Washington to Baltimore, Boston to its suburbs and then to Worcester, from Nuremberg to its suburb of Fürth in 1834, from Brussels to Mechelen in 1835, from the summer palace town of Tsarskoe Selo to St. Petersburg, and by 1851 in India, 1855 across Panama, 1857 in Argentina, and 1872 from Tokyo to Yokohama. In the 1850s, mileage began to increase significantly: World railroad construction had amounted to 4,700 miles by 1840; then 19,200 by 1850; 43,299 by 1860; 63,300 by 1870; 101,100 ten years later by 1880; 152,200 by 1890. By 1850, US rail mileage was close to 8,600 miles; by 1861, 30,600, with 21,000 in the North (of which

11,000 in the midwestern states from Ohio to Kansas, Missouri, and Minnesota), and 9,500 in the South. By the end of the century world rail mileage was close to half a million miles, of which the United States had 185,000, while Britain, Germany, France, and European Russia had about 25,000 to 30,000 each.[58]

These were extraordinary developments, less because they displaced canal and turnpike traffic at first, but because they increased speed and incentivized technological breakthroughs. "Breasting the wind and light, the shower and sunshine, away and still away, [the steam train] rolls and roars, fierce and rapid, smooth and certain." "We believe that the steam engine, upon land, is to be one of the most valuable agents of the present age, because it is swifter than the greyhound, and powerful as a thousand horses, because it has no passions and no motive, because it is guided by its directors, because it runs and never tires, because it may be applied to so many uses, and expanded to any strength."[59] The technologies entailed in turn a vast expansion of iron (and later steel) production and fashioning—a far more power-intensive process than textiles required and one in turn calling for the extraction of huge amounts of coal and ore (Table 1.2). Britain would forge ahead into this era of heavy machinery and by the 1860s iron ships, developing new techniques for smelting iron and then purifying it into steel, requiring ever-larger tonnages of coal and coke. Britain, however, would increasingly share its economic preeminence with Germany and the United States. They increased the demand for coal, then for steel, which in turn required expansion of rail service to haul the coal and ore.

Building railways required organizing large pools of investors. Coordinating rail lines over long distances encouraged decentralized modular management techniques as well as centralized supervision. The early short trains moved slowly but much faster than lurching coaches. Before the railroad, almost a week was required to cover the 380 miles from Pittsburgh to New York; by 1860 it was a day's journey. Midcentury wars—the large brutal combats that marked the seam dividing the first half the century from the second: Crimea, the American Civil War, the German wars of unification—accelerated the technology of moving individuals, large groups of soldiers, and their equipment. Pullman sleeping cars became an attainable upper-middle-class luxury in the late 1860s, brought into American public consciousness by Lincoln's funeral train. Transporting dead cows or swine en masse was a greater challenge. The development of refrigerator

TABLE 1.2

Production of coal, pig iron, and raw steel (in millions of metric tons)

	UK	Germany	USA
Coal			
1830	22.8	1.8	0.8
1870	112.0	26.4	36.3
1910	269.0	152 + 70 lignite	473.0
Pig iron			
1830	0.69	0.11	0.17
1870	6.06	1.26	1.69
1910	10.57	13.17	27.10
Raw steel			
1870	0.334	0.13	0.77
1890	3.64	2.10	4.34
1910	6.48	13.10	25.71

Sources: British and German Statistics from B. R. Mitchell, *European Historical Statistics, 1750–1970* (London: Macmillan, 1978), tables D2, D7, and D8. The German figures separated their significant lignite production from the aggregated bituminous and anthracite output *(Steinkohl).* Anthracite and bituminous coals provide approximately the same range of BTU per ton; the calorific content of lignite ranges from about 30 to 50 percent of the higher grades. US statistics from *Historical Statistics of the United States, Earliest Times to the Present: Millennial Edition,* ed. Susan B. Carter, Scott Sigmund Gartner, Michael R. Haines, Alan L. Olmstead, Richard Sutch, and Gavin Wright (New York: Cambridge University Press, 2006). For coal, data has been aggregated from tables Db67 (anthracite) and Db60 (bituminous); pig iron data can be found in table Db74; and raw steel data can be found in table Dd399. The original figures for US coal and raw steel were given in short tons (= 2,000 lb) and have been converted, for purposes of comparison, to metric tons (= 1,000 kg or 2,200 lb).

cars during the 1880s enabled the railroads to move dressed meat to eastern centers of urban population from vast interior pastures and slaughtering depots (themselves now mechanized, with carcasses traveling on overhead chains to be butchered progressively at successive work stations). The invention of a practical compressed-air brake allowed these now longer trains to operate at higher speeds with their huge momentum under control from the locomotive.

The railroad influenced political organization in two fundamental ways— first by reinforcing the credibility of the nation-state as a cohesive arena of collective decision making, second by enabling and favoring new coalitions of historical actors to seize leadership within states. The future prime minister of Piedmont and the statesman instrumental in Italian unification, the liberal Count Camillo Benso di Cavour, understood the impact: "The steam engine is a discovery that can only be compared in terms of the magnitude of its consequences with that of printing or even better the American continent. The influence of railroads will extend itself throughout the universe. In those countries that have attained a high degree of civilization, they will impart to industry tremendous growth; their economic results will be magnificent from the outset and they will accelerate the progressive movement of society. But the moral effects must be even greater that their material effects in our eyes, and especially notable in those nations that are currently lagging in their ascent as modern peoples. For them the railroads will be more than a means of enrichment, but a powerful weapon with whose aid they will overcome the retarding forces that are holding them in a baleful state of industrial and political infancy."[60]

So, too, the Prussian state officials, contemplating their state strung from the Belgian to the Russian border across the plains and woods, understood that the railroad would knit together a geographical structure that had little inherent unity; and the military elite understood that it would allow troops to be moved from one frontier to another. By 1870 Prussia possessed an armature of railroad lines that complemented the institutions being created for greater state cohesion and potential leadership of an emerging German national unit. The Italians set to building lines from north to south as soon as they could after unification, although the fiscal burden bore heavily on the peasantry of the south and helped ignite an endemic rebellion. For Canada, the early railroads posed an existential dilemma. Business and political leaders had to either get the state to underwrite costs and link western settlements to Montreal and thence to the New York railroads and Atlantic ports, or let the fledgling Canadian nation risk separating into units that would be connected southward to the various US states. Because Britain had opened its markets to wheat from all sources and not just its own overseas dominions, the outlets were urgent. The first major decision came in 1849, when a railroad guarantee act facilitated the construction of railroad links to the New York Central, allowing Canadian grain to get to ice-free ports. The Montreal-to-Boston line opened two years later. For those countries that spanned a continent—the United States, Canada, and later the Russian Empire—national political and commercial ambitions led pro-railroad coalitions to advocate that tracks should span the immense distances from East to West (as for Argentina and Chile, north–south construction was likewise compelling). Once its Civil War ended, the United States sutured together its first transcontinental line in 1869. A decade and a half later, completion of the Canadian Pacific Railroad in 1885 could be celebrated as the great Canadian national epic. It may well have been a defensive response to the transcontinental US rail lines.[61] The Russian state laid down its trans-Siberian line only in the first years of the twentieth century, but the fiscal exertions that were required aroused strong opposition to the reformist prime minister, Count Sergei Witte, who determinedly pressed the project forward. In China, the railroad advocates could not find the same support. An early line in Beijing was removed; the 1876 British-built line from Shanghai to nearby Wusong offended the government's sense of sovereignty and was destroyed the next year. Reform-minded officials understood the stakes and outlined the consequences. Xue Fucheng despairingly reported that "all the European countries are competing with one another for wealth and strength and their rise to prosperity is rapid. What they rely upon are steamships and railroads . . . if the system of railways trains is not used, China can never be rich and strong." He understood the impact on prices: America built railroads whenever it opened untilled land: and one could travel from New York to San Francisco ten times as rapidly as one might under Chinese conditions and at one-tenth the price. But if China should adopt the railroad, "then distant areas could be brought near, the stagnant could be made to flow, the expense could be saved, and the scattered could be concentrated." And as other officials warned, Japan was following these policies with aggressive intent.[62]

Railroads appealed to private investors and rulers alike. Above all they appealed to investors when the state guaranteed the returns, as it did in Canada from 1849, and in France under the Second Empire, which struck bargains with the six major lines radiating outward from Paris, as did the Third Republic in the 1880s. Railroads were major investments, but they were immensely profitable because national governments provided indirect subsidies, whether through tax concessions, guarantees of interest on the bonds issued, or help in acquiring land. The United States and again the Canadians, in their second phase of development, offered alternate square-mile tracts along the right-of way, often with valuable mineral rights, but also designed to tempt settlers. As the rulers of imperial possessions, the British would build railroads across India for purposes of defense as well as development. Late developers imported capital and technology. Sultan Abdülhamid (1878–1908) in the Ottoman Empire, and Porfirio Díaz (his almost exact contemporary as authoritarian president of Mexico from 1878 to 1911), worked with the Germans and Americans, respectively.

Railroad construction shaped the internal political coalitions that dominated states with representative institutions, or at least stock exchanges. With state guarantees, railroad consortia attracted both those groups that controlled financial capital and those agrarian elites who could mobilize the wealth of commodity production. Even before the American Civil War the outlines had emerged, as powerful railroad interests supported by Illinois Democratic Party senator Stephen Douglas bowed to Southern party members to secure the territorial administration in the West that was seen as the prerequisite for investing in further rail lines. The Kansas-Nebraska Act of 1854 sponsored by Douglas and eloquently opposed by Abraham Lincoln stipulated that local voters should be able to legalize slavery in their respective territories despite the earlier prohibition on allowing it to be instituted so far north. Douglas and the railroads won the issue temporarily, only to inflame the underlying national conflict over slavery. Within a decade the railroad sutured together Chicago and its agrarian hinterland but further divided the country. Ironically, the North's extensive rail development helped it prevail in the great war that Lincoln was to conduct against the secessionist South. Rail lines let the North project force into the central areas of Georgia, Tennessee, and the Mississippi Valley, and slowly choke the Confederacy. The great spurt in Southern railroads began in the years after 1865, although the crisis of 1873 interrupted the progress. When it resumed, Northern capital played a far larger role, especially the Illinois Central Railroad's domination of the Mississippi Valley.

The planter class slowly learned a lesson. Plantation owners teamed up with Northern industrial interests to extend railroads into the ex-Confederate states and simultaneously to undermine the Northern commitment to Reconstruction and subject the African-American workforce on the land to new modalities of subjection. As in many countries, railroad investment opportunities would draw together "old" elites from the land and the "new men" who had risen in industry. This was true in Europe, North and South America, and Europe's colonies. Political elites (some elected and some career bureaucrats), landed magnates and city bankers, and a great mass of smaller investors swept by enthusiasm for profits and technology formed a new iron triangle that would dominate politics.[63]

Of course, at the local level, men of property and wealth usually controlled the labor and conditions of life of those who depended on them. In villages the world over, the major landowners enjoyed power, and deference—by which is meant that general respect their tenants or village residents showed them without continual compulsion. Alexis de Tocqueville relates how in 1848 in France—a country, after all, that had had a major revolution, and repeated minor ones—the peasants on his land came to solicit his advice on exercising the new right to vote. Fifty years later the Italian Marxist theorist Antonio Gramsci would develop the concept of ideological "hegemony," by which he meant the general acceptance of law and private property and the existing social structure on the part of even those who were at the bottom of the economic pyramid, which was the true cement of domination—"soft power" applied to class relations. US conditions probably allowed the least deference, at least outside the coercive framework of African-American slavery. Eastern European, Balkan, and Ottoman societies incorporated more. Peasants touched their brows or kissed their landlord's hem. In Japan until the Meiji "revolution," ostentatious bowing before noble samurai was expected of peasants, and consequences could be severe if it was not provided. The intervention of peasants into East Asian politics remained confined to periodic upheaval and resistance.

Power at the regional level (whether in American states, French departments, German duchies, and so on), and at the central level, rested with traditional elites, but it had been challenged in the 1830s and 1840s by the new men of substance, whether of industrial and commercial wealth, professional degrees, or bureaucratic employment. European analysts then and since termed them bourgeois, or sometimes middle class, although that designation often described a more modest stratum. The 1848 revolutions had seen these elements try to seize power, but retreat with their own internal divisions. The politics of the 1850s and 1860s, however, became transformational but along new lines. Where political parties had become important they became less ideologically coherent. British

Tories split on the fundamental issue of tariffs, American Whigs on slavery. Even where there were no parties, political elites would divide over issues of industrial modernization and political centralization—whether in Mexico, Japan, Italy, or Prussia. This would create the worldwide alignments that struggled to remake or preserve the societies in the decades that followed.

Wars of National Reconstitution

The reconstitution of states was not a peaceful process. It entailed violence and warfare on all continents, although to a lesser degree in Africa as of midcentury. In some cases long-constituted nations took up arms once again. Whereas in Central Europe political publics felt that their nations already existed on a spiritual plane—"The nation exists in the same way that the individual does, and has no need of a people or a Parliament to proclaim the fact," Francesco Crispi wrote the venerated Italian nationalist propagandist Giuseppe Mazzini in March 1865[64]—in Latin America the long struggles for independence in the 1820s had left armies, churchmen, planters, and cattlemen yet to form coherent republics. This was a process that emerged from warfare rather than preceding it.[65] Between the mid-1850s and mid-1860s, the British were fighting in Russia, struggling to suppress a major rebellion in India, engaging in combats on the coast of China, and sporadically intervening in Latin America. The French were fighting in the same war in Russia, the same campaign in China, and then in a major expedition in Mexico. The United States, which had invaded Mexico in the 1840s, was sending military expeditions throughout Central America, landing forces in Uruguay and Argentina, and then consuming its men and energies in its Civil War. Many of the wars were national, as state builders consolidated their new territories through armed struggle, whether to overcome foreign resistance or forge sentiments of unity at home. Other conflicts were internal or "civil," contests of force over crucial issues of who would rule at home and on what principles once compromise had broken down. Some wars had aspects of both sorts. The old landed empires—Habsburg and Ottoman—proved particularly vulnerable as aspirations for national state building became more intense among subject populations. These geopolitical assemblages were embroiled in recurrent conflicts in which foreign states joined indigenous nationalities in campaigns against the imperial center. Russia fared better: after initial defeat in the Crimean War against Britain, France, and Savoy, it could expand at the expense of the Ottomans and Central Asian khanates.

Historians of Europe sometimes downplay the importance of the wars of reconstitution in comparison either with the twenty-five years of warfare that involved the French Revolution and Napoleonic expansion between 1792 and 1815 or with the two world wars in the first half of the twentieth century. It is true that warfare abated for a generation after 1815, although the contests for independence in Latin America and European portions of the Ottoman Empire flared anew in the 1820s and 1830s. Armed conflicts that might best be termed wars of European expansion led to the French conquest of Algeria in 1830 and the 1842 Anglo-Chinese clash in the southern Chinese river deltas—the so-called Opium War of 1842. At the same time that the British took up the Chinese challenge to their commercial rights in Guangzhou, they were pushing toward the Indus River valley in the states of western India, although they penetrated by a politics of alliance with local princes and rajas as much as by any show of force. Nonetheless, the politics of expansion led them into the first Afghan war of 1846. Wars of European or "white" expansion against the indigenous confederations of the Americas, Africa, and Central Asia would resume in the 1860s and 1870s, far from the capitals of their own home territories. They represented a transitional sort of conflict—wars in part to expand the power of the encroaching states, but simultaneously campaigns that suggested a new genocidal type of assault that would flourish in the twentieth century. Increasingly wars of national reconstitution were also wars of tribal destruction.

Of course, there was tremendous variety in terms of size and scope, troops committed, and duration. But these wars involved efforts to change the bases and organization of class and national solidarity. Dynastic claims, which had been so prominent in European conflicts through the eighteenth century, still played a role in the Carlist civil war in Spain in the 1830s and served as a pretext in the Franco-Prussian War of 1870 but otherwise were superseded. Some wars arose from rebellion or efforts at secession; others involved efforts at annexation or sought centralization of territorial authority. Not that they were always conceived of in those terms, but these became the implicit or explicit stakes.

A climactic war of national unification: An illustration of German troops bombarding Paris in the fall of 1870. After the American Civil War, the Franco-Prussian War was the largest of the nation-building conflicts that marked the middle decades of the nineteenth century. The Germans' rapid victory startled observers and allowed Otto von Bismarck to complete the architecture of the unified German Empire, while the defeat led the French to replace their Second Empire with a besieged Third Republic. (Library of Congress)

The critic can object: are not all wars in some sense wars of national reconstitution? Certainly the wars of the French Revolution and Napoleon involved great changes in the management of Napoleon's satellite states, as many learned from the advantages that French national mobilization seemed to confer. The wars in Europe and the Americas from 1792 to 1830 wiped out a great deal of territorial administration by the Church, enlisted new educated elites in administration, opened up the higher military ranks to talented commanders, let the British wrest decisive maritime hegemony, and mobilized large armies. Still, they were often conceived of as consequences of radical and revolutionary upheaval or later of Bonaparte's insatiable ambition; and at their conclusion there would be a major effort to restabilize a hierarchical order based on the class and constitutional equilibria of the late eighteenth century and a somewhat patched-up balance of power. The rulers who finally won on the continent even envisaged a restoration based on strengthened Christian principles, the Holy Alliance. Only in the Americas could self-made military commanders such as Andrew Jackson or Simón Bolívar challenge the imagery of a restored agrarian order in favor of populist republics.

The wars of national reconstitution from the late 1840s to the late 1870s shared some of these traits. But there was no would-be hegemonic emperor at their center and no radical ideology. They became wars for or against an encroaching nation-state order, efforts to complete the work of secularization and to challenge multiethnic empire. They were wars to survive in a world of war and of warring national states. Insofar as they led to international efforts designed to mitigate the violence, such as organization of the Red Cross of 1864 (and shortly thereafter the Red Crescent), they primarily laid down the ground rules for future war. Some of these struggles are listed in Table 1.3.

The European conflicts and the American Civil War represented armed struggles to impose—or to oppose—the construction of states built on reconstituted national or imperial principles against forces that defended a traditional social and political organization. They might also be called wars of modernization in that regardless of their intent or motivation, they resulted in societal arrangements closer to ones that prevail today. They would be followed by several decades in which the very nation-states consolidated in midcentury would turn their mobilized energies and technical prowess out to the "periphery." These produced the defensive struggles by nomadic confederations at the perimeters of white settlement that were mentioned the introduction, but other confrontations as well, through the 1880s and continuing until the end of the century, struggles marked by savagery on both sides: the American Indian resistance against US control of the Missouri Valley region, and the Apaches' battles in the Southwest in the 1880s; the British conquest of the Zulu state's resistance against British control in South Africa; the doomed effort by the Central Asian khanates against Russian control of Central Asian steppes and highlands; thereafter the quasi-genocidal Argentine conquest of Patagonia and the ongoing sporadic resistance in Yucatán of the Maya against the Mexican national authorities. But there were also wars of conquest against the small states of the perimeter. The War of the Triple Alliance against Paraguay included elements of racialized warfare that

TABLE 1.3

Wars of national reconstitution

1845–1847	War of Swiss national consolidation (Sonderbund War).
1846–1848	US-Texan-Mexican war for control of northern Mexican territory.
1848–1849	War for the control of northern Italy: Piedmont and volunteers against Austria.
1849	Austro-Russian war to suppress Magyar rebellion against Habsburg rule.
1850–1864	Yangzi Valley war between secessionist Taiping state and Chinese Empire.
1853–1855	Anglo-French-Piedmontese war in the Crimea to limit Russian power in the Black Sea and Ottoman arenas. Settlement at Congress of Paris.
1856–1857	British suppressions of military insurrections in India and enhancement of colonial control.
1856–1860	Second Opium or Arrow War: Britain and France extract further Chinese acceptance of extraterritoriality regime.
1858–1860	Civil war ("War of the Reform") in Mexico.
1858–1860	Rebellions in Ottoman Near East; sectarian strife in Mt. Lebanon, Beirut, Damascus.
1859–1860	Franco/Savoy-Austrian war to remove northern Italy from Austrian control, carried out in conjunction with Garibaldian intervention to wrest south Italy from the Bourbon regime.
1860s	The "Brigandage" in southern Italy: continuing guerrilla attacks against the new Italian administration/occupation; finally suppressed with fierce reprisals by the new Kingdom. Unsuccessful Garibaldian campaigns against Rome in 1862 and 1867.
1861–1865	US war to repress secession of Confederate States.
1863–1866	French expeditionary force to seize control of Mexico. Mexican civil war.
1864	War of German Confederation against Denmark over nationality of Schleswig. Leads to 1866 Austro-Prussian war for leadership in German Central Europe and Prussian-Italian-Austrian war to remove Austrians from Venetia and Alpine regions.
1864–1870	War of the Triple Alliance: Paraguay loses 80,000 inhabitants, or half its male population, age 13–60, and 40 percent of its territory to Brazil, Argentina, and Uruguay.
1866–1869	Unsuccessful Cretan (Greek) revolt against Ottomans.
1867–1868	Japanese civil war: Tokugawa adherents defeated by Meiji national forces.
1870–1871	Franco-Prussian war for territorial rearrangements and to unify North and South Germany under Prussia.

(continued)

TABLE 1.3

Wars of national reconstitution *(continued)*

1875–1878	Russian defeat of Ottomans in support of Bulgarian independence struggle. Treaty of San Stefano and, later, a revised general European settlement at Congress of Berlin.

Source: Brian Holden Reid, *The Civil War and the Wars of the Nineteenth Century* (New York: HarperCollins / Smithsonian Books, 2006).

Note: The list is partial and omits some secessionist episodes, as in Spain (1873), but includes China's unsuccessful efforts to resist European pressure.

may have led to the highest national death rates of any modern war, perhaps 50 percent of the prewar population. Paraguay, though, was still a well-organized state with diplomatic representation.

Once the conquest of the perimeter and its peoples was largely accomplished—a result that US citizens called the closing of the frontier—the twentieth century would begin with the great wars (1894–1923) between contending imperial states—some ascending in power, others confronting once again, as they had a generation earlier, difficult internal crises.

Although they mobilized less manpower and exacted a lower level of casualties from participants (except for the Taiping uprising and American Civil War) than the Napoleonic wars or the First World War, the midcentury wars of national reconstitution could become protracted, often involving wars of position, sieges, and long fronts. Bismarck was correct about the iron as well as the blood. The victors in these struggles drew on the resources of the Industrial Revolution: breech-loading rifles and the early versions of rapid-fire repeating guns, more-deadly artillery, ironclad ships, and the gunboats that proved decisive in river fighting. Prototype submarines and the early torpedo (invented by a British engineer in Austrian Trieste) made their appearance. Most important was the development of the railroads, which could move masses of soldiers with relative speed. This signaled the difference between the American Civil War and the wars of German unification, on the one hand, and the great Chinese civil war, the Taiping rebellion, which, though it began much earlier, would be settled in the same years of the 1860s. The Chinese fighting, though it featured massive sanguinary massacres, saw units of five to fifteen thousand troops ferried east and west on the Yangzi; the American fighting brought armies of over a hundred thousand to bear by means of the railroad, as well as sea and river communications.[66]

Clear-sighted military attachés sent to observe these great conflicts or sometimes seconded to assist in them could discern another fact: although railroads might deploy armies more rapidly and in greater numbers, and modern artillery might reduce old-style fortifications, the defense could tenaciously dig in, as did Confederate General Robert E. Lee in Virginia. In some respects the brilliant victory of Prussia over Austria in the summer of 1866 was misleading. Although it was decisive for the ascendancy of Prussia and the German national state, the Prussian triumph at Königgrätz (Sadowa) in Moravia resulted from relatively old-style tactics of a line offensive that was successful against a decrepit adversary. As the most astute observer, Archduke Albrecht of Austria, observed, the Prussians devolved responsibility on corps officers whereas his own imperial army organization impeded responsibility at all levels.[67] Encouraging small-unit initiative remained the key to battlefield success from earlier French victories under Napoleon to later German triumphs in 1940, and the approach would deeply influence Israeli doctrine long after 1945.

Just as fundamental a lesson was that that modern war was often decided away from the battlefield, in those organizations required for the state mobilization of power. The Prussians had pioneered the general staff, a military think tank whose officers served both as a central planning office and as operational consultants with the battlefield units. The very grinding nature of the warfare also meant that state agencies—to procure matériel, supervise transport, supply and arsenals, organize credit and finance, and develop medical services—had to be organized or enlarged. The toll taken by projectiles led to reorganization of military hospitals: Florence Nightingale's work for the British army in Crimea, and the US Sanitary Commission's tending to Northern wounded in the American Civil War.[68] And armies had to promote their gifted organizers and engineers and not only dashing horsemen or those who had family connections. For countries (including the British) that had clung to older methods of recruiting their officer corps—such as the purchase of commissions—it was realized that professional training and accreditation had to be stepped up.

Most crucially, perhaps, the wars of national reconstitution reintroduced ideas and practices that suggested unarmed citizens were participants in the armed conflicts. Previous wars had never lacked for the deliberate burning of buildings and ports, and, unofficially at least, pillage and rape. And the great wars of 1789–1815 had mobilized civilian levees—most notably by the French after 1793, but then in imitation by the Prussians in 1813–1814. Warfare must, it was realized outside Great Britain, place young males under the obligation to serve their countries. As part of this democratization of warfare, however, the idea emerged that the civilian population had a responsibility for causing or continuing war. Again the French Revolution had evoked the nation in arms, but the corollary idea of the nation as a target was never made explicit. General William Tecumseh Sherman decided that economic devastation in a prosperous keystone region of the Confederacy would shorten the North's struggle to defeat its adversary. Germans invading France in 1870 were convinced that French civilians would take up arms as irregular forces or *franc-tireurs,* and faced considerable guerrilla activity after subduing the official armies of Napoleon III.

In short, warfare was central to the reorganization of states, nations, and empires in the mid-nineteenth century. British North America (Canada) was the one exception, perhaps, and it had gone to the brink in the 1830s. One cannot conceive of the modern nation-state, in the form that has prevailed since the 1850s or at least from the 1850s into the 1970s, without taking into account the applications of armed force—the use of explosives, lethal flying metal splinters, maiming of young bodies, and destruction of property—that accompanied it. Nineteenth-century liberal nation builders as well as the generals, who could themselves be moved and dismayed by the suffering, were willing to pay that price. Others, less sensitive, seemed positively to welcome the exercise as a manly exercise. Wars that were a path to empire were simultaneously struggles to reaffirm a gendered supremacy at home. Certainly that was part of their result, until, at least in the twentieth century, one had to enlist women in too many related efforts. In any case, the indispensability of violence can be ignored no more than one can leave out of account the role of at least localized genocidal policies in the maintenance of empire. In that sense the nineteenth century would flow into the twentieth, as we shall see subsequently. And of course, most of those taking the initiative in these policies believed the price was necessary and worth paying. To understand the bargains, we must avoid imposing our humanistic scruples of the late twentieth century. Just as terrorists today still remain convinced that individual lives cannot be allowed to get in the way of higher principles and loyalties, for the mid-nineteenth century, history increasingly was seen as a providential juggernaut: a steamroller of civilization and higher cultures that had to triumph over lower ones.

For God *or* Country

Open the era with an almost comic-opera civil war of three weeks in November 1847, in which seven of the predominantly Catholic cantons of Switzerland, who had formed their own "separate alliance" or Sonderbund to resist what they saw as Protestant centralization, were invaded and defeated by the Protestant forces. The victorious invaders lost 60 dead and 385 wounded; the defeated Catholics had 26 dead and 114 wounded. The Sonderbund forces had coalesced in 1843 against the efforts by the Protestant Radical party to strengthen the constitution of the confederation as well as to close and secularize Catholic monasteries. When the canton of Lucerne invited Jesuits to establish a center, Protestant irregulars had taken up arms, the Catholics organized their internal alliance, and the war finally erupted four years later. Swiss unity and neutrality had been inscribed in the European order at Vienna in 1815, so secession was hardly an alternative. The Protestant victory, however, led to a strengthened confederation and the ascent of commercial and secular forces.

The alignment of forces in the struggle was not new. Loyal Catholics had felt on the defensive against the secularizing state since the Enlightenment and the French Revolution. In Spain the liberals who had pushed through a constitution at Cádiz in 1812—to be abrogated by the restored Bourbon monarch, Ferdinand VII—returned to influence with the accession of Queen Christina as regent for her daughter Isabella in 1833, provoking the Catholic traditionalists of Navarre in the Pyrenees to take up arms on behalf of the brother of the late king. The resulting Carlist War lasted six years and became a major issue in European diplomacy. Loyal churchgoers in the former Catholic archbishopric of Cologne, under French rule after 1795, then assigned to Prussia's Rhine Province in 1815, had demonstrated against Berlin's effort to secure a compliant archbishop in

1840. The division was indicative—state supporters of secular or Protestant policies provoking a pro-papal resistance on the part of Catholic traditionalists (so-called Ultra montanist, because of the adherents' alleged loyalty to the religious authority across the Alps).

Did the emerging nation-states and the Catholic Church have to go separate ways? The greatest and most inspiring prophet of nationalism in Italy, Mazzini, had seen the nation as a divine association that might coexist with religious institutions. But over the next two generations the continental European nation-state—in Prussian Germany, the Third Republic, the Kingdom of Sardinia (Savoy or Piedmont), and then united Italy (which occupied the papal territories in 1870)—would be reconstructed, centralized, and secularized at the expense of a papacy that increasingly set its standard against modern liberalism and state education. In Mexico the same conflicts would be enacted on an epic scale. Monastic lands beckoned state treasuries and would-be bourgeois purchasers at repeated intervals: originally in Iberia and Ibero-America in the 1760s, then in France during the Revolution, and in the Germanies, Naples, and Spain during the Napoleonic occupations, in Spain again during the 1830s, and in Piedmont under Cavour's liberal auspices in the 1850s. But it was not just land that was at stake. Despite a few romantic populists such as Félicité Lamennais, the Roman clergy was increasingly boxed into conservative stances, especially under the papacy of Pius IX (1846–1878), who had been forced to flee Rome during the revolution of 1848, and then found the papal states (stretching across central Italy up to Bologna and the Romagna) progressively annexed by the new Kingdom of Italy. In 1864 the papacy's "Syllabus of Errors" would insist that it was wrong for Catholics to accept the teachings of liberalism; in 1870–1871, the Vatican Council would insist that the pope was infallible in issues of faith and morals. There was no room for democracy within the Church or in the wider world. The French authoritarian Catholic Louis Veuillot admitted that the Church wanted freedom of speech to propagate its doctrines but believed in denying it to others. Rome saw the new world of nineteenth-century statehood as a force for despoliation—which it often was—and the indoctrination of children in atheism. Protestantism was just as bad, given Prussia's campaign against Austria—the natural protector of the papacy, unfortunately ejected from Italy after 1859—and then Bismarck's war against the Church in the 1870s, one he christened as a struggle for civilization *(Kulturkampf)* and that involved the dissolution and expulsion of monastic orders, including the Prussian Jesuits. In Iberia, Freemasons supposedly threatened the Church as the occult center of the secular network, a belief that remained powerful through the dictatorship of Francisco Franco until the mid-1970s.

From the other side of this epic squaring off, state officials and liberals beheld a reactionary special interest seeking to block the rights of conscience, the freedom of the press and speech, and modern financial administration. Educational systems would become the battleground after 1870. Suffering as a "prisoner in the Vatican" after the Italians took Rome as their capital, smarting from the eclipse of Catholic loyalists after the establishment of the Third Republic in the same year, out of power in Mexico, prosecuted in Germany (until Bismarck shifted his allies in 1878–1879), beleaguered Catholics would establish votive churches, such as the basilica of Sacré-Coeur on the hill of Montmartre in Paris, to atone for the transgressions of their impious polities. (Emperor Franz Joseph would erect a neo-Gothic specimen on the Ringstrasse in Vienna, to atone for an anarchist's stabbing of his beloved wife, Elisabeth, known as "Sissi.") The secular state, defiantly male and aggressive, would face a Church that, as during the Catholic revival in Ireland, increasingly reconstructed its parish life around the role of women. And not just women nuns, but middle-class women who would tend to charities and good works, and occasionally adolescent girls of rural milieu, who, moved perhaps by the political martyrdom of their Church as explained in their Sunday homilies, claimed to see and speak with the Virgin—at Marpingen in the Rhineland, Lourdes in the French Pyrenees, and later Fátima in Portugal.[69]

But if the blessed mother of Jesus could cure thousands of afflicted pilgrims who came to these sacred sites, she could not really roll back the advances of the liberal state and its administrative and commercial reforms. Her new churches memorialized the inexorable setback to her claims within the nation-state, just as the brief tribal victories at the Little Bighorn or the Zulu battlefields were in their way monuments to the defeat of the resistance at the frontiers of its expansion. Protestant or secular, male and militant, restlessly commercial, building railroads and buying new and improved artillery, rifles, and naval vessels, the nation-state advanced. Whether its commercial energies would ensure that these politically divided territorial units would vie in peace, or whether their military instincts (strengthened by the wars that had accompanied their creation) would lead to catastrophic combat, had yet to be decided. Certainly there were commentators who predicted each of these dénouements.

It is correct, but too simple, to group the new loyalties that were to prevail as those of nationalism. Nationalism—an idea originally of elites in search of a primitive and vital people who would be summoned to take on political form, establish a territory and government—had been placed on the European agenda by the French Revolution and then the Napoleonic wars. By midway through his period of rule, Napoleon I, the emperor of the French, was provoking opponents speaking the language of nationalist resistance. The Spanish partisans of the exiled Bourbon dynasty, the constitutionalists of Cádiz, and the popular forces or ex-Bourbon soldiers in the guerrilla movements that mobilized in the peninsula formed one manifestation. The philosopher Johann Gottlieb Fichte, lecturing in Berlin under French occupation, claimed to address a German "nation." The Italian writers aspiring to political independence for their lands began to advocate the reform not just of Austrian Lombardy, or Naples, but of Italy as a political unit. Some of the intellectual and military leaders from Prussia and smaller states envisaged not just a Prussian revival (although that might serve as a beginning for their aspirations), and not just a revived confederal organization for Central Europe, but a German nation. The Americans who went to war against the British in 1812 and thought of annexing Canada, or a few years later Cuba, struck a new chord of national truculence.

Of course the emerging ideas went back further. Concepts of the state as an international actor, as a force that must liberate itself from Church control, were intense since the Renaissance. The eighteenth century restored notions of the *Volk* as a vital people who had collectively formed languages, inspired epic poems (in one celebrated case, the supposed Scottish epic "Ossian" simply invented), and gathered folk and fairy tales, most famously those collected in the post Napoleonic years by the Grimm brothers, who also incurred political persecution for their democratic sentiments. The Romantic sensibility of the era just strengthened the appeal of this new sentiment, which could be nourished by literature, poetry, and opera as well as inspiring oratory. Students and other activists formed associations of Young Italy or Young America by the 1830s. In Germany, angered at the repressive censorship that Metternich had imposed on the German Confederation in the Carlsbad Decrees of 1819, students celebrated the tercentenary of Luther's original challenge to Roman Catholic authority, and in 1832 staged a patriotic gathering at the Saxon castle where Luther had found a sanctuary.[70]

But it was easier to dream a nation than to form one. The Italian effort failed in both 1848 and 1849. Theorists had proposed schemes for the pope to become president of an Italian federation; others just called for federation. The young monarch of Savoy, Charles Albert, envisaged that he might take the command of the revolutionary agitation that swept the cities of Italy under Austrian rule; he raised an army, crossed the river border into Lombardy, and was soundly defeated. Rebels in Venice had better luck and could declare a republic and maintain it within the city until August 1849. But the Habsburg court recovered from its indecisiveness by the fall of 1848 as the young Franz Joseph took the throne under the tutelage of determined aristocratic political advisers and generals. Austria was still large and powerful, held the key north–south river routes and their fortifications in northern Italy, and was not prepared to relinquish the provinces it had held even before the Congress of Vienna. In the spring of 1849, Charles Albert took up arms again, and was defeated anew and compelled to abdicate. Habsburg troops forced the surrender of Venice. Facing a renewed Magyar revolution, the Austrians got help from the Russians to suppress the revolutionary and secessionist regime in Budapest. Liberal nationalists had to bide their time. Many, including Lajos Kossuth, Carl Schurz, and Richard Wagner, fled permanently or temporarily into exile. Others accepted the straitened limits of populist politics and would join the new middle-of-the road forces willing to compromise with the post-1848 leadership, whether liberal as in Piedmont, or pragmatic as in Prussia. Many devoted their energies to supporting railroad development and agricultural improvement societies. Scientific agriculture as much as any rising industry looked to the soil as well as the territory. Cavour was a gentry farmer. The horse fairs and annual exhibitions of scientific husbandry and agriculture offered in effect a form of surrogate politics in contexts where national politics was either not yet or no longer an option—as in Ireland, Poland, and Italy during the 1850s.[71]

The reactionary aftermath of 1848 was bitter, but it would be relatively brief. Counterrevolutionaries, whether in Paris after the June Days of 1848 or in the recaptured territories of the Veneto, Hungary, and revolutionary Vienna, would shoot their opponents generously, but might pardon them by 1850–1851. Radicals changed their mentality. In 1849 the Russian revolutionary exile Alexander Herzen wrote to his son and readership in Russia, "I see the inevitable downfall of the old Europe and mourn nothing that exists, neither the heights attained by her education nor her institutions." And he rhetorically asked, "Why then do I stay *here*? I stay because the struggle is going on here. Here in spite of the blood and tears, social problems are being worked out and painful and burning as the suffering here is, it is articulate. The struggle is open and above board. No one hides. Woe betide the vanquished but at least they will have given battle." Twenty years later he wrote his erstwhile co-radical Mikhail Bakunin, who was still a partisan of revolutionary upheaval:

> You have not changed much, though sorely tried by life. . . . And if I have changed, remember that *everything has changed*. We have seen the frightful example of a bloody insurrection which, at a moment of rage and despair [he was referring to the June Days of 1848], took to the barricades and only then realized that it had no banner. . . . But what would have happened if the barricades had triumphed? Could those formidable combatants, at the age of twenty[,] have given voice to all that lay in their hearts? Their testament does not contain a single constructive, organic idea, and economic errors unlike the political ones which have an indirect effect, lead directly and deeply, to ruin, stagnation, and starvation. . . . Even if our whole bourgeois world were blown to bits, some sort of bourgeois world would arise after the smoke had dissipated and the ruins had been cleared away.[72]

And so it did.

Controlled Transformation

The national agenda was far more widespread than in Europe alone. In 1853 the American naval commander Matthew Perry anchored his squadron of four ships outside today's Tokyo Bay to open negotiations with the Japanese government, which had no naval force to counter the Americans. Washington demanded guarantees for the safety of shipwrecked sailors and commercial access to the largely self-enclosed society. With the acquisition of California from Mexico and recognition of the Oregon claims by Great Britain, the North American republic was a Pacific power by the end of the 1840s. Its vessels plied a vigorous commerce with China; Japan offered coaling stations and its own goods and lay athwart the trading route. Perry's visit followed several unsuccessful attempts to win access; for since the early years of the Tokugawa shogunate Japan had been shut down to the world with the exception of a Japanese outpost at Nagasaki at its southern tip.

Perry's menacing visit exposed what would become a fifteen-year crisis for the Tokugawa regime (the so-called *bakufu* or military administration), named after the warlord Tokugawa Ieyasu, the last of a string of three strongmen, who by 1603 after incessant campaigning had imposed a new sort of settlement on the ancient monarchy wracked by civil wars and feudal disaggregation. The imperial line, preserved with its feckless court nobility at Kyoto, had ensured ideological cohesion but little else. Policy was dictated by the shogun at Edo (later Tokyo), an office that had remained in the same family for 250 years. The realm was divided into about ninety autonomous domains or *han,* each ruled by a *daimyō* and a class of military and bureaucratic retainers or samurai entitled to bear arms and to exact visible deference from town merchants and peasants. Blood relatives of the Tokugawa line and those *daimyō* who had joined forces with the ascendant shoguns before 1603, the *fudai,* controlled the inner domains proximate to Kyoto and Edo. Those who submitted after 1603, the *tozama* or outer *daimyō,* were allocated about 40 percent of the lands farther north or south in the archipelago. In return for their domainal autonomy the *daimyō* were required to keep close family members at the shogun's court at Edo and reside there for half of each year with many of their samurai retainers. These great and frequent processions of the *daimyō* back and forth from their domains filled the roads of Japan, made Edo into a center of trade, personal services, and consumer goods, a lively theater and pleasure scene, and at perhaps a million permanent residents (estimates vary) by the eighteenth century, a rival to London, Paris, and Constantinople. The residencies consumed up to half the revenue that the domainal lords could raise from their peasantry. But the more consequential action was taking place within the further domains such as Tosa, Chōshū, and Satsuma, where European technologies and administrative methods were being studied and emulated without the resistance of a conservative court bureaucracy such as paralyzed equivalent initiatives in China.

Where reforming *daimyō,* such as Mōri Yoshichika of Chōshū and Shimazu Nariakira of Satsuma, could prevail, they prepared their domains to challenge the conservative forces of the shogunate. The reformist *daimyō* efforts to modernize these territories and a more strident resistance to the threat of foreign encroachment went hand in hand.

But the American visit of 1853 posed the fundamental question: must Japan open to the Western world or should it shut down and rely on a conservative reassertion of its isolation and self-stratification? It crystallized the division between the conservative forces of the shogunate, who sought to preserve the old regime, and the impatient nationalists of the outer *han,* who believed that the kingdom must modernize to withstand the foreigner and forestall the regime of extraterritorial possessions that the British and French were imposing on the Chinese. The diaries of the fledgling British diplomat Ernest Satow reveal the growing violence of this confrontation as young, impatient samurai resorted to assassinating political leaders they thought too compliant toward the foreigners.[73] By 1867 the reformers of Chōshū, Satsuma, and Tosa had gained domination at the court. After marching on Edo with their armies, they forced the shogun to renounce his offices and "restore" governing power to the young Meiji emperor, who would henceforth speak for their policies. There would be further resistance in the northern island of Hokkaidō in 1869 and a doomed rebellion by diehard conservatives (one of whom, Saigō Takimori, enjoyed popularity as an honest and faithful reformer) in 1877.

The Meiji Restoration was in fact a controlled transformation from above, but with a radical impact. Japan entered one of those intense periods of rapid absorption of successful foreign models that periodically marked its history— whether centuries earlier with respect to China or later after defeat by the United States in 1945. Within a few years of 1867, the new oligarchy decreed a sweeping series of reforms. They eliminated the samurai class as a legal order and prohibited the traditional right to wear short and long swords. They transformed the old *han* into new provinces, each of which was to be governed by an imperial appointee as governor (prefect), and they fobbed off the old *daimyō* by placing them in a house of peers. Feudal dues were ended, and the *daimyō* landlords compensated by issues of government bonds that provided revenue from interest. (Russia had chosen this method of compensation when the state eliminated serfdom in 1861 and placed noble lands into the control of village communes.) They started to develop shipyards and arsenals and began a more intensive program of sending bright students abroad for technical and medical education. Within a generation the country transformed itself, determined not only to avoid national humiliation but to play the imperialist game itself, seeking enclaves in China and predominant influence over the Korean court. The Japanese state entered the nation-state system as a determined and successful participant.

Only by 1890, as the Japanese elite began to claim an assertive role in the East Asian arena, would they broaden the national project by bringing in a broader citizenry. Scrutinizing European constitutions for guidance, the now-aging Meiji reformers chose the German model, not the British, American, or French patterns that granted a broad role for elected legislatures. The new Meiji constitution allowed the monarch and his civil servants a strong role in keeping parliamentary institutions within bounds: the new prime minister held his office at the pleasure of the emperor; the military leadership was given key cabinet roles as ministers of war and navy, and the army remained immune from parliamentary scrutiny. The Imperial Rescript on education of 1890 envisaged that the imperial state would in effect breathe life into an imperial citizenry through patriotic education and state-sponsored piety.[74]

Historians and sociologists have long groped for ways to characterize experiences such as Japan's, just as they had for revolutionary upheavals such as the French. For over a century Marxist theory seemed to offer a plausible, if often contested, framework. Marxist-derived explanations tended to view the agents for change as exponents of a bourgeois or middle-class world that advocated economic development, market forces, and universal legal norms against the feudal and agrarian elites of the past. The growth of commerce and early industry generated new group interests, which demanded and ultimately attained a greater political and legal role, not smoothly but through a series of revolutionary upheavals, just as ultimately, proponents often believed, it would bring the working classes to power in a new era of collective property.[75] Those who contested this historical description emphasized that often members of older aristocracies led the reform effort and pointed to the conservative aspirations of those taking up arms. This is not a debate to be resolved in a brief historical chapter. Marxian analyses serve perhaps most usefully to reveal the similarity among radical trans-formative processes, but less persuasively as detailed explanations for their indi-vidual trajectories. They have often been most insightful when their advocates, including Marx himself and his collaborator, Friedrich Engels, had to account for events that did not follow their early templates, such as the French and German revolutions of 1848.[76] Faced with the decisive role of the Japanese nationalist samurai (or the Prussian elite), analysts have often sought to describe the late nineteenth-century transformation as modernization from above. "From above" is correct in that national leaders, sometimes ministers, sometimes monarchs, pushed through important reforms that undermined the "feudal" institutions of an older regime. Nonetheless, broad-based popular agitation and stubborn loyalties to village and local rights were never absent. The Japanese leaders them-selves engaged in hard and vigorous debate over their policies, even if outsiders rarely saw the hard infighting in these years (in contrast to the assassinations that marked the 1850s and again the 1930s). Modernization from above, in fact, was perhaps the most widespread strategy for preserving state viability in an era whose statesmen understood that collective existence required fiscal efficiency, in-dustrial and military modernization, and a dedication to competition. Thus, mili-tary challenges often advanced administrative centralization, as in earlier centuries they had compelled fiscal centralization. Other examples of this approach took place—with less decisive results, however—in the Ottoman Empire, in Egypt, later in the Russian Empire, for a period in Mexico, and in Thailand. Sometimes the term is applied to the new unified German "empire" that Bismarck worked to make a powerful German nation-state.

In fact, modernization from above is a rather loose term and, as we shall see, can be applied to at least two or three varieties of experience. The classical model of this process referred to a strategy for old empires and states that relied heavily on the traditional structures of religion and landlord domination over peasants, but found themselves threatened from abroad, especially by the most corrosive social force loose in the mid-nineteenth century: British financial and industrial capitalism, along with the burgeoning trade of energetic entrepreneurs (and their supportive regimes) in Europe and the United States. To respond, the determined and ambitious administrators of these states believed they had, in effect, to create citizens by edict and to harness their productive energies with state-sponsored industry. This meant in turn linking families and individuals directly to the state and diminishing the control of their landlords. Religious authority might remain useful in the process, but the political autonomy of religious authorities was to be subordinated to the secular administration with more or less success. Japan, Russia, Turkey were all examples. In late imperial China, the reformers who attempted such endeavors after 1860 tended to be outweighed by the residual power of traditional court policies. The ancient Chinese state claimed too much conservative legitimacy. It would take a revolution to clear away resistance, and even then the emerging reformers confronted very resistant patterns of popular inertia and entrenched privilege.

But modernization from above is a term that can also describe a more temporary recourse of states that had less powerful or venerable regimes in place. Several major states with robust traditions of popular participation in legislatures and at the local level resorted to a few decades of rapid industrialization and military reforms as a consequence of the civil strife and war of the mid-nineteenth century. If in the first category summarized above, civil servants attempted to compensate for an underdeveloped civil society and little democratization at the national level, in this second group they attempted to overcome the policy stalemates that resulted from regimes already democratic, but deeply divided over fundamental issues. Naturally enough, this second set of experiences included significant varieties of transformation. In France the population accepted the downgrading of the national assembly by Louis Napoleon (soon crowned as Napoleon III), who helped to superintend almost two decades of economic development and ambitious foreign interventions, which finally brought him down. In Mexico another developmental dictator supported by a national elite (and foreign investors) emerged out of midcentury conflicts over reform and then invasion, as in Mexico. In the United States, the Republican Party pushed through the end to slavery, opened the western lands to free homesteading, and encouraged industrial development from the end of the 1850s into the 1890s.

Such a recourse to controlled transformation was compatible with regimes that already gave a large scope to electoral participation. In the United States the transformations resulted from the challenge of war, which in turn derived from the deep conflicts over which system of labor and economy would prevail in the gigantic acquisitions of land at the time of the Mexican War. The founders of the American Republic had compromised on the issue of slavery when they created their constitution in the late 1780s. They had agreed to let the institution continue—otherwise there would never have been a United States—but prohibit the importation of slaves after twenty years. This prohibition helped make the breeding of slaves for use in the newer states of the Gulf a lucrative commerce in its own right. But what was to be the regime in the lands opened west of the Mississippi? The effort at a stable compromise in 1820, which would have allowed slavery to be installed in Missouri, but otherwise only in territory south of Missouri's latitude (36°30′), proved unviable.

Northern farmers and laboring men could not tolerate the expansion of a system they felt threatened their own livelihood and national future. The economic stakes became higher as the factory looms of Lancashire and the American North multiplied their demand for raw cotton, even as the ideological and moral issues were sharpened. Southerners felt their peculiar institution was under threat from the new parties that were emerging from the development-oriented Whig coalition of the 1830s and 1840s, whether the dissenting antislavery Democrats, or the "conscience Whigs" in 1848, such as Abraham Lincoln, or the Free-Soilers in 1852 and the Republican Party in 1856. The older veterans of the Senate, Henry Clay, Daniel Webster, and John C. Calhoun, had engineered another compromise in 1850, which would let slavery exist in Texas and the District of Columbia, but not in California. Most objectionably to Northern adversaries, it required the return of escaped slaves and provided a fee for their recovery. The Free-Soilers and then the new Republicans saw a militant South demanding an unlimited extension of slavery—a conclusion strengthened by the Kansas-Nebraska Act and then by the US Supreme Court's 1857 *Dred Scott* decision, which ruled not only that Scott, a slave, had not gained a claim on freedom through his master's having brought him into a free state, but that persons of color had no claim on the constitutional rights provided for white Americans. Antislavery senatorial candidate Abraham Lincoln and incumbent senator Stephen Douglas squared off in a series of fundamental debates on race and the frayed territorial compromises on slavery in the Illinois campaign of 1858; Douglas won reelection, but Lincoln emerged as the Republican nominee for the presidential contest of 1860.

The race took place against the threat of growing sectional violence. A radicalized midwestern farmer, John Brown, already a participant in the Kansas skirmishes over slavery, attempted to seize a federal arsenal and ignite a slave revolt in northern Virginia in 1859 and was executed in December. Excited Southerners declared they would leave the Union if the Republican candidate, Lincoln, won the presidential election of 1860, which he did with 40 percent of the popular vote but a clear electoral-vote majority, in a four-way race. Advocates of secession opened debates in the legislatures of the Southern states, where the firebrands of South Carolina in the lead urged establishing an independent slave-holding republic. They bombarded the federal military base at Fort Sumter in Charleston, South Carolina, when Lincoln sent a flotilla to supply it in April 1861. The armed clash swayed the debate in Virginia, and eleven states voted to join the secession as units of the Confederate States of America.

The ensuing four-year war, which would cost the two sides together about 700,000 dead—a percentage of young men comparable to later casualty rates among Europeans in the First World War—sealed the transformation of the North American nation-state. The war itself was a slow and ponderous affair. If one measured the resources each side brought, the Union was clearly superior in population, industrial power, and railroad resources. It possessed the legitimacy of almost seventy-five years of statehood. Lincoln's call for troops brought an enthusiastic response. Nonetheless, the Confederacy was a large region and it had apparently only to keep the North at bay to secure its independence. However, a protracted war would also devastate its economy and reduce it materially. Its major cash crop, whose British sales had enriched the planter class in the 1850s, would probably remain bottled up because the Northern navy could blockade its major ports. The Union must be discouraged sufficiently to make it cease its effort to compel Confederate surrender.

The fighting began on the East Coast. The Southern capital at Richmond was only 150 miles from Washington. Initial combat revealed that the Southern armies were well led and resourceful. The attempt to land troops on the James Peninsula and then march inland toward Richmond failed because of the excessive caution of the commander, General George B. McClelland. The central valley of Virginia and the upper Potomac hills became an area of frequent combat but inconclusive gains. A major bloody victory in Antietam in western Maryland in

September 1862 let Lincoln issue the Emancipation Proclamation, which declared slaves under Southern control to be free men. But this was a promise to liberate precisely those over whom the North had no control.

Heavy fighting also took place during 1862 and 1863 in Tennessee. The tributaries of the Mississippi that flowed through Tennessee would allow the Northern troops to penetrate the cotton states of Georgia, Alabama, and Mississippi. But again the battles oscillated. Border states that did not secede—Kentucky, Maryland—still had Southern sympathies but remained under the military thumb of the North. By 1862 Union forces occupied the coastal islands of Georgia and took New Orleans from the sea, imposing an occupation regime on Louisiana. A year later General Ulysses Grant secured Northern control over the Mississippi Valley by compelling the surrender of Vicksburg, which meant that Texas was separated from the main body of the Confederacy and the north–south transportation axis of the western confederacy was closed. The Southern wager on advancing in the east into Pennsylvania (and further) had initial promising results—precisely at a moment when antiwar sentiment was becoming strong among the immigrant working class of New York, now feeling the grip of conscription. But the defeat at Gettysburg in July 1863 meant that henceforth the South must fight on the defensive.

Still it took almost another two years to force the surrender of an increasingly devastated Confederacy. Lincoln finally found a determined, tough commanding general in Grant, but Grant advanced slowly. The 1864 fighting in Virginia was immensely costly. More promising, General Sherman swung from Tennessee into Georgia, purposefully devastating the countryside as he advanced. He captured Atlanta, then moved toward the coast at Augusta, then headed north through the Carolinas. His army converged with Grant's near Richmond in the spring of 1865 and forced the remnants of the Confederate armies to surrender. The South was devastated. Its black labor force was now legally free, and many were fleeing from their plantations. Food was meager. Railroads and housing were often destroyed. Marauding bands of looters terrorized parts of the countryside. The war devastated the Southern economy; reduced the influence of its formerly slave-holding elite, but expanded the role of the reestablished central government and eventually united Southern and Northern industrial leaders in their determination to extract wealth from technology as well as cotton and wheat.[77]

Unfortunately the outcome of the war solved neither the issue of racial prejudice nor that of economic viability. Although they were legally emancipated, the black families of the South did not receive title to land, but continued as tenants where they had labored as slaves. Compelled to turn to their former masters for credit to plant their yearly cotton crop, much of which had to be surrendered to defray their debt and rent—the American "sharecropping" version of a rural pattern widespread at many times and places—many were reduced to an unremitting cycle of debt dependency. For about a decade Northern troops occupied the South, enforced voting without racial discrimination, and seemed ready to impose a regime of racial equality. But blacks were poor, the legislatures were resented, and white vigilantes often imposed local tyrannies based on nocturnal terror. The Republicans in the Congress tired of the conflict, and to secure victory in the deadlocked presidential election of 1876 agreed to remove the remaining troops. Within two decades the blacks were largely excluded from the ballot, intimidated by the white-hooded Ku Klux Klan, and reduced to subservience. Efforts to unite poor whites and blacks against the "Bourbon" white elites were usually trumped by racial demagogy. By the 1890s the former Confederacy would join such Eastern European regions as Hungary and Romania as one-party landlord-dominated states, where legalized servitude had been replaced by ethnic coercion, peasant impoverishment, rigged voting rights, de facto peonage, and exaggerated ideologies of national purity.[78]

The large geographical units to the south and north of the United States—Mexico and Canada—also underwent major transformations that combined institutional transformation, settlement of their vast territories, economic development, and consolidation of a new elite. The Mexican Republic was fated to develop, as one of its leaders quipped, so far from God, so close to the United States. Of course, it began from a different starting point: three centuries as a colony of a Catholic monarchy with a powerful church and centralized monastic settlements; an Indian population that recovered demographically during the long seventeenth and eighteenth centuries; and whites proud of their Spanish descent even as many intermarried and produced a large population of mixed or "mestizo" ethnicity. The independence movement was ignited by a radicalized clerical leadership in 1810 but was soon suppressed by the Spanish. It was successfully resumed a decade later by ambitious military leaders—some claiming traditions of a populist and decentralizing left, others pressing the centralizing and briefly (under Augustín de Iturbide) imperial claims of the right. Iturbide, who had helped Spanish forces defeat the revolutionaries of 1810, led the new rebellion when Madrid fell under the control of the liberals in 1820, claiming the title of emperor until exiled and ultimately executed. However, the continuing turbulence and warfare undermined the prosperity achieved at the end of the era of Bourbon reform. Catholic conservatives and liberal anticlericals replaced each other in power as the cynical and populist military strongman, General Antonio López Santa Anna, repeatedly switched sides, claimed the presidency, or pushed forward candidates he hoped to control.[79]

As the strongman in charge of a pro-Catholic conservative dictatorship in 1836, the general could not prevent the secession of Texas, but he fended off a French expedition to Veracruz in 1838 and briefly restored some of his luster. He returned to lead a weakened state that still claimed vast territories in the American Southwest although it only nominally controlled Anglophone Texas settlers and the feared Comanche federations of the borderlands. The Comanches' devastating raiding, carried out both to secure livestock and to exact vengeance, exposed the fragile hold of the Mexican state over its northern territory, including the contested area in today's southern Texas that led ambitious Texans and American nationalists—President James K. Polk in the lead—to press extensive border claims. Santa Anna's recourse to war in 1846 was an abject failure, and the Republic of Mexico had to surrender large swaths of territory to Washington.

This war on the margins of the settled world had profound ramifications for both republics: for the United States it undermined the 1820 Missouri compromise on the extension of slavery; in Mexico, following another conservative coup by Santa Anna, it opened the way to the Revolution of Ayutla and the great liberal anticlerical government under Benito Juárez of the second half of the 1850s. The constitution of 1857 outlined the constitution of a liberal and secular state with constitutional liberties and civil marriage. The Lerdo Law of 1856 pushed through a rigorous secularization of church properties but also the abolition of all corporate property, including the communal rights or *fueros* and collective holdings, *ejidos,* that still prevailed in many rural and Indian communities. In effect they carried through the last of the eighteenth-century revolutions, deeply dividing the country and igniting a three-year civil war, the War of the Reform, followed in turn by French invasion. Napoleon III believed he might take advantage of the turmoil (and of the United States' great internal conflict in the 1860s) to try to set up an imperial state under a Habsburg cousin, Maximilian of Austria. Maximilian found significant support among those resentful of Juárez's reforms, but the Juárez government rallied, and after the Battle of Puebla the French withdrew, leaving their well-meaning creature to be defeated and then executed. Liberal government meant an end to the threat of military dictatorship although not to the periodic warlordism that would grip the country from time to time.

Liberal government, even when headed by an Indian, too often meant incomprehension, not of the almost mystical pre-Columbian legacy, but of the social and economic organization that many still chose. The ramifications made themselves felt in the southeastern corner of the republic, the Yucatán Peninsula. Yucatán *ladinos* (including creoles and mestizos but not Indians) had attempted to secede from the republic following the turmoil of the late 1830s, but had to come to terms in the early 1840s, only to have the port city of Campeche (vulnerable to US gunships) seek its own independence, which was then followed by a renewed secessionist uprising in the interior. In January 1847 the Indians, economically hard-pressed by the country's attack on communal rights, including water claims, staged an uprising soon seen in the most lurid images of race war and cannibalism. *Ladino* Yucatán seemed lost to the Indians by 1849–1850, but Santa Anna ground down the Mayan rebels by 1855. The liberals who ousted the general had no more tolerance for the indigenous vision of government and common property, and suppressed renewed revolt, even selling some of the defeated insurrectionists into Cuban slavery. Still, rebellion continued to smolder beyond the *ladino* cities, rooted in own quasi state of "the Cross" through the rest of the century.[80] Indifferent government gave way to the tightening control of the president chosen in 1876, Porfirio Díaz, who would subdue the opposition and rally a group of *científicos,* or business elites, who worked with American and British investors to lay down a modern railroad system.

Díaz would rule for almost 35 years, until a new generation threw off his autocratic regime. During that period Mexico would advance industrially, although with firms dominated by foreign capital. It would remain poor (in fact it had regressed in comparative economic terms since the late eighteenth century), but less poor; Catholic, but secular in its institutions; recognizing in theory its indigenous heritage, but indifferent to its current condition. The elements its history wove together—wars of national consolidation, hardheaded leaders who dominated politics and simultaneously the channels for capital, and the new railroads and industry; the persistence of popular religiosity at the village level, but the secularization of church lands; reform of the educational system to take it out of Church hands; a free market in land that undermined any residual collective rights of the indigenous population; the use of railroads to knit together a vast, if largely arid, territory—were in fact the ingredients that transformed the mid- and late nineteenth-century state. But like other Latin American states, it had to rely on British, and later on US, capital and its elite had fundamentally divided over ideological alternatives.

Further to the south, the dream of a unified South American republic had fallen apart during the wars of independence led by Bolívar and José de San Martín. But all the Spanish-speaking lands remained with powerful armies, underdeveloped national or local assemblies, and a tradition of military strongmen and powerful landlords. The era of the independence struggle also tended to divide the successor elites into conservatives who wished to preserve relatively strong "centralist" institutions with respect for the Church, and "federalists," who saw themselves as liberals and supporters of decentralization and access to British capital. In effect, the Latin American republics froze, until deep into the nineteenth century, in the kind of confrontation that briefly separated American Federalists and the Jeffersonian Democratic Republicans in the late 1790s—but with the confusing difference that in South America the term *federalist* signified the decentralized option that Jefferson and Madison defended toward 1800. And no Latin American statesman could have said, as Jefferson said of Republicans and Federalists in 1801, we are all centralists, we are all federalists.

In Argentina the dictator Juan Manuel de Rosas had drawn on the backing of the independent cattlemen of the pampas, the vast grazing lands around Buenos Aires, to intimidate the liberals in the port city, who sought to maintain their leadership of the republic and their commercial connections with the British. Nominally a federalist, Rosas and his provincial supporters established a dictatorship during the 1830s and 1840s that depended increasingly on violence and terroristic elimination of his enemies and was ousted only in 1852. Like Andrew Jackson to the north, Rosas made his reputation fighting the indigenous inhabitants. But unlike the US president, he never had to contend with the former colonial power's armies. Nor did he ever have to come to terms with an emerging popular democratic movement as Jackson did. Finally he estranged even his own rancher supporters, who had benefited from his grants of little rural despotisms, by the costs of his wars and the conflicts with France and Britain over control of Río de la Plata trade. The victory of the *porteño* (Buenos Aires) British-oriented liberal elite under Bartolomé Mitre, Domingo Sarmiento, and Nicolás Avellaneda in the 1860s and 1870s brought the victory of liberal principles, British investment and railroad development, and an agrarian-export prosperity, followed by a massive immigration of southern European labor. A generation of cohesive state development followed, but Argentina remained a polity where a reactionary military and *caudillo* legacy remained a jagged ideological alternative. In Colombia, too, a conflict between military and liberals set the pattern for decades of civil strife. Army officers and churchmen who had sought to continue the Spanish ruling institutions described themselves as centralist; the liberals tended to speak for states or provincial rights. Politics seesawed between the two.

Brazil's economic and ideological conflicts were softer. The legacy of the Portuguese court and the presence of Braganza dynasty heirs as emperors from 1822 to 1889, as well as the unity needed to maintain a slave population, helped form a coherent oligarchy. So too did the coffee boom and the common intellectual formation of many in civil law and then as state administrators—a contrast with the theological and anticlerical conflicts inherited elsewhere in the Catholic Americas. The state cohered although its project remained administration, not development. The liberals' moves in the 1870s toward abolition of slavery did mobilize the conservative opposition of the coffee provinces in the south, but the liberals included sugar interests in the northeast and no major confrontation of economic interests compelled either political extremism or grand state wagers on one sector or another. The landed elites fed the state bureaucracy.[81]

The United States completed its first east–west railroad line four years after its Civil War ended. For Canada the equivalent epic accomplishment followed in the 1880s with the building of the Canadian Pacific. The history of its rail-roads and its political federation had been intertwined for a generation. Following rebellions in 1837 against the British colonial government in French Lower Canada and the Anglophone Tory oligarchy of Upper Canada, the British mission of Lord Durham recommended self-government and unification of the two provinces into a Canadian Union. The financial strains of building the Grand Trunk railway designed to link the St. Lawrence's goods to US ocean ports, and US revocation of free trade for Canadian products, caused financial strains and exacerbated the tension between the linguistic communities. A series of conferences and negotiations in the mid-1860s produced the British North America Act and the creation of the self-governing Dominion of Canada under the Crown and comprising a new federation that redivided the old Upper and Lower Canadas and attracted the maritime provinces, and provided a basis for adhesion of the western lands. The Anglophone elements saw the hope for national domination; the Francophones secured control of a provincial unit, including the cities of Montreal and Quebec.

It is instructive to think of the alternatives that might have been. Suppose Lee had won at Gettysburg in July 1863, for example, then marched toward New York, discouraged the North and allowed a peace-minded Democratic Party to eke out a victory in the presidential election of 1864 and negotiate a settlement that allowed at least de facto autonomy within a regionally decentralized United States—united though in name only. A secessionist Confederate States would have had a social structure more akin to that of Brazil. It would have formed in effect part of a Caribbean geopolitical unit based for several decades more on plantation agriculture and servile labor. The southwestern territories won two decades earlier from Mexico would have remained dependencies of this southern slave republic, and California might ultimately have been divided between its once-Hispanic south and its Pacific-oriented north. Far-fetched? That depends upon whether we believe all counterfactuals are far-fetched by the very fact that they did not come to pass. Some historians, myself included, are more willing to live, so to speak, in the hypothetical or subjunctive mode. The point is that the political and social units that shaped global institutions in fact rested on particular outcomes that came together in a decisive series of events. As the poet Robert Frost wrote, the road not taken made all the difference. From 1850 to 1880, alternatives were progressively shut down by virtue of the advance of evolutionary ideas, the progress of technology based on iron, steel, and coal, the emerging social groups that grew in tandem within these innovations, and the military decisions that these impacted.

Given the variety of experiences that revolution or modernization from above can refer to, I prefer the very loose term *controlled transformation*—a process in which a group of ambitious and powerful men, whether political leaders or economically powerful, or often both, attempted to direct policy to achieve a more vigorous national development. They could attempt this within the shell of ancient empires (where they encountered fierce conservative resistance), or under the ground rules of popular elections. Without the new opportunities of railroad and communications, and rapid-fire weaponry, they would have found their moments less favorable. Without the widespread belief in the inevitability, and even the "hygiene" (as one Italian imperialist termed it), of military conflict, they would also have played a less obtrusive role. And of course they reinforced the charged ambiance of war and industrialization that made their policies seem so essential and natural. Bismarck was right: the great issues of the day were to be resolved by blood and iron—and by strong and determined national strategists such as himself.

In the Middle of Europe

From at least the Treaties of Westphalia in 1648 through German reunification in 1990, the state structures of Central Europe have been, in effect, part of an implicit European constitution, central to issues of war and peace and the representation of ethnic communities. The Habsburg empire rested on two dominant national groups—its German-speaking west, then including today's Austria and the hilly perimeter of Bohemia and Moravia (today's Czech Republic), and, to the east, in the kingdom of Hungary, the Magyar-speaking landlord class who dominated an extensive countryside through a county organization with courthouse politics, not so different, as noted, from the plantation class in the American South. Instead of black slaves, the Magyars drew on peasant laborers—in some districts Ukrainians, Poles, Slovaks, or Romanians—who were still enserfed until 1848. Even in the second half of the nineteenth century, after serfdom had formally ended, they constructed a voting system that ensured that the Slavic groups and Romanians would not capture significant political power. Geographically the kingdom of Hungary contained today's Slovakia, western Romania, and today's Croatia. Outside the kingdom of Hungary and its Austro-Bohemian heartland, the dynasty also ruled Lombardy, with its capital Milan, and Tuscany, and, from 1797 to 1866, Venice and its hinterland. To the northeast the Habsburgs ruled today's Slovenia and beyond the Carpathians the plains of southern Poland or Galicia with the city of Lemberg (later Polish Lwów and today's Ukrainian L'viv), taken during the Polish partitions, and even the region of Czernowitz, taken from the Ottomans. When the remains of the Holy Roman Empire had been dissolved under Napoleon's pressure, the Habsburg rulers had reconstituted their diverse territories as the Austrian Empire, not as a unified unit but with different constitutional arrangements. All in all there were about ten different linguistic units, not including the dense Yiddish-speaking Jewish populations in Galicia. Between then and 1945, the Jews would emigrate or disappear in the Holocaust, and the three million Germans of Bohemia and Moravia would be expelled at the end of World War II, as would millions of Germans from the then eastern territories of Prussia further north. But major territorial and border changes would take place earlier, in the late 1860s and at the end of World War I in 1918–1919, as well.

The Habsburg empire thus comprised many linguistic groups. Increasingly they would feel the attractions of nationalism, the notion that they each should be able to govern their own communities in a national state. Or at least their intellectual and political leaders had this conviction. In fact many of the population spoke two or more languages—the local vernacular at home and in the village, but German or Hungarian in the more public world of officialdom, and in the armies. And forming new states would not be easy in areas where populations were mixed. It was in the interest of the rulers to hold back the belief in nationalism, which would tear apart this patchwork into a welter of contending peoples and places. And even if the dynasty was a German one, it would survive only by leading a multiethnic unit; its rulers learned Hungarian and Italian as well as the French so current in European diplomacy. The Austrian chancellor from 1810 to 1848, Prince Klemens von Metternich, understood the potential vulnerabilities of his state, large with respect to its population of fifty million but vulnerable in its site and its multiple ethnicities. But he also understood how to leverage Austrian power. The tsar of Russia and the king of the major state in northern Germany, Prussia (which had a significant Polish-speaking minority in the east), shared a common interest in social and territorial stability in the early years after the Congress of Vienna. They signed a common program of religiously based stability, the Holy Alliance, consulted together with British and French in periodic "congresses" on the state of Europe, and through 1849 agreed to act in common against revolutionary outbreaks. And they established a German Confederation—a loose structure that included the German territories of Austria and Prussia as well as the smaller German states that emerged from the Holy Roman Empire. Austria and Prussia alternated in the presidency of this unit. And the whole geopolitical machinery was in effect anchored by the implicit power of Russian armies, which supported Metternich's program of conservative stabilization. Notably, in 1848–1849, when the Hungarians had threatened to successfully wrest their independence, Russian armies had intervened to help the Austrians suppress the revolt.

But within a generation of 1815 the structures were increasingly fragile. The sentiment of German nationalism and Italian nationalism grew among the growing middle-class elements of the region, in particular among younger literate students. Demonstrations on days of historical significance, monuments of national allegorical figures—a Germania, for instance—celebrations of Italy or Germany in literature increased. Moreover, the Prussian kingdom's officialdom grew restive with the deference to Austria that the system entailed. The western parts of the kingdom grew as coal and iron production increased. They had inaugurated basic education for their village population in the eighteenth century. The monarchs' policy of religious toleration helped attract qualified Huguenot and other persecuted minorities. After defeat by Napoleon, they had adopted a French system of universal military conscription. They recovered and augmented their territory in 1815 as a member of the coalition against Bonaparte. Smaller in population than Austria, Prussia had a vigorously growing economy and its cities, including Berlin, were increasing in size. As early as 1819 its civil servants designed a customs union, or Zollverein, for their own state of Prussia that eliminated the internal tariffs, and in the decades to come they signed up the other midsize states in this free-trade area. The Habsburg realms not only faced internal tensions; increasingly their claim to control the German Confederation was under challenge.

So too the Italian territories in Lombardy and Venetia increasingly chafed under Habsburg rule, and many of the middle-class elements in central and northern Italy developed schemes to unite an emerging Italian nation. Many intellectuals, poets, and writers took up the cause, which was still suppressed by the Austrian authorities and other conservative rulers in the divided peninsula. But the ferment of ideas and discussion was to become known as the Resurgence or Risorgimento. Memoirs of anti-Austrian agitation and schemes for unification crystallized discussion. Nationalism was increasingly chic—British Romantic poets wrote lyrics for the Greek rebellion of the 1820s. Poles, too, had national aspirations, and soon the Czech-speaking intellectuals of Bohemia would as well, as would various southern Slav groups. But they were more directly under Habsburg control. German nationalism could prosper because of the divergence between Prussia and Austria, and the growing attractiveness of nationalism to the elites of the other states.

How was national unification to be achieved? In 1848–1849, the revolutionaries had tried and failed. The mass uprisings and demonstrations in Italy, Central Europe, and Paris threatened a social revolution and soon alienated the socially respectable middle classes. Moreover, the Habsburg court rallied and its generals suppressed the uprisings in the various cities—Vienna, Prague, Budapest, and Venice—one by one. As noted above, the king of Sardinia, who took up the national cause, was defeated twice, first in 1848 and then in 1849. When the Hungarian revolutionaries took up arms again in 1849, the tsar's troops obligingly intervened, and their leader, Kossuth, was left to become a salon hero in America. The Roman revolution, in which Mazzini served as one of the three triumvirs, frightened the pope and was suppressed in 1850 by the newly elected president of the French Republic, Louis Napoleon, who wanted to please Catholics at home. The Frankfurt Assembly could not solve the conundrum of Central European organization—the reviving conservative forces in Austria, led by the tough-minded prince Felix zu Schwarzenberg, brusquely told the Frankfurt liberals that Austria would enter a Germanic federation only with all its territories, including the Hungarian and Polish domains, or not at all. The Prussian monarch, approached as a second-best alternative, refused to offend the Habsburgs and take a crown that depended on popular legitimacy. The nationalist and revolutionary enthusiasts of 1848 were scattered and suppressed after their second wave of uprisings in 1849. Prussian troops dissolved the remnants of the Frankfurt National Assembly in early 1850.

But nationalist aspirations were quieted less than a decade. By the 1850s, Central Europe was in flux anew. First of all, economies rebounded vigorously: railroad construction and industrial development surged ahead, in Prussia and in France, as in the Americas. Even the Prussian court was prepared to adopt a more assertive policy. The tsar vetoed early plans in 1850 and 1851 for a Prussian-led union of North Germany as potentially too unsettling; St. Petersburg did not want to undermine Austria's conservative presence in Central Europe. But within Prussia the Zollverein and railroads advanced; now, too, there was a Prussian legislature since 1848, which allowed middle-class liberals a forum. In Piedmont, with its capital in Turin, the new monarch was willing to abandon the sleepy clerical conservatism of previous decades, and under the constitution of 1848 (the "Statuto") a vigorous liberal elite, under the leadership of Count Camillo Cavour, sought to emulate British parliamentary practice and French anticlericalism. The kingdom secularized Church and monastic lands and pressed forward with various reforms. Increasingly Piedmont became the hope of the Italian nationalists for leadership in unification. Earlier republican ideas, or the notion of an Italian federation under the presidency of the pope, were abandoned as unrealistic and juvenile. Moreover, Pius IX, who had begun his papacy in 1846 as a possible liberal reformer but was scarred by the Roman revolution, would gravitate toward condemning liberalism and nationalism. The Italian National Movement that was founded in 1859 united a determined cohort of middle-class and aristocratic supporters in the northern and central towns of the peninsula. No longer students or activist members of the secret *carbonari,* they were now a bourgeois movement. Similarly in Germany, the national enthusiasts confessed that they had been too generous and idealistic in 1848; they must accept the states that existed as a basis for action and work with the princes. The restored state structure of Central Europe was cracking open and the initial repressive reaction loosening up in the late 1850s. In Prussia the restored monarch Frederick William IV—who had refused a "crown from the gutter" (that is, from the Frankfurt parliament)—was removed as insane in 1858, and his brother was made regent (to inherit the Prussian throne as William I in 1862). No liberal, he did, though, appoint a new cabinet that backed off from the harsh approach following the revolution and called for new Landtag elections, inaugurating a period of renewed political discussion, the so-called New Era.

With respect to ideology and social origins, nationalists were prepared to abandon republicanism and find monarchical patrons, whether in Turin or Berlin. They were certainly not prepared to embrace socialism. But how should they solve their geopolitical dilemma of Austrian power, seconded by the tsar and prepared to intervene in Germany, Bohemia, and northern Italy? Cavour's strategy was to persuade Bonaparte (now after a coup d'état in 1851, and a plebiscite the next year, governing as Napoleon III, emperor of the French) to take up the Italian cause. Napoleon III fancied himself the champion of nationalities, but he was also preserving the rule of the pope in the middle of Italy.

It was the Crimean War of 1853–1855 that transformed the international political possibilities. Ostensibly this was an arcane struggle, fought by the French to protect their influence in the Levant and the Roman Catholic religious guardianship of Jerusalem against Russian Orthodox claims over the same holy places. But for London the underlying preoccupation was Russian pressure on the Ottoman Empire, weakened by earlier losses in its European territory, the earlier campaigns of Muhammad Ali, and probably by the ramifications of its own effort at reforms, the Tanzimat. St. Petersburg aspired to military hegemony in the Black Sea and the Straits of Marmara, and free entry into the Mediterranean; London saw a threat to its own maritime role and was determined to keep the Ottoman Empire a viable structure. As discussed above, the war—largely fought for control of the ports on the Crimean Peninsula—turned out to be a protracted and messy struggle, revealing the weaknesses of both sides. It also revealed the overextension of the Austrian Empire. The Russians expected that Vienna would repay its help in suppressing revolution in 1849 by interdicting any Anglo-French military movement in the Balkans; instead the Austrians occupied the Danubian provinces the Russians agreed to vacate. But Cavour in Turin threw in Piedmont's forces with the British and French, hoping that in the peace settlement to follow, London and Paris would compel Austria to surrender its hold in northern Italy. Fearing the loss of its Italian provinces, the Austrians sought to appease the French and British by "tilting" toward them and threatening

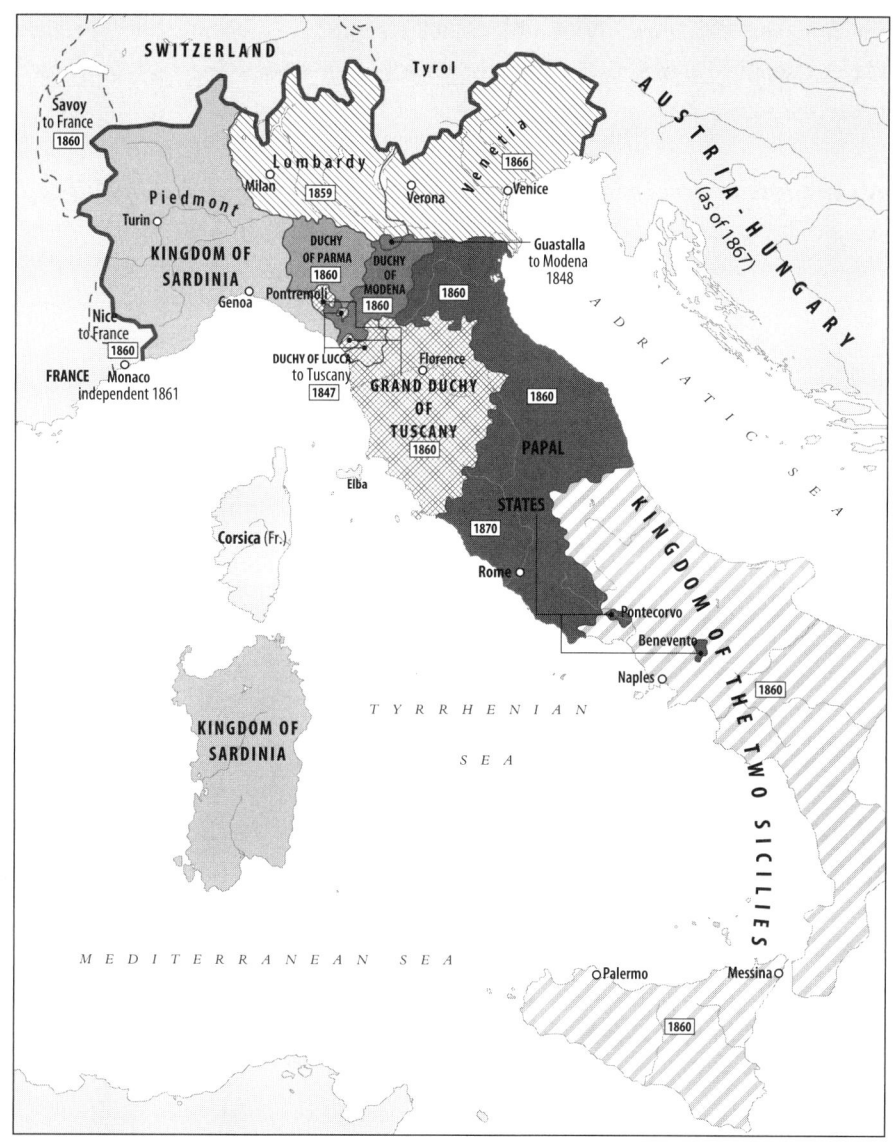

SWITZERLAND

Savoy
to France
1860

Tyrol

AUSTRIA-HUNGARY
(as of 1867)

Lombardy

Piedmont

Milan

1859

Venetia

1866

Verona

Venice

Turin

KINGDOM OF
SARDINIA

Genoa

DUCHY
OF PARMA
1860

DUCHY
OF
MODENA
1860

Guastalla
to Modena
1848

Pontremoli

1860

Nice
to France
1860

FRANCE

Monaco
independent 1861

DUCHY OF LUCCA
to Tuscany
1847

Florence

GRAND DUCHY
OF
TUSCANY
1860

1860

PAPAL

STATES

1870

Rome

ADRIATIC SEA

Corsica (Fr.)

Elba

Pontecorvo

Benevento

Naples

1860

KINGDOM OF
SARDINIA

TYRRHENIAN

SEA

KINGDOM OF THE TWO SICILIES

MEDITERRANEAN SEA

Palermo

Messina

1860

Cartographic teleology: The advance of the modern nation-state, as seen in Italy, 1815–1870.

the Russians with intervention unless they accepted their enemies' peace terms. Cavour would be disillusioned at the 1856 Congress of Paris that concluded peace; he received no concrete commitment from Napoleon III or London to take up the question of Piedmont's aspirations to unite northern Italy against Austria. On the other hand, Russian policy makers were angered by Vienna's apparent ingratitude. They had to accept that the clauses kept them from reconstituting a naval force in the Black Sea; the Straits to the Mediterranean were closed to them. If challenged anew, Vienna could not count on St. Petersburg's help. Prussia's star rose instead. Under the young Bismarck's forceful advocacy, Prussia adopted strict neutrality and made it clear that France could not intervene in Russian Poland across its territory.

Although Cavour was disappointed at Paris, events were in the sort of flux that occurs only once a generation. Within three years Napoleon would align himself with Savoy. The emperor wanted a dynastic marriage with the princess of Savoy for his heir. The groom was unattractive and brutish; King Victor Emmanuel would not compel his daughter to the union, but she accepted her patriotic duty. In addition an assassination attempt on the emperor by an Italian radical, ostensibly frustrated by the opposition to unification, raised issues of personal security. By early 1859 the French pressed Vienna into war. The two major battles, Magenta and Solferino, were bloody confrontations, signaling the shape of the new warfare. Napoleon concluded a quick peace; the Austrians conceded Lombardy (the province around Milan) to Paris, which retroceded it to Italy. Venice was to remain Austrian until 1866, when it would be joined to Italy as a result of Prussia's victory over Austria. And in return, the kingdom of Savoy ceded to France the region of Nice and the area around Lake Geneva that had been part of its own territory. Cavour won more than Lombardy, however. By this time the pro-Piedmontese liberals throughout Italy—men of substance and socially conservative, though usually liberal advocates of parliamentary politics— were organizing a movement in all the small states of the Po Valley and Central Italy; and a wave of plebiscites ratified uniting these states with Savoy into a new Kingdom of Italy. Napoleon III's troops still prevented annexing the province of Rome, although the papal province of Bologna would join Italy, as would Tuscany. Once the Franco-Austrian peace was concluded, the big question remained the fate of the Kingdom of the Two Sicilies, that is, the Kingdom of Naples, encom-

A nationalist icon: A depiction of the "handshake of Teano," the meeting between Giuseppe Garibaldi and King Victor Emmanuel of Savoy north of Naples on October 26, 1860. Garibaldi, originally an advocate of a republican unification for Italy, had forced the withdrawal of the Bourbon monarch from Sicily and Naples, but he agreed, for the cause of unity, to recognize Prime Minister Camillo Benso, Count of Cavour, and Victor Emmanuel's monarchical framework that was being extended southward from Turin. Five months later, Victor Emmanuel was proclaimed king of a (mostly) united Italy. (Private Collection / The Stapleton Collection / The Bridgeman Art Library)

passing all of southern Italy and Sicily. The Neapolitan Bourbons had been restored after the brief revolution of 1848; now in 1860 they were to fall definitively to a new revolution, supported by the dashing republican leader Garibaldi and his "Thousand." The question was, would the democratic republican leaders of the revolution in Sicily and Naples unite the region with the north? Cavour's Piedmont was a constitutional state, but with a limited suffrage and clearly conservative—Garibaldi and his lieutenants envisaged for a while a radical republic in the south that would oust the landlords, with feudal privileges and loyalties. But Garibaldi decided to yield control for the sake of a larger Italy, and in early 1861 the king of Savoy became the monarch of a united Italy. Venice would be gained in 1866, the province and city of Rome in 1870, the northern region of Trent and Bolzano, Trieste, only in 1918. Garibaldi would be disillusioned in the Turin parliament, would bitterly denounce the cession of Nice, and bitterly attacked Cavour, who although only in his fifties was ill and would shortly die. Garibaldi would attempt several invasions of Roman territory in the 1860s, only to be checked by Italian troops. Only when Napoleon III faced the Prussian invasion of 1870 would he remove his garrisons from Rome, which allowed the new kingdom to take the ancient capital.

Cavour and his close colleagues who brought about the unification of the Italian state were in effect gentry—largely gentlemen landowners, who admired Victorian liberalism and its ability for a public-spirited oligarchy to manage a country through a parliament and a moderate monarchy. The group of unifiers would become known in the early 1860s as the Right, and later the Old Right, but they quickly offered coalition privileges to those who termed themselves the Left, also middle-class men who sought a broader electorate but worked within the gradualist paradigm of state building. As of 1862 they formed a "marriage" or *connubio;* by 1882, the Left would win the elections. The Left then invited their defeated adversaries from the Right to "transform" themselves into liberals like themselves, a process of glossing over ideological differences that would characterize the governance of the state into the twentieth century. *Trasformismo* had a cost. The Italian state remained perhaps too cozy; it viewed its peasant masses as sullen adversaries, and the 1860s were spent combatting widespread peasant resistance (the *brigantaggio*) in Sicily, which cost more lives than the wars of unification. A great inquest in 1874 revealed how impoverished the rural masses remained in the Po Valley lands as well as in the south. But the unifiers were, perhaps understandably enough, also preoccupied by making their new state a viable contender in European great-power politics. That meant completing the north–south railroad lines and having a military—both of which entailed heavy taxes on milling wheat, to be borne primarily by the masses. The more radical Left, those who flocked to Garibaldi and his southern lieutenant Crispi, remained outside the system until the 1880s. So, too, did the upper reaches of the aristocracy in both the north and the south: the novelist Giuseppe di Lampedusa memorably re-evoked their quasi-feudal world in *The Leopard.* And so, too, did the

Catholic faithful, who were instructed by their clergy not to participate in the regime that had taken Rome and confiscated their properties, leaving only the Vatican territory. Until 1900 or so they remained aloof from politics, then gradually were allowed by the Vatican to vote for the Liberals and even to run "clerical" candidates to keep the socialists from power.

The Italian process contrasted with what was occurring in northern Germany. There too in 1858–1859, middle-class nationalism and Prussian administrators saw the chance to take up the German national banner with themselves in the lead. But whereas the Piedmontese monarchy accepted a British-style constitutional role, the Prussian monarchs were habituated to far more executive authority and drew on a stronger identification with the military, which had a more powerful role in government. The new king in fact wanted to strengthen his professional army and diminish the role that the liberal militia had come to claim. In 1861–1862, he urged an army enlargement and reorganization that the liberals resisted for ideological and fiscal reasons. Not having the votes to ram it through the Prussian Landtag, under the advice of his generals he summoned Otto von Bismarck to take the office of minister president. Bismarck was also a noble, a Prussian *Junker,* who in 1848 had been resolutely conservative and supportive of Austria's role in the Confederation. In the interim he had served as ambassador to Russia and as Prussian representative on the Diet, where he came to resent the Austrian leadership. Bismarck came to Berlin and was willing to collect the necessary taxes without parliamentary approval, in effect an unconstitutional recourse, although he found the legal authorities to justify it on dubious grounds. The Prussian Liberals were incensed, but within a few years Bismarck had managed national military victories that would reconcile them. The German-speaking province of Holstein with its port, Kiel, was nominally a fief of the Danish king, but concurrently a member of the German Confederation. The Confederation Diet deputized Austria and Prussia jointly to compel the new king of Denmark to renounce succession plans for removing Holstein from the Confederation so that he could preserve its traditional administrative unity with the neighboring Danish province of Schleswig. At the conclusion of the short war in 1864, Denmark had to concede both duchies to the Austrians and Prussians as agents for the Confederation, an administrative condominium doomed to conflict and one that enabled Bismarck to provoke a war with Austria two years later.

By the mid-1860s Austria rightly understood that Bismarck wanted to expel Vienna from any significant role in the non-Habsburg German territories. Austrian forces, however, proved ill prepared and in the brief war that ensued lost decisively to the Prussians at Königgrätz (Sadová) in early July 1866. Austria sued for peace to avoid further losing battles on the road to Vienna.

Bismarck exacted no territories from the Habsburgs, but forced the end of the German Confederation in which they had shared power. Prussia won the right to organize the north German states in a North German Federation, with a parliament. The southern states of Bavaria and Baden remained outside, but were compelled to sign a military alliance that would subordinate their armies to Berlin's in case of another war. Bismarck did get to annex German territories within the North—the wealthy city of Frankfurt and the north-central city of Hannover, among others. His Italian allies were awarded Austrian Venetia despite having lost a naval battle in the Mediterranean. Just as important as the success in external policy, Bismarck won the retroactive parliamentary approval for his tax measures and the army expansion. The Liberals, enthusiastic supporters of a united Germany, saw the minister president as filling their dreams of 1848. Their voting bloc divided into those willing to approve his policies—known henceforth as National Liberals and including some of the ambitious members of the annexed state government of Hannover—and the smaller number of those who refused to support him, the so-called Progressives. Bismarck expected a rapid completion of German unification with the absorption of Bavaria, Baden, and Württemberg, states now outside any regional federation. But he underestimated the growing Roman Catholic resistance to his program. Catholics were concentrated in the south and Prussia's own Rhine provinces and Silesia in the southeast. The Catholics identified with Austria as a guardian of Catholic interests and they feared the triumph of a state identified with Protestantism.

But the chancellor knew how to exploit these divisions: Catholic hostility made Protestant Liberal support even stronger than it would have been, and within a few years the Prussian leader was willing to wager on a third military adventure, this time a risky war against Napoleon III's France. By exploiting various issues, the German leader made Napoleon appear as an enemy determined to block German unification and even conspiring to seize the duchy of Luxemburg.

The French emperor was facing a rising tide of political opposition at home and felt he could ill afford to appear weak and indecisive. A pretext for war was found in a contest over Spanish politics. Spanish parliamentary and military forces were trying to stabilize a new regime after deposing Queen Isabella in 1868; the parliament rejected a republic and with General Prim sought to find a suitable monarchical candidate, inviting a cousin of the Prussian Hohenzollerns. The French objected; the Prussian royal family was willing to renounce the project, but Bismarck released a brusque edited version of the negotiations—the so-called Ems telegram—that aroused Prussian national feelings, and angered the French court. Goaded on by the hawks in Paris (whom his wife favored), Napoleon III declared war—and, to the astonishment of European observers, lost disastrously. A French general surrendered the major fortress in Metz; the emperor himself had to surrender an army on the battlefield at Sedan on September 2, 1870. The republican opposition in Paris declared the regime over and installed a de facto government that was divided among republicans, Bourbon monarchists, and supporters of the emperor—who, as a Prussian prisoner, was allowed to go into exile in London. As Prussian troops moved on Paris, the city itself rose again against the new legislature that was convened at Versailles, and for many months installed a revolutionary commune. The assembly, under a conservative republican, Adolphe Thiers, negotiated a peace with Prussia, which cost it an indemnity—soon paid—and the provinces of Alsace and Lorraine on the border, which Germany would hold until its own defeat in World War I, forty-eight years later. The Paris Commune remained besieged, cold, and near famine through the winter of 1871, until the Assembly finally retook it in the spring, executing thousands of the Communards and exiling others to New Caledonia. Only five years later would the provisional government formally recognize that it was a republic with a president as a chief executive (who was deprived of any real power) and a National Assembly that governed the country through a civil service.

Bismarck, however, knew how to exploit the victory and the rush of nationalist enthusiasm Germans enjoyed. The southern states were bound to Prussia by the alliances negotiated after 1866. In January 1871 the German parliamentary delegates, enjoying a victory session in the palace of Versailles, voted that the king of Prussia should become at the same time "German Emperor." Essentially

Bismarck used the institutions he had designed for the interim North German Confederation in 1867, but with the addition of the south German states. The resulting governmental structure was a compromise amalgam of popular and executive instruments. Prussia and the other states retained their Diets or Landtags. The minister president of Prussia became the German chancellor. He alone appeared before the German legislature; there was no collective cabinet responsibility as in Britain, and he held power at the pleasure of the emperor, just as in Prussia he held power at the pleasure of the king. The military ministers were important members of the council of ministers (as would be the case in Japan), and the military budget was debated only every seven years. Nonetheless, Bismarck did agree that the new Reichstag (like the old Customs Union parliament and interim North German Diet) should be elected by universal manhood suffrage. (An upper chamber with restricted powers, the Bundesrat, was based on state delegates.) This meant that one organ in the German constitutional structure had a franchise as democratic as the American Congress and the new French Chamber of Deputies. But it could not vote to unseat the chancellor; all it could do was make his life difficult by paralyzing the budget process. Moreover, even as he sought to placate a Reichstag majority in which, over time, liberal and working-class representatives increased with industrial development, the chancellor–minister president had to pass a Prussian state budget a few blocks away in the Prussian House of Deputies (and a Prussian House of Peers) that had a far more conservative majority. For until defeat in the First World War, Prussia retained a "three class" suffrage that gave wealthy voters a far greater proportional share of the delegates than the nonwealthy.

Bismarck had the force and the prestige to navigate within the system, but his successors found the task a growing challenge. After the end of the Third Reich, historians tended to stress the autocratic side of the empire—the potential for a willful emperor and powerful military officers to intervene in politics—but recent scholarship has emphasized the vigorous quality of political debate that marked national and local life. Until the end of the 1870s it pleased Bismarck to work with the National Liberals and to rally them against supposed threats from the disgruntled Catholics and the emerging working-class Social Democratic movement. By the end of the 1870s, Germany unified its legal codes and its monetary systems; it retained conscription and the strongest army in Europe. Its industrial development, spearheaded by the coal and steel concentrations of the Ruhr and newly annexed Lorraine, rapidly made it the preeminent industrial power of the continent, and it would overtake Britain in steel output by the 1890s. Bismarck declared that Germany was a satiated state and wanted to be a force for stability, but the annexation of Alsace and Lorraine had made it difficult to win a real reconciliation with France.

The Austrian Empire underwent its own structural consolidation after its defeat in 1866. While the new realists among the Magyar nobility had (until 1918) shelved the goal of absolute independence from Vienna, its leaders under Ferenc Deák exploited the Austrian defeat to extract a large degree of autonomy under the terms of the 1867 Ausgleich or Compromise. Henceforth, the Habsburg empire would be a dual federation: the emperor "of" the lands in the west (Austria, Bohemia, and Moravia) would be king "in" Hungary, and the country would become the hyphenated Austria-Hungary or Dual Monarchy. Dualism brought a precarious degree of state consolidation to each half of the structure, but the two "historic peoples" each faced fractious nationalities in their respective regions. The Magyars would govern their large half the country through a rigged suffrage, much as white United States citizens in the former Confederate States of America would dominate their region. Within the kingdom, Croatia enjoyed its own partially autonomous status. Linking the two halves of the Dual Monarchy was a common foreign office, a common army and navy, with German still accepted as a language of command, and a commercial trade treaty, to be reviewed every decade, that connected the grain-growing lands of Hungary with the more industrial regions of Bohemia and Austria. Austria still retained Trieste as its port on the Adriatic Sea; Hungary held the ports of Pola (today's Croatian Pula) and Fiume or Rijeka on the Adriatic. The Hungarian parliament, restricted in suffrage until 1911, divided between more or less nationalist elements; the Reichsrat in Vienna, which united the western half, would break down into Social Democrats, Liberals, eventually Catholic populists (Christian Socials), pan-Germans, and strong components of Czech and Polish deputies who fought over the linguistic rights of their respective nationalities and the control of school budgets. Civil servants were expected to use German in reports to Vienna, the local vernacular with the citizenry dominant in the respective areas. Language issues for schools—perhaps familiar to Americans accustomed to disputes about bilingualism—continued to vex the Austrian half.

It was unclear what to call the western half: strictly speaking, Austria was only part of the unit; the emperor retained a confusing series of sovereign titles over the various provinces (of which Bohemia was listed as a kingdom and Upper and Lower Austria as Archduchies). The designation "imperial and royal," *"kaiserlich und königlich"* or *"k. und k.,"* became the term applied to officials, flags, consulates, and so forth of the whole realm. The western half was sometimes unofficially referred to as Cisleithania—the lands "this side" of the little river Leith that formed part of the border with Hungary. Officially it remained the lands represented in the Reichsrat. As ethnic nationalism increased, the structure came under greater and greater stress, although the Austrian Social Democratic Party and the Jewish population, who understood the dangers of German and Magyar, Polish, or Romanian nationalism, remained the most loyal to the dynasty as the unifying and hopefully moderating force. Historians have often viewed what also became known as Austria-Hungary as a doomed state, but it fought for four long years in World War I before finally fracturing. Its armed forces were rarely victorious unless acting together with the German military, but they functioned as a unit despite their recruits' linguistic diversity. Its bureaucrats seemed addicted to a ponderous formalism, but they successfully represented the presence of the monarchy and its elaborate legalism. And curiously enough within this ramshackle compromise between modern prenational (and postnational) elements, likewise between parliamentary state and military-bureaucratic empire, the boldest experiments in music, philosophy, and psychiatry could flourish.[82]

The World of the 1870s

The world of the 1870s had been transformed—not by revolution, but by strong leaders, realists who believed in railroads, property, economic development, and national power, and the inevitability of conflict and competition. Of course there were major differences. The Italians who moved their capital to Rome in 1870 (after an interim six years in Florence, which had followed Turin) knew that they had chosen a course different from that of the Germans and Prussians. Their parliament was more influential; they felt the Prussians glorified war. But they too identified with a national state. The unifiers who were constructing the new Japanese national state felt a kinship with the Germans—like them, they saw the monarchy and its civil servants and its military leaders as crucial for their state, and they were emulating the industrialization as quickly as they could, sending their promising diplomats and generals to study in the West. The Brazilians and Argentines, who had cooperated (with the Uruguayans) in almost obliterating the Paraguayan Republic, which defied their access to the great rivers from the interior, depended much more on Britain's commercial influence. But they overcame the old conflicts to a degree, rallied (to use the Brazilian motto) around the Comtean ideas of "order and progress." Brazil, huge and decentralized under the emperors elevated from the exiled Portuguese royal line, slowly moved to abolish slavery and with it the empire. Canada was completing its railroad network and negotiating a united Dominion. Vigorous US growth came at a price. The Republican Party in the United States was determined to favor manufacturing with a tariff and open up the West to farmers, ranchers, and miners—thereby forging a coalition that would run the country for several decades once it had abandoned its radicals' effort to remake the ex-Confederacy. But in the opportunities that abounded for farmers, industrialists, and even southern landlords in the railroads and the trans-Mississippi West, blacks, Indians, and the contract laborers from East Asia would remain severely disadvantaged, if not victims. Even the French Republic, which had installed a powerful Assembly, would advance its railroad network and a state-run secularized school system, with a centralized prefectural system.

So throughout much of the "civilized" world—understood as Europe with its American outliers, the British dominions, and the ambitious Japanese— states were trump. The recipe for governing was to develop their territory, keep power in the hands of men of science, expertise, and property, and prepare for a continuing military rivalry. And to resist the archaic blandishments of communalism, dangerously close to anarchism and syndicalism, whether manifesting itself as a program to found government on village communes and collective property, advocated only by formerly servile peasants or indigenous tribes, and reject the new working-class claims to trade-union and syndical power. And to resist, too, any supranational claims to religious authority, whether from the Roman Catholic hierarchy in the West or the 'ulama' in the Islamic world or Buddhist monasteries in Asia.

Of course, there were laggards in this process. China remained a victim: the British and French had gone to war again in 1860 and forced more concessions; the Taiping had sapped imperial strength—the power of the Confucian state and the growing impoverishment of its peasant masses prevented an effective response, though not the effort. The Ottomans, who had lost Egypt and most of their Balkan territories, faced the severest self-contradictions: if they adopted modern principles of secular Ottoman citizenship, they undermined the religious communalism that had been the basis of the Empire when it was on the rise. They found it hard to mobilize economic resources and extract revenues. As in the case of China, and to a degree Latin America, where mineral extraction, commodity exports, and the coastal port activities generated wealth, foreigners would control much of the process and slow down self-development. Britain revealed some of the same pressure to modernize a political and educational system that had not been compelled to reform by radical shocks or military defeat. Between the 1830s and the 1870s, Britain too would adopt crucial reforms—a less paternalist approach to poverty, the reform of its military (abolishing purchase of commissions), free trade, key municipal reform—and rationalization of its great Indian possession after suppression of the rebellion of 1857. So, too, the Russians proceeded less dramatically, but did abolish serfdom and started toward representative institutions in the 1860s and 1870s. The transcontinental Russian railroad would have to wait until the end of the nineteenth century, as would the loosening of the communal hold over village lands, and a national parliament came only in 1905. Britain, in effect, could modernize without radically transforming its state–society balance; in Russia the state remained powerful enough and its adherents conservative enough that modernization came slowly. But all these states were on a new trajectory by 1870, and so was their intellectual and cultural patrimony. With such transformations it was to be expected that the pressure to dominate and control would press even more drastically into the colonial peripheries, and the instrumentalities for control at home would rely even more on science and measurement, steel and steam and communication. It would be both gritty and glitzy, ferociously innovative, but factual as well.

But yet, the 1870s disclosed a collection of states still spread out in their institutional and ideological transformations. Some remained hostage to their continuing multicultural divisions. The old empires—Austro-Hungarian and Ottoman, Russian to a lesser degree—had to balance ethnic or religious diversity even as they sought to modernize for the harsh international competition that had threatened them since the late eighteenth century. The once opulent Mughal Empire had finally disappeared in 1858 at the hands of its feeble princes and persistently encroaching British adversaries after the collapse of the Indian rebellion. The so-called Raj—which after 1876–1877 became officially the Empire of India under the Empress Victoria—found it expedient to preserve its patchwork territories and diverse communities, including the approximately five hundred princely states preserved alongside the directly ruled presidencies and other jurisdictions represented in London by the secretary of state for India and administered from Calcutta by the governor general or viceroy. The Manchu state with its allogenic dynasty could hardly embrace an unrestrained Chinese nationalism, but its loyal officials found Confucian traditions based on the classics and a virtuous gentry too limited to carry through a successful reform program. The Germans and Japanese seemed to understand that if they morphed imperial legacies into efficient military and bureaucratic government, they might retain the nominal trappings of empire. And countries formally democratic at home understood conversely that the currency of power in the world of states was to develop empire abroad.

Historians have always emphasized the violent confrontations between highly organized states as the material of traditional "diplomatic" history. But the contentious world of rival states was also united in its pressure on the fragmented communities at its edges, or sometimes within its territories, whom they perceived to be obstacles to progress and civilization. These alternative communities were often desperately poor, lived sometimes in a symbiotic relationship with their animals, and periodically renewed the religions of empire, whether Christian or Muslim or Hindu, with the voices of local prophets, dissident priests, austere Sufi mystics, and healers. They were remnants, but persistent remnants—the Maya of the Yucatán borderland; the *vaqueiros* or herders of the Brazilian scrublands of the northeast known as the Sertão, who resisted the new encroaching republic in 1896; the American Indian nations slowly compressed into reservations; the gypsies of Andalusia and Romania; the Chechens of the Cauca-sus; the Pashtuns at the northwest frontier of the Raj and other societies of Cen-tral Asia; the tribesmen of highland Burma; Uighurs of Xinjiang; and numer-ous other peoples. Some, such as the Tasmanians, were largely exterminated as early as the 1820s and 1830s; others later, as the Indians of Patagonia in the 1880s; still others, such as the Herero in German colonial territory, decimated in the early years of the twentieth century—as many had been in the earlier expansion of overseas empire after 1500. Many would be absorbed in encroaching cities and territories; still others managed to persist in jungle or highland sanctuaries too daunting for the victorious—waiting for chiliastic redemption or even later to be discovered and often called back to mediated life by anthropologists. Their fate caught the attention of novelists at the time and is being deservedly recov-ered by contemporary historians. But we must carry on with the progress of those who continually pushed out at their once immune domains.

3. The Human Zoo

KEEP bad news in perspective. . . . Nine days after Custer's detachment faced swift annihilation at the Little Bighorn, the United States celebrated the hundredth anniversary of its original Independence Day. As part of the centennial year, Philadelphia entrepreneurs organized the largest world's fair to date, from May 10 to November 10. President Ulysses Grant and Brazilian emperor Dom Pedro, the last monarch resident in the Western Hemisphere, opened the celebratory exhibits of technology and agricultural bounty by switching on the immense Corliss Steam Engine in Machinery Hall. Steam and iron caught the imagination of the ten-million-odd visitors who came to the Exposition. Alexander Bell's telephone, patented two months earlier, was also on exhibit. Two years later an even larger world exposition opened on the Champ-de-Mars in Paris, the meadow on which the Eiffel Tower would arise for another ever-larger world's fair eleven years later.[83] Again, marvels of engineering—but also a "human zoo" or "negro village," where four hundred indigenous peoples were put on exhibit in reconstructions of their supposed habitats.

The 1870s saw human zoos set up in cities throughout Europe, including Hamburg, Warsaw, Barcelona, and London—tribal specimens displayed in the most un-nomadic conditions possible: as objects for vicarious tourism and occasionally study. The zoos presupposed the hierarchies of civilization: spectators confirmed to themselves and their children that they were superior; exhibitors had to acquire, transport, and then supply and manage these arenas of domesticated encounter. What those exhibited thought is hard to know. We would be hasty to attribute humiliation or anger. They were in a service occupation, perhaps like actors, although the terms of their recruitment and service could be rigorous, as a recent historian of the world's fairs reminds us. They were on stage, not in a cage. Perhaps they retained their own sense of superiority to the elaborately clad visitors who came to see their miniature habitats.[84]

Confronting the Primitive

Establishing allegorical meanings is, of course, a cheap trick for historians as well as literary scholars. Seek and ye shall find. Still, controlling colonial and urban environments, keeping potential savages safely fixed to their own turf, ensuring minimal welfare for all while reinforcing the visible signs of hierarchy, finding appropriate rules for what a contemporary German writer has called today's "human zoo,"[85] marked the evolution of states and governments from the 1870s until the outbreak of the First World War. The zoos were reassuring; they suggested that the "primitive forces" of humanity—supposedly fundamentally differentiated by color and other racial characteristics, only semigoverned in their native habitats, untutored in the basic civilizing concept of private property—could be mastered and even made grateful for their subjection. The darker forces at home, whether racial in the Western Hemisphere or working class in the industrializing world, were more threatening. As late as 1871 they mounted a revolutionary regime in Paris, the Commune, established in the besieged capital of France by the radicals who resisted the new Third Republic's willingness to make peace with the German forces bivouacked to the east of the city. The Commune would soon come to represent, through both the suffering the city underwent and the hostages the regime would execute—the heart of darkness at home. In fact, within a few decades the major threat posed by the organized proletariat no longer seemed to be insurrection—the aging Friedrich Engels recognized that revolutionary aspirations would not prevail on the barricades—but the emerging Socialist and Social Democratic political parties throughout the West.

The peasant masses of southern and Eastern Europe also represented a reservoir of primitive and dark forces. Insofar as they could be woven into a social drama of integration and peaceful acceptance, analogous to the human zoo, it was through the appreciation of folklore and folk art, which flourished in this period. Human differentiation and classification also contributed to heroic scholarly achievements in the social sciences. Motivated in some instances by an assumption of inequality, in others by a cosmopolitan effort to understand difference without presupposing inferiority, late nineteenth-century anthropologists and archeologists acquired new knowledge of remote times and places. Whereas social observers a century earlier had traced curious customs and recognized that far-flung empires were as civilized as their own, the later nineteenth century pressed ahead with concepts of social structure, kinship, and religious organization. Empire allowed a collection of splendid artifacts—often entire architectural elements without parallel, to be accumulated in Paris, London, Berlin, St. Petersburg, and eventually New York.[86]

For the white middle classes of Europe and the Americas, technological angst and second thoughts about their destined global domination were usually remote through the 1880s. By the end of the century, darker preoccupations and an edgier awareness would surface as the "positivist" confidence of the previous generation yielded to critiques of empire, social activists exposed the squalid living conditions of the tenements, and the barely coded artworks referred to as "symbolist" suggested deep sexual insecurities. As the writer Rudyard Kipling understood, empire was precarious ("Lest we forget") and the perennially gloomy Henry Adams questioned machine civilization.[87] Still, the artists and intellectuals of Europe, the Americas, and Japan had not yet crossed Freud's threshold of frank insistence on Oedipal jealousy and infant sexuality. Some depicted hooded messengers of death; others, intimations of castration. Painters and composers had not entirely cast loose from the reassuring conventions of representation and tonality as they would after 1905; the world of art stood on the cusp of modernism. Intellectuals in China and India and the colonies had not yet developed sustained revolutionary critiques of imperialism. Massacres of stubborn peoples targeted by the hubris of empire—adherents of the Mahdi of the Sudan, the Armenians in the Ottoman realms in 1896–1897, the Filipinos who resisted US takeover of their islands from the Spanish, the Ovaherero in German Southwest Africa in 1905–1906, the Formosans (Taiwanese) taken over by Japanese administrators in 1895—aroused some regrets and criticism but little effective counteraction. Anti-imperialists in the United States may have braked further territorial acquisitions by force after 1898 (although the Danish Virgin Islands were purchased in 1916); the difficulties incurred in subjugating the Boer republics sobered the British; and the German policies of genocidal suppression in the later Namibia provoked parliamentary opposition, but faits accomplis were not to be undone. The unfortunate excesses of violence amounted to what President Theodore Roosevelt called the "attendant cruelties" of progress. And TR did not even consider the reduction of forest to rubber plantation or slash-and-burn sugar cultivation.[88] They took place on the margins.

And yet—even if the macho statesmen of the late nineteenth century resisted making the connection—the "pacification," and sometimes massacre, on the perimeter was related to those triumphant displays of progress in the great expositions and the ever greater confidence in modern statehood. The late nineteenth-century state was a triumph of the positivist spirit, of the materialist forces of civilization, of the social-scientific counting of populations and measurement of territory, of progress and the future. Nonetheless, it often appeared hostage to potentially the darker forces of its own proletariat, the ignorant and church-besotted peasantry of its countryside, and sometimes threatened even by its own emasculating women. The issue of female rule produced a constitutional crisis in mid-nineteenth-century Hawai'i; was accommodated in late-Victorian Britain, in effect, by desexing the widowed monarch; troubled late-imperial institutions in tsarist Russia and Qing China; and also emerged in growing claims for suffrage. Before World War I women would get the right to vote in New Zealand in 1893, Australia in 1902, Finland in 1907, and Norway in 1913, as well as in the American western states. US women won the suffrage for national elections in 1920, Britain admitted women to the polls in stages from 1911 to 1928; the Weimar Republic from its beginnings in 1919. France finally consented after World War II in 1944, and the Swiss at the federal level in 1971.

How to master these encroaching claims for political representation and participation—whether through repression and arbitrary rule, or through progressive concessions and greater inclusiveness—was the great political issue that hovered over the late nineteenth- and early twentieth-century state.

Statehood and Governmentality

When Americans talked about states, unless they had attended German universities they usually referred to the territorial subdivisions of their country. In Europe the state was a collective abstraction, referring to the legal authorities that claimed the right to legislate, enforce, and administer. The British did not use the term instinctively; French and Germans did. Other cultures had rough equivalents that referred to polity or rule, such as the Hindi raj. Having a state in the nineteenth century was an attribute of an allegedly advanced people. Colonies were allegedly not ready to claim it, but it was perhaps the highest attribute of rationality. Revived in the early nineteenth century, above all by the philosopher Georg Friedrich Wilhelm Hegel, the celebration of statehood had become a Prussian juridical specialty, a doctrine that served a new sovereign unit constructed almost mechanistically across diverse German- (and Polish-) speaking territories. By midcentury, heavy treatises of *Staatslehre* and *Rechtslehre,* the doctrines of the State and of law, had become legal and constitutional specialties of German-speaking Europe. Friedrich Julius Stahl from the 1830s, Otto von Gierke and the Swiss jurist Johann Caspar Bluntschli in midcentury, Georg Jellinek by the end of the century, were among those contributing to the genre. Some attributed to the ruling agencies and to the law an ethical and philosophical loftiness, a spiritual reality that the associations and markets of civil society allegedly could not quite possess. "The state is a moral being and it has moral tasks in life," Bluntschli insisted.[89] Civil society, so the eighteenth-century Scottish philosophers, including Adam Ferguson and Adam Smith, had argued, remained associations of interests aspiring to wealth and public happiness. Continentals felt these aspirations remained inferior, whereas the state was an association of ideals, ethics, and law. Historians used to ascribe to these German thinkers some of the blame for Nazism (ironically, Stahl and Jellinek came from Jewish backgrounds), but in fact National Socialism—insofar as it could claim any intellectual pedigree— would draw on different theories, more attuned to national and ethnic celebration as well as to the gut belief that politics was war by other means. In fact, Jellinek, a liberal, denied any metaphysical reality to the state, insisting rather that the state was a legal creation that could play an active role in regulating society and the economy. States did what private associations could do—deliver the mail, build railroads, provide education, relieve poverty—but rendered these public functions.[90]

All these treatises took care to differentiate the legal structure that was the state from the bundle of historically or linguistically formed allegiances that comprised the nation. Conceptually they also separated the state from the society it regulated. But there were important dissenters by the late nineteenth century. The idea of society had moved beyond just the notion of either a politically oriented "public" or an undifferentiated "people." Society implied a population structured according to their interests and allegiances or what today might be termed identities. These might include religious preferences, regional and local loyalties, and class and occupational affiliations, which, it was implied, took shape independent of state action. Society was often depicted spatially: it was organized from the bottom up, not from the top down, or it constituted an intermediate layer of connections more extensive than family and kinship and less powerful than the state. By the late nineteenth century some legal theorists were suggesting that these functional groups should provide the basis of the legal order. Ideas of transcendent state sovereignty should give way to a compact among interests and groups, collectively endowed with legislative power. Dismayed by the revolutionary turmoil of 1848 and after in Prussia, German liberal Rudolph Gneist looked to political administration and the development of British parliamentary representation for pragmatic representation, while Otto von Gierke examined German medieval guilds to find models of self-government. A generation later Léon Duguit, the French admirer of Comte's earlier positivism, argued that an authentic legal order had to express the "interdependence" of modern social interests, not the abstract and fictitious notions of natural rights. "Yes, the state is dead, or rather what is dying is its Roman, royal, Jacobin, Napoleonic or collectivist form, which in all these diverse aspects, has been only one form of the state." What he saw arriving was not a state as traditionally conceived but a government of technical representatives based on professions and elimination of class conflict. The American "pluralists" of the early twentieth century argued similarly that politics rested on interest-group negotiations, not on constitutional forms.[91]

Social scientists have often tried to distinguish between strong and weak states. The strong state "penetrated" society and could allegedly shape it by extensive measurement and regulation; neither wealthy elites nor organized masses effectively challenged its authority: think Prussia. The weak state's authority might be extensively flouted, subverted, or ignored by families and associations: think Italy. But the dichotomy remains too clumsy. The relationship of state and society—insofar as these abstractions correspond with the messy anatomy of human institutions—is a crucial variable for understanding history and politics, but a robust state and a strong society could complement each other. No state protected accumulated family wealth more than Great Britain; the state could be strong because it so fitted the agenda of its great families. If social discipline was inculcated and family cohesion emphasized, as in China, state authority might thereby benefit at times but evaporate at other times. The same held for Russia. And then again, did a strong bureaucracy serve as the instrument for a strong state, or did it develop into a powerful special interest blocking any projects for the general interest? The relationship of state and society thus remains complex and often paradoxical—nonetheless, the authorities we routinely aggregate as the state did become more ambitious about shaping the everyday attributes of the societies they governed in the late nineteenth and early twentieth centuries. They envisaged a more encompassing and interventionist agenda, and the results they sought entailed a different sense of mission. The good ruler in the eighteenth century might define his objective in terms of felicity or happiness or the preservation of order. The good bureaucrat in late nineteenth might think in terms of energy or hygiene.[92]

Masses of people had no provision if business cycles threw them out of work; they had no access to medical care; their old age was dependent on family support. Did not the state have constructive missions? Without the state, they would experience not picturesque village assistance, but misery. Without the state, their water and food supplies would be sources of disease. It was logical that American and some British social reformers admired the emerging welfare state regulation of Bismarck's (and his successors') Germany. As Jellinek wrote, "The economic and spiritual life of the people is advanced by laws and legal compulsion, that is social results are brought about through governmental power. . . . Through their common rule, subjects become comrades. The advancement of communal purposes through social means has become the task of the state to an increasing degree. . . . The state has become the most powerful social factor, the strongest protector and advancer of the common interest."[93] They found in the German municipalities, Prussian state commercial ministries, and national Protestant church Diet, offices that claimed state power to limit child and women's labor and provide social insurance for the disabled and elderly, at a time when American courts struck down this sort of legislation.[94] Whether or not one judges the state today as an abusive concentration of bureaucratic interference with individual freedom, the historian must recognize that as states were melted down and formed anew from 1850 to 1880, they seemed to represent civilization and progress.

The doctrines of the state found receptive audiences in far-flung soils, certainly among the aging Japanese leaders of the Meiji Restoration, who in the 1880s and 1890s wanted to endow the regime they had constructed with lofty conservative principles, including constitutional arrangements borrowed from Germany, which limited the scope of the new Diet, entrenched the influence of the military leadership, and exalted the monarch with an Imperial Rescript of 1893.[95] Latin American conservatives and military spokesmen found the ideas congenial, for they prized the authority of the central state, which as a creation of colonial elites had often remained a precarious attainment. Roman Catholic authoritarians invoked the Church's mission to enforce authority, but they also liked the idea of an authoritarian state, as did right-wing nationalists in Italy who imported Hegelian idealists with enthusiasm at the end of the century. In the Ottoman, Russian, and Qing empires, the doctrines certainly found approval, but they were hard to nativize because the German concept of the state was so transcendent that it might undermine the very real institutional claims of the monarch. The Japanese emperor might fade into the abstraction of the realm that the new ruling elite wanted to strengthen. It was harder to bypass the Russian tsar, although his civil service and their authority (the *gosudarstvo*) might become the object of loyalty for some. The conservative Chinese reformers seeking to rescue the fraying Qing state translated Hegel but turned more readily to the ancient Confucian and Neo-Confucian ideals that aligned the family, the gentry, and the emperor in a cosmic sense of duty. And in the Islamic world, including the Ottoman Empire, the religious mission of rulers overshadowed so strict an emphasis on law, abstract and compelling in its own secular transcendence. The mission of the Ottoman clan (and later the Turkic ethnic core) also made their familial or ethnic claims too strong for the state as such to legitimize authoritarian rule.

After the twentieth-century experience of states (or parties that governed states) whose leaders claimed to have the knowledge and good intentions to wield great power over individuals and associations, the effort to apply legislative power for alleviating social inequality or enhancing environmental benefits—controlling floods, increasing the yields of agriculture and husbandry, and so on—suggests an enterprise that ran amok. The distortions that arose from state ambitions, even those benevolently intended, and of course those that single-mindedly sought to control and regulate inherently variable distributions of people, environment, and property, now dominate many of the historical narratives and political analyses. A large literature, exemplified by the work of theorist Michel Foucault (d. 1984) and the political anthropologist James C. Scott, now proposes that knowledge of society—whether codified in the form of censuses or cartography, or pursued for public health reasons or even public education—was not just the prerequisite of social control, but designed precisely to achieve it. Knowledge is power, Francis Bacon, the early exponent of scientific observation, had written in the sixteenth century, and by the eighteenth century "useful knowledge" had become the goal of the broad Western movement called the Enlightenment. The alternative to "reason" seemed to be prejudice, backwardness, and superstition, still too often institutionalized by organized religion. But critics then and since have emphasized instead that social knowledge leads to the abuse of power even if applied benevolently. Knowledge, in this view, provides not just power but domination.[96]

But from the mid-nineteenth century to the mid-twentieth, state power seemed hardly so suspect. Anarchists and anarcho-syndicalists might propose that local associations could replace central government and large corporations. They wanted to build organizations from the workshop or village "upward," delegating only a minimum of authority to national governments. For two months, from late March through late May 1871, exponents of anarchist concepts, alongside other radicals, played a role in the Commune that seized power in Paris, which had been besieged since the preceding fall, first by the Germans, then by the newly elected conservative National Assembly that convened in nearby Versailles. The Commune would leave a reputation for revolutionary misery and terror, but its violence paled before the massive repression exacted when the city was finally recaptured. In Spain, also racked by revolution from 1868, the briefly established republic of 1873–1874 went through a "Federalist" episode of decentralization, confronting, moreover, a wave of local "cantonalist" uprisings in the southeast that sought even more total autonomy.

Of course, there was no direct causality that linked the anarchist uprisings in Paris and Spain's cities of the early 1870s with the episodes of tribal resistance on the margins of European expansion a few years later, which we cited in the introduction above. Nonetheless, along with the nomadic struggles on the periphery of empire, these doomed spasms of spontaneity in Europe also demonstrated that in the world of the 1870s the organized national or imperial state was trump. Thirty years earlier liberals and radicals had aspired to create nation-states that would reconcile impulses of emancipation with collective self-determination. After 1870 they found that the states they had wished for served a different spirit of organization and national competition. Francisco Pi y Margall, the scholarly theorist of grassroots government who served briefly as president of the disintegrating First Spanish Republic in 1873, would spend the next quarter-century of his life as a historian and parliamentary deputy for the republican opposition and a defender of autonomy for Cuba. Sitting Bull lived out the post-Custer years on a reservation—each a surviving witness to a vision of collective life that the modern state had effectively rendered obsolete.

Anarchism did not go quietly into the night, however. After military restoration of the Spanish monarchy in 1874 and a cozy agreement for party alternation in the parliamentary elections, Spanish anarchists put their energies into organizing agricultural cooperatives and a union federation, the CNT (National Confederation of Labor), which patiently built its strength in the Andalusian countryside and eventually among the urban workforce of Barcelona. It sent delegates to the national parliament but refused to join any governing coalition until the second Republic, installed in 1931, was challenged by the right-wing military uprising of 1936. Spanish anarchism was exceptional in its embrace of patient and collective organization. Elsewhere the doctrine attracted impatient terrorists who believed in the power of "the deed." By the 1880s and 1890s, terrorist zealots were resorting to assassination to destroy the state, claiming the lives of Tsar Alexander II in 1881, the French and American presidents in 1894 and 1901, the empress of Austria and queen of Italy. Still, these violent gestures did not succeed in arresting the strengthening of central governments, and they were disavowed by most revolutionaries, Marxist or otherwise.[97] Other advocates of working-class advancement, such as the European social-democratic parties emerging by the 1890s, believed that "capturing" the state and using it to pass such reforms as minimum wages, enhanced social insurance, stricter safety measures, and limitation on factory hours, was a more promising strategy for advancing social justice. To be sure, faithful Marxist revolutionaries condemned this "reformist" stance at the congresses of the second Socialist International, but until the eve of World War I, it attracted increasing numbers of adherents, especially among trade unionists, who played a large role in socialist parties.

Nevertheless—let's get real. For all the recent histories that suggest the state became exponentially more ambitious and powerful in controlling its citizens, nineteenth-century governments still hardly "penetrated" society. Empires left administrative power in the hands of local notables; vast areas of sparsely populated countryside had virtually no police forces. Factory owners faced virtually no challenge to their power within their enterprises. Western states taxed their citizens extraordinarily lightly; liberals had rolled back the heavy burdens that the wars of the eighteenth century and then the Napoleonic era had necessitated. Above all, as we shall see, in those offshore preserves of arbitrary power—the colonies, formal and informal, of the British, French, Spanish, Dutch, Germans, Italians, Portuguese, and later the Japanese and Americans—remote states assigned coercive power to private agents. The extortionate loan, the power to evict and to fire, sometimes the lash, the knout, the switch, and the bamboo rod, not the rational state, ensured social order and the investment opportunities that would be one of the incentives for development. (The other remained the precapitalist motive of expanding strategic power for the home country and its state.) The development of European empire rested upon this happy compatibility of motivations.

But this fabric of local and non-state authority would be significantly encroached upon from the 1860s for the next century. Not entirely, to be sure, and often least significantly in those great imperial superstructures run by the Habsburgs, Romanovs, Ottomans, and Qing. Elsewhere, having rebuilt nations, the vigorous administrative elites of the late nineteenth century and twentieth, could rebuild states. To these efforts we apply a term proposed only recently: *governmentality*. Governmentality has become a fashionable concept in the social sciences and has begun to seep into historical accounts as well. Its recent use derives from the French social theorist Michel Foucault, who applied it to describe the growing administrative and pastoral capacity of the Catholic Church in the late Middle Ages and then post-Renaissance political units to regulate the behavior of those living within their borders. The Church had the mission of tending "souls" and providing the nurturing institutions that would ensure their salvation; the state would take over this welfarist mission. Foucault separated the pursuit of governability from that of sovereignty. Sovereignty, or state authority in the abstract, he suggested, was the concern of sixteenth-century thinkers, such as Machiavelli, but from the seventeenth and particularly the eighteenth century, officials were preeminently concerned with the health and prosperity of their populations. Tracts on national economies, epidemics, and trade displaced the disquisitions on the rights of the ruler. Statistics and measurement, and the regulation (or deregulation) of national economies, became the instruments for advancing the well-being of the population.[98] In effect the nineteenth century recapitulated the transition that Foucault described from the seventeenth-century theorists of sovereignty and power to the eighteenth-century Physiocrats, cameralists, and administrative cadres, who inscribed prosperity, growth, and health of their societies as preeminent state objectives.

The discipline of sociology emerged in part as a response to the recurrent threat of revolution and working-class mass action: ideology was supposedly to yield to science, or so conservative scholars argued. The Paris popular upheaval in June 1848 (and then again the Commune in 1870) led Hippolyte Taine to displace what he felt was destructive ideology with scientific management of society through sociology.[99] In Britain Herbert Spencer applied what he believed were the lessons of Darwinism to reject any efforts at what he insisted was collectivist interference with the healthy evolution of society. His disciple in the United States, William Graham Sumner of Yale, likewise condemned social legislation as disastrous interference with the market. Émile Durkheim was in a far more liberal political camp, but also insisted on "social facts" to be measured statistically; and one of the major facts he analyzed was "suicide," which he treated not merely as a psychological collapse but as a societal disease that testified to an underlying condition of social disintegration he termed anomie. Whether on the left or the right, however, the new state possibilities of intervention depended on postulating an organic society that could be measured and shaped. This new confidence in the measurability of social relationships took its name from Auguste Comte's doctrine of positivism—a confidence in the observability of natural and social phenomena that characterized the statesmen and intellectuals of the 1870s and 1880s but would erode and dissipate, at least in high culture, by the 1890s and the first decade of the twentieth century.

The new states, having been created and re-created by the 1870s, turned essentially to projects of modernization and the transformation of their societies. Numbers were the epistemological foundations of these projects. In itself this was not new. Whenever the accumulation (and avoidance) of old taxes had to be replaced—as early as the "Single Whip" reform of the Ming dynasty, or whenever a ruler acquired a new territory—property surveys followed (recall the Domesday Book of William the Conqueror). Romanovs, Ottomans, and other monarchs needed to know their boundaries and their resources. Abbatial and manorial administrators, the trustees of Muslim pious foundations, Chinese gentry, and thereafter Italian and Dutch cities had to provide for public works and military expenditures. William Petty had pioneered efforts by means of "political arithmetick" to measure the wealth of the British kingdom in the late seventeenth century. The politics went on unabated; the arithmetic became more detailed. The brilliant mathematicians of the Bernoulli family, along with the French Huguenot Abraham de Moivre and later the German Carl Friedrich Gauss, developed the theoretical groundwork for statistical inference from the seventeenth into the nineteenth century, although governments clung to counting and eschewed sampling until the US Census of 2000. Censuses had ancient roots—Jesus had been born in the course of one—but they became far more widespread and important.[100]

The censuses were numbers fixed to territorial locations—mapped quantities. The eighteenth century had seen a proliferation of cadastres—maps of landholding and domains surveyed with an eye toward imposing taxes more systematically. Trigonometry and triangulation underlay the new techniques of measurement on the global surface as it had for celestial navigation. Rectangular grids provided the representation for locating the resources of specific sites. The British in Ireland and India undertook major geographical surveys of their still-colonial spaces; the Mexican states undertook geographical surveys as well. In 1877, President Porfirio Díaz established a cartographic commission to establish a master map, and chose a geographer who had experience in cadastral and geographic surveys, but the enterprise was underfunded and subject to imprecise local knowledge, and generally lagged behind the equivalent work carried out in British India or France. Still, its ambitions corresponded to the positivist hopes of the Porfirian state: modernization from above, clarification of property, of lines of communication, goals that by 1896 had shifted significantly from the military considerations that dominated when the project was begun.[101] Half a world away, among a Chinese administrative elite beset by intimations of weakness and decline, the geographer's impulse also served the desire for state strengthening as the researchers interested in "practical statecraft" turned to learning about the western regions as a Qing achievement in which to take pride (especially because control over the maritime frontier was dominated by foreigners). But real differentiation of a geographic focus had to await the Republican era, when Japanese territorial seizures focused attention on the threat, not just to sovereignty, but national space.[102]

Fixing people in space was crucial for control as well as for taxation or military defense. Foucault again emphasized the trend in Western societies to discipline social deviance by the confinement of vagrants and the insane.[103] By the New Poor Law of 1834, the British would establish the Workhouse, not the parish or village treasury, as the recourse for those who had no other support. More generally the new states depended upon fixed population: recall the defeat of the nomad challenge of the 1870s. James Scott's paean to the evasive tribes of the upland colonies of Southeast Asia is a testimony to their powers to move physically; running away or melting into dense forests and high mountains was sometimes the most effective strategy of resistance.[104] When migration was no longer possible, collective ownership might preserve a sort of countercultural capacity to white colonizers or middle-class development, although at the cost of conventional economic development. The capacity of indigenous peoples to shift their resource base and resist tethering to agricultural allotments they had the right to sell individually remained a fundamental challenge to the modern state. The United States, which had established and progressively reduced tribal reservation land, decided on a policy of allotment to individuals and families by the Dawes Act of 1887. This allowed further reduction of "excess" reservation land, and then a disaster for tribal society once unrestricted sales could take place. But society as a whole was intended to be counted, located, and surveyed, a task that Francis Amasa Walker, president of the Massachusetts Institute of Technology, made his own with the 1874 publication of the *Statistical Analysis of the United States,* a compendium of positivist social information based upon the 1870 Census, which he had directed. Ironically, the project of fixing abode seemed urgent at the moment when mass migration from Europe to North and South America multiplied, at a time, too, when Chinese poured into Southeast Asia and, along with the Japanese, crossed Pacific shores. The new instrumentality of passports and labor booklets, as well as the agencies set up to inscribe the migrants, was the states' response.[105]

But consider again the new cartography. Perhaps its distinguishing feature, derived from the spatial imagination of the late nineteenth century, was the assignment of potential resources to the territorial grids. In this sense it matched the new understanding of electromagnetic physics developed at the same time by James Clerk Maxwell. Every point in physical space was a point in an energy field and could be assigned a proportional quantity of energy potential. So too in the emerging statistical counting every point had a quantity of human energy resources linked to it. The surveys and the censuses both counted them and assigned them a location. Thus nomadism and even collective rights of ownership— American Indian migrations and reservations in the US case—threatened the rationality of the modern state. On the other hand, immigration and the westward movement of the population enhanced the energy potential of previously empty areas. The empty areas of the United States, the Arid Regions, would also find their great cartographic description.[106]

Walker recognized that Americans did not like to be questioned and counted, but expressed confidence that in 1880 they had "outgrown the little, paltry, bigoted construction of the Constitution, which, in 1850, questioned in Congress the right of the people of the United States to learn whatever they might please to know regarding their own numbers, condition, and resources."[107] By 1900 the American Economic Association elected as its president Richard Ely, who rejected laissez-faire sociology and admired Bismarck's nascent welfare state in Germany. He was in sympathy with the president of Johns Hopkins, who brought German graduate education methods—specialized research in laboratories and seminars—to the United States. They spoke for experts, for quantitative knowledge, and for the state. They also represented a heightened role for gender differentiation. The engineering profession, then like other specializations developing their credentialing organizations and claiming expertise and status, was a career for men, although the Census hired women, who would soon become highly represented in the clerical profession.[108]

The military experience of the mid-century wars of reunification had shaped many of these men in an almost existential way. It had put their lives on the line at a formative age, made them serious, and tested manhood. Manliness was a critical theme of the last decades of the nineteenth century and the first one of the twentieth. In a chapter on the state it may seem excessive to speculate on the roles of male companionship and homoeroticism, but the themes surface—whether in big game hunting, the French and British military excursions into the interior of Africa, the menacing females of symbolist fin-de-siècle painting or, to take an achievement of naturalism, the rowers of Thomas Eakins. But if a subterranean temptation, such gender uncertainty was vigorously suppressed by rites of passage from which men such as Roosevelt and Eakins emerged. The unexamined life is not worth living, but in a pre-Freudian era the excessively examined life could seem paralyzing. Imperialism and masculine vigor beckoned as a vocation; white manliness was critical—to be formed in sports and hunting large animals in remote locations. A French nationalist Pierre Coubertin would organize the 1896 revival of the Olympic games; Robert Baden-Powell would found the Boy Scouts and encourage military expansion.

Two later monuments to Theodore Roosevelt celebrate the diverse themes flowing together. The visitor to Theodore Roosevelt Island, in the Potomac in Washington, DC, will come upon the oversize bronze orator with his aphorisms on tablets behind him—one of which ("The State") offers his precepts for political life. The visitor to the Museum of Natural History on Central Park West in Manhattan will also find TR, again in imperial bronze but now on horseback being led by an American Indian in tribal regalia and a black African—a 1940 rendition by James Earle Fraser, most famous for his noble but exhausted Indian on horseback *(The End of the Trail).* The tourist who contemplates the 1898 bronze statue of the Meiji generation conservative Saigō Takimori near Tokyo's Ueno railway station encounters the robust nationalist in Samurai garb with his beloved dog. Saigō, too, was a military expansionist, hoping to provoke a war to conquer Korea in 1874. But he was also a dyed-in-the-wool conservative, sometimes supporting but often opposing the reforms that were transforming Japan in his lifetime and finally persuaded to lead an unsuccessful uprising in 1877 that cost him his life. TR rode up San Juan Hill, sought to regulate laissez-faire celebration of capitalism, and pressed for American entrance into the First World

War. A generation apart, the Japanese dismayed by modernity, the American embracing it, both were fulfilled by militant nationalism.

"Teddy" exemplified the synthesis of vitalism, reform, and frank imperialism. For all the volatility of this mix, it was still compatible with the reorganized state's emphasis on measuring human resources. In an age of social Darwinism this meant categorization by type as well just by quantity. Racial typology emerged; the nascent criminology depended on profiling by body type—an effort made most notorious by Italian statistician Cesare Lombroso, who felt that earlobes revealed criminal types. Measuring made sense because of underlying "type"—a preoccupation that at the end of the twentieth century might be refined as the idea of "risk" as supposedly determined by genetic factors. Mass migrations and the arrival of diverse ethnic groups—whether the Irish in England and the United States, Italians and Spaniards in France, southern and Eastern Europeans (including the Jewish migrations from Russia and Galicia) in the United States, Italians in Argentina, Chinese and Japanese in the American West, the plantation labor recruited for the colonial plantations of Malaya and southeast Asia, or the Indians relocated to South Africa—meant a confrontation with groups that sometimes seemed to bring unrest and crime and different physiques. In an era of economic expansion and industrialization, migration could not be halted, was necessary—but it required control and counting, and intensified inter-ethnic prejudices. Anti-Semitism became more virulent as one consequence, increased too by the economic adversity encountered by agricultural producers from 1873 to 1896, when deflationary pressure meant that financial interests—banks and ostensibly Jewish creditors—led to openly anti-Jewish agitation in Central and Eastern Europe, France, and the United States, as social discrimination became more prevalent. Wherever there were sizable numbers of middle-class migrants and merchants, vulnerability increased. Not that these prejudices halted the trends toward the mobility of peoples and capital; rather, they provided evidence that, short of major war, the geographic and social mobility would not be reversed. Migration and measurement increased together; the modern state could not halt the flows but it sought to classify them.

Time measurement was another project for the modernizing agenda. The development of east–west railroads made the problem critical. Sun time meant that watches had constantly to be adjusted for travel. Paris was 9 minutes and 20 seconds ahead of London, Bombay 41 minutes behind Madras. In 1884, representatives of governments, railroads, and organizations concerned with standardizing time met in Washington, DC, and Paris and demarcated the twenty-four time zones (each ideally 15 degrees of latitude although with variations for local land masses), within each of which the same time would prevail. All but the French agreed that the Greenwich Observatory near London, which served to anchor the Meridian or degree zero of longitude, might serve as the midpoint of Greenwich Mean Time, and twenty years later the French gave in. But stubborn reluctance persisted, worldwide, to abandoning the local time, usually reckoned by the sun's zenith, for the uniform hour imposed across the time zone. Local time was long-standing, governed working hours, and often was conspicuously displayed on public clocks. Where religious exercises, such as the five calls to prayer for faithful Muslims, were keyed to the divisions of daylight, which varied with the seasons, the coexistence of old and new time became even more complex. But to impose standard time was seen as modern and progressive. The effort preoccupied Sultan Abdülhamid II (1878–1908), who erected clock towers in key cities designed to send the empire's message to his "Well Protected Domains," a measure perceived by traditionalists as another example of his despotic centralization of power.[109]

Governing by Party

Governing was different from governmentality. The French said, "to govern was to choose." Ultimately decisions had to be made or fudged, which meant, as it still does, essentially postponed until they were resolved incrementally. Today's neologism, *governmentality,* curiously enough, has sometimes implied that to govern wisely was not to have to choose. Such prized public outcomes in the early twentieth century as "national efficiency" or "the one best way" might emerge as a result of knowledge, not electoral contests. Science, technology, or the psychology of human manipulation would allow a painless form of government that was self-justifying. Legitimacy supposedly would flow from the wisdom of the result, not from the process by which it was enacted—the old dream of rule by philosopher-kings, but now philosopher-technicians. But despite this dream, continually refreshed by different generations of social thinkers—even today, as we shall see in conclusion—policies had to be decided, states had to be governed. Would railroads be built? Were armies and naval forces to be expanded? Until what age and under whose auspices would children be schooled? What prerogatives might traditional religious establishments retain? So how were choices made?

In theory at least, the new states created at midcentury, like the ones constructed earlier, were countries in which representative assemblies played a large role. Piedmont and Italy, Austria, Germany, and Japan had introduced them between 1848 and 1890. Other old empires were holdouts: Russia claimed to be an autocracy, and a parliament was introduced only during the revolutionary turmoil of 1905; the Ottoman Empire established a parliament in 1908, Iran after its revolution in 1906, China in 1912. With few exceptions only males could vote on the national level before World War I. Until 1885 in Britain, property qualifications narrowed the suffrage, and varying forms of tax requirements helped keep peasants and proletarians from exercising any sort of proportional voting rights in many areas of Europe and the United States. In the kingdom of Hungary, the suffrage was rigged to keep non-Magyars (and poor ones too) from achieving parliamentary representation. So too the American South excluded black voters by virtue of poll taxes and literacy requirements (also used in Italy until 1912). Southern Europe, parts of Latin America, and the southern United States might best be described as areas in which political argumentation played itself out within a racially pure ruling class that dominated regional and sometimes national legislatures. Sometimes, if even this pattern of privileged parliamentarism seemed too fragile to prevent the advance of popular claimants, private violence could easily be organized: atrocities against Armenians in the Ottoman Empire, lynching in the old Confederate states, and Cossack pogroms against Jewish settlements in 1890–1910 might ensure that challengers to newly refurbished "traditions" were cowed into submission. Thus reinforced by occasional exemplary violence, the structures of domination allowed a parliamentary oratory to flourish, replete with glorious defenses of liberty, appeals to national and regional pride, and defense of the highly inegalitarian social status quo.

The discrepancy between words and deeds also afflicted those parliaments that more adequately reflected popular classes and opinions, as in France and the

United States. No matter how broad the suffrage, the parliaments were dogged by corruption. The public financing of railroad lines, the speculative real estate booms in the expanding capital and industrial cities, the fusion of old agricultural elites with the new wealth of industry and finance and their search for compliant legislators meant that the parliamentary politics of the late 1870s through the 1890s was riddled with scandal. Typical disorders included Tammany Hall—the Democratic Party "machine" in New York—and other US political cliques, the French corruption associated with the selling of honors from the president's office and with the bribery used by the Panama canal development company, bank scandals in Italy, and payoffs by colonial interests.

The institution that dominated the systems of government was one that written democratic constitutions would not explicitly mention until the mid-twentieth century in Germany, that is, the competitive political party. The party was an association of individuals and the groups who stood behind them dedicated to governing on the basis of shared principles, material interests, and just for the sake of holding power and keeping opponents out of office. "Party" interests existed in the ancient world and in the city-state republics of medieval Europe, but they often could not agree on policy without proscription, assassination, and civil war. In the modern era, the point of parties was precisely to settle affairs, often by a principle of alternation in power, without the need for repeated imprisonment, exile, and political murder. In its modern career, party originated in the postrevolutionary regimes of Britain in the late seventeenth and eighteenth centuries and in the former American colonies in the 1780s and 1790s, sometimes as rival associations of elites took organized rival networks of supporters—often with the claim to be the legitimate heirs of a profound historical transformation. Rulers and those who felt excluded from such associations often saw the constellations of adversaries as cabals or conspiracies. Distinguishing party from conspiracy was perhaps the signal achievement of Anglo-American government in the hundred years from 1720 to 1820. That distinction meant that men might disagree over policies—war or peace, favoring of landed or commercial interests, defending or diminishing the claims of religious institutions, imposing taxation or not—without seeing each other as traitors or usurpers.

This distinction did not come easily: in periods of acute turmoil it was hard to accept that the opposition did not intend to betray the state and its vital interests.

A war for independence, as in North America, usually created a body of "patriots," and when their common adversary was no longer present and they differed among each other, suspicions of sell-out and betrayal were hard to overcome. The United States overcame a major hurdle when in 1800 it was recognized that one group of former revolutionaries had emerged to challenge another, and took over major offices without a protest or civil strife. The French Revolution got to this stage only after an interval of dictatorial rule by violence (frankly called Terror) in supposed defense of democratic principles against domestic and foreign enemies. The weakened institutions established to prevent such a recurrence—the so-called Directory from 1795 to 1799—suffered repeated coups and canceled elections until finally overthrown by military conspiracy that installed Napoleon with increasing dictatorial prerogatives. The British rulers of the same period used political trials to establish conservative conformity and subdue those sympathetic to the French radicals with whom they were at war. The United States seemed ready to go down that route briefly before the elections of 1800 arrested the process. Gradually party was seen as the key instrument, not only of achieving political rule, but of limiting political violence. It was a key invention of the modern state.

Party as an instrument of government advanced in a major way in the late nineteenth century, and the United States seemed to be the key innovator. Whereas in the mid-nineteenth century in Britain or the early years of the French Third Republic, parties seemed to fission and dissolve, certainly between elections, by the 1870s and 1880s they developed into continuing associations, managed often by professionals with permanent offices, and as important for local politics as for national politics. Political "machines" came to be the major force for organizing arenas where the suffrage was wide and cut across diverse classes and interests. Tammany Hall was renowned as the Democratic Party machine that organized the immigrant vote in New York City. The Birmingham Caucus of Joseph Chamberlain emerged by the 1890s. Sociologists such as Max Weber and the Russian Moisei Ostrogorski studied the American political machine with great interest. The party manager and professional appeared to be a new type; the American primary or British "caucus," a disturbing nonconstitutional innovation that had the potential to corrupt disinterested government. Roberto Michels, a German-Italian student of Weber, argued that parties of the left were all the more prone to entrench oligarchies within their own ranks.[110]

The British- and American-style parties spread to the continent. By the late 1860s party was becoming important in Bismarck's Customs Union Parliament (Zollparlament) and North German Confederation—his institutional way-stations between the defeat of Austria in 1866 and the German Empire founded in 1871. Catholics, concentrated in Bavaria and the Rhineland and Prussian Silesia, feared being dominated in a Protestant state once Austria no longer had a voice in Central European government. They coalesced and soon formed a "Center Party" to defend their interests. Although persecuted by anticlerical legislation, they would soon become a mainstay of government in the German Empire, thereafter the Weimar Republic, and even the German Federal Republic after 1949. Ideologically flexible, they could form coalitions with conservatives to their right or liberals to their left. On the left of the spectrum, German Social Democrats had diverse origins. Ferdinand Lasalle founded the formal party in 1869 to compete in the Bismarckian state; Marxists comprised one strand, but not the only one. Swinging from his decade-long hostility to Catholic political organization (the so-called *Kulturkampf* or struggle over civilization), which had been combined with a reliance on nationalist liberal support, Bismarck decided to outlaw the Social Democrats in 1878, after an assassination attempt on the emperor, and to govern on the basis of a coalition of Catholics and Conservatives. Only after the old chancellor's dismissal by William II in 1890 could the Social Democratic Party (SPD) reemerge legally—to become by 1912 the largest group in the Reichstag—intent no longer on revolution in the streets but on capturing power in the parliament. Austrian Social Democrats followed suit. French Socialists remained divided between different ideological strands, but were urged by the International to merge and did so as the French Section of the Workers' International party (SFIO) in 1905. Meanwhile the French non-Socialist left had organized itself as the Radical Socialist Party in 1901 (it was fairly centrist) as a consequence of the Dreyfus affair. Parties usually had an official daily paper or at least a newspaper that tended to support their views and interpretations. Increasingly candidates for office had to be approved by the central office or, as in the United States, by a system of conventions.

The reality of political parties was disturbing to many. Again Weber made a contrast between an old style of politics where eminent leaders offered their services at elections *(Honoratiorenpolitik),* and the new one of mass politics where party government with its backroom deals and professional organization really took government in hand. By the first decade of the new century, party government seemed to be the inevitable product of modern "mass society," by which was meant not a revolutionary or socialist movement, but the dominance of the anonymous urban citizenry, working often in clerical and retail jobs and swayed by irrational appeals to national glory. Corruption seemed to go naturally with this view of a mass society governed by highly organized political parties. Was it democracy?

Parties could function in different ways. In Latin America they still froze some of the divisions that persisted after the wars of independence from Spain. Confrontations of centralist conservatives and liberal federalists (the advocates of limited centralization and more extensive regional powers) often produced coups d'état (*pronunciamentos* or *golpes*) and periods of harsh violence. The presence of strong military leaders fed this tendency. Political parties, whether in Chile, Columbia, Mexico, or Argentina, in sum remained frozen in a situation of continuing potential civil war, as had pertained long ago in the Roman Republic. In most other arenas, however, parties were content to share out the spoils of governing. In this case parties might be nominally distinct but rather similar in terms of ideology and social support. In Spain, for instance, Antonio Cánovas, the conservative prime minister who finally brought the civil wars and coups d'état of 1868–1873 under control, helped work out a monarchical restoration under whose terms liberals and conservatives agreed to alternative power with each four-year parliamentary session. This *turno politico* really meant politics was directed by a rather narrow governing class. Italy remained committed to parliamentary government; it was accepted that the monarch would choose as a prime minister only a leader who could assemble a majority in the lower house—a consensual arrangement challenged before the advent of interwar fascism only briefly from 1898–1900. The heirs to the unifiers, the expansive Liberal Party, had leaders and wings respectively more or less committed to suffrage reform and broadening the tax base, who held power at different times. Ideological challengers on the left (originally republicans and radicals and later socialists) or on the right (new strident nationalists) were largely marginalized. In Hungary, after the great constitutional settlement that provided autonomy in 1867 (the Ausgleich), liberals also dominated although conservative challengers were important in debate. Japanese constitutional government was imported gradually by the aging Meiji oligarchs (the Genrō). In 1890 they adopted a German-style constitution that bestowed a limited role on a new Diet. After an unruly beginning, the emerging post-Meiji generation produced a rudimentary political differentiation among the elite and two party associations, Kenseito and Seiyu-kai, that were oriented around rival leaders.

Such systems functioned as oligarchies, good for sharing patronage in normal times but prone to breakdown. The elites in Hungary, Italy, and Argentina tended to envision themselves as a sort of idealized mid-nineteenth-century British ruling class, cultivated and deferred to. But like their counterparts in Britain, they found their cozy politics challenged by bitter personal rivalries and the emerging challenges of working-class demands, and the popular passions of foreign policy that they sought to manipulate in their favor. Systems of nominal alternation (as in Spain), single-party electoral domination (as in the American South), or continued absorption of earlier opposition groups ("transformism," as in Italy), required large reservoirs of consistently loyal voters responsive to favors, personal fealty, or ethnic allegiances. American Southern Democrats and Hungarian or Italian liberals were thus hardly liberal—they were the leaders of political oligarchies who hoped to preserve power without wrenching changes. Early welfare legislation, such as that introduced by Bismarck in Germany in the 1880s and then advanced by the left and many occupational groups, became a major cause for political division, though more so in other countries where it enjoyed less conservative patronage, as did new land and income taxes. As controversies over social legislation grew, the issue of widening the franchise became important. Italian politics functioned because masses of the southern peasantry could not vote because of the literacy requirement. England faced harsh issues of whether Ireland should achieve home rule. New and ambitious political leaders decided they could prevail by more-ideological appeals to the masses. The mayor of Vienna, Karl Lueger, was successful in building a machine of Christian Socials, who claimed to govern Austria for the popular classes against the reactionaries and the nefarious Jews. Anti-Semitism and other ethnic appeals became more strident.

The difficulty was that toward the end of the century in the West, the old politics seemed increasingly under stress. On the one hand, the spread of industrialism—of labor in mines and factories and with machines—created an activist working class. It moved all sorts of occupational safety and pension issues into the forefront of politics. Even more disturbing was the emergence by the twentieth century of parties with new total claims, who did not believe they should share power, such as the Committee for Union and Progress in Turkey and the Russian Bolsheviks. After the revolution of 1908 in the Ottoman Empire, the Young Turks, as the revolutionaries were dubbed, preached a restoration of ethnic Turkish domination. It was hard to organize the slow-moving, clientelistic decentralized empire with such a force.

But even when parties seemed to function smoothly, the contrast between the rhetoric of liberal parliamentarism and its shabby reality ensured that a harsh critical analysis would emerge. By the 1880s trenchant critiques of democracy were emerging from the European Right with Italian writers taking the lead. (The term *Right* is chosen because the writers scorned government by liberalism or discussion in favor of rule by elites and also believed that an emerging social democracy was really just another hypocritical claim to exercise bureaucratized power.) These new critics from the Right no longer invoked the old traditions of the Church or praised paternalist and wise elites, as had conservatives almost a century earlier. Instead they pointed to the discrepancy between liberal ideals and corrupt reality to suggest that elites had always and would always rule, no matter what the nominal form of the government. Pasquale Turiello argued that the continuing poverty of the Italian south proved that liberal government had failed the masses; Italy needed instead a great new national cause, perhaps a new war, to ensure national solidarity. Gaetano Mosca's *Theory of the Governed* (1881) argued that the masses could never rule; elites would always be in charge. Vilfredo Pareto, teaching economics at the University of Lausanne in Switzerland, and known today for his statistical concepts, was the most cynical: his *Socialist Systems* (1902) argued that for all their claims on behalf of democratic reform, the Socialists were just a new elite advancing a Marxist ideology designed to ensure their own narrow rule. Mussolini briefly attended his lectures. The once republican poet Giosuè Carducci attacked the supposed reality of the new state and evoked the vultures flying over Rome.[111]

French writers also contributed to the new antidemocratic critiques and added to them an extreme nationalism and anti-Semitism. The French Right learned that even in an age of mass suffrage, a populist nationalism could win them votes: General Georges Boulanger at the end of the 1880s ran and won in several of the parliamentary districts. His adherents wanted him to seize power, but he lost his nerve and fled to Brussels, where he committed suicide. Still, the episode testified to the role that nationalism could play. The success, too, of Edmond Drumont's rabble-rousing anti-Semitic newspaper revealed the power of prejudice and demagogy. The Panama Scandal of the early 1890s, and the Dreyfus affair—in which a Jewish army officer was repeatedly prosecuted for espionage even after it was clear that he had been framed—ignited a broad-based distrust of Jews. Maurice Barrès suggested in his novel *The Uprooted* and other writings that the Republican system and the influx of foreigners, among them French Jews, were corrupting the village virtues on which French history had been built. Charles Maurras's Action Française, a movement and a newspaper, violently attacked Jews, extolled military nationalism, and urged that an authoritarian monarch replace the Republic, which he habitually referred to as "the slut" *(la gueuse)*. Although the Right lost national elections in 1898 and 1905, they became fashionable purveyors of doctrine among students and made many inroads in the national capital.

By the late 1870s nationalism manifested itself as a doctrine aspiring more to territorial aggrandizement than to linguistic or communal self-determination. This transformation of an ideology that had accompanied liberal and revolutionary aspirations into a set of xenophobic attitudes by which antiliberal leaders sought to organize mass constituencies was a fundamental development of the late nineteenth century. Poles might aspire to recover a national state wiped off the map a century earlier. Within the Austro-Hungarian Empire there were still champions of ethnic self-determination and even secession. But nationalism no longer manifested itself in Western Europe as a romantic enthusiasm for grouping the members of a language group or an ancient territory. After all, Germany and Italy had already achieved unity and Romania, Bulgaria, and Serbia were recognized as sovereign nation-states. Their imagined communities were no longer imagined; they (or their nationalist elites) were merely dissatisfied with the territory they currently held. Even Austria-Hungary seemed to settle into a constitutional equilibrium that satisfied Hungarians as well as Germans.

The economic strains of the era from 1873 to 1896 also intensified national competition. The growth of grain imports from the Western Hemisphere—the United States, Canada, and Argentina—after the American Civil War and the expansion of continent-wide railroad systems meant stagnant or depressed prices for farmers and intensified the sense of national competition for markets. The absence of new gold discoveries between 1849 and 1896, in an age when currencies were being keyed to gold and the United States was "redeeming" its paper currency from the Civil War, meant a deflationary pressure on prices for over two decades, which in turn made credit dearer for farmers. National tariffs imposed on imported grains, and on behalf of domestic manufacturers, seemed the logical answer and also allowed log-rolling bargains between the spokesmen for farmers and for industry. The Republican Party in the United States had urged and inaugurated tariff protection since its inception in the 1850s; Bismarck instituted a tariff in 1879, and it was significantly raised under his nationalist successors in 1897. The duties provided needed revenue at the national level, but also facilitated cooperation between rye growers and industrialists who were often arrayed in hostile parties: Conservatives and National Liberals. But not only the Right passed tariffs: the incoming coalition of the Left in Italy sought to confirm its power by passing a protective tariff in 1882, and the centrist coalition in France would pass its first tariff on foreign grains in 1892. Only Great Britain resisted tariffs in the last decades of the nineteenth century; and Britain certainly did not resist the other great trend that intensified the sense of national competition—the search for exclusive colonial domains.

The Colonizing State and the Colonial State

What does the great scramble to partition Africa and Asia and seize exclusive territorial domains overseas tell us about the state? We discuss the pattern of domination established overseas, the colonial state, below. But was the state of the colonizers decisively impacted by the experience of imperialism? How did acquisition of an overseas empire change the European, Japanese, or American regime? The question is not easy to answer. Max Weber asked in the 1890s what significance German political unification would possess if the country did not go on to develop an overseas empire.[112] Late nineteenth-century expansion followed upon the satisfaction taken throughout Europe in national success and power that followed the preceding period of nation-state construction but then seemed necessary to confirm it. For a few decades at midcentury, acquisition of overseas territory seemed less compelling than earlier or later. The British had acquired the Cape Colony at the Congress of Vienna. The French invaded Algeria in 1830. At midcentury British policy makers expressed no great urge to expand their political domains, since their economic prowess as bankers and manufacturers seemed to ensure their easy superiority in markets and states overseas. By the 1870s, competition—political and economic—was perceived as harsher and pervasive, so that by the 1880s and 1890s remaining territory was quickly arrogated.

Historians a generation ago could easily demonstrate that there was no master plan, no timetable, and even, they suggested, no intention. The British Empire was supposedly created, so John Robert Seeley had written in his influential 1883 lectures, *The Expansion of England,* in "a fit of absence of mind." Hardly: the tracks were laid—empire had been the aspiration of large states throughout history; the wars of 1850–1870 showed that power and territory were important. Napoleon III was muscling into Vietnam and even seeking to conquer Mexico. Disraeli and other conservatives signaled the need actually to control land masses (and the people that went with them). Seeley cautiously affirmed the imperial vocation and its beneficial impact on the lands London ruled, and vast areas of Asia and Africa beckoned. The great rivers that ran from their remote interiors to the sea—the Nile, the Niger, the Congo, the Zambezi in Africa, and the Mekong and Irrawaddy in Southeast Asia—allowed European gunboats to penetrate far inland, just as earlier the St. Lawrence, the Hudson, the Mississippi, Orinoco, and Amazon had opened up the Americas, and even earlier the oceans had allowed overseas exploration. Against his supposed intention, Prime Minister Gladstone intervened in Alexandria and Cairo in 1882 to enforce the claims of British bondholders who had financed construction of the Suez Canal. By the 1890s British troops were conquering the Sudan hundreds of miles up river ostensibly to quell the disorder that always broke out beyond their last line of penetration.

A year before the British seizure of Egypt, the French moved east from Algeria to take over Tunisia—nominally a remote province of the Ottomans, but in fact a quasi state where Jewish and Italian traders lived among the Bedouin and Arab populations—and the competitive consuls of France, Italy, and Britain sought to interest their governments in seizing control. The French moved first, from Algeria, and established a protectorate by the Treaty of Bardo in 1881, which angered the Italians, who had their eyes on this prize across the Mediterranean. French expansion in Africa depended less on river routes. Like the Muslim conquerors of earlier centuries, they knew how to expand across the vast dry lands of the Sahara and Sahel, relying on oases and a tough corps of mercenary soldiers—the French Foreign Legion—as well as their own colorful detachments of Zouaves. In the decades from the 1830s to 1890s they took over a large Central African domain, from Senegal and the Ivory Coast to Chad, then turned toward an "inkblot" strategy of penetrating the sultanate of Morocco in the new century. The Russians also penetrated an inland terrain: the khanates of the Caucuses and of the Oxus River highlands of Central Asia. Ultimately by the 1880s the Italians would establish a foothold on the East Coast of Africa, first in Somalia and Eritrea, and then would endeavor unsuccessfully (until 1935–1936) to subjugate Ethiopia. Ambitious Meiji statesmen eyed the poor and isolated Korean kingdom as well as the Manchurian littoral. American overseas ambitions excited the owners of sugar plantations in Hawai'i and fruit plantations in Central America (as before the Civil War they had stimulated cotton plantation owners in the deep South) and the fervent Presbyterians who wanted their gospel spread and women educated throughout Asia.

The years 1882–1885 comprised a crucial period of commitment to "the scramble." The stories of remote missionaries in the interior or ambitious national claimants on the coast helped create a favorable opinion for intervention at home. Bismarck, always a continental thinker, had little use for African colonies but decided it was easier to yield to the nationalist enthusiasm and his explorers' faits accomplis. Germany moved into Togo and Cameroon on the West Coast, the large territory of Southwest Africa (today's Namibia), and a swath of East Africa (today's Tanzania). The Berlin Conference of 1884–1885 also adjusted boundary claims for the coastal colonies and in effect confirmed the partition of coastal black Africa as a European cooperative project, just as the Congress of Berlin seven years earlier had established the recognition of states at the expense of the retreating Ottoman Empire as a project under Western European tutelage. Whereas the 1878 Congress of Berlin had sought to regularize the claims of newly emerging nations at the expense of a weakened but venerable Ottoman sovereign, the 1884 Berlin Conference was an effort for Europeans to expand without internecine warfare in a region they deemed to be devoid of sovereign claimants. The later National Socialist legal theorist, Carl Schmitt—we will return to his cold-blooded lucidity later—was at least partially correct when he described the international law that arose from the conference (as it had earlier from other colonial arbitrations) as a project designed to ensure European despoliation without conflict. What happened in the vast interior escaped control. Vast territories, supposedly ceded to European agents by indigenous chiefs, fell into a hazy legal status between commercial control and state sovereignty. In the months before and after the conference, Leopold II, king of Belgium, won American and then British recognition to transform his Association Internationale Africaine (AIC) into the Congo Free State, which his uncontrolled managers transformed into a gigantic tropical gulag devoted to the excruciating harvesting of rubber from the tall vines of the jungle. This scandalous behavior in what was virtually Leopold's personal colonial domain finally led the other European powers to compel its takeover by the Belgian state in 1908. In the interim the French and British carved up the huge regions of West Africa, Germans established colonies on both coasts, the Portuguese pressed inward from their old coastal outposts, and British settlers and generals reached the central great lakes from north and south. Thousands of miles of frontiers were drawn and adjusted. Leviathan 2.0, so laboriously reconstructed in its ancient, settled habitations, could allow itself fantastic windfalls of appropriation.[113]

At the same time the French, who a century earlier had withdrawn from India, now under Napoleon III pressed for outposts in the wealthy Southeast Asian states of today's Vietnam. Vietnam had a stormy history of kingdoms that at times recognized the nominal overlordship of the Chinese emperors, but then had revolted and insisted on their own independence. Consider for a moment the welter of states around the Indian Ocean, the Bay of Bengal, and the South China Sea. Here lay the region of the globe that, from the fifteenth century to

the twentieth, was most saturated—or at least on a par with the middle of
Europe between France and Russia—by claims of sovereignty, sometimes overlapping, sometimes fiercely exclusive, usually contested. Mughal, Portuguese,
British, and French imperial claims impinged on a succession of sultanates and
monarchies and overlapping religious loyalties—Muslim, Buddhist, and Christian. Mughal sovereignty decomposed during the eighteenth and mid-nineteenth
centuries; London's claims expanded in the West and East as British agents
pushed from India into Singapore, Malaya, and lowland Burma by the 1840s,
and into the highlands by the 1880s, all the while consolidating their hold on the
west of India (today's Pakistan) and its northwest territories. Between the late
1850s and early 1860s, the French secured new extraterritorial enclaves in China
and took over Cochin China (southern Vietnam), then in the 1880s absorbed
Annam in the center and, after war with China, Tonkin in the north, as well as
Laos and Cambodia in the western interior of the Mekong River watershed. Thailand preserved its independent monarchy because it served as a buffer between the
two expanding European powers and perspicacious monarchs pushed through a
sustained course of institutional reforms. The Dutch, who had outposts in Sumatra and Java (including the settlement of Batavia, today's Jakarta), pressed east
across the Indonesian archipelago, finally subduing the Bali monarchy in 1906.

Meanwhile the United States opted for a course of annexations from the late
1890s: American sugar planters helped engineer a takeover of the Hawai'ian
monarchy between 1893 and 1900, and although Democratic president Grover
Cleveland resisted annexation, William McKinley supported the local planters.
The 1898 war with Spain yielded a protectorate over Cuba and the cession of the
Philippine archipelago as well as island bases on the routes to China. China was
too huge and developed to be taken over, but Europeans and the ambitious Japanese secured territorial enclaves with rights to impose their own legal jurisdictions. Rivalries moved to the northeast Pacific region by the mid-1890s, in part
because the feeble Korean state became the objective of Chinese, Japanese, and
Russian ambitions. China viewed Korea as a tributary kingdom; Japan moved to
claim trading rights and undermine Beijing's residual suzerainty. By the summer
of 1894 a familiar escalation of incidents led to war between China and Japan,
with the surprising victory of the latter. As a result of its victory, Japan annexed
the island of Formosa (Taiwan), imposed a massive indemnity upon Beijing, and

secured recognition of their rights in Korea, which it would add formally to its overseas possessions in 1910. Their initial annexation of Port Arthur and the Liaodong Peninsula had to be renounced in the face of French, German, and primarily Russian pressure, the so-called Triple Intervention. St. Petersburg would itself annex Port Arthur in 1898; the British and Germans would secure new enclaves on the Shandong Peninsula, Jiaozhou and Weihaiwei. These events hastened the anti-foreign turbulence in a beset China, where the nationalist societies known as Boxers mobilized in Shandong and by the summer of 1900 besieged the foreign legations and missionaries in Beijing. The Dowager Empress Cixi, who had reversed reformist initiatives and imprisoned the young emperor in 1898, threw in her lot with the Boxers, but the Chinese and Manchu generals divided over what stance to take. An eight-nation expeditionary force of up to about 50,000 European, Japanese, and US soldiers crushed the revolt, suppressed the societies, and imposed another indemnity on the hapless court. Who might represent the nation in this huge but possibly decomposing polity: a Manchu court torn between traditionalists and reformers? or nationalists angered by a feckless dynasty and apparently rapacious foreigners?

These were momentous developments that came thick and fast and of course provoked major debates about causation as well as policy. Within a few decades, European states joined by Japan and the United States had claimed the right to rule hundreds of millions of people throughout Asia and Africa. The area they enclosed and bordered was many times the size in area of their own national territories, and it was often ceded in dubious and coerced claims. From one viewpoint, colonial territories were acquired as strategic resources for their imperial states in the struggle against other imperial states. Until recently those who wrote that history have not paid much attention to what was happening within the societies being subjugated and reorganized. They have focused on the confrontations and transactions among the colonizers, and for generations they have argued as to whether economic or political causation was fundamental.

Marxian notions in particular aroused efforts at refutation from diplomatic historians who stressed either traditional political rivalries or sometimes the role of missionaries—a dispute that was caught up in the greater ideological confrontations of the Cold War. Marx, and after him Rosa Luxemburg and other theorists, maintained that the falling rate of profit at home led to the search for more

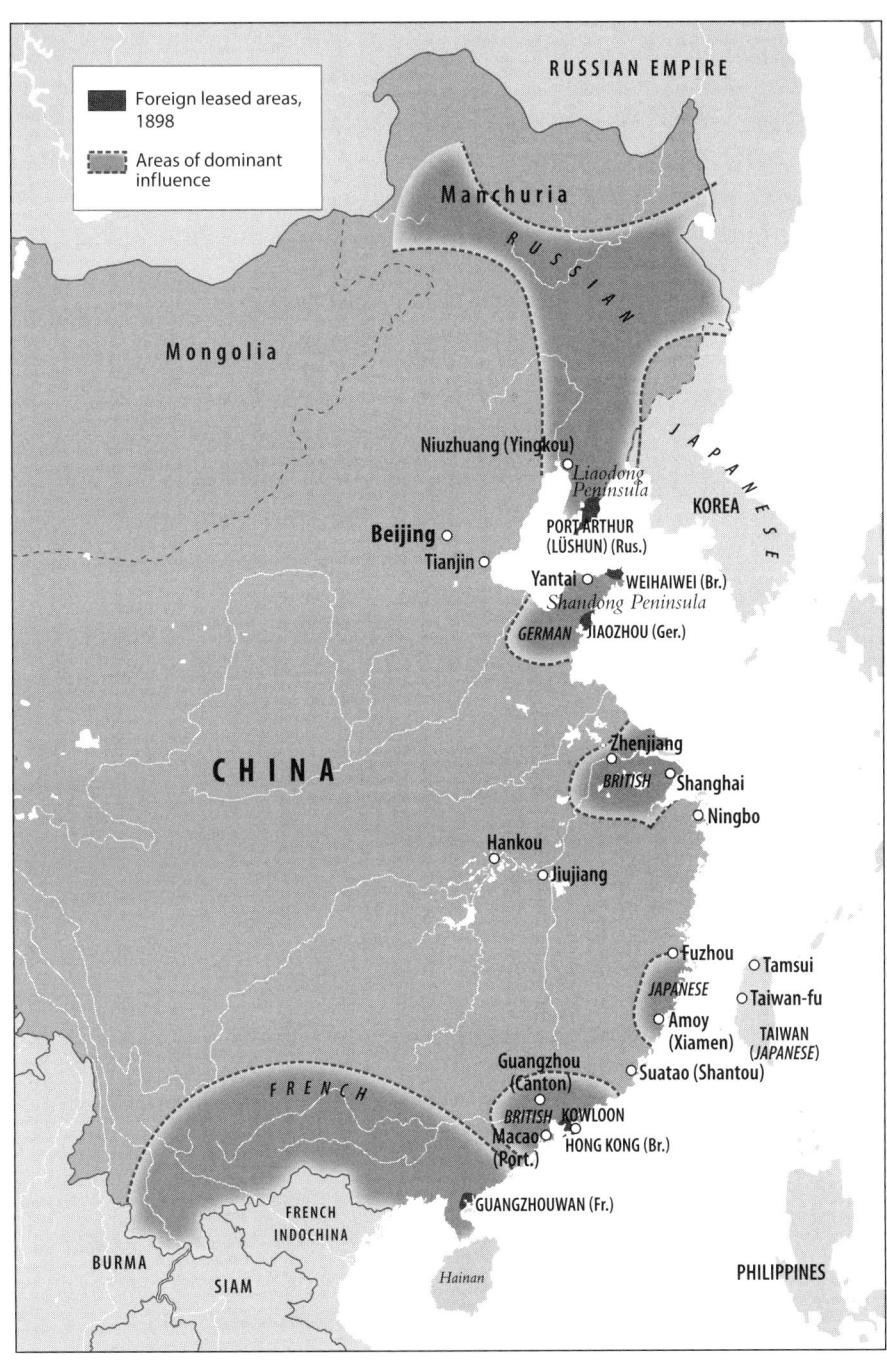

Legend:

■ Foreign leased areas, 1898

▨ Areas of dominant influence

RUSSIAN EMPIRE

Manchuria

RUSSIAN

Mongolia

Niuzhuang (Yingkou)

Liaodong Peninsula

KOREA

JAPANESE

PORT ARTHUR (LÜSHUN) (Rus.)

Beijing

Tianjin

Yantai   WEIHAIWEI (Br.)

Shandong Peninsula

GERMAN   JIAOZHOU (Ger.)

CHINA

Zhenjiang

BRITISH   Shanghai

Ningbo

Hankou

Jiujiang

Fuzhou   Tamsui

JAPANESE   Taiwan-fu

Amoy (Xiamen)   TAIWAN (JAPANESE)

Guangzhou (Canton)

Suatao (Shantou)

FRENCH

BRITISH   KOWLOON

Macao (Port.)   HONG KONG (Br.)

GUANGZHOUWAN (Fr.)

FRENCH INDOCHINA

BURMA

SIAM

Hainan

PHILIPPINES

Foreign penetration of China, ca. 1900.

profitable investment abroad in areas still predominantly nonindustrialized. Thereafter, states or monopoly enterprises—sometimes combinations of banks and industry fused in what Social Democratic theorist Rudolf Hilferding called finance capital—would press their states to establish exclusive zones for their own advantage. After the outbreak of World War I, the Russian Bolshevik leader in exile, V. I. Lenin, claimed that imperialism was in fact just the highest stage of capitalism and would have to lead to a major war.[114]

A related view suggests that governing elites adopted programs of imperialism because their societies were increasingly racked by social division at home and they calculated that expansion might divert domestic conflict into foreign adventures. Hans Ulrich Wehler's study of Bismarck's imperialism a generation ago argued that the chancellor's acceptance of colonialism placed his licensing of colonies in the framework of a German state under the stresses of industrialization.[115] Certainly many advocates of empire, some of them on the right but not all, looked to empire precisely to counteract doctrines of class conflict. British Tories, such as Alfred Milner, wanted a program of social imperialism, as did charismatic pastor Friedrich Naumann of the German Progressive Party. Italian imperialists and nationalists such as Enrico Corradini suggested that their own working class should recognize that Italy was itself a proletarian nation and fall into line behind the industrialists and intellectuals who wanted to advance the agenda of empire and military preparedness.

Not all Marxist theories had to lead like Lenin's to the notion that such imperialist rivalry had to culminate in a great war. Karl Kautsky suggested that imperialist powers might arrive at a "super-imperialism" or peaceful partition of the colonial world. Kautsky's argument suggested in fact the perspective that has become the major approach in the last few decades' study of colonial empires, namely, that we should interpret imperialism not as the extension of European rivalries but as a common European confrontation with the Third World. This point of view suggested that colonialism could be understood as a common enterprise of the advanced states and economies in the Northern Hemisphere with respect to the less resistant states in Asia, Africa, the Caribbean, and the Pacific.

The notion that the colonizers confronted the colonized in some encompassing global binary relationship, more important than the nationalist rivalries that divided them, has in fact emerged as a dominant interpretation of the imperialist era.

Social segregation, sexual exploitation, and political disenfranchisement lay at the base of the colonial relationship, in this view. But not only in the colonies: European institutions, concepts of citizenship, gender relations, and labor, it has been argued, were shaped decisively by Europe's experience as colonizer, just as the world of the indigenous inhabitants was structured by the experience of being colonized. To expand from the Indian historiography of "subaltern studies," all relationships were supposedly stunted by the experience of colonial subjection. Subsequent scholarship has suggested that this framework perhaps involves too radical a confrontation of colonizer and colonized and thus perhaps makes the experience of the colonized too passive and homogeneous.[116] The colonial territory offered the colonizing power natural resources, minerals, and agricultural goods, and specifically tropical assets that his constricted and colder territories at home could not provide. And the colonized subject essentially offered labor power at costs far below what domestic workers imposed and sometimes with less quarrelsome attitudes. Eventually they could bargain with their masters and extract concessions that by the mid-twentieth century would undermine the colonial relationship.[117] But that stage was hardly anticipated in the late nineteenth century.

Beyond the resources of territory and inexpensive labor, beyond any pride in a civilizing mission, the colonizing state provided status and prestige. Small powers along with large powers felt a sense of mission. The architecture of an imperial capital made aesthetic claims. The massive ministries of Justice and Foreign Affairs in Brussels testified to the fact that a small power controlled vast overseas resources. In the case of Belgium, moreover, the overseas mission helped cement the two linguistic communities: the French Walloons staffed the colonial bureaucracies at home; the Flemish took up office in Africa. Empire did provide a dividend of cohesiveness and grandeur as long as one did not have to fight a long war to preserve it. Britain and France did extract from their dependent populations loyalties they could draw on in the two world wars ahead. For better or worse the colonizing state could never be just an agency for providing domestic services at home. Whether this was valuable or instead the source of needless violence and illusory grandeur cannot be decided by adding up the costs and benefits. For a country such as Portugal, the empire may well have provided an excuse not to modernize and to remain less developed. By the mid-twentieth century the costs appeared excessive for many citizens of Britain and France.

As for the colonial state—that is, the regime put into place to govern the large territory and diverse populations taken over—it rested on particular sets of institutions and processes. To seek one model is misleading, because the administrations used in the regions of sub-Saharan Africa, for instance, where wealth derived from mining and the authorities ruled over many different "tribes," differed from those in settler colonies with significant European populations and in the post-1919 states carved out of Ottoman regions. Nonetheless, some commonalities existed, and the admittedly overabstracted colonial state remained a dominant force over vast areas of the world in a period of increasing stateness and governmentality. Africa retained only four sovereign countries by 1895: the ancient kingdom of Ethiopia, Liberia, the white Boer Republics of South Africa, and Morocco. The Boers would have to accept inclusion in the British Union of South Africa and the Moroccans would become a French colony by 1912. Complex confederations had contested Africa since earlier eras but fell to European rule: the Asante kingdom in Ghana, the Buganda kingdom, Shaka's Zulu state, and Samouri Touré's Wassoulu empire in Mali as late as the 1880s. Less extensive tribal communities had negotiated their trading and their security for centuries with the European settlers of the coast and river valleys. A poor and weak Korea, once the source of so much Japanese culture and nominally in a tributary relationship with China, was taken over by the Japanese between 1905 and 1910. The mini-kingdoms of Oceana would also be annexed, as would the Caribbean states. In Central Asia, Iran and Afghanistan evaded annexation if not great political pressure.

The colonial state was run by administrators or proconsuls who had vast amounts of discretionary power. They were expected, however, to cover their costs of administration, if not, as in India, to send a stream of payments back home; and most of their meager budgets went to police and measures designed for security. They could not simply govern without reference to the indigenous peoples whose labor they needed and respect they demanded, so generally they administered through favored intermediaries. Mahmood Mamdani stresses that in Africa the state became bifurcated: into rural areas where the British ruled through chiefs, and urban areas where they had to confront a more complex social scale.[118] The rural chain of command amounted to a new form of despotism; colonial rule elsewhere had to become more subtle and, in effect, a series of transactions made by co-opting native intermediaries. There was a major distinction between tribal societies where political forms were not readily recognizable to the European conquerors, on the one hand, and the subordinate sultanates of the Dutch East Indies or the extraterritorial enclaves in China, on the other. The term *colonial state* takes us only so far in understanding the structure of the British Raj—that huge possession of the crown (including today's Pakistan and Bangladesh)—where London administered a major portion through Calcutta, the Madras and Bombay presidencies, and almost five hundred rulers as successor to the Mughals whose hold on the north of the subcontinent had evaporated as the British moved west from Bengal and added to the disintegrative momentum.[119] Still, a colonial regime it was: by 1900 the Indian Civil Service comprised about a thousand administrators, of which about forty were Indian, no surprise since the entrance exams were given in Britain. Of the related administrative corps, about half of the approximately ten thousand were Indian or Anglo-Indian, but in the lower-paying ranks. The local courts and counsels were opening to Indians—although the British resisted trial under Indian judges.[120] Sovereignty, foreign policy, command of the army, and the monetary system remained in British hands. Europeans confronted the Indians, the Chinese whom they controlled, and the Southeast Asians with both contempt for their subordination and fascination with their culture and artifacts. Europeans tended to divide between those who believed the natives were children and potentially rebels, and those who for humanitarian, religious, cultural, or other reasons respected their civilization. This led to clashes among policy makers and administrators. The tough-minded who counseled sternness (often the military but not always) had contempt for the naive liberal native sympathizers who would undermine colonial rule by "the series of ineffectual compromises . . . the lamentable vacillations in facing open sedition or veiled rebellion."[121]

Africa was a study literally in black and white, although even there colonial rulers drew distinctions and lines, just as the technocrats of immigration did in America. The British encountered noble warriors (Masai), tall and attractive, versus bulkier West Africans; likewise they separated martial races in the Punjab (Sikhs) from the darker-skinned Tamils; the Belgians ascribed differences to the Hutu and Tutsi, which would lead to catastrophe many decades after their colonial rule collapsed in Rwanda. To be sure, what was taking place in the colonies

In charge of empire: George Nathaniel, Lord Curzon, in his regalia as viceroy of India (1898–1905). Curzon was a staunch defender of the British presence in India, with all its ceremonial grandeur, and was convinced that Britain and Russia were destined for a contest of empires—"the great game"—in Persia and Central Asia. His aristocratic demeanor probably precluded a later nod as Conservative prime minister, but he served as foreign secretary from 1919 to 1924. (Library of Congress)

ran in parallel with the reinforcement of racism in the colonizing societies, as Jim Crow legislation was imposed in the United States from the 1890s on, as old-stock Americans reacted to the new Japanese and Chinese labor and even to the Eastern European (Catholic and Jewish) migrants. For many in Europe the emerging proletariat represented the same dark threat as did natives: after the Paris Commune of 1870, the mass execution of the Communards was followed by the exile of many to New Caledonia, where another dangerous class existed.[122]

The colonies devalued life on the basis of race, but the racial separation was an aspect of the general classificatory mania and search for new hierarchies to replace old that characterized the late nineteenth century. So the modern state developed out of that dialectical thrust—inevitable democratization and wider communication, but reconfigured pyramids of status and authority. The brilliant Polish writer of the late twentieth century, Stanisław Lem (d. 2006) has a delicious short story about a German SS officer who after the collapse of the Third Reich seeks refuge in a remote corner of Argentina, where he organizes a miniature state among his fellow fugitives. But entranced with absolute authority, he disdains reproducing the National Socialist regime as too vulgar and populist and aspires to recreate the court of Louis XVI, insisting that his fellow mass murderers all pretend to speak French and conduct elaborate court rituals in a desolate geographic milieu that mocks the effort and finally leads to the downfall of the experiment.[123] It is doubtful that Lem was thinking of the colonial state when he wrote his fantasy, but it captures something about many of the states throughout the world in the late nineteenth and early twentieth centuries. They were theaters of ceremony—Edward VII's coronation as emperor in Delhi in 1903 claimed about 0.5 percent of the public revenue (imagine a $20 billion inauguration ceremony in today's Washington), and other grandiose state visits followed.[124] Lem's parody fails us, though, in that his obsessed leaders establish no relationship with the indigenous elite; they are self-absorbed, whereas the key to colonial rule was the selection of native chiefs or sheiks in a process of "indirect rule," most famously outlined by the British proconsul in Nigeria, Frederick Lugard, and France's Marshal Hubert Lyautey.[125]

And although not founded by mass murderers, the conditions under which colonies were established could encourage mass murder, as some advocates accepted without qualms. "Again, another conclusion from our proposition in reference to the mission of the Teutonic nations," wrote a contemporary legal theorist,

> must be that they are called to carry the political civilization of the modern world into those parts of the world inhabited by unpolitical and barbaric races, *i.e.* they must have a colonial policy . . . the larger part of the surface of the globe is inhabited by populations which have not succeeded in establishing civilized states, which have in fact no capacity to accomplish such a work, and which must, therefore, remain in a state of barbarism or semibarbarism, unless the political nations undertake the work of state organization for them. . . . There is no human right to the status of barbarism. . . . The civilized state may righteously go still further than the exercise of force in imposing organization. If the barbaric populations resist the same, *à la outrance,* the civilized state may clear the territory of their presence and make it the abode of civilized man. . . . It violates thereby no rights of these populations which are not petty and trifling in comparison with its transcendent right and duty to establish political and legal order elsewhere.

The self-described Teuton who buried this license for genocide in his major treatise on the state was in fact no German, but the leading Columbia University professor of constitutional law.[126]

The German general Lothar von Trotha put down the Herero uprising in German Southwest Africa by driving the insurgents and their families into the desert, where it was obvious they must perish. The Americans who took over the Philippines pursued the insurrectionary forces of General Aguinaldo with a war against the population. The Italians ferociously suppressed the Libyan tribes whose territory they took from the distant Turks in 1911; General Reginald Dyer famously emptied his machine guns against assembled Indians in Amritsar in 1919; the British made air attacks on Bedouin tribesmen a successful tactic of border control in their new possessions in the Middle East in the early 1920s, while the French bombarded Damascus a few years later; the Italians used poison gas against the Ethiopians whose land Mussolini coveted; and in 1945, as the war was ending in Europe, French troops killed perhaps 6,000 Algerians in wanton reprisals, perhaps many more, in inland Sétif after Muslim protests turned violent and took 100 European lives. But the casualties were far away; the

Resistance to empire: Hendrik Witbooi, ca. 1900. Witbooi, a well-educated and effective guerrilla leader, was born and educated in the northern Cape Colony in 1830 to a family of Nama tribal leaders. Migrating north to southwest Africa, he concluded a peace with the traditionally rival Herero to oppose the ambitious German colonial effort. From the 1890s until his death in combat in 1905, he led the combined Nama-Herero revolt, which was finally crushed by the genocidal tactics of the hard-line German commander. (Getty Images)

peoples were dark and fanatic; each incident was an unfortunate exception in a narrative of progress; dominion could not be dismantled—even the tenderhearted agreed—without a catastrophe for civilization.

For many of the administrators and settlers, the natives were children; they had to be taught lessons. Baron Ferdinand von Richthofen, rector of the University of Berlin and China explorer (although his initial encounters with Chinese may have come during his years in California), referred to the relationship between a master and his dog; the colonial administrator must punish all challenges to authority immediately.[127] British General Barrow, who headed the British expedition to suppress residual Boxer presence, explained his decision to blow up the white porcelain pagoda of the Beijing Bada temple complex: if Christians did not destroy the landmark, the Chinese would consider their gods more powerful. As German general Alfred von Waldersee noted, retributive beheadings of Qing officials (not Boxers themselves) by enlisted Chinese executioners were an exercise in "moral influence of far-reaching importance."[128] It is customary to balance these episodes against the hospitals or railroads and occasional schools that the European attempted. The colonial state could become a developmental state if it made sense to its masters. The Japanese built a vigorous, though often brutal, colonial empire from 1895 to 1945, and in Manchuria in particular nurtured economic and industrial development, whether coal mines or soy farming.[129] Still there was something essential to the enterprise in the relationship of arbitrary and, if need be, unfettered power far from the daily supervision of the state at home. Distancing was crucial to the exercise of power and to its ultimate legitimation, resting as it did on the racial or ethnic distance that separated the colonizer and the colonized, and making the colonial state a potential zone of day-to-day violence. Joseph Conrad has left us one essential allegory: *Heart of Darkness*—once again the fusion of violence, empire, and coming of age. Almost sixty years later the Nigerian writer Chinua Achebe left another tale, *Things Fall Apart,* from the viewpoint of the disoriented subject. Not all these stories were allegories in which violence had to follow from absolute power. E. M Forster's *Passage to India* is fraught instead with the inability to achieve personal friendship across the divide of the colonizer and the colonized; and there are many other stories of prejudice and encounter where the two sides wish for the unmediated relationship of equals but cannot achieve it given the insuperable differences of authority.

It would be tempting to conclude that the colonial state was the arena in which all the prerogatives of power earlier inherent in Western statehood could be exercised once they were no longer permissible at home—that is, that it allowed all the surviving impulses of domination to find an outlet at a time when they had to yield to democratic forms and public opinion within the colonizing state. The colonial state permitted the ceremonial staging of sovereignty and unchallenged rule. It allowed the articulation of fantasies of racial differentiation that Europeans sometimes felt with respect to their own urban masses or even peasants, and that many Americans felt toward their former black slaves and new contracted labor. In an era when the concept of equal citizenship was inscribed as the norm for the Western state or those regimes that aspired to be modern, the colonial state represented the exceptionalism permitted for global governance. It established enclaves of untrammeled power but it also allowed men of science and sensibility to see the commonalities of culture that they attempted to convey at home by studies in anthropology. This is all true, although it necessarily simplifies the myriad encounters of colonial farmers, businessmen, and soldiers with the people they were assigned to rule. In fact, the colonial state—insofar as we can speak usefully about this generalization—was an immensely complex and contradiction-ridden enterprise. Wherever whites confronted the "other," they confronted "themselves." The "other" became the fashionable historically discursive term during the 1960s, but the colonial subject was never simply just the other. And the colonial state was both different from the state at home but still a domain where its possibilities for sovereignty, authority, legislation, and violence might be tested. Ultimately what happened in the colonies in the way of violence and domination and exploitation did not just stay in the colonies. And it would never have happened in the colonies had it not been dreamed of at home.

4. States of Exception

"SOVEREIGN is he who decides on the state of exception." Forget the nice descriptions of the legal order, so German political theorist Carl Schmitt was arguing in 1921: sovereignty belonged to whoever had the authority to set aside the law.[130] Schmitt, however, did not mean just de facto power: sovereignty was a metalegal status that evaded the constraints of the constitution. Schmitt, who would live almost a century, into the 1980s, was never free of a desire to transgress bourgeois norms; and he aspired to be the poster boy for counterrevolutionary legal and political theory in the decade after World War I and then the court theorist for the Nazis. His formula became all too relevant for so many states in the twentieth century, as they coped with civil strife, revolution, depression, and war. The state of exception or emergency arose when the legal or even constitutional order, with all its protections for citizens' rights, could not provide for confronting a threat to the nation and had to be suspended. It was the moment when the ruler had to act according to what since Machiavelli was called *raison d'état* or just the moment that President George W. Bush appealed to when he called himself, doubtless without benefit of reading Schmitt, "the decider."[131]

Twentieth-century history was marked by states of exception; and the states created in those states of exception could prove exceptional in their claims and their brutality. For Schmitt, however, they were not exceptional as such, for ultimately every state had to be exceptional and politics always took place in the interstices where law failed to reach—in a democracy above all. For democracy—as he would emphasize in his writings that we return to below—was not about human rights, not about resolving policy alternatives through discussion (which liberalism celebrated), but about a people defining and protecting its identity, about who constituted "us" and who "them." In that sense Schmitt's heirs are still around, shorn usually of totalitarian temptations but tending to see public life as constituted by irreducible ethnic antagonisms usually in the form of immigration from Asia, Africa, and (in the US case) Latin America. Between the world wars they talked about the bourgeoisie and the proletariat, kulaks and collectives, Jews and Germans. And of course, they didn't just talk. Threatened, as they saw it, by fundamental internal adversaries, they moved to eliminate them.

Schmitt's formula alerts us that the twentieth-century state (and many specific states in particular) might follow two agendas, conceptually separate but often entangled, one that might be labeled "soft," the other "hard." The soft agenda involved expanding the policies associated with Foucault's idea of governmentality and the modernization of society. Expansion of activity along these lines would lead to the contemporary welfare state as gradually elaborated from the occupational safety legislation, pension provisions, and early social insurance begun in Europe during the nineteenth century and significantly enlarged during the post–World War II era. In this role states acted to shape society as they provided for education, investment in infrastructure, and regulation of the economy. As they competed internationally during the Cold War, states also took on commitments to modernization and development. Soft agendas did not renounce large social goals, and critics from Friedrich Hayek to James Scott have argued that the soft agenda could be as quietly coercive as the more brutal hard agenda. Still, facing a tax for future pension payments or being subject to compulsory trade-union dues hardly seems comparable to interrogation by the Gestapo. The "hard" agenda was precisely the one that invoked "exception" and emergency—political activity as a response to war, revolution, and unrest. States were not at leisure to just pursue the development of their societies: issues of sovereignty, identity, and violence intruded into history with renewed urgency once again as preeminent concerns in the first half of the twentieth century. They had been such in the seventeenth century, but had been gradually displaced by the Enlightenment's focus on civil society. As Schmitt realized, Hobbes was back.

Even for nations normally liberal at home, the hard agenda, the regime of "exception," intruded in two key sets of activities. One, as we have seen, was colonial administration; the other was the state at war. Colonial administrators and their restive subjects understood that sovereignty was or must become the underlying stake in the imperial world—sovereignty over acquired subjects, sovereignty vis-à-vis potential rival colonizers. Maintaining sovereignty, however, involved what French colonial advocates termed "valorization" of their "possessions," that is, modernizing and developing their economic potential whether in terms of commodities or manpower. But so too, colonial intellectuals and civil servants believed that modernization, pursuing wealth and power, was a prerequisite for standing up to the European powers. In the Pacific region, Japan's experience taught important lessons for both sides: The Meiji reformers had consciously and successfully chosen modernization to resist possible quasi colonization. But they were reconstructing nationhood precisely in an era when most successful statesmen believed that civilizations were divided into the vigorous and the feeble. They entered a world of states "red in tooth and claw," and believed their own teeth and claws needed to be as sharp as any other, and thus went on within the same generation to quickly create their own Asian empire. After Japan's victory over China in 1895, which the European powers moved to limit and then exploit for their own aims, the subsequent rivalry with Russia for preeminence in Korea led to the Russo-Japanese War of 1904–1905 and the first major modern military setback dealt to a European empire by an Asian power. Japan destroyed the Russian fleet, but the ground war bogged down in the sieges around Port Arthur and Dalian (Dairen), finally to be mediated by President Theodore Roosevelt in remote Portsmouth, New Hampshire. Japan won Russia's rights over Manchurian ports and Sakhalin and other islands, and enough of a free hand to be able to annex Korea in 1910. Tokyo's new empire rested on both the harsh exercise of power and an agenda for development of Manchurian and to a lesser extent Taiwanese and Korean resources. Chinese reformers and revolutionaries seeking asylum in Tokyo were to learn a lot from Japan in the decade after their defeat at its hands. Given the vortex of imperial conflict that opened up where Korean and Manchu weakness sucked in Russia, Japan, and indirectly the Western powers, there is a case to be made for dating twentieth-century international history from the conflict of 1895.[132]

Consider the impact of the wars (including the Cold War) that would stretch through most of the twentieth century more generally. The fiscal exigencies of war in the seventeenth and eighteenth centuries had helped create Leviathan 1.0: that is, the dynastic territorial state, insistent on sovereignty, determined if possible to override local privileges, intent on developing its economic resources and infrastructure. The wars of the mid-nineteenth century, we have seen, were instrumental for the territorial and governmental consolidation of Leviathan 2.0.

So too the great wars of the twentieth century played a fundamental role. Even as they originated in large measure from the expansionist role that the reinvented nineteenth-century nation-state found so compelling, so the world wars further impelled these states to mobilize their economies and societies to unprecedented degrees. War justified the accretion of power at home, and it beckoned the more ruthless leaders of the new century as a paradigm for seizing and exercising it. Readers of this book will have spent their lives in states whose claims on individual lives and ambitions to regulate their welfare, often their abodes, and sometimes even their demographic continuity and permissible utterances, were fundamentally enhanced by the world wars and Cold War struggles.

The experience of the two world wars in fact conflated the agendas of development and sovereignty. The states engaged in those long conflicts had to mobilize mass armies, coordinate their industries, their transports, and their medical and social services, and negotiate with their labor organizations to an unprecedented degree. Market mechanisms to allocate scarce manpower or raw materials had chaotic and inflationary results and were largely set aside for allocation by committees of the sectors involved. New ministries of munitions compelled industrialists who had resisted unions to accept trilateral bargaining among state bureaucrats and sometimes generals, unions, and employer confederations. Women emerged into the sphere of nondomestic work to an unprecedented degree. The warfare state became a proto-welfare state, but equipped with degrees of compulsion that were truly exceptional. The British Defense of the Realm Act (DORA) passed in August 1914 essentially turned over to the government the power to do what it thought necessary to prosecute the war. Powerful unspoken expectations of decent and liberal behavior persisted in Britain, and it was taken for granted that such a delegation of authority would not be used to prosecute political speech unless it challenged the war effort. The need to administer pensions and medical benefits prolonged the expansion of many of these services into the postwar eras. Although the interference with price and market mechanisms was generally rolled back after World War I, the Great Depression and the Second World War made some of the innovations into permanent features. If power in every state was defined by what happened during the exception, states of exception were no longer so exceptional.[133]

The rise of the warfare state: Canadian women workers operating machine tools in a munitions factory, September 1916. Canada and the Dominions entered the war alongside "the mother country" in 1914, and as in other belligerent nations where men were called to combat service, women took up traditionally male occupations. (Getty Images)

Finally the two agendas manifested themselves in the extraordinary role that military rule continued to play throughout the world, certainly until the 1980s. Outside the colonial world, the governing institution that had seemed conspicuously to triumph in the course of the nineteenth century—arriving finally in Japan in 1890, in Russia in 1905, in China in 1910—was the legislative assembly or parliament. But parliaments, as conservative critics such as Schmitt or earlier Gaetano Mosca pointed out, found it hard to act decisively in their role as assemblies, and, for what decisions they could reach, relied either on a committee system or on the party leaders who organized their majorities. As of 1900, competing parties were still more clublike than cohesive, although first in the United States and then Britain, where electoral campaigns focused periodically on choosing the chief executive as well as parliamentary delegates, the parties became permanent regime fixtures with professional staffs and affiliated newspapers. But where these procedures were weak or very recent, or even nonexistent, twentieth-century development brought instead the paramount role of the single encompassing party or rule by the military.

Military rule and single-party dictatorship seemed to confirm Carl Schmitt's tough lesson that real authority emerges only outside the constitution. The sovereign was the army or the authoritarian party. Or was this true only in the short run? Military rule could guarantee neither national unity nor, certainly, internal pacification. In those large countries in which weak national regimes were breaking down under the pressure of imperialist encroachment or economic stagnation, territorial fragmentation or warlordism was a recurrent danger. Even when a unified military controlled the whole national territory, it found prolonged rule by bayonet frustrating. Increasingly it had to meet the needs of civil society—the realm of rivalries between capital and labor, free-trade and protectionist sectors, the restless voices of religious organizations, the media, and culture—and thus to enter the world of policy debate and pluralism. Some military rulers sought to do so by continued force, others by sponsoring authoritarian national parties. Decades later the generals and the dictators would find they were incompetent to deal with complex societies. They would not really know how to manage religious yearnings, consumer aspirations, and the technology of the computer age. They offered authoritarian solutions that were hard to prolong when the era of iron and steel was augmented by silicon and software. But their dismantling is the story of our own age, not the segment of time considered here.

Crises of Representation

Only in the sheltered bourgeois enclaves of Vienna or Paris or the discreet banks and clubs of London did it take the First World War to shatter the *douceur de vie* of the nineteenth century. From the mid-1890s on, the world of states—already reorganized in the second third of the nineteenth century, then freighted with ambitious agendas of development at home and expansion abroad—entered stormy waters and generated new, eventually terrifying experiments. Episodes of upheaval came thick and fast. Review some of them as they would have made the gray columns of the metropolitan newspapers: famine in India and a revival of

A synthesis of culture, wealth, and power: The inauguration of the Paris Opera season at the Palais Garnier, ca. 1890–1900. The sumptuous Paris Opera House, designed by Charles Garnier and constructed in the 1860s in the opulent Beaux-Arts style of the Second Empire, served, like its counterparts elsewhere, as a public showplace for the wealthy bourgeoisie, who came to play a major political role in the late nineteenth century throughout Europe and the Americas. (Library of Congress)

anti-British violence from the late 1880s; global depression in 1893 and a mobilization of protest movements in Italy and the United States and major strikes throughout Europe. Cascading wars again—between China and Japan in 1895, between Greece and Turkey in 1896–1897, between the United States and Spain in 1898, between Britain and the Boers in 1900–1902, between Russia and Japan in 1904–1905, between Italy and the Ottomans in 1911, between the Balkan states and the Ottomans in 1912, and then among the Balkans in 1913—wars that brought the growing tendency to massacre civilians: Armenians in the Ottoman Empire in 1897, Africans in the German colonies in 1905, Bosnians and Albanians in the Balkans in 1911–1912. Although the wars themselves still took place "far away" from Western Europe and North America, the powers at the center extended their network of fateful alliances or commitments: between French and Russians after 1894, British and Japanese in 1902, British and French in 1904, British and Russians in 1907.

Starting with the Russo-Japanese confrontation, Niall Ferguson has chronicled what he aptly calls the twentieth century's "war of the world," which he finds fundamentally a product of racial or ethnic conflict.[134] Certainly distinctions of race were held to justify imperialism and, often, license atrocities. But war did not always arise from these distinctions, and certainly not the most destructive wars between the European powers. Crucial, I believe, were the political deficiencies of empire and the continuing sense of vulnerability they inculcated among those who championed them most ardently. Conflicts arose from imperial elites on the defensive (Ottoman, Habsburg, Chinese, and British) and those more assertive (Japanese and German). Empires were praised as bringing peace within their far-flung frontiers and remote territories. But although they might defer internal violence and even war with each other, they could never do so indefinitely. The bills came due after 1900.

As in all revolutionary eras, legitimacy was at stake, and actually was wearing thin in many places by the 1890s. Legitimacy implies that authority does not rely on power alone; it rests on a moral basis that commands respect and obedience without continued coercion. By the end of the nineteenth century, legitimate states had to be representative to some degree; they had to act on behalf of the expressed or imputed interests of what the Victorians termed "public opinion." In the United States and Western Europe that had long meant deferring to a parliament and respecting individual rights. In the American democracy, President Lincoln put the idea most expansively: "government of the people, by the people, and for the people." By the turn of the twentieth century, representing "society" as a complex aggregation of identities and interests became the basis for legitimacy. But it was becoming harder and harder for states to represent the often conflicting interests within society.

This was true not only for autocratic states, but for countries that prided themselves on their civilized attainments, including the role played by an enlightened public opinion. The campaigns for enlarged suffrage were the most visible effort to encompass an enlarged sense of society. The European states managed slowly to concede broader manhood suffrage in the later nineteenth and earlier twentieth centuries. Sometimes conservative parties wagered that by enfranchising the broader middle class they might strengthen their domestic position (as did the British Tories in 1867); sometimes conservatives and reformers both calculated that reform would stabilize the society as a whole and their respective positions (as in Italy in 1912). Sometimes bureaucratic rulers calculated they could use broader suffrage to limit the influence of powerful elites, as when the Habsburg ministers pressed a major general suffrage on the two halves of Austria-Hungary. Sometimes political leaders conceded to massive demonstrations, as in Belgium in 1913. Often, though, there was resistance. Prussian conservatives and the monarch resisted demands to transform the franchise in the Prussian legislature from one skewed toward the wealthy to a more general one-man, one-vote system until they felt the need to enhance working-class support during the latter phases of the First World War. In Russia a mass suffrage conceded during the year of revolution in 1905 was progressively clawed back until the fall of the monarchy in 1917. And both Left and Right might resist the claims of new groups (as with women's suffrage or African-American suffrage in the US South). Suffrage alone, moreover, did not determine the strength or absence of democratic institutions and culture. Different parliaments had different degrees of power vis-à-vis their heads of state or military and bureaucracy. National political institutions could be located along axes that ran from democratic participation (as in Third Republic France) through various admixtures of elite influence reserved for ancient families and bureaucrats, ranging from the more liberal to the less, such as Britain and Germany or Japan. (Local and regional authority might be ranged along a similar continuum, but might also fall at a different point.)

However, a single aggregate scale for ranking democracy (such as Freedom House tries to calculate for today's governments) would have made little sense. Some states remained what might be labeled *constitutionally segmented,* no matter what their written charters provided for. They were effectively divided into one sector of the adult population that was admitted to political participation and one or more that remained excluded. With respect to gender most polities were segmented until later in the twentieth century, but even disregarding the disadvantaging of women, other politics were segmented by regional "backwardness" and ethnic or racial exclusion. The Italian state was governed by a liberal parliamentary class that indulged in electoral competition north of Rome but depended on patronage, clientelism, and landowners' strength in the south as a sort of ballast to limit the destabilizing impact of these rivalries in the north. American politics remained segmented by race. The US Republican Party ended its brief effort to enforce ex-slaves' newly enacted political rights by the late 1870s as part of a deal to keep control of the presidency. The dualist electoral settlement that allowed manhood suffrage in the North even for recent immigrants while enforcing racial exclusion from the vote in the South permitted the country to achieve sectional "reconciliation" at the cost of acquiescing in Jim Crow segregationist legislation and local repression by unofficial lynch law. In the atmosphere that prevailed, white Americans in the North as well as the South wearily accepted the view that African-Americans were not yet "ready" for equal citizenship—it was the equivalent of European colonial attitudes toward their Asian and African subjects, and in effect the pool of black labor provided the human resources of a nonterritorial colony. The reunited United States also enjoyed the great geographical resource of western lands as a stabilizing outlet for national energy. Then, too, the massive influx of European migrants tended to focus their efforts at ethnic representation though state and city political machines rather than insist on prominence at the national level. Neither did they pose "radical" demands: northern or Eastern European workers recreated the emerging social democratic parties of Europe in a few locations, but largely streamed into the US alternatives already available, whether the Democratic Party organizations in northern cities, or the more radical Populist currents in the

West. Even so, middle-class urban reformers, largely of northern European ethnic stock, sought to stabilize their hold in cities by taking governance out of the hand of electoral machines and turning them over to professional urban managers. The settlement underlying US politics in the late nineteenth century consisted of a balance whereby the Republican Party usually captured a weak national government that sustained a protectionist tariff while allowing the Democratic Party to exploit the politics of the industrial cities and the reservoir of Southern white voters. Farmers in the South and West challenged the compromise in the 1890s but failed to dislodge it.

Racial segmentation also prevailed in the new Union of South Africa, where the whites who ruled constituted only a minority of the population. In effect the South African War (Boer War), which pitted the ambitious forces of white South African mining interests, backed by more than a hundred thousand British troops (and a strategy of forced removals and confinement of the Afrikaans-speaking rural families), against the agrarian Boer Republics, ended with an implicit compromise worked out between 1902 and 1910. The Afrikaans-speaking republics were forced to accept inclusion in a British Union of South Africa and an active policy of British administrative penetration under Alfred Milner. However, the British left the Boer republics a great deal of home rule and made no effort to challenge the segregationist political and social system they had constructed. In the Cape Colony, the white population of under a quarter of the whole constituted 85 percent of the electorate; in Natal, where the whites constituted 8 percent of a once Zulu-dominated region, they would make up 99 percent of the electorate. A mistaken belief that the Boers believed in a rugged democracy as well as the importance of South Africa for the British war effort against German colonial armies after 1914 (and the personal role that Boer leader Jan Smuts achieved) made it hard for London to contest the South Africans' racial state, especially because so many English shared the underlying premises of African racial inferiority.[135]

Segmented regimes formed one type of implicit constitution. Other implicit constitutional settlements opened up states to extensive foreign influence—military, economic, or pedagogic and cultural. The term *semicolonialism* has been used to describe the reserve power that European powers possessed in China, but authority could be less formally enshrined.[136] In Latin America's large republics, the ritualized party competition among elites separated those oriented toward commercial and financial ties with foreign lenders, notably Great Britain, from those claiming the traditionalist power of military, church, and landed property. Expansion of export commodities—coffee in Brazil, beef and wheat in Argentina, minerals from the Andes—strengthened the liberals and allowed a relatively cozy sharing of power and influence after civil war and violence. Brazil's new republic (and with it the compensated ending of slavery by 1889) benefited from the coffee boom and agreement on a highly decentralized federal system. Only in the interwar period, as the prices of commodities fell and new political leaders sought to broaden the political base to include manual workers or indigenous peoples, did these equilibria irrevocably break down and populist strongmen, often drawn from the military, emerge.

Once white male suffrage became generalized, regulation of the economy became more urgent. Trade unions and working-class associations had faced political restrictions in the 1870s and 1880s on the European continent, the United States, and Mexico. The First International Workingman's Association had disintegrated after the Paris Commune; Bismarck had outlawed the German Social Democratic Party in 1878; the US Knights of Labor disintegrated after the Haymarket bombing and trial in 1886; striking workers had to face soldiers and judges in many countries. But a Second International emerged in 1889; the SPD was relegalized in 1890, and the organizing of workers increased in scope and intensity. Strike activity increased in all the industrializing countries, and after 1905 the strikes were often for greater political influence, and not merely higher wages. Russia's 1905 revolution helped to galvanize activism in Germany and France. Some of the labor movements' spokesmen envisaged that workplace organizations could displace elected legislatures and even socialist parties to become the basis for a new democratic politics. At the time of the 1905 revolution, Bolshevik leaders would describe workers "councils" (or *soviets* in Russian) as the avant-garde of a proletarian order. Such anarcho-syndicalism seemed even to infect British trade unions, formerly the most oriented on narrower demands for safety legislation or wage increases. Visions of a social war exhilarated some on the left—see Jack London's lurid description of the battle for Chicago in *The Iron Heel* (1908). Conversely, the prospect obviously frightened conservatives, many of whom expected a bloody upheaval akin to their folk memories of the

Paris siege and Commune. But even more ominously the coming Armageddon gave some writers a jolt of adrenalin, as they believed it would reinvigorate a tired and decadent social order. Georges Sorel, the engineer in Paris, and Vilfredo Pareto, the Italian economist teaching in Lausanne (as well as the young Italian student Benito Mussolini, who audited some of his lecturers), anticipated the coming clashes with gusto, just as the contemporary artistic movement of Italian Futurists looked forward to a cleansing hygienic war. Privileged French university students allegedly believed that a new war would be preferable to "perpetual waiting." Liberalism was hostage to ennui as well as social cleavages.[137]

Even harder to reconcile than proletarian class demands or the literati's impatience with political compromise were the demands for national representation within multiethnic units. The Irish, who in the early nineteenth century had been given seats in the British parliament at a time when only Protestants (largely landowners) might serve, wanted "home rule" or national autonomy with an Irish parliament, but Protestant loyalists resisted and compelled the Conservative Party and the British parliament to delay. Both sides were on the verge of resorting to armed force by the early twentieth century. Although a third home-rule bill was finally passed on the eve of World War I, it was shelved until the issue of the Protestant counties (Ulster) might be resolved. This did not happen until a period of Irish national insurgency and police suppression (the Black and Tan war) followed in the early 1920s and a segment of the nationalist Sinn Fein rebels were willing to settle for an "Irish Free State" without the northern counties comprising Ulster. Austria-Hungary and the Ottomans faced far wider ethnic rebellions than did the British. National groups progressively hived off the Ottomans in the early nineteenth century (Greece, Serbia, Romania), then the 1870s (Bulgaria), or were taken over by other imperial contenders, as in North Africa. As for the world's largest colony, British India remained under sufficient control to tamp down calls for greater national representation. India, of course, was ruled as an empire, by a government sent from London. It had no mass white population, but the legacy of multiple pre-British state structures and the failure in 1857 of rebellion (which was never fully articulated as a national upheaval) kept the national challenge relatively weak until after the world war. The Indian National Congress was a group that had a long-term vision but practiced short-term accommodation and gradualist inclusion in local organs, especially the judicial system. It was an irony of the British Empire that the coronation of a new monarch could be celebrated with the greatest pomp in New Delhi in 1910, even as Irish factions were moving toward violence almost next door to London.

Representation, furthermore, was a complex activity in its own right, no matter how much of a society it encompassed. The spatial metaphor that envisaged a state above trying to react to society below was misleadingly simple. Political demands did not simply flow "upward" from society to the state. Ambitious reformers pondered how states that had themselves been transformed in the nineteenth century should transform society in turn—that is, regulate it, develop it, improve and remake it. The states that emerged in the nineteenth century had a special relationship with technological modernity; they needed breech-loading and rapid-firing guns, heavier cannon; they needed velocity, railroads, and rapid communication, the telegraph, the undersea cable, eventually the radio. Beyond their requirements for material infrastructure, states had to educate citizens and to improve their health and vigor, even perhaps through the new concept of "eugenics," or restricted breeding.

Thus the late nineteenth-century state was not, could not be, an institution built for static equilibrium. It had to ensure the development of its civilian economy, not just its military. In Britain and later in the United States, governments might rely more on the inherent vigor of civil society than direction by the state. Americans viewed their economic enterprises and their multiple associations as both the beneficiaries and the sources of modernization. The protective tariff and the distribution of national lands to railroads and homesteaders (who would be clients of the railroads) meant significant state promotion of economic development. Canada was not so different in this respect. The French and later the German, Japanese, and Russian states felt they had to intervene to a greater degree, but began at different moments, the French before their great revolution, the Germans and Japanese during the mid-nineteenth century, the Russians at the end—more rapidly and impressively than other states. Russia, still an autocracy until 1905, and guided by Sergei Witte from 1893, embarked on the trans-Siberian railroad, a program whose costs aroused aristocratic opposition and the impatience of the faction anxious to keep Korea out of Japanese influence. The monarch yielded to the pressure and eased Witte into a more ceremonial role, only to recall him in 1905 to cope with the aftermath of the war with Japan and the revolutionary agitation that had followed his removal. Failure to modernize could cost territory and erode sovereignty, even if outright colonization was avoided, as was vividly demonstrated in the case of China, which had to grant extraterritorial enclaves where the Western powers retained local legal rights, and the Ottoman Empire, which was compelled to cede "capitularies," or legal immunities, to foreigners.

Modernization, however, provoked resistance from traditionalists at home and sometimes preemptive intervention from the Western powers. When Chinese administrators began an effort to reform within the permitted parameters of Confucian values in the 1860s after a second war, now with France as well as Britain, they faced disabling court intrigues, as did the "hundred-day" reform interlude of 1898, stymied by the empress dowager, and the attempts to institute local, then national, elections after 1905. Japanese reformers fared better. Alerted by the concessions and territory extracted by Britain from the Chinese in 1842 and warned by their own experience of having to open five "treaty ports" to the Americans in 1858, reform-oriented samurai began a nationalist mobilization against the perceived weakness of the Tokugawa shogunate. Conservatives were less successful in blocking reforms in Japan than in China. The court was not in the same position to play personal politics; rather, the emperor stood to gain in influence from reform. In Japan, moreover, the central state did not penetrate the autonomous domains *(han)* of the reform-minded *daimyō* and their samurai officials, who could in effect run laboratories of rationalization. No state examination system elevated Confucian and Neo-Confucian hierarchical concepts into a portal for public service; the Japanese military traditions were conservative but allowed for emulation of modern science and technology.

Other authoritarian rulers could also save their countries from being carved up or absorbed if they were skillful and willing to modernize institutions and infrastructure. Chulalongkorn of Thailand (ruling as King Rama V, 1868–1910, almost the same span as the Meiji emperor) managed to play off the British in Burma against the more threatening French in Indochina, formed a functionally organized cabinet, reformed the military, fiscal system, and national education system, and extended rail and telegraph lines throughout the kingdom. Emperor Menelik II of Ethiopia (1889–1909/1913) ruled a poorer

Modernization for national survival: King Chulalongkorn of Thailand posing with the crown prince and presumably some of his seventy-seven children, ca. 1900. A contemporary of the reforming Meiji emperor in Japan, Chulalongkorn abolished slavery, modernized the Thai government, military, and judicial and educational systems, and preserved the country's independence vis-à-vis the British in Burma to the west and the French in Indochina to the east. (© Hulton-Deutsch Collection / Corbis)

domain, but inflicted stunning defeats on Italian forces and established a ministerial system.[138]

Global Revolution

Norman Angell had the courage to suggest in his 1910 study of international capitalism, *The Great Illusion,* that what historians today call the first globalization—the dense and rapidly thickening web of economic and financial ties among nations in the early twentieth century—should preclude major war. He overestimated the strength of interests and underestimated the force of alliances. Globalization did not compel peace.

Without needing to predict the future in 1916, Vladimir Lenin could write that the first globalization (which he interpreted as imperialism) had had to bring about a great war. We can't say he was wrong—but we can't confirm that he was right either.

The proposition that can be defended is that globalization helped produce revolution as regimes collapsed across Mexico, Eurasia, and China. This meant that revolution came not to the industrial societies of Western Europe and North America (except when military defeat discredited their rulers) but to the large, vulnerable states that were attracting the attention of imperialist rivals and the capital they brought with them. Skip over the machinations of American sugar interests in the Caribbean and Hawai'i and even the Cuban uprising against Spanish rule in Cuba at the outset of the period in the 1890s. But pay attention to the Boxer uprising in China in 1900 and the collapse of Manchu rule in 1911, to Russia's months of tumult during 1905 and then the regime changes of 1917, to Iran's constitutional revolution of 1906–1909, the Young Turks' uprising in 1908 and the fragmentation of the Ottoman state a decade later; and then to the layered rebellions in Mexico, unfolding over a decade from 1910 to 1920.

Widely separated geographically, these revolutions had each its own sources and history, but they also were products directly or indirectly of encroaching strategic rivalries and foreign investors seeking profits from local resources or investments and favorably supervised by their regimes at home. With some exception made for imperial Russia, the regimes under attack seemed to have become subservient to foreign power and foreign capital. To be sure, the foreigners' economic activity (and accompanying schools and churches, engineering and financial expertise) brought significant economic growth. Rail lines expanded by multiples; oil wells came into production, new banks channeled capital into a flurry of overseas companies; investors in London, Paris, Berlin, Vienna, and New York created local wealth even as they siphoned off significant shares for their bondholders. Socially, they nurtured in the process both a class of enriched local mediators, and countervailing forces of intellectuals, journalists, religious leaders, and military officers, who beheld a sellout of authentic national or imperial traditions. Thus, radical ferment grew apace, sometimes organized in clandestine societies, sometimes in barracks and clubs, among circles of intellectuals and newspaper editors, and professional military officers and cadets.

These developments produced the inconsistencies of early twentieth-century revolution: Resentments and frustration were intensely nationalist because they reacted to the progress of global and international capital. Revolutionaries called for modernization along Western lines but often drew on the primitive strength of religious traditionalism. Uprisings originated less among deprived workers and peasants than among nativist elites outraged by military defeat and by authorities who seemed complicit in national dependency and even humiliation.[139] But the elites that were prompted to organize and assert new programs—in Mexico by disputed elections, in the Ottoman Empire by the growth of Balkan nationalisms, in China by Qing humiliations—ended up triggering massive upheavals and civil strife. Nationalist in aspiration, they produced ten to twenty years of regional armies and territorial fragmentation. At the end of the eighteenth century, revolutions had begun as contests inside particular states, which then triggered international intervention from larger powers. Those conflicts had been articulated in the emerging language of rights and entitlements bequeathed to Americans today in their founding charters. At the end of the nineteenth century, however, the revolutionary situations developed in response to perceived transnational abuses of power arising when foreign governments and investors allied with local elites seemingly to exploit local labor or extract local wealth. Out of these transnational alignments emerged the language of imperialism and underdevelopment.

From another perspective, the amazing global spectacle of failed parliamentarism, military intervention and warlordism, coup and countercoup, and the penetration of sprawling but penetrated societies by rival capitalists and would-be colonizers, formed a delayed and defective version of the successful national reconstitutions of the mid-nineteenth century. Determined elites and strong states had emerged out of the mid-nineteenth century furnace. Partial projects of modernization, conflicting ideologies and decomposing sovereignties seemed to afflict those half a century later who had not made the earlier transition as they hurtled toward protracted revolution and civil wars. Ironically enough, these belated decomposing states would help drag the successful national constructions of half a century earlier into the great war that overtook them all: strong and viable states and crumbling empires together.

. . .

Of course, to go from a situation fraught with antagonism to actual uprisings involved the interplay of contingency and personality. In particular, the political classes of each population were growing impatient with long-term rulers or family that seemed unwilling to listen to calls for reform. In Russia the tsarina and in China the empress dowager seemed to manipulate the feckless males who held the nominal imperial title. In Mexico and the Ottoman Empire, the aging patriarchs, both arriving in power in 1876, had promoted economic development, but became increasingly domineering and autocratic. Sultan Abdülhamid II, increasingly viewed as an aging despot relying on police spies, would be ousted after thirty years in 1908, in a coup that only made his empire more prey to territorial dismemberment. Porfirio Díaz would have to stand down in 1910.

Yet these autocrats had decisively pressed in particular for major expansion of their nations' railroads—as had the Russian bureaucrats in the same period. Railroads in effect provided the sinews and axons of globalization: they enhanced the idea of a unified territory; they allowed the development of interior markets, or the transport of distant soldiers; they required the standardization of timekeeping. Early railroads in the 1840s and 1850s had helped increase revolutionary and national pressures, whether in Prussia, where a parliament was to be summoned for their financing, or in Illinois, where they opened up the plains for wheat growing and destabilized the precarious compromises on slavery. Now railroads brought the transformative pressures of global finance and investment and the development of long-distance markets into the perimeters of the developed world. Railroads were the complement of frontiers: defending frontiers was the precondition of state sovereignty since the seventeenth century—the frontier had been the prerequisite for Leviathan 1.0. The railroad promised to make the interior space of the national state a unit, economically and socially as well as politically. It was, in effect, the principal symbol of Leviathan 2.0. But it exacted a price, often a fiscal one that bore heavily on a population and required new levels of taxation as in Russia, or new degrees of foreign investment as in Mexico and the Ottoman realms. And it exposed the mechanisms of the semideveloped states into which it penetrated as insufficient to realize the promises of progress it tantalizingly held out. Finally, it created new coalitions of the privileged, composed of new and old investors, and new coalitions of protesters who felt they were being exploited by those who controlled monopoly access to privilege and power.

Ironically, however, national revolutions that erupted in reaction to global pressures often remained regionally fragmented. National parliamentary politics was quickly eclipsed. The arenas of revolution were often local, and integrated national movements emerged only after protracted and brutal military conflict. Power gravitated to rival military commanders, sometimes seeking to contest the country as a whole, sometimes just establishing their own territory. The existence of rival armies and local military rule or warlordism, often supported by dominant foreign patrons, remained a logical outcome, at least for a long intervening period of conflict. Such regional fighting often proved particularly brutal as feelings of betrayal and counterbetrayal ran high. Combat shaded into long-term feuding. Regional commanders did not always take prisoners—what should they do with them?—even if they accepted turncoats. The laws of war, weak in most circumstances, did not often temper internal combat. The leaders who seized local power might be generous, but they could also be impulsive and vengeful. Alternatively, new and ruthless parties might claim that they alone could channel the true revolutionary forces. These confrontations were often beset by internal contradiction: they mobilized working classes who were internationalist in their outlooks and middle-class or elite reformers who spoke the language of nationalism. But they were also revolts in predominantly rural countries where landlords continued to dominate the countryside, while their tenants wanted control of the land either for their households or, in parts of Russia and Mexico, for their village communes. Belated revolution, many on the left believed, meant peasant revolution—heroic and apocalyptic as in one of Diego Rivera's or Orozco's murals. In fact, countryside forces could not push through revolutionary settlements without linking up to townspeople, whether middle-class or working-class. Intellectuals and journalists, merchants and financial intermediaries, remained critical, just as religious leaders in Iran remained crucial urban-based participants. Cities and countryside forces had to reach some sort of accommodation for success.

. . .

The Russian revolution of 1905 was in effect the last of the great European revolutions since 1789, though it was provoked by the fiscal and social strains brought on by the conflict with Japan over East Asian expansion. As in the aftermath of the Crimean War, when the authorities eliminated serfdom, Russia had to make accommodations when it was overstretched. In this case the demonstrations of February 1905 and the gunfire of Bloody Sunday opened a continuing wave of protest and strikes and party formation that finally led to the tsar's agreement in October to summon a parliament or Duma. This was hardly surprising: Russia was an anomaly in the world of developed states, clinging to theoretical autocracy, which meant in effect rule by an aristocratic bureaucracy. German liberal observers, who had complacently viewed their own country as far more progressive than tsarist "despotism," were astonished to see that the Russians had acquired at a stroke a national assembly unhampered by the reactionary reserve powers that the unequal Prussian electoral system allowed. This achievement, however, was hardly to be maintained; the suffrage would be rolled back; the Dumas successively prorogued, even as social conflict increased and the financial strains of preparing for possible European conflict grew. Still, 1905 outlined the spectrum of parties—Bolsheviks, social democratic Mensheviks, agrarian "Social Revolutionary" populists oriented toward the peasants, middle-class liberals (so-called Kadets, eloquent but limited to the professional classes), and conservative "Octobrists"—that would fill the Russian political space until all were silenced after the Bolsheviks seized power at the end of 1917. The year 1905 also stimulated a decade of cultural innovation, fervent political and social debate, and continuing industrial advance.

. . .

Iran's "constitutional revolution" of 1905–1909 took place in the shadow of the revolutionary unrest that undermined neighboring Russia and the Ottoman Empire and the larger international balance of power. Iran, the stagnant remnant of a long-lived and once brilliant empire, was ruled by the Qajar dynasty, clinging to decisive power in a country that was perhaps a third or more "tribal" and in which religious authorities played a significant political role. Shi'a clerics, dominant in Iran, traditionally stayed more distant from secular authority than did Sunni, and they increasingly denounced Qajar family tyranny, even as they remained hostile to the secularism of emerging intellectuals. Neighboring Russia tended to take its own predominant influence for granted, especially because it helped train the shah's military units. Great Britain, long concerned about Russian expansion and its supposed threat to India, had long sought commercial advantages in Iran, but was increasingly preoccupied since 1890 with Germany's rise to global power. The dynasty was torn between concessions to the British for the sake of economic development and reliance on the Russians for military stability. Following an abortive grant of extensive privileges in 1872 for railroad building, the shah allowed the British to found a bank of issue in the 1880s, and granted a national tobacco monopoly to British subjects in the early 1890s—all concessions, of course, that enriched those close to the court. Tobacco, however, was a broadly based economic activity, and the concession led to "the first successful mass protest in modern Iran, combining '*ulama*', modernists, merchants, and townspeople in a coordinated movement against government policy."[140] The shah was assassinated in 1896, and the new shah, Muzaffar al-Din, found himself compelled to replace his conservative minister in 1903. The Russian revolutionary agitation during 1905 also spilled over to Iran: the Azeri region of Azerbaijan on the west of the Caspian that was divided between Russia and Iran proved a ready conduit for social democratic and Islamic organizational efforts, and protests roiled Tehran.

British and Russian interests were converging on a moderate solution for Iranian unrest. The Russian authorities were seeking to contain agitation at home, and like the British perceived a rising German threat, especially as Berlin seemed to be gaining military and economic influence in the Ottoman Empire. Both the British and the Russians sought to become patrons of the Islamic opposition and its call for a *majlis* or parliament. The 1905 standoff of protesters and the shah led the clerics to flee to Qum and the merchants to shut their markets. By August 1906, almost a year after the tsar had conceded a Duma, the shah agreed to convoke a legislature. The assembly was soon transformed from the role that conservative clerics envisaged for it, as a Muslim congress, to a national parliament in which minority religions would also be represented, even if the elections left it safely in the hands of clerics and wealthy merchants. Election of the *majlis*, however, meant that the struggle for constitutional government was only half over; the question of its future role was still open. A reluctant shah signed the fundamental laws in December 1906, but died shortly after, and divided *majlis* members prepared a contest for the all-important "supplement," which was to determine the power of the prime minister and the official role of religion. Advocates of freedom of conscience, journalists, and Western-oriented aristocrats spoke on behalf of parliamentary rights while the new shah, Muhammad Ali, and conservative clerics, who wanted to retain a large role for religious law, resisted. After a temporizing prime minister was assassinated in August 1907, the shah gave way and the constitutional supplement was passed in October, providing for a balance of executive and parliamentary power but with a council of religious notables to ensure that civil legislation conformed to Muslim law, or shariʿa.

As long as the Russian authorities, cautioned by their own revolution although progressively limiting liberal gains, and the British worked together, they could secure the triumph of the moderate constitutionalists in Tehran and the consolidation of their respective interests. Thus motivated, the two great powers reached a crucial accord in 1907 that effectively suspended London's long-standing wariness of Russian imperial ambitions. The Anglo-Russian Convention provided for the nominal preservation of Iranian territorial integrity while recognizing a predominantly Russian sphere in the north and a British sphere in the south, where British exploration for oil was successful a year later. Iranian public opinion understandably beheld it as de facto partition, signed on their own soil. The agreement also forestalled rivalry over the northwest frontier of India and either side's takeover of Afghanistan. Thus the two powers adjourned their potential conflicts in Central Asia, facilitating in turn the emergence of the Triple Entente with their mutual partner, France, and potentially confronting together the Austro-German alliance in Europe and the colonial world. But having been guaranteed that Russia would not partition Iran and would not threaten Britain's frontier zone in India, London seemed to withdraw from active policy in Iran, while the Russian ambassador now urged a hard line on the shah, who deployed Cossack-led troops to shut down the parliament in 1908 after continued street agitation.

Counterrevolution was not the last word, however, and European politics impacted again. Pro-German Young Turks staged a revolution in Constantinople; Berlin in 1909 compelled a humiliating Russian confirmation of Austria's annexation of Bosnia; and Russia decided it needed British cooperation, given the threatening international situation. Again working together in Iran, the two

powers could urge a compromise constitutional settlement, which restored the
majlis. Clerical conservatives recovered the theoretical right of religious review
of legislation, but the provision was never implemented. The victory of secular
liberalism remained provisional and precarious, however. When the Iranians
brought in an American financial expert, William Morgan Schuster, to establish
a modern revenue service, the Russians demanded his dismissal, on the grounds
that the Anglo-Russian Convention gave the powers the final say over such an
appointment, and marched on Tehran when the *majlis* resisted. The cabinet gave
way, dismissed Schuster, and dissolved the *majlis* in December 1911. The constitution remained but no new elections followed until 1914. Russian forces and
the Azerbaijani revolutionary movements after 1917 dominated the northern
half of the country, until the new Bolsheviks decided British trade was more
important than insisting on heavy-handed control in Iran. They agreed to withdraw their troops. The British may have sponsored the coup d'état of 1921 led by
the imposing military commander Reza Khan, who seized supreme power as
shah in late 1925 and inaugurated the Pahlavi rule that lasted until the Islamic
revolution of 1979.[141]

. . .

Iran was a poor and backward region compared with the Ottoman Empire, although Iranian intellectuals remembered when their empires had fought each
other on a level of parity. Seeking to weather the international opprobrium that
the attempted repression of the Balkan rebellions of 1875 had aroused, the new
Sultan Abdülhamid II (1876–1909) first summoned a new parliament in 1876,
then prorogued it and suspended the new constitution within little more than a
year as Russia intervened militarily to support the hard-pressed Bulgarian uprising. Over the next three decades the sultan tightened a repressive political regime even as he sought to modernize economic and military institutions and
develop the sleepy southern provinces of the empire. Istanbul's reform from
above, however, led to incompatible ideological programs for sustaining a multinational empire: an effort, on the one hand, to woo Arabic Muslim elites, and,
on the other, to advance a Turkic national movement, the Committee on Union
and Progress (CUP), or Young Turks, particularly concerned about the influence of Greeks and Armenians. With the reduction of his European domains
(formal cession of Romania, Serbia, Bosnia, Bulgaria, and Macedonia in 1856 and

1878), the new sultan began to stress an ideology of Pan-Islamism. Finances were the weak point: attempts to collect taxes in a decade of world economic downturn had helped to provoke the 1875 Bulgarian rebellion and the disastrous war with Russia. Part of the Berlin settlement involved establishing an international public debt oversight (Public Debt Administration) in 1881.

The sultan's efforts to consolidate his position by development in the Arab provinces and emphasis of his Muslim role, however, were destined to create vulnerability in the remaining European regions of the empire, long a site of its more capable administrators and soldiers. Rebellion and assassination seethed in ethnically and religiously mixed Macedonia, where the neighboring Balkan states and European interests all saw their opportunities. Tax revolts were erupting in Anatolia. The British and Russian monarchs, whose countries had recently negotiated their division of interests in Iran, met at Reval in June 1908, to discuss, so it was believed, intervention in Macedonia. Istanbul's humiliating feebleness provoked a nationalist reaction among so-called Young Turk officers stationed in Salonika, who formally constituted a Committee on Union and Progress, and mutinied to compel Abdülhamid to reinstate constitutional rights and parliament in summer 1908, and then ousted him a year later.[142] The sultan who succeeded him remained a powerless monarch, appointing the ministers that the parties and military who had led the last uprising or coup d'état imposed in the final acts of Ottoman constitutionalism until mid-1913.

CUP adherents had diverse aims: Ottomanism or a restoration of imperial control, including the compulsory teaching of Turkish, may have been dominant; some members advocated decentralization and perhaps dismantling into ethnic units; others were attracted to the idea of Turkic national leadership. Some were secularists and Westernizers; others advocated reasserting the commitment to Islam. All wanted a vigorous restoration of direction and an end to the temporizing, corruption, and clientelism they were convinced was rotting the legacy of a once great power. What they achieved, however, was an interval of coup and countercoup.

Open elections based on territory seated a parliament that was half non-Turkish. There was a CUP majority but a strong liberal opposition; and resentment grew against CUP domination. After the assassination of an opposition newspaper editor, there followed a counterrevolutionary mutiny and the potential debacle of the CUP in mid-April 1909, only to be reversed when Salonica military units of the Committee marched on the capital and forced reinstatement of the Young Turk government. The renewed CUP regime quickly lost power to military commanders and a reunited liberal opposition after it had been discredited by the Italian seizure of Libya and an uprising of Albanian Muslims. Still, CUP strength in the provinces allowed it to dissolve the parliament and win a resounding victory in 1912, only to be ousted by a military coalition, the "Saviour Officers," later in the year. The military saviors did not save European Turkish territory from the Balkan League of Serbs, Bulgarians, Montenegrins, and Greeks, who exploited Ottoman disarray to attack in October. Only their mutual jealousies let Constantinople recover the small strip of European coast that Turkey controls today. But the overall military humiliations of the Balkan wars gave the CUP a chance to reseize power and defend it from a counterputsch in the spring of 1913. Assassination of their vizier provided a pretext to impose authoritarian control and hammer the liberal opposition through arrests, show trials, and harsh sentences. Young Turk foreign policy was an opportunistic search for an ally: the British rejected the overture, while William II accepted it—fantasizing that the Caliphate might encourage Britain's Muslim subjects to revolt. CUP generals took over the ministry of war and the navy, brought the empire into the European war in late 1914, and made the infamous decision to massacre the Armenian minority a year later. The cadets and intellectuals who a decade earlier had organized to renew the empire ended up with a triumvirate that would ultimately destroy it.

The military option seemed initially to stabilize Turkish politics. Remarkably, the army that had so thoroughly disintegrated in the Balkan War of 1912—because of long neglect by Abdülhamid, according to German observers—was made into a relatively efficient force by 1914–1915 under German military advisers. But the pressures of a long war on four fronts (the Dardanelles, the Caucuses, Mesopotamia, and the Palestinian coast) took its toll. The empire was left as a rump state after the end of the world war: with ruinous inflation and debts, the last feeble sultan holed up in Constantinople with Greeks and British on the Ionian coast, and Italians seeking their own slice of territory. The Arab-speaking territories were carved up into British and French provinces, an Armenian state, and autonomous Kurdistan, created in eastern Anatolia, with international

From empire to nation: Mustafa Kemal Atatürk in 1923. Kemal appears here as the successful Turkish military leader
who has forced the end of the Ottoman Sultanate and negotiated with France and Great Britain the revised Treaty of Lausanne, which stabilized his country in its present borders. He
is not yet wearing a business suit and homburg. The relentless
authoritarian modernizer and secularizer of his country accepted the title *Atatürk* (Father of the Turks) in 1934. (Private
Collection / Roger-Viollet, Paris / The Bridgeman Art Library)

control of the Dardanelles and of Ottoman finances. Confronted with the humiliation of the Treaty of Sèvres, a nationalist parliament rallied in Ankara as the
Grand National Assembly of Turkey, while the vigorous military commander
Mustafa Kemal, who had assumed ever greater organizational and command
responsibilities in the war, emerged as the leader of a resurgent resistance. Over
the next three years the nationalists secured Soviet recognition, reconquered

Armenian territory, and eliminated serious rivalries in the West to Kemal's authority. The French came to terms over the Syrian-Turkish border, and in 1922 Kemal smashed the Greek-British forces and compelled a new treaty of Lausanne by 1923, remembered today preeminently for the massive exchange of Greek and Turkish populations it stipulated. The Sultanate and Caliphate were separated; the sultan was declared to have vacated his post and the office was abolished. The Caliphate did not survive long, neither did religious schools. The Assembly officially declared Turkey a republic and elected Kemal as president. The Law for the Unification of Education established the secular state, although it recognized Islam as its official religion. In April 1923 Kemal founded the People's Party, which, to preempt an emerging opposition, reorganized as the Republican People's Party (RPP); by the early 1930s, after a brief interval of allowing a tolerated opposition, he began a concerted drive to make the ruling party into the exclusive instrument for changing society and state. Conservatives and traditionalists remained resistant to the reforms, which included changes in dress and the status of women. By 1934 Kemal took the title Atatürk, or father of the Turks, and the RPP was theoretically fused with state offices in the following year. Atatürk, though, resisted following the totalitarian model as it was gaining strength around him and preserved scope for private capitalists, but his death in 1938 and the approach of the war left Turkey with an uneasy balance between a semitolerated opposition and a powerful military-supported statist party.[143]

. . .

Consider finally the two revolutions at geographic extremes from the heartlands of Eurasia: in Mexico and China—the one the product of a state repeatedly contested by Europeans and North Americans; the other a sprawling empire that seemed, in the fears of its reformers, ready to be sliced apart like a watermelon. Developing states remained vulnerable because economic growth and modernization accentuated rather than overcame failures of representation. As president, Porfirio Díaz (1876–1910) progressively tightened an authoritarian regime after the long era of civil war and foreign intervention in Mexico, favoring a privileged circle of beneficiaries, including regional party bosses, industrialists, and large land and ranch owners. The ruling group became known collectively as the *científicos* because of the economic growth they supervised as they opened up the country to European and American investment in industry, mining, and railroads. But outsize rewards flowed to the favored elite. The first decade of the new century produced a host of dissatisfied claimants to a voice in government: the liberal middle classes, who had benefited from economic advance, a growing urban working class in the northern industries, spokesmen for Indian communal rights that had been eroded since the liberal victories of the 1850s, and rival generals. Díaz cracked down harshly on the labor unions; middle-class entrepreneurs resented the foreign-owned firms that remained closed to them; powerful regional families took offense at the clients Díaz favored. The increase in foreign investment (with inflationary price rises and a sharp drop in real wages in the North) gave way to an economic downturn in the wake of the US panic of 1907. The oligarchy managed to win its rigged congressional elections with implausible unanimity in 1910. Still, revolution seemed excluded by most observers—as it usually does on the eve of great uprisings, from 1789 to Eastern Europe in 1989 and Egypt in 2011—until a local uprising broke out in Chihuahua at the end of 1910. The leader of the opposition, Francisco Madero, a wealthy rancher who had denounced the regime, threw in his lot with the rebels, then accepted an agreement that provided for a now-deserted Díaz to resign before the presidential election of October 1911. Madero was triumphant, but political and territorial decomposition followed—it was not a coherent social revolution, but, so John Womack argues, "a struggle for power, in which different revolutionary factions contended not only against the old regime and foreign concerns, but also, often more so, against each other, over matters as deep as class and as shallow as envy." Looking at the results, "the victorious faction managed to dominate peasant movements and labour unions for the promotion of selected American and native businesses."[144]

This does not mean that different groups had no conflicting interests; they were as staunchly defended as anywhere else in this turbulent decade. But they remained unaggregated, concentrated on one or more of the regionally based armies (and often fragmented at even more local levels) that coalesced around the successive leaders seeking power. Victoriano Huerta removed Madero (murdered after stepping down) on behalf of conservative forces, including the Church, but resigned in mid-July 1915 before the threatened advance of forces led by Venustiano Carranza and Pancho Villa—the gifted military commander in

Chihuahua who in late 1913 initiated a program of land redistribution. Carranza's and Villa's delegates met at the October 1914 convention at Aguascalientes, and Villa persuaded Emiliano Zapata to commit his southern army in return for further land reform, outlined in Zapata's Plan of Ayala, the most extensive agrarian program of the revolution. Zapata and Villa met as revolutionary heroes in Mexico City in late November 1914, but the strategically crucial Carranza-Villa agreement soon dissolved in acrimony. Aguascalientes had called on both leaders to stand down their military forces and renounce their own candidacy for the vacant presidency. Each imputed bad faith to the other; by 1915 their armies were involved in the fiercest fighting of the revolutionary decade.

Were there issues as well as ambitions that divided Carranza and Villa? According to Villa's biographer, a long-term historian of the revolution, they divided over the contrasting attitudes that had separated centralists and federalists in the preceding century: Carranza spoke for disciplined authority and control emanating from the capital, Villa for an improvised regionalism.[145] As of 1915, Villa was more willing to deal with President Wilson's efforts to control Mexican outcomes and ensure continuing oil supplies. But fortunes and alignments could change rapidly. Villa's friendly relations with the American representatives in Mexico and his military fortunes turned sour in late 1915. Although Carranza had been a staunch nationalistic opponent of Wilson's expedition to Veracruz in 1914, once Villa attempted his raids on US soil and the United States entered the war with Germany, the White House endorsed Carranza's presidency. Zapata's alliance with Villa also frayed, and he was killed shortly after the brief, exuberant triumph in Mexico City. Carranza was elected president and inaugurated a constitution in 1917; and by late 1920 his military ally, Álvaro Obregón from Sonora succeeded him and began the work of reconsolidating the greatly indebted Mexican economy—providing an interval of stabilization at a moment, too, when bourgeois normalization was returning to Europe and its colonies after the global upheavals of 1917–1921. Obregón did continue the distribution of hacienda lands to smaller proprietors or communal *ejidos,* although rather selectively where this program had helped to ignite revolution, as in Zapata's home state of Morelos. He also sponsored the energetic educational reforms of José Vasconcelos, the *spiritus rector* of the revolutionary state, who helped create the mythic history of Indian-Hispanic cultural fusion through school expansion, murals, and mobilization of the populist intellectuals. Obregón's successor, Plutarco Elías Calles, supervised a major anticlerical campaign worthy of the struggles a century earlier and provoked a tenacious pro-clerical Cristero uprising by rural Church adherents. Then his four-year term as president ended in 1928, and the election again of Obregón (to be assassinated a day later) threatened a shift to the left, Calles as unofficial godfather of the emerging regime managed to organize the major vehicle for stabilization, the Partido Nacional Revolucionario (PNR), the predecessor to the Partido Revolucionario Institucional (PRI) that would govern until the 1990s.[146]

. . .

Halfway around the world, in China, the regime finally fell only in 1911 after seventy years of defeats to foreigners, exhausting rebellion, and continued infringements of sovereignty, all of which culminated in a wave of setbacks in the 1890s and paralyzing court politics. The defeat by Japan in 1895 and the renewed Western scramble for further territorial concessions finally jolted a widespread but contested intellectual opening—forcibly stifled, however, by the empress dowager's countercoup against the young emperor and his radical advisers—only to throw her support to the nationalist organizations known as Boxers who attacked the Beijing legations and provoked a united foreign intervention. Still, the years from 1898 to the final Qing abdication were an epoch of extraordinary reformist effort, which could not be kept under conservative gentry control nor ultimately held in check by the Europeans. The ancient examination system that had structured elite access to rule was removed in 1905; meanwhile reformers were asking for inauguration of a hierarchy of local assemblies as well as a national parliament.[147] The Confucian ideologies appealed to in earlier reform efforts were superseded by images of modernization and of Darwinist national competition, already seen by many Chinese as successful in Japan. Impatient exiles (such as Sun Yat-sen) and military leaders converged to launch what, from the vantage of the centennial of the 1911 revolution, can be interpreted as a long trajectory that would lead, via the Republic (1911–1949), then devastating war and civil war and the vast costs of Mao's revolution, to Deng Xiaoping's emulation of capitalism.[148]

In China, the parliament established in Beijing fell under the influence of Yuan Shikai, the talented military (and police) leader, who was tempted to claim the imperial throne but died by 1916. His death led to a dozen years of rival claims and the emergence of powerful warlords who imposed de facto territorial governments, collected or extorted "tax" revenues, raised peasant armies, and joined shifting "cliques" or alliances, holding out longest in the Manchurian area around the Liaodong Peninsula, where the Japanese held the key ports and railroads since their wars with China (1894–1995) and Russia (1904–1905). The Japanese could help finance the leading northern warlord, Zhang Zuolin, in return for his deference to their own position, but he was ousted in 1928 after a failed effort to reorganize central-state politics in Beijing. The revolutionary forces in the south under the ambitious Chiang Kai-shek set up their own rival base, entrusting subordinate power to the graduates of the new Whampoa military academy. Chiang was more than a general: he inherited Sun Yat-sen's Guomindang (GMD, or National People's Party) and drew on Russian Bolshevik aid and counsel to create an authoritarian party. Bolshevik leaders in Moscow sharply divided on the issue of whether to instruct the Chinese Communist Party (CCP) to work with Chiang or challenge him. Stalin, seeking in the mid-1920s to establish his own succession at home against Trotsky and other possible rivals who urged autonomy for the CCP, insisted on subordinating the CCP to the GMD. The policy led to catastrophe in 1926–1927, for as his power increased Chiang turned on his former Communist allies and destroyed part of the party, murdering thousands first in Shanghai, then in Wuhan and Nanjing—leaving the remnants to retreat from Shanghai, and ultimately in the 1930s to trek thousands of miles to establish their mountain sanctuary under Mao Zedong in Yan'an in Shaanxi Province.

Despite the fragmentation, violence, and confusing succession of the revolutionary decade in China, the turbulence involved more than just the final denouement of a massive state structure hammered by foreigners and increasingly unable to overcome an ossified ideology, vast population increase, and ecological catastrophes and impoverishment. It also allowed a belated but energetic effort to merge traditional cultural resources with models of development frenetically taken from abroad. Warlords continued to contend for power around Beijing and in Japanese-occupied Manchuria, but by the end of the 1920s Chiang's army, and party—now drawing on German rather than Russian advisers—seemed poised to take Beijing (a development, as explained below, that would lead the ambitious Japanese military government of the region to establish the "puppet state" of Manchukuo under the nominal rule of the last deposed Qing emperor, "Henry" Pu Yi). Ultimately neither Chinese army leaders nor the revolutionary parties could impose a clear success without some fusing of effort, reflected still today in the strong role that the People's Liberation Army plays in the Communist state.[149]

Generally economic growth and development have been viewed as an asset in the path to political liberalism. During the Cold War most American social scientists did not doubt that they went together. Perhaps this was true in eras when development had homegrown roots, but the remarkable economic and financial advances of the era from 1895 to 1914, as they unfolded in the context of global inequality that marked the age of high imperialism, could not ensure liberal outcomes. The epochal revolutions in Russia, China, Mexico, Iran, and Turkey certainly mobilized masses of rural families and workers as well as urban dwellers across all classes. They awoke new currents of nationalism and encouraged cultural awakening: intellectuals envisaged awakening nations, but were also stimulated by the very awakenings they sought to advance and shape. But the mass forces, and the breadth of the social and religious movements whose volunteers descended from their homes into the city squares across half the world, were not easily contained by constitutional and parliamentary debates. As these raw and vigorous, sometimes violent, ideological transformations worked themselves out, usually over a span of at least two or three decades, it was the determined cadres of committed parties and military corps that disciplined their sometimes generous but often intolerant forces. The twentieth-century world that emerged from the wave of global revolution was a more participatory one, but not necessarily a freer one. Or more precisely, the bonds of private subjection—to landlords, local bosses, mine and factory owners—were exchanged often, not for liberal values (which seemed to reinforce private bonds of subjection for so many), but for the bonds of public discipline. Ironically enough, it was the very countries that were exponents of liberalism at home, but also convinced of the civic virtues of economic expansion, that helped plunge the huge countries outside Europe (and its offshoots) into the turbulence of foreign-controlled development, revolutionary protest, and military and one-party solutions. Sixty or seventy years later these experiments—their own disfunctionality having been repeatedly demonstrated in the years after consolidation in the 1920s—might finally be yielding to the sort of world that their early exponents envisaged.

Politics as War

No one can say what would have been the upshot of this widespread turbulence had war not broken out in Europe in 1914 and then developed into a protracted and unprecedented conflict. Where economic and voting issues were at stake, gradual compromise might have had a chance: suffrage reform and welfare legislation were all emerging before 1914. An unruly Russian republic might have settled down as of 1920. Racial minorities in the United States and South Africa might have had to wait a long time to secure voting and civil rights—as they did in fact. Nationalist aspirations might not have waited so long, and it is hard to envisage their solution without local violence—precisely the situation, however, that did ignite general war in summer 1914. The Habsburgs could not easily make their territories into a confederation of nationalities. The Germans within the Austrian half might have allowed it, but Hungarians would have resisted, and whether the Romanians and South Slavs outside the empire would have accepted such a compromise for their own irredenta within is doubtful. Would a restored and sovereign Polish nation have emerged without war? To review the alternatives is to realize that at best local clashes were hard to avoid even if better crisis management might have avoided the fatal great-power involvement that made a new Balkan crisis into World War I. Would the Ottoman state—led since 1908 by a party that feared subversion from all the non-Turkic peoples it attempted to control—have avoided continued war and decomposition? The British government's imperial compromise in South Asia with upper-class Hindus and Muslims would have gradually come undone, as it did from the 1930s on.

Historians conventionally describe decolonization as a sequel to the Second World War, an epochal transformation, compelled in part by their European rulers' interim defeat and financial exhaustion. In fact, the points of inflection came earlier. By the end of the 1920s a new generation of young nationalists came to the fore, impatient with their elders' clientelistic bargains with European rules. The economic crisis of the 1930s then brought its misery not only to Europe and North America but to the colonial economies as well. It added widespread labor unrest, in cities and on plantations, to nationalist sentiments as a potent challenge to the colonial state. By the mid-1930s, the alternatives were escalating violence or reform efforts that must ultimately lead to far more self-government than reformers wished to admit.[150] Of course, the interwar economic crisis itself might not have assumed such proportions without the disruptions of international finance and trade that the war of 1914–1918 left behind. Historical causation is always cumulative and sequential.

Stability and representation without multiparty democracy might have served many states. Single-party rule, such as emerged in Mexico and later in many postcolonial states, might have provided transitional stability for divided polities. Not all single parties must be repressive structures; some allow outside groups to dissent and can serve—at least for a generation or two—to represent different social currents and ideas. World War I did not preclude such outcomes. Nonetheless, even before the war, more radical party claims suggested a different outcome for some of the states in difficulty. The Russian Social-Democrat V. I. Lenin argued in his 1902 tract, *What Is to Be Done?* (echoing the title of a Russian radical's celebrated appeal forty years earlier), that revolution required a centralized political party demanding unswerving discipline. The single party allegedly spoke for the proletariat, endowed the working class with revolutionary consciousness, and was thus summoned to impose revolutionary dictatorship in their name.[151] Later Lenin seemed briefly to entertain the idea that a Bolshevik utopia might ultimately lead to the end of the traditional state, but the hard politics outlined in his 1902 essay remained the agenda for the foreseeable future. The Bolshevik Party would guide the authoritarian dictatorship that would grip Russia (and its reorganized empire) from the civil war of 1917 to 1921 through the death of Lenin's successor, Joseph Stalin, in March 1953—and, with a softer mix of surveillance and punishment, for another thirty-some years until the late 1980s.

French Jacobins had outlined a concept of revolutionary terror and the ruthless elimination of enemies under Robespierre, but the Jacobins had improvised dictatorship and a theory of republican virtue to rationalize the harsh measures they were imposing. On the basis of Marx's historical dramaturgy of class conflict, Lenin transformed the ad hoc Jacobin rationalizations of 1792–1794 into a doctrine of long-term revolution long before he could impose power. Even more

The promise of the proletariat: A poster from 1920 depicting Russian leader Vladimir Lenin addressing workers against an industrial backdrop at a moment when the Bolsheviks still felt that their revolution might spread to the West. The caption, which reads, "A specter is roaming across Europe, the specter of communism," echoes the famous opening lines of Karl Marx and Friedrich Engels's *Communist Manifesto* of 1848. (Museum of the Revolution, Moscow / The Bridgeman Art Library)

disturbing than his own authoritarian claims was the assent that this theory of party dictatorship could win from many Western intellectuals. After the Revolution, sympathizers abroad claimed that the Soviet homeland after 1917 was isolated and beleaguered and the only site where the socialist revolution existed in practice. Any questioning of its policies must be subordinated to the cause of its survival, as defined by the leaders in Moscow.

No one can understand the history of twentieth-century political debate and experience without working through the problem of Communist obedience. Did the Communist intellectuals and the nonparty sympathizers ("fellow travelers," to use the later term) somehow crave self-abasement, as critics such as the Polish exile Czesław Miłosz later suggested with his fable of the magic pills that made them happily yield to the charms of totalitarian power?[152] Was it the merciless logic imposed, as they believed, by the unyielding laws of history? Good communists took pride in their commitment to a disciplined body that demanded obedience even as it reassured members that they alone understood and were advancing the inexorable processes of history. In his 1922 essay *History and Class Consciousness,* the Communist philosopher Georg Lukács—who after a subsequent generation of Stalinist repression would actually strive to moderate dictatorship in 1956 Hungary—set out the dialectical logic of a party dictatorship already emerging in Russia as the Bolsheviks shut down alternative parties, established their Cheka or secret police, and used military force to suppress the Kronstadt fortress mutiny: "The forms of freedom in bourgeois organizations are nothing but a 'false consciousness' of an actual unfreedom.... Only when this is understood can our earlier paradox be resolved: ... the unconditional absorption of the total personality in the praxis of the movement, was the only possible way of bringing about an authentic freedom." Praxis meant discipline and subservience, but to policies that in the long run had to be objectively correct (although errors might be made from day to day). "The question of discipline is then, on the one hand, an elementary practical problem for the party, an indispensable precondition for its effective functioning.... The Communist Party must exist as an independent organization so that the proletariat may be able to see its own class consciousness given historical shape.... [T]he fact that it is a fighting party presupposes its possession of a correct theory, for otherwise the consequences of a false theory would soon destroy it."[153] Such reasoning and commitment could justify the visceral hatred of "bourgeois" privilege, the vituperative attacks on social democratic critics and rivals, the Nazi-Soviet pact of 1939, and the show trials and executions of the 1930s and the 1950s. Nonetheless, it is not enough to recite a record of intellectual and sometimes moral debasement; the historian has to account for how the communist vocation could appear so compelling to so many adherents. They attributed their choices to the disasters they felt capitalism was accumulating, whether the carnage of the First World War or the mass unemployment and misery before which bourgeois statesmen seemed so hopeless. For them communism alone offered a viable alternative to the fascist violence that no other parties effectively opposed, to the colonial rule that the Western countries seemed determined to perpetuate, and, in the United States, to the deep-seated racism that neither mainstream political party would challenge.

Admittedly, too, the lives actually constructed in the Russian society that the Party aspired to transform were far more diverse and disorderly, negotiated during an era of vast economic and social transformation, crowded, communal, and demanding, accompanied by bewildering policy shifts—and not to be simply understood as a neat working-out of dialectics. Still, at the time Lukács was claiming this higher freedom, he was well aware that the Leninist party ruling the Soviet Union had purged—that is, at this time, expelled—tens of thousands of its early members and shut down all other party organizations as a conclusion drawn from its supposedly privileged insights into historical necessity. By the time Stalin consolidated his personal power, the term *purge* would also entail the waves of mass arrests, long sentences to the forced-labor camps of the gulag with mortality rates estimated at up to 25 percent annually, or execution in obscurity—one reasoned estimate suggests that over seven hundred thousand did not return. Historians have debated whether the impulse to purify the party and the organizations of culture, administration, the military and economic life came from Stalin's own continual distrust of the revolutionary movement or responded to enthusiasms and impatience from the rank and file. In any case these convulsive waves of lives blighted or destroyed came to be seen as the characteristic phenomenon of the regime.[154]

The Soviet Party would create the Soviet Union in 1922 and would impose allied parties in Eastern Europe from 1945 until the end of the 1980s, although there would be differing degrees of compliance. (Yugoslavia became a communist dictatorship, although it broke with the Soviet bloc in 1948.) Party structures that demanded the same discipline would govern China, North Korea, Vietnam, and Cambodia for parts of the second half of the twentieth century and seek to take power in many other states. Even where that possibility was remote, as in Britain and the United States, Soviet party emissaries would often ask local members to engage in clandestine espionage on behalf of Moscow. Even the fascist parties, and the National Socialist Party, who ran a system just as cruel, did not make party membership as such so central a component of exacting total commitment. And although by the outbreak of World War II, in 1939, the rulers of Germany were running a chain of perhaps eight hundred concentration camps, most of them small labor dependencies of the notorious large *Lager,* such as Dachau, Sachsenhausen, Buchenwald, Belsen, and Mauthausen, they filled them with close to a million opponents and not usually their own membership. There were two waves of the collective arrests and punishments we term "purges": the liquidation of the Sturmabteilung (SA) leadership (and other potential opponents) initiated on June 30, 1934, and the roundup, arrest, and execution of the army, civil service, and remaining democratic elements implicated in the assassination attempt of July 20, 1944. Each wave was on the order of a thousand; executions were far fewer. This is not to suggest a gentle state: tens of thousands passed through interrogation and detention, further tens of thousands of "handicapped"—so-called life unworthy of life—were murdered in state hospitals, tens of thousands of German soldiers would be executed by their own army during the war, and, all told, millions of Jews, non-Jewish Poles, Roma and Sinti, Russian prisoners of war, and captured Soviet party officials and others were liquidated in occupied Europe.[155]

For the Bolsheviks, class war remained a vivid doctrine; but the term usually referred to a rather impersonal process taking place through collectivization of agriculture from the late 1920s and of industrial production during the 1930s. When national groups resisted, as in Ukraine, then class war took on dimensions of genocidal starvation, as in the early 1920s and again with even greater force at the end of the decade and into the thirties. Warfare in the sense of military combat became central to the Soviet experience in the civil and Polish wars from 1918 to 1921 and after the German invasion of 1941; Marx and Engels had been keen observers of the mid-nineteenth-century wars of national reconstitution. But warfare as a dimension of human experience did not play a central ideological role in European Marxism-Leninism. This would change with the anticolonial struggles in Asia and Africa after 1945, as Communist leaders such as Ho Chi Minh, Vo Nguyen Giap, and Mao Zedong affirmed that peasant struggles and guerrilla warfare were central to the historical process of workers' emancipation.

However, another ideological constellation emerging from the First World War did place the experience of combat front and center in personal and political life. Fascists affirmed not only that war was an experience important for manhood (that belief had long had advocates), but that politics at its most basic must be akin to war, was in fact a form of war itself. War called forth the essentials demanded by manhood: loyalty and comradeship, command and obedience, and courage. Soldiers sacrificed themselves for their nation and for their fellow comrades. Liberal politicians in World War I had stayed at home, immune from danger, chatting away in their feckless parliaments while the youth of their societies were consumed in distant battlefields. War, the Prussian general Carl von Clausewitz had written, should be thought of as politics—as the pursuit of rational policy, by other means. Wasn't it true, though, to think of politics as war by other means? Insofar as there was a common content to the doctrines we think of as fascist (and here I am including National Socialism), it lay in this belief. Political life must be waged as a struggle, a search to dominate, not just legislate. It was adversarial and hard, it demanded obedience to a party and leader just as military organization did, and often its leaders and cadres donned quasi-military uniforms for party gatherings.

Several variants of this stance developed, diverse in key respects but elaborated around this common belief. Fascists and Nazis often claimed to despise abstract ideas, but intellectuals competed to elaborate their doctrines, and some were serious thinkers. Fascism originally claimed to be revolutionary and highly nationalist: from Mussolini's organization of the Fascio di Combattimento in March 1919, to Hitler's call for a National Revolution, to French fascists' belief that they needed a revolution against bourgeois morality. Fascists and National Socialists alike knew what they were against: certainly the organized parties and labor unions affiliated with Social Democracy, and the liberal democratic parties inherited from the nineteenth century. Toward organized political Catholicism they remained more open, disdainful in Germany but willing to compromise, and ultimately courting the church in Italy with concessions on education and marriage that abandoned the claims of the earlier liberal state.

· · ·

Fascism and communism cannot be appreciated just as fixed doctrines. They claimed to be revolutionary movements before they seized power. Generally the fascists considered Bolshevism as their most fundamental ideological adversary, but occasionally the two groups cooperated opportunistically, as during the crisis of the German Republic in the early 1930s. They both rejected the premises of political liberalism as developed since the late eighteenth century. Both claimed

Collapse of the German military machine: An improvised trench filled with German dead after the hard fighting of late July 1918 as French and Americans retook the Soissons region in the Second Battle of the Marne. The French would lose 1.3 million, the Germans 1.8 million, in a war that made military discipline, mass suffering, injury, economic devastation, and death an unexpected denouement of nineteenth-century European "civilization." (Private Collection / Ken Welsh / The Bridgeman Art Library)

to leave bourgeois sentiment behind—the communists in favor of a new proletarian collectivism, the fascists on behalf of a contradictory mix of values rooted in the ancestral soil but also in the modern claims of technological innovation. Georges Sorel, the French theorist of revolutionary violence and a self-professed despiser of the bourgeois humanism he traced to the Enlightenment, outlined a regime of "syndicates," or unions of producers cutting across capital and labor, before the First World War. Only political combat, not necessarily sanguinary, based on "myth" or grand abstractions of Armageddon, could renew society.[156] Sorel would welcome Lenin in his postwar editions; the Italian syndicalists (some of whom spent time organizing workers as "Wobblies" in the American West before World War I) and antidemocratic Right would read Sorel. But this common prewar source could invigorate political movements: constructing a state on their basis, as we shall see, required further ideas and more repressive decrees. Both fascism and Bolshevism would emphasize the single party, with its mass youth organizations and suborned cultural associations, as the instrument for seizing and exercising power. Once safely in power, however, their leaders would discipline their parties so that they took on more and more personal authority, even if they exercised it inconsistently. Both parties in power would seek to shape civil society and actually claim to remake "man." They would alternate periods of "normal" authority and the proud achievement of "consensus" with convulsive efforts to revivify their original dynamism, whether through party purges in the Soviet Union or preparations for national expansion and war in Italy and Germany. Both systems exalted the grand enterprise or project, some of which were merely hollow theatricality (the March on Rome itself) and others really transformative—the clearing of malarial lands around Rome, the German autobahns, or the industrialization of the Donets Basin, Magnetogorsk, the huge hydroelectric stations, and ultimately the rearmament programs in Germany and Russia.[157] The "project" admittedly was a fixation wider than the fascist and communist states—they shared it with many regimes before and after and certainly in the 1930s, including the New Deal.

Fascist and communist movements emerged at a common historical moment— as between 1917 and 1923 political momentum arced in a trajectory from Left to Right. The Bolshevik seizure of power reinforced a worldwide explosion of radical claims—whether by industrial workers and the left in Europe or fledgling anticolonial movements in Asia. Protests against a peace settlement that seemed to backtrack from Wilsonian rhetoric sent students and intellectuals into the streets of Beijing on May 4, 1919. In India, workers were striking in Punjabi cotton mills and protesting the British refusal to relax wartime martial law. Radicalized labor unions struck throughout Western Europe. Self-declared communists seized power briefly in Bavaria and in Hungary. But while the Bolsheviks held on in Russia, the worldwide moment of the left passed. In the United States there was a crackdown on radical publications and recent socialist immigrants. Communist uprisings in 1921 and 1923 Germany proved fiascos—the right came back, not only in authoritarian form in Hungary, Italy, and Spain, but as a reorganized bourgeois order in which industry and state authorities stabilized Western Europe, and the colonial powers reasserted their authority from the Middle East to South Asia.[158]

Mussolini's small movement had no success in its original effort to win parliamentary seats in the November 1919 elections. But extralegal action became a more promising way to win adherents in the turbulent political and labor conditions of postwar northern Italy. Public-service strikes were frequent; workers staged sit-down stoppages in the industries of Milan and Turin; socialists organized agricultural laborers and imposed new labor contracts on resentful landowners, while militant Catholic priests encouraged small peasant proprietors to unionize. For the proprietors and lawyers and industrialists of northern Italy, it seemed that revolution was gathering momentum from the ground up. At the same time, returning veterans felt that their recent military service was devalued. The nationalist poet Gabriele D'Annunzio organized a group of nationalist soldiers and seized the former Habsburg port of Fiume on the Adriatic, which they feared would be awarded by the Allies to the new Yugoslav state. The government in Rome did not approve but feared the repercussions of ejecting him. Mussolini and his early adherents could observe that grassroots nationalist activism, resentment at local labor militancy, and the weakness of Rome's policing power in the provinces gave him an opportunity to implant fascism on the basis of local "squads" that would shatter the local unions and socialist party administrations. The emerging fascist movement thus won key support from the agrarian elites of the agriculturally rich Po Valley during 1920–1922, as their local black-shirted "squads" drove into towns to beat up local labor organizers and devastate the union or party headquarters. The militias went from trashing union halls to invading city halls, compelling the cabinets in Rome—divided on whether to exploit fascist violence against the Left or to attempt to reimpose law and order—to suspend socialist town councils and appoint commissioners. By 1921 Mussolini had created enough of a force to reorganize his movement as the National Fascist Party and claim a place alongside the amorphous liberal groups in the electoral coalition of 1921, winning thirty-five seats in the new Chamber of Deputies (the lower and decision-making house of the parliament ever since 1848). By the autumn of 1922 he seemed the indispensable partner for the more conservative groupings of the loose coalition that still described itself as "liberal," and he was threatening to extend to the south of Italy the same quasi-insurrectionary movement his lieutenants had installed in the north.

Mussolini and his sympathizers exploited a final liberal coalition crisis by preparations for a march on Rome by his black-shirted columns when the king called him to be prime minister at the end of October 1922. For two years he governed supposedly as a legal prime minister, and held elections in April 1924 under a revised voting law that guaranteed his supporters almost two-thirds of the Chamber. But the habits of revolutionary violence among his youthful troops were not easily disciplined, and the younger radicals in his ranks feared he might become just another party leader. Despite the coalition's majority, the old parties and parliamentary deputies that had supported him threatened to desert after close lieutenants were implicated in the kidnapping and beating to death of an opposition socialist leader, Giacomo Matteotti, who had denounced campaign violence. As the liberal politicians and journalists chided him, while his young radical supporters urged a "second revolution," Mussolini decided that he would have to choose between his party base and political defeat. In early 1925 he imposed emergency legislation to control the press and arrest opposition leaders. The twilight liberalism of 1922 to 1924 was ended.

Over the next few years the regime leaders installed the institutions of a fascist state: a political tribunal, extensive secret police spying and eventually arrest of the opposition, and a Grand Council of Fascism that combined Fascist Party officials and cabinet ministers in a supposed fusion of the state with the single party. The new institutions reflected the contribution of Alfredo Rocco, who had come from the far-right Nationalist Party that had emphasized turn-of-the-century functional legal theory, and would in the mid-1920s design the political tribunal and press for an unchallenged state.

What observers often identified as the distinctive contribution of the Fascist state (aside from its alleged fusion with a single party) was the replacement of parliamentary by functional or occupational representation. This took place by stages from the mid-1920s to the mid-thirties. Although socialist and Catholic trade unions were marginalized, there was a tradition of fascist unions (called syndicates, as unions were in French, too), who did occasionally stand up to employers. Their leaders had emerged from the prewar syndicalist movement and had been active in organizing Italian dockworkers, and had sometimes even migrated to the American West as labor organizers, before returning with the war and becoming enthusiasts of Mussolini. A major strike of northern steelworkers in the spring of 1925 proved their last quasi-independent labor action under the Fascist regime. The strike was ended; the labor representatives were centralized into a single official Fascist union federation whose official status was to be recognized by the employers grouped in the Italian Confederation of Industry—now reorganized themselves as the Fascist Confederation of Industry. When the new Fascist labor federation appeared to claim too much influence, it was split again three years later into various occupational groups. Meanwhile, representatives of the different industrial sectors and the service, medical, hospitality, agricultural, and other divisions of the economy were organized into official syndicates to be grouped by the 1930s into a network of corporations.

But in many ways the Fascist state represented continuity with the older liberal institutions. Mussolini's title remained "Head of Government" (prime minister), even though unofficially he became known as "Il Duce," or the leader. The king remained the head of state and finally exercised his prerogative to dismiss Mussolini as the wager on joining Hitler in the second war threatened disastrous invasion by the Allies in the summer of 1943. To enhance his own domestic position at the end of the 1920s, Mussolini actually retreated from the secular claims of the Italian liberal state and signed the 1929 Lateran Pact with the Vatican, which restored Church control over marriage, installed crucifixes in schoolrooms, and recognized the sovereign ministate of the Vatican. By the 1930s, Mussolini could take pride in having achieved a certain "consensus" at home. Political adversaries went into exile or, if arrested at home, were punished largely by being sent into forced residence in remote southern villages *(confino)*. There were only a handful of executions, largely imposed for assassination efforts. Most of the violence—beatings, some fatal, castor oil, the devastation of Socialist and trade-union offices—took place in unofficial clashes on the road to power. Franco's military dictatorship after seizing power, later the Argentine generals and General Pinochet in Chile, would accumulate far more corpses, with arrests and illegal torture and murder in the tens of thousands.

But those were presented as emergency interventions. Fascists claimed that their mission was not just to defeat communists, but to rule as the stewards for an entire historical epoch: the Nazis talked of a thousand-year Reich. Fascism would somehow fulfill man in a way the program of liberal individualism and party pluralism never could. Fascism, so Rocco agued, was rectifying the terrible wrong turn that history had taken in 1789 when the French Revolution had enshrined the rights of man and the citizen. But it did not claim to reject democracy in the name just of tradition and monarchy, as, for instance, such rightist authoritarian groups as Action Française did in France. It was not merely reactionary: it was designed to institute a new historical stage that Mussolini—borrowing a term from his detractors of the early 1920s—made into a particular merit: it aspired to be "totalitarian." Fascist doctrine had evolved significantly since Mussolini's demand for revolutionary renewal in 1919: now fascism was presented as a regime that reestablished a state that transcended individual or even group interests. How does the fascist state differ from the liberal state, Rocco asked rhetorically: "The fascist state is the state that realizes to the maximum the power and cohesion of the juridical organization of society. And society, according to the fascist concept, is not just a sum of individuals but an organism that has its own life and ends that transcend those of the individuals and its own spiritual and historical value. The state too . . . is an organism distinct from the citizens who compose it at any moment: it has its own life and its own ends superior to those of individuals and to which ends must be subordinated." As Mussolini put it in his contribution to the authoritative Treccani Encyclopedia in 1932: "for the fascist everything is in the state and nothing human or spiritual exists—even less so, can have value—outside the state."[159] Men and women fulfilled their potential, not as individuals with inalienable rights, but as members of a nation and subjects of a state with obligations and duties, among which was military virtue. Politics was a form of war, but designed to prepare for war: better a day as a lion than a year as a jackal. Mussolini thought periodically to posture as a man of peace, but the ideology was connected with military virtues. He resorted to force over the Dodecanese Islands with Greece, and in 1935–1936 provoked a war with Abyssinia, using air power and poison gas. He muscled in on Albania in 1937 and after casting his lot in with Hitler declared war on France in 1940, occupying Nice.

In practice the state was far from totalitarian in the sense of unremitting control through terror that later critics suggested was essential. The Church continued as a sanctioned presence although the Party sought to undermine its youth organization, Catholic Action. The family was glorified and the Party encouraged child bearing for the Duce, but the family was also a node of resistance to state claims. Later apologists ridiculed the pretenses of the leader and his regime, in effect presenting the experience as a form of *opera buffa,* distasteful but hardly to be taken seriously. Such a view, however, underestimates its novelty, its brutality on the path to power, its determination to silence those who did not agree. Like the glorious baroque edifices of Rome, façade was crucial to fascist politics—but like them, too, there was an authenticity to its grandiose style.[160]

The Italian model was influential and would be imitated. In 1923 the Spanish monarch installed General Miguel Primo de Rivera as a dictator, calling him "my Mussolini," but this was in the tradition of nineteenth-century strongmen—there was no ideological ambition. In Argentina the military took over in 1930, and its army strongman, General José Félix Uriburu, came close to asserting the fascist claims of transcendent leadership and encouraging a nationalist and authoritarian movement.[161] More durably, the Brazilian civilian political leader Getúlio Vargas seized power in the same year in Brazil, created a "New State" with authoritarian corporatist institutions, until ousted in 1945 as fascism seemed to crumble the world over, but was then elected president in 1950, governed as a nationalist dictator until 1954, when, faced with impending overthrow, he took his own life. António de Oliveira Salazar became prime minister in the Portuguese military dictatorship that had seized power from the republic in 1926 and instituted his "New State" from 1933 until 1968, administering a Catholic authoritarian corporatism, tenaciously holding Portugal's colonies, and becoming a NATO ally.

The variant of fascism that came to power in Germany was different in key respects. Hitler understood the sort of power Mussolini was striving for, and like him adopted the paramilitary uniform—the boots, the colored shirts—and the paramilitary organization. He learned from his unsuccessful "Beer Hall Putsch" in 1923 that no matter how divided the Weimar Republic might be, if the army stood behind the enforcement of the law, he could not seize power by force. During the years of economic and political stabilization from 1924 through 1929, his movement seemed destined to wither away, but the economic difficulties of the Protestant countryside (and the demagogic campaign at the end of the 1920s against a revised reparations plan) started raising his local voting totals even before the world depression struck in 1929 and 1930. Like Mussolini he railed against the system, pouring scorn on the divisions among parties that led to unwieldy policy compromises over welfare or foreign and military policy. Proportional representation meant that the postwar Italian Chamber and the Weimar Republic's Reichstag were afflicted with party fragments that found it hard to coalesce into stable majorities and oppositions. When the world depression began to take its toll on employment after 1930 and no majority could be found to finance unemployment insurance, the president and chancellor had to resort to constitutionally sanctioned decree provisions (under the fateful Article 48 of the Weimar Constitution) for passing the budget. Under such conditions Communists on the left and Hitler's National Socialists on the right (though that term hardly conveyed their radicalism) could rail against "the system." They could always denounce the reparations payments imposed after the Versailles Treaty, and even the mitigation of obligations embodied in the Dawes Plan of 1924 and the Young Plan of 1930. They could claim that the postwar Eastern borders (and the Polish Corridor that separated East Prussia from the rest of Germany) had to be rectified. And differing fundamentally from the Italian Fascists (until 1938), Nazis could excoriate the Jews as a racial minority responsible for these evils and fundamentally hostile to German interests. Although some Nazi adherents and propagandists found enough to attack without specific reference to Germany's Jewish misfortune, anti-Semitism remained a core element of the movement just as it had infected much of the other parties' discourse as well—it was the political lingua franca of the right in Central and Eastern Europe. Jews supposedly controlled banks and journalism, infiltrated the university and the-ater, exploited the peasantry, and ultimately defiled the blood of the gentile women they took to bed.

After two years of parliamentary paralysis and elections in 1930, July 1932, and November 1932, which saw the Nazi parliamentary delegation rise to almost 40 percent of the Reichstag (and brought them to coalitions in some key state governments), the political system of the Weimar Republic fell apart. Rival chancellor candidates torpedoed each other and called in army generals to claim that the country might become indefensible. The paramilitary party militias fought in weekend city brawls, suggesting that civil war might threaten at home. The coterie around the aging president Field Marshall von Hindenburg suggested that only Hitler's appointment might provide stability and that in power he would be controlled by traditional conservative circles from the economy and the military. They underestimated his skill and dynamic populism. Hitler moved far quicker than Mussolini had, although he benefited from the fascist model. Appointed as chancellor of a right-wing coalition on January 30, 1933, he dissolved the Reichstag and called new elections, which would yield the National Socialists 43 percent (but not a majority) of the votes after a month of charged political events. The party used the successful arson attack against the Reichstag building in late February (blamed on the Communists by the Nazis, then attributed to a Nazi provocation by the left outside Germany, but probably the work of a Dutch anarchist) as a pretext to arrest the Communist deputies and clamp down on the press. What Hitler sought was a constitution-amending majority of two-thirds of the parliament for a grant of decree power, tempered only by the proviso that the Reichstag would in theory remain free to reassert its role. Formally the Weimar Constitution remained in place; but this new Enabling Act served in effect as a charter for expanding domination. Having removed the Communist delegation, he came to an agreement with the Catholic Center and the Vatican. In return for a Concordat with Berlin, guaranteeing the Church's religious presence, the Center Party abstained on the decisive vote, leaving only the Social Democrats in opposition and securing the needed two-thirds majority.

In the same crowded weeks the regime set up its first two concentration camps outside Munich and Berlin—Dachau and Oranienburg—to hold political prisoners (not yet Jews as such) without formal trial. Storm troopers led a boycott of Jewish stores. Over the next months the government would announce control over the press, "reform" the civil service by removing Jews from government employment and teaching positions, press the political parties to dissolve themselves—the SPD executive went into exile—replace elected state legislatures with appointed commissioners, and announce the so-called fusion of party and state. This achieved, Hitler, like Mussolini in the late 1920s, actually tended to subordinate Party autonomy. The hopes of Nazi radicals to push through a second revolution based on the SA—an aspiration the professional army viewed with contempt and alarm—was cut short on June 30, 1934, when the SA leadership, a few Nazi dissidents, and several earlier political leaders were summarily executed. The army returned the favor in August when Federal president Hindenburg died and Hitler won army approval to combine the offices of head of state and head of government with the titles *Führer* and *Reichskanzler,* an accumulation of powers that Mussolini never achieved. Soldiers henceforth were to swear an oath of personal loyalty to Adolf Hitler.[162]

The process of consolidating hitherto unheard-of power against a background of racial demagogy punctuated by violence and the abrogation of civil liberties apparently made the regime more and more popular. Hitler walked out of the stalled disarmament talks in Geneva in late 1933 and held a plebiscite to approve his decision and overall course, and won the first of his staggering votes of approval—of over 90 percent. Unemployment dropped and businessmen invested again, knowing that they faced no real opposition from the official German Labor Front. In 1935 the Saarland voted to rejoin Germany after fifteen years of enforced separation; in the same year Hitler abrogated the military clauses of the Versailles Treaty, announced the resumption of conscription and a German air force, and in March 1936 moved troops into the demilitarized zones bordering and west of the Rhine River, all moves that destroyed the clauses of the 1919 peace treaty designed to provide Germany's neighbors with military security. In 1938 he could triumphantly annex his native Austria after its precarious republic, as we shall see, had eliminated its own democratic institutions. By legislation announced at the Nuremberg rally in 1935, Jews had been defined as a separate group within the Reich—subjects still of a German state that humiliated and harassed them, but not citizens of the German Reich. Persecution was intensified in 1938 with the pogroms and confiscations of Reich Crystal Night, as Nazi policies radicalized in general. After annexing Austria, then convincing the British and French governments to browbeat Czechoslovakia to cede its German-populated Sudetenland rim, awarded at the Munich conference in October 1938, thereafter annexing the western Czech lands of Bohemia and Moravia in March 1939, and finally securing the neutrality of the Soviet Union in August, Hitler invaded Poland on September 1, 1939. By this time even Neville Chamberlain's government decided that he must be opposed and together with France responded with a declaration of war. Not, however, before Hitler had ominously announced at the beginning of 1939 that if war came, it would be the fault of the Jews and must lead to their destruction. Britain and France, however, had no effective concept for mounting an offensive against the Germans in Eastern or Western Europe and instead met disastrous defeat when German forces struck in Scandinavia, the Low Countries, and France by mid-1940.

Hitler's government was recognizably fascist with its uniformed Party supposedly fused with state offices, the paramilitary paraphernalia, the even more ruthless and rapid silencing of any legal opposition, the abolition of formally independent labor organizations—although, as in Italy, the government unions occasionally tried to stand up against employers. Organizationally it was a confusing regime; Hitler did not like clear lines of authority, and different organizations competed for his favor. The long-standing cabinet ministries continued and pursued the activities of the German bureaucracy. However, police functions that normally were tucked into the state governments were soon accumulated with confusing overlapping jurisdiction into the Prussian secret political police (Geheime Staatspolizei, or Gestapo) headed by Hermann Goering in his capacity as head of the Prussian government, then folded into the Federal Security Main Office (Reichssicherheitshauptamt), which became the commanding agency for the new Security Services, or SS, that came under the command of Heinrich Himmler, seconded by Reinhard Heydrich. In turn the SS would eventually dissolve into three divisions—the secret police, the military units that fought in the field during the war, and the units that ran greater Germany's concentration camps and the new extermination centers sited in formerly Polish territory (Chełmno, the first, constructed in late 1941, then Bełżec, Treblinka, Sobibór,

Dictatorship and adulation: Adolf Hitler thronged by admirers at a 1938 rally. At this moment, when the National Socialist leader was probably at the zenith of his charismatic popularity, Germans were enjoying a rearmament boom, had remilitarized the Rhineland, had annexed Austria, and were about to wrest the Sudetenland from Czechoslovakia. Adulation went with absolute power: tens of thousands of those who expressed their opposition were already in brutal concentration camps; German Jews were being systematically degraded and expropriated. (Private Collection / Peter Newark Military Pictures / The Bridgeman Art Library)

Majdanek, and Auschwitz, enlarged from an IG Farben labor camp by an extermination facility at adjacent Birkenau). Several million Soviet prisoners of war, opponents from the European resistance movements, Roma and Sinti, homosexuals, and millions of Jews who were systematically rounded up from Western Europe, the Mediterranean lands, occupied Poland, and Hungary, would be expropriated, abused, and murdered.

Hitler removed the long-term career diplomat Konstantin von Neurath as foreign minister to replace him with a compliant Nazi, Joachim von Ribbentrop, in 1938, and the once elitist agency effectively enlisted in the service of Nazi objectives, whether preparing to liquidate the states of Central Europe or later to facilitate the deportation of Jews. Hitler removed the top army officers under the pretext of a trumped-up homosexual scandal, installed a far more compliant commander in chief, and made himself the effective minister of defense. In 1936 he overruled the economics minister, Hjalmar Schacht, who insisted on the financial limits to rearmament, and appointed a Four Year Plan office to rearm the country within four years. Hermann Goering became commissioner for the Four Year Plan, adding it to his functions as minister for the new Luftwaffe. As part of the armament effort, he established a special agency called simply Organization Todt after its director, Fritz Todt, which took on increasingly more power in the war and, after Todt died in a plane crash, was taken over by the ambitious architect Albert Speer, who effectively became economic tsar after 1942. The war also meant the growth of a huge directorate for the six to eight million foreign workers, either recruited or forcibly moved to work in German factories. And throughout, the Ministry of Public Enlightenment, or propaganda, headed by Joseph Goebbels, extended its influence over the organization of the media and the world of art and music.

Of course, these offices headed by ambitious men who had no compunctions about the conscription of millions of foreigners and the despoliation and eventual murder of Jews, were bound to clash. Goebbels and Goering, and later Goering, Goebbels, Party head Martin Bormann, and Speer, eyed each other's authority warily. Hitler tried to avoid coming down definitively on one side or another; he left few unambiguous directives; he knew that the zealous satraps would anticipate his general intentions. Ultimate power was compatible with

Major concentration and extermination camps in Germany and German-occupied territory during World War II. The principal death camps appear in italics.

quasi-anarchic administrative practice. This paradox has led some historians to judge him as a "weak dictator"; but the term doesn't do justice to what was stake. The dictatorship could be unsystematic; it allowed vast amounts of personal influence to accumulate under officials and it also allowed interstices where intellectual and religious and artistic life could continue somewhat undisturbed unless opponents felt compelled to make a public fuss. Given, for instance, the long-standing German cultural achievements in the musical sphere, control of musical programs and commentary was naturally a potentially important arena for patronage and generating ideology; but after a while the government essentially

A last stand for fascism: Anti-aircraft tracer shells illuminating the night sky above Algiers during a German air raid in the winter of 1943. Algeria as a possession of Vichy France had fallen to Anglo-American and Free French troops in the first major Allied landing against the Axis in November 1942; German and Italian troops remained in waning control of Libya and Tunisia to the east until the spring of 1943. (National Archives, photo no. 111-SC-182285)

gave up higher ambitions and focused on providing "entertainment" music. Goebbels condemned jazz as "Nigger Music," but underground bars continued to play it and semi-alienated youth danced to swing.[163]

· · ·

The paradox of strong overriding goals and administrative sloppiness was not confined to Germany or to fascist dictatorships. The American New Deal revealed a similar rivalry of powerful figures ensconced in different and often rival agencies: some created early on as the National Recovery Administration (NRA), the Works Progress Administration (WPA), the Public Works Administration (PWA), and so on, known collectively as "Alphabet Soup." Faced with powerfully defended policy alternatives, Franklin Roosevelt, like Hitler, preferred to put off clear decisions in favor of trying to compromise administrative decision. The point is that the Great Depression and then the world war (including the rearmament efforts that led up it), which presented large and powerful states with immense new challenges, met with ad hoc policy responses. Franklin Roosevelt, the outstanding democratic world leader of this challenging era, usually buoyant and generous in spirit, and Adolf Hitler, with his warped agenda of conquest and elimination, were motivated by totally different spirits, but their administrative responses to difficult government agendas had some similarities.

German state officials and those in the private sector seeking influence had to become Nazi Party members, as in Italy they had to join the Fascist Party. But alongside the various state agencies were those of the Nazi Party—its powerful Secretariat and its regional administrative officers of Gauleiter. In both Germany and Italy the Party waxed and waned in influence. The fusion of party and state was a slogan for both regimes, but Mussolini and Hitler soon sought to deprive the respective parties of real influence and make them instead into effective transmission belts of the authority they established. Neither leader was prepared to tolerate a "second revolution" that would have displaced the army for the party militia. Still, there were many parallel offices, and when Germany got deeper into a war whose demands it had not totally calculated, the government relied more on the Party Gauleiter and officials to organize welfare and civil defense functions. As Secretary of the Party Bormann thus became an influential figure. Preparation for war and wartime itself only increased the welter of organizations.

Although the Nazis learned from the Italians, and deep into the war Hitler retained a certain respect for Mussolini as a sort of ideological godfather, significant differences, too, separated the two fascisms—and not only the central anti-Jewish fixation in the German regime. In contrast to Italian fascist ideology, which exalted the state's absolute authority and an implacable legal order, Hitler's lawyers stressed the personal arbitrary power of the Führer as the expression of the *Volksgemeinschaft* or national, even racial, community and attributed to so-called Führer decrees, even casual ones, supreme legal authority. Let us call it a theory of legal "vitalism," an effort to attribute the most arbitrary authority to a living leader who personified the will of the national community, not to be fixed within the boundaries of any independent legal framework.

The most notable German thinker whose ideas helped prepare for such a theory (although he never would have formally elaborated it) was Carl Schmitt, mentioned earlier in discussion of the nature of sovereign decision. Schmitt (alas) was a powerful legal mind. He had made his reputation in the controversies over the nature of law, parliamentarism, and democracy early in the Weimar Republic, arguing among other points that what constituted the realm of politics, including democratic politics, was the existential opposition of an enemy. Schmitt was sophisticated, persuasive, steeped in the classics and in the tradition of the fierce Catholic authoritarians of the nineteenth century—Joseph de Maistre, Louis de Bonald, and Juan Donoso Cortés, who believed that the revolution of 1789 was fallen mankind's recapitulation of Satan's rebellion against God. He was hopeful of being taken up by the Nazis as their official thinker, but ultimately was too intellectually arrogant to make headway in their crude infighting. The political unit he believed fundamental was not the state, which so many German conservatives and Italian fascists emphasized, but the political community— once the polis, now the nation—that coalesced in opposition to its adversaries. Politics thus was about us versus them, friends versus foes. True democracy was not the same as the endless discussion that parliamentary liberalism praised, but the regime that followed from the fundamental identity of a people. In fact, he argued, parliaments no longer served even as arenas for free and rational discussion, as earlier British liberalism had postulated, but only for the representation of concrete interests already determined before discussion began.[164] Weimar constitutionalism was a defective mixture of liberal and democratic elements, a diagnosis he believed was confirmed by the paralysis of the Weimar parliament in the early 1930s, when he called for a democratic dictator.

Such views of course set Schmitt against the liberal theorists who believed that the essence of law had to lie in its general applicability, its underlying rationality and values. But Schmitt also rejected the German school of legal positivism, which said that the power to impose a law replaced any discussion of inherent normative legitimacy. He implied further that those ideas of international law based on universal values and treaties were utopian. As it was becoming clear under Allied bombs that the Third Reich was doomed and his ideas would be discredited, he turned to argue in his astringent way that international law was a doctrine Europeans had devised to keep themselves from quarreling as they appropriated the territories of the non-European world. This sort of international doctrine, he claimed, was realistic; it presumed a geopolitics of large but finite territorial empires and thus justified Nazi *Grossraumpolitik*. At the same time, however, it likewise ruled out America's Wilsonian claims of supposedly universal values as well as the former British commitment to market liberalism, both claims to global ambitions that he felt were far more nakedly imperialist in scope than Germany's claims in Europe.[165]

. . .

It was dismaying but hardly remarkable that fascism seemed to have a privileged insight into the future as the Great Depression became longer and more devastating, and as the framework of the Versailles Treaty was abandoned piece by piece. Above all in Central and East Central Europe, where the French and the British no longer seemed set on helping the smaller countries, themselves sometimes obsessed with nationalist issues, to remain independent of their large authoritarian neighbors.[166] Austria, the German-speaking remnant of the Habsburg empire (leaving aside the Germans of the Bohemian Sudetenland), was ideologically divided between the Socialists, largely entrenched in Vienna and industrial upper Austria, and the deeply Catholic and conservative rural population organized by the Christian-Social Party. By the end of the 1920s, a quasi-fascist "Fatherland Front" emerged as a political contender, and contending party militias clashed in the streets. In response to the Fatherland Front, the older Christian Socials sought to retain hegemony on the right by transforming the parliament into a fascist-like chamber of corporations. The Socialists feared that the Austrian Right was prepared to liquidate the remnants of liberalism and unadvisedly began their own revolt in February 1934, only to be forcibly suppressed and jailed if they did not scurry into exile in Prague. For the next four years, the Christian Socials sought to run an authoritarian state that Mussolini could patronize. Impatient Austrian Nazi admirers of Hitler attempted to seize power in a coup in July 1934 and assassinated the chancellor. They failed in their effort—in part because Mussolini made it clear that he was not ready to countenance an enlarged Germany on his Alpine border. Over the next four years, however, semi-independent and semifascist Austria lost his protection. In 1936, angered by the West's opposition to his invasion of Ethiopia, the Italian dictator decided to become a German partner in the so-called Axis, a move that let Hitler gradually put more and more pressure on Vienna until outright annexation or Anschluss in March 1938.

Meanwhile, the Polish military transformed their republic into a military regime step by step; dictators took power in the Baltic States. Hungary, which had been governed as an authoritarian state but with continuing parliament and some degree of open debate since the counterrevolution of 1919, vacillated between the fans of England or France, who hoped to keep a semi-open government of discussion (so long as the establishment was not seriously threatened) and the outright admirers of Hitler's Germany. The king of Greece placed dictatorial power in the hands of General Ioannis Metaxas in 1936. Czechoslovakia remained a parliamentary regime under the venerated Tomáš Masaryk, but after his death the internal stresses made its crises difficult, and the three million Germans in the Sudeten mountain rimland increasingly fell under the demagogic leadership of a pro-Nazi politician who presented their conditions as supposedly intolerable. By 1938 Hitler was determined to destroy the Czech republic, and the crisis he and the Sudeten Germans inflamed persuaded the English Tories, as mentioned above, that the only solution was to cede the geographic region to Germany.

The Spanish Republic that had been instituted on the wave of antimonarchical municipal elections of 1931 became increasingly polarized. Its conservative forces who governed from 1934 to 1936 sought to roll back the measures for secularizing education and regional autonomy that the left had enacted from 1931 to 1933. An ill-conceived socialist uprising (a strategic miscalculation parallel to the 1934 uprising in Vienna a half year earlier) brought right-wing suppression, which in turn prompted the organization of a Popular Front, which now included Communist alongside Socialist and left-liberal parliamentary candidates, in both France and Spain. Blessed by Moscow, but against a backdrop of growing street clashes, the Popular Front won elections in Spain and then France (and in Chile in 1938) on a broad platform of opposition to fascism and advocacy of pro-labor reforms. Spain in particular descended into a period of conflict and what seemed to conservatives and Church authorities to be intolerable violence, and a military uprising, coordinated for July 1936, managed to seize the garrisons in about half the country. The resulting full-scale civil war became the emblematic ideological clash of the decade, drawing in Soviet-supported International Brigades and major Italian and German military aid on the Republican and insurgent Nationalist sides, respectively. After two and a half years of fighting, the authoritarian coalition of monarchists, military, and fascists, organized by General Franco's Falange, prevailed. Tens of thousands of the left went into exile; and even more faced prison and firing squads. To be sure, democracy was maintained in Britain, France, Scandinavia, and the Low Countries. But increasingly it looked as if the vital political forces of the epoch were those that spoke for disciplined collectives, that praised or practiced war, and that had no compunction about locking up or even murdering dissenters.

· · ·

The fact that on the other side of the globe Japanese armed forces had delivered the first major blow to the League-supervised order of collective security in September 1931 made the rise of nationalist authoritarianism all the more menacing. For the Japanese military, their bases on the Liaodong Peninsula in Guangdong Province seemed the key to controlling Manchuria, which in turn seemed essential to safeguard their Korean colony and keep Soviet Russia at bay and China deferential. All the more urgency, they reasoned, for their local army units to expand their beachhead on the Manchurian mainland, especially with Chiang's growing assertion of control in the north of historic China. Careful planning led to a staged bomb attack on the South Manchurian Railway the Japanese administered and a decisive response: the military occupation of southern Manchuria. The Manchurian "incident," quickly endorsed by the minister of war in Tokyo, was equally an attack on the forces of moderation in Japan, and the cabinet accepted the fait accompli. Those parties and leaders who had been willing to build a cooperative international order in the twenties, including moderate ministers drawn from the military, lost influence and occasionally their lives to impatient military radicals. Over the course of 1932, a cowed Tokyo cabinet decided to reorganize Manchuria as the supposedly sovereign state of Manchukuo and install the last Manchu emperor, Pu Yi, as its "puppet" sovereign. League condemnation led Tokyo to withdraw from the organization in March 1933, about nine months before Berlin followed suit, allegedly over dissatisfaction with Franco-British refusal at the League's Disarmament Conference to reduce their armed forces to parity with the German military.

Whether Japan in the 1930s became a fascist regime or not has been repeatedly debated. Perhaps it was not, in a formal canonic sense, if the criteria require a fascist party that will take over and transform a state, but its rulers gradually imposed a very coercive militarized regime that glorified emperor and state and conquest. At home in Japan, military influence tightened over the government: the brief interlude where parliamentary politics remained active, known as Taishō Democracy (named after the reign of the Taishō emperor from 1912 to 1926) withered with the onset of the world depression. Younger officers, drawn from rural areas that were suffering agricultural poverty, and hard-line expansionists criticized decadent bourgeois liberalism and the lively urban culture and political debate of the twenties, much as did the Nazis in Germany. The nationalists aspired to a "Shōwa restoration," where power and property would be taken from the politicians and corrupt capitalists and would supposedly be restored to the new young Shōwa emperor, Hirohito. Attempted coups d'état by radical nationalist officers (known by their dates: 5-15 in 1932, and 2-26 in 1936), marked by the assassination of politicians, pushed divided cabinets ever further toward nationalist and authoritarian policies. Even though putschists (and the inspirational ideologue Kita Ikki) were executed, moderates were cowed into silence or imprisoned. The main political parties were dissolved while the rulers organized a supportive national movement, if not a formal party; the Imperial Rule Assistance Association trained youth in the military virtues (which came to include merciless treatment of enemies), elevated the state Shintō national religion that glorified the emperor, and claimed an Asian racial superiority. The new governments seemed divided by the 1930s between those suave nationalists, preeminently Prince Konoe Fumimaro, who felt it prudent to expand into Asia gradually so as not to arouse the British and Americans, and those military leaders who were convinced that a larger war with the Westerners and with the resurgent Chinese Republic was just a matter of time. Among the latter, General Ishiwara Kanji, instrumental in planning the Manchurian incident, envisioned wider and wider warfare, while Tōjō Hideki would emerge as a political leader and serve as the premier who would preside over Japan's fateful enlargement of East Asian hostilities against Britain and the United States in December 1941.[167]

That step, however, culminated the self-fulfilling logic of continued aggression to safeguard the expansion already undertaken: war necessitated by war. Concerned with Chiang's efforts to modernize a Chinese republic that drew on some similar national convictions, the Japanese launched an invasion of the

Flawed bravado? Chiang Kai-shek addressing a rally in Hankou in 1938. The generalissimo, heir to Sun Yat-sen's nationalist party, the Guomindang (GMD), used radio, the decisive medium for political leaders of the 1930s, an era of mass politics. China's authoritarian Nationalist government tried to wage a desperate war against the full-scale Japanese invasion that had escalated the year before. (Getty Images)

historic Chinese provinces in 1937. By 1940, deeply engaged in China, Tokyo announced adhesion to the Rome–Berlin Axis and later to the German–Italian Pact of Steel, and awaited the outcome of the war in Europe to resolve whether, as some military planners wished, to march north from Manchuria against the Soviet Union or, as the ultimately prevailing strategy envisioned, to strike south at the European colonial dominions of Southeast Asia. Moscow's free hand obtained by its Nonaggression Pact with Hitler, as well as the evident strength of Soviet armed forces demonstrated by some major border skirmishes with Japan, and the weakness of the resource-rich Dutch and French colonial possessions (whose governments had been decisively defeated in Europe in spring 1940), made the "southern way" all the more beckoning. American insistence that

Japan pull back, not only from the bases pried from the French in Vietnam but from China itself, seemed to compel a fundamental choice between humiliation or readiness for wider war. The fact that the Dutch East Indies promised the oil required by its military once the United States effectively embargoed American exports to Japan made the option of widening the war again seem compelling. Unfortunately for Tokyo, expansion south entailed preemptive strikes against British and American bases—once again war necessitated by war. From the vantage of the early 1940s, China presented Japanese leaders with a dilemma similar to that which the Soviet Union posed for Hitler, even though China lacked Russia's tremendous offensive capacity. Still, it was a vast society whose domination the Japanese believed the prerequisite for continental leadership, but whose resilience drew them into far more costly efforts than foreseen and ultimately drew in an overseas adversary with far greater resources than their own.

As of the mid-1930s, trends were already sufficiently ominous to make either defeat at the hands of fascism or resistance alongside the communists the terrible choice for many intellectuals. American democracy seemed too remote, unconcerned with the wider world, and was itself suffering from mass unemployment. Fortunately the mass of Western public opinion resisted such apocalyptic thinking, clinging perhaps too long to hopes of muddling through, indulging in what the poet W. H. Auden would call the hopes of a "low, dishonest decade," but committed understandably enough to states that resisted the total politicization of private life and sometimes even dared to experiment with progressive social legislation. The Soviet Union claimed to be on the opposing side of the spectrum from fascism but developed a control of society that was fully as pervasive and repressive, and was probably the most thoroughly penetrating of all the dictatorships. The novelist André Gide, a left sympathizer, went to Russia in 1936 and wrote that nowhere else in the world was thought and liberty more controlled— not even in Nazi Germany. George Orwell came to understand the Stalinist pervasive concern for ruthless control of the left in the Spanish Civil War.[168] Nonetheless, Western communists and their supporters could still argue (as would Jean-Paul Sartre after the war) that the Soviet Union embodied the hopes and aspirations of the world proletariat and had to be supported. The Soviet Union was also a declared dictatorship (which supposedly, according to its 1936 constitution, was a perfect democracy).

World War II in Asia: Japanese tanks, still light and primitive, advancing rapidly as Japan invades southward from its Manchurian colony into China proper during 1937 and 1938. World War II began in Asia; by the time it started in Europe, Japan controlled a broad coastal strip of China, while the Chinese Nationalists settled down in Chongqing in the upper Yangzi Valley and the Communist forces in their stronghold in northwest Yan'an. The populations trapped between the two armies increasingly suffered famine, inflation, and disease. (© SZ Photo / The Bridgeman Art Library)

Even more completely than in Italy and Germany, the agencies of the Russian state were subjected to the party acting frankly as a dictatorship of (or at least on behalf of) the proletariat. Until the reforms of Mikhail Gorbachev in the 1980s, the Russian leader served as first secretary of the Communist Party of the Soviet Union (CPSU). As was the case in Italy and Germany, the dictator himself accumulated tremendous personal authority, but Stalin would never have dared to delegate party leadership to another comrade, whereas Mussolini and Hitler both did. The German and Italian state apparatuses retained some autonomy and tradition; after the civil war and the 1920s, when the Party still recruited older officials willing to serve the Bolshevik regime, this was harder in Russia. Party officials would serve alongside commanding officers in the army during World War II, sometimes resented and subject to execution if captured. The potential rivals to the First Secretary were also party positions—for a while in the 1920s the leadership of the Communist International, which rivaled the People's Commissariat for Foreign Affairs, and increasingly the leadership of the successive political police agencies. The presidency of the Soviet Union was more of a ceremonial position. No state parliamentary organ as such remained; in theory the constituent assembly and Duma had belonged to a bourgeois state that had been displaced. The Party Congress, the smaller Central Committee, and the ruling Politburo remained the legislative organs. The Party Congress, supposedly the supreme organ although really designed to acclaim the decisions of Politburo and Central Committee, was chosen by election among Party members. It seems paradoxical, but communist states always devoted great attention to noncompetitive elections; for they served not to choose among alternative personalities or policies, but to mobilize and reinvigorate the faithful.

Historians used to separate the Leninist period (1917–1923) and the subsequent years of changing rival "triumvirates" (1924–1929) from the arbitrary and terroristic rule under Stalin, who managed to secure his own undivided control by 1930–1931. But although Stalin's mind was filled with dark conspiracies and the apparatus of state terror did reach unprecedented heights in the mid- to late 1930s, the authoritarian potential of the state manifested itself early on. Nonetheless, the early period of the regime existed under conditions of civil war and the hostility of Britain, France, and the United States. Sympathetic observers could interpret Lenin's regime as the state of "exception" that the theorist Carl

Schmitt had defined as the crucible of sovereignty. By the time Lenin died, after prolonged disabling by a stroke, the "white" or counterrevolutionary armies, supported by the Western states, had been defeated, and the government had backed away from the ruinous economic collectivism they imposed under conditions of civil war and had introduced the New Economic Policy or NEP (a partial restoration of market conditions and foreign investment). Briefly through the late 1920s, Moscow and Petrograd were home to experimental theater and futurist art, which attracted Western intellectuals, all the more so as the world economic crisis tightened its hold on the capitalist world as the thirties began.

But such an equilibrium, which might have left the Soviet Union, like Mexico, to stabilize its broad upheaval under a "big tent" one-party regime that held on to positions of power but without operating a police dictatorship, did not come to pass. There were historical, personal, and societal reasons. The rivalry bequeathed by a disabled Lenin meant that venomous rivalries developed above all between Trotsky and Stalin. Trotsky was of Jewish background, traveled, a theorist of revolution. Stalin was indigenous, a gifted in-fighter with intellectual ambitions, who saw his comrades as rivals and potential conspirators. From the end of the 1920s he accumulated power that transcended even the institutional supremacy that leadership of the party (and thereby also the state) should have bestowed. He was feared and adored. All the totalitarian leaders exercised a strong component of personalist rule—Hitler and Mussolini felt it necessary to communicate directly; Stalin less so—he was remote but watchful like some vigilant patriarchal deity.

There were differences rooted in institutions as well. Of all the authoritarian states—not counting the Chinese Republican regime—Russia had had the shortest experience with representative institutions. Italy had had a parliamentary government since 1860 and Germany since 1870. The Russian Duma had sat only from 1905 until 1917 and its suffrage had been increasingly constricted. Local self-government had been vigorous in Germany and northern Italy. In addition, the Soviet Union inherited a social structure that frustrated the Bolsheviks from the outset—a massive peasantry that they regarded as a hostile and backward force. As one of their programmatic slogans during the interim republic from March to November 1917, the Bolsheviks had promised peasants the right to take over the land they cultivated as their own property. But individualized landholdings were not the ultimate form of property they envisaged, nor did small peasant holdings promise to be very productive. The economic task, as they saw it, was to raise the productivity of the agrarian sector and move the labor power released to cities for industrial development. Peasant proprietors, moreover, would always confront the Bolsheviks as a massive and sullen opposition. Some Bolsheviks, preeminently Nikolai Bukharin, advocated at least a long period of letting the peasants sell their output on a private market and retain their holdings. Preoccupied with securing his domestic supremacy, Stalin turned on any gradualist policies at the end of the twenties. After attacking the internationalist Left in 1928, he turned on the so-called rightist leadership and declared that no cooperation was possible with Social Democrats in Europe, a policy that had disastrous consequences for German democracy. And whether as a corollary or out of doctrinal conviction, Stalin also reversed the economic compromises of the earlier 1920s and introduced a policy of collectivization in the countryside. Peasant holdings were merged into collective farms that were to retain control of tractors and implements. For over a year, the Communists wrought a devastating revolution in the countryside before they had to ease up. In Ukraine in particular there was harsh opposition, and Stalin effectively blockaded the province for 1931–1932, using mass famine as a means to smash its inhabitants' resistance.[169] In the same period he embarked on the first Five Year Plan, which nationalized industry and shut down the private economy, even as the government embarked on vast industrialization projects in the Donets Basin (Donbass). Workers were essentially conscripted in harsh conditions to build steel mills and hydroelectric installations. Youth were recruited as young communists to work on the Moscow metro, and at the most coercive end of the spectrum of labor mobilization, political prisoners would be sent to the Arctic for construction of the White Sea Canal.

Soviet industrial growth advanced rapidly during the first Five-Year Plan of 1932–1937 during the gray era when the capitalist economies were mired in the Great Depression. It remained robust during the second Five Year Plan, designed to run from 1937 until 1942, at a time the Soviets moved many industrial plants back from western Russia, where they were vulnerable to German attack, to the Urals. Economic planning by the end of the 1930s came to appeal to many on the non-Communist left in the West. Whether the quality of Soviet output kept pace with the quantitative indices has been debated; certainly the agricultural sector did not advance—it remained a vastly underproductive and probably hostile, if silenced, sector of the country. The standard of living was far lower than in Central Europe. But even more, the regime embarked on a vast upheaval of its own supporters—a purge of the large Communist Party (several million strong), dismissing thousands, sending tens or hundreds of thousands to prison camps under appalling conditions, and culminating in show trials, where the old comrades of Stalin, and about half of his general staff, would be forced into degrading and absurd confessions, and shot, or sentenced to long terms of forced labor. And yet this regime and this dictator, who so misread Hitler's intentions in 1941, was able to mobilize unfathomable national loyalties—to Russia if not to Communism—to withstand the massive German attack and survive vast losses of territory, to incur huge sacrifices of military and civilian lives, and defeat the German military apparatus. Without Soviet efforts the Nazis might well have ruled the European continent far longer than they did. Unless they used atomic weapons on Germany after 1945, Britain and the United States would have remained offshore antagonists for decades and democracy might have flickered even more precariously than it did. The inhabitants of Eastern Europe had to pay their own heavy price for that victory over the decades from 1945 into the 1980s, but by the late 1930s there were no good choices.

Estimates of Soviet victims vary—from about seven hundred thousand officially recorded as executed or deported to labor camps, which saw mortality rates of up to one-third of their inmates each year, to millions who perished as entire peoples were deprived of food or sent into forced migrations. Only the catastrophic German invasion and the war, with its additional twenty million or more casualties, may have abated the war Stalin conducted at home. Historians have debated whether he was responding to party enthusiasts who wanted some vast upheaval or whether he engineered the purges. It may not matter. After the war, as Boris Pasternak recorded in the conclusion of his novel *Doctor Zhivago*, some hoped for a more normal life amid the devastation that had to be repaired, and for a few years it appeared as the worst of the terror was over. But by 1947 and 1948, the same mechanism of denunciation and show trial descended on the countries of Eastern Europe, where the Russians had helped install communist governments. When Marshall Tito of Yugoslavia—certainly as "pure" a

Marxist-Leninist as the Soviet leader—decided not to accept Cominform "discipline," that is, not to align himself with the new international communist bureau that the Soviet Union organized in 1947 to replace the Communist International it had dissolved during the war, he was denounced by the Soviets as a traitor. Titoism became as evil as Trotskyism, a deviation in league with American capitalism just as Trotsky had supposedly connived with German fascism. By 1952 Stalin's residual anti-Semitism seemed to be building up to a purge directed at the three million Jewish inhabitants of the Soviet Union, who had remained beyond the reach of Nazi killing squads; and he may have been planning to deport them all to a Soviet Jewish homeland. His Jewish physicians, it was alleged, had plotted to poison him. Only the dictator's death, supposedly by natural causes, averted this impending purge and possible forced resettlement. Gradually his successors—fearing each other, but combining to liquidate the head of the secret service, whom they all feared most—unwound the worst of the excesses, though hardly the party-state. Nikita Khrushchev's "Secret Speech" at the Twentieth Party Congress of the CPSU in 1956 finally dared to suggest that the great leader had yielded to paranoid fantasy and some woeful policy choices. Khrushchev, himself caught up like his fellow survivors as an accomplice in the ruthless policies of the 1930s, intended at least in part to exculpate the party that would continue to rule. Still, it was the first real tremor in a series of shocks that over the next thirty-five years would gradually reveal how flawed the regime had become.

Political Pathology

As Western political analysts and commentators confronted the human wreckage produced by the German and Soviet regimes, they sought to make intellectual sense of these orgies of civic destruction. Marxist theorists and historians sought to separate the two: the Germans and Italians operated terrorist and thuggish regimes that had basically left the capitalist order intact, whereas the Russians were creating socialism, and if they had committed excesses, this was because they had taken power in a backward country. According to the "vulgar" theories propagated by the Third International (that is, those Marxists who had rallied to the Soviet regime), fascism was just the most brutal strategy for "monopoly capital" to retain power. Dissident Marxists suggested with more subtlety that fascists were politically autonomous: as "Bonapartist" regimes they arose when the different sectors of the bourgeoisie were paralyzed by rivalries.[170] Still, fascists and Nazis were allegedly spurious revolutionaries because they left intact the basis of capitalist society. Later students of the fascist economy at war suggested that in fact the regime so limited the choices of entrepreneurs by controlling their investment possibilities that it represented a grave incursion into capitalism. Marxist critics in the 1930s and 1940s such as Franz Neumann and Herbert Marcuse sought to claim that the Third Reich was not in fact a state— that it was just the expression of the strongest naked interests inside Germany, whether industry, party bosses, or the military, and that the balance of power might evolve. This was not just a Marxist analysis. For a while Franklin Roosevelt and the New Deal shared such a view: at the end of the 1930s the administration argued that fascism amounted to unrestrained private monopoly power.[171] It was true that fascists rarely sought to nationalize industries unless to bail them out or develop new production. Nazi leaders did praise industrial capitalism, engineering, and innovation, although they were demeaning about finance, which they thought exploitative and often dominated by Jewish interests. But their regime was not just a puppet in the hands of monopoly capitalists. They certainly ran a state.

It also flouts ordinary language to insist that a German regime that quickly abolished parties, acquired dictatorial power, imposed legal restrictions against Jews not seen since the pre-Napoleonic era, locked its adversaries up in brutal facilities without trial, or often guillotined them after trial, was not revolutionary. Beyond the authorities who established hundreds of labor and concentration camps, many Germans thought in fact that they were reachieving a happy society of full employment, a warm communal feeling of the *Volksgemeinschaft* or ethnic community, marked, for instance, by the Christmas collection for the poor (the *Winterhilfe*) or the sharing of an occasional simple stew *(Eintopf)* or workers' cruises and other well-organized leisure activities (*Kraft durch Freude* and the Italian *dopolavoro*) to demonstrate interclass solidarity. It was not the least achievement of the party to get ordinary Germans to look away from the brutality of the regime, the humiliation and then the disappearance of the opposition parties and then of the Jews. Germany was awakening, casting off the supposed shackles of Versailles; one legislative restriction or another was placed on its willing or cautiously grumbling citizens, but did not the United States also impose racial segregation and make it clear that resorts and parks were reserved for whites? *Kristallnacht*—the organized burning and destruction of synagogues across Germany on November 9, 1938—caused some disquiet; it was clearly outright arson and violence visible in cities and towns throughout their civilized country. By then anti-Semitism had become a national ideological tenet: the Jew was enemy to the German, and any isolated dissent to this policy might be dangerous. With rare exceptions, even Christian pastors acquiesced. The regime had gone on first to humiliate and despoil and force into emigration as many German Jews as possible, then to seize the remainder of the Jews in all the lands they swept into, to transport them to the extermination factories constructed in occupied Poland, and murder them, sometimes after exploiting their labor, sometimes without any effort to do so. If for a while German policy makers did not think beyond putting the western Polish Jews into ghettos where they could manipulate mass malnutrition and let nature take its course, with the conquests of 1941 they decided they must act more proactively, first by mass machine-gunning, then by extermination camps.

This seemed different from the Soviet experience to many intellectuals. Certainly there was residual anti-Semitism in Russia and Poland, but the Russians condemned anti-Semitism as a bourgeois nationalist ideology. Even at its worst they had Jewish old communists; and many of the communist leaders of Poland and Hungary and Czechoslovakia who found asylum in Moscow or elsewhere were identified as Jews by the countrymen who hated their role in clamping down communism in 1946–1947. Nazism had this central preoccupation with an almost atavistic ideology—which in fact had long been central to rightist forces, hostile to capitalism and socialism and liberalism, throughout Central and Eastern Europe. Communism as an ideology was also "internationalist"—it aspired to proletarian or Marxist revolutions throughout the world as conditions became ripe, but war on nationalist grounds it condemned. Nazism—and perhaps Italian fascism—was so tied up with the celebration of martial virtue that it wanted war for fulfillment, whereas there was no equivalent Soviet eschatology. (Which did not prevent Stalin from building a massive air force and a fine tank corps.)

Leviathan's perversion: Bales of hair from female prisoners numbered for shipment to Germany, found by the Soviets at the liberation of the Auschwitz-Birkenau concentration camp, January 27, 1945. Hair was shorn from prisoners, sometimes at arrival; sometimes, as at Treblinka, before gassing; sometimes from corpses, to be used for cloth, rope, mattress stuffing, insulation for boots, and more. (United States Holocaust Memorial Museum, courtesy of National Archives and Records Administration, College Park / Belarusian State Archive of Documentary Film and Photography / Dokumentationsarchiv des Oesterreichischen Widerstandes)

But was ideology what counted? Perhaps intellectuals on the left might be excused for not understanding that the famine in the Ukraine, with its millions of victims, derived from Moscow's decision to cut off imports of food. The Italian and other consuls were not deceived, but their reports were buried in the Foreign Offices.[172] Certainly political thinkers would give particular concern to differences of dogma between the ideologies, just as once church leaders sniffed for heresy in disputes over the real presence in the Eucharist or the similitude versus equality of God and son. Still, the realization grew with the Stalinist years, and then with the opening of the Cold War, that what the regimes shared in practice united them as significantly as the ideological enmity divided them. Both fascism and communism were based on the claim of a single party to capture and then exercise power (more completely even in a postrevolutionary Russia than in Germany and Italy, where bureaucratic agencies remained relatively immune); their adherents shared the tendency to adulate the single leader, to attribute legal status to his pronouncements, and even to anticipate what further uniformity he might wish to impose even before he had articulated it himself.[173]

Of course, not only totalitarian states demonstrated the intolerance of opposition and the idea that it must be suppressed and silenced by censorship and punishment. There were and would be plenty of ordinary tyrannies and even murderous despotisms. Idi Amin ran a homicidal regime in Uganda in the 1970s; Reza Shah Pahlavi governed with a zealous political police; the Argentine military would murder many thousands of students and potential opponents. What distinguished the totalitarian state was its reliance supposedly on a collective instrument of transformation. The party-state supposedly entertained grandiose projects—in physical infrastructure, reeducation, and refashioning the nation as an ethnic unit (in Germany), as the heir of empire (as in Italy), or as the homeland of a historical process of inevitable change (as in the Soviet Union). Not only did the state claim that power vis-à-vis supposed individual rights (which it claimed to be really protected), but it did so by elevating the political police into a key component of rule. The Russians founded the Cheka early in the revolution as "sword and shield" of the revolution. It morphed into increasingly pervasive intelligence and police agencies continually reorganized into commissariats and ministries—the GPU, folded into the NKVD during the 1930s, divided into the MVD and KGB in the 1950s—huge enterprises that ran the vast "gulag archipelago" in Russia or the concentration camps in Germany with their hundreds of forced-labor subsidiaries, all established before the extermination centers were constructed on conquered Polish territory. Still, there was a difference in those selected. The German state tended to define known enemies—those who dissented, who spoke out or leafleted their opposition, and ultimately all who were Jewish. The "ordinary" citizen who kept his opinions to himself was relatively safe until wartime came. In the Soviet Union arrest often seemed arbitrary and random. As later in Mao's China and Pol Pot's Cambodia, the Soviet Union invented categories of guilt: prosperity as a peasant, family background and connections, political moderation, so that the spectators who escaped the suspect categories might be spurred into rituals of denunciation, complicity, and identification with the regime. Gazing at these nightmarish landscapes of terror, what an early postwar French writer called "l'univers concentrationnaire," the concentration-camp universe, the historian of the state must ask: Were they the perverted culmination of centuries-long claims of state sovereignty, or instead the dark cloaca of private brutality where ideas of public rationality, so long a supposed property of the modern state, never penetrated—or perhaps a coexistence of law and total arbitrariness that the German critic Ernst Fraenkel memorably termed the "dual state"?[174]

Public awareness in the West of what twentieth-century dictatorship entailed culminated in the Cold War before the death of Stalin. By the 1950s, analysts who emphasized the similarities between Nazism and Communism seemed more incisive than those who still tried to redeem the "idea" of Soviet socialism by emphasizing the theoretical differences. The defenders insisted that ultimately state socialism (the name I prefer to mere socialism) would transform itself and that the liberal states that were colonial powers had to take responsibility for the equally grievous sins of colonialism and racism. When pressed, they also contended that ultimately only the Soviet Union had enabled the defeat of Hitler's Germany. Those who argued by body count and not ideas argued that in fact the twentieth century had created a new paradigm of politics and the state— that of the totalitarian party-state with tremendous ambition and the willingness to sacrifice millions of individuals to its cause.

Some of the analysts excelled in describing the subjective experience of the dedicated Communist—easier to convey to Anglo-American or continental European readers because so many premises of the ideology seemed to spring from a common Enlightenment liberalism. Of the writers who sought to analyze the institutional experience, Hannah Arendt remains the most challenging and original. For all the particular comparisons or imputed origins the reader can quarrel with, Arendt understood the centrality of the imperialist experience to the ideologies of dehumanization, and likewise the importance of anti-Semitism to Central European doctrines. She identified the role of party and terror and attempted to analyze the totalitarian society as one of isolated atomization that destroyed solidarities outside the state. She probably credited the regimes with too much efficacy in reducing men and women to isolated beings—social networks remained to challenge all these regimes, which did not so much shatter and destroy associative life as penetrated it and subverted it.[175]

The label *totalitarian* has left a set of controversies. Were the states really so total? They did not succeed in changing human nature; after the decades of the harshest repression softened, Russians still craved the church; the Chinese still treasured family. A non-Jew could retain his irony and skepticism in Hitler's Germany if he didn't insist on publicly sporting it. When liberated from the harsh practices of dictatorship, people seemed anxious to dismantle the experiences; the number of neo-Nazis, outright fascists, and those willing to plunge Russia or China back into untrammeled violence was small. And yet the term—difficult and problematic as it was, and certainly when applied to the fatigued late socialist regimes of the 1970s and 1980s—was an effort to capture a basic state experience, that of the hyper state, or, to use the term that followed from Schmitt's decisionism, the exceptional state. The totalitarian state—related to the wartime state and the revolutionary state, both of which were usually deemed finite in time—was the most extreme application of an instrumentality remobilized in the 1860s and 1870s to take advantage of new communications to build cohesive national communities or overseas empires. It represented the desire to have a powerful transformative agenda—to do positive projects with government and not just quietly administer. But it also sprang from the pervasive conviction that government and social change had to be mobilized in a world of enemies who wanted you frustrated if not killed. Again, politics was war, had no choice but to be war.

The world wars—and then the long-term struggles in the colonial world, either to retain colonies or to shake off colonial powers—made these projects of magnifying power even more plausible. For wartime states took on many characteristics that in peacetime would be thought verging on tyranny: the commandeering of young men for dangerous labor, the imposing of restrictions on entrepreneurs so they produced what was needed for the national struggle, the fanning of public and patriotic loyalties, the persecution of dissent from policy, and even in liberal societies, a new recourse to mass detention. Wartime states were dismantled when the justifications disappeared—but they were part of the twentieth century; for they made liberals and democrats believe too that states

could legitimately claim an exalted power of decision. All this had been prefig-
ured in earlier situations: the French revolutionaries' wars against the monarchs
of 1793–1803 or their own enemies within the country; the Paraguayan total
war of 1864–1870; the berserk kingdom of the Taipings; von Trotha's campaign
against the Herero; the Turkish massacres of Greeks and Armenians. The reper-
tories of military commitment lay at hand, so it was hardly surprising they could
be seized on when wars were in abeyance. Were the states of exception, then, no
more than wartime states erected on a permanent basis? Was their treatment of
opposition as racially different, as colonies within their borders, no different
from their treatment of colonial subjects?

In fact, they were more absolute. Colonial massacres and colonial genocide
followed what local settlers and soldiers believed was resistance. They were an
effort to rule a subjugated people by terror. Some of the labor practices in the
colonies rested on a willingness to impose inhumane discipline; they bore some
similarity to what Nazi Germany would impose on the "slave laborers" recruited
or dragooned from other countries. But the hyper-regimes at home rested on the
idea that this sort of mastery, absolute hegemony, suspension of the liberal rules,
glorification of decisions and devaluation of discussion, accorded with the way
men and women should live throughout their lives. They extended to one's own
nation the notion of differentiated humanity that race and war made "natural"
when confronting others. They demonstrated that the practices that arose in
"natural" situations—confronting people of color, confronting invaders—were
not just grounded in racial difference or the exceptionalism of wartime antagonism, but a lurking project of purification within.[176] With these projects history
reached a state claim that was exceptional. Perhaps resorting to the metaphor of
our title, it was no longer 2.0, but somewhere between 2.1 and 2.9. Our postscript
will suggest what might constitute Leviathan 3.0. But first we must recall that
not every twentieth-century state was a state of exception.

Although the conduct of the Second World War itself demonstrated that all
major belligerents must become states of exception for the duration, the outcome of the war suggested more hopefully that the earlier states of exception
might in retrospect come to seem exceptional states. Communist rule would be
advanced by Soviet armies; colonial struggles would be intensified; but the war
also revealed possibilities for democratic renewal. Franklin Roosevelt enunciated

war aims, inscribed in the Four Freedoms and the Atlantic Charter proclaimed after his August 1941 shipboard meeting with Winston Churchill, which looked toward the restoration of democracy, human rights, and even a minimum of material well-being. The Resistance forces inside the occupied countries issued charters that echoed similar aspirations for political and economic democracy. Resistance groups also called for a regeneration of their nations as communities of emancipation in a language rarely heard since the days of Mazzini. Two of the major European leaders, who without the war would have seemed merely archaic nationalists, provided precisely the inspiration needed to stand up to Germany: Churchill as prime minister from 1940 to 1945, and Charles de Gaulle, resistance leader in British exile until France was liberated. Their respective defiant stances ensured that they found each other hard to bear, but together they (and Christian Democratic conservatives on the continent such as Konrad Adenauer and Alcide De Gasperi) suggested that a decent postwar conservatism might also reemerge. Neither Churchill nor de Gaulle was prepared to contemplate the renunciation of empire; nonetheless their anticolonial adversaries insisted that their countries were ready to fight for independence, and the European leaders had to yield—if only after prolonged conflicts in British Malaya and Kenya, and bitter wars for the French in Vietnam and Algeria. To be sure, pro-Soviet Communist leaders sought to instrumentalize the Resistance struggles on behalf of their postwar influence and to discredit opponents. (So did monarchist authoritarians, although with less success.) "People's Democracy" became Moscow's slogan for compliant postwar regimes. Nonetheless, new possibilities for political cooperation and discourse beckoned, to be achieved in Western Europe, including West Germany and Italy, and even Japan within a few years, and in Eastern Europe only after another half century.

A Glance Ahead: From the States of Exception to the Renormalized State

The fascist party-state ended with the war it had unsuccessfully launched. Its authoritarian militarist kin continued in Spain and Portugal, and it would reassert itself in Latin America and parts of Asia and Africa and the Middle East and briefly in Greece during later decades. The Communist party-state in Russia and Eastern Europe would become less harsh but still aspire to undisputed control into the 1980s. By the 1960s, however, the dominant regime in Europe, North America, and Japan was the "welfare state"—not fundamentally different from the extension of the European liberal or even conservative regime of the late nineteenth and early twentieth centuries but with more extensive social insurance and often ownership of key infrastructural enterprises. Its antecedents could be traced to church and town provisions for taking charge of orphans and the old. In the nineteenth century, occupational safety measures were added as well as legislation designed to prevent the worst abuses of the early factories and to establish minimal ages for those entering them. The growth of industrial towns made misery more visible than it was in rural households. It also made socialist schemes for collective insurance more plausible and to Europe's conservatives more threatening, hence often prompted new welfarist responses. Bismarck is credited with legislating state provisions for old age and infirmity. Civil servants developed self-insurance schemes. Some states, such as the Prussian, had a more active role; others left assistance to families and churches and occupational benevolent associations. After the American Civil War and the First World War, the legacy of social needs of disabled veterans and widowed wives compelled national responses. By the new century, Europe's reformist Left had tried to set its own stamp on these schemes, as in the British Liberals' program of 1906–1914, the policies developed by the Swedish social democratic coalitions of the 1930s, and the national responses that were a centerpiece of the American New Deal.

From these patchworks it was an easy transition to envisage states that took a comprehensive role in ensuring minimal standards of income and insurance against the social risks of unemployment, old age, and (outside the United States at least) disease. This agenda marked the report commissioned by the British minister Kingsley Martin from the social reformer William Beveridge during World War II, which outlined a notion of "cradle to grave" support that would overcome poverty and provide access to education and health. Out of these experiences would come the welfare state—the accepted mix of private economic ownership and social guarantees that tended to mark the policies once peace returned to Europe in 1945.

As it developed, the welfare state tended to converge with other remedies for economic distress and perhaps economic inequality that the Great Depression of the 1930s had made acute. It would supervise social compacts between labor unions and representatives of industry—an initiative that had taken shape during World War I, had been made compulsory by fascist and occupation regimes in World War II, and was now to be encouraged as a normal political activity. Ideas of national planning had become popular on the left in the 1930s and were instituted for wartime industries as a matter of course by the British, Americans, and Germans. After the war, the French instituted an agency for indicative planning headed by Jean Monnet. It did not own the constituent firms but could provide strategic incentives of capital for modernization. The state, so the democratic and social democratic left urged in Western Europe, should run key industries: certainly the banks of issue, probably the railroads (the French Popular Front had nationalized their rail network), and perhaps the mines. The Labour Party had inserted a commitment to public ownership of what became known at the commanding heights of the economy as Point IV of their Party Program in 1918; and when they came to power in 1945 they nationalized the steel industry, the rail system, road transport, and the coal mines, and by 1948 they established the National Health Service.

All these measures after the Second World War tended to be associated with the democratic and social democratic Left. Trade Unions and leftist parties, after all, had gained a decisive voice in politics by their moral and wartime contribution to the defeat of fascism. Conservative opponents were often in eclipse because of their role in collaborationist regimes. But conservatives often generated or inherited similar policies, and had often had a paternalist ideology of social protection. The leading French welfare initiative for family allowances had grown out of Catholic and employer concepts for regional or occupational *caisses*. The German Christian Democrats differentiated themselves from the National Socialists but championed concepts of ordo-liberalism, which stipulated embedding competitive industries and business in a broader social order that provided for extensive welfare provisions and an overall milieu of a very structured and highly organized social market economy, not so different from what postwar Japan was developing. The Italian Christian Democrats inherited a massive state holding company—the Institute for Industrial Reconstruction, or IRI—which the fascists had created as they bailed out and took over massive shares of Italian coal, steel, and chemical firms and the Italian petroleum industry. A new elite of government planners and technocrats developed to supervise the Italian economic "miracle" of the 1950s and 1960s.[177]

The welfare state and mixed economies seemed to provide political consensus for a generation, and then from the 1970s were the object of criticism and deregulation. That forms the subject of another history. Perhaps the most comprehensive single index for the role of the renormalized state was the proportion of national spending (national income or, viewed from the production side, gross domestic product) that went through government hands, for investment in infrastructure, military expenses, and transfer payments or entitlement programs. It has been estimated that the French Ancien Régime of the late eighteenth century was spending perhaps up to 25 percent of national income on its armed forces, its roads and canals, the expenses of the Court, and the interest to bondholders. Welfare was left largely to Church institutions. But nineteenth-century government in Western Europe was largely cheap government. As World War I approached, Britain and Germany may have had public expenditures of about 12 to 18 percent divided among armaments, infrastructure and education, and national debt service. The First World War drove up state expenses drastically—up to perhaps 40 percent in France (although much was covered by foreign loans), perhaps 45 to 50 percent in Britain and Germany. This vast expansion of state claims could be covered only partially by taxation; most was taken in the form of loans, some directly from citizens, but mostly from the central bank—what today we call quantitative expansion—which raised prices and transferred purchasing power through inflation. State claims dropped off after the war, although never to the levels seen earlier, because many delayed claims of tending to disabled soldiers and soldiers' families remained. The Great Depression forced expansion of unemployment assistance, so that the Western states of the late 1930s were probably spending a quarter of their national output; with rearmament starting drastically in Germany in 1936, in Japan perhaps earlier, in France and Britain by 1938, and in the United States by 1940, the shares went up again. By the middle of the Second World War, the United States was probably spending 45 percent, the Russians and Germans well over 50 percent, and of those sums, the largest share was going to military and war-related expenses. Again, the state share retreated after the end of the war, although Britain spent large sums on fighting colonial wars. The United States helped finance the French struggles, but by the late 1960s and 1970s, the expansion of social programs, welfare states, and university systems was increasing the ratios for a third time, up to 50 percent, and slightly more in West Germany, the Netherlands, and Scandinavia, but now prevailingly for social welfare and transfer expenses, as military budgets had fallen to below 5 percent of most countries' budgets. Some retrenchment in the 1980s has led to profiles of normal state expenditure at perhaps the 40 to 50 percent level. The United States, with smaller public sectors, spends probably about a third of its national income at all levels of government. The renormalized welfare state thus remains an active constituent of citizens' lives.

But the welfare state in its North American, Western European, and British dominion model was only one of three prevalent types. As of the 1950s and 1960s, the "socialist world," which passed almost all the national product (local garden crops or handicrafts sometimes excepted) through state hands, furnished an alternative and apparently still viable model. State socialism relied less on terror, although dissidents were hardly tolerated. The socialist state became increasingly bureaucratized, and the economic energies they possessed went largely into military innovation. The Soviet Union had to spend perhaps twice the share of public expenditure (perhaps 40 percent of the budget and up to 20 percent of GDP), compared to the United States, to remain a feared nuclear-armed adversary. The crisis of this system is also a subsequent story. So-called Third World states, which pursued a developmental model, followed different strategies. India remained attracted by the model of state socialism (even as it continued to admire village self-sufficiency as praised by its early architect of resistance, Gandhi.) Other states borrowed models inconsistently, but in most of them until the 1970s, state-owned pilot industrial sectors remained attractive, as they did for petroleum in Mexico, Brazil, and the Middle East. Japan, on the other hand, followed two decades later by other East Asian states, wagered on immense work effort being harnessed to technologically advanced consumer products, including automobiles and later electronics. Family networks remained important as connective tissue among the most elaborate alliances of banks and manufacturers.

As for political apparatus, the third state model, growing alongside the Western renormalized welfare state and the seemingly stable single-party states of the socialist world, remained that of military rule. Government by military officers would remain a frequent recourse throughout Asia, Africa, and Latin America. Soldier-rulers were a prevalent form of regime since antiquity, with or without empire—justified always on the notion that emergency conditions required intervention. As we have seen, armies were often the logical winners of a revolutionary process if civilians could not arrive at unity. When civilian leaders were corrupt or paralyzed, then military leaders, perceiving themselves as the best and most dedicated core of the community, had to step in. Military organizations were by essence nondemocratic, structured for obedience, sometimes subject to civilian control, but often considering themselves more devoted to state and nation than the corrupt civilians they booted out (or locked up and occasionally hanged). Sometimes the generals or colonels returned power to civilians, but having once seized power, their renewed intervention usually threatened. The creation of the Pakistani state by partition in 1947 would collect the northwestern military castes of the Raj and give them their own domain from tribal highlands to teeming coastal and Indus River cities for repeated interventions.

Mustafa Kemal Atatürk had provided one of the most convincing models of such rule—creating a secular and modernizing republic in the 1920s and 1930s. And although after his death the Turkish army relinquished control, it intervened at several points into the 1960s when it feared the principles of his secular nationalist state (and their role in it) were precarious. Eastern Europe had seen the military take control of Poland, Greece, Romania, and the Baltic States in the 1930s. The Thai monarch threw in his lot with military saviors in 1932, and the Thai army remained a frequent presence in that country's governance thereafter. General Franco ruled Spain for almost forty years after his coup and civil war victory in the late 1930s. Independent Egypt fell under military control in 1952, perhaps to emerge from it in the current day.

The Argentine military cultivated its own state within a state, proud of its large territory, blessed by Catholic bishops, angry at the ultra-Europeanist cosmopolitanism of the capital. General Uriburu seized power in 1930; and the military's stalwart authoritarians remained distrustful even of their own gifted demagogue, Juan Perón, who knew how to solicit mass loyalties on behalf of their continued influence. After Perón no longer seemed to serve them, they would intervene more brutally than ever in the 1970s. Hardly lagging, the Brazilian military took power in the late 1960s, the Uruguayan military would impose its own terror against urban guerrillas, and the Chilean military would oust Salvador Allende in 1973. The Indonesian military moved preemptively against a feared Communist uprising in the mid-1960s and probably massacred several hundred thousand suspected opponents. Washington's perception of US national interest during the Cold War ensured American tolerance and perhaps encouragement of these authoritarian initiatives.

Generals remained attractive candidates for civilian posts in the United States, and three major commanders of the Second World War played key roles in the postwar period—Dwight Eisenhower, the European commander, served as an eminently civilian president in the 1950s, and General George C. Marshall, wartime chief of staff, as an eminently civilian secretary of defense and of state. The third, General Douglas MacArthur, on the other hand, raised the first major challenge to civilian supremacy by his public dissenting policies concerning the Korean War but was decisively removed by President Truman. In the late twentieth century military governments emerged in two milieus. In the postcolonial states they were significant in Nigeria, Indonesia, and Pakistan, and, as noted, seized power when a radical left seemed to threaten (Indonesia). They were not absent in Europe (Spain, Greece), but seemed slated for extinction there. Military regimes could be taken as relatively benign interventions when normal states had lost control and communities descended into civil war and cycles of revenge that could not be stanched. The "dirty wars" of the 1970s produced levels of internal brutality that rivaled more formal fascist regimes. And sometimes military tyrants revealed paranoid tendencies that outran even their ideologically motivated harshness (as, for instance, in Iraq, Uganda, Libya, and Sierra Leone).[178]

Still, it would be historically wrong to end with such deformations of statehood. By the 1990s states were becoming more responsive to claims of justice and human rights. Just as globalization had helped to bring revolution eighty years earlier, it also brought benchmarks of progress that could not be gainsaid by the 1990s. The idea of bringing tyrants to an international bar of justice advanced, as did the sense that states must examine their dark and repressive episodes through so-called truth commissions. So, too, did the conviction that to be modern was not to march in mass formations but to travel, discuss, and allow international scrutiny and to develop new structures for policy making across borders. Finally, the fact that there were some leaders of truly heroic willingness to work for reconciliation, such as Nelson Mandela, meant hope and deserved celebration. Yet it also indicated that states were again in flux: statehood seemed almost universal by the end of the twentieth century, but states also claimed less exclusive power as regional associations were established, and nongovernmental actors took on functions of transnational governance. Still, there can be no endpoint for summing up; the long century of modern statehood merges into the continuing record of an ancient and persevering institution, sometimes oppressive, sometimes emancipatory, continually contested and transformed.

Toward Leviathan 3.0?

In the 1980s and 1990s the Eastern European Communist regimes, South Africa's Apartheid state, and the military dictatorships in Latin America transformed themselves into recognizable democracies. Economic strains, restrained leadership, and mass protest all played a role in these remarkable nonviolent transitions. The Soviet Union at least started down that path. This great wave of liberalization forms part of a subsequent history. It was nurtured by prosperity and by the dawning realization of how much private fulfillment had been postponed or diverted by the public demands of the years from 1914 through the 1950s. Perhaps it was connected to the progressive advent of intimate communication technologies that replaced the mass publics of the cinema and the radio harangue from the 1930s and 1940s: first by the family audiences for television in the 1950s and 1960s, then by the transistor and integrated circuit and software innovations that would sweep young people and their music through the era of the Walkman, to cell phones and the Internet. By the 1980s, European and American elections registered a general reaction against, not just abusive and pathological states, but state authority in general. Conservatives argued that the state was inimical to liberty no matter how democratic. And it appeared as if one might be able to outsource its functions, devolve them on what would be called the sphere of civil society.

Was there to be a Leviathan 3.0, which might in fact not be Leviathan in any recognizable sense but a form of functional association, as envisaged by many thinkers in the nineteenth and twentieth century? Many analysts in the 1970s and 1980s, myself included, had believed that the direct state-supervised negotiations among interest groups such as unions and employers—what was called corporatism or neo-corporatism—was slated to play a large role in public regulation. But such a role, so theorists of corporatism believed, would allegedly serve to replace the free market more than the state. They were as surprised by the revival of the liberal market as a form of economic regulation under Reagan and Thatcher (and then continued under parties of the left) as by the collapse of state socialism, which was in fact a related phenomenon.

Since the 1990s, the idea of governance has shimmered as the possible alternative to the state. It suggests a different outcome from what corporatism was intended to achieve. *Governance* as a term aims to sublimate politics, not economics. And rather than arriving at public outcomes through negotiations among class or interest-group representatives, governance has tended to imply that consensus can be found among disinterested experts, that is, experts who are advocates not for their own interests, but for the public welfare of humanity (or sometimes animals). Governance implied that regulation would emerge from the recommendations of NGOs and communities of knowledge. This process was not democracy per se. Schmitt had a point: democracy rested on a perceived community—a group of people who claimed an identity (perhaps territorial, perhaps ethnic, linguistic, or religious). But Schmitt implied that such an identity could exist only when a boundary separated friend from foe, us from them, whether they were within a territory or outside. By the late twentieth century, however, contemporary politics often encountered peoples with a sense of self-identification and a sense of loyalty to more than one territory, communities we term diasporas. Nonetheless Schmitt would certainly have recognized the heightened security measures we all live with today as testimony to the underlying realism of his views. Democracies, he would have argued, needed the state because their citizens had to be preoccupied by the danger that all outsiders and not just terrorists represented. Perhaps (as I, for one, hope) there are less security-oriented reasons-of-state and reasons for states.

· · ·

We started this history of the modern state at the Little Bighorn in the 1870s with peoples who preserved a plastic sense of territory, of land that was theirs but with an ill-defined border; and we end by evoking communities that might be post-territorial. "Citizens beyond borders?" But how could one organize government for such transnational communities? Perhaps democracy might be dismantled into human rights plus experts. Information on the web, private providers such as the media or Google, might play a larger public role. Still the contemporary world had institutions that collectively covered the globe, held elections, maintained armies, entered alliances, and attempted to control trade or conditions of work. The term *governance,* which had become so popular by the end of the twentieth century and continued to fascinate social scientists and foundations, testified to the hope for government without "stateness"—as if policy making might no longer require aggregating preferences and finally wagering on one choice or another, but could take place by consensus and the force of rational discussion. Disaggregate state offices, such as courts and regulators, and enmesh them into "global government networks," argued a leading advocate, and the result would be actually to enhance state power. Foundations, university elites, social scientists, men and women of goodwill loved the idea of governance—which suggested transparent and self-justifying administration without stateness and without tears.[179] Governance was the utopia of the Masters of Public Policy.

No historian can envisage the future, or futures. Contending nations and empires—now with the addition of the Asian powers among others—may yet reassert old patterns of rivalry that reinforce state structures. Regional associations such as the European Union may play a larger role. States currently seem to have a bad reputation. Whether tyrants or compulsive bureaucrats, their managers see the need to classify, count, and control. But as Hobbes and Hannah Arendt had stressed in their different ways, being stateless was often a worse fate: States protected vulnerable individuals and communities. They provided the legal carapace for the soft-bodied creatures of humanity, lying exposed to the cruel and rapacious or even just the profit-seeking or zealous. Power and violence do not disappear when states are feeble; rather they are exercised without the restraint of law. Teens pressed into trafficking may fear the law but are ultimately victims of state absence, not presence. Being stateless in Gaza or, even worse, in Darfur in the first decade of the twenty-first century was not an enviable condition.

Between the mid-nineteenth and mid-twentieth centuries, states had recreated themselves in many ways: They had fought for territorial cohesion; enlisted the middle classes, consolidated territory, subjugated "nomadic" or tribal peoples, and turned on each other in unparalleled wars. They had experimented with revolutionary parties whose members were intoxicated by visions of transformation through violence and had virtually worshipped the most brutal of leaders. And finally they had sought normalcy and a precarious equilibrium with the ever more powerful forces of the economy. Of course, states were the inherited creations of individuals, communities, and parties infused by ideas, interests, and perhaps even instincts. They acted through policies and instrumentalities that they could not fully control. We can work to diminish their constraints or their tutelage. But the needs and ambitions that created them will remain in some hands or others, and certain questions will not disappear—not only Hobbes's question: What is life like without the state? But also Aristotle's question: Do we control the state by the one, the many, or the few? Or the question posed by the American founders: How do we run it for the welfare of us all? These issues abide.

·[two]·

Empires and the Reach of the Global

Tony Ballantyne and Antoinette Burton

Introduction

BETWEEN 1870 and 1945 the violent growth of imperial regimes and the fierce struggles against colonialism that unfolded in many places repeatedly redrew the world map, both literally and metaphorically. Frantic scrambles for land and resources, colonial wars, and sustained campaigns of imperial pacification resulted in the proliferation and growth of imperial systems throughout the period: by the 1930s, almost 85 percent of the world's territory either was part of an imperial system or, as in the case of much of Latin America, had formerly been European colonial holdings.[1] Empires were powerful agents that played a key role in determining the differential material conditions, social opportunities, and cultural capacities of various human communities. Even those states and social collectives that were able to deflect this imperial onrush or that successfully cast off colonial rule were not untouched by empire: they frequently faced diplomatic and economic pressure as imperial powers worked hard to "open" them up to the pull of international trade and global markets.

In this period, imperial statesman and colonial administrators had considerable power to redefine the boundaries of their empires and to inscribe national borders. These powers were most famously exercised in the Berlin Conference of 1884–1885, which created new regulations for European trade in Africa and formally defined European territorial holdings and spheres of influence in that continent. By the end of the nineteenth century, Liberia and Abyssinia were the only African states that were not claimed by a European state. Even if the precisely drawn maps of European imperial powers did not always translate to real colonial power on the ground, they are potent reminders of how the dynamic of empire building reconstructed worldviews and geopolitical realities. European empires created a kind of "cartographic imagination" that was central in the emergence of how the domain of "the global" was understood during the nineteenth and twentieth centuries.[2]

In this chapter we examine some of the ways in which empires shaped and reshaped global cultural formations. But rather than offering a simple story of the growth and decline of the imperial systems constructed by European nation-states like Great Britain, France, and Germany, we seek to reframe imperial history as a—partially, fitfully, and at times imperfectly—global history. We explore the spatial logics of modern imperial systems, trace the forms of interconnectedness they produced, and highlight the fundamentally uneven character of the socio-economic, cultural, and political configurations they enabled.[3] Capturing the scale, proportionality, and meaning of these imperial transformations remains one of the most challenging tasks facing historians invested in reconstructing the operation of colonial power and specifying the reach of globalizing processes. Doing so requires not just that we reckon with the global dimension of empires—and their globalizing effects—but that we also address the limits of their territorial reach and remain wary of European assertions of cultural exceptionalism as well. For although European empires claimed the greatest share of territory and resources, imperial aspirations and the fruits of colonialism were widely shared in the decades either side of 1900: after all, the Qajar, Ottoman, and Qing empires persisted into the early twentieth century, Japan built an extensive territorial empire in Asia and the Pacific between 1905 and 1945, and the United States, Australia, and New Zealand—all offshoots of British imperialism—set about building empires of their own.

The period under consideration was, of course, one in which the world's empires underwent rapid expansion and contraction. It was an extended moment, in other words, during which imperial power was recalibrated, with significant consequences for the character and scope of the global. The expansive territorial empires that had shaped Eurasia for centuries were hollowed out in this period. The Ottoman Empire, which was founded at the close of the thirteenth century CE, lost key European territories in the wake of the Russo-Turkish War of 1877–1878 and relinquished Libya after the Italo-Turkish War (1911–1912). When the Ottomans joined the Central Powers at the outbreak of World War I, Britain further undercut Ottoman power by annexing Cyprus as well as Sudan and Egypt, where the Ottomans had exercised considerable influence during the nineteenth century. After the occupation of Istanbul by Britain and France at the end of the war, the remnants of the Ottoman Empire were partitioned and distributed, stripping the Ottomans of their extensive territorial holdings in the Arab world and creating the Republic of Turkey. During the same period the dominance of the Qajars, who had exercised authority in Persia from the close of the eighteenth century, was slowly eroded by British and Russian influence. The occupation of Persia by Russian, British, and Ottoman troops during World War I marked the end of effective Qajar rule. Farther east, Qing authority in China was increasingly shaken by internal social unrest, and the future of the empire was called directly into question after the Sino-Japanese War of 1894–1895 revealed the extent to which China's political power and military capacity had lagged behind its rivals. By 1900, Qing authorities were under great pressure from a range of imperial powers who sought unfettered access to Chinese markets: in that year the Empress Dowager Cixi supported the Boxer Rebellion, which targeted violence against European missionaries and Chinese Christian converts as it attempted to expel "foreign devils" from China and fortify traditional authority. The defeat of the Boxer forces by the army of the Eight-Nation Alliance (Austria-Hungary, France, Germany, Italy, Japan, Russia, the United Kingdom, and the United States) was a clear sign of China's growing vulnerability. Against the backdrop of prolonged political instability and natural disasters, the Chinese Revolution of 1911 dismantled the Qing Empire, creating a new Republic of China.

While these land-based empires declined sharply, the authority of the Russian Empire was relatively stable until 1917, and in the wake of the revolution of that year, Soviet empire building attempted to fortify Moscow's imperial hold on Central Asia. Generally speaking, Russia had a firm grip on the lands it had long exercised its control over in the west and south—including the eastern half of Poland, Ukraine, Belarus, Moldova, Finland, Armenia, and Georgia. These areas were integral to the overall functioning of the empire: Ukraine, for example, provided the empire with the bulk of its wheat. These imperial regions not only provided valuable resources, they were also subject to sustained campaigns of Russification, built around policies that actively suppressed regional languages and local cultures. Under tsarist rule, Russian authority in Central Asia was consolidated through large-scale schemes where Russian colonists were encouraged to migrate to the frontiers of the empire and "settle," enacting social change through the sheer force of numbers and the transplantation of Russian culture

Tekke tribespeople and Russians standing near the Trans-Caspian Railway in Turkmenistan, October 1918. The railway, the construction of which began in 1879, facilitated both the deployment of Russian military resources and the export of large amounts of cotton from Central Asia to Russia. It was a vital element of imperial infrastructure that helped reshape the economic, political, and cultural terrain of Central Asia. (© Maynard Owen Williams / National Geographic Society / Corbis)

to the steppes. Although these Central Asian lands were firmly locked into, and consistently provided vital resources and markets for, the Russian economy, nationalist movements and uprisings openly challenged both Russian and Soviet authority.

Western European nations were particularly prominent in the global race for colonies in the final decades of the nineteenth century. The "Scramble for Africa" saw Italy, Spain, Portugal, the United Kingdom, France, Germany, and, more indirectly, Belgium all claiming colonial territory in Africa in the final decades of the nineteenth century. Africa—specifically Congo and Rwanda-Burundi—remained the focus of Belgian imperial activity, initially through the International African Association founded by King Leopold II to operate in the

Congo; but the other European powers maintained globally ambitious empires. France, for example, was an influential imperial power in north, west, and central Africa by 1900. In the north its holdings included Algeria, Tunisia, and, after 1912, Morocco. French West Africa was established as a federation of eight colonial territories in 1904, while French East Africa was established in 1910 as an administrative structure to control four colonial territories stretching north from the Congo River to the Sahara. French Somaliland provided a colonial foothold in the Horn of Africa, and from 1890 the empire incorporated Madagascar as a protectorate. In Asia, France retained control of its footholds in India—Pondichéry and Mahé—as well as Cambodia and Cochin China, the southern third of Vietnam, which had come under French control in the 1860s. Later it added the territories of Tonkin, Annam, and Laos. In the Pacific, France exercised imperial authority over New Caledonia and French Polynesia, and it shared joint control of the New Hebrides with Britain. In the wake of World War I, French holdings were further extended as France gained mandates over parts of the former Ottoman Empire (modern Syria and Lebanon) as well as the former German colonies of Cameroon and Togo.

Great Britain had long been France's chief imperial rival on the global stage. In 1870 it already boasted an extensive maritime empire, and its colonies included India, Burma, Ceylon, Malaya and the Straits Settlements, Singapore, Hong Kong, Australia, New Zealand, Canada, Trinidad, Tobago, the Windward and Leeward Islands, British Honduras, Jamaica, the Bahamas, Barbados, Sierra Leone, the British Gold Coast (modern Ghana), British Guiana, the Falklands, and parts of South Africa. During the later nineteenth century, British imperial ambition was primarily focused on Africa. By 1900 it had added significant African holdings to its imperial system and consolidated some older footholds: these colonies included The Gambia, Zanzibar, British Somaliland, Anglo-Egyptian Sudan, Nyasaland, Nigeria, British East Africa, and Southern Rhodesia. From 1882 Egypt had been a de facto British colonial protectorate, a status that was confirmed in 1914. In the later nineteenth century, Britain also enlarged its Asian and Pacific empire, adding Brunei, North Borneo, Sarawak, Fiji, the Gilbert and Ellice Islands, and the Kingdom of Tonga in 1900. During the twentieth century the empire was in constant flux. In 1902, at the end of the second South African War (Boer War), British influence was extended and consolidated in South Africa, and in 1910 the Union of South Africa unified the two former independent Boer republics with the British-dominated Cape Province and Natal. As this colonial authority was cemented, Britain began to hand some Pacific protectorates and colonies over to Australia and New Zealand, British colonies that had imperial aspirations of their own. After protracted conflict, Ireland, which had been incorporated into the United Kingdom in 1801, was partitioned in 1922. Twenty-six counties made up the new independent Republic of Ireland while six counties in Ulster exercised "home rule" within the United Kingdom. At the same time, however, Britain gained influence in the Middle East as Palestine and Transjordan became British mandates under the League of Nations. By 1930, Britain controlled a vast and scattered global empire.

After Germany's unification in 1871, the idea of a colonial empire became increasingly important as an indicator of Germany's national power. German colonialism was grafted onto an earlier tradition of German-speaking adventurers and companies developing commercial enterprises in West and East Africa, the Samoan Islands, and New Guinea. These provided the basis for Germany's formal colonial holdings. During the Scramble for Africa, Germany made some prominent acquisitions, including German South West Africa, German East Africa, and German West Africa, which was subsequently split into Togoland and Cameroon. In the Pacific, Germany's presence was built around the Marshall, Mariana, and Caroline Islands, German New Guinea, the Bismarck Archipelago, and Nauru, as well as German Samoa. World War I marked the end of this empire: some German colonies were seized by rivals at the outset of the war, while the remaining territories were redistributed among France, Belgium, the United Kingdom, Australia, New Zealand, and Japan under the provision of Article 22 of the Treaty of Versailles. Of course, this did not mark the end of Germany's drive for new lands, as the rapid conquest of Europe by the armies of Nazi Germany between 1939 and 1941 was energized by imperial aspirations. The German state not only wanted to access the resources of its European neighbors and rivals, but conquest was also propelled by a drive to open up *Lebensraum* (living space) for Germans, who would transplant their supposedly superior language, culture, and racial stock into territories in the east that had previously been dominated by non-German peoples. Germany's ultimate defeat in 1945 not only shattered these imperial dreams, but was also central in stimulating new critical reflection on the connections between racial thought and empire building.

In the 1880s Italy joined the European imperialist "club" as it gained African bridgeheads in Eritrea and Italian Somaliland. Its imperial dreams were then largely focused on Ethiopia, but these were initially blunted by the Italian army's humiliating defeat by Ethiopian forces in 1896. In 1911 the empire was further extended by the invasion of Libya. Under the leadership of the fascist Benito Mussolini, Italy's ambitions in Ethiopia were finally realized in 1936 and that newly acquired colony was merged with Eritrea and Italian Somaliland to form Italian East Africa. In 1939 Mussolini ordered the invasion of Albania, which was added to the empire as a protectorate. With Mussolini's deposition in 1943 and the opening of secret negotiations with the Allied command, the Italian empire began to be quickly dismantled as World War II drew to a close.

Thus many European states were energetic empire builders between 1870 and 1945. Conversely, in the later nineteenth century Spain and Portugal, who drove Europe's influence forward in the sixteenth and seventeenth centuries, were no longer dominant global powers. Even after Central and South American states claimed their independence from the Iberian powers during the first decades of the nineteenth century, though, both Spain and Portugal remained committed to empire building. In the 1860s Spain made several unsuccessful attempts to extend its imperial reach. Nevertheless, it continued to control important "New World" colonies in Cuba and Puerto Rico and exercise the colonial authority it had held over Guam and the Philippines since the sixteenth century. By the close of the nineteenth century, however, the Spanish empire was in tatters as Cuba won its independence and Guam, Puerto Rico, and the Philippines were ceded to the United States after the Spanish-American War of 1898. By the early twentieth century, Spanish imperial influence was restricted to parts of northwest Africa. By 1900 the Portuguese empire was also greatly reduced in size and significance. Portugal's recognition of Brazilian independence in 1822 had greatly eroded its global power. It retained significant footholds in Africa, with its key colonies of Portuguese West Africa and Portuguese East Africa (Mozambique). It also held some influence in Asia and the West Pacific, with footholds in India, in Goa, Daman, and Diu, as well as in Macao and Portuguese Timor (now the Democratic Republic of Timor-Leste). The imperial decline of the Dutch, who

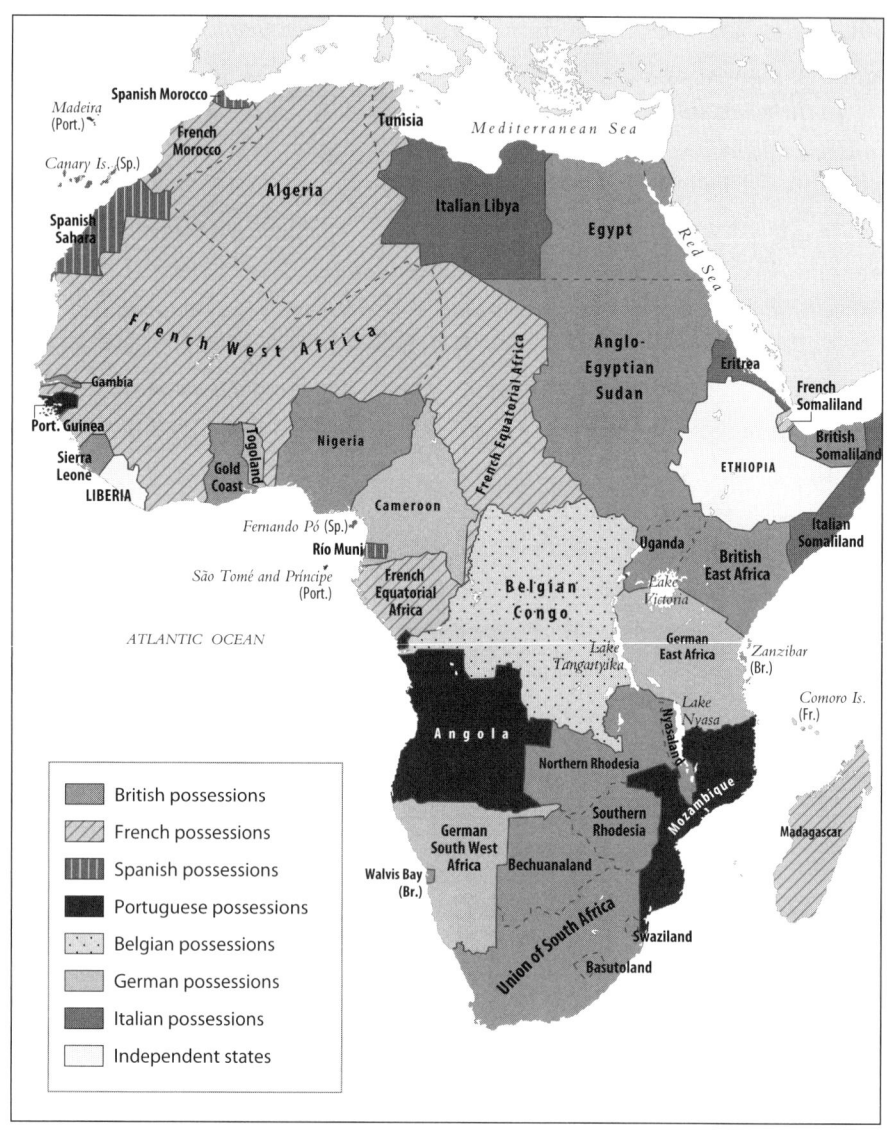

Madeira (Port.)

Canary Is. (Sp.)

Spanish Morocco

French Morocco

Tunisia

Mediterranean Sea

Algeria

Italian Libya

Egypt

Red Sea

Spanish Sahara

French West Africa

Gambia

Port. Guinea

Sierra Leone

LIBERIA

Gold Coast

Togoland

Nigeria

Anglo-Egyptian Sudan

Eritrea

French Somaliland

British Somaliland

ETHIOPIA

Italian Somaliland

Cameroon

Fernando Pó (Sp.)

Río Muni

São Tomé and Príncipe (Port.)

French Equatorial Africa

French Equatorial Africa

Uganda

Belgian Congo

Lake Victoria

British East Africa

ATLANTIC OCEAN

German East Africa

Lake Tanganyika

Zanzibar (Br.)

Lake Nyasa

Comoro Is. (Fr.)

Angola

Nyasaland

Northern Rhodesia

Southern Rhodesia

Mozambique

Madagascar

German South West Africa

Walvis Bay (Br.)

Bechuanaland

Swaziland

Union of South Africa

Basutoland

British possessions

French possessions

Spanish possessions

Portuguese possessions

Belgian possessions

German possessions

Italian possessions

Independent states

European colonies in Africa, 1914.

had been so powerful in the seventeenth and early eighteenth centuries, was a long process with major colonies being lost during the Napoleonic wars. The Dutch Asian empire was substantially reduced with the concession of Malacca and its Indian colonial footholds to Britain in the 1820s. This retraction continued in our period, with the sale of the Dutch colony of the Gold Coast to Britain in 1871. The scattered colonies that made up the Dutch empire in the New World—Suriname, Sint Maarten, and Curaçao and its dependencies—stagnated after the abolition of slavery in the Dutch colonies in 1863. Only in the Dutch East Indies, which would later become Indonesia, did Dutch imperial power expand as new territories beyond Java were brought under Dutch control between 1873 and 1920 and the colonial state worked hard to support the production of new commodities like rubber, tea, and cinchona as well as the extraction of oil to meet the demand of an industrializing Europe.

The effective decline of the Iberian powers and, to a lesser extent, the Dutch empire on the global stage is brought into particular relief by the rise of the United States of America. The United States, of course, had been born out of older traditions of European empire building, and the rapid extension of settlement and American sovereignty into the trans-Mississippi west during the nineteenth century can be seen as a type of settler colonialism. In 1867 the United States purchased Alaska from Russia, and this marked a significant enlargement of both territory and geographical ambition. The overthrow of the Hawai'ian queen Liliuokalani in 1893 in a coup d'état backed by American commercial interests opened the way for American annexation of Hawai'i in 1898. In that same year the Spanish-American War marked the most blatant exercise of American military power on the world stage: in a swift succession of military and naval victories, the United States established its military advantages over its European rival. Victory in the war with Spain brought the United States possession of the Philippines, Puerto Rico, and Guam and made Cuba an American protectorate in 1903. The empire was further enlarged in the early twentieth century with the United States assuming control of American Samoa (1900), the Panama Canal Zone (1903), and the US Virgin Islands (1917).

In many ways Japan's rise was even more spectacular than that of the United States. In the second half of the nineteenth century, Japan engaged with new ideas, technologies, and political models after two centuries of isolation. After the first Sino-Japanese war, Qing China ceded Taiwan to Japan in 1895. The clear ascendancy of the Japanese fleet over its Russian counterpart in the war of 1904–1905 opened the way for Japan's annexation of Korea in 1910. A new wave of empire building commenced in 1931, when Japan invaded the rest of Manchuria. Manchuria provided a base from which Japan attempted to push its influence west toward Russia and south toward China. The signing of the Tripartite Pact with Germany and Italy in September 1940 provided a new framework for Japan's imperial ambition: it actively sought to extend its influence into Southeast Asia and the Pacific as well as East Asia. After its surprise attack on Pearl Harbor in December 1941, Japan launched a sustained campaign to build a maritime empire in the western Pacific. Its forces quickly captured Malaya, Singapore, and Burma. They also pushed into Borneo, Java, Sumatra, and Dutch New Guinea in search of oil and other resources. Japan established a network of landing strips, ports, and military outposts in Melanesia and Micronesia, hoping to secure its strategic advantage over Allied forces and open up new sites for imperial extraction to support the war effort and the Japanese economy. Ultimately, however, Allied forces clawed back these gains and Japan's hold on its recently acquired colonies proved to be short-lived. At the end of the war Japan was also forced to relinquish control over its more established colonial holdings in Taiwan, Korea, and Manchuria.

As this sketch of different empires suggests, the period between 1870 and 1945 was characterized by sustained and intensive imperial activity that remapped significant portions of the globe. In the space of seventy-five years, a comparatively short time in world history, some powerful imperial orders collapsed while other regimes rapidly extended their reach and in the process created new and accelerated forms of cross-cultural exchange, extraction, and interdependence. Even as these systems induced change in existing cultural formations and created new patterns of exchange and circulation, they faced a constant range of challenges, confronted resistant nationalisms, and, on many occasions, resorted to the use of force to assert colonial control. But the persistent anxieties of colonial regimes over the nature of the "native mind" and the fragility of their own power is a telling reminder that such control was never total or uncontested. In this period, it became clear that the nature and consequences of empire were subject to open struggles and that colonized peoples could exploit the gaps in colonial structures and the contradictions within imperial orders that promised to civilize but were grounded in repression and violence.[4]

Just as individual colonies were always in process—subject to endless initiatives to reform, uplift, and reorder—the larger imperial systems they were part of were never fully self-contained or hermetically sealed systems. Though it was clearer to contemporaries who lived through this period than it has been to many historians of modern empires, traffic of various kinds linked empires. Migrant workers, missionaries, social reformers, highly educated professionals, and humble pilgrims, as well as money, commodities, technologies, and even diseases, moved among imperial systems. In some key domains—such as environmental science, medicine, and social policy formation—there was coordinated collaboration between empires, while complex flows of printed texts and popular cultural artifacts meant that some ideas moved easily across imperial boundaries.[5] At the same time, imperial powers both aspirant and ascendant cast a watchful eye on each other, monitoring borders and boundaries, markets and military activity in ways that begin to suggest the parameters of an incipient, if anxious, *imperial world order* by the 1880s. In this chapter, then, we attempt to trace this imperial globality in both its temporal and its spatial dimensions, seeing it as the interplay of multiple regimes that were simultaneously, but unevenly, distributed across the surface of the world: competing with each other for territory, sovereignty, strategic advantage, extractable resources, and cultural influence.

Although the late nineteenth century has often been understood as a unique moment of imperial birth, consolidation, and hegemony (the so-called new imperialism), in fact the empires of this period did not emerge suddenly, nor were they sui generis; rather they grew out of, mimicked, and even cannibalized older imperial ways of seeing, thinking, and acting. Modern imperial regimes remained heavily dependent on the capital—both symbolic and real—that had accumulated from earlier empires, stretching from the early modern period back to the classical antecedents in Greece and especially Rome. In this sense, historians' tendency to demarcate this moment of empire building as clear and distinct tends to occlude the deep continuities of form and structure and reproduces the fiction that European empires in particular were providentially acquired during the late nineteenth century.

For students of imperialism interested in understanding how the empire and the globe came to be articulated, this exceptionalist vision has several limitations. First, it centers Europe—and England within it—at the heart of the modern imperial story. What were in fact very particular imperial histories are frequently seen as exemplifying the history of modern empires writ large. Such a presumption fails to account for the *longue durée* of, say, Muslim empires, the power and durability of successive Chinese imperial dynasties, the centrality of empire building to the consolidation of Russia's vast Eurasian reach, or the potency of modern Japanese colonialism. Just as significantly, this Anglocentric reading tends to emphasize "absolute distinctions" among empires and—proceeding directly from the racial presumptions at the heart of British power—claims exceptionality for itself, if not for its American "successor."[6] The limits of Anglocentric models are increasingly clear: for all its claims to hegemony among empires as well as within its own, the British Empire was not the only globalizing agent at work in this period. In fact, an imperial system like Germany's is actually more comparable to the Russian, the Ottoman, and the Austrian than to its contemporary British rival between 1870 and 1918. Placing these competing global visions in a single frame while continuing to account for the geopolitical power of British imperialism is one of the challenges of any narrative of empire and globe in this period.[7]

Second, the "high noon" periodization obscures the work of sub-imperial formations both within dominant empires, like the Raj in the larger project of the British Empire, or alongside them, such as the so-called Comanche Empire that had developed in the late eighteenth and early nineteenth centuries on the borderlands of the emergent imperial system of the United States.[8] These kinds of imperial formations, which by their very nature were multiethnic, sutured together various sites and communities into new forms of interdependence that cannot simply be explained through a narrative that frames the story of empires as the story of "European expansion" or the "West and the Rest." The metropole–colony binary that has organized so much writing on empires fails to illuminate the complex commercial arrangements, knowledge networks, and political affiliations that developed within and frequently spilt out of imperial systems. Simple binaries do not help us understand the movements of goods, money, and information that connected Hyderabad and Shikarpur in Sind to diasporic merchants who traveled within and beyond the British Empire to establish enclaves that were scattered from Kōbe to Panama, Bukhara to Manila to Cairo. Nor do they help us make sense of the remittance flows and the expansive religious networks established by Sikh and Tamil migrants who moved along and across imperial transportation routes to Southeast Asia, Australasia, and beyond. These kinds of complex entanglements alert us to the complexity of imperial structures, to the multiple forms of interdependence that shaped colonial encounters on the ground in this period, and, in the case of transoceanic diaspora histories, to the impact of old global *ecumenes* as well.[9]

Third, narratives that see empires and modernity as markers of European particularity, if not exceptionalism, have produced a radically simplified geography of imperial influence. They tend to presume that European imperial metropoles were the sites of innovation and energy from which subject peoples received enlightenment and other benefits of "civilization," rather viewing them as sites that also *received* a range of economic, policy, and social innovations and were, in turn, made and remade by them. It is increasingly clear that the geographies of empire and modernity were entwined: that plantations, colonies, distant trading posts, and mission stations at the frontiers of empires were locations where some of the key characteristic practices, habits, and ideologies of modernity were fashioned or refined. The integrative work of imperial networks that linked frontiers to imperial centers meant that the developing global order was energized by a constant cultural traffic across modern imperial cultural landscapes—landscapes shaped by print culture, the mass production of goods and advertisements, and, of course, the steamship, the railway, and the telegraph. Citizens of the world—and those who aimed to be considered such—were becoming increasingly "at home with the empire" as imperial citizenship and modernity came to be understood as one and the same. The tensions of empire that resulted were the product of the uneasy proximities of colonizers and colonized on the ground, in the imaginative realm, and in the variegated spaces in between.[10]

In part because we are focusing on the temporal framework of the nineteenth and twentieth centuries, it is worth underscoring that, like modernity itself, the enlarged commercial and industrial capacity that underpinned Europe's aggressive reach into the world from the 1870s was also an effect of earlier colonial moments and long imperial histories. In the German colonies—from Qingdao to

Samoa to South West Africa—there are direct connections between *precolonial* travelogues and ethnographies and later colonial policies. In purely economic terms, Europe's newfound ascendancy on the global economic stage in the later eighteenth century was the product of the "New World windfalls" produced by early modern empire building impulses that allowed a resource-poor Europe to escape its economic and environmental constraints.[11] But the first truly global age of imperialism that emerged from the 1760s, which encompassed the Pacific Ocean as well as Africa, Asia, the Islamic world and the Americas, was not merely a precursor to later imperial "greatness."[12] As Richard Drayton has so succinctly put it, "the Old World was tugged into the modern by the New." Drayton emphasizes that New World models of labor discipline and time measurement were engendered by colonial plantations and transplanted to the factories of industrializing Europe.[13] Like all good capitalist commodities, modern time arrived in the metropole shorn of evidence of its imperial roots but no less implicated in colonial political economies.

Our understandings of empire and modernity are further complicated if we open up our geographical ambit wider still, to recognize the persistence of Muslim empires, abiding imperial contests in key transition zones like North Africa, Mesopotamia, and Central Asia, and the centrality of the question of empire to East Asian modernities. When we factor phenomena like the Qing conquest of Central Asia—along with the spatial, economic, geopolitical, and even historiographical innovations and reconfigurations it entailed—into our genealogy of the period under consideration, we begin to appreciate both what taking a longer view of imperial history on a global stage can yield as well as how important it is to think beyond Europe as the measure of imperial state building around 1900. Indeed, the long-distance connections and imperial systems that have been at the heart of Central Asian history anticipated a global imperial world in ways that are only beginning to be fully appreciated and that promise to reorient the routines of researching and teaching both empire and world history.[14]

There is a danger of this move—one that rematerializes imperial antecedents of modern global phenomena—being simply absorbed into debates over the local and the global. To be sure, the local has to be addressed, not least because allowing particulars on the ground to be subsumed in a kind of placeless global landscape reproduces the very mechanisms of cultural erasure that imperialisms have frequently relied upon. It is also true that not all localities were firmly linked into the imperial or the global—a point that work by Africanists makes with compelling clarity. Whether we consider peanut farmers in Niumi, The Gambia, who were both linked to and at times insouciant about world markets, or the disinterest of Asante women in missionaries' attempts to impose regimes of bodily hygiene, it is clear that that global imperial regimes often failed in their attempts to encompass local communities within broad patterns of economic and cultural exchange.[15] Not surprisingly, the view of empire and of globalization from Africa is distinctive for its rejection of totalizing views of both imperial power and globalization. For African historians like Frederick Cooper, the local was often already global, shaped not necessarily by transnational vectors but by long-standing and dynamic interregional influences: being only partially integrated into the "imperial global," as he argues, hardly equates with complete isolation. For anthropologists of Africa like James Ferguson, the insistence on convergence—of goods and influences, especially via "flows"—as a measure of globality also tends to perpetually and presumptively marginalize Africa, despite its regional diversity and intercontinental traffic across the millennia.[16] Similar arguments could be made about the Pacific, a region that has largely been marginal to both international debates over globalization and world historical scholarship. This marginality reflects outsiders' understandings of both scale—Pacific islands seem small and scattered when measured by Eurasian or American standards—and geography. The vast Pacific Ocean has typically seemed like a barrier that has "isolated" the region from the main currents of world history: yet, for the peoples of Oceania, the sea instead was a highway that linked neighbors into circuits of exchange, and their visions of history are full of encounters, travel, and cultural change. In other words, connection had always been a feature of life in Oceania; the arrival of European imperial agents did not initiate cross-cultural contact, but rather violently, if incompletely, reoriented and reordered preexisting patterns of exchange and interdependence.[17]

In our view, these examples are useful because they remind us that "evidence" of globality is a prerequisite for incorporation into global history. In other words, the ideological presumptions of what "looks global" go a long way toward shaping who gets absorbed into the narratives of world history; but globalization is not the necessary or natural destination for all modern histories.[18] If they act as a break on teleological interpretations of globalization, these critical postures also underscore the questions of proportionality with which we are concerned. When, where, and under what conditions was the global actually constructed by the imperial? Equally importantly, to what degree were imperial conditions themselves shaped by other nonimperial global forces? In our current moment, examples of such disarticulation may seem counterintuitive, but they nonetheless abound. Take, for example, the growing coordination of immigration restriction policy and response to the rapid extension of Chinese migrant networks across the Pacific world or the processes that ended slavery in German East Africa on the threshold of the Great War in spite of, rather than because of, colonial intervention.[19] In both these cases, empire was a factor, even a historical agent, but it did not necessarily play a primary or determinative role. And if we are to assess the impact of empire on global developments, we must be careful not to ascribe the outcome of every event, idea, practice, or policy to an inevitably imperial global hegemony without attention to the kind of contingencies and ruptures to which we understand all histories to be subject.

Phenomena like Chinese diasporic networks and the campaigns to end slavery depended as critically on earlier histories of empire building, long-distance trade, and global religious impulses as they did on the events and transformations of our chosen period here. As we indicated above, empires capitalized continuously on earlier connections, extending and enhancing the scale of premodern networks and drawing them into the circuits of the larger imperial or global systems. And here we want to suggest that the global is not some kind of preexisting category waiting to be filled or the inevitable destination of all imperial power. Rather, our task is to illustrate that empires in this period were regimes invested in creating geographically expansive markets, politically portable forms of government, and civilizational identities that aspired to interconnectedness and interdependence. During this extended historical moment, the spaces of the imperialized world came to be understood and valorized as *global*—a term occasionally used at the time but which nonetheless has analytical possibilities retrospectively if we are cautious about specifying its territorial remit. For sometimes the imperial global was, in fact, intercolonial, as in the manifold connections that directly linked settler colonies such as South Africa, Australia, and New Zealand or the linkages that developed between India and British territories in Southeast Asia as well as South and East Africa. Sometimes it was inter-imperial, as in the deep ideological continuities between British and American colonial rule; the movement of indentured workers from the New Hebrides to British-controlled colonies like Western Samoa, Queensland, and Fiji, and French colonies like Tahiti, New Caledonia, and Hawaii (both before and after its annexation); or the emergence of Pan-Asianism at the conjuncture between British and Japanese imperial orders; and even the interdependence that developed between indigenous New Caledonian activists and Australian communists.

Rarely was the "imperial global" comprehensive and all-encompassing, in the sense of reaching everyone on the globe or impacting or penetrating the full scope of colonized societies. In this sense, the articulation of empire and the global marks out a particular kind of uneven development. The imperial global was less an accelerating juggernaut than a set of intermittently integrative processes that shared no single common motor, processes that reflected the vagaries of conjuncture and divergence, of appetite and indifference, of intentionality and inertia. Critical histories of the global like ours will not only be sensitive to the role of imperial power in making the global, therefore, but will also track the limits of imperial reach and the anxieties and vulnerabilities of imperial authority as well. This is not to say that we subscribe to the "fit of absence of mind" account of how empires were established; quite the contrary. We embrace, rather, the "chaotic pluralism" argument that John Darwin has nominated as a possible explanation for how Western imperialism, at any rate, achieved the hegemonies it did in the nineteenth and twentieth centuries.[20]

Following the work of postcolonial critics, we adhere to the global not as an a priori category but as a positioning device: an interpretive framework that enables us to position empire in relationship to an emergent and even halting or unfinished global set of processes rather than a territorially given set of coordinates.[21] This move, which draws from both feminist/queer theory and postcolonial criticism, has at least three methodological consequences. The first is to signal our skepticism about the teleology of the terrain of the global. By resisting the temptation to presume that all histories end up as global, we can better capture the historical conditions that nurtured relationships between empires and other globalizing agents without presuming a natural or even fateful affinity between the two. Its second function is to illustrate the ways in which colonial regimes and imperial systems looked very different from different points in space and different social locations: to get outside the view from the imperial center (whether London or Istanbul, Tokyo or Paris) is to view the assemblage of global empires from a variety of angles. So, for example, the operation of Ottoman authority was experienced very differently in Yemen or Iraq than it was in Istanbul itself; just as the experiences of Han Chinese and Melanesian populations colonized by the Japanese had very different inflections due to the application of Japanese racial thought in its imperial domains. Thirdly, we seek to embed the study of imperial relations both in the very real specificities of place but also from an angle of vision that captures the texture of the social and the cultural, not simply as lived experience but as part of the structural conditions of empire building and global connectedness. Here we are indebted to geographers who are at pains to remind us about the importance, and historical specificities, of space at all scalar levels—from the hospital to the mission station, from the law to the body of the child, the day laborer, the rebel.

We insist that these microlevel histories reveal the deep contingencies of imperial global systems and tensions of the kind produced by the collision between the weight of local difference (or indifference) and the reterritorializing nature of imperial power. Imperial histories are replete with this: from the rise of the Deoband school of South Asian Islam, which attempted to reorient Muslim life by reasserting cultural continuity and teaching early Islamic principles against the backdrop of colonial modernization, to Maori prophetic leaders, who actively separated their followers from the trappings of modernity as they attempted to replicate the transformations enacted by the Old Testament's Abraham and Moses. Or in a place like Tianjin, China, where multiple empires had concessionary privileges, locals who navigated the power structures understood them not as competing local or imperial or global spaces but as a matrix of all three.[22] In other words, we see empires not as coherent wholes that can be recovered in their seamlessness, but rather as the accumulation of often incommensurate fragments that interrupt the claim to homogeneity that the global tends to promise.

The homogeneity we are writing against is enabled by imperial histories that fail to move beyond a top-down approach and insist on genealogies of the contemporary imperial moment focusing on high politics derivative of Euro-American political thought. We are wary of imperial histories that fail to reflect the imprint of the colonized, not simply because we believe there is ample evidence to show how and why they were coauthors of imperial social, political, cultural, and economic orders, but also because of the ways in which those processes developed practices and ideas of indigenous sovereignty among native peoples with implications for resistance and decolonization on a global scale. Anticolonial nationalists in this period may not have all communicated or known each other, but the parallels between movements are as striking as the resemblances between and among imperial orders themselves. No self-respecting account of the imperial global in this period can afford to ignore or sidestep the work that critics of empire in colonial "locales" and imperial metropoles undertook, because that work actively helped to create and ultimately to unravel the old global order that pre-1945 imperial powers attempted to put and keep in place. The appropriation of technology, the reconfiguration of space and place, and the will to imagine a community of transnational anti-imperial solidarities were absolutely consequential to the fate of the global world order in this period—as events like the Treaty of Versailles, the conquest of Manchuria, and the imperial border-crossing of anticolonials like Ho Chi Minh and Subhas Chandra Bose illustrate.

The importance of anticolonial nationalism also recodes our view of the nation-state, a form of political organization that, despite attempts at international governmentality like the League of Nations or at transregional political formations like the Caliphate movement, was increasingly authoritative on the global stage in this period. Instead of seeing nation-states as simply the projection of European models out into the colonial sphere, we emphasize the centrality of imperial mobility, colonial communication systems, and anticolonial nationalism in molding the shape and character of individual nation-states and the global nation-state system. At the same time, imperial economic competition compelled nation-states to define themselves increasingly as global policemen, regulating migration and controlling movement across borders with increasingly strict citizenship mechanisms, established through complex legislation and technologies like passports, visas, and identity cards. The strong nation-state was in many ways the effect of these apparatuses, which were elaborated, in turn, in the face of escalating connections: the capacity to control borders and people was the sine qua non of its definition, in both demographic and spatial terms. Nor were the leaders of anticolonial movements immune to these exigencies, as the Indian National

Congress's preoccupation with expatriate Indians in South Africa and elsewhere testifies. In this sense, the models of sovereignty and territoriality that "native critics" of empire elaborated revealed the growing inescapability of the nation-state as a model for political organization and the cultural imagination.

In the sections that follow we seek to foreground the particular, contingent, and dynamic relationships between different scales of social organization, political activity, and intellectual work in order to assess the parameters of the global in the age of empires. We are particularly interested in the ways in which forms of connection and circulation—from the operation of railway networks to international conferences, from the distribution of newspapers to the spread of diseases—throw multiple scales and dimensions of historical experience into bold relief. Even as we demonstrate how these forms and pathways helped to shape the global, our analysis consistently emphasizes the unevenness, fragility, and incompleteness of these linkages. By proceeding thus we hope to bring the histories of connection and contention, interdependence and independence, accommodation and resistance, together within the same frame. We are convinced it is within these coexisting histories that the texture of human experience is found and that particular manifestations of modern imperial and global culture take shape. Questions of gender and sexuality, race and ethnicity, class and status, are crucial to this project, not simply because they have to be accounted for but because they were utterly instrumental to how empires unfolded. Far from being marginal to the operations of imperial geopolitics, bodily practices and intimate relations of various kinds were deeply implicated in the inequalities and power struggles of colonialism.

We begin in Section 1 by examining modern empires as primarily, if not exclusively, territorializing projects: place-making regimes whose spatial logics had local and regional consequence and whose cultural forms (military barracks, the railway carriage, the imperial home) add up to a historically particular global model of "culture" and "civilization." In Section 2 we focus on the history of communication, transportation, and various forms of economic connection. While these may be thought of as the staple of an older style of "imperial history," we believe that they are crucial elements for any work that seeks to unpack the relationships between empire building and the emergence of the global—not least because they were instrumental in the rescaling of time and place that empires aspired to, whether European, Muslim, or Asian. Section 3 takes on the question of geopolitics, tracking the work of imperial agents and anticolonial subjects in the making of the new world order that participants in the postcolonial conference at Bandung were compelled to grapple with. Here we are interested as much in provincializing Britain in the story of modern imperialism as we are in centering the ideological and political work of empire's opponents and enemies. Such a move entails revising conventional views of the spatial order of the period, both to account for the roles of Russia, Japan, and the United States as imperial powers and to register the ways in which anti-imperial engagement and resistance shaped the fate of the post-1945 world. It also means remaining vigilant about historicizing the fitful and uneven development of the imperial global and skeptical about its world-historical inevitability—then and now.

One risk of arguing for empire as a kind of GPS (Global Positioning System)— even tongue in cheek—is that we imagine that ours is the view from the historiographical equivalent of Google Sphere. While we have tried to educate ourselves out of the corral of British imperial spaces and places—with all the baggage that entails—ultimately we must cop to our training, our intellectual knowledge base, and the politics of our locations. The latter are admittedly "Western," though in the case of New Zealand not self-evidently so; and they are primarily Anglophone in orientation, a fact that exerts real limits on the variety of histories we can access and put into play as part of our assessment of the limits and possibilities of a global imperial order. There is no getting beyond the materiality of one's location and its impact on one's perspectives and methods; but this does not mean that there is no possibility of directing a self-critical, and critically analytical, optic toward it and proffering new forms of historical thinking and doing from there. We hereby acknowledge our errors of commission and omission as well as the limits of our analytical interpretations. We do so not out of defeatism or from a desire to avoid accountability but out of a commitment to both the project of radical critique in an age of Anglo-American imperial aggression *and* a genuine sense of humility about the limits of the knowable world in an age of apparently boundless globality.

1. *Reterritorializing Empires*

HISTORICALLY, the building of empires was about the wresting of land—whether through military might, economic encroachment, or purposeful settlement—from its traditional owners or imperial rivals and accumulating these pieces of territory in an extended economic and political system. Newly acquired lands might offer strategic advantage, access to lucrative markets, or valuable supplies of labor. They might also allow the colonizing power to exploit profitable resources or commodities as well as a taxable population. At a fundamental level, empire building was about the extraction of rent, revenue, and resources from land overtaken. The strings of colonies, protectorates, and trading enclaves built up by imperial powers between 1870 and 1945 were routinely depicted through globes, maps, and atlases. Territorial accumulation became both a symbolic and material index of national power and international standing: advocates of colonialism in recently unified nation-states of Germany and Italy as well as in Meiji Japan gave particularly strong expression to the idea that an extensive empire was a crucial indicator of a nation's strength and modernity.

Thus empire building between 1870 and 1945 was grounded in acts of deterritorialization and reterritorialization. Put even more simply, all modern empires lived and died not just by the sword, but by territorial imperatives as well. Although this proposition may seem self-evident, it is worth dwelling on, in part because within the new political and technological orders spawned by forms of globalization at the dawn of the twenty-first century—with their supposed "flatness" or "placelessness"—the territoriality of modern imperial formations can be lost. It would be unwise, of course, to suggest that the sprawling empires of this period always had a hands-on, terra firma grasp of all their colonial possessions and subjects. It would be equally foolhardy to claim that the age of territorial empires is over: as we well know, a wide variety of raw materials remains the motivation for acts of imperial aggression large and small. Nevertheless, when viewed against contemporary networks of communication and the "virtual" nature of much imperial power at the dawn of the twenty-first century, the ways in which imperial regimes imagined and managed the spaces of empire between 1870 and 1945 begin to look historically distinctive. This period not only witnessed the establishment and consolidation of particular forms of territorial imperialism: it also gave rise to specifically spatial idioms of imperial power that carried with them a number of ideological presumptions about the benefits of imperial rule and its civilizing capacities. Those presumptions were vulnerable to influence, appropriation, and resistance by all kinds of actors, colonized and colonizers alike.

Indeed, histories of modern empires must address their spatial ambitions and aspirations in both material and symbolic terms, especially if the historical particularity of empire building between 1870 and 1945 is to be reckoned with. To be sure, the centrality of territorial acquisition, expropriation, and transformation is not unique to modern empires. From the Romans to the Mongols, from the Ottomans to the conquistadores, from Timur to Suleiman and beyond, one of the chief outcomes of the imperial impulse—whether out of religious, commercial, or political motivation—has been the acquisition of new spaces and their transformation into new places marked by the structural and cultural imprint of the new imperial power. At the most literal level, a phenomenon like the Mongol takeover of Eurasia—where powerful horses, military might, and the imposition of the *yassa* (legal code) allowed Genghis Khan and his successors to assert their dominance from Yangzhou to Budapest with unprecedented velocity—illustrates the sheer spatial ambition of premodern empire building, however loosely bound the collection of conquered lands ended up being. And in the wake of Genghis Khan there were more purposeful early modern articulations of imperial territoriality as well. For what are Gugong (the Ming and Qing Dynasties' "Forbidden City") or Fatehpur Sikri (Akbar's red sandstone wonder) if not epic expressions of empire's territorial reach and spatial ambition before modernity? Few, if any, modern empires built architectural equivalents to these palatial capitals—and when they did, as in the case of Edwin Luytens's New Delhi, they invariably had to accommodate the blueprints of previous imperial designs. Indeed, grafting one space upon another, whether cartographically or imaginatively or both (as Christopher Columbus infamously did when he saw Hispaniola and mistook it for "the Indies") is perhaps one of signature moves of would-be imperial powers.

Indeed, the history of imperialism abounds with examples of such grafting, as the British appropriation of Mughal forms in India and the French reworking of Ottoman techniques in Algeria—to name just two—so powerfully suggest. Beginning with Columbus's misapprehension, such examples remind us that colonizing powers never entered empty, history-less spaces, and they testify to how older imperial histories have been routinely sutured into emergent colonial formations.

Like those that had come before, modern imperial states understood the power of mapping empire's presence in spaces large and small. Whether in British India or on the Russian steppe, modern empires felt an impetus to measure and map territory in ever greater detail, in order to rationalize conquest in scientific and managerial terms. Modern imperial maps and modern imperial spaces linked spatial planning to state power more tightly than previously and by the middle of the nineteenth century were increasingly interested in mapping the spatial configurations of race, gender, and other manifestations of cultural difference. This is not to say that a deep concern with cultural difference was not legible before the nineteenth century. World maps produced in the early modern West were routinely ornamented by images depicting connubial figures and "native" peoples in various states of dress and undress, thus marking out the overlap between the conquest of territory and the sexual imagination. And it would be hard to gainsay the ways that the Inquisition, as one territorially far-reaching example of ecclesiastical imperium, left its imprint on the bodies of victims black and brown and red, in many cases using their sexual relationships as the basis for persecution in the enclosed spaces of the torture chamber and the very public spaces of the auto-da-fé.[23] But historians generally agree that the nineteenth century witnessed an acceleration of conviction about the fixity of biological race and a concomitant concern about the dangers of intermixture, whether in social or sexual intercourse, to imperial security *tout court*.[24] At the same time, knowledge was increasingly collected and ordered to produce detailed pictures of social organization within each colony. Dictionaries and grammars of local languages, maps and city plans, censuses and collations of statistics measuring everything from trade patterns to the average height of particular populations were crucial instruments that allowed administrators to "know the country" they ruled over.[25] Through these forms of colonial knowledge and the growing coercive power of modern states, empire builders attempted to keep a close watch over the intimate domain: policing these lines of connection was frequently a difficult undertaking, but nevertheless was a routine concern of many colonial regimes.

The dominance of racialized notions of space in imperial policy and ambition is amply evident, for instance, in both the microprocesses and the macrodiscourses of the post–World War I period. For example, the Amritsar massacre in 1919, which left at least 379 Punjabis dead, dramatized British anxieties over the racial ordering of space in colonial cities. The mixing of villagers and politically active urbanites at Jallianwalla Bagh, a large public garden and gathering place adjacent to the precincts of the Golden Temple, caused leading British officials in Punjab considerable anxiety in the wake of an assault on a white woman and against the backdrop of widespread disruptions to imperial communication networks and rumors about the possibility of a rising against British rule. The British brigadier Reginald Dyer, who gave the order to open fire on the crowd, claimed that he was facing the seeds of an uprising, and he justified his actions as upholding an increasingly precarious imperial authority. The massacre at Jallianwalla Bagh not only laid bare the anxieties of the small cadre of British administrators who were dependent on large numbers of Indian soldiers, clerks, and minor state functionaries as they ruled over a vast Indian empire, it also quickly came to stand for the brutality that was born out of an imperial desire to exert control over the social and political lives of colonized peoples.[26]

To take another example from the European context, the interweaving of space, race, and empire was striking in the context of German nationalist thought. From the 1890s the German ethnographer and geographer Friedrich Ratzel argued not only that Germany should seek to extend its naval power and overseas possessions, but that Germans should also strive to fashion a strong state that would naturally expand. This expansionist drive, he argued, should extend Germany's territorial borders and spread German culture into Eastern Europe. After Ratzel's death in 1904, the notion of *Lebensraum* that was central to his discussion of the growth and decay of states not only became an important element in German scholarly debate but also was woven into discussions of Germany's imperial potential. By 1933 a starkly racialized version of *Lebensraum* underpinned Adolf Hitler's arguments for the ruthless colonization and Germanization of Eastern Europe.[27]

Recent research has suggested that the Nazi state's weaving together of race and geography also drew upon colonial antecedents, especially from German South West Africa. Jürgen Zimmerer has demonstrated that colonial administrators in German South West Africa strove to fashion a *Rassentrennung* (racial division) between German colonists and Africans, primarily through the creation of a cheap African labor supply shorn of legal rights. The racial logic that underpinned this strategy energized a violent and genocidal war against the Herero and Nama peoples between 1904 and 1908, which reduced their populations by at least 80 percent and 50 percent, respectively. This campaign saw colonial administrators advocating the systematic destruction of local infrastructure, the deployment of "extreme terror" in the execution of the war against both fighters and their families, and the use of "concentration camps" for prisoners. These models were significant templates for Nazi practices, as they were transported back to Europe by some young colonial administrators who later served in the Nazi state and were transmitted through scientific networks that gave racial theories produced out of colonial knowledge greater purchase within learned metropolitan circles.[28] In justifying the invasion of the Soviet Union in 1941, Adolf Hitler himself explicitly invoked another set of colonial models to explain the thrust of Nazi policy: "The Russian territory is our India, and just as the English rule India with a handful of people, so will we govern this, our colonial territory. We will supply the Ukrainians with headscarves, glass chains as jewelry, and whatever else colonial peoples like." German military advances were to redraw the demographic map of Russia and Eastern Europe and, as Hitler explained, the "German Volk [people]" were "to expand into this territory."[29]

These examples remind us that the global reorderings enacted by empires between 1870 and 1945 depended on a host of projects where anxieties over space and cultural difference coalesced, not only in attempts to regulate the ways in which different populations related on the ground in colonial locations but also in efforts to create and protect what was perceived as a superior metropolitan cultural order. Collaborators and enemies of imperial regimes, for their part, also understood the stakes of these spatializing projects, and they manipulated and challenged imperial power accordingly. Although it is notoriously difficult to read intentionality off of communal historical events like the gathering at Jallianwalla Bagh, at least some of those who gathered in that enclosed space understood that they were defying imperial territoriality at a time of imperial crisis. Indian nationalist leaders had long been aware of the ways in which British colonialism rested on the reordering of space along the lines of race and gender. Mohandas K. Gandhi himself had been central in the agitations against the laws that restricted the movements of nonwhite groups in South Africa and was highly cognizant of the ways in which British colonialism in South Asia rested on a raft of spatial exclusions and hierarchies that divided the British rulers from their India subjects. Even his celebrated Salt March from Sabarmati Ashram to Dandi in 1930 challenged the ways in which the unequal legal edifice of colonialism rested on a spatial logic. The Salt Act of 1882 had given the British colonial government a monopoly on the processing, distribution, and selling of salt. This legislation restricted the handling of salt to officially sanctioned salt depots in order to undercut small-scale local gathering and distribution of the commodity. By simply gathering the naturally occurring salt from the seashore at Dandi, Gandhi defied this monopoly and literally asserted the right of Indians to handle a commodity that was deeply embedded in the routines of daily life. Madhu Kishwar has observed that this campaign offered a new spatial vision of politics as it tied the kitchen to the nation, suggesting that the most basic elements of domestic life rested at the heart of the struggle against colonialism.[30] The brilliance of Gandhi's salt *satyagraha* was that it asserted Indian autonomy while also imagining sites like the Dharasana Salt Works in Gujarat, which his followers marched upon following the march to Dandi, as sites of colonial domination.

Gandhi's *satyagraha* campaigns were a potent demonstration that indigenous apprehensions of space and the persistence of native lifeways could provide the basis for challenging colonialism and, in so doing, revealed the very limits of territorial empire. This is not to discount the tremendous violence visited upon colonized peoples in the name of imperial necessity and global preeminence. But attending to the histories of imperial struggle literally on the ground reminds us of how and why the dramas of imperial encounter in this period were profoundly territorial in nature. Empire was, in other words, about the embodied unevenness of territorial ambition and resistance in the context of imperial systems that sought to impose their power across the globe.

This section focuses on some specific cultural, political, economic, and social spaces that played a central role in the reconfigurations wrought by the particularly aggressive age of empire building that emerged from 1870. After exploring some of the broad connections between space and the question of cultural difference in imperial regimes, our analysis turns to the ways in which imperial military activity produced some distinctive new sites for cross-cultural engagement as well as how these armies reshaped relationships between colonized communities and their homelands. We then examine the particular importance of the question of space in the work of missionaries and the impact of spatial arrangements on labor regimes. This opens up a broader exploration of the symbolic and material significance of the "home" as a site for colonial transformations. Ultimately we are interested in exploring both the complex cultural traffic that brought these contestations over space in the colonies back "home" to imperial metropoles and the extent to which indigenous communities were able to exercise influence in these struggles over the meaning of space.

Thinking about Imperial Space

Drawing largely on the expertise of geographers and the theoretical apparatus provided by Michel Foucault and Pierre Bourdieu, historians have developed a repertoire of terms and concepts over the last two decades that enable us to appreciate what is at stake in historicizing the spatial order of empires. Some of this terminology originated in earlier historiographies that had varying stakes in the concept of empire. The word *frontier* is a case in point. So, for example, Frederick Jackson Turner's famous "frontier thesis"—first delivered as a paper at a session of the American Historical Association held at the World's Columbian Exposition in 1893 and later incorporated into his 1921 book, *The Frontier in American History*—recognized the process of westward expansion and settlement as a function of "colonization" but generally emphasized the way in which the frontier experience shaped the American republican tradition rather than the consequences of territorial conquest or interracial violence. This meant that Turner's narrative really focused on how European migrants to the United States became Americanized rather than exploring the ways in which the frontier functioned as a permeable and fluid space of cross-cultural engagement and struggle. Of course, *frontier* is a fraught term well beyond Turner; yet its power to conjure colonial struggles over land makes it an important *imperial* technology rather than simply a spatial one. Similarly, for historians of Australia the idea of the frontier has long been a staple metaphor for conjuring both the spatial limits of settler colonialism and the cultural manifestations of that phenomenon (as in "frontier masculinity"), though the expressly colonial or postcolonial interpretive contexts had been muted until the work of scholars like Henry Reynolds focused attention on both the centrality of violence to colonization and strategic forms of resistance mobilized by Aboriginal communities in the face of white encroachment.[31]

The same may be said for the term *borderlands*. Used most prominently perhaps in North American historiography, the concept of borderlands is a way of marking the outer limits of settlement and expansion and signifying the culturally mixed and heteroglot spaces that frequently developed at the boundaries of states and empires. The idea of "borderlands" also allows processes and events that transect or blur national boundaries to be historicized: whether these are the shifting formations of indigenous communities from Florida to California or the eruption of "transnational warriors" who dared to traverse and transgress the porous yet highly politicized border inscribed between the United States and Mexico.[32] Although the idea of "borderlands" can undoubtedly illuminate the development of relationships between the United States and Mexico, which suggests that it should be key element in the reappraisal of American empire building, the concept's historiographical roots lie in early modern conquest narratives, and the imperial context of this powerfully spatial concept is not always to the fore. This may be in part because historians making use of terms like *frontier* and *borderland* typically frame their studies within the dynamics of nation making rather than in terms of their dynamic relationship to broader imperial systems as such. This is especially true in the case of indigenous histories that, while obviously mindful of the operations of imperial power, have tended to be as concerned with recovering elements of cultural continuity and underscoring the self-contained spaces of "local" life, political economy, and culture. The shifting deployment of terms like *frontier* and *borderland* is a salutary reminder that spatial terminology itself is no guarantor of elaborate spatial analysis.

In contrast, the analytical capability of terms like *frontier* and *borderland* is being brought to bear in historiographies where questions of empire and colonialism have frequently been neglected. This is most evident in current work on the territoriality of the Russian and Soviet empires; indeed, of all the borderlands of empire, Central Asia has been among the least historicized, at least until recently.[33] A phrase like "the Great Game," which is probably the most recognizable term for the Central Asian context, arose in the nineteenth century to describe the ongoing conflict between the tsarist and British empires over the land between British India and Russia. Mobilized first by an obscure English traveler and made famous by Rudyard Kipling's *Kim,* it remains a popular way of conjuring the stakes of imperial contest over vast expanses of desert and mountain, with the Khyber Pass—that winding and often fatal road between Peshawar and Kabul—serving as the most enduring symbol of Central Asian landscapes and communities that have proven hard to incorporate into any stable and durable imperial order. Russo-British rivalry over this patch was understood in strategically spatial terms, with Afghanistan routinely seen as a staging ground for Russia's invasion of India—a fear that provoked no fewer than three Anglo-Afghan wars between 1838 and 1919. But the concept of borderlands is equally apt, not only because it draws attention to the multiethnic communities that were annexed at the frontiers of Russian and then Soviet territory, but because it signifies the liminal spaces through which colonized elites had to move and negotiate power with imperial officials. As in other imperial contexts, "these imperial borderlands ... were not incidental to Russia. Their existence—and their subjugation—helped define Russia and Russianness in very tangible ways that are lost to analysis if Russia is seen as a unitary state."[34]

The contingency of metropolitan imperial regimes on the so-called edges of empire—yet another profitable idiom for historicizing the space and place of imperial power—is something to which we shall return in greater depth below.[35] Meanwhile, thanks in large measure to the work of environmental historians, the category of borderlands has allowed for an opening out into the larger space of "nature" more generally, thereby enabling students of colonialism to appreciate how the natural landscape (bush, forest, riverbank, swamp, and cane field) and the imperialized one (aboriginal reserve, game preserve, plantation, port, and colonial monument) helped to map local encounters even as they choreographed those encounters in the tangled histories of transnational and global spatial formations. Alfred Crosby's model of "ecological imperialism" captures some of these dynamics, emphasizing the place of biological exchanges and ecological transformation in enabling imperial ambition to become territorial sovereignty, but it tends to erase the complexity of indigenous understandings and uses of the natural world prior to conquest; and it does not necessarily do justice to the complex interweaving of colonized and colonizer interests in the transformation of the landscape that frequently was the basis of imperial contest and colonial struggle.[36] The systematic deforestation of Manchuria by Japanese mining and lumber companies—in the service of the interests of the imperial state—in the interwar period is just one of many examples that might be given to illustrate the ecological and economic consequences of imperial intrusion. Stories of this kind of decimation and depletion are legion, and they need to be understood as exemplars of the uneven geography of capitalist development that identified lands at the edge of imperial formations as spaces ripe for exploitation and extraction. Dramatic acts of environmental transformation were therefore not just manifestations of modernity's rapacious hunger for energy, commodities, and material wealth, but also were frequently generated by imperial ideologies that operated from the metaphorical presumption that colonial spaces and their inhabitants were wild and uncultured, waiting to be tamed. Yet especially in recent work, historians have been keen to place their narratives of environmental imperialism in the context of local, regional, and national struggles, in part so that colonial territories can be understood not simply as surfaces over which imperial power inevitably marched but as "meeting up places" in which a variety of historical subjects, in admittedly asymmetrical positions of power, nonetheless fought over the distribution of resources and over the nature of place itself.[37] That tribal and aboriginal peoples had competing spatial regimes suggests too that the territorializing practices to which colonizers made recourse did not merely produce *reactive* spatial claims on the part of natives, but rather threw into bold relief the variety of cartographic idioms imperial officials and subjects alike mobilized in the modern age.

One consequence of empire was a heightened sense of geographical identity for metropolitan imperial cultures as well as those enmeshed in the everyday struggles of colonial life at the edge of the empire. We know, for example, that by the 1850s "the empire" and the "globe" had been stitched together in the British public's imagination because of the popularity of imperial exhibitions and widespread circulation of maps, atlases, and globes that graphically depicted the growing reach of British territorial sovereignty and cultural influence extended by traders, settlers, and missionaries. Most Britons living between the 1890s and the end of World War II were only indirectly connected with the empire, but no doubt a sizable proportion of them knew that it was Cecil Rhodes's ambition to paint the world red as a result of school geography lessons that dramatized the spatial ambition of the age. This spatial ambition was constantly reiterated in the popular visual culture that represented the empire to British people: the global span of the empire was graphically depicted on objects from tea towels to playing cards, cake tins to board games.

Understanding empires as spatial and spatializing structures means that the power of terms like *frontier, borderland, edge,* and *landscape* resides not simply in their capacity to illuminate corners of imperial and colonial history heretofore unheeded. They also reveal just how critical space was, as both a material and an imaginative resource, to the operation of imperial domination, both symbolic and real. Both Chinese and dogs (and bicycles) were prohibited in parks in British-controlled Shanghai, though debate over whether there was actually a sign that read "No Dogs or Chinese Allowed" has continued to fuel heated debate about the convergence between race, imperial power, and space.[38] As powerful as it is, this example of imperial segregation—with its echoes of the Jim Crow South ("No Negroes Allowed"), the urban United States ("No Irish Allowed"), and colonial Natal ("No Indians Allowed")—should not lead us to an easy equation of imperial privilege with whiteness, as this would occlude other forms of racial hierarchies internal to Asian empires and articulated through local and often confessional idioms. We can see this in the case of Zou Rong, a young Han Chinese writer educated in Japan who subsequently lived beyond the full reach of the Qing imperial authorities in a foreign concession in Shanghai. He published a tract in 1903 that was fiercely critical of the Qing Dynasty's Manchu rulers. He expressed his revolutionary rage in racial and spatial terms, imagining a time when China's majority Han population would "emerge from the Eighteen levels of Hell and rise to the Thirty Three Mansions of Heaven . . . to arrive at their zenith—revolution."[39] Students, traders, migrants, and travelers across the globe gave voice to similar critiques, viewing the overthrow of racial degradation as a foundational justification for revolution against imperial oppressors, from the West and East alike. The year 1903 was also when W. E. B. Du Bois published *The*

Souls of Black Folk, in which he addressed the problem of the "color line" that separated black and white Americans. The nearly simultaneous publication of these texts speaks to the global entanglements of race and space that were critical to both the stability of imperial rule and the energies behind resistance to it.

The Military-Imperial Complex

Imperial garrisons remain a key element of contemporary realpolitik, and their continued existence is an important spur to a consideration of the centrality of the military in underwriting the projection of imperial authority. But their histories also remind us how empires created distinctions between native and imperial places while simultaneously encouraging indigenous communities to accept the legitimacy of these new spatial orders. Of course, armed conflict itself reordered space: imperial armies left their imprint on the landscape in manifold ways. In the wake of open conflict, the battlefield could serve as a source of imperial or anti-imperial memory, whether it was officially commemorated or not. Imperial armies and their generals may often have been ignorant of the indigenous meanings of battle sites, but those who did understand them often capitalized on them to shore up the spatial symbolism of their victory. This was certainly the intention of Lord George Nathaniel Curzon, who became viceroy of India in 1905. He set out to pay homage to the Mughal past by restoring a number of tombs and sacred places with the express ambition of signaling the worthiness, and the spatial symbolism, of Britain's imperial guardianship. The Dutch carried out a similar project of spatial appropriation in turn-of-the-century Klungkung, the home of the volcanic Mount Agung, "considered by the Balinese to be 'the navel of the world.'"[40]

With the rise of modern technology in warfare, it was increasingly likely that conflict would devastate local landscapes and with them local economies and populations. In East and South West Africa, German colonial forces came not to see the landscape as an obstacle to their operations, but rather imagined it as a vehicle through which they could achieve their aims. When soldiers burned villages and fields, destroyed cattle and plundered food reserves, they were aiming for "the total destruction of the indigenous population's means of life"—tactics that were a direct response to "flexible" and successful indigenous guerilla strategy.[41]

The natural world, of course, not only became a target of imperial coercion but also was at the heart of cross-cultural contestation. European colonial forest and wildlife policy catalyzed outright revolt in the Maji-Maji Rebellion in the German colony of Tanganyika. Colonial officials pressured local peasants to produce cotton for export, and this demand, together with imperial encroachment on the political economy of ivory, the closing off of hunting frontiers, and anxieties over their ancestral shrines, fed deep-seated anxieties among a range of local communities. Here colonialism effectively attempted to close off the forests—disrupting traditional African economic practices and curtailing access to culturally valued sites. These intrusions led a wide range of communities to take up arms against colonial rule in a two-year war in the forest from 1905.[42] Elsewhere, as on the northwest frontier in British India, anticolonial guerrillas on the border routinely raided local food and livestock holdings, eroding the wealth of already vulnerable communities in order to sustain their own campaigns against imperial power.

Such examples suggest that the struggles over landscape and resources intensified as imperial regimes extended their global reach and "deliberate environmental warfare" became an increasingly important aspect of these modern conflicts. In numerous contexts, colonial governments attempted to consolidate their power and extend their economic resources by reorganizing the relationships between communities and the land: whether we think of drive to clear *jangli* (wild) lands in India and turn nomadic communities into sedentary tax-paying cultivators, the transplantation of techniques, seeds, fertilizers, and management practices from Japan to Korea and Taiwan to enable these colonies to be transformed into granaries for the Japanese imperial system, or even the British imperial soldier-settlement schemes that quickened the pace of deforestation in Canada and Australasia. The relationship between the military and imperial government with respect to the environment could be more or less formal, and more or less successful in terms of imperial security, of course, depending on the context. "Frontier colonization" of the kind that happened on the Russian steppe, and which disrupted and displaced so many (mostly Muslim) communities and "resettled" so many different populations (including Jews), was propelled by the butt of a rifle as well by the growl of the empty stomach. In Turkestan, peasants could be armed by a military governor and hence could approximate settler-soldiers, but that could also be a fleeting status when the gift of the rifle was withdrawn for the sake of "imperial security." The Indian Forestry Service, which combined principles of conservation with imperatives of exploitation, regularly hired ex-army men; these linkages deepened in times of war when the extractive interests of the Forestry Service were called upon by colonial officials responding to the exigencies of maintaining a global imperial army. The same combination of bureaucratic oversight and quasi-military forest clearing occurred in French colonial Indochina, where by the 1920s the colonial project to dredge and clear the Mekong Delta was the third-largest earthmoving exercise in human history (behind the construction of the Panama and Suez canals). This undertaking was designed to improve coastal agriculture and facilitate more effective commerce and communication, but it was also celebrated by the French as evidence of the improving power of colonial rule in the face of rising anticolonial sentiment.[43]

Far from being contained to episodic battles or short-term wars, imperial militarism brought with it, then, long-lasting spatial consequences. In addition to being a major player in the shaping and reshaping of the colonial environment, imperial military complexes were also fiscal and bureaucratic organisms. They could reorganize conquered territories formally and informally, through centralized mechanisms or more haphazardly, in comparative isolation or concert with commercial interests. From the Roman Empire onward, camp followers have helped to guarantee that the military space on the ground is never the exclusive purview of official personnel. Across the global territories of the nineteenth- and twentieth-century empires, barracks abutted a variety of neighborhood and community formations, sponsoring all manner of encounters between soldiers and civilians, buyers and sellers, doctors and patients, children and adults, women and men. In these encounters, existing cultural identifications were affirmed (where soldiers were identified as Sikh, Pathan, Maori, or Kamba) even as new relationships were created. Highland soldiers, whether in Montreal or the Punjab, delighted in the spectacle their "exotic" garb created across the barracks line; Private Fred Bly of the 72nd Seaforth regiment remembered fondly how his uniform had brought not just stares but "all sorts of eatables and drinkables" from the locals when he was stationed in British-occupied Bloemfontein during the South African War.[44] These kinds of social relationships were formalized in World War I and World War II when significant enterprises developed in imperial port cities and way stations, as new restaurants, sightseeing ventures, and brothels developed to allow colonial soldiers en route to the battlefields of North Africa and Europe to encounter the "exotic." Such fraternization across physical and socially symbolic space was not limited to soldiers in arms. Men like Maurice Tinkler and Harry Dirpsose were members of the Shanghai military police in the interwar years. Former army men, they regularly transgressed the white–yellow boundary that structured the International Settlement and were just as routinely called on to intervene in the social lives of English aristocrats and Chinese servants—work that took them far from the police station and into the recesses of imperial Shanghailander life.[45]

It was rare enough in this period for barracks and garrisons to serve as sites for mutiny, as happened at Yen-bay in 1930, when Vietnamese troops killed their French superiors and took control of the town. That kind of open resistance invariably resulted in brutal suppression, but in Yen-bay it also ignited anticolonial feeling among Vietnamese students and workers (and a minority of French intellectuals) in the ensuing months and years.[46] As historians have been suggesting in the last decade or so, imperial armies and their bureaucratic apparatus have done more than leave carnage or the remnants of battle or even the detritus of military tourism in their wake. Not only have they impacted the spatial order of local and regional political economies, they have contributed to the racial and sexual orders of those domains as well. The site of the cantonment—permanent or semipermanent military quarters—is perhaps the most telling in this regard. Established primarily in the context of the British Raj (India, Pakistan, and Sri Lanka), cantonments served as a locus for commercial, medical, and sexual contact between colonizer and colonized—a locus whose spatial parameters shaped the nature and character of that contact in myriad ways. As with all ostensibly "military" spaces, the boundaries of the cantonment were at once regulated and porous: soldiers and local natives came and went in ways that were formally overseen, but they also developed strategies that were less susceptible to surveillance. With the legislation of a variety of contagious diseases acts in the 1860s and onward, cantonments became a scene of increased scrutiny. Native women who were deemed prostitutes were compelled to register as such and submit to medical examination in order to guarantee that that they were physically "clean" and would not transmit disease to European soldiers who frequented them. Already a space of racialized and sexualized encounter, this legal provision made the cantonment a place of hygienic discipline as well. Thanks to the work of Anglo-American women missionaries, it became a theater of metropolitan imagination as well. Their reports of the horrors of prostitution and their insistence that the British Empire's military should not be permitted to license such behaviors created a public scandal at home, materializing what had been heretofore invisible territories of rule for a Victorian imperial public readily sensationalized by both sex and empire in the name of respectability and reform.

Nor was the question of sexual encounter in the context of the imperial military complex limited to the British Empire. American occupation forces in the Philippines, Haiti, Japan, and a variety of other imperial "outposts" drafted local women to serve the sexual needs of American troops in state-inspected brothels, even as they constructed discourses about the immorality of those women that were linked to deep-seated presumptions about racial difference. Given the patriarchal bargain at the heart of all modern empires, it can hardly be surprising that at moments of the transfer of power—as when American military rule was established in postwar Korea—there was more continuity than discontinuity in the sexual economy. One long-standing spatial consequence has been the long life of "camptowns" (in Korean, *gijchon*) with ongoing effects on local populations across several generations. American women in postwar occupied Japan, like their British forerunners in the debates over the Contagious Diseases Acts, also got involved in public discussions about the impact of this situation on the "civilizing mission" of the United States, which in turn galvanized political opinion at home. In spatial terms, then, the specter of interracial sex and the social and political anxieties it caused allowed imperialists at home and in situ to map a new relationship between metropole and colony via sexualized forms of reference and to draw occupied territories into new imaginative, and highly gendered, landscapes.[47]

Needless to say, these were not issues unique to Western imperialism. As in the case of comfort women—those women forced into sexual slavery by the Japanese military—the combination of soldiers' perceived sexual needs and the presumptions about the sexual availability and disposability of colonized women that underpinned imperial rule created a variety of coercive spaces of encounter with far-reaching implications for the project of empire and for postcolonial societies as well. This can and should be seen as part of Japan's "one-body" project for Korea: a grim metaphor for assimilation at all scales of being. We would not like to suggest, of course, that bounded military spaces were the only places where interracial sexual contact took place. For one thing, they were generative of other spaces—like the brothel, the contagious disease examination room, the streetwalker's ambit—where contact occurred and was in turn policed. And we need only think of a treaty port like Shanghai, which was governed in part by Western powers, in part by Asian and Western business interests, to appreciate how complex the boundaries enabled by colonialism and semicolonialism might be. In fact, port cities across the world—from Marseilles to Suva, from South-ampton to Port-au-Prince—were spaces where soldiers, sailors, and military per-sonnel of all kinds had opportunities to experience the pleasures and the dangers of both heterosexual and homosexual encounters. Nor were these encounters just about white men and their nonwhite partners. The seduction of the African *tirailleur* in the streets of Marseille was a mild obsession of interwar French observers and generated "a web of regulations" limiting how prostitutes could solicit, even speak to, men on the street.[48] It was precisely the liminality of such militarized zones, their capacity for seepage into regular, quotidian spaces of imperial and colonial life, that made reformers of all kinds into disciplinarians of the male and female body, colonized and colonizer alike.

Evangelizing Space

Missionaries were among the chief sponsors of imperial contact and one-to-one encounter in this period. Although a variety of clerical orders dispatched the faithful from Western Europe across the world from the earliest days of Christianity, the nineteenth century inaugurated a period of accelerated mis-sionary activity and missionary visibility. During this period missionary he-roes like David Livingstone—the Scottish Congregationalist missionary whose exploration of central and southern Africa between 1854 and 1873 transfixed international audiences—were celebrated by metropolitan print media for demonstrating how evangelism served what Victorians called the "the three Cs" of empire: Christianity, Civilization, and Commerce. Those triple com-mitments involved Western missionaries in a variety of power relationships with colonized peoples and, as histories of the missionary project have been at

Hermannsburg Mission, Northern Territory, Australia, 1930. This mission, established by German Lutheran missionaries in the 1870s, remained an important site for cross-cultural engagement into the middle of the twentieth century. It was troubled by poor funding, disease, and the legacies of Aboriginal dispossession. (© E. O. Hoppé / Corbis)

pains to demonstrate, often in an angular relationship with both their superiors at home and the official imperial enterprise—in ways that could throw the very bases of metropolitan policy and power into question.[49] The growing influence of indigenous evangelists attached to missions and the emergence of vibrant native churches, especially in Africa and the Pacific, meant that Christianity's global reach was profoundly extended between 1870 and 1945. But conversion depended on complex acts of linguistic and cultural translation by both missionaries and indigenous peoples: in other words, Christianity's spread was grounded in its vernacularization and indigenization. The growing numbers of nonwhite colonized peoples who identified themselves as Christians in this period also complicated the cultural terrain of empires. Native Christians were not only adept at using the Bible to question the inequalities of colonialism, but at a fundamental level their cultural visibility also challenged the easy equations that some Europeans frequently made between Christianity and whiteness.[50]

Against the backdrop of the imperial globalization of Christianity, the ideological work of race was as complex as it is important. Not only was it bound up
with presumptions about the right gender order that should obtain in colonial
places, it was shaped as much, if not more so, by class-specific ideas about hygiene, literacy, and political rights—questions that missionaries invariably took
up as they tried to propagate the faith among native communities. Nor was the
movement of such ideas necessarily one-directional. Missionary work perhaps best
exemplifies the ways in which the colonial experience beamed a host of ideals—
about work, domesticity, conjugality, and virtue—modified by the messy entanglements of the mission station and classroom back "home." These complex
flows were in turn internalized in domestic culture and became a natural part of
the cultural landscape. So, for example, missionary men and women might have
arrived in the colonies with certain expectations of what "savages" looked and
acted like, but those presumptions would have already been shaped by their apprehensions of a "savage" working class at home. Given the feedback loop that
travel and missionary literature enjoyed, and helped to shape, readers in metropolitan spaces from London to Moscow and beyond had access to images of all
kinds of natives, savages, aborigines, and heathen from the tribal hills of India to
the Russian Caucasus.[51]

In turn, images of converted natives were mobilized in reforming efforts, and
they became instruments that could be deployed in contests over sexual morality, work discipline, and the nature of "true faith" at home. Moreover, depending
on their own class status (which was most often of the lower to middling sort),
missionaries may have viewed indigenous marriage practices through the lens of
an aspirant (as opposed to fully accomplished) bourgeois identity. Frequently
this was an identity that would have been consolidated precisely as a result of
their encounter with native polygamy, for example, and imported with renewed
vigor and conviction in London or Paris or the farmlands of the American Midwest. Histories of these kinds of "counterflows to colonialism" challenge conventional notions of how the movement from imperial to colonial space worked in
theory and practice and allow us to reimagine what the map of imperial power
looked like on the ground in the nineteenth and twentieth centuries.[52]

Despite the rich and growing literature on missionary work and empire, the
spatial arrangements of the mission station—which was often the geographical

center of formal and informal mission settlement—are rarely attended to. Mission stations articulated a visually and experientially powerful claim to local lands and communities by laying out the spaces of evangelism and their concomitant social services. At the same time, mission stations were marked off in expressly territorial terms from the "native spaces" that surrounded them. From these bridgeheads missionaries launched their campaigns for reform and conversion: they disrupted traditional forms of self-government, realigned local and regional work patterns, and, not least, sought to refashion a wide variety of indigenous domestic, child-rearing, healing, and bodily practices. This is not to say, of course, that missionary control of hearts and minds and even bodies was total. Missionaries across the globe engaged in compromises and hybrid solutions to the problem of "native conversion." As a consequence, mission stations typically were contradictory spaces. They were celebrated as sites of religious and cultural transformation, but in reality they were never were entirely free or independent of local practices and beliefs. Mission stations became locations where missionary teachings coexisted with long-standing indigenous cosmologies as well as new localized forms of Christianity popularized by native converts and evangelists. In many cases missionaries worked hard to delineate clear boundaries between the holy and moral spaces of their compounds and the remainder of "white society," boundaries that were demarcated by fences and policed through a close attention to who was entering and leaving through the station's gates. The mission station, with its multiple functions, its power to shape the nature and character of the imperial encounter, and above all its intrusive physical presence on the landscape, was a crucial instrument of imperial power, even when missionaries found themselves at cross-purposes with specific national-imperial agendas.

In fact, the spatial logic of the mission varied significantly from place to place, empire to empire, even denomination to denomination. There was just a handful of Christian mission schools in Taiwan at the moment of Japanese takeover, and imperial officials moved quickly to bring them under control; after 1905 pressure for conformity to a series of metropolitan regulations intensified, which effectively sidelined missionary education there. At Omsk on the Russian steppe, there were eight or nine different posts *(stany),* with a central coordinator and a staff of thirty in 1900 to accomplish "the staggering task" of anchoring orthodoxy among native populations. Some *stany* might have a school or a hostel, but these were unevenly distributed across the landscape; and given the harsh weather conditions, mission outreach was seasonal. Elsewhere, the mission station and the mission settlement, while related, were not necessarily coterminous spatially. The latter was largely if not exclusively residential, whereas the former could be semicommercial as well as pedagogical, both literally and figuratively. Educational opportunity was clearly the biggest draw at the mission station; instruction in the basics ("reading, writing and a little arithmetic," as one Jesuit father in Africa put it) was accompanied by emphasis on good manners and "moral cleanliness," rooted in the genuine desire to make better subjects of colonized peoples. But education also took place on a physical landscape where the stability of mission stations stood in stark contrast to the decimation of native lands, communal and otherwise. At Chishawasha in Mashonaland, missionary work was literally bound up with imperial occupation. In the 1890s, for example, Cecil Rhodes made grants to Methodists and awarded the Jesuits twelve thousand acres of farmland and in exchange for their assurance that missionary schools would be established in villages and that native headmen would help to guarantee attendance. Not only were local livelihoods held hostage to the fortunes of the mission station and its ancillaries, but by the 1920s the elaborate sites of the Jesuit Chishawasha Mission posed a stark contrast to the burnt homes and fields and confiscated cattle and crops in both Mashonaland and Matabeleland. Access to Western education here created a species of debt peonage in which territorial imperatives were paramount. "For people coming to settle on our farms," wrote the Jesuit father Francis Richartz, "I . . . stake the condition that they must send their children to school—or I will not have them."[53]

This case is arguably unusual, if not unique: it is rare enough that the connections between the interests of colonial state power and of missionary space were so bald or so evident. On the other hand, in many colonial spaces missions dominated the provision of Western education, a fact that gave them considerable leverage and that dramatized the social, economic, and political power of the mission station and especially the mission school. If we think about the literal route to those places—the journey to the school, the dress code required for crossing the threshold of the classroom, the embodied experience of the boy or girl seeking education or the mother looking for help for a sick infant—we gain an appreciation for just how keenly the reterritorialization that mission work aimed to accomplish might have been felt in this instance of colonial encounter. For some girls living under colonialism, the road to school was a metaphor for the relationship between tradition and modernity. For others, like Serah Mukabi, who feared the hyenas along the route to her mission school in Thogono (Kenya) and whose father threatened to kill her because he was so opposed to women's education, it was literally a hard and dangerous walk.[54]

Once there, the interiors of the mission station were absolutely consequential, not just to the processes of evangelization and conversion, but equally to the broader civilizing project. One very particular example is instructive: that of the dormitory of the mission school. A space to sleep, the dorm also functioned as a boundary between home life and school routine and, in the case of native girls, as a barrier to unwanted physical contact from male relatives and peers and even protection against early marriage. Given the possibility of predatory male teachers, it was not an entirely safe space either, especially (if not only) for girls. If the mission station was a porous space where local natives could mix with white missionaries somewhat freely, it was also the prototypically segregated and regulated space for native women. That regulation involved not just same-sex classrooms and gender-specific curriculum, but an almost exclusive focus on training in the domestic arts and sciences. In this sense, as a spatial complex the mission station articulated what imperial evangelization was all about: the reproduction of very specific geographies in native communities—with the reordered indigenized version of the Western bourgeois Christian home chief among them.

Spaces of Work

Given the centrality of colonial labor to the functioning of the imperial world system, it makes sense that spaces of work should be counted among the most important sites of encounter, conflict, resistance, and negotiation. If the plantation is the most obvious site for examining these kinds of experiences, its long life beyond the formal emancipation of slaves is often glossed over in accounts of modern Western imperialism. So, for example, slavery was done away with by the British Parliament of 1834, but as a legal category it was not abolished in Zanzibar until 1897 and in Kenya not until 1907. And contrary to the dominant grand narratives of British historiography, the economic entanglements of the slave trade persisted long after the 1830s for both ex-slaves and profiteers. Escape from the plantation—from its cartographies of work, coercion, and routine—was as slow in historical terms as it was uneven in spatial terms. As physical spaces, plantation properties remained the focus of agrarian production after emancipation but they competed for ex-slaves' attention not only with their own plots, but with a myriad of economic opportunities beyond the plantation's boundaries. Nor were attempts to bend workers' will to demands of plantation owners always successful. Colonial governments in East Africa, for example, engaged in a variety of strategies to try to keep plantations profitable: strategies that involved migrant labor and that led in turn to the emergence to racial hierarchies of value based on perceived strengths and weaknesses of various African groups, comparisons that typically favored the Nyamwezi, adept traders and hunters from the region between Lake Victoria and Lake Rukwa.[55]

The association of plantation work with slavery and hence with blackness *tout court* had a long history before the twentieth century, of course. In the French Caribbean, for example, "noir" was equivalent not simply to slave but to someone who worked in the physical space of the plantation.[56] What the Nyamwezi case underscores is that the dominance of free labor created spatial parameters for the consolidation of new racialized systems of colonial and imperial labor. Emancipation did not bring an end to the use of coercion and exploitation in imperial work spaces, nor did it curtail arguments that used cultural difference to argue that particular peoples (races, tribes, religious communities, and clans) were particularly suited to specific times of heavy physical labor. Thus the formal end of slavery did not prompt a broader reassessment of the fundamental cultural categories that ordered the division of labor in most colonies. As historians of women and gender have also been at pains to emphasize, the transition to free labor made women's work more invisible than ever as "the claims to masculine entitlement forged through revolutionary struggles to end slavery . . . ensured the persistence of gender inequality in postslave societies."[57]

Both the parameters of that postslave world and its gendered, racialized dimensions are enlarged when we consider the Indian Ocean as a space through which hundreds of thousands of indentured bodies—mainly male—circulated in the wake of slavery's abolition, spurred by new settlement patterns up and down the African coast and harnessed to new forms of labor organization in

South Africa. The traffic in male laborers between the interior of India and "Zululand" in the latter part of the nineteenth century created a corridor of reserve labor as well as a set of sub-imperial political economies that illustrate the variety and the constantly shifting geographical character of the racialized configurations in the world of imperial work. Indian indentured laborers, of course, were also crucial in the functioning of post-emancipation plantation economies in the Caribbean and the Pacific. Between 1879 and 1916 over sixty thousand men from Uttar Pradesh and Bihar in India were shipped to Fiji to work on the sugarcane plantations that the British developed as the economic base of the colony after the cession of Fiji's sovereignty to the United Kingdom in 1874. The British governor of Fiji, Sir Arthur Gordon, a former governor of Mauritius and Trinidad, believed that Fijians were in danger of being marginalized in the same manner as Aborigines and Maori, and he constructed a system of governance designed to fortify the indigenous community, which had been already severely affected by disease and land loss to incoming white capitalists. Gordon imposed heavy restrictions on the employment of native Fijians as laborers, effectively prevented sales of native lands, and implemented a system of indirect rule that fortified preexisting indigenous systems of governance. On the other hand, Gordon championed the use of indentured Indian labor, and in many ways Fiji's development rested on the exploitation of these South Asian workers. This bifurcated economic and cultural system was in time further complicated by the arrival of significant numbers of free Punjabi and Gujarati migrants who became important figures in the commercial life of the colony and whose presence called into question some of the basic racial presuppositions that ordered the colony's unique social formation.[58]

If post-emancipation plantations were spaces that were heavily dependent on migration and mobility, colonial diamond mines were much more bounded, the transportation routes and the migration of laborers to and from them notwithstanding. The comparatively enclosed character not just of mining work but also of social intercourse in and around the pits created spaces for all manner of sexual encounters between African men and boys in places like Kimberley in the 1880s, where small huts were gradually replaced by hostels where a dozen or more men might share bunks. The impact of rumors and more formal allegations of *nkotshana,* the practice of taking "boy wives" that colonial officials understood

Kimberley Diamond Mine, Kimberley, South Africa, ca. 1890–1905. This mine was established after the "New Rush" of 1871. By 1873 the nearby township of Kimberley was the second-largest settlement in South Africa. Massive numbers of laborers were deployed in the mining operations. (Library of Congress)

as sodomy, was not limited to South Africa; concerns about such encounters were rife among officials in Mozambique and were linked to the importation of thousands of Chinese laborers to Africa for work in the mines by the turn of the century as well. In the Transkei Territories in the late 1920s, "(gold)mine marriages" were ignored by company officials, feared and scorned by missionaries, and considered "unspeakable" by urban African male elites.[59]

While diamonds and gold were pivotal in the world economy in this period, coal was also a crucial tributary of global capitalism, especially in the context of two twentieth-century imperial wars. In the Ottoman Empire, conditions at the surface of mines were almost as grim as those below: shelters were makeshift and horrific accidents were not limited to the mine itself. In the British imperial context, the precincts of the coal mine were sites where a variety of encounters played out, often in highly gendered ways. Indian nationalists in the interwar period saw work by women underground not only as calling into question some basic cultural assumptions about gender but also as threatening India's aspirations to civilizational parity with Britain. But at the same time, the mine was a place where presumptions about white imperial masculinity operated in tension with colonial men's convictions about their autonomy and respectability. This was especially true in places like Nigeria, where mining officials understood their role as making "men" into "boys," where "the emasculation of African men was a core tenet of colliery managerial practices," and where "racism was an organizing principle of authority in the colonial labor process." Protests sparked by these conditions were organized and effective, not least because they caught the attention of the state by demonstrating that colonial workers were not as pliable as the agents of imperial capitalism might wish, but also because they demonstrated to local communities that modernizing work had its own political and social capital. Through desertion, strike action, and perhaps most significantly, the creation of a variety of spaces where miner-financed social welfare activities flourished (schools, hospitals, meeting houses), the coal miners at the Enugu Government Colliery staged performances of a particularly African industrial masculinity that gave the lie to racialist discourses of African laziness and had consequences for "native," regional, and international labor struggles.[60]

Despite the importance of female colonial labor in a range of social spaces— from the coal mine to the kitchen, the school to the brothel—to metropolitan observers in the British, French, Russia, Ottoman, or Japanese empires, the colonial worker typically remained presumptively male. Victorian readers of London-based periodicals may have occasionally seen images of an Indian female tea-plantation worker or indeed an Irish woman agricultural laborer, but as in the historiography on empire and work until very recently, the laboring body was muscular, tireless, even machine-like: all masculine qualities and all mobilized to render the worker as nothing but body. By the turn of the twentieth century nearly 40 percent of tea plantation workers in Assam were women, partly as the result of the aggressive recruitment of single women—a project with its own spatial practices and geographical ambits. Needless to say, conditions on the plantations and in the physical spaces of the tea gardens were instrumental to the high mortality rates among workers. The incapacity of overburdened and physically exploited women workers to breed more tea-pickers was consequential to the success of global output of a highly lucrative colonial enterprise like tea cultivation. Even more significantly, given the ways in which "free" male post-emancipation labor has been mobile and women have been considered immobile, there is much to be done both to historicize the gendered implications of colonial work and to rematerialize the various spaces of colonized women's labor. Much of that labor was undoubtedly agricultural, if not plantation labor per se. The peasant household was not limited to the family abode, and colonial women across a variety of imperial terrains did "not only the actual work of cultivation or supervision but also petty commodity production, gathering and foraging, food processing, retail and even waged work"—family labor, some or all of which might fall within the shadow of the actual family home.[61] As in Europe, the family economy blurred the boundaries between home and work. The predominance of women silk workers in the Ottoman Empire is one of many examples that demonstrates how crucial they were to household economic stability, and not just as extra-income producers. The advent of the textile industry in places like British India—by 1900 there were eighty-six mills in the Bombay Presidency, for example—brought women into historically new and culturally alien spaces with profound consequences for both the stability of imperial rule and the direction of anti-imperial politics. As with the mines, factories were both self-contained spaces with dangers from which women were believed to need protection and porous sites with tentacled pathways (railway, roads) that might lead women astray or encourage an excess of independent action and thinking.

In terms of sheer numbers, colonized women who worked as laborers far exceeded those privileged few who had access to Western education and managed to get trained and find work as midwives, doctors, or teachers. For those elites, the meaning of spaces like the nursery, the hospital, and the classroom were inflected by gender. Colonial men who dared to defy the spatial parameters of professionalism by training as educators or doctors undoubtedly faced racial prejudice at work; colonial women who did so bore what is now widely recognized as the added burden of being doubly out of place—of being a native in a European or Japanese world and of being a woman in a man's world. Nor was this challenge limited to the spaces of the hospital ward or the classroom. As we have seen in the case of Serah Mukabi above, getting to and from those spaces, traversing the material and the symbolic boundaries that imperialized terrains repeatedly threw up, shaped the nature and character of their mobility in ways that have left their mark. And needless to say, if the colonial worker was viewed primarily as male, the sex worker was viewed exclusively as female and colonially "native," even where, as in British India, for example, Eurasian women and Jewish women also numbered among the ranks of prostitutes. As objects of imperial scrutiny, anxiety, and reform, female sex workers were as critical to the functioning of empires as they were central to the quest for moral authority that imperial officials sought to harness through the regulation of their hardworking, mobile, and often diseased bodies.[62]

Empire at Home

Among the most ideologically charged—and materially transformed—spaces of imperial encounter in this period was the home. As sites of labor, biological and social reproduction, consumption and violence, the colonial house and home were rarely the idyllic spaces invoked by social reformers or the bourgeois metropolitan imagination. Economic pressures and demographic constraints meant that these dwellings were often at odds with the idealized vision of the cultivated home where the "angel of the house" presided and protected the family from the worldliness of public life with all its vulgarity and corruption. Feminist historians have successfully challenged the gendered dichotomies of home (female) versus work (male) by demonstrating how structurally embedded nineteenth- and twentieth-century households were in the political economy of the nation and how national, imperial, and anticolonial debates left their mark on domestic lives and subjectivities. In fact, one of the most significant and analytically flexible categories to emerge with a renewed emphasis from recent imperial history and colonial/postcolonial studies is "domesticity." This concept has become indispensable because historians have insisted on understanding it as a spatial category with the capacity to open out onto *and* to open up a host of traditional rubrics (work, politics, the economy) that have not been seen as domains either of women or of gendered interpretive possibility—or have been so only comparatively recently, historiographically speaking. This is especially germane because the period between 1870 and 1945 marked not only the greatest extent of Europe's imperial reach but also the apex of a certain globally powerful notion of bourgeois respectability. This was an aspirant social formation framed around deeply gendered and racially specific forms of domesticity that served as the template for civilizational progress and achievement in ways that plotted men, women, and children very deliberately in relation to household space. The precincts of the domestic were, in short, a constitutive feature of imperial and colonial encounters in the context of global modernity, so much so that it may not be too much to speak of empires as carriers of ideas and practices of a domesticity that circulated globally and were under debate from Algiers to Zanzibar, Sheffield to Sydney.

The portability of metropolitan ideals to the colonies was a staple of imperial history well before the subject of domesticity erupted on the scene in the 1980s. There are few more evocative images than that of the English woman setting up a full-scale tea service in the middle of a (usually geographically unspecified) "jungle." This was an image made believable by Maud Diver and other late-Victorian writers who tried to capture the phenomenon of the "compleat Indian housekeeper" whose dominion in the home was thought to be its own form of an imperial military maneuver, whether home was suburban London or in the shadow of Government House, Calcutta. A host of other contemporaries colluded in this presumption, from missionaries to travel writers to imperial officials. Most, if not all, of these commentators took the nuclear family and the European middle-class household as their model for what "natives" should aspire to if they wished to demonstrate their capacity to resemble—by approximation, if not by complete identification—Western family forms and, ultimately, to participate in Western political forms as well. In colonial India, the ideal of companionate marriage was held up as the pathway for natives who wished to realize their social and political aspirations for self-government. This model was juxtaposed against the extended familial arrangements and especially the practices of early marriage and polygamy that were believed to be rampant among the "heathen races." It is worth underscoring here that the colonial reformist vision of companionate marriage was a conjugal ideal with very particular spatial prescriptions as well. For not only should Indian women be educated so that they could come out of purdah (seclusion) and join their husbands as equals—thereby offering demonstrable evidence of those husbands' legitimacy as men, by bourgeois European standards—they should also arrange their everyday household routines so that their education (typically in the "science" of motherhood and domestic life) would in turn allow them to reorganize the gendered spatial conventions that ordered both the Hindu and the Muslim home. In concrete terms, this meant eating at table with their husbands and children, supervising the servants, and moving effortlessly across the threshold of home into the public, social, and often political worlds of men. Those worlds were increasingly "mixed," not just in terms of men and women, but (however unevenly and uneasily) in terms of race as well, especially in Indian cities and their immediate suburbs. Thus, not only were the spaces of domesticity remade inside the colonial household, they extended well beyond the physical spaces of house and home, giving the lie to the limits of the domestic and its apparent disconnect from politics in its micro and macro forms.

Critics of the new imperial history in the British context have been eager to see connections made between what they persistently view as cultural domains, like domesticity, and the putatively "real" spaces of power like politics at the institutional level. The career of W. C. Bonnerjee, first president of the Indian National Congress and a passionate modernizer when it came to the lives of his wife and his daughters, would appear to ratify the claim that the precincts of domesticity need to be viewed in as capacious an analytical frame as possible. For Bonnerjee worked hard to rearrange the internal dynamics of his family household so that his wife could assume a companionate role. This rearrangement helped to consolidate his political success in nationalist politics, even as his wife, Hemangini, appears to have been an unwilling and even quietly resistant subject of his reformist plans. This South Asian example does more than illustrate the constitutive role that domesticity played in reterritorializing the Raj. It also challenges the presumption that models of metropolitan domesticity were simply transplanted from Britain to the colonies. Elite Indian men like Bonnerjee, who aspired to political participation and even self-government, actively participated in the reshaping of European ideals, and they by no means applied them wholesale: their attempts to produce a specifically Indian colonial "resolution" to the woman question had spatial consequences that Indian women themselves reacted to, engaged with, and also helped to shape. What this suggests, among other things, is that the territorializing power of empire was not the possession only of

British officials and reformers, as indigenous adherents to patriarchy could and did share ideological and strategic space when it came to securing a place for domesticity in the workings of imperial power.[63]

House and home mapped the overlap between domains of the cultural, social, and political in other ways as well. In the context of European imperialism, white women traveling through or living in colonial territories appeared to be breaking taboos by crossing into new "frontiers" on behalf of their sex. In addition, they were often critical to the redrawing of lines of division between black and white, especially given the prevalence of fears of miscegenation in such settings. Servants were clearly a key node of contact and exchange. In Indonesia as in many other imperial locales, domestic servants were the only colonial people Dutch women routinely met in daily life. Popular household manuals in Java recommended a minimum of seven domestics, and the majority of household workers were women, even though there were other forms of labor available to them.[64] The presence of children in the European households of empire further complicated this tense environment: at least until a certain age, they were often in the charge of native servants, with whom they might become quite intimate. These intimacies interrupted the racialized demarcations of internal household space in ways that shaped not only "imperial motherhood" but of course those children's apprehensions of appropriate or desirable colonial distance as adolescents and in later life. The removal of European children to metropolitan boarding schools at a certain age also profoundly shaped the colonial household and reminds us how contingent the organization of labor and the shape of colonial institutions were on the rhythms of imperial family life. Beyond their responsibility for European children, domestic servants routinely challenged the spatial segregation of urban colonial cities and their rural outposts even as they were coerced into new and emergent forms of apartheid inside the European home. As late as the 1970s in South Africa the internal colonialism of the middle-class "English" household persisted as more than a vestigial trace: not only were domestic workers segregated at the back of the main house, they ate substandard food and were allotted limited provisions (like toilet paper)—even as, whether men or women, they might be subject to the sexual depredations or everyday violence of the master or mistress.[65]

The household was also, of course, the site of complex kinship systems, both entrenched and mobile—a phenomenon that some imperial officials and ethnographers (whether employed by the imperial state or not) grasped to a greater or lesser degree. Disruptions of those systems in spatial terms could be radical, as in the case of child removal in the Australian case, where Aboriginal families were viewed as spaces of "physical moral danger and neglect." These representations had concrete and terrible outcomes as they were deployed to justify breaking the circle of indigenous family life and eventuated in the painful legacy of the "Stolen Generations." That these practices served the aims and work of the state, there can be little doubt: Aboriginal children were expelled from state schools in early twentieth-century Katanning, in Western Australia, as part of a larger effort to clear the wheat belt and to respond to shifting heightened local concern about the presence of poor Aboriginals among dominant communities anxious about the preservation of white schools and hospitals.[66] Incursions into familial space could also be more subtle, as when missionaries and their ancillaries tried to move into the household domain by serving as tutors in matters of domestic hygiene and child care. Significantly, in terms of assessing the reach of colonial power in spatial terms, such efforts were not so much resisted or ignored as they were seen to be irrelevant to the lives of the women and children they were targeting. So in the matrilineal society of colonial Asante, women interviewed about the impact of missionary work on their child-bearing practices effectively shrugged off the suggestion that their home spaces had been colonized—a very real pedagogical lesson about the limits of imperial reterritorializing in theory and practice.[67]

At Home in the Empire?

As scholars have been at pains to show over the last two decades, empire was never merely a phenomenon that took place "out there" without its real and symbolic effects being felt, seen, and lived "at home." In the context of Euro-American empires, the very grid of home and away that writers, officials, and administrators used to map the relationship between metropole and colony suggests the constitutive role that convictions about the "domestic" and its spatial importance had in shaping national and imperial imaginations. Inevitably perhaps, the rubrics that scholars have used for describing relationships of exchange and circulation have been spatial: whether they speak of "networks" or "circuits" or "flows" and "reverse flows," historians of modern empires have been acutely aware of empires' reterritorializing power, not just on the ground in colonial settings, but at the very hearts of Western empires as well. Debates in the historiography of the British Empire about the unevenness of imperialism's reach into "domestic" spheres are indicative of the high stakes of this reterritorializing legacy. This new work raises critical questions about where the nation ends and the empire begins, investing "home" and "away" with new historiographical meanings. These exchanges also demonstrate the continuing generative power of imperialism's spatial ambitions in the context of a globalizing world where students of the past are seeking genealogies for the contemporary present in the transnational spaces of earlier imperial moments. As we have suggested in our introduction, the relationship of imperialism to globalization is of course also a matter of great debate. If globality itself has entailed a redrawing of geopolitical space in ways that question the viability of discrete nation-states as arbiters of capital accumulation, military force, and the mobility of goods and people, attention to the dynamic relationship of domestic space and imperial power helps us at the very least to appreciate in historical terms how and why the reach of empires was so consequential to the making of the modern world.

Most obviously, the processes of global commodification that nineteenth- and twentieth-century empires brought into being transformed the spaces of "home." Here again, and especially in the context of contemporary discourses about the newness of late twentieth-century globalization, it is important to underscore that the period 1870 to 1945 accelerated transnational economic connections and sutured them to a variety of globalizing capitalist work regimes, forms of accumulation, and mechanisms of delivery and consumption. Early modern history provides examples of transregional entrepreneurship, the Chinese commercial empire being the most prominent example and the career of the eighteenth-century Cantonese merchant Howqua being among the most compelling, if not representative. A scion of one of the top trading families in China, Howqua advanced millions of silver dollars to far-flung merchants and through his profits helped to shore up the Chinese Empire during the ill-fated Opium Wars just before his death in 1843. As significantly for our purposes, his portrait hung in the East India Hall of Fame in Salem, Massachusetts, reflecting the extent to which New England merchants keen to enter the China trade were dependent on his favor and assistance.[68] Although the political economies of East Asia were worlds away, North American elites in the postrevolutionary period had dramatic evidence of their dependency on global forces and, however remotely, on the fortunes of a powerful Cantonese moneylender as well. By the later nineteenth century, the global circulation of goods was even more visible to consumers and empire builders alike. Workers in Glasgow who manufactured machinery used in the West Indies would have been able to glimpse the embeddedness of imperial circuitry in global capital. Port workers, warehousemen, and carriers as well as financiers would have understood how Canadian wheat, Iranian oil, Indian spices, Australian wool, New Zealand butter, Egyptian cotton, and Argentine meat both reflected and helped sustain Britain's aspirations for global dominance.[69]

The visibility of imperial goods at home in late Victorian Britain did not simply grow out of the increasing marketing of imperial goods, but it was also partly a legacy of the very public agitation against the slave trade, a movement with deep roots in the eighteenth century. Opponents of the trafficking in slaves and plantation slavery made the daily effects of "exotic" commodities like tobacco, coffee, and especially sugar consumption in the metropole a critical part of their abolition rhetoric and practice, with middle-class women taking the lead in targeting the female householder as the key to putting an end to the oppression of her African and Caribbean "sisters." Slave and ex-slave men and women also labored in Britain to make clear the high price of slavery to provincial and urban offices alike. Their role in enabling Britons to visualize the horrors of the slave system has only recently begun to be fully recognized, while their work in making visible the links between slavery and imperialism is only beginning to be acknowledged. Victorian "national" memory figured sugar and slavery as among the most visible effects of empire at home, but they were by no means the only ones. Much less anxiety was expressed over the more familiar commodities that flowed in increasing volumes from the white dominions to Britain: high proportions of the wheat, lamb, beef, butter, and cheese consumed by Britons were produced in Australia, New Zealand, and Canada. Not only was this imperial commodity trade integral to the modern British diet, it also was pivotal in shaping the economic and ecological transformation of those colonies, ensuring that they would primarily develop as "farms for empire" until well after 1945.[70]

While advertisements for these colonial commodities offered familiar images—featuring white farmers working the fields of temperate colonies—goods from the tropics were generally marketed and packaged as exotic for European markets. From the "oriental bazaar" of Liberty's department store to the advertisements for Pears soap that showed "little sambos," the connections between capitalism, empire, and cultural difference were routinely made manifest in Britain through material goods and print culture. They were no less visible to consumers in the Third Republic in France, where advertisements, packaging, and signage were important vectors through which ideas about France's African, Asian, and Pacific colonial subjects reached metropolitan consumers.[71] In the United States, where "empire" was a less commonly recognized fact of life (then and now), the consumption of foreign goods was seen as evidence of cosmopolitanism, investment in America's overseas enterprises, and even patriotism, if not of manifest destiny itself. By the twentieth century, middle-class homes across a host of imperial sites might exhibit signs of imperial consumption not just as marks of status, but equally as marks of respectability, as the interior "Uzbek" design of interwar Soviet homes illustrates. Whether or not great numbers of the metropolitan public in London or New York or Moscow were consciously aware of it, goods extracted from or produced in the colonies made domestic political economies imperial and made it increasingly difficult to envision the national as a segregated or independent domain—especially when boycotts and other disputes over the control of colonial resources or labor erupted into the public sphere "at home." In turn, colonial goods and forms of cultural taste circulated broadly within imperial systems, moving back out from the metropole to other colonial sites and directly between colonies. These flows meant that Indian fabrics and spices as well as Chinese porcelain and lacquerware, as well as tea from both regions, became staples of middle-class material culture in colonies as distant as Australia and New Zealand.[72]

Colonial subjects and ex-colonial peoples also wandered all over the map in this period, and many of them crisscrossed the world, moving between metropole and colony and back again as well as between colonial spaces, reterritorializing empire through their search for educational opportunities, employment, and even travel. Travelers are the easiest to spot because of the accounts they left of their journeys showing the imperial gaze to which they were subject and which they returned with equal ethnographic force. "Occidentalists" like the celebrated Ottoman writer Ahmed Midhat who visited the exhibitions and cities of Europe not only reversed that imperial gaze, they offered readers at home a glimpse of Western "civilization" through the prism of Ottoman modernity, representing European progress even as they critiqued bourgeois social and sexual mores. Exhibitions were a major draw for colonial peoples, some of whom appeared as part of the exhibitionary spectacle while others, like the Javanese Raden Ayu Kartini, actively supported their cultural and economic endeavors. Her embrace of the Dutch National Exhibition of Women's Labor in The Hague in 1898 was controversial, not least because she breached racial hierarchies by seeking solidarity with her white Dutch "sisters." Those colonials who sought or ended up with a political education, informal or formal, at the metropolitan "heart of empire"—like such figures of world-historical importance as Gandhi and Ho Chi Minh—defied the odds, carving cosmopolitan careers out of imperial systems with opportunity structures that were profoundly shaped by exclusionary logics and intricate hierarchies organized around race.[73]

The case of Ho Chi Minh is particularly instructive here. An early member of the Union Intercoloniale (founded 1923), he used its newspaper *La Paria* to think through his ideas about French colonialism, all the while using the streets of the metropole—and the highly racialized geographies of "Paris blanc et noir"— as his schoolroom.[74] Lamine Senghor and his African compatriots appropriated French domestic space and the republican tradition similarly as part of a larger field of interwar discursive and political struggle over who counted as French and where the boundaries of the nation ended and the empire began.[75] As for Gandhi in London and Johannesburg, questions of race and space—and the ways that they shaped gendered conventions of aspiring political subjects—were at the heart of these contestations, whether the site was the railway car, the vegetarian restaurant, or the halls of senates and parliaments. Elite subjects like these were certainly not representative of the hundreds of thousands who came from the "outposts" of empire to seek their fortunes its very heart. But as will be evident in Section 3, those from the colonies who did rise to prominence challenged more than just the presumption that "natives" were unequipped for self-governance.

Ho Chi Minh of the Republic of Vietnam in discussion with Marius Moutet, French minister of the colonies in the Colonial Ministry, Paris, ca. 1946. Ho Chi Minh not only played a pivotal role in the struggle for Vietnamese independence, but he also fashioned important connections with other anticolonial leaders. (Popperfoto / Getty Images)

Through public careers, extensive networking, and a variety of legislative interventions they anticipated new, scarcely imagined geographies of postcolonial power and, in doing so, revealed both the presumptive whiteness (and masculinity) of imperial power no less than the vulnerabilities to which its boundaries were continuously subject.

Natives Making and Seizing Space

Imperial officials seeking to manage indigenous populations utilized a variety of mechanisms for reterritorializing extant spatial relations both deliberately (as in the case of colonial cantonments) and somewhat less purposefully (as in the case of the diamond mines). Regardless of the level of intentionality, those who sought to impose imperial power from the metropolitan center or on the ground in the colonies had to reckon with already existing forms of spatial practice, whether they were dealing with the marketplace, the jute factory, or the residential neighborhoods of "natives." The stakes of such practices were made evident both in moments of political crisis, such as the one generated in late imperial China in 1898 when "native-place lodges" were instrumental to the formation of Beijing political societies, or in the routinized rituals of colonial life, religious or secular— as in the Shinto shrine celebrations in early twentieth-century Seoul.[76] The effective "tribalization" of Aboriginal peoples in New South Wales and Western Australia, the growth of the reservation system for native Americans in North America, and the emergence of apartheid in the new Union of South Africa— these all suggest how critical the spatial imaginary and its material realities were considered to be for the achievement of dominance by a variety of colonial states. In some cases, as in Ramahyuck (Victoria, Australia), the aim of the Moravian mission was expressly to create a "didactic landscape," one that would not only exhibit the virtues of hygienic living but "redefine Aboriginal peoples as individuals" by wrenching them from their kin-based contexts and, it was hoped, create a historically new form of self-consciousness in them.[77] Such didacticism could have startling results. When Ranavalona III, queen of Madagascar, surrendered her royal palace to French soldiers in 1895, what she carried into exile was "the costly sedan chair King Radama II had received from Emperor Napoleon III"—just one of many Western-style accoutrements designed to teach members of the Imerina dynasty how to adapt native space to European colonialism.[78]

Among the many questions this history raises is the extent to which native communities internalized these imperial visions of the meaning of space and, more generally, what impact coercive spatial reorganization had on native daily life and on the shape of anticolonial resistance. One scholar of Australian Aboriginal communities has deemed this the segregation versus social autonomy dilemma. While it is difficult to reduce the vast historiographies of indigeneity to any one binary, this one does begin to capture the dynamics at work in native space-making in the face of colonial incursions that not only resulted in long-term dispossession but also attempted to impose new visions of the nature and meaning of space.[79] The story of Lily Moya, a pseudonym given to a young Xhosa girl by the South African historian Shula Marks, is a case in point. As a young student seeking an education from a prospective English benefactor in the late 1940s, Lily's social trajectory was both restricted by the white colonial society to whose educational domains she wanted access *and* partly, though not fully, determined by the norms of that society.[80] There is no doubt, of course, that the parameters of that Xhosa world were shaped inexorably by the fact of apartheid, itself a deeply spatialized articulation of racist and sexist power; nor were the two worlds of the apartheid system hermetically sealed. As students of Native American histories in the context of New World empires have argued, settlers and indigenous people created "mutually comprehensible" worlds in which "systems of meaning and of exchange" overlapped, conflicted, and were ultimately stitched together in an uneven and often precarious fashion.[81] The challenge for those of us interested in more fully understanding what role the social cartographies of empire played in shaping the character of imperial power is to ask how we measure the historical significance, not just of the contact and contest born out of empires, but equally of the continued viability of native lifeways in both the autonomous and segregated spaces that were a consequential effect of imperial authority and power.

We believe this requires attention to formal mechanisms of colonization without overestimating their reach. It requires recognition of the persistence and adaptability of indigenous spatial practices without romanticizing them merely as static traditionalism. As we have suggested here, contests over space-making in and around the native "home" are very useful for appreciating the limits of imperial power and the tenacity of indigenous forms of knowledge about the proper organization of domestic space, especially where the gendered division of the household was concerned. In many respects the history of the Raj is best understood through this frame. Well before Gandhi made *swadeshi* (lit. "one's own land": the purchase of Indian-made goods) a geopolitical mantra and the *ashram* (settlements organized around a guru) an alternative site of anticolonial resistance, British officials, missionaries, and nationalist bodies like the Indian National Congress argued over the merits of a reformed upper-caste Hindu household. In these contestations, subjects like *sati* (ritualistic widow burning), child marriage, and the ability of widows to remarry were often proxies for larger debates about whether self-government in the political arena needed to be preceded by evidence that Indian men were fit to govern their own homes. The lineaments of similar debates are recognizable in early twentieth-century Egyptian nationalist discussions of purdah, in which Egyptian women and feminists took the lead in an attempt to connect spatial emancipation and mobility with the national movement's wider claims about anticolonial struggle.

If both of these examples reflect a shared bourgeois idiom, nationalist formations that did not derive from middle-class formations also had the politics of space at their core. This is perhaps most clear in the Mau Mau Rebellion in colonial Kenya. This uprising was energized by Kikuyu concerns over their greatly diminished landholdings under British rule and their steady drift into wage labor. Like nonwhite South Africans, the mobility of Kenyans had been radically circumscribed. The Native Registration Amendment Ordinance of 1920 had required all Kenyans over the age of 15 to carry a *kipande,* an identity document that allowed colonial officials to record the employment history of black workers and to restrict their movement across the landscape. Mau Mau aspirations were grounded in a desire to recover social autonomy and have the lands that were now locked up by white farmers returned to Kenyans: their agenda was grounded in a radical remaking and decolonization of colonial space. This agenda sparked a violent and coercive response: Mau Mau rebels were swiftly tried and condemned by colonial courts that made extensive use of the death penalty. Those acquitted were sent to special "camps" for reeducation while others were confined in "emergency villages" encircled by razor wire. The British use of summary execution, the widespread use of torture, and the confinement of colonized groups on a massive scale are perhaps the most telling evidence of the anxieties and anger that colonists expressed in the face of native groups who strove to reclaim colonial space.[82]

As tempting as it is to dwell on the most dramatic examples of anticolonial nationalism to drive home our point about the importance of space in the ways in which imperial powers set about remaking colonized domains, we also want to materialize some of the ways in which quotidian events illustrate the uneven pressure that imperial power and its agents, however determined they were to transform local people into legible imperial subjects, exercised on the ground in this period. This understanding does not reflect a presumption about the untrammeled authenticity of "native" community making, but is instead shaped by

The Maori prophet Rua Kenana in 1908. Rua, one of the most influential Maori prophetic leaders, challenged the British colonization of New Zealand. His followers called themselves Iharaira (Israelites), and they worked with Rua to construct a "City of God" at Maungapohatu. This initiative was an impediment to the extension of state power and drew Rua into protracted conflict with the New Zealand government. (James Cowan Collection, Alexander Turnbull Library, Wellington, NZ)

two decades of careful archival work that have allowed many historians to map the very uneven social and political terrains of colonial societies. In early twentieth-century New Zealand, for example, the prophet Rua Kenana established a community named the "City of God" under the sacred mountain Maungapohatu in the isolated Urewara district of the North Island. While Rua's prophetic visions combined Old Testament teachings with Maori tradition, he promised his followers that he would quickly develop the economic base of the community. This development would come not only through the reclaiming of lands confiscated by the colonial state, but also through the operation of a mining company and the creation of new transportation routes that would link the Urewara to the rest of the colony and the world beyond. This vision of economic development failed: the roads and railways were not built, and the population of the community had plummeted by the start of World War I. Even after colonial police raided Maungapohatu in 1916, killing two local men, Rua remained committed to both his prophetic vision of restoring Maori land and developing the region's economy. Neither happened within his lifetime: when he died in 1937, no roads had been completed and his followers remained impoverished.[83]

The vision of Rua Kenana encompasses many of the issues that are explored in greater depth in Sections 2 and 3, including the significance of imperial communication and transportation networks and the ways in which small communities were increasingly drawn into political struggles over the legitimacy of imperial orders. In this section we have made a case that the growth of global imperial systems between 1870 and 1945 invested questions of space with new urgency and that, in particular, imperial orders were shaped by the ways in which they laced together understandings of cultural difference and imperial space. Throughout we have stressed that imperial visions were never easily fashioned into on-the-ground realities and that real colonial spaces and real colonized peoples forced the reworking and reshaping of many plans for the construction of carefully ordered colonial modernities. Nevertheless, there is no doubt that key colonial spaces—the barracks, the mission station, the home, the plantation, the mine— did real work in transforming both the cultural and the spatial sensibilities of colonized groups and in producing a series of debates and practices that had a truly global reach. We develop this argument further in Section 2 as we examine the ways imperial communication networks enabled the reconfiguration of space and allowed the increasingly rapid and efficient dissemination of ideas and arguments between colonial sites and across imperial systems. These integrative processes had unexpected consequences, however, as we make clear in Section 3, where we offer another perspective on the question of space as we examine how the growing connections between colonies enabled the emergence of new transnational networks of correspondence and solidarity that would energize the fight against empire and influence the shape of global geopolitics in the wake of World War II.

2. *Remaking the World*

DURING the final third of the nineteenth century, imperial orders took on a new shape and quality. The technologies associated with steam power and electricity were increasingly central in the commercial practices, political regimes, and cultural debates of both European and non-European empires. It was only after 1870 that the steam locomotive, steamship, and telegraph finally overtook the horse, sailing ship, and messenger as the key means of communication on the global stage. These innovations allowed empire builders to import larger volumes of raw materials from their colonies with greater speed and at lower cost and also meant that it was cheaper to export greater amounts of finished goods back to colonial markets. As the "new imperialism" aggressively absorbed territories and incorporated distant lands into proliferating imperial systems, basic food plants, raw materials for industry, highly valued commodities, intricate machinery, delicate finished goods, commercial information, political news, and new ideas moved across greater distances, with greater frequency, and at greater speed. For contemporaries there was little doubt about the global significance of these developments. As the French free-trade politician Yves Guyot observed in 1885, colonial politics had the capacity to create ports, canals, and railroads "sur tous les points du monde."[84]

In this section our focus is on the interdependence between empire building and communication in the emergence of an increasingly integrated global order from 1870 into the early twentieth century. Our concern with the development of technologies and cross-cultural connections reflects the centrality of these issues within intellectual debates, political struggles, and cultural formations that unfolded across the globe in this period. Karl Marx suggested that railways, locomotives, and telegraphs were "organs of human will over nature" that made available to industrial nations "the power of knowledge, objectified."[85] These technologies were fundamental to a rapaciously expansionist industrial order and were at the heart of the imperial systems that both fed and were shaped by this form of economic organization. Railways and telegraphs are prime examples of technologies that were embedded in complex systems of interrelated machinery, infrastructure, and institutions and that were dependent on a sophisticated assemblage of practices and processes which were undertaken at great speed and with great regularity. Requiring massive investments of capital and labor, detailed planning, extensive maintenance, and substantial managerial systems, these communication complexes became core elements of imperial practice from 1870.

Technology and Imperial Modernity

These complex technological systems frequently depended on colonial forms of bonded or semibonded labor—a new kind of imperial-industrial proletariat. They were also energized by incursions not just into colonized landscapes but into local political economies, community practices, and the recesses of the colonized self. This era, which began with the advance of the steamship and ended with the advent of airline travel as the ultimate expression of modern mobility, witnessed a series of technological developments that revolutionized the capacity of Westerners to get to remote and "exotic" places for a variety of purposes: philanthropy, tourism, reform, or a combination of all three. If the impulse behind the development of these new modes of transportation and transnational connection was economic, driven by the quest for markets and raw materials, one globally far-reaching result was the transformation of social relations between colonizer and colonized. These forms of mobility produced new sites of collision between those who worked the "lines of the nation" and those who glided through the nation and across the empire on them.[86] Elite women—in Britain, France, Japan, China, Russia—were, arguably, the greatest beneficiaries of the freedom of movement that such technological advancement enabled, whereas subaltern subjects were increasingly locked in their social positions as laborers or as objects of increasingly elaborate state mechanisms that policed mobility and citizenship.

The growing global ascendancy of these modes of communication and forms of connection played a primary role in the production of a volatile, shifting, and partially overlapping series of imperial cultural orders. These orders were powerful—capable of mustering large military forces, harnessing vast workforces, and deploying increasingly sophisticated and professionalized instruments of surveillance and coercion—but they were constantly in process, being remade by new technologies, the push and pull of markets, and the brute struggles over access to resources, rights, and power that were at the heart of colonial encounters. These imperial orders were always in flux because they depended on laboring bodies who did not always acquiesce in the emergence of the new global industrial order and who, when they did, sought inclusion in it in ways that challenged the racial and gender hierarchies that comprised it from Paris to Beijing, Siberia to San Francisco. Given their work in the making of the railroads on several continents, it is not too much to say that Asian laborers were critical to the processes by which the world was connected in this period. Although the always-in-process nature of imperial social formations is most often associated with histories of imperial culture and identity, the case that empires were never discreet, fully self-contained systems can readily be made for the infrastructure of empires as well.[87] This was particularly true in an age where imperial orders were increasingly dependent on international commerce, the construction of capital-intensive infrastructure, transportation and communication systems, and highly mobile colonial workforces that linked colonies to their neighbors as well as to the imperial metropole.

At first glance it would seem that within such a context, the work of empire was increasingly disembodied—social communication, commercial transactions, and ideological contests that were previously grounded in personal contact were increasingly routinized in forms that were depersonalized, bureaucratized, and mechanized. Perhaps the clearest example of a kind of modern imperial bureaucracy comes from America's policy in the Philippines, where colonial authority rested upon the close surveillance of local populations and the construction of large bodies of data. This undertaking was based on an innovative complex of information technologies, including extensive telegraph and telephone networks, the widespread use of photography to document the colonized population, and the rapid production and efficient management of information through the use of the typewriter and numbered files. These technologies were at the forefront of America's attempt to assert its authority over the Philippines in the face of sustained challenges from a revolutionary national army, militant unions, messianic peasant leaders, and Muslim separatists. The Division of Military Information was at the forefront of this campaign, and it generated a vast amount of information about these various rebellious groups, information that was organized through a system of notecards that recorded data about each individual believed to be opposed to American rule. A particularly striking example of this kind of imperial bureaucratic modernity was developed during the pacification of the capital city, Manila, as the American-created metropolitan police force also produced a vast archive of information about the colonized population: within two decades it had amassed alphabetized file cards, with photographs and a range of information, for two hundred thousand individuals, around 70 percent of the city's population.[88]

Nevertheless this system—with its photographers, clerks, policemen, and intelligence officers—reminds us that technologies were not free-floating and their use was directed and determined by human choice and agency. Of course, one of the great underhistoricized stories of imperial systems of communication and transportation is that colonial bodies were the raw materials that enabled the creation of these systems of connection. Industrial capitalists deployed indentured workers, new migrants, low-caste laborers, and seminomadic tribespeople to fell timber, drain swamps, and reshape the land to make way for the highways of empire: telegraph lines, railway routes, road networks, and port facilities. It was primarily nonwhite workers who did the heavy lifting of empire, who carried out the most arduous and debilitating tasks. As a result of their position in racialized hierarchies of labor, nonwhite workers were most vulnerable. They were most often the bodies felled by diseases like cholera and influenza, which trains and steamships carried across borders and oceans at astonishing rates of speed. This is to say nothing of the ailments, chronic and otherwise, produced by proximity to the raw materials and by-products of industrial production, including dust, splinters, and fumes. As substances such as these entered the bodies of workers, they gave the incorporation of industrial-imperial modernity a whole new embodied set of meanings.[89]

While imperial power remained grounded in the ability of the colonizer to deploy the disciplinary power of violence (or its threat) against the colonized, the mechanisms of colonial governance, the ways in which imperial trade was conducted, and the nature of the imperial imagination were reshaped by the exploitative possibilities offered by industrial technologies and the truly global reach of capitalism. Here we outline the ways in which some of these transformations unfolded, paying close attention to questions of time and space, coercion and consent. Our analysis begins by sketching the growing convergences between empire and industry before examining the divergent patterns of technological development in three empires: the British, the Japanese, and the Ottoman. We argue that technology was fundamental in determining the actual shape and organization of imperial regimes, as well as being at the heart of the debates over the political, moral, and spiritual consequences of empire building. We then offer some reflections on the uneven nature of these integrative forces, stressing the ways in which imperial networks and cross-cultural connections produced differential outcomes and new inequalities. Wherever possible we seek to understand the cultural consequences of such unevenness on the ground and how common people, especially colonized workers, shaped the material and symbolic forms that global technological modernity assumed in the context of empire. This section concludes by highlighting some of the unexpected consequences of these new forms of imperial connection in a range of domains, from religious practice to the history of disease. We stress a key political consequence of the integrative work of colonialism and communications, the globalization of the nation-state model, placing particular emphasis on the roles of technology and mobility in naturalizing the nation as the primary unit of unit of political organization on the global stage by 1914.

Canals, Commerce, and Communications

The 1860s saw a striking convergence between technological change, commercial expansion, and empire building. Even as European colonial authority was called into question by recurrent crises—most notably in the Caribbean, New Zealand, and Canada—imperial commercial and communication systems expanded, realigning economic and political activity. In the 1860s telegraphs, railways, and steamships became routine elements of imperial activity as they assumed greater significance after the uprising against British rule in India in 1857–1858. These technologies were prominent in discussions of the causes of the rebellion and weaknesses of the colonial state. And they were fundamental to the reconstruction of British authority in the wake of rebellion, as private contractors and the state itself undertook massive construction projects, rapidly expanding both the telegraph and rail networks. This rebellion revealed that colonial regimes needed to develop swift means of communication and extensive transport networks to enable the effective deployment of military resources. In light of this, many colonial states worked hard to extend the infrastructure of rail lines and stations, telegraphs and telegraph offices, roads and bridges, that was increasingly central to their power. As such, technological breakdown, when it occurred, stymied even the most phlegmatic of metropolitan observers. As the London correspondent for the *New York Times* wrote in June 1895, "Not a word has been obtainable during the week about the Russian invasion of Manchuria. There are no telegraphs anywhere near, it is true, but we ought to have had news of some sort by this time, unless it is being officially kept back." Palpably frustrated by the breakdown of information technology, the *Times* lamented this "tax upon the public patience" of those eager for news of Manchuria's fate.[90]

At the same time, European empires developed increasingly dense and extensive commercial, communication, and transportation linkages that knitted together distant ports, markets, and way stations. France, for example, extended its imperial commerce as it forced Saigon to open to imperial trade in 1860; and as France asserted its authority over Tonkin, Annam, and Cochin China during the 1860s, it increasingly controlled trade between these regions in key commodities such as rice. French communications networks expanded rapidly, creating an alternative set of linkages between London and Hong Kong in 1863 and extending France's commercial connections in northeast Africa, Arabia, and Persia. New companies and initiatives also pushed imperial influence and European enterprise into the Middle East and parts of Africa. In 1864 both the French Messageries Impériales and the British Peninsular and Oriental Steam Navigation Company (P&O) opened new services that linked Cape Town to Aden. Across imperial systems, a range of new port facilities and dock companies emerged; rapid development expanded the capacity of Shanghai, Hong Kong, Singapore, Karachi, and Yokohama, establishing a new commercial matrix that would shape global enterprise up to World War I and beyond.[91] The important technological advances that improved the efficiency of steamships, increasing their cargo capacity while markedly reducing their fuel use, were an important spur for these innovations.

It was the completion of the Suez Canal in 1869, however, that was both a potent symbol and a foundation of the reworking of imperial communication and transportation in an age when the reach of European power became truly global. In 1854 Ferdinand de Lesseps, a former French diplomat, obtained a concession from Said Pasha, the Ottoman governor of Egypt, to create a company to construct a canal between the Mediterranean and the Gulf of Suez on the Red Sea. Working with plans created by Austrian engineer Alois Negrelli and financed by French capital, de Lesseps oversaw the eleven-year construction project, which relied heavily on forced labor drawn from Egypt, North Africa, and the Arab world. Despite initial international skepticism about the project, the canal proved a great success after its opening in November 1869 and quickly became a vital commercial and strategic corridor, allowing ships to move between Europe and Asia without circumnavigating Africa. In 1875 the British government, with funding from the Rothschild bank, purchased Egypt's share in the canal after Muhammad Said Pasha's successor, Ismail Pasha, was crippled by debt. Britain's expenditure of four million pounds sterling reflected an awareness of the canal's significance for the British economy and empire: although the Liberal press of British provinces was critical of the investment, Britain's new stake in the canal was celebrated by conservative commentators and most colonial opinion makers, who saw the canal as an imperial highway, even though the majority of the canal's shares remained in French hands. For British observers, the canal itself became an embodiment of modernity—a monument to the power of engineering and capitalist financing—that stood in stark contrast to an Egypt that was seen as unable to achieve full modernity because of the weight of its ancient heritage and the supposed effects of Islam.[92]

The Suez Canal greatly reduced transportation times between Europe and Asia, as it effectively cut the distance between London and Mumbai by 41 percent, London and Colombo by 36 percent, and London and Singapore by 29 percent.[93] The resulting growth of shipping in the Red Sea revived old ports and energized local markets. The canal was also central in imperial strategy and international diplomacy. British strategists believed that the canal was central in securing the "safety of the empire," as it allowed the quick deployment of military resources. This meant that the Suez Canal as well as Britain's naval bases in the Mediterranean and the Red Sea remained central in British imperial strategy until World War II (and beyond). The canal, which had a telegraph line running alongside the waterway, was also central in communication from India to Britain.

Sir Richard Temple, former governor of the Bombay Presidency, noted that this line meant that "in a few minutes intelligence is flashed across the intervening oceans and continents, deciding the profit or loss on critical transactions."[94] The importance of the canal and its telegraph encouraged entrepreneurs and imperial speculators to develop schemes for the construction of a canal and telegraph network across the Central American isthmus in the hope that it would be another lucrative conduit for global trade and a new communication route that might further advance American as well as British and French interests. Although the Panama Canal was not completed until 1914, from the 1870s it captured the imaginations of financiers, who set about developing elaborate plans for the construction of a complex communication network combining telegraphs, rail lines, and the canal. A concession for the construction of these linkages was granted by Peru in 1874, some six years before de Lesseps oversaw the initial unsuccessful attempts to excavate a pathway for the canal in 1880, reflecting the growing belief that the Suez Canal was a template that could be replicated to imperial benefit elsewhere.[95]

As this suggests, the success of the Suez Canal was not only central in recalibrating space and time within the French and British empires but also pivotal in reshaping commerce and communication at a global level. The construction of the canal marks an important rupture in maritime history: it reconfigured the sea-lanes and transformed the nature of ships themselves. It stimulated shipbuilding and further tipped the technological balance toward steam. From the canal's opening to 1914, maritime technology underwent a remarkable transformation as wooden-hulled sailing ships, which still dominated the worlds' oceans in 1870, were quickly displaced by iron-hulled, and then especially steel-hulled, steamers. Advances in industrial metal production encouraged these shifts, but they were also spurred by the peculiarities of the canal and their effects on shipping patterns. In particular, the unreliable winds of the Red Sea and the high price of towing within the canal meant that it really functioned as a conduit for steam-powered ships only. The sinking of the French barque *Noel,* the first sailing vessel that entered the canal, was a portent of the demise of the sailing ship on the oceanic routes between Europe and Asia.[96]

Moreover, in enabling the fast passage of vessels over great distances, the canal cemented the primacy of speed within shipping industries, a further nail in

The opening of the Suez Canal, 1869. For contemporaries the canal was a powerful demonstration of the ability of European powers to accelerate travel and tighten economic connections. The canal helped to boost the dominance of steam power and British maritime ascendancy. (Getty Images)

the coffin of the clipper ships that were still a key feature of "Eastern trade" in 1869. By the middle of the 1870s, steamships were carrying the vast majority of high-value commodities (such as tea, ginger, and cotton) as well as a growing percentage of bulky lower-value commodities (such as rice and jute). They were also forging new commercial linkages, being used in the importation of refrigerated meat from Australasia and Argentina to Britain and Europe, a trade that shaped the economic development and environmental transformation of Argentina, Australia, and New Zealand for at least a century. This lucrative trade, which meant that these lands developed as farms for empire, is just one example of the ways global trade grew and diversified between 1869 and 1914. In 1913 world trade had grown to ten times what it had been in 1850, stabilizing at a level that would remain fairly static until the outbreak of World War II. In fact, in the early twentieth century, long-distance shipping was extremely efficient and affordable: in 1910 the average price of long-distance freight was 20 percent lower than had been in 1869 and one-third of what rates would be in 1920. It is very important to note, however, that the canal did little to benefit Egypt itself. Even though the canal project stimulated urbanization and commercial growth in the Suez Isthmus and encouraged the growth of local road networks, the wealth generated by the canal mainly went to Britain and France, and ultimately the canal impeded rather than helped Egypt's economic development: this engine that recalibrated the geography of empire actually marginalized Egypt even as it made the region central to international communication.[97]

Not surprisingly, given its material and symbolic importance as a key global node of power and circulation, the canal became a key site of contention in international rivalries, especially during times of war. During World War II, Axis airpower in the eastern Mediterranean effectively blockaded the canal between 1940 and 1943, forcing Allied ships to travel around the Cape of Good Hope, significantly disrupting the movement of troops, arms, and supplies. At the same time, Allied forces worked hard to shore up the canal's defenses, deploying elaborate networks of searchlights to mislead and disorient Luftwaffe bomber crews. Equally importantly, however, the Suez Canal was the site of worker protest and nationalist agitation in the heady days of 1919 and after, when foreign canal workers and union supporters with anti-British sentiments combined to make common cause in ways that alarmed British imperial officials at the highest levels, including General Edmund Allenby. Striking workers alarmed the French and British alike precisely because they exhibited an inter-ethnic solidarity energized by Egyptian nationalist forces. What resulted was nothing less than "the birth of a workers' revolution in the midst of a nationalist revolution."[98]

Communications and Force

The interconnected developments of the Suez Canal and the global dominance of the steamship were key in securing British paramountcy before World War I. The global reach of the Royal Navy was a fundamental element in Britain's ability to hold an expansive maritime empire together, but its dominance on the seas also reflected its domination of steamship production. Between 1890 and 1914 Britain built two-thirds of the world's ships. Britain in effect controlled the production of the bulk of ships for other nations, and itself possessed the world's largest commercial fleet.[99] British naval power was vitally important in protecting long-distance trade networks and existing colonies, but it also enabled the growing reach of British power. In Africa, side-wheel survey ships and small steamers as well as gunboats were the instruments that enabled British traders, missionaries, and military expeditions to penetrate beyond the narrow littoral that had been the normal domain of European activity before the 1880s.

At the same time, the rapid expansion of the submarine cable network between 1870 and 1914 was a key structural development that underwrote the rapid expansion of British authority and reshaped the nature of colonial power. Coastal telegraphs and telegraph stations were increasingly central to British imperial strategy in Africa after the humiliations of the Anglo-Zulu War in 1879. In response to the lobbying of politicians and merchants in the settler colonies, a transpacific cable between Canada and Australasia was also connected, part of the drive to construct an "all red route"—a communication network entirely under British control—that encircled the world. But the growing reach of telegraphic communication was slow to constrain the actions of imperial proconsuls on the frontiers of empire. The new medium did not fundamentally recast the Colonial Office's bureaucratic procedures, and "men on the spot" on the frontier proved adept at crafting telegraph messages designed to win authorization for their own actions and policies. In many ways the telegraph's impact was stronger in the commercial and cultural domains, where it was a ubiquitous element in the emergent news services and patterns of journalistic exchange that were central features of the imperial press system that emerged from the 1870s.[100] The impact of the telegraph on the domain of culture anticipated some of the main consequences of the rise of radio during the first part of the twentieth century, as the

British Broadcasting Corporation (BBC) emerged as an important cohesive force that informed Britons about the colonies as well as linked disparate parts of the empire despite the differences of race, language, and accent.[101]

Although these forms of communication and connection were fundamentally important in threading together the constituent parts of imperial systems, we must remember that all empires ultimately rely on the deployment of force (or at least the threat of force). From 1870, Britain and other European powers harnessed industrial technology to military uses, discovering that the application of science and technology could produce increasingly fast, powerful, and efficient killing machines. World War I was a horrific staging of the destructive capacity of these new technologies, as machine guns, tanks, and chemical weapons were key elements of the battlefield repertoire. But some of these technologies had been deployed on colonial frontiers in the previous decades. Most notably, the Maxim gun—a state-of-the-art belt-fed machine gun capable of firing five hundred rounds per minute—emerged as a potent weapon in "little wars" that were fought on colonial frontiers, where small British forces sought to imprint their authority over large areas and the substantial armies that tribal leaders could muster. This weapon was routinely deployed after its first use in The Gambia (1888) and was pivotal in the spectacular victories of British forces at Shangani River (1893) and Omdurman during the reconquest of the Sudan (1898). At Omdurman, Field Marshall Herbert Kitchener's forces, who had traveled to the battlefield on river steamers and by railway, met a much larger Sudanese force armed with rifles and a large arsenal of artillery; but the rapid fire of the machine guns deployed by the British infantry and on gunboats gave the British a decisive advantage. C. A. Bayly has reminded us that British global power ultimately rested in that nation's ability to kill imperial rivals and colonized peoples, an ability that was increasingly underpinned by industrial military technology.[102] The London-based poet Hilaire Belloc famously satirized the centrality of military technology—and white imperial self-confidence—to British paramountcy: "Whatever happens, we have got / the Maxim gun and they have not."[103] But metropolitan authorities knew only too well that superior military technology was no guarantor of imperial success on the ground, as Zulu strategic brilliance under Cetewayo and Boer guerrilla warfare two decades later so palpably demonstrated.

An early Maxim gun operated by the British Royal Navy during the Transvaal, or First Boer, War, 1880–1881. This weapon was both a potent agent of colonial domination and a symbol of the confluence of industrial technology and imperial might. (Private Collection / Ken Welsh / The Bridgeman Art Library)

After 1870, steam and electricity were also central to the economic development of all British colonial economies. In Britain's tropical colonies, railways were crucial instruments for accessing valued commodities and bringing finished goods and labor to the large port cities that were vital nodes in the imperial system. In India, massive rail networks connected even the smallest market town or resource bulking-point with the imperial economy. At the same time, the railway emerged as an important strategic tool in the "Great Game" with Russia in the northwest of India and Central Asia. India's railway network was seen as a vital tool in combating the growing reach of Russian imperial power in Central Asia, influence that was embodied in the extension of its Caspian and Trans-Caspian Railways. This Indian system, which eclipsed the size of the British metropolitan network in 1895, was well known for its technical sophistication, its impressive bridges spanning South Asia's large waterways, and its strict management. As Manu Goswami has pointed out, while the colonial Indian network connected interior commercial centers to the coast, its lines often cut across existing routes and lines of movement, supplanting some well-established market towns and important waterways.[104] As a result, new patterns of intra- and interregional economic inequality were produced, and these quickly solidified around the iron arteries of empire. These transformations underscore that Britain's investment in India's railways reflected a deep-seated desire to reorient India's economy outward and was central in reconfiguring a sophisticated textile exporting economy into a key source of raw materials and as outlet for British-made goods. Conversely, Britain's African colonies (with the exception of South Africa) had sparse and undercapitalized networks that were developed much later than India's. In some notable instances, such as the development of the African copper belt in the early twentieth century, new rail networks were constructed to connect mines to key ports. Generally, however, these lines were expensive and inefficient. Tropical Africa was never welded as firmly into the British Empire (or any European empire) as India was.[105]

For Britain's settler colonies, railways were powerful engines for economic advancement, encouraging the extension of cultivation and settlement by colonists as well as connecting farms, mines, and goldfields in the interior to port cities and the imperial economy. In Australia the expansion of railways enabled the conversion of the grasslands of southeastern and southwestern Australia into grain-growing regions for export. Farther north in Queensland, the limited number of navigable waterways, a sparse transportation network, and a lack of capital for wharf development constrained the expansion of the sugar industry in the final third of the nineteenth century. These impediments were largely removed with the extension of the rail network in the first decade of the twentieth century.[106] The extension of rail was also a high priority for the development of New Zealand's colonial economy. New Zealand's main rail network effectively connected major ports and urban centers, but even in the late nineteenth century, travel to and from many smaller provincial towns relied on local roads punctuated by dangerous river crossings and mountain passes.

These technologies were also central in the consolidation of political affiliations, especially in the settler colonies that were granted responsible government in the mid-nineteenth century. Railway politics were the backdrop for Confederation in Canada in 1867 and remained a crucial point of alliance building and conflict as national politics took shape. In New Zealand, the expansion of the railway network and the lucrative benefits that flowed from state contracts were a powerful centralizing force after the abolition of the provinces in the 1870s, but provincial loyalties remained strong until the early twentieth century. Across the Tasman Sea in Australia the strength of the states, which had constructed self-contained communication networks, inhibited the development of deep national cultural connections and a coherent national identity. The Australian colonies had cooperated in establishing interstate telegraphic communications from 1858, but developing a coherent national rail infrastructure with a common gauge was a slow and difficult process.[107]

While these nationalizing projects helped consolidate distinctive colonial forms of cultural identification, there were also strong connections between work, technology, and the emergence of new political ideologies. In Dunedin, an early site of industrial development in Australasia, railway workshops were key sites where new progressive labor ideologies were formulated by workers, but these visions of work and socialism were couched in a language of "brotherhood," which marginalized the sisters and mothers of the workers, women who themselves were precocious advocates for women's suffrage.[108] Many of the leaders who harnessed this language in national politics, and as the underpinnings of New Zealand's pioneering social reforms at the turn of the twentieth century, also were key architects of anti-Asian legislation, championed New Zealand's imperial ambitions in the Pacific, and supported initiatives designed to crush the power of Maori healers and prophets. In New South Wales, railway technologies also bonded communities of railway workers in highly gendered ways, with women, mainly workers' wives, expressing a marked distaste for the grit and grime of "the iron horse."[109]

Railway politics also became the subject of intense racial conflict. In late nineteenth-century New Zealand, influential Maori leaders attempted to prevent the extension of the rail network into regions where Maori still retained effective control of resources and the land, revealing a strong awareness of the connections between communications, capitalism, and the effectiveness of colonial power. Meanwhile, the vast local labor forces mobilized by the British in South Asia proved adept in challenging the aspirations of British managers and contesting their working conditions. These workers drew upon a range of tactics, including dictating the length and rhythm of labor, using petitions and letter writing, declaring informal "go-slows" or formal strikes, and fleeing worksites at the outbreak of disease or in response to shifts in managerial expectations.[110] Questions of race were also central in the organization of labor aboard steamships. By the early twentieth century, maritime labor opportunities within Euro-American empires were increasingly closed off to nonwhite workers. The economic advantages and sociopolitical alliances that sailors of Asian and African origin had enjoyed a century earlier were systematically undermined at the end of the nineteenth century. A new racial order was calcifying where shipowners, maritime bureaucrats, and officers wove together the languages of race and gender to justify the exploitation of nonwhite workers and their increasing economic and political marginalization. This process was not restricted to shipboard life alone, but was also made manifest in legislation that was designed to constrain both the mobility and the citizenship of nonwhite maritime workers.[111]

The Politics of Connectivity

In light of these developments, it is hardly surprising that the growth of colonial communications occupied a central position in British discourses on empire. Cecil Rhodes, whose career was built around an enthusiasm for railway building as well as the wealth generated from mining, argued for the construction of a "Cairo-to-Cape" railway under British control: this scheme foundered on logistical problems and a lack of official enthusiasm, but Rhodes's vision was a telling instance of how deeply technology and imperial thought were interwoven by the close of the nineteenth century. J. R. Seeley, the Regius Professor of History at Cambridge, clearly articulated this imbrication in his famous lectures published as *The Expansion of England* (1883). Seeley argued: "Science has given to the political organism a new circulation, which is steam, and a new nervous system, which is electricity." These technologies, he argued, required a fundamental reconsideration of imperial organization: "They make it in the first place possible actually to realise the old utopia of a Greater Britain, and at the same time they make it almost necessary to do."[112] The growth of telegraph, steamer routes, and railways as arteries that fed an aggressively expansionist imperial system meant that by the 1880s the globe had emerged as an obvious level for British political analysis. Although Seeley's vision of an integrated global British state was never achieved, his work articulated the recalibration of British thought and theory by the application of industrial technology to imperial development.

What the imperial men who oversaw these developments could not perhaps have anticipated was how women would appropriate them to fuel their imperial ambition. Mary Kingsley's exploration of Africa, famously captured in her 1895 book *Travels in West Africa,* depended on steam power not simply as a mode of transport but as the very platform from which her imperial ethnography was launched. Her trip from Gabon up the Ogooué River was crammed with observations of the flora, the fauna, and "black deck-passengers galore," with whom she mingled with a combination of unease and excitement. Her description of the nocturnal routine of the ship is worth quoting in full:

> Silence falls upon the black passengers, who assume recumbent positions on the deck, and suffer. All the things from under the saloon seats come out and dance together, and play puss-in-the-corner, after the fashion of loose gear when there is any sea on. As the night comes down, the scene becomes more and more picturesque. The moonlit sea, shimmering and breaking on the darkened shore, the black forest and the hills silhouetted against the star-powdered purple sky, and, at my feet, the engine-room stoke-hole, lit with the rose-coloured glow from its furnace, showing by the great wood fire the two nearly naked Krumen stokers, shining like polished bronze in their perspiration, as they throw in on to the fire the billets of red wood that look like freshly-cut chunks of flesh. The white engineer hovers round the mouth of the pit, shouting down directions and ever and anon plunging down the little iron ladder to carry them out himself. At intervals he stands on the rail with his head craned round the edge of the sun deck to listen to the captain, who is up on the little deck above, for there is no telegraph to the engines, and our gallant commander's voice is not strong. While the white engineer is roosting on the rail, the black engineer comes partially up the ladder and gazes hard at me; so I give him a wad of tobacco, and he plainly regards me as inspired, for of course that was what he wanted. Remember that whenever you see a man, black or white, filled with a nameless longing, it is tobacco he requires. Grim despair accompanied by a

gusty temper indicates something wrong with his pipe, in which case offer him a straightened-out hairpin. The black engineer having got his tobacco, goes below to the stoke-hole again and smokes a short clay as black and as strong as himself. The captain affects an immense churchwarden. How he gets through life, waving it about as he does, without smashing it every two minutes, I cannot make out.[113]

Though this is scarcely the utopia of Greater Britain that Seeley and his kind imagined, the image of Mary Kingsley sharing tobacco with the African engineer surely suggests the possibility of whole new worlds of encounter, contact, exchange—not to mention a historically unprecedented variety of worldly confidence unique to the late Victorian imperial feminine traveler.

White women throughout the British Empire capitalized on the opportunities that technological advance proffered in more ways than one. Like the young Miss Golightly of Anthony Trollope's 1857 novel, *The Three Clerks,* they were minor but significant investors in railway stock. Add to this George Eliot (Mary Anne Evans)'s investments in, and profits from, companies like the Great Indian Peninsular Railway, and we appreciate the embeddedness of the world of literary culture in trajectories of empire, as well as the role of middle-class British women in the imperial corporate economy.[114] Over and above the way rail and steam fostered more mobility for affluent women from the later nineteenth century, "world" travel quickly became an essential dimension of the "New Woman." The new mixed and public spaces of the railway car and train platform were a major source of anxiety about gendered modernity, for colonized and colonizing patriarchs alike. As in the Jim Crow South, they were viewed as nothing less than vehicles for the "miscegenation of modernity."[115]

And yet women traveled. Of particular interest in the British imperial context is the way white settler women capitalized on these new opportunities, traveling from Sydney and Wellington via Colombo and Aden to Britain and consolidating their sense of themselves as imperial subjects in the process. Their voyage "home" to London also often cultivated in them a sense of feminist internationalism, enabled by networking in the metropolis and across the Pacific world—experiences that brought them into contact with Aboriginal and Asian women under the aegis of global sisterhood. In this sense, rail and steam allowed them to claim what they viewed as their racial destiny—citizenship in the world—even as their encounters with activist women black, yellow, and brown unsettled notions of colonizer and colonized and required that they understand how and why the world of women tilted as much on a Pacific axis as it did on an imperial one.

Japan's Railway Imperialism

Railways, telegraphs, and steamships were central in imperial orders between the 1860s and 1945, whether these were long-established imperial states that exercised authority over a contiguous landmass (such as the Ottoman Empire, Qing China, or imperial Russia) or maritime empires where one state exercised authority over a range of colonies (for example, the British, French, and Japanese empires). Building on our earlier discussion of the place of technology and transport in British expansion, we extend our analysis here to an assessment of the development of these systems of connection within two other imperial regimes, which contrast with the British case. Where Britain possessed a long-standing and resurgent maritime empire, our first example, the Japanese empire, was the product of a condensed process of industrialization and aggressive territorial aggrandizement. Our second example is the Ottoman Empire, the most durable of the Muslim "gunpowder" states, which directly confronted the extending reach of European imperial aspiration and influence. Our discussion focuses on how these communication and transportation technologies were implicated in imperial rule, the various ways in which they shaped the basic contours of imperial economic relationships, and their centrality in determining relationships between various empires. In the British case, the rapid proliferation and extension of these networks built upon earlier imperial foundations and were molded by complex economic traffic between established colonies, new imperial frontiers and zones of influence, and the imperial metropole itself. Conversely, in the Japanese case, empire building developed within a context of rapid political change, the beginnings of an economic revolution, and extensive experimentation with new technologies. But the links between new imperial aspirations and railway policy were nonetheless crystal clear, if not from the start of the Meiji period, then certainly from the end of the century— so much so that a Tokyo magazine writer in 1899 could observe almost casually, "the means of extending one's territory without the use of troops . . . is railway policy."[116]

The emergence of such conviction about the efficiency of railway imperialism is instructive. In the wake of the "opening up" of Japan's ports through the force of American guns and diplomacy in the later 1850s, Japan abandoned the *sakoku* (seclusion) policy that had been a foundation of the Edo shogunate. The fleets of "black ships" that Commodore Matthew Perry brought to the Japanese coast in July 1853 and February 1854 triggered a mix of interest and alarm among the Japanese elite. The "gifts"—a variety of state-of-the-art weapons, telegraphic equipment, a small-scale but functional steam train, and a circular section of rail—that Perry offered the emperor were a potent demonstration of Western industrial prowess and American military might. Japanese officials, who had exhibited a long-standing interest in Western medicine and technology, studied these objects closely; scholars and military men debated their value and produced detailed sketches of the operation of a Colt revolver and a cavalry rifle.[117]

Immediately after Perry's initial visit, a range of bureaucrats, warlords, and scholars based in the various political domains that made up Japan explored the possibilities and implications of Perry's "gifts." An important set of plans was drawn up for the establishment of an institution that would guide Japan's exploration of new industrial and military technologies, the Bansho Shirabesho (Office for the Investigation of Barbarian Books). This center for learning was directed to assess the military strength, technological development, and strategic aspirations of Japan's rivals, as well as to translate books on "bombardment," "fortifications," "building warships," "machinery," and "products." The establishment of the Bansho Shirabesho initiated a substantial reorganization of knowledge production within Japan and of Japan's engagement with the world. Attempts to develop new forms of knowledge gained greater purchase after the Meiji restoration in 1868, which centralized authority and allowed the construction of nationalized knowledges that were directed by state impetus and oversight. The development of new communication and transportation systems was a key component of the Meiji state's attempts to build a "rich country, strong army."

From the moment of Perry's arrival, Japan had experimented with telegraphic technology, and by 1895 more than four thousand miles of lines and a complex network of telegraph offices had been established. With British assistance and capital—shaped by a desire to secure its position as Japan's key trading partner—the first Japanese railway line was opened in 1872, linking Tokyo to the port of Yokohama. Between 1872 and 1912, the Meiji state oversaw the building of a large and increasingly sophisticated rail network, while local entrepreneurs established numerous local light-rail lines. The construction of these networks drew heavily on foreign-produced locomotives, expertise, and capital, but local experiments with steam and rail continued at a steady pace. After the outbreak of World War I, rail development was increasingly driven from within Japan. These transportation systems connected with a host of ports that were served by a range of international as well as Japanese shipping companies, such as the Mitsubishi line, which increasingly asserted dominance over the expanding coastal shipping network at the same time as it established new connections to Hong Kong and other regional hubs.[118]

The extension of these networks was a crucial element in the nationalization of culture. They promoted the movement of individuals and ideas, facilitated the dissemination of state ideology, and reinforced new ideas about "Japaneseness" as a modern identity. As in Europe and the United States, the urban commuter railway served as the nexus between residential development, work, and leisure, integrating masses of people into a new social and cultural order. In Japan as elsewhere, it could be a site of commercial exchange, an opportunity for sexual encounter (wanted and unwanted), a subject of literary preoccupation, and a site of political protest. The dialectic of intimacy and alienation was, it seems, a common, if not a global, effect of modernization via railroad. As a major force in the imperializing of Japan beyond its "national" borders, the rails had a unique capacity to conjure imperial identity as well. Processes of assimilation and identification via the railroad had particular impact on those territories that had been integrated into the Japanese state only in the Meiji period, such as the Ryūkyū Archipelago (including Okinawa) and the "land of the Ainu" (Hokkaidō). Once these regions were incorporated into the state and discourses on national culture, peoples like the Ainu and Okinawans were increasingly seen as "backward" elements within the nation, rather than as "foreigners": this in turn reinforced the desire to modernize these communities and their environments, drawing them ever more firmly into the fold of an industrializing nation. Clearly, modern technological innovation was essential to the workings of racialization through which metropolitan Japanese pathologized internal others (the Ainu) and proximate others (the Chinese). Not only that, but even with the railways, travel could be hard, accommodations primitive, and national prestige fragile. This was what the Japanese traveler Ōgoshi Heiriku learned on a fin-de-siècle trip to Manchuria—where, he discovered, Japanese were still not allowed to travel on Russian trains.[119]

Beyond the boundaries of the nation, new technologies and communication networks were equally important in the Japanese drive to remake its place in the world. Colonies and resource frontiers were of special economic value to Japan, given that the Japanese archipelago had a finite amount of agricultural land, limited natural resources, and a dense population. Until the conclusion of the Sino-Japanese war in 1895, Japan had been self-sufficient in one key commodity: coal. But the depletion of Japanese coal stocks due to the growth of its factories and furnaces during that conflict meant that it was increasingly dependent on coal sourced from Manchuria, Korea, and Sakhalin Island. It was hunger for this energy source for industrialization that helped stoke Japanese imperial interests in north Asia. Korea and Manchuria became primary sources of high-quality coal for Japan's growing industrial sector.[120] As it attempted to secure its interests in these regions, Japan quickly asserted its control over both communication and transportation networks. Even before Japan formally annexed Korea, the Japanese controlled the major commercial and military rail lines that made up the peninsula's rail network. During the 1904–1905 Russo-Japanese War, Japan monopolized Korea's road network to serve the ends of military transportation and, reflecting an awareness of the military value of telegraphy, seized control of Korea's telegraph system. These networks were ultimately integral to the maintenance of Japan's authority in Korea after it was formally annexed in 1910. Interestingly, opposition to railways in Korea tended to focus on the ways in which Japanese rationalization worked, and it came from Japanese settlers and Korean collaborators, who sought a greater role in management and supervision. They staged a sit-in in 1903 and effectively won the competition for freight when the Railway Bureau conceded them a virtual monopoly in the transport industry.[121]

Manchuria was of particular importance in Japan's economic development and the region was a quintessential "railway colony"—a phenomenon that conjures the "binary mode of territorial and informal colonization" characteristic of Japanese imperial governmentality in unique and spectacular ways.[122] The South

Manchurian Railway—a key transportation route and conduit for commerce and communication—was the heart of Japan's enterprise. The extension and improvement of the line enabled it to carry high-density traffic and was a powerful stimulus to mining and manufacturing: as a result, the region quickly became a key supplier of raw cotton and iron ore. The Japanese state and entrepreneurs invested heavily in the venture and reaped substantial profits. The railway company also supported a wide range of research activities, and Manchuria was seen by the Japanese as an important frontier where ideas about race, culture, and environment could be tested and experiments into new processing and manufacturing techniques could be carried out. Significantly, it was the site of investment also for the Russian Empire, which had been instrumental to its initial construction—and of popular hostility as well. Hence the attempts of the Boxers, with the help of the Qing court, to destroy the railway line and prevent further Russian military encroachment. Indeed, railway sabotage was crucial to the Boxer Rebellion, which included the murder of European railway engineers and missionaries proximate to the fray. Thirty years later, in 1931, the Guangdong army detonated the railway track near the Chinese military base in Fengtian, an act that inaugurated a dramatic and prolonged firefight along the South Manchurian Railway, which Japanese readers followed with intense interest in the nation's newspapers as the fate of rail lines and the direction of the war hung in the balance.[123]

With time, Japan's colonial holdings became increasingly important: they accepted growing amounts of Japanese exports, were dominated by swelling populations of Japanese officials, merchants, and settlers, and were crucial to sustaining the metropole itself. This was particularly true in terms of staple crops: in 1910 Korea supplied Japan with seventeen thousand tons of rice; by the mid-1930s this contribution to Japan's food supply had expanded to 1.5 million tons as colonial authorities pushed the extension of rice cultivation and became more aggressive in their expropriation of the crop. In a similar vein, the combination of technological advancement and imperial expansion created the conditions for the rapid creation of a large pelagic fishing enterprise that was fundamental in supplying a key element of the Japanese diet.[124]

Japanese administrators believed that colonies should be harnessed to serve metropolitan economic interests. To these ends, Japanese colonial rulers worked hard to effect wide-ranging transformations in supposedly "underdeveloped" regions that had been incorporated into the empire. In the Liaodong Peninsula in northeast China (which was under Japanese rule from 1905 to 1945), Japanese rulers not only attempted to impose their authority (suppressing local "bandits") and secure peaceable relations with local populations, but they also encouraged the expansion of cultivation, the transfer of technology (especially with relation to farming), and the expansion of the market. These innovations were underpinned by a desire to make the peninsula a productive part of the empire and were driven by a colonial regime that excluded locals from the political process and made ready use of the coercive power of the empire. But even as the products of the peninsula were drawn into an increasingly rapacious imperial economy, the improved rail networks, the deployment of new technologies, and the application of fertilizer meant that the region's productive capacity eclipsed that of other parts of China. This transformation was a clear sign that China's waning political power and economic frailties were connected to its belated and partial attempts to grapple with the new industrial technologies championed by both its European and its Japanese rivals.[125]

Japan's recognition of the value of communications technology reflected the rapid transformation of its military power and strategic interests. In the Japanese case, there were close connections between industrialization and the rise of imperial aspirations. The desire to establish Japan's credentials as a modern nation and a power on the international stage were important stimuli to the extension of its economic influence and territorial reach. Technological development was an important precondition for the rapid expansion of its military capacity during the Meiji period and its military successes against China in 1895 and Russia in 1904. From the late 1860s, Japan invested heavily in developing its military capacity within a new industrial framework: drawing upon Western scientific models and making extensive use of foreign experts (from Britain, France, Italy, the Netherlands, and Belgium), new furnaces, arsenals, shipyards, and drydocks were constructed. By the mid-1880s, the Japanese were no longer producing wooden ships and had successfully established factories that were producing large numbers of explosives, artillery shells, machine guns, and large cannon.[126]

In turn, the success of the Japanese military in these conflicts against China and Russia stimulated the development of new technologies and was a powerful spur to the extension of industrial production. Wars against China and Russia, as well as the Meiji state's "strong army" policy, provided sustained impetus to Japan's shipbuilding, production of armaments, and development of machine tools. In the wake of its victory over China, influential Japanese military leaders and politicians increasingly argued that military technology, especially naval technology, was fundamental to Japan's future. These officials appealed to nationalist sentiment and imperial aspirations, as they argued Japan had to develop a potent blue-water fleet, not only to ensure national security in age of aggressive European colonialism, but also as a foundation for Japan's status as a regional power. Some of these concerns echoed contemporary developments in Germany. In the final decades of the nineteenth century, an influential cohort of politicians and officials argued that, given Germany's growing industrial might, a strong navy was vital to the nation's future, especially to avoid being eclipsed by its European rivals. Naval power was seen as essential if Germany was to build an empire, outflank its European rivals, and compete with Britain on the world stage. The construction of a strong German navy was also seen to have real political benefits. As a truly national institution, it would not only protect the recently consolidated German nation but also stimulate a patriotism that would help the Germans foreground their common nationality and transcend religious and regional divides.[127]

In Japan, where strong arguments linked sea power to the standing of the nation, the state's embrace of technology and its commitment to the development of its military capacity sowed the seeds for the Japanese navy's spectacular rout of the Russian Baltic Fleet in May 1905. The development of Japan's military capacity before 1914 further laid the foundation for the transformation of the Japanese economy in the interwar period, which saw the rapid expansion of Japan's industrial capacity, the refinement of its military technologies, and the growth of new forms of enterprise, especially in heavy industry and chemical production.[128]

Japan's expanding industrial and military capacity, as well as its growing influence on the world stage, colored its perceptions of the peoples and lands in Asia and the Pacific. During the Meiji and Taishō periods, Nan'yō—"the South Seas"—were actively reimagined as an important space for Japan's future by various intellectual and political figures. The southern Pacific was seen as a site for potential Japanese emigration, a region where Japan could acquire territory and enlarge its standing as an imperial power, as well as a largely untapped resource frontier brimming with valuable materials that could be easily exploited by the resource-poor Japanese state.[129] In 1915 the South Seas Association was established with government backing to promote the expansion of Japan's economic and cultural presence in Southeast Asia and the Pacific. Japan enlarged its interest in the region after it gained control of Micronesia during World War I. Japan's expanding presence in these western Pacific islands was championed by the navy and was considered to be of great strategic value in the 1930s, as Japan was increasingly mindful of its strategic position relative to the United States. In these southernmost portions of the empire, advocates of Japanese imperialism believed, Japan was ruling over people who were radically different in cultural and racial terms. Whereas Koreans, Taiwanese, and Chinese populations under Japanese rule were seen as belonging to the same broad cultural group, the peoples of the island Pacific were believed to be extremely primitive and, as such, required strict rule and extensive indoctrination in "civilized" values consonant with imperial citizenship.[130] These islands were connected to Japan and its colonies: shipping routes, newspapers, and radio circulated images of these distant lands and peoples back to Japan, while these media were also central to the imperial project of fully integrating these islands into the mesh of empire. By the 1940s, on the international stage Japanese ideologues and diplomats increasingly articulated a vision of their national and imperial future as being based in a "Greater East Asia Co-prosperity Sphere." This was to be a regional economic complex headed by Japan, which would free Asians from the threat of European and American imperial aggression. It is crucial to remember, however, that this distinctive vision of the international order was underpinned by the transportation, communication, and political networks Japan had fashioned in northern, East, and Southeast Asia and the western Pacific and ultimately reflected the confidence Japan had gained from its industrialization and the rapid extension of its imperial reach from the Meiji period on.

Ottoman Innovation and the Tracks of Empire

Japan's transformation between the 1850s and World War I was a powerful and attractive model for many intellectuals and reformers in the Ottoman Empire.

Japan's new standing on the international stage suggested not only that modernization could progress at considerable pace, but also that European power could be successfully challenged by non-European states. Many Turkish military leaders drew particular inspiration from the Japanese defeat of Russia in 1904–1905, believing that Japan demonstrated that technological expertise and military prowess could be gained without comprising distinctive moral and social values.[131]

For these Turkish thinkers, industrial development, military improvement, and the strength of connections between the constituent parts of the Ottoman Empire were important issues that would define the future of their community. Unlike Japan, however, the Ottoman state exercised authority over a long-established empire; it had an extensive history of cross-cultural contacts; and it did not have the buffer of the open ocean protecting it from its rivals, as the sprawling Ottoman domains shared borders with a range of the empire's European rivals and their colonial possessions. In other words, the contingencies of geography and history gave questions of industry and empire a particular inflection in the Ottoman world.

While the question of the Ottoman Empire's relationships with Europe was a central issue shaping the development of its communication and transportation networks, these technologies were also seen as an important instrument for ensuring the integrity of the empire, for the promotion of trade and exchange, and for enabling the mobility of troops, administrators, scholars, and pilgrims. Although by 1847 Sultan Abdülmecid I saw the possibilities that telegraphy offered state practice, the first substantial Ottoman lines developed during the Crimean War as part of a coordinated effort between the British, French, and Ottoman regimes. Despite the sultan's enthusiastic support of the new technology, the pashas of the Ottoman provinces, who were fearful that it would allow the Ottoman center to develop a more detailed knowledge of local affairs and strengthen the power of the sultan at their expense, initially opposed it. Despite this, the Ottoman telegraph network quadrupled in the 1860s to encompass over fifteen thousand miles of line in 1869. Growth of this network not only linked key political and commercial centers within Ottoman domains, but it was also shaped by the influence of British capital and strategy, as lines that traversed the Ottoman lands were designed to connect to British India, reflecting the strategic value placed on telegraph communication in the wake of the 1857–1858 rebellion. In addition, in certain parts of the Ottoman Empire—especially in Hejaz and Yemen—Ottoman communications were still routed through British-owned lines and stations in British-controlled Egypt. This dependence was cast off with the inauguration of a new and extremely expensive network that linked all the major administrative centers in the Transjordan region in 1901. The main line was subsequently doubled and new stations were added to the network as Sultan Abdülhamid II was impressed with the efficiency and strategic value of the new lines. But the sultan's opponents also seized on the political utility of the telegraph network. Provincial townsfolk and merchants used the new technology to swiftly communicate their petitions to Istanbul, and the reformist Young Turks saw the telegraph as an important instrument for the reform and modernization of the Turkish nation. Women telegraph operators were among those who filled the streets of Ottoman cities, taking part in and helping—through shopping, looking, and riding the streetcars—to shape the character of secular public life.[132]

Railways were even more significant than the telegraph in Ottoman attempts to modernize. By 1850 the Ottoman state was aware of the challenges that the rise of steam power and European industrialization posed, and embarked on a concerted effort to harness the empire's coal resources to supply its growing factories, its imperial fleet, and the fledgling rail network that was inaugurated in 1856. Railways were of particular significance within this large land-based empire that incorporated a wide variety of environments and widely dispersed markets. The massive capacity of trains pulled by steam locomotives meant that a significant long-distance trade in grains developed and the agricultural potential of the fertile regions in the interior of the empire could be effectively tapped for the first time. Lines were constructed to serve both commercial and strategic concerns. The Oriental Railway, which connected Istanbul to Sofia and Edirne, and Edirne to Salonica, in the 1870s and 1880s, linked key imperial markets. In a minor but telling example of the interconnection of production and transportation and its gendered character, the development of rug factories in Turkey was accelerated by the incursion of the railway into the interior—which in turn stimulated employment for women, albeit of the low-paid variety. But the actual routing of lines was dictated by strategic concerns and the desire to be able to deploy the empire's troops quickly and effectively. Railway projects were also heavily symbolic. In 1900 Sultan Abdülhamid II announced the construction of a new rail line that would run from Damascus to Medina and Mecca, a massive project designed to enable pilgrims on the Hajj to reach Islam's sacred cities and to demonstrate the sultan's commitment to the ties of faith and culture that connect the Muslim world. This project reflected a general Ottoman strategy to associate the railway and telegraph, which some Muslim critics dismissed as products of the infidel, with the authority of the sultan and the maintenance of Islam itself. In stunning contrast, it was against the backdrop of a train station in Cairo in 1923 that Huda Shaarawi launched her anti-veil movement, thereby dramatizing, if only by allusion, the contrast between the mobility of modernity and the fixity of harem as emblems of Egyptian women's particular colonial and nationalist dilemma.[133]

Despite the emphasis that successive Ottoman rulers placed on the railway, the Ottoman network ultimately developed slowly and unevenly. At one level this reflected the varying economic capacity of the regions and the differential rates with which Ottoman subjects embraced rail travel. The lines in Anatolia and the Balkans were relatively heavily used both by passengers and for freight, whereas the railways in Arab domains did not carry large volumes of either. Overall, however, the Ottoman rail system was relatively underdeveloped. The network was based around a limited number of trunk lines and not the kind of dense mesh that characterized British India or even the proliferation of feeder lines found in many other colonies and in the European lands that used to be part of the Ottoman Empire. Concentrated networks did develop in former Ottoman domains, such as Egypt, and some feeder networks developed around ports like Beirut and İzmir, but generally it was a "thin" system that had only moderate reach into the imperial hinterland. Indeed, the lateness of trains and the general inefficiency of modern transport were not uncommonly satirized in the early twentieth-century Ottoman press. At the outbreak of World War I, the network remained patchy in both quality and coverage. During the war the Turkish army frequently faced persistent logistical difficulties as the rail network had limited reach across Anatolia and stretched only forty-five miles east of Ankara. The gaps within the system meant that soldiers had often to rely on camels, boats, and their own feet as they moved to marshaling points and engagements. These limitations did not, however, prevent the Ottoman authorities from carrying out a program of Armenian "relocation," which authorized the deportation of Armenians and the seizing of their property, as Armenians were identified as a threat to the security of the empire. Eyewitness reports testify to the role of the Baghdad railway and its staff in this genocidal drive to redefine the ethnic composition of the empire, a project that culminated in the extermination of over one million Armenians.[134]

While the patchiness of the Ottoman transportation networks contributed to the eventual dissolution of the empire, ultimately the nature of Ottoman economic development was the primary cause of the hollowing out of centralized authority. The extensive public works programs that developed in the second half of the nineteenth century were an important engine of economic development. Significant advances were made in the development of communications technology, steam power, factories, and new machinery, but these innovations were unevenly distributed in the empire. Economic modernization was produced at greater speed in larger cities, but these technologies had much less impact in provincial towns and among the large peasant population that was the demographic backbone of the empire. Most importantly, the pattern of development was dictated by the Ottoman's dependence on international funding and scientific innovation. Much railway construction was reliant on foreign capital: German capital was particularly important, financing the important Anatolian rail line. Ottoman infrastructure and industrial capacity increasingly fell under European control as well: European financing was also central in developing ports, tram networks, and factories.[135]

At the same time, the growing numbers of steamships visiting Ottoman ports and the expansion of rail networks meant that Ottoman markets were increasingly opened up to European goods: regions like Syria were flooded by European-produced textiles at the end of the nineteenth century. This reliance on imported finished goods was compounded by the opening of the Suez Canal, which enabled vast imports of silk from the Far East, undercutting the production of Ottoman silk at centers such as Bursa. These transport networks also meant that the Ottoman Empire was increasingly locked into a European agricultural market and basic agricultural goods made up around three-quarters of the empire's exports.[136] In other words, Ottoman workers produced basic foodstuffs and raw goods for export to the industrialized nations of Europe, while Ottoman consumers increasingly purchased imported processed foods (such as refined flour and sugar), manufactured goods, and luxury products. In light of this pattern, by 1914 the empire "assumed the character of a European economic appendage."[137] Because of this economic decline, the attempts of successive sultans to build military capacity and establish a state-of the-art navy (which included a submarine from 1886) foundered. The dream of rapid modernization and imperial strength that Japan offered was unattainable for the Ottoman state, and the ultimate failure of Ottoman industrialization was made clear with the empire's dissolution in 1922.

Remaking Time and Space

If we shift our gaze beyond the development of individual imperial systems to focus on the broader development of these connective technologies, it is clear that from the 1860s imperial regimes worked hard to make their communication and transportation networks larger, denser, faster, and more efficient. Steam power and electricity drove environmental transformation, the extension and intensification of industrial production, and the expanding investments in military technology that were common features of imperial regimes between 1870 and 1945. But the nature and outcomes of these transformations were irregular. The empires' wire and steel networks, which knitted the continents together, were extended at different speeds and transformed various regions in different ways. Both geography and economics shaped these patterns. Regions that had few natural anchorages or insufficient resources for the construction of artificial harbors, or were too distant from high-traffic shipping lanes, developed fewer port facilities and benefited much less from international trade. This was particularly the case in Africa, where high-quality ports were developed only in regions that were firmly incorporated into European empires and where substantial capital had been invested in port infrastructure. While Egypt, Tunisia, Algeria, and South Africa had several significant ports each, most large cities in tropical Africa either lacked natural harbors or drew insufficient capital from their imperial masters for the development of high-capacity port facilities.[138] Railways did become important elements in African colonial culture, but the continent's rail networks lacked the quality and density of South Asia's. Railway development in

Africa was patchy, in both coverage and the successful execution of projects. Railways were rarely constructed to serve African communities or to link major population centers; instead they were instruments that allowed valuable raw materials—rubber, cotton, copper, gold, diamonds, and groundnut and palm oils—to be moved from the interior to port cities from where they were shipped to European markets.[139] These patterns meant that even as Europe's intrusion into Africa was geared to the expropriation of African resources, Western technology and culture were never as deeply embedded into many local cultures as they were in those colonies where colonial rule was accompanied by a dense mesh of new communication networks. But in light of this we should not read Africa, or even tropical Africa, as a unique case: instead we should remember that the work of empires was always asymmetrical in its nature, producing spatially and socially differentiated outcomes.

One of the most important of these outcomes was the reconfiguration of time and space. It is well established, of course, that industrialization transformed European experience and understandings of both space and time. There is strong evidence that the growth of European productivity was the outcome of a reorganization of labor and time from the middle of the eighteenth century. New industrial technologies also reshaped popular understandings of time as European workers increasingly internalized the disciplines of clock time and factory whistles. Most importantly, the steam locomotive and the extension of rail networks revolutionized European and North American apprehensions of speed and distance as old perceptions of space, formed by an earlier and long-standing technological order, were torn asunder by the power of steam. Train travel and the increasing acceleration of other forms of communication—from the electric telegraph to the daily newspaper—led to a widespread sense that industrialization had resulted in what contemporaries termed the "annihilation of space and time," seemingly reducing distances and bringing points in space closer together with great speed.[140]

The globalization of steam-powered travel on the back of imperial systems meant that from 1870 most societies in the world were exposed to these cultural shifts. Even in Africa, which as we have seen had relatively small, patchy, and slow communication networks, the technologies brought by colonialism did reconfigure space. The trip from Mombasa to Uganda, for example, traditionally may have taken up to a year to complete on foot, but in an age of train travel, it could be completed in two to four days.[141] In those parts of Africa where there were few or no railways, another industrial form of transportation—the bicycle—became a key feature of the colonial landscape for colonial rulers and Africans alike, achieving some acceleration of social movement but with little attendant recalibration of temporal perception.[142] Another important marker of the shifts in temporal perception that empire and industrialization wrought on the world stage was the globalization of the pocket watch and the growing dissemination of this technology beyond the European and North American middle classes to their counterparts in Asia, Africa, and Latin America.

Perhaps the most telling evidence of how the combined effects of industrialization and empire building reordered temporality was the standardization of time at a global level. The United Kingdom was the first country to impose a standard time system. With the growth of rail travel, there was a greater need to organize time to ensure the coordination of the movements of trains and to guarantee the accuracy of timetables. By 1855, most public clocks in Britain were set to London's Greenwich Mean Time. This standardization across Britain encouraged the commodification of time. Not only did pocket watches and family clocks become more common, but time itself was a commodity. The most famous time-seller in Britain was the "Greenwich Time Lady," Ruth Belville, the daughter of an assistant of Greenwich Observatory, who used a subscription service to sell Greenwich Time, which was calibrated on a weekly basis on her fine pocket watch, to Londoners.[143]

It was not until 1880, however, that the legal system caught up with this popular move toward standardization with the passage of the Statutes (Definition of Time) Act. Larger nations comprising regions that significantly diverged regarding "solar time," such as the United States, faced even more serious problems. In 1883 American railways implemented a system of standardized time zones, breaking away from the "local reckoning" that had been previously dominant, but it was only in August 1918 that Congress passed the Standard Time Act. In 1884, long before the US government adopted a standard national time, forty-one delegates from twenty-five nations met in Washington, DC, for the International Meridian Conference. The speed of telegraphic communication and steamships had made it clear that international standards for the measurement of time and space were needed, and the conference fixed an international meridian and international time zones. This issue was particularly pressing for large maritime empires, which hoped that the standardization of time would aid the daily function of commerce and imperial administration. The conference delegates agreed that Greenwich, which already functioned as Britain's standard-setter, would serve as a global meridian and that all longitude would be calculated both east and west from this meridian. Thereafter, Greenwich Mean Time functioned as a global baseline from which international time zones were established, creating a unified system that has become the international standard.

As the measurement of time was standardized, the conviction that imperial centers represented both the present and the future, whereas colonized spaces represented backwardness and the past, not only persisted but was strengthened. The technology of the daguerreotype in particular and the apparatus of modern photography more generally enabled cultural difference to be coded visually into scenes of apparent temporal distance, enhanced by "native" costume and nakedness either total or partial. Women and children were the invariable (though by no means exclusive) foci of these forms of appropriative technological innovation, even when colonized men were in charge of the lens. With the arrival of moving pictures around the turn of the twentieth century, the capacity for time to mean space, for the past to mean the remote, was at once accelerated and fixed for metropolitan audiences increasingly desirous of evidence of their own racial and civilizational superiority in a post-1918 world. If the difficulty of Britain's victory over the Boers by 1902 and Japan's defeat of Russia in 1905 were not evidence enough, the critical support provided to the allies by troops of color in World War I and the fevered nationalist movements at Versailles spoke volumes about the finite global possibilities of modern imperial power. By the interwar period, would-be imperialists who wanted "native views" could have them virtually, beyond the constraint of time and space, via film. Though the movies certainly delivered colonized spaces and people from myriad perspectives, among the most common was via the view from the steamboat or the train window.[144]

Indeed, apprehensions of space and more particularly of scale were transformed by industry and empire as the linkages that technology aspired to create came into more widespread view. Most importantly, the completion of the Suez Canal and the paramountcy of steamers reconfigured space, giving rise to a new geography of shipping, as ports developed to meet the needs of expanding long-distance shipping and were themselves reconfigured by steam power, iron, and concrete. New ports sprang up and were built on a grand scale by imperial rulers confident of the further growth of shipping in the age of steam: Singapore, Hong Kong, Dakar, and Karachi became significant hubs. Port Said, at the entrance of the Suez Canal, emerged as the world's premier coaling station for steamers, but other ports, like Montevideo in Uruguay and Las Palmas in the Canaries also rose in economic and strategic significance because of their new prominence as refueling sites. Steam eroded the significance of some long-established ports: after the Suez Canal opened, Calcutta was increasingly overshadowed by Mumbai, and increasingly the commercial and political weight of British India moved gradually toward the west and its premier port.[145]

Just as locomotives and steamships effectively compressed space as they greatly reduced travel times, various social groups also experienced the compression of space differently. Some colonized communities who lived in close proximity to new transportation networks were unable to access them because of their social status, long-standing economic marginalization, or a recent decline in their standing.[146] This divergence was made especially clear in some colonial cities, where the physical organization of space and its attendant social morphology was fundamentally shaped by the locations of rail lines, stations, wharves and the factories that supported these industrial transport technologies. Laura Bear's work on the culture of Indian railways has demonstrated the ways in which these new technologies and their associated labor patterns were central in creating new and highly spatialized hierarchies of race and gender. Disciplining the railway family was a crucial dimension of the railway colony project, not least because the spaces it gave rise to rendered unstable both racial distinctions and, therewith, that most prized of imperial exports, domestic respectability.[147] The conjunctures between communication networks and the geography of cultural difference were striking features of newly established port cities such as Suva in Fiji as well as in long-established cities like Lahore in Punjab and Ajmer in Rajasthan, which were profoundly reordered after their incorporation into the colonial rail network. In these cities, the railways had a transformative power, shaping patterns of industrialization, residential development, and the organization of public space. Indeed, imperialists from Korea to Cairo saw the railroad itself as the model colonizer, delivering the civilizing mission via modern technology while stoking the extractive colonial economy as well.[148]

Thus the "annihilation of distance," or at least the greater speed of movement and communication experienced by most societies by 1900, had a variety of unexpected consequences. The transport networks constructed by colonial states, which were typically committed to modernization and imperial strategic interests, were a key factor in the popularization of pilgrimage. According to a popular early twentieth-century railway song in Japan from the memoir of Japanese poet Takamure Itsue heading to Shikoku on pilgrimage, "when you ride this train you'll go a thousand *ri* in just an instant."[149] Rail quickly also became central in the local, regional, and interregional journeys to sacred sites and temples that were a central element of South Asian religious practice. Some railway lines were routed so that they effectively served pilgrimage sites, and by the third quarter of the nineteenth-century railway travel was firmly embedded within the pilgrimage experience of many South Asians. This new form of transport encouraged the faithful to undertake more long-distance pilgrimages, prompted more women to undertake pilgrimages as they saw trains as secure and reliable, and in effect reshaped the frequency, quality, and organization of ritual activity within South Asia as a whole. In a similar vein, new technologies and imperial transportation services helped bring about the end of the traditional Hajj, which had relied on long-established overland routes, caravan transport, and the use of sail power where necessary. The crossing from the ports of Egypt and North Africa to the Hejaz were always a feature of the movement of pilgrims toward Mecca, but in the age of steam many of these crossings were reduced from over thirty days to just three. The increased speed of this crossing encouraged, in turn, an increase in the number of travelers making the journey. Interestingly, Nawab Sikander Begum, hereditary ruler of the state of Bhopal who traveled to Mecca with a retinue of hundreds in 1863–1864 and published her account in 1870, chose not to mention the part of her journey traversed by rail, and scarcely mentioned the sea journey either. In addition to accelerating the movement of pilgrims, steam power also reordered traditional routes. Jidda, on Saudi Arabia's Red Sea coast, emerged as the key gateway port in the age of steam and the city was transformed by the new status and commerce that it enjoyed. European steamship companies serving such ports made handsome profits and were keen to increase the volume of traffic from imperial ports and cultivate the popularity of pilgrimage.[150]

The modern Hajj brings us to another key consequence of the reordering of time and space. The increased volume of pilgrims and the growing numbers traveling from India's Ganges Valley, where cholera was endemic, not only had devastating effects on the population of Hejaz, which was increasingly exposed to the disease, but also caused widespread concern among European imperial powers. In light of a deep-seated fear that Europe would be devastated by an epidemic carried by pilgrims, international conferences were called on the Hajj and European powers worked with the Ottoman authorities to regulate the movement of pilgrims and the sanitary regimes to be implemented during the Hajj. These conferences reflected contemporary awareness that imperial networks became key vectors through which environmental transformations were enacted as they stitched together previously disparate lands and communities. Road networks, which were increasingly extensive in most frontier regions, facilitated the flow of seeds and weeds along multiple vectors. There was nothing new in this, as roads had been central agents of epidemiological integration in Eurasian history, but these imperial networks connected inland communities and frontier zones to an increased number of market towns and port cities, linking the most distant settlements into a "common market" of microbes produced by large-scale imperial formations and long-distance trade.[151] Most importantly, bicycles, trains, steamships, and automobiles allowed pathogens to move across space at greater speed, fundamentally reshaping the epidemiological profile of many diseases.

The biological consequences of the suturing of these transportation technologies into imperial networks was well demonstrated by the great epidemics that shook the world in this period. The 1889–1890 influenza pandemic moved quickly across the globe, spreading at great speed through the dense rail networks of Europe and North America. The new railworks and steamer connections fashioned by empires allowed this disease to reach out into more distant lands: colonial port cities like Tunis, Cape Town, Algiers, and Hong Kong were key nodes from where the virus spread out along local shipping lanes, roads, and rail networks. Those regions that were only lightly integrated into imperial networks were largely inoculated against the virus. In Eurasia the influenza largely moved from west to east and, given the shape of routes in Eurasia, moved slowly across the eastern frontier of the Russian Empire, moving very slowly toward Siberia and delaying its arrival in Manchuria and Korea. The connections between imperial transportation and the movement of disease were even more forcefully demonstrated with the influenza pandemic of 1918. As War World I drew to a close, large numbers of soldiers, sailors, and military workers were transported from combat zones to their homelands. These travelers carried the virus—which had taken root in the battlefields of Europe as the war came to a close—along rail and steam routes to every nation that supplied combatants. The efficiency of these forms of transport meant that the virus subsequently spread out to those countries and communities that had little or no connection to the conflict. Because of the extended reach of steamships, in the American colony of Guam, the French colony of Tahiti, and Western Samoa (which was under New Zealand's jurisdiction from the end of the war) indigenous communities suffered extremely high mortality rates.[152] Meanwhile, in British India the relationship between railways and the dissemination of disease was subject to frequent discussion: there was strong evidence that plague traveled along railway routes, a point highlighted by a range of Indian nationalists.[153]

Gandhi's Traveling Incarceration

Among the most strident critiques of the consequences of empire and industrialization was Gandhi's *Hind Swaraj,* drafted in 1909 and published in 1910.[154] Presented in the form of a dialog between Reader and Editor, Gandhi offered his scathing critique of "civilization" and "colonialism" through the voice of Editor. Editor argued that railways were a key component of the "disease" of civilization and were an instrument that "had impoverished our country." He suggested that they were not "gifts" but rather colonial tools that helped cement Britain's "hold on India." The rail networks had not elevated India, but instead had caused misery: they increased the frequency of famines, carried germs from place to place, and destabilized the social order by breaking down the "natural segregation" that had previously shaped Indian society. In short, railways were instruments of evil, allowing "bad men [to] fulfill their evil designs with greater rapidity." This recalibration of time had spiritual and moral effects: "Good travels at a snail's pace."[155]

Gandhi's infamous encounter with the physical and social limits of the segregated railway carriage in 1890s South Africa reminds us that the new cultural and technological order crafted by colonial regimes was never passively accepted; rather it was subject to appropriation, frequent challenge, and open resistance. This can be clearly seen in the Ottoman Empire, where symbols of Westernization were both criticized and physically attacked. For example, an anonymous Ottoman-Turkish text, probably drafted by a minor religious thinker from the provinces toward the close of the nineteenth century, railed against Western schools, factories, railways, and telegraphs. The author was especially critical of these new forms of mobility, suggesting that they allowed humans to achieve their desired goals with less effort, time, and thought. As a result, these technologies encouraged humans to undervalue experience and to develop conceited souls as they became dependent on created things rather than on God, became caught up in worldliness and desire, and cast aside the truths of the Quran. The social and religious consequences of the adoption of these technologies introduced into the Islamic world by "unbelievers" were far-reaching: in fostering human arrogance and the negligence of sincere devotion, they gave rise to spiritual disobedience, widespread sin, and the total corruption of the moral order.[156] Yakup Bektas had shown that this kind of position was common among those Ottoman subjects "skeptical of the Christian-Western world" who viewed the telegraph as "an infidel, satanic invention." This critique rejected Western technology on the grounds that it had a demoralizing effect, but also because "the telegraph entailed a spatial framework that contrasted with the traditional view of geographical space and distance."[157]

Other Ottoman opponents of Westernization relied on physical rather than textual resistance. The expanding telegraphic network was subject to attack in many rural areas as poles were removed and materials were stripped, reflecting a mix of ideological opposition to the new technology as well as a local hunger for scarce raw materials. As a result, the Ottoman government implemented a system of annual subsidies to chieftains who undertook to prevent these abuses of the system as well as establishing special guards (*çavuslar*) to protect the network as a whole. This initiative, however, was unable to suppress hostility toward Western technologies in southern portions of the empire. The extension of railways under the Ottomans and the new centrality of steam transport in the movement of pilgrims angered Bedouin tribes whose livelihoods had long been dependent on providing camels to pilgrims. Resentful of their constrained economic prospects and the Ottoman state's withdrawal of a subsidy to protect pilgrims, Bedouins rose up in open revolt in 1909. These same groups subsequently provided crucial support to the Arab revolt against Ottoman authority in 1916, an uprising that focused much of its attention on attacking the Hejaz Railway.[158]

Nationalist critiques of innovations in imperial communications also reveal the connections between communication and the growing naturalization of the nation-state. Even though empires constructed global networks, some imperial thinkers were encouraged to consider the possibilities of constructing global states, and nationalist ideologues frequently drew inspiration from other critiques of colonialism, the primacy of the nation-state was finally secured in the second half of the nineteenth century. The transference of these industrial technologies and the creation of new communication networks were central in giving shape to colonies within the putative form of the nation-state. Benedict Anderson has famously drawn our attention to the pivotal role of newspapers in producing imagined communities, though even these depended on other technologies (especially the telegraph and railway).[159]

Nations were not simply produced by the circulation of cultural representations, but were also molded by the shape of transportation and communication pathways along which commodities, capital, and workers moved on a regular basis.[160] A crucial precondition of the process of nation building was the lacing together of preexisting regional economies, and railways in particular were central in giving economic patterns a national shape. Railways not only recalibrated trade in key commodities within regions (such as the rice trade in Bengal) but were simultaneously central in the production of a national market for food grains in colonial India. The integration of transport networks was often central in the political process of nation building: this was particularly clear in Nigeria, where the linking up of the previously distinct railroad systems in the north and the south preceded the political fusion of the protectorates and functioned as the primary means of colonial state formation.

Not only did rail and telegraph networks provide the core spatial structure for many nations that came into being under colonial regimes, but they were also fundamentally important in the cultural processes that helped naturalize the nation-state as a political unit and fortified the large-scale identifications that are required for nationalism to successfully take root. Even as they were critical of the many of the outcomes of railway construction, Gandhi and other nationalists saw the railways as an indispensable instrument for their cause and a crucial element in the unification of an extremely diverse population into a coherent citizenry. It is also clear that in settler colonies, railway journeys and the emergence of popular commercialized leisure were central in producing emergent ideas of colonial citizenship, fortifying new understandings of race, landscape, and nationality.[161] In other words, transportation and communication were pivotal in producing the symmetries among economic organization, political identification, and cultural cohesiveness that were central in the production of the nation-state. The centrality of these technologies at a global level by 1900 helps explain not only how the idea of the nation-state was globalized but also why the content of nationalisms were remarkably consistent in widely different colonial contexts. Even as nationalist leaders insisted on the uniqueness and difference of their communities, they did so through idioms and narratives that shared many common features. As early as 1914 imperial globalization had arguably cemented the authority of the nation in the non-Western world at the same time as a conflict between European powers quickly transformed into the world's first truly global conflict waged with industrial technologies.

In light of the evidence we have presented here, we are wary of attempts either to disentangle empire and "globalizing forces" in this period or to bind them too tightly together. This wariness stems not from a conviction that all globalization was imperial in its nature, but rather from historical evidence that over the course of five centuries the shape of the various global overlays—communication and transportation networks, flows of capital and commodities, missionary institutions and pilgrimage routes, the movements of scholars and the printed word— had been molded by the boundaries, ideologies, and practices of imperial regimes in a host of ways. Moreover, not only were forms of interregional connection operating from the 1870s on, conditioned by these structures fashioned in earlier imperial moments, but they were constantly being remade by new imperial aspirations, international conflicts that were threaded through with imperial concerns (even when they were not necessarily imperial in nature), and by the efforts of various individuals and groups to overturn, resist, and subvert the march of empire. In an age of global imperialism, the world was continually remade by these struggles, and its hegemonies were never either self-evident or complete, in the sense of being finished in time or total in space. Empire and globalization were not synonymous, but the processes of empire building and the weight of imperial legacies gave shape to the connections that linked regions, communities, and states into new and often unexpected forms of connection and interdependence.

This threading together of human communities raised questions about identity and difference in new and pressing ways: even as the economies and infrastructures of nations were increasingly interwoven, nationalist leaders insisted on the uniqueness and particularity of their political community. Ironically, of course, these ideologues articulated these supposedly singular identities through a common set of images, objects, symbols, and narratives. As will become clear in Section 3, questions of space, political change, and transnational connection were at the heart of the struggle over the politics of empire and imperial power across the first half of the twentieth century. Whether via contact or collision, contemporaries were able to see, to appreciate, and to act on such linkages because of the structural transformations sponsored by technological development, new patterns of circulation, and ongoing processes of cultural transfer and adaptation in a world that had been radically, if unevenly, remade by global imperial systems.

3. *Global Empires, Transnational Connections*

IN APRIL 1955, representatives of 29 independent Asian and African countries convened in Bandung, Indonesia, in "the first intercontinental conference of coloured peoples in the history of mankind."[162] Sponsored by the recently independent nations of Burma, Ceylon, India, Indonesia, and Pakistan, Bandung became shorthand for utopian hopes about the future of "Third World" solidarities in the wake of decolonization and in the context of the Korean War and the superpower ambitions of the Soviet Union and America. Although Bandung took place a decade after the end of the period we are discussing, scholars who wish to understand the full historical meaning of empire, colonial encounters, and decolonization must account for how and why African-Asian solidarity and nonalignment became watchwords of the postcolonial Cold War—as well as how anti-imperial movements structured the histories of the later nineteenth and early twentieth century. Using Bandung as a touchstone serves several methodological purposes. First, it allows us to center the history of anticolonial activists and movements, big and small, at the heart of our account of imperialism during this period, a period that is often framed as a story of imperial growth and decay where the key players are European or American and where decolonization is primarily seen as the outcome of the ideological shifts and economic crises that developed in the West after World War II. Instead we see the period from 1870 to 1945, and especially the years 1918–1945, as a time when colonized peoples worked hard to wrest power and authority from imperial governments loathe to "grant" independence except when faced with the inevitability of defeat at the hands of diverse opponents, from nationalist leaders to "guerillas," from "terrorists" to those colonized subjects who worked hard to maintain their language, cultural practices, and limited political rights in the face of imperial power. Second, it enables us to appreciate the ways in which the Bandung Conference itself was the culmination of decades of transnational connection between and among colonial peoples rather than the inaugural moment of African-

Asian solidarity. Rather than seeing Bandung as an originary moment, this approach foregrounds the long histories of intercolonial connection, collaboration, and of course also friction. Last but not least, thinking backward from Bandung makes it possible to track not just the flow of people and policies between metropole and colony but also the movement of ideas and political platforms below the imperial surface, if you will. It allows us to historicize the ways in which a variety of actors, nationalist and otherwise, across the imperialized globe of the nineteenth and especially the twentieth century linked up rhetorically, symbolically, and even organizationally. Some of these were well-known elite figures; others have become so in the context of postcolonial history; while others remain obscure, and instructively so, insofar as their histories fly below the radar even of the intersection of global, local, regional, and imperial histories. In highlighting these often-neglected "encounters" between colonized peoples, we are suggesting that the period 1870–1945 not only was a high point of imperial reach but, equally, marked the emergence of new kinds of intercolonial connections and solidarities. These new political forms were central in the global political terrain during the second half of the twentieth century and, arguably, were central in structuring the new imperialisms of the twentieth century.

By figuring the Bandung Conference as emblematic of the broader reshaping of the global political order, we aim to challenge what is often, and unaccountably, viewed as a sharp break between the Cold War and what came before. At the very least we want to suggest new chronologies that, rather than privileging the "Scramble for Africa" and World War II as bookends, emphasize the 1890s and the interwar years as watersheds in the geopolitical restructuring that enabled the Bandung Conference to emerge as a historical possibility. Needless to say, our call for the recognition of a different temporal frame—one that underscores continuities as well as fissures between the apparent chasm of the pre- and post-1945 periods—does not aim to cast doubt on the power or the historically unprecedented accomplishments of anti-imperial movements. Nor do we wish to fetishize the Bandung Conference itself as the apotheosis of postcolonial harmony and interracial brotherhood: there were now-famous internal currents of disagreement and dissension among the delegates and their leaders at the conference itself. Indeed, what Sukarno, the first president of Indonesia, said in his opening remarks about the relationship between the West and "the rest"—notably, that "great chasms yawn between nations and groups of nations"—might just as easily have been said about the relationship between Jawaharlal Nehru, the prime minister of India, and Zhou Enlai, premier of the People's Republic of China, or between Zhou and Sir John Kotelawala, prime minister of Ceylon, over leadership and peaceful coexistence, particularly with respect to the conference's position on the USSR and its semicolonial satellites.[163]

What is significant is that such disagreements and the transnational bonds they cut across were by no means new to the postwar world. They grew organically, if not necessarily predictably, out of the wreckage of older imperialisms, the contests among recently postcolonial states, and the aspirations of newly energized imperial powers—in part because they were the inheritance of the "globally articulated imperial structure" of the mid-twentieth-century world.[164] Gender as an embodied experience together with the idea of "woman" as a reformist platform for the claims of imperialists and nationalists alike was critical to how new global structures were articulated in this period. Indeed, gender's simultaneously discursive and material presence—and its entanglement with racialized ideas and practices—was a clear marker of how empire building imprinted modernity. In anticolonial thought and practice, the emergence of women as political, economic, and cultural agents in their own right occurred against a backdrop of a "woman question" that turned women and even some feminists into icons of tradition or modernity or both, despite the fact that in many cases they were in the process of forging new movements claiming rights at a global level. The Bandung Conference—with its success in bringing together ex-colonial peoples to debate the ramifications of their sovereignty and solidarity on the world stage *and* its virtually exclusively masculinist take on the new world order—can be read as both a harbinger of the fractious global order of the late twentieth century as well as a key product of the global reach of anticolonial resistance to the violence and repression of modern Western imperialism.

Empires Ascendant

Standard narratives of the period between Henry Morton Stanley's journey down the Congo River and the height of the Great War emphasize the ascendancy of Western European empires especially: a claim that, at a basic level, it would be hard to contradict. In terms of territorial expansion alone, a range of European powers did extend their spatial reach significantly, if not exponentially, during these years. European armies, diplomats, and adventurers succeeded in bringing a variety of social, cultural, linguistic, and religious communities under direct imperial rule (especially in Africa) or into a variety of imperial spheres of influence and informal control (especially in East Asia and Latin America). In terms of sheer numbers (whether the calculus is subject bodies or square miles), Britain outpaced its European rivals significantly between 1870 and 1914, with the result that the British imperial experience has become emblematic in historiographical terms of "the imperial encounter" *tout court*. If the litmus test for imperial global-imperial power is economic dominance, Britain's preeminence at the close of the nineteenth century was not challenged. At the heart of the "developing capitalist core" both in the West and in the world, Britain was undoubtedly the center of the imperial globe. Within Britain, England served as the fulcrum for industrial production and commercial consumption and, within England, London functioned as the center of a vast empire of financial services that encompassed the globe, even allowing for comparative decline after 1900.[165] Equally significant, the structural conditions that Britain had long established for realizing profits from its Asian imperial territories, where both full and semicolonial power was operative, meant that aspiring empires like Japan were compelled to grapple with British imperial foundations as they sought to enhance their own economic and territorial power. This is not to say that Japanese imperialism was merely reactive to or derivative of Western empires; instead, it was compelled to stake its claim to global power in waters—treaty port waters, to be precise—already well-navigated by European interests and shaped, at the end of the nineteenth century, by centuries of British imperial enterprise. In many respects, nations and empires aiming to be global players and to exert domination over local or indigenous peoples had first, or at least simultaneously, to deal with the specter, whether diplomatic, military, or economic, of British power. As empire building became a key marker of a nation's economic and cultural capacity, Britain, for its part, was also faced with competitors on all sides as well as resistance from below. "The Ottoman sultan, the Meiji emperor, the Russian tsar, the Hapsburg emperor . . . all looked to each other to see . . . [how to play] the role of 'civilized monarchy'" as their respective officials eyed the others' bureaucracies, militaries, and imperial/civil societies.[166]

Thus, it is a truism worth perhaps repeating: imperial "encounters" in the late nineteenth and early twentieth centuries occurred on multiple fronts, engaging colonizer, colonized, and would-be colonizer in a wide variety of asymmetrical relationships of power.

These asymmetries are less visible—as indeed is the vulnerability of European hegemony—than they should be when one holds to the argument that the history of the British Empire ought to remain near the heart of global accounts of imperialism in the modern period. There is no denying, then, that in terms of technological development and economic prowess (in almost every register in which that might be assessed), the British Empire was critical to the definition, in practical and symbolic terms, of modern imperialism as such. In this sense, the appellation *anglo-globalization* is not without merit as a characterization of the processes that restructured many economies, polities, and cultures in the period 1870–1945 and laid the foundation of our contemporary moment.[167] And yet, recognition of the British Empire's centrality to the establishment of a certain species of globality need not mean that we should see British imperialism as a static, fully accomplished, or (worse yet) teleologically hegemonic phenomenon untouched by either the threat of competitors or the specter of native resistance from within.

The case of the South African War of 1899–1902 is apposite here. Although the conflict fed into and was shaped by the shifting imperial alignments of Britain, France, Russia, and Germany, the war itself was precipitated by the eruption of intra-ethnic rivalries—between African groups as well Afrikaner and English colonists—on the South African frontier. When read against these multiple contexts, this fin-de-siècle contest must be understood as the result of the complex set of divergent strategic imperatives and cultural aspirations that were produced by the intersection of competing imperial visions with the complexities produced by a long tradition of cross-cultural engagement and colonialism on the ground. As the clash between English and Afrikaner armies played it, it became clear to many observers that this was not simply a small colonial war of local significance, but was rather a conflict with global ramifications.[168]

Events in South Africa not only resonated within English and European high politics, but they were central to debates over race, nationhood, and the bonds of empire throughout the British colonies. The British campaigns against the Afrikaners drew on colonial manpower, with white soldiers from Canada, Australia, and New Zealand serving alongside British troops. Even though small cliques of settler intellectuals and politicians in both Australia and New Zealand were fashioning increasingly confident nationalist traditions, the opportunity to serve the empire that the war provided was embraced with great enthusiasm by the majority of colonists. But the desire of many Maori communities to demonstrate their loyalty to the queen and to the empire, opened up a series of contentious debates over race after the Colonial Office declined the offer of Maori military manpower conveyed by the New Zealand premier Richard John Seddon. This British decision, together with the experience of mobilizing an expeditionary force and the reality of losing soldiers in an imperial conflict, fed colonial nationalism and further militarized the culture of British settler colonies. The conflict in South Africa raised complex issues in Ireland, which formally remained part of the "Union" of the United Kingdom of Ireland and Great Britain, but where there was a strong sense that Ireland was in effect a British colony. Although the politicians who represented Irish constituencies in Westminster praised the efforts of the Irish soldiers who fought as part of the British war effort, there was widespread agitation against British military recruitment in Ireland during the war. Many of the Irish settlers in South Africa fought alongside the Afrikaners against the British army. And despite its explicitly Protestant theological underpinnings, Afrikaner nationalism remained an important inspiration and reference point for Irish nationalists into the 1920s and beyond.[169]

The end result of the South African War was a pyrrhic victory for the British. Its ultimate "success" on the ground came at enormous cost, in terms of dead and wounded, capital expenditure, and with respect to imperial confidence as the new century dawned. This complex balance sheet suggests how unstable "British imperialism" actually was even at one of its most self-consciously jingoistic moments. The relatively poor performance of British soldiers in South Africa fed into a set of metropolitan exchanges about the bodily fitness of the British race, not just for global rule but also for sustained cultural reproduction. The journalist Arnold White mixed jingoism with popular science in a series of thirty-three articles in the *Weekly Sun* that highlighted the large number of potential recruits for the British campaign in South Africa who were rejected because they were physically unfit for service. White's fears over the future of the nation were widely shared. At the start of the twentieth century, Fabian socialists like Sidney Webb and the pioneering eugenicist Karl Pearson were united by their deep concern with the strength of the nation. For Pearson, who aggressively applied Darwin's idea of the "struggle for existence" to the social domain, empire building was central to the fortitude of the nation. He believed that colonialism not only allowed Britain to extend its power by defeating "inferior races" but also kept the body of the nation strong through the exertion of war. These arguments about race and nation were strongly inflected by the language and politics of gender. Even as he supported women's enfranchisement, Pearson suggested that the nation would be strengthened if traditional gender roles were reinforced: the "primary duty of the woman," he suggested, was "to rear strong and healthy children, and the primary duty of the man to carry arms in its [the nation's] defence."[170] The depth of these worries over the physique and character of Britons in the wake of the war in South Africa was such that Parliament established an Interdepartmental Committee on Physical Deterioration in 1904. Nor was Britain the only place where such debates were prominent. Fin-de-siècle French fears of depopulation in this period were laced with anxiety about all manner of immigrants. These were part of a wide-ranging political discourse about the "the color of liberty," its relationship to conjugality, and its links to *métissage* in the Third Republic. In this same period in Japan, sex and social control were thought to be not just intimately related, but critical to imperial governmentality at the level of the reproductive body, an overtly nationalist tradition of thought that drew heavily on European and especially German scholarly and scientific work on sexuality.[171]

For our purposes, it is as crucial to recognize that the South African War was also a key political moment beyond the boundaries of British power. The global communication networks surveyed in Section 2 meant that news from South Africa traveled widely and swiftly. Reports on the struggles between the Afrikaners and British imperial forces were carried in newspapers across the globe and were widely debated by philosophers, politicians, and diplomats. Afrikaner attempts to resist British dominance won support from an otherwise unlikely coalition of Russian and German nationalists, French-Canadian separatists, and prominent Marxists, such as Karl Kautsky. Seeking more detailed information than could be found in telegrams and editorials, the Russian state used the war to collate extensive military intelligence on the British army to equip itself for an

A French political cartoon depicting a Boer woman enraged by the death of children at a British concentration camp during the South African War. This image, one of a series printed in the French satirical journal *L'Assiette au beurre* during 1901, offered a scathing critique of British policy. (Getty Images)

imagined future conflict. In 1899 Russia sent engineers and military agents to South Africa to gather information, and additional intelligence was produced by the Russian officers who volunteered in the Afrikaner armies.[172] At the same time, Chinese intellectuals monitored events in South Africa in the late 1890s alongside those in the Philippines, not only because they were concerned about a resurgent "Anglo-American" imperialism but also because they understood their own global possibilities to be at stake in these conflicts. Afrikaner attempts to assert their sovereignty in the face of British imperial power were followed closely in China at a moment when the relationship between ethnicity, political power, and the nature of the nation itself were subject to an open debate that was explicitly global in its range. Afrikaner aspirations functioned as a kind of political mirror through which Chinese observers could reflect on the nature of Manchu authority, the ethnic constitution of Chineseness, and the relationship between politics and the state.[173] This Chinese engagement with Africa, a region that had long been at the very margins of Chinese cultural and historical consciousness, reminds us of both the inescapable globality of politics around 1900 and how important anticolonial resistance was in principle and in practice to debates over the nature of the nation.

Using the South African war to resituate the British Empire in the complex of nodes in which it historically operated reorients our understanding of what the global arena looked like from outside the precincts of the British imperial experience. If nothing else, it reminds us that in the last quarter of the long nineteenth century there was a host of players on the global stage jockeying for elbow room. Within this context, non-European states espoused many of the same justifications for territorial expansion as their European counterparts, and they had their eye as much on other global imperial powers as they did on the indigenous people they aimed to colonize. This understanding unseats the easy equation of imperialism with Europe or the West, or indeed claims that preoccupations with cultural difference, in all its multivalent forms, were primarily or even uniquely Western phenomena. The geographies of imperial systems around 1914 cannot be forced into simple binary models. At the same time, however, it is striking the extent to which the economic aspirations and cultural logics of various imperial systems shared common preoccupations and aspirations.

The Russian experiment in Tashkent is a case in point. The quest to be recognized as equivalent to the Western powers was a huge motivating factor in the imposition of administrative rule in Central Asia. Officials like Governor General K. P. Kaufman sought to impress both Moscow and Paris while maintaining authority over subject Muslim communities as he set about modernizing Turkestan. Campaigns such as Kaufman's drive to reform the city of Tashkent were at least in part designed to showcase Russia's capacity for civilizing native populations through all the canonical means: sanitation, education, and, of course, the imperially designed ceremonial occasion. As we shall see in greater detail below, the boundaries Kaufman and his successors tried to establish and the reform projects they strove to carry out met with both local collaboration and outright resistance. This evidence reminds us that the predicaments of improvement were common to features of the imperial encounter in this period, even as these predicaments played out in different ways in different locales. Meanwhile the common comparison in colonial Tashkent of Sart traders—Turkicized inhabitants of Central Asian regional urban centers—with European Jews, both of whom were viewed as preternaturally unhygienic, reveals the ways in which local hierarchies of difference were laced into broader discourses on difference, which were at least in part shaped by imperial projects elsewhere. While it might be too much to suggest that pogroms and Muslim persecution emanated from the same national/ imperial cauldron, inter-imperial echoes like these must give us pause when we think about cordoning off non-Western empires from histories and theories of European nation building and colonialism. Although organized campaigns against the veil and other material expressions of Muslim identity were carried out only later by a Soviet regime determined to revolutionize Central Asia (especially Uzbekistan), women's agency was crucial to the ways in which imperial power unfolded—and was contested—in places like Tashkent well before the interwar period, where lower-class Russian women blamed tsarist officials for food shortages even as they attacked Central Asian merchants with stones on the eve of 1917.[174]

British power and ambition drove much of what would be considered imperial territorial aggrandizement in this period, due to Whitehall's fixation on both the long-term security of the Indian empire and the related drive to establish a corridor of power from the Cape of Good Hope to the Mediterranean. This was globally apparent throughout the 1880s. The desire to contain, pressure, and rival Britain was clear after the 1884–1885 Berlin Conference, organized by Otto von Bismarck, chancellor of Germany. In particular it was a powerful spur to Kaiser Wilhelm's fin-de-siècle *weltpolitik,* which aimed to rival British imperial aspirations on the global stage. The German desire for imperial power drove a massive expansion in German military capacity from 1897. This was particularly focused on the navy, which Kaiser Wilhelm believed could pose a significant threat to British power in the North Sea and could therefore shift the global balance of power between Britain and Germany. The Kaiser's *weltpolitik* also catalyzed a popular nationalism that proved politically useful for elite interest groups who hoped to secure the young nation against the threats supposedly posed by the dangers of democratization and socialism. A small but significant number of Germans, including some influential female writers and feminists, were more broadly drawn to the idea of an aggressive German foreign policy, a stronger commitment to the Germanization of Polish regions of Prussia, and a global territorial empire.[175] This kind of imperial vision was underwritten by an assumption that more territory was needed to ensure the economic security and cultural vitality of the German people. In 1904 one exponent of German empire building starkly articulated this desire: "We must have lands, new lands!"[176] Of course, this enthusiasm for extending Germany's territorial reach and cultural power was to have fateful consequences for colonized peoples and the future history of total war.

But the most historically accurate way to view these contests for imperial hegemony is not simply through a competitively nationalist frame. For one thing, such an approach casts the history of imperial encounters in a purely international framework. Not only does this prevent us from understanding how deeply enmeshed the scramble for Africa was in an emerging global field of imperial power, it potentially obscures our ability to look beyond the arenas of diplomacy and the military for other sites of consequential imperial encounters. As elaborated earlier, the late nineteenth century was a moment when the spatial reach of imperial power was in the process of being consistently remapped, from the garrison to the forest, from the mission school to the metropolitan parlor, from the Colonial Office to the compound of the diamond mine. And as we shall see, across a range of imperial regimes in this period, imperial states attempted to extend their reach into regional, local, and quotidian spaces for the sake of "civilizing" their subjects and, of course, protecting soldiers and settlers and thereby securing their hold on conquered peoples and places. Holding to the top-down, nation-state model of Western imperial rivalry makes it difficult to appreciate how crucial the more local and intimate colonial encounters were to aspirations to global power.

Nowhere are such designs more spectacularly apparent than in discourses and practices aimed at controlling sexuality and the body. Significantly, a major locus of these projects was the military itself, which was preoccupied with the dangers of sexually transmitted disease and miscegenation as consequences of contact between soldiers and native women. In the British imperial context this resulted in the creation of a series of Contagious Diseases Acts, from India to Queensland to the Straits Settlements. In the context of the Meiji imperial state it meant the licensing of an official system of brothels (comfort houses) that was part and parcel of a modern imperial health regime. Some of the key principles that underwrote this regimen were articulated in the 1889 text *Kokka eisei genri* (The Principles of State Hygiene) by Gotō Shimpei, a leading doctor, colonial administrator, and advocate of public health. Gotō imagined the Japanese state and its colonial territories as a biological entity, a body, that required careful observation and cultivation. While he encouraged individual citizens to embrace "enlightened" bodily practices, his vision required an interventionist state to assume responsibility for the creation of a distinctive hygienic modernity. This model placed significant emphasis on sexual hygiene and had profound ramifications for colonial municipal governance, the policing of cross-cultural sexual contact, and the regulation of "comfort women" into the twentieth century.[177]

If imperial ascendancy before 1915 meant the incorporation of territories and bodies into an increasingly avaricious set of colonial regimes, it also meant increasing "spheres of influence" as well. In this respect, the Berlin Conference did not cap imperial ambition but fed it. The 1890s witnessed the steady progress of a variety of "creeping" colonialisms. Whether it was the Japanese in Korea and Fujian, Germany in Qingdao, or the Italian invasion of Ethiopia, the fin-de-siècle years saw imperial powers relentlessly seeking advantage and influence. But Italy's humiliating defeat in Ethiopia, like Spain's capitulation to the United States in 1898, made it clear that the stakes were high in the Great Game of imperial power. Nor was outward expansion the full extent of colonizing projects in this decade. Inside some already established imperial states, particularly white settler colonies, measures were also afoot to secure specifically racialized political regimes—through reservations (in the continental United States), passbook procedures (South Africa), and white supremacist legislation (the White Australia Policy of 1901)—that would solidify new forms of white privilege that had enduring power into the second half of the twentieth century. Women and children were particularly vulnerable within these racially stratified projects, and even as social reformers and feminists drew new attention to the "woman question" at a global level, the divergence between the opportunities and experiences of white and nonwhite women were typically consolidated rather than overthrown. Global histories of imperial encounters require us, in other words, to trace and to historicize imperial ambition before 1915 through a kaleidoscope of inter-imperial and cross-status exchanges and rivalries. Rather than simply a transnational emphasis, these new global histories of imperialism also necessitate a multilayered, *multiaxial* approach for apprehending the structures of trans-imperial contact that this period set into motion.

Not incidentally, such a globalized view of imperial design would have undoubtedly been clear to contemporary observers in a number of imperial and colonial locations. The explosion of print culture in the final quarter of the nineteenth century enabled the apprehension of a variety of imagined communities at the doorstep of newspaper readers in Paris, Delhi, Shanghai, Cairo, Moscow, and Istanbul. The "world of journalism" and the growing array of genres—from "penny dreadfuls" to missionary tracts, travel narratives to illustrated periodicals—that reached popular audiences delivered imperial encounters in all their diversity to expanding readerships, as literacy spread rapidly and became a key element of modernity. By reading the news or immersing themselves in a popular tale of empire, both male and female readers were able to transport themselves to "other places" and to learn something about "other" peoples. Printed texts brought news about distant lands and strange peoples to recently colonized peoples, who frequently assembled an image of human variation and the pattern of world history through simple missionary narratives, school texts, and newspaper stories. At the same time, reading functioned as an important element in the fashioning of metropolitan and cosmopolitan subjectivities as readers in major centers defined themselves in part through their imaginative encounters with peripheries, both national and imperial.[178]

This growing entanglement with print shaped regional linguistic traditions, national languages, and an increasingly powerful global English, which encircled the globe from Hawaii to New South Wales, Bengal to Alexandria, Wales to Jamaica. Travel writing, with all its ethnographic affect and semiscientific authority, was the most common delivery system for the making of imperial cosmopolites, whether authors or readers. It functioned among elites across empires from east to west and back again as a legitimating political and social reform vehicle—even as it worked to naturalize imperial expansion, whether Qing, French, or British.[179] The details of the native body, whether male or female, offered opportunities for mapping both cultural affinities and differences in colonial space. As Arakawa Gorō, a member of the Japanese Diet who visited Korea in 1905, observed after cataloging native hair, dress, coloring, and physique, declared: "if you . . . did not look carefully . . . you might think that the Japanese and Koreans are the same type of human being."[180] In an interesting example of countercolonial flow, some Turkish and Egyptian litterateurs—like those behind the publication of *Misr al-Qahira* and *al-Urwa al-Wuthqa* in Paris—published their journals in Europe itself, where from the 1890s Turkish journalism in particular flourished. In this way metropolitan readers of all kinds bore witness to the geopolitical realities and uncertainties of global imperial power, as did some colonial readers. When Auguste Robinet, the Algerian-born author of the popular *pied-noir* literary figure Cayagous, had his character meet the anti-Dreyfusard Édouard Drumont in 1898, he dramatized the proximity of colonial politics to domestic ones. He also made clear how critical both colonial opinion *and* the imperial encounters at the heart of business of empire building were for all groups embroiled in the drama of empire, at home and on the peripheries as well.[181]

Anti-Imperial Sentiment before 1915

In 1871 the existing political configuration of the French world was explicitly challenged. The Paris Commune saw a socialist government briefly installed in the French capital by workers disgruntled in the wake of France's defeat by Prussia. In Algiers, French colonists launched a republican uprising styled as the "Commune of Algiers," but their dreams of Algerian autonomy were swiftly crushed by the threat of French military power. It proved more difficult, however, to reassert French control over the rest of the country as the Kabyles, mountain dwellers in eastern Algeria, sparked a revolt against the French colonial state over incursions into their land. French imperial officials considered the ancestral domain of the Kabyles, Kabylie, to be critical in their quest for colonial resources, but equally because it offered a pedagogical lesson to colonial peoples that French territorial conquest would be total. This struggle is useful as a starting point for a discussion of the character and direction of anti-imperial resistance before the twentieth century. In the first instance, it reminds us of the overlap between metropolitan political time lines and colonial ones, a pattern evident certainly in the British case, where major moments in domestic political culture were often framed by, if not also responsive to, unrest in colonial possessions. In the French context the uprisings in Haiti and Guadeloupe that occurred in the era of the French Revolution and the twentieth-century anticolonial movements coming out of North Africa are perhaps better known than this nineteenth-century example. Yet both Kabyl and Arab resistance in the long shadow of 1830 are clearly critical to an appreciation of the nature of changing shape of French colonialism over the *longue durée*. This is especially the case as the war against indigenous populations—in the Arab case, against the Muslim leader Abdul Qadir—went on for the better part of two decades, a fact that suggests that French imperial hegemony, such as it was, was hard-won and that native resistance was tenacious and multifaceted. The Kabyl example is also useful because it represents peasant action directly responsive to land seizure and encroachment and because it did not cease with the suppression of the 1871 outbreak but continued sporadically across the rest of the century. These eruptions were typically in reaction to specific legislative enactments by the colonial state, but their effects could be far-reaching: most obviously, the 1945 Sétif (Petite Kabylie) uprising helped to fuel the eventual Algerian war of independence. Whether in Ireland, the Antipodes, the American West, Africa, or India in the half century before the outbreak of the Great War, unrest directed at the imperial state and its local representatives by colonized peasants or rural laborers accounts for a large proportion of anticolonial activities in this period, even as they sometimes laid the tentacled foundations for anticolonial and decolonizing struggles.[182]

In some significant instances, indigenous peoples could oppose land policy via representative institutions. While a sequence of Maori prophet-warriors (like Te Kooti) and prophetic advocates of nonviolence (such as Te Whiti) believed that God's favor would ultimately overthrow the colonial order, other leaders like the Ngai Tahu chief H. K. Taiaroa used their parliamentary positions to criticize the operation of colonial governance and protect the interests of their communities. In the global context such formal political representation for indigenous communities was the exception rather than the rule. Of course, given gendered limitations attached to the franchise in most polities, the formal political rights of colonized women were typically meager or nonexistent. But this is not to say that colonized women were not concerned with the questions of politics or engaged in political struggles. Where land was a symbol of tribal or communal unity as well as a crucial source of economic sustenance and political authority, as in late nineteenth-century Kenya, women's work could be essential in a host of domains, from livestock ownership to provisioning work parties to spiritual exorcism, even if there was no formal space for Kenyan women in the political process. Elsewhere women's power and authority were significantly refigured against the backdrop of expanding commodity production, as in colonial Asante. Thus, in Africa, colonized women were constantly engaged with political questions, as they responded to white government officials, missionaries, and colonial capitalists as well as to their own chiefs and elders. These multiple engagements meant that cultural visions that various groups of African women articulated frequently were ambivalent and contradictory as they tried to balance their own community's interests with the competing pressures placed on them by politically powerful groups. Their relationships to imperial power were paradigmatic, in other words, of the multiaxial encounters produced in the messy and uneven terrains of global empires—and of the routine protests against the highly gendered regimes that imperial powers put in place through policy and practice.[183]

In the end, the oppositional practices of most colonized subjects remained invisible or appeared inconsequential to contemporaries beyond native communities themselves. In colonial Australia, for example, Aboriginal resistance to their dispossession was sustained and widespread, but its small-scale organizational basis meant that colonists could deny its existence and it typically remained beyond the lines of sight of officials securely based in Sydney, Melbourne, or London. But some of these very localized contests over land rights and usage sparked bloody massacres, punitive raids, and the confiscation of long-held native lands. In the Australian case, the basic freedoms of Aboriginal communities were heavily circumscribed by both state and, after 1901, federal law. At the level of the law and high politics, the very existence of indigenous communities could be denied through the theory of *terra nullius,* a legitimating myth of the colonization of Australia that held that Aborigines did not work or own the land and such were a people without sovereignty or political rights.[184] But on the ground in frontier areas, the persistent resistance of Aboriginal communities to the rapid extension of pastoralism and mining frequently spilled over into interracial violence and the "normalization of brutality" as an instrument of colonial control.[185] Many social reformers, both in the colonies and in the imperial metropoles, decried colonial violence. Only a few commentators, however, connected wars and murder to colonialism's rapacious hunger for resources or the racial logic that underpinned colonial violence. More typically, social critics hoped to construct a better type of imperialism, one that was grounded in the cultivation of spiritual and moral improvement as well as economic advance. Essentially the hope was to redeem empire, to fashion a beneficent colonialism: this was a powerful line of argument when many supporters of empire building continued to believe that extensive territorial empires were a sign of providential favor. Harnessing native women's reproductive and productive labor to the "higher ends" of building stable families was crucial to this process of legitimation, as was the constrictive "loving protection" of those white women reformers who sought to rescue them *from* the grip of cultural subordination and marginalizing national policies.[186] Increasingly in the twentieth century, these white reformers also pushed beyond imperial boundaries to utilize the power of an international ethic of social reform, if not anticolonialism, as well.

It is clear that, due in part to these routine anxieties about colonialism and the extensive and more sensational international coverage attracted by imperial atrocities such as those enacted by the agents of King Leopold II of Belgium in the Congo, the quest for usable resources underpinned the aggressive quest for imperial power. Whether they were seeking essential goods like rubber from the Congo, luxuries like diamonds from the South African mines, or Aboriginal land, colonizers frequently came into direct conflict with native people when they tried to exercise authority over valued resources. For colonized populations, the surveyor, the manager, and the merchant embodied colonial authority and their subordination as much as the jackboot of the imperial soldier.

Of course, territorial conquest and annexation are the most self-evident explanatory factors in the emergence of anti-imperial resistance, and the history of that global phenomenon in the prewar period can be readily understood as reactive in the most basic sense. When Menelik II of Ethiopia and Tippu Tip of Zanzibar repelled European incursions, for example, they did so defensively to maintain their own power and to keep their kingdoms free from colonization, as did the African tribes who conducted the Swahili war in 1892 against the Belgians. What we might call "defensive agency" could occur on more fronts than imperial contests over territory, as the career of Zaynab (Laila) bint Shaykh Muhammad (ca. 1850–1904) suggests. The daughter of an influential Algerian Sufi educational reformer, Laila fought not just the suspicions of the French colonial regime about the educational activities of her father's Sufi Lodge,) but also her cousin's attempts to wrest succession to her father's work and holdings. While this was a classic case of native women facing the collaboration of indigenous and colonial patriarchies, Laila mobilized both Muslim dignitaries and reform-minded French administrators in her struggle to preserve her own power and to fortify, literally and figuratively, her father's spiritual work. But in Africa as elsewhere, the determination of imperial powers to extend their territorial influence and reach was also often itself a defensive reaction. Colonial encroachments and frontier wars sometimes arose from anxieties produced by an encounter with "indigenous grammars of power and authority" in addition to a more basic hunger for land and resources.[187]

There is not, in other words, a facile or easily generalizable formula of cause and effect when it comes to historicizing anti-imperial episodes, which might range from the killing of an English magistrate (like the murder of Hamilton Hope by the Mpondomise chief Mhlontlo at Sulenkama in South Africa in 1880) to an out-and-out revolution of the kind led against the Spanish and then the United States in the Philippines by Emilio Aguinaldo from 1896. Captured by the United States in 1901, Aguinaldo recognized US sovereignty in the Philippines, in contrast with some of his countrymen who continued to resist the occupation. Nor were anticolonial agents circumscribed by the territorial limits of those empires to which they were subject. This was particularly clear in the earlier career of the great Filipino polymath and novelist José Rizal, who undertook medical training in Madrid, Paris, and Heidelberg, mixed with leading ethnologists in Berlin, traveled widely in Europe, Japan, and the United States, and lived in Hong Kong before returning to the Philippines, where he was a leading social reformer and advocate of independence until he died in 1896.[188]

As importantly, across the colonized world resistance and conflicts played out on an everyday basis in fields, at wharves, in factories, schools, and prisons.

Emilio Aguinaldo (seated third from right) with other insurgent leaders in the Philippines during the Philippine-American War, ca. 1900. Aguinaldo was an influential leader of the revolution against Spanish colonial rule and in the subsequent resistance against American colonial occupation. (National Archives, photo no. 391-PI-34)

In these struggles, subject peoples sometimes engaged imperial power and its representatives directly, but more frequently these challenges were careful and indirect, not always prominent or fully legible in the historical record. The kinds of insurgencies that grew up in the Caribbean around the festival tradition of Hosay illustrate the indirectness as well as the power of such quotidian and episodic struggles. Transplanted to the Caribbean by South Asian indentured workers, the late-Victorian Hosay was an indigenized version of the remembrance of Muharram, when Shiʿa Muslims commemorated the killing of Husayn ibn Ali, the grandson of the prophet Muhammad. In places like Trinidad, Hosay involved a procession from the plantation along a local route that brought Chinese merchants, Portuguese traders, African revelers, and "coolie" workers together. The convergence of these public parades with labor unrest and strikes did not reflect any concerted attempt to undercut the authority of the colonial state. But the spectacle of such a polyglot movement through colonized space fed fears about the tenuousness of the authority of local planters and colonial officials. In 1884, against the backdrop of a downturn in the sugar market and widespread industrial action in Trinidad, British authorities resolved to prevent Hosay processions made up of Indian plantation workers from entering the town of San Fernando. After blockading the processions and reading the Riot Act, which defined the parade as an unlawful assembly, British soldiers opened fire on unarmed and shocked participants, killing at least twelve and wounding over a hundred.[189]

Sites like Trinidad, which had been under British colonial control since 1797, demonstrate many of the complexities that developed in the wake of the end of the transatlantic slave trade and the emancipation of slaves. In Trinidad slaves were emancipated in 1838; but this did not mark the end of exploitation. Trinidad planters worked hard to source cheap labor, whether from Chinese workers, free West Africans and former slaves from the Lesser Antilles, or poor Portuguese workers from the island of Madeira. Ultimately, however, indentured workers from South Asia, recruited principally from the rural poor in Bengal, Orissa, Uttar Pradesh, and Bihar, were the key source of labor on sugar and cacao estates. These workers were prone to exploitation and only a few prospered at the end of their indenture; individuals like Haji Gokool Meah, who became a successful merchant, plantation owner, and industrialist in Trinidad, were atypical.[190] Trinidad's heterogeneous and polyglot labor forces remind us that the global territories of empire in the "age of emancipation" were sites for remarkable stories about the intertwining of slavery and freedom, bonded labor and anticapitalist, anticolonial resistance.

Many of these stories remain obscured as much by the challenges of excavating the complexly, unevenly transnational circuits of migration and mobility as by the emphasis on elites and anti-imperialists motivated by or engaged in "high" geopolitics. These global spaces were breeding grounds for organized forms of anticolonial sentiment at the end of the nineteenth century, even if the majority of full-fledged nationalist movements did not achieve their ends until the interwar period. The Indian National Congress (1885) and the African National Congress (1912) were each born in the tumultuous decades before 1915. Key leaders of both organizations—Mahatma Gandhi and Pixley ka Isaka Seme—were trained barristers whose experiences as legal practitioners and as colonial subjects were to have world-historical ramifications for the long-term fate of modern empires. For Gandhi it was displacement from the Indian subcontinent and the discovery of himself as a raced, second-class subject (first in Britain, then in South Africa) that helped to catapult him to the center of a nonviolent resistance movement. Seme's nationalist thought was shaped by his cosmopolitan travel and education in the United States and England as well as his experience of the hardening racial boundaries in South Africa on his return from England in 1910. He had an expansive view of the ability of nonwhite South Africans to challenge colonial rule and their capacity for driving forward the broader transformation of Africa as a whole. As with Western forms of nationalism, anticolonial nationalist aspirations were far from provincial. To the contrary, though they grew out of the forms of civil society produced by and antecedent to imperial conquest, they were shaped as much by the kinds of multiple encounters that entangled imperial powers, though those entanglements were clearly not of their making. Most often they articulated their nationalist ideas and formulated their anti-imperialist strategies with a variety of audiences in mind: fellow colonial subjects, who in turn might espouse a multiplicity of religious/ethnic identities and an equally diverse set of class positions; imperial overlords; competing imperial powers; and even fellow revolutionaries or critics across the increasingly interconnected imperial world. Though less of a household name in this period than Gandhi, the West African nationalist J. E. Casely-Hayford exemplified these distinctive new forms of intellectual and cultural engagements on a global front. His 1911 *Ethiopia Unbound* can be read as evidence of the kind of visionary anticolonial political thought that circulated widely in the immediate prewar period, not least because it addressed not just his fellow Africans but African-Americans and even the subjugated Irish through an aspiration for racial emancipation.[191]

That rubric drew women of color, colonized and "free," into public debates about race uplift and into equally public action, both reformist and more directly oppositional to imperial power. Late nineteenth-century African-American women like Anna Erskine in Sierra Leone modeled a very specific kind of female emancipation, one that emphasized Christian respectability and educational attainment inside colonial institutions that were at once developmentalist and accommodationist. Others, like Madie Hall Xuma, threw their lot in with the African National Congress at the moment of accelerating nationalist militancy. Still others, like interwar African-American suffragists, made connections with Caribbean feminists, albeit in the context of the uneven power relations created by American imperialism.[192]

Although some colonized or subject peoples sought solidarity with fellow travelers, this was not universally or uniformly the case. Irish republicanism in the nineteenth century is an interesting case. Men like Thomas Davis and John Mitchel of the Young Ireland movement helped legitimate anti-imperialism as a strand of nationalist discourse. Michael Davitt, a self-avowed socialist and anti-imperialist, wrote sympathetically about Egyptian independence and the fate of Russian Jews but championed Afrikaners over native Africans in his writings about the South African War. Keir Hardie, the British Labour Party leader who traveled to India and South Africa in 1907–1908, occupied an only slightly more complex position when he supported contemporary Indian nationalists and British policy in the Transvaal but played to white settlers' fears that "coloured labour" was a threat to their economic and political agendas. Meanwhile, imperial states were not above collaborating with each other to keep the radical possibilities of incipient nationalism in check. So the French and the Japanese colluded to harass Tran Trong Khac while he studied in Shimbu in 1908; he went on to study in China and Germany and in so doing, illuminated the global paths to Vietnamese independence in this early period.[193]

If these kinds of connections flourished in the first decade of the twentieth century, their roots lay in the 1890s. In that decade the geopolitical equilibrium aimed at by the world's imperial powers was seriously compromised—in part because empires old and new were increasingly cheek by jowl, if not supplanted or superimposed, from the Caribbean to the treaty ports to the Cape Colony to the Russian steppe. This awareness was clearly articulated by the Cuban writer, publisher, and revolutionary philosopher José Martí. Before his death in battle against the forces of the Spanish Empire in Cuba in 1895, Martí advocated complete independence from Spain for Cuba, an argument that dismissed the Home Rule (Autonomista) Party as too conciliatory toward the colonial authorities. He also warned against the imperial aspirations of the United States of America, arguing that a multiracial democratic republic was the only legitimate foundation for

Cuba's future.[194] These arguments, which were informed by Martí's extensive travels in America, the Caribbean, and the United States and his conviction that strong cultural sensibilities unified Latin America, repudiated both Spanish and American empire building. Martí's writings and politics are a potent reminder of the intellectual labor that underpinned late nineteenth-century nationalist projects and the kinds of transimperial hinges that anticolonial movements turned on in the 1890s. If we rematerialize the structure of imperial systems around 1900, we see with particular vividness that the world in which opponents of empire worked was a set of globally articulated moving parts though which images and arguments about empire were disseminated, translated, and localized with great speed.[195]

At the turn of the new century, some critics of empire aimed to reform from within as well. These included subscribers to the Indian National Congress, who sent a representative to Britain's Parliament in the 1890s, and "the Three Pashas," whose 1908 revolution occurred in the midst of a constitutional crisis at the heart of the Ottoman Empire. In Iran too in this period, a constitutional crisis precipitated a revolution by forces that secured the new constitution against the backdrop of accelerating imperial designs on Tehran. Both the tsarist army and British imperial officialdom looked on menacingly, waiting to pounce on the spoils of the failed experiment. Meanwhile, Iranian women boycotted European textiles at virtually the same moment that Indian women participated in *swadeshi* protests. These kinds of parallel nationalist developments called forth specific forms of gendered participation in the public sphere even as they contributed to the creation of new female, even feminist, subjectivities.[196]

Metaphorically speaking, young Turks everywhere were inspired by events in Istanbul and Iran. Contemporaries of all kinds, including anti-imperialists in metropolitan centers, also saw a range of similarities in the politics that developed in the wake of the creation of the Union of South Africa in 1910, the struggles in Ireland after its incorporation into the United Kingdom as a consequence of the Act of Union in 1801, and between Pan-Africanism and Zionism. Others drew parallels between the experiences of Africa and Asia, a connection embodied by the *African Times and Orient Review,* run by the Egyptian Sudanese Dusé Mohamed Ali from London. In many ways, the occasion of the Universal Race Congresses in London in 1911 dramatizes our argument about the challenges of centering the British Empire in the story of this period. At least one contemporary, D. S. Margoliouth, professor of Arabic at Oxford, reminded observers that for all its claims to primacy, it had been preceded by a number of important congresses elsewhere, including the Congress of the Young Turkish Party in Paris in 1902 and the failed Pan Islamic Congress in Cairo in 1907. Not unlike the Bandung Conference, the Universal Race Congress bore the imprint of earlier meetings, both large and small; it drew on and further enabled collaborations between people of color; and it demonstrated the possibilities of transnational solidarity. Though centered in London, its networks extended to "many global points," some of which destabilized the imperial certainties of the Raj—as did Iranian delegate Yahya Dawlatabadi and Riza Tevfik from Turkey, when they challenged both European imperial hegemony and, in Tevfik's case, Aryan civilizational superiority.[197]

Like both their pro-imperial counterparts and the less-privileged colonial subjects struggling against colonial rule, these arguments and self-representations were complex and "multidirectional": counterhegemonic and nativist, anticolonial and internally colonial (as Tevfik was with respect to the non-Turkish populations of the multiethnic Ottoman Empire), transnational and cross-imperial. And like a number of nationalists of this era, they brought hierarchies of scale and value to their "progressive" agendas, including their attitudes toward women, who even when viewed as companionate were not accorded the possibility of emancipation qua women, but instead were seen as nationalist women inside a fairly narrow script. Women themselves exhibited a global vision imprinted with transimperial references and, inevitably, their own civilizational biases as well. For example, the first Iranian women's magazine, *Danesh (Knowledge),* observed in 1911 that Iranian women were "as good as Ottomans and better than Zulus" with respect to conjugal practices and the marital experience.[198] Regardless of women's participation in the framing of these discussions, of course, the honor of woman through marriage and reproduction was a major nationalist preoccupation in ways that are only just beginning to be fully appreciated, and that underscore the collusion of patriarchies across the putative nationalist/imperialist divide.

The International Council of Women and the International Woman Suffrage Alliance, for their part, embedded principles of national self-determination in their platform in ways that engaged international power dynamics across a

Susan B. Anthony (seated second from left) and Elizabeth Cady Stanton (seated fourth from left) and the executive committee that arranged the First International Council of Women in 1888. This meeting in Washington, DC, marked the emergence of an influential tradition of feminist internationalism, which increasingly grappled with questions relating to the connections between women's rights, race, and empire. (© Corbis)

rank and file whose subjects were part of several different empires, British and Habsburg included. Suffragists in the Habsburg empire struggled to come to terms with how to address the multiethnic character of their movement and the constitutional divisions that entailed.[199] Although their work in nationalist organizations and in collective anti-imperial bodies largely awaited the postwar period, women with distinctively anticolonial platforms were active in both their "local" colonial contexts and beyond before 1915. They also embodied the particularly gendered challenges of criticizing patriarchy in "traditional" communities and the prejudices of the colonial state—confronting the collaboration between the two in the process. Pandita Ramabai, the social reformer and founder of a home for widows in India, articulated this powerful combination in ways that cost her dearly in India, despite her success abroad and the high profile of the institutions she was able to found and support, like the Mukti Mission outside Pune, Maharashtra. She had a marginal relationship with the Indian National Congress, reflecting a structural predicament experienced by many nationalist women as they sought to negotiate a place for their concerns within the broader currents of anticolonial movements.[200] In this respect, the political culture of imperial dissent produced by colonial elites in and around the turn of the century anticipated Bandung, its solidarities and its limitations, in quite prophetic ways.

Global 1919 and After

There is little doubt that the First World War saw the end of a particular form of global power and the beginning of historically new articulations of geopolitical reasoning and strategizing. Old empires crumbled while comparatively young nationalisms gained confidence from mass support and psychic energy from their own gradual successes. In terms of imperial history, the emergence on the international scene of an ambitious Asian empire in the form of Japan is perhaps the most significant development of the post-Versailles period. It was a phenomenon noted not just by Western imperial powers but also by a variety of "subject" observers—mostly famously by W. E. B. Du Bois, whose admiration grew in the wake of the Russo-Japanese War (and waned by the 1930s when the racially exclusive character of Tokyo's global vision was increasingly apparent). The interwar years were absolutely decisive, in short, for the fate of global imperial politics in the twentieth century and beyond. It is worth dwelling for a moment on the fact that by the end of the event-filled year of 1919, the world tilted, if not turned, on a different axis than it had before. In nearly every quarter of the developing and developed world, the social and political order was challenged as liberals and radicals, victims of colonial power, and anticolonial visionaries pushed the limits of the possible with the intention of capitalizing on the promises of liberal internationalism, Bolshevism, and the possibilities of postwar realignment to realize their political, economic, social, and cultural aims.[201]

One way of assessing this tectonic shift is to consider the claims that multiple constituencies made on the Versailles treaty proceedings and the effects of the failures of Egyptian, Indian, Chinese, and Korean nationalists on the fate of anticolonial movements and revolutions in those places. Activists from regions outside the West drew on the Wilsonian ideal of national self-determination as enshrined in his Fourteen Points speech. They deployed this ideal as the basis for arguments about their right to participate in the shaping of the terms of the postwar order, specifically at the moment of its reconfiguration in 1919 but more generally as part of what they viewed as a watershed moment in the history of geopolitics. So, for example, Saad Zaghloul of Egypt and Lala Lajpat Rai of India were actively engaged in campaigns to present their respective anti-imperial cases directly to Woodrow Wilson. They used established networks to broadcast both the opening that they believed Versailles represented and their own convictions about how and why nationalists should harness the liberal ideals that were being used as the putative basis for the postwar settlement to advance their own programs for self-government. Although they, along with Syngman Rhee of Korea and Wellington Koo of China, were the public face of this effort, they each represented deeper nationalist constituencies, whose energies and organizational frameworks they drew on to advance their claims for independence. In the process, they articulated varying degrees of admiration for the United States as an exemplar of civilization, liberty, and global leadership.[202]

Wilson, for his part, used the work of non-Western movements to justify his own agenda at Versailles without taking full account of the ramifications of Indian or Chinese logics or, for that matter, of the implications of his particular brand of liberal internationalism for the maintenance of conventional Western imperial power. Nor should we overlook the critical role played by an imperializing Japan in laying claim not simply to a place at the table at Versailles in 1919 but to a kind of racial equivalence with white Europeans on the basis of its imperial success over Russia in 1904–1905. These claims were reinforced by the conviction of civilizational superiority and racial supremacy produced out of its own colonial projects. Despite Japan's claims, the discussions at Versailles were characterized by a series of "empty chairs," for although twenty-seven nations were represented, the negotiations were directed in the first instance by the United States, France, Great Britain, Italy, and Japan, and ultimately the agreement was driven by British prime minister David Lloyd George, French prime minister Georges Clemenceau, and American president Woodrow Wilson. Thus, it is not

Zaghlul Pasha, Egyptian nationalist leader, ca. 1910. An influential bureaucrat and politician during the British occupation of Egypt, Zaghlul was exiled by the British after demanding recognition of the unity and independence of Sudan and Egypt at the Paris Peace Conference of 1918. He was influential during the Egyptian Revolution of 1919 and, in 1924, was the prime minister of the Egyptian government formed by his Wafd Party. (Popperfoto / Getty Images)

sufficient to say that as nationalism emerged, imperialism was challenged, or that the differences between imperial power and anticolonial nationalisms grew starker because of Versailles. What shifted in visible and "felt" ways was the very internal logic of what had masqueraded as disinterested internationalism but was in fact liberal *imperial* internationalism. This shift played out in a variety of domains, including the intellectual and ideological. What characterizes both African and Indian nationalisms in the wake of the Great War and its aftermath is nothing less than a frontal assault on European claims to both technological and moral superiority and hence to that central plank of modern empire building: the civilizing mission. Women who met at The Hague in 1915 and eventually in the Women's International League for Peace and Freedom in 1919 also failed to grapple with the ramifications of empire building for the construction of international solidarities. Consisting of mainly European delegates, both of these meetings struggled with the limits of their global aspirations, in part because they could not recognize their own Eurocentrism, even when it was pointed out to them by colonized women, either close up or from afar.[203]

But what, in the end, was the relationship between the failure of anticolonial efforts and the uprisings in various imperial territories in 1919? Any answer to that question requires a recognition that from the point of view of anticolonialism on the ground, Versailles served as a catalyst rather than root cause. It provided a rallying point around which critics of empire could test the application of "new" theories of global order to their own proto-nationalist movements. Nor did the players involved necessarily represent the full spectrum of anticolonial opinion in their respective movements. Indeed, in the case of India, Rai was part of a much larger constellation of anti-imperial critics, many of whom had affiliations with the Indian National Congress. Though Rai's location as an exile in the United States offered him a powerful vantage point from which to address Wilsonian rhetoric, his tactics were also opposed by more than one contemporary. Meanwhile, the events at Amritsar—where British troops fired on Punjabis who gathered to celebrate the traditional spring festival of Baisakhi—are not traceable even indirectly back to Versailles, though the disillusion produced by the failure of self-determination at Paris undoubtedly contributed to the long-term movement toward *Purna Swaraj* (complete independence). At Amritsar, imperial discipline in the wake of a colonial "riot" was deeply implicated in the protection of white women's bodies and the links between sexual boundaries and the hierarchies of the colonial order; the Paris Peace Conference was worlds away. The same may be said for China, where the May Fourth Movement erupted in the wake of bitter disappointment at Versailles but was driven by several decades of reform aimed at transforming the precarious Qing regime. In this sense, Versailles—where the concession of former German colonies to Japan fed larger concerns about the further aggrandizement of Japanese imperial power—offered an influential rearticulation of imperial power, but that power was simultaneously being tested and reworked on the ground in a range of colonial sites in the face of a range of quite localized pressures.[204]

If 1919 was a pivotal moment, then, not all of its eventfulness can be tracked to Versailles and its aftershocks. Even approaches that set up anticolonial nationalists against a new imperial world order cannot necessarily capture the complex alliances and—as in the case of Faisal I, who led the Arab delegation to Versailles and subsequently became the king of Greater Syria and later Iraq—the collaborations between "nationalist" advocates and Western powers. Indeed, if we were really to understand this period of imperial instability and fractious encounter looking back from Bandung, with that event's "rhizomal networks" in mind, it is possible to identify key convergences and moments that were particularly influential in shaping the global imperial order. One such moment was 1913. That year witnessed land acts in South Africa and California—both major pieces of segregationist legislation with world-historical consequences for multiple imperial regimes. It was also the year of the first meeting of the Arab Congress in Paris, and of the inauguration of the Bantu Women's League.

Needless to say, the Bolshevik Revolution of 1917 also altered the global imperial landscape in immeasurable ways. In addition to enabling a Soviet empire whose territorial reach and economic power would rival its twentieth-century competitors, the 1917 revolution opened an alternative model of political power and social organization that had considerable appeal for Indian and especially Chinese nationalists as it became clear that liberal internationalism was failing to reconfigure the global political system. The Comintern (also Third International), founded in 1919 and the sponsor of seven congresses in the interwar period, was a key player here. If we viewed the interwar period from the pivot of the Comintern-sponsored Baku Congress of 1920, where global anticolonial revolution was debated by delegates from India, China, Turkey, Azerbaijan, and Persia, we would glimpse the anti-imperialist aspirations of Bolshevism in Asia and beyond. Although the Comintern did not live much beyond the late 1930s, one of its affiliates, the League Against Imperialism, was expressly designed to link anticolonial movements in Africa, Asia, and Latin America. Despite the work of the Senegalese nationalist Lamine Senghor and the League's French sections, the League developed only tenuous links with black Africa in this period and influential European communists viewed its efforts with increasing skepticism. Despite the ultimate failure of the League, interwar black internationalism looked as much to Moscow as anywhere else. This investment grew in part out of a disillusion with the liberal internationalism of Versailles that was predicated on total exclusion of subjugated peoples from the mechanisms through which it created its mandates, as Marcus Garvey and other "new Negro" intellectuals were determined to point out. The global vision and influence of leaders like Garvey reached into Aboriginal activist communities from the 1920s to the 1950s, leaving no doubt as to the globality of the black American and Pan-African political movements or, conversely, the cosmopolitan sensibility of some influential strands of Aboriginal activism. These traditions of critique remind us that class struggle and anticapitalist protest were critical to the transnational anti-imperial impulse in the interwar period. The publication *The Negro Worker* aimed at spreading Comintern propaganda to black workers in the United States, the West Indies, and Africa—often under covers like *The Missionary Voice,* a prop designed to facilitate its distribution.[205]

As well, there were upheavals in and around 1919—like the foundation of the Irish Republic and the creation of the Anglo-Irish Treaty—whose origins had only tangential relationships with events at Versailles. As with anticolonial agitation elsewhere, Irish republicanism had a long variegated history and was shaped by a variety of imperial encounters at all levels that at once preceded and were transformed by the interwar years. The Dail's "Message to the Free Nations of the World," released during its first meeting in January 1919, claimed, "The race, the language, the customs and traditions of Ireland are radically distinct from the English. Ireland is one of the most ancient nations in Europe, and she has preserved her national integrity, vigorous and intact, through seven centuries of foreign oppression." This certainly bears traces of Versailles rhetoric.[206] What is clear is that in the wake of Versailles, imperialism of all species—Western, Asian, and Eurasian—tried to adjust to new ideological configurations and territorial conditions. This new context was produced by the internationalization of nationalism as well as by those anticolonial ideologies and actors who traversed the landscapes in and between empires and had encounters that would shape their future careers. The formative impact of 1919 on Mao Zedong is probably the best-known example of this: his scornful response to the "robbers" of Versailles helps explain the kind of leader he became and the geopolitical vision he articulated at Bandung and elsewhere. Less well known, perhaps, are the conditions that the interwar years created for figures like Senghor and Nguyen Ai Quoc (Ho Chi Minh), whose work in Paris in the 1920s, in part through the Union Intercoloniale, respectively laid critical foundations for the *négritude* movement and anti-French colonial movements in Vietnam.[207]

Even less well attended to, until recently, has been the role of both women and gender in shaping the very categories of anticolonial sentiment and activism in the years around 1919. European women played a role in the shaping of the postwar mandate system, imprinting a combination of social improvement and authoritarian rule on the Permanent Mandates Commission of the League of Nations and most often ratifying the geopolitical order, not challenging it.[208] Fighting against gender prejudice could lead to a critique of race prejudice and even to activism against segregation. This was the case for the British journalist and novelist Winifred Holtby, who became a strong advocate for struggling black workers in South Africa and a fierce critic of the complicity between humanitarian reform and imperial power, but this kind of vision was the exception rather than the rule. In Egypt and India, women took the lead in making claims for the urgency of national self-determination and for the centrality of feminist questions—on conjugality, biopolitics, suffrage, education, public activism, and social service—to aspiring postcolonial nations. In this sense, and especially given the use they made of their own transnational networks of connection and publicity, they made significant contributions to increasingly visible arguments about the illegitimacy of imperialism on the nineteenth-century model. These gains were made despite the Orientalist rhetorics to which they were subjected by Western feminists, like those in the International Alliance of Women where the concept of "global sisterhood" was structured from the outset by presumptions about the civilizational superiority of Europe and by anti-Islamic sentiment. Meanwhile, in the interwar years throughout the Middle East, Arab women were increasingly mobilized by their commitment to the cause of Palestinian nationalism, and this public mobilization was a key element in the emergence of an organized Arab feminist movement. At the same time they often laid claim to individual rights as the basis for their participation in new or emergent political communities in ways that could bring them into collision with the "precarious universality" of male nationalist discourses and aspirations.[209] This was especially true in contexts (like Syria and Lebanon) where imperial power (French, British, Ottoman, Arab nationalist) was in flux following Versailles. In these contexts even non-elite women were able to take advantage of the "crisis of paternity" that was the common ground of imperial and nationalist leaders who attempted to shape a new idiom of social rights for specific constituents, albeit inside an enduringly colonial welfare state. Indeed, the lead-up to war and its immediate aftermath created opportunities for welfare activism spearheaded by nationalists in and outside Europe, with women of all classes petitioning their respective imperial states and interpreting the social crisis in nationalist and often feminist terms. Family politics in all its gendered dimensions, and with its ramifications for both the domestic basis of modern state practice and nationalist ideology, was critical to this moment in Egypt, if not more generally through the Middle East.[210] Such phenomena unfolded unevenly across the post-1919 world, and gains for women and a range of subaltern actors could be both partial and short-lived. But they begin to indicate some of the ways in which the interwar period, with its new solidarities and its capacity for lateral as well as vertical connections, would anticipate rather than simply set the stage for Bandung.

Interwar Intercolonialisms

Historians have only recently begun to grapple with the transnational underpinnings of anticolonial nationalism. This belated exploration of connections tells us more about the optics through which both the period between the wars and its imperial dimensions have been historicized than it does about the geopolitical significance of intercolonial and transcolonial relationships. There was no dearth of cross-referentiality about "analogous" colonial sites between imperial powers. China was routinely seen as the Balkans of the Far East, for instance, and the Japanese saw parallels between their settler colonial projects in East Asia and those of the Zionists in Palestine.[211] These kinds of parallels and echoes were identified more frequently in the interwar period, when long-distance communication networks were extended and operated with greater speed, when new systems of ethnographic knowledge collection and production were in operation, and new political regimes—such as the Soviet Union—were more invested than ever in the question of comparison across colonial sites.[212]

And as we have seen, links between anti-imperial figures and nationalist movements were not new post-1919. For decades (if not centuries), enemies of empire had traveled, collaborated, organized, argued, and planned—thereby proliferating imaginative and unlooked-for forms of "imperial encounter." Such encounters may have begun as responses to empire in its various geographical, discursive, and material incarnations, but by the 1920s at the very latest, anticolonial activists had created a terrain of anti-imperial global critique of which neither they nor even colonial states had a panoptical view, but which is evident to us now if we read across insular imperial histories and equally inward-looking nationalist historiographies.

That they did so chiefly, if not exclusively, in imperial capitals is also telling. Although the majority of nationalist leaders primarily sought imperial reform, not outright independence, before World War I, some thinkers and activists positioned at the very heart of imperial systems routinely discussed how they might begin the process of dismantling empires. Among the best known of these was Gandhi, whose travels and travails at the heart of the empire in the 1880s, as well as in its more distant locations (South Africa) in the 1890s, predated the Roundtable Conferences of the 1930s and did more than lay the groundwork for his anti-imperial program. Like José Rizal, the cosmopolitan Philippine patriot and imperial critic who traversed the globe, and King Khama III, the African chief who traveled to London in the 1890s to protest Cecil Rhodes's grand schemes for Africa, Gandhi's Victorian experiences are in many ways paradigmatic of the role of mobility in shaping challenges to imperial power at the center. When ranged against the wide array of colonial people on the move between and across any number of imperial regimes, in other words, Gandhi's cosmopolitanism does not look so exceptional. His experiences and the platforms of critique they enabled gained new momentum in the wake of Versailles and the subsequent failure of liberal internationalism. Across European, Russian, and Asian empires, radicals and revolutionaries transgressed geographical boundaries and created new spaces of encounter aimed at bringing down global imperial structures—if not collectively, then at the very least in parallel and in concert.

Several dimensions of this emergent and often halting transcoloniality require our attention. First is the long history of material foundations upon which both solidarities and suspicions between colonized peoples were based. Well before the twentieth century there was a vibrant "world of working-class polyculturalism" spanning the Caribbean, Africa, and South Asia. This reflected transference and "mixture" that the political economies and labor markets of the British Empire gave rise to.[213] As the practice of Muharram in Natal (or "Coolie Christmas") makes clear, such mixture was a double-edged sword. While Muharram was traditionally pivotal in the Shiʿa Muslim calendar, in Natal it brought together a range of Muslims and Hindus and drew on the sensibilities of both communities. While the festival was an important element in the construction of a working-class pan-Indianness, it did not preclude either internecine clashes or sexual violence. So although this festival helped build the cultural basis of a distinctively Indian anticolonialism in Natal, in the short term it also kindled animosity between racial groups, while its long-term consequences included a further calcifying of racial hierarchies in colonial regimes.[214]

In contexts where the colonial state was "faced with the combined rage" of ethnically diverse anti-imperial actors (whether directed at economic targets or expressed in cultural terms, or both), conditions that might have nurtured solidarity were made difficult, if not impossible, by officials for whom "divide and conquer" was the governing axiom. Struggling against empire from below was complicated, in other words, by the encounter on the ground not just between colonizer and colonized but often between multiple colonizers, especially where imperial frontiers intersected (as in Central Asia and the Caucasus) or where competing concessionary states met (like the city Tianjin, in north China, "home" to multiple imperial interests). In other words, the global political terrains of empires were barriers to transcolonial alliances even as they potentially enabled the creation of new anticolonial solidarities. Nevertheless, important points of connection did exist, some entailing quite consequential results, as with African-Americans' involvement in the Mexican revolution, between 1910 and 1920. Such linkages were not, of course, made only between colonized peoples; they could be established and exercised by anti-imperialists from inside the precincts of dominant power as well. When the suffragist Marion Wallace Dunlop undertook a hunger strike in London's Holloway Prison, her act was the ultimate embodiment of transnational anticolonial cross-hatchings, drawing as it did on Indian, Irish, and even Russian traditions and practices—a species of "mad bravery" that speaks to how powerfully motivating awareness of common forms of struggle might be.[215]

The figure of W. E. B. Du Bois, whose journalism, fictional writing, and political discourse articulated one of the most globally aspirant modes of African-Asian solidarity at the beginning of the pre–World War I period, is the exemplar of the kind of possibility that might materialize from the common struggle against the "color bar regimes" established by colonial rule.[216] Du Bois's work, with its transnational vision not just for African-Americans but for Africa in what he imagined to be an ultimately postcolonial world, testifies to the angles of vision it was possible to take up in relationship to imperial globality. These possibilities were perhaps most tellingly encapsulated when Du Bois compared the streets of Shanghai to those of Mississippi and challenged Chinese bankers to resist "the domination of European capital."[217] The possibilities (and constraints) of ideological and political alliances across the color line are also suggested by the impact of the early Soviet empire on Du Bois and Langston Hughes, Claude Mackay, and Paul Robeson. The "Soviet archive of Black America"—of literary writings, cartoons, political tracts—allows us to glimpse the complexities of alliance and dis-identification. These dynamics were clear in the ways Hughes came to view Soviet interventions in Muslim women's veiling practices as a metaphor for racial emancipation, in ways that complicate Hughes's own vision of the relationship between politics and desire: the "sexual politics of black internationalism," in short.[218]

Although we know less about his sexual politics, the same politically motivated mobility marked the early career of Ho Chi Minh, whose political work in Paris and Moscow linked him not just with European radicals but also with fellow anticolonial travelers. His role in the foundation of the Union Intercoloniale (IU) in Paris in the early 1920s grew out of his association with Annamite patriots but it also connected him with nationalists from Madagascar, with whom he founded the newspaper *La Paria*. The Union Intercoloniale included North Africans and West Indians, but it was by no means an unproblematic space of solidarity; the Africans felt the "arrogance" and condescension of the Vietnamese, who in any case wanted to revert to their own group where they could speak their own language. As significantly, Ho Chi Minh also traveled to China during its post-1919 revolutionary fervor; he attended demonstrations where the British fired on Chinese protesters, and he participated in the Society of the Oppressed Peoples of Asia, which professed Vietnamese solidarity with the Chinese cause.[219]

That the majority of these peripatetic intercolonialists were men reminds us that although empires created new spaces across which elite women could travel, their mobility was still limited in comparison to their male counterparts who dominated twentieth-century nationalist movements. Stressing the primacy of transnational connections in women's political work can tend to occlude the efforts of women like Nguyen Thi Giang, a contemporary of Ho's and an activist-worker in the women's section of the Viet Nam Quoc Dan Dang (Vietnamese Nationalist Party). The partner of the revolutionary Nguyen Thai Hoc, who was executed for his role in the Yen Bai uprising in 1930 in French Indochina, she committed suicide shortly after he met his fate.[220] Where activist women met beyond their national borders, they did so most often in the context of "international" suffrage and social reform organizations that were mostly unselfconsciously Euro- or Anglocentric, even though they faced criticism as subjects of imperial powers. At the International Alliance of Women Conference in Istanbul in 1935, an Arab correspondent "warned women from the great powers that 'no amount of effort on your part will ever achieve your high aim while imperialism reigns in any corner of the world.'"[221] Meanwhile, women in the Middle East had already gathered at several "Eastern congresses" to debate suffrage and social and political rights, once in Damascus and once in Tehran—not simply in response to Western feminists but also in purposeful dialogue with post-Versailles discourses about internationalism in an attempt to make a place for their own versions of modernity in the interwar world. At the very same moment, women like the Chinese writer Dan Di were trying to think the idea of a "new" woman in the context of Japanese imperial occupation, for which she achieved some fame but ultimately imprisonment on suspicion of anti-Japanese activities. If she had ties to or felt a sense of solidarity with contemporary anti-imperial women, this is a story that has yet to be written.[222]

Given that historians have only recently expressed a commitment to genuine transnational analysis, it is likely that a range of other significant connections and trajectories will surface in the coming years. Recent work has begun to push beyond well-known colonial elites to recover the careers of modestly well-heeled figures like Lowe Kong Meng, a Penang-born businessman who was extremely active in Chinese communities in Australia and who capitalized on imperial networks to protest racial exclusion practices, or Ras Makonnen, who owned teashops, restaurants, and nightclubs in Britain and was a pioneering advocate of Pan-Africanism. Makonnen's establishments served as the sites of multiple inter-colonial encounters—between African nationalists and between Pan-Africanists (as Makonnen was) and Indian nationalists as well.[223] Despite many strategic and political sympathies—including engagement with Gandhian strategies of anticolonial resistance—proto-black nationalists were suspicious of the role of Indian troops in supporting the British Empire and its interests, as well as of Neh-ru's apparent blindness to the challenges this raised to African-Asian solidarity. Debates and other forms of public exchange and interconnection occurred within the walls of the Cosmopolitan, Makonnen's Manchester restaurant, where asso-ciational links between opponents of empire were productive of conflict as well as unity and comradeship. Like Makonnen, the Bengali revolutionary Rash Behari Bose was as much an institution as an individual. He fled to Japan from India after playing a leading role in the failed Ghadar Conspiracy that aimed to initiate a mutiny in India in February 1915 and became a leading Indian propo-nent of Pan-Asianism. This vision was consolidated by his marriage to Toshiko, the daughter of the progressive Japanese Protestants Sōma Aizō and Sōma Kokkō. Their Nakamuraya bakery in Shinjuku, famous for its introduction of Indian-style "curry rice," echoed Ras Makonnen's Cosmopolitan as it functioned as a kind of cosmopolitan salon for spiritualists, White Russians, and Indian exiles like Bose.[224] Bose's Pan-Asianism invariably involved anti-British activity, and he promoted "Asian international union" in Indian exile circles in Japan. Ananda Mohan Sahay, Bose's contemporary, founded a branch of the Indian National Congress in Kōbe in 1929, and he was supported by Pan-Asianists who presumed Asia to be underpinned by a civilizational unity that transcended cultural and

A portrait of Lowe Kong Meng, in Melbourne, Australia, 1866. Kong Meng was a successful merchant with global connections, a prominent public figure in the state of Victoria, and an ardent defender of the rights of Chinese immigrants. Fluent in both French and English, he was the author of several important petitions and pamphlets critical of exclusionary legislation that targeted the Chinese. (Ebenezer and David Syme, State Library of Victoria)

racial barriers—though this was a minor formation inside the movement. Significantly, some of Bose's Japanese supporters were also involved in Korean "reform," signaling how even Pan-Asianism with global anticolonial sympathies could "embody a devotion to Japanese Empire and grievances about a weak Asia."[225]

It is crucial, then, to recognize that transcolonial encounters were always inflected by interregional dynamics with long histories that predated, as well as intersected with, the terrains of Western and Asian empires. In this sense, the much-vaunted friendship between Indian poet and philosopher Rabindranath Tagore and Japanese art critic and curator Okakura Tenshin has to be understood not merely as a meeting of minds and of aesthetic movements but as evidence of how intra-Asian economies of affiliation and cultural belonging could be shot through with competing hierarchies of civilizational value. These tensions were especially significant in the context of a very publicly, if not globally, staged philosophical and intellectual relationship.[226] This is all the more important because some Japanese, at least, who were influenced by Okakura did not come to share his pacifist viewpoints. For them, "Asianism" meant not just Japan as the first among equals but Japan as warrior against the West, with a defeated United States a major goal. This aspiration took shape before Versailles, in the long shadow of a "smaller" but nonetheless geopolitically powerful Russo-Japanese War. Without putting too fine a point on it, those who might sympathize with anticolonial nationalism in one context might be seen as colonizers or colonial sympathizers in another.[227]

A complex matrix of interrelationality, mutual suspicion, and interdependence persistently played out in South Africa between Africans and South Asians in the 1930s and 1940s in ways that presaged many of the cohesions and tensions that defined African-Asian solidarity at the Bandung Conference. One exemplar of this is the Durban riots of 1949, which grew out of decades-long anti-apartheid struggles by both Africans and Indians against the colonial and, subsequently, the National Party state. The famous "three doctors' pact" of 1947—which joined Dr. A. B. Xuma, president of the African National Congress, Dr. G. M. Naicker, president of the Natal Indian Congress, and Dr. Y. M. Dadoo, president of the Transvaal Indian Congress in a very public declaration of cooperative commitment "between the African and Indian peoples"—was seriously jeopardized by the riots, which were sparked by an encounter between an African teenager and an Indian market stall merchant. The ensuing violence revealed tensions between Africans and Indians rooted in the asymmetries of a racialized political economy on the ground. These tensions were to leave their imprint on the anti-apartheid movement for years to come, though in ways that postcolonial theorists, caught up perhaps in a utopian vision of African-Asian solidarity, have not fully acknowledged. Women—South African Indian, "native," and "coloured"—may not have been visible at the forefront of these struggles, but they did actively participate in the shaping of the anticolonial and anti-apartheid movements. They protested pass laws and landownership legislation and were eventually elected to the executive committee of the ANC, as in the case of Lilian Ngoyi.[228] Just as tellingly, they were instrumental in shaping how those struggles—with their complex, intertwined, and as yet not fully historicized racial and gendered politics—were remembered and are being memorialized in the late twentieth and early twenty-first centuries. To be sure, these relationships unfolded in the context of white supremacist ideology, policy, state formation, and military force, and they were made and remade in that cauldron as much as they were by anticolonial sympathy. As with the male-dominated movements of African-Asian "solidarity," like those on offer at Bandung, these are not stories of unproblematic transracial alliance or self-evident political unity of the kind imagined by Du Bois even as late as 1947.[229] But they do remind us of the multifaceted nature of imperial encounter in the decades leading up to the postcolonial world, as well as the agency of colonized people in shaping its fate.

Bandung and Before

If all modernities—national, colonial, imperial, anti-imperial, and nationalist—were formed "in a complex regional matrix" of institutions, exchanges, and debates, we need to be aware of the limits of the nation-state as way of organizing our understanding of cultural change between 1870 and 1945. It is precisely the connections that made up these regional matrices and the unevenly global reach of empires that should be at the heart of truly a global history of both imperialism and anti-imperialism in the late nineteenth and twentieth centuries.[230] This means historians must be aware of the key continuities within significant global regions (such as South or East Asia), seek to reconstruct the importance of the cultural connections *between* colonies, and study the relationships between particular imperial metropoles and their colonies. But the story of anticolonialism between 1870 and 1945 also suggests that it is important for historians to capture the deliberate, fleeting, accidental, and at times utterly improbable connections of actors high and low *between empires* as well.[231] In the case of Bandung, this kind of approach also entails bringing three scholarly literatures—the new British imperial history, the history of internationalism, and postcolonial studies—more resolutely into dialogue. These bodies of work must also begin to pivot on different axes as well. The most critically engaged work in British imperial studies must strive to deprovincialize the histories of the British Empire and especially of the Raj by setting them alongside the histories of other contemporary empires in order to more fully appreciate what global imperial modernity meant. Work on internationalism must, at the same time, be much more attentive to the question of imperialism and the significance of the connections between anticolonial movements. And postcolonial studies must critically assess and even deflate some of the overblown emancipatory claims of anticolonial nationalisms by underscoring the many dimensions of their chauvinistic presumptions and their uneasy, uneven momentum toward the vision of Third World solidarity being tried out at Bandung. This includes mounting a rigorous and historically embedded critique of what recent interlocutors have revived as "the Bandung spirit."[232] Ideally these histories of the global will operate "at the micro-level of colonial practices in their minutiae"[233] while also illuminating the macro level of anticolonial practices in all their gendered, racialized, and classed contingencies. Reconstructing the connections between local struggles and global structures, exploring the ways in which specific events had unforeseen ramifications across space and time, and producing histories that explore both the reach and the limits of anticolonial cosmopolitanism will allow us to begin to fully appreciate the complex texture of the global struggle over empire building and its consequences. By pursuing such questions, we will have a much sharper appreciation of the place of the imperial global in the making of modernity.

·[THREE]·

Migrations and Belongings

Dirk Hoerder

Introduction

TO TAKE a worldwide perspective on migrations and belongings, we must raise a question of definition: How are migration systems and macroregions defined? We must also ask a question of periodization: How do long-lasting migration systems fit into the time frame of industrialization, transformation, and crisis from the 1870s to the end of the Second World War?[1]

Critiquing the traditional Atlantocentric perspective common in "the West," Adam McKeown has argued that three large-scale long-distance migrations in the century from the 1840s to 1940 need to be addressed and compared:

- 55–58 million to the Americas, mainly from Europe (the Atlantic migration system) and in smaller numbers (2.5 million of the total) also from Africa as well as China, India, and Japan;
- 48–52 million to Southeast Asia, the Indian Ocean Rims, and the South Pacific, mainly from India and southern China (the China Seas–Indian Ocean–Plantation Belt migration system) and in smaller numbers (4 million of the total) from Africa, Europe, northeastern Asia, and West Asia or the Middle East;
- 46–51 million to Manchuria, Siberia, Central Asia, and Japan, mainly
    1. from northeastern China (the north China-to-Manchuria migration system) and
    2. in the Russo-Siberian migration system from Russia.[2]

In addition,

- from 1807 to the 1870s, another 2 million Africans were force-migrated to the Americas (from a total of 12.4 million shipped and, after the deaths of the Middle Passage, over 9 million arriving in the early sixteenth century to the 1870s); and
- about 1 million colonizer migrants (administrators, soldiers, merchants and personnel) from Europe to the acquired territories.[3]

·[435]·

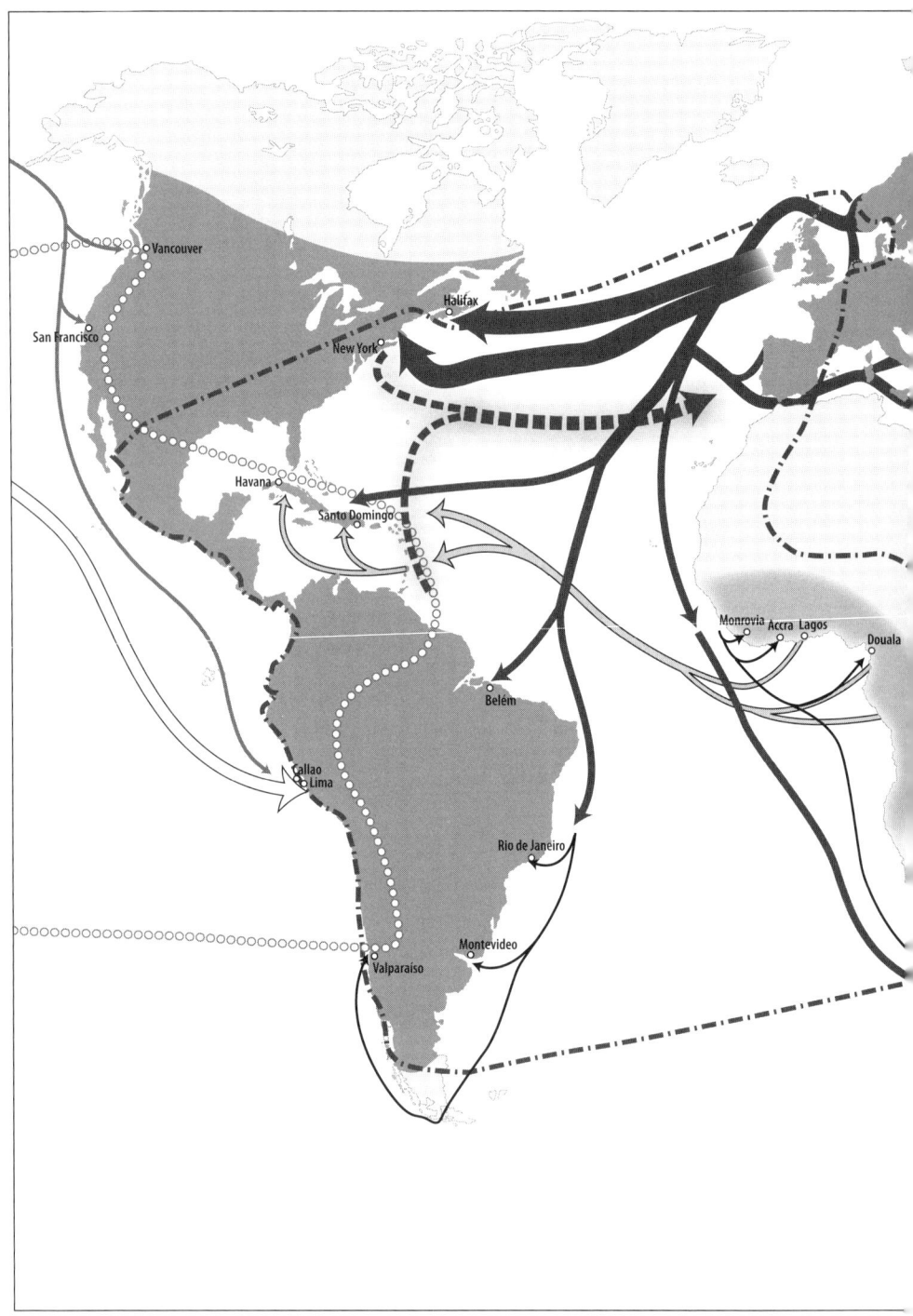

Global systems of migration, 1840–1940.

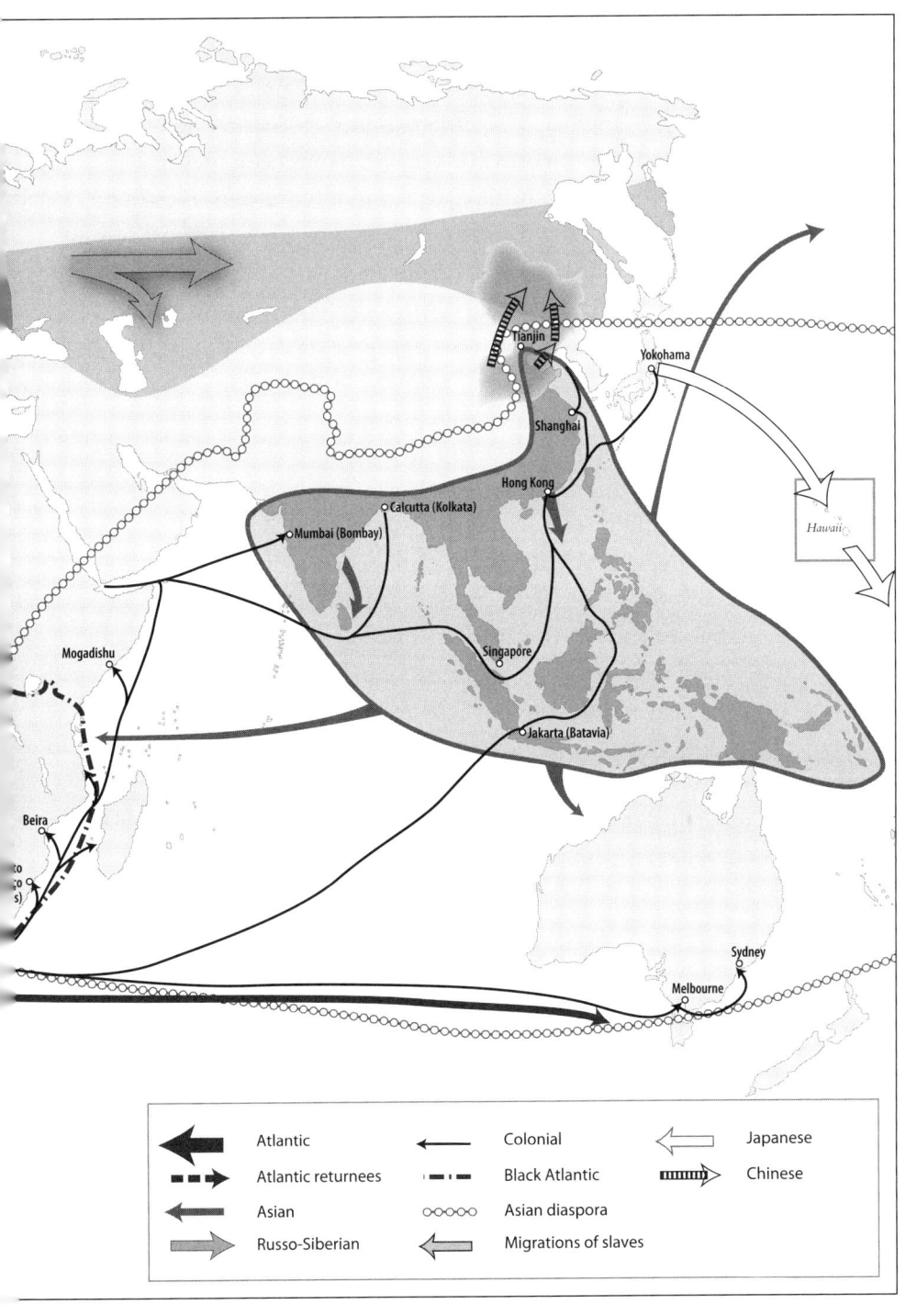

	Atlantic		Colonial		Japanese
	Atlantic returnees		Black Atlantic		Chinese
	Asian		Asian diaspora		
	Russo-Siberian		Migrations of slaves		

Tianjin

Yokohama

Shanghai

Hong Kong

Calcutta (Kolkata)

Mumbai (Bombay)

Hawaii

Mogadishu

Singapore

Jakarta (Batavia)

Beira

Sydney

Melbourne

The figures are still being debated, because they compare transoceanic movements and northern Asia's land-based migrations. If intracontinental land-based migrations in Europe and the Americas are included, numbers for these macroregions are far higher. But inclusion of regional and interregional migrations within the whole of the Qing Empire or any other macroregions also massively increases numbers. Each and every individual migrant also left behind his or her family—on all of whom the departure impacted. Large-scale migrations were a global phenomenon connecting societies and states that were in the process of defining themselves as nations with deeply engrained national identities—imagined and constructed ones, in fact.[4]

Transglobal migratory movements emerged over century-long periods or in the first half of the nineteenth century. These continuities will be outlined to examine the developments in the several distinct macroregions of the globe. To begin a discussion of *global* migrations and regional identities from the North Atlantic and Mediterranean worlds reflects both an adherence to the traditional perspective centered on Europe and North America, as well as these states' worldwide imperialism by armed force, economic penetration, and an ideology of the superiority of white people—or, in terms of the times, white men. Since the early sixteenth century, colonization and imperial rule involved migrations of white administrators, soldiers, and investors or their personnel. The black Atlantic's forced migrations, which did come to an end in the 1870s, had depleted sub-Saharan Africa of about 12.4 million men, women, and children before 1810, and the descendants of survivors continued to shape the economies and societies of the Americas.[5] In the world of the Indian Ocean, the migrations of free men and women and, from the 1830s, of indentured servants—never more than 10 percent of the total South Asian migration, though white racializing views labeled all of these migrants "coolies"—established a macroregion of trade and cultural exchange. The indentured and free men and women sustained production in Plantation Belts imposed by European investors.[6] In the Far East—or from a North American transpacific perspective, in the west—nineteenth-century imperial China was weakening both internally and externally. Its many regions were the arenas of expanding populations, many millions of which migrated to fertile lands and growing cities.[7] In the North Atlantic world the period 1870 to 1945 encompasses the apogee of both intracontinental and transatlantic migrations, beginning in the early decades of the nineteenth century, at the height of industrialization. It also comprises the self-paralysis of Europe during two world wars that were in many respects European wars, whose aftermaths changed the massive labor migrations that had begun before 1914 into massive refugee migrations, from 1914 to the late 1940s.[8]

Each perspective or positioning implies a point of view, particular or partisan, and marginalizes others of the many viewpoints available. Challenging a Euro- and US-centric perspective, we can discern five major migration systems across the globe in the nineteenth century, with some beginning centuries earlier:

- the dual North and South "white" Atlantic system connecting Europe and the Americas, as well as Europe with its colonies, beginning in the early fifteenth century, reaching its apogee from the 1880s to 1914, and ending in the mid-1950s;
- the African slave, or black Atlantic, migration system, beginning in the 1440s, reaching its apogee in the eighteenth and nineteenth centuries, and ending in the 1870s;
- the system of migration of Asian men and women, both free and under indenture—often within the framework of power relations imposed by the British or other European empires and US capital investments on colonies—as well as its transpacific extensions to the Americas;
- the Russo-Siberian system composed of both high-volume, often circular, rural-to-urban migrations within European Russia and settlement of trans-Caspian and southern Siberian regions, as well as some emigration to North America and in-migration from Western Europe;
- a fifth system, the North China-to-Manchuria system, commencing in the late nineteenth century and assuming large proportions in the 1920s and 1930s.[9]

A migration system, on the level of empirical observation and geographical space, is a cluster of moves between a region of origin and a receiving region that continues over a long period of time. It is distinct from nonclustered multidirectional migrations. Gross and net quantity of migration flows, continuity over time, and ratio per thousand population may be studied on this level. Across macroregions (and similarly across meso- and microregions), migration systems connect distinct societies with a labor surplus to others with a demand for additional laborers or, from the view of the migrating men and women, more options. (The connection may also involve densely settled agricultural regions of out-migration with regions less densely settled but never empty.) The regions of origin and of destination are each characterized by the ratio of rural to urban populations, by degree of industrialization and urbanization, by political structures and current policies, by social hierarchies and the impermeability of dividing lines between classes or status groups, by specific educational, value, and belief systems, by ethnic composition and demographic factors (infant mortality, marriage patterns, dependency ratio, age structure), by gendered and intergenerational role ascriptions, and by traditions of internal, medium-distance, and long-distance migrations. These complex structures and processes are often simplified into general push-and-pull-factors. Because economic sectors and regions transcend state borders, and because migrants in pursuit of their life-course decisions often cross political borders, states are not a useful unit of analysis for the nineteenth century and earlier. However, with the invention of passports in the late nineteenth century and mainly in the first two decades of the twentieth century, as well as with exclusionary policies based on racial ascriptions, states increased their role in establishing a framework, or migration regimes, for migrants' departure or entry.[10]

Macroregions are empirically determined, interconnected, and related spaces. They provide a human-agency-based spatial frame of analysis that cannot be achieved by using fixed units of physical geography, like continents, or the fixed borders of polities. Europe's regions—Iberian, then Mediterranean, Atlantic littoral, northern, west central, and east central—became one migration space in the nineteenth century both internally and as regards out-migration. Eastern tsarist Europe remained a separate region connected to southern Siberia by eastward out-migration. The divide between the Atlantic and the Russo-Siberian system along the Dnepr River was crossed eastward or westward by comparatively small numbers. Asia's four macroregions—South Asia, Southeast Asia, China with North Asia, and the Japanese islands—remained distinct spaces but were connected through sea-lanes. From Southeast Asia, migrations extended to the Pacific islands, including the islands of Australia and New Zealand. A further region, the cultures of the Eastern Mediterranean and the Persian Gulf or West Asia, is best discussed as a hinge region connecting Mediterranean Europe, the Russian and Ottoman Black Sea littorals, and North Africa with the Indian Ocean's littoral societies and their products. Africa's spaces include the distinct Arab and Kabyl Mediterranean North, the littoral societies of the Indian and the Atlantic Ocean and a central landlocked region. The Americas, Anglo North and Latin South, contain a French-language region in the St. Lawrence Valley, the culturally interactive Caribbean, and the Greater US Southwest and Mexican Northwest in which Spanish and English mingle.

Periodization, as is obvious in this synthesis, varies between the macroregions; and the 1870s, in most regional migration systems, reflect continuities rather than breaking points. In the 1870s, about six decades after European governments decided to end the slave trade, slave merchants did indeed cease to buy and sell human beings. They did so more for economic reasons than for any respect of law. In the white Atlantic, the age of revolution, counterrevolution, and Napoleonic imperial warfare—extending from the 1760s in some of the British North American colonies to the reestablishment of a reactionary dynastic order in Europe at the 1815 Congress of Vienna—slowed transatlantic mobility. Migrations resumed in 1816–1817, partly induced by a particularly harsh winter, and grew steadily in conjunction with economic growth or slowed during periods of recession and the American Civil War, 1861–1865. From the 1870s and 1880s, the "proletarian mass migration" reached new heights. This Atlantic migration system came to a sudden halt in 1914 and reemerged for a decade each after 1918 and 1945. In South Asia and in the southern provinces of the Qing Empire, indentured servitude was introduced or assumed larger proportions in the 1830s. Almost a century later, India's nationalist leaders used the weakening of imperial Britain in 1914–1918 to negotiate an end to British rule, which was achieved de facto by the 1930s. Migrations in most of China, influenced by the British Opium Wars, after around 1840, which massively increased opium sales and indebtedness, show no particular caesura in the 1870s. However, in the north, the Shandong-to-Manchuria migrations began. In contrast to the continuities characterizing the 1870s, the end of the Second World War changed the parameters of (refugee) migrations almost everywhere in the world, and the decade after 1945 is characterized by resettlement of refugees and displaced persons (DPs)—people who had been moved to forced labor, internment camps, or other confinement by the warring Axis powers, Japan included. At armistice, they found themselves wherever they had been deposited, with limited means to return home.

This discussion focuses on the developments from the 1870s. Section 1 discusses preceding migration and migration-related developments across the globe and establishes patterns and processes specific to regions and societies. Section 2 turns to contemporary concepts of belonging and identities and to theorizations and interpretations of migrations. Section 3 describes and analyzes migrations in the Atlantic economies, in the world's Plantation Belt and mining nodes, and in all other macroregions from the 1870s to the 1910s or, depending on the region, the 1930s. Section 4 turns to twentieth-century (refugee) migrations induced by 1910s warfare and related to the 1930s Great Depression and includes intellectual migrations that contributed to a global critique of colonialism and racism. Finally, Section 5 discusses the consequences of the displacements and migrations of the Second World War for the subsequent decade.

Languages imply connotations, and scholars are socialized into them in childhood. Hidden viewpoints of languages, mother tongues spoken in fatherlands, also need to be brought into the open for critical assessment. Common usage has it that "wars break out"—they are declared, sometimes prepared. Governments are involved, and refugee migrants are aware of this. Historians need terminologies that do not imply interpretations. Migration history has been written in an emigration/immigration dichotomy. Both terms imply unidirectional permanent moves. In a further ideologization, nationalist historians often assumed that emigrants were a loss to the nation or even committed treason to a constructed national identity. Immigrants have been viewed as uncultured and uprooted, in need of immersion into a melting pot to become new and better human beings. In contrast, the term *migration* is open as to direction, number of moves, return, and variants of acculturation processes. Migration experiences and choices, it still needs to be emphasized, were gendered. In specific periods, varying by region, more women than men moved. Another problem occurs when terms with different connotations are used for similar phenomena or when one term is used for distinct phenomena. Forced African migrations have been subsumed under the catch-all label *slavery,* but they encompassed (1) forced migrations that, in the Americas and the Plantation Belt, led to a status as "chattel"—labor forces commodified as property without personality; (2) traditional rights-in-persons dependency relationships within Africa; and (3) service bondage in Asia in households, as soldiers, or as highly educated business or court administrators. *Bondage,* the generic term, and associated mobilities involve serfdom in Europe, forced labor in 1930s Fascist Germany and the Stalinist Soviet Union, and subsequently in apartheid South Africa, or bound status in Chinese societies. The binary juxtaposition of free and unfree migrations hides a continuum from voluntary to involuntary. The problematic connotations of bounded categories like "free," "coolie," or "slave" skew analyses. Most "free" migrants—from Europe to the Americas, for example—were forced to leave by severe economic constraints. They departed from known impossibilities to perceived options, but never to "unlimited opportunities." Bound migrants, whether slaves or coolies, are often assumed to have been passive (or to have been deprived of the possibility to act on their own). But all bound and constrained migrants (except for young children) came fully socialized and have created cultures. Migrants come with developed personalities even if they must adjust under extreme constraints.[11]

1. A Longue-Durée *Perspective*

SCHOLARS have often given priority to white migrants who moved westward across the Atlantic, based on the assumption that they migrated in singular quantity, an assumption that is not born out by the data. In fact, the numerically small migrations from Western Europe and, later, from the United States into the colonized regions of the world were of far larger global economic and mobilizing impact. The Europeans' economic activities and aggressiveness, or simply their imposition of rule, set in motion local, regional, or even empire-wide migrations. None of the colonizer powers did ever imagine a reversal of migratory directions, a future of decolonization that would result in mass movements—for example, of Indonesians to the Netherlands, of West Africans to France, of Jamaicans to Britain, or of Puerto Ricans the United States. In conjunction with other factors the long-term effects of the colonizer migrations still determine many patterns of present postcolonial migrations.

When humanist and Enlightenment thinkers in Europe began to connect the issues of inalienable human rights to human bondage, whether in regimes of serfdom or of slavery, economic transformations were beginning to change the character of work and some employers started to discuss the advantages of permanently bound versus flexibly hired labor forces. At the same time, bound human beings, who had never accepted any legitimacy of enslavement as chattel, had established subcultures under bondage that gave them collective strength, and they were aware that withdrawal and resistance would undercut the plantation regime's productivity.[12] In Europe, serfdom, which was intended to immobilize large segments of the regionally diverse peasant populations, was also more complex and involved mobility: When nobles favored hunting over husbandry, fewer serfs were needed; when they intensified agriculture, bound peasant families had to be attracted; when neighboring cities offered escape from *corvée* labor, serfs fled.[13] In Spanish America, slavery involved the forced mobilization of segments of the many West, Central, and East African peoples, as

·[444]·

well as of many of the Native American peoples, and their immobilization at the destination.[14]

The resistance of bound men and women, the Enlightenment debates over human rights, and the discussions about perceived benefits of free or bound labor impacted deeply on human mobility in the frame of power relations. Europe's sedentary *latifundia* lords and their migrating cousins, the plantation owners in the colonized world (later augmented by those of US origin), demanded a supply of workers as cheap and as tractable as possible. If Africans could no longer be enslaved, could Europe's underclasses be induced to migrate to subtropical or tropical climates? Could laborers from colonized Asian societies be recruited, under pressure if necessary? Investors in plantations considered recruitment by incentive, whether bonuses or high wages, expensive and thus detrimental to profits. They lobbied for state mobilization of workers under indenture or from Europe with assisted passage to shift cost from the private sector to taxpayers. Class interests and struggles, racializations and resistance, and reformatting of patterns of thought on "the human condition" impacted decisions to migrate.[15]

Forced Migration in the Black Atlantic

After two centuries of transatlantic slave migrations, mulattoes and Negroes in French Saint-Domingue / Haiti cast off their yoke once, in the interactive white and black Atlantics, concepts of government by social contract were discussed in pre-revolutionary France, and concepts of self-determined lives were discussed by enslaved Africans. Ideas, carried by travelers and migrants from France, brought class distinctions between *grands blancs, petits blancs,* and *gens de couleur* to a crisis. Together the three groups accounted for less than 10 percent of the population. Segments of the other 90 percent, the approximately half a million slaves of African birth or origin, held distinct views. Slaves who as servants lived at the interface between white and black spheres were conversant with both discourses and could negotiate between them. Men and women recently force-migrated from Africa knew of lifeways other than those imposed by the slave regime. Whites, resident or migrant, opposed the extension of human rights to the colonies; mulattoes demanded it, with the support of the French *Amis des Noirs*—a group that Paul Gilroy overlooked in his book *Black Atlantic*. Slaves began self-liberation in August 1791; France's National Assembly liberated chattel slaves only in 1793. When Napoleon, under the influence of the French-Caribbean mixed-ancestry transatlantically mobile planter class, reinstituted slavery, the force-migrated and self-freed Africans defeated the force-migrated forty thousand soldiers of the invading French army. After Haiti's independence, many of the free families left the plantations to pursue subsistence agriculture and self-determined lives. The resulting collapse of the sugar-plantation-based economy gave a competitive advantage to British-controlled Jamaica, where slave imports increased and slave labor continued to the 1830s.[16]

Planters, fearful of losing their purchased labor force, and thus their investments, almost frantically tried to recruit labor wherever possible: poor Europeans, Asians who could be indentured, free or semibound Africans. Economically, it was the price of labor that counted, not the color of skin. In the early 1800s, trial shipments of indentured Chinese laborers from Portuguese Macao were sent to British Trinidad and to Portuguese Brazil. More than half a century later, planters in Hawai'i would also experiment, asking for shipments, alphabetically, of "fertilizer" and "Filipinos," and having poor Portuguese and poor Japanese migrants work alongside each other.

Although the slave trade was banned from 1807–1808 in Europe and the United States, and although enforcement of this ban by the British Navy began in 1815, Brazil accepted the policy only in the mid-1850s and the trade's de facto end came as late as the 1870s. In these decades some 1.9 million men and women—"pieces" in the Spanish expression—were force-migrated. It needs to be recalled that, up to the 1820s, more Africans than Europeans came to the Americas, and one-half to two-thirds of the Europeans came under indentures rather than as free persons. Black and white, men and women, carried their cultural and spiritual practices with them. Often of Animist or Islamic faith, they continuously added African elements to the Afro-Euro-American Creole cultures. In mid-nineteenth-century Rio de Janeiro, some eighty thousand slaves accounted for almost 40 percent of the population, and two-thirds of these had been born in Africa. In the United States, on the other hand, where slave imports did end and population increase came by procreation, African-Americans were the most creolized in culture.

The British imperial government abolished slavery in 1834 but—to satisfy planters' demands—tacked on a four-year "apprenticeship"; in the French colonies abolition came in 1846. Latecomers as regards to ending slavery were the Dutch colonies (1873), the remnants of the Spanish colonies (Cuba in 1880 with a six-year "apprenticeship" added on), and the two largest independent slaveholding states, the United States and Brazil. Their slavery regimes lasted to 1863–1865 and 1888, respectively—some 85 to 110 years after the Declaration of Human Rights in France and later than the tsarist empire's abolition of serfdom in 1861. As early as 1776, the classic exposition of new middle-class—not capitalist—economic doctrines, Adam Smith's *The Wealth of Nations,* had called slavery an economic anachronism not competitive with free labor. Afro- and Euro-Creoles understood the plantation regime's economy of theft of the rewards of labor. US slaves called flight "stealing oneself," and French planters described a slave's purchase of his or her own freedom as "vendre un nègre à lui-même."

In the Caribbean, where marginal agricultural land was accessible by short-distance migration, many of the freed Afro-Caribbean families refused wage labor. To replace slaves, planters in the British Empire hired African-origin men and women migrating within the Americas or freed from slave ships, European "free" labor migrants who left home societies that did not provide sustenance, and Asian contract labor migrants bound for time. As regards African-origin workers, Euro-Caribbean and mulatto planters first attempted to continue bondage in the form of apprenticeship or indenture. Next they tried local—i.e., Caribbean—free labor, which, in terms of cost of migration, was cheapest. In Caribbean inter-island migrations, hundreds of thousands moved according to wage levels, working conditions, and legal status. In a third strategy, planters indentured Africans freed from slave ships whom imperial authorities wanted to earn their keep. About forty thousand were debarked in the Caribbean and British Guiana before the mid-1860s. Many fled and joined free Afro-Caribbean communities. Planters also attempted to recruit free US Afro-Creoles, and some did migrate to the less-racist island societies. Planters recruited free Kru from West Africa, especially Sierra Leone, but once the first migrants returned home and reported on working conditions, no further enlistments could be obtained.[17]

Planters' experiments with white labor began in the mid-1830s and—like Asian indenture—assumed larger proportions in the 1840s: Irish and English,

French, Germans, Maltese, and Portuguese—many of them "black" Cape Verdeans. Some workers abandoned plantation labor as soon as possible and turned to small trading, often in competition and conflict with local Afro-Caribbeans. From Asia, some 270,000 Chinese reached Cuba, Peru, and other Latin American economies, and about half a million South Asians came to the Caribbean colonies and the Guyanas. Yucatan Amerindian prisoners and their wives, as well as peons sold by Mexican Euro-Creole *hacendados,* were carried to Cuba before 1860. Polyglot interracial societies emerged, homogenized on each island, and divided into states that developed a regional sense of identity. Across color lines class solidarities were forged. The Caribbean segment of the black and white Atlantics became many-colored.[18]

The slave-labor regime immobilized workers at their destination for as long as their owners could use them profitably. However, as in European serfdom, involuntary mobility also continued. When the US cotton economy moved from the Atlantic seaboard to the Mississippi's riparian states, the free planter migrants forced their bound labor to follow. Slaves considered refractory were sold "down" the Mississippi River to regions where discipline was harsher and exploitation more brutal. In the Caribbean, the shift of the center of sugar production from Haiti to Jamaica to Cuba involved forced and voluntary mobility. In Brazil, the removal of plantation economies from the northeast to the southeast and the expansion of mining ever farther inland involved mobility of slave and free blacks. "Fugitives"—refugees from forced labor, manumitted slaves, and those who had purchased their freedom—were able to move according to their goals in the frames of economic and racialized constraints and options. With the end of slavery in the Atlantic world at the advance of industrialization, African-Americans' mobility, except in the United States, did increase—provided there were known options for earning a living elsewhere and provided racism did not prevent self-determined lives. In Brazil, African-origin men and women could and did move, as others did in the Caribbean inter-island migrations. In the United States, out-migration from the South was delayed until after 1900 and the "Great Migration" began only during World War I.[19]

Asian Migrations and the Regime of Indenture

In terms of culture, economics, and migration, the eastern part of the triconti-nental European-African-Asian world consisted of macroregions distinct to a degree that it makes no analytical sense to aggregate all data and discussions into a generic Asia or to construct generic "Asians" as migrants. We will deal with South Asia (British India and Ceylon / Sri Lanka), with Southeast Asia from Burma to Sumatra and beyond, with China, and with Japan. Although for a long time the Atlantic and Pacific Oceans were separating expanses, the Indian Ocean and the Strait of Malacca connected the many littorals to the seas east-ward between the islands and northward along the coast of the mainland and the Japanese isles.[20]

The intrusion of tiny numbers of Europeans into the vibrant, multidirec-tional, and intensely traveled routes of the Indian Ocean trade emporia and into the Southeast and East Asian seas changed labor demands—on a modest scale at first, in larger proportions once plantation economies were institutionalized, and massively under nineteenth-century imperialism. Steamships, introduced since the 1830s, and the Suez Canal, opened in 1869, changed the region's acces-sibility from the world economy's core. In the 1850s, when Western European capitals established Łódź in Russian Poland as a textile center, a first cotton mill opened in Mumbai (Bombay)—in both cases sizable regional labor migration networks developed. Distant politics and warfare impacted on local economies globally: During the American Civil War, Britain's Manchester mills substi-tuted Indian for American cotton imports. Thus, for five years laborers in India's plantations were in great demand, then after the end of war none were hired. In terms of family economies, a boom in one segment of the global economy and a related bust in another, often distant, segment translates into employment or underemployment, overwork or undernourishment, and, often, migration and dislocation.

African Slavery in the Indian Ocean World

In most of the Asian societies, resident local people or short-distance and inter-regional migrants formed the labor forces. Bound and free East African men and women came or were brought to the Indies, the Malaya Peninsula, and the Southeast Asian islands as sailors or as servants for ruling, merchant, or noble families. In the worlds of the Eastern Mediterranean and the Indian Ocean, slaves came from a wide variety of regions and cultural origins: Africans, Turks, Circassians. In extended merchant families, slaves became a kind of nonrelated kin varying in position from menial service in households, laborers on business premises, to educated and highly placed clerks. In contractual labor arrangements, slaves kept part of their incomes, and if successful could in turn own slaves, become substantial property owners, and purchase their freedom. Slave and free women might intermingle in the same household or court as wives and concubines. Children of a free father—including those by a master of a domestic slave from exploitative sexual relations—assumed his status and were of equal standing with the children of free wives. By giving birth, their slave mothers improved their status and could no longer be sold or alienated by the master-husband. Dependency relationships that placed restrictions on sale and bondage were part of everyday social life rather than a marker of segregation. The impossibility of return as well as the comparatively benign nature of the system of slavery in this region, enjoined by the Koran, legitimized the system to a degree that flight and revolt were rare. Cultures merged and slave mothers or nannies might tell children bedside stories about free lives in their culture of origin, their (forced) migration trajectory, and the culture of residence. Hierarchical mixed societies rather than regimes of segregation emerged.[21]

Migrations in South Asia

The many societies on the South Asian subcontinent and in Ceylon have been described as sedentary by British imperial scholars, Kingsley Davis in particular. This culturally insensitive view overlooks the fact that Hindu views of kinship consider people in a village community as related and thus prohibited from marrying each other. Brides had to translocate in short-distance migration to a neighboring community. Courts and wealthy households attracted teachers, artists, and artisans in long-distance moves. To mitigate land shortages, people of the plains migrated into hilly regions, thereby displacing men and women from the "hill tribes." The many-cultured port cities were nodes of interurban circulation.

The London-based East India Company, a multinational or global player in modern terms, and the British Empire as the period's "superpower" restructured many of South Asia's societies, and the global cotton economy restructured local producing families' lives. Imperial regulations of the 1790s affected Bengal, Bihar, and Orissa in the north, regulations of the 1810s affected societies the south and, after its annexation in the later 1840s, the Punjab. These regulations and subsequent legislation introduced new land revenue systems, which grafted the role of English landlords onto Indian societies, made men from local elites tax collectors, and permitted alienation of village lands. As a result, a new class of landlords as well as middlemen, moneylenders, and tax farmers (*zamindars*) emerged, dependent on and allied with the temporarily resident colonial administrator-overlord migrants. Within a few decades these measures destroyed the traditional village community, with its precarious balance between population, agriculture, and handicrafts. A report to the British Parliament admitted that massive distress forced families to migrate or become vagrants.

In Punjab, a region of stable population and balanced economy, the British administrators expanded the irrigation system, made land a transferable asset, and required taxes to be paid in cash. The extension of cultivation and land sales drew or forced villagers into a money and market economy. Peasant families who perceived opportunities needed loans for investments, and good crops encouraged, just as poor harvests necessitated, borrowing. Rural indebtedness grew fast. Then the new railways brought cheap factory goods, displacing the rural peasant-artisan families. Out-migration became a necessity. Punjabi men became British "colonial auxiliaries"—clerks, policemen, soldiers—and labor migrants. Sikh men might be stationed locally or sent to Hong Kong, Singapore, and Malaya. They thus came to know other parts of India and of the empire—white Australia and Canada, for example—and initiated self-sustaining migrations. The railroads carried off men for wage work as far as the port of Calcutta (Kolkata), from where they could leave for Malaya or even North America. Women had no similar options.

Indian cloths, family-produced, enchanted European consumers by their colors and moderate price. In India's southeast such families owned land and thus derived income from two sources. This traditional risk diversification permitted flexible income substitution in unpredictable markets. When European purchasers increased demand, the weavers' decision to increase returns implied longer daily working hours and increased family labor. It alienated the families from their land. Food purchases and wages paid to hired labor necessitated larger cash flows. The artisan-farmer families entered debt relationships. At the same time, in Britain the mechanization of spinning and weaving began to permit production at a cost below that of family labor in India. Capitalist and state forces combined: policies levied prohibitive taxes on export of India's artisanal products but permitted free entry of British goods. Until 1800 London's Spital-fields weavers had suffered from Indian imports; by 1850 Indian village produc-tion had been destroyed. Single women, appropriately called "spinsters," could no longer gain subsistence; whole families starved to death. This deindustrializa-tion of village handicrafts and the parallel refeudalization of land ownership and tax farming pauperized whole regions' populations, which, as "agricultural pro-letariats," were forced to migrate to wherever subsistence was available. Just at this time the empire-wide plantocracy needed semibound labor.[22]

Southeast Asia, China, and the Chinese Diaspora

In the spice-producing and resource-rich Malaya and Southeast Asian islands, the European state-supported armed colonizer merchants, investors, and power-wielding administrators had long relied on forced local labor. Because "locals" could use their resources—knowledge of the terrain and supportive networks—to refuse waged labor and to resist force, bound labor was imported and immo-bilized at the point of arrival. The Spanish colonizers of the Philippines had carried enslaved laborers across the Pacific as far as New Spain in the Americas. The Dutch intruders' regional system of forced labor became globalized under the British Empire's expansion. Existing local migration systems were intensified and new ones created.

In the societies farther north, China's and Japan's imperial courts had pro-hibited emigration since the fifteenth century. In the case of China, mobile mer-chants, artisans, and laborers in particular from the southern provinces of Fujian and Guangdong had traditionally resided temporarily in outposts along the sea-lanes. Over time the "overseas Chinese"—a modern term—became a settled dia-sporic network extending to Manila, Bantam, and Malacca. A second network involved the "western ocean" connecting to Japan and Korea; a third one emerged in the "eastern ocean" in response to invitations by Siamese rulers to assume positions as foreign traders under royal monopoly. In Siam's capital, Chinese from the east and Muslims from the west lived in distinct quarters; others—Portuguese, Javanese, Malays, Makassarese, and Pegu—lived outside of the walls, each group administered by a speaker of its own choosing. Such communal living and self-administration was the practice in most of the Indian Ocean's port cities.

The community in Manila, Philippines, formed the second-largest overseas community after the Siam-Chinese. Like that of the Spanish, the Chinese community was almost exclusively male. Informal unions or marriages with native women initiated a process of ethnogenesis: a mestizo population emerged. The diasporic Chinese became cultural mediators and economic middlemen for the European in-migrants who lacked languages, cultural skills, and capability for intercultural exchange. In the mixed society of Luzon, Hispanicized *indio* culture, to use the Spanish term for local people, ranked lowest, and Chinese and Spanish competed for status, because both considered themselves as originating in a high culture. Over time, the Chinese-Philippine mestizo population assumed economic leadership, provided natives with credit, and—seizing land in case of defaults—expanded their urban-based economy to landholder status. By 1850, when the Spanish once again restricted Chinese migrants' activities, it was this native-born mestizo elite, rather than the marginal European elite, who profited.[23]

Given the high quality of Chinese goods and the vast array of goods produced, British and other foreign merchants had little to sell for whatever they wanted to buy. Opium sales would rectify their balance of trade—and opium could be mass-produced in India. When a regional Chinese administrator seized the cargos and burned them in 1839, the British Empire went to war. The resulting reintroduction of opium into the trade would also impoverish large numbers of Chinese, who were then sold, or had to sell themselves or their children or wives, into indentured labor. Parallel to peasant pauperization in India, the policy created the Chinese segment of a labor reservoir for work across the colonized world. To the migrants' image of being "heathens"—that is, of a different religion—the image of "opium dens" was added. As indemnity for the cost of the aggression, the British Empire extracted from imperial China territorial rights to Hong

Kong. Rural-to-urban and interurban migrants increased the city's population from four thousand in 1842 to about two hundred thousand by 1900—colonizer entrepôts were poles of attraction.[24]

Within China, where many-directional migrations were of long tradition, several factors increased mobility in the mid-nineteenth century. As in Europe, population growth was fast, from 300 million in 1790 to 420 million in 1850. While the price of rice, the main food staple, increased tenfold, inflation reduced incomes; the government's devaluation of copper, the circulating medium, in regard to silver as the taxpaying medium further undercut peasant families' precarious living conditions. From about 1860 on, a policy of increasing production in industries created jobs but was hampered by inefficiencies of bureaucratic control. Widespread social discontent, political unrest, and ethnic antagonisms, some of them fused with issues of religion, caused large-scale dislocations. Uprisings throughout the 1840s, the Taiping and Muslim rebellions and their repression 1851–1864 and 1855–1873, and warlordism sent people fleeing to search for subsistence elsewhere.[25]

Chinese overseas migrants traditionally came from the coastal provinces of Guangdong and Fujian (including from Chaozhou and Amoy and surroundings, and Hokkien-speakers), as well as from the island of Hainan and from among the internally migrant Hakka. The provinces' population density reached one person per quarter acre. The British Empire tapped this reservoir when, in 1860, it imposed the principle of "free emigration" on the Chinese state. Middlemen sent indentured and free migrants far beyond the limits of the traditional diaspora. In reaction, in 1868 the Chinese government ended its policy of disregard for emigrants, regulated the "coolie" trade, opened consulates, and sought ties to Chinese overseas merchants whose social capital as middlemen it had shunned while all Western powers had benefited from it. Diaspora Chinese sent remittances to their "emigrant communities" of origin, in many of which only women, children, and the elderly remained. Sequential migration led Chinese, like all migrants, to clusters of kin and friends at particular locations in the three main destinations: Southeast Asia as the easiest migration route; Latin America, particularly Cuba and Peru; and the United States and Canada as the most costly destinations.[26]

Migration in and out of Japan

Japan's government, after closing the society to foreigners in the 1640s, had always kept Deshima (an island in the port of Nagasaki) open to Dutch traders to acquire knowledge and products deemed useful. A squadron of US gunboats forced admission of American and European merchants in 1854. In contrast to China's entrenched bureaucrats, Japan's new Meiji era administration (1868–1912) embarked on a program of "restoration" of the nation to economic and military power. To finance this urban modernization, the regime taxed and uprooted agrarian populations. Increasingly powerful, Japan succeeded by the 1890s in abrogating the unequal treaties, granting extraterritorial rights to Western merchants. The government hired influential "guest workers" from the West: advisory British military officers replaced the samurai warrior class with a soldiery of commoners; US engineers and missionaries, by providing technical assistance, opened entryways for industry; German- and Harvard-trained men helped develop a strategy of imperialist expansion undergirded by a doctrine of Japanese genetic superiority and a xenophobic chauvinism. Dislocated peasant men and women in turn migrated to Hawai'i and the Americas.[27]

The Institutionalization of Indentured Servitude

When colonizer governments abolished the African slave migration system between 1807 and the 1870s, planters from Java via Réunion to Trinidad and Cuba, mine owners in Malaya and South Africa, guano pit entrepreneurs in Peru, and others demanded from these governments new manageable workers with low reproduction costs. Attempts to recruit Europeans foundered because these shunned semibondage and selected destinations in temperate zones with free wage labor and democratic-capitalist institutions.

Succumbing to planters' interests, the British and newly imperial[28] French colonizer states imposed a regime of indentured labor, a "second slavery," on men and women in their Asian territories. Beginning informally in the 1820s, British imperial legislation buttressed the system in 1834, the year of abolition of slavery. Indigenous forms began earlier and lasted longer in the Chinese realm. The French recruited workers in Indochina, and slavers kidnapped men and women from Pacific islands, Fiji in particular. The term *coolie,* which symbolized cheap and despised laborers among Western white capitalists and working-class organizations alike, meant "bitter strength" in Chinese and "wage for menial work" in Tamil. Recruits came from impoverished rural families and urban underclasses. In transoceanic migrations, free or "passenger" migrants moved along the circuits of the indentured workers and established supply networks for food and clothing. Larger numbers moved internally to regions of mining and factory work with the help, or under the tutelage, of labor recruiters.

Recruitment involved deception and force: idealized descriptions of working conditions, deliberate tricking into debt bondage, agent-induced gambling in China, self-pawning, or clan fighting. To be "shanghaied," a term used by sailors when enlisted against their will, derives from this practice of kidnapping. In southern China, middlemen or "snakes" controlled recruitment; in India, the colonizing British mobilized migrants and, only after much abuse, appointed "protectors of emigrants." In Meiji Japan the government attempted to recruit suitable workers and prevent exploitation by distant employers.

Travel to destinations across the Asian seas took a few days or weeks, whereas the Calcutta-to-Caribbean trip lasted about six months. Before the 1850s, America-bound Chinese on British and Spanish vessels suffered mortality rates of up to 12 percent. The introduction of steamships in about 1865 lowered mortality, and the reduction of fares and travel time resulted in vastly larger numbers of migrants. During the sea voyage from India, involuntary rites of passage replaced village and family social ties with labor agents' control. This partial deculturation, in the eyes of Europeans, turned people of many specific regional cultures into generic bound workers. While caste, class, and custom lost some validity, faith remained a marker—Hindu, Muslim, Sikh, Jain, Christian. And the multilingual composition—Urdu, Hindi, Bengali, Tamil, Telugu, Punjabi, Gujarati, and others—necessitated the development of a South Asian creole, usage of a non–South Asian lingua franca, or assimilation into the largest language group at a particular destination. Similarly, Chinese laborers spoke mutually unintelligible dialects and had to develop a language of cross-cultural communication.

Of the 2.5 million Chinese who left for Asian destinations in the nineteenth century, no more than one-eighth were indentured laborers in the literal sense. A second group, under the "credit-ticket system," owed travel cost to kin, previous migrants, or merchants. Free migrants relied on diasporic networks for selection of destinations—within the limitations imposed by economic constraints: Burma, Malaya, the Dutch East Indies, Siam, French Indochina, the Philippines, and the Pacific islands. Less than a million Chinese, most of whom paid their own way, left the Asian orbit for Australia, Latin American economies, and North America.[29]

The mass of India's transoceanic migrants—only 10 percent of whom were indentured—came from a northern belt extending from Bengal through Bihar to Uttar Pradesh and from a southeastern coastal belt from Orissa to Madras (Chennai). To the mid-1850s, recruiters targeted mainly non-Hindu aboriginal people, the poor of the ports, and the lowest castes. Many were famine victims with no prospects of reinsertion into labor markets or social positions. Recruitment followed patterns of ethnoculture and skills. In Burma, Bengalis provided clerical workers; sweepers came from Nellore; middle-class Tamils worked as clerks; Telugus from the Coromandel coast provided the labor for mills and other factories. The first of four outbound routes, to Burma, Malaya, and Ceylon, involved an estimated six million, most of whom returned. On the second route, small numbers of merchants, often with families, migrated to traditional centers of trade in East Africa and to new contract worker settlements. On the third route, the British brought Indians as "imperial auxiliaries" to Malaya as administrators, to Hong Kong as policemen, and to other possessions. Finally, on the fourth route, about 1.5 million contract workers were transported to destinations outside of Asia: one-third each to Mauritius and the Caribbean, one-tenth to Natal, the others to East Africa, the Indian Ocean, or the Pacific islands. After 1870, long-distance moves increased.

Most contract migrants were healthy young men, exploitable in the prime of their strength. Migration of women depended on restrictions in societies of origin as well as at the destination. The ratio of women was lowest among Chinese; among migrants destined for Latin America, a mere 1 percent were women. To counter the low rate among Indian migrants, the British government set a quota of 25 percent women among outbound workers. The actual percentage grew to just over 30 percent in the early 1890s. All societies of departure placed restrictions on women's migration. Among employers in the receiving economies, attitudes to women depended on labor force requirements and gendered role ascriptions.

Where men were encouraged to stay, as in Trinidad, women were viewed as a stabilizing factor. The Australian government, expecting male workers to leave at the end of their contract, excluded women and children from entry to prevent permanent settlement. The slow pace of community formation among indentured laborers was related to the low rate of women. Transoceanic family lives impacted on gender roles and the raising and education of children.

Migration under indenture as well as of credit-ticket and free passenger migrants to the Pacific coast of the Americas began in the mid-1840s. Free Chinese came with the California and Fraser River gold rushes. Though free Chinese laborers were in great demand for railroad construction to the 1870s or 1880s, anti-Asian racism in North America led to unsuccessful attempts to restrict the hiring of Chinese workers. The period from the 1870s to the 1920s, from the introduction of steamship transport to the stepwise end of the Indian variant of the regime of indentured servitude, would form the apogee of this labor migration regime.[30]

Transatlantic Connections

Migrations to the Americas, usually viewed as transatlantic, also involved transpacific crossings. Within Europe internal migrations preceded and accompanied the emigration, and within the Americas intracontinental moves contributed to settlement patterns—for example, northbound in New Spain to the regions that were to become the US Southwest. Colonization from California to the Bering Strait had been undertaken, in terms of empires, by Creoles and Spanish from New Spain, by British coming via the Pacific from East Asia, and by Russians from Siberia. The northern Pacific coast was Amerindian in culture and so were California and the Greater Southwest before the latter became Hispanic (Spanish-Indian mestizo) and before the first English- or French-speaking migrants arrived. Immigrants from New Spain reached New Mexico decades earlier than religious migrants settled in what they called New England.

On the West Coast of North America, Russian and Siberian fur traders, entrepreneurs, and fishermen, accompanied by Aleut hunters, came as far south as San Francisco Bay. Thousands of Chinese settled in Hawai'i, a few dozen sailors and skilled workers reached Vancouver Island in the 1790s. The latter were employees of the British East India Company engaged in a global competition with both Spanish transpacific shipping and its rival megacorporation, the Hudson's Bay Company, whose migrant traders came across the Atlantic. The first transpacific arrivals remained few, but from the mid-1840s the second phase of the Pacific migration system—after the sixteenth- and seventeenth-century connection from Spanish Manila to New Spain—brought Chinese and, later, Japanese settlers and workers. Their eastbound mobility and their labor helped build the transcontinental railroads that would facilitate European-origin westbound migrations in the 1870s and 1880s.[31]

The Atlantic world's age of revolution impacted deeply on migrations in Europe. Changes in societies and, more so, two decades of warfare interrupted goal-directed migrations within Europe and to the Americas. The contrast between the new republican United States and the reimposed dynastic rule in Europe created a dual discourse of hope: Individuals and families began to consider improving their personal life chances by transatlantic migration; and collectively, reformers and, later, reform parties struggled for better conditions and called upon people to stay. Finally, a new emphasis on ethnic-national cultures, a democratizing move challenging the nobilities' trans-European culture, began to make "the people," often constructed as families tilling the soil, the *referent* for statewide national cultures. The "nationalization" of the largest and most powerful ethnocultural group in a particular region often forced smaller groups of different cultures living in the same territory to consider emigration. The European war commenced in 1792 with the revolutionary attempt to export France's republican model into neighboring dynasties' realms and the counter-revolutionary old order's aggression to contain the French Revolution; it continued with Napoleon's imperialist expansion as far as Egypt and Moscow, his plantocracy-induced attempt to recapture Haiti, and the intra-European wars of "liberation" from French-Napoleonic rule. Large numbers of men and women were displaced; more than half a million soldiers were marched into Russia; defeated units, disabled men, and stragglers were left behind. Soldiers, depopulating fertile countrysides, might return as settlers with their families after the war. When in 1815 a backward-looking dynastic order was reestablished, defeated revolutionaries and reformers turned to the United States. Arrivals would skyrocket in the 1870s and 1880s.

Before independence of thirteen of the British colonies, European immigration to colonial North America peaked with some 15,000 arriving annually in the fifteen years before 1775: Protestant Irish, Scots, English, and German-speakers were the main groups. About three-fifths of these, under indentures, had to work off the cost of the ocean passage by three to seven years of bound labor. However, the largest group of newcomers were 85,000 enslaved Africans. Given the imperial structures of rule and shipping connections as well as language affinity, migrants from the Western and Northern European cultures moved to the northern regions from the St. Lawrence Valley to the Carolinas. Few French-speakers migrated because, the society's Catholicity notwithstanding, couples traditionally limited their fertility to two children and thus no surplus rural population without land emerged. Those from the Iberian Peninsula moved to Florida, New Spain, or Brazil. Portugal's global reach influenced its migrants' destinations: By 1800, 1.8 million European-born and Creole-born Portuguese lived in Brazil, as compared to 400,000 on the Atlantic islands, 80,000 to 100,000 in Equatorial Africa, and 120,000 or fewer in Asia. To the 1870s, the Atlantic migration system remained a dual one, from Western and Northern Europe to North America and from Iberian and Mediterranean Europe to South America, with some interaction in the Caribbean.

From the Atlantic world's two major revolutionary societies, the United States and France, supporters of the old order departed by their own choice or had to flee. Nobles and segments of the clergy spread to courts and monasteries in neighboring dynastic states. From the new United States, supporters of the Crown (loyalists) left for British North America (Canada) or moved to Britain and other parts of the empire. The French Revolution, which, from a guillotine-centered view, was far more violent than the American, displaced only the small nobility and clergy. The split in American society divided the urban and rural middle classes and sent hundreds of thousands fleeing.

Interregional migrations made colonial and revolutionary North America a mobile society: circuits to sell redemptioners (indentured servants who would redeem their liberty), migration from New England to Nova Scotia or westward to the Ohio Valley, sale and forced migration of slaves, deportation and return of Acadians, the mass flight or emigration of loyalists. Of the German-language soldiers (Hessians), traded by their sovereigns to the British for service in North

America, some deserters and many of those taken as prisoners of war decided to stay and settle. Like voluntary migrants they took advantage of the local options. With those who returned to Hessia came about two hundred African-Americans who had enlisted in the Hessian regiments.[32]

In the new United States and in the reestablished multiple German states, farming families could not settle all of their children on the parents' land. Wherever a family on a subsistence farm raised more than two children into adulthood, the "surplus" had to migrate. From the southwestern German states people had migrated eastward down the Danube to the fertile south Russian plains from which previous Ottoman-ruled peoples had been sent fleeing. From the 1820s, they changed destination: via the Rhine River and Dutch ports to North America. There, a perceived shortage of land east of the Allegheny Mountains had led to demands that the British government open the Ohio Valley, protected by the Proclamation of 1763 as native people's (Indian) territory. Speculators and settlers moved into the region, annexed to the United States without the consent of the native people living there. Americans' and Europeans' settlement migrations generated refugee migrations of agricultural and hunting families and whole societies of Native Americans, who, from the late 1860s to the 1890s, were either killed or confined to reservations.

At its founding the United States had a population of 3.9 million, consisting of English (49 percent), enslaved and a small number of free African people (20 percent), Germans and Scots (7 percent each), Scots-Irish and Irish, Walloons and Dutch, French, Swedish and other Scandinavians, and Spanish. Men and women from Minorca, Livorno, and Greece settled in Florida. Religious refugees included Pietists, Moravians, Huguenots, Mennonites, and Old Order Amish. The society, later constructed as a homogeneous "Anglo America," had heterogeneous origins and was multicultural from the start. From 1790 to 1820, just under a quarter million migrants arrived; from 1820 to 1840, three-quarters of a million; in 1841–1850, 1.7 million; and in the last decade before the American Civil War, 2.6 million. Because US government statisticians counted only arrivals, these gross figures need to be adjusted for return migration to Europe. Actual return was low in times of sailing vessels, but after steamships came into use in the 1870s, rates of return increased to one-third of the arrivals.[33]

In bicultural English- and French-language British North America (Canada after 1867), migration followed similar patterns. Its prairie West, inaccessible across the Canadian Shield, was settled from the 1870s. The third North American country, Spanish-language Mexico (independent since 1821), attracted few migrants: given the large haciendas, no "free" land was available for peasant settlers; the laws of the 1850s deprived the sizable native population of much of their land and created a mobile reservoir of wage laborers. An insurgency by those loyal to Spanish rule in the late 1820s and a European French-led invasion in the 1860s resulted in strong antiforeigner sentiments. The whole of the North American migration region achieved its final territorial and political-social shape in 1867. British North America became the Dominion of Canada. The United States— after annexation of almost half of Mexico in 1848 and 1853—purchased Alaska and began its post–Civil War Reconstruction. Mexico defeated the European invaders and began a period of reform under President Juarez in the 1870s.[34]

In postrevolutionary Europe, a changing and expanding economic order demanded flexible labor. As a result, states began to emancipate their agrarian serf families from bondage between 1762 (Savoy) and 1861 (Russia). The former serfs, with few or no means, had to compensate their former lords for the loss of *corvée* labor and fees. Like Mexican native peoples deprived of their land, and like freed US slaves without compensation for the labor of generations, reduced landholdings and cash payments forced emancipated—and emaciated—peasants and their children to migrate within Europe or, if they could afford it, to the four frontier societies of the Americas: Canada, the United States, Brazil, or Argentina. The portrayal of their settlement as one broad and continuous westward movement across North America or into South America's interior glosses over the multi-directional nineteenth-century internal migrations. The Euro-American creoles' and immigrants' advance required the construction of roads, railroads, and, in the northern part, canals. Such earthworks mobilized unskilled labor locally and from afar and, after completion, facilitated travel of further migrants—from the 1870s the transcontinental railroads were completed.

Internal migrations in North America included mobility across the US-Canada and US-Mexico borders both into and out of the United States. In New England, newcomers from old England introduced textile machinery. Mills, requiring waterpower, were located in places with no previous settlement and attracted farm families' daughters, whose brothers often migrated west to lands more fertile than the local hills. From the 1840s on, factory owners replaced the "girls" migrating within the region by transatlantically mobile Irish families whom British colonialism and famine forced to leave and by Catholic French-Canadian families from the St. Lawrence Valley, where high numbers of children, slow industrialization, and a backward-looking regime of the Catholic Church hindered the development of job opportunities. In the southern United States, the cotton plantation economy—free owners and enslaved workers—shifted from exhausted soils along the tidewater via the piedmont of the Alleghenies to lands east of the Mississippi. From the late 1860s, high urban demand for labor induced an east- or northbound migration of supernumerary farm children to Pittsburgh, Chicago, and the many other industrial, commercial, and transportation nodes.[35]

Among the South American receiving societies, Brazil, as the largest, experienced a first post-independence phase of European migration from the 1820s to the 1860s, a period during which African slaves continued to be imported. German, Italian, and Polish settlers came to the coffee plantations of Rio Grande do Sul on the southern border, where investors had relocated because of soil exhaustion north of Rio de Janeiro. A second phase with vastly increased in-migration, departures, and transatlantic circular migrations began in the 1870s. In Argentina, too, the takeoff of in-migration came in the last third of the nineteenth century.[36]

To put into perspective the hopes for a better life in the Americas and the volume of migration, we have to remind ourselves that in the European context, Vienna was viewed as an El Dorado, Paris as a city of freedom, the German Ruhr district and London as providing multiple opportunities. Regardless of continent and destination, migrants valued the increase in choice when wages were paid in cash rather than in kind. The transatlantic migrations, beginning after 1815 and accelerating from Western and Northern Europe in the 1840s, created the frame and the ethnocultural neighborhoods and transatlantic family branches that, from the 1870s on, provided the proletarian mass migrants with first anchor points.

The Russo-Siberian Migration System

European Russia and its Siberian and Central Asian regions were arenas of several migration orbits: southern Russia, Siberia, and the Amur borderlands, northwestern European Russia. In a long struggle with the Ottoman Empire, tsarist armies expanded the state's territory to the Black Sea, subdued local Asian peoples, and opened the region for settlement of Ukrainian peasant families, and then also, from 1763 on, for southwest German-language peasants and religious refugees, Mennonites in particular. A kind of homestead law provided the migrants with land. These West Central Europeans could keep their faith and language and establish their own schools. Five decades later, authorities ended the admission of German-speakers because southeast European and Slavic migrants appeared to integrate better. Then potential eastbound migrants turned westward; from the 1880s, with revocation of privileges, Russian Mennonite and other German-language families would move in secondary migrations to North America.

Its huge distance away and its harsh living conditions made Siberia, in the view of tsarist authorities, ideal for penal colonies: An estimated hundred thousand Polish "rebels," fifty thousand Russian political exiles, and forty thousand criminals were sent there before 1914. About five thousand women, some with children, joined their deported husbands. To the contested border with China, the government sent troops and settlers. Peasants moved to southern Siberia on their own because of "free" land from which native people had been displaced and because thereby—turning distance to their advantage—they (almost) left the reach of tax collectors and other government officials.[37]

European Russia (which since the late eighteenth century included one-third of Poland as well as the Baltic peoples) had attracted or even invited Western European migrants for investment, technical expertise, commercial connections, and artisanal skills, as well as for military service. Because the Russian nobility owned the enserfed peasants and looked down on commercial activities, no indigenous middle and proletarian classes could develop: Migrants became an "inserted" middle class of different cultures and languages. For this very reason, Polish rulers had invited persecuted Jews from Western Europe to settle in their realms centuries earlier. The Ashkenazi Jewish culture had emerged from both these invitations and the West European pogroms.

From the early nineteenth century, the range of activities and regions of settlement open to Jews became ever more restricted. In 1804, Jews were designated as an urban people and ordered to leave the countryside—half a million men, women, and children were affected. In the mid-nineteenth century, further restrictions followed and the "May Laws" of 1882 prohibited settlement in rural areas altogether. From 1835 they were limited to a "pale of settlement": the traditional communities in Poland, Belorussia-Lithuania, and Ukraine, as well as areas in the Baltic provinces and regions of southern "New Russia." In the Kingdom of Poland, where the Jewish population almost tripled from 1816 to 1865, exclusionary legislation prevented Jews from living in many of the larger cities. The enforced and yet restricted mobility contributed to their concentration in stagnating small towns. In all of Russia, the Jewish population increased by 156 percent the three decades before 1867, a vast reservoir for outbound migrations. The pogroms of the 1880s provided the trigger.

In the early decades of industrialization, before the emancipation of serfs in 1861, common laborers and workers for the new industries needed to be recruited from among serfs. In the northern *obrok* system, serf duties had been monetized. Serfs paid their owners an annual sum from income obtained by sale of crops, cottage production, or labor migration. Some owners even helped their serfs to find city labor. Cottage production and seasonal migration resulted in higher literacy rates. In the south central belt with fertile soils and sufficient rain, the lords needed servile labor throughout the year and, under the *barschina* system, immobilized serfs by means of high work obligations. In St. Petersburg, founded in 1703 with the help of in-migrating Dutch drainage experts and German-language artisans, the temporary migrating servile labor force accounted for one-third of the 450,000 inhabitants around 1840. Such mobile rural people lost their utility once industrial production in the 1860s and 1870s began to require training and skills. The government first initiated programs to train local labor with the help of in-migrating foreign experts, and then it adjusted the structure of society in order to reduce the need for foreigners. Toward the end of the nineteenth century, due to the nobility, who were jealous of the position of West European migrants with social and human capital, and to Russian nationalism, immigrant foreigners lost their protected status. At the same time exchanges with Western Europe, French culture in particular, remained intense.

Late nineteenth-century European Russia was an industrializing society. Land shortages and cash crises were exacerbated by a near-doubling of the population of 68.5 million in 1850 to 126 million in all of Russia in 1897. Families' adjustment of child-bearing patterns to new socioeconomic circumstances achieved results only a generation later. Relative rural overpopulation resulted in migration and proletarianization, voluntary for those who desired wage incomes, involuntary for those who would have preferred to remain on the land. Romanov Russia, like the Hohenzollern territories east of the Elbe and the Danubian sections of the Habsburg monarchy, was characterized by a feudal-bourgeois type of socioeconomic development that contrasted with the bourgeois-capitalist ways of Western Europe and North America. These vast agrarian regions in the three semifeudal empires became reservoirs of labor through internal migration to Russian industry, through seasonal migration to German and Austrian agriculture and industry, and through emigration for other parts of Europe and North America.[38]

Peasant emancipation did not make men and women independent. Each village commune *(mir)* held land collectively, reallocated this commonwealth among its male "souls" annually, and was collectively responsible for payment of taxes, for redemption payments to former lords, and for sending recruits to the army. Out-migrating men remained part of the community, needed passes for seasonal or multiannual absence, and were expected to return for spring sowing or harvest work. Such seasonal migrants had to be fed in the village in winter, and they also returned during slumps in employment. Later, men who renounced their rights to land could leave permanently, but with no urban social security system in place, few chose this option. In the decade after emancipation (1861–1870), some thirteen million men migrated for one year or less. In the next decades migration increased continuously.[39]

In terms of mobility across the globe, the completion of networks of railroad lines with port cities and the introduction of steamships in the 1870s vastly increased the speed and volume of travel, though in view of the population growth not necessarily the rates of mobility. The improved means of transport and communication affected the outbound mass movements from Europe as well as return migration from the Americas—the "proletarian mass migration" began. Similarly, there was a quick growth in the mass migration of bound proletarianized men and women in the Indian Ocean and the Plantation Belt under a regime of temporary bondage imposed mainly by the British Empire. The ending of permanent bondage of serfs in Europe between the early 1800s and the 1860s, and of slaves in the Americas by the 1880s, permitted mobility, but it was constrained by color of skin: white Europeans could move regionally across Europe, transatlantically, or worldwide, but people of black African origin could move only regionally within the Americas. Population growth in almost all regions of the world sent people searching for "free"—that is, less densely settled—land and, far more so, for wage work. In East Asia, the same migratory potential also resulted in mass outbound mobility. Most African peoples' mobility remained constrained or controlled by the European colonizer states and the investor migrants or their personnel.

2. The Global and the Local

THE OUTLINE of migrations before the beginning of industrialization and transformation demonstrates that the movement of people as much as of goods was global then, and in fact even earlier. "Globalization" has a far longer history than the early twenty-first-century catchword suggests. To analyze movement of people, we need an understanding of the scope of regions across the globe that migrants connected, and a differentiation of categories of migration. We also need to understand systematically how migrant agency developed in the context of the society of birth, and how migrants developed belongings and identifications or—in an earlier interpretation—had national identities. Finally, we need to ask how migrants inserted themselves at their destination, if there was only one, or during the several layovers and at multiple points of arrival.

The approach of an older migration historiography involved a "progress of history" perspective, which usually neglected allegedly backward societies of departure, began at the port of entry, and assumed that only highly developed societies attract migrants. Most historical writing was generated in receiving countries, especially those of the Atlantic world, so a self-congratulatory tone emerged. Migrations within Europe, with few exceptions, began to attract interest only in the 1980s. Migrations elsewhere were studied in separate historiographical slots. The US Ellis Island approach to migration history saw "free" Europeans arrive with cultural baggage to be deposited before entering a melting pot. It subsumed other migrants under the labels *coolie* and *slave,* designations that connote passivity and even inferiority. No comparative approach or scholarly exchange with historians of the Chinese diaspora and its migrations or those of the Indian Ocean emerged.[40]

European immigrants arriving in North America at Ellis Island Immigration Station in New York Harbor, ca. 1904. Ellis Island, an entry gate for immigrants from Europe since 1892, was considered both an "island of hope" and an "island of tears." Very few immigrants were rejected, because European officials had already refused departure to those deemed not admissible. But while waiting for inspection, immigrants still felt fear that they might be excluded. (Library of Congress)

Spaces of Mobility

In the above survey, geographic denominations, whether continents or oceans, have been reconfigured as major socioeconomic regions with locational references such as the Atlantic economies, the Plantation Belt, and the several distinct cultural regions of Asia. Physical geography, except as hindering or facilitating mobility, has little meaning for migrants. What is important is how particular locations are imbued with meaning, "home" or "better opportunities," and how societies experienced as constraining are being connected with others assumed or known to provide better options. Geographic *places* thus become lived social *spaces* and, in Arjun Appadurai's term, *scapes*. Beyond the spatialization of physical geography by social and economic life, a land-scape or a sea-scape is lived space imbued with meaning, is a fixed geography in flexible frames of interpretation. Migrants' writings show how a person leaving his or her space of birth and socialization appropriates new landscapes or sea-lanes into the familiar frame of reference for geographies or, if they do not fit, may label them "strange," "alien," or "exotic" rather than expand or change the frame of reference.

An Italian or Chinese migrant, for example, leaving a family plot far inland from the emigration port will experience the first leg of the route—on foot, cart, or carrier animal—as slow, the landscape as familiar. The bustle of the port will seem unfamiliar, hectic, difficult to decipher. The voyage across the Atlantic or the China Seas will be short, at least in memory, because nothing of interest is being recorded. What for mariners is a sea-lane, for a rural or urban migrant is an empty expanse. If arriving from Genoa in New York, he or she will see the El-trains and report back to friends and family that trains are going over the roofs of houses. Among the recipients, such a piece of information is difficult to place within the customary frame of reference: "at home," only birds fly over roofs. If arriving from Guangdong in Manila, merchants would have mental maps connecting the trading ports, artisans would concern themselves with similarities and differences between their neighborhoods. Geographies and their social usages are developed in people's minds and emerge as comprehensive scapes. Because such mental understanding and appropriation of spaces changes constantly, scholars have introduced the concept of "processual geographies" to counter the traditional notion of fixed place.[41]

For historians of migration, as for those of the movement of goods, the transport connections between different spaces matter as much as to migrants and traders. Such connectivity was overlooked in bordered nation-state approaches to history from top down, from nonmigrating statesmen's and historians' viewpoints. State approaches add fixed territorial boundaries to fixed geographies and, in the nation-state version, add national-cultural boundaries as a third fixed dividing line. Nation-state historiographies separate themselves from neighboring communities and societies or distant linked ones. If some 150 million men and women migrated in the three major migration systems quantified by McKeown, 320 million across international border from the 1840s to the 1940s, and additional hundreds of millions moved medium distance across international borders, nation-state historiography would need to incorporate them as much into their narratives as economic sectors extending across the world. Where was the cotton, necessary to clothe statesmen and commoners alike, grown, how was it transported, where was it processed? How did plantation, mining, and factory workers and investors and their overseers, clerks, and technicians move to satisfy the demand for cloth or, at courts, for luxury goods?[42]

To understand interconnectedness, scholars have criticized the reification of dividing borders, the vagueness of "global" expanses, the simplification of a "global village." People are socialized during infancy, childhood, and adolescence into the space and value systems of their locality of birth in family, local society, and regional or statewide educational institutions. Separating themselves from the parental household in their late teens, they tend to search for jobs (or tillable land) or professional options in the region familiar to them or in others accessible through information feedback. They may have to take into account statewide labor markets and regulations. Thus, the local, the regional, and the statewide form three sequential layers of socialization and experience. The economic sphere, in which they search for an income-providing occupation, does not necessarily stop at the borders of their state of birth. Meso- or macroregions, the interconnected Caribbean islands or Europe's landmass, for example, are accessible through road, rail, and shipping connections. Thus, scholars need to establish empirically the extent of migrant geographies, spaces, and scapes. For 1870 as a specific point in time, for example, it makes no sense to speak of generic "European" migrants: Those from the western and west-central regions of Europe had moved for generations to particular destinations afar and had connected them in mental maps; those from southern segments had moved to different locations and had established their specific information flows; those from northern regions were relative newcomers to transoceanic expanses. Similarly, the regions of recruitment of indentured laborers and the regions of departure of migrants in India shifted over time, expanded and contracted as did the destinations. For each period, spaces of migration and their micro-, meso-, or macroregional extent need to be delineated, because social geographies are in flux.[43]

Conceptually, research distinguishes between *inter*-state and *trans*-border moves: the "inter" posits two distinct entities, usually polities, as in "international;" the "trans" emphasizes continuities and overlapping spaces. The validity of the recent conceptualization of "transnational" needs to be questioned. In its original formulation it was applied to migrants since the 1990s, a period in which nation-states lost some of their hold on societal developments and much of their hold over economies. In the later nineteenth century, most migrants originated not in nation-states but in empires—the Qing, Romanov, Habsburg, Hohenzollern, and Windsor realms, the labels of which were being nationalized into China, Russia, Austria-Hungary, Germany, Britain—though every one of them contained many peoples and the Habsburg empire called itself a "state of many peoples" *(Vielvölkerstaat).*

The term *transcultural* provides a comprehensive meaning for movements between societies, regardless of geographic distance traversed: translocal, transregional, transnational or trans-state, transoceanic. Although ideologues of the nation-state, historians included, posited migration as occurring from nation to ethnic enclave in another nation, 94 percent of the European-origin migrants arriving in the United States in the early twentieth century traveled from their place of birth or a previous migration destination to friends and kin in a particular locality in the United States. They migrated in family and friendship networks between urban neighborhoods or villages and, in the frame of family economies as well as individual aspirations, between mesoregional or national economies. Self-determined migrations and recruitment of indentured workers also connected specific regions of India or China to particular regions and localities in the Plantation Belt. A recent approach calls such migrations "glocal"—connecting local social spaces in one society with specific spaces in another across the globe. Family economies may thus connect individuals and constraining frames with opportunity structures across locations in several continents or macroregions. An early twentieth-century southern Chinese peasant family might thus establish a second base on Canada's Pacific coast and perhaps branch out to inland cities. People sought options on the basis of information provided by reliable members of their network at destinations to which possibilities of travel existed. Only in some states' overblown mythologies did they reach for "unlimited opportunities."[44]

A Typology of Migrations

Both everyday language and scholarly terminologies aggregate multiple migrations into undifferentiated, often implicitly value-laden catch-all terms. Views of migrants common in the United States and the neo-Europes saw hardy men (without mention of hardy women) colonize assumedly virgin rural regions and bequeath the land to generations of children: white-skinned Europeans as cultivators of wooded wilderness and prairie grasslands. The earlier residents held different views of such intrusions, which often turned them into refugees. The designation "proletarian mass migration" for the Atlantic world's decades from the 1870s to 1914 implies that all migrants were urban workers.

A comprehensive approach analyzes migrants' decisions and trajectories—within institutional frames—in a spectrum from free to forced, from local to intercontinental, from seasonal to permanent, as well as in terms of the range of goals to be achieved at the destination. Within each and every type, gendering is required: men and women are assigned different roles, have different experiences and different goals. Intergenerational aspects also need to be included. A classification along the free/unfree or self-willed/bound axis yields the following categories:

- free migrants who decide when to depart and where to go according to their own desires and life-projects on the basis of trustworthy information available within the frames societies and states impose;
- labor migrants, the "free" transatlantic migrants of the late nineteenth century and of the late twentieth-century South-to-North migrations, who, however, live under often severe economic constraints and thus decide to depart "self-willed" under duress;
- bound-labor migrants who have to sell their labor for a number of years because of poverty (European and Asian indentured servants and credit-ticket migrants);
- forced-labor migrants who are enslaved for menial work for life (Africans in the Atlantic world), who are enslaved for service or intellectual labor (Africans

in the Indian Ocean world and people elsewhere), who are bound for a certain period of their life against their will (South Africa under apartheid), or who are corralled by force and interned for an indeterminate period (Nazi Germany, imperialist Japan, the Stalinist Soviet Union);

- involuntary migrants displaced by political intolerance (exiles), by religious intolerance (religious refugees), or by other causes like ethnocultural or gender-based inequalities;
- refugees from war and other violence;
- persons displaced by ecological disasters whether natural or human-made, the latter meaning *men*-made.[45]

Transatlantic and transpacific migrants of the turn of the twentieth century—like Third-to-First-World migrants of the turn of the twenty-first century—made and make decisions "free" *under the constraints of economic conditions* that leave no room for life-projects or even survival. Their "home" may be a society that is unfair and unsupportable, that does not permit sustainable lives. Institutionalized restrictions of colonialism, imperialism, and racism constrained decisions; gendered restrictions and sexism were intended to prevent women from making their own decisions. Children have to follow parents even though they may resent being separated from friends and other family. On the other hand, parents may migrate and accept a downward move during their own lifetime to improve, in a middle-range perspective, the life chances of their children; men may migrate to better provide for their wives. "Free" decisions are framed, in the double meaning, by systems of reference at best and massive constraints at worst. Involuntary migrants, refugees and exiles, depart under political, ethnoracial, gender, or other persecution; because of warfare within or between states; social ostracism or fundamentalist religious pressures; tradition-bound stagnation or other. Usually refugees hope to return if conditions improve in their society of birth. Forced migrants are torn out of their social environments by military, police, or private entrepreneurs, whether raiders for forced laborers, slave catchers, or traffickers in the sex trade.

Distance of migration may be short, medium, or long. Migration of long geographic distances may lead to similar occupations and cultural environments: Indian Ocean port cities were part of transoceanic commercial and migration networks with similar labor practices and trading protocols; rural young men heading for work on another continent often remained in earthwork and lived among migrant compatriots. Similarly, geographic proximity does not necessarily imply cultural proximity. Young peasant women moving to domestic labor in middle-class households of nearby towns and cities face transitions across class and status lines. In the past, greater distance often involved higher travel cost in terms of both transportation and time. Cost also depends on means of transport; land-bound voyaging was usually more expensive than water-borne ship travel. Patterns of travel became time-compressed in the 1870s with the introduction of steamships and again from the mid-1950s with air travel.

As regards intended duration, migration might be seasonal, annual, multi-annual, for working life, or permanent. In agricultural societies across the globe, men and women, sometimes with their children, migrated and migrate seasonally to harvest work or to food processing, temporarily to mines or factories, or multi-annually to a distant branch of an internationally active company, whether a multinational textile company of the late nineteenth century or a 1920s automobile firm, or to domestic service and caregiving work. People might leave for a number of years to gain additional experience in a craft or at a university, to set up a branch of a family business, or for income-generating reasons. Migrants often plan to stay for only a number of years, but both poor labor markets "at home" and adjustment to the receiving society may induce them to extend their sojourn. Thus some, wanting to return, become unwillingly permanent migrants. Others adjust and stay as unintentionally permanent migrants.

From the 1870s to the 1930s, about one-third of the migrants to the United States, labeled "immigrants" in public and in research terminologies, returned to Europe, more to Asia. They were temporary or, to use a modern problem-laden term, "guest" workers. Most of the indentured servants from Asian societies returned to their respective regions of departure, but some—jointly with free passenger migrants—formed communities at the destinations, whether Indians in Natal and the Caribbean or Chinese in Malaya and the Americas. In the Atlantic migrations, two-fifths of the migrants were women; after 1930 women accounted for just over 50 percent. In migrations within the Indian Ocean and the seas of East and Southeast Asia their share was lower. However, when men decided to stay and form communities and, because of racial and ethnic hierarchies, could not marry women from the resident cultural groups, marriage migration increased the ratio of women, and families began to be formed through transoceanic correspondence.[46]

In the three-quarters of a century from 1870 to 1945, inter-state agricultural settlement migrations remained limited; inter-state bound and free labor migrations accounted for the majority of the long-distance moves; migrations of professionals were small in number. *Intra*-state migrations related to urbanization and industrialization were far larger in volume than *inter*-state ones. In many cities across the urbanizing segments of the globe, more than half of the population had not been born there. Small, but extremely powerful, were the migrations of white men (and some women) from the European to the colonized segments of the globe. Their armed political and economic domination resulted in intensification of colonial penetration and of mobilization of working men and women of colors other than white for the plantations and mines across the subtropical and tropical segments of the globe.

A Systems Approach to Migration

To understand the complexity of migrant men and women's agency in local and society-wide frames as well as during their trajectories between societies, historians have developed a systems approach. This comprehensive theoretical-methodological frame incorporates causational and incidental factors and outcomes as well as multiple rationalities. Specifically, it connects migration patterns and decisions in terms of (1) the society of departure in local, regional, statewide, and global frames; (2) the actual move across distance given an era's means of transportation and communication; (3) the society or societies of destination again in micro-, meso-, and macroregional perspectives; and (4) linkages between the communities in which migrants spent or spend part of their lives. Its interdisciplinary and transcultural character permits analyses of the structures and institutions—which constantly evolve and thus could be called processual structures and structured processes. It also permits analytical inclusion of the discursive frames of migration in the societies of origin and of arrival in particular local or regional variants. It deals with all aspects, including industrialization, urbanization, social stratification, gender roles and family economies, demographic characteristics, political situation and developments, educational institutions, religious or other belief systems, ethnocultural composition, and traditions of short- and long-distance migrations. The approach emphasizes lived culture and indicates how the interrelated economic, social, political, and technological forces converge into migrants' cultural "habitus" and whole way of life.[47] The systems approach analyzes societies as they reshape within the global hierarchy of domination, dependency, and development. Societies and economies have been and are linked globally through families spread across several countries.

The systems approach analyzes the impact of out-migration on families and societies of departure and of in-migration on receiving societies and specific communities. What did out-migration mean for agricultural villages, whole agrarian regions, or urban neighborhoods, whether in China or in Europe? The decisions of millions of men and women to depart change communities and societies of origin as much as those in which they establish transitory or permanent homes. This agency approach needs to be modified in the cases of forced, indentured, or enslaved workers, as well as refugee migrants who are deprived of agency at the time of departure. But their postmigration survival and insertion depends on choices, even if under severely constraining conditions. Slave acculturation resulted in African-origin cultures in the Americas, and refugees impacted on labor markets and social customs, whether Koreans under Japan's occupation or German Jews in 1930s Turkey. People act in their own perceived best interest but do so under conditions not of their own making but imposed by historical developments and power structures.

Precipitating and facilitating factors for migration include rigid stratification and class structures that prevent upward mobility or choice of economic activity. Established patterns of mobility ease departures because potential migrants may rely on information and, often, on guides. People traveling from Hong Kong to San Francisco or Vancouver, from rural village communities to St. Petersburg, or from small towns to Buenos Aires, follow clearly, if often orally, demarcated routes. The self-reinforcing attractiveness of migration systems emerges from information generated and easily accessible. Distances to be traversed, cultural affinities, possibilities (and cost) of regular return, congruence of skills and job openings inform migration decisions rather than imagined future wealth.

Societal arrangements and processes always impact on migration, but states' roles changed dramatically from emigration regulation or prohibition, until the mid-nineteenth century in many dynastic states, to immigration controls in the late nineteenth and early twentieth-century Atlantic world and subsequently elsewhere. The introduction of state-issued passports changed a travel document from a permit to pass a port of entry into an instrument to exclude those of other cultures, colors of skin, or class. It took decades for states to fully enforce such controls. Asians—women at first—were restricted from North America in the mid-1870s; for Europeans, regulations were tightened but near-exclusion came only in the 1920s; along the US-Mexican border, patrols initiated in the mid-1920s were meant to limit the movement of "brown" people out of Mexico but several economic sectors in the United States depended on their labor. In Europe, passport laws were operationalized faster. In a side effect, they made 1930s flight from fascist states difficult as states denied entry to refugees without papers. Under national chauvinism, especially under fascism, and in cases of corrupt political elites, whole states have become refugee-generating apparatuses. Oppressive and self-enriching political elites lose the trust of large segments of the society.

High rates of out-migration change states and societies. In phases of demographic transition, emigration might decrease pressure on labor markets and permit wages to rise and standards of living to improve. Thus, societies might become more stable. But out-migration may also reduce the need to create jobs or to reform constraining structures and thus exacerbate tensions. Policy makers and administrators feared loss of tax revenues and army recruits as well as loss of women able to bear children for the state's armies; others wanted to rid their polity of what they considered surplus populations. Only recently has the social cost of emigration been conceptualized: Families and societies "invest" in raising and educating (as yet unproductive) children. These, as adults, "repay" intrafamily and intrasocietal investment by intergenerational transfer of the cost of caring for the "dependent" young and old. This "compact between generations" is broken when people withdraw from the obligation by emigrating. Working-age migrants take their accumulated individual and social capital with them. States of birth cannot recover social costs, and states of destination, getting trained and educated men and women "for free," benefit from their productivity and taxes. This has been called "development aid" given by poorer societies to more-developed societies.

Out-migration deprives societies of departure of part of the human capital that, given the respective state's economic stage of development, often cannot be used there. Emigrants may send back remittances and thus contribute both to their family's budget and to the state's foreign currency reserves. The budgets of some sending states, such as late nineteenth-century Italy, have depended and still depend on individual migrants' remittances. Though some economists and politicians have extolled investment opportunities provided by such transfers, the recipient families often need such funds to prevent their daily lives from sliding below subsistence level. Migrants may also transfer ideas through communication or return in person. Such innovation may improve stagnant economies, but elites benefiting from the old state of affairs often impede or prevent change and reform.

The actual process of transition to a location in another society may be extended over time, compressed into a few days, or delayed if, for example, refugees are stacked away in camps rather than being able to restructure their lives. Obstacles to departure include cost of travel, which needs to be related to the days, months, or years of work it takes to procure the sum necessary. During the period of voyaging, formerly extended, no income may be earned. Emigration regulations may pose barriers; the barriers posed by immigration restrictions might be almost insurmountable. Racial barriers erected in the Anglo-American and European societies against "people of color" made entry difficult. Inducements include prepaid tickets sent by earlier migrants or, in the case of indentured migrants, contractually guaranteed return fare. Even more so, they include accurate information on the trip and the availability of income-generating positions after arrival.

Arrangements for travel are made on the basis of information sent by prior migrants, with the help of guides from the community, or by labor recruiters. For centuries, "travel agencies" arranged package tours: medieval Christian pilgrims destined for Jerusalem or Muslim Hajj pilgrims are examples. From the mid-nineteenth century, migrants across Europe contracted with the local representative of a reliable agency connected to the distant shipping and railroad companies; contract laborers in India or China would approach a recruiting office that would also take charge of the trip. Change of trains and embarkation was done under supervision of the agencies' personnel—the voyage was as organized like modern group tourism.

Some migrants move stepwise, first as far as their limited funds take them— perhaps to a job-providing city, ideally the port (in the present: the airport) of future departure. For some, the need to earn money for the next leg of the trip was an unwelcome delay, for others a welcome stopover for a first adjustment. Travel experiences and emotional coping vary from person to person. To gauge the capabilities required of migrants, we need to be aware that many nineteenth-century emigrants had never seen a train or a ship before they stepped aboard one. Accounts reflect both easygoing confidence and bewilderment. From the imposition of immigration controls, admission procedures were fraught with fears of rejection. Even the US rules, liberal for migrants from Asia to the mid-1870s and for those from Europe to 1917, were difficult to negotiate because of frequent administrative changes, lack of precise information, and sometimes abusive treatment. Such regulations had a gendered impact: women faced more administrative harassment than men.

Migrants live and, if self-willed, decide at both ends of their trajectory, comparing labor markets and other income-generating options. They select perceived increased options in a place accessible given their means and where they expect to be able to communicate, given their language. Far more migrants moved to a neighboring city or job-providing mine, plantation, or other site than crossed oceans. The intercontinental connections directed them to communities of previous migrants of the same language. Job-providing economies of destination for the period of imperialism—as for other periods—need to be placed in the global as well as mesoregional hierarchies of political and economic power relations. The sociopolitical frames of the receiving societies need to be analyzed with the same comprehensiveness as those of the societies of departure.[48]

National Identities, Societal Belongings, Identifications

If territorially bordered states or culturally bordered nations were not the primary identification of migrants, two questions demand answers: Why has a nation-state approach been so dominant in migration history? Why do receiving societies refer to migrants by labeling them according to national origin? States do have an impact on research because they collect data on mobility, but often only at international borders and not about internal migrations. Such data lump together people of different regions, dialects, and social attributes, aggregate those of majority with those of minority cultures, and often do not count women separately. Important as they are, the data provide only a skewed image of the composition of migrant populations and of overall mobility. Scholars using nation-state-produced data necessarily use nation-state terminologies for the people they are analyzing. In public discourse in receiving societies, the variety of cultures within states-of-origin is usually not known: migrants from India became generic "Hindoos," those from a particular region in China generic "Chinese," and German-speakers from the many different regions generic "Germans" or, misnamed, "Dutch." Such naming implies ascription of national identities. It emerged in the nineteenth-century climate of opinion: first, in the emergence of (middle-class) national consciousness in juxtaposition to status-centered nobility's cultures and dynastic interests; second, in the self-organization of the middle classes in the national revolutions of 1848–1849; and third, in the aggressive national chauvinisms. National descriptors are further complicated by the development of the Russian, German, Austrian, and English descriptors within empires that comprised many peoples. In the colonized regions the colonizer/colonized or white/colored dichotomies were the main demarcation lines.

In much writing the *early* nineteenth-century national consciousness, a pride in group culture, has been conflated with the *late* nineteenth-century nations' chauvinism and the self-assertion of "minority" cultures. Such authors saw imperial structures as given and depicted struggles for self-rule as disruptive and responsible for the refugee-generating warfare of the early twentieth century. Legitimate affirmation of group culture (internally differentiated by gender, generation, age, class, and region) became oppressive when a polity's largest ethnic group not only designated itself "nation" but also denigrated all other cultures in the same territory as "minorities." The creation of such cultural hierarchies stood diametrically opposed to the age of revolution's political human-rights concept of each and every human being as equal before the law. The contradiction notwithstanding, political practice and political theory merged the concepts into the nation-state construct in which citizens were equal before the law—unless they were of non-national culture, of lower-class status, or of female gender. Equal rights were extended to lower-class men from the turn of the twentieth century, to women from the 1920s. In the same period, men and women from marginalized cultural groups migrated to states granting, if not equal, then at least better, status.

Migrants depart with regional cultural practices. In the later nineteenth century these did become homogenized to some degree within nation-states, but national chauvinism in Europe's empires exacerbated ethnocultural differentiations. In their society of destination, migrants would cherish the language, food habits, and other practices of everyday life they brought with them. But they would discard the society of origin's emperor worship, class hierarchies, or, if women, gender hierarchies. Migrants thus show both cultural affinities to previous ways of life and clear dislikes of the unacceptable aspects. Rather than arriving with a national identity, they came with cultural practices and with goals for life-projects that they could not realize "at home." (This is similar for migrants at the turn of the twenty-first century from, for example, Indonesia or West African states, who migrate to neighboring states, Europe, or North America.)

Recent scholarship avoids the term *national identity* as an analytical category but continues to analyze its ascriptive functions. It asks how people identify themselves and discusses multiple identifications. It explores how migrants relate to new structures, institutions, communities, and ways of life: it studies *belongings* rather than identities. Migrant self-organization validates this approach: migrants from the Qing Empire might have been labeled "Chinese," but they organized themselves by home region and family group; migrants from Europe might have been labeled Hungarians, but they organized themselves by regional cultural affinity. Faith and class or status also played a role in postmigration self-organization. The receiving society's institutions, once said to demand unconditional surrender of previous culture or "assimilation" to a new national identity, provide embeddedness (or marginalization). Newcomers are not "in limbo" or even "uprooted" (unless refugees or forced migrants), but they acquire knowledge of the new changeable structures, cultural practices, and institutional processes only gradually. Once the concepts of a fixed "identity" and the paradigm of nation-to-ethnic-enclave migrations are abandoned, steps toward participation may be empirically observed and analyzed. Acculturation is the process of selectively fusing old and new ways of life, coming to terms with societal structures and political institutions, and thus developing new identifications and belongings.

Transitions are facilitated by supportive migrant or ethnocultural patterns of self-help in mutual aid associations or by cultural clustering in ethnocultural neighborhoods. The formerly used term "ethnic ghetto" implied nation-rooted genetic or bloodline identity and suggested a self-segregation of migrants incapable of dealing with the "new world" around them. "Ghetto" may also be a reference, more empirically grounded, to segregation into slots of inferiority by the receiving society. Ethnocultural communities rarely achieve "institutional completeness," because its adult members leave its confines daily for their workplaces and the younger ones for schools. Individuals and families constantly negotiate the demands of their life-projects in the frame of both new structures and options and cherished aspects of pre-migration ways of life. They negotiate between community cohesion and the political strength it may provide and openness to the many options the receiving society at large provides. No "New England" or "New Spain," no "Chinatown," "Little Italy," or "Little Manila" ever replicated the society of departure. All emerged from negotiation and compromises with the new environment. Outside observers saw ethnic enclaves emerge, segregation of migrants by the receiving society was frequent, and self-segregation into neighborhoods and communities facilitated acculturation. However, as data for Chicago show in detail, the perceived mono-ethnic communities were, in fact, on the street level, areas of geographically mixed settlement where such mixing implied contact but not integrated social networks.[49]

Some groups have been said to form diasporic consciousnesses, a conceptualization that originates from the historic Greek and Jewish dispersions. Ancient Greek migrations, however, involved a fusion of several cultures, with the Persian and Egyptian cultures in particular. Hellenism thus was an Eastern Mediterranean syncretic culture and as such original rather than Greek-diasporic. From the Jews' expulsions, migrations, and persecutions an ideal-type "diaspora" may be deduced if also differentiated: People defined by religion, everyday practices, cultural ways of expression (high literacy), and—perhaps—genetic similarity because of intermarriage migrate under duress (destruction of the Second Temple by the in-migrant Roman rulers): westward to southern Europe and northern Africa, eastward to the Indian Ocean littorals. As diaspora they were defined by a shared memory of a cultural-geographic homeland and by communication between the different communities in the many regions of arrival. This connectedness differentiates diasporas from ethnic enclaves. However, rather than coalesce into a single diaspora, migrants of Jewish faith differentiated into a Sephardic community and an Ashkenazi community, as well as into distinct other groups in Asia and elsewhere. Distinctiveness, including different dialects, may overshadow connectedness. Most nineteenth-century migrant communities did not develop strong global connectedness. Italian, Polish, and Scottish migrants spread worldwide but did not always remain connected. Imperial administrative channels rather than diasporic community formation connected the worldwide British and French colonizer personnel. The multidirectional migration of southern Chinese is better analyzed by region of destination—Nanyang (southeast insular Asia), Australia, the Latin American and Anglo-American Pacific coasts.[50]

The late nineteenth-century intensification of nationalism, in the two complementary variants of armed nation-states and expansionist chauvinist ideologies, has had major consequences as regards emigration (release from membership, expulsion) and immigration (admission, imposed assimilation). Many states with a relative surplus population, that is, men and women who would not find jobs to support themselves, were happy to see the departure of such potential for militant change. Some placed obstacles in the way of men who, it was posited, should be available to die for their country in military service. European states with resident "minority" cultures increased emigration of these by reducing educational opportunities in other than the majority language, by disadvantaging economic development in peripheral regions, and by not providing equal access to state institutions and labor markets. Furthermore, with increasing demands for self-rule among peoples of the Balkans, of divided Poland, and of the western tsarist empire, people of unwanted religions, like Jews in Russia, or of unwanted cultures, like Slovaks in Hungary, began to be persecuted or, in the case of the Habsburg-Ottoman military frontier, to be deported: Populations that did not fit the construct of monocultural nation-states had to be eliminated. Such state violence has been called "ethnic cleansing" of a national home, though there is no reason to assume monocultural nations to be cleaner than many-cultured societies. Some states, reaching beyond their territorial borders, began to use "their" emigrant nationals as a bridgehead for economic and cultural penetration of receiving societies. Such instrumentalized people became "enemy aliens" to be interned or deported in wartime. "The growth of the modern nation-state implied not only the naming of certain peoples as enemies of the nation, but also the expulsion of significant groups for whom the state would or could not assume responsibility." The First World War "schooled the new masters" of nation-state apparatuses: "Civilians could become dangerous enemies . . . , it was best to eject unwanted [groups]." Under such conditions proactive departure as "free" migrants helped people survive.[51]

In receiving societies, too, migrants considered to be of different status under dynastic rule began to be treated as Other and marginalized. An exception is the treatment of newcomers from Europe in Latin America, where they were considered racially more desirable than resident native people, and in Australia, where they were needed to make the country economically viable. Admission restrictions first excluded those who could be identified by color of skin and who were genetically constructed as "race," that is, as inferior. Jewish ghettoization and Asian exclusion became the prototypes. Next, Anglo-Saxon and Teutonic ideologues, buttressed by so-called scientific racism, agitated for exclusion of the darker or olive "races" of Europe, East and South Europeans as well as the Irish, who, colonized and Catholic, were less than "white." From the 1880s newcomers and resident "minorities" were subject to acculturation pressures, whether in America, Canada, Germany, Russia, or Austria. The Welsh and Scots had been Anglicized centuries earlier. Such pressures induced earlier migrants who, under the eighteenth century's different incorporation regime, had been granted the privilege to practice their religion and speak their language—groups like Mennonites in the tsarist realm, for example—to depart in secondary migrations to more flexible societies. At the apogee of nationalism, democratic-republican states' attempts to enforce assimilation replaced absolutist dynastic societies' acceptance of pluralism among a ruler's subjects.[52]

Cultural and racial hierarchies—but no nation-state ideology—also existed in other segments of the world. In the many South Asian societies, lighter color of skin was considered a mark of status; in parts of China the migrant Hakka people suffered from marginalization; imperialist Japan pursued a policy of superiority that relegated Koreans, Manchurians, and Chinese to an inferior position. At the turn of the twentieth century, racialized identity politics became instruments of refugee-generation and of in-migrant segregation. In a complex interaction, migrant-generating nation-state policies were paralleled by migrant-segregating or exclusionist policies of migrant-receiving nation-states. Across the world, but in the Atlantic economies in particular, labor migrants became a segregated underclass with no equal access to the institutions of the state to which their taxes contributed. Around 1900, Jews, Slavs, or Mediterraneans who did not find acceptance could blend in only over generations. As residents after migration, they remained "foreigners," were subject to "alien laws," and could be deported. Under earlier societal frameworks, migrants had been able to find a slot or be granted a status that permitted economic activities and, often, cultural expression. The most-cited cases are Huguenots in Europe and Chinese in Southeast Asia. Policies that marginalized migrants as Other made insertion, acculturation, and belonging difficult. Although in the 1920s some criticism of exclusion, (scientific) racism, and discrimination was voiced, the onset of the Great Depression increased support for restrictions. New attitudes would emerge in reaction to the racism of fascist European and corporatist Japanese expansion and its immense refugee generation and death toll.[53]

It needs to be added that the transition to nation-states also could have positive implications for belongings. Societies could provide for, at first, limited participation in policy making that did create "belongings." People did develop an affinity to their nation of birth if cultural-structural practices changed to provide increased options and more equality. The in-migrant receiving societies, in particular the Anglo–North American societies, many countries in Latin America, and Australia, pursued integrative policies for white men and their female and child-age dependents. After decolonization from the 1950s on, Western political scientists and political advisers would transport the analytically untenable nation-state concept to the newly independent states, most of which combined peoples of many cultures.

Color-Coded Colonials and Bound Bodies

Debates about citizenship and belonging had their counterpart in a body-parts approach to migrants. The calls for additional "hands," "muscles," or "braceros" indicates as much, and so does the sexual exploitation of women and, perhaps, men. The emaciated bodies of "coolies" attest to the physical aspects of migration, and European workingmen brutalized by company thugs in the United States felt they had been "raped" and noted that they were forced to sell their bodies on a "flesh market." In contrast, British middle-class "boys" in their twenties or even thirties migrated to the white Dominions where outdoor physical labor would "make a man" out of them. Furthermore, all exclusionist movements argued by color of skin, genes, and bloodlines. Men and women were reduced to bodies in oppressive migration regimes.

While "at home" the Western colonizer societies denied or, under the impact of both workers' and women's militancy across borders, debated the political and human rights of workers and women, discrimination was exacerbated in the colonized segments of the world where skin or the color of it entered into the establishment of hierarchies. Colonizer personnel, predominantly male, in Senegal, India, or Indochina, for example, had to construct all indigenous people as inferior and unfit for inclusion. The construction of nationals and colonials was inextricably entwined. Strong men from self-styled advanced nations were ruling weak colonized peoples, the imperial ideologues asserted. The subalterns, trained to observe the masters so as not to incur their wrath, did observe them. They saw men without the knowledge of the society's language of communication; men who extolled their own culture but totally lacked understanding of the culture into which they had been sent; men with sexuality but without women; men who could not or would not do their own housework. The colonizer migrants were caught in many contradictions, as Ann Stoler and others have pointed out—that is why firepower was so important to their sending states.[54]

Earlier historiography written in terms of empire overlooked the construction of masculinity and gender roles. The strong men knew that they lacked stamina for plantation or mining work or even the will to make their own tea. Because women from their own culture, in the everyday sexism of the times that considered women the weaker sex and fit only for service tasks, were not available, men from the indigenous people had to be ordered or forced do such work. To fit this role ascription they had to be demasculinized and constructed as weak, as effeminate, as unable to act by and speak for themselves. The "manly Englishman" (and any other colonizer man) constructed the "effeminate Bengali" (or any other colonial man), to use Mrinalini Sinha's felicitous phrase.[55]

British officials, for example, in Burma, considered the empire to be engaged in a "human experiment to sweep away the cowardly, the inefficient, the weak." Colonial men had to become "strong," able to confront the world, if necessary "savage" and ready to destroy: "He must learn to be a man." That was what seasoned army officers and administrators in the colonies also told their younger countrymen who, sent off from their familiar surroundings by their families and the state to do duty in contexts alien to them, were deprived of emotional comfort and embeddedness. When colonial men did struggle to push others aside, as in the First Indian War for Independence (the "Mutiny" of 1857, in British parlance), they were gunned down. A future US president, Theodore Roosevelt, went out as Rough Rider to gain Cuba for US planters. Japanese officers in 1930s China saw the Chinese as weaklings to be shunted aside to make room for the more manly and ruthless conquering men. Imperial and capitalist strategists, like those of Latin American mestizo ruling classes, relied on constructions of men's bodies.

If colonizer countries exported young men, young women could not marry. British population planners sent off "surplus women," those who would not find husbands "at home," to become "imperial mothers" in the colonies. Other women migrated by their own choice and for their own purposes. Wives of ranking colonizer administrators were part of the ritual display of power in many subjugated regions. Depending on empire or period, the imperial planners of colonial rule at first encouraged men's unions with native women. Concubinage was considered medically less dangerous than consorting with prostitutes. The bodies of colonized women were to be available for colonizing men. Japanese military planners drafted Korean women as prostitutes for soldiers.

However, consensual relationships between migrant men and resident women of different skin colors were not to the liking of white Church authorities. Imperial Christian missionaries insisted on white-to-white monogamous church-celebrated marriage and underpinned their dogma by stigmatizing women of colors other than white as squaws, as promiscuous and dirty. They did not interfere when plantation owners and their overseers refused to assume the wage expense of 1:1 ratios of productive to reproductive labor by excluding women from labor recruitment. In view of the low wages, men could not afford to bring unemployed wives. Some policy makers, in Australia for example, admitted that such separating of husband and wife by admission of male laborers only was inhumane. But they did not change the system, because "colored" children born to "coolie" couples on Australian soil would be British citizens, and it was feared that, if they were boys, when they grew up they would partner with white women.

Exclusion based on skin color as a phenotypic marker was treated like it was a necessity for the white race's existence. It was not sex but the potential life-giving consequences that caused racial exclusion. Individual identifications and identity ascriptions were contingent on global power relations mediated by migrating colonizer personnel.[56]

The "anthropology of empire" involves analysis of the construction of Others in gendered and sexualized terms—sexual violence and exploitation included. However, the relationships also involve consensual unions and the concomitant cultural exchanges, "tender ties" on the "intimate frontiers of empire," as Sylvia Van Kirk noted. The regime of bound-labor migration, which deprived the predominantly male labor force of the option to develop cultural and, through family procreation, intergenerational communities, was the reverse side of nation-building processes based on families in which mothers inculcated national virtues into children. Neither Polish harvest laborers in imperial Germany nor Indian plantation laborers in the British Empire could migrate as families. Nation-states' regimes of migrant admission and exclusion, both to the metropole and to the colonies, were deeply gendered and racialized.[57]

To summarize, the comprehensive or systems approach to migration requires that the society of origin, as a frame of state and nation, as a region, and as a locality of origin, is studied in its whole layered complexity to understand the individual and social capital migrants have at departure and the networks in which they act. This society needs to be placed in global perspective as regards job and income opportunities as well as racial and ethnic hierarchies and interstate power relations. Within each group, gender roles and relations determine both options to migrate as well as discriminations and income differentials. In some societies children and young adolescents have to migrate and need to be studied separately. Only a gendered approach can explain the formation of intergenerational communities. In a second step, the trajectory to the society of destination sets frames for subsequent insertion and acculturation. Migrants departing by their own choice in a frame of information flows and established migration corridors have a better chance to adjust to the demands of the receiving economy than those sent under contract or by force. Again power relations are highly important, and even "free" migrants move under constraints. Finally, the receiving societies need to be studied in the same comprehensiveness and same differentiation between statewide, regional, and local. If migration occurs within or into colonies, hierarchies of color of skin ("race") and colonizer views of the bodies of the colonized impact on degrees of exploitation or of agency. Migrations question the "container" view of states, and unlike nonmoving residents, migrants acquire familiarity with more than one way of life.

3. Migrations, Free and Bound

MIGRATORY developments followed different time lines in the major cultural macroregions, but in the 1860s and 1870s they coalesced in both new coherence in some regions and accelerated change in others. Transoceanic migratory movements expanded rapidly with the introduction of steamships in the 1870s. Industrial development, urbanization, and increased production in the Plantation Belt's "factories in the field" (as Carey McWilliams and Eric Wolf pointedly called plantations) accelerated demand for labor. "Taylorization"—the breaking down of factory manufacturing processes into simple, repetitive tasks—changed the character of many tasks from skilled to semi- or unskilled, and thus labor migrants with different predispositions were in demand and regions of recruitment changed accordingly.[58]

The Atlantic world's political economy consolidated. In Europe, industrialization extended to East Central regions and European Russia. As latecomers, the fragmented Italies and Germanies embarked on industrial expansion and unified as nation-states, though the German-language peoples, due to the German-Hohenzollern and Austrian-Habsburg rivalry, became two nations. The continental empires ceded neither to middle-class-driven nation building nor to their internally subjected peoples' demands for self-administration. Instead, they engaged in the all-out warfare of 1914–1918 and, outdated as their structures were, self-destroyed. Vast refugee migrations accompanied their disintegration. In North America, the three continental states consolidated while the Caribbean societies remained colonized. The American Civil War—only twelve years after the war of aggression against Mexico—cemented unity and abolished the old-style plantation regime. As early as the 1840s, when settlement of the western regions accelerated, only one-third of the immigrants were settlers; artisans and skilled workers accounted for another third, and unskilled workers, agrarian laborers, and domestics for the last third. Canada, achieving Dominion status in 1867, extended its territory from coast to coast and attracted both agricultural settlers and urban workers. Immigration of farm families ended in the United States in the 1890s, in Canada in the 1920s. The Estados Unidos Mexicanos, having lost half its territory to the United States of America in 1848 and 1853, repelled a European French-led invasion and, under President Benito Juarez, embarked on a policy of (limited) social reform. The deprivation of the *indios* of much of their land forced them into internal cityward migrations, and thus no need for working-class in-migration arose. Immigrant or absentee European and US investors took advantage of the surplus labor force, but from the end of the nineteenth century ever larger numbers of Mexicans would migrate northward.[59]

In the many Caribbean societies, European influence declined while that of the United States grew, in particular in consequence of the war against Spain in 1898 and the resulting annexation of Puerto Rico and the establishment of a protectorate over Cuba. After the abolition of slavery in the British Empire in the 1830s, sugar production had shifted from Jamaica to Cuba's slave-worked, partly US-owned plantations. Steam-powered sugar mills turned Cuba into one of the foremost industrializing and urbanized countries in the world, and it became the sixth-largest receiver of immigrants from Europe and the largest receiver of Cantonese bound workers after the abolition of slavery.

Central and South America's states and societies experienced uneven development. The Pacific coast and Andean regions stagnated, the Atlantic seaboards and the accessible interiors, with plantation and mining regions, expanded rapidly, with Brazil and Argentina at the forefront. Iberian, but in particular Italian, as well as some West and East Central European migrants provided man- and womanpower as well as technical and cultural expertise. Urban growth relied mainly on European migration. Liberated ex-slaves, native peoples, and earlier immigrant rural settlers stayed put and thus, in relative terms, declined. When they did move to the cities later, they—like natives in Central America and Mexico—arrived as latecomers and formed a social stratum below the recent European migrants. Because much of the investment came first from Britain and then the United States, economic decision making did not necessarily have societal and country-wide development at its center. Thus, in the long run these countries underwent a relative decline in comparison to the economies and polities of the northern Atlantic. Migration declined accordingly.[60]

Africa, often overlooked as part of the Atlantic world, became the object of the continuing British, new French, and late Belgian and German imperialist greed. The new rulers and their labor demands for new extractive economies replaced slave catching and slave export with displacement and involuntary migration. In French North Africa, British Kenya, and the British Dominion of South Africa, immigrant European agricultural settlers displaced resident peasant populations. The investors and intruders established regionally varying regimes of forced labor that mobilized or immobilized men and women according to decisions made in the European and, again later, US cores.

Across the Plantation Belt the demand for labor, whether temporarily bound, permanently bound through debt peonage, or free and cheap, had resulted both in recruitment drives in impoverished segments of Europe—Ireland, Poland, and southern Italy, for example—and in the imposition of the indenture system on Asian populations. The latter were transported westward as far as East Africa and the Caribbean, within the Indian Ocean to the plantation islands and littorals, eastward to Malaya and Australia, and transpacifically as far as the Americas.

In West Asia and Egypt, the Ottoman Empire and its formerly well-structured cohabitation of many peoples was challenged by unsuccessful demands for self-rule and successful imposition of British or French zones of influence: Egyptian cotton and Iraqi oil were annexed to the North Atlantic's industrial economy. In British-ruled South Asia, demands for independence increased. Concentration of production and intensification of mining spurred vast migrations. These followed patterns of imperial rule and investment as much as local cultural and economic exigencies. Japan pursued its own distinct political economy, a dynastic-corporate regime of Western-style modernization, which forced overtaxed peasants into internal and outbound migration. From southern China a transpacific migratory connection emerged from the mid-1840s on and, expanding to additional regions of origin, accelerated from the 1870s.

In the northern Asian segments of China and Russia, as well as in European Russia, there developed internal patterns of migration as well as some transoceanic out-migrations. Mainly laboring men and women of peasant background moved. In addition, rural families migrated from European Russia to southern Siberia, and a new mass migration from northern China to Manchuria continued earlier traditions of rural-to-rural migrations. Urbanization, especially of the Harbin region, made distinctions between agricultural and industrial migrations fluid. Elsewhere, small numbers of peasants still moved to farming regions, and some states and ideologues of white people's expansion as late as the 1920s advocated colonization migrations of Europe's and North America's surplus farming families (labeled peasant "stock") to ever more marginal farming regions—but such schemes remained rhetoric.[61]

The havoc and destruction of World War I temporarily ended transatlantic migrations. They resumed after 1918, the increasing US restrictions notwithstanding, but were cut short by the Great Depression after 1929. In the black Atlantic, small-scale reverse migrations from the Americas to Africa began. The 1930s also witnessed the first arrival of West and North African sailors and workers in France, as well as educational migrations of the sons of upper-class families from the colonies to France and Great Britain. The Plantation Belt's labor regime changed with the gradual abolition of indentured servitude in the 1920s and the collapse of world markets in the 1930s. Thus, depending on macroregion, the period of mass labor migrations lasted into the mid-1910s or into the 1930s. All bound as well as self-willed labor migrations were accompanied by numerically smaller free migrations of middle-class men and women.

A Mobility Transition?

During the so-called demographic transition, when population growth and economic growth do not match, families and unmarried young people have to depart. Infant survival rates and life expectancy of adults increase, but birth rates have not yet declined nor have labor markets expanded. This, if called a "mobility transition," implies lower mobility in earlier decades and centuries. Recent research indicates that rather than a vague "modernization" in some regions, improvements in transport routes and speed accelerated mobility. Demographic expansion occurred in Europe and China from the mid-eighteenth to the late nineteenth century. Only France, where couples had limited their number of children far earlier, remained an exception.[62] (This demographic change is occurring in many Arab, African, and Asian societies in the present.) In 150 years after 1750, Europe's population tripled to 430 million and its share of the world's population grew from one-sixth to one-quarter. People in family units, particularly adolescents ready to leave the parental household, correct such demographic-economic imbalances by migrating from spaces with a surplus of livelihood-seeking men and women to spaces with a demand for additional workers or thinly settled land, often constructed as "free land." In the late nineteenth century, demand for labor was limited in the European cities of the societies of their birth but high in societies a continent away. Patterns of migration usually begin interregionally and as rural-to-urban moves within a language region before they become long-distance and international. Migration is a learning process, and routes need to be established and extended. Once a society's labor markets expand to provide sufficient options for wage work, departure rates decline. This was the case in Western Europe from the 1890s; in Italy and Eastern Europe, migration began in the 1880s and continued to the caesura of World War I.[63]

The conceptual shift from textile and food production to the steel and iron industries as indicators of a modernization in nation-states and their economies has obscured the causes and effects of migration as well as the gendered divisions of labor. Work and consumption in the home are little affected by tons of steel produced. But imports of cheap grains mass-produced by immigrant farmers and laborers, whether wheat in Europe or rice in Asia, wrought havoc on family farm economies. The resulting agricultural crisis of the 1880s and 1890s forced millions of small peasant families to depart from their plots and head for jobs in the new industries. This "proletarian" mass migration involved rural men and women with little or no land, the towns' lower classes, and urban workers—it was a proletarianizing rather than a proletarian migration.[64]

The transition-by-migration from rural to industrial tasks was facilitated by the initial stage of industrial mass production in food and garments: mills for cane sugar in the Caribbean and for beet sugar in East Central Europe, sewing machines for producing clothing—for which most women had the skills. The conveyor belt began as a disassembly line in the slaughterhouses from Chicago to Kansas City. Rural men and women who had done their own food conservation and slaughtering on small farms moved to seasonal canning and year-round meat-packing in large firms. On a small family farm, slaughtering a pig provided a feast and food for the winter, but slaughtering on a production line was gruesome work. Such mass production in the fields of the plains and in the factories of new metropoles reduced food prices worldwide and caused more and more families to depart from marginal lands. Similarly, investment in cotton plantations in the southern United States, Egypt, Uganda, India, and elsewhere, and investment in cloth factories, whether in Manchester or Mumbai, Lowell or Łódź, demanded quick and permanent changes in allocation of family labor, whether Irish, Dutch, Egyptian, Tamil, or Burmese. Men and women, from adolescence on, responded with myriads of back-and-forth, circular, temporary, and permanent moves.

The Proletarianizing Mass Migrations

With the concentration of production in hand-powered manufacture and machine-powered factories, the protoindustrial period's transfer of raw materials or semifinished goods to sedentary cottage dwellers with spare time and a need for cash income reversed to self-transfer of such working families to centralized job locations. In addition, rural men moved to work in local infrastructural improvements, and women continued their migration to domestic labor in nearby towns and cities. Railroads and steamships permitted such workers to move intercontinentally: Some twenty million from Europe to the United States from 1880 to 1914, of which about six million returned to Europe. These migrants, considered "unskilled," were skilled agriculturalists and household managers in the economies they left and inexperienced only in the factory production they entered.[65]

The mass migrations to farm and factory labor targeted the mass-producing plains from southern Russia to North America and from Argentina to Australia as well as the mass-producing factories from St. Petersburg to Chicago to Buenos Aires. When East German landlords converted to machinery, drove out their tenants, and imported Polish seasonal laborers, North American second-generation immigrant farming families hired these displaced tenants-turned-migrant-laborers, and industrial employers, also descended from earlier immigrants, hired them for Taylorized (simplified) tasks in machine-driven production. In the societies of departure, home and subsistence producers, usually women, became dramatically aware of the futility of their labors when factory-produced cloth came to be available cheaply in a nearby store. To supply a family with cloth demanded a winter's work—but its purchase required cash at the very time when the agricultural crisis of the 1880s reduced family incomes. The crisis of

Men and women on a transatlantic vessel's crowded lower deck, mid-ocean, ca. 1890. Sharing expectations as well as uncertainties about their destination, passengers often banded together as
"ship sisters" or "ship brothers." Images like this one, however, are not always what they seem. Joseph Stieglitz's famous photo "The Steerage," for example, shows migrants returning to Europe
from the United States. Around 1900, about one-third of all migrants to the New World returned.
(Library of Congress)

"free" time and empty tables forced individuals and whole regional populations to reorient their lifestyles and their attitudes to migration.

The combination of human agency and socioeconomic frames may be illustrated by migration from Italy. The almost fourteen million men and women who departed from 1876 to 1914, and the further four million from 1915 to 1930, selected as destinations Western Europe (44 percent), North America (30 percent), Brazil and Argentina (22 percent), and other places (4 percent). Craftsmen followed traditional routes to France and Germany; rural migrants compared work offered by East Elbian and Argentinian landowners and found working conditions in Germany's East worse and train fare over the Alps more expensive than transatlantic fares. The latter were cheapest to the United States, but those who could afford it went to Latin America because there, comparatively, prospects were better, language problems smaller, cultural adjustment easier, upward mobility higher. From North America one-third of the migrants returned to Italy—they came as temporary workers, not as immigrants. "Unskilled" men and women skillfully evaluated life chances in several regions of the Atlantic world. Migrants' remittances— through deposit in banks—funded industrialization of the Milan-Turin-Genoa triangle. Family economies in villages were "glocal," and remittances supported mesoregional development.[66]

In the society/economy of destination, migrants faced complex stratified and segmented labor markets. Jobs in the primary growing, capital-intensive, concentrated sector offered relatively high wages, good working conditions, and stable employment. Only a few migrants, like skilled German workers and English mechanics, could reach for such jobs, whether in Budapest or Chicago. In the secondary stagnating, competitive sector with irregular employment, low pay, and unpleasant working conditions, migrants were hired regardless of cultural origin or nationality. A tertiary marginal or ghetto sector demanded and provided high flexibility. Migrants could enter only those labor market segments commensurate with their skills or lack thereof, their communication capabilities or problems, and their cultural Otherness. Furthermore, labor markets were segregated by gender, ethnicity, color of skin, and sometimes religion. Only some segments offered transatlantic internationalized access—the labor markets were heavily racialized.[67]

Jobs provided migrants with the initial income and basis for survival. Culture provided links to others—permitted community formation and expansion of individual human capital by development of social capital. Contrary to Karl Marx's assumption, migrant men and women had more to lose than chains: To avoid the loss of regionally specific ethno-class or race-class cultures, and thereby individual practices of belonging, they based their support organizations and material life on transferable aspects of the culture of origin within the frame of the receiving society. Adjustment to new societies and labor movements involved multiple and gendered negotiations and compromises. The working-class migrants were transculturally mobile, but they were not necessarily a conscious internationally minded proletariat.[68]

Europe's Cores and Peripheries

The oft-repeated juxtaposition of labor-exporting European (emigration) and labor-importing North American (immigration) countries skews the evidence. Europe itself was divided into a labor-importing core and a labor-exporting periphery. Industrialized England, the Netherlands and Belgium, France, the west and central German regions, lower Austria, Bohemia, and Switzerland attracted migrants first from surrounding agricultural regions, then from Europe's periphery. Great Britain and the Germanies as well Belgium and sections of Austria exported settlers and workers at the same time. England drew workers mainly from its Irish colony, Switzerland from Italy (earlier from Germany), France from most of its neighboring countries and Poland, and Germany from Poland and Italy. The peripheral societies of Ireland, Portugal and Spain, Italy and southeastern Europe, the Polish and Jewish territories, as well as the Scandinavian countries supplied labor. People's identifications, rather than being based on membership in a nation, emerged from a search for options to earn a living.[69]

State-propounded ideologies of national identity notwithstanding, some population planners attempted to rid their country of "undesirables," including political or religious dissidents, "the poor" in general, underemployed proletarians, and people considered deficient for other reasons: deportation of dissidents and criminals from Russia to Siberia; of paupers and criminals from Western Europe to America and Australia; Great Britain's program of shipping off unmarried women, orphaned children, and lightly disabled soldiers; US deportations of alleged socialists and revolutionaries during the "Red Scare" (or "white fear") around 1920.

Nationalist economic elites forced people to depart because institutionalized relations between capital and labor did not provide for sustainable lives, and people of minority cultures were deprived of access to societal resources by cultural elites.

Intra-European labor migrations were vastly larger than outbound ones: At the height of the transatlantic migrations, only 5 percent of all Austro-Hungarian migrants left the empire for other European economies or North America; 95 percent moved internally, with Prague and Vienna being the largest receivers. Many of the expanding manufacturing towns in Europe still resembled industrial islands in an agrarian world and thus drew on work-age populations from the countryside: ethnoculturally similar but economically distant peasant people. In the ethnoculturally stratified eastern cities, ethnically distinct from local peasants, multilingual working classes emerged.[70]

Regions of industrial investment, like Lancashire in England or the Ruhr district in Germany, or investment-attracting rural towns, like Łódź, attracted people in transition from rural to industrial patterns of earning a livelihood. Capital cities, because of political linkages, the nobility's consumption patterns, and bourgeois investments, attracted heterogeneous migrants. Vienna, linked by railroads to the Germanies and by Danube shipping to the Black Sea, exerted its pull over Bohemia, Moravia, Slovakia, the Hungarian lands, Polish-Ukrainian-Jewish Galicia, and Bukowina. Greek traders, Italian merchants, and Jewish families lived in distinct quarters. The tantalizing facades of aristocratic and bourgeois quarters suggested riches to be made, while the harsh working conditions of the factories and the poverty, pneumonia, and prostitution of the drab working-class quarters were invisible from the locations where migrants developed their expectations. Many workers came seasonally, and ethnic associations registered a membership turnover of up to 100 percent per year, as did Germany's labor unions. The proletarianizing migrations involved high mobility in a particular stage of the life cycle rather than a single and unidirectional emigration.[71]

Even though most cities were dependent on in-migration for their growth, newcomers experienced segregation and hostility from the increasingly nationalistic host societies. In Austria and Germany, assimilation pressures undercut the viability of immigrant cultures. Exclusions and, in the case of people of Jewish faith, racializations were common to all of Europe's states. In urban societies, whether London, Paris, or Berlin, racialization targeted in-migrating Italian and

Eastern European workers. The development of nations and national economies depended on migrant workers of other cultures and on their Otherization.

North America from Canada to the Caribbean

The popular adage "Go to *America*" refers to the United States, but migrants went to two states, the United States and Canada, and to several linguistic regions: French Canada, the Spanish-English US Southwest, and the creole regions of Louisiana. Mexico and the societies of the Caribbean islands, positioned as a connecting region of the Americas by patterns of migration since the 1880s as well as by patterns of US political interference and economic penetration, are best considered part of North America.

Most migrants to North America had originated in Western and Northern Europe—they were white. From the 1870s and more so from the mid-1880s, migrants originated from Eastern Europe, southern Italy, and as well as the southeastern European societies. The racial ideologies of Anglo or Teutonic whites color-coded them as dark, swarthy, or olive. The ideology of US racial identity, and to a lesser degree Anglo-Canadian racial identity, led to restrictions against in-migration of "yellow races" from Asia and, after 1924, of nonwhite Europeans. Lynch violence (sometimes called "lynch law" in the peculiar parlance of national discourse) and lack of migration traditions kept black African-Americans tied to the southern states into the 1880s. "Brown" migration from Mexico remained limited before 1900 and was hardly discussed in public. Canada, with its demand for prairie settlers and urban workers, kept its doors open for Europeans through the 1920s.[72]

In the United States, nineteenth-century economic and demographic development was characterized by a sequence of large-volume internal migrations. Westward migrations did not serve as a safety valve that defused class conflict; instead urbanization attracted young surplus rural people, as it did in Europe. From the early 1900s, "bonanza farms" or corporate *latifundia* displaced settler families, and flight from the land accelerated in the 1930s during the Great Depression. Pushed by pogroms and disenfranchisement, the southern ex-slaves' children began to migrate to northern urban jobs, about one hundred thousand net in the decade before 1900. When immigration from Europe came to an involuntary stop in 1914, the African-Americans' "Great Migration" became a

A Chinese poem carved into the wall of the Angel Island Immigration Station in San Francisco Bay. Angel Island, the Ellis Island of the Pacific coast, often served more as an interrogation station and a detention center than as an entry gate. Asian immigrants arriving at Angel Island were frequently detained upon arrival, the victims of exclusionary and discriminatory policies. Many of the migrants expressed their sorrow and anger by carving elaborate poems into the wooden walls of the station. (Carol M. Highsmith's America, Library of Congress, Prints and Photographs Division)

proletarianizing mass movement involving about one million men and women from 1916 to 1920, or almost 10 percent of the 10.4 million black citizens.[73]

In addition to the multicultural cities, rural regions were made bicultural by the presence of migrants, and the international northern and southern borderlines became borderlands in which people moved back and forth. From the St. Lawrence Valley, Canadian French-speakers came to New England's Anglo-owned textile mills. English-Canadians settled in Michigan, the Prairies, and Washington state; US farmers accounted for the largest number of in-migrants in Canada's prairies. The border along the 49th parallel was permeable, it was but an imaginary line. A German-Scandinavian belt with distinct linguistic practices and with Ukrainians on the Canadian side emerged, as did a Hispanic Spanish-English belt along the Mexican border.[74]

The United States of Mexico, while part of the Atlantic economies and cultures, remained distinct as regards migration. Not only were few labor migrants needed, due to the government's disenfranchisement of the *indios,* but the incursions of Spanish royalists in the 1820s, of US armies in the mid-1840s, of French-led European troops in the 1860s, and since then of powerful British, US, French, and German investors, created an antiforeigner sentiment that, for the Americas, was singular. The mid-nineteenth-century urbanization and land "reform" (dispossession of native peoples) accelerated the internal cityward migrations of the dispossessed but segregated them by racialization. Capital influx from the United States, accompanied by investors and migrants with technical skills, also mobilized dispossessed rural Mexicans. Increasing numbers headed for the United States during the disturbances of the anti-Porfiriato revolution after 1910 and during the burgeoning US labor demands of World War I. From the 1940s on, the United States recruited large numbers of *braceros.* Already by the 1920s Mexican and Canadian migrants entered the same labor markets in Detroit factories and Michigan mining.[75]

From the 1890s to the 1930s, a North American migration region emerged. Borders were porous, and when European migration was being reduced, the "backdoor" for Mexicans—a "front door" for them—was left ajar. American planters with capital moved to Cuba, Mexico, and elsewhere. Railroad and transportation impresarios developed the Mexican and Isthmus of Panama railroads, not always based on sound engineering expertise. Canada, in addition to being a country of immigration, became a transit country for Europeans: 2.6 million moved to the United States between 1871 and 1930. Only a tiny percentage of both US- and Canada-bound migrants crossed the Pacific from Asia.

In the 1920s, low cotton prices pushed white families out of the US South's rural economy. Most headed for California and became migrant agricultural laborers. In the 1920s, mechanization beyond the scope of family investments, exacerbated in some regions by drought, displaced people from family farms. During the Great Depression, first-generation European and Mexican migrants returned to their societies of birth. Because of continuing racism, a small but vocal "Back to Africa" movement emerged from the United States as well as from Brazil and the Caribbean. Along the Pacific coast—as in Mexico, Peru, and eastern Siberia—Chinese migrant or immigrant workers had become part of the respective

DIRK HOERDER

proletariats. The working-class diasporas from Europe and Asia overlapped in North and South America, where they joined forces or competed with free black and white labor.

Framed by such global connections, the Caribbean served as a hinge region between North, Central, and northern South America. Several of its societies, Cuba and Trinidad in particular, received Cantonese and Indian indentured workers and free migrants. After the end of slavery, African-Caribbeans' migration was at first limited to the Caribbean area. US-bound migration grew parallel to US investment in the island economies. In the early twentieth century, the Panama Canal's construction sites became a major destination, attracting several tens of thousands of free and contracted Barbadian, Jamaican, Guadeloupean, and Martinican migrants. US investments in plantations increased seasonal mobility and expanded the catchment area to Costa Rica and Nicaragua. By the 1930s the Caribbean plantation regimes had become political regimes—"banana republics" under the remote control of multinational corporations. Caribbean migrants in the United States developed a cosmopolitan cultural expressiveness, centered on New York's Harlem and connected to Paris, France. African-American and African-Caribbean music began to attract white audiences; cultural fusion was a consequence of migration.[76]

South America

About one-fifth of the fifty to fifty-five million transatlantic migrants headed for South America.[77] Their numbers grew after 1850, rose rapidly from 1885 to 1914, stagnated in the interwar years, and resumed for a decade after 1945. Most originated in the Mediterranean cultures, especially Italy, Spain, and Portugal. Argentina and Brazil received almost four-fifths of the newcomers, Cuba 14 percent—in all three of these societies the patterns and composition of migration and the labor regimes changed after the abolition of slavery. Around 1900, Italian migrants modified the Euro-Atlantic migration patterns and increasingly selected North American destinations. Thus, the Mediterranean- and Atlantic-European departure areas and the several receiving areas in the Americas became integrated. Self-selection of migrants channeled people to destinations according to their social profiles and the receiving society's economies.

An oil-drilling team of Portuguese immigrants in Patagonia, Argentina, 1907. Most photographs of immigrants show men, but women accounted for about 40 percent of the Atlantic crossings. Communities of immigrant men and women, often with children, emerged throughout the Americas from Patagonia to Alaska. (Patagonia Mosaic Project, Dickinson College)

Migrations internal to Latin America increased when ex-slave families left plantations, first in a process of moving to or forming villages, and then in medium-distance cityward migrations. Plantation owners and the governments they dominated experimented with various labor recruitment schemes before they settled on free migrants from Europe. In the Latin American scheme of skin color gradation, European working-class immigrants held a competitive advantage over local workers of mixed origin, and these over African-origin workers. However, no US-style segregation into black and white ever developed or, given the many-colored *castas,* could develop. The societies of the Guyanas and the Pacific coast, like those of the Caribbean, also included contract laborers and free migrants from Asia. After exclusion from North America, Japanese immigrants came to Brazil and Peru, often as families. Internal migration to states and migration between states involved women moving independently to domestic service. Although economic growth had been high for more than half a century after the independences, migrants at the turn of the twentieth century reached economies of "expansion without development," societies experiencing urbanization without further industrialization. Still, wages compared favorably to transportation cost and to living expenses in the cultures of origin, but harsh working conditions on plantations resulted in high rates of secondary rural-to-urban migrations and of return.[78]

In Argentina, which pursued a policy of encouraging in-migration of both agricultural and industrial labor, about 6 million Europeans arrived from 1869 to 1914, and 2.7 million returned; by 1914 the Argentinian population had more than quadrupled to 7.9 million, 58 percent of whom were foreign-born or the children of immigrants. Agrarian settlement resembled that of plains across the world, with railways constructed by private companies using British capital, government subsidies, and immigrant labor. After the mid-1890s it was no longer possible, even for hardworking families, to advance to independent landownership. Argentina had no frontier of settlement. Its only city, Buenos Aires, had a Spanish elite, Italian bourgeois and lower middle-classes, and multiethnic shantytowns. In the latter the tango and *lunfardo* developed, to become popular across the Western world. For six decades, 70 percent or more of the city's residents were foreign-born, a percentage twice as high as was ever reached in the United States. Half of the migrants were Italians, one-third were Spanish, 5 percent were French. Steamship fares as low as fifty dollars from Italy to Buenos Aires made the trip profitable even for seasonally commuting harvest laborers, who, because of the inverse season, could thus achieve year-round employment. In contrast to rural settlers, urban immigrant families experienced intergenerational upward mobility and immigrants could participate easily in political life.[79]

In Brazil, the post-independence phase of European migration up to the 1860s had brought German, Italian, and Polish settlers to the coffee plantations of Rio Grande do Sul, where planters had relocated because of soil exhaustion farther north. In secondary migrations many fled the miserable—literally "unsettling"— working conditions. The second phase, from 1870 to 1920, brought a total of 3.4 million, of whom 860,000 returned to Europe or moved elsewhere. Given Brazil's population size, the ratio of immigrants to native-born was always lower than in other receiving states in the Americas. African-Brazilians, as part of the multi-colored population, migrated to jobs or sharecropping. In prospering cities European labor displaced free Africans, who had to migrate to stagnating regions or take the most menial jobs. The Brazilian Euro-Creole elites engaged in a nation-building process conceived in European terms and relying on contemporary concepts of race to prevent *indio* and black peoples from accessing political or economic resources. Notions of improving the "population stock" by "crossbreeding" and "whitening" emerged. Belonging, in the minds of elites, was predicated on color.

For African-Brazilians, belonging was predicated on culture. In brotherhoods and through socioreligious practices of *candomblé* they struggled against alienation and displacement as well as the slave traders' insidious "witchcraft" that had transformed them into forced labor "across the water." The importation of slaves into the 1860s kept the institutions closely related to African multidivinity. They organized by nation, color, gender, and status to pursue material as well as spiritual goals. Portuguese-origin Brazilians were aware of cultural differences between groups of different African origins, such as the Savaru, Ardas, Hausa, Tapa, Jejé, DaGome, and Nagô. Such diversity of origin demanded search for a common language. The African languages also impacted on the official European language; some twenty-five hundred Brazilian-Portuguese words are of sub-Saharan African origin. Ethnically based working-class organizations combined slave and freed workers and organized strikes, resisted government interference, controlled quality of work, and asserted self-governance. Many members were African-born, others internal migrants from the declining sugar regions. Some, in old age, reembarked for Africa, like European-origin workers in North America who at retirement returned to their societies of birth.[80]

Migration to the Americas and the establishment of Euro-domination there has been discussed in terms of white over black and the annihilation or displacement of red people. If the imposition of a white-topped racial hierarchy was indeed a major goal, skewed sex ratios—expressed in sexual attraction as well as violence—brought forth new mixed peoples. In all of the Americas, including the northern self-labeled "white" societies, racial mixing resulted in ethnogenesis, the development of new mestizo peoples in new ecological environments. While gatekeeper ideologues of the Anglo-Protestant societies invented a myth of racial purity and whiteness, in Latin Catholic societies the hierarchized *castas* remained porous and wealth could override color. In 1920s Mexico, partly in a reaction to the arrogance of neighboring Yankees, a self-identification of *mestizaje* emerged, a blending of Europeans, Native Americas, Africans, and even some Asians. An extreme version, countering Yankee superiority fantasies, made Mexicans a "cosmic race." All migrations involve mixing, *métissage,* or *mestizaje,* and they involve new self-arrogated or ascribed hierarchies by phenotype or genes.[81]

Intercolonial Migrations

Parallel to the free-under-constraints migrations in and between the Atlantic economies, free-under-massive-constraints and unfree mass migrations occurred within the Atlantic imperial powers and were imposed by those states on people in the colonized tropical and subtropical extractive economies circling the globe.

From the Atlantic world, numerically small migrations of investors, plantation owners or inheritors, their personnel, and support personnel for such imperialist economic penetration, whether administrators, soldiers, or governing elites, converged onto the vast colonized territories and peoples and diverged into the region's many different locations and spaces. For the resulting mobilization—as well as immobilization—of labor forces, exact quantitative data are difficult to compile, given the many different recruitment regions, routes, and destinations in extended societies as well as specific economic regions. Recent scholarship indicates that the volume of intercolonial long-distance migrations equaled those of the Atlantic world and, through political and economic power relations, were intricately connected to them. Migrations within the colonies, like those within Europe and North America, come in addition—though the borderlines between free and unfree, internal and external, locally induced and colonizer-mandated are fuzzy.[82]

Again, it is necessary to reflect on images and connotations framing the thought on colonial worlds, the Plantation Belt, and nodes of mineral extraction or wood "harvesting." Geographically accurate maps of continents and territories reflect neither the economic importance nor the size of demand for labor. From a socioeconomic perspective, such maps are inaccurate and misleading. Territorially small islands like Saint-Domingue, Jamaica, and Cuba demanded more workers and, through European white planters' appropriation of the surplus of such black African labor, produced more wealth than the whole of colonial continental North America taken together. In the Indian Ocean, the islands of Mauritius and Réunion and, in the Southeast Asian seas, the so-called Spice Islands as well as Java and Sumatra had become the core of wealth production in the interest of the colonizers. In all of these, the small resident populations did not meet the intruder-investors' demand for labor. Muscled laboring bodies—there was little interest in minds and emotions—were imported like fertilizer for fields or luxury goods for the colonizer elites' homes.

Agricultural production units in the Plantation Belt, the "factories in the fields," required (and for centuries of colonization had required) as much labor, designated as unskilled, as the new factories in the cities of the Atlantic economies. Again: "unskilled" refers to repetitive tasks at the destination. Migrants, in their societies of birth, had led lives with skills that enabled them to cope with adverse conditions. That they were forced to migrate was usually due to local socioeconomic frames and imperialist impositions rather than to a lack of survival skills, although mismanagement of land and other assets could also be the cause of individuals' self-indenture or of the indenturing of family members.

In addition to the regions of the plantation regime, locations of mineral deposits and other types of extraction, like forest clear-cutting, guano digging, or rubber collecting, required labor forces from afar in order to become economically viable and profitable. *Labor force* is a neutral, production-oriented term for men and women, and often children, who wanted to lead whole lives but whose concentration in camps at centers of investment and of natural resources often involved brutal exploitation. Camp regimes need to be analyzed on a continuum from those inhabited by voluntary migrants (under economic constraints) for woodcutting or placer mining, for example, to those with forced migrants like the plantation camps in the Caribbean and the factory barracks in fascist states—both with extremely high death rates. The distinctions between a colonized region and an independent region were not always clearly defined. One region with a long tradition of voluntary migrations, North America's "Greater Southwest," from Arizona and New Mexico to Sonora and Zacatecas, underwent rapid expansion of mining in the later nineteenth century. US investors and the pliant Mexican ruler Porfirio Diaz set the frame; white US personnel exploited often skilled but brown Mexican laborers to dig silver and copper. Protesting workers were subdued by armed military units (as at the Cananea mine in 1906) or deported and dumped in the desert without water (as happened at the Bisbee mine in 1917). Cananea, at the time, also housed several thousand imported or migrant Chinese workers.[83]

Both the plantation and the mining/extracting labor forces were predominantly male, but when the male reservoir of labor for European and, later, US investments was insufficient, women were imported. Male nodes of in-migration usually became gendered communities if their sex ratios were skewed. Even where only men were employed, reproductive work needed to be done: cooking, washing of clothes, mending. Some migrating men did such work for themselves, and in isolated labor camps across the world men were hired as cooks. Elsewhere women came on their own or were brought in to do the "household" work where no households existed: mass production of food in cantinas, washing of endless piles of dirty work clothes. Women might also be brought in for sex labor or, as small businesswomen, migrate on their own account to sell provisions or their bodies (like men sold theirs to exploiters).

The plantation regions and the centers of mineral extraction, often distant from towns and transportation facilities, needed connections to centers of processing and consumption. Thus, further workers were mobilized to build dirt roads, paved roads, railroads, or waterways and the necessary hardware, carts, wagons, or rail cars. Once transportation routes were completed, the carters, canal men, and railroad men created further demand for reproduction labor. Thus, isolated productions sites, barracks for plantation and mining laborers, and solitary hostels became gendered communities. Women followed their husbands; families separated by migration were reunited, single women came to work and often to marry. Women's patterns of migration involved independent moves, sequential ones with prepaid tickets, or transport under contracts. Only the birth of children and multigenerational communities ensured continuity. Given the gendered allocation of tasks, men did often move first. The "women who stayed behind" did become a topos of public debate (as well as, belatedly, of migration research). It needs to be reemphasized that women did form their own migration connections and, when such decisions were open to them, searched for independent incomes. The labor regimes entwined the categories of class, gender, and race-ethnicity.[84]

By the last decades of the nineteenth century, the plantation, mining, and transportation complexes were becoming ever more integrated. The increasing use of machinery created a fast-growing demand for lubricating palm oil; caoutchouc plantations provided the rubber for transmission belts and tires. Capitalists and state agents sought control over territories, partly for their "natural" resources, like fertile soils or minerals, and partly to reduce resident populations to mobile labor forces. Depending on location and demand, people were immobilized for work locally, were forced to move over short or medium distances individually or in family units, or were sent into long-distance migrations—at the end of which they were immobilized again. This, too, involved a balancing of labor demand and labor supply, but it imposed the interests of investors and employers.

The consumption demands of Europe's rapidly increasing populations and the speedup of transportation through steamships and new canal connections, the Suez Canal in particular, intensified production in the extractive industries. Because neither the British- nor the French-controlled areas (nor, for that matter, the remaining Dutch and new German colonies) could be kept under control by the migrant soldiers and administrators sent from the cores, some ethnocultural groups, voluntarily or by coercion, joined the repressive apparatus of the colonizer powers. Sikh police from Punjab and Gurkha soldiers from Nepal or, in French-controlled regions, the *tirailleurs sénégalais,* are examples; Bengali administrators in Burma form another category. In the French Empire of 1930, there were 76,900 colonizer personnel controlling sixty million colonized people with the help of "colonial auxiliaries" transported about. When, in the First World War, which was predominantly a European or Euro-Atlantic war, labor forces in Britain and France shrunk through draft and death, hundreds of thousands of colonial contract laborers and soldiers were transported to Europe and to battlefields in those colonies that were drawn into the Euro-centric interimperial conflict. They labored, fought, and died for the Allied cause. Given the skewed thinking of national ideologues, demands for acceptable living conditions by indentured workers (or native working classes) had never been tolerated. But the argument that "colonials" had fought and many had died for the nation (which was not theirs) induced colonizer governments after the war to reconsider the regime of indenture.

Chinese indentured laborers carrying shells at an ammunition depot in France, 1917. During World War I, Indians, Vietnamese, Chinese, and West Africans were recruited or forced to enlist by the British and French imperial governments to support the Allied war effort. Some, like the *tirailleurs sénégalais,* served on active duty. (Private Collection / Peter Newark Pictures / The Bridgeman Art Library)

Indentured, Credit-Ticket, and Self-Paying Migrants

With the establishment of the indenture system in British India, in Imperial China in the period of the Unequal Treaties, and in Fiji, as well as in other specific regions, workers, like the free-under-constraints European migrants, had been socialized in particular cultural systems of meaning, languages or dialects, and socio-scapes. Those leaving through ports have been counted; those walking or being walked on land have not necessarily been counted—thus quantitative data are inaccurate. For terminological clarity and empirical soundness, forced migrant labor in Africa will be discussed below.

By status, three major categories of migrants in the colonial circuits need to be discerned: (1) those coming under indenture or contractual debt relationships, (2) those coming on loans for their fare, and (3) self-paying (passenger) migrants. Indentures of Indians from the eastern coastal regions, of Chinese from the southern provinces and later the northeastern provinces, as well as of those recruited or kidnapped from Fiji and other Pacific islands, lasted usually five years with no option to change the contract. Not all arrangements guaranteed return fare. Lack of funds for return, exploitative pay conditions, overcharging by company or plantation stores, nonwork because of illness or pregnancy, all might contribute to involuntary reindenture. A new contract could also be signed voluntarily, either because working life in all its aspects was acceptable or because conditions in the place of origin, "home," were unacceptable. Reindenture might also be a strategy to accumulate savings and establish a small business within the region of indenture or a nearby town. Second, in a different arrangement, people without means could migrate by taking a loan for the cost of their passage. Such "credit-ticket migrants" worked off the loan at the destination. Repayment usually involved a three-year period but could be achieved faster or under exploitative conditions might take longer. Finally, self-paying individuals or families decided on their destination and intended to establish themselves in business. The term *passenger migrant* for people from India differentiates them from "coolies" who, on the same boats, were treated like cattle. The term *merchants* for Chinese reflects the long tradition of diasporic trader migrations. Such migrants, often with wife and children, could be large merchants with wide-ranging import and export connections. They could also be artisans or small traders, migrating singly or with family labor. Some migrated in family networks in which travel costs were advanced without debt relationships but with an obligation to contribute to the family economy.[85]

Once shipping routes and regular traffic had been established, free migrants from other cultural origins could take advantage of them. Free men and, with some delay, women from Meiji Japan began to migrate in the late 1860s, and Filipinos did so after their country became a US colony in 1898. Within the orbit of Dutch colonialism in Southeast Asia, workers were recruited in Java for work on other islands. In some Pacific islands, where at first small populations were depleted by forced migration and then indentured Indians were imported, societies underwent traumatic changes.

Calculations and estimates of total numbers of migrants have varied widely. Adam McKeown's reassessment suggests a total of 48 to 52 million, divided between some 29 million Indians and 19 million Chinese as well as people from other cultures but excluding Dutch Indonesia, which was neither part of the regime of indenture nor an arena of forced long-distance outbound migrations. Less than 10 percent of the migrants came under formal indenture, but much of it occurred with financial assistance from colonial authorities or under debt obligations in the *kangani* recruitment system, under which employers sent one trusted and capable laborer, the *kangani* or *maistry*, to his home region to hire additional workers among acquaintances and dependents. More than 2 million Indians migrated as "passengers." Of Chinese from Guangdong and Fujian, less than a million indentured themselves to European employers but large numbers were bound to Chinese employers, who might be subcontractors for Europeans. Other types of contracts involved wage labor or profit sharing.

Asian destinations for migrants from India included Burma (15 million), Ceylon (8 million), Malaya/Malaysia (4 million), other ports in Southeast Asia, as well as islands in the Indian and Pacific Oceans. From among southern Chinese, up to 11 million traveled to the Straits Settlements (Penang, Singapore, and Malacca)—but one-third or more used the port only for transshipment to the Dutch Indies, Borneo, Burma, and elsewhere. Nearly 4 million headed directly for Siam, 2 to 3 million to French Indochina, over 1 million to the Dutch Indies, less than 1 million to the Philippines, and more than half a million to Australia, New Zealand, Hawai'i, and other islands in the Pacific and Indian Oceans. Destinations in Africa and the Americas included 1 million Indians to South and East Africa, and hundreds of thousands of Chinese to Latin American and the Caribbean. Contract laborers in Cuba, some 270,000, and Peru became de facto slaves. After 1900, indentured laborers for South Africa, and for Europe during World War One, came mostly from northern China's new recruitment region. For most destinations, 80 to 90 percent of the migrants returned; of Europe's transatlantic migrants, only one-third returned around 1900.[86]

In 1917–1920, British India's national leaders used the contribution of more than one million Indian soldiers and indentured workers in Britain's armies and behind the front to the 1914–1918 war effort to negotiate the end of the indenture regime. However, through voluntary or involuntary reindenture it lasted in

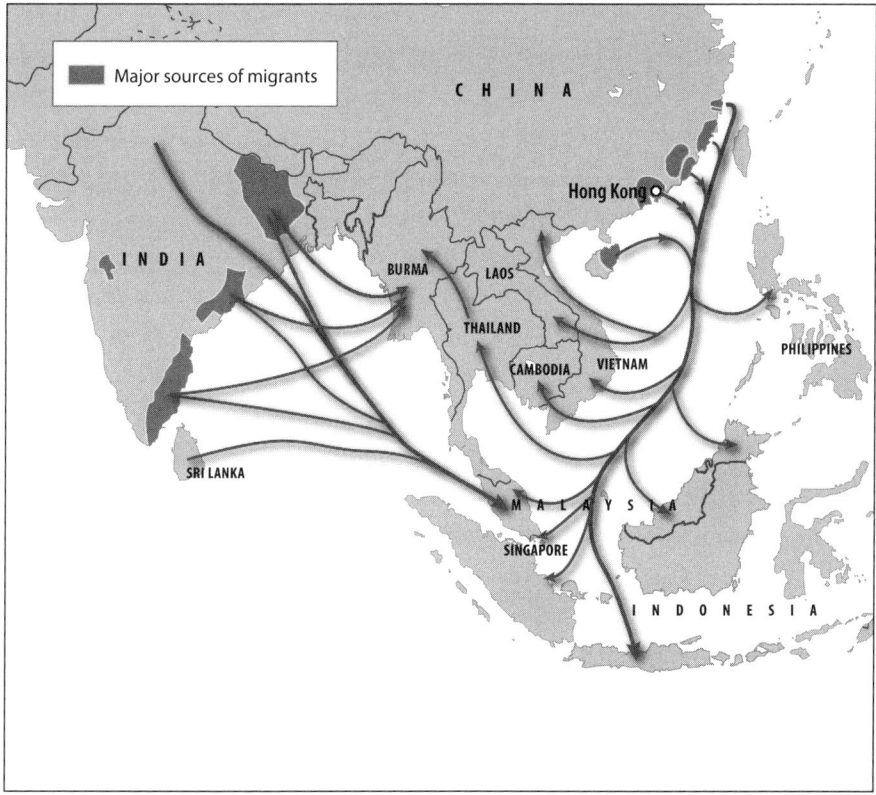

Migration to Southeast Asia, 1850–1914.

some regions into the 1920s or even 1930s. From China, in contrast, departures almost tripled between 1901–1905 and 1926–1930 to 3.3 million. The decisive break in patterns of migration in the East Asian, Southeast Asian, and Pacific macroregions came with Japan's aggression against China in July 1937.

South Africa, Mauritius, and the Malay Peninsula

Destinations within Asia included Burma, Siam, Malaya including the Straits Settlements, some Pacific islands, as well as "white Asia," Australia and New Zealand. Westward travel across the Indian Ocean reached for East and South Africa, Natal in particular. Across the Pacific or around Africa's cape, specific locations along the West Coast of the Americas and in the Caribbean could be reached. Migrants could take advantage of long-existing trading connections of Gujarati merchants to East Africa and of Malabar Coast merchants to Siam and the Malay Peninsula. Capitalists took advantage of short-term global changes. Plantation owners in Mauritius observed the collapse of Antillean sugar production following slave revolts and the abolition of slavery in the early nineteenth century, saw the marketing opportunities in continental Europe, and expanded production by importing coerced Indian labor. Migrations, trade, and investments were of oceanic, hemispheric, and global extent. Mauritius, Natal, and the Malay Peninsula will serve as examples for migrant insertion.

The Mauritian plantocracy, under the postslavery global realignments, changed its traditional voluntary contract labor to brutal exploitation of forced labor. Of the 450,000 Indians who came from 1834 to 1907, less than one-third returned. The planter-administrator complex had designed legislation, regulation, and taxation to force migrant workers to reindenture and to bar them from moving to opportunities outside of the plantation economy. They used vagrancy laws and licensing regulations that the British upper classes had applied for centuries to English working classes. This labor regime, consolidated in the "slave code" of 1867, remained in effect until 1922. However, economic changes, especially the centralization of sugar milling in the 1880s, provided job options in rural towns, to which many workers migrated. Labor militancy was punishable; labor combinations were outlawed until 1937. In Mauritius, the indenture regime was a "new system of slavery," to use Hugh Tinker's term.[87]

Conditions and structures were different in the South African colonies, especially in Natal, where some two hundred thousand South Asian men and women arrived in 1860–1911. About 75 percent stayed permanently, nearly two-fifths of them women. In 1911, when 44 percent of the community of 150,000 was African-born, only 10,000 had been able to enter commerce and a mere 729 the professions. When, after 1911, exclusion legislation ended the old-world influx and constant cultural renewal, acculturation proceeded rapidly. Some sixty-four thousand Chinese were brought to Transvaal mining under the Labor Importation Ordinance of 1903 and the Anglo-Chinese Labour Convention of 1904 as "captive" workers before abrogation of the scheme in 1906. Europeans' prejudices against "primitive" tribal people and African men's and women's sophisticated resistance combined to retard the development of an indigenous labor force. The plan was for Europeans to control the economy, an inserted and partially bound Indian laboring class to do the plantation and railway work, and Africans to be culturally and geographically marginalized.

Pursuing their own agenda, Indian migrants in Natal developed a full-fledged community. At first laborers were brought in for the newly established sugarcane economy. When early returnees' complaints about abusive treatment reduced further recruitment, a "Coolie Commission" in 1872 improved living conditions, if only minimally. Planters briefly turned to hiring free and slave Africans from Zanzibar but then again recruited Indians because they needed experienced workers. Though early migrants originated from Madras, in the 1870s most sailed from Calcutta. The volume of labor imports depended on the sugar industry's economic cycles, on particular railway construction projects, and on general depressions like that of 1866–1874. Arriving men and women were distributed along the coastal belt according to employer demand—similar, in one scholar's words, to Virginia and South Carolina in times of slavery but with a British "sugarocracy" at the top. When the British government imposed a quota of about 30 percent women migrants, planters paid the women only half the men's wages and food rations. Children were paid according to age. Women (and children) had to endure multiple abuses: women were allocated no food when no labor was available for them or when pregnancy or child care prevented them from working; employers sexually harassed them, and jealous husbands mistreated or murdered them; some women committed suicide after being sexually abused. Some resisted exploitation by "desertion"—by joining African communities. From the 1880s on, Indians also worked in coal mining and in railway construction from Witwatersrand to the coast of Natal. Railway workers often came with skills acquired in construction work in India and, after their time expired, moved to similar work in the Belgian Congo and Portuguese Angola.

Free Indians came as traders, and plantation owners had to rely on them to supply the migrant workers with food and fabrics. Shopkeepers dispersed and settled in coastal cities, plantation camps, and country towns and villages. The government culled the immigrant community of nonproductive as well as politically active members. In Durban and Pietermaritzburg the free Indian population, including independent women, survived in economic niches. Free Indian mechanics, masons, blacksmiths, and carpenters were brought in from Mauritius. In Durban's vicinity ex-indentured servants and enterprising immigrant families established truck farming and began to operate small tea or sugarcane plantations. During economic depressions the community suffered and return migration increased, but a lasting presence was established.[88]

In the other South African colonies, in contrast, African labor had been mobilized or immobilized for almost a century before Indian and Chinese contract laborers were introduced. In Transvaal the gold-mining capital, supported by a pliant government, refused to offer wages that would attract African labor from the local competitive labor market and instead tapped four other reservoirs: Africans from Portuguese Mozambique, convicts, unskilled whites, and Asian contract workers. The latter were recruited by a firm that also supplied coolie labor to Russian employers in Vladivostok. Health inspection before departure permitted selection of the fittest, and to achieve maximum exploitation the government criminalized leaving the job ("desertion"), slow work ("loafing"), and inefficient work. Racism ended recruitment of Chinese coolies after only three years, and the government decided to repatriate all.[89]

In the Malay Peninsula, which from 1870 was integrated under British rule, as well as in Burma and Siam, migrants arrived from both India and China to take advantage of mining, agricultural, trading, and imperial opportunities. The resident Malays, Thai, and Burmese, and the large numbers of multiply ethno-culturally differentiated Indians and Chinese sojourners and immigrants, with a European and Eurasian superstratification, developed new societies. In the process, the Chinese and Indian migrants expanded the economy and created jobs, often establishing themselves above the resident peoples.

When the segments of the Indic world, fragmented by three centuries of rule by competing European powers, were reintegrated into the new whole of the British Empire, comparative labor costs induced capitalists and administrators to move labor from the colonized population core, India, to other locations. Singapore's population, for example, increased eightfold to 90,700 in the four decades before 1864: 58,000 Chinese, 13,500 Malays, and 12,700 Indians. Chinese came on their own to work in tin mining or in commercial agriculture; Chinese entrepreneurs provided the capital. Depending on economic cycles, demand, and productivity, the size of this population fluctuated greatly. The contracts bound men to work off the cost of passage within a year, but overtime pay went into their own pockets. The short contracts and the large number of small employers permitted workers to use their own discretion in finding the most remunerative job. European plantation owners had intended to use Malay people as a labor force, but these were able to live off their land and had refused the indignities of wage work under foreign masters. Chinese investors were able to attract workers without government support, but European capitalists demanded public support to import labor. From among the Indian migrants, 90 percent originated from southern Tamil-speaking people, the rest from Telugu districts and the Malayalam districts of the Malabar coast. They were used in the production of coffee, sugar, tapioca, and coconut, and when, after 1900, rubber plantations expanded and oil palm cultivation increased, labor demand skyrocketed. The whole region from British Burma's Irrawaddy Delta via Siam's central plain to the French Indochinese Mekong Delta became a mass producer of rice to feed the rice-eating labor forces transported by the British across the globe.

In 1921 the multiethnic populations of Singapore and Malaya of 3.3 million included 1.6 million Malays, 1.2 million Chinese, five hundred thousand Indians, and some sixty thousand others. Ethnic ascription was as common as in other parts of the world. Malays often considered Chinese dangerous and looked upon Indians as "small people." In contrast, in the Burmese construction of foreigners, Chinese, of whom few came, were "cousins," Indians and British were "black men." The British viewed the Burmese as "happy-go-lucky people" or as the Irish of the East, and the Chinese as the Jews of the East. After 1929, overproduction of natural rubber and the worldwide depression induced British administrators to reduce Indian in-migration by quota and to ship about a hundred thousand workers back to India within a year. The colonized laborers were expendable human beings.[90]

In distinction to the South Asian diaspora of colonial auxiliaries, free migrants, and contract workers, the Chinese diaspora never became an integral part of British or other colonial empires. Its experience in Southeast Asia varied from ghetto life in Batavia and Manila to easy intermarriage and emergence of the Philippine mestizos and Indonesian *peranakan*. When the presence of women increased, community formation and a re-Sinicization began in the Nanyang, and return migration decreased. The role of the ethnic Chinese as middlemen,

Immigrants on board a junk, Singapore, ca. 1900. Singapore was the main transit port for migrants from China and India from the 1890s to the beginning of the First World War. Several hundred thousand arrived each year to work locally or to continue their journey to the Malay Peninsula or other islands in Southeast Asia. (National Archives of Singapore)

and their complete control over particular sectors of the economy, eventually resulted in anti-Sinicism and repeated violence.

Trade Connections and Migrations in South, Southeast, and East Asia

The presence of colonizers, and their creation of the Plantation Belt, which was powerfully imposed and established by the second half of the nineteenth century, in the Indian Ocean and the East and Southeast Asia seas, impacted on regions that had millennia-long traditions of seafaring mobility. It changed such traditions, permitted or enforced new labor and merchant migrations during the regime of indenture, and remolded directions of regional mobilities. To understand agency in and historical frames of the societies, it is useful to discuss some of the many intra- and interregional moves separately. Examples will be selected from the western Indian Ocean via insular Southeast Asia to Japan. Migrations and influences emanating from this macroregion extended westward to East Africa and eastward across the Pacific to the Americas.

Colonizer penetration might intensify existing local migration practices and systems; the sojourning or settling European powerful investor and administrator migrants might also induce emergence of new ones. Resident people could and did refuse to enter wage- or bound-labor relationships. They used their resources—knowledge of the terrain and supportive networks—for resistance. Imported bound laborers, lacking such resources, were more easily controlled.[91] In British India, investment and labor demand or job opportunities did not necessarily result in mobilization of resident rural people. New and growing economic sectors or locations remained unattractive; agriculture, village crafts, the caste system, early marriage, and joint family living arrangements supported sedentary ways of life.

From northwestern India, Gujarati merchants had traded with and settled in East Africa for centuries. From the southeastern Malabar coast merchants had connected to Siam and the Malay Peninsula for a millennium and a half. Because voyaging is costly in terms of both time and conveyance, merchants often establish branch firms and communities at distant places of exchange. Trade voyaging thus turns into migration, and once a trading community has been established the migrant traders begin to bring in personnel, circular migrations develop, and communities emerge and grow.[92]

The Western trade had, for example, led to settlement of merchants from the Gulf of Kutch and from Jamnagar in Zanzibar. In view of local hostility to intermingling, the merchants brought in wives and a community emerged by 1860. Its five to six thousand Hindus and Muslims fragmented, however, along ethnoreligious and occupational lines: Baluchi as soldiers of the Omani sultan, Memons from Sind in shipping and fishing, Parsi merchants, Hindu trading castes—Baniyas, Bhatias, Lohanas, and Shia Muslims, as well as Daudi Bohoras, Ismaili Khojas, Isthnasteris, and Goan Catholics. Ethnoreligious-professional traditions framed agency: Hindus usually returned when they had accumulated savings or wealth, whereas Muslims stayed and formed families. Return also depended on the world economy. It grew when American cloth undersold Indian cloth and when the British enforced the ban on Indian Ocean slave trading after 1873. In the frame of dependencies between colonizer and colonies, the Gujarati enclave, protected by the Omani sultanate, did in the 1870s become a conduit for British influence and, over time, for colonizer ascendancy. Distinct vertical links of each of the South Asian ethnoreligious groups to the British in Mumbai hindered horizontal Indian-cultured homogenization in the community. Mumbai's commercial expansion resulted in increased Gujarati in-migration, and Gujarati became the community's lingua franca. The privileged and thus distinct status granted by the Omani sultanate prevented indigenization. The immigrants remained an outpost of the Gujarat in East Africa and in the later nineteenth century pursued a strategy of Westernization to improve their position toward the power-wielding colonizer and to enlarge their commercial circuits.[93]

In most of the littoral societies of the Indian Ocean, in the interior of Africa, Arabia, and India, and in China, long-extant bondage continued. In many African societies rights-in-person slavery kept dependents within a family, yet deteriorating economic circumstances might always result in transfer to a creditor or sale to a trader. In most of India's family economies and hierarchies parents might alienate children, and the larger socioeconomic power structures implied servitude of poorer social groups. In Bihar, loans to the poor gave lenders the right to their services. Children born into such service relationships could be sold, leased, mortgaged, or transferred with land until debts were repaid. In Madras, rural laborers and servants became virtual serfs of landlords when unable to repay loans. Such practices intensified under British rule. In Southeast Asia and the Indonesian archipelago, customs of slavery, debt bondage, and forced labor of war captives were as varied as the societies. All involved involuntary mobility under slavery-like conditions or as members of a restricted underclass.[94]

In South Asia, including British India, middle- and long-distance internal free and contract migration was, it has been argued, small in proportion to total population if compared to Western Europe, European Russia, or North America. According to the 1891 census, which, it must be emphasized, did not include international migrations, 89 percent of the population resided in the district of birth, 97 percent in the province of birth. Such data underestimate intraprovincial long-distance moves—the subcontinent is as large as West, South, and East Central Europe taken together. The data also exclude women's marriage migrations and marriage-ancillary migrations of servants who accompanied brides from wealthy families or of needy female kin who accompanied brides from poor families. Birthing migration, the custom of women in many South Asian cultures to return to their parents' home for the first child's birth, added to sojourning mobility. If men migrated to distant jobs, marriage migration could follow the routes of labor migration.

Under the distinct but related Indian and British economic developments, four major internal migration systems emerged: (1) medium-distance northeastward migrations to Calcutta's jute mills and other industries, to Bengal's coal mines, to Assam's tea plantations, and to Bihar's indigo plantations and factories; (2) migration to urban Mumbai from a circle stretching some 300 kilometers (180 miles) in each direction; (3) in-migration from surrounding areas to Delhi, and from the same areas of the United Provinces westward to newly irrigated lands of the Punjab; (4) northward migrations from Madras into Mysore and Hyderabad as well as westward into the estate agriculture of the Ghats. In addition, numerous smaller movements crisscrossed the subcontinent and others targeted plantations in Ceylon.

Four socioeconomic types of migration may be discerned: family agricultural, to plantation labor, to mining, and cityward. Peasants, often in family units, migrated to Assam and the Canal colonies. The valleys of Assam offered fertile land, but local people resented the arrival of hundreds of thousands of Bengalis after 1900. Migrant families clustered according to faith and caste (rather than ethnicity). In-migration of young couples meant high birth rates and population increase. Indentured estate laborers migrated to tea, coffee, rubber, and cardamom plantations, especially to the tea estates of Assam, Jalpaiguri, and Darjeeling. Tea cultivation, introduced in 1840, required importation of labor beginning in the 1850s. In the single decade after 1911, Assam became the destination for 770,000 coolies. Many organized and fought for better conditions. A slump in the market in the early 1920s, due to declining exports to civil-war-torn Russia, reduced the number of workers. This migration took many forms: individual migrations for seasonal labor, migrations of entire working families, granting of small plots to in-migrating families as an inducement to stay. By the 1930s, immigrants constituted one-sixth of Assam's population. Mine workers for coalfields in West Bengal, for example, were recruited from the nearby hills since the 1870s. As long as women's underground labor was not prohibited, whole families migrated. Under the British *zamindary* system, owners of large mines acquired rights over people in neighboring villages. They created a semifeudal labor regime by combining land grants with an obligation to work a stipulated number of days in the mines.

In all of South Asia, rural-to-urban migrations, which involved larger distances than rural-to-rural migrations, accounted for nearly half of the internal moves in the early 1930s. The male-to-female ratio of 60 to 40 equaled that of transatlantic migrations. On average, 37 percent of urban residents were in-migrants, but in Mumbai their share reached 75 percent. Calcutta, which grew more slowly, counted 57 percent in-migrants in its population of 680,000 in 1891, and 64 percent of nearly 900,000 in 1911. Demand for labor was high, both because villagers had little predisposition to migrate and because people remained welded to caste-assigned trades. Once indenture declined and free migrations increased, information flows and voluntary departures replaced employer-dominated recruitment. By the early twentieth century, rural-to-urban moves integrated the northeast, Bihar, Bengal, and Arakan (coastal Burma) into one system of interconnected migrations. Elite migration involved families who wanted to be close to the British administration and have their children attend urban schools. Migrations of high and low became entwined when servants of elite migrants became anchor points for low-caste chain migrations. Internal migration occurred parallel to, not interlinked with, transoceanic migration.[95]

In Siam and the adjoining Dutch Southeast Asian islands, people traditionally followed multiple smaller intra- or inter-island migration routes. Because islanders could live off their agriculture, fishing, or local seafaring, Dutch-Javanese planters imported labor, but the colonizer authorities also forced Javanese to migrate to the "outer" islands, which from their point of view were undersupplied with labor, and even to Dutch possessions in the Caribbean. In Sumatra, tobacco cultivation relied on indentured workers. By 1934 more than half of the 1.25 million Chinese migrants lived in the outer islands; of the quarter million European immigrants, 80 percent lived in Java, where connections to the metropoles were best.[96]

Japan in the 1870s began a policy of expansion and industrialization. In a first step, the government established settlements on the near-empty and chilly island of Hokkaido in the north and on the southern, densely populated subtropical Ryukyu Islands, including Okinawa. Large-scale migrations from Japan's densely settled main island increased Hokkaido's Japanese population from 60,000 in 1860 to 2.4 million in 1920. Okinawans, on the other hand, migrated in small numbers to Japan proper and later to the new colonies. Imperial authorities did not consider the islands' natives as equal to "Japanese proper," nor did they consider the migrating Japanese as equal to those staying in the core island—just as American colonists had never been accepted as equals by the British or the Spanish cores. A second, aggressive move, also in the 1870s, opened long-secluded Korea to influence and migration from Japan. Japan annexed Korea in 1910 and invaded Manchuria in 1931. This colonization project involved a strategy to rid society of the ex-samurai warrior class, demoted to commoners, by sending them as soldiers to other countries.

Industrialization generated considerable internal migration, especially short-distance migration of rural people to towns and urban agglomerations. After liberalization of emigration regulations, migrants established themselves in Hawai'i and along the Pacific coast of the Americas. When anti-Asian hate campaigns and exclusionary regulations in the United States and Canada made entry and settlement difficult, Japanese migrants shifted their destination to Peru and

Brazil. Only a small percentage moved as contract laborers; in contrast to imperial China, the government cared for Japanese laborers abroad and, if protection proved impossible, attempted to prevent their emigration. The volume of migration remained small. In 1937 there were 40,000 Japanese living in other noncolonized Asian states, 207,000 in Hawaii and North America, and 227,000 in Latin America. Japanese migrants became part of the government's project to extend Japan's influence abroad. Thus, self-willed migrations became an aspect of imperialist strategies.[97]

Transpacific Distances, Connections, and Racializations

After the first phase of the Pacific migration system, which had connected the Philippines with New Spain from the 1570s to the mid-seventeenth century, commercial connections within the Spanish imperial sphere continued but, during a two-century-long hiatus, involved almost no migration. The distances of the Pacific Ocean were not easily traversed. Even though the Indian Ocean and the Southeast and East Asian seas were connecting waters, the Pacific remained a dividing ocean. Via well-traveled routes from the Indian Ocean to the Atlantic, a first few hundred indentured laborers had been shipped to Caribbean and Brazilian plantations in the early 1800s. The Pacific migration system's second phase evolved in connection with intra-Asian migrations. It thus resembled the emergence of the Atlantic system. Merchants, prospectors, and free laborers developed small communities in Hawai'i and along the Pacific coast of the Americas. Since the 1840s indentured Chinese and Indian laborers were transported to the Caribbean and South America, and free migrants and subsequently credit-ticket migrants came to North America. From the 1880s, Japanese, Koreans, and Filipinos also migrated—though at this time race-based exclusion began to hamper this mobility.

From around 1800, the Polynesian-settled Hawai'ian Islands, halfway across the Pacific, became the destination of migrants from continental Asia as well as of a few Europeans. Both Chinese and Western capital-owning migrants established plantations, but the demand for sugar in California gave US planters a competitive advantage after midcentury. This they buttressed by positioning themselves as advisors to the Hawai'ian rulers and thereby marginalizing Chinese planters. Until the 1870s, Hawai'ians made up most of the plantation labor force. But from the 1850s on, indentured Chinese, including some women, labored alongside South Sea Islanders and Japanese, Norwegians, and Germans, as well Portuguese from Madeira. Because of harsh conditions, many of the latter moved on to the Macao- or Sino-Portuguese communities in California. After the United States annexed Hawai'i in 1898 and the extension of the Asian exclusion laws, migration declined and the two major communities stabilized. The Chinese community, numbering twenty to thirty thousand, had its own institutions and ethnic enterprises. From marriage with either Chinese or local women, a mixed second generation emerged. Its rice cultivation economy expanded to market gardening. The Japanese community grew and came to account for about 40 percent of the islands' population by 1930. Independent farming families leased land, and workers labored on European- and US-owned plantations. When these workers struck for better working conditions in 1909, the Chinese, Filipino, and Portuguese working-class diasporas did not yet support them; ethnocultural specifics still ranked over class solidarity. An internationally mixed labor force and a differently mixed entrepreneurial class had emerged.[98]

From the late 1830s, the Caribbean and circum-Caribbean mainland colonies became the destination of South Asians, indentured under the British Empire's labor allocation across the globe. French planters in Guadeloupe, Martinique, and French Guiana imported hundreds of laborers from colonized Asia; the Dutch recruited 33,000 workers from Java for Surinam. Such contract workers labored alongside African creoles and slaves from the Congo and East Africa liberated from slave ships but forced to "redeem" the cost of their liberation. A total of about 1.75 million voluntary and enslaved workers reached the Caribbean from 1811 to 1916: perhaps 800,000 Africans, 550,000 Asian Indians of whom fewer than one-third returned, and 270,000 Chinese who were sent to Spanish Cuba or Puerto Rico. In addition, 60,000 or fewer free African and 200,000 European migrants came. In the context of empire, 80 percent of the more than half a million laborers sent to Britain's island and mainland possessions came from India, and in British Guiana, Trinidad, and Jamaica, free communities emerged by the 1870s. Among the offspring of East Indians who had migrated to the West Indies, the salience of caste declined. Their chances for community formation were better than those of the Chinese because more women were present. South

Asians, mobile within the region, became peasant proprietors, shopkeepers, or import-export merchants. An affluent urban elite emerged, and by the early twentieth century the first Indian-Caribbeans were elected to legislatures.

For Chaozhou, Hokkien-speaking, and Cantonese indentured workers, in contrast, options were few. Recruited for Cuba, Jamaica, Trinidad, and Guiana at below-subsistence wages, many were forced to reindenture. Those in Spanish Cuba were virtual slaves. Spanish merchants, engaged in contraband slave trading, attempted to cut their losses by shifting to the legal trade in coolies. Recruitment of families was considered desirable because children, like women, were contractually bound to work alongside the men in the family. Planters estimated mortality, including suicides, at a rate said to be the highest in the world, at 10 percent per year; others have estimated it to have been higher. An international French and American commission revealed forced recruitment, transport in prisonlike ships, and twelve-hour workdays. Without guaranteed return passage and without money to bribe officials for a passport permitting departure, the survivors became perpetual contract laborers. The few who gained freedom dispersed to wherever they perceived opportunities, sold their labor in self-organized work gangs, or became marginal retailers, artisans, and domestics. Some established themselves in vegetable farming and oyster fishing. A few elite men opened larger trading establishments or owned cocoa estates. In the early twentieth century, the Trinidad community and separately the Havana Chinese established contacts with California Chinese. Acculturation of Asian migrants to the Euro-African-Amerindian heterogeneity proceeded by gradual change of language, intermarriage or liaison, and emergence of a community of mixed ancestry.[99]

A few South American economies—Peru, Nicaragua, Brazil—also recruited Cantonese, Hawai'ian, and Japanese laborers. In Peru, which attracted investors from Britain, America, Germany, and Italy, working conditions resembled those in Cuba. Hawai'ian and Japanese workers on plantations, in internal improvement projects, and in the digging of bird manure (guano) for export died in large numbers. Hostility against Asians abated somewhat when Japanese men fought in the Peruvian army during a boundary dispute with Ecuador. Subsequently a thriving community emerged, but during the Great Depression in the 1930s, many of the descendants, especially of Brazilian Japanese, migrated back.[100]

In North America, the first Chinese arrived in the context of the early transatlantic US-China trade. When transpacific migrations of free Chinese began with the gold rushes—California in 1848, British Columbia in 1858, and Alaska later—a direct route connected Hong Kong to Vancouver. In California, racist legislators imposed a "foreign miners' head tax" on Chinese as well as on Mexican prospectors. These entrepreneurs, adventurers, and service workers formed a nucleus that attracted credit-ticket migrants and contract laborers for transcontinental railway construction. The migrants worked in industries, in independent market gardening, or as sharecroppers, and, along the coast and in the Rockies, as miners, in fishing, and in canneries, as well as in niches like abalone fishing. Some moved to Louisiana and Gulf of Mexico fisheries, others were hired for southern plantations after the end of slavery, and a few traveled to eastern factories before the depression of 1873. Because wealthy Chinese occupied positions as ethnic leaders and middlemen in the credit-ticket business, hierarchies were strong and exploitation was frequent. The small US-Japanese community expanded after 1890, and Filipinos and East Indians became part of this migration. Total immigration from the Asian Rim to the Pacific Rim, in 1850–1920, amounted in the United States to 320,000 Chinese, 240,000 Japanese, 30,000 from "other Asia," 10,000 Pacific Islanders, and 44,000 Australians and New Zealanders. These gross figures include multiple migrations. In Canada, the census of 1921 listed 39,600 Chinese, 15,900 Japanese, and 10,500 "East Indians." Compared to European migration in the Atlantic system, in the Pacific system numbers were small. The demand for cheap labor in the United States remained high after the Asian restriction, which did not apply to the colony of the Philippines, but Filipinos continued to come and recruitment of Mexicans for work began around 1900.[101]

In all of the societies of the Americas, migrants from Asia kept diasporic ties to their cultures of origin. When racism in the Anglo-American societies was operationalized in restriction regulations beginning in 1875, migrants circumvented the bureaucrats' Great (paper) Walls. By creating "paper" sons and daughters, dependents migrating with false documents and assumed identities, the migrants breached the state-fabricated racist regulations. Such irregular migration, which lasted into the 1930s, permitted communities to remain stable. Racists demanded independence for the Philippines so that Filipinos and Filipinas might also be excluded. Once again nation-state ideologues refused to

Indian immigrants debarred from entry to Canada on board the *Komagata Maru,* Vancouver Bay, 1914. Though British subjects, regardless of skin color, were free to move throughout the British Empire, the Canadian government used bureaucratic subterfuge to prevent entry. The most famous case involved the 376 passengers of the *Komagata Maru.* Erroneously labeled "Hindoos," most of the would-be migrants were Sikhs. All but twenty were sent back. (Library and Archives of Canada, PA-034015)

accept working-class human beings as equal. They did accept comradeship in arms, and in 1943 the United States relaxed restrictions against the Chinese because China had fought as an ally in the Second World War, which began in 1937 in Asia.

Peasant Migrations and Mobility in China and Manchuria

The century-long traditions of outbound migration from Guangdong and Fujian provinces had involved the diaspora formation in Southeast Asia, or Nanyang, and the migration of indentured workers. The vast and differentiated inland regions had been arenas for peasant settlement migrations, refugee moves from famines and, from the mid-nineteenth century in particular, from internal warfare and rebellions. Early industrial development from the 1860s on did not achieve a scale that provided jobs in sufficient numbers. Increased trade, expansion of coal mining, and establishment of shipyards and factories induced internal migration of skilled laborers and technicians. Construction of railways and ports absorbed surplus labor, but once new transportation systems became operative the vast numbers of men previously engaged in porterage and barge pulling were thrown out of work. The introduction of steam power into a social economy based on human power caused immensely larger unemployment than economies based on animal-powered transport incurred. Furthermore, as in Europe, population growth was rapid. In European societies that were unwilling to undertake structural reforms, the possibility of emigrating provided people with options elsewhere; in contrast, except for the two southern provinces the Chinese had neither traditions of emigration nor, before the late 1890s, a railroad network connecting to port cities, nor a political and discursive frame that would encourage emigration. From the 1880s there developed a new northbound, mass-migration system from Shandong to Manchuria. In these very decades, the terms of trade imposed by the European colonizing powers dislocated large numbers of Chinese.

Toward the end of the nineteenth century, emigration began from the provinces of the northern littoral, first under indenture or credit-ticket practices. Men were recruited as contract laborers for Russian Siberia and for South African mining. Early twentieth-century railway construction in the northern plains increased information flows and provided outbound transportation in the impoverished agricultural provinces of Zhili, Shandong, and Henan. In Zhili, climatic conditions and short growing seasons prevented predictable crop yields; in Shandong, where better conditions prevailed, floods were a constant threat. An estimated nine to ten million people died or fled during the drought and famine of 1876–1879.[102]

In a macroregional context, Sakhalin, Korea, and Manchuria became contested territories after the Russian Empire incorporated the Far East into its territories: two competing powerful neighboring states and a northern Chinese peasant population with too little land even for mere subsistence. North of the

Amur River, settlement of and interaction between Chinese and Russian migrants had developed over two centuries when eastbound migrations from European Russia extended to the Amur and the port of Vladivostok. Japan, seeking access to China's presumed markets, attacked in 1895, annexed Taiwan and the Pescadores Islands, and "leased" the northern territories (renamed Kantoshu) with Port Arthur (Lüshun) and Dalian in Liaoning Province. In 1905 it defeated Russia and annexed South Sakhalin (renamed Karafuto). Korea, at first a protectorate, was annexed in 1910 and Manchuria and Inner Mongolia became part of Japan's zone of influence. Under Japan's corporatist military-economic rule, mining and industrial production increased. Labor was needed, and in the view of Chinese peasants, land was but thinly settled.

The Treaty of Shimonoseki in 1895 opened China's northern ports to European and Japanese imports. Cheap machine-spun cotton cloth increased demand for cash while home production collapsed. Only those with the initial means to migrate could depart in family units or hope for a potential cash flow of individual emigrant remittances. As everywhere, the most impoverished could not move. The limited educational institutions of the villages and province were further reduced when students left temporarily and teachers and journalists joined the diasporic communities. Northbound transportation became cheaper and faster; Manchuria appeared closer. The whole northeastern Asian region, but Manchuria in particular, became the destination for 28 to 33 million Chinese, 2 million Koreans, but just over half a million Japanese—far fewer than the Japanese government's colonizing project had envisioned. Japanese migrants, under the empire's protection, took possession of Korea's cultivated agricultural land and allocated urban jobs to themselves. In consequence, especially in the 1930s, about 2.5 million Koreans migrated or were "induced" to migrate to militarizing and industrializing Japan as laborers of inferior status.

Chinese internal migration as well as emigration involved people speaking many different, often mutually unintelligible, local dialects. In addition, about 10 percent of China's population were "minorities"—conceptualized as such only in 1930s China—of more than fifty nationalities: Muslim Turkic-speaking peoples from the Uighurs to the Kazakhs in Central Asia, Mongolian and Tibetan people in Mongolia and the Himalayas, Koreans and Manchu in the north. Through internal migration, Beijing accommodated small communities or seasonal populations of maritime Arab Muslim traders, Turkic Muslims from Samarkand, and nomad Mongol traders. Commercial connections reached deep into the interior; the Muslims of Inner Mongolia, for example, grew tobacco for the British American Tobacco Company. Mongolia was targeted by the Chinese government's colonization policies. Men with limited means migrated for seasonal labor, younger sons of peasant families moved, whole peasant families resettled. As everywhere, families with limited means were separated because some members, usually the male head of the household, departed to earn cash income afar. Alienation, experience of mobility, and bilingualism induced younger men to remain in towns as interpreters. Markets and new railways connected the nomad and pioneer economies to the core.

Migration to Manchuria, vastly larger, began in the mid-nineteenth century when northern Chinese had settled in the Liao River valley, then moved to regions north of Mukden and Harbin. Construction of railroads, eastbound from Beijing to Suiyuan and northbound to Harbin, provided mass transportation. Impoverished families, however, had to walk hundreds of miles and build homes out of sun-dried mud bricks with a mud roof on brush—similar to European newcomers' sod houses in North America's prairies. Manchuria's population doubled from fifteen million in 1911 to thirty million in 1931. Into the 1920s, China's government encouraged and assisted migration; private companies or administrative bodies held and sold land. To the mid-1920s, three-quarters of the half-million seasonal workers returned annually to their families in Shandong or Zhili. Thereafter railway-stimulated in-migration increased to a million per year and permanent settlement grew through family migration. Most originated from Shandong Province and migrated voluntarily in the framework of continued droughts, famine, and internal war. The mass migration to "Manchukuo," the region's name under Japanese rule after March 1, 1932, provided Japanese-run coal mines, railway construction, and cities with workers via the Japan-controlled South Manchurian Railway from the port of Dairen to Mukden, Jilin, and Harbin.

In Mongolia, cultural interaction was the rule; in Manchuria, by sheer numbers the Chinese immigrants absorbed the local Manchu. The newcomers formed classic urban immigrant communities in which families from the same region or village of origin settled close to each other, founded mutual aid societies, banded together in vigilante-type groups to keep order under frontier conditions, and established credit arrangements to avoid moneylenders. Because settlement was compact, the frontier moved ahead slowly. New railroads, banks, and market crops facilitated settlement; Confucian concepts of family, of ancestral spirits related to land, and of sons' duties toward living and deceased parents retarded change. By 1940, Manchuria's population of 43.2 million consisted of 36.8 million Chinese, 2.7 million Manchu, 1.1 million Mongols, 1.45 million Koreans, 0.85 million Japanese, as well as Russians and others. The ubiquitous population planners estimated that Manchuria could still absorb a further 30 million immigrants. However, Japan's aggression against China in 1937, the beginning of World War II, turned mass labor into mass refugee migrations. The postwar change of regimes in China from nationalist to communist, as well as the need to rebuild the war-devastated country and resettle the internal refugees, ended the recent pattern of northward and the traditional pattern of southward migration.[103]

Industrializing European Russia and Its Siberian Frontier

At the turn from the nineteenth to the twentieth century, the Russo-Siberian migration system involved (1) large-scale, mostly seasonal rural-to-urban migrations in European Russia of tens of millions; (2) increasing "internal emigration" of peasant families but also of workers to southern Siberia as far as the Amur River, the Sino-Russian border; and (3) from the 1880s, emigration to North America, predominantly of Jews, Poles, and Ukrainians.

Since emancipation in 1861, peasant families increasingly migrated to southern Siberian and trans-Caspian cultivable lands, and from the 1880s, parallel to the Canadian West, the mining frontier became a magnet. Transcontinental railroads facilitated movement since the 1880s. Similarities between the United States and imperial Russia were many: The "Great American Desert" had been considered as uninhabitable as Siberia. The US and Canadian governments encouraged migration through homestead acts, in 1862 and 1872, respectively, as did Russia from the mid-eighteenth century and again under Pyotr Stolypin's policies of 1906–1911. Migrants settled contiguous tracts of land and created social systems more equal and more dynamic than those of their home villages. In the United

States, Mormons fled westward; in Russia, Old Believers moved eastward. Under Russification policies—as part of the Northern Hemisphere's nationalist surge in the latter nineteenth century—Russian Doukhobors, other religious dissenters, and south Russian German-language Mennonites migrated to Canada and the United States to escape religious persecution and national homogenization. Some 150,000 departed for North America from 1899 to 1914, and more left in the 1920s, fleeing policies of atheism and collectivism.

In the Russo-Siberian migration system, during the decades from 1880 to 1914 and into the 1920s, some ten million men and women individually or as families moved eastward and southward—the same period in which some twenty million Europeans, Jews and Ukrainians from Russia included, migrated westward. In the 1890s an average of forty-two thousand people arrived in Siberia annually; of these, less than 2 percent were deportees. Many of the political exiles were highly educated and socially responsible men and women who became teachers and nurses in Siberian villages and towns neglected by the distant government in Moscow. By 1911, First Peoples accounted for a mere 10 percent of the total Siberian population of 9.4 million. The immigrants and their descendants, mainly Russians, Ukrainians, and Ruthenians, concentrated along a belt of land six hundred kilometers wide in western and central Siberia. Settlement was easier for the estimated four million settlers in the trans-Caspian and trans-Aral regions and Kazakhstan. In Central and East Asia, Russian and Chinese migrants interacted with peasants living in interspersed but separate villages. The Amur River became a trade artery, Chinese merchants and artisans moved to Vladivostok, and Chinese migrants as unskilled laborers on the Trans-Siberian Railway worked alongside skilled workers from Germany and Italy in a labor force that was 25 percent foreign. In the Amur gold fields, Chinese contract workers made up 15 percent of the labor force in 1900, and 76 percent in 1915. By 1910, one hundred thousand Chinese, some skilled workers or urban artisans, lived in the Russian Far East. Like pidgin English in California gold prospecting, a Russo-Chinese pidgin became the lingua franca. Discrimination prevented Chinese from owning land or staking claims. Racism notwithstanding, intermarriage was widespread. While Russian administrators, of white mentality, attempted to restrict the "yellow peril," the whole regional economy depended on immigrants and became a meeting ground for Eurasian peoples.[104]

Internal rural-to-urban migration after emancipation in European Russia is well documented. The communities of origin, which shared responsibilities for taxes, kept detailed records of the temporarily absent. In the decade after 1870, almost forty million migration permits were issued—almost all for a year or less. At the time of the first empire-wide census in 1897, 9.4 million men and women (11.7 and 8.0 percent of their respective shares of the population) had moved away from their province of birth. The net figures do not reflect gross moves: multiple migrations, departure and return before the census date, emigration, rural-to-urban migration within the populous Moscow and St. Petersburg provinces, and other intraprovincial migration. The provinces of Moscow, the central industrial region, and St. Petersburg, as well as the four provinces of the Donbass and Urals industrial belt, received the bulk of the internal migrants. In 1897 almost three-quarters of Moscow's one million inhabitants and St. Petersburg's 1.25 million were migrants. All other provinces had negative migration balances. Low out-migration characterized the three Baltic provinces (subsequently Estonia and Latvia) because of the language differences. Many rural families followed the almost worldwide pattern of gender-specific allocation of labor resources: male wage labor at a distance and female double-load farm labor at home as an income-diversification strategy when cash rather than exchange came to characterize trade.

Temporary rural-to-urban mass migration influenced family relations as well as peasant, worker, and gendered mentalities, workloads, and self-organization. Men and women migrated jointly to the rural and mining zones of the Donbass and the Urals, but more than 80 percent of the urban migrants were men. Most families could not afford to or did not want to leave agriculture altogether, and women staying behind had to assume their absent husbands' workload. In contrast to work, independent decision making hardly grew in view of male relatives' roles and control. As in all regions of out-migration, children of such bifurcated households hardly ever saw their fathers. Women visiting their husbands in the cities got a glimpse of urban life and male working-class standards of living, the latter probably no inducement to follow. However, women who did migrate acculturated quickly to urban life, took factory jobs, and married late. Neighborhood support, shared traditions of everyday life, and festive customs eased the transition. In self-organized *arteli,* collective units of life, the men cooked together or hired one woman to do the work for many, elected a leader, and regulated their affairs. There were high levels of geographic, job, and residential fluctuation. Thirteen percent of Moscow's inhabitants of 1882 had arrived in the preceding year, requiring institutions similar to the village *mir,* and the *artel* was a democratic as well as a constraining frame.

Proletarianization occurred over generations. Serfs and emancipated peasants first became seasonal labor migrants, then, with longer sojourns in the factories, peasant-workers still bound to the village. When ties loosened, they changed to worker-peasants, and their urban-born sons and daughters would be urban workers, proletarians. However, due to the *mir* system and the bifurcated families, children were usually raised in the rural world, distant from urban working-class environments. They would have to begin the cycle again, with each generation of workers socialized anew into factory life, whether in Russia, North America, or Western Europe. Migrants who did not return to their village origins developed both craft skills and proletarian mentalities, and they or their children could enter skilled positions. More recent migrants had to take unskilled jobs that provided lower incomes.[105]

In a third movement Jews, Poles, Ukrainians, and Baltic peoples migrated westward into the Atlantic migration system. Jointly, Jewish and Polish migrants accounted for 68 percent of emigration from tsarist Russia to North America; others included Belorussians and Ukrainians (11 percent), Lithuanians (9 percent), Finns (7 percent), and Russian-Germans and Mennonites who left after their privileges were withdrawn (5 percent). From 1830 to 1860 only about thirty thousand of the tsar's subjects left the empire westbound; from 1860 to 1914, 4.5 million followed. Of special groups of migrants, the Polish political emigration ended with the last rebellion (struggle for independence) in 1863–1864. Activists were sent to Siberia; some seven to eight thousand refugees headed for Paris and England. The émigrés became a nucleus for later Polish labor migrants. Russian reformers and revolutionaries also emigrated and emerged as a kind of society-in-exile, a "second Russia abroad." Militants who returned during the revolution of 1905 were soon forced into exile again; fleeing revolutionary Jewish workers increased the US-bound migrations. Of young Russian women, barred from universities, some five to six thousand migrated to Swiss universities from 1882 to 1913. Most planned to return and devote themselves to medical and charitable work among peasants and perhaps the urban poor.

A family of Jewish immigrant shoemakers in Paris, 1920. In the face of escalating violence and increasing social, political, and economic restriction, two million Jews emigrated from Russia between 1880 and 1914. Many settled in Europe's metropoles: Berlin, Paris, London. Others continued to North America. (Mémorial de la Shoah / CDJC)

Labor migrants from the Jewish Pale of Settlement, Russian-occupied Polish lands, and Ukraine headed to West European cities, Berlin, Paris, and London in particular, and to North American cities, from Montreal via New York to Pennsylvania. From Ukraine agricultural settler families also migrated to Canada's prairies. Of the world's Jewish population an estimated three-quarters lived in Eastern Europe. The 750,000 to 900,000 Jews of the late eighteenth century had increased to 5.2 million in Russia and 2 million in other parts of East and East Central Europe by the end of the nineteenth century. Early marriage, combined with large numbers of children, explains this increase, which was more than twice the empire's average population growth. Internal migrations from the stagnating northeastern borderlands of the former Polish-Lithuanian Commonwealth targeted Russia's southern provinces. Briefly, the government recruited Jewish families as settlers for agricultural regions. In contrast, some cities, such as Kiev, continued the medieval discrimination and barred in-migration. Again others, like the thriving, relatively new port of Odessa (founded in 1794), with a mere 250 Jewish inhabitants in 1795 but 152,000 in 1904, saw a vibrant Jewish culture emerge. Pogroms in the 1870s and severely restrictive legislation accelerated the mass exodus that transferred elements of the cultures of the small shtetl or urban Odessa to North America. World War I brought all movement to a standstill, and the Russian Revolution of 1917 changed all parameters of action.[106]

Mediterranean Africa, the Persian Gulf, and Sub-Saharan Africa

In the cultures of the Eastern Mediterranean, Mediterranean Africa, and the Persian Gulf (West Asia, North Africa, Arabia), the stability the Ottoman Empire was being challenged and the imperialist governments of Britain and France began to expand their influence into the region. In the core of the Ottoman Empire, multiethnic coexistence became more tenuous as administrators' inability or venality grew, as did aspirations for self-rule among Armenians and many other peoples.[107] In the Ottoman's former Mediterranean African realm, port and trading cities declined when the centuries-long ascent of Mediterranean Europe began, and subsequently economic activity shifted to the Atlantic. According to political-economic aspirations, imposed European domination, and migration

DIRK HOERDER

patterns, four regions emerged: Egypt and the Omani state, Ethiopia, the Nilotic Sudan, and North Africa.

Egypt and the Omani state asserted influence over Arabia while, at mid-nineteenth century, British and French migrant entrepreneurs infused the Egyptian elites with concepts of Western-type modernization and inserted capital for construction of the Suez Canal. In the early 1870s, vast infrastructural projects as well as cotton cultivation—partly in response to the interruption of cotton supply from the secessionist US states in the 1860s—mobilized rural workers and marginal peasant families. A nationalist movement among the rising elites and antiforeigner riots among urban populations countered the impositions of the European immigrants and states. Ethiopia, coveted by the English and French, was militarily colonized by Italy after 1882. When the state, in a late colonizing attempt, planned to send Italian settler families, the millions of Italian migrants preferred the Americas and, in small numbers, destinations around the world. Even the fascist expansion of the 1920s and 1930s could not change this pattern. The Nilotic Sudan remained contested ground as a catchment area for slaves until, in the 1870s, the slave trade from the upper Nile region was abolished officially if not in practice.

In North Africa, the French state conquered Algeria and Tunisia after 1830, while Morocco remained independent until 1912. More than one hundred thousand agricultural settlers came. Labeled "French," they were of Spanish, Italian, Maltese, Swiss, Prussian, Bavarian, and Hessian background. The French government feared the mass in-migration of rural poor to Paris—some twenty-five thousand to thirty-five thousand added themselves to the one million Parisians annually. It planned to transport some hundred thousand of these *classes dangereuses* to Algeria, but only fifteen thousand could be corralled and shipped. The colonization process displaced resident Arab and Kabyl people. New regulations in the 1870s—when the tsarist government reclassified the position of Jews—reduced Muslim land rights and additional *colons,* including many French citizens of Jewish faith, came from Europe. Some 630,000 Europeans lived in Algeria by 1901. A Native Code serving the interests of the colonizers regulated and restricted local people's migration. Along with the long-term decline of the southern Mediterranean littoral and the impoverishment created by colonizer impositions, epidemics and famines reduced native North African populations.[108]

·[540]·

South Africa, the one other agricultural colony established by the Dutch, had been annexed by Britain in 1806. In contrast to the homogenization of immigrant settlers in Algeria, the Dutch and the British remained distinct and antagonistic. They fought over land and control of the native labor force. The resulting segmented and color-coded society provided a stark contrast to Latin American many-colored ethnogenesis. Against the Dutch-Afrikaners the British passed Aliens Expulsion and Aliens Immigration Restriction acts in the 1890s; the Transvaal Afrikaner (Boer) government in turn discriminated against British subjects. For the resulting war, the British Empire sent some 300,000 troops and, in the course of it, deported some 120,000 Afrikaner women and children to camps. Deportation as a British imperial strategy had been used against French-speaking Acadians in the North American colonies in the 1750s and was to be used against Kikuyu and Kabaka in East Africa in the 1950s.

Immigrant European farmers imposed restrictions on the resident Khoi, and by the mid-nineteenth century the government imposed segregation. From the 1860s the colonizers imported indentured workers from India and from China's northern provinces. With the discovery of diamonds in 1866 and of gold in 1886, the demand for mine labor, investment capital, and skilled gem cutters expanded massively. A niche economy connected the mines to Dutch-Jewish diamond experts in Amsterdam. Cities grew by leaps and bounds: Johannesburg's population, zero in 1886, by 1899 numbered one hundred thousand from across southern Africa and fifty thousand from across Europe. The diamond mines' migrant owners housed the migrant workers in closed compounds both for purposes of control and to permit them to carry wages home. At first the arrangement suited migrants to a degree that employers could rely on self-recruitment. In the last decades of the nineteenth century, African men from Portuguese Mozambique and other neighboring colonies joined the mine labor force. In these migrations ethnic identifications were reshaped by interaction, and male and female cultures—separated by migration and compound housing—evolved along distinct paths. By the 1930s the three hundred thousand mine workers formed a distinct ethnic class. It no longer included migrants from Asia, because the government of the Union of South Africa, established in 1910, immediately excluded migrant labor from Asia. Australia, too, upon receiving Dominion status, had announced a white Australia policy in 1901.[109]

In East and West Africa, the actual end of the slave trade in the 1870s was paralleled by the British, French, Belgian, and German governments' quest for colonies. In the east the British government and merchants imposed their influence on Zanzibar, in part through the immigrants from India; Germans and British established mainland settler colonies. In the west, the French colonizers—after resistance from the Mandinka state and conquest in 1898—relied on traditional chiefs and on competition between them rather than on the integrative Islamic religious structures. The British government, in contrast, sent costly administrative personnel from the core. Both systems succeeded in dividing African peoples into frenchified or anglicized elites and traditional-culture urban lower classes and hinterland dwellers. Because labor was difficult to recruit, colonizer employers and colonizer missionaries combined forces to teach their values of work and to train skilled craftsmen and orderly housewives. Africans, however, adapted some of the Europeans' resources, like written languages, to their own purposes. Women missionaries, who migrated out of their home society's gender hierarchies, helped African women to undercut male authority. In some regions—among the Soninke, for example—itinerant traders, perceiving demand for labor, relayed information back to their communities and free migration ensued. The empires also extracted labor, and colonizer-appointed chiefs shifted the burden of compulsory labor to weaker members of a society. In the German and the Portuguese southwest, rulers and their male supporters, who traditionally had raided weaker peoples for cattle, held colonizers at some distance by becoming their extended arms. They raided villages for labor and delivered captive men and women to the colonizers. In West Africa, the British administrators—with regional variations—demanded compulsory work from men aged fifteen to fifty and women aged fifteen to forty-five. Wage incentives, if offered at all, were low—among East Africa's Kikuyu, for example, far lower than income from independent farming.

Regional patterns of migration depended on traditions, power impositions, and new patterns of mobility. In traditional market-oriented economies, like groundnut production in Senegal, migratory patterns existed previous to and independent of colonial rule. In the Ngoni and Ngonde societies of the Great Lakes area, gender hierarchies kept women in bondage, and in the 1880s and 1890s Bemba "entrepreneurial brigandage" captured women and children to be handed over to traders. Many such women fled to return to their people or to migrate independently. In Kenya, the British colonizers alienated Kikuyu land, and in consequence the number of migrant laborers grew from 5,000 in 1903 to 120,000 in 1923. Kikuyu and other people protected themselves by developing market agriculture in crops that did not lend themselves to economies of scale and thus remained outside of colonizer interest. Infrastructural projects like the building of the Uganda railway from Mombasa to Nairobi, begun in 1896, demanded large labor forces: in this case a mere 107 European technicians, overseers, and tavern keepers; 6,000 Indians, including 4,800 Punjabi Muslim coolies, 300 soldiers, and 1,100 Baluchi and Arab merchants; and 17,400 Swahili-speakers, comprising 14,600 free persons, 2,650 slaves, and 150 prisoners. Over the next years, some 35,000 indentured workers were imported, mainly from the commercially related villages and towns along the Gulf of Cambay. Asian immigrants to East Africa amounted to 54,400 by 1921. Denied the right to acquire land, they entered the trades.[110]

From Africa's many regions of fragile ecology, those impoverished by drought or other natural disasters migrated first. Caught in a web of power relationships between wage-appropriating local rulers and exploitative colonizers, by the 1920s people developed working-class militancy and collective action. Information about destinations permitted increased agency and migration over larger distances. In hinterlands, the coming of Asian-origin immigrant or traditional African traders created new expectations and a resulting need for cash. Wage incomes permitted escape from oppressive parents or societies, choice of marriage partners, and increase in prestige. On the other hand, centripetal forces remained strong. Women-and-child families remained behind; rural ways of life were stabilized by infusion of cash. Jobs within walking distance kept migrants in their own systems of orientation. African labor migration resembles migrations elsewhere in the world. Contact with European workers, often marred by racism, could also infuse European-style ethnic-class consciousness. French Guinean soldiers who fought in Europe in World War I carried back socialist ideas and organized the Conakry dockworkers' strikes in 1918 and 1919.

At the beginning of the twentieth century, the European presence in Africa was politically all-powerful, economically intrusive, culturally transformative as regards elites, but numerically weak. Settlement clusters were limited to 750,000

European immigrants and their descendants in Algeria (less than 14 percent of the population), 1.25 million in South Africa and Rhodesia (22 percent of the population), and 24,000 in Portuguese Angola and Mozambique. Unknown to contemporaries, decolonization was only a few decades away.

Migrating Colonizers

Labor migrations have usually been discussed in terms of options or of exploitation. Migrations of agrarian settlers have been discussed in terms of soils to be cultivated. Migrations of imperial personnel were disregarded as comparatively small or, in an older version, endowed with a civilizing mission. However, colonizer personnel migrations are of particular importance in terms of interest groups, gender, and constructions of "white," not merely over "black" but over all "coloreds," in processes of racialization and categorization of peoples as Other. Language needs to be used carefully: the white-over-black color scheme, from a different perspective, could read "pale trumps colorful" and connotations would change.

When the French state in the 1870s embarked on a new imperial strategy or "mission," its body politic—the middle classes—had just been humbled, forced into submission, by Prussia's victorious aggression. France's elite, unable to beat up the Teutons, turned to putting down the French working class (deportation of the Communards), French Jews (as in the Dreyfus affair), and peoples in Africa, Indochina, and Caledonia. Several wars later, in 1945, after five years of Fascist German occupation and considerable cooperation, collaborating French men turned against French women who had fallen in (carnal) love with German soldiers and humbled them: a ritual to regain their manhood. The aspects of maleness in British migration and statesmanship have been discussed above. Politics, warfare, and migration are bodied and gendered processes and involve strategies. This kind of manhood—both inside the nation and outside of it in the colonies—was conceived in terms not of humanity but of self-aggrandizement and bullying. Maleness implied the capability to put down weaker Others.

The white or paleface colonizer states' middle classes and ruling elites were internally segmented. Patterns of access to "national" state offices and specific cultural practices made hierarchies of class and gender as well as of ethnicity and race integral parts of "democratic" polities, whether called the "mother country" or the "fatherland." The constructed homogeneity of "the English," for example, was, as some contemporary and most recent scholarship of colonialism and imperialism has noted, intended for the benefit of a small group of profiteers, whether merchants and financiers in the metropole or Caribbean planters, South African mine owners, or Kenyan settlers. Implementing policies of imperial expansion, decided upon by statesmen, enormously increased state expenses for military men and equipment—all paid for with public funds. On the periphery, ambitious colonizer personnel generated their own expansive and enriching tactics. The Belgian king turned the Congo colony into his private fief; military officers did the same in French Sudan. It may be argued that, at the time, this colonial order was so entwined with the politics and economies of colonizer countries that its sudden abolition might have involved the collapse of imperial economies, regardless of the state involved.

Who gained advantages by or profited from which political stratagems depended on social customs and political processes in a particular state and society. The British gentry and nobility who could not provide for younger sons' lifestyles in keeping with the family name sent many of them into colonial service to live off government-paid, tax-funded incomes. Colonial administrations and armies, as James Mill, a Scottish Englightenment thinker, commented, provided "a vast system of outdoor relief" for the male children of the wealthy. Not having been brought up with business acumen, a trade, or professional expertise, most were unable to support themselves. The less competent were sent off by their families— just as Russian peasant communes rid themselves of their least productive members by detailing them into the decade-long army service. From the Netherlands, men with incomplete schooling and those labeled misfits by their families left. Such separation from or abandonment by birth families, as well as the life in all-male communities far from the world of childhood socialization, often involved emotional deprivation that was passed on as brutality against weaker subordinates and subalterns. For some family-sent colonizer migrants, mental disease resulted; the British in India hid their insane in asylums because their visibility to the colonized would have undercut the myth of the white man's superiority.

On the other hand, numerous military or administrative colonizer officials did come with education and what, in their own societies, were major capabilities.

These, however, they had to put to use in societies they did not know, often did not understand, and usually made no effort to learn the language of. Their ethnological, geographical, botanical, or other studies have received acclaim and, in many ways, advanced knowledge. However, the cultural specimens they sent home were taken without the consent of the individual owners or social users. To take the statue of a Buddha or a Dogon mask for purposes of study and exhibition is like taking a Madonna from a Christian church. Thus the venerable British Museum contains "the loot" of British imperial expansion; a similar museum in Paris changed its original name, Musée Permanent des Colonies (opened in 1931), to Musée de la France d'outre-mer (1935) and then to Musée des Arts Africains et Océaniens (1960). Collecting material from and studying other, less powerful peoples has had a complex history—as critical anthropologists, like Michel Leiris in France and others elsewhere, pointed out as early as the 1930s.

Educated segments of the colonizer states' middle classes—university and school teachers, for example—showed great interest in other cultures and carved them into academic subjects. In the process they also provided themselves with securely tenured positions. Journalists and authors sold texts and photographic images about the distant "possessions"; the British Colonial Office instituted a Visual Instruction Committee after 1902. Scholars in geography, history, languages, and surveying methods formed learned societies to supply practical knowledge. To elevate their contribution and make themselves indispensable, many of these intellectual gatekeepers participated in the construction of "scientific" racism and, in an "imaginary ethnography," viewed other cultures through their own preconceptions. They "Orientalized" non-European societies, to use Edward Saïd's term.[111] The Other was seen and (mis)understood through the grids of meaning of the power-wielding intruders or, neutrally, outsiders. This skewed data collection or image production emerging from colonizer migrations has deeply influenced scholarly interpretation and analysis. For lack of other data, scholars of the present often have to rely on such collections and even on colonizer categorizations.

The quantitative data would have been available: With the change from permanently bound to temporarily bound or free-under-constraints migration, the Africa-to-the-Americas slave migration was abolished but still involved almost two million men and women in the nineteenth century. As partial replacement, the new British-imposed Asian indenture system became part of the other partially bound or free-under-constraints migration and, like the North Atlantic Europe-to-the-Americas system, involved some fifty million men and women. The equally large out-migration from north China began only in the 1880s and, with the exception of a very limited transoceanic migration under indenture, remained transcontinental. Also transcontinental was the Russo-Siberian and trans-Caspian system, with perhaps ten million involved, a system that would expand massively under Stalinism and last to the mid-1950s. In China, India, Europe, North America, and European Russia, vastly more men and women migrated internally from regions with a surplus of labor to developing urban, mining, or industrial regions. Such internal migration also occurred in Latin America, given uneven regional development, and in Africa, southern and northern, for the same reason but under colonizer impositions. All of these mass migrations involved men and women who formed families, and with few exceptions the gender ratio became balanced at the latest in the second generation. Demographic data about births—that is, "natural" population growth (as if growth by migration were unnatural)—were available all along. The view that migration is a "male thing" stemmed from gender-biased minds—research of the last two decades based on vital records and port statistics has provided the aggregate statistics.[112]

4. Migrations during War and Depression

FROM around 1900 to the 1930s the nationalization of Europe's many-cultured dynastic states—the Habsburg, Hohenzollern, Romanov, and Ottoman empires in particular—resulted in both refugee migrations and deportations of whole population segments. At first, imposition of the dominance of one ethnocultural group labeled "the nation" occurred within empires under such notions as "Germanization" or "the Turkish nation." This new domineering approach was to the detriment of numerically smaller ethnocultural groups who were labeled "minorities." At the empires' collapse in 1918, nation-states were carved out of imperial territories from regions with historically mixed settlements of peoples of many cultures. Talking heads of the times propounded the strength of their respective state in competition with neighboring ones and the importance of racial superiority. Only the League of Nations and a very few scholars addressed the refugee-generating consequences of the transition from empires to nations.[113] From Russification to Americanization, new conformity-demanding nationalism emerged across the Atlantic world—and, under Western hegemony, would become the organizing principle of former colonies after independence from the late 1940s on.

The internal changes in the Ottoman Empire, hastened by the British and French Empires' intrusion into the region, involved a new nationalism of the Turkish people. This replaced traditional interreligious and multiethnic coexistence. In the same vein, the growing intransigence of the dominant German-speakers of the Habsburg empire undercut the polity's multiple cultural-regional structures. The demands of these empires' many peoples for self-rule were quashed. Old empires and new nation-states came to advocate an "un-mixing of peoples" by involuntary mass migrations. On the two ends of the Eurasian landmass, the brinksmanship of Hohenzollern Germany (world war from 1914) and the imperialist strategies of Meiji Japan (from the war against China in 1895) were instrumental in disrupting the mass labor migrations and in generating mass refugee migrations. Contemporaries discussed the defeat of (white) tsarist Russia by (nonwhite) Meiji Japan in 1905—with arms bought from the West—in terms of race domination. Japan's aggressive expansion changed the parameters of migration in Asia and, in intention but more so in propaganda, involved a reassertion of Asia's self-determination against European and US imperialism. In this constellation, the British Empire and the reemergent French Empire (from 1830, but especially since the 1870s), in their turn, refused to grant self-administration or independence to any but "white" colonies, the new Dominions. This imperial intransigence generated massive waves of refugees, first in the Northern Hemisphere to the late 1940s, and then in the Southern Hemisphere during and after the wars for independence from 1947 on.

In the course of their colonization, European settler and investor migrants had displaced resident or regionally mobile peoples. European peasant families from densely populated sedentary societies moved to what seemed to them thinly settled regions. Such view is never shared by those "thinly" settled: Native Americans in North America, Aborigines in Australia and New Zealand, native peoples in South Africa and, from the 1870s, East Africa. White newcomers displaced not only nomadic hunter-gatherers, as their rhetoric liked to suggest, but resident agricultural peoples. Likewise, the northward migrations of Chinese overwhelmed local Manchurians. In the 1920s, the Atlantic world's transition to industrial and urban patterns of life notwithstanding, some ideologues of white peoples' settlement in other peoples' "underused" regions suggested reducing what they considered urban congestion by further rural settlement projects in a global belt from Canada's northern Alberta via Manchuria's lowlands to southern Siberia; in a Latin American south-to-north belt along the eastern foothills of the Andes; in an African belt of cool subtropical highlands from Transvaal to Kenya; as well as in sections of Australia, Tasmania, and New Zealand. Even though all of these regions were distant from transport facilities, provisions, and markets, the population planners rhapsodized about a global "pioneer fringe" with virgin soils to be put under the plow. Influenced by racist and sexist eugenics, they divided the "white" race by extolling the virility of strong and healthy men and denigrating "slack" workers and "sickly people (especially women)." This migration planning involved a gendered "culling" of populations.[114]

One of the many migration-connected transitions of the interwar years in-volved a little-studied change of images: the United States, settled and urbanized as well as imperialist, became less attractive to migrants who wanted to build new societies (and the United States also sharply restricted immigration from dark Eastern Europe and olive Southern Europe). In contrast, the new Soviet Union seemed to provide vast urban-industrial frontiers as well as Siberian mining and rural frontiers full of opportunities for enterprising migrants. The project of building a new proletarian-democratic society—in the years before the Stalinist purges—offered hope and options to militants. The Soviet Union with Siberia appeared as "the other America." From the mid-1920s, with postwar economic recovery, its industrial growth did attract migrants who expected to arrive in a promising workers' republic. This image replaced the nineteenth-century hopes for an ideal American republic. To escape racism, some African-Americans from the South fled to pioneer cotton growing in Kazakhstan. Frontier opportunities, pioneer achievements, and powerful machines reflected the promises of a "youth-ful" culture—just as did a "young Europe" a century earlier and as "Young Turks" struggled for at the same time. The vision ended with the Soviet forced-labor camps of the 1930s and the Axis Powers' invasion in 1941.[115]

The late nineteenth-century realignment of imperial hegemony in the region of the contracting Ottoman Empire and the emergence of Japan as a new power-ful empire initiated both refugee generation and forced-labor migrations of people designated as inferior. The declining European empires' transcontinental war-fare, in 1914–1918, with the involvement of the newly—and differently—imperial United States from 1917, produced tens of millions of refugees and the deporta-tion of peoples designated as "non-national" from their historic spaces of settle-ment. "Statesmen," by treaties, moved borders over them and changed their citi-zen status overnight from members to aliens. New forced-labor regimes were buttressed by internal militarization of societies in Africa's recently colonized segments, Europe's fascist states, the Soviet Union as a whole, Japan's internal and external economies, and South Africa. However, at the same time a combi-nation of educational-intellectual and labor migrants moving from colonies to cores developed the foundations for anticolonial concepts and projects. Hardly noticed by white colonizers, these were to turn into movements for indepen-dence after World War II. Most involved armed struggles because the colonizer powers, though weakened, refused to withdraw, and thus from the 1950s mass refugee generation shifted from Europe to the Southern Hemisphere.

Disintegrating and Emerging Empires

The political implementation of race-based nation-building projects in the old empires involved expulsion of whole peoples—Otherized from being accepted subjects of a dynasty to being non-nationals.[116] Historic interethnic patterns of migration and settlement were characteristic to all borderlands: the Romance-German borderlands from Belgium to Alsace; East Central Europe from the Baltic via the Polish-Lithuanian-Russian-German to the Polish-Ukrainian-Russian spaces; and the region from the Balkans via Anatolia to the Caucasus. Millennia of migrations had left mosaics of interspersed and cohabitating groups.[117] From the 1860s, emerging nationalist governments claimed territories of neighboring states under the pretense of incorporating co-nationals into their home. The wars of expansion and national unification of Prussia in the 1860s to 1871 and subsequent national chauvinism sent Czechs fleeing, made French Alsatians Germans, brought the expulsion of 80,000 Germans from France, and caused the departure of 130,000 Alsatians for France after annexation. Subsequently, in the east Prussia expelled 85,000 Poles. The Romanov empire's Russification sent Jewish, Mennonite, Lutheran, and Catholic German-speakers to seek shelter by westbound moves to North America. Definition of groups as minorities with lesser rights and less access to a society's resources and labor markets forced individuals and families to depart under duress. In Britain, the Alien Act of 1905 discriminated against proletarian migrants, in particular those of Russian-Jewish background.[118] Governments withdrew ordinary rights from culturally unwanted residents and denationalized them. Thus deprived of their documents of travel, they had to be relieved by the League of Nations High Commissioner on Refugees, Fridtjof Nansen, who invented the "Nansen Passport" in 1922 as a non-national travel document.

In the Ottoman Empire ethnoculturally and religiously defined peoples had lived in separate social slots (*millet* and *mahalle*) in structured and legally secure cohabitation. Since the eighteenth century, tsarist Russia's annexation of Ottoman lands had sent multiethnic Muslims fleeing, between one and two million by the 1890s. The Ottomans resettled Circassians and Chechens to Palestine to serve as border guards against Bedouin incursions. In the Balkans, the Greek people's self-rule, British, French, and Austro-Hungarian interventions, a new Turkish nationalism, and liberation struggles of resident peoples caused flight or emigration. The multiethnic and multireligious population of Istanbul doubled from the influx of Bosnian-Muslim refugees.

After 1900 the Young Turks movement called for a secular, homogenized nation-state without protected status for ethnoreligious groups. At the time of the establishment of the Turkish state, Armenians and Kurds were denied independent statehood and peoples of intercultural regions were "un-mixed." When the Christian autocephalous Armenians sought social progress, the Turkish government feared demands for autonomy. The presence of proselytizing US Protestant missionaries was seen as further imperial meddling. During World War I, Ottoman hard-liners had hundreds of thousands of Armenians deported to the Syrian and Mesopotamian deserts. In the new Soviet Union an Armenian republic was created in 1918; it had to accommodate about half a million refugees, and within a year an estimated 10 percent of its population died of starvation and epidemics. A European and North American refugee diaspora of Armenians emerged.[119]

Between Greece and Turkey, a government-imposed population exchange was legitimized by the "great powers" and left the 1.25 million Greek and 400,000 Turkish "repatriates" impoverished. The population planners neither consulted those selected for repatriation nor prepared accommodations for the "imported" co-nationals. A Turko-Bulgarian Agreement of 1925 decreed the "voluntary" exchange of Turks from Bulgaria and Bulgarians from Turkey. Such nation-state mandated migrations involved more than a million men, women, and children in the region in the 1920s and 1930s. In the western Balkans, the post-1918 new South Slav or Yugoslav state combined Serbs and Croats, Bosnian Muslims and Montenegrins, Slovenes and Dalmatians. The policies of un-mixing of peoples sprang from nationalist ideologies in which ethnocultural and ethnoreligious lifestyles were perceived as badges of political loyalty or disloyalty.[120]

Under a League of Nations mandate, formerly Ottoman Syria and Palestine were administered by the French and British governments, respectively. Palestine, according to the Balfour Declaration of November 1917, was to become "a national home" for the Jewish people without infringements on the civil and religious rights of resident Muslim and Christian peoples. Competition for land and other resources made this multicultured and interfaith region conflict-prone. In North Africa the realignment into Arab states did not involve population exchanges, but the British in Egypt had requisitioned forced laborers during wartime. When Egypt's nationalist elites responded with a project for independence, the British government deported the elite to Malta. In the Ottoman and Romanov realms, on the other hand, the British had fanned the nationalist sentiments of non-Turkish and non-Russian peoples to consolidate their hold on oil production from the Caspian Sea to Persia and to implement anti-Bolshevik policies. In the frame of Turkish nationalism and British imperialism the Ottoman Empire's dissolution turned some 8.5 million people into refugees. The region's political-territorial structures and cultural interactions have remained conflict-prone into the early twenty-first century.

Imperial Japan expanded its reach by warfare against Russia, China, and Korea starting in 1895, just as the United States had done half a century earlier against Mexico and, also in the 1890s, against Spain. With the help of hired Western advisers, the Meiji government modernized the army and pursued three expansionist strategies: modernization to win the allegiance of the population of annexed Taiwan; territorial and migratory competition in Russia's Far East; and domination, of Korea first, then Manchuria, and finally China. Taiwan, as a food-producing appendage, became a laboratory for agricultural, social, and fiscal improvements. Japanese administrators established security of landholdings and, in distinction to Western colonizers, did not introduce a plantation mode of production. Taiwanese small and middle producers benefited. Sakhalin, a contested territory with economic potential, attracted Russian newcomers who had to compete with Chinese, Korean, and Japanese migrants. The Russians, though nationals, were far from their home base, so in-migrating Chinese merchants and Japanese fishermen held a competitive advantage. According to the 1926 Russian census, one-fifth of its Far East population was of East Asian origin. South Sakhalin, valued because of its natural resources and strategic location, was annexed by Japan and renamed Karafuto. Its Japanese population of twelve thousand in 1906, working in manufacturing, commerce, and transportation, had grown to over four hundred thousand four decades later.

In Korea, in contrast to Taiwan, imperial Japan's takeover of the peasant farming economy came as a shock. Under the slogan of modernization, Japan's Society for Eastern Colonization confiscated family land for forced mass cultivation of export crops. Koreans, forced to live on inferior grains, migrated or fled to Manchuria or Russian Siberia. Japanese citizenship was imposed on them, as was modernized health care. The latter resulted in population growth at the very time when ten million "surplus" Japanese were sent to Korea, whose population density had been underestimated by Japan's population planners. The same happened in other occupied territories: two million were sent to Formosa. No sturdy agricultural pioneers, the staple of imperialist rhetoric, migrated; instead the migrants were small traders, artisans, shopkeepers, and adventurous merchants. Migration was a male middle-class and lower-middle-class project. A few women came as wives, midwives, and prostitutes. Most migrants gravitated to the cities, some became landlords. The Japanese government's rural settlement project was undercut by migrants' choice of Brazil, Peru, Hawaii, and the Philippines as destinations.

In contrast to the historic Ottoman concept of cohabitation of self-administering ethnoreligious groups within one economic-political frame, Meiji expansion employed Japanization to weld the colonized to the colonizers. Administrative personnel were sent from Japan, and Japanese education was given to sons of the Taiwanese and Korean middle classes. A Japanese-inspired youth movement was created in Korea to capitalize on intrasocietal generational differences. In all occupied regions—including, after 1937, China—the Japanese military and colonizer personnel considered "locals" as inferiors to be used to fulfill military-industrial-imperial purposes or, if women, to provide sexual services to the occupation forces.[121]

Trans-European Warfare, 1914–1918

The Habsburg and Hohenzollern imperial bureaucracies as well as general German-culture nationalism—in Austrian and German variants—refused cultural and political autonomy to "minorities." From the 1860s, Hohenzollern Germany's unifying and expansionist warfare rearranged borders over people. Southeastern Europe was unsettled by conflict between the Habsburg and Ottoman empires as well as the expansionist aspirations of semi-independent Serbia.

Many of the region's peoples demanded self-rule, but it was not evident which groups, culturally akin, formed a people. Were Macedonians a distinct people or were they Greeks? Were people in Kosovo Serb, Albanian, or a distinct group? Conflicts intensified in the 1870s. From the late nineteenth century the tsarist empire's Russification policy, which affected East Central European Baltic and Slavic peoples, as well as German-Germanization and Austrian-Germanization, attempted to deculturate the many other peoples of the imperial territories. In addition to the intracontinental conflicts, France and the United Kingdom rejected German expansion into "their" Africa and Asia, feared its new navy on the high seas, and opposed the Habsburg-Austrian ambitions in and beyond the Danube region. A minor incident in 1914 was used to declare all-out war.

The first twentieth-century European internecine war, which in its ramifications in Africa became a world war, did not "break out" but was a calculated strategy. Some sixty million men were mobilized and marched about. Women took their jobs in the aggressor or "home" states. In August 1914, about five million Europeans did not live in their state of birth. Overnight their status changed from guest, labor migrant, or immigrant to "hostile alien" or "citizen of an enemy nation": they could be interned, expelled, or repatriated. The majority, migrating workers, experienced a renationalization of the internationalized labor markets. Prevented from returning, they became captive labor forces in the Axis power states. On the side of the Allies, France relied on the labor of some 230,000 Spanish, 135,000 North Africans, Vietnamese, and Chinese, as well as neighboring Belgians or distant Malagasies. Great Britain mobilized 1.2 million non-European soldiers, mainly in India but also in northern China, and France 0.6 million mainly in North and West Africa. Thus the colonized segments of the empires supplied men and materials to the Allies, or colonial overlords, and in consequence could accelerate their process of self-liberation. The German Reich, an importer of predominantly male labor from Eastern Europe since 1885, declared as one of its war aims the achievement of permanent empire-style control over this reservoir of labor.[122]

The warfare cast the civilian populations first of Belgium, then of Poland, the Baltic provinces, and western Russia, as well as those in southeastern Europe, into nightmares of dislocation, starvation, and death. Armies and displaced civilians foraged on people who were struggling to survive. Within three months,

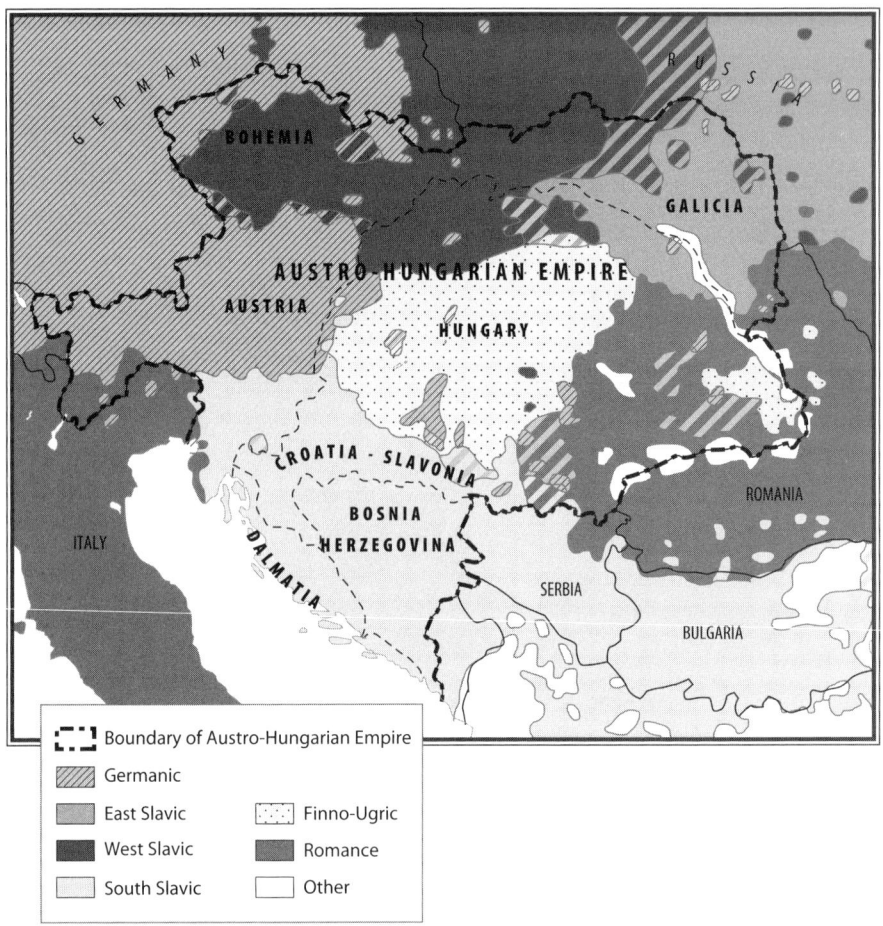

Primary ethnolinguistic groups in the Austro-Hungarian Empire, ca. 1900.

one-fifth of the Belgian population of about seven million were refugees in the Netherlands, France, and Great Britain. Of Serbia's population of three million, one-third were refugees, one-tenth were in the army, another tenth were in camps in Hungary and Bulgaria, often as forced laborers. Typhus killed 150,000. All over Europe, families fled advancing armies, the actual lines of fire, or the reach of distant artillery. In conquered regions, military administrators and civilian authorities expelled groups whose loyalty they questioned, whether Poles from

Germany or Jews with their Yiddish-German dialect and descendants of German immigrants from Russia.

Russia's populations were particularly exposed to uprooting. To slow down the advance of German armies, retreating Russian forces pursued a scorched-earth policy. In late 1915 Russia counted 2.7 million refugees, half a year later 5 million. The 1917 armistice between Germany and Russia sent hundreds of thousands of demobilized, wounded, and sick soldiers in search of families or shelter. By the early 1920s, some 1.5 million children who had lost their parents by separation or death were said to wander about. Male and female workers who had been drafted into the war industries were let go or escaped; those who had been deported from German-occupied territories to forced labor had to find their way back. After October 1917 the Russian Revolution sent a comparatively small number of political exiles, refugee aristocrats, and bourgeois entrepreneurs into westward flight. The subsequent internal wars of 1918–1921 pitted royalists, liberals, and revolutionaries against each other and involved Ukrainian and other national liberation movements. Defeated troops, politicians, and antirevolutionary families fled northward to Finland and the Baltic states, southward to Istanbul, Syria, and Palestine, and westward to France in particular. In the East in China, Harbin and later Shanghai became centers of perhaps sixty thousand exiles. A decade and a half later, both cities were to shelter Jewish refugees from Nazi Germany. Émigré colonies also emerged in Turkestan, Manchuria, and Mongolia.[123]

After the war, prisoners of war had to be repatriated: two million Germans from the Allies, forced laborers from the Reich, Russian prisoners from Austria and Germany, and many others. The peace treaty established new states out of the self-destructed empires. Spokespeople of millions of transatlantic migrants from the empires' disadvantaged peripheries supported independence movements and lobbied in Washington for support. Because large parts of Europe had historically mixed populations, the new borders mandated by the peace treaty forced some five million to change residence between states. The new Baltic and Polish states became the destination of returning prewar emigrants, wartime displaced, and conationals from outside the new borderlines. According to official data, Poland, which had been divided for a century and a half among Russia, Prussia, and Austria, and devastated by the armies of all of the belligerents, received 1.25 million

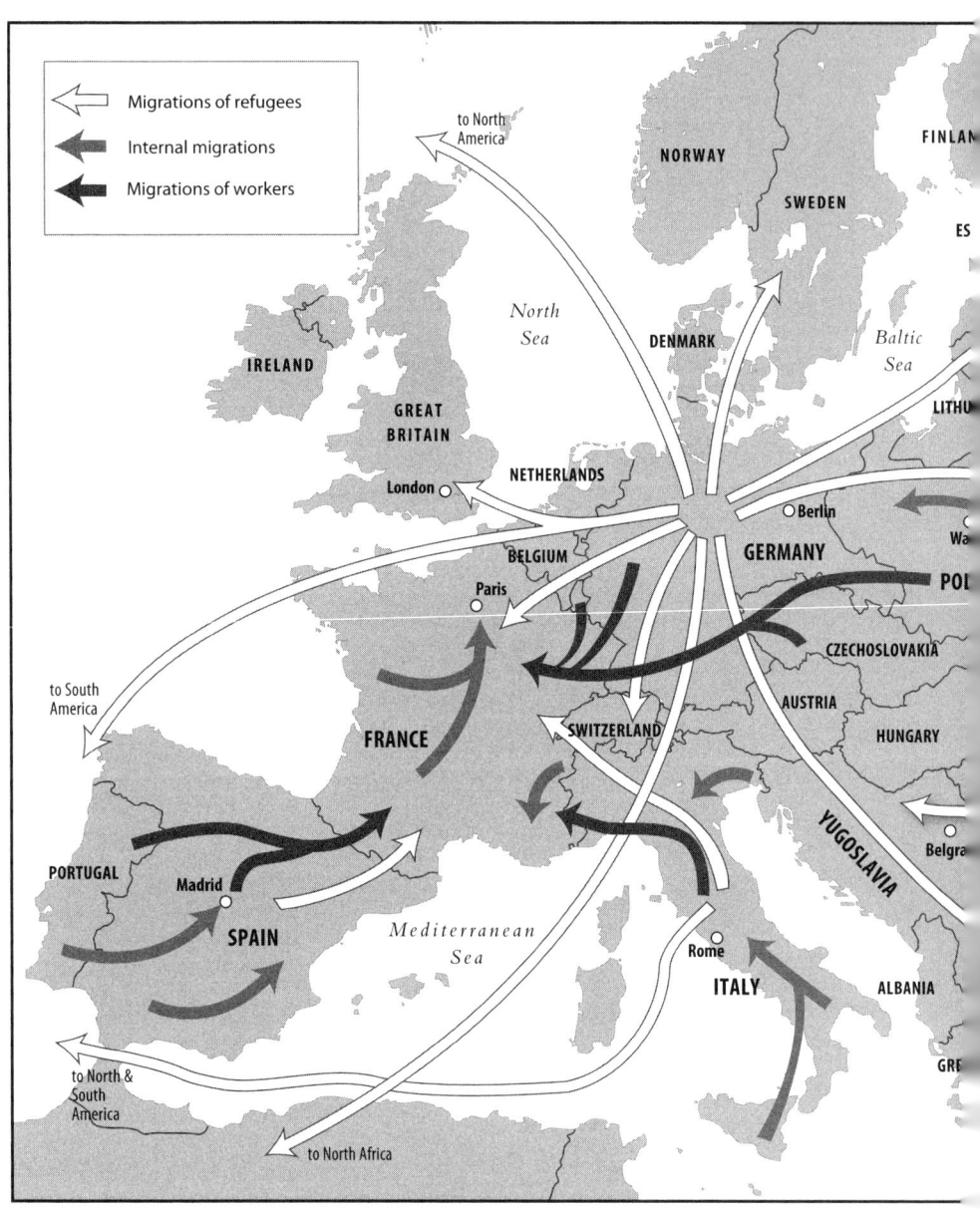

Patterns of migration and flight in Europe, 1914–1939.

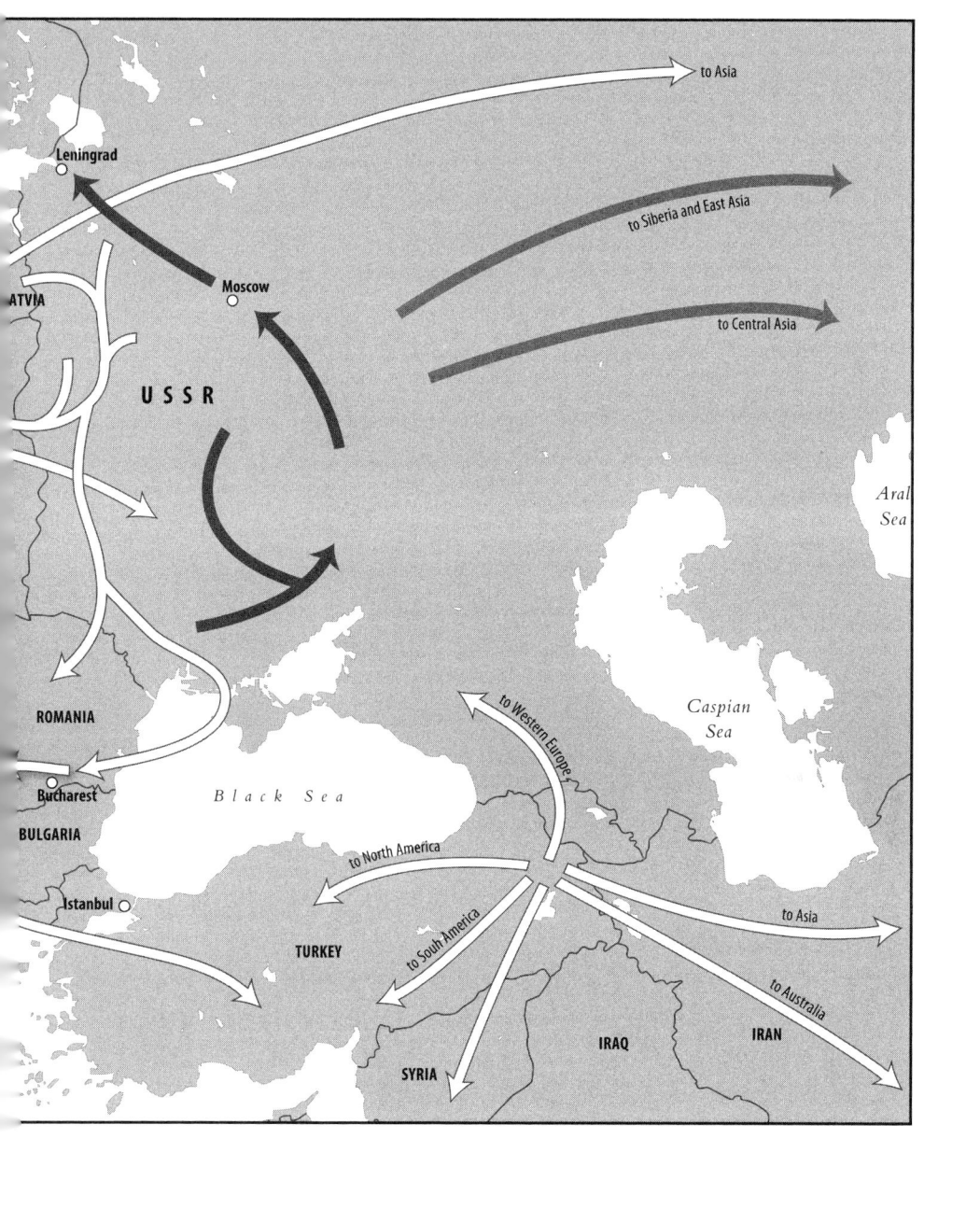

to Asia

to Siberia and East Asia

to Central Asia

Leningrad

Moscow

ATVIA

U S S R

Aral Sea

Caspian Sea

ROMANIA

to Western Europe

Black Sea

Bucharest

BULGARIA

to North America

Istanbul

TURKEY

to South America

to Asia

to Australia

SYRIA

IRAQ

IRAN

returning refugees by 1920, received another 700,000 returnees by 1923, and expected a further 300,000. Hungary in its new borders received Magyar ethnics from Romania (140,000), from Czechoslovakia (57,000), and from Yugoslavia (37,000), while it expelled Hungarian-Germans. Across the war-ravaged lands, displaced civilians and demobilized soldiers returned to villages that no longer existed, to towns of which only ruins remained.[124]

The peace treaty advocated self-determination of peoples in contrast to prewar imperial domination. However, how were borders to be drawn? Centuries of migration and interaction had made almost all of East Central Europe and parts of Western Europe patchworks of interspersed settlements. None of the new states was monocultural; borders were drawn without regard to mosaics of historic settlement; people who stayed put found themselves in ethnically different states. Only national gatekeepers professed certainty about a nation's historic ethnic territories—the areas they claimed often happened to be rich in natural resources. Postwar establishment of such "nation-states" left more than twenty million people outside of the state of their ethnocultural cousins: (1) "Minorities," who in their compact, if small, territories formed the majority, could attempt to stay; (2) small groups could opt for the recently created "home" nation and leave; (3) those who did not fit the newly constructed nations could be expelled or exchanged for others considered fitting; (4) those deemed unacceptable by any state became stateless, trapped wherever they happened to lose citizen status. Multiple identities were considered a threat to the monocultures of nation-states. For the culturally reconfigured men and women, nationhood complicated lives. Borderlines between groups were fuzzy, people often rudimentarily multilingual. Nationalism was the fundamentalism of the period. There were few discourses of respect for other cultures or multicultural interaction—in fact, their existence in the past had been exorcised from memory.

In the interwar years thousands of migrants from North America returned to help build political institutions and to invest in the economies of "their" states, while tens of thousands left the devastated lands for the Americas. From Britain, in a last empire-migration scheme, population planners sent unemployed civilians and demobilized soldiers to "white" Dominions—men to marginal farms, women into domestic service. Working-class families emigrated after the lost general strike of 1926. To reduce ethnic antagonisms, some states improved minority rights, others pursued homogenization policies. Of the former empires, Austria became a small state without further pretensions while Germany's elites retrenched but schemed for new expansions.

In Germany, the post–World War I narrative construction of displacement and resettlement of East European German-origin groups was instrumentalized for aggression in 1939. Official terminology divided German people into those living in the Reich, *Reichsdeutsche,* those living adjacent but outside its borders, *Grenzdeutsche,* and those living farther east or southeast, *Auslandsdeutsche* or *Volksdeutsche*—descendants of three centuries of migrations. The new post-1918 German Republic included 1.5 million non-Germans, mostly Poles, and 1.3 million German-origin expellees and "voluntary" departees from Alsace, Poland, and Gdánsk (Danzig) in a population of 62.4 million. After 1933 the Nazi government augmented estimates of *Grenzdeutsche* to 10 million and began its annexation with the Sudeten region of Czechoslovakia (population 3.5 million) in 1938. Poland's and Hungary's ruling elites also began annexations. Trans-European warfare followed.[125]

Population Displacement in the Interwar Years

In the Soviet Union, wartime devastation resulted in a disastrous decline of food supplies, millions died, and hunger migrations emptied the cities. When agricultural output increased under the New Economic Policy, 1921–1927, migratory directions reversed and industrial production resumed. After 1923 substantial population growth induced large-scale rural-to-urban migrations. The Jewish population, freed from restrictions, dispersed. Between 1926 and 1939 approximately five million migrants crossed the Urals eastbound or moved southeastward into the Central Asian peoples' republics—especially Kazakhstan, Turkestan, and Kyrgyzstan. Fewer than one-sixth still came as peasant settlers; all others were labor migrants on their way to industrial and mining frontiers. However, after 1928, when collectivization of agriculture expropriated peasants, a second mass flight from starvation, particularly in Ukraine as well as from undersupplied cities, involved millions and caused high death rates. To permit self-administration of ethnocultural groups, the Soviet government established autonomous regions or states for several of the many peoples—the Armenian republic, Birobidzhan as a Jewish enclave, and rearrangement of settlement patterns among Uzbeks, Kirgiz, and Kazakhs, to name only a few. However, in Kazakh agricultural regions self-styled "superior" Russian settler migrants appropriated lands, and in 1928 the government opened Kazakhstan to Russian settlers. The constitution of 1936 reduced self-determination of non-Russian peoples, and non-Russian peoples deemed disloyal to the Bolshevik state were deported from ancient settlement regions to Central Asia. To take the case of the Crimean Tatars, many of whom had emigrated after the Crimean Peninsula passed from Ottoman to tsarist rule, starvation in the period of the civil wars after 1917 and in particular during the state-enforced export of grain in 1921 led to death and flight, collectivization implied deportation, and the Stalinist purges led to deportation and, often, execution of non-Russian peoples' intellectual leaders.[126]

In Spain, Italy, and Germany, fascist governments caused renewed flight even before people who had been displaced by World War I were integrated. Especially during the 1930s, democratic elites fled into exile. The fascist regimes aimed at intellectual decapitation of their societies and of subjected peoples. Those fleeing had few options, both because of immigration barriers in the rest of the Western world and because of the collapse of economies during the Great Depression. Italian fascists derisively called the émigrés from liberal elites, militant unions, socialist or anarchist parties, artists and intellectuals *fuorusciti,* "foreign fellows," just as German socialists had once been labeled "fellows without a fatherland." From 1918 to 1926, 1.5 million Italian workers continued prewar migratory patterns, then the Fascist government criminalized emigration without permission. Some nine hundred thousand Italians lived in France, the main destination, until their vibrant culture was destroyed under German occupation in 1939.

In Spain, a rebellion of army officers pitted the modernizing coastal and northern populations against the elites of the stagnant, reactionary agricultural areas. When the Fascist generals sent Moroccan, "Moorish" soldiers to fight the Republic, a racist imagery of atrocity-committing North Africans emerged. Some forty-five thousand radicals and democrats from across Europe, North America, and the Soviet Union fought for the Republic; the German and Italian Fascist governments sent "volunteers" in support of the insurgents. By August 1938, two million refugees from Fascist-controlled areas had reached Republican Spain, and after the Republic's collapse some 450,000 soldiers and civilians fled to France, where almost 390,000 refugees from Nazi Germany had already arrived.

Nazi Germany in 1933 implemented a boycott of German-Jewish businesses and professionals and expelled ten to twenty thousand Eastern European Jews. Within a year some sixty-five thousand Jewish and Christian notables and cultural leaders had fled. Because only about 1 percent of the population was "non-Aryan," German racism has been called "anti-Semitism without Jews." By 1938 some two hundred thousand impoverished Jewish and non-Jewish refugees had arrived in receiving societies, which could ill afford, or were unwilling, to offer support. The refugee-generating fascist states were surrounded by refugee-refusing democratic states in which anti-Semitism was pronounced. In 1930, 3.3 million Jews lived in Poland, 3 million in Russia, about 1.2 million in Romania and Hungary, as well as 525,000 in Germany and 180,000 in Austria. By 1939 the United States had admitted a mere 8,600 refugees, and Canadian bureaucrats had closed the doors. At the July 1938 refugee conference in Evian, France, US diplomats avoided any swift help by insisting on procedural negotiation through a new Intergovernmental Committee on Refugees, and Western anti-Semitic ideologues suggested deportation of Jews to French Madagascar, North Borneo, the Dominican Republic, British Guiana, Cyprus, the Philippines, the Belgian Congo, and other destinations. Only the Soviet Union, Turkey, some Eastern European states, and China admitted refugees. The some eighteen thousand Jewish refugees who reached Harbin and cosmopolitan Shanghai could stay after Japan's takeover. In Palestine arriving refugees displaced local Arabs. When the German armies began to advance in 1939, a second flight carried those who had taken refuge in neighboring countries farther afield.

After the German occupation of Poland in September 1939, German Jews were first transported there to be utilized as an inferior laboring population. In a second phase, this resettlement region was to be "cleaned" of human beings of Mosaic religion. The deportees were deported again, this time to the ghettos of Polish cities where overcrowding and planned starvation caused high mortality. An estimated 200,000 to 350,000 reached the nonoccupied Soviet Union and, among neutral countries, Turkey became the most important transit route. The third deportation, labeled the "final solution," brought about six million men, women, and children to camps were they were to be worked to death in the

German industry's war production or exterminated immediately. In the end, one branch of the German-language family, the Yiddish-speakers, had nearly been exterminated.[127]

Forced Migrations

Parallel to the ethnocultural relocations, governments restricted working-class migrations through the 1920s and the Great Depression of the 1930s: entry restrictions were enacted to reduce international mobility; in many countries unemployed men, and sometimes women, were relocated to relief camps; labor activists and many of the unemployed were deported. State bureaucracies could use forced laborers on sites to which no free workers would migrate, and could shift them to wherever need arose. Relocation was cheap. Workers could be forced to construct their own camps, they received minimal wages, if any, and in economies with scarce consumer goods their confinement decreased consumption. If knowledge about forced labor was public, the system could be used to intimidate free workers. In the Americas, the US government deported labor organizers and radicals to the Soviet Union after 1917 and Mexican workers to Mexico in the 1930s. Peonage, forced labor because of alleged debt, though outlawed, continued to be imposed on African-American and Mexican-American laborers. In 1920s Canada, male harvest laborers and female domestics were sent to their destinations under police guard to work off assisted-passage contracts. In the interior of South America, the peonage system resembled slavery and landowners held the right to the part-time labor of natives. In several North African Arab states, slavery continued to be practiced, though on paper most Muslim states from Morocco to Afghanistan abolished slavery in the interwar years. Experts estimated that there were about three million slaves, worldwide, in 1930.[128]

European states, during World War I, militarized labor regimes. France relied on colonial labor and forcibly drafted African soldiers. Britain imposed compulsory labor on colonial populations, as in Uganda. Indentured workers from China and Vietnam were sent to Britain and France. After the postwar depression and a temporary closing of the borders, France became Europe's most important destination of labor migrants, with almost two million arriving. They replaced the 1.35 million French soldiers—10 percent of the adult male population—killed in the war. When Italian peasants came to settle villages emptied of men by the wartime carnage, nationalists prohibited their arrival to reserve national soil for an "undiluted" French nation—the soil in fact was bought up by an emerging agribusiness. Polish workers, recruited by employers, had no right to change jobs or demand better conditions. Soaring unemployment after 1929, when three million Poles, Belgians, Italians, and Polish-Germans resided in the country, caused the Right to mount a campaign of xenophobia. Fascist Spain outlawed unions and workers' parties—control over workers lasted to the system's demise in 1975.

Russia, fifth among the world's industrial powers before 1914, had to reconstruct its destroyed economy, relocate industrial centers, and deal with famines. It reached prewar production levels only in 1928. The policies of the Soviet state economy were contradictory. Collectivization was to reduce the need for rural labor, but bureaucratic mismanagement and poor urban living conditions reduced out-migration and some ideologues feared infiltration of rurals as a "class-alien element" into what they constructed as the proletariat. Labor migrations were voluntary, and in the first of five phases of migration, rural-to-urban mobility assumed unprecedented proportions: 1 million annually before 1926, 2.6 million annually from 1927 to 1930, 4.3 million in 1931; by 1939 the Soviet urban population had more than doubled and had been "ruralized," because two-fifths had arrived from the countryside in twelve years. After Stalin's "Great Turning Point" in 1928, in a second phase of migration, forced collectivization sent peasants fleeing, often to industrial work; many, especially from non-Russian peoples, were shipped to deadly labor camps. During the third, consolidating, phase before 1938, some 250,000 skilled factory workers and communist educational cadres were sent to rural areas to introduce mechanization, teach reading and writing to illiterate villagers, and inculcate a new consciousness. Within five years, 12.5 million new wage workers were drawn into the urban labor forces. But free migration still failed to fill demand, and in a fourth phase, starting in February 1930, the state terminated unemployment benefits and assigned jobs by a passport system that was compulsory for urban laboring men and women. From the mid-1930s, the fifth and last migration phase involved forced recruitment, captive labor for lumbering and road and railroad construction, and the transfer of whole factories before the German armies' advance. The labor camps, gulags, were controlled by the police (NKVD). Recent research indicates that there were 2.9 to 3.5 million forced laborers in 1941, about one-tenth of them women, and at least 750,000 Polish and other deportees. Other estimates reach as high as 20 million during the peak of the system. The system was exposed in 1956 and abolished in 1960.[129]

The German Reich's labor regime had relied on harsh internal control over foreign workers since the 1880s. By 1900 the Reich ranked second among labor-importing countries. It required Eastern European workers to carry passes and expelled those who changed jobs without permission. Russian and Austrian Poles were forced to depart during a "closure period" each winter, both to prevent permanent settlement and to free agricultural employers from paying them wages. This twenty-five-year-long first phase, for reasons of German nationalist ideology and cultural purity, established the policy of a rotary labor force. The second phase, in 1914–1918, involved forced labor: with the declaration of war the 1.3 million foreign workers were prohibited from leaving, and the food rations for these "working classes of non-German nationality" were kept at starvation levels. The third phase, the 1920s, involved a "governmentalization" of labor markets, but only a few foreign workers were present. In a fourth phase, the new Nazi government restricted freedom of movement of German laborers and channeled "racially different" laborers to sectors with poor working conditions. From 1936 the state assumed complete control over mobility. Even though ideological constructions of racial purity had precluded recruitment abroad, preparation for war led the Nazi government to import agricultural laborers from Poland, where unemployment stood at 40 percent. The occupation of Poland initiated the fifth phase with a compulsory levy of 1 million Polish workers, half of them to be women, in early 1940. Eastern Europe's allegedly "subhuman" peoples became essential for the Aryan war economy. Western European civilians and prisoners of war were conscripted for labor, some 1.2 million within a year. Civilian foreign workers included Italians, Belgians, and Yugoslavs. After the attack on the Soviet Union in June 1941, employment of Russians, Byelorussians, Ukrainians, and men and women from many other ethnicities was forbidden, but by 1942 the policy was reversed. *Ostarbeiter* were captured and transported to industrial sites in the occupied and "home" territories. At the end of the war, some 1.9 million POWs and 5.7 million civilian foreign workers, about one-third of them women, slaved in Germany, as did six hundred thousand men and women in concentration camps. Together, they accounted for 20 percent of the labor force.[130]

In Japan, militarization of the economy and society increased from the mid-1920s. State bureaucrats and employer organizations determined labor relations, the National Essence Society and the Harmonization Society advocated corporatist cooperation of capital and labor, the near-fascist New Order for Labor regime was mitigated by wartime welfare legislation. Workers in the recently occupied colonies had to produce industrial and military supplies under the control of a "directive minority" of Japanese managerial personnel. Korean peasants were uprooted to form an urban industrial, low-skill, mobile proletariat. From the populous southern provinces many had to move to Japan, where in 1917 through 1929, 1.2 million arrived and 850,000 returned. By 1945, more than 10 percent of the Korean population worked outside of Korea, and another 20 percent had been drafted for urban work or were otherwise uprooted. A type of identity-destroying labor forced Korean women to work in "comfort stations" as prostitutes for Japanese soldiers. In Manchukuo the Japanese military constructed heavy industry close to the mines in the middle of an agricultural subsistence economy of recent immigrants from China. High wages and, under Great Depression conditions, an abundant labor supply resulted in free labor markets except for ethnicized immigration policies that preferred Korean and Japanese workers over Chinese. By 1940, 1.4 million workers had been imported from Korea's north. Within Japan, policy makers allocated labor according to priorities of the military. Since 1941, labor reserves were managed centrally. In 1942 skilled workers and technicians were prohibited from changing jobs and employers were prohibited from offering wage incentives to "steal" technicians from other factories. In the occupied territories civilian and POW labor was conscripted. At the end of the war Japan's regime of forced-labor migration came to an end, but South Africa initiated a similar system a few years later to conscript Africans under its version of superior and inferior peoples in the regime of apartheid.[131]

In many of the colonized regions across the world, labor recruitment through force and taxation had been replaced by cash-related voluntary migrations.

Commercial relations and mining operations—as expressions of global capitalist relationships—had penetrated deeply from ports as places of contact into hinterlands, or, from the point of those who lived there, into people's primary living spaces. Ever more transactions involved money rather than exchange, and money came from wage labor or sale of crops. With the Great Depression the demand for raw materials, and thus for labor, collapsed. At the beginning of the 1930s the population of the new towns in the copper-mining region of Northern Rhodesia and in older towns in the Belgian Congo as well as elsewhere shrank dramatically. Laboring men—and their families, if these had joined them—migrated (or drifted) back to the land to eke out their subsistence. In the northern Nigerian tin mines, wages fell rapidly, but due to the collapse of grain prices living standards did not decline as much. Surplus workers left or subsisted on income from a few days of work per week—given the by-then established cash nexus, they could not simply withdraw from wage labor. Given the power relations, the colonizers' tax rate did not fall as much as wages. As a result, in some regions whole economies collapsed, creating migrant populations in search of food or jobs. In Malayan tin mines the situation was similar. The labor recruiters, *kangani,* were no longer sent back to their home villages to recruit from a reservoir that, again under the cash nexus, was waiting to be recruited. From the rubber areas Indian workers were deported home. Thus the social costs of the Great Depression were shifted to the home communities. Across the colonies that produced raw materials, workers who had been forced to migrate in the interest of capitalist production were sent back when the capitalist system temporarily collapsed. Stable prospects for gaining income through migration demand stable economic conditions. While much of contemporary debates centered on the dramatic conditions in the First World's banking centers, dramatic food shortages imperiled most migrant families' lifeways and chances for survival.[132]

Flight, Expulsion, and Population Transfers during World War II

In 1937 the next worldwide war began with Japan's aggression against China, called the "Second Sino-Japanese War," and in 1939 with the German aggressions in Europe. When the United States became a belligerent in 1941, the two wars, from a perspective of military efforts and political alliances, became a world war, but population movements remained largely separate. By 1945 hundreds of millions had been forced into flight or relocation camps. Population planners, who had shifted around human beings as laboring or surplus populations, reduced them to "human material." The peculiar construction of allegiance and duty to a nation in wartime made dissenters and pacifists persecuted citizens to be deported to camps, even in democratic states.

Japan's preparation for war had involved small-scale elite in-migrations and large-scale rhetoric. While military advisers were invited from Europe and the United States, military preparedness was justified as being of pan-Asian interest— Japan's expansion would counter European imperialism. In fact, Japan coveted China's raw materials and other resources, including human labor, and its (postwar) markets. Starting in 1937 it seized Shanghai and occupied large parts of China. After the fall of Nanjing, the Nationalists' capital, Japan's army massacred, raped, and looted, killing some three hundred thousand. In the countryside, both retreating Chinese and aggressing Japanese armies drove off peasants in scorched-earth campaigns or through the flooding of plains. In less than a year, a hundred million Chinese had become refugees and an estimated twelve million had fled as far as the western provinces of Yunnan, Guizhou, and Sichuan. The International Refugee Organization evacuated the small numbers of Europeans from China while Jewish refugees from Fascist persecution in Europe continued to arrive via Siberia.

In December 1941 Japan expanded the war to Southeast Asia and the Pacific by bombing the US fleet in Hawaii and occupying the Philippines, Hong Kong, Malaya, French Indochina, British Burma, Dutch Indonesia, and most of the Pacific islands. From Burma, as one example, about half a million Indians fled, perhaps fifty thousand dying en route. Bombing raids resulted in urban flight from Calcutta, and in Japan, in turn, urban populations were ordered to move to the countryside to escape Allied bombing and to produce food. After mid-1942, the Western Allies and China forced Japanese armies into slow retreat and surviving refugees followed the armies to return to former homes, many of which no longer existed.[133]

In Europe, the German and Soviet attack on Poland caused a first mass flight toward Warsaw, across the Baltic Sea, and through Hungary or Romania for

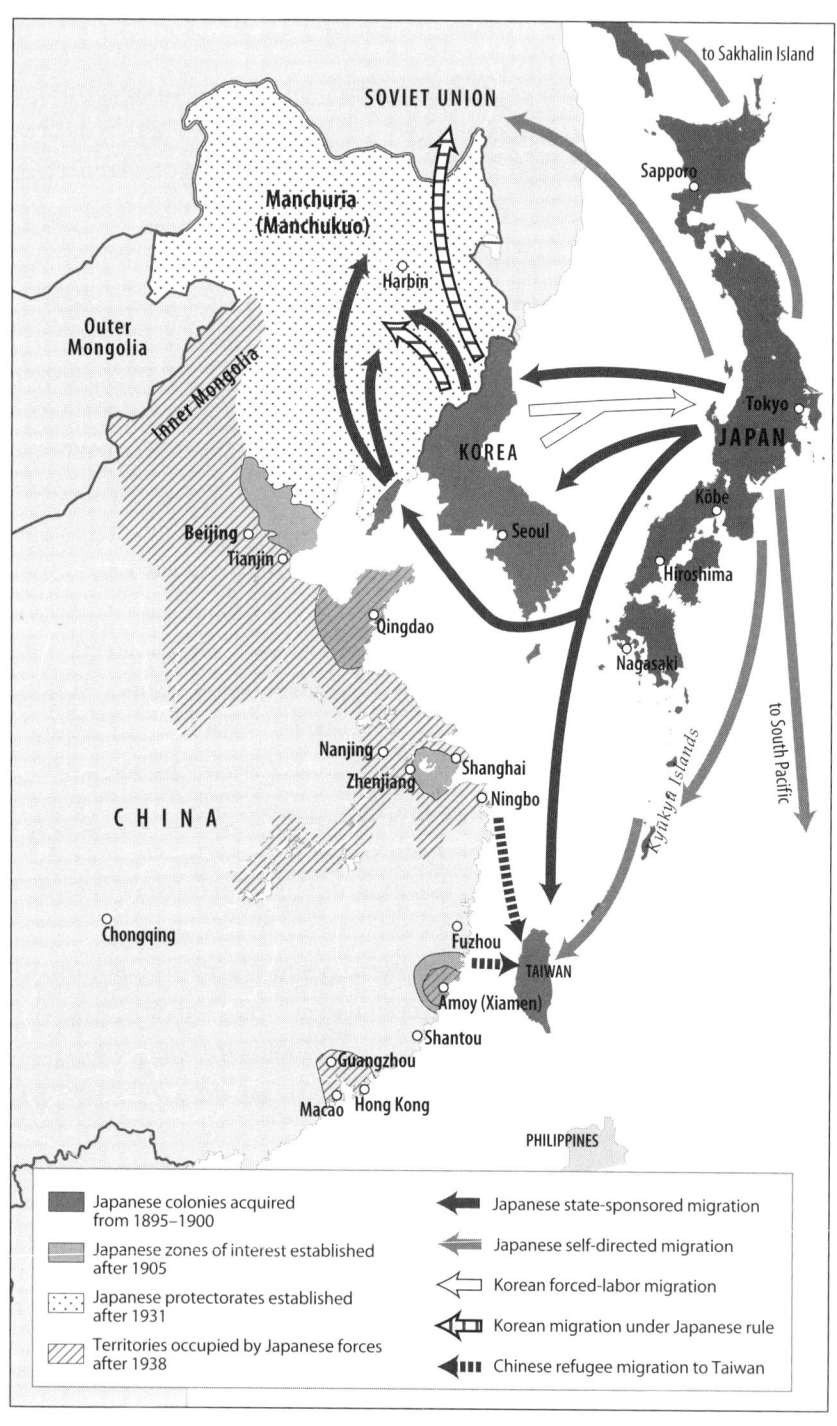

to Sakhalin Island

SOVIET UNION

Manchuria
(Manchukuo)

Sapporo

Harbin

Outer
Mongolia

Inner Mongolia

Tokyo
JAPAN

KOREA

Kōbe

Beijing
Tianjin

Seoul

Hiroshima

Qingdao

Nagasaki

Nanjing
Zhenjiang

Shanghai

CHINA

Ningbo

Kyūkyū Islands

to South Pacific

Chongqing

Fuzhou

TAIWAN

Amoy (Xiamen)

Shantou

Guangzhou

Macao   Hong Kong

PHILIPPINES

■	Japanese colonies acquired from 1895–1900	◀ Japanese state-sponsored migration
▨	Japanese zones of interest established after 1905	◀ Japanese self-directed migration
⋯	Japanese protectorates established after 1931	◁ Korean forced-labor migration
⫽	Territories occupied by Japanese forces after 1938	◁ Korean migration under Japanese rule
		◀⃫ Chinese refugee migration to Taiwan

Migrations within the Japanese Empire, 1890–1940.

evacuation via the Middle Eastern British zone of influence. Information about German troops' atrocities sent Jews fleeing across the lines of the Soviet army. After the USSR occupied Finland's Karelia Province, it deported 420,000 to 450,000 Karelian Finns to the rest of Finland, where 11 percent of the population were refugees. More than half of them returned when Finnish troops retook Karelia in 1941, only to flee again before a renewed Soviet advance in 1944. In and from France Jews fled; in the Scandinavian countries citizens transported some of them to neutral Sweden to ensure their survival. Shortly after the westward aggression, 2 million French, 2 million Belgian, 70,000 Luxembourger, and 50,000 Dutch refugees were near destitution according to Red Cross estimates.

The Nazi bureaucracy had planned major population transfers of allegedly inferior West Slavic peoples eastward and of allegedly superior Aryan Germans into the vacated lands. Other, "lesser" peoples were to cooperate with the Reich or be used as reservoirs of cheap labor. The "General Plan East" ordered "resettlement" of 80 to 85 percent of all Poles, 75 percent of the Byelorussians, 65 percent of the Ukrainians, and 50 percent of the Czechs in interior Russia or Siberia. However, the German military, overextended from the beginning, needed "colonial auxiliaries" and resorted to local regimentation of labor. The Nazi administrative machine, intending to expand the contiguous German-settled territories five hundred kilometers eastward, divided occupied Poland into a resettlement area for Germans and a vast Polish-settled labor camp. A total of 1.2 million "Slavic" Poles were deported, at a rate of 10,000 a day. ("Potential German" Poles—designated as such by the occupation forces—could support the Nazi regime as soldiers.) In the vacated lands, diasporic German-background people from eastern and southeastern Europe were to be resettled: some 500,000 were uprooted in a region extending from the Baltic states to Bessarabia. Another 750,000 trekked westward in the next years. By the time Soviet armies advanced, most were still in camps, only a fraction had been resettled. They commenced another trek westward or, when overtaken, were deported eastward.

Soviet bureaucrats, equally unconcerned about life courses, considered many non-Russian peoples "unreliable," either because of avowed Nazi sympathies of elite segments or because they had been oppressed as minorities in the Stalinist empire. Deportations toward the interior or further east ensued: peoples from the recently occupied Baltic and Polish states, refugees from the advance of the

German armies, the 1.4 million German-origin people of Russian citizenship, as well as peoples of the Caucasus, the Crimea (Tatars especially, as well as Greeks and Bulgarians), Transcaucasia, and the Caspian steppes. The USSR's massive program of transplanting industry toward and beyond the Ural Mountains as a means of self-defense for relocated workers and families meant abominable working conditions, worse living conditions, and high death tolls. Few alternatives existed: from Odessa, Moscow, and Leningrad alone, more than a million people fled or were evacuated when the German armies advanced. Still certain of victory, the German occupiers debated whether to starve whole populations, transport survivors to the Russian interior, or permit a "humanitarian" rescue by the Red Cross for resettlement somewhere else.

In southeastern Europe, where the Reich, Italy, Hungary, and Bulgaria had divided Yugoslavia among themselves, Slovenians were exchanged for German-background people, Serbs were expelled from dispersed settlements, Macedonians were expelled or Bulgarianized, and Romanians were sent into flight. The subsequent advance of Soviet armies meant new relocations; the retreat of German armies meant the flight of collaborators from among Ukrainians and other nationalities as well as anti-Soviet Cossacks. When the Soviet army reached the prewar German borders, an estimated fourteen million refugees lived behind their lines, not counting those moving before the advancing army.

Mobilization of men for nation-state armies and their interment as prisoners of war in other nation-states are not usually considered in terms of population transfer. However, they involved involuntary mobility and interaction. POWs, forced to work in the war industries and agriculture of the capturing power, interacted with local populations. During the war, when no Allied shipping was made available to transport refugee Jews out of Europe, four hundred thousand German POWs could be shipped to the United States—most returned, some emigrated subsequently. Prisoners of war from many nationalities labored throughout Germany in agriculture, mining, or factories, and German POWs labored in France and Russia. German civilians and Allied prisoners of war faced the same air raids. Germans, who worked alongside forced laborers until 1945, a mere decade later would work alongside guest workers. Would attitudes be transferred?[134]

Intellectual Migrations

Just as colonizer migrations, small in number, have frequently been left on the sidelines of research, the limited migrations of the colonized through exile or for education have been neglected by scholars. They were of major impact. As temporary migrants, many of the intellectual leaders, statesmen, and militant fighters for independence could compare life in the colonies with life in the metropoles. Most had studied there, some received education by missionaries, a few had worked there. As prospective elites they were given privileged access to colonizer-framed education in missionary schools and in universities of Great Britain and France. There, pronouncements about the equality of all the monarch's subjects or about the integrative role of French culture notwithstanding, they experienced second-class status or even racist deprecation. Two generations, of the late nineteenth and early twentieth centuries and of the 1920s and 1930s, experienced the humanist and democratic intellectual debates as well as racializing practices. Most of the intercultural migrants formed worldviews and militancy by a fusion of their own colonized culture with Western colonizer cultures. They became reformers or radicals, nationalists, socialists or communists. Educational migration familiarized them with two cultures and provided the strategic capital to comprehend and critique colonizer rhetoric and policies in ways understandable in their societies as well as by the colonizers. They became spokespersons for independence early in the twentieth century, in the interwar years, and during decolonization.

Intellectual exchanges had been part of early contact and later colonizing, especially in the cases of complex societies that, at least initially, could influence the character of intercultural contact. In Asia, Japan and China pursued different, yet similar, courses. Japan, said to be closed before the 1850s, had always kept abreast of the latest developments in Europe through a regulated Dutch enclave in Deshima, Nagasaki. The Meiji reformers invited Western experts for colonizing agricultural development of the northern islands and for training a new army. In contrast, the Chinese court's intellectual-cultural self-sufficiency (and, perhaps, arrogance) had abrogated the scholarly contacts epitomized in the seventeenth-century presence of Jesuits and their partial Sinicization. To deal with the increasing dominance of treaty powers, the government invited US and

European advisors late in the nineteenth century. Many of China's reformers and future leaders migrated for educational purposes or had to go into exile. Sun Yat-sen (1866–1935), one of the founders of the Guomindang and first president of the Republic, had lived in Hawai'i, studied in Hong Kong, and been in exile in Japan, Europe, the United States, and Canada. General Chiang Kai-shek (1887–1975) trained and served in Japan's army in 1907–1911. He staffed Nationalist China's military academies with German and Russian instructors, and his cabinet included Harvard-trained ministers.

Women were part of these elite migrations, and the well-studied three Soong sisters may serve as examples. Their father, a Hakka Chinese, had been educated as a Methodist minister in the United States and had become wealthy in part through Bible sales. He sent his daughters to the United States for their education at Wesleyan College in Georgia. All three became politically powerful and were internationally connected. Soong Ch'ing-ling in 1949 founded the well-known international magazine *China Today* with Israel Epstein, who came from a Polish-Jewish family of labor radicals; his mother had been exiled and his father had worked in Japan. Soong May-ling—"Madam Chiang" after her marriage to Chiang Kai-Shek—became China's foremost spokesperson in the United States and in 1943 was instrumental in ending the exclusion of Chinese immigrants from the United States, which had been first instituted in the 1880s. Such contacts ended after the Communist takeover in China in 1949 and during the mind-numbing Cold War period of the 1950s in the West.

A Vietnamese young man named Nguyen Sinh Cung strove for education and as a kitchen helper departed on a vessel in 1911 for a work-study trajectory in the United States, Great Britain, and France, combining menial jobs with self-education in public libraries. He petitioned for Vietnam's independence during the Peace Conference of 1918–1919, and under the assumed name Ho Chi Minh became the leader of Indochina's struggle for independence from French rule and drafted North Vietnam's constitutions using the US Declaration of Independence as a reference. Like many colonial political intellectuals and leaders, he espoused a cultural-economic nationalism but was radicalized by the West's continuing unabashed colonial exploitation combined with grand human rights rhetoric.

In South Asia, "British India" in the colonizers' naming, the colonizers introduced Western science and English history into higher education from 1835.

Sons, and to some degree daughters, of the colonized elites were to appreciate the rational and impartial government in general and England as a place of law, culture, rationality, and model literary texts in particular. By the 1880s almost half a million had graduated, and increasing numbers migrated to England (as well as to the United States, France, Germany, and the Soviet Union) for university education. Fifty years later, the British census listed seven thousand Indians in England and Wales, of which the seafaring labor migrants of the London port's lascar community were only a tiny minority. The best-known educational migrants included Dadabhai Naoroji (1825–1917), called the architect of Indian nationalism; Mahatma Gandhi (1869–1947) and Jawaharlal Nehru (1889–1964), who studied Law at the Inns of Court; Rabindranath Tagore (1861–1941), who studied at University College; Aurobindo Ghose (1872–1950), temporarily an extremist who experienced a "denationalization" and a return to Hindu culture; Bhimrao Ambedkar (1891–1956), a social revolutionary leader of the caste of untouchables and coauthor of independent India's constitution; Vinayak Damodar Savarkar (1883–1966), one of the earliest proponents of revolutionary terrorism to achieve independence; and Subhas Chandra Bose (1897–1945), an activist in the 1920s noncooperation movement. This elite congregated in India House in London and, when persecuted, moved their center to Paris. Others, influenced by the revolutionary writings of the American colonies in the 1770s, attempted to foster Indians' independence from their places of exile in the United States only to be prosecuted by US attorneys. In the context of international power rivalries, again others sought support in Germany or the Soviet Union. Several attended the seminal 1907 Stuttgart conference of the Second Socialist International. Arriving in the West, some realized that they could recite the British counties but not India's states—colonizer schooling had not considered India's history noteworthy. By living in "the West" they understood Orientalism before Edward Saïd created the term, and they established contact with European and American advocates of equality of cultures, agrarian reform, and socialist sharing. In contrast to most colonizers, they, as colonized, learned to compare the two (or more) sociocultural systems in which they lived and to analyze the gap between the rhetoric of Euro-civilization and its practices.

From African and Caribbean Francophone colonies, black students migrated to France, and in the 1920s and 1930s—after Africans had had to fight and work for France in World War I—a sailor and worker community emerged in Marseille. In the mid-1920s the sisters Paulette, Andrée, and Jeanne Nardal from Martinique established a salon in Paris as a center of debate and literary development where Antillean, US, and West African intellectuals met. Paulette Nardal, a feminist as much as an African-Caribbean "culturalist," and Leo Sajou from Haiti founded the short-lived *Revue du Monde Noir* in 1931 and published African-Americans like Claude MacKay and Langston Hughes. The migrants included Léopold Sédar Senghor (1906–2001) from Senegal, Aimé Césaire (1913–2008) from Martinique, and Léon-Gontran Damas (1912–1978) from French Guiana. Senghor served in the French army and was a prisoner of war of fascist Germany and thus experienced French culture as well as militarism, German fascism, and European warfare. The Association des Étudiants Martiniquais en France in 1934 began to publish *L'Étudiant martiniquais* but renamed it *L'Étudiant noir* in 1935 to indicate the Atlantic-wide reach of the African communities. In addition, numerous African-Americans migrated to Paris to escape racism. Influenced by both Haiti's role in the age of revolution and the Harlem Renaissance of the 1920s and 1930s, Césaire and Senghor in a reappropriation of the derogative term *nègre* developed the concept of *négritude* as conveying African identity and culture juxtaposed to colonialism and racism but using the French language and recognizing (French-) European cultural achievements. The concept was self-assertive and integrative, and it aimed at teaching white Europeans. Alioune Diop (1910–1980) founded the influential *Présence africaine* in 1947, perhaps the most influential journal to place black culture before a white audience on a par. Cheikh Anta Diop (1923–1986) also lived in Paris and was to become one of the foremost African scholars, controversial because of his racializing views of African history that remained a counterimage to European self-racialization. Many of these students became leaders in West Africa and the Caribbean.

Starting from the colonized/colonizer dichotomy, these intellectual migrants developed a critique of racism and imperialism. Another migrating group approached the issue of class and took a decidedly leftist, socialist or communist, approach to working-class and racial equality. George Padmore (1902–1959) may almost serve as prototype. Born in Trinidad, he migrated to study at Fisk and Howard Universities in the United States, then moved to Moscow where, under the auspices of the Communist International of Labour Union, he joined the leaderships of its Negro Bureau and the International Trade Union Committee of Negro Workers. Continuing to London, he cooperated with Guyanese historian C. L. R. James (1901–1989) in Pan-African and working-class activities and helped organize the 1945 Pan-African Conference in Manchester, which discussed an agenda for decolonization: independence for the "British West Indies" and for African colonies. Trinidadian Eric Eustace Williams (1911–1981) became first a historian of slavery and of the connection between capitalism and colonial underdevelopment, then prime minister of Trinidad.

In these networks these students who would become intellectual leaders received their socialization and education. They could contextualize colonized societies worldwide. At universities and law schools they developed a spectrum of approaches to change and fight unequal colonizer–colonized, white–black, or British–Indian relationships. They struggled to free the workers of capitalist and colonized societies from oppression and, occasionally, to demand equal rights for women. Observing industrial change and urbanization, they developed concepts for a transition to independence that incorporated economic development and universal human rights—the ideas of the Age of Enlightenment freed from Eurocentrism and whites-only provincialism. They were the initiators of the many decolonization movements that would gain global dimensions from the late 1940s.

At the same time intellectuals and literati, socialized in the recently democratic Germany, had to flee Fascism and continue their work as expatriates, briefly in other European countries, then mainly in the United States and, for a smaller number, in Brazil and in Mexico. They were designated as un-German by the Fascist rulers and their student youth organizations. Some moved to Los Angeles and continued to write or to influence the film industry: Fritz Lang (Hollywood), Thomas Mann (Princeton and Pacific Palisades), and Bertolt Brecht, who, called before the House Un-American Activities Committee in 1947, fled to Switzerland. In theater, Erwin Piscator stayed in New York. The social scientists, psychologists, and literary scholars of the interdisciplinary Institute of Social Research in Frankfurt am Main (founded in 1923), after a brief relocation to Geneva, Switzerland, moved to New York, where scholars at Columbia University provided an affiliation, as did the New School of Social Research, founded in 1919 after Columbia University, like many other US institutions, demanded nationalist loyalty oaths from its faculty. The New School's graduate program began in 1933 as a university of exiles, a shelter for scholars rescued—partially with funds from the Rockefeller Foundation—from all over occupied Europe. Theodor W. Adorno, Hannah Arendt, Erich Fromm, Aron Gurwitsch, Max Horkheimer, Hans Jonas, Herbert Marcuse, Leo Strauss, Max Wertheimer, and others were associated with it. Their lasting contribution was "critical theory," an approach to scholarship that rejects positivism and national narratives for a critical understanding of societies, their material basis and cultural superstructure, and an awareness of the relatedness of knowledge and interests. The French-language École Libre des Hautes Études was also associated with the New School.[135]

As a postscript it might be added that many of the European theoreticians of postcolonialism also emerged from circuits of migration. From the 1930s to the 1950s they experienced hierarchized interaction between colonized groups or subalterns, ready to rebel, and colonizers clinging to an imperial regime without vision, without moral foundation, and—after 1945—without the military power to support their superior position. Of the French-language theorists, Roland Barthes had lived in Romania and Egypt, Frantz Fanon in Martinique and Algeria, Jacques Derrida and Pierre Bourdieu in Algeria. Other theorists experienced two (or more) social regimes in one society: Antonio Gramsci and Mikhail Bakhtin lived through (and suffered from) the transformation of their societies' governments to Fascism and Stalinism, respectively. Michel Foucault observed the multiple discourses of schizophrenic men and women and of those who did not live according to assigned sex roles. In Britain, Stuart Hall and Catherine Hall, the former being of a color of skin other than white and of Jamaican origin, questioned imperial and national discourses. By their physical displacement or replacement, they came to live dual or multiple perspectives and thus enabled themselves to replace monocultural foundational stories and nation-state ideologies with the multiple perspectives of discourse theory. The political-societal transition of decolonization became an academic transition from nationalist historiographies to transcultural societal studies. Migrating common people throughout the ages had to negotiate two or more systems of reference and of everyday life.[136]

5. The Aftermath of War and Decolonization

THE IMMEDIATE aftermath of the Second World War gave rise to two major migrations. First was the migration of refugees, prisoners of war, forced laborers, prewar imperial colonizer migrants, and soldiers who needed to be repatriated or needed to be resettled, if "home" had been destroyed or new postwar governments made return undesirable and, perhaps, life-threatening. Second was the migration of laborers who were needed to rebuild destroyed economies. Two other important migrations were the consequence of persecutions: the migration of people of Jewish faith to Israel and the flight of Palestinians. Finally, postwar migrations also included multiple moves resulting from decolonization and forced migration of labor to meet the needs of the new regime in South Africa.

Repatriations, Expulsions, Resettlement

After the atomic bombs were dropped on Hiroshima and Nagasaki and Japan surrendered, the internment and repatriation of the 6.5 million Japanese abroad began. The population of Karafuto (South Sakhalin Island) had become 93 percent Japanese; Nan'yō's population of 132,000 included 81,000 Japanese; in continental China, Japanese migrants had remained few; in Taiwan they accounted for 6 percent of the population; some 800,000 Japanese lived in Korea. In Europe, many displaced persons (DPs), whom the Allies estimated to total eighteen million in May 1945, walked home over hundreds of kilometers—as Chinese refugees did. Repatriation, often to homes in ruins, was completed by the end of 1946 in both macroregions. Some, however, remained in camps: Jews with no home, Baltic and Ukrainian people who had collaborated with the German occupation, East Europeans who refused to return to Stalinist Russia or other newly communist states. Nonreturning DPs did not received citizenship; in Europe they became "stateless," in Japan they were "third-country nationals."

From Japan more than a million Koreans repatriated to South Korea, another hundred thousand accepted a repatriation offer by North Korea; those remaining in Japan faced continued discrimination. At the war's beginning, Japanese migrants in the United States and Canada and their locally born children and grandchildren suffered from the warfare though living a continent off. After Japan's attack on Pearl Harbor, the migrants who purposely had left Japan became "enemy aliens." Constructed as a military threat, harassed under continuing racism, and owning modest property that could be confiscated by their Euro-American neighbors, most were relocated. Canada's security bureaucrats had all Japanese and Japanese-Canadians living within one hundred miles of the coast removed to the interior; their confiscated properties were sold. Of the 275,000 men and women of Japanese birth or ancestry in the United States and Hawai'i, more than a 100,000 were relocated to desert concentration camps. Four decades later, the US government acknowledged that the measure "was not justified by military necessity" but due to "race prejudice, war hysteria, and a failure of political leadership."

In China, warfare continued. The Nationalists (Guomindang) and the Communists received support from the Western and Soviet blocs, respectively. Thus, refugee generation continued, resettlement was delayed. The establishment of a Communist government in 1949 resulted in Nationalists' mass flight to Hong Kong as a British enclave and to Taiwan. Another 340,000 refugees, landowners, and students in particular, headed for neighboring countries, mostly to Burma and in small numbers to Laos and Portuguese Macao. In Taiwan the some two million newcomers, in an occupation-type move, overthrew societal and economic institutions. Hong Kong's population, 1.6 million in 1941, doubled by 1961. Refugees arriving in Southeast Asian countries could receive help from the diasporic Chinese, often distant family members. By mid-1953 the "Overseas Chinese" numbered 13.4 million in sixteen countries or enclaves, with another 300,000 in the Americas, Oceania, Africa, and Europe. In the Southeast Asian segment of the subsequent Cold War world, several "nationalist" movements—a misnomer, given the multiethnic population in each and every region—labeled diasporic Chinese a bridgehead of "Communist" China and targeted them for reprisals or even ferocious massacres. Many were forced to flee to the People's Republic, Taiwan, or Hong Kong or seek admission to countries with existing Chinese communities like the United States, Canada, Britain, or the Netherlands. Subsequently, abolition of racialized admission criteria in Canada (1962–1963) and in the United States (1965) made a new phase of large-scale migrations from Asia to North America possible.[137]

At the end of the war in Europe, where the number of refugees amounted to thirty million and number of dead fifty-five to sixty million, the Allies committed themselves to create conditions that would enable all refugees and displaced persons to return. In the West this was a guise for not accepting the dislocated and, from the side of Soviet Russia, a guise for depriving refugees of a choice in where to begin new lives. In the Soviet zone of liberation and occupation, given the destruction of infrastructure, refugees at first had to move by themselves. So did men and women in the post-armistice havoc of the Western zones. In the latter areas, civilian refugees, forced laborers, and Jewish survivors from the death camps, named "displaced persons" to distinguish them from POWs and demobilized soldiers, received some support from aid organizations, and several hundreds of thousands were resettled in the United States, Canada, and Australia. Polish soldiers elected to stay in Great Britain. Some two hundred thousand DPs, so-called hardcore cases, remained in West Germany as "stateless." The perhaps one million surviving men and women of Jewish faith received no recognition of their special needs after witnessing and surviving the Holocaust. Palestine remained closed because Britain had to balance Arab and Jewish interests. By the end of 1946 in Poland, where anti-Semitism remained rampant, 170,000 survivors had fled to territories administered by the Western Allies. Their hopes for admission to North America foundered on quota limitations, and "repatriation" to Palestine, the home of Muslim Arabs, emerged but slowly. The callous British request that the USSR settle Jews in Birobidzhan, the Soviet Jewish autonomous region in Central Asia, elicited but an equally callous query by the USSR government about empty spaces in the British Empire.

In the aftermath of the war, people continued to be expelled and shifted around by governments because of their allegiances during the war, ethnocultural prejudices, or redesigned "national" territories. Some 12.5 million refugees and expellees from the many eastern German and diasporic German cultures reached the four zones of Germany between 1945 and 1949. Their insertion, initially de facto segregation, was achieved only over time and under government pressure. East of the new German border, 4.5 million Poles settled, dislocated five years before by German occupation forces or fleeing from those eastern territories annexed by the USSR after the war. From 1939 to 1949 the Polish people were subjected to some twenty-five million resettlement and deportation moves, with many being shunted about repeatedly.[138]

In the Soviet Union's southern regions, where segments of some indigenous peoples had attempted to achieve independence during the war, some six hundred thousand to one million men and women of many cultures were deported, and the prewar autonomous republics of the Crimean Tatars, the Kalmyk, the Chechen, and the Ingush were not reestablished. In-migrating Russian ethnics profited economically; Russian and Ukrainian peasants were brought in to cultivate the vacated farmlands. The territories newly acquired from Finnish Karelia, along the Polish-Byelorussian-Ukrainian borderlands to Romanian Bessarabia—like southern Sakhalin Island retaken from Japan—were vacated by flight and population transfer and resettled with Russian migrants. Many acquired deportees' possessions without having to pay recompense. In addition, a lively and mobile postwar youth movement contributed to the reallocation of individuals from the many peoples.

In East Central and southeastern Europe, Hungarians fled from Transylvania, which became part of redesigned Romania. Greece, wracked by civil war, in the fall of 1949 counted some seven hundred thousand refugees in a population of seven million. Men and women of the Yugoslav peoples fled from each other or fled from the area of mixed settlement of Venetia-Giulia and Trieste, contested between Italy and Yugoslavia. When Italian-occupied Dalmatia was reincorporated into Yugoslavia, some three hundred thousand ethnic Italians, one-third of the total population, left. From Africa, Italians who had settled in Tunisia and Ethiopia returned. Aid to refugees, at first provided by the UN Relief and Rehabilitation Administration, was coordinated by the International Refugee Organization (IRO) after December 1946. Refugee movements involved family migrations, often female-headed because men were soldiers, prisoners of war, or dead.[139]

Women's postwar migrations included departures as "war brides." The United States, to take the major recipient state as an example, had sent sixteen million men for combat or war-related activities into fifty-seven countries. Nonfraternization policies toward enemy populations were quickly undercut by human relations. From 1942 to 1952 an estimated one million soldiers married local women, and hundreds of thousands of war brides reached the United States—only occasionally did a groom remain in his wife's country. Forty-one thousand Canadian soldiers married overseas, mostly to British women. Japanese brides of US men had little hope for a lasting union because the US exclusion laws prevented them from immigrating—and African-American soldiers could not marry European women because of miscegenation laws. On the whole, however, politically mandated ethnonational hierarchies were undercut in everyday contact, through principles of humanity, and by emotional-sexual relations. In the United States, the war brides were to become the ethnocultural nuclei for postwar migrations.[140]

From destroyed Europe, emigration resumed. The Dutch government supported emigration for fear of overpopulation; the establishment of communist governments in East Central Europe caused people to flee. Because no economic recovery seemed in sight, many people headed for societies not ravaged by war. Net out-migration from Europe in 1946–1955 amounted to 4.5 million and was directed primarily to Canada, the United States, South America (from southern Europe), and Australia, as well as Israel.

Postwar Reconstruction and the Need for Workers

From Western Europe to East Asia, devastated countries needed to be rebuilt, demobilized soldiers had to be reintegrated, industrial workers whose factories lay in ruins needed to be employed, and the gendered division of work had to be renegotiated as a result of women having migrated to industrial jobs when men were off as soldiers. In most societies, women were displaced from their wartime jobs, but their new economic clout allowed them to protest and organize. Types of migration became fluid: After the war some 30,000 German POWs were assigned to work in Belgian coal mines and 1.75 million to work in France. When return became possible, 20 percent of those in France turned the forced assignment into a migration decision and opted to stay. Elsewhere demobilized nonnational soldiers or POWs decided to remain in the society of demobilization rather than return to home societies that were in ruins and that, often against their interests, had sent them into war.

The North American societies had to reintegrate millions of soldiers, migrants arriving from economies in ruin, and war brides. In Europe policy makers encouraged or retarded labor migrations. The West German labor allocation bureaucracies refused exit permits to able-bodied male prospective migrants in order to retain a labor force for reconstruction. The conservative Italian government encouraged departures to rid itself of radical and unemployed working-class voters. By the early 1950s, fast economic growth in northwestern Europe and slow development in southern Europe made imbalances of manpower evident. Governments negotiated treaties to permit controlled inter-state mobility of laborers with an implied obligation to return. The "guest worker" system came into being. In 1950s North America, Canada continued to rely on immigrants, especially from southern Europe; the United States recruited Mexican workers under the Bracero Program, expecting them to return. For ideological reasons, the communist states in East Central Europe, the Soviet Union, and the People's Republic of China permitted neither emigration nor immigration. Japan, for racist reasons, also pursued a non-immigration policy. Thus, systems of labor were redesigned. The transatlantic system came to a standstill by the mid-1950s, except for the migrations from southern Europe to Canada. A decade later there evolved a transpacific system of labor, investor, and student migration that often involved sequential family migrations. In the socialist world, bordered by the Iron Curtain in the West and Japan's exclusionism in the East, migrations remained internal to states, although later there were small-scale movements between neighboring states, such as Poland and Hungary.[141]

Jewish and Arab Migrations

For Jewish refugees from anti-Semitism and survivors of the Holocaust, *aliyah* to Arab-settled Palestine meant ascending to the place of religious roots. It had been a spiritual and, from about 1900, a religio-nationalist state-building project. Before 1914, only 60,000 of 2.75 million Jewish migrants worldwide selected Palestine as destination, and in the interwar years, 1919–1939, only some 345,000 chose the agricultural settlement projects. In the next five years, 45,000 refugees from fascism arrived. The United Nations' November 1947 partition of Palestine envisaged a Jewish state with an Arab "minority" of almost 400,000, or 42.5

percent of the population. Statehood of Israel (1948), Israel's discrimination against the Arab-Muslim populations, the several Arab-Israel military campaigns, and state-organized Jewish immigration generated new Muslim refugee populations, some 330,000 by late 1948, some 0.9 million to 1.2 million in 1950 according to the UN Relief and Works Agency. Israel became a major region of both immigration and refugee generation. At first Holocaust survivors arrived, some 150,000 Europeans of Jewish faith. Next came an estimated 200,000 North African, Arabian Peninsula, and Iraqi men and women of Jewish faith and, according to the high rabbinate's labeling, of Jewish genetic descent through the mother's line. Third, a new exodus from Eastern Europe's rampant anti-Semitism, in 1950–1951, brought 425,000. Israel's admission and citizenship policies became as exclusionist as postwar Germany's—admission followed bloodline descent.[142]

Racialized Labor Mobility in South Africa

After the forced-labor regimes of Germany, the Soviet Union, and Japan, the white South African government began similar policies. Before 1940 the state's increasingly interventionist Euro-origin segment expelled Chinese contract workers, restricted Indian workers, and imposed a system of labor controls and pass laws on Africans. Its restriction, since 1913, of Africans to reserves, "Homelands" or "Bantustans," brought involuntary relocation of two to three million people from territories designated for whites. In 1948, partly in reaction to labor militancy, apartheid was institutionalized under a "white supremacy" doctrine. All aspects of life were racialized: mixed marriages were prohibited (1949), interracial sexual contacts outlawed (1950), identity checks established (1952). The labor regime forced Africans to work for European-origin employers, to migrate seasonally or for extended periods of time, to leave families behind and live in camps. The powerful mining core and many utility companies drew their labor forces from a marginalized countryside. The state, which was interventionist regarding workers, guaranteed industry's labor system and, with adaptations for women and children's labor, that of white farmers. Concomitantly labor recruitment expanded to a subcontinental scale.[143]

Decolonization and Reverse Migrations

During the interwar period, movements for self-rule or full independence had gained momentum in many colonized societies. From the beginning of war in Asia in 1937, the Euro-American colonizer powers in need of support and soldiers came up with promises for various forms of postwar partnership or independence to India (1940), Burma (1945), the Philippines (1946), and other colonies. In Africa, recruitment of soldiers, in particular by the French government in exile, was not accompanied by any negotiations for postwar rights. After the war, the political-structural frame was one of outdated and crumbling empires unwilling to negotiate transition to a new order. In consequence, wars for independence began in the 1950s—Kenya, Algeria, West Africa, to name only a few. Refugee generation and population displacement by construction of independent nation-states and imposition of arbitrary borderlines followed the European model.

Japan's and Nazi Germany's attempts at empire building, Europe's internal warfare, and US intervention left the imperial systems in shambles. French, Dutch, and US attempts to reestablish colonial rule or zones of influence in Asia only prolonged processes of dislocation. In postwar Korea, for example, a moderate prewar collaborationist elite stood opposed to an anticolonial, left-oriented elite, trained in underground activities or exile. The former was aging and established, the latter young and dynamic. Prosecution of collaborators initiated partial elite displacement, and warfare between the Communist north (population 9 million) and the West-influenced south (population 21 million) resulted in southward flight of 1.8 million.

In British India, the colonizer–colonized dualism turned into tripartite British-Hindu-Muslim negotiations, which in 1947 divided the subcontinent into (Hindu) India and (Muslim) West and East Pakistan. The 389 million people spoke fifteen official, twenty-four regional, and twenty-three indigenous languages as well as some seven hundred dialects, and thus the term *Indian* as an ethnic or cultural descriptor remained a creation of outside observer-rulers. The bulk of the Muslims, 22 percent of the population, were agriculturalists; the Hindus were predominantly shopkeepers, moneylenders, or workers in cloth and other factories. All negotiators accepted that partition would involve a projected exchange of four million men, women, and children. From Karachi, long free of intercommunal violence, almost one-third of the population departed, mainly Hindus in commerce. In the Punjab's interspersed settlements of Muslims, Sikhs, and Hindus, atrocities and massacres occurred. In the exchange between West and East Bengal (India and East Pakistan), 1.2 million of a population of 20 million Hindus and 8 million Muslims left eastbound and 4.8 million of 32 million Muslims and 10 million Hindus moved westward. Governments and armies began to speed up the movement to reduce the danger of epidemics and to resettle people in time for sowing and harvesting, to reduce the danger of famines. By the end of 1947, the two religion-based states had exchanged 7.3 million men, women, and children. An estimated one million died during the treks. Women were particularly liable to attack and robbery because they carried their traditional marriage gifts of gold and jewelry. By 1951, refugees had increased to 14.5 million. Regional populations had thus to some degree been homogenized by religion, but cultural and linguistic heterogeneity remained. State formation was a costly process for refugees.

In independent Burma (1948), in-migrating Chinese technicians who had filled the vacancies left by the flight of British Indians in 1942 faced riots after allegations that the People's Republic of China supported the state's "minority" peoples. The Karen had unsuccessfully attempted to create their own state in the late 1940s, and the Mon opposed the central government in the 1950s. In Malaya/ Malaysia, which achieved independence from 1946 to 1963, a small nationalist-communist uprising was quelled by British troops in 1950 but some five hundred thousand Chinese agriculturalists were forced to resettle in order to deprive the insurgents of their produce. In Indochina (later Cambodia, Laos, and Vietnam) France reestablished colonial rule only to be defeated in a war of independence. At the time of the 1954 cease-fire, which divided the country into a nationalist-communist north and a Buddhist, Catholic-ruled, US-dependent south, 140,000 civilians opted to move to North Vietnam (population 16 million) while 860,000 moved to South Vietnam (population 11.5 million). Two more decades of warfare created further millions of refugees. French-ruled Siam/Thailand, which had survived the war years as an ally of Japan, became a refugee-receiving country.

The Netherlands East Indies declared independence immediately after Japan's surrender. British and Dutch troops, instead of interning the Japanese, fought the Indonesian People's Army. Of 240,000 residents designated as "European," more than four-fifths were of Dutch origin (1930 figures). The label veiled the other, Asian, side: 70 percent were Indos of mixed parentage. Before independence, achieved in 1949, the highest social strata left; subsequently some 15 percent of the Indos opted for Indonesian citizenship, while about one hundred thousand colonial auxiliaries, middle-level officials, and military men and their families were evacuated to the Netherlands. Most had never been there before, some did not speak Dutch and were, like the Ambonese, nonwhite. In 1957 Indonesia expelled the remaining Dutch nationals and expropriated Dutch agricultural properties.

Other wars for independence resulted in further multiple refugee streams. First, colonizers, on the defensive, deported populations; in the 1950s, the British resettled half a million Chinese in Malaya, tens of thousands of Kikuyu from Nairobi, and the Kabaka from Buganda, and the French uprooted Algerian peasants. Second, wars for independence dislocated people of whole regions. Third, in many post-independence societies factional wars between different political groups, as in Angola and Mozambique, or between divided societies, as in Vietnam and Korea, displaced millions. Conflicts exacerbated by intervention of the US and USSR superpowers or former colonial overlords took the highest death tolls and created the largest refugee movements.

Independence ended both the temporary assignments of administrators and soldiers in colonies of exploitation and the privileged position of farming families in colonies of settlement. Many would emigrate, some in immediate flight, others over time. They saw their political power crumble, their economic calculations collapse, their lifestyles vanish, and "their" subaltern native labor rise to citizenship. Most were locally born (creoles) and had never known the society of origin. Furthermore, colonial auxiliaries had to leave, whether recruited locally as in French Algeria, distributed across an empire as the Sikhs, or pitting minority against majority populations as in the case of Indochina's Hmong, whose pro-colonizer policing role made them liable to retribution from the newly sovereign people. Finally, men, women, and children of genetically mixed ancestry as well as elites with cultural affinity to a core found themselves in precarious positions. Withdrawal of elites, whether owners of capital, of skills, or of knowledge, could create havoc in the new economies. After independence, many of the new nationalist elites, in the face of multiethnic populations, pursued European-inspired models of state formation that placed one cultural group as "nation" in hegemonic position. In the metropoles the arrival of some 5.5 to 8.5 million Italian, French, British, Belgian, Dutch, and other white colonials and of nonwhite auxiliaries (before 1975) created new tensions and initiated the transition to multicolored and multicultured peoples.

The frame for further developments was set by the mid-1950s. In 1955 the Bandung, Indonesia, Conference of Non-Aligned Countries coincided with the publication of Aimé Césaire's "Discours sur le colonialisme" in the famous journal *Présence africaine* (Paris). African and Asian migrants' presence in the white world, with its many antecedents, would increase in the next decades. Former colonizer–colonized relations became migratory connections. These served life-course projects rather than nations' power interests. The migrations of the second half of the twentieth century and of the turn of the twenty-first century had their origins in the imperialist period. Although there are no figures on total short-distance, intra-state, cross-border, and transcontinental or transoceanic migrations, the extremely high levels of mobility worldwide, from the 1870s to 1945, indicate that state mobilizations and constraints, global economic inequalities, and power hierarchies mobilized and immobilized hundreds of millions.[144]

·[FOUR]·

Commodity Chains in a Global Economy

Steven C. Topik and Allen Wells

Introduction

THE seven decades after 1870 have been labeled the "Second Industrial Revolution," the "Era of High Imperialism," the "Great Acceleration," and the "Great Transformation."[1] By any measure the global economy underwent a remarkable transformation. Thanks to unprecedented gains in industrial and agricultural productivity, an exponential increase in commerce, investment, and immigration, and sweeping improvements to transportation, communication, and distribution, the world's population doubled, trade more than quadrupled, and output multiplied fivefold. New monetary and property standards, nascent multinational corporations, and international conventions and organizations facilitated such fundamental changes. Many people, however, experienced the grim side of these developments: It was also an era of colonialism, racism, and an unprecedented concentration of wealth. A succession of deadly wars and the degradation of landscapes ensured that these improvements in productivity came at a high cost.

It was a time when the principles of liberal economic thought were first systematically applied to parts of the international economy and when "globalization" first became clearly manifest.[2] But globalization did not mean that everyone was brought into lockstep with Europe and North America. Although the logic of capitalist investment and trade imposed themselves in ever more parts of the world, heterogeneity and diversity also became more striking. There were many ways to respond to similar market pressures. While international trade, prices, and technologies affected most everyone, people often felt the impacts differently, in ways that may have had greater cultural or political resonance than economic.

We will illustrate the evolving dimensions, contradictions, and functions of the world market during this period by focusing on the material and conceptual sinews of trade and the commodities that tied together continents and fueled commerce. We do not reify the economy. In fact, the world market was "a rather abstract, theoretical fiction" with great variations and cyclical swings.[3] But our studies of the international trade of wheat, rice, hard fibers, rubber, sugar, coffee, tea, cacao, and other commodities will show that it is a useful concept in appreciating the movement of enormous amounts of goods and capital, as well as millions of people. Market forces operated through humans in varied, unpredictable, and even contradictory ways, reflecting local customs and past lessons as much as contemporaneous opportunities.

We begin with how historians have conceived of our period, and then turn to an overview of the world economy and its characteristics between 1870 and 1945. After painting with a broad brush the contours of the Great Divergence—the growing gulf between the haves and those who had little—we examine the apparent contradictions that emerged between liberalism and state capitalism or socialism, laissez-faire individualism and organized capitalism, free trade and colonialism, and the irony of creative destruction and its environmental implications. After a brief visit to the cotton-driven First Industrial Revolution we discuss the Second Industrial Revolution and its defining characteristics. Then we explore the sinews of the world economy in greater detail: the legal frameworks, monetary standards, shipping, canals, rails, and telegraphs, and the changing sources of energy that fostered ever-larger markets. That is followed by discussions of industrial linkages to copper and industrial metals, oil, and rubber that were made possible by key advances in transportation and communication.

After this extended overview of economic framework, we turn to the heart of our story, the various commodity chains that carried the bulk of cross-border commerce: staples such as grains, especially wheat and rice, and the hard fibers needed to package them; and stimulants like sugar, coffee, tea, chocolate, and tobacco. These agricultural products were not just marginal luxuries. By 1913 food made up more than a quarter of world exports, and grains and stimulants were truly global in their reach.[4] Other commodities will be addressed for comparative purposes.

Although historians generally distinguish the period 1870–1914, an era of relatively free trade and export-led growth, from the following three decades, which wrestled with world wars, depressions, and growing state intervention in economic matters, we examine the entire seventy-five years because so many of the dynamics, aspirations, and assumptions were linked. Although overall world trade expanded until 1914, stagnated in the 1920s, and shrank dramatically during the 1930s, disputes between liberalism and protectionism, industrialism and agrarianism, and public and private interests marked all seven decades.

Historical Disagreements

Was it the best of times or the worst of times? Scholars have characterized this three-quarters of a century in strikingly different ways. For Whig historians, defenders of empire, or champions of free trade, it was a time of progressive diffusion that spread the benefits of civilization and brought God and the written word to benighted peoples. This is the Henry Stanley, Teddy Roosevelt, and Jules Verne eighty-days-around-the-world version of modernity, which had Europeans and neo-Europeans, such as those in North America, Australia, and Argentina, "discovering" and improving all with which they came into contact. To apologists, this was a time of expanding freedoms—of trade, worship, and scientific research.

Contemporaries who rued the consequences of what was often cast as social Darwinism saw the titanic struggle between fit and unfit races, winners and losers, in much darker hues. Here one thinks of Joseph Conrad ruing in *Heart of Darkness* that "the conquest of the earth, which mostly means the taking it away from those who have a different complexion or slightly flatter noses than ourselves, is not a pretty thing when you look into it too much." The light-skinned, in European and North American minds, brought progress and development, all too often orchestrated by the terrible killing power of the automatic guns that permitted the great issues of the day to be decided, as Prussia's prime minister Otto von Bismarck predicted in 1862, "by blood and iron."

Some commentators and scholars have stressed technological innovations and the growth of markets (though not necessarily unfettered markets). Sometimes these improvements were seen as the teleological triumph of reason and science. According to this view, technical progress imposed itself on ever more people in ever more distant parts of the world. But the machine was not neutral. It was seen as a "civilizer" that proved the superiority of Western Europeans.[5] Proponents contended that reason, race, technology, and prosperity were inextricably tied together.

Yet reason and "racial science" also gave rise to an unreasonable "Age of Extremes" that discarded liberalism for a "triumph of the will," and substituted totalitarianism for laissez-faire. In the United States, racism became widespread and politically volatile in the wake of the abolition of slavery and the end of Reconstruction.[6] In the theories of US eugenicists German Nazis found reinforcement for their racial ideology and practices, leading to the cruel and bloody Holocaust that spread through Central and Eastern Europe.

Gazing from a Eurocentric perspective, the historian Eric Hobsbawm characterized the time as the "Age of Empire," while the Marxist theorist Rudolf Hilferding labeled it the period of "Finance Capital."[7] To leftist militants like Nikolai Bukharin and Vladimir Lenin, it was the era of "monopoly capitalism." Rather than a world open to progress shaped through a freer diffusion of trade, capital, and technology, this historical conjuncture, such critics fulminated, was rent by imperial possessions, monopolies, and cartels.

Perhaps surprisingly, outside of Europe the most dynamic regions generally were not part of formal empires. Indeed, recent research has underlined the importance of Asian entrepreneurship and inter-Asian trade in the East Asian industrial model that emerged in our period. Trade *within* Asia grew faster than in any other region in the world. Even those that were colonial subjects, like Australia, Canada, and South Africa, effectively won their independence in this period. India would not be far behind, achieving its freedom in 1947. So if formal empire made its mark on our seventy-five years, it also wrote its final chapters. Moreover, if the economic theories of John Gallagher and Ronald Robinson are to be accepted, "free-trade imperialism" motivated empire builders. This hotly contested perspective would inspire a rash of studies on neocolonialism, dependency theory, and world systems that complicates our understandings of methods of formal and informal colonial rule.[8]

Our approach acknowledges the central role that Western European and North American capitalists, laborers, and technology played in the metamorphosis of world trade and finance and agrees that entrepreneurs on both sides of the North Atlantic were fundamental to the era's profound transformations. As historian Jürgen Osterhammel recently observed: "The history of the nineteenth century was massively made in and by Europeans.... Never before had Europe generated a similar excess of innovation and initiative, while at the same time unleashing overpowering force and arrogance." But we agree with him that European exceptionalism has been exaggerated.[9] Not all changes originated from or were dictated by European and North American capitalists. The world beyond Western Europe and North America was hardly an undifferentiated "Third World" that continued to meander along in time-honored ways. Despite widespread representations of the non-Europeanized world as "Oriental" in this period, in fact radically differentiated economic transformations occurred in many parts of the globe between 1870 and 1945.

As Say's Law had pronounced a century before, products created their own demand. Or, in the words of Brazilian diplomat J. F. de Barros Pimental, "A century ago, the public pressured to have the commodities. In modern times, we observe the pressure of goods over the public. It is the inverse system: provisions [dominate] over populations. The globe's inhabitants do not search for goods as much as products seek consumers."[10] So what was produced in overseas agrarian areas not only responded to the appetites of affluent industrializing areas but shaped their tastes and notions of "decent" standards of living. The imported became centerpieces of national identity and class definition, from tea and wheat in the United Kingdom to coffee and sugar in the United States and Germany.[11] Thorstein Veblen may have ridiculed "conspicuous consumption," but goods that were previously undreamed of suddenly became status symbols or markers of modernity for the fortunate. Over time these goods filtered down to the general public and became mass necessities.

The vastly intensified labor of the working class also funded diversions of the leisure class that spread across borders: sumptuous retreats sprung up in Marienbad, Bohemia, and Battle Creek, Michigan; sin cities emerged in Casablanca, Havana, Shanghai, and Rio de Janeiro, and overseas tours led by the British Thomas Cook Company and travel guides written by the German Baedeker company catalyzed a global tourist industry. Leisure became commodified into manufactured things that could be exported: cheap publications like dime store novels and newspapers, player pianos and music rolls, records, Victrolas and other phonographs, and, of course, moving pictures. Tropical products, like chocolate, coffee, bananas, and tea, also fed these newfound leisure pursuits.

Why Study Commodities?

Tracing the evolution of a number of commodity chains during this era illuminates how agricultural, pastoral, and mineral-producing areas of the world—many in Latin America, Asia, Oceania, and Africa—were linked commercially to Western European and North American financiers, industrialists, and consumers. Commodity chains reveal connections among people who were distant and unfamiliar to each other; they linked inhabitants of different continents with markedly diverse lifestyles and cultures, who sometimes worked under contrasting modes of production. Rather than concentrate exclusively on diffusion or homogenization brought about by the industrial center imposing itself on an agrarian periphery, as many economic histories of this period have done, we study commodity circuits to demonstrate the inherent variety and interplay of world commerce and the contributions of the areas outside of Europe and North America.

Defining a "commodity" is no easy task, given the thorny nature of scholarship on this subject. The Ricardian or Marxian definition posits a commodity as a good produced for exchange to create profit, rather than one strictly made for use by its maker. The value of the commodity was determined by consumers rather than by its producer. We prefer this broad definition to the more restricted one recently in vogue with economists and businessmen who think of commodities only as raw materials or, more specifically, bulk undifferentiated and unbranded goods. To us, commodities were the result of dynamic and contingent processes of commodification, what some sociologists call "value chains," which sometimes included producers, processors, transporters, exporters, wholesalers, and retailers. Anthropologists, however, remind us to take into account cultural differences in how commodities have been perceived and utilized over time. They were not always market-bound tradable things. Things moved in and out of a commodity state, appreciated as much for their practical uses, their lore, and their symbolic value as for their roles in exchange and accumulation. They also had gendered meanings determined by households and subcultures as much as by individuals.[12] Because this was such a transitional moment in the global economy's expansion, in one locale goods could sometimes be produced solely for exchange, whereas in another the same product carried locally generated cultural and symbolic significance. World history enables us to understand how malleable commodities and their social roles were, just as we hope to show how the movement of these goods reveals the contours of world history.

To be sure, commodities often acquired new meanings and uses as they traversed oceans and were turned into imaginative new products. But it was also true that in the original producing areas the significance and even the essence of these "goods" (we use the term recognizing its imbedded and sometimes inaccurate value judgment, given that sometimes these goods were bad for producers or consumers) were altered as they were bent to the needs of foreign and domestic consumers. Examining the transformation of primary goods into finished products illuminates the workings of the world economy, because it requires consideration of a host of legal, technological, political, and social institutions that facilitated and accompanied such changes. Therefore, we first consider the conventions necessary for trade to flow and blossom, *before* entering into a detailed discussion of the commodity chains.

We pay particular attention to commodities that transcended national borders, even though the vast majority of economic activity in the world before 1945 was still dedicated to home and local production. It is impossible to consider the bewildering array of goods that circulated globally during this era, so we will concentrate on a few key products that were representative of the diversity of agricultural, mining, intermediary, and industrial processes.

We have chosen these products not because they were new to the world economy in 1870. Most, in fact, were not; some had already traveled internationally for centuries. Rather, they were selected because they were some of the most valuable globally traded products of the time. They not only fulfilled new social, cultural, and economic roles and elicited remarkable technological and institutional innovations, but they confounded some of the basic assumptions that contemporaries held about world trade. They allow us to follow goods from where they were grown, mined, or raised, to their processing and transformation for the market as they were packaged, branded, advertised, and placed in stores and stalls, to their final consumption in distant lands in remarkably different forms with usually quite different social meanings. Following these commodity circuits provides a heuristic device for understanding the complexities of global integration during this crucial era.

·[599]·

1. Transformations

GIVEN the sweeping changes that occurred, it is not surprising that winners and losers littered the new economic playing field. British, US, German, and French trade, capital, technology, and spheres of influence spread across the globe while eminent older empires such as the Ottoman, Chinese, Austro-Hungarian, Spanish, and Portuguese declined and fragmented. Western Europe, North America, Russia, Japan, and some parts of Latin America fared relatively well. Africa, the Middle East, and most of Asia (significantly, areas most afflicted by colonialism) fared less well. Clearly, transformations were far from uniform.

Even on the more prosperous continents, economies did not grow steadily and predictably. Intensified capitalist relations led to more frequent and destabilizing booms and busts, deflations and inflations. It was only in this period that economists began to theorize that economic cycles were inherent to capitalism. The economic concept of "cycles of accumulation," in which dramatic downturns ultimately and painfully cleared the way for later growth spurts, would come later. More unsettling to investors and producers alike, the economies most closely involved in international trade and finance found themselves most affected by global ups and downs. The seventy-five years after 1870 were marked by the first worldwide depression in the early 1870s, a downturn that lasted into the 1890s, followed by a European *belle époque* from the late 1890s until 1913 (save for the 1907 panic), unsettled conditions in the wake of World War I, and then what was, at least until recently, the most devastating and longest-lasting international commercial and financial crisis the world had ever experienced, the Great Depression. And just as the global economy was digging itself out, the pernicious effects of World War II would cripple huge swaths of the globe.[13]

Not only were sharp contrasts evident in different parts of the world, but their temporal character ensured that the benefits of "progress" were far from obvious for contemporaries. Preceding generations had bequeathed cultures of

violence, unfree labor, cumbersome concepts of property and wealth, and monopolized markets to the denizens of this new age. Indeed, critics like Lenin,
Bukharin, Rosa Luxemburg, and Hilferding asserted that such "market imper-
fections" (to borrow a concept from liberal economics) were not just anachro-
nisms or anomalies, but fundamental to the expansion of imperialism and
industrial capitalism. Closer integration to the world market did not necessarily
mean shared values, social structures, or prosperity. The pressures of the international economy may have melded together local peoples and markets, but they
also wrought fissures and fragmentation in areas newly affected by world commerce. In some regions, market integration offered greater productivity, choice,
and convenience to many. Elsewhere, market expansion resembled military campaigns imposed at the end of a bayonet at frightening cost.

If this era was the high tide of private property, privatization of land, and
less-restrictive trade, it also witnessed the birth of the "organized capitalism" of
trusts, cartels, and conglomerates, as well as socialist and fascist command
economies. Hobsbawm has noted: "Still, it does not much matter what we call it
('corporation capitalism,' 'organized capitalism,' etc.), so long as it is agreed—
and it must be—that combination advanced at the expense of market competition, business corporations at the expense of private firms, big business and large
enterprise at the expense of smaller; and that this concentration implied a tendency towards oligopoly."[14] Even in South and East Asia, where family firms and
partnerships continued to be the predominant form of business organization,
there was a tendency toward concentration, just as there was in Latin America
with its large plantations and relative handfuls of enormous mines, banks, and
factories.

Certainly, new technologies rewarded economies of scale and scope while
permitting centralized supervision and international coordination of an unprecedented order.[15] But the impetus to control these markets mocked ideologues
who preached the virtues of individualism and competition. This gave rise to
political movements, such as the Populists in the United States and anarchism
and socialism elsewhere, that denounced large banks and corporations and sought
more cooperative or communal endeavors. Their actions reflected what economic
theorist Karl Polanyi called the reformist "double movement" or what Marx
referred to as revolutionary "contradictions," as states, groups, and individuals

sometimes moved to mitigate or overturn the consequences of intensified market relations.

And for all of these new forms of organization and responses to rapid change, we should remember that many of the world's inhabitants were still peasants living in rural villages, often with communal forms of landownership. For them the rush of events in the center of the world economy could be a distant rumble, though often they came to feel its aftershocks.

Striking contrasts frequently were evident within the same country, as skyscrapers in modernized city centers were juxtaposed with sod or wattle-and-daub huts in the countryside. The differences in power, wealth, lifestyle, health, and labor systems often became so great that the rural and the urban were treated as separate realms and the populations as almost racially distinct. Over time some of the contrasts diminished in the more affluent areas as primary cities colonized their hinterlands, and in the process transmitted technological advances and social institutions, while absorbing ever more migrants from the countryside.

Difference imposed itself not only in lifestyle, but also more intimately in the quality and length of life itself. Unlike the post–World War II period, the areas of fastest population growth prior to 1945, such as the United Kingdom, Western Europe, and North America, were also the areas of rapid economic growth. In the United States, life expectancy began to grow quickly after 1870, jumping from forty-five years at birth for white males to sixty-five years in 1939–1941, a remarkable advance given that the total population was ballooning. Despite crushing wars, Scandinavia and other countries from Northern and Central Europe like Germany and the Netherlands reached life expectancies of sixty years by 1945. European offshoots, like Australia and New Zealand, experienced some of the most dramatic gains in longevity, attaining an average of sixty-seven years by the end of World War II. Latin Americans, with the exception of Argentines and Uruguayans, did not enjoy such demographic improvement. Most of them could expect to live only into their forties. In Africa and Asia (outside of Japan), where most of the world's people lived, population grew more slowly *and* the average person often could not expect to live past the age of thirty or forty.[16] So global life spans grew at historically unprecedented rates in some locales but so too did the gap in life expectancy between those in the richer countries and those in the poorer. Even within the same country, differences in longevity grew, as advances in sanitation and public health initially were concentrated in the cities. The medical discoveries of this period offered to the affluent included commodified and branded miracle drugs, such as aspirin, penicillin, and quinine, and increasingly modern practices from professionalized physicians and nurses. The poor continued to rely on folk remedies and shamans or simply suffered and died.

Constructive Destruction?

Distress and economic progress were not simply sad coincidences; they were often causally linked as they accompanied the carving up of Asia, Africa, and the Middle East by European powers. As Hilaire Belloc wrote in a sardonic ode to the colonial *mentalité,* the Europeans won out abroad—particularly in Africa—not so much because of the brilliance of their civilizations or the strength of their faith, but because: "Whatever happens, we have got / the Maxim gun, and they have not." Although the full poem was in fact a searing indictment of colonialism, it did correctly point to Europeans' military advantage, if not their moral superiority.

Over time, however, the diffusion of weapons by arms dealers and states undercut the early edge of the armed. Outlaws also took advantage: Chicago's policemen feared that "Tommy guns," first designed for trench warfare during World War I, might fall into the hands of Al Capone's mobsters. The Plains Indians and later the Apache in the US Southwest used rifles not just for hunting but also for raiding and self-defense. Revolutionists as well as militaries used dynamite to explosive effect.

Weapons industries reflected the contradictions of science and industrialization. Modern weaponry integrated precision engineering, standardization, assembly-line manufacturing, and automatic technology with durable and light materials to create potent engines of slaughter. When economist Joseph Schumpeter extolled capitalism's "creative destruction," he saw it as a virtue that removed barriers to rapid progress.[17] Perhaps he did not take into account that some of the largest corporations to arise from the Industrial Revolution, companies like Colt, DuPont, Siemens, IG Farben, and Krupp, profited handsomely from building devastating weapons of destruction. By the end of World War II, guns were capable of hitting targets miles away, guided missiles could fly over the English Channel, and airplanes were dropping powerful bombs, culminating in the atomic bombs dropped on Hiroshima and Nagasaki. Tragically, morality did not keep step with scientific "progress."[18]

When applied to livestock, the killing technology of Chicago's stockyards lowered the price of meat, making it available to the working class in the most affluent cities. At the same time, the "disassembly lines" of Chicago's Armour and Swift meat-processing plants were scientifically efficient means of terminating millions of animals' lives and transforming their skinned, cut-up carcasses into dozens of new commodities, from meat to shoes and buttons. These multinational corporations, which spread their operations to Latin America and beyond in the 1920s, used everything but the squeal in their merciless creative deconstruction that was the precursor to the industrial assembly line.[19]

A particularly striking example of the contradictions of technology was Alfred Nobel's inspired invention of dynamite. Mixing nitroglycerine and silica, he arrived at an explosive that not only was much more powerful than gunpowder, but, when joined to his invention of the blasting cap, was safe and controlled. The result was a godsend to miners, tunnelers, and builders more generally because it made their professions much safer. Dynamite went global not only because the more stable explosive could travel safely but also because Nobel's firm built dynamite factories in many countries. Although his invention was useful in the building and construction trades, he was denounced as a merchant of death. But as a pacifist, Alfred was earnestly distressed about the destructive genie he had let out of the bottle. Nobel willed a sizable part of his $9 million fortune to reward constructive scientific and other intellectual advances with a major prize. Perhaps the most ironic part of his penance was the creation of the Nobel Peace Prize, funded by explosives earnings.[20] Construction and destruction, peace and war danced to unpredictable rhythms in volatile couplings.

The Great Divergence

This era magnified what historian Kenneth Pomeranz has called "the Great Divergence." Taking exception to the conventional wisdom, at least in the West, that Europe had enjoyed wealth and technology superior to the rest of the world since the Middle Ages, Pomeranz contends that the West's margin over Asia materialized only after 1750 and then more for economic and geographic reasons than for cultural or racial ones. Thereafter, wealth, technology, and military power became concentrated among a few countries and in a few corporations in one corner of the world to a degree that had never before been experienced.[21] By 1880 the developed world's per capita income was about double that in the "Third World." It was to be over three times as high by 1914 and reached a five-fold difference by 1950, despite the devastation Western Europe experienced during World War II.[22]

Indeed, the wars brought about a divergence even within the developed economies, because such burgeoning economies as the United States, Canada, Australia, New Zealand, and Argentina were spared the ravages of war. The United States' per capita gross domestic product (GDP) jumped from a fourfold advantage over the average of "the periphery" in 1870 to almost ninefold in 1950, while Western Europe's lead grew more slowly from 3.5-fold to 4.7.[23] The democratically impoverishing Great Depression and World War II would lessen the divergence somewhat, but nonetheless in 1945 it was still far greater than it had been in 1870. Even these shocking numbers mute the reality of the gaping divide. The world's richest entrepreneurs and robber barons controlled more wealth than many small countries.

Sharp differences did not just stand out between countries on distant continents. Even within the same country immense inequalities were apparent, though not as great as those between richer and poorer countries. This Gilded Age saw plutocrats in enormous estates lighting cigars with five-dollar bills while millions of hungry proletarians huddled in teeming, filthy slums.[24] Tropical plantations may have provided delights such as coffee, sugar, and bananas, for the first time available to the new urban class of consumers in Western Europe and North America, but planters' ostentatious mansions were ringed by peasant huts or barracks and hungry, barefoot children, all too often hidden from the view of a well-armed *patrón*. Meanwhile, many people, particularly in Africa and Asia, continued to till their land and tend to their livestock as they had for as long as anyone could remember.

Contemporaries attributed this chasm to differences of race, religion, or climate, or to a clash of civilizations. The global divide was viewed as a confrontation of civilization versus barbarism not only by self-satisfied European and North American plutocrats but by many elites in the periphery. By the end of the period, explanatory concepts such as "underdevelopment" and "imperialism" began to replace the older cultural, religious, or racialist distinctions. Despite the urge to spread Western ways and homogenize the world during these years, *difference,* often growing differences, marked the gap between the daily lives of the globe's impoverished populace and those who benefited from the era's changes.[25]

Environment as Resource and Victim

Although our chapter concentrates on human involvement in the world economy, we would be remiss if we overlooked the collective impact of humans' explosive new productivity and trade on the natural environment. Economic growth and medical advances helped the world's population expand at the fastest rate in history to that point, doubling from 1.2 billion people to 2.5 billion in seventy-five years, and, as noted, in many areas life expectancy increased. Coupled with peoples' expanding ability to produce—total world output grew 500 percent by some estimates—and a growing appetite to consume, as well as the capability to access remote areas because of improved infrastructure, "nature" was losing its domain. While virgin prairies and grasslands were put to the plow, yielding bountiful returns, human intrusions also brought on disasters. Irrigation may have turned some deserts into fertile fields, but overfarming and grazing transformed once-prosperous lands into dust bowls.

Movement by actors in the world economy into formerly uninhabited areas had contradictory consequences. As Europeans and North Americans encountered parts of the globe formerly unknown to them in the Amazon, the American West, central Africa, and Siberia, plant and animal extinctions became commonplace. Development for some species often spelled tragedy for others.

Conservationists like John Muir in the United States began to see the threat of human sprawl and fought to maintain "pristine" nature. But they were unusual. In most places a "primitive accumulation" occurred in which the flora and fauna were treated as resources for human use and profit. "Darkest Africa," for example, became a natural bounty rather than a wilderness. Its great herds of elephants were slaughtered for their tusks just as the millions of buffaloes of the North American prairies were sent to near extinction. Brazil's vast coastal forest, the Mata Atlântica, was felled. And on the oceans, humans overran many islands. There, as well as on the continents, exotic species were introduced with occasional disastrous consequences for indigenous creatures and plants.[26]

Human audacity was not new, of course. For millennia some people thought their gods had bequeathed them ownership of the beasts and plants. Civilization and suzerainty had by definition long been equated to the domination of nature.[27] What changed was not ideas but rather how technocrats and scientists began developing techniques for massive frontal assaults on nature. Environmental degradation went hand in hand with commodification. Human societies with markets increasingly became market societies dominated by the urge to sell and buy in ever more parts of the world. Land, forests, and wildlife increasingly were perceived either as private property or as barriers to progress. This capitalization of nature in turn demanded new legal institutions, titles, financial instruments, and exchanges.

Cotton and the First Industrial Revolution

By 1870 the First Industrial Revolution had already caused cheap cotton textiles to replace precious metals, spices, silks, sugar, and tobacco as the principal engine of long-distance trade, though international commerce in all these commodities, with the exception of spices, grew rapidly throughout our period. The steam-powered loom, fed by Welsh and British coal, and Eli Whitney's cotton gin had revolutionized textile and clothing manufacturing. Where cotton had provided a mere 4 percent of clothing in the United Kingdom and the United States in 1793, a century later it had reached 75 percent. That this industrial powerhouse was fed by slave labor in North American cotton fields appeared to augur its demise once Abraham Lincoln abolished slavery. After all, on the brink of the American Civil War, the United States provided two-thirds of the world's total supply and fully 80 percent of the cotton manufactured in Britain.[28]

But cotton growers in the United States and elsewhere came to realize that they did not need slaves. King Cotton would continue to drive the economy of the southern United States after the Emancipation Proclamation, thanks to debt peonage, but now producers in Egypt and India, who took advantage of peasants, sharecroppers, and debt peons, could offer competition, thanks to even lower labor costs. By the last decades of the nineteenth century cotton was no longer the engine of world trade, because many areas, from Brazil and Mexico to South Africa, Uganda, and China, now grew their own. For the period 1860–1887, cotton ranked ninth in the value of seaborne trade, valued at less than one-fifth of grains or sugar and less than one-fourth of coffee. US exports of cotton regained antebellum levels by 1880 and doubled by 1895, but stagnated thereafter. The swelling US domestic market for textiles compensated somewhat for declining foreign demand, but domestic cotton production grew slowly and inconsistently, as it did worldwide. It would soon encounter stiff competition from other natural and synthetic fibers.[29]

As textile manufacture matured, investors from the first industrialized countries as well as native entrepreneurs in Latin America, Southern and Eastern Europe, and Asia, especially Japan and India, imported machinery and set up their own factories. They then appealed to their governments for tariff protection, further reducing the international circulation of textiles though increasing sales of machinery from the core to the periphery. This was the first stage of what became more generally known after 1930 as import substitution industrialization (ISI). Cotton was an early victim of what economist Raymond Vernon termed the "product cycle": the life trajectory of a new technology that initially provided great monopoly rents to "first movers" who first mastered more-efficient techniques and expanded markets.[30] While continuing to profit, first movers of cotton manufacturing lost their international advantage and their dynamism as the technology diffused. We will see this pattern repeated over and over again in areas as disparate as steel smelting and the telegraph and commodities from grains to rubber. New products demanding different raw materials from far-flung parts of the globe would take the baton in a global relay race to lead the continued expansion of the world economy.

Free Trade

The battle over tariffs on international trade was of enormous import for the course of world commerce. In 1870 Britain clearly enjoyed a privileged position in the world market thanks to its industrial head start in cotton textiles and other products, domination of global shipping, prosperous and sophisticated financial system, and access to imperial markets. There was little wonder, then, that British statesmen and politicians were quick to invoke classical economists like Adam Smith and David Ricardo on the advantages of free trade and the invisible hand of the market. Although one could attribute the concept of laissez-faire to earlier French Physiocrats, economic liberalism by our period spoke with a British accent. Her Majesty's imperial officials, as well as British investors, wage-earning workers, and consumers, all came to see advantages in lower duties on trade.[31] England's economic missionaries set out to convince statesmen and borrowers across the globe of the necessity of the gold standard, low tariff duties, limited government, and the primacy of the private sector—all of which would benefit British manufacturers, merchants, and bankers as well as their empire.

Political leaders and capitalists in other countries could be excused for not being as enamored of free trade. The unequal distribution of global capital led many governments to be suspicious of its benefits. Even in regions that enjoyed the most success in this age of export-led growth, such as the Americas, or later industrial giants such as Germany, Russia, and Japan, there was heated debate about the wisdom of open markets and privatization. Protectionism continued to vie with free trade, as defensive-minded political elites developed sophisticated economic discourses in favor of greater autarky.[32] Some statesmen sought to extend the idea of a tariff barrier to entire regions under the aegis of commercial unions. Each major economic power flirted with such unions: the French created their own union with other "Latin" countries, the United States' policy of Pan-Americanism tried to coordinate trade in its imagined "backyard," Britian would build its own imperial preferences in the 1920s and 1930s, the Germans followed suit in Central Europe, while the Japanese imposed their economic will on their regional neighbors.

Elsewhere there were efforts to protect narrower markets. In Latin America, protectionist lobbies exercised great weight in Brazil, Peru, and Mexico at the end of the nineteenth century.[33] Moreover, regional strongmen or *caudillos,* who still exercised considerable sway as late as the 1870s and 1880s, were key actors in the struggle to marshal resources. *Caudillos* acted like warlords in China or chieftains in Africa, who themselves were fervent advocates of local autonomy, even if sometimes that was seen as a step toward eventual greater regional unity.

So it is no surprise that warfare and political upheavals hindered economic development and investment. As a result, the export performance of most of Latin America remained shaky until the last decades of the nineteenth century and most of Africa and Asia fared even worse.[34]

Although some of Latin America's national leaders were among the most fervent disciples of the Manchester School's free-trade policies, conditions in that hemisphere necessitated responses different from those in England. In the "New World" the economies demanded significant state interventions, not only in transportation, banking, and public utilities, but also in the key export sectors, such as coffee and rubber. Nonetheless, liberalism continued to be an ideological and rhetorical desideratum of state policy even if it was obeyed more in the breach than in practice. They spoke liberalism; they acted interventionism.

The desirability of free trade also proved controversial in the United States. The defeat of the Confederacy in 1865, after the United States' bloodiest conflict, failed to put to rest divisive debates over the tariff, which continued to be a contentious matter for the nation's two major political parties. The Democrats were especially wary of big government, and Populists and then Progressive Republicans demanded greater state intervention in the economy. These parties remained suspicious of foreign investment even as it flooded into the country. Anti-British sentiment became so inflamed that the United States and Britain only narrowly escaped war in the early 1890s.[35]

For the most part, Canadians did not share such anti-British feelings (with the notable exception of the Québécois), but they pursued a middle ground, seeking freer trade by reducing their colonial ties while still remaining a part of the Commonwealth. Freer trade, however, meant turning away from London. The majority of their trade shifted from the United Kingdom south to the United States in these years. In 1870 Canada imported over half of its consumption goods from the United Kingdom and only a third from the United States; by 1911 just a quarter of its imports came from the British and 61 percent came from its southern neighbor.

Canada's experience contrasted rather sharply with those of other British colonies, such as Australia, New Zealand, and South Africa, which received over half their imports from Britain. Around half of Canadian exports, on the other hand, continued to go to Britain. They surpassed Australia but were considerably lower than New Zealand, and South Africa, which sent over three-quarters of their exports to the United Kingdom.[36] India, South Africa, and Rhodesia had success in the international market, but all three were under the aegis of British colonialism and paid a price in terms of severe internal inequalities.

The situation was different in most of Asia and Africa, which had not been subjected as thoroughly to British or Iberian influence. There, tribal and village authorities meant fragmented sovereignties; the great majority of the population consisted of subsistence peasants and herders who probably did not find foreign trade appealing. In such locales, European powers frequently attempted to foster monetary markets by statute or through force of arms. Even Japan, which was the most successful Asian economy at industrializing and expanding trade, abandoned its efforts at integration into the world economy to seek a self-contained imperial trading unit, the Greater East Asia Co-prosperity Sphere, once the Great Depression made its government wary of free markets.

It would require the near collapse of international trade and capital flows during the First World War and then the Great Depression of the 1930s to force major changes in commercial and financial thinking. Only then did theory catch up with the piecemeal policies of politicians engaged in crisis management. The severe dislocations of trade and financial flows generated new ways of understanding the global economy and of appreciating new roles for states.[37] Initially the advent of state planning was largely unplanned and unsought. This occurred in both agricultural and industrial export economies. After the First World War the leading powers, with the exception of the USSR, attempted to return to classical liberal economics by reinstating the gold standard and lowering barriers to trade and international investment. However, the Soviet Union and parts of Eastern Europe that increasingly fell into its orbit after the war turned to state planning for ideological reasons as well as for survival. During the 1930s the self-regulating market ceased to regulate itself even in Western Europe as commodity prices and trade dropped precipitously. In the face of deflation, unsettled financial markets, and political unrest, even European and North American governments turned to protecting home industries and widened the scope of public investment and regulation.

Exporting countries attempted to follow suit. Domestic markets in most of Latin America, for instance, already had expanded and diversified considerably under export-led growth. Consequently, ISI became increasingly attractive as a means of lessening reliance on imports. Politicized and radicalized urban workers, and, in a few countries such as Mexico, peasants and workers in the export sectors, demanded greater state attentiveness and a social safety net.[38] Similar statist efforts occurred in India and in Japan's sphere of influence, which included its colonies of Korea and Formosa as well as its growing influence over Southeast Asia and China. The Keynesian Revolution, even if it was not yet called that, began to challenge free-market liberalism in theory and practice.

The Second Industrial Revolution

The late nineteenth and early twentieth centuries were at once a natural extension of the First Industrial Revolution and a fundamental break with the past. A bevy of changes occurred in everything from the materials utilized, the sources of energy, the organization of production and business, the application of science, the nature of the most dynamic sectors, and even the nations now commanding the heights of this new wave of industrialization. Whereas the English had gained their head start in the eighteenth century through the application of coal to develop steam power, after 1870 they gradually ceded leadership to the United States and Germany. Although coal, steam, and iron continued to be important, now oil, electricity, and steel took precedence. Chemists became as important as engineers as they created aniline dyes, dynamite, and nitrates for fertilizers and munitions. Scientifically based, capital-intensive technology led not only to newer, more efficient, and larger-scale production methods, but to new materials such as rubber, steel, and cement, and new industries, such as weapons, electronics, the telegraph, the typewriter, the bicycle, and the automobile. Many of these new materials and products rewarded economies of scale. Assembly lines with continuous-flow production and standardized interchangeable parts eventually led in some places to the "American System" and Frederick Taylor's concept of "scientific management" predicated on greater efficiencies (what critics viewed as greater labor exploitation) through enhanced work norms and time-and-motion controls.

Other mass-produced products, particularly foods and medicines, were now packaged, branded, and advertised to facilitate their conquest of global markets.

By the post–World War II era, consumers in the West craved goods that were not even dreamed of in 1870; farmers and peasants for the first time could imagine buying factory-made clothes or store-bought foodstuffs that heretofore had characterized city life. The advent of department stores (and the consumer credit they extended) in the late nineteenth century in Western Europe and the United States, like Le Bon Marché, Harrods, Selfridges, Macy's, Marshall Field's, and Wanamaker's, and catalog stores, such as Montgomery Ward and Sears, Roebuck & Co., began to widen the market for ready-made mass clothing.[39]

Even though the growth of the world economy was no longer driven primarily by cotton, the British continued to be a driving force behind its expansion. By revolutionizing production and transportation technologies and expanding credit mechanisms, the United Kingdom and Ireland were responsible in the latter half of the 1870s for almost 40 percent of the world's manufactured exports. To export finished products, they had to import raw materials for their factories as well as food and drink for their growing urban populations, because their climate and the limited fertility of their land could not sustain them. That is why almost two-thirds of world trade in the forty years before 1913 was in primary products. The United Kingdom and Ireland accounted for just under a third (and northwestern Europe another 40 percent) of all imports of primary products. The world economy was driven by the relatively small islands of the United Kingdom and a cramped northwestern Europe, which were monetized and dependent on the outside world. Competition in the factories of Manchester, London, and Sheffield and on the European continent dropped export prices of manufactured goods, creating accelerated demand abroad. At the same time the gnawing British appetite for food and raw-material imports at least initially raised prices in agricultural exporting countries while London cemented its position as the world's banking and finance center.[40]

The pound sterling, which became the official unit of the British gold standard in 1821, replaced the Spanish, Mexican, and Peruvian peso in most countries by the 1870s, to eventually become the currency standard for world trade. This greatly reduced transaction costs and facilitated lending. As London became the world's commercial *and* financial center, the United Kingdom could sustain for a while the lead it had taken in the First Industrial Revolution (see Table 4.1, p. 619).

Britain's need for raw materials and food for its booming factories and population meant huge trade deficits. It financed this imbalance from its "invisible" earnings achieved through interest on commercial and public loans, profits on foreign direct investments, shipping and insurance charges, and currency exchange transactions. Historian Niall Ferguson does not exaggerate Britain's preeminent role as the motor of world trade when he writes: "Yet the fact remains that no organization in history has done more to promote the free movement of goods, capital and labour than the British Empire in the nineteenth and early twentieth centuries."[41]

States, Markets, and Monopolies

Despite the dreams and aspirations of the most radical champions of liberalism and the free market, turn-of-the-century economies were not unregulated. Expensive and far-reaching new technologies demanded public oversight of the private sector. States played an important role in subsidizing, regulating, and in some cases constructing costly infrastructure to lubricate the wheels of commerce. This was also true in some of the export economies in Latin America, Asia, Oceania, and, to a lesser extent, Africa that were more recently integrated into the world market.[42] Elsewhere, traditional modalities of trade remained largely uninterrupted, and, not surprisingly, states' presence in the economy was barely noticed.

The roles of merchants, officials, and information itself evolved in response to the evolution of the market. Even as late as 1870 most specialized knowledge of the market was local, sporadic, and heterogeneous, controlled mostly by specific actors at different points in a commodity chain—growers, traders, transporters, processors, dealers, wholesalers, retailers, and peddlers. Closely held information on trade and personal relations of trust aided the continued importance of ethnic and familial trading diasporas, such as the Cantonese, Tamil, Gujarati, Sindhi, Persian, Hadhrami, Armenian, Syro-Lebanese, Moroccan Jewish, Basque, Scottish, and Ashkenazi Jewish networks.[43]

Over time, information became more widely disseminated, systematic, and standardized, first by merchants and shippers, then by trade gazettes, newspapers, wire services, and commodity and stock exchanges. The telegraph that began linking distant contiguous areas and the undersea cable that tied together continents sparked the need for commercial, legal, and scientific conventions. European languages—French for diplomacy, German for science, and English for business—supplemented by the forces of colonialism and imperialism, became widely used among anonymous elites across the globe. Even areas that did not experience colonialism directly, like Japan, introduced modern conventions, but with their own twists. But the urge to "modernize" (another word and concept that became fashionable in this period) did not always connote the desire to homogenize. Outside forces were often perceived as pernicious and malignant. Reaction to them frequently inhibited diffusion rather than encouraging it.

There is ample debate among economic historians about whether this era of globalization primarily meant the growth of the free market, secure property rights, liberalism, the gold standard, and free trade, or whether it was characterized more by imperial and domestic government intervention and the emergence of monopolies. In fact, both were in evidence. Consolidation and monopoly were particularly noticeable in modern transportation sectors like railroads and steamships, in communication marvels like the telegraph, and in heavy industries dependent upon government contracts, such as armaments. It was also found where new energy forms and systems were utilized, such as oil and electricity, and with certain new raw materials that governments deemed to be of strategic value, like rubber. Standard Oil controlled over 90 percent of the oil refined in the United States in 1880, US Steel at the turn of the century produced almost two-thirds of the industry's steel, while the Rhine-Westphalian Coal Syndicate controlled the same share of coal in Germany.[44]

Concentration also emerged in intermediary capital goods sectors, such as machinery that was sold to manufacturers rather than to consumers, who remained blissfully unaware of the components that went into these goods. Among the pioneering machinery firms, notes business historian Alfred Chandler, "rarely did more than a handful of competitors succeed in obtaining a significant share of the national and international markets. These industries quickly became and remained oligopolistic or monopolistic."[45]

Much more evident to the general public in North America and Western Europe was that "bigness" was an indelible characteristic of such industries as perishable food and drugs, because processors found ways to profit from economies of scale and scope. Linking vertically between agricultural production (which they only occasionally did themselves), purchasing, processing, packaging, and distribution, some enormous, highly capitalized corporations that we are still familiar with today, such as the United Fruit Company, British Tobacco, Coca-Cola, Wrigley, and Quaker Oats, created international commodity chains within their firms to sell recently created products for mass markets.[46]

Huge corporations dominated not just because of technological imperatives or market demands. Financiers, who previously had profited from loans to governments and other financial instruments, emerged as key brokers who were best placed to take advantage of the more felicitous business climate. With the passage of joint-stock-company and limited-liability laws, financiers created large commercial banks that pooled the small investments of rentiers and the middle class to promote new innovative undertakings and expansions, all the while assembling trusts to restrain competition.

These enormous companies often had stockholders and even directors and managers from a number of countries, so increasingly they carried multiple passports. Although Lenin thought that nationalism and consolidation characterized the highest stage of capitalism and that they would lead the dominant imperialist nations to war among themselves, in fact multinational companies often preferred to cooperate with their international business associates rather than with their national compatriots. J. P. Morgan underwrote huge US combinations through his father's London-based company; the Rothschilds had banks headquartered in five countries; the American-based General Electric (GE) and the German firm Siemens undertook mutual projects; and French and British banks jointly underwrote loans. The governments of the countries in which these firms operated now were faced with divided loyalties. The new international scope created challenges for multinational corporations like Standard Oil in Austria, which found itself "caught between the international markets in which they operated and the national governments whose support they sometimes needed to protect their extended operations."[47]

Transnationalism was furthered by multinational corporations, bilateral and multilateral treaties between and among states, and international familial diasporas. This was also the beginning of what today are known as nongovernmental organizations (NGOs). Internationalists, sometimes working for "one world," banded together for causes as disparate as the conservation of nature, poverty relief, and health care.[48]

It should be noted that multinational combinations reigned among illicit organizations as well, hiding from government watchdogs rather than utilizing them. This was the era of the rise of immigrant street gangs, of some Chinese *tongs* that veered into illicit enterprises, and then later the internationalization of the Italian Mafia, which became an economic force with which to reckon.[49]

New technologies and capital accumulation also created what economic historian Alexander Gerschenkron termed "the relative advantages of backwardness." Formerly "backward" economies such as Russia, Germany, and Japan did not need, he argued, to follow in lockstep Britain's blueprint for industrialization. Government oversight and foreign-financed and imported technology would help them leapfrog forward. Sometimes being very backward proved advantageous because, as economic historian David Landes has observed, "the greater the gap, the greater the gain for those who leap it."[50] Backward countries could grow faster than the early leaders because they could avoid their mistakes and take advantage of successful technologies as well as more plentiful international capital available for investment. Argentina, Australia, and Canada found their minimal colonial heritages and the dearth of inhabitants salutary once the world economy stimulated the demand, the means, and the investments to farm their fertile fields and transport their produce.

Advanced forms of capitalism were sometimes embedded in rural and poor settings where they were slow to spread and share their benefits. For instance, Mexico's export-led economy during Porfirio Díaz's dictatorship (1876–1911), which featured raw materials and staple goods, was characterized by crony capitalism, either by multinational companies and banks composed entirely of external capitalists or syndicates of politically connected foreign and domestic investors.[51] Argentina, Brazil, Chile, and Canada witnessed the presence of well-capitalized European or North American firms in transport and urban utilities, mining, banking, and the grain and beef industries. The domestic industrialization of Meiji Japan was aided by the weakening of the samurai oligarchy through land reform, but now concentration took another form, as *zaibatsus* or large financial cliques were created that worked closely with the state. But in this instance capital and management were domestic, though with foreign advice.[52]

Economic change also brought with it new social tensions that occasionally erupted in violence and radical political upheaval. The state–capitalist alliance in Mexico, for example, provoked the first social revolution of the twentieth century, and rapid industrialization in Russia (and the disastrous consequences of the First World War) helped bring the Bolsheviks to power. Statist development in Japan spawned Asia's first imperialist power during the Age of Empire.[53] In China, European capital and technology were largely concentrated in neocolonial treaty ports under the authority of European powers. They contributed to unrest that overthrew the empire in 1911. Anti-European nationalism (and opposition to the occupying Japanese) would later stimulate the rise of the Communists and their ultimate triumph at the end of our period.

Foreign Investment

The world had never seen as much foreign investment as was put in circulation between 1870 and 1929. This vast expansion of surplus wealth, monetary instruments, stocks, bonds, and loans encouraged more individual and corporate investment abroad. Although states supervised and regulated investments, it was the private sector, not states, that was responsible for the increase. Even when states borrowed to balance their budgets, pay debts, or invest in infrastructure, the lenders were usually a handful of international bankers. The banks making the loans were almost all Western European until the 1920s, when some US banks began placing loans abroad. Much of the capital raised in London, for example, was continental European, with smaller amounts coming from the Western Hemisphere, as well as India or Australia.[54] In addition, we do not know how much was invested by members of ethnic diasporas who never registered officially or how much went into partnerships rather than corporations. We do know that the stock offers often were as reflective of dreams or schemes as of concrete wealth. Nonetheless, they give us a general idea of the prodigious increase in international financial flows. Foreign investment surged from over £6 billion in 1870 to £23 billion in 1900 and £43 billion in 1914 (see Tables 4.1 and 4.2).

We should note that although much of this capital was invested in infrastructure and helped subsidize the public sector, some of it merely kept corrupt

TABLE 4.1

Distribution of foreign investment, 1914, by investing regions (in pounds sterling)

	Amount invested	% of total
Britain	4,100,000,000	43
France	1,900,000,000	20
Germany	1,200,000,000	13
Belgium, Netherlands, and Switzerland	1,100,000,000	12
United States	700,000,000	7
Other	500,000,000	5
Total	9,500,000,000	100

Source: A. G. Kenwood and A. L. Lougheed, *The Growth of the International Economy, 1820–2000,* 4th ed. (London: Routledge, 1999), 27.

TABLE 4.2

Distribution of foreign investment, 1914, by recipient regions (in pounds sterling)

	Amount invested	% of total
Europe	2,500,000,000	27
North America	2,300,000,000	24
Latin America	1,800,000,000	19
Asia	1,500,000,000	16
Africa	830,000,000	9
Oceania	500,000,000	5
Total	9,420,000,000	100

Source: A. G. Kenwood and A. L. Lougheed, *The Growth of the International Economy, 1820–2000,* 4th ed. (London: Routledge, 1999), 27.

despots in power, enriching their families and cronies, or it enabled members of the political class or wealthy elites and corporations to buy up local assets and lands. And although foreign investment brought with it bridges, roads, and even schools, it also ensured the longevity of colonial or neocolonial regimes that sustained inequality as much as gunboats and troops ever did.

·[619]·

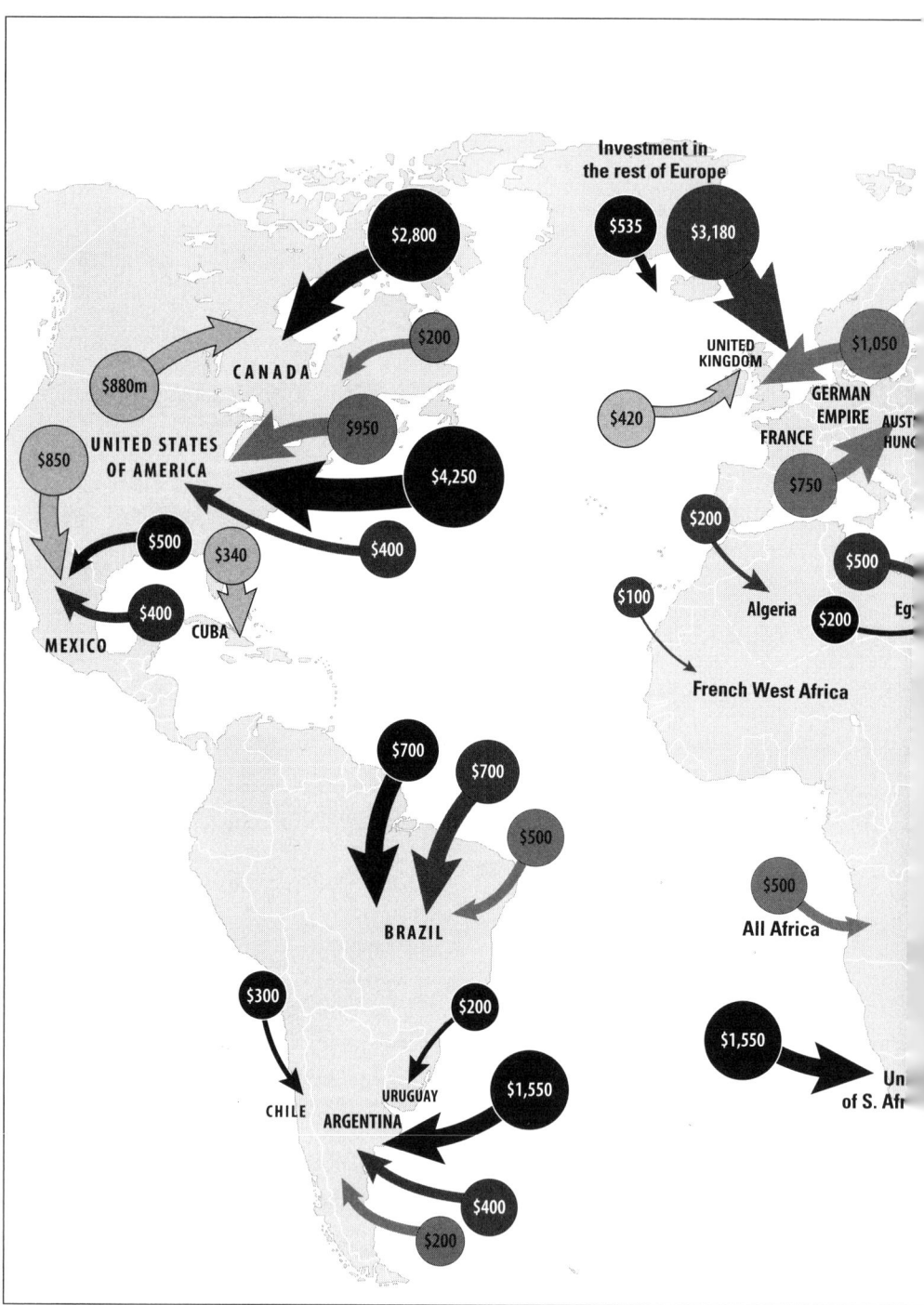

Patterns of foreign investment, 1914.

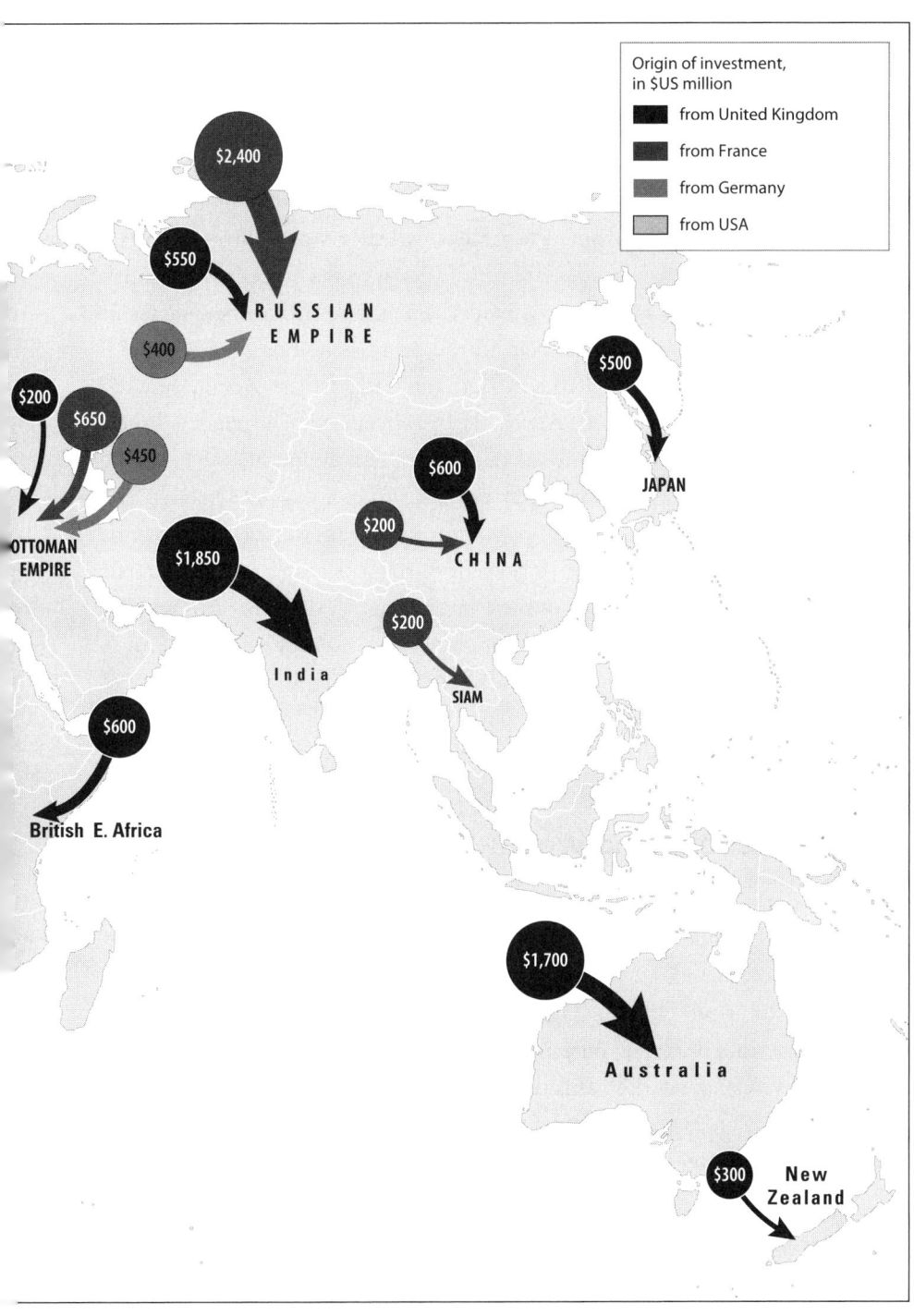

Origin of investment,
in $US million

■ from United Kingdom
■ from France
■ from Germany
□ from USA

$2,400

$550

$400

RUSSIAN
EMPIRE

$500

$200

$650

$450

$600

$200

JAPAN

OTTOMAN
EMPIRE

$1,850

$200

CHINA

India

$200

SIAM

$600

British E. Africa

$1,700

Australia

$300

New
Zealand

Over time the British found that their financial prowess had its limits and that London could not extend its reach into every corner of the world. Unwilling to protect its home market, the British gradually fell behind in the new chemical, electronic, and oil-based technologies, areas dominated by United States and German trusts and cartels. By 1913 the British share of global manufactured exports had fallen from 37.8 percent, where it stood thirty-five years earlier, to 25.3 percent; two decades later it was down to 19.5 percent. The British concentrated their trade ever more within their empire: from one-quarter of trade in 1871–1875, it rose to 41 percent in the depression years of 1934–1939.[55] Even within the empire, the United Kingdom ran trade deficits overall, showing positive balances only with South Africa. So Britain ceased being the workshop of the world, becoming instead its banker, investor, and shipper.

The same gradual retrenchment was evident in portfolio investments. The four decades after 1870 were a golden period for European overseas investments. Between that year and 1914, fully 40 percent of the world's foreign investment was British.[56] Surprisingly, in view of the conventional wisdom that this was the Age of Empire, European investors did not prefer to invest in their own colonies. Instead they focused on government bonds, railroads, ports, and urban improvements in independent regions like the United States and Latin America. Only after the First World War did Britain concentrate its investments in its colonies.

Comparing Worldwide Production

Some parts of the world remained rather marginal to international markets. Notwithstanding the imperialist scramble for Africa in the last decades of the nineteenth century, that continent remained peripheral to world production (roughly 4 percent of total production). However, its population grew faster than the world's average, and per capita output outstripped its accelerated birth rate, more than doubling per capita GDP. This reflected a move from subsistence to market-oriented production as much as it demonstrated an absolute increase in production. In aggregate terms there were some hubs of export growth on the periphery, such as South Africa with its diamond and gold bonanzas. But in the main, growth was won at the cost of extreme inequality and exploitation as white settler enclaves and homegrown collaborator elites enjoyed privileged positions in Europe's sub-Saharan colonies.

Relative to the expansion in Europe and the Americas, Asia—with the exception of Japan—lost ground. Its share of world population, production, and international commerce declined. The fall was most notable in China. It was bad enough that the venerable empire was divided by warlords and foreign enclaves, and wracked by revolutions from the Taiping to the overthrow of the emperor in 1911, civil war between the Guomindang and the Communists, and Japanese invasion. But in addition its main exports, such as tea and silk, were either replaced by production elsewhere—tea in India and Ceylon (Sri Lanka), and silk in Japan and Italy—or, as with silk, replaced by synthetics, particularly North American and European rayon.[57]

We should add a note of caution about these findings, however. Calculating Asia's relative decline in the world economy underlines the danger in assuming that exports were an accurate measure of economic progress. China lagged behind in absolute and per capita exports in part because its large population had created large domestic markets and dense settlement. It lacked marginal unpopulated areas appropriate to production of goods for Europe and North America—the main importers in this era.

Nonetheless, in a few products there were impressive export advancements worth noting. Indian cotton and textiles, tea, rice, and jute were world leaders, as were Indonesian (mainly Javanese) rubber, sugar, and tea and Malaysian rubber and tin. And opium was certainly one of the world's most valuable exports (in monetary terms). These crops and extractive undertakings were mostly successful in formerly marginal areas, like India's Assam district for tea, the Irrawaddy Delta for rice, Burma for jute, and Malaysia and Sumatra for rubber.

Moreover, it is plausible that the inward orientation of most Chinese, Japanese, and Indian production and the institutions and the skills they learned from this were ultimately to the good. Considered a detriment in the age of exports, they may have ultimately prepared these countries for dramatic explosions of exports that occurred in the last quarter of the twentieth century.[58]

The proof that prior development was often a disadvantage in export production is the fact that the areas that recorded the greatest aggregate gains were the sparsely populated Americas and some areas in the Pacific. Known as "new" or "vacant" areas, "neo-Europes," "settler colonies," or "Western offshoots," the United States, Canada, Australia, and New Zealand grew from a negligible share in 1820 to 10 percent of world output in 1870, then more than doubled their percentage of output by 1913, and reached almost a third of world production by 1950.[59] Per capita GDP jumped more than fourfold, reaching an estimated $9,288 (in 1990 US dollars), by far the highest level in history to that point and more than twice the level of Western Europe in 1950. We must bear in mind that in addition to enjoying favorable natural resource endowments, small native populations (important as the denominator in calculating per capita income and production), access to vast quantities of immigrants and capital, and in several notable cases the advantage of adopting the latest world technology under the umbrella of British free trade, neo-European lands benefited immeasurably because they avoided the world wars. Although hundreds of thousands of their soldiers died in those gruesome struggles, they benefited indirectly from the economic devastation experienced by their main competitors and trade partners. In particular the United States, which transformed itself from a debtor nation to a creditor, would, more than any other country, benefit from the Great War's deleterious impact on Europe.

Similarly, Latin America avoided the world wars and prospered from its export boom, more than tripling its share of output. Certainly Argentina and Uruguay's unparalleled success contributed greatly to that outcome. But many other nations throughout the region, such as Brazil, Chile, Colombia, Cuba, Mexico, Central America, and Venezuela, enjoyed more limited export booms. Latin America's per capita GDP grew 3.5-fold, reaching one of the world's highest totals by 1950. If Latin America "fell behind," as one influential volume has argued, it fell behind only the most prosperous economies of the world.[60] Some parts of Latin America, with their burgeoning markets and emerging native bourgeoisies, compared quite favorably with areas of Europe. Indeed, Argentina and Uruguay were among world leaders in both per capita income and trade after the turn of the century, while Cuba's economy, thanks to sugar and a welcoming market in the United States, also flourished. Chilean exports (first nitrates and then copper), Peruvian guano and nitrates, Bolivian tin, Mexican industrial metals and oil, and Brazilian coffee and rubber were all world leaders (see Tables 4.3 and 4.4).

TABLE 4.3

World GDP per capita, regional averages (in 1990 international dollars)

	1820	1870	1913	1950
Western Europe	1,232	1,974	3,473	4,594
Eastern Europe	636	871	1,527	2,120
USSR	689	943	1,488	2,834
Western offshoots (USA+)	1,201	2,431	5,257	9,288
Latin America	659	698	1,511	2,554
Japan	669	737	1,387	1,926
Asia (except Japan)	575	543	640	635
Africa	418	444	585	852
World	667	867	1,510	2,114

Sources: Gene Shackman, Ya-Lin Liu, and Xun Wang, "Context of Change in the Twenty-First Century," http://gsociology.icaap.org/report/longterm.html; and Angus Maddison, *The World Economy* (Paris: Development Centre of the Organization for Economic Co-operation and Development, 2006), table B-21.

We should caution that aggregate world economic data are "ballpark guesstimates" and are ideologically biased. Wealth is presumed to be measured by monetary market transactions. Gross National Product really measures Gross National Monetized Transactions. Self-sufficient production of goods and services, from peasant farming and animal husbandry to domestic activities and barter, were not counted unless sold for money in a market where data was collected. So wealth and productivity became synonymous with commodification of goods and labor. Calculating them accurately relied on sufficiently strong, interested, and wide-reaching states that collected data. In supposedly "underdeveloped" areas, which for most of our period entailed the majority of the Earth's human population, data on economic activity was infrequently compiled, tabulated, monetized, or credited.

Another problem with data is the implicit assumption that increasing production or market activity was synonymous with improving welfare. As any reader of Charles Dickens's novels of the Industrial Revolution, such as *Hard Times,* Victor Hugo's *Les Misérables,* or the works of historian E. P. Thompson knows, rapid economic growth was usually attended by the appropriation of the labor and land of significant portions of the working classes. Their absolute welfare

TABLE 4.4

Economic output and population, by area (in 1990 international dollars)

	1820		1870		1913		1950	
	% of world economic output	% of world population	% of world economic output	% of world population	% of world economic output	% of world population	% of world economic output	% of world population
Western Europe	23.57	12.80	33.61	14.80	33.52	14.60	26.26	12.10
Eastern Europe	3.33	3.50	4.13	4.10	4.49	4.40	3.47	3.50
USSR	5.43	5.30	7.59	7.00	8.59	8.70	9.56	7.10
Western offshoots (USA+)	1.94	1.10	10.18	3.60	21.65	6.20	30.65	7.00
Latin America	2.01	2.00	2.53	3.10	4.49	4.50	7.94	6.60
Japan	2.99	3.00	2.30	2.70	2.65	2.90	3.02	3.30
Asia (except Japan)	56.25	65.30	36.02	57.50	21.91	51.70	15.45	51.40
Africa	2.99	7.10	3.65	7.10	2.69	7.00	3.64	9.00

Sources: Gene Shackman, Ya-Lin Liu, and Xun Wang, "Context of Change in the Twenty-First Century," http://gsociology.icaap.org/report/longterm.html; and Angus Maddison, *The World Economy* (Paris: Development Centre of the Organization for Economic Co-operation and Development, 2006), table B-21.

declined, at least in the short run, and this was true not only in cities. The "vacant" or "newly settled" areas also experienced land appropriations through military campaigns that forcibly moved the indigenous populations off their lands in the last decades of the nineteenth century, such as Argentina's Conquest of the Desert, Chile's war against the Mapuche, and the United States' campaigns in the Midwest and West. More privately run attacks were carried out in the Australian Outback, New Zealand, and Mexico's northern deserts. Gross national product (GNP) in these areas grew even while entire ethnicities were exterminated or corralled onto reservations.

2. The Sinews of Trade

GREED, desire, labor, capital, and sophisticated technology were not enough to catapult the world economy on a path to sustained development. As economic historians Douglass North and Lance Davis have shown, the creation and timing of economic institutions and infrastructure played a significant role and fostered path dependency, making some outcomes much more likely than others. Global expansion also often demanded large systemic investments and international agreements. In this section we discuss key underpinnings of the international economy, including currency standards; improvements to infrastructure, such as shipping, canals, railroads, autos, and airplanes, and the oil and rubber that they required; and vastly expanded communications networks, especially the telegraph, transoceanic cables, and radios, and the electric, copper, and aluminum industries that both resulted from them and facilitated their rapid expansion.

Currency

The standardization of currencies was especially critical to the growth of commercial markets. The British pound sterling was the premier currency in the world economy, but in 1870 it was far from hegemonic. A bimetal silver/gold standard still reigned throughout much of Europe with the creation in 1865 of the Latin Monetary Union by France, Belgium, Italy, and Switzerland. The union was French emperor Napoleon III's brainchild, designed to counter London's monetary clout. It later added Spain, Greece, Romania, Austria-Hungary, Bulgaria, Venezuela, and Serbia and Montenegro. The United States was officially bimetal as a result of the Sherman Silver Purchase Act of 1890. Latin American countries were mostly on the silver standard, thanks to the widespread circulation of Mexico's peso, as were most Asian currencies. Of course, the silver–gold divide refers to international and governmental transactions, because most of the world's inhabitants still lived largely outside a money economy, engaging mainly in subsistence or barter economies, where often natural goods such as bricks of tea, cocoa beans, salt, cowry shells, cattle, or cloth served as markers of value.

Nonetheless, monetization grew rapidly as governments minted the gold and silver bonanzas discovered in California (1848), Australia (1852), South Africa's Transvaal (1886), the Yukon in Canada (1898), Russia from the Urals to Siberia and the Amur region, and silver in Nevada and Colorado in the United States (1850s–1870s). Silver finds dwarfed gold discoveries, so silver's relative price dropped, which persuaded many bimetal countries such as France and its counterparts in the Latin Monetary Union and the United States to eventually make the move to the gold standard. The United States attempted to tie its new colonies to the dollar by sending out financial missions (and gunboats) to Latin America as well as to China to craft a "dollar diplomacy" that enhanced Wall Street's global financial position. Some countries such as Brazil had inconvertible currencies whose value was based on faith in the government but not backed by precious metals (except for brief, partial experiments). Merchant notes and bills of lading served as unofficial currency; by the twentieth century bank checks backed by private bank deposits began to circulate. China also enjoyed a rapid growth of paper currency that facilitated the spread of the money economy, domestic regional trade, and lower transaction costs. When the Great Depression disrupted the world economy, some aspiring empires, such as Japan, Germany, and the Soviet Union, responded to the crisis by creating trade currencies for bilateral exchanges.[61]

For all of these challenges to the pound sterling, the gold standard (whereby national currencies were convertible to gold) came to dominate in world trade and finance and played a significant role in their unparalleled expansion up to 1914. Issuing governments therefore had to store ample gold to back their currency. That was a boon to international trade, because foreign commerce would be the means of procuring gold for the vast majority of the world's countries that did not mine sufficient gold for their own needs. Balance of payments deficits would have to be addressed by adjusting prices or by reducing imports to avoid a gold drain and resulting currency depreciation. Governments could issue only as much currency as they had gold, so their actions were greatly circumscribed by international trade and finance. The private sector engaged in international exchanges, which supplied gold via trade surpluses. Private companies' political power was therefore strengthened. Because of the gold standard currency, exchanges were more certain and cheaper, facilitating commerce and international lending. This was known as the "self-regulating market."[62] Underpinning the gold standard was the desire to defend the value of money and therefore the assets of creditors and the wealthy by preventing inflation.

The drawback to the standard was that it was pro-cyclical. When the economy was thriving, money was abundant. But when there was an international downturn, governments could not issue more currency to prime the pump of economic activity. Prolonged slumps resulted. The world economy rode out the 1870s depression and the 1907 scare on the gold standard, but the First World War caused many countries to abandon it as world trade ground to a halt. Germany was the most crippled by war reparations and a historically unprecedented inflation.[63] Some forty countries returned to gold during the 1920s, but the 1929 financial crisis and the ensuing depression of international trade caused the British to abandon the standard in 1931. Others soon followed. Efforts to return to the gold standard after 1945 were halfhearted. The world would never return to the hegemony of the gold standard of the pre-1914 years, yet the world economy would boom as never before. Apparently gold was not essential to prosperous international trade after all.

Shipping

If the standardization of currencies was of paramount importance, so, too, was the slew of infrastructural improvements that made their staccato-like appearance during these seven decades. The steamship was long considered one of the key markers of the transportation revolution. It *was* important, but its impact was not felt until the last third of the nineteenth century, yet freight rates had been declining since 1815.[64] Long-distance trade was already expanding rapidly before the conversion to steam, because of a combination of political, scientific, technical, and commercial improvements—such as the reduction of piracy; the elimination of navigation laws that had impeded multilateral shipping; the improvement of navigational instruments and nautical maps and an enhanced knowledge of winds and currents; the ability to build larger, more seaworthy transoceanic sailing ships; and the reduction of idle time in port. In the East, improved ports and their connections to their hinterlands were constructed in Alexandria, Mumbai (Bombay), Cape Town, and Calcutta (Kolkata), while new harbors were built at Aden, Port Said, and Singapore—to mention only the largest. In the Americas, a modernized Vera Cruz in Mexico, Belém, Manaus, Rio de Janeiro, and Santos in Brazil, Buenos Aires in Argentina, as well as Havana, Cuba, joined newly improved ports in New York, New Orleans, and San Francisco in the United States.

For Britain's manufactured products to flood first neighboring countries and then more distant ones and stimulate imports in return, the cost of transport had to fall and the capacity to carry large loads quickly and predictably had to grow. British sailing ships had dominated the seas before the First Industrial Revolution, so most of the nineteenth-century sea trade continued to be powered by wind on ships owned and manned by the British. As late as 1880, three times as much large-scale waterborne freight traveled by sail as by steam. With small loads, sailing ships had a much greater advantage. However, beginning in the 1880s steam came to drive ever-larger freighters built increasingly of steel rather than wood. Technical advances in steamships, such as the screw propeller, the iron and then (after 1880) the steel hull, the surface condenser, and the compound engine, made steamships lighter and more durable. These improvements enhanced carrying capacity and required less than a fifth as much coal, freeing up additional space for cargo. Steamers could now travel substantially greater distances without needing to refuel. The leading imperial powers, such as Britain, Germany, and the United States, which also held some of the world's largest coal reserves, established coaling stations on remote islands to provision the steamer trade.[65]

World trade and shipping in large vessels (over a hundred tons) grew at similar rates between 1881 and 1913. Both would stagnate in the 1930s and, of course, fall during the wars. Ship construction became increasingly mechanized and inexpensive, so that shipyards continued to serve as some of the largest manufactories of their time, just as some steamers were among the most capital-intensive machines of the era. By the end of our period, tanker ships were developed to transport oil, thereby clinching the transition from coal-fed steam power to oil-fueled steam power and finally petroleum-driven internal combustion engines.[66]

In addition to becoming bigger, faster, and safer, ships were transformed to serve and stimulate the growth of major new industries. The refrigeration of ships in the last quarter of the nineteenth century, for instance, permitted the rapid growth of the chilled and frozen meat industries. By the turn of the century, bananas also were benefiting from refrigerated ships to eventually become the leading internationally traded fruit, and would integrate formerly marginal areas of Central America and the Caribbean into the world market.[67]

Technological inventions and institutional innovations meant that in the period 1871–1914, when global trade underwent such spectacular growth, freight rates for commodities declined the fastest on the busiest oceanic routes because of fierce competition.[68] Before this revolution in shipbuilding technology, with freight rates declining, the rising cost of constructing a ship would have dissuaded investors from risking more capital in yet more expensive ships. Now shipping companies were forced to spend on more efficient ships and facilities, recouping the additional expense with the greater carrying capacity of the new ships and paying for it with lower-priced loans from international bankers.

Competition alone was not a sufficient motor of change. Some shipping companies received government subsidies to carry the mail, deliver colonial officials, or maintain merchant marine fleets as a backup in times of war. Also, many shipping companies were early conglomerates that also engaged in insurance, banking, and commerce on their own accounts, so what was a commercial loss for the shipping company could be a savings for a company's trading arm. In some cases, such as the Grace Line and later the United Fruit Company's Great White Fleet, the line's main purpose was to carry the company's cargo. Such multipurpose agricultural companies also built ports and increased the number of plantations they owned to develop new commodities like bananas and pineapples.[69]

This swelling of ship size and economies of scale that accompanied it meant ships were the most expensive capital goods of the era. But they would not have been economically feasible unless markets for goods and port facilities were large and efficient enough to unload and sell the goods. During the era of the spice trade, the simultaneous arrival of two ships could drive down the price of a precious commodity by glutting the tiny specialty market. But now a revolution in port facilities and land transport, often publicly financed or underwritten, as well as advances in warehousing and marketing, accompanied the dramatic explosion of shipping capacity. Multiple large shipments could be landed at the same time and still be profitable. Transport efficiency was coupled with remarkable changes in wholesale and retail marketing and distribution to satisfy swelling consumer cravings for overseas goods. Standards and prices for goods coming from myriad origins were increasingly negotiated at commodity exchanges that arose in key ports. All of these marketing innovations sped up turnaround time for shippers. This justified increased investments in ever-larger ships. Now mercantile corporations could maximize their use of the larger carrying capacity rather than suffer their ships' idling in ports, slowly being emptied or awaiting new return cargo.[70]

To take advantage of ever more commodious ships, the nature of the freight carried also changed. Early on, luxuries such as precious metals, spices, skins, and cloth that fetched high prices abroad drove long-distance trade. Now bulk commodities, goods that had a high volume-to-value ratio, such as coal, meat, and grains and tropical goods like chocolate, coffee, and bananas, became profitable to ship across oceans. The greater certainty of travel time under steam meant that goods that spoiled easily could now successfully traverse the seas, reaching large moneyed populations.

Still, the interrelationship between marketing economies and institutions (the cost of getting goods to the retail customer), freight economies, and the emergence of new long-distance cargo advantaged a relatively small part of the globe. Western European factories required ever more raw materials like cotton and lumber and fuel such as coal and later oil. Their populations could afford (and required as they left their farms) basic foodstuffs like wheat and more luxurious treats like sugar, coffee, and tea.

Those goods were exported mostly from a relatively small number of sparsely settled areas. Outside of densely populated Western Europe, the most dynamic economic regions were frontiers that were land rich and people poor. In these areas the cost and reliability of shipping became all the more important. Their few inhabitants meant land was relatively cheap in monetary terms (although often purchased with the blood of the indigenous peoples pushed off their tribal lands and of native animals) and labor was dear. Enjoying the greater productivity of fertile, well-watered lands, agricultural crops could be grown relatively inexpensively and shipped to Europe economically. However, the Europe-bound ships with their holds filled with coffee, cotton, or wheat had to return to the "vacant" agricultural lands where demand from the sparse and often poorly paid population was insufficient to fill them. They either filled up with ballast with little economic value or offered cheap fares to northern and southern Europeans who were being crowded off their lands at home. The passengers in turn worked the fields opening in the neo-Europes and provided a market for export of goods and capital from Western Europe. Thus, the freight revolution played a large role in the great transoceanic movement of peoples, most notably the movement of millions of Europeans to the United States, Canada, Argentina, Australia, Brazil, and New Zealand. As our discussion of grain, sugar, coffee, and tea commodity chains will show, sometimes the ships bound for the Far East and the circum-Caribbean contained Chinese coolies or Indian contract workers who benefited less from the change in latitude than immigrants bound to more temperate climes.

Lower transport costs that had enticed immigrants to less-populated areas also carried relatively cheap imports that competed successfully with local manufacturing and handicrafts. This undercut peasant agriculture and handicrafts in more established, crowded countries such as India and Eastern Europe, "freeing" population for emigration. So in its early phase during the nineteenth century, the Industrial Revolutions in Western Europe and the eastern United States contributed to the deindustrialization or the rerouting of goods to other parts of the world and the international movement of people.[71]

During their golden age the British had a near monopoly on building freighters because of their head start in shipyards, the steel and coal industries, and capital markets. In 1888 the British merchant marine had secured almost half the world's carrying power (the United States added another quarter of the total but it was mostly dedicated to domestic freight).[72] As late as 1918 the British steamer fleet was still 12 percent larger than the merchant fleets of all other European countries combined.[73]

The United States was slow to make its mark in international shipping after midcentury because between its Civil War and the early twentieth century its ships retreated from the Atlantic trade. Instead it concentrated on coastal and internal waterways such as the Great Lakes and the Mississippi, while its transoceanic cargo traveled on Western European ships—even if the goods were exported from tropical ports to the United States. Even for its trade in the Pacific, where the US navy had opened ports in Japan and Korea, little public incentive was given to shipping. In 1882 total US federal subsidies were only one-quarter the size of those of an empire not known for its maritime prowess, Austria-Hungary. Where US ships had carried most of their country's cargo before the Civil War, they fell to about 40 percent in 1870 and down to about 20 percent by 1900, where it remained until the 1930s. Then the Great Depression and especially World War II permitted North American ships to gain dominance. By 1945 they plied the seas with almost two-thirds of the world's tonnage, an amount that had grown tenfold since 1870.[74]

Imperial as well as commercial motives drove the shipping revolution, because ships were the paramount means of projecting national power and influence overseas. The merchant marine served as an adjunct to navies and was essential to the building of Western European, North American, and Japanese empires. US admiral Alfred Thayer Mahan had pushed for a "New Navy" already in the 1880s, underlining his view in his influential 1892 tome, tellingly entitled *The Influence of Sea Power upon History*. In 1911 First Lord of the Admiralty Winston Churchill championed the conversion of the British navy from coal to oil on similarly grandiose grounds: "The whole race and Empire, the whole treasure accumulated during the many centuries of sacrifice and achievement, would perish and be swept utterly away if our naval supremacy were to be impaired." Domination of the seas was critical, in his mind, to empire: "Mastery itself was the prize of the venture."[75] In the decades before World War I, as Germany also embraced the idea that strong navies signaled national power, German-British rivalry produced accelerated naval building in both countries.

States did not have a monopoly on the militarization of shipping. Private global arms dealers rose to prominence during these years. Merchant and financier Charles Flint was a member of the covert international fraternity of ship and weapons traders. As a private citizen he brokered deals to provide ships and modern weapons with, among others, an Ottoman sultan, the Japanese emperor, and republican presidents of Peru, Chile, Venezuela, and Brazil.[76]

Only some of the largest countries outside of Europe—Brazil, Argentina, and Chile—could afford to build, subsidize, and nationalize domestic merchant marines. In the cases of Brazil and Chile, they also ran large state-owned shipping companies (Lloyd Brasileiro and Compañia Sud-America de Vapores, respectively) that carried some freight internationally.[77] Domestic shipbuilding gained from their demand because they placed orders for ships and repairs with national as well as foreign shipyards. But the British merchant fleet clearly overshadowed their efforts.

The major exception to this model of European domination, as in so many other areas, was Japan, which moved quickly to address its deficiencies. During the prior two centuries of Tokugawa rule, ports had been all but closed off from foreign ships. Japan's geography, with its numerous islands and inland sea, and its precocious political capital (Edo, today known as Tokyo, already had a million inhabitants by 1800), had conspired against the creation of a modern merchant marine. But consternation over the British defeat of the ostensibly mighty Chinese fleet in the Opium Wars during the 1840s and 1850s, as well as the unanticipated appearance of Commodore Matthew Perry's American warships in Japanese waters in 1853, persuaded leaders that they had to modernize their maritime industries.

Close ties between strategic government concerns and the construction of a formidable merchant marine first became apparent in the Japanese attempt to conquer Formosa (today Taiwan) in 1874. The Japanese government purchased thirteen modern steamships to carry soldiers and gave them to a private company, Yūbin Kisen Mitsubishi Kaisha, contracted to carry out the invasion. The company initially had a monopoly on international trade as it opened service to Shanghai. After a merger in 1885 created Nippon Yūsen Kabushiki Kaisha (NYK), it became an entirely private company with routes to Korea, Asiatic Russia, India, and China. Over seventy local Japanese shipping concerns were merged in 1887 thanks to government subventions creating Ōsaka Shōsen Kaisha (OSK), which initially operated mainly in Japan and then branched out to Korea.

The connection between the maritime industry and war was further demonstrated in the Sino-Japanese War of 1894–1895 when the Japanese imperial government purchased fourteen ships and added them to the NYK fleet. At first these fleets relied to a considerable extent on imported ships, steamers from England and sailing ships from the United States. Gradually the government passed legislation that encouraged the growth of the domestic shipbuilding industry, insisting on the construction of larger vessels and inducing their shipping lines to purchase them. The naval buildup had military as well as economic purposes. It brought a Japanese victory against Russia in 1905 that surprised Western observers. After the war, capital and experienced shipbuilders shifted to the private sector. By 1910 half of the new merchant ships were built in Japan, giving rise to some of the world's largest and most sophisticated shipyards.[78]

Elsewhere in the Indian Ocean as well as in the Red and South China Seas, domestic non-Euro-American shipping was relegated to smaller sailing ships such as Chinese junks, Arab dhows, and Japanese *wasen*. Hence, in this most densely populated area of the world, coastal shipping—which could have excluded foreign merchant marines and stimulated domestic industry and commerce—was uncertain and expensive.

Besides Japan and Great Britain, all other major island complexes (Indonesia, Australia, Philippines, Madagascar, Cuba, and the rest of the Caribbean), for whom a domestic merchant marine would have stimulated commerce and development, were colonies. Their colonial masters were not interested in cultivating potential shipping rivals. The other major non-European export economies, such as Argentina and Brazil, focused on trade with Europe rather than developing domestic markets that could be served by national freighters.

Domination of high-volume freight by a dozen countries not only provided the world leaders a competitive advantage in terms of profits and lower costs, but also allowed them to develop insurance companies, large warehouses, and intelligence about freight and long-distance business conditions. Indeed, before the oceanic telegraphs, mail ships were the principal source of international news. The early steamship lines received large subsidies precisely so they would deliver the mail. Faster ships also meant greater international intimacy. Where mail and freight took six weeks to travel from England to Calcutta in 1840, by World War I the time had been cut to less than twelve days. Australia also was brought closer. From 125 days required to reach it from England at the beginning of the nineteenth century, the trip fell to a month a century later. The Dutch, who had required a year to reach their colony in Indonesia in the seventeenth century and still over a hundred days in 1850, could reach it in a month by 1900.[79] So shipping advances not only increased trade, they bound colonial systems more closely together.

Shipping advances also brought the Americas closer to Europe in travel time. Where sailing packets had required twenty-one days to reach Europe from the United States in the mid-nineteenth century, steamships could make the crossing in nine to ten days, which was reduced further to five or six days by the 1880s.[80]

Canals

The unprecedented drop in the duration of ship voyages occurred because of changes on land as well as on the seas. Canals initially had been built to connect domestic markets, such as the Grand Canal in China and the Yangzi and Pearl River Deltas, canals in northern Italy and the Netherlands, and the dense riverine and canal systems in England, France, and Germany. In the United States, the Erie Canal connected New York City with the Great Lakes and eventually, through the Chicago River, down the Mississippi River. Because they issued out to oceanic ports, the interior waterways often made vast areas accessible to international trade.[81] However, generally they were narrow, so they inhibited economies of scale. They consequently lost trade to the railroad and motorized road vehicles. Sometimes, as with the Chinese Grand Canal, state budgetary decisions deprived the canals of maintenance funds.[82]

Most spectacular was the engineering feat that had been first accomplished in the days of Egypt's pharaohs, the Suez Canal. Designed by former French consul to Egypt Ferdinand de Lesseps and financed largely by French capital, this 119-mile-long passage finally connected the Red Sea to the Mediterranean (though bypassing the Nile) in 1869. Intended to assert French commercial and political control over Africa, the Middle East, and the Indian Ocean, the canal succeeded in stimulating international commerce beyond de Lesseps's wildest dreams. But it did not enhance French imperial aspirations, nor did it reorient the world economy from the North Atlantic back to the Mediterranean as was hoped. After the canal's opening in the 1880s, British ships accounted for 80 percent of the tonnage that passed through it. Their domination of Suez traffic declined over time, but as late as 1940 they still controlled over half the total passing through the canal.[83] Equally disappointing to the French imperialists was the British occupation of Egypt in 1882–1936. British control of the canal would be relinquished only in 1956.

Although ships needed two and a half days to pass through the canal and it could not accommodate the largest steamers, this was compensated by the great savings in time on the overall voyage—a 41 percent time reduction between London and Mumbai and a 26 percent drop between London and Hong Kong. (Australia benefited little from the canal because the circum-African route was not a great detour to the land down under.)

The other great canal of our period was built in Panama. The dream of avoiding the difficult and dangerous rounding of Cape Horn had inspired mariners dating back to 1521, when Ferdinand Magellan found his way through the straits named after him and located the long route from the Atlantic to the Pacific. But this dream became both possible and a pressing matter only when gold was discovered in California in 1848. Adventurers with gold fever would not wait for the slow wagon trains or the only somewhat faster rounding of the Horn. Routes across Central America became popular. With the United States now bicoastal, a canal became an important tool of national defense and fundamental in the building of a North American national market.

The same magnet that had attracted Magellan—the fabled China market—and the desire of French expansionists such as Napoleon III to establish a continental American colony (Mexicans defeated his effort to place Maximilian I on their throne in 1867) attracted the first serious effort at canal building. To the chagrin of North Americans, it was the French, not the Yankees, who initiated the project. Their success at Suez induced international investors to found a Panama canal company and bankroll it with the impressive sum of more than US$400 million. Unfortunately, de Lesseps attempted to apply the lessons learned in Suez, which proved ill-suited to the Americas. Although the Isthmus of Panama was less than half the distance of the Suez project (50 miles compared to 119 miles), the Panama Canal would have to be cut through dense jungle with torrential rains and a peak that rose to 360 feet above sea level rather than through flat desert sand as in Suez. That first company went bankrupt seven years after building was initiated, and its successor also failed. In 1902 the French company sold its canal works and its concession from the Colombian government to the US government. The Colombian Senate, wary of the United States' designs on Latin America made evident in the 1898 Spanish-American War, refused to permit the United States to take over the canal works. Proving Colombian concerns warranted, US naval forces then supported a rebellion that declared Panama independent. A French representative of the French canal company not only signed a treaty in the name of Panama and sold the nascent canal works but also ceded a fifty-five-square-mile canal zone over which the United States would exercise sovereignty for seventy-six years.[84]

As at Suez, this massive feat of engineering that greased the path of globalization began as a nationalist effort at empire building. The canal itself was built between 1904 and 1914 at an enormous cost in human lives and funds. The most expensive construction project in United States history up to that point, it cost around US$400 million. Less often mentioned is that the building of the canal cost twenty-five thousand to thirty-five thousand lives. The workers were mainly people of African descent from nearby Panama, Colombia, Jamaica, and Barbados. The North American enclave that developed in the Canal Zone had much in common with British settler colonies in Africa. Historian Julie Greene notes that the Canal Zone was characterized by "large-scale mobilization and segregation of labor, special rewards and recognition of citizenship rights for certain (skilled, white) workers and a suppression of political dissent and forms of collective organizing deemed radical."[85] The canal's completion, hailed as a key step in the United States' move past continentalism to globalism, was celebrated in San Francisco at its Panama-Pacific International Exposition in 1915. But there was no remembering the workers or Panama at the festivities. The linkage between commerce and empire could not have been clearer. As the editors of *World's Work* proclaimed, the canal represented "the evolution of a new America. Our splendid isolation is gone . . . we have become a colonial power with possessions in both oceans. And now we open under our own control one of the great trade routes of the world."[86]

Great hopes for developing Panama and the tropics in general were held out by US expansionists. Although earlier efforts at settling defeated southern Confederates in Brazil and Mexico after the Civil War had largely failed, medical advances such as the discovery of the effects of quinine, derived from the bark of the cinchona tree, and the isolation of the mosquito as the carrier of malaria and yellow fever made the tropics more hospitable to white European and North American colonial administrators and investors. The medical advances were tested and applied at the canals in Suez and Panama, attempted at dependencies such as

Freetown, Liberia, and successfully implemented in Cuba during the US occupation after the conclusion of the Spanish-American War. Nonetheless, relatively few North American investors or colonists settled in the tropics. The most ambitious attempt, Fordlandia in the Amazon, was a complete failure.[87]

In both shipping and canal building, Great Power *realpolitik* and imperial pretensions wrestled with the forces of the marketplace. On the one hand, the greater capacity, speed, efficiency, and certainty of shipping stimulated trade, information, and competition. On the other hand, shipping lines experienced the same efforts at reducing competition that we will see in many other highly capitalized strategic areas of the world economy. For freight companies, the solution was shipping conventions (or collusion, as their critics scoffed) that coordinated the freight business through quotas and rate fixing. The conventions resulted from a transformation in the nature of ship ownership.

Where traditionally ships had been owned by groups of merchants, either as individuals or as a group such as the East India Company, the greater capital demands of steamships required well-endowed corporations, often benefiting from the protection of joint-stock legislation. Indeed, the British Parliament first created the protection of limited liability in 1855 with railroads, shipping companies, and banks in mind.[88] With this legislation corporations gained juridical identity separate from that of their stockholders. The investor was liable only for the amount of his investment, not for other company debts. Many pietistic Protestants found this shirking of responsibility reprehensible. Others, like Baptist John D. Rockefeller, considered it a welcome opportunity to get rich using other people's money. Despite an outcry, the legislation passed and the idea spread elsewhere as European and North and South American countries soon followed suit because this mechanism vastly facilitated the pooling of large amounts of capital, protected enormous long-term investments, and aided anonymous stock transactions.

The relatively small number and great investments of huge freight companies, as well as falling freight prices because of global competition inspired by the Suez Canal, convinced some companies to create international conventions or cartels. These agreements made the high fixed costs of maintaining existing fleets affordable and allowed participants to keep up with technological advances in this rapidly changing industry. Steam companies that belonged to the same cartel agreed to maintain rates rather than compete on price. They also agreed to honor deferred rebates to customers who used only ships within the conference, an early-day loyalty or frequent flyer card. The first convention began in the European Calcutta route in 1875. A China convention began in 1879 and a West-Africa-London agreement in 1894. Various conventions also operated in South America among European steamers. British courts ruled the conventions legal in part because they did not successfully monopolize the traffic. Unscheduled "tramp" freighters that opportunistically steamed to wherever sufficient cargo or passengers awaited them were able to ignore the conventions and charge lower fares. In 1900 tramps constituted a third of world sea-bound cargo capacity, so they put a sizable dent in the conventions' ability to control pricing.[89]

Railroads

Just as steam drove the First Industrial Revolution in production and transformed navigation, it also powered railroads. Railroads did not begin as a means of exporting or importing goods. Instead, they began their practical applications in Britain in the 1820s to assist the burgeoning coal industry. A fortunate confluence of mechanical power and fuel to transport the coal via the railroad to more distant factories ensured England's primacy in rails and industry. Although the railroad revolution is usually associated with the First Industrial Revolution, it in fact spurred the second one as well. In Europe alone as many miles of track were laid in 1880–1913 as had been put down in the heroic pioneer railway age of 1850–1880. Outside of Europe, tracks were laid down at an even faster pace. World rail mileage multiplied fourfold between 1870 and 1910 and grew again by half to 1930, despite the destruction caused by the Great War. However, the Great Depression, World War II, and the advent of the automobile and truck would all but stop the railroad age. Worldwide track fell by 1945, mainly because of its decline in the United States (see Table 4.5).

The railroad's impact up to 1913 is hard to exaggerate. The usually reserved Hobsbawm waxes lyrical: "But by far the largest and most powerful engines of the nineteenth century were the most visible and audible of all. These were the 100,000 railway locomotives (200–450 HP), pulling their almost 2¾ million carriages and wagons in long trains under the banners of smoke."[90] Even if some

TABLE 4.5

World railroad mileage, by continent, 1840–1945 (in thousands of miles)

	1840		1870		1901		1910		1930		1945	
	Miles	%	Miles	%	Miles	%	Miles	%	Miles	%	Miles	%
Europe[a]	2.6	47.0	65.4	50.1	181.8	35.6	212.1	33.1	236.9	25.0	252.9	26.9
(UK)	2.4	43.6	21.5	16.4	30.4	5.9	32.2	5.0	32.6	3.4	32.0	3.4
North America[b]	2.8	51.0	55.4	42.5	216.7	42.5	265.8	41.5	471.6	50.0	440.6	46.8
Latin America[b]	0.1	2.0	2.4	1.8	29.1	5.7	60.7	9.5	78.7	8.3	83.0	8.8
Asia w/o India	0	0	0.3	0.2	12.0	2.4	27.2	4.3	44.8	4.7	49.9	5.3
(India)	0	0	4.8	3.8	25.5	5.0	32.3	5.0	42.5	4.5	40.8	4.3
Asia	0	0	5.1	4.0	37.5	7.4	59.5	9.3	87.3	9.2	90.7	9.6
Oceania	0	0	1.1	0.8	—	—	19.3	3.0	31.2	3.3	31.8	3.4
Africa	0	0	1.1	0.8	12.5	2.5	23.0	3.6	40.8	4.3	42.4	4.5
World	5.5		130.5		510.5		640.4		946.5		941.4	

Sources: A. G. Kenwood and A. L. Lougheed, *The Growth of the International Economy, 1820–2000*, 4th ed. (London: Routledge, 1999), 13. For 1901: *Railroad Gazette*, May 30 and June 6, 1902. For 1910: A. Russell Bond and Albert A. Hopkins, *Scientific American Reference Book: A Manual for the Office, Household and Shop* (New York: Munn and Co., 1915). For 1930 and 1945, figures were calculated from B. R. Mitchell, *International Historical Statistics: Africa, Asia and Oceania, 1750–2005*, 5th ed. (Basingstoke, UK: Palgrave Macmillan, 2007), 713–728; B. R. Mitchell, *International Historical Statistics: Europe, 1750–2000*, 6th ed. (Basingstoke, UK: Palgrave Macmillan, 2007), 675–681; B. R. Mitchell, *International Historical Statistics: The Americas and Australasia* (London: Macmillan, 1983); and Bureau of the Census, *Historical Statistics of the United States: Colonial Times to 1957* (Washington, DC: Bureau of the Census, 1960), 429.

a. Europe includes Russia and the Soviet Union, but not Turkey.

b. Mexico is included with Latin America, not North America.

economic historians such as Robert Fogel cast doubt on railroads' centrality in spurring US industrialization, it is clear that railroads fundamentally altered transport costs and travel time while adding enormous backward and forward linkages (see Table 4.6). They were the largest industrial corporations of the era, with the most factory workers and the largest investment of capital. Moreover, as Alfred Chandler has eloquently demonstrated, they played a significant role in pioneering the managerial revolution of vast new corporations while expanding the white-collar (female as well as male) portion of the workforce. Rail technology not only bound together British markets (which had already been well served by intricate canal systems), but it provided an extremely important export product as well as a basis for British financial investments abroad. In 1913 fully 41 percent of British overseas investment was directly placed in railroad construction, and a good share of its loans to foreign governments also financed railroads.[91]

Over time, exporting the technology undercut Britain's first-mover advantages as other, larger countries with less-developed waterways were better able to take advantage of the iron rail. As a result, Britain's portion had already fallen from nearly half the world's rail in 1840 to only one-sixth in 1870. By 1910 the United Kingdom held only 5 percent of the world's rail network.

That former British colony, the United States, was the first overseas area to apply and adapt British technology and capital. It had surpassed Britain's rail network already by 1840 and in fact had more track than all of the rest of the world combined at that early date. This was done with outside help, particularly that of the British; in 1914 some 57 percent of the US foreign debt was held in railroad securities abroad, over half of them held by British capital. Germany also passed England by 1873 in the amount of track laid; France caught up with Britain in 1888.[92] Over time the initial leaders built dense networks, causing profits on new lines to decline; their capitalists sought out other sectors or railroads in other lands.

The new areas with their vast expanses and dispersed populations demonstrated the "relative advantages of backwardness." They were the natural beneficiaries of the railroads and more efficient shipping after 1870. In that year the United States' total of 53,000 miles of track already was more than 50 percent greater than the total combined of Britain, Germany, and France. Sixty years later the US rail network (431,000 miles) was more than four times as extensive

TABLE 4.6

Net tons-miles of goods carried, 1871–1939 (in millions of miles)

	India	France	Germany	Britain	Russia/USSR	United States
1871–1874	4.2	51.6	—	181.8	21.4	—
1890–1894	27.0	96.2	219.0	308.5	76.2	—
1900–1904	45.3	83.2	378.8	435.9	166.0	650.1
1910–1914	74.0	117.8	613.1	533.4	163.0	1,075.8
1920–1924	92.8	164.0	358.7	318.3	49.0	1,233.6
1935–1939	120.3	143.6	516.8	284.8	491.0	938.8

Sources: Daniel R. Headrick, *The Tentacles of Progress* (New York: Oxford University Press), 57. For the United States, figures are calculated from Bureau of the Census, *Historical Statistics of the United States: Colonial Times to 1957* (Washington, DC: Bureau of the Census, 1960), 431.

as those of the three major European industrial powers combined, and Canada had more than any of the European industrial giants. Areas of older settlement, such as Russia (which joined the Soviet Union in 1922) and India, were rewarded by British and French investments that built up their networks to 49,000 and 44,000 miles, respectively.[93] Even Latin America, with its sparse population and fertile fields, had some 61,000 miles of track by 1910, more than all of Asia and three times Africa's total.[94] As in the case in North America, these lines bolstered the domestic market for national producers. As Table 4.5 demonstrates, newcomers like the United States, Argentina, Australia, and Canada overshadowed former world powers, like Portugal, Spain, and Turkey. China had virtually no track at the end of the nineteenth century and only 9,000 miles by 1930. Fears that the railroad threatened China's embattled sovereignty, particularly in the interior, undercut official support for track. Given the Japanese invasion and internal civil war, the effective total was probably even smaller in 1945.[95]

Integration or Fragmentation?

As often as not, railroads were conquering tools of nation or empire building. They as much *created* markets as responded to them. The longest lines early on required state aid because they were not initially profitable. They often passed through areas virtually devoid of passengers, as, for example, did the transcontinental Union Pacific in the United States (1869), the Canadian Pacific that connected Ontario to Vancouver (1886), and the Trans-Siberian Railroad that connected Moscow to Vladivostok in 1905. (The Paris-to-Istanbul Orient Express, 1889, and the Berlin-Baghdad Railroad, finished only in 1940, were more about connecting empires than controlling marginal areas.) Even when the lines remained in only one country, they spurred international trade by permitting goods farther from the coasts to find foreign markets and for imports to have access to ever-denser markets in the interiors. This was particularly true of Western Europe and the United States. Hamburg, Bremen, Amsterdam, Rotterdam, Le Havre, Trieste, Marseille, New York, Chicago, New Orleans, and San Francisco, as well as numerous other ports, connected to land, canal, and sea networks that reached across borders into the interior. Rail lines also served major ports elsewhere, such as Sydney, Melbourne, Buenos Aires, Montevideo, Alexandria, and Cape Town.[96] The railroads also sped up port activities, as rail lines were built right up to the docks and warehouses to reduce bottlenecks that had hindered trade.

Not all rail systems integrated domestic markets, however. Many of the systems built later were designed to service export enclaves—passing through sweltering deserts, as in Arica, Chile, a center for nitrates and copper; dizzying heights, like the Lima-La Oroya–Cerro de Pasco, which climbed the Andes to silver, copper, zinc, and lead mines in Peru; or steaming jungles, like the Madeira-Mamoré Railway that connected the Brazilian rubber forests of Acre to the Amazon River and eventually to the Bolivian highlands. Less of an engineering feat but no less vital were the two rail lines (of differing gauges, of course) in Yucatán in Mexico that connected the port of Progreso, an outlet for henequen fiber, to the state capital of Mérida. These lines often tied their hinterlands more closely into foreign markets than to domestic ones. Some of these were not just successful conduits for exports but engineering marvels, scaling cliffs, tunneling through towering mountains, or snaking through tropical rainforests. But these agents of civilization were built with the blood and on the backs of thousands of laborers, many of them imported from the Caribbean, India, and China.

Other ambitious lines that were intended to integrate neighboring national markets, such as Brazilian railways that passed through Uruguay into Argentina, failed to reorient the overseas export focus. This sadly learned reality would abort the Pan-American Railroad intended to run from Canada to Argentina. The only lines that successfully linked international American markets were those that extended north from the United States to Canada and south to Mexico. Both were intended to exchange raw materials (lumber, grains, and hides from Canada, and silver, gold, copper, and nickel from Mexico) for US finished goods. In the short run they reinforced the export orientation of those two US neighbors and did little to grow domestic markets.[97]

There were important exceptions, however. Monterrey, Mexico, which was conveniently located close to iron deposits on the Mexican National Railroad, became the country's northern industrial center. Mostly specializing in consumer products like cigarettes and a new drink from the Anglo-Saxon north, beer, Monterrey also developed the only advanced steel industry in Latin America during our period. It grew trying to satisfy the demand from the booming railroad sector for rail, bridges, and some moving stock.[98]

Railroads in Argentina and Brazil also succeeded in strengthening their domestic markets, albeit in different ways. In Argentina the rail system reinforced the national dominance of Buenos Aires, won at the cost of repeated civil wars in the nineteenth century and a massive infusion of foreign, principally British, investments. As the country's main port, commercial and financial center, and national capital, Buenos Aires enjoyed the advantages of primacy. In fact, early on it was a global city like New York, London, or Shanghai, with most of its population foreign-born or first generation and many important corporations and banks establishing branches there to serve its prosperous population. As one of the world's richest countries in terms of per capita income on the eve of World War I and with a well-integrated rail system, Argentina's domestic consumer goods factories were concentrated between Buenos Aires and Rosario.[99]

Brazil's coastal settlement dictated that there were numerous competing port cities, each serving different hinterlands. Although the political advantage of Rio de Janeiro city led to an early head start in the railroad age, by the 1890s the coffee boom enhanced the clout of São Paulo (both city and state). Though never becoming the country's political capital, São Paulo became the national commercial, financial, and eventually by the 1920s, industrial center. Its capitalists financed railroads throughout the state and in the adjoining states of Paraná,

Goiás, and Mato Grosso, and diverted some of Rio de Janeiro's trade with the country's largest state, Minas Gerais. In São Paulo itself, the booming export economy led to domestic regional integration by 1945. The northeast, Amazon, and southwest regions would have to wait decades for highways to tie them to the prosperous southeast.[100]

Some landlocked capitals were connected to their coasts, but the impetus behind the initiatives was made clear when the railroads *began* at the ports. The line that started in Djibouti in French Somaliland in 1897 did not reach Ethiopia's capital of Addis Ababa until twenty years later because of the wariness of Ethiopia's king Menelik II, who feared French colonial designs. The European-financed railway helped his Shoan government based in Addis Ababa to assert internal colonialism by conquering neighboring peoples such as the Oromo and the Harari. The central Ethiopian government formed a national state by sending out coffee and other goods by rail in exchange for weapons and ammunition. This allowed Ethiopia and Liberia to be the only areas in Africa that remained free of European colonialism (except for a brief Italian occupation).

The Uganda Railroad, which started at the port of Mombasa and reached Lake Victoria in Kenya in 1901, was quite different. A European colonial project, it later completed its 562 miles to Kampala, Uganda, and to Nairobi. But its effects contrasted strikingly with those of the Djibouti line. To make the British line to Lake Victoria pay for itself, English settlers were summoned and given fertile lands in the highlands and a monopoly over coffee production, which was forbidden to native peoples. The one hundred white settlers in Kenya in 1903 became one thousand in 1914 and reached about three thousand in 1942. Small but consequential in number, by the time of World War II they controlled some 6.3 million acres. By the 1920s most of the able-bodied agricultural peoples, like the Kikuyu and the Luo, were working under semicoercive conditions for European settlers. English modernizers disdained their colonial subjects. As Sir Charles Eliot, the British Commissioner of the East Africa Protectorate, blithely observed in 1905: "We have in East Africa the rare experience of dealing with a tabula rasa, an almost untouched and sparsely inhabited country, where we can do as we wish, to regulate immigration and open or close the door as seems best."[101] Indian laborers who were imported there to help build the railroad remained and became important economic actors in both countries. Whites, together with Indian immigrants, came to control the economy and the majority of exports as Kenya became one of Africa's main coffee producers and one of its most racially divided colonies.[102] With racially based marketing and regulatory boards as well as land rights and taxes, this was clearly not liberal, free-trade capitalism. The railroad did not create an imitation England in northeast Africa.

Nor did Uganda come to look like England, but the impetus was to create capitalist labor and land relations and monetized commercial transactions that would benefit the indigenous people. Even the coffee growers and cotton growers were mainly natives. Of course, the revenues raised from the production of these commodities strengthened the colonial state as well.

German East Africa (today Tanzania, Burundi, and Rwanda) also was transformed by the new rail opening to the Indian Ocean, and it, too, became a significant coffee exporter. It was a German colony until the end of World War I, when part of it passed to British control and part to Belgian. Unlike the situation in Kenya, missionaries and then colonial officials sought to incorporate the indigenous population into export commodity production by privatizing land ownership and overseeing peasant production. Coffee and cotton growing remained under majority African control. Because coffee was indigenous in Tanganyika, as in Ethiopia, local peasants undertook most of the cultivation on their own fields.[103]

The railroads, however, were slow to serve internal commerce in Africa. Ethiopia's entire system, which was a mere 193 miles in 1903, reached 490 miles by 1917 and remained at that small number at the end of our period. Goods were still carried by camel and horse caravans, so movement within the country remained slow, expensive, and unreliable. Uganda's system was even smaller, not surpassing 330 miles of track by 1945. Kenya had 640 miles of track by 1916 and increased it to 1,300 in 1945.[104] But paved roads were scarce, in part to protect the railroad's monopoly on long-distance trade. These railways were umbilical cords between the interior and the outside world, not projects for internal development.

The British dominion of South Africa, which Britain seized from the Boers and Zulus in numerous battles after 1877 and officially after a bloody South African war (Second Boer War) and compromise in 1902, received almost a third of the modest 28,500 miles of track laid in Africa by 1914. By 1945 its share had grown to 40 percent of Africa's total of 31,763 miles of track. (No other sub-Saharan colony had one-tenth of South Africa's rail total at the end of our period.) This racially segregated but mineral-blessed colony with abundant diamonds and gold was a prime destination for British capital. By 1913 it received some £370 million (more than US$1.8 billion), almost as much as Australia and New Zealand combined, or India and Ceylon combined, though it had only 2 percent the population of the latter (and was about equal in population to Australia and New Zealand).[105] The railway system had economic and state-building objectives: it connected the diamond and gold mines of the interior with the ports and tied together the Boer interior with the British south. In this it resembled the rail line from the coast to Rhodesia's copper mines. It was also supposed to be Cecil Rhodes's centerpiece to his proposed "Red Line from Cape Town to Cairo"—British railroads that would connect Africa from south to north. But that ambitious plan, like the abortive line from French Algeria to Niger, never became a reality.

This underlines the close relationship between colonialism and railroad building *in certain colonies*. For the most part, the white settler colonies or former colonies, such as Australia, Canada, South Africa, and the United States, received most of the rail. The exceptions were the areas close to Europe (North Africa) or the United States (Mexico and Cuba) and India. In Latin America, which Table 4.5 shows was a major area of railroad building, most of the lines were constructed either in areas closely tied to the North American economy or in countries with large European immigration, such as Argentina, Uruguay, and southern Brazil. The other major exception was India, which by 1920 surpassed the rail mileage of Britain, Germany, and France. Its rather dense rail system was more used for moving passengers, who preferred the cheapest and least profitable seats, than for freight. It also spurred little industrialization, unlike the other major lines.[106]

In almost all countries, rate schedules favored large-scale international commerce over less-voluminous local trade. Fares from the interior to ports were cheaper than between two interior stations and large-scale and long-distance rail shipments received generous discounts and rebates while small, short-distance cargo did not.

Not all state leaders welcomed the railroad. We have already mentioned Chinese imperial reluctance. Similarly, in India some leaders feared the change accompanying domestic development. The Nizam of Hyderabad was appalled that the steel rail would "upset all orthodox notions [and] make the popular mind gyrate or swing backwards and forwards with the movement like that of children at a fair." Despite the fact that he "dreaded the British government and disliked its civilization," he submitted to the British plans for a railroad because he felt that a railroad would provide "the only strong tower where he could in extremity take refuge."[107]

So in certain places and at some times, the railroad maintained subservience and inequality as much as it brought advancement. Historian Daniel Headrick concludes that the railroads in India created "the great transformation of India from congeries of traditional states into something new on the subcontinent: modern underdeveloped nation-states."[108] Similarly, the world's most populous country, China, built a rail system one-quarter the size of India's by 1942, some 19,300 kilometers. For the most part it connected ports with their hinterlands rather than integrating the country, with the important exception of the line from the capital in Beijing to Guangzhou (Canton).

The unevenness of rail growth meant that Asia and Africa, which together in 1913 held over 60 percent of the world's population, in 1945 enjoyed only about 13 percent of the world's rail lines. Vast areas in Asia with hundreds of millions of people were strangers to the rail. Two-thirds of Asia's railway miles lay in India and Japan alone. We must recognize, however, that even in a vast country like China, which built relatively little rail compared to world leaders, the iron track had an enormous impact. Some interior crops like cotton and tobacco could now be exported, and the risks and time for internal transactions was greatly reduced in key areas. The completion of the Beijing-to-Hankou line, for instance, reduced the time it took to travel from Guangzhou to Beijing from 90 days at the turn of the century to 3.3 days by 1936. Even areas not on the line were affected by connections via ship, so that by one estimate the time it took to travel from Beijing to the outer perimeter of the country fell by 84 percent.[109] This, of course, demonstrated the primacy of state interests over export considerations.

In more fortunate areas, the iron connections of ports with the domestic interior were sometimes seen as triumphs of modernization and nation building. Many railway stations, such as Paris's Gare d'Orsay, London's St. Pancras Station, or New York's Grand Central Station, were built as gorgeous and elegant monuments to progress. They were emblems of a modern age that forcefully demonstrated humans' power not only to subdue nature but to erase distance and space. Visitors praised the stations, and the telegraph offices that accompanied them, as the nerve centers of global cities.[110]

Critics, however, saw the steam locomotive as a Trojan horse that permitted foreign capital, technology, and arms to conquer regional politicians, indigenous peoples, and different ways of life. Rail systems were disparaged with epithets such as "suction pumps" or "tentacles." They also upset and transformed economic calculations, political allegiances, and local and national identities.

Iron and Steel

In addition to reducing travel time and costs and creating access to places that formerly were out of bounds, railroads had multiplier effects on other areas of the world economy. They reflected and sped the technological breakthroughs in the creation of first iron and then steel. Both metals had long been used by humans, but their modern contributions came first during the First Industrial Revolution. Iron and then steel track, locomotives, and bridges created a huge market and stimulated technical improvements. Iron had served for the first four decades of the railway age, but proved to be too weak and vulnerable to weather. Steel, which was of poor quality until the Bessemer and Siemens-Martin processes were developed at the end of the 1850s, soon transformed transport infrastructure. The connection between the railroad and the steel industry was intimate. In 1848 a quarter of the puddled iron production of England and Wales had gone into rails. In the United States, the connection with steel was even stronger. Until the 1890s more than half of all US steel went into rails.[111]

Although a number of countries made iron and steel by the end of the nineteenth century, few of them could compete with the handful of modern industrial steel producers, such as Britain, Germany, Belgium, Russia, and the United States, who supplied the vast majority of the world's track. With constant technological improvements and great economies of scale, the steel industries were concentrated in the hands of a few enormous corporations (or, as in the case of the Soviet Union, state companies). For example, in 1901 J. P. Morgan bought out Andrew Carnegie and brought together seven steel and tin companies to form the United States Steel Corporation. Capitalized at US$1.4 billion, it was up to that point the largest corporation in the history of the world, producing two-thirds of all the steel in the United States. To demonstrate how significant this was, the United States produced, on average, over 40 percent of the world's steel in 1909–1913 and more than half in 1925 and 1926 as war-driven demand sparked a rapid rise in output. France, Germany, and the United Kingdom contributed another third of world steel production in those years, but destruction brought on by the First World War reduced their share to about 28 percent in 1925 and 1926. By 1938 the United States still produced 35 percent of world steel, which was matched by the combined output of the three main European producers. The Soviet Union and Japan were the only other major steel manufacturers, with Russia jumping from 6 percent of the total in 1909–1913 to 13 percent under the Communists in 1941, which put it third in the world, and Japan producing almost six million metric tons in 1937, making it the world's fifth-largest steelmaker. In both the Soviet Union and Japan, the steel industry was not only fomented by the state but also largely controlled by it for strategic as well as economic reasons.[112] All the other countries in the world combined to manufacture under a quarter of global steel, usually in relatively small, inefficient factories.

India and Mexico were exceptional cases. The former was a British colony and the latter an economic appendage of the United States. India had a long history of steelmaking, but was so inefficient that even the state-run railroads imported almost all their steel from Britain and Belgium. One of India's most famous entrepreneurs, Jamshedji Nusserwanji Tata, who had made his first fortune in textiles, financed the Tata Iron and Steel Company (TISCO), which came to life while World War I cut off competing iron and steel imports. Protected by first the crisis in the world market and then the colonial government, TISCO increased its share of the Indian steel market to 73 percent by 1938, when it was producing virtually all the rail purchased in India.[113] Still, compared to the main steel powers, it was a minor concern. Mexicans in Monterrey, Mexico, developed the Fundidora de Hierro to supply steel track, bridges, and girders for the country's expanding transportation system. It did not export. Financed by local capital, it became a regional growth pole, but again its output was minimal by world standards.[114]

Other countries with major rail lines, like Brazil and Argentina, were slow to build steel industries, though their military leaders and outspoken nationalists called for state-led factories. Brazilian president Artur Bernardes proclaimed in his 1926 message to Brazil's Congress that a steel industry "is the primary condition of our economic autonomy."[115] His successor, Getúlio Vargas, would make the state-run Volta Redonda steel mill a major part of his development policy, though by then the automobile and other steel products loomed more important than the railroad. Because of its rich ore deposits, Brazil would become a major steel producer after World War II. Argentina had to overcome greater geographic disadvantages and was slower to build its steel factories.

Where railroads did not give birth to modern steel industries, they sometimes had other linkages to domestic producers in the form of demand for wood for ties, trestles, and railway cars. Locomotives, the most technologically advanced component of rail systems, still were almost all imported from the United States and Western Europe. The railroad's most important developmental contribution was to build the domestic market, although in some places that just made imports more accessible. But that link to the world economy has probably been exaggerated. Early estimates that most of Mexico's and Brazil's freight traffic was for exports have been reassessed. Even those lines built with European and US markets in mind wound up building up the domestic market for food, clothing, and some durable goods.[116]

Three examples taken from the richest independent successful export economies—Argentina, Brazil, and Mexico—demonstrate the iron horse's varied consequences. Argentina, effectively an honorary part of the British Commonwealth until World War II because of the preponderant influence of British capital and trade, had the most successful of the independent export-oriented economies prior to 1945. Argentines spent extravagantly on imports because of the high wages their sparse labor force commanded, inexpensive imports delivered by the modern port and railroad facilities built at Buenos Aires, and low duties charged by its laissez-faire government. Over time, domestic industries grew, however. Tariffs were set at first to simply raise government revenues for operating expenses. Over time they increasingly financed developmental goals and became more protective as factory owners and workers gained political clout. The same was true for Brazil and Mexico. By World War I, despite pronouncements of fervent faith in free trade, their tariffs were among the highest in the world.[117] From there on out, exports would continuously fall as a share of GNP, reflecting the relative growth of domestic economies.

Just as railroads did not bring free trade to most countries, neither did they guarantee private enterprise. Although the first countries to enter the rail age, such as Great Britain and the United States, relied on private companies, those enterprises had received generous (critics thought, too generous) subsidies, land grants, tax breaks, or guaranteed profits. Latecomers amplified government assistance as railroads came to be seen not only as an economic benefit, but also as a defensive necessity (against either external attack or internal revolt), a lure for foreign investment, a symbol of modernity and civilization, and the glue that held countries together. So essential did they become, that when railway companies faced bankruptcy during recessions, governments nationalized them. This was done not only to keep the trains running and the cities provisioned, but also to maintain the country's international credit and the strength of its currency. As a result, governments dedicated in theory to laissez-faire, such as in Brazil and Mexico, nationalized their principal railways before World War I.[118]

We emphasize, however, that outside of the Soviet Union, state interventions in strategic infrastructure (railroads, shipping, roads, public utilities) were not primarily socialist acts. It is true, though, that there was social pressure for public participation in the infrastructure: railroad workers were sometimes the most vocal and radical sector of the working class, socialists usually advocated nationalization, and urban passengers occasionally rioted about high fares and bad service. Although the nationalization of railroads usually was not socialist-inspired, neither were states acting as public capitalists. Most of the nationalized railroads ran at a deficit in order to subsidize the private sector by providing low-cost services. State interventions were usually seen as temporary remedies intended to shore up the private sector with public funds, though nationalist pique at foreign-owned companies also played a role. Both were involved in Brazil and Mexico, where the federal governments bought control of most of the rail lines before World War I. Even colonial India, certainly no hotbed of radicalism, nationalized its railways to escape the burden of interest guarantees, but allowed private companies to continue to run them. For more strategic reasons, the Turkish government nationalized lines in the wake of the dissolution of the Ottoman Empire after the First World War. The Great Depression later encouraged Germany and other European countries and colonies to assert or expand state control over railroads. Even the British, who had mastered the railroad age with private companies, nationalized their trains after World War II as Labour won power.

The Automobile

The automobile was to the twentieth century what the railroad had been the nineteenth; emblematic of individual speed and power, it competed with the railroad in the most affluent countries. Numerous inventors in the United States, England, France, Germany, and Italy busily improved the automobile as cheaper fuel for it became more readily available. The growth of demand was astronomical, particularly in the United States, which not only had steel for the chassis and copper and aluminum for the engine, but was the world's leading producer of oil and gasoline at the turn of the century. From 8,000 registered autos in 1885, the number jumped to 902,000 in 1912. As Henry Ford perfected the assembly line in Deerfield, Michigan, the growth really became spectacular. By 1920 the number had grown tenfold to 9.2 million motor vehicles, and continued upward. Then Alfred P. Sloan and General Motors (GM) began to stress mass distribution and offered a choice of models. With yearly changes, they appealed to fashion as well as price and convenience. This allowed GM to surpass Ford as the world's largest producer in the 1920s. Workers in the United States built 2 to 3.7 million new cars a year in the 1920s and 1930s, with the high reaching 4.4 million in 1929, a total that would not be matched again for twenty years. Because Henry Ford had introduced the "Fordist" policy of paying the stupendous wage of five dollars a day (and regimenting workers so they would not unionize) and offered relatively inexpensive cars, the sector created a great swell of consumer and fiscal linkages as well as the backward and forward supplies needed to construct cars and serve them.[119] Despite Ford's efforts to the contrary, autoworkers, along with coal miners, became some of the most powerful and politically influential unionized trades in the United States and Western Europe.

In 1929 the United States had 78 percent of all the cars in the entire world. Almost all the rest were in Western Europe, but there they were far less in use. In 1938 the United States had one car for every 3.9 inhabitants, Britain had one for every 22 people, France one for 28, Germany one for 98, and Italy one for every 151. In Asia, only Japan produced a significant number of autos, and this only

Model T Fords lining 42nd Street in 1918. Little more than two decades after the first automobiles were manufactured, New York's Manhattan was already experiencing traffic jams. Efficient production by Ford and then General Motors turned the auto into a mass product. As Western Europe joined the automobile age, demand for rubber, oil, and steel exploded. (© Kadel & Herbert / National Geographic Society / Corbis)

after the First World War. They had only one car for every 1,195 inhabitants in 1938.[120]

The overwhelming dominance of North Americans in this new sector was even greater than that astounding percentage indicates, because the major US auto companies exported abroad. The value of US auto and parts exports shot up from $11 million in 1910 to $303 million in 1920, making them a leading manufactured export.[121]

However, exports flattened out thereafter because of war in Europe and because the leading firms bought up foreign companies. In 1928, Germany's leading automobile company was Opel, which belonged to GM, while Ford was Germany's third-largest producer. British Ford became a major player in the United Kingdom. Elsewhere the major Detroit companies began to set up assembly plants to circumvent tariffs established to protect domestic producers. In Brazil, Ford had already built an assembly plant in 1920. It was followed quickly by GM.[122]

Most of the world's trucks, buses, tractors, and motorcycles were also in the United States, carrying freight and working the fields as well as moving people. (As late as 1950, 85 percent of Europe's agricultural horsepower was supplied by horses.)[123] The surge of motorized vehicles in the United States not only helped urbanization, but also cemented North American agriculture's position as the most capital intensive and most labor efficient in the world, characteristics that will be more fully illustrated in the section on wheat ahead.

The sociological effect of the internal combustion engine in our period was ambiguous. In the few countries where it proliferated, the automobile emphasized the individual or family unit over the collective, which the railroad and streetcar served. However, the internal combustion engine also drove a rapidly expanding fleet of buses that served large groups with fixed routes and schedules. Where the auto stressed private ownership, urban bus lines were often municipally owned or at least regulated. And paved roads were a mutual public good.

The Airplane

The human dream of joining the birds in flight was finally realized in our era. Beginning with (depending on your national loyalty) the Brazilian Alberto Santos Dumont, who brought to life Jules Verne's fiction by flying a dirigible in Paris in 1901 and made the first public flight in Europe in a fixed-wing aircraft in 1906, or the North American Wright Brothers, whose light aircraft had a sustained, though brief, flight in Kitty Hawk, North Carolina, in 1903, air travel captured the public's imagination. Before the 1930s, however, it was more spectacle or military weapon—combatants built some two hundred thousand planes during the First World War—than commercially useful. Its day would come, even more than the auto, after 1945.[124]

As with so many other technologies, the early leaders were North Americans and Germans. The latter had already sent a few planes over the channel to bomb England during the First World War. Longer international distances followed for peaceful purposes as three aircraft succeeded in crossing the North Atlantic to the United States by 1919. Germans developed the radio navigation system in the 1920s to permit flying with minimal visibility.[125] Still, their expense, danger, and small carrying capacity meant that airplanes were little used internationally for commercial purposes until the 1930s, though they were extremely helpful for local flights in vast countries with poor road and railroad networks, such as Brazil, Colombia, and Mexico. Native capitalists initiated many smaller lines.[126] The first aircraft to be commercially viable internationally was in fact the German Zeppelin Company's hydrogen airship, which made 144 transatlantic two-day crossings in the first part of the 1930s. Though the airships were profitable initially because of the considerable cargo they could carry, they were doomed by improvements by their competitors, fixed-wing aircraft, combined with a few tragic accidents when the hydrogen gasbags that kept them aloft ignited.

Airboats replaced zeppelins for international flights; they were hours and days faster than ships. Only a few activities could pay the freight for this more costly means of transport. In the United States and to a lesser extent in Western Europe, airmail was the main customer. Banks in particular were interested in hurrying checks to be cashed so they would not lose interest. Sometimes planes were used to literally drop bags of money to meet payroll in dangerous areas, such as the oil fields of Tampico, Mexico. In certain places time was money, and so money (as well as time) flew. For largely commercial reasons, the US government subsidized airmail. Pan American Airlines in particular took advantage of the 1928 Kelly Foreign Air Mail Act to assemble routes down to and around Central and South America, connecting to Europe via the Caribbean and West Africa, and by 1937 crossing to China via Hawai'i. Because of its size, population, and wealth, the United States was also able to develop the world's densest domestic air industry, just as it had the most developed railroad and road networks.[127] And, as with other US transportation systems, it was private commercial companies, albeit with government assistance, that forged the path for the global aeronautical industry.

Although Germans, the second most active in the air, were interested in the airplane more for military applications, the privately owned Condor Syndicate, a forerunner of Lufthansa, developed air companies in Brazil (VARIG) and Colombia (SCADTA). Until the rise of the Nazi Party, the Soviet and German governments connected Europe with Asia through the Deutsche Russische Luftverkehrsgesellschaft.[128] Thanks to the German treaty port of Qingdao, Lufthansa was also an early leader in China.

The British saw the airplane as a means of tying together their vast empire, but it advantaged the neo-Europes. Unlike the Dutch, who early on encouraged KLM to connect with the Dutch East Indies (Indonesia), and the French, who developed air travel in Indochina through what became Air France in 1933, the British were discouraged from creating a South Asian air network by India's well-developed rail system. As R. E. G. Davies observes: "Throughout the 1920s, India seemed, in fact, to be regarded by Great Britain as a mere staging point on the route to the Far East and to Australia."[129] In fact, the first successful air company in India was planned and financed by an Indian, J. R. D. Tata.[130] Soviets shared all of these motivations for air travel, but added the symbolic importance of a fast, modern transport for the world's first anti-imperialist, communist country.

Although commerce motivated some of the first private airlines, strategic considerations growing out of both world wars, as well as nation building and colonial impulses, provoked startling growth in aircraft and aviation technology. Headrick has recently pointed out the key role played by airplanes in colonial and neocolonial wars, ranging from the Italians in Libya and Ethiopia to the North Americans in Mexico and Nicaragua. "Air control" gave the colonizers a great advantage up to the end of our period.[131]

State aid was fundamental to the figurative and literal explosion of the air industry and travel. By 1947, the cost of crossing the Atlantic was low enough that a GI sergeant was able to afford to fly Gertrude Topik from Paris to New York, helping to ensure that one of the authors of this chapter would be born in America a couple of years later.

Telegraphs, Underwater Cables, and Radios

Just as steamers, locomotives, cars, and planes powered by steam and fossil fuels bound the world more closely together by vastly accelerating the speed with which goods and people moved, the telegraph wire shrank the world via electricity. The "Victorian Internet," as Tom Standage has nicknamed the telegraph, sparked a conceptual revolution, shaking notions of time and space.[132] But it also opened a great gulf between those connected to its hurried and harried rhythms and those who continued to work at the pace of natural time. Communication of news, orders, commodity, stock and gold prices, and interest rates was made possible by revolutionary advances in the use of electricity, which became one of the foundational cornerstones of the Second Industrial Revolution. As with railroads and steamships (and later telephones), the telegraph demanded systems with large capital investments, coordination through private agreements, and government regulations. At first tying together national markets and polities, it soon became the adhesive of the global market, serving commercial, political, and military purposes simultaneously. The dark side of connectivity was discovered in 1873 when the rapidly transmitted news of financial crises in Europe and the United States provoked the first global depression, which affected all countries and colonies that were closely tied into world capital and commodity markets.

The telegraph, like the railroad and steamers, played a vital role in consolidating rival colonial and neocolonial systems. But its high costs and vast range made international cooperation economically advisable. As Dwayne Winseck and Robert Pike observe, the global telegraph system, "like most other capital intensive industries, continued to contain a complex admixture of collaboration, competition, and conflict, self-interest and opportunism, private enterprise and state interventions."[133] International cartels, consortia, joint investments from different countries, and mixed public and private investments capitalized and coordinated these singularly far-flung enormous enterprises. Thus began the modern era of multinational corporations.[134]

Electricity had been known as early as the eighteenth century, but it remained a little-used curiosity until the nineteenth century. Building on the work of many European and American scientists, the Englishman William

Fothergill Cooke established the first commercial telegraph in 1837. It was used in London on the Great Western Railway, symbolizing the link between these two revolutionary technologies. Cooke's contemporary, the North American Samuel Morse, developed a more successful telegraph system (and code), which was operational by 1846, connecting New York with Washington and demonstrating its close ties to political and commercial nation building. Soon thereafter, a multitude of telegraph systems based on competing technologies arose. Finally, some order and standards were brought to the fledgling industry in upstate New York and in the Old West with the creation of the Western Telegraph Union in 1856. Traveling largely along the beds of railroads and generously aided by federal funds inspired by the Civil War's strategic needs, the telegraph crossed the United States to California by 1861, driving the Pony Express out of business. Two major private companies, Western Union and American Telegraph Company (which would become AT&T when it added telephones), coordinated and dominated the national network.

Europeans, split into dozens of states and languages, required more strenuous efforts at coordination, because the telegraph was of limited use if it could not tap into neighboring networks in small though prosperous countries like Belgium, Great Britain, and the Netherlands or splintered principalities like Germany before 1871 and Italy before nationhood in 1861. Indeed, international commerce played a large role in stimulating later, denser domestic networks.

Telegraphs eventually stretched over the national territories of Western Europe and North America, followed by Latin America and the colonial areas of Asia and Africa, representing a leap for communications, as the ruling classes of distant countries and continents could remain in contact. The advent of international wire services like Reuters in England, Havas in France, the Associated Press in the United States, and Wolff in Germany provided world news (really the news of the part of the globe they thought was important in Western Europe, North America, and various global cities) to the daily newspapers that were beginning to attract mass readerships in major metropolises.[135] They moved in the direction of homogenizing tastes, prices, and technical and scientific advances, though there was resistance as well as acquiescence. Scandals, riots, and disasters as well as celebrities and fashion became known throughout the Western urbane world, which included overseas outposts such as Rio de Janeiro, Cape Town,

Mumbai, and Shanghai. The military joined the intelligence gained from the telegraph with the Maxim gun and rapid deployments on the railroad to subject many formerly autonomous peoples to more-centralized rule. Both government and private enterprise could expand their reach and concentrate power and surveillance. In addition to spurring commerce and homogenizing market prices, the form of business organization was changed as corporations and cartels could synchronize over distant geographic stretches now that they were wired into the telegraph grid.

As with the other revolutionary technologies, at first the telegraph gave great advantages to Western Europe and North America. In 1870, Western Europeans sent some 40.6 million telegrams (over half from Germany, France, and the United Kingdom) and the United States sent 9 million, while in Africa the telegraph was possessed only by the French colony of Algeria, which sent a mere 263,000 telegrams; the only Asian country to enjoy the telegraph was India, which sent 577,000 telegrams.[136]

By 1913 the gap had narrowed, in good part because, as with the railroad, the colonial powers and their capitalist classes invested abroad. By then Europeans were sending 329 million telegrams, and US residents transmitted about half that number. Though still greatly lagging, Africans sent some 17 million telegrams (three-quarters of them from the Mediterranean countries of Algeria and Egypt, together with South Africa), and Asia 60 million, two-thirds being sent by Japan and its colonies and one-quarter by India. Chinese sent only some 4 million inland telegrams as late as 1935. As with other revolutionary technologies, the Japanese state played a central role in inviting in English technicians in 1869 to build the state-run telegraph system. They were quickly able to adapt the telegraph to Japanese characters, creating a dual Japanese-English, forty-two-character system.[137]

If the Japanese system was built for defensive and state-building purposes, the Indian network was constructed as an instrument of colonial domination. Already in 1858 the British chief commissioner of the Punjab, John Lawrence, had thankfully announced that "the telegraph saved India" (for the British) by allowing them to mobilize troops against anticolonial disturbances.[138]

By 1930 the gap between the first builders and the followers declined because Europeans and North Americans were turning to the telephone and using the telegraph less. Asian telegrams grew some 40 percent in number but remained concentrated in Japan and India. China's telegraph system mainly tied together the European treaty ports, though eventually lines ran into the countryside and smaller cities. Other densely populated areas such as Indonesia and Indochina lagged behind China.[139]

The telegraph did not initially democratize communications, because it was expensive to build, maintain, and protect. In the beginning it was also terribly costly to use, so only the most affluent sent (curt) telegrams. In 1890, when a dollar a day was a good wage, a telegram from London to the United States or Canada cost US$0.25 *per word*. The previous sentence would have cost a worker six days' pay. And that was the cheapest rate! A telegram to India was US$1.00 a word, to Brazil US$1.50, to Australia US$2.37, and to South Africa during its gold rush, US$40 a word![140] Those sending telegrams to South Africa had to literally weigh their words in gold. The telegraph's laggard introduction into many of the most densely populated—and often least affluent—areas meant that local culture and languages retained autonomy longer there.

On the other hand, the telegraph was useful in mobilizing troops of central authorities against local or regional resistance, so in many places the wire reinforced the power of the few over the many. It was not pure coincidence that one of the first acts by local rebels was to cut the telegraph wire. But alas, the wires could be easily strung up again. The first Englishman to oversee Japan's telegraph in 1870 remarked lightheartedly: "Beyond a few of the poles being slashed by fanatical samurai who must find some use for their swords, there was no evidence of hostility on the part of the people."[141]

Underwater cables that bound together continents by erasing oceans were the sorts of modern miracles that so inspired contemporary Verne's science fiction. They represented the greatest conceptual leap in communications until satellites began bouncing back radio signals in the 1960s. Cables connected international markets, leading to commodity exchanges that set global standards and prices while encouraging competition.

Joining areas with underwater cable started small, crossing the English Channel between France and England in 1851. This was made possible by the merging of two nineteenth-century miracle products: copper wire, which transmitted electrical impulses with little loss to heat, and rubber, which insulated the copper and protected it from water. The first form of latex, gutta-percha, had been sent to England as an experimental colonial export from Malaya. In addition to learning that it served as a fine bottle stopper, which advanced the incipient carbonated water industry, and later that it could serve as the core of golf balls, scientists discovered gutta-percha's more important ability to provide electrical insulation while being durable and unappetizing to marine life.

But this was not an easy technology to master, because the early cables often broke soon after being laid on the ocean's floor. That is exactly what happened to the 1857, 1858, and 1865 cables laid across the Atlantic by a steamship specially constructed to lay out cable underwater. Finally in 1866 the first successful transatlantic submarine cable went into operation.

Other submarine cables soon followed. Brazil connected with Portugal via Senegal and the Cape Verde Islands in 1875, with other South American countries joining in to take advantage of the transatlantic cable over the next two decades. The Caribbean was connected to Europe via the North Atlantic cable through the United States and Canada. Wire spreading south from Texas linked up Mexico and Central America down to Peru by 1882, and indirectly reached South America's east coast urban centers.

Already by 1868 London reached Mumbai via telegraph passing through Ottoman and Persian lands and waters, but telegrams took more than seven days and were subject to foreign scrutiny. For political and commercial security, plans for an all-English line (known as "all-red") led to the Eastern Telegraph line connecting with India by 1870. Imperial arrogance also motivated the all-red system. The colonial mindset was blatant in a petition by Mumbai merchants who objected that their connection to London "passes through . . . foreign territory, much of it wild and uncivilized [the Ottoman and Persian Empires!], where European management cannot be brought to bear, and where ignorant and untrained native officers are alone obtainable."[142] "Civilized" British lines continued to reach east to Indochina, China, and Japan and south to Indonesia and Australia.

Sub-Saharan Africa was swept into the world of telegraph by a combination of several forces. Interest in booming Argentina and Brazil had motivated the laying of cable from Lisbon to Senegal and across to Recife. The 1870s diamond strike in Kimberley, South Africa, and the 1880s gold rush in Witwatersrand had whetted the appetite of imperialists like Rhodes. Other European powers developed the same craving that led to unprecedented conferences in Berlin in 1884 and 1885 that carved up Africa, leaving 90 percent of the territory officially under European control. Conquest, at least on the maps in European administrative offices, generated a hunger for control and knowledge. Political, diplomatic, and economic urges led to the connection of the most affluent areas to the European colonial powers beginning in 1886 with the joint-effort African Direct Telegraph Company.

With every continent connected to Europe, the globe was finally girded in 1902 when a submarine cable linked the Americas and Asia. It stretched from San Francisco to the US Pacific territories of Hawaii, Guam, and the Philippines. From there it linked to the Asian mainland and Oceania.

For the telegraph networks to function efficiently, international coordination was necessary. Because early on each country used a different system, messages had to be transcribed, translated, and handed over at the borders. They were then retransmitted over the telegraph network of the neighboring country, causing delays, errors, and additional costs. After numerous bilateral agreements in the 1850s between countries seeking telegraph connections, a conference of twenty European countries created the International Telegraph Union in 1865. It facilitated further standards and procedures as newcomers to the telegraph world joined in. Continents became connected by the submarine telegraph before many countries developed internal networks.

Telegraph wires began to lose some of their usefulness with the wireless inventions of the Italian physicist Guglielmo Marconi. Not only were these a boon to naval communications, they laid the groundwork for the radio on land and later in the air. A Nobel Prize–winning scientist, Marconi was also an astute businessman who quickly commercialized his discoveries, as did other heroic entrepreneur-scientists of this era such as Alexander Graham Bell, Thomas Edison, Ford, Nobel, and Werner von Siemens. By 1901 Marconi's English corporation sent signals across the Atlantic Ocean, and six years later a transatlantic wireless service had been established. By 1906 an international telegraphy conference in Berlin signed the first International Radiotelegraph Convention.

Marconi's invention gave rise to the radio, which would democratize access to information even among the illiterate once electricity and then the battery found their way to poorer countries and once commercial broadcasting began transmitting news and entertainment. In many countries that would happen only after the Second World War. Initially, however, as with the other major inventions discussed, the wireless radio and then broadcasting companies were concentrated in the wealthier countries, expanding the divide in lifestyles by social class and country until the 1930s.

The radio, like the earlier telegraph and telephone, was a communication system that demanded large investments in coordinated networks. This was unsurprising because it was developed by people who sought to perfect the telegraph and the railroad and who had mastered electrical generation and its applications such as lighting and power. Some of the giant electronics corporations that would put their mark on the consumer and industrial advances of the twentieth century were involved in the radio's earliest days. In the United States this included General Electric (GE), which resulted from the 1892 merger of Edison's company with the Thomson-Houston Electric Company; Westinghouse Electric, which began with the air brake for trains; and American Telegraph and Telephone (AT&T).

This was a sector more characterized by collaboration than by unrestrained competition. After Thomson and GE merged, the new GE pooled its patents with Westinghouse, effectively cornering the large and rapidly growing electronics industry. These two firms joined with AT&T in 1919 at the urging of the US government to form the Radio Corporation of America (RCA) to accelerate the diffusion of the radio. RCA bought out the originator of wireless telegraph in the United States, the American Marconi.

Forces were also joined in radio broadcasting. Westinghouse established the first commercial radio station, KDKA in Pittsburgh, in 1920, followed by GE's WGY in 1922 in Schenectady, New York. RCA combined with GE and Westinghouse to form the National Broadcasting Corporation (NBC) in 1926, linking forty-eight radio stations. Two years later the Columbia Broadcasting Corporation (CBS) followed. To regulate them, the Federal Radio Commission was created in 1927. By 1928 Americans from coast to coast could hear "The Lone Ranger" on radios that were created by Westinghouse and GE and distributed by RCA and Western Electric (which had begun the telegraph boom a half century earlier).[143] The radio swept through the United States like a hurricane.

Already in 1925, 10 percent of households had radios; five years later nearly 50 percent had one. By 1945 almost 90 percent of US households listened to the radio, as mass production and consumer credit dropped its cost and turned it into a necessity.

But most other countries did not adopt the US radio model based on large private corporations. National governments established major broadcasting companies like the British Broadcasting Corporation and Japan's NHK. France had a combination of public and private broadcasters. In Germany, private companies began broadcasting, but the national Post Ministry had to have a majority share in them. Similarly, in Brazil the *Hora do Brasil* was created, a one-hour time slot during which only a central government program could be broadcast. The Soviet government had complete control of USSR radio.

The radio was used initially for educational purposes but soon was turned to commercial popular culture and to political education. An early student of mass communications and its unfortunate possibilities was the Nazi propaganda minister, Josef Goebbels, who introduced the production of relatively cheap *Volksempfänger* receivers so the country could hear the Nazi version of the "Big Lie." Communication and truth did not necessarily come together. Radios quickly spread through the richer countries. In France, for instance, there were already some five million radios by 1939. Sales of radio equipment in the United States reached $843 million in 1929, a fourteen-fold increase in just eight years![144]

These early radio companies became household names in the United States, Western Europe, and parts of Latin America. They soon became enormous conglomerates producing everything from electrical capital goods to generators and transmission lines, electric trains and trolleys, movie projectors, consumer goods, such as lightbulbs, and by the 1920s refrigerators, electric ranges, and washing machines. These more expensive goods spread more slowly than the radio. Significant international trade goods, their export declined as they were increasingly manufactured in the overseas consuming countries, at first by branches of the European and North American corporations and then, by the 1930s, by protected domestic factories. Still, incomes were too low and the prices too high for electronic domestic goods to enter the mass market in many places outside of the most affluent countries and some major cities. Their heyday would come after the 1950s.

Telephones also were electronic instruments, but they became the monopoly of a different company, Bell Telephone. The Scottish inventor Alexander Graham Bell was trying to improve the telegraph when in 1876 he invented in Boston the device that would speak the telegraph's demise. When it was combined with the mouthpiece invented by Thomas Edison, it could reach the immediate area around the caller. By 1904 there were already three million telephones in operation in the United States. De Forest's triode vacuum tube made possible a phone call from New York to San Francisco by 1915.

But the telephone was slow to bind continents, because the technology to amplify speech sufficiently to send it long distances lagged behind. The first transatlantic call was made only in 1927 from New York to London. A three-minute call, done by wireless radio, cost the then-princely sum of seventy-five dollars, making it economically impractical. Telephone cables were not laid across the Atlantic until 1955. Because telephones required an expensive system to be useful, they were slow to internationalize. They were concentrated in Western Europe and North America, where each had some 26 million telephones in service by 1945. Africa lagged behind with some 400,000 phones for the entire continent, as did Asia, with some 1.7 million, more than two-thirds of them in Japan.[145] Sparsely populated Oceania had 1.1 million telephones.

A few giant companies in Europe also moved away from the telegraph and accompanying electronics into consumer goods. The Thomson-Houston Company that merged with GE established subsidiaries in England and France that became, after mergers there, the largest companies in those two large markets.

Germany experienced the most remarkable advance in the electrical sector, a key to its *Wirtschaftswunder* (economic miracle). Between 1890 and 1913 the electrical industrial sector grew at an astounding 9.75 percent a year. By the eve of the First World War, Germany produced 20 percent more electricity than Great Britain, France, and Italy combined. (In part to generate electricity, Germans increased coal production almost eightfold between 1870 and 1913, and jumped in industrial production fivefold, so that Germany's primary exports were no longer raw materials but instead finished and semifinished goods.)[146]

A few gigantic corporations that became world leaders characterized Germany's electrical sector. Edison's German affiliate created what became the precursor to the Allgemeine Elektricitäts-Gesellschaft (AEG), one of the largest electrical firms in Germany and in the world. Also in Germany, another giant corporation, Siemens, had begun with the telegraph in 1847, then moved to the undersea cable, to the telephone by 1877, and then power generation. Siemens followed the same path as US electrical companies by moving downstream into consumer appliances by the 1920s. It took a more active role than the other electrical companies in producing instruments of war, in 1944 going so far as to design the V2 rocket, which was an extension of its experience in the nascent airplane industry.[147]

Initially the large electrical multinationals participated in the public utility companies that arose in major cities in Latin America and Eastern Europe and to a lesser extent in Africa and Asia near the end of the nineteenth century. The British tended to invest in stand-alone companies organized for specific locations, such as the S. Pearson electrical generating company in Mexico and Brazilian Light and Power in Rio and São Paulo, while US and German investors like GE, Westinghouse, Siemens, and AEG, the Swiss Brown, Boveri & Co., and the Swedish Allmänna Svenska Elektriska AB (ASEA) won power, lighting, and tram concessions in numerous major cities. Sometimes, as in Rio de Janeiro, they replaced smaller predecessors that had launched power companies with local capital. Usually the giant foreign firms sold off their power companies once they were up and running, because the daily demands of light and power generation and the political problems of dissatisfied consumers and municipal governments they entailed were too different from these companies' core competencies.[148]

Other holding companies arose to take advantage of their access to European capital—most had intimate ties to large European or US banks—and technology to run public utility companies in many countries. The Belgian Compagnie Belge des Chemins de Fer Réunis, for example, spread its investments in tramways and railroads from Belgium, France, and Greece to as far away as Russia, Turkey, China, Congo, and Egypt, and even to the Americas in Argentina and Chile.[149] The Western European and North American early movers in electricity also were usually the first to win concessions in countries outside the core. The main exception was again Japan, which used mostly national capital supplemented by government assistance. Even in Japan, however, foreign participation in the electrical area was greater than in any other sector because of the systems' bulky demands and the patented technology's sophistication.[150] (In the other major Asian "independent" country, China, modern public utilities were found mostly in the European- and Japanese-controlled treaty ports, where companies from those countries built and ran the light, power, and trams just as they did in their Asian and African colonies.)

Because of their great capital requirements and strategic economic importance, many public utility companies eventually were taken over by national or local public entities. The Soviet Union expropriated foreign power and light companies, and a couple of decades later the Turkish government bought up the French-owned public utilities.[151] Even in the United States, where suspicion of state intervention was strong, calls for public regulation and even operation of utility companies began to resonate. The federally funded and run Tennessee Valley Authority (TVA) began building dams and generators in 1934 to supply light and power to underserved areas in eight states that bordered the valley. Serving mostly as a wholesale provider of electrical power as well as a development program, the TVA became the largest power generator in the country, but it distributed power through municipal, state, and private companies.[152] Only after World War II would state-run public power, light, and transport companies become the worldwide norm.

The site of the greatest gap in inequality for the Americas, Europe, Oceania, and parts of Asia and Africa was not between countries but within countries. Public utilities made the qualitative difference between urban living and life in the countryside much greater than it had been before electricity. Particularly with the rise of public street lighting and movie theaters, the "bright lights of the big city" meant more than the conquest of the night. It meant greater leisure opportunities, perceived "culture," and social standing.[153] With the urban populations being the best educated, most politically attuned, and most socially dangerous because of their capacity to organize and riot, governments concentrated funding for mass public utilities in cities. Of course, their dense residential patterns also made urban dwellers easier to reach with public services. And health concerns over epidemics of contagious diseases made sanitation a generalized concern.

Copper and Other Metals

So far we have stressed electricity's role in the Second Industrial Revolution's transformation of communications, light, and power. But electricity's newfound roles created demand for other economic activities that stimulated international trade. Employing economist Albert Hirschman's concept of "backward linkages," that is, prior activities necessary for later industrial production, we briefly survey the new needs and possibilities that arose for copper and aluminum.

Humans have found important uses for copper, which nature has widely distributed across the globe, since at least the Bronze Age (bronze is an alloy of copper and tin). Copper is an important raw material for implements and weapons. However, it fell out of favor as harder and more abundant iron took its place. Before the electrical age it was used mainly for coins and jewelry. But copper's ability to conduct electricity made it the logical source for wire (including telegraph and telephone lines) and motors.

In our period copper became essential in the most industrialized and prosperous countries that introduced electricity. Demand was so great that copper production grew twenty-four-fold between 1870 and 1938. One of the leaders in the electrical revolution, the United States, had the good fortune to have the some of the world's richest deposits in accessible areas, such as Michigan's Upper Peninsula and later Butte, Montana, and the Southwest. At the outset of our period the United States produced only one-seventh of the world's copper, barely a third of Chile's or Europe's output. Within fourteen years, US output had grown over eightfold to surpass all other copper-mining countries. By 1913 the United States mined more than 80 percent of the world's copper ore and smelted 60 percent of its output as production jumped another fivefold. Of its competitors, only Chile, Spain, and Russia had mines of any size.[154]

The sector continued to grow rapidly and diversify geographically after the First World War. While US production stagnated so that its share fell to one-third of world output, Canadian and Chilean mines doubled their output. Production in the Belgian Congo (today the Democratic Republic of Congo) and Rhodesia (today Zimbabwe) allowed Africa to become a major colonial copper producer, rising to over 20 percent of world output by 1938.[155]

The European electrical companies had to turn overseas for their necessary copper, because production in Spain and the USSR, which held the richest European copper deposits, could not satisfy demand. Some companies, such as the German giant Metallgesellschaft, invested in US mines through its subsidiary American Metal. Others partnered in colonies or other countries, or imported copper from third parties. In all cases, copper, used for the spread of the mass-produced electrical products, was characterized by oligopoly.[156] This apparent paradox was in fact almost a rule: widespread industrialized products aimed at the masses tended to oligopoly.

Technological advances had created synergies and demanded economies of scale. Vast copper mines became possible in the twentieth century as nitroglycerin was used to blow open pit mines and steam shovels and power drills were devised to exploit them. They built some of the largest mines ever made, usually in remote, sparsely populated areas. The cost of moving workers to these sites, purchasing heavy moving equipment, and laying rail to them meant that only a few companies with close ties to bankers and financiers were able to prosper. For this reason capitalists, like the Rothschilds, J. P. Morgan, and the Guggenheims, and major German banks like Deutsche Bank came to dominate the sector, with interests in numerous countries in the Americas, Europe, and Africa.[157]

Refining technology as well as mining costs led to domination by a handful of firms. Electricity not only needed copper to travel efficiently, it also provided the solution for cheap copper smelting through the "electrolytic revolution." New high-power generators developed in 1891 had to be large to be profitable. As a result, only twelve huge new modern smelters were built in the United States between 1891 and 1910. That was enough to produce a fivefold increase in copper production in the United States by 1914. The five largest copper producers in 1948 were the same as in 1917: Anaconda Copper, Phelps Dodge, American Smelting and Refining, Kennecott, and American Metal. These companies were among the first US multinationals (with the exception of earlier railroads in Mexico, and sugar and fruit in the tropics like United Fruit) to invest abroad; they built vast mines and smelting plants in Mexico, Peru, and Chile.[158]

Although some of the corporations attempted to establish company towns abroad to bring to their workers the "American way of life" (including perceived Protestant morality to order the private lives of their employees), they also unintentionally exported an unsought cultural value: the class struggle. Miners were some of the most politically active and organized workers in Mexico, Peru, and Chile. They created some of the most successful labor unions and helped launch leftist political parties in Chile. The 1906 strike in the Cananea copper mine in Sonora, Mexico, has been seen as a catalyst of the Mexican Revolution. Indeed, the argument has been strongly made by historian John Hart that anti-imperialist sentiments sparked by the flood of foreign investment after the later 1890s was a key to the revolution's outbreak, a position contested by many other historians.[159]

Certainly other copper mines did not explode in violence. But they did sometimes underpin the great divergence in lifestyle that was growing. Dennis Kortheuer has written about this clash of cultures in his study of the French Rothschild-owned El Boleo mine in Baja California. Illiterate miners from Mexico's heartland were brought to tunnel deep into the mountains of Santa Rosalia for copper that transmitted electricity for power, spread the written word through the telegraph, and lit the night in the United States. But the diggers had only dim candles to guide them through the dark caverns, because electricity was slow to reach the mine.[160]

It should be noted that the hunt for copper had the side effect of increased mining of zinc, nickel, silver, and lead. These minerals appeared naturally together with copper deposits, so that miners exploited them all and their worldwide use grew exponentially.

Electricity and copper also led to the expansion of a metal that would become important in the twentieth century, aluminum. To provide electricity in the United States, an enormous generator was built at Niagara Falls, New York. The energy generated by the falls' hydroelectric power attracted to the area some of the largest mineral and industrial processing plants, including heavy industries and food processing. The predecessor of the Aluminum Company of America (Alcoa) with financing from the Mellons, the leading venture capitalists in the United States, built a giant aluminum plant in 1895 at Niagara Falls to exploit the electrolytic process, which had been invented nine years earlier to reduce alumina (bauxite) into aluminum. It allowed the price of a pound of aluminum to drop from twelve dollars to thirty-two cents, turning the formerly costly product into an essential industrial input. This would earn Alcoa a monopoly position throughout the Western Hemisphere.[161] In Europe four firms produced 95 percent of all aluminum before World War I. Still a specialty metal, aluminum would become increasingly important for use in petroleum-based vehicles like the automobile and the airplane, and would find its way into packaging and household appliances, its use skyrocketing during and after World War II.

Petroleum

Rock oil (petroleum) became a major new source of energy during the Second Industrial Revolution, though its true era of triumph came only after 1945 when it would overshadow coal. Still, already in the first decades of the twentieth century the race to develop and dominate world petroleum products, sources, and markets created some of the largest and most dynamic corporations in North America and Western Europe. It also sparked imperial rivalries among the Great Powers in areas formerly marginal to the world economy, like Central Asia and the Middle East. Petroleum would revolutionize transportation by introducing the automobile and the airplane.

In 1870, however, it was still not of major importance. Though petroleum had been known for thousands of years for its medicinal qualities and as an illuminant, the rather rare and volatile seepage sites where it appeared were too few to make it a major global resource. The breakthrough came when in 1859 an American, Edwin Drake, applied drilling technology initially developed for salt mining to seek pools of oil in the state of Pennsylvania. Turning oil into kerosene created an important international commodity.

One company, Standard Oil, controlled 90 percent of the refining capacity of kerosene by 1879. The company's prosaic name—by today's standards—was taken to connote a uniform, reliable commodity. They sought to set the country's and then the world's *standard* for oil products. Three years later Standard created the first "trust," a legal entity that combined numerous companies under a single management. It produced one-quarter of the world's kerosene. Through pipelines, special arrangements with the railroads, and eventually its own fleet of steamers and sailing ships, Standard came to control much of the distribution as well. Only later did it drill for oil.

Its founder and mastermind, John D. Rockefeller, was an enemy of "unbridled competition," preferring instead organized capitalism. He declared, "The day of the combination is here to stay. Individualism has gone, never to return."[162] Eventually Standard Oil would succeed so well at assimilating or crushing its competition that it became the largest corporation in the world.

That is, it was the largest until muckraker journalist Ida Tarbell aroused public outrage at Standard's market power. Amid an unprecedented wave of trust formation in the United States that witnessed the birth of 234 trusts worth $6 billion just between 1898 and 1904, Standard Oil refined over three-quarters of all US crude oil, four-fifths of its kerosene, and nine-tenths of its railroad lubricating oil. Outcries by Progressives led President William Howard Taft and Congress to take on the Standard Oil "octopus," breaking the trust in 1909 into eight different entities. But that was something of a pyrrhic victory. The successor firms continued to cooperate with each other. They did so well that most of them saw their share values double within a year of dissolution and continued to grow thereafter.[163]

Although most kerosene was used within the United States, the oil industry had an international orientation from its inception. Kerosene became the leading US manufactured export by the 1880s.[164] "Cracking" petroleum also yielded other valuable products: naphtha, asphalt, diesel, fuel oil, lubricants, petroleum jelly, paraffin, and last but not least, gasoline.

Gasoline's rise to prominence proved a godsend. It saved Standard from going the way of whale oil and beeswax producers when the demand for kerosene dwindled in the wake of Edison's 1879 invention of a reliable lightbulb and its diffusion as cities began installing electric lighting. In 1885 there were 250,000 lightbulbs in use; just seventeen years later there were 18 million. The automobile and the navies' and commercial ships' conversion from coal to fuel oil created massive new demand. By 1910 Standard Oil was selling more gasoline than kerosene.[165]

Thirsty vehicles did not drive the international race for oil. After all, the United States, which had by far the most cars, trucks, and planes, was self-sufficient in petroleum because of its rich strikes in Pennsylvania, California, Louisiana, Oklahoma, and Texas. After a brief scare at the end of the First World War, when a survey incorrectly predicted that the United States would run out of oil, there was no fear of insufficient domestic proven reserves. American oil companies looked abroad more because of fear of European competition.

Western European powers found no oil at home. On the continent only Romania had some. But as Churchill had said, the British needed oil, though more as a ship fuel than for cars. Without the navy, he intoned somewhat melodramatically, "the whole fortunes of our race and Empire . . . would be swept utterly away." More pointedly, he warned, "If we cannot get oil we cannot get corn and we cannot get cotton and we cannot get one thousand and one other commodities necessary for the preservation of the economic energies of Great Britain."[166]

Of course, the British, who imported and exported so much, were particularly vulnerable. But in the twentieth century the French, Germans, and Japanese also became concerned about access to oil, not only as a fuel but also as a raw material for so many different products. Initially petroleum was treated much as other commodities, with individual entrepreneurs such as the Nobels staking out the great strikes such as Baku in southern Russia.[167] The Rothschilds soon joined in, as did the Englishmen Marcus and Samuel Samuel. Eventually the major states became concerned with control of what was becoming not only a precious commodity but also a strategic one. The Dutch struck oil in Indonesia and created the Royal Dutch Company, which soon merged with British Shell, which initially had imported Russian oil but then entered Romania. A little later the newly expanded company bought up the Mexican Eagle Oil Company. After the merger the new firm was known as Royal Dutch Shell. In Japan the strategic implications of oil became increasingly acute in the decade before World War II. With no oil production of its own, Japan was largely reliant on supplies from the United States. Japanese engineers unsuccessfully drilled for oil in their new colony of Manchukuo in the 1930s and increasingly dreamed of building a "co-prosperity sphere" in Southeast Asia that would provide reliable access to oil sources.

A British-educated and Turkish-born Armenian go-between, Calouste Gulbenkian, played a crucial role in expanding the race for oil into the Middle East. He secured the concession to oil in Persia (today Iran), where oil was discovered in 1908. The breakup of the Ottoman Empire, Germany's ally, after its defeat in World War I, left the Middle East open to competition between the British and the French. (The German and Japanese dependence on oil from companies flying the flag of competing Great Powers would encourage their invasions of the Soviet Union and Indonesia during the next major war.) Recognizing its strategic importance for India and the rest of the British South Asian Empire, and particularly for supplying the British navy in the Indian Ocean, the British Admiralty and Parliament invested in the Anglo-Persian Oil Company. Later renamed British Petroleum, the corporation came to be an arm of the British government, implementing imperial policy as well as becoming enormously profitable to its other stockholders. Other Middle East kingdoms and emirates such as Iraq, Kuwait, and Saudi Arabia, which came largely under US influence, were only beginning commercial oil production in 1945.

Even before moving into the Middle East, US oil companies like Standard as well as wildcatters like Edward Doheny and the British Eagle Company had found ample oil in Mexico. When the Mexican Revolution broke out and foreign-owned oil concessions were menaced by nationalist regimes, Standard looked south to Venezuela. By 1938 when Mexican president Lázaro Cárdenas decreed the nationalization of oil companies, Mexico was no longer a leading international producer. Its production had been mostly channeled to domestic needs as Mexico's industrialization drive recovered from revolutionary upheaval.[168]

Mexico was not the first country to nationalize a viable oil industry. The Soviet Union had already done so. There the issue was not only one of anticapitalist principle, but also the fact that Communist activist and later dictator Joseph Stalin had gotten his start as a radical organizer in the oil fields of Baku. Elsewhere state takeovers of oil companies became common after World War II. Nationalist populists in Iran, Mexico, and Bolivia would take control of their oil sectors. Others would be undertaken by pro-capitalist and socially reactionary monarchies as in Saudi Arabia and Kuwait. By then the major oil corporations that initially fought the nationalization in Mexico, and later (1954) of BP by Iran, learned that they could live with and profit from state oil companies. The public–private divide has always been hazy in oil, as in many other strategic, capital- and technology-intensive commodities.

Rubber

For the marriage of the auto and oil to succeed, a third commodity was needed: rubber. Roads were usually dirt and rutted from wagon wheels. For the auto to attract users, the ride had to be more comfortable. Even once asphalt and macadam pavement spread, something else was needed. Rubber, which had been known for thousands of years in Central America for ball games, was turned to broader uses in the early nineteenth century when in 1844 Charles Goodyear invented the "vulcanization" process of removing sulfur from the crude product. Once treated, rubber remained malleable and became stronger and reliable; now it was neither brittle in the cold nor melting in the heat. Rubber had been used for erasers to rub out mistakes (from which its name derived) and for golf balls. Soon it became widely used in overcoats, boots, and even condoms, because of its waterproof properties. But demand and supply were small. Goodyear died a poor man, his name appropriated by others who founded a major rubber company thirty years after his death.

The next invention, which also was the key to an industrial empire and which pushed forward wheeled transport, was the pneumatic tire, invented by a Scottish physician, James Dunlop, in 1888. Dunlop also made little money from his invention of the inflatable tire, as he sold the patent and his name to what became a leading rubber company. The pneumatic tire was instrumental in the bicycle craze of the 1880s and 1890s. Two- and three-wheel human-powered vehicles spread around the world because they were relatively cheap and fast.

However, the pneumatic rubber tire had to wait two decades before it was successfully applied to automobiles. Rubber tires with inflatable inner tubes greatly improved the ride of autos and bicycles, but they faced the continuing problem of wear and tear. The poor construction of the first tires, combined with limited paved roads, meant that the average car needed eight tires a year, quite an expense. Within a few years, though, tire life improved sixfold because of technical advances in production and public investments in better dirt and paved roads. In the United States the surfaced mileage of rural road and municipal streets doubled between 1904 and 1914, reaching over 300,000 miles. Federal and state highways to connect cities added an additional 250,000 miles by 1938.[169] European paving also advanced rapidly. Petroleum, then, provided not only the gasoline to power autos and the oil to lubricate them, but the asphalt to pave their roads.

The bicycle and automobile revolutions stimulated great appetites for rubber—US imports jumped 25-fold between 1900 and 1929. Although latex is provided by many different plants, the boom centered on a variety of rubber species found in the Amazon Basin. Nature had graced Brazil with a natural world monopoly of *Hevea brasiliensis* rubber until about 1908, which allowed it to enjoy a bonanza as prices doubled between 1900 and 1910 even while the volume of exports continued to climb. Rubber trailed only coffee as Brazil's main export between 1890 and 1920.[170]

This stroke of luck caught the imagination of international observers, with stories of the great tenor Enrico Caruso performing in the elegant Manaus opera house a thousand kilometers upriver from the Atlantic, where the city's elite imported lavishly from Europe and sent out their laundry to France. But Brazil's fabulous experience during its rubber boom wound up an early episode of what later became known as "the Dutch disease." Nature had given Brazil stands of latex-bearing trees but had located them in an inhospitable and sparsely populated area. The boom would be short-lived.

Skyrocketing foreign demand and prices provoked an invasion of the tropics by thousands of rubber *seringueiros* (tappers), mostly men from Brazil's impoverished Northeast, in a hunt for stands of rubber trees. Supplied with hatchets and tin cups, each man collected latex by tapping trees along long roads in the jungle, about a hundred trees to the worker, and then cured it over a smoky fire. This was extraction or hunting and gathering rather than production; the trees soon tapped out because the inexperienced gatherers often cut too deeply into them, and new trees had to be found. Merchants, who had provided advances in the form of provisions and loans to attract many of the tappers, paddled or steamed up the tributaries of the Amazon to collect the scattered bits of cured rubber, but this did not revolutionize the production process. There were no economies of scale. In fact there emerged diseconomies because gathering could be increased only by extensive rather than intensive harvesting, that is, only by expanding geographically. Consequently, the more they produced, the further the *seringueiros* were from their Brazilian depots and European and United States markets. And many of the workers were more indentured servants or even slaves than they were proletarians. Except for frontier trading towns and a couple of modern, electrified outposts of European culture like Manaus and Belem, the rubber trade left little of permanence on the landscape. Its main geopolitical consequences were Brazil's purchase of the Bolivian province of Acre and its diplomatic consolidation of its borders with Amazon neighbors such as Peru, Colombia, Venezuela, and the French, Dutch, and British colonies in the Guyanas.[171]

Brazil's central role in the rubber economy was not a problem for the Americans and Western Europeans craving rubber, as long as auto production grew slowly. But as we have seen, Henry Ford's widely imitated inventions on the assembly line

A worker tapping a rubber tree with a machete, probably in Brazil before the bust of rubber's boom in 1912. Hundreds of thousands of migrants from coastal Brazil poured into the Amazon rain forest to use simple tapping techniques to harvest the sap of several latex-producing trees and plants. As the market for bicycle and automobile tires expanded, both foreign demand and prices for rubber skyrocketed, provoking an invasion of the tropics by thousands of rubber *seringueiros* (tappers). (Library of Congress)

caused an explosion in the number of tire-greedy cars. Synthetic rubber was a complex proposition that defeated Edison's best efforts and yielded only a partial answer from DuPont. A major chemical company that had begun producing gunpowder by 1802, DuPont imitated some of the magic that German chemists were performing across the Atlantic in 1938, creating neoprene and nylon, which, together with cotton and steel, would become the main ingredients of tires. But before 1945 rubber was still so important to transportation that it was considered a vital strategic material.[172] Japanese goals in World War II were, in large part, the conquest of not only oil-producing but also rubber-growing areas.

Asia became involved in the world of rubber by imperial design, not by natural accident. Henry Wickham, a British adventurer and sometime employee of the Foreign Office, managed in 1876 to secretly export from Brazil seeds of the *Hevea brasiliensis* and bring them to Kew Gardens in England. There rubber seedlings were raised and then sent to Ceylon and later on to Malaysia and Indonesia. This was a very dangerous and difficult process, little helped by the minimal assistance offered by the miserly British Foreign Office. Wickham's rewards were as sparse as the vitriol heaped on him by Brazilian nationalists was thick.[173] But within thirty years his scheme had succeeded in fomenting South Asian colonial rubber plantations funded by British and Dutch capital and worked by locals and indentured laborers from India and China. By 1912 their rubber exports exceeded Brazil's and within a couple of years overshadowed Brazilian natural extraction. By 1925 Asian plantations and small farms produced sixteen times more than Brazilian tappers.

Because rubber grew in fertile, populated areas of the East Indies, "native rubber" grown on small family plots of a couple of acres came to surpass plantation rubber. Rubber was the cash crop, but grew alongside food crops like rice, so growers were buffered from international market prices in that they could devote more family labor to consumption crops rather than rubber when prices fell. Political resistance was as important as economic logic in reducing the role of rubber estates and the scale of landholding, however. In Sumatra, Ann Stoler has shown, opposition to the Japanese invasion and seizure of lands led to small-holdings. But, she argues, these holdings ultimately were "brought within the vortex of capitalist control."[174] Auto companies could now buy plenty of rubber and benefit from continually falling prices. Even auto companies in Brazil now imported rubber from Asia.

Perhaps the grimmest episode of the rubber boom afflicted central Africa. Leopold II, king of the Belgians, was awarded a free hand over the Congo Free State by other European powers at the Berlin Conference in 1885, supposedly to squash slavery there and bring civilization. Rubber (and ivory and mineral) exports certainly increased, but not enough to affect the world market much. The brutal, neo-slave-labor regime under Belgian colonialism, however, may have killed off as many as a fifth of the local population. It provoked international outrage from the likes of the Irish journalist Roger Casement, and it inspired Joseph Conrad's *Heart of Darkness*. Rubber profits built imposing structures in Belgium but brought death and disfigurement to Congolese workers.[175]

North American tire producers like Goodrich, Goodyear, and US Rubber were satisfied with the European domination of rubber supply, but some, like Harvey Firestone, feared that a British-Dutch cartel would drive prices back up. This, in fact, was attempted in the early 1920s under the British Stevenson Plan. The Dutch, however, refused to go along with price fixing, so an open market resumed after 1926.

Concern with British and Dutch control of the world rubber market led to some intriguing, but ultimately failed, experiments. The most famous was Henry Ford's "Fordlandia," a plantation and company town in the Brazilian Amazon. Despite serious efforts, the plan was defeated, not by governments or markets but by tiny pests that feasted on the leaves of the plantation's densely regimented rows of trees. It turned out that rubber could not be grown on plantations in Brazil, not only because of the scarcity of cheap labor but also because rubber was *native*, not exotic. Being indigenous, it was host to native insects and diseases that had developed along with rubber. In South Asia, neither had arisen, so trees could be planted close together. When joined with the large, poor, and accessible peasant populations of Malaysia, Indonesia, India, and China, conditions were ripe for successful plantation monoculture.

Efforts to exploit a different organic source for latex, the guayule bush, had only limited success. Farmers in northern Mexico and, in a little known episode, Japanese-Americans interned in the Manzanar concentration camp in California, cultivated guayule. These experiments were put to rest by political pressures and the success of petroleum-based rubber synthetics.[176]

Harvey Firestone had more success with his rubber plantation in Liberia, and efforts were made to plant in the Philippines. But production never made a dent in US demand. As with other key imports such as sugar and coffee, US policy preferred imports from closer "neocolonial" producers over a concerted effort to establish production in the Philippines colony.

3. Commodity Chains

SO FAR we have taken a rather traditional approach to the economic history of our period by outlining the sinews of the world economy in the period 1870–1945, its transportation, communications, and energy sectors, as well as by surveying the main industrial raw materials of the Second Industrial Revolution. Now to diverge from more Eurocentric studies, we turn to some key international *agricultural* commodities, such as wheat and rice, as well as stimulants, like sugar, tobacco, coffee, and tea. Examining the chains associated with these commodities will illustrate the particularities of change over time, the international variations, and the different effects within producing and consuming countries. We will see that participants in each commodity chain developed their own logic according to a wide set of conditions. Moreover, the nature of the relationships and exchanges in the chain usually changed because of technological innovations and ecological constraints.

The commodity chain approach makes us sensitive to the fact that there was not *one* world market, but myriad, often segmented, and ever-evolving markets. First movers were not guaranteed continued success. They often succumbed at a later moment to rivals. The US automobile industry's loss of dominance to Japanese and European producers in our day is just one poignant contemporary example that head starts were not necessarily insurmountable. Loss of advantage occurred in agricultural and extractive industries as well. Brazilian rubber, Indian jute, Mexican henequen, Chilean nitrates, Indonesian coffee, and even British textiles bore witness to a corporation's rapid changes in fortune. One economic historian has aptly called this merry-go-round of commodity boom and bust the "commodity lottery," underlining the role of chance as well as design.[177]

Moreover, market power, the ability to control the flow and prices of a commodity, rested with different actors along the chain at different times and places.[178] Indeed, the same commodity often participated in several chains with different end uses and destinations. This was the case when the Peruvian and

Bolivian coca leaf, which inured Andean peasants to high-altitude sickness when chewed or drunk as a tea domestically, was converted to cocaine (and grown in Java) to become a local anesthesia for surgeries in Europe, the United States, and Japan, to flavor the soft drink Coca-Cola, and later to become a recreational drug in the cities of North America and Western Europe. Social and political attitudes also evolved, from seeing coca as a traditional marker of indigenous identity and an aid to strenuous labor of the working class; to viewing cocaine as a sign of modernity, a heroic medical commodity of the late nineteenth century, and a mainstay of the emerging pharmaceutical industry; to finally labeling the substance as an outlaw and international pariah today.[179]

As pointed out already, we do not assume that the world outside of Western Europe and North America was "peripheral" to the world economy. On occasion Latin Americans, and to a lesser extent Asians and Africans, were the price makers and developed the cutting-edge production technology. The global South—or at least enclaves in it—was sometimes dynamic and prosperous.

We intend to question the agricultural/industrial divide so common to traditional "modernization" accounts of this period. It is a remnant of an Orientalist or tropicalist worldview that implies a sharp break between "the West and the rest." Too often it is assumed that agriculture required sweat while industry demanded mechanization and capital. Agriculture is seen as nature's bounty, as the result of natural resource endowment, a crude raw material, while industry is seen as instead reflecting human innovation.[180] Consequently, agriculture is seen as growing incrementally over time, simply applying traditional methods to wider swaths of land, rainfall, and sunshine; industry, in contrast, develops, invariably bringing something new and creative to the production process.

The divide between agriculture and industry was much narrower than that dichotomy implies. Prometheus inspired both.[181] The processing of agricultural goods took place in the fields *and* in the factories. Steam, electric, and petroleum-driven machines for processing and transporting came to the countryside. There were remarkable botanical, chemical, and mechanical innovations in the rural sector, some of which would shape industrial processes in urban centers.

Indeed, agro-industry, which had existed already for four hundred years in the form of the sugar plantation complex, took firm root in numerous regions of the post-1870 world. Production of primary products almost tripled in the period 1880–1913, accounting for almost two-thirds of international trade by World War I.[182] This swelling of primary products complemented industrialization because Western Europe's urbanization and population growth increasingly led it to turn overseas for food and raw materials. Not surprisingly, then, by 1914 six of the world's richest countries in per capita terms were largely exporters of primary products: Argentina, Australia, Canada, New Zealand, Sweden, and the United States.[183]

At the start of our period, long-distance trade tended to be exchanges of exotics, goods that could be grown, harvested, or mined only in certain ecological niches. To bear transport costs and market transaction costs, they needed to have a high value-to-weight ratio. Before the widespread usage of steamships and refrigeration, and certainly before air transport, the goods had to be durable and relatively imperishable. Table 4.7 shows an estimate for the value of seaborne merchandise.

TABLE 4.7

Seaborne merchandise, 1860–1887, by value (in millions of pounds sterling)

Merchandise	Value
Coal	410
Iron	480
Timber	660
Grain	1,050
Sugar	1,130
Petroleum	180
Cotton	180
Salt	18
Wine	510
Coffee	840
Meat	560
Sundries	24,982
Total	31,000

Source: Michael G. Mulhall, *The Dictionary of Statistics,* 4th ed. (London: G. Routledge and Sons, 1899), 130.

Although the large share that is not discriminated by item diminishes the analysis, Table 4.7 covers the most valuable transcontinental commodities. Those with high weight-to-value ratios, like coal, iron, timber, and even cotton, were less likely to travel long distances. The world market clearly was not based simply on utility. Otherwise the value of coal, iron, and timber would have far exceeded that of sugar and coffee, and clean water would have been perhaps the leading commodity.

Grains

The global market for wheat, which was one of the world's most important and geographically far-flung commodities and enjoyed some of the most advanced agricultural technology, provides a major case study of globalization in this period. The sheer magnitude of the wheat trade defies easy description, and the enormous amounts of grain in transit during this era stimulated all kinds of businesses related to transportation, storage, and marketing. This year-round crop developed a dense network of businesses related to transport and storage; it gave rise to standardized grading and a futures market that turned grains (and later many other commodities) into monetary abstractions; it led to innovations in processing, marketing, and advertising; and it brought boomlets to a variety of hard-fiber producers whose products were needed for binder twine. Most importantly, wheat, together with rice, fed cities throughout the world. So successful was it that even historic rice eaters like the Chinese and Japanese and coarse-grain consumers in Eastern Europe and the Middle East turned increasingly to wheat, often imported wheat. The most prominent wheat frontiers had a striking similarity: all were land-abundant and labor-scarce. But each region responded to those resource allocations differently, despite producing for an increasingly well-integrated national and international market. Wheat's central place in the world economy demands that we give it special attention. Its contrast with the other staff of life, rice, leads us to also give the Asian grain detailed study.

"Give us this day our daily bread" took on a whole new meaning between 1870 and 1945, thanks to a revolution in the global grains trade. The diet of millions of consumers worldwide was profoundly altered and enriched as declining grain prices and improvements in modern milling not only permitted consumers to

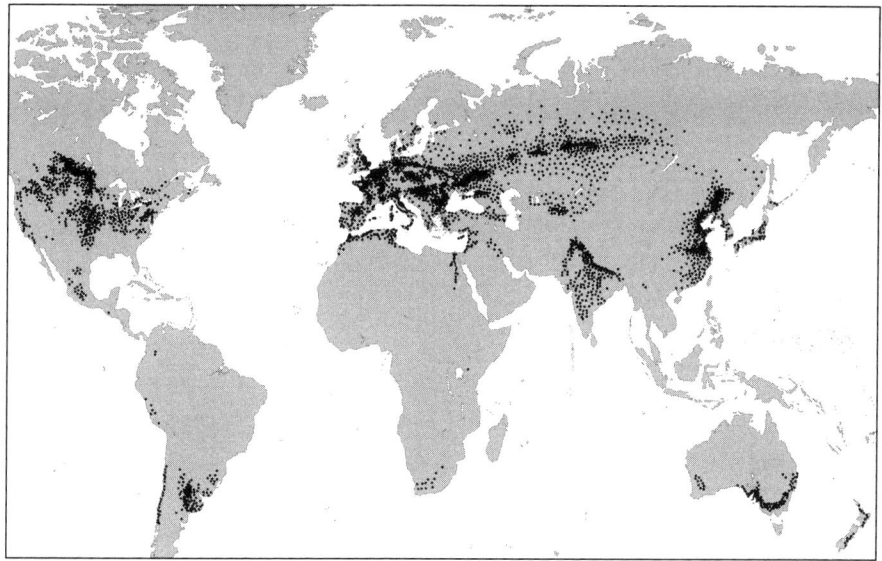

Global production of wheat, ca. 1913–1925.

choose from an assortment of bread flours and rice, but for the first time brought to the tables of the middle and working classes a seemingly endless array of pastas, crackers, biscuits, and ready-to-eat breakfast foods.

Pegging the start of a global grains trade is a matter of some scholarly dispute. Some fix it as early as the 1830s and point to falling cereal prices in Europe during that decade as evidence that continental farmers were responding to the distant drumbeat of competition abroad.[184] Although Russian grain exports via the Black Sea port of Odessa had served European markets for much of the first half of the nineteenth century, prior to the repeal of the (British) Corn Laws in 1846 most countries remained largely self-sufficient in bread grains.[185] Grain price differentials between homegrown and imported grains may have been on the decline over the following decades, but it was after 1870 that a veritable tidal wave of cheap wheat, coarse grains (rye, barley, oats, and corn), rice, linseed, and alfalfa began moving across continents and seas, altering what Europe's proletarians ate while sending its farmers clamoring for relief.

Always a bastion of protectionism, continental Europe refused to go down without a fight. Determined to defend their tradition-bound farmers from the onslaught of cheap cereals from temperate settler societies on the Canadian and US prairies, the Argentine pampas, as well as the fields of Russia, Romania, India, and Australia, Western and Central European governments imposed stiff tariffs to stanch the flow of imported grains and to cushion the impact of falling prices on their farmers.

France's response was typical. Always a family affair, as late as 1921, 85 percent of its farms were twenty-five acres or less. French farmers were generally reluctant to embrace change or adopt new technologies, yet they insisted on government protection to insulate them from more efficient competition from abroad. And they were a very effective lobby. Politicians invariably came to their rescue: one observer wrote, "There is no tolerance by the French government of the proposition that wheat might be more cheaply imported. Every reduction of the wheat area is regarded as a national disaster."[186]

Interestingly, doubts about the relative merits of the trade were voiced not just in Europe. Even experts in countries dedicated to grain exports expressed reservations. Writing in 1867, an Australian extension agent pointed out: "To produce cereals largely beyond our own requirements for home consumption . . . will prove an extremely hazardous speculation . . . sending grain out of the country . . . is like selling a portion of our birthright—the soil's fertility."[187]

Doubting Thomases and populist protectionism, so prevalent for much of the 1870s and 1880s, however, were powerless in face of the onrushing market revolution. The continent's breadbasket increasingly was outsourced as population growth in Europe outpaced cereal production during the late nineteenth and early twentieth centuries. Once proudly self-reliant, Central and Western Europe by World War I were importing more than 30 percent of their wheat needs.

In Great Britain, where the dogma of free trade was not just empty rhetoric, little prompting was required. In 1883 *The Economist* did not seem troubled in the slightest by a growing dependence on imported grain:[188]

People think of the old days when the British harvest really fed the British people. Now we have to go further afield. A good wheat harvest is still as much needed as ever to feed our closely packed population. But it is the harvest already turning brown in the scorching sun of Canada and the Western States— the wheat already ripe in India and California, not the growth alone of the

Eastern counties and of Lincolnshire, that will be summoned to feed the hungry mouth of London and Lancashire.

Wheat acreage dipped from three and a half million acres to under two million acres in a little more than thirty years. By 1914, 80 percent of the United Kingdom's wheat and flour consumption came from abroad. Britain may have built tariff walls around its Commonwealth to keep other commodities out after World War I, but it arguably did more to sustain the global grains trade than any other nation, just as it was at the center of the tea and sugar trades. Between 1909 and 1937 Great Britain alone absorbed 30 to 40 percent of the world's wheat exports. That gave British grain importers, as one expert opined, "commanding importance" in the setting of international grain prices.[189]

Reduced transportation and insurance costs, low land and labor costs, the mechanization of agriculture, and a host of technological and scientific improvements in the cultivation, harvesting, transport, and marketing of grains all contributed to what economic historians refer to as "dramatic price convergence" in the global grain market. Improvements such as the standardization of grain varieties, inspection protocols, the increased usage of commercial as well as natural fertilizers (such as animal manure and clover), the periodic rotating in of crops that restored nutrients to the soil, like alfalfa and maize, and the adoption of early-maturing and hardier, drought- and rust- (or mold-) resistant varieties all prompted greater market integration and heightened productivity.

Plant breeders scoured the world in search of varieties that met local needs and created hybrids that combined the best attributes of different strains. As a recent study of biological innovation has demonstrated, specimens from the old periphery of cereal producers in Eastern Europe, Russia, and North Africa became the genetic building blocks for new varieties that then flourished in the settler societies of the Americas and Australasia. But scientific experimentation traveled no predictable path, as new hybrids moved in multiple directions. "By the early twentieth century the new generations of successful European wheats—distinct varieties tailored for the United Kingdom, France, Germany, or Italy—often contained germplasm introduced from North America and Australia." Plant breeders were celebrated for their accomplishments; for instance, the likeness of Australia's William Farrer, the nation's foremost wheat scientist, who experimented with "130 varieties of wheat under cultivation and had made approximately 1,500 crosses," appeared on Australia's two-dollar bill.[190]

Beginning in the 1830s, revolutionary advances in labor-saving farm implement machinery replaced the scythe and sickle. Cyrus McCormick's mechanical reaper, John Deere's steep plows, the twine or self-binding harvester that automatically gathered the grain up in sheaves, and the combined harvester-thresher (or combine) all increased productivity. The combine, powered by the internal combustion engine and petroleum, which first made its appearance in the 1890s, could cut a ten- to fifteen-foot swath through grain fields, lopping off the heads of the yellow stalks and sweeping "through miles upon miles of ripened grain." One knowledgeable writer waxed enthusiastic about this new machinery.[191]

> [It is] the most wonderful of modern harvest machinery; it not only cuts, gathers, threshes, and cleans the wheat, but even sacks the grain without a touch from man's hand; the only human labor is sewing up the sacks . . . one man can easily operate this machine, with a boy to ride the lead horse, and in one day it is possible to cut and thresh the grain from six to ten acres.

Estimates had the combine saving 3.6 to 5.4 cents a bushel.[192] The tractor, which followed soon on its heels, continued the mechanization mania.

These new machines made economic sense only where large areas of grain could be harvested, privileging land-extensive, labor-scarce regions like the North American prairies, the Argentine pampas, and southern and western Australia. As late as 1914 only 270 combine harvesters were manufactured in the United States; fifteen years later, 36,957 had been built. Similarly, the numbers of tractors on North American farms skyrocketed from 30,000 in 1916 to 850,000 twelve years later. Cereal production, as a result, became a much more capital-intensive undertaking. Fewer workers and draft animals were needed, the per-acre cost of harvesting was slashed, but much larger acreage was required to justify the expense.[193] Traditional grain producers, who had an abundance of labor or lacked an open frontier or the necessary infrastructure, chose not to mechanize, putting them at a decided disadvantage with their competitors.

Thanks to the telegraph and the transatlantic cable, international sales "that were formerly awaited for two or three months are now flashed by electricity over the whole world during the same day on which they are made."[194] Farmers, dealers, and speculators in the Americas or Australia had at their fingertips specialized and detailed data on how much wheat was in storage worldwide, what and how much was "afloat" on the oceans, and what their Russian or Indian competitors' prospects were for the next harvest (or harvests). Price differences between the home market and the grain exporter, which might have been ignored prior the advent of the cable, now presented golden opportunities for merchants and speculators.[195] As one observer noted in 1912:[196]

> If a telegram is received saying that the monsoon in India is overdue; that the drought in Kansas has been broken; that a swarm of grasshoppers has been seen in Manitoba; that a hot wind is blowing in Argentina; that navigation on the Danube is unusually early; that bad roads in the Red River Valley are preventing delivery; that ocean freights to China have risen; or that Australian grain "to arrive" is freely offered in London, prices rise or fall to a degree that corresponds to the importance attached to the news.

On one level this made farmers and traders more vulnerable to price fluctuations around the globe, but that susceptibility, as we shall see, would lead to the creation of futures markets that (at least in theory) spread risks and helped diminish the volatility of cereal markets. A new class of professional speculators emerged, willing to assume risks previously considered unacceptable to local and regional grain dealers or farmers.[197]

As a result, the price differential between British and American wheat tumbled from 54 percent in 1870 to zero at the onset of World War I, while barley and oats price gaps dropped from 46 percent to 11 percent and 138 percent to 28 percent, respectively, over the same time frame. Small- and medium-size European grain farmers, unlike their North and South American counterparts, may have been more reluctant to invest in American-made McCormick reapers and Deering binders, but they realized that their productivity had to improve and their costs had to be cut if they hoped to meet the competition and remain solvent. Rather than emulate their mechanized competitors, many European peasants either voted with their feet and headed across the seas to seek employment out on the burgeoning grain frontiers or switched to other cash crops, which, thanks to the liberal adoption of guano and nitrate fertilizers imported from Peru and Chile, respectively, were more remunerative.[198] The Americas benefited either way. The immigrants went mostly to the United States or South America, and until German chemists synthesized nitrates at the end of the nineteenth century, Peru and Chile enjoyed enormous windfall profits from their guano and nitrate exports, which for a while strengthened both states and gave a push to economic development. It also radicalized labor and introduced nationalist politics.[199]

Clearly this global cereal market did not exist in a vacuum; a rise in one grain's prices could trigger a corresponding increase in the price of another, especially in locales where the markets for different cereals converged. Given the enormous size of the wheat market, it became, in effect, the price leader of the trade in all grains. Under normal market conditions there was a correlation between its price and that of other coarse grains, such as barley and rye. But the same appeared to be true about wheat's relationship to rice, two grains that heretofore had catered to different clienteles. It may be an overstatement to argue, as one scholar does, that "rice and wheat were not separate markets, but together formed a basic market for food grains," but more so than in the past, price and availability, rather than preference, dictated what people ate.[200]

Improvements in water-powered milling during this period not only resulted in the grinding of more flour but improved the taste and extended the shelf life of certain varieties of wheat, opening the eyes and palates of German and Russian peasants, who were now more willing to supplement their customary allegiance to rye. The same could be said for Japanese and Chinese consumers, who continued to express a cultural and gustatory preference for rice but now were complementing their diet by producing and importing vast quantities of wheat for noodles. As anthropologist Sidney Mintz notes, preferences in diet and food habits are unpredictable and shift and change over time. "These addings-on and gradual eliminations are often hard to explain, for they proceed against a substantial, persisting stability of diet at the same time."[201] Prior to World War I, China imported 2,000 metric tons of wheat; by 1930 it was purchasing 580,000 metric tons a year; during the same time frame Japan almost quadrupled its imports from 93,000 to 350,000 metric tons. Japanese policy makers were so alarmed at this influx that they made food self-sufficiency a priority, and by 1935 domestic wheat production had increased by 60 percent.[202]

Wheat was the most valued and easily shipped of the boxcar lot of grains, and during this period wheat and rice became staples of preference for four out

of five of the earth's inhabitants. Remarkably adaptive to heat, cold, and different soil types, wheat could be grown just about anywhere, from Sitka, Alaska, to
Patagonia, save for the hot, low-lying regions of the tropics. Wheat even prospered at the equator; Ecuadorian and Colombian farmers successfully raised the
crop in upland regions. It was almost indifferent to soil type, so long as the ground
retained moisture. One expert was only slightly exaggerating when he opined, "It
is as much at home in the sands of North Africa as in the 'black lands' of Russia."[203]
The only region where wheat was ungrowable was the lowland, monsoon belt in
Asia, where it was shunted to highland areas.[204]

Wheat farming was not without its challenges. Susceptible to inclement
weather, winterkill, blight, rust, and insects, it encouraged farmers in temperate
regions to diversify their holdings. Even so, frontier production would not be
denied, as farmers overcame each of nature's challenges and world exports surged
nearly sixfold from 130.5 million bushels in 1873–1874 to a peak of 747.9 million
bushels in 1924–1929. Ultimately, with the notable exception of many parts of
Latin America and Africa where maize still held sway, wheat's transcendence
would relegate the other coarse grains to animal fodder (although barley was
used to make beverages).[205]

By the end of World War II, more than forty countries were producing the
ubiquitous grain, but, perhaps surprisingly, only a relative handful were active
participants in the global grains trade.[206] China was the exception that proved the
rule. Although statistics must be used with care, one estimate of China's annual
wheat crop in the early 1930s was five hundred million bushels, making it one of
the three largest wheat producers at the time. Yet little of that entered international trade markets. So production was not always synonymous with exports.[207]

It was, more than anything, the rise of an urban, industrial working class
during the Second Industrial Revolution in Europe and the United States that
helps explain this surge in demand and the export of enormous quantities of
wheat from the grain frontiers. One might expect that falling wheat prices would
eventually discourage producers in neo-Europes, but such was not the case. The
worldwide growth of demand for bread flours, fueled by population growth and
lower grain prices, meant that except for certain moments in the 1870s and then
again in the early 1890s, the demand for wheat and flour continued to outstrip
supply up until 1930. As a result, neo-Europes continued to increase acreage

throughout the period. Prior to World War I, enhanced yield per acre best explains increases in productivity, but after the war a spike in planted acreage accounts for the increase in world wheat production.[208]

The Great Depression would put an end to this era of expansion, as gluts, production quotas, and higher tariff walls prompted a time of reckoning for grain farmers. Protectionism was back in vogue, as government or quasi-governmental control boards monitored transactions, provided farmers with subsidies, and established strict rules to limit the acreage planted with certain grains. Moreover, European colonials gave preference to their dependencies. In 1933 an International Wheat Agreement was reached by eighteen European countries and the big-four exporters to set export quotas and reduce acreage. But the best efforts of diplomats to regularize production were for naught, undermined by the absence of an enforcement mechanism. It was the mid-1930s dust bowl in North America, not international agreements, that (tragically for some) reduced the glut of surplus grain.[209]

It may be surprising that government regulation in some cases spurred greater productivity and capitalization though its intent was to insulate farmers from depressed markets. During the New Deal, economic historian Sally Clarke contends, farm sector productivity soared. American farmers, taking advantage of stable grain prices, new sources of credit, and changes in marketing by farm implement manufacturers, invested increasingly in tractors, combines, and trucks. Regulatory agencies gave farmers much-needed breathing space by providing long-term security against price fluctuations in the grain market. With prices stabilized, farmers were not as concerned about savings and more willing to assume debt.[210]

At a time when increasing numbers of rural Americans moved to urban areas in search of employment and the number of farms diminished, the size and scope of the remaining farms increased significantly. By investing in biological and chemical inputs, such as hybrid seeds, insecticides, herbicides, and chemical fertilizers, US farmers, despite operating under the constraints of bad economic times, were more willing to invest in costly machinery than they had been during the 1920s. Of course, taking on such heavy debts was a complex calculus. As Clarke notes, farmers not only replaced their horses and oxen with machines, but when they invested in a tractor, farmers made not one but a series of decisions.[211] Now they needed to buy fuel, lubricants, and repair parts rather than raise feed for horses. Horses no longer supplied manure; the farmers had to switch to commercial fertilizers. Moreover, they often needed to purchase additional land to better realize the machinery's cost savings. Thus, the capital-intensive, mega family farms that Americans are so familiar with today were the product not only of market forces, but also of calculated governmental strategies to bolster grain prices, credit, and productivity.

Given the ebb and flow of business cycles and wars, it is not surprising that there was a shakeout in the export trade during this period. Prior to World War I, Russia, Argentina, Australia, Canada, and the United States dominated grain exports. The Russian case illustrates just how difficult it was to maintain market share in such a competitive market. Before the war, Russian peasants continued to produce and consume rye for the domestic market. But wheat and barley were cultivated for export on the southern steppes on large estates and by wealthier peasants (who supplemented their holdings by leasing lands) on modest properties on the northern shore of the Black Sea where the black soil, even without the benefit of manure or fallowing, was so rich that it sustained higher yields. "Production for export, in competition with young countries of extensive farming," according to an agricultural economist writing in 1930, "did not contribute to intensification, especially in a country of small peasant farmers which, owing to the scattering of its production, was at a disadvantage with its competitors on the world market." The railroad gradually usurped river and canal transport, and storage elevators began to pop up at railheads in the late 1880s. But inspections and grading were not mandated, resulting in dirtier, damaged grain that fetched lower prices on the market. As a result, samples had to be sent abroad before foreign buyers agreed to the transaction. By the onset of World War I, exports of wheat were in decline, while lower-value barley exports were on the rise—not a harbinger of future success. Just as significant, Russian wheat exports to England, always its principal market, were losing out to competition from the Americas and Australia.[212]

Even so, Russia maintained its position as the world's largest wheat exporter in the years leading up to the First World War. But it had to rebuild its agrarian sector from the ground up after the 1917 Bolshevik Revolution and subsequent civil war, as production fell by almost half, prompting a virtual cessation of Soviet exports. The Revolution and its aftershocks also prompted a massive agrarian reform; large estates were broken up and turned into cooperatives and state farms, and the number of peasant households increased dramatically—from twelve million in 1905 to twenty million by 1924.

Desperate for foreign exchange and anxious to regain its preeminent position in the grains trade, the Soviet Union went so far as to collaborate with a New York-based capitalist philanthropy, the American Jewish Joint Distribution Committee, to move more than 150,000 Russian Jews from towns and cities in the Pale of Settlement in western Russia to the rich, black soils of the Crimean steppes and the southern Ukraine. From 1924 to 1938, the Soviets made available nearly two million acres of land, while the philanthropy provided $17 million in aid, tractors, and water-drilling equipment as well as their expertise in crop rotation and high-yield seed varieties. Although initially successful, the partnership between these strange bedfellows foundered during the 1930s, a casualty of Stalin's collectivization and industrialization impulse, the purges of the mid-1930s, and growing Stalinist xenophobia.[213] In the short term, collectivization proved profoundly disruptive to the wheat sector. Significant deficiencies in infrastructure, animal power, and farm implement machinery, coupled with a growing domestic population that consumed ever-greater quantities of grain, hamstrung the Soviet Union's effort to recapture its export markets.[214]

The Soviet Union's dislocation and devastation during and after World War I would be a windfall for the other four principal exporters, who during the interwar period collectively gobbled up Russia's prewar share of the market. During the War to End All Wars, the six great European powers had lost sixty million men, and the continent's soil fertility had been impaired. The result was a precipitous decline in continental cereal production and a fundamental reordering of the international grain market. Cereal producers untouched by the fighting leaped to the forefront. By 1929, Canada, the United States, Argentina, and Australia had cornered more than 90 percent of the market (see Table 4.8). European and Soviet agriculture did recover somewhat, although the latter would never regain its prewar position in the trade. But European cereal producers could

TABLE 4.8

The principal wheat-exporting countries, by market share, 1909–1929

Country	Market share (%)
1909–1914	
Russia	24.5
USA	16.4
Danubian countries[a]	16.2
Canada	14.2
Argentina	12.6
Australia	8.2
India	7.5
1924–1929	
Canada	38.8
USA	22.4
Argentina	19.4
Australia	12.1
Danubian countries[a]	4.6
Soviet Union	1.6
India	1.1

Source: World Agriculture: An International Survey (London: Oxford University Press, 1932), 75.

a. Principally Romania, but the figure also includes exports from other Eastern European countries.

not match their rivals when it came to yield, scale of production, capitalization, mechanization, or infrastructure. Still, economic nationalism and self-sufficiency continued to be championed across the continent, despite (or perhaps because of) their competitors' considerable comparative advantage.[215]

The United States had such a massive domestic market that it—along with China, among the major grain producers—was not reliant on exports. The population of the United States grew from 50.1 million in 1880 to 131.7 million sixty years later; more significantly for US farmers, during the same period urban centers grew from 14.1 million to 74.4 million. By 1940 more than 55 percent of the population lived in urban areas, a fivefold increase since 1880. In fact, as urban demand and population increased, the US domestic market garnered an increasingly larger share of the country's wheat sales. Exports fell accordingly from 23 percent of production in 1922–1927 to a mere 0.3 percent in 1932–1937.[216] That, coupled with high tariffs, made it difficult for competitors to crack the protected US market. By contrast, sparsely populated Canada and Argentina had much smaller home markets and had little choice but to ship their wheat and flour greater distances across the Atlantic, thereby incurring higher costs.

And distances mattered. Even though the US grain producers turned inward during this period, they and their Canadian neighbors had a powerful advantage over other wheat producers. Whereas Canadian and American producers only had to ship their grain exports 3,000 miles, it was 12,000 miles from Sydney to Liverpool and 6,500 miles between Buenos Aires and Great Britain. Grain shipments on clipper ships from California to England traveled 14,000 miles around Cape Horn and took four to five months. Even factoring in the time it took to ship wheat from the prairies to the Eastern Seaboard, Southern Hemisphere wheat, whether from the Southern Cone or from Australia, could take two to three times as long to reach market as wheat from its North American rivals. Australia could not have been a major player in the trade if not for improvements in shipbuilding techniques, the opening of the Suez Canal, and the adoption of the Great Circle Route in the 1850s, which took advantage of more favorable winds and currents between England and Australia, reducing the trip from 120 to 90 days. Steamships with larger carrying capacities replaced clipper ships in this long-distance trade after the 1880s.[217]

Despite such handicaps, expanding grain frontiers found ready markets in Western, Central, and Northern Europe, the Far East, Egypt, South Africa, and New Zealand. Unlike for most commodities, demand for wheat, as a necessary staple, was remarkably inelastic and remained predictably consistent despite frequent price swings; per capita consumption, with some minor variation, hovered around 2.5 bushels even during the depths of the Great Depression. The wheat market may have been susceptible to sharp fluctuations in price and periodic gluts, but that did little to affect overall production levels from year to year. Wheat was not immune, though, to the generalized slump in commodity prices during the mid-1870s, the early 1890s, and after 1920. As one agricultural survey noted in 1932, it was not overproduction but the importers' lack of purchasing power that precipitated the crisis; "the root of the farmer's difficulties lay in the general financial situation and in the general dislocation of international trade."[218]

The sheer magnitude of the wheat trade defies easy description: the average carrying capacity of boxcars in the United States during the late nineteenth century was eleven hundred bushels, and it was not unusual for trains to "haul sixty such cars." Minneapolis, which milled more flour than any other US regional distribution center, received upward of ninety million bushels annually, but that paled in comparison to its northern neighbor Winnipeg, which regularly handled more than double that amount.[219]

Great Lakes whaleback steamers, resembling Viking longboats, transported flour from Minneapolis or grain from Duluth or Chicago, carrying cargoes containing as much as three to four hundred thousand bushels. Transatlantic sailing ships, which once dominated the grains trade, gradually gave way to steam liners and tramps during the last few decades of the nineteenth century, because it was so much more cost-effective and efficient to move the vast quantities of grain by steamship. Tramps could carry the harvest of fifteen thousand acres of wheat land, while ocean liners could hold twice that. Within the Americas, however, the iron horse soon eclipsed water transport. In the United States alone, by 1876, 83 percent of all the grain transported to the Eastern Seaboard was sent by rail.[220]

More than any other improvement, the railroad opened up grain frontiers in settler societies, giving wheat farmers a cheaper and more efficient way to get their product to market and making it cost-effective to open up new lands for development. In some cases, development-minded politicians gave railway companies vast expanses of frontier lands as a subsidy, which the companies then made available to would-be farmers. Now instead of having to farm near fertile river valleys, farms sprung up along recently opened railway corridors. Farmers' expectations were raised as costs fell. Grain producers now thought in terms of filling boxcars instead of sacks of grain. "By the Civil War," as environmental historian William Cronon notes, railroads "could pull enormous loads at better than twenty miles per hour on end—far longer than horses or people could move a tiny fraction of that load at less than half that speed." Because railroads had such high fixed costs and because the costs of loading and unloading grain were the same whether the boxcar was hauled a short or a long distance, railway companies stood to realize larger profits (or smaller losses) on longer journeys. To encourage such long-distance shipments, railways offered discounts to more-distant grain farmers.[221]

Railway companies became just as reliant on hauling grain as wheat farmers were on the railroad. In Argentina alone grain was nearly 40 percent of total freight tonnage. This transport revolution also redirected the flows of grains. In the United States, Chicago became not only the gateway to the West, but the point of departure for midwestern and western grain shipments to the Eastern Seaboard and beyond. The same phenomenon developed over the next few decades, with minor variations, in Canada, Argentina, and Australia. In some cases governments proactively assisted their farmers by pressuring railway companies to cut freight charges. In Canada, where grain had to be transported great distances, policy makers drove down freight rates so that their farmers' wheat remained competitive, but in Argentina, where grain was carried hundreds rather thousands of miles to the ports of Rosario, Bahía Blanca, and Buenos Aires, the state was reluctant to pressure its British-owned railway companies.[222]

Given the enormous amounts of grain on the move, methods of storing and transferring the grain from rail to ship became indispensable. In the United States, railway companies, grain dealers, cooperatives, and in some cases individual farmers built massive wooden elevators at local and regional markets, at railheads, and at primary distribution centers. They not only loaded and unloaded the grain from and to wagons, boxcars, and the holds of ships, but stored, cleaned, dried, and gathered the wheat. Cronon has called the steam-powered elevator, which got the grain "off the backs of individual workers and into automatic machinery," the most important innovation "in the history of American agriculture." Henceforth, grain entering primary markets like Chicago had to be sackless—"in this way corn or wheat were more like liquids than solids, like golden streams that flowed like water."[223]

Chicago became a first mover in the construction of terminal elevators, giving it a tremendous advantage over its rivals. "They [Chicago's distribution centers] can receive and ship 430,000 bushels in ten hours ... in busy seasons these figures are often doubled by running nights." Public and private warehouses in that city could hold upward of fifty-six million bushels of grain, a study of wheat reported in 1912. Once it was inside the giant elevator bins, "workers

Unloading grain at the Great Northern Railroad elevator in Buffalo, New York, ca. 1900. Given the enormous amounts of grain on the move, methods of storing, cleaning, drying, and transferring the grain became indispensable. Major flour corporations built multiple manufacturing plants closer to the sources of production and sought out sites that reduced their transaction costs. Thanks to the rise in importance of the Great Lakes as a conduit for western US and Canadian wheat, and the abundance of cheap electrical power from Niagara Falls, by 1930 Buffalo was the world's leading milling center. (Library of Congress)

could deliver grain to a waiting ship or railway car simply by opening a chute at the bottom of the building and letting gravity do the rest of the work." The cost of moving a bushel of grain from railroad to ship was half a cent.[224]

The advent of the elevator, railroad, and the steamship (and the resulting fall in freight charges and insurance costs) meant that land considered marginal at best for wheat cultivation was now considered ripe for expansion. In North America the frontier moved ever westward, as Minnesota, the Dakotas, and Kansas replaced Illinois, Indiana, Wisconsin, and Ohio as the top wheat-producing states. Across the northern border, Saskatchewan replaced its more eastern neighbors as the premier provincial producer on the Canadian prairies.[225]

Breadbasket Variations

The new grain frontiers were by definition land-abundant and labor-scarce, historically considered unattractive backwaters before their future was synchronized to the wheat boom. At first glance, two of these new breadbaskets, Argentina and Canada, appear to have much in common. Both recently had achieved nationhood; each sought to replicate the path followed by US grain farmers; each had at its disposal vast public lands well suited for cultivation once indigenous groups had been summarily pushed out of the way, put on reservations, or annihilated; both featured highly speculative land markets that drove up prices; in each case, the railway system, which was initially paid for, built, and managed in the main by British companies, proved indispensable, not just in getting grain to market but in opening up new lands for cultivation; each enticed European immigrants to populate their rural hinterlands; they welcomed mechanization; and for the most part both fed the same market, Great Britain.

Yet even though they shared similar resource endowments, these temperate frontier societies are a study in contrasts, evolving in markedly different ways. Ever since Frederick Jackson Turner, scholars have debated whether frontiers, acting as a kind of demographic escape valve, fostered the yeoman farmer and a more egalitarian ethic. Theorists have posited that a tradition of family farms that took hold on the Great Plains and the Canadian prairies helped to inculcate a democratic and populist ethos. But not all grain frontiers were created alike, nor did they evolve in the same way. Argentina privileged large landed estates, tenancy, and an authoritarian tradition (as did Chile, Romania, Russia, and India). Argentine dependency theorists and some Canadian staples theorists contend that external forces (in Argentina's case, often in collusion with native landholding oligarchs) provide the best explanation for the failure of these vast regions, over the long haul, to live up to their potential. But Argentina and Canada were both reliant on British capital and markets, yet they took demonstrably different paths. It is the internal dynamic—land tenure, labor relations, infrastructure, and government policies—that best explains why and how different settler societies responded the way that they did to the global grain market.[226]

Pastoral pursuits—cattle and sheep farming—had dominated rural life in Argentina prior to the 1880s boom in cereal production. Fresh off a successful military campaign against Indians in the late 1870s that added 175,000 square miles to the national domain, the Argentine state moved aggressively to open up its great plains, or pampas, which extend in a large semicircle three hundred to four hundred miles south, west, and north of the national capital, Buenos Aires. Even though Argentina tried to emulate the US yeoman-farmer homesteading model, its bureaucrats had little appreciation for the value of regulation and oversight. Because of official negligence, coupled with easy credit and outright fraud, a speculative land market emerged on the pampas that privileged large landholdings at the expense of family farms.

Some elite families, who initially had catered to the hides and jerked beef markets and then switched over the course of the nineteenth century to wool and beef production, gobbled up tens of thousands of hectares of land on the pampas. They were responding to the dramatic expansion of the international chilled mutton and beef market made possible by *frigorificos,* refrigerated steamships that brought relatively good-quality meat to Europe and especially England beginning at the end of the nineteenth century. So valuable did this become that some of the largest packing companies in the world, like Chicago's Armour and Swift, built plants in Argentina. They took advantage of new canning technology that used tin containers to preserve meat. Ultimately the packing industry would transform politics in Argentina as meat packers became some of the most unionized and militant workers in the country and a foundation of Peronism.[227]

But in 1924 the rural elite still ruled. In Buenos Aires Province, fourteen families owned more than 100,000 hectares each; one family alone acquired 412,000 hectares. As historian Jeremy Adelman writes, "the Argentine frontier, unlike its North American counterpart, was not an empty land on which the State could create a society of owner-producing agrarian units. Grazing antedated the movement to enclosure, and was a lucrative enterprise."[228] Because the State did not impede the concentration of land, cattle barons sold off their sizable patrimonies only when land prices were on the rise. Yet even if property relations precluded homesteading, that did not mean that Argentine ranchers were irrational or inefficient. Cereal production always had to compete with a prosperous cattle economy.[229]

Wheat would have to earn its pride of place on the pampas; skeptical cattle ranchers only grudgingly turned portions of their holdings over to agriculture in response to rising world grain prices. In their eyes, farming was always a secondary activity, a safety valve to turn to when beef prices were depressed. This prioritizing of ranching is perhaps also explained by the greater capitalization and labor inputs required by grain. And even after it became the nation's chief source of foreign exchange, wheat still had to vie with a number of additional rivals, including sheep, maize, alfalfa, and flax or linseed. Despite this crowded field of competitors, attractive wheat prices, state-sponsored European immigration, and government subventions for railway construction led to a surge in wheat production in the 1890s. Between 1890 and 1910, wheat acreage increased nearly fivefold from 3.2 million to 15 million, and by 1914 no settlement on the pampas was more than twenty miles from a railroad, making the region competitive with the US Midwest wheat bowl. Despite the considerable revenues wheat generated, the nation's skewed land-tenure regimen and the oligarchy's political clout made certain that this precocious newcomer never challenged ranching for primacy. No presidential administration between 1880 and 1930 enacted any substantive policies to aid wheat agriculture; land reform for smallholders was out of the question.[230]

Breaking the pampa sod was so labor intensive and costly that, to contain labor costs, cattle barons leased portions of their ranches to tenants. This reliance on tenancy was highly unusual; the wheat produced by its principal competitors was predicated on family farms.[231] Startup costs for Argentine tenants were modest. They, in turn, hired seasonal workers at harvest time, not infrequently "swallows" *(golondrinas)* who had emigrated from Italy or Spain to seed the crop or work the harvest and then return home. Government policies were redesigned to address the labor market, rather than to encourage immigrants to become settlers on the land. *Golondrinas,* who earned three to six times the wages of Argentine peons, traveled to Argentina after the fall harvest in Europe, worked through to February, and then returned home in time to plant in the spring. One should be careful not to overstate the importance of *golondrinas* for agricultural production; recent scholarship has documented the increasingly important role played by the domestic urban and rural labor sectors, which complemented imported labor on the pampas.[232] Nonetheless, the Argentine model of seasonal international labor migration for agricultural workers would not be imitated anywhere else until Mexican workers were hired in the United States under the US government-sponsored Bracero program during and after World War II (though temporary—if not seasonal—workers were brought a shorter distance overseas from India to work in tea in the neighboring British colony of Ceylon, as also happened with Haitian workers in Cuban sugar). Only in Argentina was agricultural labor sufficiently remunerative, because of labor shortages, and transport sufficiently cheap, because of vast exports, that this system of interoceanic commutes could work.

It may seem counterintuitive, but immigrant tenants turned out to be tough negotiators; they demanded land at low rents, and if ranchers did not comply, they had several good options. They could pack up after a few years and seek out lease arrangements on other ranches, return home, or seek employment in Argentina's urban centers. But tenancy also was beneficial to ranchers, giving them the flexibility they desired to respond to the vagaries of the market. During the 1920s, when beef prices collapsed, many ranchers converted their properties into grain farms, while others rented out parts of their cattle ranches and carried over their tenants' lease contracts.[233] When beef prices rebounded, however, more land reverted to pasture.

Argentines also eagerly embraced mechanization on the wheat frontier; 1,112 combines were imported in 1921, and by 1929 imports had reached 15,000. But a snapshot of "modern" Argentine wheat farming offers some jarring inconsistencies. A Canadian traveler writing in 1938 noted: "Among these southern and southeastern European tenant farmers one finds the paradox of a mud hut with a bench, a table, and a bed for furniture, but outside a combine harvester, a tractor and a motor truck of the latest models." To tenants, machines were mobile assets they could take with them if or when their current contract ran out. By 1936, combines harvested more than 65 percent of the wheat crop.[234] In fact, the Argentine pampas mechanized faster than its northern rival; Canadian family farms were slow to adopt the combine-harvester. The Canadian government actually worsened matters for its own farmers by setting extremely high tariffs on agricultural machinery to protect its farm implement manufacturers. That kept the costs of mechanization artificially high at home. But farm implement manufacturers, anxious to export their wares abroad, sold their machines overseas for well below what Canadian prairie farmers had to pay. The result was that Ottawa was "subsidizing the Argentine or Australian wheat farmer to assist him in competing with the Canadian wheat farmer in world markets."[235]

The absence of granaries in Argentina meant that marketing began right after harvest. The grain was transported in jute bags and then hauled along pitted country roads by enormous two- or four-wheeled carts with eight-foot wheels. Two-wheelers were hauled by up to twelve to fifteen horses or mules or by eight to sixteen oxen. Only the largest grain dealers had warehouses, so small farmers had to be content with piling wheat outside where it was exposed to the weather.[236] The inability to build an effective marketing system would plague Argentine grain farmers for decades to come.

The pampas had a warmer climate (with little danger of frost or snowfall except in the southernmost districts of Buenos Aires Province) and more fertile soil than the Canadian prairies, and lower labor costs, and its farms had the added advantage of being within two hundred miles of the nation's principal port, Buenos Aires. Their farmers did not have to absorb the cost of transporting their grain by rail across the continent, as their North American rivals did. But Argentines did not make the most of their natural advantages; unlike Canadians, they neglected to invest in agricultural research and education, and so their infrastructure lagged behind that of their competitors.[237]

Unlike in Argentina, where landowners had so many options about what to produce, wheat was king in Canada, the source of 50 to 75 percent of prairie farmers' cash income during the interwar period. A turn-of-the-century Canadian economist estimated that wheat was three times more important to Canada than it was to Argentina or Australia.[238] The fundamental difference between the two breadbaskets was that family farms predominated in Canada. To understand why such different paths were taken in what were in 1914 two of the world's richest countries, we must consider what each region looked like on the eve of their coterminous wheat booms. Unlike the pampas, where ranching on a large scale was a well-established way of life dating back to the early 1800s, the Canadian prairies offered thousands of square miles of open lands that ambitious policy makers were intent on populating and developing with white farmers.[239]

Canadian lawmakers thought they had an imaginative solution to the problem of populating the frontier in which the risks as well as the rewards could be shared with private interests. Ottawa doled out huge chunks of national lands to two companies, the Canadian Pacific Railway and the Hudson Bay Company, which would in turn sell off that land to homesteaders. But the companies could not entice enough settlers to move to the prairies. Despite the railways' arrival in the western prairies, a raft of liberal land legislation, and a variety of inducements to colonists, Canadians and foreign immigrants were initially reluctant to take advantage of the public and private lands made available to them.

Cheap land was not enough. The principal problem was that the United States was a much more attractive option to European immigrants. Settlers did not begin to flock to the Canadian prairies until the mid-1890s, when a bevy of scientific and technological enhancements persuaded immigrants from abroad and migrants from the United States that grain farming north of the border was viable.

First, there was discovered a new strain of hard wheat, Red Fife, that matured twenty days earlier than the next earliest maturing variety—no small matter to prairie farmers who had to cope with the persistent threat of frost in late August and early September. At the same time, innovations in milling techniques made it possible to grind heartier, quicker-ripening varieties like Red Fife into flour.

Two additional innovations clinched wheat's rosy future on the prairies: surface mulching, a moisture-conserving technique that inhibited evaporation on the arid prairies; and dry-farming, which coupled summer fallowing with spring soil compaction to prevent "the passage of the moisture from the sub-surface to the surface by capillary action, thereby trapping the moisture on the soil, so that while the land lay idle, its moisture content would rise—theoretically to a level to sustain crops for at least two successive years."[240]

Recent arrivals from the States were more interested in obtaining a quick return on their investment and took advantage of surging land prices to flip their wheat farms rather than patiently waiting to build up livestock herds. The capital needs for a mixed regimen of livestock and grain were too great for most family-owned farms to bear on the prairies. Moreover, unlike in Argentina, government policies consistently privileged farming at the expense of ranching. Coupled with a speculative land boom that attracted American migrants from the

"Western Canada, the New El Dorado," a promotional poster produced by the Canadian Department of Immigration, ca. 1890–1920. The Canadian prairies were considered a veritable *tabula rasa*—thousands of square miles of open lands that ambitious policy makers were intent on populating and transforming into wheat farms. The government made extensive public lands available to the Canadian Pacific Railway Company and the Hudson Bay Company, which in turn sold the tracts at low cost to Canadians and European immigrants. (Library and Archives of Canada, C-085854)

Dakotas, Montana, and Wisconsin to move across the border, wheat farming took off. Interestingly, speculation did not concentrate land in the hands of a few, as it did in Argentina. Once locked in, wheat farmers found it disadvantageous to shift out of wheat.[241]

Canadian farmers were well aware of the pernicious effects of monoculture, but they felt they had good reasons for sticking with wheat. As one defensive Saskatoon farmer put it:[242]

> I know perfectly well that continuous wheat-farming exhausts the soil, but I know that stock-raising, or at any rate dairy-farming, means continuous and hard work, and I know too wheat-growing requires less capital and less labor and gives bigger returns, and though there is a disadvantage in having all one's eggs in one basket, I am to take the risk and go on growing wheat until the soil will grow it no longer, and then I shall sell out to the tenderfoot and move west.

As a result, wheat became the engine driving Canadian exports. Between 1890 and 1916, the number of farms on the prairies increased from 31,000 to 218,000, while improved acreage soared from 1.4 million to 34.3 million acres. Ultimately, after the frontier had reached its limits, the ecological consequences of monoculture would become all too apparent, but from 1890 to 1945, sowing wheat on the prairies made good economic sense.

Although the Argentine and Canadian governments both aggressively sought European immigrants to populate their hinterlands, their objectives and policies were very different. Argentina's immigration policies were much less selective, because they were not predicated on creating a permanent rural landholding class. Initially Argentine policy makers wanted to attract northern European immigrants, but they quickly settled on southern Europeans, who came cheaper and were willing to work seasonally. Canada's immigration policies were much more restrictive and ethnically discriminating. Ottawa was less interested in creating a fluid and efficient labor market and was more intent on creating family farms on the prairie.

Another salient difference between these two large wheat producers was the cooperative ethic that crystallized on the prairies. The Scandinavian, British, and Central European immigrants who established family farms on the prairies had experience with consumer cooperatives in Europe and, being capital-poor, were willing to pool their resources. By the 1920s the cooperative movement, which pooled members' grain sales, stored their grain, and functioned as a mutual aid association, was firmly entrenched in the wheat-growing districts of western Canada. In contrast, ephemeral tenancy arrangements on the pampas did not lend themselves to collaboration. As a result, Canadian farmers' standard of living and quality of life improved markedly during the 1920s, far exceeding any improvement for their Argentine counterparts.

This brief comparative sketch of these twin breadbaskets illustrates that not all grain producers were created alike, nor did they evolve in the same way. Despite similar resource endowments, domestic forces—such as land tenure, labor systems, and state policies—shaped how Argentina and Canada responded to a highly competitive global grain trade.

Imperial ambitions also tried to shape the grain sectors of colonies. British India's wheat producers on the dry plains of the Punjab were greatly aided by the opening of the Suez Canal in 1873, but railways were slow to make headway across the subcontinent and "the traveler still saw the long lines of camels that were silently and majestically treading their way through the night across the plains to the seaports, in successful competition with the railroads as grain carriers."[243] Although India never satiated the United Kingdom's appetite for grain, it was not for lack of trying. British entrepreneurs invested heavily in railways and canals in the Ganges and Indus River valleys where wheat had been grown for centuries, but much of the wheat they produced stayed at home to feed India's burgeoning population, and the trains mostly carried Indian passengers.[244]

The planting and harvesting of wheat may have been a seasonal preoccupation for farmers, but the trade itself barely enjoyed a respite. Somewhere around the globe farmers were harvesting wheat each and every month of the year, making it possible to stagger the arrival of wheat and flour shipments to ensure that Europeans and other importing nations would not go hungry (see Table 4.9).

One observer of the trade writing in 1911 described when and from where Europeans got their daily bread.[245]

For the greater part of the year there is surplus wheat awaiting shipment on some port on the American coasts, by January and February the wheat exports

TABLE 4.9

The global wheat harvest calendar

Month(s)	Harvest area
January	Australia, New Zealand, Chile
February–March	Upper Egypt and India
April	Lower Egypt, India, Syria, Cyprus, Persia, Asia Minor, Mexico, Cuba
May	Texas, Algeria, Central Asia, China, Japan, Morocco
June	Western, midwestern, and southern USA, Turkey, Greece, Italy, Spain, Portugal, southern France
July	Midwestern USA, northern Canada, Romania, Bulgaria, Austria, Hungary, southern Russia, Germany, Switzerland, southern England
August	Midwestern USA, southern Canada, Colombia, Belgium, Netherlands, Great Britain, Denmark, Poland, central Russia
September–October	Scotland, Norway, northern Russia
November	Peru, South Africa, northern Argentina
December	Argentina, Burma, Australia

Source: *The Crop Reporter,* 1899, cited in Peter Dondlinger, *The Book of Wheat: An Economic History and Practical Manual of the Wheat Industry* (New York: Orange, Judd Co., 1912).

from the Pacific coast of the United States have begun to arrive in Europe in considerable quantities; in March, the wheat ships from Argentina and Uruguay are arriving in Europe with their first cargoes of importance; winter wheat of the United States first reaches the ports of Western Europe in August; U.S. spring wheat begins to cross the Atlantic in considerable quantities in October, and Canada spring wheat in November.

To the serendipitous constellation of forces that propelled the transformation of the international grain market, we must add one more critical enhancement that arguably was more critical in propelling the expansion of the trade than any other single factor—the futures market.

Hedging Futures

Futures not only greased the wheels of credit, they sustained a continuous, year-round market, thus making possible the sale of much larger quantities of grain than ever before.[246] The principal innovation was to facilitate future delivery of grain through standardized contracts. Now farmers, millers, jobbers, and exporters had an incentive to store grain throughout the year. By buying a bushel of wheat that did not yet exist, a merchant was not only taking a risk, but also reinventing the concept of property rights. As we shall see, commodities like wheat became useful tools to gamble on, whether or not that bushel of grain ever left the farm. Along with its contemporary, the cotton exchange, the grains futures market laid the foundation for a dizzying array of commodity futures markets, for everything from pork bellies to orange juice and coffee. Multimillion-dollar transactions among strangers continents apart soon replaced a handshake between a farmer and a wholesale jobber. Moreover, futures contracts also acted as a hedge against volatile prices, always the bane of grain markets.

To accomplish this, private grain exchanges, like the Chicago Board of Trade (CBT), imposed a uniform system of weights and measures (with penalties prescribed for offenders) to bring order to what had been a very decentralized and unregulated market. As one expert put it in 1911, without futures markets "the grain trade would be chaos."[247]

In 1856 the CBT set quality standards for three types of wheat. That seemingly simple step proved revolutionary. If a shipment of grain received a certain grade, it could be mixed in elevators or boxcars with other shipments of the same grade. For all intents and purposes it was considered identical. Now when farmers or grain dealers shipped their grain to market, they obtained a receipt that they or anyone else could redeem for payment. These contracts allowed farmers to secure credit from their local bank by simply presenting a "to arrive" contract to the lender, specifying that a certain amount of grain would be delivered at a specified date in the future. These markets proved so successful at increasing sales of grain, raising capital, and managing the trade that a futures market was added in Liverpool in 1883 and in Buenos Aires in 1908.

A futures market could not have come about if warehouse, boxcar, or elevator receipts for specific lots of grain did not mean the same thing in Liverpool as in

New South Wales. When an elevator receipt was as good as the bushels of wheat it represented, then and only then was it possible to buy a contract for the future delivery of a good and be reasonably certain that the buyer would get what he was promised. By 1860 the CBT had identified ten different grades of wheat; quality standards were soon mandated for other coarse grains. By the mid-1880s, the volume of Chicago's futures market was fifteen to twenty times as large as the city's actual grain sales, strong evidence that it was the pieces of paper, not wheat or corn, that speculators were buying.[248]

Because futures contracts had less to do with the sale of the commodity and more to do with the price of those goods at a future date, speculators gambled on whether or how much grain prices would rise or fall. Such arbitrage and fungible grain receipts, of course, could not have become a reality unless sufficient storage capacity, financing, and the necessary transportation and communication infrastructure existed to permit continuous deliveries of grain year-round. Whereas in the past, grain dealers had to build in a substantial margin of five to ten cents a bushel to guard against prices dropping, now, thanks to the opportunities for arbitrage and the standardization of the trade that made it possible, margins were reduced considerably to perhaps a penny per bushel. By trading in futures, at a certain price for a certain grade of grain, risks were shifted theoretically from the farmer and dealer to the speculator, who then offset his exposure by hedging transactions to insure against losses.

Justice Oliver Wendell Holmes welcomed this innovation, noting that, although "speculation does result in evil consequences," governments should be prudent about if and when they meddled in the operation of these markets. In his mind, these self-regulating institutions were proof positive that capitalism had matured.[249] Farmers on the plains likely would find much to disagree with in Justice Holmes's survival-of-the-fittest mentality. Holmes's assertion that "the success of the strong" induced "imitation by the weak" was, however, more than just elitist rhetoric. It reflected a liberal worldview that held that markets control people rather than the other way around.

Unfettered markets, however, invited abuse. After all, the two markets—the actual grain market and the futures market—were, in fact, linked to each other, as tenuous as those ties might seem to be. This became all too apparent when bulls, speculators confident that prices would rise, attempted to "corner" the market. A corner might begin harmlessly enough with bulls quietly buying up futures contracts just before the harvest season, when supplies were at their lowest. Then they would move into the actual grain market, buying up sizable quantities of "spot" wheat as well. Now bulls had control of both present and future supplies of grain. If this was accomplished surreptitiously enough, unsuspecting bears, those who believed that future prices would fall, could be caught unawares. If a bear speculator could not make good on his futures contracts and deliver the grain, he had little choice but to buy grain from bulls who now dictated prices. If bears failed to fulfill their contracts, they could be subject to legal action, their reputations ruined.

Corners, however, entailed significant risks for bulls too. Those stockpiles of actual grain had to be disposed of eventually; holding on to such large quantities of grain indefinitely was costly, but selling them off was risky because putting all that grain up for sale meant that high prices could not be sustained. If bulls could not sell off their grain before prices fell below what they bought the grain for, they faced major losses.

At first glance, the winners or losers of a corner appeared to be confined to speculators playing the futures market. But there were residual effects that could either help or harm all those connected to the grains trade. Any time a market was intentionally distorted, it undermined confidence up and down the grain chain. Successive corners so infuriated the German government that it banned futures trading on the Berlin Exchange in 1897. Most efforts to regulate the trade, however, proved ineffectual; speculators simply picked up and moved their business to another exchange. Meanwhile, farmers and dealers watched helplessly as prices fluctuated up and down with little apparent connection to supply and demand.[250]

With so much out of their control, it is understandable why growers organized to defend their interests by establishing cooperatives like the Grange and by backing populist politicians. They had little faith in the market and little trust in bankers or railroad tycoons. Grading was a subjective matter at best. Farmers were convinced that unscrupulous speculators, railway and elevator operators, and state grain inspectors were conspiring to lowball their grain.

Sealing and Resealing Boxcars

Given the daunting scale of the trade and the relative speed with which it covered enormous distances, oversight to maintain standards and inhibit fraud was essential and increasingly sophisticated. The time and money spent on the maintenance of these protocols were a testament to the cereal trade's budding professionalization and the potential for abuse. Unscrupulous jobbers invariably tried to hide "plugged" (inferior, dirty, or damaged) grain underneath better-quality grain in railway cars or in grain elevators. Too much was at stake for farmers, brokers, millers, railway and elevator operators, shippers, millers, futures traders, and consumers to allow any one of the principals too much latitude.[251]

The linchpin of protocol enforcement in the United States was the state inspector. Walking encyclopedias of wheat minutiae, inspectors had the exacting task of evaluating grain for "color, soundness, and the plumpness of the kernel" in each and every boxcar that arrived at major distribution centers. They tested the weight and determined the grade, providing written justification for their assessment.

Invariably there were complaints from both sellers and buyers about the grades assigned. Elevator operators and railway companies were the usual suspects, accused of mixing grades and tampering with weight scales. Grain making the long forced march across the heartland might be inspected anywhere from three to six times. During a busy time of year, it was not unheard of for a million to a million and a half bushels a day to be inspected and weighed at the Duluth, Minnesota, distribution center. In general, inspection delayed the shipment of grain by one day, so inspection was clearly not too meticulous.[252]

Elsewhere government oversight was lacking. In Argentina, for instance, no state inspection protocol was in place; instead, representatives of buyers would appear at railway stations and personally inspect the jute bags hauled by peons to railway cars "by means of a 'tryer,' a pointed tube that is thrust into each bag bringing out a section of its contents." Buyers often would fix their own standards to the grain, guaranteeing greater variability and more complaints.[253]

The absence of standards put outliers at a competitive disadvantage, as uniformity was prized. But there were limits to this drive for standardization. Wheat may have dominated the diet of much of the world during this era, but certain regions asserted their preference for one or more of its rivals. Barley was king in North Africa; maize the staple of choice in much of the Americas and Africa;[254] rye held sway despite inroads made by wheat in Eastern and Central Europe; and, of course, rice, with the exception of some parts of China and India, had no peer in South, Southeast, and East Asia. With the exception of rice, wherever wheat was preeminent the grains that were its competitors were consigned largely to livestock fodder.

From Millstones to Minneapolis

Consumption of flour increased dramatically during this period, thanks to a slew of innovations that altered the production, distribution, and marketing of bread. Sadly, there were casualties. Millers in particular became an endangered species, as the mass production of flour transformed what had been craft into an industry.

For centuries the making of flour rested in the hands of experienced millers. To mill wheat, skilled artisans furrowed their sandstone millstones with sharp edges, set the stones close together, and ran them at a very high speed. The objective was to grind once through as fine as possible. Popular wisdom had it that millstones were quirky and temperamental, supposedly feminine traits.[255] Only the most practiced millers, who understood their particular stones' idiosyncrasies, could coax sufficient quantity and superior quality out of such finicky machinery.

Beginning in the 1870s a series of innovations was introduced in flour mills springing up along the banks of the Mississippi River near Minneapolis, Minnesota. Taking advantage of the thunderous waterpower cascading down the Falls of St. Anthony, Charles Pillsbury and Cadwallader Washburn's mills refined and improved upon Hungarian and French techniques of milling, and in the process radically transformed how flour was produced worldwide.[256]

In this case, necessity was the mother of invention. Minneapolis millers had ready access to hard spring wheat in their home state and the neighboring Dakotas. This variety, although higher in protein and more gluten-rich than its chief competitor, winter wheat, was harder to grind and more difficult to sift to remove impurities. The most notable change the Minneapolis manufacturers made was to switch from millstones to automatic steel rollers, a modification that produced superior, cleaner, and more uniform flour in greater quantities at reduced costs. The corrugated rollers did 30 percent more work but required 47 percent less power. Where millstones had to be redressed twice a week, the steel rollers ran for months without the need for adjustment.[257]

New techniques were developed to recover valuable elements of the kernel left on the mill floor. Termed "gradual reduction," these extra steps necessitated additional machinery, oversight, and, of course, expense, but gains in productivity more than offset the added cost. Milling now was entirely mechanized and automatic; "from raw material to finished product the stock is treated without the direct intervention of human hands."[258] Gradual reduction demanded copious amounts of energy. New sources of power—first steam and then electricity— were adopted over a period of time to sustain the more complex industrial plants.

At first critics ridiculed Cadwallader Washburn for sinking the unheard of sum of one hundred thousand dollars into his first mill. Even though "Washburn's Folly" experienced some costly growing pains, it was the entrepreneur who enjoyed the last laugh.[259] The innovations were a revelation, especially for farmers in Minnesota, Dakota, and Canada; formerly unpopular with millers and bakers, hard spring wheat was now the bread flour of choice at home and in Europe. Flour produced in Minneapolis by the "New Process," as it was called, produced 12.5 percent more bread, on average, than the best winter wheat flours on the market. Milling capacity skyrocketed. In 1870 a large mill might produce two hundred barrels of flour a day; two decades later, three out of four Minnesota mills were producing more than a thousand barrels a day.

Better-capitalized, high-capacity mills bought their wheat in bulk from farmers and elevator operators and benefited from rebates and an array of transit privileges from railway and shipping companies.[260] Economies of scale also enabled big mills to better service the burgeoning overseas market. By the turn of the century, Minneapolis millers were shipping out sixteen million barrels a year and the city could lay claim to being the greatest flour producer in the world.

Critical to Minneapolis's ascendancy was its commitment to export its flour abroad, especially to Great Britain. By 1880 the United Kingdom absorbed three-fifths of US flour exports; Minneapolis exports alone rose from one million barrels in 1881 to 4.7 million barrels in 1900, much of it to the United Kingdom. In addition Minneapolis flour found its way to Western Europe, Hong Kong, the Philippines, Cuba, Brazil, Haiti, and Jamaica.[261]

The New Process consigned the age-old craft of artisanal milling to the dust-bin of history. It also led to a fundamental reorganization of the flour-milling industry. Experienced millers now found work in large factories as mill managers, while captains of industry with no prior experience in the business took control. Over time Pillsbury's and Washburn's flour mills became two of the world's largest manufacturers, and their brands of flour (Pillsbury and Gold Medal, respectively) not only became mainstays in North American pantries, but were aggressively marketed abroad.[262] Not surprisingly, the high costs associated with mass production and the smaller mills' inability to compete with industry giants at virtually every phase of the commodity chain signaled the death knell for smaller flour mills. In Minneapolis alone, by 1890 four corporations had secured 87 percent of the city's milling capacity.[263]

Foreign investors thought they knew a profitable undertaking when they saw it. Pillsbury, already a well-known brand in England, attracted the interest of a British syndicate in 1889. The syndicate had invested heavily in US railroads and breweries and now turned its attention to flour milling. The investors took control of three of Pillsbury's mills, two additional Minneapolis flour mills, two waterpower companies, and the Minneapolis and Northern Elevator Company. Charles Pillsbury did retain managerial control of the flour mill itself and held significant stock in the new company. As with other Gilded Age industries, however, combinations in the flour business met with considerable resistance and sometimes collapsed under their own weight. Overbuilding, gluts in production, price cutting, low profits, and fierce competition undermined the conglomerates' efforts to corner the market. The British intervention in the Minneapolis flour market proved relatively short-lived. In 1924 the Pillsbury family and other American investors refinanced and absorbed the British holding company.[264]

Despite the obstacles, the lure of consolidation proved irresistible for Washburn's successors at Washburn-Crosby. In 1928 General Mills was born in a massive merger of milling companies in the US Midwest, Southwest, and far West. The conglomerate absorbed twenty-seven companies from sixteen states, making it for that time the largest flour-milling company in the world.[265] (In the United States the name "General" came to signify dominant rather than ordinary, as enormous corporations such as General Motors, General Electric, and General Foods arose.)

Although economic historians disagree on why these combinations occurred during the Gilded Age and what their relative impact was at home and abroad, they generally concur that such consolidations were part of a "managerial revolution"—a revolution that would effectively alter the structures of all kinds of businesses throughout the world.[266]

These capital-intensive industries proved effective only if they fashioned an efficient managerial hierarchy that coordinated purchasing, pricing, production, and marketing. Salaried managers developed long-term and short-term strategies to integrate their enterprise vertically. Integrating "backward," they secured access to raw materials; linking "forward," they created a modern, responsive sales organization to market their goods and services efficiently.[267] General Mills' predecessor, Washburn-Crosby, went national as early as 1882, opening up a sales office in Boston, and it was the first to buy advertising space for its product—in the *Ladies Home Journal* in 1893.[268]

Competition reared its head abroad as European governments turned increasingly protectionist and raised tariffs, while making a greater effort to import more of their flour from their colonies, or, in the case of the United Kingdom, from Commonwealth nations. Nor did it take long for English millers to adopt the New Process; by 1905 Great Britain, always the United States' best customer, was importing only half as much flour as it had in the previous two decades. Canadian manufacturers like Ogilvie Flour Mills moved into the British market. Indeed, the heyday of US flour exports proved short-lived, as exports declined from twelve million barrels a year in 1911–1914 to a low of less than five million barrels during the Great Depression.[269]

Branding and packaging became two cornerstones of the flour industry's efforts to beat competitors. Pillsbury and General Mills' determination to brand their own flours met with success, proving that they could market their products directly to the consumer. In this way, they bypassed nettlesome jobbers who heretofore had promoted their own brands and dictated their needs to the manufacturers. The goal of branding was to connote uniformity and reliability to the consumer. Pillsbury's XXXX brand, for instance, was consciously chosen to invoke medieval bakers who had marked their flour for communion wafers with crosses. Packaging size was reduced over time to 2.5-pound bags to better service retail customers. Wholesale and retail markets became more segmented over time, owing to the growing demand for different types of flour (e.g., whole wheat, cracked wheat, oat flour, cornmeal, and buckwheat flour) destined for home use and commercial baking. Increasingly, manufacturers were asked to blend flours to precise bakery specifications.[270]

The massive amounts of wheat processed meant that science became the new standard of expertise. Whereas flour buyers in the past had judged the raw material by color, odor, and appearance, now flour's chemical properties (especially its gluten content) were subjected to rigorous testing in factory laboratories. Large batches of wheat emanating from different sources, even if they were of the same general quality, varied in moisture and protein content. Ensuring uniformity under these conditions was not without its challenges. The wheat first had to be tempered or conditioned by adding or subtracting moisture, and then impurities were removed before grinding could begin, all under the watchful eye of experienced technicians.[271]

Technicians also were preoccupied with the flour's color, because dealers and customers apparently judged quality by its whiteness. Artificially bleached flour first made its appearance in England in 1879 and then in the United States in 1904, as nitrogen peroxide was applied to the flour to make it appear whiter.[272] It soon became the industry standard, despite protests from critics who claimed it was unfit for human consumption. Although the milling industry spent vast sums to rebut the charges and publicized their technical reports, which insisted that bleaching did not alter the flour's basic properties, Progressive-era reformers passed the Pure Food and Drug Act in 1906, which mandated that bleached flour had to be so labeled.[273] Gadfly journalist Dorothy Thompson did not hold back, lambasting the white-flour bread marketed by commercial bakers as "a sickly, bleached-blonde, airy, quick-staling, crustless, sweetish, sticky mass."[274]

Mass production was unkind to millworkers, as conditions inside the mills were straight out of Dickens's *Hard Times*. A labyrinth of conveyers, elevators, chutes, and clattering machines, the new flour mills were an assault on the senses. The noise was deafening, "the persistent sweetish smell and taste cloying," working in the summer was especially stifling, and the flour dust lingering in the air not only made it difficult to breathe but proved hazardous to workers' health.[275] Multiple operations in succession generated vast quantities of flour dust inside the factory walls. In one of the largest Minneapolis mills, "three thousand pounds of dust were collected every day from two dust rooms on a floor underneath the millstones." Unchecked, flour dust—"air so thick that one often could not see a light bulb ten feet away"—in the poorly ventilated factories prompted a host of pulmonary and respiratory problems for workers, including shortness of breath and a chronic "miller's cough," better known as mixed dust fibrosis.[276]

Under the "right" conditions, the New Process mills could turn deadly in the blink of an eye. To address the dust problem, initially mill owners placed exhaust fans in the different rooms of the factory, but this solution proved lethal because the dust "under favorable conditions will ignite and burn so rapidly that the gases released have explosive force."[277] This increased the potential for mill fires so much that insurers were reluctant to underwrite policies for flour mills.

On May 2, 1878, the Washburn "A" mill in Minneapolis blew. The force of the explosion was so great that it blasted the roof hundreds of feet into the air, leveling the building and razing three neighboring mills as well. Eighteen men were killed in the explosion, fourteen in the Washburn mill alone. The explosion destroyed half of the city's milling capacity, but within a year Washburn had built a new mill, adding specially designed dust-collecting machines to "minimize the fire danger." The entrepreneur kept adding new plants, and by 1881 flour production in his factories had doubled.[278] But it did not take long before Minneapolis's hegemonic position in the industry was challenged. With wheat farms scattered all over North America and beyond, by the 1920s it was no longer cost-effective to ship grain to one central point. Mills sprang up in regions where consumption was greatest. Moreover, railroads, increasingly under criticism for cozying up to manufacturers, raised rates to flour mills, making lake shipping a more attractive option.

In response, the major flour corporations branched out, building multiple manufacturing plants closer to the sources of production. They also sought out sites that reduced their transaction costs. Thanks to the rise in importance of the Great Lakes as a conduit for western US and Canadian wheat and the abundance of cheap electrical power from Niagara Falls, by 1930 Buffalo, New York, was the leading milling center in the world.[279]

Despite the periodic upheavals in the flour industry, manufacturers, farmers, merchants, and speculators all shared a common goal—consumers needed to eat more grains. They invested copious sums in education and marketing to convince global consumers that it was in their enlightened self-interest to alter their diets.

Uneeda to Eat More Crackers

The age of industrial capitalism implied a never-ending stream of mass-produced goods.[280] As scarcity gave way to abundance and factories churned out ever-greater numbers and varieties of finished goods, patterns of consumption and methods of encouraging that consumption changed as well. Progress was at hand; gluts and overproduction, advertisers argued, could be overcome simply through their formidable powers of persuasion. Advertising agencies were on a mission "to compose a new chapter of civilization." As an arrogant copywriter explained, "It is a great responsibility to mold the daily lives of millions of our fellow men, and I am persuaded that we are second only to statesmen and editors in power for good."[281]

According to cultural historian Jackson Lears, advertisers, who sought national and increasingly international markets for their corporate clients, promised the public a "magical self-transformation through the ritual of purchase."[282] In this vein, not-so-subliminal messages were spread that grains and flour meant much more than just sustenance; their daily consumption augured well for an individual's self-worth. Those consuming the right product would work harder, be more efficient, and set themselves apart from their peers. A turn-of-the-century Quaker Oats advertising campaign promised their product would "put its whole strength into your system," while a later advertisement insisted in intense alliteration that "lovers of Quaker Oats" were "wide-awakes, active and ambitious, whether they were seven or seventy. . . . Lovers of life eat them liberally. Lovers of languor don't."[283] Although the rest of the world was slow to adopt American innovations in the branding and marketing of food products manufactured by massive corporations, these trends would reach worldwide by the 1960s.

Consumption habits also changed remarkably during this period as diets, especially for urban dwellers, diversified considerably. As early as the 1890s in the United States, food-processing companies "single-handedly destroyed the traditional American breakfast."[284] The rise of Kellogg's "Corn Flakes" and Post's "Toasties" meant less bacon and beans in the morning and more carbohydrate-carrying grains in American diets. These products were initially marketed to the middle class as more healthful; in fact, Corn Flakes were created as a vegetarian alternative at a religious sanatorium in Battle Creek, Michigan. Charles W. Post, who created his own breakfast cereal company to challenge the primacy of Kellogg's, was a former patient at that same sanatorium and was so enamored with the concept of healthy breakfast foods that he began marketing his "Grape-Nuts" as "brain food." It did not take long before cereals were touted as cures for everything from malaria to consumption, and even loose teeth. Post preyed on concerned mothers, asking them, "Are you bringing up your children properly?" Not to worry, Post informed housewives, Grape-Nuts contained "iron, calcium, phosphorus and other mineral elements that are taken right up as vital food by the millions of cells in the body."[285] Breakfast cereals, a dietary marker of American identity, would also begin to spread internationally both before and in the decades after World War II.

In their efforts to spread the gospel that grains were good for the body and the soul, flour manufacturers were aided by advancements in packaging, especially the industry-wide transition from paper bags to paperboard folding boxes. The latter were less likely to rip during shipment, thereby minimizing spoilage. Cardboard boxes also protected their contents better, making them much more attractive for products like crackers. Finally, they were well suited for printing and were attractive for store displays. It was the Quaker Oats Company that pioneered the concept of selling its products in "small, clean, distinctive packages," which today is in evidence worldwide.[286]

American and European per capita consumption of flour, however, nosedived after the First World War. The average American consumed only a little over two-thirds as much flour as he or she did in 1900. The decline was triggered by a number of factors—wartime conservation edicts that educated consumers to save wheat and eat different foods; increased consumption of milk, sugar, and vegetables; commercial bakers' doctoring of flour with nonflour ingredients; dieting; and mechanical bread slicing. One study published in 1952 concluded that "over the last fifty years, almost no factor worked in the direction of increasing flour consumption."[287]

Baseball superstar Babe Ruth eating Puffed Wheat breakfast cereal in a publicity photograph, 1930. Prodigious advertising budgets of companies like Quaker Oats and Pillsbury made new products household names, especially when nationally known celebrities, like the "Sultan of Swat," George Herman Ruth, trumpeted their value. While many ads targeted housewives, others, like this one, were geared to their husbands and children. (Getty Images North America)

Even though nutritionists were well aware by the 1920s of the inherent deficiencies of white flour, and consumers were informed of the need to supplement their diets accordingly with fruits, vegetables, meats, and dairy products, it was very difficult for health officials to overcome the impact of huge advertising campaigns by the food-processing industry. A heady mix of vitamin scientists and Hollywood celebrities sold Americans on how wholesome white wheat flour was. An industry consultant came before a congressional committee to rail against "the pernicious teachings of food faddists who have sought to make people afraid of white flour bread."[288] The companies went so far as to ingratiate themselves with the public school systems and women's organizations by hiring teams of home economists to give demonstrations, buy up ad space in the *Journal of Home Economics,* and provide educational materials that testified to the wholesomeness and nutritional value of their products.

No matter the contradictory health claims, what these mass-produced foods had going for them, of course, was convenience, catchy packaging, and advertising. Companies initiated the sort of market research that would become accepted practice around the world. They conducted studies of the "instinctive likes and dislikes of buyers" as their marketing departments labored over the shape, color, and the texture of the packaging and how it would be displayed in stores.[289] Slogans that were "easily read, easily remembered and distinctive" sold these brand names to the American public. For instance, Washburn-Crosby implemented an aggressive advertising campaign featuring the slogan "Eventually—Why Not Now," which was plastered on countless billboards along railway routes. Not to be outdone, their rival Pillsbury shot back a response to Gold Medal's rhetorical query on its own billboards, "Because Pillsbury's Best."[290]

Manufacturers realized that their market was gendered. They reached out to housewives to sell their flour and one only had to glance at the data to understand why. By the 1920s, researchers were estimating that women purchased at least four-fifths of the total products acquired by families. To better target them, market researchers distributed questionnaires and took surveys to assemble "a portrait of the housewife." Advertising agencies sought answers to all that transpired in the home, pioneering "the statistical surveillance of private life, a practice that would become central to the maintenance of managerial cultural hegemony."[291] Who better to watch and then sell their wares to than the "average" woman? But as historian Jennifer Scanlon has noted, for advertising agencies in the United States, typical was synonymous with female, white, and middle-class.[292]

Washburn-Crosby came up with the ingenious gimmick of the larger-than-life persona of Betty Crocker, a fictional character who answered questions and shared recipes with American housewives. Soon the ubiquitous Crocker, "the embodiment of old-fashioned neighborliness," was a fixture in newspapers and magazines and on the radio, validating women's place in the domestic sphere.[293] Cooking schools were launched across the country, and twenty-one home economists were hired to work in Betty Crocker kitchens to test and demonstrate Gold Medal Flour. "Betty" would respond to up to four thousand letters a day from housewives about the intricacies of baking, and her radio show, *Betty Crocker School of the Air,* was a hit.[294] Small wonder that General Mills' Betty was once voted the second-best-known woman in America, taking a backseat only to Eleanor Roosevelt.[295]

In the 1920s the radio eclipsed print journalism and billboards as the preferred mode of transmission. Catchy singing radio commercials were unveiled; the lyrics of an early jingle for Wheaties was short and to the point:[296]

> Have you tried Wheaties?
> They're whole wheat with all of the bran.
> Won't you try Wheaties?
> For wheat is the best food of man.

With women won over, marketers turned their attention to husbands and children. General Mills not only sponsored action-packed radio shows like *Jack Armstrong, All-American Boy* to better appeal to male listeners, both young and old, but they produced and wrote the serials, all the while shamelessly plugging their products. Even so, Wheaties really did not become a household word until the company strategically associated its product with sports to appeal to consumer masculinity. The coined slogan "Breakfast of Champions" was advertised by sportsmen, such as heavyweight champion boxer Jack Dempsey, Olympic swimming champion Johnny Weissmuller, and tennis star Don Budge.[297]

Some of the industry's first movers were enormously successful and used their monopsonistic position in their markets to buy out their competitors and establish market dominance. The National Biscuit Company (NABISCO), for instance, thanks in large part to its flagship Uneeda Biscuit soda cracker, was one such corporate heavyweight, accounting for an astonishing 70 percent of industry sales. A clever name was not enough, however; the company wrapped its crackers in colorful, hygienic packaging and then cut out the wholesalers by building its own sales team and selling right to grocers. The cracker's taste was secondary to marketers. Advertisements featured a rain-slicker-clad boy carrying his prized package of crackers in a downpour, safely protected from the elements by a double-sealed package. That plus a prodigious advertising budget made the cracker a household name as Americans were persuaded they had multiple reasons to need large quantities of Uneeda Biscuit crackers.[298]

Food-processing companies, however, soon came to realize that there were limits to what consumers would eat and that an increase in consumption of one item often came at the expense of others. In this zero-sum game, industry magnates had to get the attention of consumers, no matter the cost. A flour millers' trade association, which trumpeted the virtues of grains, called on consumers to "Eat More Wheat" during the 1920s. This far-ranging campaign, which sought to arrest the decline in per capita consumption of flour, was as imaginative as it was multifaceted.[299]

Advertising and corporate research and development departments worked synergistically; the former, for instance, provided timely data to the latter, which was constantly in search of new product lines. Millers began grinding a drought-resistant, rust-resistant durum variety grown initially in Eastern Europe and then transplanted to the Dakotas. By 1919 the durum wheat crop averaged forty million bushels annually in the United States alone, and flour manufacturers were not far behind in trumpeting the virtues of macaroni products. Manufacturers touted the nutritional value of their pasta products in their trade publication *Macaroni Journal* and crusaded nationwide for a Friday "Macaroni Day." As a flour company president self-servingly noted: "Such new products represent an increase in the consumption of grains as food; they actually compete less with other cereal products than with types of foodstuffs outside their own field."[300] European companies were not far behind their American counterparts in conjuring up catchy ad campaigns to sell their products.

Not all grain products during this era experienced such a revolution in marketing and advertising. These techniques were little used, for instance, in selling rice. But in other respects, rice's commodity chain complemented rather than competed with the wheat trade. The rice chain demonstrates that the existence of technological and infrastructural innovations during this period did not in and of themselves guarantee that growers would embrace such changes.

Rice as Contrarian

Unlike grain farmers in settler societies, rice growers in South, Southeast, and East Asia, with few exceptions, chose not to substitute machines for human and animal power, nor did they adopt chemical fertilizers or allocate funds for agricultural extension services.[301] Given the choice to invest in labor or machinery, rice farmers chose the former. It is not that rice and mechanization were or are incompatible; in this period, rice cultivators in the United States, Australia, and southern Europe adopted the latest farm machinery to sow and harvest their crops. In the United States rice was cultivated in the same highly mechanized manner as wheat and other grains; farmers employed combines, tractors, and even airplanes. Japanese rice farmers also were quick to adopt beneficial technology, replacing treadle irrigation wheels with small diesel and electric pumps when they were first made available in the 1920s. In fact, the pumps dramatically transformed rice production in Japan, reducing labor requirements on the Saga Plain from seventy worker-days per hectare in 1909 to twenty-two worker-days in 1932 while doubling production. But the great majority of rice farmers had very plausible reasons for eschewing new technologies and investing their energies (and profits) elsewhere.

The difference in ecology, the idiosyncrasies of wet-rice growing, and the diminutive size of the large majority of rice plots in monsoon Asia best explain why peasants stuck with the traditional tools of the trade and looked for other ways to enhance productivity. Much of the prime wet-rice land was in deltas, along coastal strips and river basins. Such land was boggy at best, usually silts and silky sands, soils where the wheels of machines could not gain traction. The machines that best tolerated such muddy conditions were those that floated and did not require adhesion.

Rice, like wheat, prospered in different ecological zones; for instance, it could be grown on hills or mountains without the need for irrigation or surface water. Upland rice, however, was cultivated in sparsely settled regions and constituted only a small proportion of the world's rice crop. Roughly 90 percent of global production during this period was lowland rice, which thrives in the hot lowland tropics with abundant rainfall and enough water to either naturally or artificially flood fields.[302]

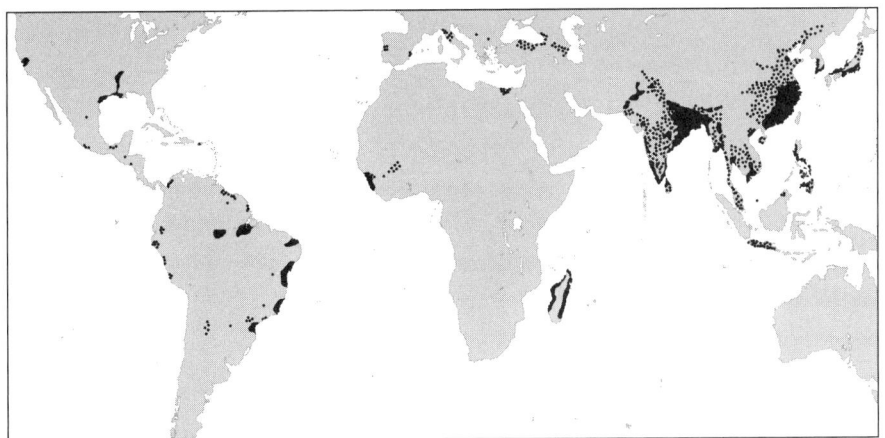

Global production of rice, ca. 1913–1925.

Lowland rice, unlike wheat, had few competitors in the tropics and subtropics; only millet, sorghum, and maize would tolerate such heat and moisture, and then only in areas of modest summer rainfall. Paddy rice in monsoon Asia also had another intrinsic advantage over its rivals: it grew "under water," so it was relatively impervious to pests, disease, and, of course, drought.[303]

Unlike settler societies where labor was scarce and emphasis was placed on substituting machinery for labor, Asian agrarian economies had the luxury of drawing on an abundance of skilled manual workers. Instead of mechanizing, growers focused on improving rice yields. When sufficient labor was available, wet-rice growers in well-watered areas often could realize two or three crops a year. As a recent survey of rice economies noted: "It is no coincidence that the most densely populated agricultural regions of the world, Java, the Tonkin delta (present day Vietnam) and the lower Yangtze provinces of China, all have a centuries-long tradition of intensive wet-rice farming. No wheat growing areas can sustain such numerous populations."[304] Multicropping also enabled farmers to grow different varieties in any one season, to minimize risks and cater to niche markets. Moreover, rice had a higher yield-to-seed ratio than wheat, barley, or rye, so conserving seed grain at the end of harvest season was not as much of a hardship for peasants as it was for European and American wheat growers.

Another striking contrast between wet rice and other grains was that yields could actually increase in the same paddy from year to year and then stabilize over time "because water seepage alters the chemical composition and structure of the different soil layers in a process known as pozdolisation."[305] Soil type was much less important to wet-rice farmers than proper irrigation and drainage. Whereas soil from grain or dry-rice farming lost its fertility after a period of time if manure or fertilizers were not utilized, the reverse was true with wet-rice farming. Small wonder rice farmers preferred to farm old paddies rather than break in new ones.

Not all rice-growing regions required irrigation. The fertile deltas of Burma, Siam, and Vietnam, the three principal rice-exporting areas of the world during the late nineteenth and early twentieth centuries, employed much less irrigation than Japan and southern China, where land was scarce and population pressure demanded that yields be maximized. Rivers overflowed the delta banks at least once a year, depositing rich alluvial silts that replenished the soil and permitted rice to be grown year after year with little need for fertilizer or the rotation of crops. Unfortunately, these three prime exporting regions in Southeast Asia were on the same marketing schedule. With harvests occurring simultaneously, the result was "intensified competition and consequent (downward) pressure on prices, with adverse effects upon returns to growers and government revenues."[306] Because more than fifty million peasants' livelihoods were tied to rice production, price fluctuations or declining yields often had dire consequences.

Even where irrigation was in vogue, methods of addressing constraints varied. Chinese rice farmers focused on multicropping and early-maturing varieties of rice. Their Japanese counterparts adopted varieties that responded well to fertilization, as Japan "coaxed" farmers in its colonial possessions in Formosa and Korea to plant in new lands for cultivation after World War I.

Rice was produced and circulated largely within Asia during this period. India and China were the largest producers, but almost all of their production fed domestic consumption. Because most rice was consumed locally or regionally, and because rice milling was far simpler than milling wheat into flour, the transport, storage, marketing, and milling of rice did not follow the pattern of wheat. Harvested or paddy rice was transported to mills by oxcart or on workers' backs; rice that had to be conveyed longer distances was shipped by water transport. Railroads, such stalwart conveyors of wheat and other coarse grains, were utilized to carry rice in Japan and India, which as we have seen had Asia's best rail networks, but other rice regions made the most of water transport. Storage facilities were rudimentary at best, so rice was milled soon after harvest.

Rice-milling establishments varied considerably, "[ranging from a] farmer's hand-operated 'woodpecker,' which merely removed hulls to a large power-driven establishment employing many laborers and equipped with machines that hull, skin, polish, and coat the rice."[307] Suffice it to say, even the largest rice-milling factories in Rangoon, Burma, paled in comparison to the size and output of Pillsbury's massive Minneapolis flour mills.

The establishment of a uniform set of weights and measures proved elusive. Even where varieties were categorized, price quotations were limited to the nominal classifications high-, middle-, and low-quality, with considerable variability found at different rice exchanges. According to a study published by the Stanford University Food Research Institute in 1940:[308]

> The buyer of paddy rice . . . must learn to know as best he can from experience the quality of rice grown from one region to another and by many individuals. In the absence of marketing standards, trading necessarily becomes a highly individualistic matter. Trading risks are therefore large . . . [and] the spread between producers and retailers prices tends to be high.

Prior to World War II, Asia accounted for 93 percent of global rice exports, but the continent also absorbed three-quarters of the imports and, taking into account subsistence rice farming, probably consumed over 90 percent of the world's rice. Just as there were a few prominent exporters in the wheat trade, Burma, French Indochina or Cochin China, Siam (present-day Thailand), Korea, and Formosa dominated the rice trade. Exports steadily grew throughout the late nineteenth and early twentieth centuries. By 1940 Burma was exporting 3 million tons of rice annually, while Indochina, Siam, and Korea shipped out 1 to 1.3 million tons a year. Japan imported the most rice—on average 1.7 million tons annually, with almost all of it after the mid-1920s coming from its colonies in Korea and Formosa. Japan privileged these colonies by placing import restrictions on "foreign" rice imports. British India was the next-largest importer, taking in 1.5 million tons annually, with the British colonies of Ceylon and Malaya each garnering half a million tons of foreign rice a year. Chinese imports fluctuated greatly from year to year, owing to the unpredictability of domestic rice harvests.

Just as Western national governments became increasingly protectionist as commodity prices declined in the 1920s and 1930s, nationalistic Asian governments also promoted food self-sufficiency at home to preserve favorable balances of payment and to protect domestic rice production. In some cases governments even encouraged their citizens to consume less rice to promote self-sufficiency. Because the level of urbanization—outside of Japan—was low in Asia, imports were less crucial than in much more urbanized Western Europe. Despite the growing tendency toward protectionism, rice exporters, with the notable exception of Burma, which saw its European market shrink precipitously, held their own during the Great Depression, especially when compared to wheat-exporting countries. As one comparative study noted:[309]

> Rice exports increased more rapidly than wheat exports in the period before 1930, declined relatively less on impact of the world depression, and ... [from 1936 to 1938] rice stood moderately above their immediate pre-Depression level while wheat exports fell by nearly a fourth. With rice, enough import markets expanded to offset those that contracted; with wheat, the policies of self-sufficiency were much more general and more restrictive upon world trade.

The rice trade's ability to weather the volatile interwar period is especially noteworthy given that wheat was becoming progressively cheaper in relation to rice (see Table 4.10). Asian demographic growth, which far outpaced rice production and ensured demand, partially explains the rice trade's resiliency under such difficult conditions. Perhaps another reason was that up until 1935 one of its major importers, China, acted as a stabilizing influence by importing more heavily when rice prices were lower and buying up less from external markets when prices shot up. Because China was such a major force in the rice trade, such elasticity kept rice prices worldwide in check. This held true until 1935, when the Chinese government moved aggressively to protect its home market, causing rice imports to decline significantly.

Each of the principal exporters serviced a discrete market and by and large stuck to it. Burmese rice went to England, where a portion of it was re-exported

TABLE 4.10

Indexed wheat and rice prices on British markets, 1867–1939

	Average wheat price	Average rice price	Ratio of wheat to rice
1867–1877	100	100	1.00
1878–1887	75.5	80	0.94
1890–1899	54	63	0.86
1904–1913	61	77	0.79
1922–1930	89.5	152	0.59
1931–1939	48	93	0.57

Source: V. D. Wickizer and M. K. Bennett, *The Rice Economy of Monsoon Asia* (Palo Alto, CA: Stanford University Food Research Institute, 1941), 137.

Notes: Indexed average for the period 1867–1877 = 100.

Average wheat price represents the British and American price for the period.

Average rice price represents the average price of cargoes arriving from Rangoon, Burma.

to the rest of Europe, the West Indies, and Africa. Prior to World War I, rice from Burma, which was part of India from 1852 until 1937, was sold only in Asian markets during times of famine. After 1937 most of its "exports" went to other Indian ports and were then re-exported to East Africa, British Malaya, and Ceylon. But the rice seldom flowed to East Asia. On the other hand, exports from Siam and Cochin China (later southern Vietnam) were earmarked for Japan, China, the Philippines, the Dutch East Indies, the Malay Peninsula, and Java, although the French market bought up rice produced by its colonials, especially during years when East Asian markets contracted.

Interestingly, as the period wore on and as ever-larger amounts of wheat and coarse grains went to the European continent from grain frontiers, less rice was shipped to Europe from Asian exporters. Instead, rice was shipped from the ports of Rangoon, Bangkok, and Saigon to growing Asian markets or it now bypassed England and was exported directly from the rice frontiers to the West Indies and Africa. Before paddy rice was exported, it needed to be cleaned and polished because this made it keep better. Owing to the dearth of storage in producing countries, rice was bagged for overseas transport, rather than shipped in bulk the way that wheat and the other coarse grains were.

The focus on the export trade, however, obscures a lively domestic rice trade that existed in some countries, mainly flowing from countryside to the city. Bengali rice, for example, was shipped largely westward in India, while surplus rice from southern China was shipped to China's northern provinces.

Although it is true that rice was cultivated globally—Spain and Italy were Europe's largest producers, the US South and Brazil dominated production in the Americas, and Egypt and Sierra Leone monopolized African rice production—taken together, non-Asian rice never amounted to much; less than 5 percent of world production was grown outside of monsoon Asia on the eve of World War II. Or to put it another way, the output of the United States and Brazil together was less than that of the smallest Asian producer, Formosa. It was not until the 1930s that Africa and the United States began to export significant quantities of rice.

It may seem counterintuitive, but the three deltas in Southeast Asia—the Irrawaddy-Sittaung (Burma), the Chao Phraya (Siam), and the Mekong (Vietnam)—dominated the export trade to Europe and China, even though rice yields in these regions were historically low (and showed no upward trend until after World War II). Compared to other major rice producers, their double-cropping and fertilizer use was minimal, agricultural education and infrastructure lagged, and what irrigation existed was qualitatively inferior to methods used in East Asia. On these new frontiers, however, rice was grown on larger farms for export.

What these Southeast Asian delta frontiers had in common with settler societies in the Americas and Australia was an abundance of new lands available for cultivation and significant in-migration. These expanding rice frontiers also were characterized by colonial interventions, often with unintended consequences. A fascinating illustration was Lower Burma. Colonial administrators immediately recognized the untapped economic potential of the Irrawaddy-Sittaung Delta region. What had been a sparsely populated, underdeveloped backwater of the British Empire would become over the course of the next fifty years the world's largest rice-exporting area. Colonial authorities invested considerable sums to improve rail and water transport and to establish technical education, credit institutions, and public works projects.

But imperial plans did not go according to script. British officials initially encouraged the development of small landholdings in the delta region, in the belief that independent peasants, many of them transplanted from the "dry" districts of Upper Burma, would improve and extend their properties in a way that large landowners, who were, in the minds of the British, little more than glorified rent collectors, would not. Because this was relatively untouched territory, where no preexisting land tenure system had established roots, officials believed it would be possible to develop a rural economy that favored independent proprietors who received the profits and where the "rent surplus went to the state rather than to intermediaries."[310] To promote this, squatters, taking advantage of familial labor, were given titles to lands after they had occupied and paid taxes on their holdings for twelve years. Hundreds of thousands of Burmese migrants, making the most of their opportunities, made a successful transition from subsistence farming to export production. Marketing of the trade, for most of the part, stayed in Burmese hands, although increasing numbers of southern Indian immigrants moved to Rangoon and began to participate in all aspects of the export trade.

Peasants dominated rice cultivation in the Irrawaddy-Sittaung Delta until well into the first decades of the twentieth century as production grew exponentially. But as yields stagnated and the rice frontier closed after World War I, land values increased. Moneylenders, rice brokers, and millers who had advanced credit to smallholders in return for their paddy rice, began to acquire properties, often as a result of foreclosures on mortgages. Debt burdens mounted, and peasants lost their lands and became tenants on large estates. As historian Michael Adas explains, "the social and economic position of a small segment of Delta society, the large landholders, improved substantially, while the solvency and wellbeing of the great majority of persons engaged in agricultural production was gradually undermined."[311] A system designed to promote economic growth, rice exports, and imperial revenues, and in which Burmese farmers, middlemen, and entrepreneurs were all active participants, became progressively less balanced. During the Great Depression the delta region was especially hard hit. Rice monoculture left landless tenants in desperate straits. Rural unrest and the Japanese occupation only compounded their plight.

Cochin China presents a different model of colonial economic development. Although the region was sparsely populated when the French first arrived in the mid-nineteenth century, over the next seventy years under French rule, rice cultivation increased fourfold as peasants flocked to the region from the northern provinces. The colonial administration invested heavily in water control, constructing a sophisticated system of canals. To recoup some of their costs, colonial administrators sold large expanses of land to French nationals and companies. By 1930, rice lands were concentrated in the hands of some 120 French colonists who among themselves held approximately one hundred thousand hectares of land. Recently arrived tenant farmers were given ten-hectare plots on these estates in return for a portion of their rice.

In Cochin China and other delta regions, cultivated rice lands were owned by landlords who advanced money and supplies to tenants at usurious rates of interest in return for a portion of their crop. Much of the rice crop was mortgaged out even before it was planted. Soon after the harvest, growers had to settle up with landlords or merchants to meet their obligations. Unlike wheat farmers, rice farmers were all too often in the dark about market prices, rates of interest, the cost of supplies advanced to them, and the weight of their crop.

In Japan the government took an active role in marketing and financing the crop. Rice exchanges were established in all of Japan's major cities, but in this case it was the government, not the private sector (as in the West), that administered the trade. In stark contrast to the Chicago Board of Trade and other Western commodity exchanges, speculation was discouraged.

The rice trade, then, in virtually every meaningful way, ran counter to the other grain trades. Export markets were more regional and remained remarkably consistent over time. South and Southeastern Asian exporters serviced Asian markets first and foremost; although countries in North and South America, Africa, and Europe produced rice, much of it was destined for home markets. Because several of the largest exporters essentially planted and harvested rice on the same timetable, and because storage facilities in the principal exporting regions were remarkably underdeveloped, large quantities of rice flooded the market at the same time, inevitably depressing prices. The business of rice trading was much more rudimentary than the grains trade; there was much less standardization, processing functioned on a much smaller scale, markets were not as integrated, transportation and storage infrastructure were glaringly deficient, and speculation, which had such a dramatic impact on investment, capitalization, and price differentials in the West, was a nonfactor in Asian rice markets.

Although not averse to new technologies, fertilizers, or scientific experimentation, rice growers understandably invested more time and capital into increasing yields through multicropping than through mechanization. The presence of dense populations and the ability of rice to reward ever more workers by increasing yields mitigated the need to embrace costly machinery. Rice had been and continued to be a peasant-cultivated crop. Even in the southeastern deltas, where large farms predominated, tenants, who leased lands from large landowners or companies, cultivated rice.

Still, there were some significant similarities that warrant mention. Open rice and grain frontiers prompted migration and the concentration of land and wealth in the hands of a few (though in other, less export-oriented areas, rice permitted the continuation of small peasant plots.) But given how fertile the deltas were, there was less need for substantive investment in irrigation or other technologies. As we have seen, formal and informal colonial relationships mattered in both trades; mother countries privileged their dependencies. Interestingly, consumers preferred their grains, whether rice, wheat, or other coarse grains, "white"—nutrition be damned!

Ripple Effects

The growth of a global grains trade had multiplier effects that facilitated the growth of other products and industries vital to the production, processing, marketing, and consumption of the trade.[312] Some of these products, and the processes needed to transform them into useful inputs, dramatically transformed those regions of the world that cultivated and manufactured these items. Hard fibers proved indispensable to the grains revolution and in turn became creatures of that trade. The life histories of several hard fibers illustrate how commodity chains were forged, how and why they flourished, and ultimately how each one proved unable to sustain its position in its respective market during this tumultuous age. The fates of entrepreneurs and peasants in such disparate regions as the Bengal region of eastern India, the Yucatán Peninsula in Mexico, and the East Indies were tied not only to the world market price of their commodities and to those of their chief competitors, but to the roller-coaster, boom-and-bust cycles of the grains and rice to which they owed their existence.

A competitive hard-fibers trade developed during the nineteenth and twentieth centuries as new fibers were introduced to manufacturers—each with its own strengths, weaknesses, and particular applications. Each new fiber jockeyed with more established rivals, and eventually the market became more segmented. Some versatile fibers had multiple applications and benefited from the growing complexity of the global market; others were confined essentially to a specific submarket. Each new fiber was first subjected to intense chemical scrutiny, followed by controlled cultivation investigations at agricultural experiment stations, before a lengthy apprenticeship in the market. In general, each hard fiber gained ascendancy in the market for the better part of a century, as each enjoyed a brief Ricardian comparative advantage. Although in some cases new uses were found or new cultivation or processing techniques were employed to postpone the inevitable denouement, bona fide development for the regions that produced these crops proved illusory. These export economies simply did not generate sufficient forward or backward linkages to prompt sustained economic growth. Hard-fiber sectors in Africa, Asia, or Latin America never acted as growth multipliers, nor did they prompt economic integration for the host countries. This was particularly serious because, unlike rice and grains, one can't eat hard fibers.

One inexpensive fiber useful for the storage and transport of grains and other commodities was jute (*Corchorus capsularis* and *Corchorus olitorius*). Although not so strong, durable, and elastic as other hard fibers, Indian jute was more plentiful, cheaper to produce, and easier to manufacture. It soon conquered the bagging market. Handwoven jute bags (called hessian or burlap) produced on looms in the Bengal delta region (present-day Bangladesh) had been an important cottage industry as early as the sixteenth century. Although too rough for apparel, jute found its niche as a preeminent packaging material of the age. The Dutch were the first to use the coarse fiber for coffee bags from their Java plantations in Indonesia in the 1830s. When the Crimean War cut supplies of Russian hemp and the US Civil War caused a shortage of cotton bags, the jute industry responded.

Inexpensive labor costs contributed to jute's popularity with fiber buyers. Peasants and tenants interspersed plantings of jute with rice paddy in northern and eastern Bengal, but its cultivation placed heavy demands on the labor force.

The cash crop required deep plowing, weeding, hand-cut harvesting, and then the retting of the fiber in ponds to separate the stem and the outer bark from the fiber. Brokers extended credit to growers at usurious rates—one estimate fixes the rate at never less than 36 percent—and then shipped the raw product in bales, first by boat and later by railway, to the port of Calcutta in West Bengal. By 1910 production had soared to nine hundred thousand tons a year and by the end of the Second World War, India had a virtual monopoly on the raw material. When the chairman of the Indian Jute Mills Association stated in 1915, "We want cheap jute, and lots of it," the implication was obvious: Indian jute's comparative advantage lay in its exceedingly low labor cost—in the field and in the factory.[313]

Jute was made into burlap and gunnysacks for everything from sandbags to sugar, and fertilizer to animal feeds. (Devotees of rock-and-roller Chuck Berry may recall that even "Johnny B. Goode" carried his guitar in a gunnysack.) By the mid-nineteenth century, power-driven jute mills in Dundee, Scotland, had overtaken the Indian handloom industry. The fiber's popularity soon attracted a rash of competition from manufacturers in France, Germany, Belgium, Austria, and Italy. By the end of the nineteenth century, however, Calcutta bagging manufacturers, benefiting from cheap labor and proximity to the raw product, stepped into the fray and offered serious competition to European mills. The process was relatively simple: first, raw fibers of varying length, thickness, color, and tensile strength were spun into a uniform yarn; then the yarn was woven into cloth. As early as 1875, the US consul general in Calcutta reported that local jute manufacturers were a force to be reckoned with: "There seems to be every reason to expect that Calcutta will become the great jute manufacturing center of the world."[314]

Located in and around Calcutta along the banks of the Hooghly River, jute mills were managed by Scotsmen imported from Dundee, but capitalized by a melding of British expatriate and indigenous entrepreneurs who established holding companies. Initially they catered only to domestic markets and the rice trade in nearby Burma, before marketing their bags internationally. Over time Indian capitalists increasingly assumed command of these holding companies. By the turn of the century, Calcutta and its environs had thirty-five mills with a capacity of 315,000 spindles and 15,340 looms, turning out 440,000 tons of gunny and burlap sacks.

Angry Dundee jute manufacturers pleaded with their members of Parliament to implement tariffs or quotas, fully expecting that "an upstart competitor in a dependent part of the empire could be brought to heel."[315] They were sadly mistaken. Dundee's jute makers never recaptured their preeminent position; all of their politicking could not keep Indian jute out of United Kingdom and its dependencies. The reason was that jute paid its way; after the turn of the century, sacking was frequently India's largest export earner, which helped pay for the administrative costs of empire during the Raj. This tale of two cities is an instructive example of the limitations of empire. Manufactured jute may have gotten its start near the imperial center, but it reigned triumphant in the colony. One could think of this as India's revenge. Where the First Industrial Revolution in England had undercut India's textile industry, the Second—and the growth of agricultural (rice) exports—had allowed Indian manufacturers to outcompete British rivals.

Between 1870 and the First World War, Indian gunnysack production increased from 1.8 million to just under 370 million bags annually.[316] At their zenith, the Calcutta mills employed between 250,000 and 300,000 workers, and jute constituted just under 30 percent of India's total exports. By World War I the Calcutta factories had even founded a cartel, the Indian Jute Manufacturer Association, which regulated production by buying up raw material when prices were low and storing it in warehouses until prices improved.

By the early twentieth century Calcutta's cheap and coarse gunnysacks and its higher-quality burlap bags had captured the market in Australasia, the United States, South Africa, and the Southern Cone of South America. Calcutta hegemony proved short-lived, however. During the Great Depression, European governments revived their jute industries by imposing high tariffs on imported bags. Together with the transition to bulk transport of grains and competition from paper and cotton sacks, this led to a crisis in India's jute industry. Peasant and tenant producers, by definition not well capitalized, were particularly hard hit. An economic historian, writing about the litany of ills of Bengali jute growers during the depths of the depression, painted a discouraging picture: "With no relief in sight, increasing indebtedness, consumption loans at exorbitant interests, distress sales, shortchanging, debt default, land appropriation, proliferation of pauperized sharecroppers and agricultural laborers were the mileposts on the road to debt peonage."[317]

Producing jute inexpensively became an industry-wide mantra. Producers and manufacturers had good reason to be concerned about the revolution in bulk storage and transport, newfangled synthetic substitutes, and old-fashioned protectionist strategies employed by their chief competition in Europe. The subsequent introduction of synthetic fibers, like nylon, patented by DuPont in 1934, sealed the industry's fate.

If jute found a niche in the bagging market, Philippine-grown manila *(Musa textilis)* proved to be a more than worthy adversary for Russian- and US-grown hemp *(Cannabis sativa),* which had been the raw material of preference for the making of cordage. Whalers, clippers, and eventually steamships required a seemingly endless supply of rope for rigging, cable, and towlines. The smallest schooner carried a ton of cordage; a frigate used one hundred tons. Even the advent of steamships did not curtail demand, as they still required large amounts of cordage for towlines, warps, and auxiliary sails.

By the late nineteenth century, manila, a member of the banana family, overtook hemp in the cordage trade. Extracted from the plant's bark, it was naturally resistant to saltwater, so that it did not have to be tarred like hemp. This clean fiber, introduced and tested by North American cordage manufacturers in 1818, was more durable and 25 percent stronger than tarred hemp, had greater flexibility and elasticity, weighed a third less, and carried a lower price tag. By 1860, manila, which was grown in the Kabikolan Peninsula in southeastern Luzon, was firmly entrenched in the US maritime trade, and consumption by British and other European manufacturers steadily increased. Production doubled between 1870 and 1880 alone.

The cordage industry's infatuation with manila overshadowed the introduction of a new tropical fiber. Although henequen *(Agave fourcroydes)* had been cultivated in Mexico's Yucatán Peninsula since pre-Columbian times for clothes, shoes, and hammocks, only in the late colonial period did Spanish entrepreneurs begin to recognize its broader commercial potential. Commonly, but incorrectly, known as sisal—the name of a Gulf of Mexico port from which the fiber was shipped—henequen was earmarked for low-end cordage and rigging purposes because it lacked tensile strength for heavy-duty usage.

Twice as strong, more rot-resistant, and smoother than the Yucatecan fiber, manila merited its higher price and remained the fiber of choice in the maritime market. Henequen justifiably gained a reputation as an inferior but inexpensive substitute for manila. Blends of manila and henequen were marketed as such and priced midway between the "pure" twines. Hence, the prices of these commodities were inextricably bound. Abundance or a shortage of one commodity invariably affected the rival's price.

Demand was ensured as technological advancements continued to find new industrial applications for the erstwhile rivals. Tests determined that rope offered the most economical means of conveying power. With new factories springing up throughout North America and Western Europe, manila proved ideally suited for power transmission cables and the expanding oil-drilling industry. The new application of greatest consequence for henequen (and, to a lesser extent, manila) was binder twine. Labor-intensive hand-binding had been supplanted in the early 1870s by mechanical wire binders attached to reapers. When bits of wire clogged the machinery and found their way into flour mills and animal feed, inventors built a mechanical twine knotter in the late 1870s that substituted biodegradable twine for wire, thus revolutionizing the farm-implement industry. Now a harvesting machine with two men to pick and shock the sheaf could reap twelve to fourteen acres of wheat a day, effectively doubling previous output with a substantial labor savings. The North American Deering Company and the McCormick Harvesting Machine Company, the world's largest producers of mobile agricultural machinery, quickly built their own twine binder harvesters in 1879 and 1881, respectively. Sales of mechanical grain binders soared, and by the turn of the century, henequen and manila production grew exponentially to meet the insatiable demand.

When fiber prices were high, growers and merchants made bountiful profits. Local business leaders in the Philippines and Yucatán served as conduits for British and North American brokers and manufacturers, realizing sizable profits, usually in the form of commissions and kickbacks but also from the usurious loan practices that access to foreign capital allowed them. Ideally, just as foreign investors sought to carve out a durable monopoly or "corner" on the trade, local collaborators wished to enjoy exclusively the benefits of a monopoly over communication with foreign interests controlling the market. With these limitations, it was difficult for local producers to adjust productivity and to predict prices; so local landholders were vulnerable to the repeated boom-and-bust cycles that afflicted the trade. Chronic price instability, coupled with the producers' inability to diversify, meant that these regional economies experienced severe dislocations amid sustained growth.

Yucatán was one of the economic jewels of Mexico; its henequen plantations enjoyed a dominant position in the hard-fibers market, supplying upward of 85 to 90 percent of the fiber used to make binder twine in North American cordage and twine factories. Over the last four decades of the nineteenth century, the peninsula's colonial-style haciendas were transformed into bustling modern plantations; contemporaries chronicled how cornfields and pasture had been replaced by rectilinear rows of bluish-gray spines of the agave plant. Fortunes were realized by enterprising landowners, fiber merchants, and North American cordage and binder twine manufacturers, who secured bountiful profits from the turn-of-the-century fiber boom. Locally, a "divine caste" of thirty families and a smaller subset of prosperous landowner-merchants dominated the henequen economy, transforming the state's capital city of Mérida into a beautiful showcase, while constructing opulent homes for themselves in the state capital and on their haciendas. State and national governments came to rely on tax revenues generated from this profitable export.

Like many staples, henequen was hamstrung by cutthroat competition and a fickle marketplace that constantly sought out more cost-effective supplies of hard fibers. But hard fibers did enjoy some notable advantages over other tropical commodities. Fibers were nonperishable, so production, transportation, and distribution did not have to be systematically coordinated as they did for other tropical goods. Moreover, unlike some staples, henequen was seasonless; the absence of a prescribed harvest season had important ramifications for marketing, distribution, and the labor regimen.

By 1902 the International Harvester Company, a combination of five of the largest harvesting machine companies (including McCormick and Deering), had become the world's principal buyer of raw fiber. Binder twine, manufactured in

Harvester's Chicago twine plant, was an important secondary line for Harvester, as farmers needed a regular supply of twine to operate their binders. The company made its profits by selling binding machines rather than from twine sales, so Harvester and its agents sought to keep twine prices low to make its farm implements more attractive. Historians debate the leverage that Harvester enjoyed over the market, but local agents such as Olegario Molina y Compañía in Yucatán benefited greatly from access to foreign capital. This enabled Molina to acquire mortgages, purchase credits outright, and consolidate its hold on regional communications, infrastructure, and banking—all of which guaranteed control of local fiber production and generally worked to depress the price. In the short term, the boom enriched a small group of foreign investors, merchants, and local elites in Mexico and the Philippines while the greater majority of producers and tens of thousands of laborers found themselves tied to the whims of an unforgiving market.

Inputs like land tenure patterns, labor relations, technological improvements, and marketing and credit practices were either overhauled or fine-tuned in the wake of the boom. Henequen was highly inelastic to price changes in the market. Because landowners had to wait seven years to begin harvesting their crops, they invariably based their decision to expand or contract their holdings on their ability to acquire capital. Faced with such a lag between planting and first harvest, landowners could predict neither future prices nor world market demand. As a result, supply in the short run was usually out of phase with demand.

The henequen estate had some physical resemblance to a commercial plantation—with modern machinery, narrow-gauge tramways, and land-intensive cultivation of the staple crop—but familial ownership, management, and *mentalité* continued to imbue the institution with characteristics of the pre-henequen cattle and maize hacienda. Emblematic of a rural society in the middle of a complex transition, the henequen estate is best viewed as a hybrid that illustrates some of the traits of its predecessor but reflects inevitable adjustments in land, technology, labor, and infrastructure. Moreover, a full-fledged plantation society's emergence was inhibited by lingering vestiges of the earlier institution, particularly the way in which *hacendados* confronted their labor problems.

Just as the syncretic henequen estate combined characteristics of both the traditional hacienda and the commercial plantation, its labor relations were also

Women workers operating twine-balling machines at International Harvester's mill in Chicago, Illinois, April 26, 1939. Raw henequen, manila, and sisal fiber, produced on plantations in such tropical locales as Mexico, the Philippines, and East Africa, were shipped to cordage and twine factories in the United States, Canada, and Europe. These modern, mechanized plants manufactured binder twine from these natural fibers and then sold the inexpensive product to North American and European farmers, who used it to bind sheaves of wheat. (Wisconsin Historical Society, WHi-8897)

an amalgam of various modes of coercion. Underwritten by the assistance of the state political apparatus, three complementary mechanisms of social control—isolation, coercion, and security—allowed *henequeneros* to maintain the disciplined work rhythms of monocrop production. These three strategies worked in unison to cement the structural relationship that not only suited the production requirements of management but also served the subsistence needs of workers, at least until the eve of the Mexican Revolution.

Designed by *henequeneros* to limit the workers' mobility and autonomy, the three mechanisms were often so mutually reinforcing that it is sometimes difficult to delineate where one began and the other left off. Institutions like the hacienda store, for example, served many functions. On one level, the store gave *henequeneros* a surefire mechanism for raising workers' debts (coercion). On another level, by providing basic foodstuffs and household needs, it diminished the need for resident peons to leave the property to purchase goods, thereby minimizing the chances of potentially disruptive contact between resident peons and neighboring villagers and agitators (isolation). Finally, through the sale of corn, beans, and other staples, it ensured subsistence for resident peons (security). In sum, the hacienda store was a perfect vehicle for appropriating labor in a scarce market, as it facilitated dependency and immobility while conveying a measure of convenience and security for landless peons. Henequen monoculture's fundamental security of subsistence throughout the boom, coupled with the economic demise of nearby village communities, enlisted workers for, and harnessed them to, the disciplined work rhythms of fiber production.

Gender relations on henequen estates only reinforced these complementary mechanisms. In fact, masters and peons found common ground in their perceptions of the role Maya women should play on the estates. First and foremost, they agreed on a rigid division of labor. Male debt peons toiled in the fields, performing all tasks related to planting, harvesting, and processing the fiber on the estates. If the daughters or wives occasionally worked in the fields to remove the spines from the henequen leaves after cutting (just as they had helped in the past with harvesting corn), they were accompanied by their fathers or husbands and were never paid in scrip for their labors.

Not surprisingly, women on henequen estates were relegated to the domestic sphere. Their tasks centered on rearing the family, cooking, cleaning, retrieving water from the well and firewood from the forest, bringing lunch to their husbands and sons in the fields, and tending the family garden. Ledger books occasionally listed women as domestics who worked in the landlord's "big house" or as hammock and sack makers and corn grinders, but they were not identified as henequen workers. Indeed, it appears that the fiber boom brought little change to the *campesinas'* regimen, for this strictly observed division of labor on the estates was consistent with preboom patterns. Even at the height of the fiber boom, when planters were desperate for workers, Maya women were not used in the fields.

Why did planters, who regularly complained about the scarcity of labor in the henequen zone and who did not shrink from using coercive strategies when it suited their purposes, not employ *campesinas* in the fields? By permitting the male peon to earn "wages" to provide for his family through access to corn plots and hunting and to exercise power over women in his household, the *hacendado* was securing the "loyalty" and limiting the mobility of his worker. As a consequence, families were rarely separated in the henequen zone nor does it appear that *hacendados* used the threat of separation to ensure loyalty.

This thin veneer of reciprocity formalized gender relations on the estates. When *henequeneros* arranged weddings for their peons, they provided grooms with a loan—the couple's first debt—to pay for the religious and civil ceremonies and a fiesta. The result was a complicit arrangement among males on the estate in which the master permitted the peon to preside over his own household as a subordinate patriarch. If this led to cases of domestic violence, more often than not they were handled circumspectly on the estate; rarely did grievances find their way to the local courtroom. Typically, *hacendados* and overseers put gross offenders in the hacienda jail.

Such *campesino* patriarchy, however, had limits. Often enough the *henequenero* or his overseer, exercising the humiliating "privilege" of the "right of first night," invaded the peon's hut and violated his spouse or daughter. Even though such an affront undermined the reciprocal nature of the shared sense of patriarchy, it did provide the peon with one more object lesson in where power ultimately resided on the estate. The servant would seldom take revenge on his boss; more often, we learn of unfortunate cases of misdirected rage, as peons abused their wives to reassert their dominion in the home.

Planters were reluctant to tamper with the peons' patriarchal control of their families because in the long run it suited their economic interests. As far as the *hacendado* was concerned, the principal task of Maya women was to procreate and rear the next generation of henequen workers. To permit women to work in the fields would undermine that role and upset social relations on the estate—relations that reflected the acculturated Maya's evolving cultural identity as well as the requirements of fiber production.

Thus a grim irony emerged from the henequen commodity chain: capitalistic North American wheat farmers, embedded in a democratic political system, using advanced technology on their family wheat farms, created demand for henequen in Mexico that spread and intensified coerced grueling manual labor and disrupted families in an oligarchic polity. In effect, the labor that was saved in the Midwest by mechanization was expended in Yucatán by Maya peasants working to exhaustion in the henequen fields. Ultimately the success of midwestern farmers, made possible in part by low wages in Yucatán, led them to modernize corn production and begin to export south. That, in turn, would undercut and drive down corn prices in Mexico, where maize was first domesticated.[318]

After World War I, henequen and manila found their comfortable niche challenged by a new fiber. Yucatecans were well acquainted with sisal *(Agave sisalana)*, which was indigenous to the peninsula and had long been used by artisans to make hammocks and bagging. This true sisal reached German East Africa in the 1890s, and by the 1920s sisal plantations flourished in Tanganyika and Kenya. Later Java, in the South Pacific, would commit to sisal. A formidable competitor, sisal was stronger than henequen and, unlike manila, lent itself well to defibering machines. Labor costs in these areas were even lower than in Yucatán and the Philippines; another race to the bottom. By 1927, Asian and African nations accounted for nearly half the world's hard-fiber production.

The Great Depression and the invention of the combine, which did not use twine, hurt the henequen and manila trades. Production fell precipitously; henequen exports reached a low in 1940, when they were less than one-fourth the six hundred thousand bales exported during World War I. The introduction of low-cost synthetic fibers after World War II would devastate all hard-fiber economies; indeed, reports of their demise were not exaggerated as polypropylene harvest twine gradually replaced both sisal and henequen-based baler twine as the industry standard.

To add insult to injury, the economic multiplier effects of these primary commodities were limited. The local economies were too small to transfer earnings to other productive enterprises. Hard-fiber exports, despite the great wealth generated for some in the short run, were unable to lead to self-sustaining economic development in Mexico, the Philippines, Africa, Bengal, or Java. In this, hard fibers were much less generous than wheat, whose sophisticated commodity chain helped foment industrialization by technological invention, important backward and forward linkages, labor-saving devices, and a lowered cost of living in the booming cities. The fibers were also more injurious than rice because of the widespread use of coerced labor in henequen and manila and their intense market orientation. Rice continued to mainly be for subsistence; it fed the same people who worked the paddies, though its role was more developmentalist in industrializing countries like Japan.

Stimulants

Last we include a category of goods that has usually been given insufficient attention in this period: stimulants. They are often dismissed as luxuries, "non-necessaries," or "drug foods." Some of them, such as cocaine, are even denounced as outlaw goods on the margins of booming world trade. Other stimulants, like kava, the kola nut, mate, or khat, while permitted, were popular only locally. Even when goods important to the world economy, such as sugar, coffee, and tobacco, are included, they have been derided as the "big fix" and "the big drain."[319]

Most are psychoactive, or mind- and body-altering. At certain times and in certain places they were considered illicit (sugar would have to be converted to alcohol to win such a dubious honor). Ingested for purposes other than nutrition, initially they were thought of as medicines, drugs, or spices, and soon they became associated with food and even replaced the hunger for food (though not the body's need for nutrition). In fact, they played a central role in feeding international and transcontinental trade. Some began as luxuries and ended as necessities or even industrial inputs. Others became medicines essential to health and to military operations. They were closely attached to the development of the food and pharmaceutical industries.

The goods that were important in the last third of the nineteenth century still had in common characteristics necessary for the era of slow-moving and expensive trade, loosely institutionalized markets, and incipient chemistry labs. Given the risks of oceanic travel, however, they also had to be potentially quite profitable to encourage traders to engage in long-distance commerce. They had to travel well—that is, not spoil easily—and have a high value-to-weight ratio to support transport costs. Moreover, these stimulants could be cultivated only in a limited geographic area, otherwise they would simply be grown in the country of consumption. Finally, they operated in varied cultural and religious contexts in which they played many different roles.[320]

The sometimes radical difference in climate between growers (often tropical) and consumers (mostly temperate) was usually also reflected, at least in 1870, in the strikingly distinct social and cultural settings of the people involved in the trade. By 1945, however, some of the difference between the two ends of the various commodity chains had declined as export-led growth brought development and urbanization to the most successful agricultural countries and at least urban pockets of development in the places less enmeshed in the world market.

The post-1870 period experienced new uses even for products that, like sugar, had been consumed for a long time: this was the era of urbanization, intensified labor, longer workdays, and market-oriented workers who could occasionally afford to buy imported goods. Although these goods often began as markers of distinction and status to separate the wealthy and privileged from the masses, they became necessities sometimes as important as food itself where factories and electricity imposed work discipline over laborers' biological clocks. Stimulants both induced pleasure and dulled misery.

We concentrate on sugar, tobacco, coffee, tea, and chocolate because they were among the first commodities to tie together the continents, as early as the sixteenth century, and became some of the most valuable internationally traded goods in the years 1870–1945. They highlight the contrasting and changing roles of colonialism, slavery, immigration, mechanization, and botanical improvements in cultivating areas. They also demonstrate the industrial, marketing, and financial transformations, and the growing mass appeal in consuming countries as well, allowing us to contrast production systems on different continents. Cane sugar was grown in tropical Caribbean and South American colonies but was challenged by beet sugar production in more temperate zones. Coffee in our period was overwhelmingly grown in independent countries in Latin America after an initial success in South Asian colonies; tea grew almost exclusively in Asia, at first in China and Japan but mostly in colonies by the twentieth century; and chocolate was first cultivated in independent Latin America but increasingly in African colonies after the First World War. The global reach and cultural interactions of the international economy are underlined by the fact that the word *coffee* is derived from Arabic, *tea* from a Chinese dialect, and *cacao* from the Olmecs of southern Mexico. (*Chocolate* is a corruption of the Aztec name for the beans.)

The impact of these commodities cannot be measured solely in monetary terms. Their social and political impacts were also registered in their strategic importance and the roles they played in people's everyday lives, from the crushing labor in the fields to the delight of a sweet candy, a good smoke, or a fresh brew of coffee, tea, or chocolate. Some stimulants were particularly prized during wartime.

Sugar

Sugar remained one of the most valuable commodities on the world market. Its cultivation and production were spread around the globe, because in addition to the more traditional tropical cane sugar, beet sugar started flourishing in temperate lands during the late nineteenth century. Competition between the two types of sugar provoked technological and institutional improvements that reduced the price to consumers while progressively broadening the market for both. Both types of sugar delivered cultivars, capital, migrant labor, new business forms, and new products all over the world. The economist W. Arthur Lewis notes that sugar was the only tropical crop to undergo a scientific revolution before the First World War.[321] Still, the circumstances of its production in different areas varied widely.

Characterized by innovation and dynamism, sugar was not a crop that lent itself to freedom, even though overt slavery was abolished in our period. By and large, neither labor nor commodity markets were free. Generating some of the most advanced capitalist cultivation and processing complexes in the world, sugar also relied on various forms of colonialism: international, internal, and neocolonial; coercion through a variety of means from slavery and debt peonage to indenture; corporate monopoly of land and monopsony of harvested cane; and cartels and trusts in consuming countries. Not surprisingly, sugar labor relations played a large role in inciting revolution in Haiti (1791–1804), Cuba (1860s and 1896–1898), and Mexico (1910–1917) as well as inducing radical politics in the Caribbean and elsewhere. For consumers, sugar—formerly a luxury—became an everyday spice and fuel that provided sweetness and calories. Not only were its cultivation and processing industrialized, sugar became an important ingredient in the burgeoning processed-foods industry as a sweetener and a preservative.

Sugar, specifically the species *Saccharum officinarum,* was one the first transcontinental commodities to mobilize world trade and colonialism while moving laborers across oceans. Domesticated by humans perhaps twenty-five hundred years ago, it remained of minor importance until the early modern era. Restricted by nature to areas free of frost, it was the quintessential tropical crop. The spice that had begun probably in New Guinea or Indonesia, then India, in the early modern era was moved to the Mediterranean area, where Arabs adapted processing techniques first developed for olive oil. Although sugar continued to be cultivated in India, China, and Persia, it was grown on such a small scale that it did not replace other sweeteners. In the Western world, especially in Europe, it would become what by the seventeenth century could convincingly be called, along with silver, one of the first two transatlantic commodities. Sugar replaced honey, syrups, and tree saps to become the dominant sweetener. It enjoyed the advantage of not changing the flavor of the food or drink to which it was added, and it was cheap to transport once processed, relatively imperishable, and easy to store.[322] It was also the raw material for highly coveted products like molasses and rum.

Sugar's inherent botanical characteristics were certainly responsible in part for its enormous popularity and extensive economic consequences in Europe. But demand was as important as supply. Changes occurring in Europe set the stage for the explosion of demand that started in the seventeenth century and became full-blown in the last quarter of the nineteenth century.

Sugar evolved from a spice and medicine to a marker of status.[323] Demand for it in Europe grew at a stunning 10 percent per year in the nineteenth century. The British had the greatest cravings for sugar, or at least the greatest capacity to buy it—and Europe's worst teeth. On average, each Briton ate eighteen pounds in 1800 and ninety pounds a century later.[324] Because Great Britain ended its protection of colonial sugar imports by 1846, it became the largest free import market in the world as its colonial production declined. This reflected the victory of domestic sugar refiners and candy makers over colonial and foreign planters. As historian of sugar Noël Deerr ruefully admonished: "During the whole three hundred years of the British sugar industry there has been a clash of interests between the producer and the refiner, and it is not going too far to say that there has been a tendency to reduce the former to the position of a bond servant to the latter."[325]

British duties were low or absent on low-grade sugars but high on better, more profitable sugars. Hence, colonial planters sent an industrial input that the protected refiners in Britain turned into a more profitable finished sugar product. It turned out that free trade meant the colonial grower was not protected but the home refiner was. Continental European countries like Germany and Austria as well as the United States followed the same policy, privileging the home industry over those overseas.

Sugar in the years 1870–1945 is given less scholarly attention than in the colonial slave era, but world sugar production expanded tenfold in our period, growing four times as fast as the world's population. Even once the last major cane sugar growers abolished slavery—Cuba in 1886 and Brazil in 1888—world sugar output continued to mount, quadrupling from 3.8 million tons in 1880 to 16 million tons at the outset of World War I, and as high as 27.8 million tons in 1942. The continued upsurge in production occurred not so much because sugar now relied on free wage labor, but because new forms of coercive labor, such as debt peonage and contract labor, were introduced, and the fields and mills were increasingly mechanized.[326]

The ability of the sugar trade not only to survive but to grow vertiginously after emancipation would have shocked principals of the sugar trade who had for centuries assumed that sugar required slavery. (They did not know that in Asia, free peasants grew and cut the cane.) Clearly, planters in the Americas were able to make adjustments to this radical change in the labor regime. This should not have been surprising. As historian Manuel Moreno Fraginals has shown for Cuba, some of the planters were agile capitalists, not hidebound feudal traditionalists committed to precapitalist labor forms.[327]

Despite the multitude of reformers and historians who have argued that slavery impeded industrialization, that was clearly not the case for sugar. Sugarcane was not simply a "raw material" that would be refined by factories in Europe. In one sense it was an industrial good, processed initially in situ on the plantation. But it could be considered an intermediate good because it more often than not was added to other foods and often underwent further processing in consuming countries. The processing in sugar mills to extract sucrose from the cane and then purify it—sometimes in a different installation—had required some of the most advanced chemistry, which was practiced in mills that were some of the largest enterprises of the early modern and nineteenth-century worlds. A good case has been made that sugar mills were the first modern factories in the field with large disciplined labor forces and integrated, time-sensitive processes. These factories were developed by local and often immigrant landowners and merchants as well as by absentee investors in the purportedly backward Caribbean and South America, not in the advanced centers of the Industrial Revolution.[328]

After 1870, abolition, electricity, foreign capital, and modern transport would inspire a new technical revolution. The industrial nature of sugar production meant that demand for sugar could rise at the same time that prices of cane and processed sugar *fell*. In the restricted markets of mercantilist Europe, growing demand usually had been answered by soaring prices and restricted trade. But after 1870 the competition of empires changed almost everything. As historians Bill Albert and Adrian Graves observe: "By World War I, the only aspect of sugar production which remained unchanged from the early decades of the nineteenth century was cane cutting. In all other respects there had been a complete and radical transformation."[329] The transformation was brought about not only by changes in technology and labor regime, but also by the organization of sugar firms. Economic historian Alan Dye notes, "In most instances, the industries affected by the technical changes of the second industrial revolution and the organizational innovations of the accompanying managerial revolution centered in Europe and the United States. In one industry they did not— sugar."[330] The market widened beyond the aristocracy and bourgeoisie and spread out from the largest cities to towns and villages. In England, even servants were given a weekly sugar allowance.[331] The downtrodden sailors of Her Majesty's navy received a generous rum allotment. Sugar, even when it relied on slave labor, was, as Adam Smith recognized, a capitalist enterprise that increasingly reached a mass market.

Capitalism and slavery had gone hand in hand; many of the most capitalistic of planters invested the most in slaves.[332] But sugar plantations proved to be a hybrid. In Cuba they had started using the railroad to move sugar on plantations within thirteen years of its first public use in England. Steam-powered, and then electrically powered, machines moved out to the ever-larger sugar mills in the countryside.

While welcoming technological innovation, planters did not want to dive straight into a world of free labor. Part of the solution to the end of slavery for growers was some years of "apprenticeship" of ex-slaves adopted throughout the Americas to ease the transition for planters (and extend it for laborers). With the end of the Atlantic slave trade in the first half of the nineteenth century, the colonial powers encouraged the movement of technically free but often indentured peoples from one colony—and ocean—to another. Importation of Amerindians from Mexico (in Cuba) and immigrants from India as well as Chinese and Pacific islanders (in Fiji and Australia) provided some of the hands that had previously come from Africa.

Some of the most important changes came in the last decades of the nineteenth century when slavery's demise became evident to even the most successful sugar producers. Large central mills were installed that employed the centrifugal process using vacuum pans to separate the crystals from the molasses. They greatly sped up the process and permitted undreamed-of economies of scale if provided sufficient cane to keep the boilers and centrifuges operating at full throttle. The new machinery would demand greater coordination between the harvest in the fields and processing in the mills.

In Cuba, technological innovations, combined with the devastation of the smaller mills caused by the pro-independence Ten Years War (1868–1878) and the closing of the transatlantic slave trade in midcentury, led to the establishment of large mill-plantation complexes. They were neither agricultural enterprises nor factories, strictly speaking, but rather, in the words of sociologist Fernando Ortiz, a complex "system of land, machinery, transportation, technicians, workers, capital, and people to produce sugar. It is a complete social organism, as live and complex as a city or municipality, or a baronial keep with its surrounding fief of vassals, tenants, and serfs."[333]

Until official colonialism ended in 1898, these complexes were financed by mostly by Spaniards, though with growing US investments. Then, under neocolonial independence, large US sugar corporations built giant central mills. They required fewer workers to process far more cane much more quickly and extract more sucrose. The central mills were not only more efficient; they exercised local monopsony control over the smaller sugar estates. The smaller-scale sugar land-holders, known as *colonos,* began to specialize in cultivation while sending their cane on a much improved rail system to be processed by their giant industrial neighbors. Increasingly, the US mills moved to the east end of the island where they dominated landowning. *Colonos* became their tenant farmers. Before Cuba's 1895–1898 war for independence from Spain, the slightly less than three million acres of sugar lands had been divided into ninety-one thousand estates that averaged just thirty acres each. Afterward land became so concentrated that by the 1920s, 180 huge sugar mills owned almost twenty-three thousand square kilometers of land, 20 percent of Cuba's territory! The voracious sugar sector came under the sway of US capital just as Cuba bent to North American military and political might. Already in 1896 some three-fourths of Cuba's sugar went north to the United States. By 1913 almost 80 percent of Cuba's exports went to North America.[334] Most of the economy, not just plantations but also the railroads, public utility companies, banks, and even hotels, were owned by Yankees. Sugar saw the creation of enormous foreign-owned estates, modern agro-industrial factories in the fields. The mill owners were not only factory bosses and planters, but also virtual sovereigns issuing laws and money and overseeing housing.

The botanical nature of cane sugar, with one or at most two harvests a year, and the fact that cane had to be processed within a day or two of cutting or its sugar content fell drastically, meant that factories had to process *local* cane—the cane could not be imported from elsewhere during the local off-season. As a result, the industry faced idle capacity and unemployed laborers during the dead season. Seasonal instability was exacerbated by cyclical fluctuations of world prices caused by rain, drought, and hurricanes. This was in the context of a secular price drop by half between 1870 and 1910 and then, after a spike during World War I, back down to one-quarter the 1870 price by 1930.[335] Because so much capital was invested in the sugar mills, members of the mill complex could not convert to another crop to compensate. They had to find a means to improve efficiency in processing and transport, which brought further debt and reliance on external markets. Not surprisingly, some of the first literature stressing the "dependence" of exporting countries on overseas markets and capital focused on sugar and was published in this period.[336]

A sugar mill near Havana, Cuba, ca. 1904. Cuban sugar barons became world leaders in sugar production by combining the most advanced technology of the Industrial Revolution in their large steam-driven mills with efficient railroads that brought cane from huge plantations and exported processed sugar to the world. These factories in the field were serviced by the back-breaking labor of machete-wielding rural proletarians. (Library of Congress)

Cuba and to a lesser extent the Dominican Republic and the newly won US territory of Puerto Rico were the Caribbean success stories of the first part of the twentieth century. The other European former sugar colonies stagnated or lowered their sugar production while Cuba's production grew two and half times just between 1904 and 1914. By 1929 it had doubled again, though output would fall rather sharply once the Great Depression hit.[337]

The solution to reducing production costs and attending to the rapidly growing markets of North America and Western Europe was not only better machines. Agronomy also contributed. Experimental stations in Cuba, Java, and England developed through "nobilization," breeding new types of sugarcane that had higher sucrose content, were more resistant to disease, could flourish in different climates, and were easier to harvest.

In addition to both intensifying and extending sugar planting and processing in the Spanish Caribbean, the colonial regimes stimulated new areas of cane cultivation in the Indian Ocean. The more dependable and larger ships, driven by steam and the Suez Canal's opening, allowed such an inexpensive, bulk product as Indian Ocean sugar to compete with Caribbean production in the markets of Europe.

The Dutch turned to sugar once Java's coffee economy was devastated by leaf rust disease in the 1870s and 1880s. By the 1920s, Java was the second most important sugar exporter in the world, though it declined sharply with the Great Depression and a change in British sugar import duties in India. Java's sugar success stemmed from a system quite different from the Caribbean's. Using what anthropologist Clifford Geertz calls "agricultural involution," a mounting population invested increasing amounts of labor in their sugar and rice terraces to maintain food at a "minimal level."[338] Geertz viewed this as more than a colonial relationship:[339]

> There never really was, even in [Dutch East India] Company times, a Netherlands East Indies economy in an integral, analytic sense—there was just that, admittedly highly autonomous, branch of the Dutch economy which was situated in the Indies ("tropical Holland" as it sometimes was called), and cheek-by-jowl, the autonomous Indonesian economy also situated there.

Elsewhere in the East, the British applied their own capital and workers from Pacific islands to Queensland, Australia. Having assumed control of the continent from the indigenous Aborigine population in the late eighteenth century, white settlers and British capital began the sugar industry in the mid-nineteenth century. The extent to which these initial workers were voluntary or "kidnapped" is disputed, but that they were indentured seems clear. However, racism and broader imperial goals soon reshaped the Australian sugar industry. Seeking a land of small-scale *white* farmers rather than the more typical plantation model using foreign capital and brown workers, Queensland first sponsored two sugar mills to fight the oligopsony of the existing major refining companies. In 1887 milling began to be consolidated under the Colonial Sugar Refining Company

(CSR), a company intended to be Australian-owned. It backed labor legislation that sought to end indentured (brown) labor. Then legislation in 1893 created central mills managed by smallholders. Although under strictly economic free-trade calculations the Australians were not competitive, London leaders of the British Commonwealth decided to protect the white Australians through tariffs and bounties. Investments in modern cane species and advanced technology under the stewardship of state governments and the CSR led to a seventy-fold rise in Australia's sugar production between 1870 and 1910.[340]

The experience of sugar in Fiji, which became a British colony in 1874, contrasts with Australia's. In Fiji there was a substantial native population, but it was marginalized under colonialism. The sugar industry was run by British and Australian capital using labor from Britain's colony in India. Indeed, it has been argued that Fiji was a colony of Australia, at least insofar as it was the sugar sector that dominated exports. The same CSR that instituted policies that favored smallholders and invested domestically in Australia, controlled Fiji, where it employed poorly paid indentured Indians. Profits, instead of being reinvested in Fiji, were repatriated to Australia. Australian banks dominated in Fiji as well, but instead of aiding Fijian development as they did in Australia, they sent profits back to Australia.[341] This underlies a major difference in British colonial policy. In part this difference can be explained by the nature of the comparison—in one case, a small island dominated by one crop and few economic activities versus a vast diverse continent. Sugar islands were less able to develop than were continental spaces with sugar, like Brazil or Australia, that were not so wedded to monoculture.

But the distinction between Fiji (or Mauritius, Barbados, or Jamaica) and Australia also reflects the different policies and economic patterns of tropical and temperate colonies. Temperate-climate colonies (also thought of as settler and white when the local indigenous population was sufficiently marginalized, as in Australia, New Zealand, or earlier the United States and Canada) were awarded more local autonomy and far more European investments.[342] An enclave example of the settler colony on the southern tip of Africa was Natal, where whites displaced native Africans and then contracted Indian coolies. (Wages were too low to interest black South Africans.) As in Australia, at the end of the nineteenth century central mills were introduced, indentured labor was phased out, and plantations were replaced by smaller holdings.

A different form of sugar colonialism appeared in Formosa, which began producing sugar particularly under the supervision of Japanese colonial rulers. Although Formosa had prospered during a sugar boom in the early eighteenth century, its family-run farms and small mills had difficulty keeping up with advances in foreign production. After the Japanese occupied the island in 1895, Formosa's economy remained agricultural. Families continued to dominate farming, but sugar processing was modernized. Japanese conglomerates built large, advanced mills and acquired some of the sugar lands. As in Cuba, their mills controlled the native-owned sugar farms. Although unable to compete internationally, sugar once again became Formosa's leading export because it was sold duty-free within the protected Japanese market.[343]

US sugar colonialism in Hawai'i was similar. Cane was already being cultivated before the arrival of Captain Cook in the late eighteenth century, but it was chewed rather than made into sugar. Sugar production and exports rose only with the settling of North American missionaries, which also caused the native Hawai'ian population to dwindle, as the outsiders brought deadly diseases. To replace the natives, 46,000 Chinese, 180,000 Japanese, 126,000 Filipinos, as well as Portuguese and Puerto Ricans were brought in, often as semicoerced workers bound by "semi-military labor contracts."[344] Appropriated by the United States in 1893 and annexed five years later, Hawai'i became a significant sugar and pineapple source as large companies, such as Spreckels Sugar and Dole Pineapple, connected the islands ever closer to the United States under the umbrella of US protective tariffs.[345] These companies not only grew and processed their crops, but also branded and wholesaled them.

In the circum-Caribbean, colonies of the British, French, Dutch, Danish (until the purchase of the Virgin Islands by the United States in 1917), and Spanish (until 1898), and independent sugar-growing nations such as Brazil, found their sugar exports sharply declining and their exports diversifying into other crops, especially coffee, cacao, and bananas. With the exception of Cuba, which became one of the world's premier sugarcane producers, and to a lesser extent Puerto Rico and the Dominican Republic, New World cane growers turned inward, either to their colonial mother country or to the home market.

Independent Brazil turned after the abolition of slavery to the burgeoning domestic market for sugar as well as *cachaça* (cane spirits). The historiography of

Brazil laments the collapse of its sugar industry as the Northeast failed to attract immigrants and refused to permit Africans or Asians to enter as laborers after 1888 (with the exception of Japanese, who came in large numbers to the state of São Paulo in the 1920s—but to work in coffee, not sugar). *Modernization without Change* is the subtitle of one well-known study of the purported backwardness of the sugar sector. But it looked at sugar only as an export. In fact, the construction of new railroads and central mills *(usinas)* allowed the country to remain one of the world's main sugar producers after abolition. In 1945 Brazil produced 1.2 million tons, trailing only Cuba in the Americas and Java as well as beet producers Germany and Russia in world production.[346] This feat did not receive much attention, however, because the sugar was not exported; it simply remained within the country.

Mexico followed a similar trajectory as its sugar continued to be directed to the domestic market, which was protected to benefit the local elite. Sugar producers relied on the domestic workforce from Mexico's impoverished and largely indigenous center. With labor becoming scarcer or more restive, capital in the form of mechanization and rationalization—especially in processing and transporting cane—reduced the workforce. Sugar areas in both Mexico and Brazil would become hotbeds of political agitation. In 1911 Emiliano Zapata led revolutionary peasants angered at expanding sugar plantations in their home state of Morelos just south of Mexico City. Agitation in the northeast of Brazil came only in the 1960s. Of course, the sugar-inspired revolution that would rock the world brought Fidel Castro to power in Cuba in 1959.

Peru's huge export-oriented coastal sugar plantations relied mainly on some one hundred thousand Chinese contract laborers who worked under harsh coercive conditions from the mid-nineteenth century to 1874. Almost all male, this coolie population did not expand to satisfy labor demands. Gradually, indigenous workers from the Andes were convinced to work in sugar under the *enganche,* where indigenous laborers were literally hooked from their communities by contractors. But they were usually somewhat unreliable seasonal workers because they were ill-treated and because they continued to own small farms in the Sierra. Unlike the *colonos* of the Caribbean, they were not proletarians, though swelling population, grasping *hacendados,* and warfare had reduced peasant autonomy in the mountains. To supplement indigenous workers and the evaporated pool of coolie labor, the Peruvian government entered into a contract with a Japanese immigration company in 1898. Protected by the company and the Japanese legation, the 17,700 Japanese laborers who arrived to work in Peruvian sugar by 1923 were better treated than either the Chinese coolies or native Peruvians had been.[347]

In Argentina, the interior province of Tucumán, connected to the Buenos Aires area by a railroad in 1876 and protected by a high tariff, began to supply the national market and even export some. Instead of using workers of African, Indian, or Chinese origin, as in most other sugar economies, the Argentines mimicked the Peruvians and Mexicans by relying on debt peonage of indigenous Andean populations, a holdover from Spanish colonial labor systems but adapted to a new product. This system was sufficiently successful that Argentina began exporting sugar to neighboring countries, yet the Tucumán area remained one of the country's poorest provinces.[348] Sugar's success in Argentina's interior resulted from a national development project, in the sense that government railroad and tariff policy aided the elite of the landlocked northwest. But these measures did little for its workers.

The sugar policy of the US South came to resemble Argentina's. Sugar planters in Louisiana, for example, had originally grown for export when Louisiana had been part of the French Empire. But they had changed orientation to the US home market after the French sold their colony well before the American Civil War. The war created great destruction to life and property, and then the Emancipation Proclamation freed the more than two hundred thousand slaves in the sugar sector, many of whom became sharecroppers. Despite the protection of import duties and bounties, southern cane production would not grow much until the 1959 Cuban Revolution and ensuing embargo.[349]

Sugar Beets

The world sugar industry witnessed a great transformation of the trade in the nineteenth century with the development of the sugar beet, *Beta vulgaris,* which grew in temperate climates. Substitution of successful commodities, by finding new sources, new cultivars, or chemically synthesized replacements, was a common feature of the late nineteenth- and twentieth-century world economy, as we have already seen with hard fibers. In the case of sugar, the beet, a previously unimportant tuber, came to challenge cane's place as a worldwide sweetener. This was just one of the fundamental applications of German science (chemistry, agronomy, and engineering) to economic problems. Without tropical colonies or great exports, Germans had an inclination to self-reliance that would greatly affect world markets in nitrates, dyes like cochineal and indigo, rubber, and sugar. This was a result not only of German chemical prowess and sophisticated labs and universities—chemistry had been a *Lieblingswissenschaft* since the eighteenth century—but of necessity brought on by the world economy. German wool could not compete with Australian wool, German flax and hemp lost out to Mexican henequen, African sisal, and Indian jute, and their vegetable oils could not compete with petroleum jelly or margarines that used palm, soy, and peanut oil from tropical countries. The response was to improve seeds, plants, and fertilizers in agriculture and create chemical substitutes or synthetics. Their exports continued to go principally to Europe (though their imports now tended to come from the neo-Europes and tropics), but the composition of German exports changed from raw materials to finished and semifinished goods.[350] Their success at this is why the German word *ersatz* ("substitute") became part of the English vocabulary.

A German scientist, Andreas Marggraf, in 1747 became the first to extract sugar from the beet. A half century passed before research efforts led to the first sugar beet factories in Prussia, Russia, and Austria-Hungary. But it was the British blockade of Napoleonic France beginning in 1806, which drove prices for cane sugar sky-high, that encouraged the opening of more sugar beet factories. Colonial powers like the French resumed their affair with cane sugar once the blockade ended in 1815, but the Central Europeans and Russians continued to put their hopes in the beet. They bred new beet cultivars and developed processing techniques to increase sucrose content from 7 percent in the early nineteenth century to 8 percent by the 1870s, up to 11.9 percent in 1889.[351] New extraction through centrifuges beginning in the 1840s and the expanding size of mills as they became modern factories caused beet sugar production to mount.

But this is not just a story of the agronomy and technology of the beet itself. The sugar beet occupied an important place in the farm complex of the rural poor that made it economically viable. Like potatoes, the sugar beet grew in cold climates as well as warm. Densely planted, it did not require much land or many inputs. It was cultivated with a simple hoe. The beet offered side benefits because it was the highest-yielding field crop of the temperate zone in terms of volume. Its leaves as well as the pulp left over after sucrose extraction were used to feed livestock, whose manure in turn fed the beets. Beets reached maturity quickly and replenished the land with nitrogen. So rather than competing with other crops as grains did, the beet complemented them as a stage in crop rotation instead of leaving the land fallow.[352] Labor demands were not particularly time-sensitive because the ripe beet could be left in the ground until the farmer was ready to extract it. So in contrast to cane sugar—an exotic that encouraged foreign ownership, coercive labor systems, concentration of lands and profits, as well as an industrial processing plant, and imported workers—beet sugar could be more benign (though many Poles came to Saxony and many Mexicans to the US Midwest to work beet sugar in the twentieth century).

On the other hand, the advantages of beet cultivation offered few economies of scale or scope. (Sugar beets could not be used to make alcohol, for instance.) This made it socially and politically attractive in that peasants were not dislodged during the boom. On the other hand, the Prussian *Junker* landlords of Saxony combined their feudal agrarian heritage with modern industry. They retained their vast estates and turned them to the sugar beet as they invested in the most modern mills and sugar factories as well.[353] Increased output demanded more workers, who now were paid in wages rather than in kind or usufruct. By 1913 there were four hundred thousand migratory workers, mostly from Poland. The beet inverted the relationship of the state to the agricultural elite; rather than the *Junkers* dominating the state, the state subsidized the agrarian *Junkers*. To protect them, duties on imported sugar were kept high and bounties on exports, to encourage a balance-of-payments surplus, also remained high. This meant that the German consumer paid a price above the international market price for sugar while the British consumer enjoyed the treat of sugar subsidized by the German government. To protect beet growers and more importantly refiners, the German government also banished saccharin—a sugar substitute synthesized from coal tar first in 1878 by a German chemist and cheaper than beet sugar—to pharmacies as a medicine rather than a food ingredient.[354]

Beets needed government protection because they could not compete with cane on price; they were too expensive. But the governments of Prussia (and

Germany after unification in 1871), Austro-Hungary, and Russia offered bounties to encourage cultivation and exports. This was not only a state-led effort to
promote industrialization and positive trade balances. Protecting peasant farmers was also politically wise because German farmers had more than once shown
their ability and inclination to revolt. This was a particularly sensitive issue in
Germany when the expansion of cheap wheat production in Russia and in the
"vacant lands," such as Argentina and the US Midwest, drove out of business
some German wheat farmers working poorer fields. These were the same lands
that sustained the sugar beet. By the end of the nineteenth century, government
aid and peasant agriculture in France, the Netherlands, Belgium, parts of Scandinavia, and Spain were also yielding beet sugar.[355] Although beet sugar was a
national crop rather than a colonial or neocolonial one like cane, it was also the
product of state supervision and aid rather than a result of unadulterated market
forces.

Beet sugar production was embedded in what Bukharin termed "state capitalism." As with a number of other commodities, state governments cooperated
with big banks and merchant houses to create sugar-refining oligopolies and cartels. Initially beet cultivation was also concentrated in a small number of countries. Germany produced over one-third of the world's 1897 total, and together
with Austria, France, and Russia fully 86 percent of the world's beet sugar. Russia
and France mainly consumed their sugar while Germany and Austria exported
more than half of what they produced, mostly to European neighbors.[356]

In the Midwest and West of the United States, government tariff protection
encouraged beet production. But the United States, like the United Kingdom,
was still one of the world's largest importers of sugar. In 1896 sugar production
(and sundries) in the United States occupied about 3.6 million acres, less than 2
percent of total agricultural acreage, and yielded a similar share of agricultural
production by value. Sugar remained small despite the calculation that on a
returns-per-acre basis it was far more remunerative than grains, cotton, or potatoes. Only tobacco surpassed it. The reason more farmers did not embrace sugar
production was that it required an ample, cheap labor force or political protection. So the United States mostly imported cane sugar, particularly from colonial
or semicolonial areas such as Hawai'i, Puerto Rico, the Philippines, and Cuba.
But with the dawn of the twentieth century and ample government protection,

the beet industry took root, concentrating in California, Colorado, Utah, and Michigan. By 1920, after the world war and civil wars had destroyed the beet industries of Russia, damaged those of Austria and Germany, and cut world beet production in half, the United States briefly became the world's leading beet sugar producer.[357] Seeking shelter from colonial competitors, American beet growers added a loud voice to battle against American colonialism.

The Market for Sugar

Sugar production mounted steadily, albeit haltingly, in the century after 1840 (see Table 4.11). The data implied a more homogeneous and monolithic market than was in fact the case. The difference was not only between cane and beet producers, but also between the taxation regimes of states and colonies. In Great Britain, true to its free-trade doctrine at this point, sugar cost almost half as much as in protectionist Germany, Austria, and the United States (see Table 4.12).

Given that the world sugar market was divided between colonial or neocolonial empires (cane) and national state-aided systems (beet), it should come as no surprise that the world sugar market was segmented and regulated. National governments, not individual corporations, were the players. International wars, revolutions, and civil wars shifted production. Even though the British attempted to open up the world sugar market by dropping sugar duties and reducing colonial preferences, other major consuming countries did not follow suit. Their strong state presence and contradictory interests were manifested in the numerous international sugar conferences held in the years after 1870. Because sugar was so central to national and colonial government policy, and world prices were falling dramatically, it seemed natural that it would be the major European producers and colonial powers—Austria-Hungary, Belgium, France, Germany, Holland, Italy, Russia, and Spain—who attempted to regulate the world sugar market. The only non-European exception was Peru, which sent a representative to three of the ten international meetings held between 1860 and 1912.[358]

They tried to hammer out differences over bounties, tariffs, and national cartels but were frustrated by failure until the 1902 Brussels Sugar Conference. The problem was that although sugar was a valuable commodity and one of the most internationally traded goods in terms of value, it was also, as historian Horacio

Estimated world cane sugar and beet sugar production, 1841–1940 (in tons)

	Cane	Beet	Total
1841	829,000	50,929	879,929
1850	1,043,000	159,435	1,202,435
1860	1,376,000	351,602	1,727,602
1870	1,662,000	939,096	2,601,096
1880	1,883,000	1,857,210	3,740,210
1890	2,597,000	3,697,800	6,294,800
1900	5,252,987	6,005,865	11,258,855
1910	8,155,837	8,667,980	16,823,817
1913	9,661,165	9,053,561	18,714,726
1920	11,924,813	4,906,266	16,831,079
1925	15,140,542	8,617,960	23,758,502
1930	15,942,438	11,910,883	27,853,321
1935	16,598,262	10,430,394	27,028,656
1940	19,255,041	11,242,422	30,499,463

Sources: Noël Deerr, *The History of Sugar,* 2 vols. (London: Chapman and Hall, 1950), 2:490–491.

TABLE 4.12

Indexed price of sugar imports, 1888

Britain	Germany	Austria	Sweden	Belgium	USA
100	176	170	123	123	170

Source: Calculated from Michael G. Mulhall, *The Dictionary of Statistics,* 4th ed. (London: G. Routledge and Sons, 1899), 470.

Note: 100 = 17 pounds sterling, 11 pence, per ton.

Crespo has observed, one of the foods "most sensitive to strategies for national self-sufficiency" because of the high amount of calories per acre it produced. Sugar became "an article especially valued by governments in their aim to attain food autarky."[359] Domestic economies were dominated by cartels in Germany and Austria and trusts elsewhere. Other producers were offering export bounties in the attempt to enter the British market, the only free market where colonial and subsidized continental sugar competed. Even the Brussels agreement succeeded only for a few years; the Liberal Party came to power in Britain in 1905, objected to the higher prices caused by the agreement, and withdrew the United Kingdom.

World War I's destruction of European beet-growing countries drastically changed the global market. Cane growers, especially Cuba, regained their former dominance and now had to be included in conversations. But it was difficult to convince all the major sugar players to participate, even as the non-European world gained greater representation. An effort in 1931 supported by the League of Nations that included Cuba, Peru, and Java, as well as major beet growers, failed because countries that had not agreed to production quotas raised their output. A more promising agreement in London in 1937 included not only the members of the previous meetings, but also major consuming countries such as Britain and the United States, and, reflecting a true worldwide discussion, China, India, the Soviet Union, and South Africa. The agreement, however, did not come into force before World War II broke out and suspended the pact. Sugar would remain a politically sensitive commodity in the postwar years, but its role as a major international commodity declined as mineral commodities and industrial finished products dominated.

As Table 4.11 shows, cane's share of all sugar, which had fallen from 64 percent in 1870 to 41 percent in 1890, returned to over three-quarters of all production by 1940. In part this was because war destroyed beet sugar mills and displaced farmers. Also, national policies shifted as sugar became recognized as a strategic good for wartime consumption. Both the United Kingdom and the United States responded to World War I by offering tariff protection and bounties. Other producers, battered by warfare and the Great Depression, sharply reduced sugar production. As a result, although the world sugar market stagnated between 1930 and 1942, the relative global position of the two English-speaking empires advanced. The United Kingdom, Ireland, and Commonwealth producers combined to grow 12 percent of world production in 1942. The United States, when combined with its territories or colonies of Hawai'i, Puerto Rico, and the Philippines (under US control after 1898), provided 13 to 14 percent of the world total. When Cuba is added—it alone supplied more than all the British colonies, or the United States and its territories—to the other US totals because it had privileged access to the

North American market and a neocolonial relationship, the US areas produced almost a third of the world's sugar in 1930 and a quarter in 1942. Together with the United Kingdom, the two English-speaking empires supplied some 40 percent of the world's sugar at the end of our period.[360] Add the Dutch production in Java, and the three colonial powers had close to half the world's sugar output.

The boom in lower-cost, more efficient sugar production led to the creation of oligopoly in the greatest consuming countries. Sugar in the world economy was a true commodity, measured by its weight, degree of refining, and sweetness, but with little birthmark of its origins or whether it derived from cane or beet. This commodification of the final product lent itself to consolidation. A small number of large companies dominated the final processing in the largest markets. In the United States, H. O. Havemeyer oversaw the 1887 merger of eight refining companies to produce the American Sugar Refining Company. At its height in the early 1890s it controlled 90 percent of US refining. It was also politically influential, reputedly playing a large role in presidential elections and in inciting the Cuban-Spanish-American war. Other companies were created to contest its dominance, but the sector remained under oligopoly control. Although the US Sugar Company did create a brand—Domino Sugar—and Spreckels did also, as did a cooperative of Hawaiʻian producers who sold C&H sugar—the major continental European producers mostly did not. This may be because continental Europeans were slower to develop larger retail establishments or brands. There sugar was an ingredient, a sweetener, rather than an end-use product.

Even without brands, sugar did become entrenched in the daily lives of people in the most prosperous countries in North America, Western Europe, the neo-Europes and the cities of major exporting countries in Latin America. It became widespread as a sweetener in drinks (including the start of soft drinks) and as marmalade but also as a preservative and spice in processed foods. Because only the countries listed above, particularly the United States, had moved far along in the food-processing field, it was mainly in those countries that sugar became as omnipresent as it is today. Researchers included sugar as a necessity in studies of daily-life needs for artisans in England as its uses grew. Candy and treacle spread their hold on children, as we will see in our discussion of chocolate.[361] As Table 4.13 illustrates, there was a close correlation between affluent countries and high sugar consumption.[362]

TABLE 4.13

Per capita sugar consumption, 1933 (in pounds)

Country	Pounds of sugar consumed
Denmark	123
Australia	113
Great Britain	106
USA	100
Cuba	81
Argentina	63
France	55
Germany	51
South Africa	47
Brazil	46
Mexico	31
Peru	23
Japan	23
India	20
China	3
World	27

Source: Noël Deerr, *The History of Sugar,* 2 vols. (London: Chapman and Hall, 1949–1950), 2:532.

We have seen how dramatically the world sugar market changed after 1870. New species and varieties of cultivars, and innovations in agronomy, chemistry, and engineering, brought sugar production to every continent save Antarctica. Laborers varied from slaves, apprentices, and indentured workers, to plantation proletarians, smallholders, and peasants. The market for sugar, although one of the oldest, largest, and most valuable, was clearly not an open one. Colonial (or to include post-1898 Cuba, neocolonial) logics regimented the cane sugar markets while national development logics drove the beet sugar markets. In some parts of the world, cane and beet competed on price because their taste was identical. However, the largest consuming areas were caught up in what were essentially colonial or national development projects. Their criteria were much more political than economic.

Coffee

Because tens of millions of people in the Americas, Europe, Africa, and Asia have been intimately involved in growing, trading, transporting, processing, marketing, and consuming coffee, it is more than just a case that illustrates broader trends. Coffee itself has been central to the expansion of the world economy; it was not only one of the most valuable commodities in international commerce, in much of this period exceeded only by grains and sugar, but it was the most popular legal drug. For centuries it has truly been a *global* trade good because its intolerance of frost demanded that it be grown exclusively in the tropics or semitropics, but its cost and psychoactive effects meant that since the end of the eighteenth century it has been consumed mostly in richer and colder, caffeine-craving Western Europe and North America.

Coffee embodied the diversity and contradictions of the world economy. In the cultivating countries coffee was viewed mostly as an agricultural export commodity demanding traditional manual labor and natural resources: sun, soil, rain. In the developed consuming countries it appeared as a modern labor-intensifying, sociable brain food disembodied from its agrarian past. So in the global South, coffee meant the plantation and the farm, while in the North it meant the industrial assembly line and coffeehouse as well as the domestic break-fast table. Like sugar, a taste for coffee had intensified colonialism in the early modern period. By 1870, however, the crops were grown mainly in independent countries, particularly Brazil. Coffee sales and consumption helped sustain states by providing revenue and energizing armies while coffee cultivation sparked revolts against other states and landowners.

The coffee species that became internationally popular, *Coffea arabica,* originated in what is today Ethiopia, where it grew natively in the wild. Over one hundred species of *Coffea* (and thousands of varieties) have been identified, yet only one species was widely popular in 1870. The popularity of arabica and its global diffusion were human decisions, which, as the name implies, began not in Ethiopia but across the Red Sea in Yemen.

We would not be discussing coffee had not the coffee *drink* gained popularity before 1500 in Yemen, where coffee was planted in the mountains and became a trade good.[363] Although it was also chewed, fried, and infused as a tea

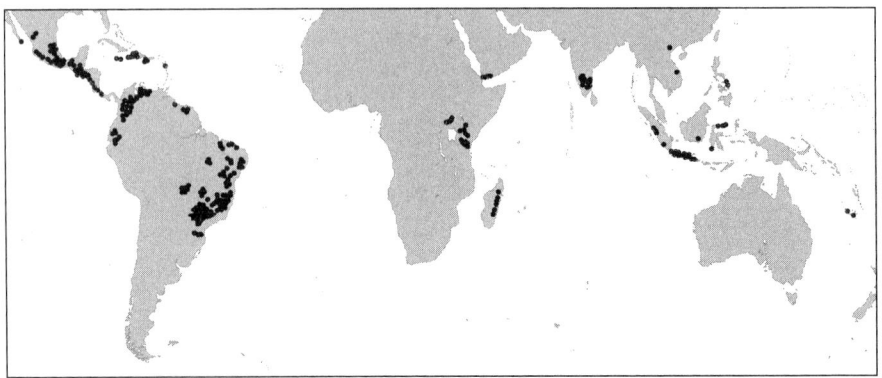

Global production of coffee, ca. 1925.

using *Coffea* cherry husks, the Sufi of Yemen made a drink out of the roasted cherry pit or "bean," which was much less perishable than other parts of the plant. This taste choice would prepare coffee for its precocious long-distance trade. Until the twentieth century, coffee—unlike grains and rice—was produced overwhelmingly for export.

Clearly, the coffee trade was not a European invention. Only after more than two centuries of an Arab-centered international market did British, Dutch, and French monopoly companies become involved as an extension of their spice trades.[364] By 1770 more than 80 percent of the world's production originated in the Americas. It was almost all arabica, but traders had to be aware of the differences in provenance. Because of relatively slow transport, poor packaging, and crude processing and brewing, differences in the "quality" of the beans remained at the level of visual inspection—that is, color and defects of the beans. The lore of provenance and appearance continued to dominate grading and pricing well into the twentieth century as *cupping*—actually tasting coffee brewed from a roasted sample—was slow to gain favor. This, and rudimentary international systems of credit and information, at first strengthened trade diasporas of ethnic minorities and family firms, because personal reputation underlay coffee transactions.

By the second half of the nineteenth century the trade was centered in the Americas. Asia, particularly Java and Ceylon, and some African colonies had raised their combined coffee exports to about one-third of international trade in

1860. But the coffee disease *Hemileia vastatrix* struck, driving their exports back to 5 percent of world trade by 1913; they remained low (13 percent) through 1945.[365] As mentioned, these areas turned to producing sugar and rubber and, as will be seen, tea.

The market for coffee, an urban luxury good at the beginning of the nineteenth century, remained small until the last third of the century. Only green arabica coffee beans were sold until technological innovations allowed the marketing of roasted, ground, and canned beans at the end of the nineteenth century. But even just selling green beans, coffee cultivation proliferated. Commercial competition also accelerated as traders from numerous European nationalities and the United States began transporting and selling beans. The price spreads between cultivators were as large as 100 percent, and because of varied taxation policies and differing freight rates, retail prices also varied widely by nation and region.[366] Early on, green coffee was sold at auction in Europe by consignment merchants who dealt in mixed cargos. They had some idea of the amount of coffee that was reaching port but were not aware of the extent of the crop awaiting harvest. The relatively small and dispersed market was volatile. Merchants and shippers—who were often the same people—governed the trade and attempted local corners.

Merchants and planters were the main entrepreneurs in expanding the coffee trade, because unlike in sugar, European states did not play a major part in stimulating production after the middle of the nineteenth century. Even though it still was produced with coerced labor, coffee was one of the "freest" markets in the world in the sense that the colonial powers dropped out of the trade.

Dutch Java's production fell sharply after leaf rust disease attacked trees beginning in the 1870s. It returned to a position of prominence only in the late twentieth century after independence.[367] In the Americas, the Dutch preferred to serve as traders and shippers; they never developed or expanded their small colonies. The British preferred the mercantilist possibilities in exploiting the Chinese and then the Indian tea trades over protecting their colonial coffee production in Jamaica, Kenya, and Uganda. The Spanish and Portuguese colonial masters preferred cacao, so Iberian Americans had to wait until well after early nineteenth-century independence and Angolans well into the twentieth century to become significant coffee producers. Although the French were fond of coffee, they had to turn to the open world market once Haitians—the world's largest coffee exporters at the time—won their bloody fight for independence in 1804; French colonies in Africa, particularly the Côte d'Ivoire, became major coffee exporters only after World War II. The decline of colonialism in coffee production meant that when states reasserted their control over the world coffee market, they did so only in the twentieth century, and the actors were independent American nations, not European colonial regimes.

Coffee and sugar were treated differently in the nineteenth-century Age of Empire because coffee's low technological demands meant that an independent former colony, Brazil, could begin producing on an unprecedented scale. Cheap, fertile, virgin land combined with rudimentary tools and machinery and abundant and relatively inexpensive slaves (due to the proximity of Africa) allowed Brazil to cause world coffee prices to plummet after 1820. Prices remained low until the last quarter of the century. Low prices and continually expanding production stimulated demand.

Brazil's success was not because of European colonial know-how. Brazil emerged as the world's major coffee exporter only after it threw off the Portuguese yoke in 1822. In fact, colonial policy had favored sugar but hindered coffee. More important to Brazil's rise to caffeinated dominance than independence were exogenous changes in the world market: the collapse of the world leader, Haiti; desire among the swelling European and later US urban consumers for stimulants; and internationally available capital and eventually labor.

Brazilian production not only largely *satisfied* growing world demand, Brazilians *stimulated and transformed* the place of coffee in overseas cafés and homes. The dependency view of agricultural producers as servants or providers of brute labor-power, willingly serving up the fruit of their labor to thirsty European buyers who were the masters of the trade, misconstrues the nature of the relationship. Brazilians, either native-born, African, or Portuguese immigrants, developed new production techniques, discovered productive cultivars, constructed an elaborate domestic transportation network in a geographically unpromising setting, and developed market standards and financial instruments. Unlike the case in other commodities we have reviewed, such as rice and sugar, in which colonialism played a major role, for coffee, independent Brazilians outproduced all colonial growers.

To give their due to the *dependentistas* who argue that Western Europeans called the tune during the nineteenth-century export boom, Brazilians benefited in the nineteenth century because of British dominance in the form of inexpensive and reliable shipping and insurance, loans, infrastructural investments, and the protection of its sea routes. So although the tea-drinking British did not export or import much coffee from their own colonies after the middle of the nineteenth century, they exported and re-exported a lot of coffee from Brazil to the United States and continental Europe. Even so, British merchants' significant presence in the coffee trade was a minority share. Most coffee exports went to the two other fastest-industrializing countries in the world, the United States and Germany, whose merchants, along with the French, gained increasing control of the trade. The same was true with British banks, which lost their dominance of financing the coffee trade to other Europeans and native Brazilian banks by the end of the nineteenth century, as they did with railroads, many of which were nationalized by the Brazilian state or financed by local capitalists.[368]

Even with Brazil, Ceylon, and Java greatly expanding world coffee production in the first half of the nineteenth century, the essential nature of the commodity chain remained the same. All the coffee exported was still green arabica sent overseas by consignment merchants, who in turn provided planters (though not peasants) with the working capital to bring crops to port. Larger plantations set the standards for cultivation, though smaller-scale slave-worked holdings in Brazil and coerced peasant production in Java successfully competed. Unscheduled sailing ships carried coffee packed in leather pouches or cotton and jute bags to major markets, where it was often sold at auction to wholesalers. Roasting, grinding, and brewing were still done in the home or in the coffeehouse. The centuries-old frying pan and mortar and pestle remained the tools of the trade for most consumers until the twentieth century.

The creation of the liberal export economy in the Americas, which contrasted with and complemented expanding European colonialism in Africa, Asia, and Oceania, transformed the nature of the demand for coffee. At first a noble, and then a bourgeois, beverage before 1800, coffee was transformed into a mass drink in the most industrialized and prosperous countries in the last part of the nineteenth century. The slaves of Brazil (until abolition in 1888) slaked the thirst of the factory workers of the industrial countries, particularly in the United States, the German and Austrian realms, and the Netherlands.

Europeans had already changed the nature of the coffee drink in the eighteenth century when Viennese and Parisians added sugar and milk and the French and Dutch began growing it in the circum-Caribbean. These acts not only would make coffee acceptable to Christians, by Europeanizing it, but would later make coffee (and, as we will see, tea) into a popular drink for the working class. In addition to its natural psychoactive properties, which reduced the sense of hunger and sleepiness while releasing adrenalin, coffee also offered the physiological advantages of being a digestive and a diuretic, and of being safe because the water was boiled before consumption. Moreover, calories and nutrition in the form of sugar and milk were now added. Although the international trade in milk would have to wait until companies like Borden, Carnation, and Nestlé developed less-perishable condensed and evaporated milk, the vast expansion of sugar production and the dramatic drop in its price greatly stimulated coffee consumption among the less advantaged in urban Western Europe and the United States.[369]

Brazil, which produced over half the world's coffee by 1850, was responsible for about 80 percent of the unprecedented expansion of world coffee production in the nineteenth century. In the exceptional year of 1906 Brazilians *produced almost five times as much as the rest of the world combined.* And this was no marginal market. For the quarter century 1860–1887, the value of coffee trailed only grains and sugar in seaborne merchandise.[370] Coffee continued for the rest of our period to be one of the world's most valuable internationally traded commodities.

How did this happen? Brazil's remarkable expansion of the world coffee economy and the increase in the trade's breadth and complexity resulted from a unique confluence of Brazil's natural endowments; externalities such as the availability of foreign laborers in Africa—until the Atlantic slave trade was abolished in 1850—and in southern Europe after Brazilian slavery was outlawed in 1888; economies brought by revolutionary advances in transportation and communication technology; and fundamental transformations in the coffee business in the United States and Western Europe.

The explosion of coffee sales during the first three quarters of the nineteenth century had not been brought about by new production methods.[371] Only in the

Workers picking coffee berries in Brazil, ca. 1900–1923. Between 1888, when slavery was abolished in Brazil, and 1933, nearly three million immigrants from southern Europe, especially Italy and Portugal, entered Brazil, mostly to work in the coffee fields. Whole families were given the use of plots of land, and some pay, in exchange for labor in the coffee plantations. This *colono* system allowed Brazil to produce over three-quarters of the world's coffee in the period between 1880 and 1945. (Library of Congress)

last quarter of the century did cultivating, harvesting, and processing transition out of the same sort of slave labor Brazilian planters had previously used for sugar. But the vastness of its plantations and industrial-scale harvesting, which lowered both the cost and the quality of coffee, were new.

Technological improvements were more evident in transportation than in cultivation. Beginning in 1854 and intensifying after the 1870s, the Brazilian coffee zones of Rio de Janeiro, Minas Gerais, and São Paulo states experienced the largest rail growth of any coffee-based economy. In 1889, when the monarchy was overthrown, the system extended about six thousand miles; at the turn of the century it was ninety-five hundred miles and had grown again by half by the beginning of World War I. Although compared to the industrialized countries of Western Europe and North America this total seemed puny, it towered over all other coffee-growing countries. In Latin America no other coffee-growing country had even one thousand miles of rail at the time. (Mexico had a larger network, but only a small share of it served the coffee-growing areas before World War II.) Track was scarce because other coffee growers were either small islands in the Caribbean and the Indian Ocean, or poor and often politically unstable continental areas in northern South America and Central America.[372] In Africa only Ethiopia, Kenya, Uganda, and Tanganyika were connected to their ports by rail in this period. But their coffee exports were tiny. Brazil's system stood out worldwide, being larger than the entire amount of track in Africa and all of Asia outside of India.

Even though railroads did not dramatically reduce cargo costs, because rail companies in Brazil did not offer the same sort of long-distance discounts and rebates that so benefited midwestern US and Canadian wheat growers, they did help improve the quality of coffee at port. More importantly, cheaper, more fertile lands were now accessible in the interior. This was key to Brazil's astounding success, because coffee was a frontier crop—its fields were prepared by cutting down virgin forests, the coffee trees required four to six years to reach maturity and first harvest, then after twenty years of harvests the growers moved on, leaving behind pasture or unworkable lands. Instead of fertilizing, *fazendeiros* exploited the "forest rent" of rich, untilled lands and thick composted soils. Irrigation was rarely needed. Because of the land's natural fecundity, Brazilian *fazendeiros* enjoyed some of the highest-yielding coffee trees in the world. Prus-

sian agronomist Franz Daffert called the Brazilian method *Raubbau,* or predatory agriculture.[373] Although taken aback by its nomadic destructiveness, he had
to admit that it made good economic sense in the land-rich, demographically
poor tropics.

With the vast interior within reach of the ports via the iron rail, ever-larger
amounts of the harvest could be brought to market faster, reducing interest
charges on working capital. In other words, the railroads, some of which pioneered novel engineering feats to climb the steep escarpments from the ports to
the coffee fields, allowed Brazilians to take advantage of their country's vastness
and *continue* their boom. They thereby escaped the geographic trap that had
prevented much smaller Yemen, Java, Martinique, Dutch Guiana, and Haiti
from qualitatively transforming the world market and from taking advantage of
economies of scale. The railroad also temporarily intensified the use of slaves in
coffee, partially explaining why Brazil was the last country in the Western
Hemisphere to abolish slavery, in 1888.[374]

We should note, however, that although Brazil certainly benefited from its
vastness and had some of the largest export plantations ever seen, the Italian and
Portuguese immigrants who started replacing slave laborers in the late 1880s appeared to be more self-sustaining peasants than proletarians in a factory in the
field, as in Cuban sugar or even in California's Central and Imperial Valleys. In
Brazil their main goal was to grow corn and beans for subsistence, only second-
arily paying rent for their land with the coffee trees they also tended.[375] Even
coffee trees were divided up by families, which, unlike the former slave system,
self-exploited women and children as well as men under the authority of the
family patriarch. (In other coffee areas like Java and Chiapas, Mexico, fieldwork
was done overwhelmingly by migrant men.) Over time, immigrant indentured
workers in Brazil bought their own land. Unlike in sugar, the size of the average
Brazilian coffee holding declined over time, even as the mills that processed the
beans grew. This probably explains why rural revolts were much less common in
Brazilian coffee-growing areas than in sugar fields.

Railroads were useful but not *necessary* for a coffee export economy—no
other coffee producer had much track until the twentieth century (though Costa
Rica's and Mexico's relatively short lines were important). But the great amount
of low-priced Brazilian coffee making its way to international ports on iron

tracks expanded and reconfigured the world market, because Brazil produced more than the rest of the world combined. Rail latecomers, such as Spanish American growers, then took advantage of specific niches in the larger North American and Western European markets that Brazilian rail-transported mass production had initiated. Spanish American production varied from relatively small family farms in much of Costa Rica, parts of Nicaragua, Venezuela, and parts of Colombia, to large plantations using semicoerced labor in Guatemala, southern Mexico, Nicaragua, and parts of El Salvador.[376] Growers throughout Spanish America were not able to produce as cheaply as Brazilians, but they still found buyers as North American and Western European wholesalers and roasters—particularly the Germans—blended the more expensive but higher-quality Spanish American milds with lower-cost Brazilian beans to satisfy the swelling market in the United States.[377] An important part of their formula for success, despite lacking Brazil's ample natural resources, was the use of family labor on small plots the families owned, rented, or cropped on shares. As in Brazil, they cultivated their own subsistence crops on neighboring plots and exploited the labor of the entire family. In Guatemala and southern Mexico, coffee growers also lowered costs by exploiting the coerced labor of indigenous peoples, male and female, who seasonally migrated to the fields for the harvest. As the indigenous populations grew rapidly in the twentieth century and the land they passed down and divided up became too small for subsistence, the market rather than government coercion delivered Indian workers to coffee plantations as laborers.

Coffee commodity chains grew as a side effect of transformations in the broader world economy as well as from internal dynamics. A clear case of an externality that revolutionized the relationship of Brazil's coffee (and later that of competitors) to the Atlantic world was the shipping revolution already discussed that shrank the world.[378]

Despite the fact that inexpensive and plentiful Brazilian production quenched the thirst and stimulated the wakefulness of ever more North American and European consumers, its remarkable increase in cultivation did not create a monopoly. Yes, in 1906 Brazil produced some 80 percent of the world's coffee. But the institutionalization of the market, with scheduled large steamers, railroads, warehouses, standards, futures market, and new convenience coffee products, opened North American and European ports to other Latin American producers. Rather than a zero-sum game, this was a mutual benefit for all Latin American coffee producers. In most years until the Great Depression all Latin American growers increased output. Large, inexpensive production, combined with plentiful sugar production, allowed coffee to overshadow competing caffeinated drinks such as cocoa, tea, mate, and substitutes such as chicory and grains. Latin America turned much of the Western world into coffee drinkers. In other words, Brazil was not just a passive bystander; it was a market maker and would become a price maker beginning in 1906 as the result of government price interventions.[379]

Coffee's heroic nineteenth century occurred not only because of Brazilian and gradually other Latin American production, but also because of burgeoning US and Western European consumption. The transportation revolution and lowered international transaction costs reduced the cost of the lengthiest section of the commodity chain; it also accelerated the commercial relationship between Brazil and the United States, which was strengthened by ever-closer diplomatic ties.[380] Coffee became truly a mass product for the first time in the United States, which was followed by wider consumption in Western Europe.

Coffee shippers benefited from the same efficient internal transportation system in the United States and Western Europe that so helped grain and other food sales. US per capita coffee consumption rose prodigiously even as the total population exploded. The same happened in Western Europe, so that coffee offloaded in Hamburg, Le Havre, Amsterdam, or Trieste could quickly and cheaply reach large and growing consumer markets in the interior.

US government policy also helped. The United States was the only major market to import coffee tax-free after 1832 (except in the Civil War period). Coffee taxes in Western Europe were all substantially higher because of their mercantilist traditions. Consequently, per capita consumption of coffee in the United States grew the fastest in the world, from one-eighteenth of a pound in 1783 to nine pounds a hundred years later. The US population's fifteen-fold explosion in that century meant that total coffee imports grew by 2,400 times. Half of the growth in world consumption in the nineteenth century was due to increased US purchases.[381] Almost all of the rest was in Western Europe, especially in the north. Coffee producers were very fortunate to find such favor in the

A coffee seller, Tunisia, 1916. Even while the vast majority of coffee production had shifted to the Americas and consumption to the Americas and Western Europe, coffee continued to be socially important in the Middle East as it had been for almost four hundred years. This photo depicts the common sight of a street vendor serving two men. In public spaces, coffee was usually the domain of men. (National Geographic Image Collection / The Bridgeman Art Library)

countries whose incomes were growing the fastest in the world. (Coffee boosters argued that this relationship was not coincidental. It was not just that prosperity paid for coffee, but also that coffee as a brain food and labor stimulant brought about prosperity.) US per capita consumption would continue to grow, with some fits and starts, until the 1940s, but Western Europe would lag because of the crushing burden of two devastating world wars.

Demand in the nineteenth century, in both the United States and Europe, was initially both income- and price-elastic. The more people earned, the more likely they were to purchase coffee, and the lower the price, the more likely they were to buy it. This is because coffee initially was viewed as a luxury item, a sign of aristocratic and bourgeois distinction. As it became available to them at a relatively low price, lower-class urban inhabitants and eventually even rural populations chose real coffee over the ersatz coffees and teas they had previously drunk because coffee symbolized affluence and status. Perhaps surprisingly, as it became an accepted part of the working class's breakfast and even lunch in the factory canteen—that is, as it came to be viewed as a necessity—coffee purchases ceased growing faster than the population did. Coffee was one of the few major internationally traded commodities to enjoy a real price increase in the second half of the nineteenth century and still have a per capita consumption increase. In other words, people bought more and more of it even though its relative price continued to rise. Again the coffee chain benefited from an externality: the plunging price of many staples such as grains, due to overproduction, left the working classes of North America and Europe with more disposable income to buy occasional luxuries like coffee. Cheaper sugar made coffee more palatable and affordable.[382]

The rapid expansion and transformation of the US and Western European markets led to new institutions that gradually brought governance of the longer chain to importers and then to roasters. Merchants based in the growing countries lost leverage when a submarine telegraph cable in 1874 tied South America to New York and London. Information about prices, standards, and demand and supply were now published in newspapers and trade journals in consuming countries. Warehouses were built to hold a substantial share of the world's visible stocks, strengthening the market position of importers, who now knew where much of the coffee was and tried to control it.

Exporters ceased being consignment agents, becoming instead agents of importers abroad who dominated the trade and set the prices. Merchants such as the German Theodor Wille and Englishman Edward Johnston started their careers in Brazil, expanded their commercial business to other ports and countries, and moved up-country by opening offices in the coffee-growing interior. They invested in complementary activities such as insurance companies, banks, and warehouses, and reluctantly in plantations.[383] Rarely did they become roasters, however.

Eventually the roasters, who built large factories in the consuming countries, came to dominate the trade. Coffee had to be processed to the point of green or parchment coffee in the cultivating countries because the ripe cherries spoiled

STEVEN C. TOPIK AND ALLEN WELLS

too fast to be exported in that condition. Green coffee, also known as "gold coffee" *(café oro),* was durable and transportable. Although historians often treat coffee exports as a raw material, in fact they were semifinished. Until the second half of the twentieth century, the roasting and grinding had to be done in the consuming countries because the final processed product quickly lost its flavor and aroma. Once new packaging technology permitted the exportation of roasted and even ground coffee in the twentieth century, import tariffs in consuming northern countries and the market power of the roasters in the north prevented finished coffee exports.[384] In other words, geography and climate dictated that coffee was grown within twenty-five degrees of the equator and that it be initially processed there. Roasting and distribution technology in the countries with the largest, most prosperous markets for coffee dictated that final processing and marketing be done in the United States and Western Europe; later, government tariffs protected the profits of Western European and North American corporations. So different areas of the world coffee market had different comparative advantages and controlled different aspects of knowledge of the coffee trade. This was similar to sugar, where politics and market power prevented pure, highly refined imports in order to protect the position of oligopolistic refiners and distributors in the consuming countries. Neither of these huge international sectors operated in a truly unfettered market.

As the trade grew, so did the size and market power of the largest exporters. Most of them were Western European or North American firms (partnerships and corporations) with ample capital, access to credit, control of shipping fleets, and inside information from their branches, partners, or associates in the major overseas coffee markets. By the end of the nineteenth century the five largest exporters shipped over 40 percent of Brazil's exports, and the ten largest over 60 percent.[385] Oligopoly encouraged attempts to make speculative windfall profits by cornering the market, leading to some spectacular bubbles and busts. In response, and in imitation of grain dealers, merchants founded the New York Coffee Exchange in 1882 and then the exchange at Le Havre to attract trade to their ports and capital in the form of a futures market. They sought a frictionless transparent market where transactions were safe and capital was available. The exchanges institutionalized access to standardized information. Hamburg and London, also major coffee entrepôts, soon followed with major coffee exchanges.

Already in 1880 merchants were buying an idea rather than a palpable commodity, as we saw happen in the grains futures market. In that year, sixty-one million bags were bought and sold on the Hamburg futures market, when the entire world harvest was less than seven million bags! It was this sort of speculation that caused the German government to shut down the futures market for a while.

No single port dominated coffee imports in most countries, but the huge size of the US market meant that although New York continued its dominant position as lead importer of coffee, Baltimore, New Orleans, and San Francisco all imported significant amounts to serve their hinterlands.[386] The telegraph created the possibility of an integrated international commodity market and increased the market power of importers and processors in consuming countries where they had easy access to crop and price information. Prices and grades thereby became more standardized, though this was, and still is, a fairly artisanal undertaking, reflecting personal relations and tastes.

Social practices in the largest markets, the United States and Germany, very much affected the nature of demand and the ability of roasters to respond to it and to modify it. The fact that in the United States, Germany, the Netherlands, and Scandinavia, coffee was consumed in the home much more than in coffeehouses had important implications for the organization of the trade. In the United States, coffee was overwhelmingly sold in grocery stores, so a few roasting companies such as Arbuckle and the Woolson Spice Company took advantage of the invention of industrial-scale roasters in the late nineteenth century to create brand names for their roasted coffee. The proliferation of brands meant that roasters were no longer selling a commodity—the green bean—but were selling a trademarked product such as Arbuckle's *Yuban*. As with other food and drug products, from crackers and flour to soft drinks and cigarettes, advertising and other marketing tactics such as colorful cans and trading cards attempted to whet the appetite for particular brands and to appeal to the expanding retail grocery sector. They provided new information that appealed to more than "quality" or price; they appealed to the aesthetics of the can, the trading cards included in it, and to fashion. Less wealthy purchasers recycled the cans and crates in which the coffee arrived by reusing them as household implements and building materials.[387]

A Viennese coffeehouse, ca. 1900. Coffee took on a very different social role in bourgeois Vienna, the capital of the Habsburg empire, during its prosperous fin de siècle. Dapper and refined men of the middle and upper classes read newspapers and books or discussed politics and culture in elegant coffeehouses while being served by women. (© Austrian Archives / Corbis)

In the second-largest coffee market, Germany, coffee was sold in specialty stores known as "Colonial Goods" stores. Even though more than 90 percent of the coffee came from Latin America, to a considerable extent from German or German immigrant-owned plantations in Guatemala, Brazil, and Mexico, the dream of African colonies, loudly pronounced at the 1884 Berlin Conference, continued to dominate the German imagination. Some brands carried African images, often caricatures of native black people. In fact, much of Germany's and Central Europe's coffee was actually coffee substitutes like grains or chicory root, because import taxes hindered real coffee imports.[388] So when Germans consumed coffee, often they were actually drinking locally grown tubers rather than imported tropical beans. US coffee companies portrayed coffee as being inherently American by promoting brands such as "White House" with Uncle Sam as their spokesman. South America and its farmworkers were ignored. Neither the imperial German nor the republican American vision gave Latin Americans due credit.

But these appeals did sell ever more coffee. A technical breakthrough and government oversight allowed the ever-larger roasters to overtake the thousands of grocers and small roasters who sold green beans or custom roasted. Larger roasters were able to win consumer confidence in the quality of packaged beans they now could not see. The first step in winning over the suspicious buyers was vacuum sealing, which was invented in 1900. It was borrowed from a Chicago butter company, though two decades would pass before vacuum packing gained wide acceptance. By the 1920s, "convenience" started to become an important attribute of roasted coffee, just as it did in the case of other processed foods as the Jazz Age heightened the desire for speed and leisure.

But the second problem—the questionable quality of canned coffee beans—required government interventions to take command of the market away from importers, who often adulterated coffee stocks. In the United States, the Pure Food and Drug Act of 1906, based upon a British pure food law some thirty years earlier, set standards. Aimed particularly at the meat and patent medicine industries, it also decreed that imported coffee be marked according to its port of exit. Thus "Santos" became a specific type of coffee, as did "Java" or "Mocha." Germany and other Western European governments followed suit soon thereafter.

By gaining the confidence of consumers and providing mass-produced roasted coffee, large industrial roasting firms began to control the market and the chain. They lengthened the chain by industrializing and commodifying roasting and grinding, which formerly were the domain of the housewife. Brands segmented the market by selling various roasts and blends depending upon region. By 1935, 90 percent of all coffee sold in the United States was sold roasted, in branded packages. The branded coffee housewives purchased at their neighborhood grocery store was not a commodity, it was a proprietary product. In Germany, the Kaiser food chain, which began selling branded roasted coffee in 1885, had grown to 1,420 stores on the verge of World War I. Its laughing coffee pot logo spread throughout the country. The introductions of new packaging, branding, and advertising would be slower to filter to the rest of Western Europe and would take yet longer to reach Latin America and Asia, where coffee consumption was less commodified and production less industrialized.[389]

The largest roasters also integrated vertically, sending their agents into the coffee interior to purchase directly from producers and sometimes even buying plantations in growing countries. The most successful at integrating segments of the chain before World War II was the A&P chain-store empire. The company imported, roasted, canned, branded, and retailed millions of bags and cans of Eight O'Clock coffee in thousands of its own stores. With their command of "shelf space" and their increasing concentration, supermarket companies could assert ever-greater governance over the coffee commodity chain as the power of independent merchants, small-scale roasters, and shippers declined.[390] Like it was for many other transformations of processed foods commodity chains, the United States was in the forefront. Supermarkets came to most of the rest of the world only in the 1960s or later.

As a result of developments in the United States, value—in the sense of market-priced processes—was increasingly added as the housewife's unremunerated role in making coffee declined and her labors were commodified by roasters. This caused an ever-greater share of the monetary value of coffee to be added in consuming countries. A small number of US companies, such as Folgers, Maxwell House, and Hills Brothers, took advantage of marketing economies to expand regionally and finally, after World War II, nationally. They came to make the lion's share of profit in the coffee chain.

In addition to using their market power and governance of the commodity chain to gain most of the profit in the coffee trade, roasters introduced new coffee products that allowed them to add additional value. In 1901 a Japanese chemist, Katō Satori, applied to coffee a technique he had first invented for tea to create soluble (or instant) coffee. It was not very successful, commercially; "George Washington's Instant Coffee," devised in 1910 by a Belgian immigrant to the United States, fared better because of better timing. The new wonder drink arrived in time for World War I, when it was deemed by the War Department "one of the most important articles of subsistence used by the army." The Washington company's entire output was sent to US troops on the European front.[391] Once peace came, consumers reverted back to slower, but better tasting and cheaper, brewed coffee. Nonetheless, the seeds of change were planted at the end of our period when the Brazilian government, facing glutted world markets and miserable prices, appealed to the Swiss instant milk company, Nestlé, to devise a better soluble process. They introduced the world to Nescafé in 1938. It became a cherished part of soldiers' rations. Its impact would be felt after the Second World War when it gained great favor. Because instant coffee stressed convenience over taste, the cheaper, faster-growing *Coffea robusta* beans were preferred. Robusta was a different species of *Coffea* that was discovered in Central Africa in the 1860s and transported to Java and Ceylon because it resisted leaf blight better than the arabica.[392] After the end of our period, this would undercut Latin America's near monopoly on coffee cultivation as Africa and Indonesia, then much later Vietnam, rushed to plant and harvest robusta trees. Because of the large role of technology in creating instant coffee and the use of a low-quality raw material, coffee growers received an ever-smaller share of the final supermarket price for the instant coffee, just as the growers of wheat and rice, and the miners and extracters of industrial raw materials, earned a diminishing share of the final price of the finished good.

The power of the cultivating countries in the world coffee market was further undercut by the expansion of large roasting companies. Roasters' superior technology, greater efficiency, and marketing sophistication led to greater concentration of processing and distribution. By the 1950s the five largest roasters in the United States handled over one-third of all US coffee. Very large traders grew to satisfy the growing demand of roasters. According to the Federal Trade Commission, by the 1950s the top ten importers were responsible for over half of all imports.

Ten exporting houses in Brazil sent out anywhere from two-thirds to 90 percent of the exports until the 1920s and continued to control more than half after that. Because Brazil was exporting 40 to 80 percent of the world's coffee until the 1950s, and these exporting houses operated in other producing areas as well, this meant a few houses dominated world exports and information.

Government intervention had brought some governance of the chain to the producing countries in the early twentieth century. Beginning in 1906 some of Brazil's provinces held stocks off the world market to "valorize" them. Then the province of São Paulo, which single-handedly grew most of the world's coffee by the turn of the century, established in 1924 a semi-state coffee institute to oversee financing, warehousing, and sales. This led to a federal price support program in 1931. The Great Depression caused coffee demand and prices to precipitously fall and left Brazil with enormous surplus stocks on hand. The initial solution was for the Brazilian central government to burn almost ten million pounds of coffee, a year's supply for the entire world. When that did not stabilize prices, diplomacy followed.

Where an earlier effort to bring together the coffee-growing countries to defend against falling prices had failed, just as had happened with sugar and rubber, the new crisis was sufficiently dire that fourteen Latin American coffee-growing countries met to discuss their concerns. They joined together because, as one contemporary student of the sector observed: "The importance of coffee in the economic life of the American republics can hardly be exaggerated.... More than many other export commodities, the proceeds derived from its sale abroad are distributed widely among the inhabitants of the country of exports."[393] Even countries that were small exporters in the world market depended greatly on coffee for foreign exchange and government revenue. The agreement was finally consummated in 1940 because World War II blocked shipments to Europe, glutting the markets of the Americas. Washington, which had strenuously fought against Brazilian valorizations in the first decades of the century, now recognized that cooperation between the main producers and consumers was necessary. The newly created Inter-American Price Coffee Board set price controls and quotas. The 36 votes on the board were distributed between the growers (Brazil 9, Colombia 3, and others 1 each) and the main consumer (the United States—12 votes). This was the first major international agreement to include both producers and a major consumer, unless we count the sugar meetings where countries like Germany and Austria were both producers and consumers. It set a precedent for the 1961 International Coffee Agreement that would bring together the vast majority of coffee growers and consumers from all over the world.

Coffee, then, differed from other leading global commodities because of the development of extensive international coordination and the singular role played by a country from the Southern Hemisphere. Brazil's success stemmed from its natural endowments, its ability in 1822 to throw off European colonialism, and its capacity to adapt to the transformations of the world economy by taking advantage of foreign capital, technology, immigrant labor, and markets. The fact that coffee was a durable drug food that traveled well and stimulated the swelling consumer population of the urban industrializing North, combined with the power of the Brazilian postcolonial state, allowed Brazil to enjoy a position in the world economy of unprecedented strength for an agrarian exporter from the global South. Over time, however, a growing share of coffee profits would accrue to roasters and distributors in the industrialized centers.

Tea

Tea resembled coffee in that it was a stimulant with little nutritional value, it did not spoil quickly, and it traveled well. Caffeine had important psychoactive effects on the central nervous system, so coffee and tea were treated as medicines as well as beverages and were useful in leisure, labor, and combat. The two stimulants often competed for consumers, and the same companies often sold both. In both cases, the commodities destined for an international market were grown in the South by poor workers in large part for the industrial North. However, tea's history, location, business organization, and political context were worlds apart from coffee's. Where coffee had become the product of independent national states in our period, tea—formerly the monopoly of China—became a colonial product.

For at least two thousand years tea was cultivated, processed, and consumed in China. Aside from seeds taken to Japan more than a thousand years ago by Buddhist monks, tea had been a Chinese monopoly. When the Dutch and Portuguese began importing tea in the 1600s and the English a century later, China was the sole exporter and retained its monopoly until British and Dutch colonies began sending out small amounts in the middle of the century and Japan opened up in the 1860s. Tea surpassed silk to become the most valuable product of the China trade. It came to connote great wealth: "for all the tea in China."[394]

Tea, *Camellia sinensis,* was an indigenous plant. Millions of Chinese peasants (the estimate for the 1920s was four million tea cultivators) grew the crops on their own small plots, where they processed the leaves and twigs using native technology. Drying and curing had to be done almost immediately upon picking, lest the leaves rot, so peasants were also artisanal processors. They were consumers as well as producers as the drink became entwined with Chinese and Japanese culture, religion, and identity.[395]

Tea was an expensive luxury in England because of the nature of the commodity chain. The very many peasants sold to local traders who brought it to larger markets, and weeks later it found its way from the distant interior mountains to the ports. Chinese merchants dominated the trade up to the seaside ports, such as Canton and Amboy, and took a healthy cut of the profits. Cultivation practices created no economies of scale; equally problematic for an export crop, it was expensive to bring the tea out of the interior either over land, often with human carriers, or by small boats down the rivers.

The cost of the commodity was a particular problem for Europeans because the only thing they had that the Chinese wanted in trade was silver, and that was in short supply. Much of it came from the mines of Peru and Mexico across the Pacific or around the world across the Atlantic and Indian Oceans. To create a trade good that paid for tea, in the nineteenth century the English East India Company brought from India another stimulant, opium. That drug caused devastating addiction in China and provoked wars that ultimately caused the emperor to cede to Europeans treaty ports and the right to import opium. But this still did not provide Europe with sufficient low-priced tea. Even at the height of China's tea trade, at least one-half of production was consumed by the Chinese. By the 1920s, 70 to 90 percent of Chinese production was drunk at home.[396]

The solution to the problem of trying to meet rising demand was implemented in the 1800s when the English and Dutch mercantile monopolies introduced Chinese tea seed, and new scientific techniques developed in their state-run botanical gardens, into India and Java. Using domestic indentured workers or debt peons, known as coolies in India, and European capital and new technology, they began to grow tea on a plantation scale. At first they imported Chinese tea plants, because these were the most valued by the international trade and because they did not recognize that, in quality, the little-cultivated native Indian tea plant, *Camellia sinensis var. assamica,* was for industrial purposes superior to the Chinese variety. Producers in India added a fermenting process that yielded black tea, which was less common in China and Japan than green tea. Combined with low-cost sugar, the steady supply of black tea found a swelling market among the British working class, who, unlike most original Asian consumers, liked their tea sweetened.[397] Steamships and railroads now began to bring vast amounts of black tea from Assam to Calcutta. There some of the fastest ships in the British merchant marine were waiting to take the tea to Europe to enrich British stockholders in London and the British managers in India who oversaw Indian laborers.

But though the English praised their scientific technical mastery and progressive means in the new Indian field, the plantations did not use modern capitalist labor systems. It is true that the investors were capitalists and that tea became an industrial product there. Beginning in 1872 with William Jackson's tea roller, processing became increasingly mechanized. Hot-air driers, roll breakers, and even mechanical tea sorters followed.[398]

However, as with sugar, industrial processing demanded increased manual labor in agriculture. The delicate and skilled work of planting, tending, and particularly harvesting tea was still done by hand, often female hands, under conditions that Henry Cotton, chief commissioner of Assam in 1896, called "scandalous." Imported mainly from the neighboring jurisdiction of Bengal, the coolies were, in his words, "practically bond slaves . . . the period of bondage may be interminable."[399] This was coercion on a massive scale. By 1927 Assam alone had some 420,000 acres under tea with 463,847 permanent plantation coolies and another 41,176 temporary workers brought in from outside.[400]

Colonial state power to enforce low-paying labor contracts combined with surplus population and modern transportation to ignite a veritable explosion of Indian production. Whereas in 1859 there was virtually no Indian tea trade while China exported over 70 million pounds to England, forty years later Chinese exports to London had fallen by more than three-quarters to 15 million pounds while India exported three times the earlier Chinese total, almost 220 million pounds. By 1932 Indian exports reached 385 million pounds.[401] This was a bonanza for the British colonial regime, planters, and traders and a disaster for China's balance of payments. Although ever more Indians worked in tea, relatively few of them owned tea plantations in booming Assam, where half the colony's tea was grown. However, one contemporary source notes that "in Kangra, Darjeeling, the Dooars, and the Tarai fair areas are owned by Indian companies . . . in Hill Tippera all the gardens are so controlled."[402]

So successful was the tea experiment in India that British planters in the nearby colony of Ceylon (Sri Lanka) also turned to that plant once their previously prospering coffee fields were felled by leaf rust. Again the tea system was also mainly a foreign import: British planters, using British capital, imported indentured Tamil workers from southern India to plant exotic tea bushes imported from China via India to grow a drink for British and Commonwealth consumers. The native Sinhalese would have nothing to do with tea cultivation or drinking. Tea created foreign enclaves. As Roland Wenzlhuemer has observed: "With the transition from coffee to tea cultivation in Ceylon, the immigrant labour force changed in its nature. Work in the coffee estates had been seasonal. Now tea required a permanently resident labour force. . . . Social contacts between the plantation workforce and the indigenous village communities were rare and usually confined to commercial relations."[403]

British planters in Ceylon undertook a vigorous publicity program at the end of the nineteenth century to compete with Indian tea in Great Britain and to open new markets elsewhere, as in the United States. For the British public, advertisers deracinated the domesticated tea industry. They stressed how English, sanitary, disciplined, and modern their industry was. It worked. Ceylon became the second-largest tea exporter in the world, surpassing a politically troubled China in 1917. By 1933 Ceylon was exporting a quarter of the world's tea, more than twice China's exports. Other British colonists also tried their hand at planting tea, particularly in Africa. However, the tea plantations of Kenya, Uganda, Nyasaland (Malawi), and South Africa had little impact on the world market before 1945.[404]

Tea became a marker of British identity to the point that a meal, "tea," received its name and the military received tea rations. Britain in 1933 was still by far the world's largest tea importer, bringing in over half of all worldwide tea imports. It enjoyed the highest per capita annual consumption at almost ten pounds. Historians have persuasively argued that tea and sugar fueled the Industrial Revolution by sustaining the poorly paid, hardworking British industrial proletariat. Probably neither end of the commodity chain, Indian coolies or English proletarians, recognized the complementarity of their activities, which squeezed out surplus value through intensified labor to enrich capital over labor.

Tea became a glue of the British Empire. But elsewhere in the Commonwealth (the United Kingdom plus Australia, Canada, New Zealand, and South Africa), tea fueled colonialism rather than industrialism. Commonwealth mem-

Workers moving Lipton tea sacks in Ceylon (now Sri Lanka), early twentieth century. In order to sup-
plant China's tea monopoly in the second half of the nineteenth century, Britain brought more than
two million Tamils from the southern part of India to Ceylon to work in tea either seasonally or permanently. Nearly three-quarters of internationally traded tea was sold inside the British Commonwealth, especially the United Kingdom. Companies such as the British leader, Lipton, grew, cured,
transported, branded, and sold tea wholesale and retail. (© Hulton-Deutsch Collection / Corbis)

bers consumed over 70 percent of the international trade and averaged almost
seven pounds per person in the white settler areas. The indigenous Indian population had drunk tea only in the areas where it naturally occurred, like Assam,
before the British popularized it across the colony. Though it began as a white
person's habit, its popularity spread. By the 1950s India had become the world's
second-largest tea consumer.

We find a peculiar variation on British tea influence in the most prosperous neocolony of the United Kingdom, Argentina, which also showed a preference for tea over coffee. However, there, as in the south of Brazil, it was local
erva mate tea rather than the Indian import. And instead of serving as a sign

of cosmopolitanism, tea drinking in Argentina was an indigenous habit tied to Argentine rural identity. *Mate* found almost no market outside the Southern Cone.[405]

The other major tea drinker was a former British colony, the United States. Its 13 percent of world tea commerce made it the world's second-largest market, even though this translated to less than a pound per capita because Americans were as enamored of coffee as the British were of tea.[406]

The only major tea consumer outside of China and Japan not related to the British experience was China's neighbor Russia. Tea was of course important to Russian culture, with the samovar as iconic as an Orthodox icon or a bottle of vodka. Russian firms established some eighteen tea factories in China, in Hangzhou and Fujian, when the Suez Canal provided a sea route from China to the populated core of Russia via the Black Sea. Robert Gardella, studying this trade, finds that the trade in brick tea, "rightly considered as a 'manufactured' commodity, rather than simply a cash crop," led to "an impressive degree of commercialization." Nonetheless, Gardella concludes that "the premodern Chinese economy was organized to accommodate cycles of extensive commercial expansion and contraction *without* the need for structural transformation."[407] In fact, Russian imports of brick tea from China fell sharply in the wake of political troubles in both countries after the turn of the twentieth century, and because by the last quarter of the nineteenth century tea was also produced for the Russian market in neighboring Georgia.

The other major tea producers and exporters were the first Europeans to engage in the trade, the Dutch. Importing tea seeds from China and then from India, they were able to have some success in Java and later in Sumatra. Earlier efforts were stepped up, like the British in Ceylon, when leaf rust devastated their thriving coffee plantations beginning in the 1870s. In coffee's place, Dutch planters, using coerced Javanese peasants, forced tea exports to jump tenfold between 1900 and 1927. By 1933 the colony was the world's third-largest tea exporter, providing a fifth of the international trade. The cruel methods led to nationalist outcries in the Dutch East Indies (today Indonesia) and humanitarian campaigns in the Netherlands.[408]

The Japanese increased tea cultivation in their newly won colony of Formosa at the end of the century, turning it into a major exporter of oolong tea, particularly to Japan itself and to the United States. Production grew some 50 percent between the last decade of the nineteenth century and the period 1931–1940. But the system differed sharply from those used in the British and Dutch colonies. In both Japan itself and Formosa, tea was grown on small hillside plots by peasant family labor. It complemented other agriculture, such as rice growing. Improvements in yield allowed the Japanese and Formosan farmers to reduce the size of their tea fields while increasing production and devoting more land to other crops. Even though much of Japan's exports were marketed by US exporting firms, tea in Japan obeyed domestic farm logic, not an export logic as elsewhere in colonial Asia.[409]

In England, tea, which had begun in coffeehouses, became a domesticated drink served at home and drunk by men and women alike. Seen as a temperance drink, just like coffee, tea was considered by Victorians to be a civilizing beverage. Purveyors began branding different sorts of tea and retailing through grocers. Some companies, such as Lipton, purchased plantations in Ceylon, where the tea was grown and cured, and sold the tea in its chain of grocery stores in the United Kingdom and the United States, "direct from the tea garden to the tea pot." The same was done in the United States by the Great Atlantic and Pacific Tea Company (the A&P), which by the 1920s had some twenty-four hundred outlets. Americans changed the nature of tea consumption by developing a product that distressed Britons, who were more concerned with flavor, but appealed to Americans who wanted speed and convenience: tea bags. Created in 1908 by Thomas Sullivan as tiny samples for marketing purposes, tea in pouches of silk, and then cotton gauze, vastly increased the number of US tea drinkers. As Roy Moxham observed, tea bags "turned tea from being a drink of ceremony into a drink of convenience."[410] Although they took decades to follow suit, by the end of our period even Tetley, Lipton, and Twinings were producing tea bags for an ever less reluctant English public. That dramatic change in consumption practice had a similarly huge effect on production, because tea bags were filled with broken leaf or even leaf dust. The lowered common denominator put an end to finely graded teas on most tea plantations.[411] Another similar American innovation was iced tea. Drunk mainly in hot climates, it required the advent of refrigeration machines to make ice. Heavily sweetened, iced tea used low-quality leaf. The Chinese and Japanese spiritual cultural custom had become fully commodified, adapted, secularized, internationalized, and modernized.

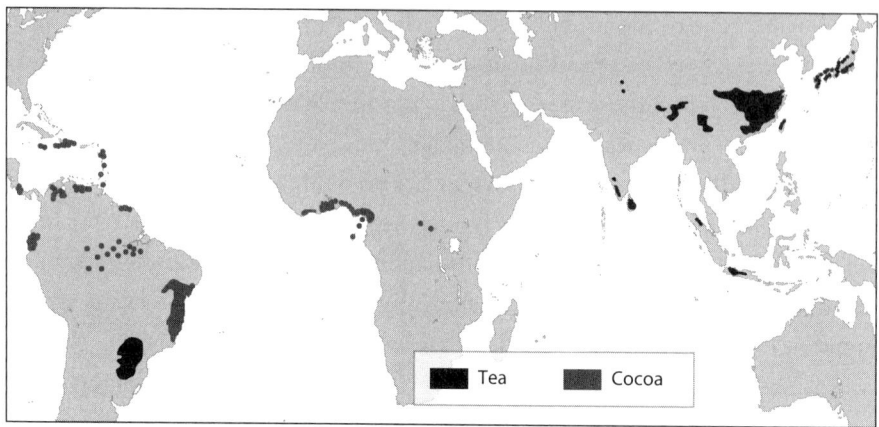

Global production of tea and cocoa, ca. 1925.

Chocolate

The last of the major stimulants that we discuss, chocolate, was native to the Americas and initially was spread overseas by the Spanish. Another tree crop with the alkaloid caffeine and to a greater extent a cousin of caffeine, theobromine, cacao traveled and stored well once harvested and processed. Domesticated by the Olmecs of southern Mexico before 1000 BCE, cacao became much later an important symbol of Aztec culture and status as the *xocoatl* trade spread long distances through Mesoamerica. It was paired with processed seeds of another indigenous Mexican plant, the orchid vanilla, which was first domesticated by the Totonac Indians of Veracruz but joined in chocolate by the Aztecs. The Spanish became fond of the drinking cacao with vanilla hot or cold, calling it "chocolate," but it was seldom eaten. Indigenous cultivation methods and indigenous farmers continued to produce the fine *criollo* beans after the Conquest in Mesoamerica. In Venezuela, the hardier and more prolific *forastero* variety found a market abroad once sugar was added.[412]

Chocolate as a drink found some favor in Western Europe, particularly in the south among the aristocracy and the wealthy, but it was unable to compete well in the north with coffee and tea, which were usually served in the same cafés or meted out by the same apothecaries. Like its competitors, cacao was thought of as a temperance beverage. Perhaps unfairly, it was branded a Catholic and a feminine drink in northern Europe; it languished until the nineteenth century when new industrial methods and new chocolate products made the *forastero* more appealing and its production spread and grew.[413]

Two of the most important inventions in transforming the world of chocolate were undertaken by Dutch and Swiss entrepreneurs. The Dutchman C. J. Van Houten in 1829 devised a means to remove the cocoa butter from the bean to create an easily soluble cocoa powder. That it was a Dutchman is not surprising, because Amsterdam was the world's main chocolate market as the Dutch Caribbean colony of Curaçao became a gateway for Venezuelan cocoa. Van Houten's process opened the door for producers of drinkable chocolate. The falling price of sugar helped increase the market for the beverage, though it was not able to compete with tea and coffee. Chocolate purveyors such as the Swiss Phillip Suchard and the Englishman John Cadbury, who began branding their drinking product in the 1820s and 1830s, adopted Van Houten's process to create a more soluble powder that was still somewhat coarse and bitter. Now coca powder became a cooking ingredient as well as a drink mix. But their dark chocolate became widely popular, and a treat for children as well as adults, only when in 1875 the Swiss Daniel Peter joined his chocolate with his neighbor Henri Nestlé's powdered milk to produce milk chocolate. Other chocolatiers, such as the Swiss Lindt and Tobler companies, spread the new product as it became increasingly a mass treat and sometimes a military provision. The American Milton Hershey was able to mass-produce inexpensive confections like "Kisses" and "Mr. Goodbar," creating in 1894 the world's largest integrated factory in Pennsylvania, where he joined milk from his local dairies and sugar from his plantation in Cuba with imported chocolate. Other manufacturers were finding reliable, inexpensive milk ever more available as legislation, refrigeration, and new hygienic practices allowed milk to be sold at a distance from dairies. Combination candy bars, often with caramel and nuts covered by chocolate, like the Clark Bar, Baby Ruth, and the Mars Company's Snickers and Milky Way bars, as well as M&Ms, spread the chocolate candy snack habit widely after the First World War.[414] Chocolate had become an input in the processed food industry.

Vanilla continued to accompany chocolate as a drink and as a food. A demanding parasite that was difficult to sustain because it was ecologically sensitive and required a specific bee, butterfly, ant, or hummingbird to pollinate, vanilla did not

A young girl discovering candy in a songbird's nest: an advertisement for Nestlé chocolate, ca. 1910. By the beginning of the twentieth century, the popularity of chocolate, which originated in Mexico and South America, had spread to Europe in the form of candy, once sugar and milk were added and cocoa butter was removed. Still grown mainly in Latin America in 1900, the majority of production would move to African colonies by 1914. Nestlé's advertisement, however, did not betray its chocolate's origins to consumers. Once the drink of Aztec warriors and later of European nobles, it had become feminized as the food for the young and the romantic. (Getty Images)

lend itself to industrial-scale production or international travel. Fortunately for consumers, small amounts could flavor a substantial amount of chocolate. Indigenous people in Veracruz, growing the orchids as a subsidiary crop, had a world monopoly until French immigrants to the state in the mid-eighteenth century discovered a way to manually pollinate the orchids. This permitted other Frenchmen to move vanilla plants to French colonies in the Indian Ocean, such as Réunion and Madagascar.[415] Its taste was spread even more after German chemists synthesized vanilla in 1874, bringing its production from the forest to the lab.

Low-priced milk chocolate created booming demand for cacao (and vanilla) just as an increasing supply of cacao permitted the rapid expansion of the low-priced confection. First, the variety of cacao employed changed because the addition of milk and sugar neutralized the bitterness of the rugged and productive *forastero* bean. The early leaders in *criollo* cacao—Mexico, Central America, and Venezuela—gradually lost their grip on the world market as they could not expand to satisfy the explosion of demand. Ecuador and some Caribbean islands, particularly Trinidad, began to send out cacao. In 1890 the international trade supplied less than 60,000 metric tons of cacao; by 1914 the trade more than quadrupled to some 280,000 metric tons. World commerce in cacao surpassed 600,000 metric tons in the 1940s. Although small in comparison to coffee's 1.5 million metric tons in the 1940s, cacao did experience an unprecedented burst of expanded cultivation. Its rate of expansion—growing tenfold in a half century—far outpaced coffee's tripling and tea's decline in those same years. The secret of this unprecedented jump in world cacao production was the colonial transplanting to Africa of *forastero* trees and a variety developed in Trinidad, *trinitario*. Begun by the Portuguese on their islands of São Tomé and Principe, cacao moved onshore to the British colony of Gold Coast (Ghana) followed by Nigeria and the French in Côte d'Ivoire. By 1914 Africa was producing most of the world's cacao, much of it on small indigenous farms. This had risen to two-thirds of the international total by the end of our period.[416] As a result, cacao was, along with palm oil, one of Africa's most important agricultural exports prior to 1945.

The nature of labor and land systems in cacao production during our period was probably even more diverse than in any other of the commodities we have studied. This is because cacao production was divided among many independent countries and colonies and, as with coffee, the scale of production actually declined, so there were more growers. William Clarence-Smith observed: "As the volume of cocoa production increased prodigiously, techniques of cultivation actually became less intensive."[417] Estates were not an efficient way to grow cacao. Nonetheless, because of uneven power and land-owning relations, estates continued to exist and even dominate in some places. But even when they did, they were not capital intensive and labor was mostly not coerced. For example, in the domestically owned estates in Ecuador, entire families of Ecuadorians were contracted for five- or six-year periods. Labor contracting was also used in the British colony of Trinidad, where the workers were often from other British Caribbean colonies as well as some indentured South Asians. The same was true in Dutch Surinam. Venezuela and Costa Rica did not have access to Asian British colonial migrants, but tapped the crowded Caribbean islands whose former sugar workers now sought other employ. The Dominican Republic and Bahia, Brazil, had sufficient local small-scale growers and workers that they did not import either capital or workers. Instead, native migrants came as wage workers, sharecroppers, or smallholders. In Chiapas, Mexico, and Guatemala, however, the indigenous Maya were subjected on some cacao plantations to the same slavelike conditions they faced on some coffee fields.

Africa displayed the most variation. Colonial regimes differed on their acceptance of slavery and coercion, though all favored colonial landowners. The British in Nigeria and the very successful Gold Coast gradually ended the slave trade and then slavery itself. Their problem was convincing the chiefs, who "used a medley of pawns, slaves and corvée labour to create their coca farms," to end coercion.[418] Still, the great majority of the colony's production was undertaken by African smallholders. The Germans in Cameroon and Togo were more permissive of labor coercion of Africans in cacao farming, as were the Spanish in Spanish Guinea and the French in Congo and Madagascar. Actual legal slavery, however, was phased out. The Portuguese may have been the most severe in ignoring the worldwide abolition movement. After abolishing slavery in 1875 in Angola, they reinstated it in the 1880s. Until 1908 thousands of slaves and contract workers were sent to São Tomé and Principe cacao farms from the Portuguese colonies of Cape Verde, Angola, and Mozambique.[419]

In the seven decades after 1870 chocolate grew as a romantic gift, a leisure drink, and a child's treat. The sweet-consuming experience clashed with the sometimes bitter reality of its global production. Over time, however, even in growing countries the scale and extent of foreign ownership of landowning tended to decline. But as with coffee and tea, the chocolate commodity chain bridged continents, straddled colonial systems, brought disproportionate profits to processors in the developed world, and became characterized by heterodox labor systems that moved in the direction of freer labor while maintaining considerable coercion in many growing areas. Science, in the form of chemistry, agronomy, and engineering, played an important role in cultivation, processing, transporting, industrializing, marketing, and distributing the stimulants.

Outlaws

A final note on our commodity chains: We have pointed to the importance of nature, technology, international politics, and social customs in creating and attending to demand. The legal apparatus of patents, copyrights, and trademarks underlay property rights and value. What we have not much discussed is the legal boundary that protected and celebrated some commodities, creating great wealth and status for their producers, while denouncing other products as outlaws. Sugar, coffee, tea, and chocolate were considered respectable and modern by most people and all governments, even when their cultivation and processing were done under troubling conditions. But other goods that had equally long histories and that were often first considered miracle medicines became marginalized. Opium, heroin—synthesized by the former dye-producing Bayer Chemical Company—cocaine, and marijuana were condemned for their addictive properties despite their valuable medicinal effects as painkillers, anesthetics, and sleep aids. Revealing the whims of regulatory agencies, at the same time as it abandoned heroin Bayer became one of the world's largest pharmaceutical corporations largely on the merits of another painkiller, aspirin. International conventions led by the United States, and gradually and reluctantly accepted by the colonial powers through the League of Nations and then the United Nations, began to successfully forbid narcotics just as other legal pharmaceuticals became enormously profitable.[420] Only in the last decades of the twentieth century would government agencies lose their control over narcotics production and imports, as cultivators in areas rather on the periphery of the world economy, such as Bolivia, Colombia, Afghanistan, and Turkey, smuggled them into the most prosperous countries. A similar effort to close down and outlaw the most popular social drug, alcohol, had already failed in our period as the US Volstead Act of 1919 was repealed in 1933. Prohibiting legal drinking had spurred bootleg production and the rise of gangsters. More importantly, too many people wanted a drink and too many government agencies wanted the revenue. Nonetheless, we still live with the porous and sometimes arbitrary international legal boundary first systematically instituted in the years before 1945.

Clearly, commodity chains were not governed just by the forces of supply and demand. They did not entirely operate in an ethical vacuum where profit and loss overshadowed concerns of justice and equity, and they could not entirely transcend cultural values. Just as it is difficult to account for taste, so it was hard to forecast the line between the legally permitted and the prohibited as new products came on the market.

. . .

The seventy-five years that followed 1870 witnessed an unprecedented explosion of production leading to heightened market transactions, many of which crossed national borders and spanned continents. Industrialization, agricultural innovation, and marketing revolutions touched most people on Earth by the 1940s. Electricity and oil joined with steam to power the world in wholly new ways, shrinking distance and abolishing the night in cities.

This could fairly be called the first era of intensified globalization. But global spread did *not* create homogeneous actors, nor was everything commodified or predictable. Our use of the commodity chains approach and our emphasis on agriculture has allowed us to outline the broader contours of these frenzied changes while at the same time highlighting the extent of variation in production systems, processing, transporting, marketing, and consumption, even for the same product, such as wheat or sugar. We have seen that commodities such as cotton, grains, and stimulants interacted in different ways with the natural environments, social systems, value regimes, market institutions, and state or colonial agencies they encountered and shaped.

These contexts of economic transactions changed over time and by geographic location. As a result, the forward and backward linkages of the commodities to other economic activities, and their consequences for providing employment and tax revenues, also varied by place and time. The heterogeneity of the world economy meant that simultaneously with the "Great Acceleration" that brought people together through intensified international economic relations made possible by accelerated transport and communications there also grew a "Great Divergence" that distributed the benefits of economic and technological advance unequally. The gulf between, on the one side, Western Europe, North America, and the "neo-Europes," and, on the other side, the rest of the world tended to widen. By using a commodity chains approach we are able to palpably connect growers, processors, shippers, and marketers on different continents even though they did not know each other at the time and did not necessarily realize that they were participating in a complex international chain.

Technological advances in communications, transportation, processing, preserving, and packaging caused an enormous expansion of the volume, speed, and content of world trade. Space was rearranged by the steamship, canals, and railroad as well as the telegraph and finally the telephone. Geography was also modified by the transoceanic transplanting of various agricultural cultivars and massive migrations of people, as humans increasingly dominated and transformed nature. In some sectors, particularly food, people began questioning what was meant by "natural" and the extent to which that was pure and wholesome or unrestrained and dangerous. Some things that were unknown or rare in 1870 became necessities for many peoples by 1945, enriching the material lives of some participants in the world economy but making them more dependent on monetized market transactions. In the most prosperous countries there arose a whole new class of market-oriented consumers and new sites for purchases, such as chain stores and department stores.

The expansion of consumption of goods was directly related to the intensification of labor. Stimulants, machines, and new agricultural techniques squeezed more labor power out of workers. Leisure increasingly became a valued commodity. Managers, investors, and workers came to think that time was money for ever more people, as clocks and electrical lighting regimented and even replaced individual biorhythms and seasonal cycles in industrialized areas. This intensification and global spread of what Jan de Vries has called the Industrious Revolution (1650–1850) was mitigated and abetted some by leaps in food and medicine production. Just as, during this era, matter and energy were shown by

Einstein to be interchangeable when enough force is brought to bear, so did labor and things appear to become fungible. Traditional labor and land conventions succumbed, if unevenly, to market forces. Markets for important commodities like wheat, coffee, tea, and hard fibers tended to regional and even worldwide price convergence while futures trading sold things that did not yet exist.

This period was not an uninterrupted monolith, a steadily rising curve of prosperity. It was pervaded by cycles, booms, and crashes, by fads and backlashes. Whereas the years up to 1914 were generally marked by the rapid rise and spread of liberalism, reduced customs duties, diminished state interference, and increasing reliance on foreign trade—particularly in the British Empire—the three decades after the eruption of world war at Sarajevo witnessed mainly a "retreat from a short brush with liberalism."[421] However, because ours is a world history not solely concentrated on the economies of the North Atlantic, we cannot fully agree with O'Rourke and Williamson that "the world economy had lost all its globalization achievement in the three decades between 1914 and 1945."[422] Although the previous price convergence dissipated and overall global trade slowed, the organizational structures—the sinews—for trade and new technologies remained.

Figuring the balance sheet for the global spread of commodity chains is tricky, because it is ambiguous. On the one hand, the changes we have examined brought the world closer together through trade, technological diffusion, and formal and informal imperialism. On the other hand, most of the benefits of the commercial revolution were concentrated in just a few places. Between 1870 and 1945 there was an unprecedented international concentration of power and wealth. The concentration centered in certain nations, mostly Western European and North American; within them was also a great class divide and continuing regional divide (think of the US South versus the US Northeast). But it would be simplistic and wrong to think the world was divided into the West versus the rest, between colonizers and colonized, or between industrialists and agriculturalists. There was ample variety and growth in the "non-West," tied to a considerable extent to their connections to the world economy. There was also significant interregional trade, as in China, that did not register in global trade statistics. There was certainly more wealth and advanced technology in global cities like Buenos Aires,

Rio de Janeiro, and Shanghai than in, not only their own hinterlands, but, say, Wales, Andalusia, or New Mexico. With the rise of agro-industry in some crops like sugar and wheat, as well as large-scale processing of the harvests, the divide between industry and agriculture/extraction often became fuzzy.

People not incorporated into the world market did not necessarily consider themselves "losers." There was notable resistance by colonial peasants and ethnic minorities such as the Maya, the Zulu, the Apache, and the Tamils who were conquered or subjugated. These people did not submit meekly. Our period witnessed a double movement of resistance leading to internal warfare and civil wars as well as more benign reforms. At the same time, many religious movements rejected the primacy of materialist market values over spiritual values, and more secular anarchists, socialists, and social democrats fought to reform or overthrow capitalism's bourgeois individualist property regimes. Ideological hegemony was contested all over the globe even though a small number of people exercised unprecedented power in this era.

The growing concentration of power derived not only from a small group of people controlling most of the capital and know-how, but also from the industrialization of destruction. Modern new weapons (machine guns, railroads, gunboats, bomber planes, and, at the end, missiles) and means of delivering them over long distances reinforced the advantages of the rich and created gigantic new markets and fortunes. Apparent economic decisions, such as the shift of ships from coal to oil or connecting colonies by telegraph, were as likely based on strategic considerations as they were motivated by the desire to maximize profit. Indeed, many of the imperial or defensive decisions to build infrastructure did not make much short-run economic sense. The celebration of the "economically rational man" was challenged by irrational and racist destruction.

Although stores and markets found their shelves and stalls filled with more and different things, growing choice did not greatly affect the lives of most people. In fact, coercion was as much a central theme of the period as was opportunity. Semi-free trade and bountiful markets resplendent with new modern goods lived in a world also marred by peonage and authoritarianism. True, this was the era of growing rights through the abolition of slavery and the first women's suffrage. Democracy was spread by liberals and social democrats. But it was also the age of pogroms in Russia and Turkey; internal wars against indigenous peoples in such areas as Argentina, northern Mexico, the US Prairie, and the Australian Outback; and more institutionalized and deadlier "racial cleansing" by German Nazis.

This period saw at its beginning the high tide of British imperialism but then witnessed London's power subsiding in the twentieth century as the United States, Germany, France, the Soviet Union/Russia, and Japan challenged its dominance. British rule had never been monolithic anyway, because its treatment of white settler colonies, such as Australia and Canada, was far different from its treatment of the brown colonies of Africa, Asia (with the partial exception of India), and the Caribbean. Independent areas such as Argentina, Uruguay, and southeastern Brazil received more British capital, trade, and technology than did most formal colonies.

Great advances in transportation and communications joined with international empires, corporations, institutions, and nongovernmental organizations to standardize weights, measures, international laws, and property rights. These in turn strengthened the private sector. Transaction costs of doing business fell dramatically in some places because of the widespread acceptance of the gold standard and large international banking syndicates, conventions, and cartels facilitated by the advent of the telegraph and then the telephone.

But even in the heyday of economic liberalism, states were fundamental to ensuring that conditions of the market prevailed. Without government interventions such as trust busting and treaties, monopoly would have triumphed over competition, stymieing innovation. Governments did not merely interfere and tax, as their loudest critics complained. Public officials also coordinated and financed the construction of infrastructure, fomented scientific advances, and tried to prevent actors from unfairly restraining trade. They also attempted to pacify and control workers. States defined and protected newly invented commodity rights by overseeing trademarks, patents, copyrights, stocks, bonds, monetary conventions, and the value of currency as well as land titles. Through their courts and jails, states were fundamental to protecting and inventing property rights, facilitating great accumulations of wealth. In some fortunate lands they also oversaw the reproduction of the labor force by beginning to enforce new health regulations, funding medical advances, and expanding educational systems.

As populations grew, migrated, and urbanized, societies moved away from natural economies and face-to-face transactions toward market commodification. The growth of anonymous and impersonal relations mediated by local markets and long-distance trade called for greater third-party—usually state—oversight. In numerous commodities, such as coffee, rubber, sugar, and tea, states attempted to join together to regulate or corner the market. The public sphere that arose in this period transformed the divide between the private and the public. In the relatively few places where there began to appear laws protecting workers—women and children as well as men—and protecting the integrity of products such as food and medicines, states helped ensure the long-run health of the economy and the society they served. In the most prosperous countries and in the Soviet Union, they also sometimes responded to labor unions by increasing regulation of the workplace. Sometimes, as in Brazilian coffee and North American wheat, farmers banded together to demand government intervention.

Moreover, for many commodities, tariffs, treaties, and imperial preferences shaped markets. State officials were as likely to be as motivated by concerns about national defense and integration, and about state building and social peace, as about maximizing the profits of the private sector or enriching specific capitalists. Religious values also impinged on secular public actions. Markets and the struggle for profit did not independently rule human actions.

The birth of the modern world showered wealth, power, unimagined products, and lifestyle possibilities on the fortunate. For many people, life expectancies and life choices improved. Urbanization, the popularization of the press, and ease of movement gave voice to many who had formerly been muted. This was the high point not only of monopolies and multinational companies but also of labor unions and international socialist movements.

We even see the beginning of concern about the treatment of the environment. But people continued to think of "nature" as natural resources meant for human use. The world's flora, fauna, and minerals seemed limitless, and human ingenuity and appetite unbounded.

At the dawn of the twentieth century, many observers enthusiastically predicted worldwide peace and prosperity because of the alleged dominance of reason and science. The Prometheus of global trade and industry promised a bright future. Then the last thirty-one years of our period were darkened by crushing war and debilitating economic depression. Tens of millions of deaths and economic stagnation brought widespread disillusionment and revolutionary fervor.

Peering back at the world of more than sixty years ago, we need to consider which are its most important legacies. This was both the triumphant era of the railroad, airplane, and radio, of mass production and mass consumption, *and* the era of wealth concentration, two world wars, the Russian Revolution, and the atomic bomb. Accelerated economic interactions led to cultural diffusion and syncretic amalgamation. Greater communication only sometimes yielded greater understanding. It was an era of sharp contrasts. The telegraph, steamship, and global markets led some people to think of One World, shorn of divisive differences. They launched the League of Nations, the International Court, Esperanto, and NGOs like the Red Cross and the Boy Scouts to traverse national borders. World fairs and the Olympics brought people together from many corners of the Earth. But the urge to compete was probably stronger than the desire to cooperate. Intensified international transactions also intensified nationalism and imperialism.

The fleshing-out of the international commodity chains of some key illustrative goods shows that the concept of "*the* market" is simplistic, that markets were more fragmented, unstable, and heterodox as new products became more valuable for different reasons. Certainly people in places geographically remote from each other began to affect each other in unexpected and unforeseen ways. Whether chaining farmers together in networks of commodity exchanges was positive or detrimental depended upon specific historical circumstances. Outcomes were not uniform, foreordained, consistent, or constant. The genie released by new energy forms, new mechanical and chemical techniques, new means of transport and communication, and new products was not necessarily benevolent or malignant. Human history and the environment in which people lived shaped the consequences of this first modern age of globalization as commodity chains linked areas and peoples that historically had limited interactions. The global forces unleashed in that period still reverberate today. As William Faulkner warned us: "The past is never dead, it is not even past."

·[FIVE]·

Transnational Currents in a Shrinking World

Emily S. Rosenberg

Introduction

"THE extension and use of railroads, steamships, telegraphs, break down nationalities and bring people geographically remote into close connection. . . .
They make the world one." So wrote David Livingstone, the famed British
missionary-explorer whose accounts of Africa became widely influential in the
West.[1] By the late nineteenth century, this commonplace sentiment echoed
throughout the world, expressed in some form or other both by those who celebrated the shrinking world and by those who feared it.

The observation that the late nineteenth-century revolutions in transportation, communication, finance, and commerce were transforming loyalties and
sensibilities, limiting or even eliminating spatial distance, animated the creation
of an ever-widening array of international and transnational networks during
the era from the mid-nineteenth to the mid-twentieth century. C. A. Bayly has
aptly called the steps toward what is now often termed globalization the "Great
Acceleration." In many older historical writings it was assumed that Europeans
shaped the onset of the "modern" age during this era and then, for better or
worse, exported its characteristics to other regions through emerging structures
of empire, trade, and cultural hegemony. Bayly, however, conceives of the world
during this era "as a complex of overlapping networks of global reach, while at
the same time acknowledging the vast differentials of power which inhered in
them." Europeans were often able to "bend to their will existing global networks," he writes. Yet "it was the parasitic and 'networked' nature of Western
domination and power which gave it such strength, binding together, and tapping into, a vast range of viable networks and aspirations."[2]

This chapter follows Bayly and other recent scholars in suggesting that although Euro-Americans played a significant role in the creation and spread of
modernity in this era, the many social and cultural networks that increasingly
crisscrossed the globe helped to coproduce and accelerate the transformations.
It recognizes that state-building projects, imperial dynamics, demographic

movements, and economic interrelationships leave significant global interconnections unexamined, and that today's dense and varied social networks and cultural entanglements have important forerunners. A wide range of new international agreements and institutions expanded the realms of intergovernmental connections. In addition, many non-state networks existed more or less independently from governments (or sometimes operated loosely through them). These networks connected people through aspiration, expertise, and affiliation of various kinds. This chapter, in short, is concerned with how transnational social and cultural currents circulated across and beyond national states and drew the world together in new ways.[3]

To begin, it will be helpful to imagine the usual territorial map of the world with pastel-colored countries and empires grouped into continents separated by blue seas. It is within the invisible assumptions of such a map that most history has been written. The conventions of professional history writing, after all, emerged in the late nineteenth century in association with the accelerated processes of state building, empire building, and mapmaking. Textbooks, for example, often use maps to illustrate the rise and fall of territorial control. Contrasting colors display the before-and-after borders of controlled or claimed realms. Examples would be the common use of before-and-after maps of World War I, the partition of Africa, the expansion of Japan in the 1930s and early 1940s, the shrinkage and then enlargement of the Soviet empire after the Bolshevik Revolution, and so forth. Such maps exemplify how history is generally taught and learned with reference to geographically bounded national states, and they exemplify the extent to which history centers on questions related to why and how those shifting borders moved. Of course, such maps are enormously helpful in visualizing the world, and one would not seek their eradication. Geographical information provides a solid basis for visualizing world history. But such maps also silently construct realms of inquiry that mostly relate to the decisions and actions of those expanding and contracting, appearing and disappearing, yellow, pink, and green entities named states.

Other kinds of maps can be, and have been, devised. If the world is mapped according to population, for example, the "sizes" of countries or regions look far different from when they are plotted according to geographic territory. Consider, further, how the world changes shape when remapped according to data on per capita income, urbanization, energy consumption, numbers of people living less than fifty miles from their place of birth, or any other of dozens of indicators. Even though less common, these kinds of maps may track historical information that seems just as important for understanding the world's past as are those more familiar maps delineating territorial borders.

This chapter tries to construct, through words, yet another kind of map that is even more intricate. Perhaps possible to conjure only in the flexible dimensions of the imagination, this map directs attention not to a particular territorial place or to the information that might be contained therein but to the dynamic connections, both visible and invisible, between and among places. Such networks and connecting flows, in all their variation, cannot literally be charted onto geographical space, but they nonetheless constitute a mental map that may recast the terrain of history writing. Livingstone and so many of his contemporaries around the world claimed to be witnessing a revolution in geographic space and the allegiances it commanded. Historians need to conjure new maps in order to capture and then raise questions about the amazing acceleration of interconnectivity that was shrinking distance and complicating identities.

The sections that follow suggest some of the interwoven pathways that might make up a mental map of social and cultural transnational history. No world or global history can be comprehensive, and this one does not attempt to cover every transnational network in every area of the world through this long and complicated era. Because the idea of transnational history remains a concept under construction, however, I have tried to map what might be some major categories and interpretive themes for these networks. I have then illustrated these with examples from throughout the world, sometimes making reference to the more conventional realms of national states ("Japan," "Argentina," "the United States," "Germany," and so on) while still attempting to hold at bay the assumptions of nation-state primacy conveyed through their naming. The focus is not primarily on separate geographies but on those flows that spanned geographical boundaries. The concern of this chapter is the fluid realm of the "trans-."

To illuminate transnational networks, the central metaphor of *currents* provides appropriate imagery for this age of electricity. The globalizing currents examined here emerge unevenly and in complex fashion. The metaphor of currents moves away from a spoke-and-wheel, center-and-periphery framework to suggest crisscrossing flows of power and an interactive, though usually asymmetrical, reciprocal dynamic.

The idea of "currents" suggests a number of associated words that serve to illuminate the global interactions analyzed here. Currents, for example, can run through circuits. They may pulse in one direction or be interactive; they may flow from point to point or charge a more generalized field. They come together in nodes, which are points of collection and retransmission. They may be conveyed along lines that may be singular or of blended and woven character. They have both a visible and an invisible quality. Currents move, connect, and draw together but are also subject to disruption, overload, and shock. Currents can be smooth, even pleasing, but always carry the danger of interruption. In short, the vocabulary of currents suggests linked contingency and variability, process and transformation rather than static structure. All of these connotations prove useful in schematizing the world as it came into being during this era of accelerating interconnections.

It seems helpful to elaborate further on some of the ways that this metaphor will do its interpretive work in the sections that follow.

1. Currents, of course, move through networks. Networks among states and interconnections among peoples often transcended boundaries and drew different nationalities and cultures together. Some of these networks were highly utilitarian and served an array of specific functions. Many new organizations, for example, sought to facilitate global connections through the international standardization of norms and through institutionalizing regulatory and legal regimes. Other networks were more visionary, linked to ideas and affiliations that their adherents held in common and wanted to project transnationally. Older world histories that centered primarily on states and empires often lost sight of the variety of visions that animated individuals who operated and held strong allegiances across political boundaries.

Global networks often transcended geographical boundaries, but they nonetheless participated in other kinds of boundary drawing. In fact, the more that some types of boundaries were challenged and erased, the more new networks might shore up others in new ways. The simultaneous erasure and creation of difference and distinction, of course, were interrelated. The language and categories of disease, gender, race, cultural affinities, religion, and science, for example, often transcended geographical boundaries at the same time as they created new grammars and registers of difference. Cultural currents could foster inclusion, exclusion, and rearrangement of human relationships; their effects could be sometimes transitory and sometimes more lasting.

2. Although global networks were not coterminous with bounded states or imperial systems or regional affiliations, neither were they free of them. Transnational currents complicate the interpretive terrain of world history along both a spatial and a chronological axis. First, the globalizing networks in this era assumed shape within the context of Western Europe's nation building, empire building, and growing economic and cultural hegemony. Nations and empires were spaces, themselves assembled through networks of various kinds, that attempted to regularize and delineate the movement of people, goods, and ideas. Secondly, in the West most conceptions of what was "global" and "international" implied an inevitable and presumably progressive universalizing of certain Western ideas and experiences. The extension and imposition of Western universalism played an important role in constituting many global networks. Thus *transnational networks developed not necessarily in opposition to the hardening boundaries of nationalism or of empire, or as a stage of progress beyond them, but sometimes as necessary counterparts to state and empire building.*

3. An examination of global currents helps direct attention to particular people who shaped the emergent networks and affiliations and who served as conduits for exchanges connecting several planes of analysis. A focus on people and their connections can help make visible how the realms of the transnational, the national, and the local intersected in ways both dangerous (for whom?) and liberating (for whom?). *Using the metaphor of currents with nodes of connectivity facilitates an analytical process that scales back and forth, seeing large and seeing small while concentrating on the interactivity and often unevenness among local, regional, and global levels.*[4]

4. Historians writing within a postcolonial sensibility have tried to break loose from the earlier era's rigid conceptions of territorial boundaries and from its teleological assumptions of geographic, racial, and class destiny. Many have sought to build a new appreciation for the networked interactivity that characterized what Mary Louise Pratt has called "contact zones." Contact zones are "social spaces where cultures meet, clash, and grapple with each other, often in

contexts of highly asymmetrical relations of power, such as colonialism, slavery, or their aftermaths." Pratt sees a shrinking world's clash of cultures not simply as a story of loss, imperialism, and oppression, but also as one about mutual borrowings, diverse if unequal forms of power, trickster reversals, possible harmonies, and substantial confusion. Anthropologist Anna Tsing suggests that, in transnational space, the global and the local meet in unpredictable encounters, which she calls moments of "friction."[5] *Within the friction of contact zones, which multiplied within the connective currents that networked the globe in this period, there was creativity as well as oppression, coproduction as well as imposition of "imperial knowledge." Currents brought diverse kinds of transformations.*

5. Thus, this chapter endorses anthropologist Arjun Appadurai's insistence that the presumed universalism of modernism nested together with diverse oppositions. *Claims of universalism and particularism bred each other; the global and the local interacted to produce uniformity as well as diversity. The world became increasingly characterized by what I will call "differentiated commonalities"— that is, commonalities that nevertheless manifested themselves differently depending on the unpredictable frictions arising from geographical, temporal, and sociocultural locations.*[6]

6. Currents also appropriately connote the age of electricity. The global spread of electricity was a feat of science, engineering, and finance that embedded almost mystical qualities within this age of rationality. It aptly exemplified *the unity between two often-dichotomized aspects of "modern" life—reason supported by exacting taxonomies and accounting practices, and emotion charged through fluid spectacularity.* By dramatically shrinking time and space, electricity's progeny—illumination, telephony, movies, and much more—all seemed one part science and one part miracle.

Concepts of "modernity" are the subjects of an enormous scholarship, of course, and this chapter develops a particular view. It projects "the modern" as emerging from two, seemingly contradictory, impulses. Promises of "order and progress" expressed one impulse. It emphasized rationality, science, engineering, corporate organization, and classification. It exalted the application of expertise and often worked to stabilize hierarchies of gender and race and geographical space. A second impulse arose within various new forms of entertainment and the changing media of mass communications. Characterized by spectacle, image, flow, surprise, and disjuncture, it appealed to a kind of emotional knowledge that was often self-styled as "popular." Science/spectacle, expertise/entertainment, order/disorder are, of course, only schematic opposites. It was within the combinations and clashes of these false poles that emerged the messy diversities and contradictions that have characterized modern life.[7]

7. The metaphor of currents whose dynamics are driven by polarities presents an even broader interpretation of modernity. Currents carry power, experience charge, and often activate their energy through polarities. Similarly, the emerging modernism of this increasingly networked era was one in which seemingly binary poles emerged as coproductive counterparts: *homogenization and differentiation, the global and the local, trans- or internationalism and nationalism, reason and spectacle. All of these sets are composed not of opposites but of nested complements that operated in creative tension with each other.*

There are dangers in any interpretive or metaphorical schema, and two of these need to be considered at the outset. Electricity brings with it a language and presumption of "enlightenment," of bringing "light" to and illuminating, "dark" continents and peoples. The metaphor itself can frame the discursive constructions of the age of electricity, hiding as much as it reveals. Authors, and readers, however, cannot escape the entrapments of language and discourse; they can only strive for the kind of critical reflection that will mitigate the hazards. In addition, the idea of mapping networks and currents may leave invisible the many people in the world who remained relatively untouched by them or who became more *dis*connected. Swaths of the earth, particularly in the interiors of Africa and Asia, may have been partially or largely "off-grid" in the transnational connectivity of the age, perhaps remaining in localized networks or perhaps intentionally self-shielded from outsider threats. Still, any idea that continental interiors held timeless people living the unchanged ways of their ancestors has proved to be an Orientalist cliché. Transnational currents could have secondary and tertiary ripple effects, touching even very remote people in uneven and unpredictable ways. In some cases the borders and restrictions that colonial rule imposed, of course, also worked to restrict networks: Colonial powers in Africa, for example, often destroyed prior long-distance trading and cultural networks. Extractive production brought some areas into greater contact with global networks of economic and social exchange while it made others more isolated. The forging of some networks thus could mean the disarticulation of others.[8] The frame of transnational currents, in short, cannot hope to capture either a connotation-free or a total story of all the localities in the world. Indeed, no schema could succeed in achieving linguistic neutrality and an accounting of all lives on the planet.

Despite potential hazards, I seek to use selective examples to show the possibilities inherent in focusing history around the dynamic, if uneven, flows of transnational currents. Focusing on five areas—international agreements and institutions, social networks and attachments, nodes of exhibition and collection, epistemic affiliations based on expertise, and the spectacular flows of mass media and consumerism—this chapter provides a tentative map for some of the transnational global connectivities that preceded the popularization of the word *globalization* in the 1960s and 1970s. These currents are diverse in character and in operation; they comprise neither a coherent global project nor a new stage of history that is beyond the national or imperial state. Although there is by now an enormous amount of research on transnational networks, their representations in this chapter are necessarily partial and contain overlapping chronologies. Chronological time is important: the kind of networks that once mostly abetted the rise of European dominance developed circuitry that helped undermine European power as the twentieth century wore on. Still, chronological time, like geographical space, is less important in this chapter than the thematic elaborations. The five themes that follow suggest that "complex interconnectivity," a term that John Tomlinson has given to the era since 1970, is no less a descriptor for the period 1870 to 1945.[9]

1. Currents of Internationalism

IN the early twentieth century, the British writer Norman Angell electrified the imaginations and hopes of people who called themselves "internationalists." A small man scarcely five feet tall who had officially dropped his given last name "Lane" to become known by his penultimate name "Angell," Norman had moved to America at the age of seventeen and headed west. In his six years in America, he worked briefly as a tutor on a southern plantation, a cowboy, a homesteader near the "fearful, weary, merciless desert" around Bakersfield, California, and a journalist.[10] From 1905 he began serving as the Paris editor for the *Daily Mail* and, after returning to England in 1912, he took up politics. Angell's short book *The Great Illusion* (1910) made him famous. Angell was a complicated man—sickly, moody, shy—but his ideas resonated internationally, and he proved to be a compelling speaker. *The Great Illusion* was translated into twenty-five languages, sold over two million copies, and briefly spurred a movement called "Norman Angellism."

The thesis of *The Great Illusion* (from which the famous antiwar film *The Grand Illusion* would later derive its mocking title) held that military clashes had become obsolete because the integration of finance and commerce in European countries made war counterproductive. Conquest, he argued, added nothing to the wealth of a nation or its citizens. Reworking the popular Darwinian beliefs of his day, Angell wrote that war "involves the survival of the less fit. . . . Warlike nations do not inherit the earth" but "represent the decaying human element" of "primitive instincts and old prejudices." In many nations of the world "Norman Angellism" had its converts. In the United States in 1913 no less a figure that the president of Stanford University, David Starr Jordan, proclaimed that war was "impossible." "The bankers will not find the money for such a fight, the industries will not maintain it, the statesmen cannot."[11]

Angellism was only one manifestation of a widespread conviction that the revolution in communications, travel, and trade would shrink the world and create greater harmony. In China, the reformist ideas of Sun Yat-sen, Kang Youwei, and Liang Qichao, for example, had taken shape from these men's late nineteenth-century travels around the world. Kang cited the telegraph, the Universal Postal Union (UPU), and international law as evidence of a trajectory from which states might one day organize themselves into a world parliament. Liang, who between 1902 and 1907 published an influential biweekly journal called the *New Citizen,* expressed the hope that emerging international news services might promote a cosmopolitanism that would eliminate national and factional hostilities.[12]

The world of the late nineteenth and early twentieth centuries did indeed see the development of newly established "international institutions," defined by some scholars today as "persistent and connected sets of rules, often affiliated with organizations, that operate across international boundaries. Institutions range from conventions to regimes to formal organizations."[13]

A seeming paradox lay at the heart of these newly institutionalized international networks. The rhetoric of internationalism often suggested that its advocates transcended "narrow" nationalism and embraced a progressive universalism that would, incrementally, come to replace national states. People who considered themselves internationalists frequently lashed out against what they regarded as excessive or militant nationalism. Yet, as the very word *international* suggests, the "national" constituted the building block of the "international" realm, and most internationalists pursued projects that created cooperative forums and regulatory regimes among bounded states—states that were consolidated along a European model.

The boundary-strengthening moves of states and of empires thus emerged not as preconditions for or in opposition to internationalism but often as its necessary accompaniments. Indeed, most of the international regulatory peace-keeping regimes that took shape in the nineteenth and twentieth centuries attracted support precisely because so many people believed they might serve, or even universalize, the interests of their national states.

A close look at the emergence of international networks dissolves any possible paradox involved in linking the emergence of "internationalism" together with the attempts to harden the delineation of national and imperial borders. In this period the most successful international institutions sprang primarily from a Euro-American impulse that sought to refashion the world into an assemblage of "advanced" states that could project and protect their imperial realms while using cooperative institutions to spread a universalistic Western ethos. Internationalism most often came dressed as a Western project, but as we will see, its visions also contained many variations that inspired movements in diverse directions, including nationalisms linked to anticolonialism.

This section positions World War I as a major watershed for internationalism. In the late nineteenth century, the promise and problems of accelerating technological change drew delegates from states together to regularize practices, particularly related to global communication and transportation. The shrinking globe also spurred ideas that international law might broaden its scope from addressing specific practices (such as navigation) to shaping larger regimes of arbitration and peacekeeping. Before the Great War, a wide variety of associations blossomed under the sunny optimism that international political institutions might keep pace with the globalization occurring in the economic and technological realms. International networks were generally elite affairs, and many Euro-American leaders assumed that nationalistic warfare had become a relic of a less enlightened past and that imperialism and internationalism would eventually uplift the globe into an era of shared "civilization" and progress.

World War I dealt a blow to such dreams. Specific internationalist projects continued, and many of the international regulatory regimes developed over the period remained as vital mechanisms that promoted the connectivities of the age. The war's destruction, however, shattered prewar optimism, and interwar internationalism seemed propelled more by fear than by hope. Could international rivalries and militarism be contained? As a greater diversity of people and ideas entered the international arena, disagreements widened rather than narrowed, and the label *internationalism* became fraught with ever more contradiction and multiplicity of meaning. As first one and then another world war wreaked its incomprehensible devastations, fewer and fewer people could assume that movement toward a common definition of "civilization" provided the inevitable telos of history.

Ordering Space and Time

In the second half of the nineteenth century, the telegraph became the most visible symbol of a shrinking and interlocking world. Facilitating communication across distances through telegraphy, a task driven by strategic and business interests, became one of the earliest arenas for the creation and coordination of international norms and practices. Underwater telegraph cables successfully spanned the English Channel in 1851 and only fifteen years later, amazingly, traversed the Atlantic Ocean. Connecting first Europe and North America, telegraphy spread into the Middle East, Asia, and Latin America during the 1870s. Britain's extension of telegraph lines from London to India in 1870, to southern Africa in the 1880s, and between Australia and Canada in the early 1900s illustrates the importance of telegraphy to imperial systems. World War I proved the telegraph's significance for national war strategies, including intelligence gathering.[14]

The International Telegraph Union, founded in Paris in 1865 and subsequently retitled the International Telecommunication Union (ITU), sought to standardize and regulate international telecommunications. International telegraph lines had adapted a version of Morse code, a system of short and long clicks that Samuel B. Morse pioneered in the United States in the 1840s for his Western Union company. The ITU made this practice its global standard. The new organization also, in time, came to allocate radio spectrum and devise procedures for international telephone calls. Europe developed an international telephone system in the 1920s, but reliable transoceanic telephone and a functioning global network did not emerge until well after World War II. In Europe, states owned telegraph and telephone services, and the United States, where ownership by private business generally prevailed, remained reluctant to join the ITU as a formal partner until after World War II. Still, the United States nonetheless sent observers and participated in various standard-setting conferences. Both states and enterprises embraced these emerging international norms that, by helping curb monopolistic or overly nationalistic practices, facilitated commercial and social connections across the entire system. The preeminent historical account of the ITU claims that, as the first genuine international organization, the ITU became the model for subsequent international bodies, including the League of Nations.[15] The ways in which telegraphy mixed national and imperial aspirations with international regulation are illustrative of emerging international regimes.

Closely related in structure and function to the ITU, the Universal Postal Union (UPU), founded initially as the General Postal Union in 1874, regular-

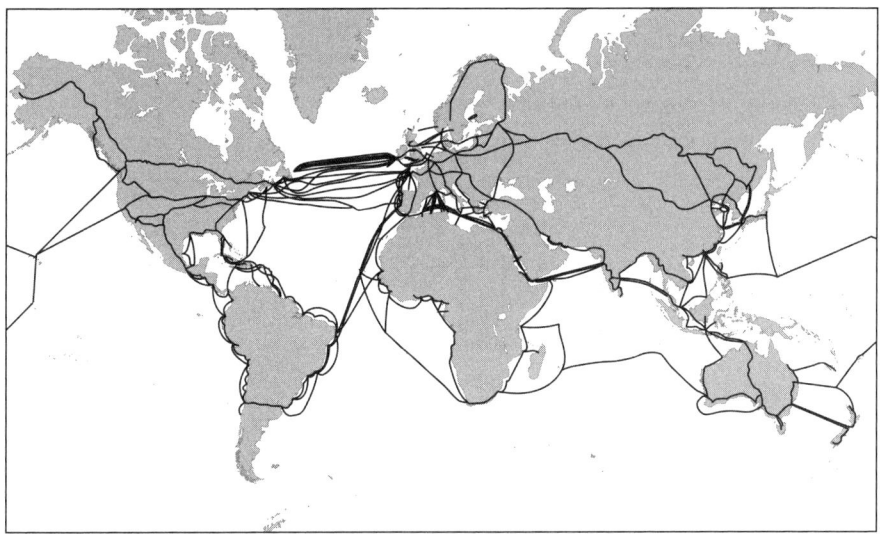

International network of major telegraph and cable lines, 1924.

ized the carrying and delivery of international mail. Nationalized, government-run postal services had emerged along with the nation-building efforts of modern states. The United States, for example, had consolidated its services into a single postal district and had, in 1863, introduced free home delivery of mail in its largest cities. Hoping to expand the possibility of correspondence worldwide, US officials then called for an international postal congress. Similarly in England, Rowland Hill's midcentury reforms had introduced inexpensive, prepaid, and uniform rates. Building on such beginnings, Heinrich von Stephan, the German postal minister who had standardized postal exchange in Bismarck's Germany, led an effort to form an ongoing international organization. In 1874, European nations, the United States, Russia, Turkey, and Egypt entered an agreement to cooperate in creating a shared postal space, and within two years Japan, Brazil, Persia, and many European colonies joined. The Union soon included every country in the world.

The Union sponsored ingenious efficiencies. Before the UPU, each country had to negotiate a separate treaty with every other; after the UPU's establishment, one treaty would link a country to the Union. Then all correspondents in the participating nations could post to each other by paying a flat, relatively inexpensive rate that did not depend on distance or on diplomatic status. Stamps of member nations were accepted for the whole international route, making additional stamps from countries along the route of transit unnecessary. Each country retained the monies it collected for international postage. As with the ITU, the UPU compellingly illustrated how national objectives dovetailed with the creation of international rule-setting and enforcement mechanisms.[16]

The rapid spread of a coherent global postal system under the UPU spurred the growth of literacy and of letter writing. It helped generate a revolution in written communication and print media. Postal reform coincided, for example, with the rise of postcards, which Austria introduced in 1869 and Germany embraced during the Franco-Prussian War of 1870–1871 to facilitate military communications. The Americans introduced a "penny postcard" in the 1870s, helping democratize letter writing by encouraging inexpensive, briefer, and more casual communication.[17] Soon advertisers discovered that efficient postal services and postcards could create bonds with customers. Mass letter writing took on a new commercial function. Book and magazine publishing also became global industries that continued targeting their elite purchasers but also developed new products to appeal to new middle- and working-class buyers. By 1914 the major industrial nations in Europe, the United States, and Japan all had mandated schooling for children up to age fourteen, and all had reached roughly 90 percent literacy fifteen years after that. International regulatory regimes often benefited the largest companies within the countries with greatest literacy rates because those firms could most easily profit from a globalizing market.

The burgeoning industry of publishing, benefiting from streamlined postal systems and a rising literacy rate, also turned to international rule setting to safeguard authors' rights and bolster markets. The Berne Convention of 1886 began to unify procedures related to literary property, and a Publishers' International Congress, formed at the end of the century, tried to secure the interests of the huge international publishing houses in Germany, France, Britain, and America.

It would be hard to overstate the importance of the revolution in print media in this era. Fueled by growing literacy, revolutions in technologies of production, and regulatory agreements, it linked people and spread ideas even as it entrenched inequalities between those who were part of the world of print and those who were not.

As international rules for electronic and written communications became standardized and more businesses and individuals broadened their contacts, the regularization of time seemed urgent. Cycles of sun and moon had governed the preindustrial world, but a predictability that transcended distance was critical to an interconnected and industrial world. In the mid-nineteenth century, as Britain and then Germany moved toward regularized time zones within their national spaces, the rules about time in the United States and most other countries remained chaotic and governed by local authorities. In 1870 Philadelphia's noon came twenty minutes after Pittsburgh's. An American train traveler from Washington to San Francisco would have to reset his or her timepiece over two hundred times in order to be current with each locality through which the train passed. Ships could not clearly communicate their positions at sea because of multiple national meridian systems; Greenwich, Paris, Berlin, Bern, Uppsala, St. Petersburg, Rome, and others each promoted its particular status as an anchor for a different prime meridian.

The new speed of railroads, shipping, and telegraphs necessitated the coordination of global space and time. Without a standard time, how could business appointments be kept; how could travelers meet; how could trains and ships stay safe? With their special need for rationalized scheduling, railroads often led the way. In the United States in 1883 railroads standardized their time zones to accord to Britain's Greenwich-based system, and most towns embraced this reform that some opponents derisively called "Vanderbilt time."

The International Meridian Conference, held a year later in Washington, DC, brought together twenty-five nations, which represented most countries in the Americas and in Europe in addition to Turkey, Japan, and Hawai'i. Although France had been committed to its Paris prime meridian (and did not accept the new system until 1911), Britain prevailed in the diplomatic wrangling. The conference accepted the Observatory of Greenwich as the initial meridian for longitude. Establishing longitudes west and east from Greenwich until they met at an "international date line" in the Pacific Ocean, the conference's technicians of time also urged the universal adoption of a standardized twenty-four-hour day. Although most of rural China, India, and elsewhere continued to use sundials and to observe a plethora of local times, over the next several decades most nations gradually adopted a system of twenty-four time zones—a system that the Meridian Conference of 1884 had discussed but not mandated.[18]

As much of the world was standardizing time, new inventions and practices readjusted how time might be valued, understood, and experienced. The telephone collapsed distance into simultaneity. Stop-action photography froze time in a moment. The electric light pushed back the hours of darkness. Railroad sleeping cars (pioneered by Pullman in the United States and Wagons-Lits in Europe) sped passengers with great comfort across much longer distances, including the fabled Orient Express route that opened from Paris to Istanbul in 1889. Automobiles spurred construction of more and better roads. The electric clock, invented in 1916, introduced a fluid motion to the second hand. Motion pictures played with time by slowing, accelerating, and punctuating it. Artistic and literary modernism broke with established traditions to toy with new sensibilities of time and space; Salvador Dalí's *The Persistence of Memory* (1931) famously bent and distorted watches that symbolized time's passage. Frederick Taylor chopped up time and motion to accelerate the work processes of industrial labor, while typewriters sped up the pace of office work. The international networks that synchronized the world and its people thus altered economic, cultural, and emotional realms, stimulating new visions of globality that sparked both hope for universalist understandings and dread of machinelike conformity.[19]

The rationalization of time gave encouragement to other standardization movements. Efforts emerged to coordinate railroad track gauges and scales. The Treaty of the Meter, signed by many industrial countries in 1875, created an International Bureau of Weights and Measures to monitor the spreading metric system. (Britain and the United States remained outside of the metric zone.) The International Electrotechnical Commission (IEC), formed in 1906 as one of the earliest nongovernmental standardizing bodies, codified electrical standards and symbols. Its 1938 International Electrotechnical Vocabulary contained over two thousand terms in English, French, German, Italian, Spanish, and Esperanto. Engineers, the new professionals who seemed to be the heroes of the era, led many of these movements toward the coordination of national, regional, and international systems. Supporting such efforts, the International Statistical Institute (ISI), founded at The Hague in 1885 as a semigovernmental organization, linked the statistical offices of various governments. The statistics gathering of the League of Nations assumed some of the ISI's tasks in the interwar era, when the trade among ninety countries began to be monitored in statistical terms. Statistical calculations emerged to track international comparisons in balance of payments, unemployment, price levels, and national income.

The expanding matrix of statistics, especially after World War I, elaborated a new branch of knowledge in which the very conception of an "economy" was national in its orientation but transnational in its scope. The Weimar Republic and the Third Reich led the way in using economic statistics as a way of engineering national power. Yet the emergence of economic analysis became itself a transnational endeavor, as professionalizing "economists" borrowed and adapted ways of examining the "economy" as a sphere separated from "politics" and "society."[20]

International standardization, dominated by European governments and the United States, cascaded from one arena of life into others.[21] Enthusiasm for the principles of uniformity and efficiency, of course, mingled with foreboding and with nostalgia for local practices. International networks emerged in tandem with localized, sometimes anti-imperial, resistance to their spread, and they also took shape within competing claims on universality among clashing national standards. Still, the importance of the standardization movements of the era can hardly be overstated. They provided the infrastructure for the spread of all kinds of transnational currents in a shrinking world.

International Networks for Sports

In a movement parallel to the ordering of communication and time, the International Olympic Committee (IOC) sought to facilitate and standardize competition in sports. French nobleman Baron Pierre de Coubertin, an early champion of the Olympic Games, convened the initial IOC in 1894, and Athens hosted the first modern games in 1896, attracting three hundred athletes from thirteen countries. The next two games became appendages of world fairs, one held in Paris in 1900 and one in St. Louis in 1904. Coubertin and the IOC then tried to establish a regularized tradition by holding games in Athens in 1906 and in London in 1908.

Coubertin promoted the Olympic Games as a way of fostering an international community around sporting events. The games, he argued, would bolster

A postcard depicting the Panathinaiko Stadium in Athens, site of the first modern Olympic Games in 1896. As international mail improved, picture postcards became a popular way of communicating without having to write long, descriptive letters. (© Rykoff Collection / Corbis)

manliness, transcend national differences, and foster respect for others. With the theme of "peaceful internationalism," he aimed to inspire young men to build strength of body and character. Such idealistic notions of transcending the state through state-sponsored competitions were consistent with the pre–World War I internationalist spirit, but critics emerged even from the beginning. Some charged that the games were insignificant, while others suggested that competitions might stir, rather than dampen, nationalism. Indeed, the games in Stockholm in 1912 foreshadowed the tensions that were mounting toward war. Moreover, sporting events tended to be the province of elite and male participants, linked as they were to presumed qualities of leadership. Controversy grew over the issue of female participation. The push to bring women into the Olympics accelerated in view of the growing popularity of the Women's World Games, held in 1922 and every four subsequent years until the late 1930s.[22]

The popularity of international sporting competitions in the early twentieth century sparked the creation of a body to oversee the worldwide game of football (soccer). The Fédération Internationale de Football Association (FIFA), founded in Paris in 1904, held an unsuccessful international competition in 1906 but established recognition for itself after a competition held in conjunction with the London Olympics of 1908. FIFA's membership expanded beyond Europe before World War I, as South Africa, Argentine, Chile, Canada, and the United States made application.

The world wars illustrated how both nationalism and internationalism became woven into the fabric of sporting events. The disruption in travel, the military enlistment of athletes, and the national hatreds generated by World War I hurt international sport. The Olympic movement and FIFA both foundered. The Olympic Games scheduled for Berlin in 1916 were not held, and the immediate postwar Olympic and FIFA matches attracted fewer nations and even less public interest than their prewar counterparts. The mid-1920s and early 1930s, however, brought some recovery. FIFA introduced the World Cup competitions in 1930, and the IOC successfully staged Olympic Games in Paris in 1924, in Amsterdam in 1928 (where female athletes finally participated in five track-and-field events), and in Los Angeles in 1932 (made famous by the amazing all-around athlete Mildred "Babe" Didrikson).[23] At the infamous Berlin Olympics of 1936, however, Adolf Hitler tried to showcase the Aryan race and German power. His ethno-nationalistic displays, very visibly challenged when the African-American Jesse Owens won four gold medals, tarnished the rhetoric of internationalism that surrounded the games.[24] The global military struggles of the World War II era postponed any revival of a supposedly harmonious "Olympic spirit." Although many scholars of the Olympics present international and national impulses as being contradictory, they clearly were also complementary. One had first to be national in order to compete in international games.

Sports projected the hegemonies found in other internationalist arrangements. Both the Olympics and football (soccer) claimed to symbolize a global community united in sport, but the organizing bodies reflected not only national loyalties but also imperial and gender allegiances. Universalized values and rules, in sports as in other domains, emanated from the powerful states and citizens who could view international rules and gatherings as being consistent with their own views. As football spread to European colonies in Africa, the Caribbean, and Asia, and as baseball spread to zones of American influence, each

colonial power portrayed the expansion of its favorite sport as the elixir that promoted civilization and manliness. Officials, missionaries, and educational initiatives in both informal and formal colonies became associated with the spread of
national sporting preferences. Gender and racial distinctions were both reinforced and challenged within the expansion of international sports.

Legal Internationalism and Arbitration

The proliferation of international institutional structures dating from the late
nineteenth century seemed to confirm the possibility that nations could develop
supranational regulatory regimes. It was only a short leap from devising specific
functional collaborations such as the ITU and the IPU to imagining that states
themselves might form leagues or federations for even more ambitious purposes,
especially legal arbitration or multilateral peacekeeping.

Some theorists proclaimed that the global networks of trade and communications would make sovereign states obsolete. In the 1860s, lawyers from various
European countries began to assert a "scientific" view of law, suggesting that
universal legal principles should gradually be codified and spread.[25] Universities
established chairs in international law, and professional gatherings of lawyers
discussed how to standardize legal systems.

Creating law for the world was bound up in the sense of civilizing mission, so
strong in the West, and fit with the evolutionary, progressive view of history that
was becoming hegemonic. The idea of an emerging legal order both spread a
sense of one-world universalism and also became a way of dividing "civilized"
nations from the "backward" areas that seemed in need of transformation. Within
this discourse of transformative universalism, the turn of the century witnessed
many attempts to develop a body of international law and to create venues for its
enforcement and for the arbitration of disputes.[26]

Most scholars agree that the emergence of the concept of international law
generally developed from the law of the sea. Hugo Grotius's interest in developing international law, for example, had stemmed from his reflections on freedom
of the seas. As the largest arena of space between and among national states, the
seas raised complicated issues of jurisdiction, and the 1913 International Convention on Safety of Life at Sea (formulated in the wake of the *Titanic* disaster)

provided an important step toward a multilateral process of lawmaking and law enforcement. This and other international legal agreements, which attempted to ensure free flow of maritime transport and to protect innocent passage through territorial waters, aimed to convert the world's waterways from arenas of conflict to safe commercial highways.

Many late nineteenth-century European politicians and jurists pursued the dream that international arbitration could replace war as a means of settling disputes. An active group of legal internationalists, operating through several influential associations, had been building a context for legal arbitration over the course of the late nineteenth century. The so-called *Alabama* Treaty of 1873 between Britain and the United States, for example, dealt with claims arising from the British-made Confederate cruiser that had sunk seventy Union ships during the American Civil War. Setting a precedent for the competence of arbitral tribunals, the treaty defined the rights and duties of neutrals and provided momentum behind the inclusion of arbitration clauses in other multilateral treaties, such as the Congo Act of 1885 and the Anti-Slavery Act of 1890.[27] In 1889 the Inter-Parliamentary Union (IPU), formed by peace activists William Randal Cremer and Frédéric Passy, joined together countries with parliaments (twenty-four by 1913) to advance methods of international arbitration.

The Hague Peace Conferences of 1899 and 1907 represented the high point of prewar internationalist attempts to substitute law and arbitration for war and force. International politicians, intellectuals, and jurists had picked up on an idea promoted by Tsar Nicholas II of Russia to hold a major international conference to standardize precepts of international law and procedures for arbitration. The idea of convening such conferences at The Hague electrified many of those who were advocating diverse forms of peace activism and international lawmaking. Henri Dunant, the founder of the Red Cross, played a significant role in persuading world powers to accept the tsar's proposal. Austrian baroness Bertha von Suttner, a prolific journalist and author of a widely translated 1889 bestseller *Die Waffen Nieder! (Lay Down Your Arms!)*, helped galvanize the burgeoning international peace movement behind the idea. She had earlier helped convince Alfred Nobel, the inventor of dynamite, to dedicate money in his will to establishing a prize for a person who would work "most effectively for the fraternization of mankind, the diminution of armies, and the promotion of

Peace Congresses."²⁸ The eccentric British journalist William Thomas Stead founded a new weekly in London called *War against War* to further his International Peace Crusade and to promote the gathering at The Hague. The Universal Peace Congress, composed of a growing number of men and women activists who met yearly to advance the cause of arms limitation, also backed the idea.

The conferences at The Hague did not simply endorse lofty goals about peace; they attempted to devise practical measures to build a structure of international law. The internationalism represented at The Hague, although limited in scope, transcended Europe and the United States to include China, Japan, Siam, Turkey, Persia, and Mexico (in the 1907 conference, seventeen other delegations from the American continent also joined the New World contingent). Delegates pursued three specific aims: to promote the peaceful settlement of disputes, to restrict the "excessive" cruelty of warfare (for example, restrictions on "dum-dum" bullets and projectiles that would harm civilians), and to limit arms races and the burdens they placed on national treasuries.

The idea of arbitration as a way not of ending but of preventing conflict may have been the most important concept to come out of meetings at The Hague, although specific problems of jurisdiction remained. Participating nations signed a convention for the Pacific Settlement of International Disputes. They created the Permanent Court of Arbitration, or World Court, which operated before the outbreak of World War I and was reconstituted after the war as the International Court of Justice (1922–1945), associated with the League of Nations. Agreements also codified laws of war, including rules for the opening of hostilities, the rights of neutral nations and persons, the status of merchant ships, and the conduct of naval and land warfare.²⁹

Set against the stirring speeches, the expectations set by the participating luminaries, and the lavish ceremonies, banquets, and press coverage, the outcomes of The Hague conferences have often been trivialized. The conferences were, after all, followed closely by outbreak of the Great War. But they did clearly tap into important characteristics of the age—the interest in establishing international standards and the vision that legal regimes could gradually transcend national borders and come to govern the behavior of states just as they governed individuals within successful states. The conferences comprised expressions both of the fear that national competition might lead to devastating warfare and of the hope that global communications and other networks might facilitate a new international order with mechanisms to keep the peace.[30]

Before the outbreak of the Great War, coinciding with the optimism that helped promote The Hague conferences, the idea that major wars had become obsolete circulated among "internationalists" around the world. New England anti-imperialist Raymond Landon Bridgman, for example, published "The First Book of World Law" in 1911. Bridgman proclaimed that "for more than a generation true world law has been growing," and he provided a compendium of agreements relating to everything from communications to sanitation to world government. He wrote that "within a comparatively short time the organization of all mankind into a political unit has advanced rapidly" and that an unwritten World Constitution of widely accepted tenets already formed the basis for an emerging World Organization.[31] In many parts of the world, as has been noted, people read Norman Angell's *The Great Illusion* and hailed him as a prophet. The "guns of August" that touched off World War I, of course, proved that nationalism easily trumped the internationalists' dreams of convergence and peace. Efforts to build international institutions, however, persisted through the war and after.

A League of Nations

The staggering casualties that the Great War inflicted on a generation of European men (almost ten million soldiers dead; perhaps twice that many wounded) seemed to confirm the folly of military contests. Although it seems clear, in retrospect, that the devastations of the Great War fostered the growth of communist and fascist authoritarianism and planted the seeds of World War II, the war initially appeared to strengthen the hands of those who advocated new international mechanisms for the peaceful settlement of disputes. The idea of a League of Nations embodied the early twentieth-century internationalist faith that liberal capitalist democracies, benign imperial administrations, and international bodies might all promote a system that would civilize the rest of the world and spread universalized norms.[32]

US president Woodrow Wilson became the most prominent voice for building a postwar peace through a kind of world federalism based upon international legal standards. His vision that collective security arrangements and "self-determination" of peoples would curb aggressive nationalism and ethnic grievances became globally influential. Wilsonian faiths, however, were fraught with contradiction. Wilson's country would never join the League of Nations, though that body is forever associated with his name, and his conception of self-determination turned out to be excruciatingly limited.

As president, Wilson had developed his ideas about internationalism as he steered his foreign policy through a series of crises with Mexico and confronted the outbreak of war in Europe in 1914. Only leagues of cooperating, democratic nations, he came to believe, could discipline the rapacious forces let loose by revolutions and wars. For the Western Hemisphere, he had proposed a Pan American Pact that would organize collective action among nations to solve wrongdoing within the hemisphere (wrongdoing to which Wilson, of course, assumed the United States would never be party, although many Latin Americans felt otherwise). The pact itself went nowhere, but after the European war began in 1914, Wilson drew closer to advisers who were generally influenced by Angell, Jordan, and others who advocated international arrangements, arms reduction, and a repudiation of nationalism as the path to peace. Once in the war, Wilson proposed his Fourteen Points (1918), a plan for a postwar reconstruction of the international system along lines that he believed would eliminate the root causes of war.[33]

Around the world, reformers and internationalists of various stripes saw in Wilson, and perhaps in the United States, a reason to believe that a new order actually could come from the sorrows of war. Two of the president's Points would have especially profound influence. One was "self-determination," a vague concept that Wilson advanced as an antidote to the instabilities raised by ethnic tensions in the old Austro-Hungarian Empire but one that colonial subjects around the world quickly embraced as a rallying cry for their own national aspirations. The second was "collective security," a concept to be embodied in a League of Nations. Conceiving of the new world-to-be in terms of individual, self-determining states that would come together in a protofederation, Wilson's vision embodied the aspirations that had buoyed so many of the internationalist currents before the war.

In some ways Wilson was an unlikely midwife to the vision that became styled as a "new diplomacy" based upon open covenants, "peace without vic-

NOT ROOM FOR BOTH

The Covenant of the League of Nations struggling to unseat the Constitution of the United States. This political cartoon, published in the *San Francisco Chronicle,* supported President Woodrow Wilson's Republican opponents, who charged that the League of Nations would curtail the nation's sovereign powers. The US Senate refused to ratify the Treaty of Versailles because the treaty established the League. (© Bettmann/Corbis)

tory," self-determination, and collective security among democratic nations. An aloof intellectual who had been president of Princeton University, Wilson had dispatched troops into Mexico, installed US military rule in Haiti, tightened US military control in the Dominican Republic, and implanted a US administration into Nicaragua. America's first southern president since before the Civil War, he had brought racial segregation to his nation's capital and had appointed many southern Democratic segregationists as top diplomats around the world.

Yet Wilson also had deep ties to international circles that advocated for labor rights, feminism, anti-imperialism, and even socialism. His blueprint for a conflict-free world of self-determining democracies and laws resonated within the agendas of many reformers throughout the world, including anticolonial leaders in China, India, Egypt, Korea, and elsewhere. Many internationalists at home and abroad, even if they decried Wilson's various compromises and rigidities, had been inspired by his belief in the concept of a league of self-determining states. Although Wilson met opposition at the 1919 Peace Conference at Versailles and then from his own Senate, which ultimately refused to ratify the Treaty of Versailles because of the article creating the League, his League of Nations exemplified many of the hopes—and contradictions—of the era's internationalists.[34]

By 1918, as old autocratic empires (Russian, Austro-Hungarian, German, and Ottoman) fell apart and a dozen new republics were proclaimed, liberal internationalists such as President Wilson hoped that postwar cooperation among emerging democratic states might vindicate the horrible costs of war. Wilson's idea that war could be an instrument for bringing stability and international understanding, however, was always delusion. From 1914 into the early 1920s, much of the world witnessed epic-scale devastation: deaths from the world war, casualties associated with the Russian, Mexican, and Chinese revolutions, ravages from influenza and other epidemic diseases, and displacements of populations associated with wartime's rising nationalism. In Europe, the self-styled seat of civilization, perhaps over fifteen million people perished from these combined causes, and this death toll affected societies and cultures in profound ways, becoming both a symbol of instability and a further cause of it.

New dictatorships, nourished by demographic dislocations and new ideologies, quickly challenged any idea of an emerging liberal republican norm. The Bolshevik revolutionary regime, which came to power in Russia in 1917, provided inspiration and support for a transnational communist movement advocating more power for working classes. It also promoted a doctrine of self-determination that, unlike Wilson's, was merged directly with anti-imperialism, thereby appealing globally to nationalists seeking independence from colonial powers. Liberal republicans in many countries, faced with postwar economic instability and threats to their power from communist movements, often moved rightward. Partly in response to the growing strength of communist parties and the weaknesses of liberal parliaments, various forms of nationalist dictatorships and fascist regimes came to Italy, Spain, and Portugal in the 1920s and to Germany and Japan in the 1930s. Corporative states with varied degrees of authoritarianism also emerged in Mexico, Brazil, Argentina, and elsewhere. The League's structure of internationalism could hardly contain such political and economic polarization—much less the virulent nationalisms within which the many consolidating dictatorships thrived. The structures of the League were ill-suited to cope with what Eric Hobsbawm called the "age of extremes" and the clashing imperial aspirations that ultranationalism nourished.

Still, the League was a significant conduit for transnational connections in the interwar period. Headquartered in Geneva, it had thirty-two original member states, and thirteen additional states were invited to join. With a structure vaguely reminiscent of the IPU and inspired by plans from The Hague Peace Conferences, the League was the first international organization devoted to a broad agenda that included arbitration of disputes, the prevention of war, and the international coordination of social and economic programs. It drew together the transnational connections that had been emerging among groups of professionals since the nineteenth century and brought them under a single international umbrella. The secretariat of the League in the early 1930s employed over seven hundred staff members from all over the world, although those from Europe were by far in the majority. The dense network of people working in League-sponsored economic, social, and cultural organizations in the interwar era probably constituted the League's most lasting impact. One scholar writes that the representations of the League at the time of its creation "conjured images of a globe crisscrossed by streams of electrical energy."[35]

Internationalist legal thinkers saw the League as the kernel that might grow into a global legal system. The Permanent Court of International Justice heard disputes between states in 1921–1940, and various League institutions worked on codifying international law, especially in the areas of communications, transportation, and arms control. The League also promoted restricting opium traffic (resulting in the Geneva Convention of 1931), protecting women from trafficking and children from exploitation, opposing the continuation of slavery, facilitating intellectual and cultural exchange, and resettling refugees.

The League's Economic and Financial Organization (EFO) extended the practice of standardization by collecting economic statistics on national economies and on the international economy as a whole. It widened its purview beyond data collection when leading nations and bankers urged active intervention to help stabilize postwar economies in crisis. Drawing upon the expertise of leading economists in Europe, the EFO began to advocate particular policies related to tariffs, trade, monetary systems, production, and poverty. It hosted the World Economic Conferences in 1927 and 1933. Although the EFO clearly failed to prevent the world from slipping into depression during the 1930s, its statistical yearbooks and networks of economists provided a basis for the creation of international economic agencies after World War II.

The League of Nations Health Organization (LNHO), formed in 1923 in response to postwar epidemics, also coordinated national policies to promote international norms. With one-third of its scientific work subsidized by the Rockefeller Foundation, the LNHO linked together public health experts from nations and regions throughout the world to collect data and to standardize statistical and epidemiological practices, such as cataloging blood types. It encouraged the establishment of public health programs globally and reported regularly on health conditions throughout the world. League-promoted sanitation programs helped lower death rates.[36]

The International Labour Organization (ILO), established in the Treaty of Versailles partly in an effort to forestall the appeal of communism in the wake of the Bolshevik Revolution, became one of the League's most activist bodies. The ILO built on a long but fairly ineffective tradition of international conferences convened by labor activists. In the 1870s leading labor reformers had begun to hold international gatherings, and an International Association for Labour Legislation (IALL) met in Paris in 1900 to informally coordinate national rules and expose countries with labor abuses. The resolutions of such international forums, however, had little impact on national legislation. The ILO, having more formalized institutional backing, accelerated efforts to advance rights for workers and labor unions. Its first annual conference in October 1919 adopted six conventions dealing with workplace safety, work hours, and protection for women and children who worked in industry. Gradually, many countries ratified the ILO's conventions, although the deepening depression of the 1930s slowed the pace of ratification. In 1926 the ILO established a supervisory system that monitored how states were applying its standards.[37]

Within the ILO, however, various approaches clashed along lines of nationality and ideology. The ILO recognized trade unions and employers as partners with national states—a tripartite form that merged "public" and "private" sectors in ways that invited disagreements. Moreover, even among pro-labor groups, the ILO was frequently beset with competing views on the style of labor activism—ranging from conservative unionists such as American Samuel Gompers to a spectrum of less accommodationist leaders. Generally the organization supported a liberal capitalist system operating through cooperating national states, however, and opposed an alternative transnational labor movement that was being promoted through the Soviet Union's Third International.

The League's relationship to colonialism was similarly uncertain, as the League both undermined and buttressed the justifications for colonialism. The war victors stripped the defeated powers, Germany and the Ottoman Empire, of their colonies and converted these holdings into mandates. This action in effect repudiated the colonialism exercised by defeated nations and provided a structure for a presumably more enlightened tutelage. Mandates were to be administered by designated "advanced" nations until ready for self-government, and the mandate administrator had to pledge to protect the "native" and minority populations and to "develop" the territory. The mandate system, however, sanctioned and rejustified foreign administration, and the League did little to interfere with the empires of the war's victors. Colonial peoples who had hoped that Wilson's calls for postwar self-determination would challenge colonial rule were bitterly disappointed. For them, the League inscribed colonialism into a Euro-centered internationalism rather than offering a more inclusive blueprint. Nationalist movements, which were growing in colonialized areas, embraced and continued to organize around the language of self-determination even as they rejected the postwar settlement that restored and relegitimized the colonial order. A new anticolonialist internationalism took shape.[38]

After the Great War and paralleling the League's efforts at standardization, countries created additional structures to establish common rules. Most of these disciplinary authorities did not threaten the sovereignty of national states but simply enhanced states' abilities to facilitate the global reach of citizens and businesses. The overriding interest of all states seemed to be in providing speed, security, and safety in international commerce and communication. The International Broadcasting Union of 1925 (later absorbed into the ITU) handled issues of newly emergent broadcast radio. The International Commission for Air Navigation and International Air Traffic Association, created in 1919, developed technical and safety standards for aircraft, although commercial aviation remained quite limited before World War II. International shipping conferences promoted agreements on maritime safety. The Hague Codification Conference of 1930 tried to settle a broad range of issues relating to how nationality and citizenship status should be determined.

Despite, or really because of, the Great War, the efforts at arms limitation also experienced some rebirth. The Washington Treaty of 1922, despite its flaws and omissions, attempted to limit certain categories of naval armaments and to curb a renewal of the pre–World War I arms race. The 1925 Geneva Protocol to the Hague Convention, a response to public outcry over the wartime use of mustard gas and fears that even more deadly agents would be developed, prohibited "the use in war of asphyxiating, poisonous or other gases, and of bacteriological methods of warfare." Sixty-one nations ultimately signed the Kellogg-Briand Pact of 1928, which outlawed war, but the multilateral agreement provided no mechanism for enforcement or determining fault. Peace movements that denounced nationalism surged in many countries during the early 1930s, even as ultranationalist fascist governments reshaped politics in Italy, Germany, and Japan and armed for war.

In 1935 the Nobel Peace Prize went to Norman Angell, the well-known peace pamphleteer of a quarter century earlier. In his acceptance speech Angell articulated the arguments that still animated those who placed their hopes for peace in international law and a League of Nations. War, he said, "is made, not usually by evil men knowing themselves to be wrong, but is the outcome of policies pursued by good men usually passionately convinced that they are right."[39] Only the application of law and the mediations of a body such as the League of Nations, he concluded, could curb the passions and the overzealous patriotism that led to violence. The optimism of Angell's earlier writings, however, only faintly echoed. Networks of internationalists no longer exuded confidence that they formed a vanguard in a natural progression by which new economic and cultural interconnections would morph into international rules and bodies that could keep the peace.

The disruptions and revolutions arising from World War I had fostered ideologies of communist and then fascist authoritarianism, and the Great Depression, which fell most heavily on parliamentary democracies and liberal capitalist regimes, strengthened the self-confidence of these dictatorships. In the early 1930s Joseph Stalin consolidated his power in the Soviet Union, fostered a famine in Ukraine that would kill perhaps three million people, and laid the foundations for institutions that, in 1937 and 1938, would carry out a Great Terror of targeted murder directed at dissenters, peasants, and members of national minorities. The year Angell accepted his prize, Italian armies invaded Ethiopia. Hitler was promoting his program to remake and "purify" Germany, and in the next few years he laid plans for an expanding German Reich in which Jews and Eastern Europeans would be "cleansed" away to make room for German settlers and "civilization." As Nazi ideology became more extreme and dedicated to warfare, these proposals hardened into the systematic implementation of a "final solution" to the "Jewish problem" through mass slaughter. By the time of Hitler's defeat in May 1945, approximately six million Jews—or two-thirds of the prewar population of European Jews—and been killed; millions of other "undesirables"— Roma, homosexuals, disabled persons, Poles and other Eastern Europeans—had also met their deaths; and documents suggest that the mass killing of non-Germans in the lands that Hitler wished to resettle to the east had just begun. Japanese leaders, also linking "civilization" with their own plans to build a settler colony, sent hundreds of thousands of farmers and technicians to develop Manchuria while their army and the notorious Unit 731, which conducted horrific human experimentation, consolidated control over inhabitants. Japan's military leaders moved into China and promised to keep extending their reach into Southeast Asia.[40]

As Angell and many of his internationalist contemporaries watched the governments of Japan and then Germany leave the League of Nations, launch their expansionist programs, and touch off a new war in Europe in September 1939, they embraced the need for collective military action against fascism. They continued to advocate for an even stronger international body that could build alliances among democracies, but they could no longer sustain the idea that the new connecting currents of the twentieth century would render war-making a "Great Illusion." Well-functioning global economic markets and effective parliamentary forms had deteriorated in tandem. The currents of transnational connections that some internationalists had once hoped would spread cooperative institutions instead swept most of the world into the vortex of a second world war. In a linked world, alliances, affiliations, ethnic and class hatreds, and research on modern war-making techniques quickly fed the global conflagration. The internationalism of the late nineteenth century turned defensive and fearful in the mid-twentieth century's increasingly interconnected, yet increasingly militarized, world.[41]

The world's second war in the twentieth century, like the first one, both curtailed and also spread global interconnections. The Great Depression and the rising tide of autarchic nationalism and regional blocs had chipped away at the institutions of the global economy, but the war also underscored, for many, the need to rebuild a functioning world system. British prime minister Winston Churchill and US president Franklin D. Roosevelt met aboard a warship in Newfoundland in August 1941 and issued a statement called the Atlantic Charter, which tried to sketch out internationalist aims for the postwar period. Endorsing lower trade barriers, global economic and social cooperation, freedom of seas, disarmament, and a fair peace, the Charter expressed standard internationalist positions. Within a few months, all of the "United Nations" of the wartime alliance accepted the Charter's principles. As the war dragged on, the importance of building transnational ties of all kinds became ever more compelling to all belligerents: access to raw materials throughout the globe proved strategically critical, as did being able to maintain global transportation and communications systems. In addition, the huge wartime mobilizations of people—for both war work and war fighting—sent millions away from their homes and introduced them to new countries and cultures. Internationalists of the interwar era—and there were by then many versions of what, specifically, internationalism should champion—still might hope for some kind of postwar reconstruction of a functional world order.

The United Nations Organization and the Bretton Woods economic agreements, created as World War II ended, emerged from both the hopes and the fears that had come to animate internationalism over the previous century. They also embodied the contradictions of earlier international agreements, bodies, and rule-setting regimes. Like the League, these institutions advanced an internationalism that often masked agendas for national and imperial advantage. The San Francisco Conference that forged the new United Nations in 1945, for example, hailed Jan Smuts for having been present at the creation of the League. Smuts spoke eloquently about the need for a new institution that would preserve justice and the "fundamental rights of man." But Smuts epitomized the imperial and racial ideology of British colonialism, and he was there to preserve its values from what he regarded as the misguided humanitarianism that might cast his own country of South Africa in a bad light. Smuts, writes Mark Mazower, was a member of the generation "who sought to prolong the life of an empire of white rule through international cooperation." Similarly, international meetings at Bretton Woods in 1944 to reconstruct the global financial system signaled the limitations, more than the promise, of new postwar cooperative institutions. Stalin refused to attend; Britain and the United States clashed; lesser countries and colonies had little voice; and the newly created financial bodies initially proved so ineffective that the British financial system veered into near collapse in the year after the war ended.[42]

. . .

In the late nineteenth century, the revolutions in communications and transportation brought by the industrial age promoted a flowering of efforts to imagine the world as a single field. At the same time, the growth of new fortunes, extracted from growing global economic networks, financed a host of international initiatives and structures designed to bring national leaders together to spread regularity of practices and common ideas about law. In the pre–World War I era, marked by the ascendancy of Western nations and dominated by transnationally networked elites, many projects on behalf of international cooperation and perpetual peace reflected an ebullient optimism about the future.

To those involved in them, the variety of international bodies that emerged from the late nineteenth century seemed to be constructing universalized values and practices that could, over time, bring nations and the people they governed into cooperative and standardized arrangements. The destruction of the twentieth-century wars and the brutalities of imperial regimes, however, showed the limitations and naïveté of such visions of universality.

The world history of convergences and "progress," which turn-of-the-century internationalists had hoped to witness and enact in the twentieth century, had turned dark by 1945. At the end of our period, the past half century seemed the story of ruin, war, depression, lost generations, and misbegotten colonial adventures. Some important infrastructure of the cooperative rule-setting regimes remained—regulations on telegraphs, mail, time, and measurement, for example, along with efforts to draw together laws and statistics—but most seemed narrowly technical matters rather than steps into some postnational or convergent future. The infant United Nations began to take up work done by the League, but the emergence of anticolonialism and a budding Cold War brought myriad challenges to the visions of earlier internationalists.

Significant voices, of course, had scoffed throughout the period at any idea that internationalism might promise a new universalistic age. Throughout the era, the rivalries sharpened by nationalism, frightening new weaponry, and hatreds bred in colonialism had provided clear-eyed warnings. Mark Twain wrote bitter essays against the self-deceptions and silences of imperialists. Joseph Conrad probed the darkness at the heart of colonial relationships. Growing anticolonial networks, their hopes spurred and then spurned by Wilsonian internationalists who talked of self-determination, coalesced to challenge Western frameworks of convergence and to amplify the voices of those who felt disenfranchised and marginalized within emerging international bodies.

International conventions and rule-making institutions thus forged important global networks, but these often favored people already endowed with economic and political power. The contradictions of "internationalism" became manifest in the bloodletting of World War I, the rise of communist and fascist authoritarianism, the brutalities of and resistances against colonialism, and the horrific destructions of World War II.

2. *Social Networking and Entangled Attachments*

SOCIAL networking among people who might be distant from each other in geography, culture, class, age, or other attributes often seems a phenomenon of the computer age, but it clearly long predates the Internet revolution. In the age of electricity, the growth of communications—mass publishing, faster and less expensive travel, telegraphy, telephone, and radio—created currents that allowed people to interact globally as never before. As has been seen, one vision of world harmony imagined a convergence of national states within rule-setting regimes such as the Hague Conventions and the League of Nations. A wider variety of non-state transnational alliances and affiliations, however, also coalesced to both bolster and challenge this form of internationalism.[43]

Social networks assuming non-state forms organized themselves around class, religion, gender, race, function, ideas, and perceived moral frameworks. They offered attachments that were transnational; that is, they pulsed above, below, and through the more formalized structures of national states, empires, and international institutions. Although today's concept of a "networked society" sometimes connotes a horizontal, nonhierarchical structure, my usage invokes the idea of social networks in a more flexible sense: they took hierarchical or horizontal shapes; they assumed forms with clear management structures or as loose associations of entangled attachments. Social networking came in all kinds of patterns.

The relationships between transnational attachments and the allegiances formed around national or imperial loyalties are complex. Participants in transnational networks often proclaimed that they stood for universalistic goals articulated against the presumed particularism of national states and empires. Yet as this section elaborates, aspirations for universal betterment could also draw on an often unstated sense of ethno-national and imperial superiority. In both the international networks discussed in the preceding section, and the transnational attachments discussed in this and following sections, the universal and the particular most commonly intertwined, and each drew strength from their tensions and coproductivity.

The historical periodization of globalization, put forth by A. G. Hopkins and others, sees it quickening in the late nineteenth century and slowing from the 1920s into the post–World War II period before resuming its rapid pace. Such a trajectory well describes economic interconnections. When examining the complex matrix of transnational social networks, however, it may be difficult to discern such a metanarrative of accelerations and decelerations. Rather, one might posit irregular patterns where some entangled attachments wax while others wane, some social networks become denser while others atrophy.

This section tries to capture the irregularity and diversity of currents rather than to characterize their overall flow. It seeks to develop notions of connection and entanglement—and of blockage and disruption. The networks and attachments that are traced below constituted no single field of transnational vision; some ran parallel, some intertwined together, some pulsed in different directions, some seem simply incommensurable. In the terrain of the transnational, historical trajectory is not a singular but a plural thing.

Language and Photography

The most fundamental building block of communication—language—became one medium that attracted transnational reformers. Ludwik Lazar Zamenhof, convinced that language divisions reinforced nationalist ideologies that led to global conflicts, attempted to create a new international language called Esperanto. Growing up as part of a Yiddish-speaking Jewish majority in a Polish town (part of the Russian Empire) in which other groups spoke Polish, Russian, and German, he was inspired to devise and publish in 1887 the first book of Esperanto grammar. The idea caught on, especially with middle-class people engaged in cross-border commerce and tourism. The language spread over the next few decades, at first primarily in Russia and Eastern Europe and then into Western Europe, the Americas, China, and Japan. Esperanto's first world congress, held in 1905 in France, attracted 688 Esperanto speakers from twenty nationalities. The World Esperanto Association, founded in 1908 by a Swiss journalist, continued to hold yearly congresses. The language became so identified with internationalism that it received considerable credibility among delegates to the League of Nations, although France blocked any official use of Esperanto on the claim that French was already a universal language. As one historian writes, the Esperanto movement displayed not just "a commitment to an ideal language" but "a theory of the purpose of language."[44]

Esperanto rode a global wave of popularity during the 1920s, a time of deep disillusionment with nationalism and war and of energetic networking on behalf of cosmopolitanism and peace. Esperanto, writes one scholar, "helped generate an ideological framework of one-worldism."[45] But the movement also divided in the 1920s, one wing becoming closely associated with socialist circles. Both wings were generally distrusted by strong nationalists, and the movement came under fire during the 1930s in Germany and Soviet Russia, precisely the countries in which it had initially been the strongest. Adolf Hitler and Joseph Stalin both disparaged the language as associated with Jews and subversion. They worked to stamp it out.

Other new methods for enlarging communication proliferated during the late nineteenth century. Louis Braille, a young boy living in Paris who had lost his eyesight, devised a system of raised dots that allowed reading by touch and thus expanded the reach of the written word to the blind. Variants of this system spread during the mid-nineteenth century, and in 1878 an international congress in Paris adopted a standard system, which was finally codified for the English-speaking world in 1932.

Such projects for humanistic language reform represented the hope that new kinds of codes might forge common meanings across all kinds of borders, facilitating understanding and peace. In this sense, photography also ranked as one of the new potentially transnational "languages" that emerged in the late nineteenth century. French photographer and balloonist Gaspard-Félix Tournachon, who adopted the name "Nader," publicly dramatized the potential of aerial photography when he flew over Paris in 1858. A few years later he launched his huge balloon *Le Géant,* which was unsuccessful but inspired the global-flight fantasies of Jules Verne. Seeing and photographing the world from on high or by traversing previously unseen territory became a preoccupation among many explorers and armchair adventure seekers who had growing access to mass-produced books and magazines.

The desire to understand the world through photography sparked a variety of significant projects in the late nineteenth century. Scottish photographer John Thompson published one of the most famous and influential early collections, *Illustrations of China and Its People* (1873), after a decade of traveling in the Far East. In it, he established some of the conventions of documentary photography.[46] *National Geographic* magazine published its first photo in 1889, and before World War I published many photo tours that brought images of the world to its growing numbers of fans. The first photos of Lhasa in Tibet, the North Pole, and Machu Picchu, and some of the earliest color photos of gardens in Belgium, for example, all appeared in *National Geographic*. France and Germany provided the early leadership in photographic techniques, and international conferences, such as the International Photographic Exhibition held in Dresden in 1909, drew photographers from many countries into technical and artistic communities. Generally these early photographers saw themselves as capturing new kinds of information that would serve the transnational development of science, social science, and civilization.

Albert Kahn, a French photographer, banker, and internationalist, perhaps best exemplified the idea that his images from autochrome photography—a portable color process—could draw the peoples of the world together in mutual understanding. From 1909 until the onset of the Great Depression, when he met financial ruin, Kahn sent photographers to more than fifty countries and collected some seventy-two thousand images, which he called "The Archives of the Planet." The archive boasted probably the earliest color photographs of Egypt's pyramids and India's Taj Mahal. It showed daily life among Kurds, Vietnamese, Brazilians, Mongolians, Europeans, and North Americans. The color pictures were, and are, stunning but the assumptions behind them were perhaps even more arresting: Kahn hoped to deploy photography as a tool that, by representing human diversity for all to see, might promote greater familiarity and peace among the world's cultures.[47]

The semiotics of photographs, however, involved more complexity than simply broadening people's visions and promoting familiarity. Kahn may have hoped that photography could be a neutral symbolic language that enhanced mutual recognition, but the meanings of photographic images necessarily emerge from the variable and unstable constructions of both producer and

A photograph from Albert Kahn's "Archives of the Planet," ca. 1920, showing Angkor Wat, the famed temple complex in Cambodia. Kahn's archives consisted of 4,000 stereoscopic plaques, 72,000 autochromes, and around 183,000 meters of film. The archives were intended to promote peace by documenting the world's people. Five cameramen supervised by French geographer Jean Brunhes shot photographs in forty-eight countries on nearly every continent. (© Musée Albert Kahn—Départment des Hauts-de-Seine, Léon Busy, photographer [A35852])

receiver. Photography's new representations of the world thus advanced no single agenda.

Photographic technologies were developed and consumed most thoroughly, for example, within the hearts of empires, and they therefore often represented an imperial perspective. A multivolume set of 468 photographs, *The People of India* (1868–1875), published in London, accompanied the first census of India (1872) and land survey of India (begun in 1878). All represented efforts to categorize colonial inhabitants and make them legible to their rulers.[48] The Ottoman Empire also became an early supporter of photography, and Sultan Abdülhamid II used photography as one method of enhancing control over his territories.[49] Around 1907 in Russia, the photographic pioneer Sergei Mikhailovich Prokudin-Gorskii began to execute a photographic survey of the Russian Empire to be shown in color slide projections. The project brought him to the attention of Tsar Nicholas II, who then gave his project official sponsorship. From 1909 to 1912 Prokudin-Gorskii traversed the various regions of Russia and sought, through his slide show, to make the diverse landscapes and peoples more familiar to Russian audiences. The tsarist regime, like other imperial rulers, recognized that picturing the empire could help constitute it as a familiar and bounded whole.

Many of the photographic projects of empires famously projected images of domination—over land, animals, and indigenous people. Some seem designed to soberly inform people back home about new lands and the civilizing role of imperial institutions. Some clearly aimed primarily to entertain. Either way, photographs helped guide audience responses to encountering cultural difference. For example, exotic and often highly sexualized women were favorites on postcards; photos of white women displaying animal trophies pictured the domination of white prowess even over native masculinity; juxtapositions of traditional lifestyles with the machines of modernity—autos, cameras, record players—became stock favorites. As also reflected in the international institutions erected at the same time, the more the world became "one," the more its many hierarchies of difference—race, gender, region—were displayed in high relief.[50]

Laura Wexler's examination of the photos by American photojournalist Francis Benjamin Johnston of US imperial adventures at the turn of the century suggests how the artifice of photography seemingly presented the "real" while inflecting imperial mission with a sense of benevolent supremacy, or what she calls "tender violence." Similarly, the US photographic archive of the building of the canal in Panama projected such imperial visions. Ernest Hallen, the US government's official photographer of the canal's construction work, who provided an extensive, systematic record of the undertaking, favored techniques that emphasized grand panoramic and panoptic perspectives.[51]

The meanings of photographs, however, were never easily contained. In examining the early US colonial period in the Philippines, Vicente Rafael has found that elites in colonies often adapted the technology of photography to project their own self-confident emergence as leaders of protonations. Rafael writes that "images emerge at times from the archives that contain certain intractable elements, peculiar details, or distinct sensibilities that do not easily fit into the visual encyclopedia of colonial rule." An examination of imperial photographic archives of Samoa in the same period likewise finds uncertain views that seem inconsistent with a stereotypically imperial gaze. Esther Gabara shows how, in the hands of Mexican and Brazilian modernists of the 1930s, photographic conventions became distorted and "errant."[52]

Kahn died during the Nazi occupation of France. By this time national states had firmly embraced photography and its successor, motion picture film, in order to highlight difference and stoke ferocity and war. The propaganda machine honed by the Nazis revolved around the use of images and rested on the understanding that photography, while thoroughly constructed, could be easily taken for "reality" and could motivate and manipulate. Nazi filmmakers excelled at crafting images that could tap existing prejudices to augment hatreds, at shaping pictures of enemies that the state could then justifiably destroy.[53] And most other nations involved in World War II joined in the project of merging film into war making. What John Dower has aptly called a "war without mercy" in the Pacific was grounded in a war of images. Photographers and filmmakers often borrowed and readapted techniques from each other along transnational networks and then used them for national ends.

The comparatively inexpensive technology of photography, let loose in a transnational world, both defied putative borders and also hardened nationalistic and imperialistic divisions. Although its images and symbolic languages produced currents that connected the globe, the meanings and effects that circulated in those currents, and remain embedded in photographic archives, proved variable and multivocal. Photography exemplifies the differentiated commonalities of this period.

Labor and Anticolonial Transnationalism

As telegraphy, postal services, mass publication, and photography accelerated global transmissions, activists espousing diverse causes could find new audiences. Transnational social networks proliferated. Sometimes entangled within the processes of state building and imperial consolidation and sometimes not, the outreach of transnational movements helped define many of the most significant global trends of the late nineteenth and early twentieth centuries.

Efforts to abolish slavery forged one of the most prominent of such networks. British abolitionists had convened a World Convention in London in 1840. From midcentury on, abolitionists from the Americas, the Caribbean, Europe, and elsewhere increasingly linked up to create a transnational antislavery movement.

Action on the level of national states remained all-important, and it would be misleading to suggest that national and imperial goals stood apart from the transnational antislavery cause. The many antislavery conventions and decrees during the latter half of the nineteenth century, after all, emerged from the specificity of national and local circumstances, such as grassroots resistance by slaves, the Civil War in the United States, variable economic changes favorable to free labor, and the triumph of liberal revolutions in particular countries. Antislavery objectives also became entangled in imperial justifications. By helping to structure a benign "civilizing" mission for colonial powers, antislavery campaigns could sometimes enhance discourses of national destiny and advance the universalistic rhetoric that dressed up assertions of imperial virtue. In the Berlin Declaration of 1885 and the Brussels Act of 1890, for example, colonial powers pledged to suppress slave trading and work toward abolition even as they were carving up parts of the world.

Transnational organizing, however, proved critical to stigmatizing slaveholding and to the longer legacies that antislavery campaigns produced. Moreover, as antislavery networks collaborated across the globe to collect and share data, other kinds of labor abuses came within their purview. Practices of contract labor, debt peonage, and trafficking in women and children, for example, often seemed analogous to, or at least on a continuum with, chattel slavery. The well-organized antislavery campaigns of the nineteenth century thus fostered collaboration among reformers on a range of issues and boosted the authority of a twentieth-century movement concerned with human rights more generally.[54]

As industrialization accelerated, attempts to improve working conditions for the burgeoning urban industrial labor forces also spawned an array of transnational efforts designed to combat what some called "wage slavery." Seeking transnational solutions to economic exploitation, labor advocates embraced the idea that workers had common interests that might supersede national loyalties. Many viewed the national state itself as a creature of the ownership class. In this vision, the goals of international peace and justice could not arise from cooperative bodies of national states until worker-led social democratic forms of governance had triumphed in every locality. Worker-based movements that tried to build transnational networks based upon class rather than nation, however, had goals that competed as much as they coalesced.

Jean Jaurès, leader of the French Socialist Party, emerged as one of the most influential leaders of the social democratic movement, which spread principally in Europe and the Western Hemisphere. In 1889 Jaurès helped found the Second International, a body that famously declared May 1 as International Labor Day. Associated with the Paris Exhibition of that year, the gathering brought working-class organizations together around a vision that transcended states. Another meeting, coinciding with the 1900 Paris Exhibition, brought two thousand delegates from sixteen countries and created an International Socialist Bureau (headquartered in Brussels) to serve as an informational clearinghouse for geographically scattered workers' organizations.

Between 1900 and 1914 Jaurès became one of the most influential advocates of working-class solidarity in the face of industrialization and rising nationalism. An electrifying speaker, at the 1912 meeting he proclaimed, "We are all opposed to those ready to deliver the multitudes to the bronze clutches of the demon of war. It is up to us, workers and socialists of every country, to make war impossible." His "Second International" met regularly until World War I, and Jaurès worked against the military draft and on behalf of general strikes in France and Germany that he hoped would force governments to negotiate with each other.[55]

Jaurès was assassinated by a nationalist in 1914 just as the Great War was beginning, but his messages continued to resonate internationally in the interwar era. Peace (between owners and workers and between nations), he had argued, was unachievable under capitalism. A socialism forged by cooperating trade unions and workers' cooperatives, by contrast, could create both a supportive political process in individual countries and a grand moral transformation. Although his Second International disbanded during the Great War, supporters reconstituted it in 1923 as the Labor and Socialist International. The Second International and its successor sought evolution, country by country, toward a transnational democratic socialist state that would express working-class interests and gradually seize ownership of production from private hands.

Attempts to build international labor solidarity, however, had competing advocates and agendas. The struggling International Labor Organization of the League of Nations, as already mentioned, tried to monitor labor reforms and empower labor unions within the existing order of national states. Socialist networks led by women such as the German Clara Zetkin spread globally from the 1890s on and generally concentrated on promoting sex-based legislation that would provide special workplace protections for women. International Women's Day, which began to be observed on March 8, 1913, emerged from efforts of socialists who wanted to honor and give greater visibility to the contributions of working women.

Anarchism and syndicalist doctrines also circulated globally. A number of factors may help explain the rapid spread of anarcho-syndicalist ideas at the turn of the century: the growth of inexpensive publication; the mass migration of Jews and Italians, two groups in which anarcho-syndicalist doctrines had become strong; the cross-border role of sailors, who spread the doctrines to port cities on many continents; and the influence of major syndicalist models, especially the CNT in Spain, the CGT in France, and the IWW in the United States. Some historians also suggest that the proliferation of dangerous occupations such as mining and sailing encouraged "virile syndicalism"—an aggressively anticapitalist masculinity that emphasized male bonding around acts of physical strength and violent resistance to authority.[56] Anarcho-syndicalism before World War I took on a local intensity especially in immigrant, urban areas of the United States and Latin America, and it also spread to East Asia through student and other exchanges. Campaigns against radicalism in many countries after World War I significantly weakened anarchism as a transnational movement, although the CNT in Spain grew stronger by successfully deploying general strikes to enlist support from much of the Spanish working class in the interwar period.

The Bolshevik Revolution in Russia in 1917 advanced yet another radical transnationalist vision. In 1919, in the midst of civil war in Russia, the Bolsheviks called for a "Third International" to be held in Moscow. Guided principally by Vladimir Lenin, the group formed the Comintern, a central governing body that would command a worldwide communist revolution. The Comintern's creation formalized the split, grown wider during the war, between pro-Soviet communist parties and those social democratic parties that had supported their nations' war efforts. A 1920 Congress of Peoples of the East, held at Baku, the capital of Soviet Azerbaijan, drew about two thousand delegates from workers' parties and anticolonial groups based in Turkey, Persia, Egypt, India, Afghanistan, Arabia, Syria, Palestine, Armenia, Georgia, Turkestan, India, China, Japan, Korea, and elsewhere. These delegates linked up to learn about the support for colonial self-determination sponsored by communist parties.[57] Africa's first two communist parties were formed in South Africa and Egypt in the early 1920s. By the early 1920s communist parties existed in most countries and continents in the world.

As Joseph Stalin began to emphasize "socialism in one state" in the mid-1920s, the Soviet Union's internationalist emphasis faded. Leon Trotsky had advocated building a transnational revolutionary movement, but his expulsion from the Soviet Union in 1928 and subsequent assassination in Mexico dramatized Stalin's nationalist turn. By 1934 Stalin accepted that communist parties would have to form "popular fronts" with social democratic parties in order to combat the rise of fascism, and the Comintern was disbanded in 1943. Meanwhile, Trotsky's followers had created a Fourth International in 1938, but their transnational movement kept splintering.[58]

Although there were persistent tensions between broader transnational connections and narrower national or ethnolinguistic loyalties, most communist or socialist labor-based movements tried to find ways to accommodate both. Lenin, for example, tried to solve the national question by establishing a purportedly federated Union of Soviet Socialist Republics (USSR). Many Marxists within the Austro-Hungarian Empire likewise imagined transforming the Habsburg monarchy into some kind of federation. Labor transnationalists, generally, spoke in universalistic terms but constructed their networks with a sensitivity to particular national loyalties.

In colonial territories the revolutionary ideology of communism, its appeal enhanced by resentments over the false promises of Wilsonian self-determination, created a transnational context that facilitated the growth of networks of anti-imperial resistance. Especially after the Great War, diverse homegrown movements drew strength from their leaders' global networks to challenge Western hegemonies. The Oriental Branch of the Workers' Communist Party, for example, operated both locally and across Asia. Trinidadian George Padmore's publication *The Negro Worker* (1928–1937) joined the advocacy of communism to anti-colonialism, and merchant seamen distributed its messages widely in Africa and elsewhere in the black diaspora.

The careers of three leaders within India's nationalist movement exemplify how anti-imperial transnational networks fostered campaigns for national self-determination. Narendra Nath Bhattacharya, known as M. N. Roy, was a transnational anti-imperial activist, a Bengali Indian revolutionary, and a political theorist. Roy had developed some of his revolutionary philosophy while in New York City, where he met his future American wife, Evelyn Trent. After traveling to the neutral nation of Mexico during World War I, Roy started what would become the Mexican Communist Party. Once the war ended, he accelerated his transnational activities, founding the Communist Party of India, serving with the Comintern for several years, and organizing to promote a revolutionary movement in China. With Trotsky's expulsion, Roy fell out of favor in Stalin's Moscow and left the Comintern and the Soviet Union. Once back in India during the 1930s, his continued commitment to transnational revolution landed him in prison, where, disillusioned by both Western democracy and communism, he began to work out his own manifesto for a future characterized by India's independence and a broad vision he called "New Humanism." His humanism, advanced as a universally applicable philosophy, emphasized scientific and critical approaches to knowledge mixed with an ethical grounding. Despite their substantial differences, Roy and Jawaharlal Nehru worked together to try to maneuver India toward independence.

Nehru had also been closely involved in transnational anti-imperial movements. In 1927 as a delegate from the Indian National Congress, he helped organize in Brussels an International Congress against Colonialism and Imperialism. Closely tied to Soviet goals, the Congress sought to connect labor movements with anticolonial leaders. Before World War II, Nehru established connections with liberation advocates in Egypt, Syria, Palestine, Iraq, and North Africa, many of whom already had established friendships with Mohandas K. Gandhi. It was Nehru who, in 1947, raised the flag of an independent India, espousing secularism and liberal, parliamentary democracy.

Gandhi's technique of nonviolent resistance to colonial rule had also gained him a transnational following. While in South Africa before World War I, he had joined with women in the large population of Indian laborers to successfully demand that the government recognize Hindu, Muslim, and Parsi marriages, which had been declared invalid.[59] Back in India, his famous Salt March campaigns of 1930–1931 brought wide attention to nonviolent resistance, and the currents from Gandhi's philosophy penetrated not only other anticolonial projects in Asia and Africa but also the often intertwined networks of Western peace activists. The War Resisters' International (WRI) and the Christian International Fellowship of Reconciliation (FOR) were only two of the many transnational organizations that helped popularize Gandhi's views among European and North American antidraft and pacifist groups before and after World War II.[60]

Gandhi and Nehru advocated the concept of *Vasudhaiva Kutumbakam,* or the world as one family. They envisioned India as a hub that could bind East Asia, South Asia, the Arab Middle East, and North Africa. The sufferings under colonialism would presumably forge bonds of sympathy that would radiate out to eventually include the world as a whole, nurturing a transnational consciousness as well as national self-determination.

Roy, Nehru, and Gandhi illustrate how India's nationalism and eventual independence became nourished within transnational networks that sought global solidarity among anticolonial movements. As Sugata Bose has written, "anticolonialism as an ideology was both tethered by the idea of homeland while strengthened by extraterritorial affiliations."[61] Like other articulations of early twentieth-century universalist ideologies—whether generated from Britain, France, Germany, the United States, or the Soviet Union—Indian leaders saw little contradiction between their own embrace of nationalism and the transnational webs they hoped to anchor and orchestrate. They proposed their own nationalist struggle as the opening wedge toward a larger global order that they claimed would emphasize justice and peace over inequality and war.

Contacts among labor and anticolonial movements circulated in many directions. Irish revolutionaries built connections to labor movements in the United States; Sikh migrants in Canada kept in touch with anticolonial activists in India; nationalists from Southeast Asia established contacts with sympathizers

Mahatma Gandhi and Sarojini Naidu on the nonviolent "Salt March" of 1930. Gandhi and Naidu, along with eighty thousand other Indians, were arrested after this campaign, which protested the British tax on salt and British rule of India. Naidu was the first Indian woman to serve as president of the Indian National Congress. (The Illustrated London News Picture Library, London, UK/ The Bridgeman Art Library)

from Africa and South Asia; Sen Katayama organized for anticolonial and communist causes in both Japan and the United States; the Paris-based Étoile Nord-Africaine connected Algerians and French supporters in agitating for independence of French North Africa; philosophical tracts and bomb-making manuals published in Paris or New York surfaced within resistance movements throughout the world. Just as national states organized international bodies and agreements, groups advocating workers' revolutions or those aspiring to throw off colonial rule and establish their own states (or non-states, in the case of anarchist-influenced movements) also forged transnational networks.[62]

Diasporic Attachments

The waves of immigration (both coerced and voluntary) that characterized this period mixed populations throughout the world and nurtured the emergence of transnational networks that followed the paths of the various diasporas. Though characterized by no single pattern and having no consistent relationship to national identities, diasporic attachments based on perceived ethnocultural ties provided important carriers of globalizing currents.

Slavery had produced an African diaspora throughout the Atlantic and some of the Pacific world. As most countries formally abolished slavery over the last two-thirds of the nineteenth century, indentured or contract laborers from the Indian subcontinent, China, and elsewhere augmented ex-slaves as cheap labor used especially in agriculture. The global diffusion of laborers from Africa and Asia, along with the histories of colonialism in most labor-exporting areas, created a milieu in which diasporic attachments often intertwined with labor solidarity and anticolonialism.

"Pan-Africanism" emerged as one of the most significant currents of diasporic transnationalism. The African-American intellectual W. E. B. Du Bois powerfully articulated how Africans, even though geographically dispersed, could become part of an emergent black nationalism. In 1900 Du Bois addressed a Pan-African Congress to call for the integrity and independence of African states. This congress, convened in London by Trinidad-born barrister Henry Sylvester-Williams, would be the first in a series of congresses that brought together delegates from Europe, the West Indies, the United States, and Africa to oppose colonialism and racism. Yet while building transnational solidarity within the African diaspora, Du Bois also advocated equality for people of African descent within the individual nations in which they resided. He advanced the idea that African-Americans had to live within a "double consciousness," an awareness of the self as distinct from the persona that dominant groups might construct. "The problem of the twentieth century," Du Bois declared in his famous 1900 speech to the congress, "is the problem of the color line." The First Universal Races Congress met in 1911 in London to build support for a global struggle against racism.[63]

The end of World War I brought new Pan-African initiatives. A Pan-African Congress of 1919 convened in Paris to coincide with the Versailles Peace Conference. Its delegates invoked Wilsonian self-determination and issued a proposal to turn Germany's former colonies in Africa into a new state, but the officials at Versailles largely ignored the effort. A fifth Pan-African Congress, held in New York in 1927, was primarily financed by Addie W. Hunton and the Women's International League for Peace and Freedom (WILPF), a sponsorship that underscored the overlapping goals of the Pan-African Congress and the WILPF, a transnational women's organization. Throughout the 1920s Du Bois, Hunton, and others consistently championed self-determination in Africa as well as equality for African-descended citizens in their own countries. Although few delegates from Africa attended international conferences during the 1920s because colonial administrations restricted their travel, groups throughout Africa formed to fight white minority rule and used new networks of communication to link their efforts to sympathizers elsewhere in the world. Padmore's *The Negro Worker,* his work as head of the Comintern's International Trade Union Committee of Negro Workers (before he renounced the Communist Party over its policies toward colonialism), and his labor organizing throughout Africa and the Caribbean during the Great Depression of the 1930s facilitated the spread of Pan-Africanism.[64]

Marcus Garvey espoused Pan-Africanism of a different kind. Born in Jamaica, where he founded the Universal Negro Improvement Association (UNIA) in 1914, Garvey brought a charismatic message of racial pride to the United States and built a huge following after World War I. From 1919 to 1922, Garvey's Black Star shipping line visited ports throughout the world and attracted enthusiastic supporters. By using black seamen as agents, Garvey established a global informational network that spawned branches of the UNIA in Africa, Australia, and the West Indies and throughout the Americas. At its height the UNIA had perhaps a thousand chapters in forty-three countries and territories. Like Du Bois and other Pan-Africanists, Garvey called for self-determination of African nations, but he rejected the assimilationist, antiracist message of Du Bois's "double consciousness." Embracing race essentialism and racial pride, Garvey preached that America was a white country and that black people needed to return to Africa and establish nations based within their own race. He tried to promote a settlement in Liberia but was jailed on mail fraud charges in 1923. In 1927 he was deported back to Jamaica, as his movement faded. The UNIA's global influence fell as quickly as it had risen, but Garvey's uncompromising message of black nationalism and pride continued to influence the Pan-African movement on several continents.[65]

The writings of Léopold Senghor, who would become the first president of Senegal, and Martinican poet Aimé Césaire helped forge a related transcontinental intellectual movement called *négritude*. Meeting in Paris during the 1930s and linked to flourishing black arts and cultural movements in Haiti and in Harlem, black intellectuals from Africa and the Caribbean sought to build a common identity that rejected assimilation, turned *nègre* into a positive word, and asserted opposition to French racism. These intellectuals did not seek political independence from France so much as creation of a more inclusive, transnational culture based on equal respect. Just as French colonialism contained both a universalizing discourse of Greater France and a particularizing discourse related to race, so *négritude*'s critique of French colonial modernity also developed a "two-fronted response." One front embraced French citizenship in the French empire and the other articulated a cultural nationalism in which mythic black-African culture and soul stood opposed to the presumed dehumanization of Western modernity.[66]

In his examination of what he called the "Black Atlantic," Paul Gilroy uses ships as a central metaphor. The displacement of Africans to other continents brought an accompanying need to hang on to memories of distant places and to see the Atlantic Ocean as a connecting highway rather than as a barrier. The circulation of people, ideas, and arts within this Black Atlantic, through people such as Du Bois, Padmore, Garvey, and Césaire, Gilroy argues, formed a sense of nationalism even under conditions of the fragmented consciousness produced by geographical and cultural displacement. People in the African diaspora, he suggests, lived with instability and juxtaposition of identity long before the advent of the term *postmodernity* in the late twentieth century.[67]

Pan-Africanism as a transnational nationalism, of course, flourished not just on the ocean currents but on the new currents of the electrical age. Du Bois's writings and his newspaper, *The Crisis,* circulated widely; Padmore's *The Negro Worker* and Garvey's newspaper *The Negro World* constituted parts of their global networks. Other giant figures in the Pan-African movement also circulated their ideas and platforms within the new networks of travel and communication: During the 1930s some of the major activists in the Pan-African movement—C. L. R. James, Claude McKay, and Paul Robeson, all of whom embraced socialism and its anticolonial agenda—were prolific writers and artists.[68] Moreover, many Africans, some of whom would later lead postcolonial governments, participated in this transnational circulation. Kwame Nkrumah attended school in the United States, spent time in London, and became the first president of Ghana. Julius Nyerere studied in Scotland before he headed the newly independent nation of Tanzania and helped found the Organization of African Unity (OAU).

Diasporic allegiances that became influential in the late nineteenth and early twentieth centuries emerged in diverse formulations, each with distinct regional characteristics depending on the density of the diaspora and the power of the grouping with which it aligned. The Gadr movement, for example, took shape in San Francisco among Sikhs who sought to mobilize migrant groups in support of an anti-imperial, anti-British uprising in India. Irish nationalists mobilized their far-flung networks with a similar goal. Chinese *tongs* spread their influence throughout immigrant communities on several continents.

Pan-ethnic or pan-national movements, however, could prove ambiguous and even deceptive. Programs to promote "Pan-Americanism" and "Pan-Asianism," for example, claimed to construct broad regional identities, but they can also be seen as tools of expansionist national states. The respective attempts by the United States (after the 1880s) and by Japan (especially in the 1930s) to create geographically proximate spheres of influence provide examples of highly nationalistic programs dressed in the garb of regional imaginaries. Both the Pan American Union and the creation of Manchukuo expressed rich regional cultural circulations of ideas about moving toward modernity but came manifested politically as client state relations or as highly asymmetrical regional associations.[69] Populations of Slavs, Ottoman Turks, Germans, and Arabs, to cite more examples, also asserted transborder identities. These movements, too, often arose from regional cultural circulations but became creatures of expansionist states and empires seeking to justify boundary claims, border transgressions, or attempts to drive away outsider populations. Regionally based transnational appeals, of course, waxed stronger when confronted by the claims of oppositional networks (for example, in liminal areas in the Balkans and the Caucuses) and when they served as useful weapons within the geopolitical rivalries of national states.

The Jewish diaspora constituted another variant of transnational attachments. In 1900, 82 percent of Jews lived in Europe, the majority in Eastern Europe; by 1939 the number had shrunk to 57 percent, with the United States and, to a lesser extent, Palestine as newly important centers of Jewish life. Jews from this increasingly globalized diaspora, itself split into Ashkenazi and Sephardic branches, played important roles in many of the intellectual currents and social movements discussed in this chapter—internationalism, anarchism, socialism, pacifism, as well as in a variety of economic, artistic, and epistemic networks. Jewish transnationalism, often fueled in tandem with a global discourse of anti-Semitism, could combine feelings of loyalty to an ethnic identity, national attachments to particular countries, and a universalism that aspired to build tolerance for difference. Although linkages forged among often far-flung Jewish communities proved important to transnational networks of all kinds, there are few common threads among them. Jewish transnational linkages were both secular and religious; they strengthened both capital and labor; they both buttressed and undermined divisions marked by nationality, empire, gender, and racial identity.

The modern nationalist movement called Zionism, however, was one transnational impetus that may be discussed in very loose analogy with Pan-Africanism, as it sought to imagine and advance a national identity within a diasporic community that held no singular or specific territory except in various constructions of memory. A movement of highly varied roots and diverse histories that began in the late nineteenth century, Zionist groups constituted an "international nationalism" that advocated the establishment of a Jewish national home in Palestine.

They gradually grew stronger in response to pogroms in Russia; to unfulfilled promises for a homeland that were made in the Balfour Declaration of 1917 and in the League of Nations' creation of a Palestinian mandate; to rising anti-Semitism in Europe during the interwar era; and finally to the Nazis' mass killing of Jews in the Holocaust. As with other diasporic groups, the longing for a grounded homeland and the transnational organizing in pursuit of that goal became bonding elements.[70]

Religious Transnationalism

Major world religions had all built strong transnational affiliations in the age that preceded the consolidation of national states. In the nineteenth century, however, state-building projects could rival and sometimes even tried to suppress such religious attachments. Moreover, the growing influence of scientific method, evolutionary thought, secularism, and Marxism seemed to challenge religious ways of knowing.

In this context of increasingly secular state building and scientific modernity, religious connections nonetheless continued to refresh themselves and even flourish. In fact, under competition from secular trends and from each other, Christianity, Judaism, Islam, Hinduism, Buddhism, Yoruba, and other groups all experienced revival and expansion. New modes of communication and the accelerating global flows of people and ideas facilitated the new energy. C. A. Bayly has argued that this period saw the consolidation of religion as a universal category of identification, and that "many modern nationalisms were themselves heavily influenced by emerging religious solidarities."[71] There were, however, always inherent tensions between religious claims to universalism and practices rooted in adaptation to local cultural traditions. The uniformities of religious doctrine came to be rendered in distinctive local ways—as differentiated commonalities.

From one perspective, Christianity could seem on the decline in our period. In the late nineteenth century Friedrich Nietzsche, son of a Lutheran pastor, articulated an influential disenchantment with Christianity, even as Karl Marx advanced a highly materialist view of the human condition. These and other philosophers challenged the basis of Christian belief from many directions in the generation before the eruption of the Great War. Then in 1914 an Orthodox-inspired killing of the archduke Francis Ferdinand, heir to the Austro-Hungarian throne and a devout Catholic, threw Europe into what became a devastating war that pitted Christian rulers against each other—the German and Austrian emperors against the British king, the Russian tsar, and finally the US president—and prompted extravagant rhetoric on every side about doing battle in the name of a Christian Lord. Just as the costs of war weakened Europe's states economically, the fighting took its toll on both the territories and the faiths of Christendom. The Russian Revolution of 1917 toppled the established Russian Orthodox Church. Persecuted Christian communities, especially of Armenians and others on the eastern frontier of the new Turkish republic, were scattered and killed as the old Ottoman Empire fell apart. Britain's hold on colonies became more precarious, and the Irish crisis pitted Catholics against Protestants. The dispirited generation that survived the devastations of the First World War emerged with all kinds of faiths shaken. After surveying the memorials to the dead from this struggle, Diarmaid MacCulloch writes, "The greatest casualty commemorated in this multitude of crosses and symbols of war is the union between Christianity and secular power: Christendom itself."[72]

Yet countervailing signs of Christianity's expansion also emerged, illustrating the contradictions of the age. From the middle of the nineteenth century appeared new visionaries, new excitements over End Times, a vibrant new Pentecostal movement in the United States, and—most importantly—an upsurge of Christian missionary fervor. Financed from private donations, Protestant missionary societies led efforts to "civilize" people around the world by saving their souls, spreading literacy (to facilitate Bible reading), and instructing people in the virtues of monogamous marriage and disciplined labor. Christianity reached into every continent.

The Salvation Army, for example, was founded in 1878 in England and grew into a worldwide network of schools, hospitals, and other institutions. Initially looked upon with suspicion by state authorities, it was later seen as a helpful tool in controlling "dangerous" populations. The Salvation Army constructed both Britain's urban poor and the "heathens" and "savages" in Britain's empire as populations in need of the social salvation it offered. Becoming an imperial force that discursively linked together both domestic and colonial social threats and remedies, the Army became active throughout the globe. It was called upon, for example, to reeducate ex-convicts in places as far-flung as Japan, Australia, South Africa, French Guiana, and elsewhere.[73]

Social-gospel Protestantism furthered the global evangelical movement. The American Student Volunteer Movement for Foreign Missions (SVM), founded in 1886, famously promised "the evangelization of the world in this generation." The SVM movement, allied with the Young Men's Christian Association (YMCA), quickly spread to Great Britain and to other countries of Western Europe and developed chapters in Syria, Egypt, China, India, and across the globe.[74]

The late nineteenth-century famines, especially in India, China, and other mission fields, assisted evangelization, as the sensational coverage of these tragedies spurred missionary activity, boosted circulation for the new missionary magazines, and prompted heartrending appeals for donations to support Christian relief efforts everywhere. In the United States, the *Christian Herald* carried out the most dramatic campaign, using the relatively new medium of photography to show graphic images of people in various stages of starvation.[75] Such images, while meant for philanthropic purposes, also worked to underscore the superiority of Christian civilizations and to suggest the need for imperial interventions. Moreover, missionaries and other humanitarian activists often invoked ideals of a shared humanity in their appeals while remaining blind to the ways in which Western imperial policies had contributed to the very calamities that altered social and ecological patterns and thus disrupted food production and availability.

By the time of the World Missionary Conference in 1910, Protestant Christianity had become a rapidly growing global network incorporating many church leaders in non-Western areas. As the faith expanded, its meanings and practices became ever more diverse. The African prophet William Wadé Harris, for example, defied colonial boundaries in 1913 to lead a transborder revival movement in West Africa that gathered perhaps one hundred thousand conversions. Harris, educated in a mission school in southeastern Liberia, spread an indigenous Christianity into areas not previously tilled by European missionaries. He urged his converts to abandon their nature spirits, which had failed to protect them from colonial conquest, and to embrace the Christian God, who could restore their sovereignty and bring access to needed knowledge and technology. Preaching accommodation with most Westerns ways but also upholding the custom of polygamy, Harris was responsible for the largest conversion to Christianity on the African continent. When Western missionaries later arrived in areas of West Africa, they were often astonished to find Harrist churches flourishing. Indeed, especially from the 1920s on, indigenous rulers and prophets throughout Africa carried out vigorous campaigns to found their own Christian churches independent of European interference.[76]

The influenza epidemic of 1918–1919 promoted the transnational growth of Christian divine-healing churches. The teachings of Faith Tabernacle Congregation, which formed in 1918 in Philadelphia, found their way to Ghana, an area also populated by many indigenous healing cults. Through pamphlets and correspondence, Faith Tabernacle's leaders promised to heal people of influenza at a time when medical authorities had neither the knowledge nor the supplies to adequately treat hard-hit populations. In Ghana, colonial authorities banned native healing cults as "witchcraft" but allowed Christian healers. As word of successful cures circulated, Faith Tabernacle's evangelism spread to include Britain's Apostolic Church and stretched into Côte d'Ivoire and Togo to become forerunners of the large Pentecostal movement that would continue to spread even after Faith Tabernacle itself declined in the mid-1920s.[77] Pentecostalism, which had its modern roots in Britain and the United States in the late nineteenth century and emphasized healing, speaking in tongues, and a direct relationship with God, became one of the most dynamic global movements in Christianity in the twentieth century.

Catholics also stepped up their involvement in social issues by accelerating a global missionary effort. Pope Leo XIII's encyclical *Rerum Novarum* (1893) placed Catholicism behind attempts to ameliorate industrialization's excesses. It championed fair wages and legal protections for workers. And in the 1920s, Pope Pius XI adopted worldwide outreach as a priority. He founded new mission centers around the globe, endorsed vigorous national churches under indigenous leadership, and consecrated six Chinese bishops and a bishop in Japan and in Vietnam—the first non-Western bishops since the eighteenth century. In addition, Catholic missionaries constituted one of the largest groups of French men and women working abroad, although they often had conflicted relationships with imperial administrators of the determinedly secular Third Republic. French imperial policy in Indochina, Polynesia, and Madagascar, for example, emerged in the crucible of discordant religious and secular goals, and indigenous communities were sometimes able to work the dissension to their own advantage.[78]

William Wadé Harris (center) with singers and fellow missionaries after a mission in the coastal town of Assinie in the French colony of Côte d'Ivoire, 1914. Prophet Harris led a mass movement that spread Christianity throughout West Africa in the early twentieth century. (Archives of Société des Missions Africains, Rome)

The transnational religious networks in this period all intertwined with their members' other affiliations—national, imperial, racial, regional. For example, in many Christian mission fields, missionaries tended to keep to their own, with ethnic and national affiliations trumping ideals of Christian unity. Social separation from racially different "native" converts was pro forma almost everywhere, and missionaries also broke down into national groups. British missionaries in Asia and Africa often found American Christians too zealous, too egalitarian, and too uncultured—the same attitudes that marked an anti-American discourse outside of the mission field as well.[79]

As Christian missions tried to "uplift" indigenous people, they developed the kinds of ambiguous relationships to colonial states that so often marked "contact zones." The Salvation Army and other mission efforts based in Britain became an important arm of policy at home and abroad. The American YMCA similarly functioned during World War I as an arm of state military power. It ran the programs for the troops sent to France and conducted anti-Bolshevik espionage in the new Soviet Union. Missionaries abetted colonialism by schooling their converts in their own social conventions related to monogamous marriage, hygienic rituals, work habits, and gender roles. Often working in volatile and insecure areas, they frequently favored forceful colonial rule as a way to facilitate order, progress, and conversion.[80]

The instabilities and injustices of colonial rule, however, could also place religious conversion at odds with the economic and political structures of empire. In China, the US YMCA's goals to improve economic conditions led some missionaries to criticize colonial powers and the foreign merchants who seemed to exploit the very people they had pledged to serve. Moreover, missionaries developed expertise in native languages, and some cultivated a sympathy based in cultural understanding. As missions involved themselves in education, health, and the preservation of languages, the basis for a locally generated articulation of ethnic identities flourished—and sometimes bolstered anticolonial movements. If missionaries could not avoid being a part, sometimes even an appendage, of an imperial presence, some nevertheless sought to ameliorate, critique, and at times actively resist it.

Moreover, the indigenous Christians who assumed positions of local leadership brought even more complexity to the fraught intersections between transnational religion and colonialism. The ambiguous historical memory surrounding Anglican missionary Bernard Mizeki provides an example. Mizeki was born in present-day Mozambique, converted to Anglicanism in Cape Town, and was dispatched to Rhodesia as a "native catechist" in the 1890s. After being stabbed by opponents in 1896, his body reportedly miraculously vanished into air. The site of the Mizeki miracle in present-day Zimbabwe came to symbolize both a despised colonial collaboration and also a growing cultural nationalism fed by annual pilgrimages with special meaning for trans-African Anglicanism.[81] Missionaries, in short, could both embody and also mediate the global inequalities of the imperial age.

Korea exemplified another twist on the intersection of anticolonialism and Christianity. After Japan seized their country in 1910, Korean Christians fused their faith with Korean national identity and developed it into a symbol of nationalist resistance against the Japanese occupation. This association helped set the stage for the later robust growth of Christianity in Korea.

As Christian revivalism spread missionaries around the world, assisted by Western economic expansion, Islam experienced a parallel surge designed to push back and halt Christianity's spread. The growth of European spheres encroaching into India, Southeast Asia, and Africa spurred Pan-Islamic networks, and the new forms of publication and communication reinforced bonds of attachment on all sides. Indeed, as Islam expanded in West Africa and, like other religions, adapted to local variations, some groups found special success by embracing the new technologies that colonialism helped introduce. Sheikh Ibrahim Niass, for example, used radio to spread his Tijani Sufi revivalism in the areas of Gambia and Senegal, and his network expanded to become one of the most important religious forces in West Africa. Roads that were improved to enhance imperial commerce also extended the reach of Muslim scholars. A Tijani dissident, Yacouba Sylla, inspired the rise of the Yacoubist movement, which became particularly powerful in Côte d'Ivoire.[82]

Transnational networks may have proved an especially congenial structure for the spread of Islam, or at least that has been an influential argument advanced since the 1970s in the scholarly work of Ira M. Lapidus. Lapidus and the others who have endorsed this view argue that the concept of a network provides a powerful "root metaphor" in a civilization that has struggled to sustain its identity under the onslaught of colonial political administrations. In this view, transnational interactions among Muslims became part of a network of practices animated by powerful symbols—the Quran and the mosque. These Islamic symbols became the focus for personal loyalty, ritual, and sacrifice in a sprawling territory controlled by mostly alien political jurisdictions.[83]

Pilgrimages helped reinforce such transnational ties of practice, and they created a common loyalty to specific and highly symbolic places. Pilgrimages, of course, may be found in all transnational religious affiliations, as they help bring diverse localized practices and beliefs into a more unified sense of community and orthodoxy. But the Hajj (pilgrimage to Mecca) proved especially important for the extensive Islamic networks that reached from western Africa, across the Middle East and South Asia, to Indonesia.

The Hajj had provided, writes Sugata Bose, a "key integrative element in the economy, religion, and culture of the Indian Ocean in the precolonial era," but the introduction of steamships and railways further consolidated its importance to the Islamic world.[84] The opening of the Suez Canal in 1869 and the offering, by British and Dutch steamships, of regular Hajj trips helped forge Pan-Islamic links among Cairo, Mecca, and Indonesia, which was emerging as the most populous Islamic country. Ottoman Sultan Abdülhamid II positioned himself as a defender of Islam against Christian encroachment and completed the strategically important Istanbul-to-Baghdad railway and the Istanbul-to-Medina railway, which also made the Hajj somewhat easier. The sultan also dispatched emissaries to many distant lands to spread Islam.

The rise of Egypt as a major crossroads within the Ottoman Empire, as a result of the Suez Canal, posed challenges for the sultan and for Pan-Islamic movements generally. The opening of the canal accelerated the movement of trade, people, and culture and drew many parts of the world together. It also facilitated the rising hegemony of European states in the Middle East and in Africa, which colonial powers began to partition in the 1880s. The mixture of Islamic and Christian influences under colonialism brought clashes but also borrowing and accommodation. Even as European encroachment and technologies changed caravanning patterns in northwest Africa, for example, Islamic law continued to structure and facilitate networks of trade and cultural exchange in that region.[85] With the demise of the Ottoman Empire after World War I, the British imperial authorities and the Saudi state gained greater territorial influence over Mecca and Medina, Islam's second holiest city. Still, Muslim networks proved adept at crossing seas and forging religious connections that state boundaries could hardly contain or control. Stronger colonial rule from the West often enhanced the oppositional appeal of Islamic practices.

Islam was split along lines of doctrinal disputes, and different movements within Islam all had transnational reach. The largely Sunni-based Salafi movement, for example, called for a return to traditional Islam that would accommodate the kind of technological and scientific modernizations taking place in Europe. From the mid-nineteenth century into the twentieth, writings by the main figures of the Salafiyya circulated especially among intellectual elites and influenced anticolonial and nationalist movements, particularly among Arab Muslims. Such Pan-Islamic appeals, closely linked to calls for Muslim societies to modernize in order to free themselves from European colonial rule, provided a basis for transnational connections as well as for militant anti-Western nationalism. At the same time, often propelled by rivalry with each other, Shi'i elites and the Naqshbandi Sufi orders also, in their own ways, promoted Islamic revitalization across and within national boundaries. All of these revitalization quests bore the imprint of both universalism and sectarianism.

Although the symbolism of the Hajj played a major integrative and symbolic role in Pan-Islamism, the numbers of actual participants remained comparatively small in this period. Before World War II, overseas pilgrims rarely surpassed 100,000. The peak year, 1927, registered around 132,000, but the global economic depression brought sharp declines thereafter. Pilgrimages were made easier by new transportation, but European imperial regimes generally regarded them with suspicion. Worried that pilgrimages might spread politically subversive ideas along with infectious diseases, colonial regulations over the Hajj proliferated, and international sanitary regulations closed key ports. Calcutta (Kolkata) was closed as a pilgrim port for thirty years, for example, after an outbreak of plague in 1896. Only in Dutch-ruled Indonesia did a colonial officer, Snouck Hurgronje, advocate facilitating well-run pilgrimages to Mecca. Hurgronje, a noted Dutch Orientalist, believed that a religious accommodation with Islam would facilitate Dutch rule and would reduce, not increase, political radicalism.[86] Moreover, splits within Muslim communities during the Hajj always had the potential to rip away at Pan-Islamic solidarity. The Wahhabi ascendancy in Saudi Arabia sometimes sparked hostility from Shi'i and Sufi pilgrims.[87]

With the rapid spread of Christianity and Islam, reform movements also reshaped Hindu, Buddhist, and Confucian traditions. As in Islam, many reform leaders called for a return to traditions that emphasized elements consistent with adapting to modernity in order to more effectively challenge outside imperial powers. Perhaps partly to counter the appeal of Christianity and Islam, these faiths became more systematized in terms of doctrine, ritual, and organization. They even took on proselytizing attributes, and they also fused with national or protonational visions. The Young Men's Buddhist Association, for example, modeled itself on the YMCA and played a role in China, Burma, and elsewhere by promoting national strengthening against European influences.

Swami Vivekananda well illustrates the intertwined spread of transnational religious impulses and nationalism. A disciple of the nineteenth-century mystic Ramakrishna, Vivekananda traveled India as a "wondering monk" and then proceeded on a world trip, visiting China, Japan, Canada, the United States, England, France, and Italy. Arriving in Chicago for the 1893 World Parliament of Religions, held in conjunction with the Columbian Exposition, Vivekananda managed to get himself accepted as a representative of India and received growing acclaim for his speeches. Presenting Hinduism as an international force that encompassed toleration for all religions, he also proclaimed the spiritual superiority of the East (especially India) over the materialism of the West. While in the West, he had reportedly remarked to a friend that he hoped to return home and "send an electric thrill" through "India's national veins."[88] Indeed, he returned to India in 1897 to be hailed as a prophet of Indian nationalism. His enthusiastic reception in the West, where he sometimes came to symbolize India's worth to the rest of the world, established him as perhaps the most important representative of Indian culture. Swami Vivekananda remained a singular figure both in the transnational spread of Hindu teachings of Vedanta and yoga and also in the creation of a sense of Indian nationalism that informed Gandhi and others.

Theosophy also stretched globally even as it promoted Indian nationalism in the 1920s. Like Vivekananda's teachings, Theosophy probably spread in the West in the context of a particularly Orientalist vision of India. Annie Besant, a British socialist who campaigned for democratic self-rule in India and was elected president of the India National Congress in 1917, embraced Theosophy and headed the Theosophical Society. Theosophical views, which embraced a kind of mystical spiritualism, helped popularize ideas of human community and essential religious unities, even though they also accommodated prevailing views of racial hierarchy.[89]

Localized religious traditions could also spread globally within specific diasporas. Wherever the African slave trade brought Africans, for example, religious practices came along, adapted, and even flourished. Specific groups of Africans, especially throughout the New World, tried to preserve and pass on beliefs and rituals. The religious culture of Yoruba, for example, thrived as *Candomblé* in Brazil and Santería in Cuba.[90]

Within major religious affiliations, transnational conversations around proper gender roles seem at least superficially similar in this era. Some Christian and Islamic reformers (women and men), for example, propounded education for women on the maternalist grounds that women's moral education was essential for nurturing future male leaders. Encouraging motherhood and modern housekeeping within the moral framework of a religious tradition dovetailed with the goals of those who advocated nation building, literacy, sanitation programs, and other attributes of modernity. Religious transnationalism, in fact, provided a powerful (though certainly not the only) framework for the women's networks that emerged in the late nineteenth century.

Worlds of Women

As with other transnational movements and affiliations, women's networks varied widely in their goals and cannot be seen as taking shape independently from other movements. Gender-based women's networks were affiliated with groups associated with labor, anticolonialism, socialism, racial solidarity, and religion, and with epistemic, artistic, and professional communities. Clearly, there was no single "women's movement" generated from any single place. Rather, there was a robust current of diverse "women's movements" flowing from multiple locations. With such variation, transnational identifications along lines of gender sometimes undercut and sometimes reinforced other demarcations of difference based on ethnicity, nationality, class, religion, and region.[91]

Many causes rallied relatively elite women who could marshal the resources to travel internationally. The more formalized transnational organizations of women were therefore heavily based in Europe, European settler colonies, and the United States. Most transnational networks, however, emerged simultaneously with local activist groups, each helping give shape to the other. Campaigns for suffrage, for a larger role in civic life, for control of prostitution and alcohol, for birth control, and for special protections for workers were a few of the strands within the larger current of women's connections.

Local and national politics provided one context for the growth of the suffrage movement, but transnational organizing offered another essential ingredient. In the United States and Great Britain, declarations advocating women's civil and political rights (along with access to higher education and to professional service) had become influential—and controversial—by the middle of the nineteenth century. The writings of Mary Wollstonecraft and John Stuart Mill had wide dissemination, first in the English-speaking world and then in translation, as did the Seneca Falls Declaration of 1848. Suffrage leaders in the United States, Britain, and France established in 1888 the International Council of Women, the first lasting transnational women's organization. Socialist groups formed the International Suffrage Alliance in 1902. Before World War I, Finland, New Zealand, Australia, and Norway granted voting rights to women (although aboriginal women were restricted in some Australian states). The important roles that women played during World War I in many countries provided additional impetus to suffrage. Denmark, Sweden, Canada, Soviet Russia, the Baltic states, Germany, Poland, Czechoslovakia, Hungary, the Netherlands, and the United States embraced women's suffrage during or just after the war. In Britain, women were granted a parliamentary vote, although fully equal suffrage did not come to Britain until 1928. Other countries, such as Burma, Turkey, and Ecuador, gave the franchise to women during the 1920s. As agitation for suffrage spread, victories seemed to beget more victories.[92]

Drawing inspiration and tactics from their globalized networks, movements for suffrage and other rights for women broadened their scope in the interwar era, expanding in Western Europe, in the old Russian, Austro-Hungarian, and Ottoman empires, in Egypt, Turkey, India, Japan, and Latin America. The First International Women's Day Celebration Conference, held in Canton in 1924, highlighted women's activism in China. One of the leading Egyptian feminists, Huda Shaarawi, famously returned from a women's conference in Rome in 1923, stood on the railroad step, drew back her veil, and received applause from the crowd of women onlookers. As founder of the Egyptian Feminist Union and its president from 1923 until 1947, she championed greater independence for women as well as national independence for Egypt. US and Cuban feminists pressed the Pan American Union to establish an Inter American Commission of Women (Comisión Interamericana de Mujeres) in 1928. Transnational peace activist Rosika Schwimmer fled postwar Hungary in 1920 for the United States, where although the Supreme Court barred her from becoming a citizen because of her highly visible involvement with the feminist peace movement, she continued her activism. In 1934 Turkey enfranchised women in national elections, a measure that radiated through Islamic networks.[93] Transnational organizations carried some of this global activism among women, while books and ideas also helped sprout local initiatives that were independent of larger organizational

Huda Shaarawi (center) and the Egyptian delegation to the Ninth International Woman Suffrage Conference in Rome, 1923. Shaarawi was the force behind the Egyptian Feminist Union, the first explicitly feminist organization in Egypt. The Union merged feminism with advocacy on behalf of anticolonial nationalism and Islamic modernity. (C. C. Catt Collection, Bryn Mawr College Library, Special Collections)

structures. Modest reformist approaches and bold transgressive acts both found encouragement within the formal and informal transnational circuits that women were forging.

For many women who struggled to gain the right to vote, national suffrage campaigns constituted less ends in themselves than means by which other social concerns might be addressed. Women in many countries led reformist causes associated specifically with women's issues. Josephine Butler led efforts to protect prostitutes in England and the British Empire, and Ghenia Avril de Sainte-Croix carried on Butler's work in France and within the League of Nations during the interwar era. Transnational efforts aimed at protecting women from becoming the victims of male vice and sexual exploitation.

Members of the Woman's Christian Temperance Union (WCTU) argued that greater political involvement by women could help protect the home by alleviating the brutalities arising from the evils of alcoholic drinks and prostitution. The WCTU, based in the United States, became one of the largest transnational women's movements, extending itself along currents of Christian connections and, mostly, within the zones of Anglo-American cultural influence. WCTU members believed that the United States was superior in its drinking habits to most of the rest of the world. Indeed, temperance crusades had successfully lowered alcoholic consumption in the United States. Moreover, the WCTU held that Christianity, efforts for peace, work against violence against laborers, and opposition to both prizefighting and animal cruelty would advance globally along with women's rights and temperance. Basing their arguments on biological essentialism, WCTU members advanced the view that women, as mothers, were natural homemakers and peacemakers, while men spread militarism and exploitative profit making. Women, in effect, were represented as the mothers of the human species and as custodians of international morality and well-being. Ian Tyrrell's global history of the WCTU traces the work of some of the thirty-eight global missionaries the WCTU dispatched to recruit women worldwide.[94]

Empowerment of women as a means to combat militarism was a common theme among transnational women's groups. Calling for a halt to conflict in Europe, an international group of women met at The Hague in 1915 and established the Women's International League for Peace and Freedom. This group quickly widened its mission to fight colonialism and racism as well as militarism, and it became one of the few interracial organizations of the interwar era—a time when views of strict racial hierarchies were still strong.

Birth control became another cause of transnational advocacy. Drawing upon European women physicians who advocated use of the vaginal diaphragm, Margaret Sanger promoted birth control in the United States and gained both acclaim and notoriety worldwide. After she met Sanger in New York in 1919, for example, Baroness Ishimoto (later Katō) Shizue returned to Japan and formed a birth control league. When Japanese authorities refused to grant Sanger a visa to visit, Sanger booked a ship to China, docked in Japan on the way, and received visitors in her stateroom. Under pressure, authorities finally permitted Sanger to

Margaret Sanger and Ishimoto (later Katō) Shizue (side by side, center), and other advocates of birth control in Japan, 1937. These two women worked in their respective countries and also globally to elevate the status of women and to give women more power over planning their families. Katō, who lived to age 104, was one of the first women elected to the Japanese Diet after women received the vote in 1946. (Sophia Smith Collection, Smith College)

undertake a speaking tour, and Ishimoto accelerated her efforts to spread Sanger's message. In the late 1930s, however, the nationalist, pro-natalist stances associated with Japan's growing militarism (as in Germany) stalled the country's prewar birth control movement.[95]

Calls for women's empowerment had an ambiguous relationship to empire building. Sometimes supporters of women's rights from the West interlaced their advocacy with imperial justifications, often pointing to practices such as sati (self-immolation), foot binding, and harem as evidence of the backwardness and injustice that colonial uplift might remedy. The harem especially became construed in much of the West as the very antithesis of respectable notions of family order and as a sign of a degenerate society that only imperial authority could stamp out.

At the same time, women in less powerful colonized territories often recognized that they were constrained through both imperial and gender inequalities. In this sense, feminism (a term that appeared in various languages in Western Europe in the late nineteenth century) and anti-imperial causes could also go hand in hand. Moreover, women's advocates from colonies could call on women from the metropole to support their causes and give them international visibility. In the 1880s and 1890s, for example, India's Pandita Ramabai appealed to networks in England and the United States to press her opposition to Hindu customs related to child marriage and sati. She also converted to Christianity. Such women's and Christian networks helped her finance her Mukti Mission, established in 1889 for the education and training of poor women, especially widows. Still, Indian feminism did not arise out of a transnational network of women so much as it sprang from local grievances and traditions and then tapped into broader networks. And these could be fragile. Pandita Ramabai's feminism so disquieted some of her British missionary sponsors that they came to see her as heretical.[96]

Global travel consistently undermined the idea that Euro-American women activists were essential in bringing greater women's equality to the rest of the world. When American Carrie Chapman Catt decided to "survey the status of women" by a global trip around the world from 1911 to 1913, she found both the expected and the unexpected. In many places she saw the disempowerment and even isolation forced upon women and commented upon women's plight in clearly Orientalist terms. But she also traveled through places, such as Rangoon, Burma (now Myanmar), where matriarchal customs meant that women voted in local elections, held property, could choose and divorce their husbands, and controlled much of the retail trade. In some places in Southeast Asia, she witnessed the decline of women's power as the influence of Islam and Christianity spread. In the end, she wrote that her trip provided "an experience so upsetting to all our preconceived notions that it is difficult to estimate its influence upon us."[97] Women's networks entangled unpredictably within the uncertain currents of transnationalism.

Transnational organizations to improve the status of women became somewhat less visible over time, especially in the West. Older women dominated these movements, and younger women seemed reluctant to join the formal associations that championed suffrage, pressed purity causes, and frequently advocated a variety of religious or political agendas.[98] Younger, particularly urban, women found attractions within another, quite different, transnational current—consumerism. "Modern girls" popped up on every continent in the early twentieth century. Like the organized transnational women's movements with which they occasionally overlapped, these "modern" women asserted an independent spirit and sought new freedoms. But they rejected the nineteenth century's world of women, one that often assumed values found in homosocial bonds, gender essentialism, and domesticity. Instead many "modern girls" gravitated toward a jazzier version of femininity that looked toward heterosexual companionship, a sporty and androgynous look, and a revamped vision of family life. This chapter's final section will examine "modern girls" and their involvement in an array of transnational "codes" spawned through consumerism. The bonds they developed were less those of affection based on gender than those woven through acts of purchase and self-presentation in an age of mass media.

The variety of aspirations projected in global women's movements reflected differing ideas about proper or natural gender roles. Definitions of masculinity and femininity and of proper sexuality, of course, varied widely around the world. As global networks intruded upon localized habits, the production of perceived gender differences and of sexual behaviors could undergo change and challenge, not always in predictable ways. Discourses of masculinity generally infused imperial ideologies, as a rhetoric of benevolent paternalism mixed with the threat of military force. Many women's organizations, as we have seen, participated in this masculine projection of empire, endorsing an extreme version of domesticity counterpoised against a presumably rational and assertive manliness. On the other hand, the new global connectivities, even in imperial realms, also provided networks within which people on both sides of colonial divides could meet, question prevailing social values, and develop alternative affiliations. In transnational space, feminists and same-sex unions might find nourishment for their opposition to rigid gender or sexual norms. Cosmopolitanism could thus challenge the very discourses of masculinity that were embedded in imperial and other hierarchical relationships. Issues of gender expectations and realms of intimacy, as Ann Stoler has elaborated, lay not outside of imperial and global politics but often at their heart.[99]

. . .

In this increasingly networked world, aesthetic currents associated with music, literature, and art may have produced some of the most intangible, yet enduring, attachments. Realism, impressionism, cubism, art nouveau, surrealism, Dadaism, and neoclassicism all drew together aesthetic movements that developed a global semiotics and, often, cosmopolitan circuits of collaborating artists and intellectuals. Paris seemed to generate an intellectual avant-garde. Its status as a transnational gathering place provided fertile soil for cross-cultural attachments based within globalized artistic communities of many kinds.

It would be impossible, however, to map all of the transnational affiliations and intellectual currents that developed in this era.[100] This section has tried to suggest examples rather than provide a comprehensive accounting, and to advance several central arguments. First, transnational affiliations almost invariably harbored tensions between universalistic and particularistic claims and goals. Second, realms of the transnational, the national, the imperial, and the local were not distinct; most people lived in them all at the same time. Global currents and the individuals involved in them shaped localized variations and vice versa; transmission lines ran in diverse directions, and the frictions among them often proved mutually constitutive.

3. *Exhibitionary Nodes*

AS popular representations of the world's geographic and human diversity spread within the increasingly dense transnational currents of the age, collecting and categorizing became a mania, as both science and entertainment tried to tame, order, and make legible the world's vast differences. The tradition of collecting "curiosities" and of assembling specimens from around the world, of course, well predated the late nineteenth century. Collectors in this era, however, displayed a distinctive faith that the sum of their assemblages would produce a system of universalized knowledge that would transcend geographical bounds. Most collectors and exhibitors saw the "facts" of their collections as building a unifying system. In Britain, writes Thomas Richards, "the administrative core of the Empire was built around knowledge-producing institutions like the British Museum, the Royal Geographical Society, the India Survey, and the universities," and collections of data promised to rationalize the empire, and the world, by ordering them into "categories of categories."[101] Such enthusiastic faith in collections of facts and artifacts emerged from a confluence of romanticism, evolutionary ideas, bureaucratic methodologies, and the rapid shrinking of time and space.

Who, however, collects what, and what is collected? Who establishes categories, and what gets categorized? The answers to such questions help map flows of power and constructions of hierarchy that once masqueraded as naturally ordained.

The mania for collection both shaped and reflected the transnational currents and power dynamics of the age. The taxonomies created within collections ordered the world's presumed differences—in national capacities, in racial and sexual characteristics, and in animal and plant hierarchies. They were implicated in structuring imperialism and in asserting national and class advantage. Collecting, cataloging, and exhibiting can assert (or simulate) control. Yet the more these exhibitionary nodes linked into broad global networks, the less their meanings could be carefully channeled. The exhibiting and collecting of this age certainly projected dominant hierarchies, but they also represented the messier attributes of "contact zones"—realms of transnational connection where what was taught and what was learned could be neither tightly disciplined nor unambiguous.

World's Fairs

World's fairs in our period perhaps best reflected the exhibitionary spirit of the age. They presumed to present tours of the world, but each was a tour confined to a constricted space, locality, and time. Fairs were shaped within the politics of individual large cities vying for attention, and they mostly represented the world as imagined by their sponsors, usually Westerners. They opened and then closed within several months. But despite their seemingly local and ephemeral nature, world's fairs constituted one of the most important nodes in the transnational currents of this period. Fairs became major cultural enterprises of global significance because their representations projected powerful imaginaries about the world, its diverse cultures, and its interconnectivity and divisions. They often left behind catalogs, collections, iconic buildings, networks of people, and memories that continued to structure perceptions of world "realities." A world's fair offered a simplified and comprehensible scale to both those who attended and those who learned indirectly about its exhibits.

A series of world's fairs stretched over the century that followed the famous Great Exhibition in London in 1851, better known as the Crystal Palace Exhibition. The idea was simple: if masses of people could not traverse the actual world, then glimpses and bits of that world could be assembled and represented to them. To showcase whatever city and country served as host, each fair attempted to contrive a compelling attraction that could both educate and entertain.[102]

The dozens of small and large fairs—held mostly in the West and deeply implicated in the emerging colonialist order—conveyed multiple meanings and by no means advanced any unified view of the world. Yet their projected imaginaries about the state of the world's peoples and history illuminate two of this chapter's prominent themes. First, the fairs mixed images of national and cultural particularism with expressions of universalism. They provided structured representations of the new imperialism of the age—a time of nationalistic excesses and decidedly hierarchical visions—but cast these visions as a harmonious coming together of disparate parts. Universal peace was a prominent theme in most of the exhibitions, but so, of course, was nationalism. Secondly, discourses of rationality often coexisted with, and even helped give definition to, a spectacularity associated with the emergence of mass mediated culture. The fairs mixed the modernist impulses of reason and classification together with projections of fantasy and spectacle.

Prince Albert, Queen Victoria's husband, who championed London's Great Exhibition of 1851, predicted that it would provide a new starting point from which all nations would thenceforth be able to direct their exertions. In a way he was right, not because it actually sparked the evolutionary global advancement that he envisioned but because it set a broad model for how visions of progress in future fairs and public spaces would be designed, articulated, and debated. It foreshadowed the themes of particularity/universalism and reason/spectacle.

The Great Exhibition was held in Hyde Park in London in a huge iron and glass "Crystal Palace" designed by Sir Joseph Paxton, a specialist in greenhouse construction. The mixture of hard iron and translucent glass provided an apt metaphor for the fair's juxtapositions of materiality and fantasy. The Crystal Palace established four categories that would come to be used in most fairs of the future: Manufacturers, Machinery, Raw Materials, and Fine Arts. Within these four areas stretched thirteen thousand exhibits from countries all over the world. Six million visitors (some crowding in on affordable "Shilling Days") attended, and the exhibition produced a surplus of revenue that, into the future, funded some of the great British museums and enterprises fostering science, design, and natural history. Celebrating the prospects for progress in both nation and world, the exhibits highlighted but at the same time claimed to efface the boundaries of nation, culture, and class.

The dominant messages of the Great Exhibition of 1851 featured the transformative impact of machinery, powered by raw materials, inspired by industrial ingenuity, and executed by skilled labor. The exhibits, of course, showcased products from Britain and its empire above all, but its larger goal seemed to project the cornucopia of goods that free trade could offer. Looms, appliances, reapers, and a host of other innovations hummed paeans to the Industrial Revolution and to global exchange. National technological advancement and international prosperity became seamless.[103]

The Great Exhibition exemplified and foreshadowed future discussions about whether such material "progress" enhanced or debased good taste and the dignity of work. Perhaps to temper the projections of power and industry, the Great Exhibition showcased print culture and "correct" design principles, displays that merged machinery into traditions of artisanry and early nineteenth-century design reform. Exhibits presented labor as ennobled in this new mechanized world. Dedicated artisans could lend their skills to modern industrial technique—if only consumers could be schooled, through such displays, to exercise sound aesthetic judgments.[104]

Visitors to the Crystal Palace encountered specific visions of how industrialization promoted a civilizing process, and of how improved standards of living might elevate personal morality and public taste. The huge glass hall hosted major concerts featuring the world's largest organ, showcased the famous tightrope walker Charles Blondin, displayed arts and architecture from ancient Egypt through the European Renaissance, held aeronautical and motor exhibitions, and exhibited various scenes from the natural world. A yachting event, which would evolve into the America's Cup competition, was held in conjunction with the Great Exhibition. Such spectacles of machine and of human achievement merged with exhibits of exquisite small-scale designs, such as those found in Sheffield knives and silver scissors, in the lace designs devised by women, in fine French porcelain, and in the printmaking arts. The Crystal Palace thus seemed providentially poised to have a positive moral and material effect on a world waiting to be reformed through the presumably enlightened conquests that many in the West believed would characterize the global expansion of commerce.

Displays from other nations brought this first modern world's fair its greatest distinction. Visitors looked with wonder at the array of agricultural products and raw materials from around the world—herbs, grains, spices, fruits, coal, and clay. From India, especially, the gorgeous jewelry, shawls, and silks highlighted an unsurpassed tradition of skilled artisanry. The global dimension of such displays fit well with the fair's larger themes of how free trade, skilled labor, and design could complement each other.

On the other hand, by implicitly mapping the world to represent differences in the physical, economic, and cultural characteristics of its nations and peoples, the Palace exhibits extended ambiguous messages. In the words of one guidebook, the displays presented not only "the different industries of nations, but that of centuries."[105] India's goods were presented as the products of a romantic and timeless tradition, as the magical offerings of an "unchanging East." Ethnographical models of India's artisans presaged the practice, in future fairs, of highlighting living showcases of human "types" from around the world. Themes of exoticism and Orientalism, suggested in the clay and wood-carved models in the Crystal Palace, would later morph into "real" anthropological displays enacting Western evolutionary science. In this sense, the "premodern crafts" provided a foil to complement and define the "modern" of British industry. But there was also the suggestion about the capacity of Britain to regenerate premodern lands while incorporating their cultural strengths. In the world of the Crystal Palace, cultural and economic exchange simultaneously destroyed and created boundaries among peoples.

For many visitors and commentators, the Great Exhibition captured a moment of optimism; reason and awe seemed to shape the wave of the future. Not everyone, however, was swept away. The exhibition touched off wide-ranging debates over the role of machines and their effects on humans. The uplifting messages of the Palace met other commentary that insisted that laborers would be losers in the spreading system of industrial capitalism. William Morris famously refused to enter the Palace. Karl Marx, among others, argued that the exhibition displayed a deleterious commodities fetish that would undermine dignity and good taste even as it rendered workers subservient to the needs of capital. Machines, many charged, would make slaves of their operators and undermine the nations who exalted them. The fair, in the words of Jeffrey A. Auerbach, was "a protean event with numerous possible meanings."[106] It not only disseminated a positive vision of a national identity based upon capitalism, free trade, and British destiny, but prompted a public debate over competing visions. The kinds of debates and ironies surrounding the Crystal Palace event would echo in subsequent global exhibitions.

The Crystal Palace had not been the first grand industrial exhibition in Europe. A series of French exhibitions, since 1798, had attracted international comment and admiration by featuring progressive techniques in agriculture and technology. In just a single decade before 1851, Berne, Madrid, Brussels, Bordeaux, St. Petersburg, Lisbon, and Paris had all featured exhibitions. But the

Crystal Palace set a new standard by opening to international exhibitors from the entire world. In its wake, others were quick to emulate, as numerous cities and countries tried similarly to put themselves in the vanguard of the globe's material and moral progress. One huge building had contained the London extravaganza, but the increasingly grandiose fairs after 1851 became vast campuses in which distinctive architectures punctuated the presentation of cultural difference even as orderly design principles worked to harmonize them.

A General Exposition in 1863 in Istanbul and another in 1869 in Cairo, celebrating the opening of the Suez Canal, were among the few held outside of Western Europe. They showcased both the Ottoman Empire and Egypt as modern nations on the European model. Writing of Cairo in 1869, the newspaper *Nil* boasted that foreigners would see the old city in a new light as the "Paris of the Orient," with "balls, concerts, vaudevilles, circuses, ballets . . . first-class hotels luxuriously furnished, entertainments and feasts."[107] From 1851 to the outbreak of the First World War, such extravaganzas and their breathless media coverage appeared somewhere on an average of every two years.

Paris alone hosted an Exposition Universelle approximately every eleven years—in 1855, 1867, 1878, 1889, 1900, and more after World War I, culminating in the spectacular 1937 exhibition that offered 250 acres of interior space. The 1878 fair, which boasted what was then a record-breaking territory of sixty-six outdoor acres, introduced new practices that future fairs would embellish. An "Avenue des Nations," resplendent with specimens of architecture from countries on every continent, seemed to offer a more extensive tour of the world than a single building could simulate. Moreover, where fine arts had played a minor role in the London Crystal Palace, the Paris exhibitions gave them highest prominence by emphasizing the French theme that successful manufacturing should depend on its integration into a tradition of fine arts. This fair attracted thirteen million paying visitors, and its promoters claimed it had been a financial bonanza in terms of the revenue gained from enhanced trade.

The 1889 Paris Exposition Universelle, a centennial celebration of the revolution of 1789, expanded upon the themes of technology, the arts, and colonialism. Being part of the Third Republic's strategy to construct a more exalted national identity and imperial agenda, the fair is most remembered for its signature gateway—the strange and then-controversial iron Eiffel Tower, the tallest

The Eiffel Tower at the Paris Exposition, 1889. Electric lights lit up the night and announced an exciting new age in which darkness, literally and symbolically, could be rolled back. (Library of Congress)

building in the world (until 1930). As with previous fairs, the architects of the 1889 exposition sought to represent the finest of French culture as well as the latest in machinery.

The world presented in the shadow of the Eiffel Tower again became a harmonious offering of difference. The American display introduced consumer innovations such as Thomas Edison's phonograph. Mexico's national pavilion, built to suggest an Aztec palace, announced the modernizing and "whitening" goals adopted by the regime of Porfirio Díaz. The Colonial Exhibition, one of the most popular exhibits, displayed France as the master of a far-flung empire that was spreading French civilization throughout the world. The Algerian and Tunisian exhibits were housed in extraordinary hybridized palaces intended to rival the lavish displays Britain had developed of India and to flaunt the wealth and accomplishment of French colonies. A *village nègre* enclosed some four hundred indigenous peoples in a live display. One visitor wrote that "the ingenious French have established colonies of savages whom they are attempting to civilize. They are the genuine article and make no mistake."[108] European fantasies about harem life turned belly dancers into the most popular and profitable attraction, drawing some two thousand spectators a day. Encounters with non-Western artistic traditions often inspired: Claude Debussy reportedly borrowed forms from the Théâtre Annamite in reworking his distinctive musical style; Paul Gauguin adapted a Japanese cloisonné-style separation of colors into his postimpressionist paintings.[109] "Exotic" subjects, it seemed, could offer creative gifts.

Americans, bidding for world recognition, also built fairs to advertise their power, ingenuity, and visions of future international leadership. At the US Centennial International Exhibition in 1876 in Philadelphia (celebrating the signing of the Declaration of Independence), some ten million visitors were treated to a spectacle that held special importance for a country whose citizens, living in a vast territory relatively insulated by two oceans, could seem removed from the wider world. The official name of the exhibition was the International Exhibition of Arts, Manufactures, and Products of the Soil and Mine. In its two hundred buildings, including an iron-and-glass Horticultural Hall designed to recall the Crystal Palace, the Centennial celebration brought together exhibits from thirty-seven nations and proudly showcased America's specialty products. A screw-making machine, a telephone, a typewriter, and Hires root beer exemplified

American inventiveness, and a Women's Building began the tradition followed in future world's fairs of celebrating the role and accomplishments of women, while safely segregating them from the male mainstream. The fair opened with a ceremony that switched on the impressive Corliss steam engine, which powered all of the other machines at the fair. Li Gui, the Chinese emissary who was interested in how Western technology might contribute to "self-strengthening" measures in China, was in awe. "Nothing can be done without machines.... All the universe seems to be the macrocosm of the machine," he wrote in the travel account of his around-the-world visit.[110]

If machinery impressed a visitor from the East, however, the exhibitions from Japan and China proved among the biggest hits for Americans. A fascination with Asia and Asian markets had burgeoned after Commodore Matthew Perry's visits to Japan in 1853 and 1854. The commercial treaties the United States subsequently signed with Japan and China spurred hopes for expansion of the trading highways that had long characterized the Pacific region. Japan erected its own separate building to show its finest traditions—intricate bronzes, showy lacquer work, artful screens, and elaborately carved figures and furniture. China's pagoda-style display featured elaborate screens, urns, and vases.

The Japanese pavilion, especially, touched off an enthrallment with the arts of the "Orient." Over the next few years a generation of American art collectors and scholars, such as Ernest Fenollosa, Edward S. Morse, and John LaFarge, would travel to Japan and elaborate a common nineteenth-century hope that the "feminine" arts of the East would marry the "masculine" industrial machinery of the West (especially North America) to complete the foreordained evolutionary course of civilization. Although some people in Asia talked about foreign devils and some people in the United States championed exclusionary policies that restricted most Chinese and Japanese immigration, this philosophical and aesthetic stance emphasized the civilizational gains that could be derived from the Pacific exchange's "marriage" of different cultural traditions. Influenced by the stylistic simplicity of Japanese open-plan and screen-wall construction at the 1893 fair in Chicago, Frank Lloyd Wright pioneered the sleek form-follows-function look of modernist architecture.

As with its predecessor in England in 1851, the Centennial Exhibition prompted expressions of awe but also of disgust and fear. One of its architects wrote of his joy at seeing that the "restless, happy crowds are flitting from point to point, and the whole looks like a fairy-land, an incantation scene, something that we wish would never pass away." But Japanese commissioner Fukui Makoto wrote, "Crowds come like sheep, run here, run there, run everywhere. One man start, one thousand follow. Nobody can see anything, nobody can do anything. All rush, push, tear, shout, make plenty noise, say damn great many times, get very tired, and go home." Henry Adams wrote to a friend: "I have registered an oath never to visit another of these vile displays. The crowd there was appalling and there was a great deal of sickness and alarm—Much typhoid is caught there and if they are not lucky, they will have yellow fever."[111]

The famous White City of the Columbian Exposition in Chicago in 1893, however, eclipsed the Philadelphia Fair in its scale, didactic ambition, spectacle, and controversy. Civic boosters allied with scientists, educators, and business interests to design elaborate displays that, presumably, would teach Americans (and foreign visitors) about the world. Opening during a severe economic downturn that threatened the stability of the social order in the United States, the fair followed the pattern of previous fairs by projecting a nationalistic confidence, unity, and ambition even as it emphasized the language of international harmony.

Like previous international fairs, the Columbian Exposition emphasized both industrial and moral progress. An array of American-made farm machines revolved around a huge globe at one end of Agricultural Hall. Full-size models of Pullman cars and locomotives presented the railroad as the harbinger of global prosperity. Elevators, pneumatic conveyors, models of ocean liners, affordable carriages, Westinghouse dynamos, long-distance phones, electric trolleys, mechanized street cleaners, Singer sewing machines, and steam-powered newspaper presses—all boasted of US ingenuity and positioned the country in the vanguard of the globe's future interconnectedness. While Westinghouse's incandescent lighting system illuminated the entire fairgrounds and its buildings, General Electric's three-ton searchlight and the seventy-eight-foot shaft of colored lights called the Edison Tower of Light demonstrated the dawn of the electrical age.

Amid these technological marvels, this so-called White City expanded upon a practice that would become a standard element for future fairs. It convened a World Congress of experts on almost every conceivable topic to advance theories promoting "progress, prosperity, unity, peace, and happiness." The Congress became a gathering place for the variety of new professions that, as the next section will show, were forging transnational epistemic communities. The exposition's grounds themselves became a demonstration, for example, of how new expertise in health and sanitation could turn a polluted and sickly urban environment into a City Beautiful. Cuban travel writer Aurelia Castillo de González looked past the United States' burgeoning imperial pretensions to praise a vision of modernity that, if imported to Latin America, she claimed would prevent imperial encroachment by showing an adoptable model of a well-planned, well-engineered, and more harmonious future.[112]

In addition to the promise of technology and the uplifting potential of applied expertise, evolutionary science was another structuring principle of the White City. The Smithsonian Institution's anthropologists avoided a seemingly random collection of interesting things and instead carefully constructed an allegorical and moral lesson about civilization and its advancement. The presentation of "racial types" and of evolutionary classifications purveyed the dubious concept of "race" and aimed to educate viewers in the emerging racial science of the day. Some races ("Anglo-Saxons") were represented as destined to lead the world while lesser races represented throwbacks in evolutionary time who needed to either die out or be tutored. The theme of purification in the White City extended from sanitation facilities to urban planning to racial science.

On the entertainment-oriented Midway, sensory temptations became associated with darker "races" who contributed song, dance, and titillation. Here, erotic female dancers and exotic cafés tempted the Americans who flocked to Chicago from cities and from farms. Little Egypt's dancers, with bare midriffs and semi-transparent skirts, presented movements that American slang labeled the "hootchy-kootchy" and brought outrage from purity crusader Anthony Comstock.[113] White Western viewers, for whom racial difference might have raised repulsion based on fears of racial or biological contagion, could relish the exotic from the safety of a White City. Although Ottoman sultan Abdülhamid II donated 1,819 photographs depicting the Ottoman Empire's natural beauty, architectural grandeur, and modern institutions, representations of Orientalist fantasies undoubtedly proved more memorable to most visitors.

The lavish spectacle, the scale of production, and the complex mixture of lofty education and bawdy entertainment combined together with a hawkish consumerism to mark the Chicago fair as quintessentially American. The fair featured soon-to-be-ubiquitous products such as postcards, hamburgers, soft drinks, and a Ferris wheel, named for George Washington Gale Ferris Jr., a Pittsburgh bridge builder who sought to create a huge metal landmark that would surpass the Paris Exposition's Eiffel Tower.

Like the fairs before it, the Columbian Exposition prompted debates over national identity. An appeal by African-Americans to construct an exhibit in the White City was denied. Women, again, had a separate building, but African-American women were similarly barred from it. Such racial exclusion prompted a series of protests and spurred African-American leaders to greater action.[114] Critics elaborated other familiar laments—the fair was too crowded, too elitist, too bawdy, too open, too restrictive. The fair projected clear themes involving technological, scientific, national, and racial destiny, but the precise meanings accorded to these themes invited discussion and controversy.

The Chicago fair foreshadowed America's arrival as a global power, and in 1898 the spirit of expansive and racialized nationalism manifested itself in foreign policy. Taking on the once-great empire of Spain, the United States embarked on what Secretary of State John Hay called a Splendid Little War, which sparked its experiment in overseas colonial acquisition. The government of Republican William McKinley justified as a war measure the annexation of Hawai'i, a territory increasingly dominated by US sugar interests. As Spain withdrew from its three-centuries-long hold on the Philippines, McKinley concluded that America's civilizing mission necessitated its colonial control over that Pacific archipelago, long an entrée to the coveted China market. In the Caribbean, which US strategic planners had slated to become an "American Mediterranean" that guarded a hoped-for Panama Canal route, the United States gained Puerto Rico as a colony and in 1903 subjected both Cuba and Panama to protectorate status.

The sense of power and colonial destiny that accompanied these imperial moves became deeply embedded in the series of extravagant US World Fairs held in Omaha in 1898, Buffalo in 1901, St. Louis in 1904 (to commemorate the Louisiana Purchase), Portland in 1905, Seattle in 1909, San Francisco and San Diego in 1915, and Philadelphia in 1926. All of these fairs, promoted by local city boosters for profit and regional status, celebrated America's emergence as an imperial and global power and introduced the nation's new colonial subjects to its increasingly skeptical citizens. The theories of racial inequality and hierarchy, advanced by physical anthropologists, appealed to dominant white interests in both political parties. As Lee D. Baker writes, "Southern interests marshaled the anthropological discourse on racial inferiority for propaganda and Jim Crow legislation, while Republican interests used the anthropological discourse on race to demonstrate that the inferior races of the Pacific and the Caribbean needed uplifting and civilizing."[115] These American imperial fairs also fed on models from perhaps the greatest world fair of all—the Paris Exposition of 1900.

The Paris Exhibition of 1900, which attracted some fifty million people, displayed colonialism at its most confident peak. A decade and a half before World War I would plunge Europe into a nightmare of debt and self-doubt, this turn-of-the-century exhibition emphasized the prospects for global peace and commercial uplift that so many Europeans then believed would provide the major themes of the twentieth century. The Eiffel Tower, built for the earlier fair, was painted yellow and bedecked with electric lights. Previous decades had seen a rise in labor organizing, strikes, and industrial strife, but the fair of 1900 projected confidence in industrial capitalism and in the mutual advancement that commercial connections might bring. In this greatest of all world's fairs, previous fair themes stood out in even bolder relief: capitalism, colonialism, and world peace wove together in an expanding arc called progress.

A Musée Social at the 1889 Paris exhibition had become celebrated for hosting international discussions related to the "social questions" raised by industrial civilization. The Musée Social's organizers for the 1900 fair, building on the model of 1889 and the Chicago fair's congresses, gathered experts together to exchange scientific information on subjects as far-ranging as fisheries, publishing, dentistry, hypnotism, philately, and public health and medicine. Their special interests, however, centered on how to deal with the insecurities of the industrial age. They sought ameliorative examples from various countries and groups. Subsections formed on protection of child workers, regulation of work conditions, wages and profit sharing, workers' and employers' associations, farm credit, workers' housing, workers' cooperatives, savings and insurance institutions, sanitation, temperance, slums, and poor relief. The industrializing nations contributed a range of models—from Germany's extensive state-provided accident and old-age insurance, to Italy's workers' cooperatives, to French displays of voluntary mutual aid organizations, to America's representations of "model" corporations and enlightened capitalism. The Paris fair offered a congress on "women's works and institutions" that discussed equal gender rights but mostly concentrated on expanding educational opportunities and on according special protections to women and child factory workers. The gathering accentuated the maternalist impulse in women's growing international networks by emphasizing women's special role to elevate and protect the less fortunate.

The fair thus facilitated transnational discussions about how to arrange the roles of the state, of labor, and of private capital. But it presented, as Daniel Rodgers writes, "no agreement on how an effective counterforce to the world of iron might be constructed. State paternalism, private paternalism, mutualism, socialism, maternalism: the shorthand phrases led toward different configurations of power and policies."[116] The Paris Fair presented a kind of smorgasbord, with no one configuration for organizing the new industrial society seeming dominant.

The colonial area within the 1900 fair stretched farther than any previous one, with even more fantastical architecture representing the pasts and futures of colonies. In the fair's conference halls and art nouveau palaces appeared no hint of the struggles and suffering from European or colonial wars, of strikes or social conflicts. Colonies seemed places of newly ordered bounty, indebted to the know-how of colonizers: the Dutch East Indies were present in three pavilions; nearly twenty French colonies or protectorates had their own displays or buildings; Americans showed off their "civilizing" missions in Cuba and in Native American mission schools. Other nations offered additional cultural and architectural contrasts: Russia contributed nine pavilions employing over three thousand people; Serbia constructed a Byzantine mansion with a display of silkworm cocoons; the Ottoman government, which had not participated in earlier Paris fairs, featured a huge neo-Islamic pavilion with a bazaar, workshops, café, military museum, and theater performing vignettes from Turkish life.[117]

The Paris exhibition of 1900, its successors in the 1920s, and the Paris Colonial Exposition of 1931 featured displays of humans as their most popular attractions. The nineteenth-century fairs had showcased colonial craftspeople and servers, but the idea of exhibiting humans blossomed as teams of anthropologists and entertainers illustrated the ideas of racial evolution that were sweeping the

West. Joseph-Arthur de Gobineau's *Essay on the Inequality of Human Races* (1853), which advanced ideas of biologically rooted racial hierarchy, reached the heights of its popularity during the first two decades of the twentieth century in both the United States and France. In line with this racialized view of the world, peoples from throughout the globe began to be imported and displayed alongside the plants and animals that were already standard fare. Humans became, in effect, zoological exhibits—and profitable ones. These "human zoos" became living catalogs of evolutionary categories, projecting tropes of primitivism and narratives about the history of the world.

Such exhibits easily slid into entertainment and demeaning caricature. The more exotic the display, the more audience it attracted. One Egyptian visitor criticized the absence of any modern Egyptian industry or intellectual contributions. An Egyptian novelist portrayed a visitor to the fair as being so embarrassed by the performance of two female Egyptian dancers that he left in shame.[118] British guidebook writer Alex M. Thompson praised the "multi-coloured dwellings of the various Asiatic and African natives. . . . Here one may sit and take tea or coffee, served by men of strange tropical nationalities, whose faces look as polished as your fire-grate at home, while . . . the 'Danse du Ventre' drones."[119]

Embracing the practice of human display, Americans at the St. Louis Fair also introduced their new colonial subjects to visitors. The largest and most popular proved to be the "Philippine Reservation," occupying a huge and lavishly arranged area that surpassed anything the British had shown for India or the French for Algeria. In the Reservation, anthropologists carefully structured the diverse people from the Philippine Islands (numbering some twelve hundred) into representations of race evolution. The progression of "primitive" peoples morphing into well-dressed and disciplined "modern" constabularies provided a visual demonstration of progressive colonialism. This theme would structure US world's fairs until the 1930s. Moreover, with each new fair in America, the exotic enticements of the Midway (soon called the Joy Zone) became ever more substantial and garish. The always popular *danse du ventre* was promoted at the San Francisco fair in a huge painting that featured a mechanically driven rotating belly.[120]

In all of the early twentieth-century fairs, colonies had their own buildings and identities, each hiding the militarized brutality, the greed, and the cultural destruction that was part of colonialism while emphasizing commercial and moral progress. British decision makers in India, for example, accorded an increasingly larger presence to lavish Indian palaces filled with opulent produce. These huge palaces exemplified the wealth that India had brought to England and also sought to show that British rule had brought progress and prosperity to India. By contrast, the epic-scale famine and poverty in the British colony had no visibility. Similarly, Australia, Canada, New Zealand, and South Africa rivaled each other to establish national distinctiveness and to show the material and cultural accomplishments attained under white rule. Decimation of aboriginal peoples had no place. France carefully crafted structures representing each and every colonial possession, with Algeria, Tunisia, and French Indochina having special visibility. Portugal, Belgium, Holland, and Japan all joined in the celebration of imperial uplift, as their displays of colonies such as Brazil and Angola, of Congo, of Indonesia, and of Formosa and Korea, respectively, grew in grandeur in each fair during the 1920s and early 1930s. Out of sight remained the violence that extracted colonial abundance.

As fairs became increasingly structured to celebrate empire, they became more and more associated with large and successful imperial powers. Spain, Germany, Russia, Austria, and other countries grew less enthusiastic about participation in fairs, and the internationalist mission of fairs became less convincing. Fairs thus simultaneously offered festivals celebrating interconnectivity and also became venues for hardening divisions among nations.

Fair-displayed colonialism and internationalism contained another central paradox: fairs supposedly celebrated human unity, but effective displays depended on highlighting differences among the world's peoples. Even as fairs supported a romanticized, one-sided vision of colonialism, the separate and lavish fair buildings fostered the constructions of distinctive colonial identities.[121] Even after the fairs, these constructions (architectural as well as cultural) often had substantial impact in the colonies. By bringing together leaders from both metropole and colony to plan and execute displays, fairs helped consolidate disparate, and independent, ethno-nationalistic identities. Moreover, the humans who were exoticized in colonial exhibits gazed back at the gazers and made their own meanings. What they might have seen or learned is hardly well documented. After the close of the fairs, some lingered outside of their homelands; some returned. But the impact of their views, as varied and particularized as they might have been, must have reflected a new awareness of cultural differentiations and fostered nationalisms of their own.

This paradox is illustrated by the instability of lines between white and non-white worlds at the 1900 Paris exhibition, where American commissioners sponsored a display on Negro Life in the United States that challenged some of the primitivist tropes so prevalent elsewhere. Organized by the African-American sociologist W. E. B. Du Bois, an array of photographs showed the world of middle-class black Americans—professionals, writers, experts—whose intellectual and cultural sophistication challenged the color line that colonialism inscribed.[122]

During the depression decade of the 1930s, the overt justifications for colonialism waned, opposition to racism grew, and human displays in colonial pavilions mostly ended. In the New York fair of 1930, for example, the theme of "Democracity" helped banish the nation's most overtly imperial displays. Still, the Chicago Fair of 1933–1934, the 1937 Paris Fair, and the New York Fair of 1939 retained many of the structural elements of past shows: the displays of self-confidence about progress, commerce, and empire; the promise of science and technology; the lavish use of electrical power for astonishing illuminations and efficient transportation; the vision of a union between art and technology. Coming in the midst of economic depression and international turmoil, this staged optimism about the future seemed more and more contrived. Moreover, the depression seemed to give a further boost to Midway entertainments. The Chicago fair's Midway featured a large dance hall, in which two hundred taxi dancers danced with visitors for a dime; a Lido theater with notorious fan dancing by Sally Rand; a Midget Village, "freak shows" in an Odditorium, an Oriental Village that boasted a Slave Mart, Flea Circus, and Monster Snake Show. The fair tradition was increasingly being given over to carnival and spectacle, still passed off as internationalism.[123]

At the Paris Fair of 1937 a two-hundred-foot mural consisting of 250 painted panels depicted the "spirit of electricity" from the Greeks to the present. Harmonizing with this theme, the United States featured its Depression-era electrical power projects (dams, rural electrification), and the Soviet Union presented electrical projects as the soul of communism. Yet in another part of the fair, Pablo Picasso created a very different mural, showing not progress but the destruction that German aircraft had rained upon the Spanish town of Guernica in a bombing raid on April 26, 1937. The growing horror of the Spanish Civil War augured greater trouble to come. As Jay Winter writes, "the two murals encapsulated the collision between hope and despair which created massive fissures in the 1937 expo itself."[124] Within a few months, both the fair and the Spanish Republic would end. And not too many months after that, the site of the fair's Tower of Peace, which stood taller than any nation's pavilion and had been inspired and sponsored by French pacifist veterans of the First World War, would itself host Hitler's military might.

Incongruities thus haunted the 1937 fair. The Spanish Republic's building stood near to the one in which the Pontifical States celebrated the fate of Catholic martyrs in Spain. The massive pavilion of Nazi Germany, designed by Albert Speer as a monument to the country's national grievances and renewed power, faced off against an imposing Soviet building topped by a seventy-five-ton monument to industrial and farm workers. Behind but also facing the German edifice stood the Land of Israel Pavilion, a Zionist statement erected by the Jews of Palestine. The League of Nations had a pavilion, and so did the Japanese, whose invasion of China had so clearly illustrated the impotence of that body.

Representations of empire were greatly diminished and moved to the periphery. The Indian representative had wished to come with national, not colonial, status, so India had no presence at this fair. Although French officials still displayed their own colonialism as the spread of republicanism, other nations no longer featured colonies and human zoos. Even before 1937, at the 1931 Colonial Exposition in Paris, the United States had allowed parts of its colonial empire— Alaska, Hawaii, Puerto Rico, the Virgin Islands, and Samoa—to represent themselves for the first time at a foreign exposition. Although the Eugenic Society sponsored a beauty pageant to feature the "Best Colonial Marriage," the days of colonialism and its optimistic portrayal at world's fairs were clearly waning.

World's fairs have been described as vehicles of local and national pride, as conveyors of ideals of peace and internationalism, as structures embedding colonial hierarchies, as opportunities for sharing expertise and cultural exchange, as places where newly consolidating and "modernizing" states could project their self-definitions, as sites where colonial subjects cultivated their own national imaginaries. They held all of these, often conflicting, meanings. Modernity, as represented in the world of fairs, emerged as more complicated than the fair boosters might have initially imagined.

The simultaneous meeting and separation of different cultures at world's fairs played out especially visibly in architecture and art. Many fairs presented arresting visual experiments in integrating Islamic influences into Western buildings and using Western styles to inspire the neo-Islamist forms that were often readapted back into the design repertoire of their host countries. Classical influences appeared strong at the Columbian Exposition and the Paris exhibition of 1900, but the Exposition Internationale des Arts Décoratifs et Industriels Modernes, held in Paris in 1925, pronounced the primacy of Art Deco with its internationally eclectic influences. The Antwerp Fair of 1930, the largest held outside of Britain and France, presented an imposing Congolese pavilion but built it in an Orientalist mode because the architects deemed African architectural forms too modest to be used for anything other than decorative motifs. The art gallery for the 1931 Paris Exposition, which became the Permanent Museum of the Colonies (today called the Museum of African and Oceanic Art), displayed art from the French colonies and also works by acclaimed French artists such as Paul Cézanne and Gauguin. These two, of course, had themselves derived inspiration, in both style and subject, from non-Western art. Such pastiche represented a world in motion and an eclecticism that drew from the contradictions between transnational and particularistic influences.

As nodes of transnational circulation for forms and ideas, fairs became spaces of complex cultural exchange. The physical and intellectual architects of fairs joined the world together even as they separated its parts. They showed that cultural contacts produced both attraction to and repulsion of difference. By mashing together incongruities and by trying to order world cultures whose interrelationships were disorderly, the fairs simultaneously constructed and deconstructed their messages. Despite the intentions of promoters and exhibitors, the modernity revealed in the fairs showed itself as unstable and highly contingent. Designed as tours of the world, fairs ended up representing something much more complicated—the chaotic look and feel of twentieth-century modernity.

Museums

World's fairs were part of what Tony Bennett calls an "exhibitionary complex" that manifested itself even more solidly in the bricks and mortar of museums.[125]

Museum professionals circulated in global networks, borrowing ideas from their counterparts in other countries and using international connections to build their collections.

German ethnologists in the late nineteenth century created the most important museums in the world in Hamburg, Berlin, Leipzig, and Munich. Their ethnographical exhibits, which became globally influential, projected the same kind of universalism and particularism that infused other imperial visions of the era. Well-traveled cosmopolitans, these ethnologists celebrated a unitary humanity and believed that only a museum could display and rationally compare the world's rich human varieties. At the same time, their museums were designed to celebrate the roles that they, their cities, and their still-consolidating nation had assumed as leaders of the new scientific internationalism. Not overly imperial in their late nineteenth-century displays, the museums nonetheless depended for their collections on the emerging imperial order and participated in pushing the "ethnographic frontiers" into areas that seemed the most exotic and "savage." If "otherness" had not been the initial vision of the global science of ethnography, it increasingly became its underlying frame.[126]

Many of the great public museums that had taken shape during the late eighteenth and early nineteenth centuries were restructured in the late nineteenth century around the (sometimes conflicting) goals of advancing scientific research and teaching the public the newest findings of natural history. London's celebrated Natural History Museum, for example, opened in 1881, and a new curator, William Henry Flower, tried to make it an important teaching institution by reorganizing its original displays into scientific lessons about evolution in the natural world.[127] London's Natural History Museum, together with the modern scientific museums in Berlin and other major capitals of Europe, established models that were broadly influential worldwide.

As in Europe, the new museums claimed to embody transnational intellectual and professional currents even as they became central symbols of imperial and national pride. Most proudly asserted both global vision and local distinctiveness. The great Latin American museum collections from this period, for example, took shape as a nationalist discourse produced within the transnational networks of curatorial expertise. Hermann Konrad Bermeister, a Prussian naturalist, directed the Museo Público in Buenos Aires for thirty years after he was hired in 1862. Ladislau Netto, a Brazilian trained at the Musée d'Histoire Naturelle in Paris, led the Museu Nacional do Rio de Janeiro. German-born Hermann von Ihering headed the Museu Paulista in São Paulo. All worked to research the geological formations of the Southern Hemisphere and to display its creatures, especially the whales from the southern seas and its huge, extinct glyptodonts.[128] A Dutch medical practitioner, J. W. B. Gunning, migrated to the Cape Colony in the late nineteenth century, became first director of the Staats-museum (later renamed the Transvaal Museum), and compiled one of the first surveys of birds of South Africa. The establishment of major museums in far-flung locations in this era exemplifies how the analytical scales of nation, empire, region, and world are best understood in interaction with each other.

In this period major museums began to separate collections for study from those for public exhibit, boosting the capacities for both. Research collections expanded as most museums became sponsors of transnational expeditions. The American Museum of Natural History, for example, sponsored fifty-seven col-lecting parties during its peak years 1929–1930. Latin American museums avidly collected fossils that provided significant evidence of paleontological connections among the continents of South America, Africa, and Australasia.[129] At the same time, exhibitions became more exciting through better taxidermy and the spread-ing practice of placing specimens against high-quality, naturalistic dioramas. Dis-plays of huge ocean mammals might hang from ceilings; the reassembled bones of enormous extinct land creatures might amaze visitors. Like the world's fairs, museums boasted their science and rationality but also cultivated the kind of spectacularity needed to attract audiences.[130]

Sometimes sensationalist displays went to extremes. Robert Peary in 1897 shipped six Eskimos to New York to be studied at the Museum of Natural History, where they were confined in a cellar. Upon the death of one man, the museum mounted his skeleton for display and refused to relinquish the bones to a son, Minik, who had also been captured and who ultimately died in New York of influenza in 1918.[131]

If the ability to assemble museum collections signified power, then the sack-ing of other people's collections loomed also as a highly symbolic challenge. The Old Imperial Garden and Palace in Beijing (Yuanming Yuan), for example, stood as one of the greatest collections in the world in the mid-nineteenth century. Not a public museum in the Western tradition, the invaluable antiquities and art held in its temples, galleries, and halls gave it great symbolic importance. Its gardens contained exquisite reproductions of famous landscapes from southern China. In 1860 French and British troops went on a looting and burning rampage, plundering Yuanming Yuan while grabbing valuable items as trophies of conquest. The goal, of course, was to humble and punish the Chinese, spread a sense of despair, and weaken the Qing court. The scar made a lasting impression on the Chinese. "Hence, for a long time to come," writes Young-tsu Wong in *A Paradise Lost,* "while appreciating the marvels of Western science and technology, they were somehow reluctant to sing praises of the moral values of the West."[132] Within China, Yuanming Yuan had once seemed the center of the world; the destruction of its collections signaled the world's reordering.

Collecting Plants

Botanical gardens also displayed the "world" to visitors and depended upon new links of global trade. Exchange of plants and of gardening aesthetics, of course, long predated the 1870s. Missionaries, traders, and travelers had become inadvertent or intentional conveyors of plants. Horticultural practices spread along with European colonizers who sought solace from strange lands by importing familiar plants arranged in familiar landscapes. Horticultural and acclimatization societies, as well as farmers in settler colonies, became imperial intermediaries. Hoping to improve the land or to introduce more profitable practices, they borrowed and adapted, sending specimens through imperial networks from one continent and context to another. Even before the middle of the nineteenth century, many Mogul gardens became Anglicized; botanic gardens and associated museums took shape in Melbourne, Calcutta, Ceylon, Trinidad, New South Wales, Hong Kong, and Canton. France established the famed Jardin d'Essai in Algiers to provide a laboratory for acclimatization efforts, and its horticulturalists subsequently experimented with Chinese yams, bamboo, and other plants that might complement those that could be grown in France.[133]

The networks of people who specialized in plant and animal exchange and in acclimatization both decreased and increased biodiversity. Gorse, a tough fire-resistant evergreen brought to New Zealand and Australia from Western Europe as a wind and fire break, proved highly invasive and choked off other species. Introduction of the carp from Germany to Nebraska, according to one historian, was "on par with the destruction of the buffalo . . . one of the most significant, federally provoked environmental catastrophes in the United States."[134] By contrast, new connections also spawned an ever-widening array of adaptations and gave rise to new horticultural aesthetics and new commercial products. American horticulturalists domesticated a scraggly plant from Mexico and renamed it the poinsettia after the American diplomat who had acquired it. Varieties of reddish poinsettia plants, perfected by a German-American grower and his Hungarian-born horticulturalist in California, became a Christmas-season phenomenon. An American dryland plant specialist, Thomas Kearney, adapted Egyptian cotton to cultivation in the deserts of California and Arizona to produce the "Pima" cotton (named for the Pima Indians who lived near Kearney's research station outside of Yuma) that became so widely used in the early twentieth century. The experimental station run by Louis Trabut at Rouiba, Algeria, forged connections with US plant breeders to help adapt figs and dates for growing in California and sisal plants for use in the dry lands of Algeria.[135]

Some collections followed networks of empire and allied themselves to specific imperial projects. Kew Gardens, for example, became one of the premier sites of botanical collection and experimentation.[136] The curators at Kew together with the Horticultural Society of London created an unrivaled collection of plants from China by sending expeditions into the hinterlands from the colonial garden in Hong Kong. (Specimens of Chinese tea plants became the basis for tea plantations in India.) Kew also established relationships with botanical stations throughout the empire, with Colonel David Prain becoming director of Kew after having been superintendent of the Calcutta Botanic Gardens, an important research center of tropical botany, and one of the authors of the thirty-seven-volume botanical survey of the empire.[137] Kew became not only a collector but also a disseminator: between 1863 and 1872, Kew sent over eight thousand plants a year abroad. And the professionals at Kew established their preeminence over the methodology and taxonomy of botanical classification into species.[138]

Botany, of course, had been an adjunct to medicine even before it became an adjunct to commerce. Kew tried to play a key role in facilitating the production of quinine, which was found to be effective against malaria and could, therefore, facilitate European expansion into Africa and elsewhere. In the early nineteenth century, Peru had tried to outlaw the export of the cinchona seeds and saplings that produced quinine, but smugglers managed to circumvent restrictions. A race to develop effective cinchona plants that could be grown in colonial plantations shadowed the larger late-nineteenth-century "Great Game" for empire. In this contest, Kew's mission was clearly imperial, as the garden's transnational network allied with the British state to develop this all-important tool.

Both in its medicinal and in its commercial aspects, the global trade in quinine helped strengthen imperial power. Half of the quinine production in Bengal, for example, went to the Governments Medical Stores, and in Madras almost all of it did. The royal near-monopoly on this vital drug greatly enhanced the leverage of the British Raj.[139] British successes in quinine cultivation, however, paled in comparison to the Dutch. More successful than Kew in nurturing plantation-adaptable cultivars, the Dutch developed quinine as a lucrative crop in their East Indies colonial possessions. By the 1930s, Dutch plantations in Java produced most of the world's quinine. Within a generation, the Peruvian plant had given rise to a global commodity chain upon which all kinds of imperial and transnational interactions depended.

Other botanical gardens besides Kew also refined methods of plant collection and made the previously strange more familiar. For example, the German-Russian Carl Maximowicz, a botanist who traveled around the world and then focused on studying the flora of Japan during the 1860s, became head of the Botanical Garden of St. Petersburg in 1869. From this position he gained the funds to employ teams of Japanese collectors to develop the institution's collection, the oldest and most prominent botanical garden in Russia.

If some gardens represented imperial interest, however, other collections emerged less from any alliance with a nation-state or empire and more from a desire to advance specific commercial, civic, or scientific projects. A brisk exchange of plants among arid regions in Australia, Hawaii, South Africa, California, and elsewhere, for example, transformed local horticultural practices in all of these places and stimulated local adaptors to create botanical collections as a way of publicizing newly available species. Civic boosters in turn-of-the-century San Diego established Balboa Park, where the irrepressible horticulturalist Kate

Sessions plotted out an array of plant borrowings that she hoped would transform the look of southern California while still being sensitive to its arid climate. Huntington Library and Gardens, established by Los Angeles railway magnate and developer Henry E. Huntington in the early twentieth century, developed a famed Desert Garden, one of the oldest collections of cacti and succulents brought from trips to Central and South America and elsewhere. A British naturalist gathered one of the most impressive private collections of orchids, bromeliads, and palms at his Jardín Botánico Lankester in Costa Rica in the 1940s. Improvements in transportation and horticultural practices allowed many private nurseries, now both famous and forgotten, to make a business in the global marketing of seeds and exotic plants, especially flowers. During the 1920s to 1940s, British plant hunter Frank Kingdon-Ward captivated readers with accounts of his exploits. His widely selling *Plant Hunting on the Edge of the World* (1930) celebrated the ways in which brave plant collectors discovered strange and exotic lands and tamed their natural offerings into familiar taxonomies and potential products. Plant prospecting and acclimatization could provide parables of the interconnected world order and its hierarchies.

Plant collection and distribution depended on global collaborations that bridged cultures and on establishment of interactive networks. Local people, after all, held access to information on the whereabouts, the characteristics, the possible propagation techniques, and potential uses of plants that might be unfamiliar to outside collectors. Even if the cultural traditions within which plants were understood seemed haphazard and unsystematic to those schooled in European taxonomies, the local oral or written descriptions could prove invaluable. British collectors who roamed the interior of China in the late nineteenth century, for example, complained about, but always used, Chinese gazetteers. Most hired Chinese collectors to assist them in areas that could turn hostile to Western foreigners. If Orientalist assumptions inflected the writings of Western collectors, their observations and practices also disrupted easy generalizations. The multiethnicity of China's regions, the deals that had to be negotiated in different locations, the ways in which even the presumed appropriation of knowledge forced hybridization—all illuminate the creation of global networks being born within the structures of unequal power.[140]

Collecting Animals

In this age of connectivity, collecting and displaying animals also expanded rapidly. Although traveling menageries of exotic animals had provided common forms of entertainment and entrepreneurial activity for centuries, animal collections in zoological parks eclipsed the appeal of menageries in the latter half of the nineteenth century, and new "scientific" zoos became expressions of the comprehensive, systematic, and global collecting that characterized the age.

Jean Delacour exemplified the transnational networks forged through collecting. He created what many regarded as the finest private zoo in the world, and his career illustrates the shift of zoos from private collections to public institutions. Especially renowned as a collector of rare birds, Delacour assembled an array of noncarnivorous animals, such as gibbons, gazelles, kangaroos, flamingos, and cranes, on his estate, Château Clères in Normandy. Owning perhaps five hundred different species of birds, he erected aviaries for smaller birds and took special care of the most rare. On his annual expeditions between 1922 to the late 1930s, especially to tropical lands, he gathered live specimens and distributed them to other collectors—some thirty thousand birds and eight thousand mammals were divided among Paris, London, and New York. Delacour published the most significant handbooks on birds for Southeast Asia and elsewhere. In 1939, on the eve of World War II, his estate was burned, and he fled to New York to work for the Bronx Zoo, the American Museum of Natural History, and eventually the Los Angeles Museum. After World War II, he labored to restore his chateau and zoological park at Clères and, upon his death, left it to the state of France.[141] Zoological parks, and aquariums, like world's fairs, natural history museums, and botanical gardens, sprang from a transnational exchange of expertise, even as they were also propelled by national, local, or personal pride in their construction.

Zoos spread as part of the transition from a rural, agricultural world to an urban, industrial one. They grew fastest in countries caught up in these changes. By 1903 a guidebook to Europe could describe sixteen zoological gardens in Germany, four in Britain, and four in France; zoos had opened also in Antwerp, Amsterdam, and Rotterdam. Under the leadership of the Bengali scientist Ram

Brahma Sanyal, the Calcutta Zoological Gardens distinguished itself both in its animal displays and its research. The first zoo in the United States, whose founders looked to European models, opened in 1874 in Philadelphia. Many other US cities followed—Kansas City, Baltimore, Providence, St. Louis, St. Paul—as civic boosters incorporated zoos along with botanical gardens into designs for new municipal parks. An official National Zoological Garden opened in Pretoria in 1916. In Europe and elsewhere, zoos often emerged from private collections (as in Delacour's case) sustained by private patronage, while in the United States they emerged from civic movements to create public parks. World's fairs began to add zoos, and these sometimes became permanent. The 1931 exhibition in Paris that housed a display of exotic animals, for example, became the basis for the zoo in the park of Vincennes. In the early twentieth century, professional zoos that tried to project a conservationist mission could be found throughout the world.[142]

Such collections turned animals into representations of both the interconnectivity of the globe and its regional diversities. Carl Hagenbeck's famous Tierpark that opened outside of Hamburg in the early twentieth century advanced new models, influential internationally, of intertwining botanical gardens, natural history displays, and animal exhibits to create broad representations of other parts of the world. Using rows of tiered enclosures in which moats and screens remained invisible to the public, the Tierpark offered an African and an Arctic "panorama" featuring animals in their "natural" habitat. After the opening of Hagenbeck's sensational exhibits in 1907, visual simulations of natural landscapes through panoramas and other features became the obligatory backdrops for animal collections and for the displays of humans *(Völkerschauen)* that Hagenbeck also featured.

Infused with the age's mania for taxonomy and distinguishing themselves from the menageries of an earlier era, zoos claimed the status of scientific displays that would encourage research and educate the public in biology and natural history. In fact, their displays increasingly offered the veneer of science more than its substance. According to the analysis of Eric Baratay and Elisabeth Hardouin-Fugier, the argument for the scientific utility of zoos was widely advanced, but actually zoos were far outpaced in scientific achievement by universities and museum laboratories.[143]

"Paradise," a wildlife panorama constructed for Carl Hagenbeck's Tierpark outside of Hamburg, 1908. Opened one year earlier, the Tierpark showed animals (and often people) in extravagant "realistic" settings and influenced the look of zoos throughout the world. (Hagenbeck-Archiv, Tierpark Hagenbeck)

Zoos struggled to balance science with spectacle. One elephant, after all, would attract more visitors than even the most complete and careful array of small mammals. Urban dwellers had become accustomed to being entertained by circus animals, traveling menageries, and exotic creatures in pubs and public parks. World's fairs also conditioned expectations of exotic sensationalism. Zoos had to compete, and the tension between scientific education and audience appeal was difficult to manage. Albert Geoffroy Saint-Hilaire, director of Paris's Jardin d'Acclimatation in the late nineteenth century, tried to advance the scientific agenda that his father and grandfather had pursued but felt forced, when faced with bankruptcy, to add sensational ethnographic exhibitions—of Nubians, Eskimos, Argentine gauchos, and dwarfs whom he named the "kingdom of Lilliput." Ota Benga, an African Pygmy, was exhibited at the Bronx Zoo briefly in 1906, but zoo directors generally tried to avoid the ethnographic displays of live people that had become so popular on world's fair midways. Most zoos never resorted to the diving horses and water-sliding elephants featured at Coney Island and other amusement parks, but zoos nevertheless steered a wobbly course between science and showmanship. When the National Zoo of the United States was established in 1889, it proclaimed its goals as both "the advancement of science" and "the recreation of the people."[144]

Zoos were often supported, in part, by visitors' fees, and one way that they attracted audiences was by simulating familiar miniworlds. They did this in a number of ways. Projecting a politics of hierarchy, zoological collections positioned the collector and audience as master over all creatures—the outrageously exotic and the commonplace, the huge and the tiny, the fearsome and the timid. They structured memorable, if biologically erroneous, lessons about social hierarchy. The lion, for example, was the "king" of beasts. They often projected a sentimentalized view of animals. Largely urban zoo-goers, after all, had little direct experience with animals and found them most interesting when they were anthropomorphized. Cages and confines became larger so they could house animals in "families" whose activities were then described to match the prevailing assumptions about human emotions and gender roles.

The explosion of zoos, large and small, created a surge in demand for "exotic" animals (zoos of the period seldom contained common farm animals). In response, dense transnational networks formed to facilitate trade in animals from distant lands, a trade that depended heavily on the growth of commercial infrastructure, such as the Suez Canal, and on colonial power. Such networks included entrepreneurs, shipping companies, local administrators, and local procurers who brokered trades, found reliable assistants, and mediated cultural misunderstandings of all kinds.

Hamburg became one of the most important nodes for animal collecting. Carl Hagenbeck, whose father had been a fishmonger in that city, began to buy animals to build his local menagerie while still a teenager and quickly branched out to broker animals throughout the world. Teaming up with some Italian explorers in the 1860s, he arranged a huge shipment of African wildlife—elephants, giraffes, ostriches, lions, hyenas—that attracted widespread publicity and made him famous. By the mid-1880s he and his family had orchestrated the collection and dispersion of over a thousand lions, three hundred camels, one hundred and fifty giraffes, tens of thousands of moneys and birds, and thousands of reptiles. His animal business became part of a larger entertainment empire that included traveling circuses and ethnographic exhibits as well as his Tierpark, which opened in 1907 and became celebrated for its "natural" settings with background panoramas.[145] In his animal-trade business, Hagenbeck also supplied the kinds of "curious" human specimens he displayed in his own circuses and zoo in Hamburg. Charles Reiche, a German immigrant to New York City, set up a similar animal-trade business near Hanover, contracted agents in Egypt and Ceylon, and supplied much of the US market. German animal dealers, in fact, dominated the global wildlife trade until World War I.[146]

After the Great War the German networks began to fall apart. Germany lost its colonies; its shipping companies suffered from the war; hoof-and-mouth disease prompted new regulations on animal importation. The expansion of demand by private collectors, amusement venues, and zoos, however, continued. A new generation of animal collectors, especially the American Frank Buck, turned collecting into a celebrity career. Buck capitalized on the decline of the German networks and spent his career gathering animals from South Asia and the East Indies. Zoos also got directly into the act, as animal-hunting expeditions brought favorable publicity. The US National Zoo's director, William M. Mann, himself headed expeditions to collect animals in Tanganyika, the Dutch East Indies, and Liberia. Seeking both publicity and animals, however, Mann's trips mainly garnered the former. On the trip to Batavia (now Jakarta), his wife's journal recorded that the group found "almost as many animal collectors in towns as animals."[147]

One of the people Mann hired in Borneo, Liang Gaddi Sang, exemplifies the global nature of animal collecting. Born in Borneo but living mostly in Siam, Gaddi was employed at various times by the governments of Malay and Siam, the US Fish Commissioner, the Crown Prince Leopold of Belgium, and the British Museum.[148]

The proliferation of zoos and the huge global trade in birds, mammals, and fish destroyed living creatures at an almost incomprehensible rate. To collector networks, natural abundance seemed limitless. If four animals died for every one successfully transported for display (and many more died once they entered their permanent confinements), most animal traders calculated only the financial loss. In fact, the huge decline in populations of certain birds and mammals could even provide new justifications for zoos, which began to emphasize preservation despite the appalling death rates that the animal trade and confinement in most zoos produced.

As the transnational circuits of animal collectors and traders became more ruthlessly efficient and threatened certain species, they generated global organizations aimed at curbing abuses. The numbers of transnational groups and agreements devoted to preservation multiplied, especially in those very countries whose citizens were most active in the destruction. During the nineteenth century, animal protection societies grew in many European and American cities, and their leaders became part of a transnational network of reformers, some of whom also embraced vegetarianism and extended their animal protection societies into colonial areas. In 1903 British and American naturalists established the Society for the Preservation of the Wild Fauna of the Empire to foster preservation in Africa. T. Gilbert Pearson, a founder of the National Audubon Society, formed the International Council for Bird Preservation in London in 1922.[149] A 1930 international convention prohibited killing certain kinds of whales, and in 1933 a Convention Relative to the Preservation of Fauna and Flora in Their Natural State was adopted.

The transnational circulation of ideas about natural preservation, however, also intertwined with discourses of nation, empire, and race. Hunters and hikers concerned with maintaining vigorous lifestyles often spearheaded efforts to establish game reserves and national parks in order to regularize rules of use. In Africa, India, and elsewhere in the colonial world, such reserves turned indigenous hunters into "poachers" on European-controlled hunting lands. In these areas, animal hunting became an important recreation for imperial officials, who collected personal trophies or built collections for imperial natural history museums. Preservation therefore often had an adverse effect on the self-sufficiency of indigenous peoples and particularly on their nutrition. Preservationists frequently invoked their special interest in the advancement of science. After considerable international pressure to protect the dwindling gorilla population and enable the work of scientific expeditions, for example, King Albert of Belgium established in the Congo in 1925 the National Park Albert, the first national park in Africa. In colonial areas, facilitating hunting and science often went hand in hand with racial restriction.

Romanticized attachments to natural settings and animals commonly constructed preservation efforts as necessary to promote national and racial destiny. In the early twentieth century in California, Germany, South Africa, and elsewhere, eugenic societies and preservationists had overlapping constituencies. The creation of national parks in Africa provides an example. Although game reserves had been established in South Africa before World War I, the upsurge of Afrikaner nationalism after the war spurred new aesthetic and practical arguments for the creation of a larger national park. Kruger National Park, which restricted use by black Africans, was created in 1926 as a white space in which white tourists could reimagine and nostalgically celebrate their ancestors' settlement of the wildlife-rich territory.[150]

Collectors and exhibitors devised fairs, museums, gardens, and zoos as nodes that they hoped might, in some tangible form, represent "the world" to viewers. Often these forms of collecting blurred together. Fairs featured museums, zoos, and gardens that sometimes became more permanent institutions. Zoos grew to feature gardens, and gardens added zoos. All exhibitions claimed to advance science, instruct visitors about the world, and entertain, even though such goals often ran at cross-purposes. Many of the conventions developed in these exhibitions also intersected with the worlds of amusement parks, movies, and popular fiction. Such collections, preponderant in the West but following networks of imperial power and trade into many other areas of the world, attempted to establish categories, to universalize knowledge, and thus to control representation. Constructed within imperial and evolutionary visions of the world, they often projected interlocking sets of hierarchies: "Civilized" Europeans who embraced science, machinery, and progress stood in evolutionary progression over primitives who would slowly change or die. The rational order imposed within gardens tamed nature's apparent anarchy. Humans stood as the masters of the animal world.

Still, networks forged by acts of collecting had more complex characteristics than simply the production of hegemonies. Collectors came from all kinds of origins and roamed the world out of all sorts of personal and sponsored motivations. Collections, after all, could be assembled in diverse places, and they could travel and change over time. Even fairs, static in time and place, involved dense webs of exchange. People, plants, animals, objects, and ideas were all on the move and, perhaps, on the move again. Adventurers, wealthy patrons, eccentrics, corporate enterprises, diverse institutes, and governments relied on global exchanges to produce their assemblages. Collecting and displaying thus involved not only dominion but myriad interactions that, on many levels, shrunk the world.

. . .

These institutions of display—fairs, museums, botanical and zoological gardens—illustrate the mutually constitutive discourses of nation, empire, and world. Imperial and national rivalries and glory propelled institutions and elites not just to draw from but also to outperform their peers. But each node of exhibition and collection took shape within and depended upon transnational circuits of expertise and acquisition.

Exhibitionary nodes also, as has been seen, combined rational classification with spectacle. They drew from the latest of scientific knowledge and technological invention but merged these wonders into the emotional pleasures honed in amusement parks. Great halls exemplifying hierarchies of classification and the disciplinary structures of professionalism were interspersed with exotic temptations projecting the unstable meanings and ambiguities compatible with porous social formations. Both reason and spectacle proved central to the cultural circulations that produced new global imaginaries. No single projection could necessarily contain or control the cacophony of cultural meanings that became a feature of the era.

4. Circuits of Expertise

THE collection of data and the sharing of technical expertise, so important to exhibitions, were hallmarks of the transnational professional associations that emerged in this era. The new professionals of the late nineteenth century generally embraced a scientific, positivistic faith: if sufficient data on a particular question could be collected, the information could then be ordered, analyzed, and used to solve problems in the natural and social worlds. In this great task, the divisions of religion, ideology, and even national loyalties might be put aside as specialists constructed common understandings of statistics and science. Nature might be engineered for human benefit; the social sphere might be reordered to eliminate gross injustice; epidemic disease might be eradicated. The new professionals, who energetically worked to build transnational epistemic communities, generally embraced the idea that global evolutionary progress could be guided by the authority of their expertise.

In the late nineteenth century, international congresses of several scientific disciplines (mathematics, statistics, chemistry, philosophy) began to meet, and many launched projects to compile international catalogs or bibliographies. At the same time, the opening of universities in Western Europe to foreign nationals contributed to transnational encounters, as did the spread of translation and publication. Through these professional connections, specializations in old and new disciplinary categories reordered the sciences, social sciences, and humanities.

Those who constructed circuits of expert knowledge claimed they could assemble observations from around the globe and extend their expertise by using far-flung networks in which localized "facts" could be compared, tested, confirmed, and connected together. Experts in the colonizing West often appeared to dominate the circuitry, but many leaders and intellectuals throughout the world also embraced ideas about improvement through science and expertise. The allure of transnational science emerged partly out of self-defense against more technically advanced opponents and partly from fascination with the idea of a universal scientific project.

Many governments encouraged their citizens to embrace transnational science and technology. The Great Reforms of Tsar Alexander II in Russia during the 1860s and 1870s sought to wed Russian nationalism to Europeanization, and midcentury Ottoman rulers also launched Tanzimat, a modernization campaign centered on military strength but also assuming broader scope. The Meiji government in Japan embraced the introduction of Western science and sent its famed forty-eight-person commission led by Iwakura Tomomi to visit the United States and the major cities of Europe during 1871–1873. This Iwakura mission produced sixty-eight volumes of diaries, documents, commentaries, and special reports designed to assess practices in the West and their applications to Japan. In China after the Taiping Rebellion, the Qing rulers and educated elites encouraged translations of basic scientific texts, such as Joseph Edkins's *Primers for Science Studies* (1886), later published as *Primers of Western Learning* (1898).[151] King Chulalongkorn of Siam embraced administrative and architectural Westernization. The Porfiriato in Mexico had its ruling elite of *científicos*. The positivists who shaped the Brazilian republic in 1891 placed the motto "Ordem e Progresso" (Order and Progress) on the country's new flag. The Japanese victory in the Russo-Japanese War of 1905 held global significance to those who aspired to resist or best Europeans through technological acquisition and adaptation. In the interwar era, nationalist leaders in India, Korea, and elsewhere sought to blend Western science and technology with their distinctive heritages. Building upon and learning from transnational communities of expertise was a global phenomenon—a "shared developmentalist project" that transcended discursive boundaries of East versus West and blurred lines between programs that could be called capitalist, corporate, socialist, statist, or some version of "national strengthening."[152]

As these examples suggest, there was a tension between transnational professionalism and national or imperial goals. Disciplinary specialization did not rule out national distinctions, and different national groups sought recognition for their particular models in the production and dissemination of knowledge. The tensions of nationalism, however, could be mediated through the circuits of experts who, even if anchored in national institutions and different cultural styles, might study in foreign universities, travel to world congresses, and exchange

A Japanese rendering of the departure from Yokohama to the United States of Japan's first extensive foreign mission, headed by Prince Iwakura Tomomi, Ambassador Extraordinary and Plenipotentiary, in 1871. Iwakura's mission, which was gone for nearly two years and studied practices that might help Japan to modernize, visited cities in the United States, Western Europe, Russia, Egypt, South and Southeast Asia, and China. (Private Collection/The Bridgeman Art Library)

views through international journals. The effects of such mediating circuits were neither predictable nor uniform. As Peter Wagner writes, "Transnational orientations could take the form of intellectual interaction, either to widen and refocus debates, or to gain a stronger position for an individual approach within the national field."[153]

Transnational epistemic communities thus could undermine national projects through hybrid borrowing or reinforce them through the hardening of differences—or they could do both at once. Louis Pasteur's breakthroughs in bacteriology, for example, boosted French national prestige, facilitated its colonial strategy, and fostered transnational research networks. As in other realms of interaction, claims to universality and to national and imperial distinctiveness often fit together. Indeed, a country's highest expression of nationalism often arose from the claims to universality embedded in its scholarly discourses.

Even as scientists imagined globalized circuits of knowledge, they constructed discourses of difference. Michael Adas has shown how in the West the use of machinery came to be an indicator of the "measure of men," the most important indicator that supposedly marked the superiority of the West over the rest. Africans, for example, were widely represented as incapable of developing a technological civilization, and Westerners who found archeological evidence of massive architectural and engineering feats, as in present day Zimbabwe, wrongly attributed such ruins to the influence of outsiders. One of the most common tropes in Western imperialist accounts involved showing some small wonder of technology (a rifle, a phonograph, a camera) to preindustrial people and describing their astonishment.[154] The acquisition of Western science and technology became an important marker of progress in the narrative that dominated professionalism.

Western historians, themselves privileging scientific and technological measures as the truest gauge of human achievement, once took for granted that modern knowledge had begun in the West and had then diffused into "backward" regions. This story of the spread of enlightenment was itself related to justifications for the colonial project.

Postcolonial critique has, however, challenged such premises. In their counternarratives, some scholars have represented networks of science and technical expertise as purveyors of abstracted and often inappropriate "imperial knowledge" that vied with more contextual and localized knowledge. Such scholarship may imply a global/local dichotomy in which the global was the imperial enemy of the local.

Other postcolonial scholars, however, have emphasized "co-production" between the transnational and local realms. They argue that even in a world of vastly unequal power and of racial and imperial hierarchies, good science depended on co-constructed circuits that could accommodate the experimentation, comparison, and collaboration that transnational connections facilitated.[155] As participants in building circuits of expertise on radio waves, for example, the Bengali scientist J. C. Bose, the Italian inventor Guglielmo Marconi, and the Serbian-American Nikola Tesla were all important to the late nineteenth-century transnational breakthroughs in research.

This section builds on the framework of coproduction. If circuits of knowledge often projected imperial and hierarchical assumptions, localized interactions also altered both findings and implementations. Even as scientists tended to endorse the idea of a common transnational language and methodology, differentiated and coproduced expressions on the ground often reshaped their sense of commonalities. While keeping in mind asymmetries of power when analyzing epistemic currents, then, the discussion that follows emphasizes to the themes of coproduction and differentiated commonalities.[156]

Scientists, Surveyors, and Engineers

In 1870 a proponent of the idea that the earth was flat bet five hundred pounds sterling that no one could scientifically prove the earth's curvature in a body of water. British naturalist and professional surveyor Alfred Russel Wallace rose to the challenge. He set up an experiment along six miles of the Bedford Level, in Norfolk, demonstrated a discrepancy in heights of objects at each end, and was judged the winner. The outcome, however, only further energized the flat-earth proponent, who denounced and sued Wallace for years into the future.[157] Flat-earthers, who retained a transnational group of supporters, could not accept the world as a globe, despite the repetition of this "Bedford Level Experiment" in many other places on into the twentieth century.

The theory of a round earth, of course, had predated Columbus's voyage, and one might have expected that the famous explorations of the seventeenth and eighteenth centuries would have worn down beliefs about a flat earth. But scientific revisions of deeply rooted "truths" about the makeup of the world never come easily.

The global spread of new scientific methods created backlash and uncertainty everywhere. What might be the implications for humans of a round earth? Or of the accumulating evidence confirming an evolutionary view of biology, another view with which Wallace was associated? Could science (with its view of how the earth and its creatures slowly evolved over far more than seven days) be reconciled with the Bible or the Quran or other spiritual systems? Despite the storms of controversy raised by such questions, prevalent even (or especially) in those areas in the forefront of scientific discovery, confidence about the reliability of scientific technique spread rapidly. Scientists (the word *scientist* was coined in the 1830s and widely used by the late nineteenth century) created webs of understandings and techniques that sought to corral the world's natural systems into arenas of specialized knowledge tamed for human use. Guided by emerging professional standards and goaded by naysayers, expertise became transnational.

To comprehend the earth in scientific terms required extensive mapping and surveying with scientific techniques such as Wallace had employed. Although the mapping of trade routes had long been commonplace, the latter half of the nineteenth century brought precision mapping on a different scale than before. In this period, experts explored and surveyed the last remaining unmapped areas of the world in the name of science and usually of empire. New techniques of triangulation produced very large-scale field surveys, and such scientific surveys often included the accumulation of detailed data on the people, animals, plants, and natural features of a region.

The scientific expeditions that surveyed and described the remaining "unknown" world produced heroic figures, especially in those national states and empires that might reap benefits. Britain's Great Trigonometrical Survey of India, for example, became one of the celebrated attempts of the early nineteenth century to create a vast archive of knowledge for imperial purposes. Then, between 1863 and 1885, Britain hired native Indians to measure and map the million-and-and half square miles of the trans-Himalayan region. Code-named "pundits," these mappers took the disguise of pilgrims and risked their lives and health to record accurate measurements of the territory, which technically belonged to China. On his first surveying trip, Nain Singh walked twelve hundred miles recording his measured steps by using specially constructed rosary beads; he subsequently won international fame and awards from the Royal Geographical Society. Pundit Sarat Chandra Das wrote two books and inspired the character of Hurree Chunder Mookerjee in *Kim,* Rudyard Kipling's famous novel about the Great Game in Central Asia. The pundit known as Kinthup (or K.P.) returned to India after four years of harrowing danger, during which he and his colleagues mapped the course of the Brahmaputra from its source into India. Although their activities had remained secret during the mapping, these and other pundits soon became highly acclaimed because their technical contributions had significantly enhanced survey techniques and their endurance epitomized imperial greatness.

European expeditions into sub-Saharan Africa also took advantage of local expertise. In trying to settle a dispute over the origin of the Nile, for example, Richard Francis Burton relied upon Arab informants while his rival John Hanning Speke relied on Ugandans. Their competition erupted into high drama when Speke shot himself in advance of a public showdown with Burton. Henry Morton Stanley's attempt to settle this controversy would explode into one of the most sensational stories of the late nineteenth century.[158]

Land surveys and scientific commissions proliferated in the late nineteenth century, as the ambitions of national states intertwined with the discourses of expertise that sought to make the whole world legible. Only governments could afford the expense that extensive triangulations entailed, and only national states had the compelling interest in developing systematic and uniform statistical information. Both Russia and the United States, for example, commissioned scientific surveys to map and consolidate knowledge about their inland empires. John Wesley Powell, who would later serve as director of the US Geological Survey, famously explored the Colorado River and Grand Canyon in the 1860s. Various US biological surveys, which preceded the creation of the Fish and Wildlife Service Bureau in 1939, were likewise guided by scientific agendas. Russian surveyors gathered information on Siberia, as well as bordering lands in Central Asia and Tibet. Napoleon III created the Scientific Commission of Mexico to "lift up this unknown world and deliver it from chaos." This commission (1864–1867), which coincided with the ill-fated French attempt to establish an empire in Mexico under Maximilian, floundered in its extravagant ambitions but did issue a lavish sixteen-volume report along with important reference works on the botany and zoology of Mexico. Mapping the most inaccessible parts of the world became "global sport in both Norway and Sweden," as competing explorers ventured north of Siberia across the Northeast Passage, north of Canada across the Northwest Passage, into Central Asia, and also entered the race to the South Pole.[159]

Colonial administration heightened the need for surveys of land and people, and each colonial power adopted some form of expert commission to collect and evaluate information on acquired territories.[160] The United States carried out extensive data collection in the Philippines after 1898. In these reports, the array of landscapes and peoples that characterized the various territories of the archipelago came to buttress the views that ranked peoples of the world into a racial hierarchy according to skin color, physical features, type of agricultural practice, and gender norms. The modernizing elites in Manila also had a stake in such surveys, as they worked to assert their own capacities for scientific administration and for larger degrees of self-governance. Even though surveys were legitimating tools of colonial states, they often attracted help from subjects who were engaged in their own nation-building and career-enhancing projects.[161]

International agreements such as the many boundary-drawing treaties of this period—for example, the Anglo-Afghan Treaty of 1875, the Canadian-US agreements, and the post–World War I territorial settlements made at Versailles—also depended on more accurate, common maps. The idea that the entire world could be "known" provided a strong pillar not only of the age's confidence in measurement but also of the conviction that the world, through science, might converge into a unified, if hierarchically ordered, whole. Mapping projects provide clear examples of how nationalism, imperialism, and transnationalism often stood not in opposition but as codependents.

As empty spaces on world maps became filled and calibrated, the history of humankind through archeology likewise became a field for global, rather than simply local, knowledge. More precisely, local knowledge interacted with and helped to shape emerging transnational disciplinary practices. German archeologists were especially important in this late nineteenth-century development. Alexander Conze became the first to include photography in reports of archaeological excavation; Carl Humann, an important developer of scientific techniques of excavation, worked throughout the Ottoman Empire and cooperated with archeologist Osman Hamdi Bey, founder of the Istanbul Archeology Museum. Teobert Maler, born of German parents, came to Mexico with an Austrian army supporting Maximilian, stayed to become a citizen of Mexico, conducted a survey of Palenque for Harvard's Peabody Museum, and devoted his life to archeological study of the Mayan civilization. Heinrich Schliemann, who had traveled to California and made a fortune in banking during the Gold Rush, conducted significant but also highly sensationalized digs to uncover the sites of Homer's Troy. In the decades before World War I, Germans developed a keen interest in the Bible as a historical text and, consequently, in Middle Eastern archeology.[162] Worldly scientists illuminated natural and human history, but their activities also often led to the plundering of local sites, the alienation of artifacts, geopolitical positioning, and even hucksterism in the name of science. The careers of these German explorer-scientists suggest the globality of this new age of investigation, as well as the uneven pace of identifying professionalized disciplinary practices.

Such examples tend to confirm that surveying and archeological missions often bent scientific knowledge toward the purpose of Westerners. Naming is one way of claiming; controlling representation (in geographic space as well as in historical time) is the most profound form of power. Still, the new cultures of professionalism were not simply one-way impositions. Building transnational circuits of knowledge rested on local expertise and on various degrees of coproduction. Moreover, globe-trotting professionals might become ever more cosmopolitan as they cultivated their abilities to thrive in unfamiliar terrain or to succeed as cultural mediators.

Engineering, often considered to be applied science, became one of the most hallowed professions in this instrumentalist age. Sandford Fleming, a Canadian born in Scotland who was a member of over seventy international societies, a surveyor and mapmaker, a champion of the Prime Meridian reform movement, and a facilitator of the transoceanic cable line across the Pacific, saw his profession of engineering as a neutral peacemaker in the social turbulence of the industrial era. In 1876 he wrote that engineers were not usually "gifted with many words" but that they did battle against "nature in her wild state" in order to "smooth the path on which others are to tread." "It is their privilege to stand between these two great forces, capital and labour, and by acting justly at all times between employer and the employed, they may hope to command the respect of those above them equally with those under them."[163] Moreover, the amazing technical feats associated with construction of the Suez Canal in the 1860s and the Panama Canal in the early twentieth century became emblematic of the claim that engineering could draw the world geographically closer together. Civil engineers working on projects such as canals, roads, and bridges were among the most active professionals to form transnational networks that were both personal and professional.

Although this ideal of the politically neutral engineer skilled in universally useful techniques circulated widely, many of the huge turn-of-the-century projects employed laboring people in ways that could scarcely "command respect" from all. The building of the Panama Canal, for example, orchestrated one of the largest, most global labor mobilizations in modern history. With jobs and compensation scales arranged according to race and nationality (West Indians received the most perilous assignments for the lowest pay), the tens of thousands of imported workers from every continent paid a huge, generally overlooked price in life and limb, even as engineers reveled in accolades. Other colonial construction projects assembled similarly global workforces, not to serve the uplifting goals so often proclaimed in professional circles but to drive down costs in the increasingly globalized labor market.[164]

As engineers did battle against "wild nature" and sometimes against cadres of laborers, their efforts were almost always justified within an entangled rationale linking service to the world with service to empire and nation. The case of India provides an example. Under the rule of both the East India Company (EIC) and then the British crown, India became a laboratory for experiments in the application of scientific and technical expertise. The construction of canals, irrigation works (for agriculture), and railroads was central to the British conception of imperial development, yet this transportation infrastructure necessitated large numbers of civil engineers who could develop methods suitable to local conditions. Before the EIC relinquished its rule of India to the crown in 1858, it had established engineering colleges at Mumbai (Bombay), Roorkee, Calcutta, Roona, and Madras. The heavy emphasis on state-directed engineering projects accelerated in the latter half of the nineteenth century (an emphasis that ironically emerged simultaneously with Britain's highly visible public promotion of laissez-faire theories). The Famine Commission of 1880 especially pressed for a range of applied specialists, operating on the village level, and suggested that their success would be a test of imperial benevolence. After more end-of-the-century famines, the new viceroy, George Curzon, proclaimed that the advancement of practical science would be his highest priority, and he created a Board of Scientific Advice that lasted until 1924. The model of state-sponsored engineering schools and ambitious projects, pioneered in India, came to be replicated in Britain itself and elsewhere in the empire. Indian graduates became part of a broad transnational network of experts from everywhere on the globe who shared ideas about technical training and infrastructure development.[165]

Britain, the United States, France, and Germany each adopted somewhat different models for the training, credentialing, and employment of engineers. More important than such differences, however, was the proliferation throughout Europe and colonial areas of technical schools, each with specializations relevant to the respective extractive and industrial strengths of each area. National and imperial rivalry thus fueled the transnational spread and exchange of technical practices. Building canals and railway beds, regulating river flow, and draining wetlands for agriculture all fit the export-oriented goals of colonial powers and often fit within the modernizing visions of elites outside of Europe as well. By the early 1880s, for example, most irrigation engineers in Egypt were Egyptians schooled in the techniques of the École Polytechnique in France, and the surplus of Egyptian-trained experts served throughout the region for decades.[166]

China's technical education likewise arose within the context of both transnational networks of expertise and nation-building imperatives. The Chinese "self-strengthening" movement, launched after the second Opium War, emphasized military technology, engineering, and basic science. The Fuzhou Naval Yard, one of the most important industrial sites in late-Qing China, hired foreigners to teach many of the technical courses related to ship building. Similarly, the expansion of its Jiangnan Arsenal, which focused on training related to technology and machinery, by 1892 produced forty-seven kinds of machinery under the supervision of foreign technicians and successfully produced rapid-firing machine guns for China's coastal defense. New schools, encouraged by the

Chinese government, embraced Western science and emphasized engineering, even as increasingly more Chinese students also studied abroad. Although China's defense industries faltered in the face of the country's declining resources and defeat in wars, they exemplify how important access to transnational networks of experts became in helping to determine which countries flourished and which floundered in the late nineteenth century. In the late 1920s and early 1930s the Nationalist government in China worked with German experts to try to shift industrial infrastructure away from treaty ports to presumably less vulnerable interior locations, but this program also stalled as war approached.[167]

Japanese scientists worked very successfully to join transnational scientific circles. Self-confidently embracing attributes of modernity, the state promoted participation in technical and professional conferences, issued the extensive reports of the Iwakura mission, and sponsored student study outside of Japan. Japan's scientists made special contributions to the science of seismology, among other fields.[168] Japan's modernizers and scientists did not regard such transnational participation as Westernization, because they sought to import Western practices not as a coherent entity but as piecemeal adaptations. The newspaper *Nihon,* published on the day the new Japanese constitution was announced in 1889, stated, "We esteem Western science, economics and industry. These, however, ought not be adopted simply because they are Western; they ought to be adopted only if they can contribute to Japan's welfare."[169] The overlap between transnational circuits and state-building projects could hardly be better expressed.

Engineering projects often focused on controlling water resources. Hydroelectric dams proliferated in the late nineteenth century, especially in the United States, Scandinavia, and the Alps, as a result of improvements in turbines and transmission lines. An era of large-scale dam building began in earnest with the construction in 1931 of Hoover Dam, which was completed in the United States in 1936 and thought to be the largest man-made structure in the world and a marvel of modern engineering. Other monster-size dams followed: Shasta Dam in California and Grand Coulee Dam in Washington. Meanwhile, American engineers were helping lead the construction of the Dneprostroi Dam in Ukraine, Soviet Union, in the late 1920s and early 1930s. General Electric Company manufactured the dam's first huge power generators. At the time of its construction, the Dneprostroi Dam claimed to be the largest in Europe. France completed the Kembs Dam in 1932 on the Rhine River, which had been a site for hydroelectric power since the late nineteenth century and would become thoroughly regulated by a dam-and-lock system after World War II. Uses of the Rhine (but unfortunately not its protection, until more recently) lay in the hands of engineers of the Rhine Commission, which, dating back to 1815, was the oldest multistate commission in Europe. In China, engineers for the Nationalist government, inspired by foreign models, as early as the 1920s began plans for a huge dam at Three Gorges on the Yangzi River (a plan ultimately carried out after 1989).[170]

Created under President Franklin Roosevelt's New Deal, the Tennessee Valley Authority (TVA) most fully reflected the vision of top-down planning for the kind of huge projects that technocrats everywhere began to associate with modernization and progress. The TVA married the promise of engineering a system of dams to regulate an entire river system with the hope of engineering human health and prosperity on a broad regional scale. Dams could bring both flood control for agricultural development and inexpensive electrical power for accelerated industrialization. Farmers and workers, region and nation would all supposedly benefit. The TVA model became globally influential, and in the next few decades millions of people would tour its system. TVA's head, David Lilienthal, popularized the idea that dams would bring progress to any country whose wild rivers were "waiting to be controlled by men." His writings were translated into many languages.[171] Although most of the large dam-building projects in the developing world, influenced by the TVA model, came after World War II and often with financing from the World Bank, American, Soviet, Nazi, and other dam-building undertakings during the 1930s confirm the importance of a transnationally influential developmentalist project not necessarily tied to particular forms of national states. From the late nineteenth century on, for example, German engineers had been reshaping the Rhine, and under the Third Reich they drained marshlands to the east while also advancing ideas about reshaping both the landscape and its people. Each state, of course, manifested the commonality of water-related developmentalism in somewhat different figurations.

Despite the disruptions associated with the First World War and the waning prestige of the German academic institutions that had often taken a lead in professionalization, the interwar era became the heyday of transnational professional associations, especially in the natural sciences. Under the auspices of the

International Research Council, formed in Brussels in 1919, international unions were formed for astronomy, biology, chemistry, geophysics, and physics in 1919, and for geography, radio science, mechanics, soil sciences, and microbiology in the 1920s. In 1931 the Research Council regrouped as the International Council of Scientific Unions (ICSU), headquartered in Paris, and continued to foster its networks. The Comintern also sponsored its own transnational professional circuits, the most important of which advocated the complementary scientific nature of the biological and physical sciences.

Walking the line between robust universalistic scientific communities and the hierarchies of empire seldom came easily outside of Europe. Most Indian scientists, for example, had experienced second-class status in British scientific and administrative circles. In 1876 Mahendra Lal Sircar consequently had helped launch the Indian Association for the Cultivation of Science (IACS), a group independent from colonial authority that eventually affiliated with the physics and chemistry department at Calcutta University. The group ultimately produced scientists who received global recognition, such as the 1930 Nobel Prize winner C. V. Raman, the first Asian scientist so honored. P. C. Ray, one of the great chemists of the turn of the century, who had been heavily influenced by developments in Germany, insisted in 1918 that "the Hindus had a very large hand in the cultivation of the experimental sciences" and wrote his monumental *A History of Hindu Chemistry* (1902–1909) to carefully document the scientific heritage of his nation, which remained under colonial rule.[172] Prominent Indian scientists, such as Ray's student Meghnad Saha, went on to advocate national advancement through the use of science for industrial promotion. Even when seeing science as wedded to particular national goals, however, Indian scientists such as Saha asserted the belief that science, as a transnational endeavor, should stand above particularity and draw the world together. Saha wrote that "rivalry amongst nations should give way to cooperative construction and the politician should hand over his functions to an international board of trained scientific industrialists, economists and eugenicists who would think in terms of the whole world."[173] Muslim and Hindu scientists sometimes formed distinct groups with different goals, but Rabindra Narayan Ghosh, who wrote on the use of scientific method, felt that cultural unity could be found in technological achievement. Without repudiating religious backgrounds, he taught, people could find common ground in scientific rationality.

The scientific and technical endeavors of this period were thus not necessarily Western impositions foisted on the unwilling. Although unequal and frequently in service of empire, professional circuits could generate sparks of transformative innovation from diverse locations. Ashis Nandy has suggested, for example, that the creative brilliance of Indian mathematician Srinivasa Aiyangar Ramanujan, who persistently resisted the kinds of proofs demanded by Cambridge professors and instead invoked Hindu deities as the agents for his mathematical breakthroughs, may have stemmed from the rich cultural cross-fertilization in his own life.[174] Epistemic currents, in short, became stronger as their architects became larger in number and more varied in background.

Agricultural and Forestry Sciences

The devastating waves of famine from the 1870s through the turn of the century, particularly in India and China, elicited calls for greater agricultural expertise. These "late Victorian holocausts," to use Mike Davis's term, seem linked to ways in which colonialist policies were changing both the global and the local economic orders. Still, governmental elites and agricultural experts from America and Europe generally promoted the idea that Western science and engineering were the solution, not the problem. Blind to ways in which interaction with the West could often devastate the complex social and economic networks that supported native production and land tenure systems, agronomists allied with engineers to build circuits of knowledge that promised to boost yields, control floods and erosion, and eliminate pests. George Curzon, for example, inaugurated a large number of experimental farms and agricultural colleges in India; a contingent of missionary–soil scientists from the United States went to work in China; Western hydrologists advised how to drain marshland and convert deltas in India and Southeast Asia into farms for rice export. As agricultural experts helped plantation agriculture spread throughout the world, more and more people became enmeshed in labor and commodity markets.[175]

Although Western agricultural experts in the early twentieth century generally worked to enhance the profits earned by export commodities, global networks that introduced new methods could also facilitate an optimal mix of new and old practices. In the Kigezi district of southwestern Uganda, unlike in much

of the colonial world, local farmers rejected colonial land policies and cash crop-
ping yet adapted new soil conservation practices that they layered onto precolonial customs. Their careful and limited interface with networks of agrarian
expertise enabled them to produce farm surpluses even as population grew.[176]

As with agricultural science, the rise of a science of forestry accompanied the
growth of colonial power. In many parts of the world, forests were common
property, or at least different groups of people had access to different uses of the
forest. However, as traditional ways broke down under the globalization of markets, forestry experts increasingly made a case for systematic, top-down intervention to curb the rapid clearing of land and the avarice for extractive products.
The claim that experts backed by the power of states would make wiser use of
resources than would local people bolstered arguments for standardizing and
even commercializing forestry practices.

Interventions in forestry, like those in agriculture, had various effects. Some
changed the land in dramatic and irreversible ways by developing methods of
intensive use that contributed to deforestation globally. Forestry science could
easily work against local groups who lived in or depended upon mixed forests.
US timber experts, for example, devised methods of systematic logging in the
colony of the Philippines. In German East Africa, one study concludes, "scientific forestry" was neither rational nor efficient but simply served the needs of
colonial extractive industries. Colonial forestry experts in Southeast Asia became both advocates and facilitators for the huge rubber plantations that came
to dominate land use there. Throughout the colonial world, European demands
to make space for plantations of sugar, rubber, pineapples, and other commodities took down mixed forests and the lives of people who depended upon them.[177]

In other cases, transnational experience helped forestry experts grasp the
important interrelationships between forests, healthy environments, and culture. The early nineteenth-century German biogeographer Alexander von Humboldt profoundly influenced nineteenth-century visions of the tropics. Born in
Prussia but living for extensive periods in the Americas and Paris, this influential transnational figure had addressed the deleterious consequences of cutting
trees from mountainsides. Of even more significance for forestry was the work of
George Perkins Marsh, the American scientist and US ambassador to Italy from
1861 to 1882. Marsh's influential books *Man and Nature* (1864) and *The Earth as*

Modified by Human Action (1874) examined the global interrelationships among forests, wildlife, watersheds, and healthy communities. His work influenced the German-born Australian acclimatizer Ferdinand von Müller, who championed horticultural connections between California and Australia and helped develop exchanges of seeds and plants, including the Australian eucalyptus varieties that became so widespread in California.[178]

Professionalized forestry services often emerged as transnational coproductions. British colonial officials made tropical forests in India a training ground, and Indian foresters subsequently helped shape forest services in New Zealand, Ceylon, Kenya, Nigeria, and elsewhere. Gifford Pinchot, the founder of the US Forest Service who had previously studied at the French forestry school in Nancy, developed the conservation doctrine of "wise use" that became widely influential in Canada, Australia, and South Africa. The forest services of the major colonial powers watched each other closely and exchanged practices.

The science of forestry thus branched in several directions—toward greater exploitation, toward enhanced sensitivity to ecological interactions, and toward coproduction of practices among colonial and local experts. As in the case of other professionalized circuits, transnational interactions became critical in shaping policies, practices, and debates that historians have too often studied only within the framework of national or imperial histories.

Science in the Social Sphere

In the nineteenth century, close observation, careful documentation, and creative experimentation rapidly changed ideas about the natural world. Alfred Russel Wallace traveled through what is now Malaysia and Indonesia in the late 1850s and early 1860s, collected 125,000 specimens, and carefully observed the differences in their characteristics. He formulated ideas about natural selection and evolutionary theory that his friend, Charles Darwin, was also developing from his famed five-year voyage (1831–1836) on HMS *Beagle*.[179] This revolution in the way scientists thought about the natural world, together with convictions about the efficacy of applying scientific techniques, began to influence what came to be called the "social" realm. In the late nineteenth century, the influence of what has been called "social Darwinism" mixed with philosophies such as

August Comte's "positivism" to influence a larger milieu that forecast evolutionary social improvement through the application of professional expertise.

Daniel T. Rodgers's *Atlantic Crossings* details how the development of industrial capitalism in Europe and North America prompted a transatlantic exchange designed to address common social problems. Intellectuals and practitioners of newly emerging professions such as political economy, sociology, and education addressed questions of public sanitation, vice, labor codes, currency, poverty, housing, disability, and old age. They also debated the role that central governments should play in redressing social ills. Could transnational groups of experts create a "social science"?

Such exchange, of course, did not mean agreement on specific matters, nor did it encompass only Western Europe and the United States. The many transnational conversations that developed over how to tackle social problems certainly did not move toward programmatic cohesion. German social insurance plans introduced in the 1880s, for example, provided an influential model that stood in sharp contrast to experiments with worker's cooperatives or to the more private, corporate-dominated welfare systems developed in the United States. The Soviet government in the interwar period advanced very different socialist models that attracted leaders of Marxist parties to Moscow for study and exchange. But even if particular models varied, the transnational epistemic disciplines now calling themselves "social sciences" did foster some common sets of referents and generally shared the conviction that the whole world, in effect, could become a giant laboratory for experiments in social improvement.[180]

This cross-fertilization of social science networks reached far beyond the Atlantic community, as modernizers in the Ottoman Empire, Japan, China, and Latin America also participated. The Meiji government in Japan after 1870 and the Turkish government of Mustafa Kemal in the interwar era, for example, carefully studied and adapted an array of international models that addressed social problems. Moreover, discussions of social policy often traveled within imperial networks affected by local conditions and also by what Ann Stoler has called the "politics of comparison" among empires. Leaders of the new Soviet Union in the interwar era proclaimed their ability to re-engineer a new social order and even to create a New Man. International conferences, world's fairs, travel, student exchange, and mass publishing created circuits that brought leaders together from around the world.

In the spirit of science, independent fact-gathering organizations burgeoned, especially in the United States. Before World War I, new institutions such as the Russell Sage Foundation, the Brookings Institution, the National Industrial Conference Board, the National Bureau of Economic Research, and the Twentieth Century Fund sought to propel an intellectual revolution based upon the practical application of expertise.[181] The League of Nations enshrined the fact-gathering mentality in its various agencies, especially those dealing with labor and health. Although there was a growing chorus of dissenters who warned against the hubris and inherently antidemocratic tendency of the enshrinement of technocratic expertise, apostles of the new age paid as little heed to the naysayers as did natural scientists to flat-earthers.

Social scientists were especially involved with educational experimentation, and "industrial education" provided one of the important new transnational models during the early twentieth century. Programs of industrial education fit well with the emerging colonial order. The Hampton Institute and the Tuskegee Institute, for example, pioneered industrial schools in the southern United States, in the US colony of the Philippines, in Haiti under US military occupation, in the protectorate of Cuba, and as part of US missionary efforts in Africa. Between 1901 and 1909 German authorities attempted to implant Tuskegee structures in Togo in order to boost cotton production for export. In the early 1920s, well-publicized commissions financed by the Phelps-Stokes Fund encouraged developing industrial education in Africa. The recommendations from these commissions found strong backing in the British colonial office and from John Dube, the president of the South African Native National Congress (later the African National Congress) and James Aggrey of the Gold Coast, who lionized Booker T. Washington's program of educational and economic development. Afro-Cubans also generally welcomed a close connection with Tuskegee because it brought broader awareness of Pan-African ties and allowed them to adapt Tuskegee's models to suit their own aspirations for upward mobility. The links between educational strategies directed toward American Indians, African-Americans, and colonial areas suggest the complex transnational intersections among progressive-era faiths in social science expertise and Christian social-gospel ideas. They also suggest how practices that transnational professional currents carried around the globe might express both Western colonialism and also the anticolonial goals of empowerment that challenged it.[182]

Racial Science

As encounters with racially different people multiplied in this shrinking age, it is hardly surprising that ideas about race figured prominently in all social science discussions. Examined transnationally, no broad brush can paint a characterization of the knowledge systems about race that prevailed from the mid-nineteenth to the mid-twentieth century. For brevity, however, one might tease out four dominant threads: a missionary discourse, a physical anthropology discourse, a discourse of culture, and a discourse exalting race mixture and local empowerment (given various labels, such as *indigenismo*). All four circulated transnationally; they also often blurred and emerged in shadings. All could be found both as justifications for empire and as elements of anti-imperial arguments. But these four competing, and sometimes overlapping, views of the role of race helped construct the language and the understandings of social science and of world history that have long shaped discussions of the past and the present.

The missionary-inspired imperial discourse, especially prevalent in the mid-nineteenth century, held out hope that racial others could be saved and transformed; that all characteristics of their culture could be purged and replaced by enforcing a universalized morality and discipline. William Holden, a British missionary among the Xhosa in Kaffraria, wrote that by breaking the power of chiefs and placing the Xhosa in educational and labor camps, British overseers could guide "the black races . . . to the highest state in the civil and ecclesiastical world." The American founder of the Carlisle Indian boarding school, Captain Richard H. Pratt, put it more succinctly: "Kill the Indian, and save the Man." The violence suggested in such views (and demonstrated in colonial warfare) dripped with sentimentality about the essential equality of humankind. People could be coerced, in effect, into joining the Christian "brotherhood of man."[183]

The "science" of race that emerged in physical anthropology toward the turn of the century did not so much replace such views as layer another set of coercive justifications beside them. If races were, in effect, different competing species, as many social Darwinists argued, then the progress of humanity depended upon the more robust and powerful race taking firm control over others and, in time, dominating the genetic pool. The "race-suicide" theories, which seem to have sparked particular panic among Anglo-American elites, propelled pro-natalist policies directed at the "better" races and policies of destruction or sterilization or draconian control directed at the "lesser." As Theodore Roosevelt proclaimed, "With much of the competition between the races reducing itself to the warfare of the cradle, no race has any chance to win a great place unless it consists of good breeders as well as of good fighters."[184]

Late nineteenth-century scientists (especially biologists and anthropologists) and medical doctors who wrote in terms of "racial type" usually presented racial mixing as degeneration within the human species. They also tended to represent successful nations and states as being ideally coterminous with racial composition. Such notions emerged especially strongly in settler colonies such as the United States, Australia, South Africa, and parts of South America. In these locations, becoming a "white" country seemed so pressing precisely because it was so problematic. Success in creating a white citizenship seemed to forecast national destiny in a "survival-of-the-fittest" world.

As Warwick Anderson and others have pointed out, however, the white body was not a stable signifier, and its biological definitions proved flexible according to location. Whiteness was frequently discussed as a matter of blood and heredity, but it was less a category of origins than a cultural category that connoted health, responsibility, and efficiency. Although *white* was an imprecise term, it nevertheless proved a useful marker in designating progress, along with a particular conception of masculinity, against its "nonwhite" opposite. To "whiten" a population also involved marginalizing, and often feminizing, nonwhite groups that were deemed to be "inefficient" or "degenerate." Racial science, empire, and global commerce all marched hand in hand to create a doctrine of "whiteness" and a racial justification critical to acquiring cheap labor.[185]

In Argentina, Chile, Mexico, Brazil, and elsewhere in Latin America, schemes to "whiten" the population through immigration became a major goal of national state building. As Juan Bautista Alberdi, the famous mid-nineteenth-century Argentine political theorist, put it in 1852, "gobernar es poblar" (to govern is to populate). As the science of race became increasingly elaborated later in the century, Alberdi's dictum seemed ever more urgent. The director of the Museu Nacional do Rio de Janeiro at the turn of the century joined other influential members of the governing elite in proposing that Brazil convert its population from black to white.[186] In Latin America, various incentive programs to attract immigrants from Europe, as well as proposals to "whiten" through modernization and efficiency, drew from and reinforced a discourse of racial hierarchy.

As some late nineteenth-century reformers sought to improve their nations by whitening, many others pursued an associated program. What if professional interventions, with assistance from state power, could strengthen the body politic by improving and standardizing *individual* white bodies? Regeneration not just of the national body but of its individual members might mean that strong white bodies would no longer be confined to temperate climates but could master the tropics and inherit the earth.

As social Darwinists regarded the ultimate triumph of white races throughout the globe as both assured by survival of the fittest and at risk if fitness were not maintained, eugenics became a transnational conversation propelled by organized networks and institutes. Francis Galton, a cousin of Charles Darwin, is regarded as one of the founders of eugenics—the idea that, because of the heritability of physical and intellectual characteristics, humans could be improved by scientific breeding. Eugenic ideas, important to the construction of states and empires, traveled rapidly within elite circles who wished to "better" their populations by preventing interracial unions and by barring the reproduction of those whose supposedly inheritable conditions (such as epilepsy, "feeble-mindedness," even alcoholism) rendered them undesirable. An international literature, circulating especially in the West, sounded alarms about a decline in fertility among European peoples, especially after the huge losses in population associated with World War I, and about the need to "strengthen" populations. This concern reflected anxieties about race and about how the growing participation of white women in public areas and workplaces outside the home might adversely affect reproductive rates.

Eugenics, however, was a big tent, and its supporters by no means all saw the world alike. One branch of eugenics (stronger in the United States, Britain, and Germany) assumed that biology and reproduction controlled destiny. Two Californians, Eugene Gosney and Paul Popenoe established the Human Betterment Foundation in 1928 and published *Sterilization for Human Betterment* (1929). Their book and other publications, which advocated eugenics through sterilization, circulated throughout the world and proved especially influential in Germany. California and Sweden became leaders in eugenic sterilization programs—many involuntary.[187] British settler populations in Kenya in the 1930s also adapted eugenic ideas and created a vigorous movement. Although widely supported by the medical profession in Kenya, the push for racially based eugenicist policies in Kenya failed after the British colonial office refused to back it.

In the Third Reich, official promotion of public hygiene, racial doctrines, and doctors' interests in medical experimentation mixed together to create a system designed to cleanse the fatherland through increasingly horrifying practices of eugenic medicine. German legislation passed shortly after Adolf Hitler seized power led to sterilization of two to four hundred thousand people. The Nazi state financed a eugenics institute, employed Hereditary Health Courts to decide on sterilization, traced the genealogies of "criminal types," and set up a racially based welfare state that targeted Jews and others who were deemed unfit for life under National Socialism. The horrific medical experiments at Auschwitz and the mass killings of Jews and other "undesirables" emerged from these ideas about "bettering" humanity through elimination of "unfit" breeders.

Historians have tried to explain how such extreme exterminationist practices emerged in Germany. Some have argued that German anthropology in the nineteenth century embraced a tolerant, humanistic, and internationalist agenda, while Anglo-American and French variants saw races ranked within an evolutionary hierarchy. In the early twentieth century, however, Anglo-American cultural anthropologists began to leave behind the physical measurement of "racial type" and accentuate the pluralism of cultural traditions. Indeed, the German-born Franz Boas and his cultural anthropology students at Columbia University saw themselves as continuing the older humanistic Germanic tradition. Germans, however, moved in the other direction—toward a more nationalistic view that became absorbed with biologically based theories of race and with "scientific" ways to measure racial distinctions.[188]

Studies have emphasized several factors behind this turn. Even in the nineteenth century the Prussian state had imagined a long-term colonial project in

Eastern Europe, and the image of inferiors in the East came to figure commonly in culture. Empire building in East Africa, especially the brutal war against the Herero people from 1904 to 1908, further contributed to a racialized vision of the nation (just as similar colonial wars fueled racial ideologies in other imperial states as well). World War I, however, proved especially critical in the development of racial ideology in Germany, for a number of reasons. First, anthropologists in Germany gained access to POW camps during the war and worked on the classification of POWs to develop a "science" that ranked humans hierarchically according to racial attributes. In addition, the great fear of typhus triggered disinfection campaigns that identified socially marginalized groups such as Jews and Eastern Europeans as vectors of disease. Campaigns for health took on an exterminationist rhetoric, as the desire to eliminate dangerous germs and pests, displaced onto their presumed hosts, justified eugenic purification. Moreover, racial discourses everywhere intersected with representations of masculinity, and post–World War I Germany developed a particularly romantic image of white soldierly masculinity. Embodied in the heroic figure of General Paul von Lettow-Vorbeck, the commander of Germany's African soldiers in the successful East African campaign, the image of the white German soldier in strong command of obedient black troops contrasted sharply with the image of "disorderly" African troops that Allied armies had used against Germany, particularly in the Ruhr Valley. Representations of the "white hero," and of black Africans as either dutifully subordinate or frighteningly threatening, fed interwar intersections among discourses of masculinity, race, and nation. Although Hitler embraced a less gentlemanly masculinity than that represented by the popular general, Nazi culture also emphasized a strong identification between restoration of "Aryan" masculinity and national strengthening. Finally, of course, in the economic environment of the 1930s Hitler was able to play upon an acute sense of national grievance against both the Versailles settlement and the economic order, a grievance blamed on all kinds of outsiders, but particularly Jews.[189]

As eugenic thinking careened to extremes in Germany, other groups of pronatalist eugenics professionals (stronger in Romance-language and Far Eastern areas) emphasized the need for ameliorative social conditions and decried coercive and grimly deterministic assumptions. The rifts between rival groups of eugenicists, different varieties of which were all connected to transnational networks, surfaced in international eugenics conferences in the interwar era. There was ongoing debate over whether racial and national regeneration should focus primarily on improving the genetic pool or on improving the surrounding environment. Different professions and people in dissimilar circumstances, of course, had different stakes in the answer.[190]

As "scientific" racism and eugenics built different constituencies, the meaning and significance of race was meeting important transnational challenges. In 1911 the Universal Races Congress, held in London, assembled fifty people from Asia, the Middle East, Europe, and the Americas to promote interracial harmony. Speakers at the conference endorsed both human universality and racial difference; they both reinforced and also denounced the idea that history was fundamentally a story of "races." This gathering had no specific outcome and was multivocal on the race question, but it did provide intellectual space for plurality and for dissenting voices of various kinds.[191]

Moreover, dominant voices within the profession of anthropology, which had once promoted the idea that humans could be arranged into clearly defined hierarchical categories, began to doubt that race defined any foundational set of characteristics. Franz Boas, as has been mentioned, moved away from the precepts of physical anthropology, with its stress on the biological grounding of racial difference. Arguing that difference was rooted in culture, not in characteristics such as skin color or skull size, Boaz and other cultural anthropologists redirected part of the discipline of anthropology away from its racialist orientation. Boas's many influential students working in the interwar period and after included Alfred L. Kroeber, Margaret Mead, African-American folklorist Zora Neale Hurston, Mexican anthropologist Manuel Gamio, and Brazilian sociologist Gilberto Freyre. In an article in the *American Anthropologist* in 1915, Kroeber advanced a list of professional principles that included "the absolute equality and identity of all human races and strains as carriers of civilization."[192]

As this culturalist view broke from the grim determinism of race essentialism, programs for "whitening" populations as a mark of social improvement lost scientific justification. But emphasizing cultural difference could still support policies of imperial coercion in order to promote the cultural transformation of the less powerful. Boas's pathbreaking book *The Mind of Primitive Man* (1911) represented primitive cultures as less complex and more intuitive than civilized ones, and the word *primitive* in popular usage came to be the antonym of *modern,* underscoring otherness and representing a gaping chasm of difference. A vogue of things "primitive" swept the West, influencing transnational artistic and cultural styles. Josephine Baker, costumed in a skirt of artificial bananas, enchanted Parisians with her seminude *danse sauvage;* Art Deco styles (often adorned with a line representation of Baker's facial features) became a worldwide sensation after Paris's Exposition des Arts Décoratifs popularized ethnic artistic forms. Antimodernists from various parts of the globe visited Mabel Dodge Luhan's dwelling in New Mexico, where they embraced the native and Mexican heritages and advanced the view that indigenous people lived lives superior to those in the modern industrial order. The appeal of primitivism rested partly on the idea that it represented a disappearing way of life. In most professional social science circles, "primitive" remained a condition that was headed for extinction in a shrinking and modernizing world.

Other social scientists inverted the paradigm of racial difference that remained so powerful within professional communities in the white West. While still presenting social science as a topic very substantially concerned with race, intellectuals such as José Vasconcelos Calderón in Mexico and Gilberto Freyre in Brazil articulated the idea that racial blending enhanced, rather than degenerated, a population. Vasconcelos, one of the most important intellectuals associated with the Mexican Revolution and Mexico's first minister of education, promoted Mexican nationalism around the idea that his country's racial mixture had produced a superior "cosmic race." Freyre, likewise, argued against the idea that Europeans had made the major contributions to Brazilian society. Instead, he saw Brazil's future as coming out of the mixing of Portuguese, Africans, and Indians. He pronounced that Brazil's "racial democracy" was perfectly consistent with evolutionary progress.[193]

Pride in racial mixture implied a new respect for local indigenous cultures and a rupture with ideas of racialized social Darwinism. A movement called *indigenismo* profoundly affected transnational discussions about race throughout the Western Hemisphere and elsewhere. Spread globally especially through the visual arts in the dramatic interwar murals of Mexican painters such as David Alfaro Siqueiros and Diego Rivera, *indigenismo* dignified the historic contributions of indigenous and mixed-raced people and foregrounded them in narra-

A detail from Diego Rivera's *The Tarascan Civilization,* 1942. This mural, which decorates the Palacio Nacional in Mexico City, honors the work, artistry, and learning of pre-Hispanic Mexico. Rivera and the other great muralists of Mexico endorsed racial equality and helped to build Mexican nationalism around pride in its indigenous past. (Palacio Nacional, Mexico City, Mexico/Giraudon/ The Bridgeman Art Library)

tives of national and civilizational progress. This kind of antiracism often found support in and traveled through transnational communist networks, which viewed racism as a barrier to working-class solidarity.

Challenges to the hierarchical, biological view of race thus came from diverse sources. Cultural anthropology challenged its scientific claims. Some intellectuals embraced indigenous influences as part of a rejection of industrial modernism. Communist parties often built class solidarity around programs to advance racial equality and anticolonialism. The transnational currents concerned with the role of race in social science thus ran in no single direction, but each drew enhanced energy from the messy, crisscrossing nature of their networks.

Municipalization of the World

Networked professionals devoted to improvement in the social realm turned attention especially to the late nineteenth century's burgeoning cities. The prevalence of cities, of course, varied widely. In 1900 nearly 40 percent of Western Europeans lived in cities or towns of over five thousand people. Although much of Africa had no settlements at all of this size, recent research has nevertheless emphasized the long-ignored importance of Africa's urban history. Some cities (especially in Europe and America) arose as major productive centers; others (such as Shanghai, Calcutta, or Buenos Aires) became significant points of distribution. A few cities, such as Chicago, boasted both industrial and commercial might. Urban elites, in any case, drew their wealth and status from a globalizing economy, and cities themselves became symbols of new transnational economic interrelationships. Industrialization and commerce, wherever in the world they appeared, spurred the quickening pace of urban life and linked cities together. These new "global cities" offered a cosmopolitanism accentuated by diverse streams of immigrants who came through in transit or who swelled their neighborhoods as resident laborers, traders, and entrepreneurs.

Most cities exhibited similar patterns. Urban living conditions accentuated divisions between rich and poor and between majority and minority ethnic groups. Inadequate water supplies and sanitary systems raised the specter of disease, which could easily slip from poor and crowded areas to threaten the health of the powerful. Upper and middle classes, no matter the region or nationality, tried to confine criminality and vice to separate zones, even as some profited from and might themselves frequent these areas. Such divisions became even more apparent in the outposts of empire, where merchants and administrators from the metropole carved out privileged sectors in which they could separate themselves and try to replicate familiar landscapes and customs. In cities, women very often made claims on public space and found both new freedoms and new perils. Consumer goods, advertising, amusement parks, sports clubs, bars, coffee shops, and movie theaters rearranged the ways people lived together. Labor radicals, anticolonial activists, bohemians, and dissenters of all kinds could find gathering places and exchange ideas, as could those transnational elites who occupied the often classical-style banks and mercantile houses. From whatever vantage point, cosmopolitan urban life with its mix of ethnicities seemed to embody both the promises and the dangers of the age.

Cities often became not just polycultural spaces but also environmentally polluted. Smokestack industrialization, particularly in urban areas close to belts of mining and smelting, belched particles that darkened skies, poisoned waters, and sickened populations. Industrial areas concentrated around certain cities in England, Belgium, Germany, Pennsylvania and Ohio in the United States, Russian Ukraine, and Osaka in Japan, and to a lesser extent in South Africa, India, South America, and Australia.[194] Such conditions prompted appeals—crafted within transnational conversations—to reorganize space, create sanitary systems, and curb industrial smoke and effluents.

Berlin and New York boasted that they led the way in electric lights, which flooded the windows of stores and made dark streets less treacherous. But electrification by no means came just to the largest cities. In the early 1870s, ten thousand gas lamps had illuminated Denver, Colorado, for example, and these were easily converted to electricity; boosters dubbed Denver America's "City of Light," without irony, and claimed that no city in the United States had better public and private lighting systems (although Buffalo, New York, and others also claimed this status).[195] Municipal lighting became an emblem of progress, of public safety, of enlightenment. Names such as the "Great White Way" and the "White City" resonated within the racial coding of the day. The transformation of localized electrical systems of the turn of the century into the large regional "power pools" of the 1920s, together with the multinational stretch of utilities companies (especially American), served national advantage and also defied national boundaries in favor of transnational connectivity. Analogizing electricity to modernity, T. P. Hughes writes that "modern electric systems have the heterogeneity of form and function that make possible the encompassing complexity [of modern life]." Energy consumption soared.[196]

It is hardly surprisingly that cities converged in some of their basic structures. Networks of communications and transportation, after all, emulated each other, and the many world's fairs served as nodes to showcase new international practices. In addition, expertise in urban planning, like that in most other professions, took on a transnational character, and planners embraced the idea that there could be a universalistic "municipal science." Demand for urban electrical networks and for the new lighthouses called forth cadres of experts, technicians, and capitalists who operated around the world to construct the circuits that supported the new age of electricity.[197] Other groups of experts, traveling both within imperial administrative networks and outside of them, specialized in port and terminal building, street design, sanitation, food inspection, and social services. Indeed, recent scholars have worked "to make urban history one of the avenues to historicize globalization."[198] The so-called global city, they point out, is not just a phenomenon of today but began to take shape in the late nineteenth century.

Even in the world's least urban continent, Africa, cities played a more important role than their number and population might suggest. The shocks of colonization changed the patterns and institutions of urban life throughout Africa. Cities had long functioned as crossroads, mostly trading posts on inland or coastal waterways. With colonization, however, specific port cities, mostly those linked to Western commercial networks, flourished, and these municipalities, unlike earlier ones, layered white metropolitan models upon already varied and culturally mixed cities. In South Africa's industrial zone of Durban, for example, formal planning began in the early twentieth century and meant replacing "slums"—the products of informal development—with formalized zones that restricted access from "disorderly" Indian and African residential areas. Modern port facilities, Western architecture, including Christian churches, racially separated zoning, regulated and "purified" housing, and uneven installations of sanitary services changed the look and operation of many African cities.[199]

The commercial, imperial, and professional networks that often linked the governance of cities throughout the globe sought to develop a scientific and universalistic approach to urban problems. Germany's zoning laws prompted emulation in many countries; Britain's Garden City Association and America's City Beautiful movement influenced ideas about how urban space might be planned to promote spiritual and physical health among urban dwellers. Urban planning laws in French-administered Morocco influenced France's own planning efforts after World War I. The Union Internationale des Villes, which first met in 1913, emerged from networks of European socialists and internationalists who wished to form a body composed of individual cities. Led by Belgian socialist Emile

Vinck, after World War I the Union became a more formalized international association, the International Union of Local Authorities, which expanded its membership into the Americas, Asia, and Africa.

Looking more closely at what Pierre-Yves Saunier called the first wave of "municipalization of the world," it seems clear that there were dense transatlantic and transpacific conversations over urban design and administration. Libraries of municipal planning in Melbourne, Australia, show that city officials there drew ideas not just from British treatises but from sources written in the United States, Mumbai, Dunedin, Toronto, and elsewhere. Daniel Burnham, the famed American architect who formed what became the world's largest architectural firm, oversaw the creation of the "White City" in Chicago, implemented projects in Manila and Baguio City, and saw his 1909 "Plan of Chicago" come to have international influence. Elites in Buenos Aires reconstructed their rapidly growing city in the late nineteenth century and styled it "The Paris of South America." In Meiji Japan in the 1880s, Tokyo also devised a plan modeled on Paris (which was not implemented); German experts helped draft the administrative structure of several Japanese cities, towns, and villages; the progressive mayor of Osaka, Seki Hajime, tried to eclectically adapt urban reforms from many countries; and the mayor of Tokyo invited famed urban expert and historian Charles Beard to advise on rebuilding after the devastating earthquake of 1923 (his recommendations had little effect). The industrial-modernist "internationalist" styles of Le Corbusier in France and Ludwig Mies van der Rohe and Walter Gropius in Germany projected a simplification of form and a rejection of ornamentation. The machine aesthetic of this design movement would influence the look of cities throughout the globe. Even while asserting unique features arising from their own heritages, then, city experts worldwide valued being part of transnational circuits that linked professionals specializing in municipal governance and design.[200]

As with other transnational movements, the "global" and the "local" in cities proved to be mutually constitutive, rather than oppositional, realms. What Michael Smith has called "transnational urbanism" foregrounds cities, with their groups of migrants, refugees, activists, entrepreneurs, and institutions, as localized sites within which transnational realms are created and enacted.[201] Combinations of borrowed forms, of local practices, and of diverse transnational networks influenced city life everywhere, even as they played out differently in each particular location. Exemplifying the theme prevalent throughout this chapter, municipal transnationalism found expression through differentiated commonalities.

Healing Bodies

Could people really thrive in transnational cities and their hinterlands? The spread of disease made port cities particularly vulnerable and challenged the circulation of goods and people on which they depended. In the last half of the nineteenth century several pandemics swept the globe. Anxieties related to health and the spread of disease mounted.[202]

The connective currents of travel and commerce could, quite suddenly, pose the gravest threats to human well-being. Cholera seemed to follow paths of infection from India, often carried by pilgrims going on Hajj to and from Mecca. Yellow fever outbreaks accelerated with sea travel and reached global proportions in the late 1870s, when they simultaneously claimed thousands of lives in Madrid, Havana, Memphis, and other cities. Bubonic plague carried by shipborne fleas and rats spread alarmingly, with almost every port city in the world experiencing outbreaks in the two decades before World War I. The influenza pandemic of 1918–1919, called the "Spanish flu" but probably originating in Kansas, may have killed fifty million people worldwide. The virulence and rapidity of such pandemics left scientists scrambling for preventions and cures. Commerce, colonialism, and civilization itself seemed to rest upon halting the global circulation of disease.

Pandemics called forth responses from teams of transnational health experts. These professionals increasingly accepted the germ theory of disease and exchanged specimens and theories. Research institutions such as the Pasteur Institute in Paris, the Robert Koch Institute in Berlin, the Lister Institute in London, and the Kitasato Institute in Japan worked on vaccines and antitoxins. By 1930, transnational efforts from a variety of labs had produced vaccines against typhoid, cholera, tuberculosis, smallpox, plague, diphtheria, and tetanus. New public health bureaucracies in many countries carried out vaccination programs and swapped knowledge about how remediation might best work at a grassroots level. Sometimes vaccination programs in colonies had low priority. British policies in

A line of people waiting to receive vaccinations in Côte d'Ivoire in the 1920s. Epidemic disease, which knew no geographic borders, spurred transnational scientific and medical efforts. Imperial governments, especially concerned with the health of their emissaries and of colonial labor forces, frequently ordered massive vaccination efforts. (Centre Historique des Archives Nationales, Paris, France/Archives Charmet/The Bridgeman Art Library)

Gambia in the first three decades of the twentieth century, for example, included no vaccination efforts even as large expenditures were made on commercial roads and canals and for courts and clubs where European merchants might relax. In many places, however, states and colonial administrators tried to institute programs of compulsory vaccination from the late nineteenth century on, although antivaccination movements formed almost everywhere to contest such exercises of power. Indeed, early vaccination procedures did involve a significant health hazard. Opposition to them at least had the salutary affect of prompting technical improvements, which made vaccinations ever safer and less painful.[203]

A string of international "sanitary conferences" during the late nineteenth century brought together delegates from Europe, the Ottoman Empire, Persia,

China, Japan, and the Americas. In 1907 the Office International d'Hygiène Publique was established as a permanent body for global coordination of health policies. Such transnational initiatives helped regularize quarantine procedures, especially applying to port cities. They also promoted sanitary projects to improve sewage and water systems in disease-prone areas. After World War I, the League of Nations Health Organization assumed some monitoring and coordinating functions.

Remedies for epidemic disease also often emerged through processes of co-production between transnational science and local experts, even if medical encounters were uneven. During the US military occupation of Cuba after 1898 and in Panama during the building of the canal, for example, US scientists built on the mosquito theory of Cuban doctor Carlos Finlay to successfully combat yellow fever and other diseases. The successful mosquito eradication measures influenced those who sought to fight disease elsewhere in the world, even as they helped justify US imperialism as necessary to contain disease.

The differences in the meanings of health and disease between China and the West also worked in various ways. Practitioners of traditional medicine in China adapted Western theory to develop their own versions of modern (but non-Western) medicine. Transnational discourses on health that circulated in China layered imperial influences from the West and from Japan alongside the desire of Chinese elites to shed the country's weaknesses by adopting concepts of hygiene that might improve the nation's fitness. Ruth Rogaski has analyzed the embrace by elites in the northern Chinese city of Tianjin of goods and practices that would advance "hygienic modernity" *(weisheng)* to improve cleanliness and hence bodily vigor. Moreover, China both borrowed from and competed with the West. Entrepreneurs in Chinese medicine, for example, waged successful marketing campaigns against Western medical companies to attract buyers in Southeast Asia. And medical knowledge and practice did not simply flow from the West to the East and South. George Soulié de Morant, who served in the French diplomatic corps in China during the first two decades of the twentieth century, became so impressed with the success of Chinese acupuncture during a cholera epidemic that he wrote major works on the technique and, during the 1930s, developed a significant following in France that would expand in the post–World War II period. As in China, instances of "medical pluralism," in which patients exhibited considerable eclecticism in choosing healing practices from an array of local and imported systems, emerged in many areas of the world, even though health-care provision was often inequitably distributed.[204]

The civilizing potential of medicine emerged as a central discourse of imperial justification from the mid-nineteenth century. Epidemic disease hindered imperial stability and infrastructure development, and colonial officials gave it high priority. Colonial rivalries added further urgency. Plant experts in all the imperial powers, for example, competed with each other to smuggle and adapt the Peruvian cinchona in order to produce sufficient quantities of the quinine needed to protect against malaria.

Medical practice, however, could also easily prove to be a site of imperial failure or of resistance to colonial authority. During the early years of French rule in Algeria, for example, imparting modern medical knowledge and administration provided a strong justification for colonialism, both morally and pragmatically. As France began to construct health-care institutions in Algeria, however, the costs and difficulties of building a comprehensive medical system began to eclipse the early optimism. Even if doctors and other personnel operating in the city of Algiers could imagine they were building a structure that would transform the colony's health, their reach into rural areas was spotty and encountered resistance. By the turn of the century, ideologies of racial inferiority had blended into the intractable problems of cost, poor administration, and jurisdictional battles among French colonists, Algerians, and the French army. Plans to train Algerians as doctors and to spread French-style medical care throughout the countryside were largely abandoned, and Algerian medical personnel, who had once supported the French effort, gradually withdrew from the networks of colonial medicine. Complaining about deep injustices in the system, the vision they had once shared with French doctors degenerated into disillusionment and resentment. At the same time, the French effort to spread health gradually devolved into an effort to segregate off the "sickness" in the body of the colony so that it could not escape through the port to contaminate or threaten healthy French cities. Not only did French medical interventions have insignificant or negative effects on the health of Algerians overall, but the French administration labeled Algeria itself as a sick state.[205]

Similarly, during the 1920s, British officials increasingly blamed Sudan's "moral and economic backwardness" on the practice of genital cutting. Spurred by a Western-based transnational movement to abolish the practice, they launched an all-out campaign to introduce "scientific" medicine and especially to change midwifery practices. By the late 1920s a "circumcision crisis" in Kenya and associated debates in the British Parliament led to even stronger directives to end practices that harmed the health of women and children throughout the empire. The interactions among colonial policy, British nurse-midwives sent to reform what were seen as detrimental Arabic cultural practices, local advocates on both sides of the issue, rising nationalism, and differing religious orientations created a complex milieu over several decades, during which genital cutting may have became more, rather than less, culturally entrenched.[206]

Disease thus provided a central cultural trope of this interconnected age, although it framed a variety of meanings. Within transnational circuits, metaphors of disease often became part of a moral discourse that marked tropical bodies as backward and hazardous and justified exogenous interventions, including colonialism. "Tropical medicine," which became a subspecialty of medical knowledge, segmented off the "tropics" as an area of danger and disease, even though the geographic boundaries were anything but clear.[207] At the same time, the sweeps of epidemic disease and famine could also threaten the Western claims of superiority that justified imperial and racial power. Within some communities swept up under colonialism, metaphors of disease could mark outsider-carriers and justify resistance to contact with imperial officials or transnational health workers. Moreover, anticolonial nationalists sometimes embraced public health programs as a way of strengthening local communities and institutions in order to counter colonial or neocolonial power. Ideas about who carried disease and who could stop it thus became parts of larger discussions. The powers of healers, like all other circuits of expertise, involved global circulations and contestations of meaning.[208]

Numerous transnational organizations in this period tackled problems related to global health. For example, the Friends (Quakers), the Catholic Church's Caritas Internationalis, and other religious-based groups led major efforts. Save the Children International concentrated on relief work to help children suffering from war and disaster. Two transnational organizations, the Red Cross and Crescent and the Rockefeller Foundation, deserve special attention because of the influential and long-lasting transnational networks they forged.

The International Committee of the Red Cross (ICRC) began as the inspiration of Swiss businessman Henri Dunant, who witnessed the bloody battle of Solferino in 1859 in northern Italy and became determined to alleviate the suffering of war. The organization adapted the design of the Swiss flag, taking as its emblem a red cross on a white background, and began to spread its services into war-torn areas. In 1877 the ICRC reluctantly agreed that the Ottoman Empire could use a crescent instead of a cross. In 1901 Dunant was awarded the first Nobel Peace Prize. A private institution headquartered in Geneva, the Red Cross and Crescent played a major role as a neutral intermediary during World War I, when it provided medical assistance and advocated improved treatment of prisoners. Through a federated structure, the Red Cross expanded internationally, gradually sprouting local chapters throughout the world.[209]

Clara Barton, who had inspired a volunteer service to soldiers during America's Civil War, helped start an American Red Cross (ARC) chapter in 1887. The ARC served military personnel during America's War of 1898 and became a semiofficial agency in 1905 when it received a charter and subsidies from Congress. Active during World War I and during the interwar era, the ARC expanded its mission beyond wartime emergencies to coordinate international disaster relief and, unlike the ICRC, tried to tackle broader issues related to sanitation reform and prevention of epidemic disease. After the great Japanese earthquake of 1923, President Calvin Coolidge asked that all American donations of food and medicine be channeled through the ARC. Despite some tensions over core mission, the International Red Cross and Crescent and the American Red Cross together provided a strong and ever-expanding global infrastructure for advocacy related to humanitarian and health concerns.[210]

Philanthropic foundations, based on the fortunes of some of American industrial barons, also became heavily involved in global health issues. Oil baron John D. Rockefeller launched a Sanitary Commission in 1909 to combat hookworm in the southern United States. He then expanded the idea by incorporating his new Rockefeller Foundation with the goal of promoting well-being throughout the world. The foundation's International Health Board (IHB), which operated for thirty-eight years after 1913, carried its anti-hookworm campaign to one billion people in fifty-two countries. It also gradually broadened its concerns to include malaria and twenty-two other diseases or health conditions.

A special yellow-fever commission, formed in 1915, led work on the eradication of mosquitoes and successfully developed a vaccine.

The work of the foundation frequently emerged from coproductive local relationships. After World War I, the foundation established a European office in Paris and courted European partners for its programs to advance basic science. The foundation built institutes of public health in some two dozen cities to train health-care workers and conduct research. It helped establish women's colleges in China, India, and Japan. In China, where the foundation developed a special interest, its China Medical Board became an independent institution in 1928 and supported the Peking Union Medical College. Using this China model, the foundation formed partnerships through grants to large medical education and research institutions in Beirut, Hong Kong, Singapore, Bangkok, and other locations.

Cadres of locally trained health workers joined the IHB's transnational network. In 1935 the Rockefeller Foundation launched a grassroots initiative to take health care and community development into rural villages in China by relying on midwives and other paramedics to bring basic care to peasants. It also supported the development of local outreach programs for rural health-care delivery at the grassroots level.

In many countries, alliances among the Rockefeller Foundation, local public health reformers, and national state-building elites shaped the programs. In Costa Rica and Brazil, for example, research on and treatment of hookworm disease and yellow fever preceded the foundation's involvement, and Rockefeller grants provided the money for local public health activists who were advocating a more vigorous role for their national governments. Many governments feared the economic consequences of epidemic disease and welcomed efforts to keep ports open and commerce flowing. Foundation money also helped local officials pay for public health educators and professionals focused on hygiene and mosquito eradication.[211]

In the British colony of Ceylon the IHB developed a demonstration project for the eradication of hookworm. Plantation owners first resisted the costly health requirements the IHB tried to enforce, but the IHB then switched course. Broadening its focus to a range of infectious diseases, it promoted educational campaigns operating on the village level, provided training for local herbal doctors, and encouraged provincial governments to create sanitary departments. From the mid-1920s, the IHB teamed up with a new generation of local leaders who advocated a grassroots approach that stressed preventive measures such as vaccinations and maternity services. This switch from curative to preventative medicine dramatically lowered mortality rates.

Any assessment of the role of scientific health professionals and philanthropic foundations depends upon specific context and can hardly be captured in a single interpretive narrative. Professional transnational medicine was, in one sense, allied with capitalist globalization; it disrupted settled ways in the name of modernization. As such, medical professionals might be seen as agents of Western medicine working on behalf of the West's imperial aims. They might also be viewed, however, as participants with local elites in a global circulation of knowledge that both coproduced possible remedies and furthered anticolonial nationalist agendas by extending the power and reach of local officials. Health programs on behalf of grassroots groups and women's empowerment proved to be important, if controversial and sometimes counterproductive, forces in many areas. Like other networks of expertise in this period, health professionals served imperialism, nationalism, local aspirations, and transnational ideals variously and often simultaneously. The currents of their expertise often asserted hierarchies of race and culture, but local impacts varied widely, as recipients of funds sometimes ignored, changed, or adapted methods to their own purposes.

. . .

The nineteenth century exhibited a faith that the transnational and neutral character of science and expertise would foster universal frameworks and propel the progressive convergence of "civilization." Over time this faith came under challenge from various directions. To many, World War I underscored the bankruptcy of the Western fascination with technological change. Chinese reformer and scholar Liang Qichao, who visited the shell-shocked European capitals just after the war, pronounced that the "peaceful" traditions of Eastern civilizations would flourish in the ruins of war-breeding Western techno-materialism. Intellectuals as diverse as Rabindranath Tagore, Muhammad Iqbal, and Liang Shuming developed parallel critiques of Western materialism and called for revivals within their own religious and cultural traditions.[212] Paris hosted a "lost generation" of artists and intellectuals who also hoped to pronounce the death of the

West's mechanical approaches to life and the natural world. These dissenters built a transnational aesthetic out of shattering conventions and revolting against formalisms of all kinds. American educator Mary Parker Follett warned that transnational networks of professional elites would breed narrowness. She wrote in *The New State* (1918), "The man who knows the 'best' society of Petrograd, Paris, London, and New York, and that only, is a narrow man because the ideals and standards of the 'best' society in London, Paris, and New York are the same. He knows life across but not down—it is a horizontal civilization instead of a vertical one, with all the lack of depth and height of everything horizontal. This man has always been among the same kind of people, his life has not been enlarged and enriched by the friction of ideas and ideals which comes from the meeting of people of different opportunities and different tastes and different standards." A flat world, she suggested, would be a provincial one.[213]

Bruno Rizzi's *La bureaucratisation du monde,* published in Paris in 1939, and James Burnham's *The Managerial Revolution,* published in New York in 1941, exemplified yet another line of critique. These two works articulated the view that the Soviet Union, Nazi Germany, and the New Deal all manifested a new bureaucratic mentality that had arisen over the past half century. Throughout the world, these two ex-Trotskyists suggested, new groups of people who claimed specialized expertise had come to exert power through governments, empires, and corporate structures. They were neither owners of production nor people of great wealth. They were managers, and they claimed ultimate authority, through the power of specialized knowledge and technical expertise, to know what was best for the public in whose name they presumed to operate. Although Rizzi and Burnham were primarily concerned with how this new class of experts had emerged within national states, their critiques of "bureaucratized" and "managerial" systems also addressed the networks of scientists, technicians, and professionals that had coalesced transnationally since the late nineteenth century.[214]

All such critiques, however, tended to exaggerate the unities within scientific and technical networks. A close look at transnational circulations suggests that circuits of expertise did not simply devise their theories and "facts" from on high and transplant them into various localities throughout the world. Rather, transnational circuit builders interacted with each other from many different geographic and social positions, and in their encounters, specific context interacted with and altered supposedly universalized laws and propositions. Science, technology, and health were neither neutral in the powers they embodied nor consistently one-sided. In a variety of configurations, they were coproduced through encounters, often unequal, between the local and the global. Expertise could both serve and also alter imperial designs; it could work in favor of nationalistic visions but also as a check against them.

If the euphoria associated with late nineteenth-century one-worldism, transnational bonding, and supposedly apolitical networks of science and engineering deflated after the Great War, the crisscrossed transnational networks that had been forged remained in place and even flourished. These "soft" networks constructed within scientific, engineering, and healing communities spanned the globe as surely as did the "hard" ones of cables, telephony, railroads, and ocean liners. The meanings carried in their currents remained complex and often contradictory, but the global reach and importance of transnational epistemic communities continued to grow, generating both broad commonalities and localized variations.

5. Spectacular Flows

THE world was shrinking, and ever more people made their way around it—for adventure, education, and even publicity. Li Gui claimed to be the first Chinese official to travel around the world and wrote an account of his 1876 trip, describing for Chinese readers parts of the world he visited: their social customs, industrial organization, and material culture. In the early 1880s King Kalakaua of Hawai'i, determined to investigate immigration and how other rulers governed, became the first ruling monarch to journey around the world and meet with other heads of state. On November 14, 1889, American journalist Elizabeth Cochrane Seaman ("Nellie Bly"), sponsored by Joseph Pulitzer's *New York World* and inspired by Jules Verne's 1873 book *Le tour du monde en quatre-vingts jours (Around the World in Eighty Days)*, left New York on a 24,899-mile trip to set a record in speed for circling the globe. Seventy-two days, six hours, eleven minutes, and fourteen seconds later, she arrived back in New York, having traveled through England, France, the Suez Canal, Ceylon, Hong Kong, and Japan. She captured loads of publicity and her coveted world record, which would be broken only a few months later by another American. Pursuing what was now a sure-fire market for globe-circling adventures and broke because of a bad investment, Mark Twain published an account of his roundabout through the British Empire called *Following the Equator* (1897). Rabindranath Tagore, the Bengali poet, undertook a global oceanic voyage in 1916, going from India to Burma to Japan to North America, and in 1924–1925 traveled from Latin America across the Indian Ocean, the Mediterranean, and the Atlantic. These were only a few of the many late nineteenth- and early twentieth-century globe-trotters whose adventures provided a sense of the vast, yet also small, new world of interconnected currents.

In such a world, adventure awaited and encounters with difference expanded imaginations. The new transnational networks, deeply imbedded in commerce and its culture of desire stimulation, altered ideas about the fixity of identity and seemed to offer possibilities of self-fashioning. Borders of all kinds, geographic, racial, and gendered, seemed more permeable and less permanent. Media technology fostered new entertainments that challenged traditions and gave rise to global networks of celebrity and consumerism.

Older histories of this era, organized around a linear teleology, emphasized the spread of the West with its supposedly rational culture of science and reason leading toward an evolutionary future called progress. Recent work in anthropology and history, however, has challenged the narrative structures that framed this view. First, transnational networks, rather than clear geographic centers, map the changes often marked as modernity. Second, scholars as diverse as the historian C. A. Bayly, the anthropologist Arjun Appadurai, and the interdisciplinary Modern Girl collective all see the emerging and networked modern world as characterized by the simultaneous (and related) creation of both uniformity and difference. Bayly's work, for example, "traces the rise of global uniformities" while emphasizing how "connections could also heighten the sense of difference, and even antagonism, between people." Appadurai calls this homogenizing and differentiating process "modernity at large." The Modern Girl project, which analyzed the nearly simultaneous emergence of "modern girls" in every part of the world in the early twentieth century, illustrates what I call differentiated commonalities as it describes the emergence of local variations within uniform global trends.[215] Third, scholars note that modernity did not represent the triumph of the rational as much as the conjuncture of the rational with a new media-driven spectacularity.

The examination of adventurers, celebrities, travel, and consumerism illustrates the networked world of differentiated commonalities and exemplifies how sensationalism—driven by a search for audience and by peoples' yearnings for self-fashioning—merged with the rationalism needed to produce market calculation and machine-driven mass culture.

Adventure

By the nineteenth and early twentieth centuries, the greatest cartographic and cataloging enterprises of the age of exploration were coming to an end. The mapping of the globe, even its remote regions, was mostly complete. But a few blank spaces remained, and the era thus featured some of the most celebrated feats of exploration. The thirst for scientific discovery had once driven geographical exploration. As the scientific justification for new discoveries diminished, however, the emerging popular media lavished increased attention on the "conquests" of the few still-uncharted places.

With the rise of mass-circulation media, adventurers who once emphasized the scientific aspects of their deeds became tempted to join forces with sensation-seeking newspapers to enhance their own fame and profit. Still claiming status as instructors about science and the natural world, many converted themselves into globe-trotting showmen and showwomen. The turn of the century remained a time of daring feats of endurance, as adventurers challenged themselves to reach the remaining unexplored terrain of arctic and high-mountain regions, but it was also a time of sensation seekers and even charlatans, for whom the seductive yearning to become a celebrity often overrode good judgment and truthful representation. "As the world got 'smaller', travelers' tales grew taller," writes Felipe Fernández-Armesto.[216]

The age of industrialization vastly improved the ability of explorers to survive in extreme environments, and increasingly more people became tempted to try. Adventurers had growing access to specialty clothing for tropical and arctic climates, to orienting devices, and to antimalarial remedies. Steam engines, iron-clad ships, railroads, and telegraphic communications eased and sped travel to more places. Various kinds of industrial power, now more than sheer physical endurance, made the world smaller and more accessible. Still, the hardships of exploration remained real enough to pack the pages of adventure stories. As surveyor-explorer Kenneth Mason writes about the hardships in the still-remote places, "there were no roads and fewer tracks; there were no maps; the people were suspicious. . . . [Mountaineers] had no mountain equipment, no ice-axes, crampons, pitons, no nylon ropes, wind-proof clothing or indestructible tents. They learnt about frostbite and snow-blindness the hard and painful way. They carried no oxygen and no Pervitine tablets."[217]

Maurice Isserman and Stewart Weaver's history of Himalayan mountaineering points out one of the central paradoxes of the expeditionary culture that emerged. "It was bound up with visions of imperial destiny that assumed the rule of white Europeans over darker-skinned Asians and drew many of its conventions from the hierarchical order of the English public school and the British Army. At

·[962]·

the same time, it harbored individual climbers who were often misfits in their own societies, romantic rebels who found a spiritual purpose and freedom in the mountains." It fostered "colonial arrogance" but also a mix of individualism and "responsibility to others."[218] The media-framed tales of adventure from this period drew from these paradoxes to create iconic sagas of moral, racial, and physical supremacy wrapped within notions of the brotherhood of hardship.

The age of extreme expeditionary culture and the golden age of popular newspapers and journals were a marriage made in heaven. Whereas nineteenth-century explorers usually worked for governments eager to publicize scientific discoveries and to press colonial territorial claims, the new breed often sought stories that could be sold. Well-publicized adventures found their way into theaters, music halls, exhibitions, "yellow journalism" in America, the "penny press" in Britain, and mass-circulation magazines such as *National Geographic.* Almost everywhere in the world the numbers of newspapers and theaters soared. Newspapers printed in China alone, for example, quadrupled from two hundred to eight hundred between 1905 and 1920. The adventure genre would become a staple of photojournalism and of the new film industry. In almost any year of this era, some spectacle-ridden adventure dominated the news everywhere that mass publications reached. Stories with audience appeal circulated feverishly within the emerging information and entertainment networks that connected empires and spanned the globe.[219]

Henry Norton Stanley's expedition best exemplified the union between mass entertainment and adventure. Stanley excelled at grafting imagined "facts" into stories of exploration, even obscuring his own birth as John Rowland in North Wales to claim that he hailed from New Orleans. Sent to Africa in 1869 by James Gordon Bennett Jr., publisher of the *New York Herald,* Stanley was to find and interview Dr. David Livingstone, the British Congregationalist missionary to Africa, explorer, and antislavery activist. Livingstone, whose motto "Christianity, Commerce, and Civilization" was subsequently inscribed into his monument at the base of Victoria Falls in Zimbabwe, had disappeared into the interior of Africa in his obsessive search for the source of the Nile River. Stanley's search for the famous man, chronicled by the newspaper, became a sensation. In November 1871 Stanley landed on the shore of Lake Tanganyika and reportedly met the ailing Livingstone with the soon-to-be-famous words, "Dr. Livingstone, I presume?"

Stanley's exclusive stories to the *Herald,* and the adventure's sensational ending (capped by the doctor's death from malaria a year and a half later), boosted the newspaper's circulation and profits.

Stanley became what the twentieth century would call a "celebrity," an emerging cultural phenomenon that sprang from the popular media's new sensational style and global interconnectivity. The Royal Geographic Society, which had sent its own expedition to try to locate Livingstone, derided Stanley's lack of scientific credentials, but London newspapers emulated the *Herald*'s profit-making formula. In 1874 the *Daily Telegraph* of London teamed up with the *Herald* to sponsor another African expedition led by Stanley and to publish his exciting accounts. The *Daily Telegraph* helped spread within the English press the fad of covering sensationalized, often brutal, adventures. The huge popularity of Stanley's writings and the many personae he projected in them also shaped the conventions of adventure writing. The Livingstone-Stanley story became, and remains, one of the most mythologized and familiar tales in the world, and Stanley's fame illustrates the emergence of globally circulated stories that interconnected mission, adventure, colonial violence, and celebrity.[220]

The writings of both the religious Livingstone and the sensationalist Stanley became influential in shaping the views of Africa presented within the global webs of popular publications. A study by Clare Pettitt raises questions about what Livingstone's (and Britain's) relationship with his African servants, Jacob Wainwright, Susi, Chuma, and Wekotani, might further illuminate. She points out that the servants exist in a historical void. They pop up here and there in photographs and scattered accounts but leave no significant trace of how their own perspectives or voices or narratives might have framed the famed Livingstone and his encounters in Africa. The "native" servants are the silent participants in an association in which only one side left the kind of accounts out of which "realities" and then histories are usually made. This era of communications, her study shows, is often not about communication at all but about the projections emanating from those who, through publication, gained access to a future audience. Transnational currents, once again, both bridged but also accentuated differences in power.[221]

National Geographic, of course, became one of the most popular purveyors of adventure and one of the most influential venues through which Americans and others learned to picture and understand the world. In 1903, for example, the magazine featured the explorations of Fanny Bullock Workman, a record-setting woman explorer, and her husband, William Hunter Workman.[222] Their many adventure books, such as *Ice-Bound Heights of the Mustagh,* helped to popularize accounts of mountain climbing in this age when men-women duos were still unusual enough to attract special attention.[223]

Striving for rewards and recognition within the new world of mass publishing came also with hazards. Otto von Ehlers, for example, wrote travelogues that became best-sellers in Germany and beyond. Spurred by success, von Ehlers tried in 1895 to cross New Guinea's central mountain range, coast to coast, but misgauged the time it might take to transverse the 150 miles. The party of forty-three ran out of food, lost their compasses, and suffered from sores made by leeches and from the red maggots that settled in them. After seven weeks, a few remaining native guides shot the Germans in an effort to secure at least their own survival. The adventure had little scientific or even imperial rationale. It showed, however, that a desire to recount a daring exploit to the vast audience that seemed eager to read tales of travail could be deadly.[224] Similarly, Joshua Slocum's *Sailing Alone around the World* (1900) told the exciting tale of Slocum's three-year, forty-six-thousand-mile journey, at age fifty. The first person to make such a trip alone, Slocum enjoyed great popularity from his book. Trying to achieve another celebrity-style feat a decade later, he disappeared at sea.

In the early twentieth century, expeditions to the North and South Poles captured the most frenzied press coverage and popular attention. In 1909 the Americans Frederick A. Cook and Robert E. Peary both claimed to have reached the North Pole (probably neither did), and two rival newspapers, the *New York Herald* and the *New York Times,* magnified the controversy to build sales through sensational stories and charges against the other. After Cook cabled that he had reached the pole, the *New York Herald* splashed the news on its entire front page with the headline "Fighting Famine and Ice, the Courageous Explorer Reaches the Great Goal." Several days later when Peary also cabled success, his sponsor, the *New York Times,* reported that "the world accepts his word without a shadow of hesitation" and quoted Peary as saying that Cook was a fraud who "has simply handed the public a gold brick." With this and other stories, according to historian Beau Riffenburgh, the *Herald*'s publisher, James

Gordon Bennett Jr., "established the role of the press in the creation of the modern image of the unknown," emphasizing not facts but exhilarating stories of rivalry, hardship, and perhaps tragedy. The global spread of newspapers and news networks was an essential component in creating the formulas of spectacularity that dominated visions of adventure by the early twentieth century.[225]

The interest in the North Pole controversy culminated in another "race to the pole," this time to Antarctica. Sixteen different expeditions from nine countries headed toward the Antarctic to gain the distinction of being first, but only two ultimately became contenders. Media again played up the stories of the hardships and rivalry. News came in 1912 that Norwegian Roald Amundsen's group had reached the Pole. Then came the gripping story of Robert Falcon Scott, Britain's most famous explorer, whose expedition had struggled to the Pole only to find that Amundsen had attained the goal several weeks earlier. On their arduous return across the glaciers, Scott and others then died from starvation and cold. Apsley Cherry-Garrard, a member of Scott's expedition, wrote one of the most vivid accounts of the travails in *The Worst Journey in the World* (1922). The greatest fame from the race to the Pole, however, came to the experienced Antarctic explorer Sir Ernest Shackleton, who had once been part of Scott's team before the two had a falling out. Shackleton's Imperial Trans-Antarctic Expedition, which embarked early in 1914 aiming to be the first to travel across Antarctica from sea to sea, suffered an almost incredible ordeal when the crew became stranded in the ice and Shackleton endured deadly conditions to rescue them. Shackleton's tale, which he published as *South* (1919), was bone-chilling adventure, and Shackleton became a legend for his remarkable endurance, dedication to his team, and truly sensational story. Amundsen, whose fame also spread, went on to explore the Northwest Passage and the North Pole region, where his plane disappeared in 1928 as he was attempting to rescue a former associate.

After the race to the poles, individuals and nations turned toward the Himalayas as the only "unconquered" place left that held significant challenge. Some called the Himalayan heights the "third pole." In the 1920s the English mountaineer George Mallory joined expeditions that claimed the goal of surveying and subduing hitherto unmapped territory in the Himalayas. Mallory, however, claimed no utilitarian purpose. Displaying his late-Victorian concern with character, he insisted that he climbed only because the mountains were there and posed a personal challenge. He thus exemplified mountaineering as being about self-discipline and self-improvement, values that were widely celebrated in this imperial age. Mallory was no sensation hunter, but his famous climbs of 1921–1924 were nonetheless sensational, and he lost his life attempting to be the first to reach Mount Everest's summit. In the dispirited post–World War I atmosphere, Mallory and other mountaineers captured world attention with their messages stressing the importance of personal fortitude. Throughout the interwar era, expeditions from all over the world made the conquest of Everest a determined goal (not achieved until 1953).[226]

Adventurers pushed not only into remaining uncharted territories but into the skies above. In July 1909, French airman Louis Blériot crossed the English Channel in an airplane in thirty-six and a half minutes, and much of Europe celebrated the achievement. The well-known Viennese author and pacifist Stefan Zweig saw flight as a positive sign. The feat, he wrote, prompted people to consider "how useless are frontiers when any plane can fly over them with ease, how provincial and artificial are customs-duties, guards and border patrols." Air flight, exclaimed Zweig, promoted "the spirit of these times which visibly seeks unity and world brotherhood!"[227] Some hoped that the very possibility of aerial bombings would deter war, and there were suggestions that the Hague Peace Conference of 1915 (which was not held) should take up the subject.

Although World War I confirmed that air flight could facilitate not just interconnection but killing, the popular fascination with flight nevertheless provided a new arena for adventure headlines. Charles Lindbergh became the greatest celebrity of the late 1920s when his 1927 solo nonstop flight across the Atlantic from Long Island to Paris drew huge crowds and global media attention. Lindbergh's good looks and his feat's celebration of individualism made him a media sensation and contributed to a decade in which adventure flying remained constantly in the news and on the movie screens. The first flight over the South Pole in 1929 brought fresh excitement to this new-style "race to the Pole." And other flying records of all kinds remained to be repeatedly set and then broken. Amelia Earhart, the decorated aviatrix who went missing during her attempt to circumnavigate the globe in 1937, added mystery and tragedy to airborne adventures. All the enormous publicity associated with these early years of flight, of course, drew from the fascination that had captured Zweig and so many others: humans

The *New York Daily News* celebrating the completion of aviator Charles Lindbergh's historic non-stop flight from New York to Paris, May 22, 1927. Crowds amassed in Times Square to hear the news of his landing in Paris, and journalists made "Lucky Lindy" into one of the best-known people on the planet. Lindbergh came to symbolize the new globalizing age of flight. (NY Daily News via Getty Images)

could now glide across geographic borders as though they did not exist; they could reach distant lands in hours rather than weeks. The shrinking of time and space had accelerated very dramatically.[228]

Back on land, or under its surface, the lure of "lost cities" beckoned to other kinds of adventurers and sensation hunters. Ruins of past civilizations from the Mycenaean to the Mayan to the Anasazi spurred searches for more, and it often was not easy to distinguish the line between scientist-archeologists and headline-hunting hucksters. In the 1870s, German archeologist Heinrich Schliemann excavated many sites that he claimed showed the historical authenticity of Homer's *Iliad* and Virgil's *Aeneid*. Although garnering great publicity, his finds were and still remain controversial because of the suspicion that he may have planted some of the more spectacular items he then uncovered. The American Hiram Bingham came upon the ruins of Machu Picchu in 1911, and he then excavated, photographed, and publicized them to the world as though he had been the first to "discover" them (which he probably was not). The Incan artifacts he encountered were crated off to Yale University.[229]

American Roy Chapman Andrews typified the showman-scientist. Andrews, a naturalist with the American Museum of Natural History, launched his famous Central Asiatic Expedition into the Gobi Desert in the early 1920s in hopes of finding evidence of earliest human evolution. Exemplifying the America of his era, he sought extensive publicity by traveling in caravans of automobiles through one of the world's most inhospitable terrains. His 1925 expedition required 125 camels and a huge support staff to carry the needed gas, oil, tires, and repair equipment for his six motor vehicles. Finding no significant ancient human remains, he did uncover troves of dinosaur fossils and eggs, many of which he dispatched to New York. His flamboyance and appropriation of fossils raised disputes over ownership with the Chinese government and produced enough complications to end his expeditions. But Andrews published book after book recounting his exploits, and some claim that he became a model for the *Indiana Jones* movies that thrilled a later generation.[230]

The famed American animal collector Frank Buck likewise displayed the flair of a vaudeville agent (which he had been) while promoting his adventures. In the interwar era, his "bring 'em back alive" books, movies, and radio shows dazzled fans worldwide with tales of his encounters with jungle animals and of his travails in transporting them to "civilization." An entire genre of Buck-inspired products—*King Kong* and its many offshoots being the most influential—plotted stories in which rare animals, native "boys," and intrepid Euro-Americans played out predictable scripts in the "jungles" of the world. The drama of such stories came not from a kill or even from a capture but from the physical and financial dangers of trying to keep the beasts alive through the process of transporting them. Frank Buck also promoted his exploits at the New York World's Fair of 1939, where his Jungleland exhibition advertised a display of thirty thousand animals and birds—vastly more than the number featured in even the largest zoo of the era.[231]

As adventurers on, above, and below the earth generated amazing stories about daring the unknown, they fed consumer appetites for even more sensational tales and pictures of distant lands. Avowedly fictional presentations of the discovery and exploration of unmapped or lost worlds boomed, as this new age of connectivity spurred imaginations to go beyond even the often exaggerated exploits of real-life adventurers. French author Jules Verne's tales of adventures under the sea, in the air, and on uncharted islands reached audiences from their first book publications during the 1870s on into the age of mass movies. Japanese writer Oshikawa Shunrō, influenced by Verne, was not translated outside of Japan, but he popularized the adventure genre in Japan just after the turn of the century. German novelist Karl May's tales set in the American West, Asia, and the Middle East sold hundreds of millions of copies in thirty-three languages. In *Lost Horizon* (1933), British author James Hilton wrote of a fictional "Shangri-La" in the forbidding Himalayas. American writer Edgar Rice Burroughs claimed that Stanley's *In Darkest Africa* was by his side as he wrote his extravagantly popular Tarzan fantasies, the first of which came out in 1912. Like Verne's tales, Burroughs's many *Tarzan* books found audiences worldwide and provided staple formulas for the new medium of movies. Meanwhile, a growing global circulation of pulp magazines and their local adaptations, which sprang up on every continent, featured adventure stories and derring-do of all kinds.

Adventures engage readers through drama. There must be physical exploits, of course, but the popularity of the adventure genre arises from the constructed narrative form. Looking at the structure of adventure stories—the hope, the hazard, and then the triumph or tragedy—reveals less about the world than about audience expectations. In short, the transnational encounters embedded in adventure accounts *seemed* to be about the world but often achieved popularity because their dramatic centers and resolutions reinforced familiar verities: the importance of nation, of empire, of manly character. They often seemed to validate notions both of shared humanity and of exceptional races, and they generally obscured the contradictions between the two.

Shows and Entertainments

Adventure stories provided the structures for most popular amusements during this period. This was the heyday of extravagant live shows that traveled the globe while purporting to represent it. During the late nineteenth and early twentieth centuries, so many larger-than-life showmen and showwomen presented the "world" to so many audiences that it is hard to grasp the scale and significance of these spectacles with which people in almost every land became familiar. Even as the disciplinary circuits of sober scientists and engineers spread around the world, these transnational networks based on fantasy and spectacle also burgeoned. Both, in a sense, depended upon each other's achievements.

Looking through the biographical and descriptive material on the great shows of the period, one is quickly struck by the superlative language. Each show is often proclaimed as the most spectacular of its day and as the model for others. It becomes clear that no spatial or chronological ranking makes sense. The art of the spectacle did not "begin" in a particular place or at a single time and then spread in some predictable way. Rather, the currents of entertainment radiated transnationally and often with a kind of simultaneity. Newspapers, migration, travel, and then film created communities of entertainers that spanned the globe, borrowed from each other, and profited from weaving ever more extravagant representations. The major entertainers of the era, discussed below, appear in no order of chronology or importance. As a group, they suggest the pervasiveness of spectacle to this age of rational categorization and also provide background against which to understand the most important transnational entertainment that emerged from the age—the motion picture.

Circuses had become one of the central diversions of the nineteenth century, and just before and after the turn of the century many great circus families attained international fame: George Sanger and Frank Bostock in Britain, Carl Hagenbeck in Germany, the Gautier family in France, Albert Salamonsky in Moscow, Herman Renz in the Netherlands.[232]

The brilliant American promoter Phineas Taylor Barnum used many of the same formulas as these great circuses of Europe. Barnum, however, added scale and also perfected the art of enabling his huge circus entourage to travel widely and rapidly. With Hagenbeck as his designated foreign agent for animal procurement, Barnum found that portrayals of the "world" and its "exotic" creatures provided a circus's most powerful draw, and he took these appeals to their limits and beyond. Barnum's "Great Ethnological Congress of Curious People from All Parts of the World" featured "uncivilized" specimens that he claimed would instruct his viewers about the world. He acquired nine aborigines in Queensland, for example, and they toured with his circus during the 1880s (along with the huge pachyderm, Jumbo). His "Congress" included bearded ladies, armless men, a Chinese giant, a Burmese dwarf, and a family of Sioux Indians.[233]

During the 1870s and 1880s the most prominent showmen in America engaged in a rivalry over elephant displays—first over which could display the greatest numbers, then the greatest in size, then the whitest. In her history of the circus in the United States, Janet Davis speculates about the power of such exotic attractions: "The modern child first glimpsed the exotic Other through circuses and toys, a formative encounter that helped make colonial hierarchies part of the 'natural' world of child's play." This world both blurred and reinforced the lines of gender, race, and class—and especially the lines between animal and human. Well-performing Indian elephants became representatives of India, and "wild" elephants became emblems of Africa. Genuinely white elephants became the most coveted creatures.

Empire building was one of Barnum's standard themes. In his hands, the 1904 Durbar of Delhi became a lavish and popular pageant. His advertisements described the Durbar with the exaggerated codes of Orientalism: "native soldiers riding upon lofty, swaying camels and preceded by the mystic priests of Buddha, leading the sacred zebus and the sacrificial cattle; there is a prince of Siam with his retinue of warriors and shapely oriental dancing girls . . . while the Potentates of the Indian kingdoms pay their tribute to the Imperial power."[234]

The presentations of "abnormality" and difference that lay at the heart of Barnum's spectacles could have many meanings. They could project American middle-class values as normative, but they could also provide tempting glimpses into very different alternative worlds. Being carried off by circus people, after all, could function either as a fearsome cautionary tale or as a tantalizing possibility.

Whatever the exact impact on the sensibilities of individual viewers, however, circus spectacles helped to standardize entertainment formulas. Even as they projected diversity, spontaneity, and surprise, their success rested upon the precision needed for replication of acts and railroad mobility. As circuses traveled from place to place, they spread attention-grabbing sensations and raised expectations for encountering the unusual. They drew viewers away from their own local frameworks and introduced the techniques of regional, national, and even international mass culture.

Regional circuses flourished within this international milieu of circus techniques and performers. In China and Japan, countries whose acrobatic techniques had influenced European circuses in the nineteenth century, troupes of acrobats performed locally and sometimes as traveling parts of European or American circuses. In South Africa after World War I, Boswell Brothers Circus and Menagerie traveled by ox-wagon and train throughout the countryside. The Great Royal Circus of India, dating from 1909, and the Great Bombay Circus, operating primarily in Punjab, attracted regional audiences during the 1920s and 1930s. Argentines and Brazilians in the early twentieth century developed *circo-teatro* shows, which combined traveling circus-style acts with musical, melodramatic, and magic-show performances. In all their variety, interconnection, and mutual borrowing, circuses came to be paradigmatic representatives of globalizing networks.

There were many turn-of-the-century extravaganzas that were related both to circuses and to world's fairs. Carl Hagenbeck, the impresario of the animal trade and developer of the much-copied Hamburg Tierpark, for example, merged together the concepts behind zoos, circuses, and exhibitions to establish a global entertainment empire. Although Hagenbeck presented his shows as part of a scientific impulse to document zoological diversity and to "authentically" represent other lands, he enthusiastically embraced the spectacle of the entertainment world. His Tierpark incorporated a dinosaur area with gigantic sculptures. Its ethnographic arena once featured a Wild West show, including forty-two Sioux Indians from the Pine Ridge Reservation in South Dakota that attracted more than a million viewers. Like Barnum's, his traveling circuses circled the globe, presenting the animals, people, and displays that had gained such a following at the Tierpark.

Imre Kiralfy, born in Austria-Hungary, became similarly famous for his extravagant productions. In the United States, Kiralfy and his brothers produced, among other things, a long-running version of Jules Verne's *Around the World in 80 Days,* which featured large female chorus lines and unusual special effects. For the Chicago Columbian Exhibition, Kiralfy staged "America," an extravaganza that grossed almost one million dollars in its seven months. After moving to London, he then built a smaller replica of Chicago's "White City" at Earl's Court and opened an "Empire of India" exhibit in 1895. The height of his career featured a huge Great White City at Shepherd's Bush in London, which hosted yearly exhibitions and the Olympic Games of 1908.[235]

Buffalo Bill Cody's Wild West traveled the world on a scale that was probably unmatched. Like the dime novels and highly mobile circuses from which Cody borrowed ideas and techniques, his Wild West shows generated enormous popularity by reinforcing the familiar formula that linked imperial destiny to the evolutionary progress of civilization. Even his show's musical background, offering such songs as "The Passing of the Red Man," advanced the message. In Cody's pageants the cowboy-hero of the American frontier became a mythic creature of unsurpassed virtue and skill who always vanquished his opponents. He was nature's nobleman: civilized and gentlemanly, yet an enemy of both savagery and of overrefinement. His drama of the triumph of civilization over barbarism seemed to have worldwide appeal.

The Wild West's popularity stemmed also from its skillful promoters and managers. Publicity stunts, larger-than-life images, and simplistic stereotypes all expanded the arts that were being perfected in the nascent advertising industry. Moreover, the mechanized precision of worldwide tours itself became part of the spectacle. Featuring sometimes as many as one thousand people, with all the horses and equipment needed to accompany them, the past represented in the Wild West inevitably met the future of Taylorized efficiency. Specially equipped trains, adapting models from the traveling circus, facilitated the logistics of quickly transporting and setting up the shows in destination after destination. The military campaigns so often celebrated in the dramas became surpassed in the show's own militarized speed and maneuverability.

In 1893 the name of the troupe became "Buffalo Bill's Wild West and Congress of Rough Riders of the World." The change signaled a transnational focus, and the show built a huge global fan base that included kings as well as commoners. Accommodating different audiences and the headlines of the day, Cody's scripts proved flexible in assigning heroes and villains. The Indians who played Cody's defeated nemesis could cue their hair to become Chinese Boxers overwhelmed by the forces of progress; celebratory reenactments of America military victory in the War of 1898 could vanquish assorted Spanish, Filipino, or Cuban foes; Russians could be flattered by epic renditions of their sweep to civilize the steppe. The romance of "The West" helped lure some Germans into dreaming of a frontier of their own in Eastern Europe. At the turn of the twentieth century, Buffalo Bill Cody might have been the most famous American in the world, and his entertainment formula shaped the production of mass culture across the media spectrum, including the new possibilities offered by film.[236]

Motion pictures truly revolutionized the transnational possibilities for show business. Developed more or less concurrently from various kinds of precursors in France, Germany, and the United States, motion picture films meant that images and stories could be projected relatively inexpensively all around the world almost simultaneously. In France the Lumière family created its first projections in 1895, and by 1899 Lumière films were being shown in Istanbul, Damascus, Jerusalem, Cairo, Mumbai, Mexico, Rio de Janeiro, Buenos Aires, Australia, Shanghai, Peking, Tokyo, and Yokohama.[237] Initially films concentrated on documenting and reporting notable events; the technology itself highlighted the spectacle of the object filmed. Most of the earliest films, only a few minutes in length, drew their appeal from collapsing both distance and class status. Popular topics showed images of celebrations that most audiences could never personally have witnessed: *Leaving Jerusalem by Railway* (1896), *The Capture of Rome, September 20, 1870* (1905), *The Coronation of Edward VII* (1902), *The Durbar at Delhi* (1912), *Carnival Scenes at Nice and Cannes* (1909). Before World War I, productions from France and Italy predominated in world markets, but few people thought in terms of national film industries. Production sprouted everywhere in the era of silent film. Distribution channels included a range of venues, from the lavish theaters that opened in every major city to the mobile screens that traveled via carts through even very remote areas of the world.

After World War I, films from America increasingly dominated global production and distribution. In older scholarship, the formulas and techniques that characterized Hollywood films were often cast as "American" and their global spread deemed "Americanization." Hollywood, however, was always a global place that had emerged within early cinema's transnational network. If Hollywood was innovative and popular in diverse localities throughout the globe, it was because filmmakers with transnational backgrounds and connections made it so. American films emerged less from the traditions of elite art (as films had in Europe) than from immigrant filmmakers who sought to develop entertainment for a diverse, multiethnic audience. Such films, especially in the silent era when language proved no barrier, perfectly suited a world market.

Hollywood's global appeal, of course, brought special advantages to investors and manufacturers in the United States. During the interwar era American companies directly owned more than half of the leading movie houses in the world, and American industries manufactured most of the film and production equipment. In 1925, American-produced films constituted approximately 95 percent of the total shown in Britain and Canada, 70 percent of those in France, and 80 percent of those in South America.[238] Japan developed a substantial film industry that retained a predominant market share in its own country, but Japanese films did not significantly figure in international distribution networks. During the 1930s especially, many national cinemas declined sharply under competition from Hollywood, depression-era conditions, and the coming of "talkies," which made it difficult for films in small-market languages to flourish.

Still, even when US companies dominated the international movie trade, the transnational currents in film culture remained strong. Some directors developed differentiated commonalities in their moviemaking, as transnational filmmaking came to display what film scholar Miriam Hanson called "vernacular modernism." The film industry boomed in India, for example, where new technologies and styles emerged from coproductive links between local innovations and the globalizing networks of production and distribution. Some thirteen hundred silent films were produced in India from 1912 to 1931. Even after "talkies" came in, the Indian industry flourished. Director Pramathesh Barua, for example, contributed his distinctive touch after study in Paris and London. His movies, wildly popular in India in the 1930s, grafted the narrative traditions, the melodrama, and the visuality of transnational film culture during India's colonial era onto some of India's own precolonial cultural forms. The popular orientation of Barua's films has brought him mixed reviews from later film critics, but he well exemplified filmmaking styles and themes that, as with many popular directors, skillfully mixed the global with the local. In interwar Shanghai, director Sun Yu also sought Chinese forms of modernity that drew from global currents. In Latin America, Argentine and Brazilian filmmakers imported equipment from France in the late nineteenth century; before World War I, Argentina, Uruguay, and Chile had developed a brisk exchange in the production and distribution of films. After the war, even in the face of relentless competition from Hollywood, Argentina produced several dozen movies a year, many featuring tango dancing. Likewise, the pre–World War II Mexican film industry became one of the strongest in the world, influenced by, and also standing apart from, nearby Hollywood.[239]

Hollywood itself became even more internationalized as directors, producers, and film technicians from many countries migrated there when threatened by the rise of fascism in Europe. Although barriers remained high against anyone not from the United States or Europe, "American" movie products of the late 1930s nonetheless emanated from one of the most cosmopolitan settings in the world. *Casablanca* (1942) provides an example: director Michael Curtiz had been born in Budapest, producer Hal Wallis in Chicago, musical creator Max Steiner in Vienna, screenplay writers Julius and Philip Epstein and cinematographer Arthur Edeson in New York City, editor Owen Marks in England, art director Carl Jules Weyl in Stuttgart. The cast featured Humphrey Bogart (New York City), Ingrid Bergman (Stockholm), Paul Henreid (Trieste), Claude Rains (London), Conrad Veidt (Potsdam), Sydney Greenstreet (Kent, England), Peter Lorre (Rózsahegy, Hungary), Madeleine Lebeau (Antony, Seine, France), Dooley Wilson (Tyler, Texas). The film's internationalism in production matched its message.

The global influence of Hollywood's motion pictures joined the spread of mass-produced magazines to set new styles of celebrity-dominated journalism. American physical culturalist and magazine impresario Bernarr Macfadden set

A portrait of Dolores del Río, transnational film star. Born María de los Dolores Asúnsolo y López Negrete in Durango, Mexico, del Río became a popular part of Hollywood's international social scene and a superstar in the industry's global movie empire during the 1920s and 1930s. Refusing to take part in films that she felt disparaged Mexico or Mexicans, and facing pressure for her leftist politics, she returned to Mexico in the 1940s to star in major Spanish-language films. (Library of Congress)

the tone. Macfadden's publishing empire, which like Hollywood in the early twentieth century developed strong appeal within America's upwardly mobile immigrant communities, included popular titles such as *Physical Culture, True Story,* and *True Romances.* The largest publisher in the United States for several decades, Macfadden developed a huge global distribution network in the first half of the twentieth century. His publications popularized a "look" of modernity that included a reliance on celebrities and confessional formats along with projections of strong bodies, eroticism, and self-fashioning.[240]

The new film and celebrity magazines helped promote global film stars. During the silent era, stars such as Clara Bow (the "it" girl) and Lillian Gish in the United States, and Ruan Lingyu and Hu Die in China helped construct and explore a variety of roles for women. Film culture spread transnationally a feminine look that often combined heavy use of cosmetics and flashy clothing styles, evoking consumerism, with an aura of independence and sexuality. In the same era, Rudolph Valentino, the Italian-American heartthrob, parlayed his ambiguous national and ethnic identification as a "Latin lover" into a sex appeal that brought him global stardom. After the advent of "talkies" in the 1930s and 1940s, many of the most popular film celebrities continued to be figures who embodied transnational appeal in diverse and often personally destructive ways—Anna May Wong, Marlene Dietrich, Rita Hayworth, Carmen Miranda. Very often, the cultural otherness depicted in European, American, and Asian cinema provided ways of suggesting new gender norms and even alternative modernities. The currents of transnational cinema, like popular culture generally, offered a complex interplay of emulation and differentiation.[241]

The medium of film, its celebrants claimed, brought the world together by depicting unfamiliar places. It projected images of New York apartments to people in Patagonia, constructed Chinese rural life for filmgoers in Paris, represented Chicago gangsters to fans in Africa. Especially in Hollywood's world, global diversity could sometimes be mastered quickly and easily. Fox's *Movietone News,* begun in 1919, took viewers "Around the World in Fifteen Minutes in Picture and Sound." Paramount News, begun in 1927, adopted a similar cosmopolitanism-but-be-quick-about-it appeal.

These glimpses of the world, of course, were highly selective and structured in formulaic and misleading ways. Many of the popular documentary films of the first three decades of the twentieth century, for example, claimed an ethnographic authority similar to that supposedly represented in world's fairs and museums. Safari films produced by Nordisk, the first Scandinavian film company, purchased bears and lions from Carl Hagenbeck to stage safaris. Everything about these films was faked, except for the animals, which were shot and killed in front of the camera. For safari and hunt films, body count (of animals) seemed a key factor in popularity. Hagenbeck himself turned toward film. He constructed his own Kino in the Tierpark, shot many films, and killed some of his most troublesome animals after staged hunts. He also allowed other filmmakers to use the dramatic backdrops of his park. Even during and just after World War I, seven different production companies shot films at the Tierpark, which became an all-purpose "foreign" background that could be outfitted to stand in for any exotic terrain in the world.[242]

Robert J. Flaherty's *Nanook of the North: A Story of Life and Love in the Actual Arctic* (1922) is considered the first feature-length documentary film. Flaherty's cameras followed, and sometimes staged, the story of an Inuit man and his family in the Canadian arctic and highlighted their traditional methods of hunting, fishing, and igloo building.[243] A box office success, *Nanook* encouraged other adventurers to try to capture the lives of premodern peoples for the movie screen. Like *Nanook,* the supposedly ethnographic documentaries of the age, however, often exaggerated their presentations by incorporating the formulas that audiences already expected from mass attractions.

The primary purpose of most documentary films, of course, was entertainment, and their formulas borrowed from those pioneered in world's fair midways, zoos, vaudeville, amusement parks, circuses, and adventure novels. Osa and Martin Johnson provide an example. They began their careers in vaudeville and then turned to nature photography and film. With their one million feet of film (their photographs formed one of the initial collections of the Museum of Natural History in New York), eighteen books, and over one hundred articles, they epitomized the way in which various new mass media intertwined to represent the world and to entertain audiences, who seemed to crave spectacles of unfamiliar cultures in a shrinking world. "This was the Africa as no civilized man had seen it," boomed the narrator of their film *Simba* (1928), produced under the auspices of the Museum of Natural History. *Congorilla* (1932), a voice declared, demonstrated "the age-old story of man emerging from savagery." Osa Johnson, in poses echoed in so many of the photos taken in this age of imperial power, frequently posed with her rifle over the animal kills. In *Simba* she contributed the crucial shot that saved the party from an elephant stampede, killed a charging rhinoceros, brought down a lion that was the object of a village hunt, and then joined the "natives" in celebrating the kill

Osa Johnson demonstrating the use of cosmetics to a group of Masai in a carefully posed photograph, 1923. Johnson, alongside her husband Martin, were American vaudevillians, explorers, photographers, and filmmakers who produced influential but highly staged images of Africa. Always on a tight budget, the Johnsons pioneered product-placement advertising in their photographs by depicting odd scenes in which they "introduced" Africans to globally marketed products such as Coca-Cola, Shell Oil, Eveready batteries, Bisquick biscuit mix, Fab detergent, and Colgate toothpaste, along with various brands of cosmetics. (© Bettmann/Corbis)

by baking an apple pie. An accomplished shooter of both guns and film, Osa domesticated exotic places and displayed the prowess of white women over both animals and the native males who also participated in the hunts. If Osa and Martin's photos and films fostered greater familiarity with the world, they did so by also reinforcing the highly contrived conventions of racial and cultural hierarchy that permeated the adventure shows of the age.[244]

By purporting to show ethnographic "realities," documentaries constructed cultural differences that could supply humor and even melodrama. One common comedic device involved highlighting the superior knowledge of whites while mocking the inadequacies of "natives." Frank Buck, one of the preeminent procurers of exotic animals for zoos and shows, for example, scored a box office hit in 1932 with his feature-length documentary *Bring 'Em Back Alive,* a film that became the cultural reference for the 1933 hit *King Kong.* One scene features a large hunting party of natives who fearfully flee when they hear a jungle noise. The audience is then treated to a shot of the accompanying white explorer, who unflappably pulls back bushes to reveal a small and harmless honey bear. In such films, the dominant subject was the white hunter-adventurer, the setting included exotic animals and peoples, and the drama came from the testing and ultimately the mastery displayed by the protagonist, an obvious symbol of Western civilization.

The world according to Hollywood's feature films also took shape within such conventions. Although the preponderance of Hollywood plots presented images of the United States, those images could become more defined when played off against a "foreign" setting. Producers found that they could easily create rather undifferentiated "foreign" locations by adding a repertoire of various exotic fixings to the same studio lot. As Hagenbeck had discovered when his Tierpark became the standard place to shoot German movies set in foreign locations, one did not need to travel around the world to make movies. Rather, a standard set of "exotic" motifs would do. Film historian Ruth Vesey points out that although Hollywood dressed residents of foreign locations in different costumes, they were generally accorded similar picturesque qualities and set against similar backgrounds. As American-produced films sought export markets, directors had to be sensitive about giving offense to any particular national group. Vesey writes that "since the foreigners' national origins were deliberately obscured, the population of Hollywood's universe came to be broadly comprised of 'Americans' and 'others.'"[245] Film viewers consequently could "travel" without the cultural, physical, or monetary discomfort of actually doing so. The world they experienced through film, however, was a carefully constructed and formulaic product that had evolved out of the mass amusements popularized in the nineteenth century.

Mass Tourism

The adventures represented in novels, the sensationalist press, and film brought visions of a shrinking world to mass audiences throughout the world. They perhaps stimulated wanderlust in many, and they schooled those tempted to stray from their familiar surroundings in the conventions of how to perceive whatever appeared strange. Buoyed by ever cheaper and faster transportation systems, mass travel began its rapid rise, at least for Europeans and Americans. In 1911 the London *Times* reported that one million Britons were visiting the continent yearly. A century before, the number had been fewer than ten thousand.[246] In 1880 about 50,000 US tourists per year traveled to Europe; thirty years later the number had mushroomed to 250,000.[247] Historians of US tourism have emphasized the huge growth in traveling to Europe and to the "Holy Land," but at the turn of the century six steamship lines also served US travelers to Asia.[248] It was within the context of this boom in mass tourism, of course, that the world's fairs flourished as an around-the-world travel destination located closer to home.

Mass travel promoted new industries that constructed their own transnational networks. Operators such as the British firm Thomas Cook, which put together some of its first tours for the Crystal Palace Exhibition of 1851, developed the global connections and specialty tours that could ease the hardships of individual travel. Cook and the Berlin-based company Stangen operated almost all over the world. Guidebooks by Baedeker in Germany, John Murray in England, and Michelin in France advised travelers on what was "important" to see in various locations worldwide. Michelin introduced the practice of according stars to favorite eateries and inns. In Germany the Nazi regime also encouraged a carefully controlled tourism designed to offer working people something other than a message of discipline and sacrifice. The "Community Strength Through Joy" agency, created in 1933, sought to build support for the regime and weaken the appeal of the Left by developing a limited but affordable menu of consumer activities and tours. By 1938 Strength Through Joy constituted the largest travel agency in Germany, with buses and twelve cruise ships. It had sent fifty-four million Germans not just on outings to well-known domestic historical and hiking sites but also on excursions to Norway, Greece, Italy, Madeira, and elsewhere.[249]

Inexpensive and easily portable Kodak cameras became signatures of the traveler. The American company Kodak democratized the medium of photography, heavily promoted travel for the middle class, and cleverly used its advertisements to instruct users in how to take engaging and enviable photos. Armed with information on tours, guides, and cameras, armies of new tourists set out on adventures and then brought their experiences and photos back home to church basements, living rooms, and community gatherings.

Women proved critical to the growth of the mass travel industry. In the United States, for example, dozens of American women, often sponsored by newspapers and magazines, wrote about their travels around the globe. The demand for such accounts in women's magazines seemed almost endless. The *Ladies Home Journal,* especially, fed the fascination for romps through the world in its many features of foreign travel and, for young girls, its around-the-world series of paper dolls that wore different national costumes. Moreover, women's travel clubs sprouted in towns all across the United States, providing armchair adventure for those who might not go themselves. For thirty years an American entrepreneur, John Stoddard, successfully marketed his "Travel Series" of lectures and travel accounts to such clubs. As members gathered to discuss different countries and cultures, the women's club culture strengthened the idea that travel was desirable, educational, and generally accessible to the broad middle class. Acts of travel, it seemed, could come from acts of study and imagination as surely as from boarding a ship or rail car.[250]

Film did the most to promote and simulate mass travel. In the new genre of the "travelogue," the Americans Burton Holmes and James A. Fitzpatrick were the kings. Holmes had begun on the lecture circuit, where he coined the word *travelogue* to describe his performances. Like Stoddard, he sold impressive numbers of volumes that interspersed his lectures with photographs. After World War I, however, Holmes took to the screen. Working for Paramount Pictures, he featured titles such as *Burton Holmes' Head Hunters* (1919) and *Torrid Tampico* (1921). Fitzpatrick's *Traveltalks* and other documentaries, which commonly played before feature films in movie palaces worldwide from the mid-1920s through the mid-1950s, perfected the formula for the travel film genre.

Fitzpatrick specialized in introducing his audience, who were presumed to live harried "modern" lives, to the presumed simple pleasures and uncomplicated customs of distant lands. In choosing his world locations, he was keenly aware of fantasies and fascinations with the "primitive." Social evolutionary thought had, of course, placed the primitive at the low end of a progressive continuum, but Fitzpatrick's formulations exalted ideas about how a rural life and closeness to nature could counterbalance the enervating influences of urban civilization. Many of his travelogues ended with the somber "and now we must say a fond farewell" (to some idyllic lifestyle) and return to the thankless pressures of "our" advanced ways. For many moviegoers, Fitzpatrick became the "Voice of the Globe."[251]

Mass travel seemed to promise enlightenment by reaching out to other lands and peoples, but the tours and travel literature often structured experiences designed to confirm Euro-American advancement set against backwardness elsewhere. Not surprisingly, Strength Through Joy's tours began each morning with swastika-draped ceremonies, emphasized racial exclusion, and contrasted the orderliness and cleanliness of German cruise ships with some of the disorderly, poverty-ridden, and darker-skinned ports of call. Travel could establish new bonds among people, but it could just as easily confirm beliefs in racial hierarchy and fuel ethnonationalism.

Consumer Codes and Advertising

The sensational display of adventure, the advent of motion pictures, and the growing appetite for mass travel were all parts of a new ethos of mass consumerism. Spreading within transnational networks, this emerging world of consumerism was not just about buying necessary goods. Rather, "mass consumerism" may be defined as a mass-production and mass-marketing system that imagines an abundance of goods within a culture that emphasizes purchasing, desire, glamour, and flexible, consumption-driven identities. Consumerism, in this usage, is as much a cultural as an economic system. It operates to establish "codes" by which particular mass-marketed items signal specific kinds of associations. The United States, with its large domestic market and adroit advertising industry, emerged as perhaps the most significant global driver of mass consumerism and its codes. The specificities of local cultures, however, also helped coproduce variants of mass consumerism within the expanding transnational networks of commodities, producers, sellers, buyers, and advertisers.

Such transnational flows were inevitably complex and often contradictory. C. A. Bayly has emphasized that colonial rule, by creating networks that introduced Western modes of speech, dress, and sociability, proved critical to the spread of consumerist codes and "modernity." So were global networks of media, which circulated publications, movies, and advertisements. It would be beyond the scope of almost any work to trace out all of the various codes projected within transnational circuits of consumption, much less to speculate on how they might have, over time, shaped the identities of people, regions, nations, empires, classes, genders, sexualities, and ethnicities. As changes in demography, communication, and trade mixed people together as never before and augmented the availability of goods, how would it be possible to represent all of the ways in which consumers might signal affiliations and identifications? Yet the significance of the mass consumer networks that emerged in this era may not be ignored just because their meanings are necessarily elusive and variable.

The consumerist-driven mixing of cultural attributes within transnational space can be described by many terms. *Assimilation* connotes the loss of one culture along with the embrace of another. *Hybridity* connotes the selective adaptation of different cultural elements into some new combination. I prefer to borrow, from linguistics, the term *code-switching,* which seems best to capture what most often occurred in the culture of transnational mass-consumer images.[252] Just as people with fluency in multiple languages may go back and forth, strategically invoking words from different languages at particular times, so consumer code-switching may also connote the going back and forth, strategically producing an assemblage, at any given time, of different cultural and political significations.

Consumer goods coded all kinds of projections and allegiances. Consider, for example, the "modern girls" in Shanghai in the 1920s who assembled their "look" from a *qipao,* high-heeled shoes, and bobbed hair. Or the rebels who fled New York for New Mexico in the 1920s and projected their antimodernist views by mixing western ranch styles with emblems of Mexican indigenous culture. Or the elite Mexican "chica moderna" who mixed European style with folkloric attire and accessories mimicked from indigenous cultures and from Europe's "exotic" representations of them. Or the zigs and zags of men's fashions. Before World War I, many urban men of affairs throughout the world embraced the simplicity and uniformity of Western-style clothes. Rejecting the complex, colorful, and often luxurious robes and coats characteristic of many indigenous styles, the simple top hat and black coat came to signal power and sobriety. Yet, especially after World War I, men in colonies often became more self-conscious about signaling pro- or anticolonial political affiliations by the degree to which they adopted Western business attire and housing styles, and many sought to retain traditional customs in clothing and dwelling. Moreover, political currents, generally controlled by men, often channeled women's fashions in significant ways. Meiji reformers in Japan mandated Western dress in the 1870s, but a nationalist revival later brought the kimono for women back into greater prominence. Soviet authorities scorned the capitalistic overtones of the women's fashion industry, favoring simple garments that facilitated work and were not provocative, but many women dreamed of having access to greater choice and style. Fashion was just one arena in which consumerist identities could be assembled and advanced.[253]

The more open particular societies were to global currents, the more consumer code-switching became a cultural style associated with modernity. Code producers, such as those involved in movies, advertising, governmental fashion policies, or movements of various kinds, helped contour the environment in which different cultural codes might be accepted or rejected. Individuals, however, also played an active role in selecting, mixing, and making meanings from the available codes. Consumerism offered the raw material for a constructed (and reconstructible) projection of self and society that drew upon transnational networks of goods and symbols. As such, it could seem both alluring and subversive.

The power of capital, of course, clearly shaped consumer culture. Commercial advertising, an increasingly transnational set of practices and businesses, became perhaps the most important global purveyor of consumer codes (along with films). From the late nineteenth century, expanding along with trade, advertising sought to foster values and lifestyle aspirations that would boost people's desires to purchase specific products. Advertising agencies became important cultural brokers, working to adapt messages across boundaries and to create what historian Daniel Boorstin called "consumption communities" that transcended geographic space.[254] Although in the twentieth century a substantial critical commentary portrayed advertising-driven mass consumption as a homogenizing influence (and often as an agent of "Americanization" or of "cultural imperialism"), more-contemporary cultural analysis has stressed the interplay between global and local and the possibilities for the often creative juxtapositions that became a mark of modernist pastiche. Advertising strategies have generally responded to pressures for both standardization (the "packaging" of buyers to sell to marketers) and diversification (the flexibility needed to appeal to diverse buyers). As with other transnational phenomena, they exemplify differentiated commonalities, even as they also may embody asymmetries in power.

American advertiser J. Walter Thompson became a leader in forging transnational networks devoted to selling. Founded in 1864 in New York, JWT opened its first branch in 1899 in London and expanded rapidly into dozens of other countries. The American model of advertising departed from the older European approaches that emphasized artistic styles associated with nineteenth-century posters. Centering the appeal of their ads on whatever was likely to make customers respond, US advertisers pioneered techniques developed within the emerging field of psychology. They employed surveys and other types of "scientific" methods to gauge and constantly improve the effectiveness of their persuasive strategies. Partly through advertising—and partly through screen images—constellations of signifying codes became recognizable throughout much of the world. JWT designed ads, used worldwide, for American auto manufacturers that featured sporty, young, unescorted women and appealed to a car's beauty as much as to its performance. It also held the accounts for many cosmetics and soap companies. Especially in the interwar era, such advertising messages constructed and spread a look of modernity that, when often mixed with localized images, aimed to stimulate desire for products, especially among women.[255]

Among urban youth throughout the world in the 1920s, consumerist modernity often seemed to come dressed with cropped hair, cigarette adornments, and fascination with jazz music, movies, cars, and dancing. These codes beckoned toward cultural reorientations, especially changing relations between men and women. They suggested approval of heterosocial relationships, that is, close friendships between men and women who were not related. They signaled the ideal of couple-formation based on individual desire and companionate marriage. In some cases, they hinted at greater acceptance for same-sex attractions. Within patriarchal systems in which male control of female sexuality was paramount, such "modern" styles could represent a threat of social breakdown or a promise of new freedoms, depending on one's perspective.

In the early twentieth century, images of "modern girls" had emerged simultaneously throughout the world as flappers, vamps, *garçonnes, moga, modeng xiaojie, kallege ladki,* schoolgirls, and *neue Frauen.* Everywhere, these were "young women with the wherewithal and desire to define themselves in excess of conventional

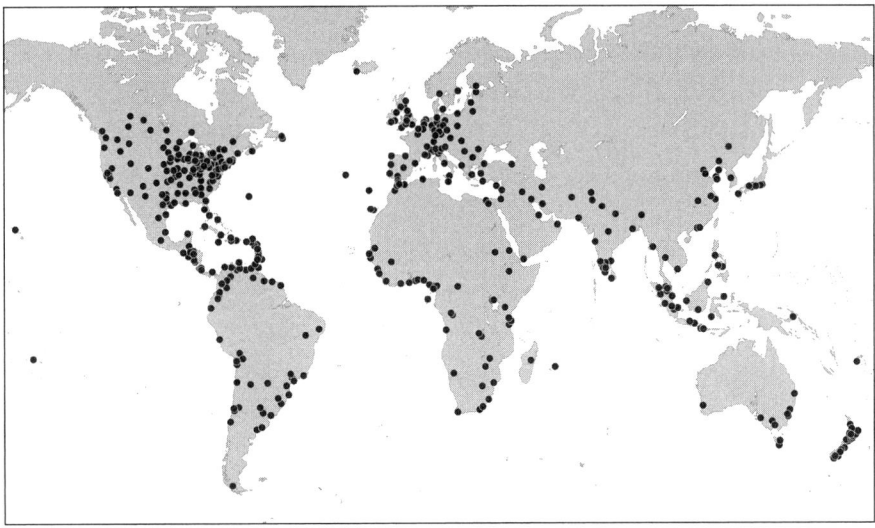

Global operations and distribution centers for the Goodyear Tire and Rubber Company, 1928. The distribution and sales of rubber tires, which accompanied the rapid spread of motorized vehicles, exemplifies the global, but uneven, spread of the automobile/consumer revolution. By the mid-1920s, US-based Goodyear was the largest rubber company in the world.

female roles and as transgressive of national, imperial, and racial boundaries." Modern girls seemed especially drawn to automobiles, which signaled independence and mobility. The 1920s became a heyday for women motorists.[256] Moreover, advertisers encouraged the love affair between women and autos. In the United States and in markets around the world, ad campaigns for the American autos that dominated global sales portrayed women as athletic, unsupervised, and fashionable. They showed women driving often simply for recreation. In different languages, they proclaimed the message that "Every Day More and More Women Drive Cars."[257]

As consumer advertising and modern-girl imagery emerged globally, contests over cultural values flared. Cultural wars over the products and entertainments associated with mass consumerism became especially contentious in the 1920s and the depression decade of the 1930s. In countries as diverse as Germany, Mexico, France, Nicaragua, Italy, China, and Japan, custodians of elite culture and groups espousing "traditional" values (especially related to gender) most loudly invoked themes of nationalism and anticonsumerism (or their own consumer-nationalism) against the proliferation of foreign consumer goods and images they regarded as degraded and feminized. The Nazi regime in Germany denounced jazz music, which it depicted as an alien and degenerate art form produced by African-Americans and Jews, and tried to develop a mass culture supposedly rooted in *völkisch* traditions. Popular "swing clubs," however, kept jazz alive, even during the outright bans of the World War II era.[258] On the contentious grounds of mass commercial culture, any particular assemblage of consumer codes could send especially evocative—and provocative—signals.

China, particularly the trading crossroads of urban Shanghai, provides a specific example of the growth of transnational mass consumerism and advertising and of how consumer codes travel. Consumer products, promoted in advertising and film images, washed into urban China during the 1920s and 1930s as American, European, and Japanese entrepreneurs sought to capitalize on the potential of the fabled "China market." At the same time, the ethos of the May Fourth era in China (1917–1921) encouraged both nationalism and an influx of Western writings, as the movement drew from a cosmopolitan spirit that sought to adapt foreign models to national goals.[259] Especially in the treaty ports and particularly in the International Settlement in Shanghai (where approximately thirty thousand foreigners lived among more than eight hundred thousand Chinese), the rapid growth of modern mass media and electrification provided the transnational infrastructure for advertising and consumer awareness. Estimates suggest that by the mid-1930s, nearly two thousand magazines reached over thirty million people in the whole of China; there were seventy-eight broadcast radio stations, and outdoor billboards were increasingly common. In Shanghai specifically, thirty-six newspapers had a combined daily circulation of nearly nine hundred thousand, and there may have been as many as thirty advertising agencies, foreign and local. Eight Hollywood studios established distribution offices in Shanghai, and by 1927 the city boasted 150 domestically owned film production companies. Dozens of gigantic movie palaces proliferated in both the International Settlement and in the Chinese City sections of Shanghai, the world's sixth-largest city. The great Art Deco structure *The Grand* accommodated an audience of two thousand people.[260]

Despite low buying power and occasional nationalist boycotts against foreign goods, the icons of Western and Japanese consumerism grew in familiarity in China. Ads for lipstick, face cream, women's fashions, and a variety of patent medicines found their way into all of these new media outlets. Women's fashions in Shanghai, taking cues from French designs and American movie stars, were popularized in the widely disseminated calendar posters. Dresses narrowed to become more fitted; hems rose; and side splits revealed legs with Western-style shoes. Hair that was bobbed or curled with new permanent-wave machines often complemented these styles.[261] The British-American Tobacco Company advertised its cigarettes on the first neon sign in Shanghai and hired local graphic artists to adapt appeals appropriately to the local setting. Although new Chinese mass consumers generally came from the affluent class, people from across the income spectrum became familiar with the look and tastes associated with mass consumerism—products such as French designer dresses, Singer sewing machines, RCA records, Colgate toothpaste, Palmolive soap, and Max Factor makeup. Shanghai's International Settlement became famous for its neon lights, night life, and entertainments. Jazz music and ballroom dancing provided the sounds and signs of a consumerist culture.

The products and images from America and the West entered China in conjunction with several other major trends: Western colonialism (with its unequal administrative authority as well as a Marxist, anti-imperialist critique of this inequality); Chinese hopes for a modernity consistent with Chinese nationalism; an often chaotic political system faced with trying to accommodate the vast geographical and ethnic diversity within China; and the emergence of an urban sensibility that challenged the intellectual status quo. Within this complex of circumstances, the semiotics of consumerist messages became shifting and ambiguous.

Karl Gerth's study of consumerism and nationalism in early twentieth-century China, *China Made,* discusses the movements that sought to promote the idea that China could become a modern nation by avoiding foreign imports and encouraging the purchase of Chinese-made fashions, foods, and fun. The development of nationalistic consumerist actions and rituals—boycotts of foreign products, exhibitions of Chinese goods, commemorations of national humiliations, and celebrations of Chinese entrepreneurs—came together under the slogan "Chinese people should consume Chinese products!"[262]

Just as consumerism could express nationalism and generate codes against foreign incursion, however, it also contributed to a cosmopolitanism that welcomed external influences. In the interwar era, Shanghai, a city often seen both as a part of but also as different from the rest of China, exemplified a hybrid worldliness. Department store display windows, calendar posters, magazine advertisements, and movie palaces complemented each other in emphasizing visuality, display, and spectatorship. Leo Ou-fan Lee argues that the respectable display of the female body became "part of a new public discourse related to modernity in everyday life."[263] The *Young Companion (Liangyu huabao),* a magazine established in Shanghai in 1925, specialized in photography and featured a "modern" woman on the cover of each issue—at first actual women and later fantasy women. Such publications exemplified the ways in which Chinese cosmopolitans adapted and rescripted cultural forms. Lee describes, for example, how Western formulas for plots in popular cinema and magazine articles were neither rejected nor appropriated outright; they were, instead, often shaped to suggest traditional Chinese narratives and values. Similarly, Chinese female film stars borrowed from Western fashions and poses, but often also conveyed independence less through sexuality than by posing with books as well-educated women. Intellectuals, after all, constituted the most enthusiastic audience for foreign cinema and were most open to the kind of new relationships between men and women that were shown on the movie screens. Although the Chinese "modern girl" of the 1920s and 1930s clearly drew upon the Japanese *moga* style, which had been heavily influenced by Hollywood, she nonetheless projected a complex imagery. For example, the *qipao,* which came to dominate fashions by the late 1920s and 1930s, provided a look that was both modern and Chinese.[264] Wen-hsin Yeh's *Shanghai Splendor,* which elaborates Shanghai's complex modernity, concludes that "not only was it possible to be simultaneously 'modern' and 'Chinese,' it was virtually imperative for a patriotic Chinese to be modern."[265]

People in interwar urban China, of course, were not alone in the complex ways in which they interacted with the spread of consumerist culture. Miriam Silverberg has analyzed how Japanese women in the interwar era used code-switching in consumer practices to articulate identity. Examining the Japanese women's magazine *Shofu no Tomo,* she points out the juxtaposition of Western products and consumer practices with distinctly Japanese aesthetics and contexts. Similarly, the contributors to the "Modern Girl Around the World" project note both the commonalities in the "modern girl" image and also the local differences. Cosmetics and soap advertisements throughout the globe confirm the proliferation of skin-whitening products and their association with sexual attractiveness and modernity; yet individual ads also show significant locally rooted differences in how the ads directed their appeals. In fashion, Parisian houses that set the pace for much of the world's fashion industry attracted an internationally oriented elite clientele, but down-scale adaptations with local twists quickly emerged and catered to larger groups with differentiated tastes.[266]

The images and practices of consumerism thus helped shape the visual environment, particularly of cosmopolitan cities; and by offering code-switching possibilities, consumerism encouraged a style of modernity characterized by pastiche and allowing for differentiated commonalities. Mass consumerism undoubtedly bolstered the power of the world's capital centers, especially those in the United States, an export powerhouse in the 1920s. But it also challenged and played with many seemingly fixed definitions, particularly those related to gender, ethnicity, sexuality, and national culture.

The emergence of an increasingly globalized mass culture may have been one of the most important characteristics of this age. Innovations in media—mass publication, traveling shows, and film—helped create the era's adventurers, entertainers, and mass marketers, whose spreading transnational networks channeled the spectacular forms and formulas that, in turn, looped back to feed the new media. Radiating through the protean and nonspatial geographies of transnationalism, the currents that carried mass cultural products mapped, unmapped, and remapped the globe. The sureties of territoriality gave way to movement and to the ever-changing configurations of connectivity.

The new worlds born within the expanding availability of images and codes could be ones of shrunken space and dissolved boundaries, but they could also be worlds that accentuated difference and incommensurability. By drawing together the world's people within representational, often moneymaking, forms of written and visual images, dissimilarities could be both muted and exaggerated. Like all of the global networks of this era, the highly symbolic realms of media worked in no simple or uniform way toward building a global audience or toward accommodating global variation.

The multiplication of consumer codes that different people could accept, reject, adapt, or combine in almost limitless patterns became a hallmark of spectacularized cultural modernity. As transnational circulation of an ever-widening variety of consumer codes spread, the possibilities for interpellation (and reinterpellation) into an increasingly broad array of cultural identifications accelerated. By code-switching to create different assemblages of consumerist goods and activities, individual and national identities could be constructed in a kind of modular fashion. Variously coded attributes could be switched on or off, combined with others, and modified in different degrees. Even as mass consumerism's main productive and profit-making centers remained firmly anchored in the West, its symbols presented an aspirational world of self-fashioning that spanned the globe.

The rise of transnational mass cultural enterprises and codes signaled the broader transformation that was at work during this era—"the move from a nineteenth-century imperial tactic of spatial discovery by occupation to one of territorial ubiquity through technology and representation."[267] The late nineteenth and early twentieth centuries' obsessions with cartography, territorial exploration, nation building, and empire building were parts of a worldview that had framed a civilizing project of global improvement marked by territorial acquisition. The seeming solidity of geographical maps provided an apt symbol of that teleological sensibility. What Charles Maier has called the "hyperstates" that embraced communism and fascism tried to use law and repression to control cultural codes they deemed threatening. So did many imperial, and anti-imperial, authorities. By the mid-twentieth century, however, the fleeting and spectacularized images of a transnational, consumerist mass culture increasingly beckoned the future. Coproduced and complex networks stood ready to invade any demarcated territory. Flows of images and other codes held potential for a continual remapping of significations and relationships. The onset of this flickering, unstable, and electronics-shaped modernity came linked, perhaps, to the rise of the United States' particular brand of global dominance in its short "American Century" (famously announced by Henry Luce in 1941), but state power could hardly control the increasingly interactive landscapes of meaning.

·   ·   ·

As the world shrank between 1870 and 1945, changes in one domain and one geography connected, often quickly and unpredictably, to transformations in numerous others. Two closing examples underscore how interconnections and disjunctures coexisted.

As entrepreneurs raced to lay oceanic telegraphic cables during the second half of the nineteenth century, the demand rose sharply for a natural rubber-like substance called gutta-percha, which could protect electric lines from seawater corrosion. Found in Southeast Asia and extracted by forest dwellers who would kill the wild trees to extract the profitable gum, the gutta-percha boom deforested land and changed the power relationships and living patterns of nearby people. This ravaging of specific Southeast Asian forestland enabled both a European-centered communications revolution and also a global network of connectivity. It helped draw people and nations together even as it created new inequalities among them.[268] Thinking simultaneously about the forest dwellers, living locally, and the near-instantaneous telegraphy, which obliterated space, helps suggest the many unpredictable interrelationships within this era's local, national, imperial, international, and transnational networks of people, goods, and ideas.

During the next generation of the communications revolution, in the first half of the twentieth century, innovators laid the production and distribution networks for motion pictures and radio. Entrepreneurs and governments understood that their efforts depended on electrical energy. Generated primarily from coal, oil, and hydroelectric dams, electricity rapidly transformed not only how people traded, traveled, and made war, but also their ability to manufacture symbol-laden images that circulated meanings, aspirations, identities, and desires. Electricity increased human energy consumption exponentially, and access to electrical energy facilitated both "hard" and "soft" power, even as two world wars highlighted the important connections between being able to produce what was "real" and "reel." Rivalries for control over energy supplies, especially oil, and over symbolic industries, especially movie production and radio, shadowed each other. Nations, colonies hoping to become nations, businesses, localized groups, and transnational organizations all engaged in complicated moves to enhance their influence in a conjoined world. Every network affected every other one. Materiality and representation, once imagined as fairly separable realms, increasingly fused together.

These two examples suggest how the new technologies of connectivity rippled globally and cascaded from realm to realm, affecting livelihoods, cultures, identities, geopolitics, and power relationships of all kinds. Such networked processes epitomize the invisible and irregular currents of global change within transnational space during this period, and they foreshadow the complexities of power that would characterize the late twentieth century and beyond.

Notes

Selected Bibliography

Contributors

Index

Notes

Introduction

1. William H. McNeill, *The Rise of the West: A History of the Human Community* (Chicago: University of Chicago Press, 1963); Immanuel Wallerstein, *The Capitalist World Economy* (Cambridge: Cambridge University Press, 1979). Critiques of Eurocentrism include Jack Goody, *The Theft of History* (Cambridge: Cambridge University Press, 2006); and Dipesh Chakrabarty, *Provincializing Europe: Postcolonial Thought and Historical Difference,* rev. ed. (Princeton, NJ: Princeton University Press, 2007).

2. Kenneth Pomeranz, *The Great Divergence: China, Europe, and the Making of the Modern World Economy* (Princeton, NJ: Princeton University Press, 2000); James Belich, *Replenishing the Earth: The Settler Revolution and the Rise of the Anglo-World, 1783–1939* (New York: Oxford University Press, 2009); Jürgen Osterhammel, *Europe, the "West" and the Civilizing Mission* (London: German Historical Institute, 2006); Osterhammel, *Geschichtswissenschaft jenseits des Nationalstaats* (Göttingen: Vandenhoeck & Ruprecht, 2001); Osterhammel, *Die Entzauberung Asiens: Europa und die asiatischen Reiche im 18. Jahrhundert,* 2nd ed. (Munich: C. H. Beck, 2010), 378; Michael Adas, *Machines as the Measure of Men: Science, Technology, and Ideologies of Western Dominance* (Ithaca, NY: Cornell University Press, 1989); Uday Singh Mehta, *Liberalism and Empire: A Study in Nineteenth-Century British Liberal Thought* (Chicago: University of Chicago Press, 1999); Jennifer Pitts, *A Turn to Empire: The Rise of Imperial Liberalism in Britain and France* (Princeton, NJ: Princeton University Press, 2005).

3. C. A. Bayly, *The Birth of the Modern World, 1780–1914* (Oxford: Blackwell, 2004), 476 (for quotations). Also see Michael Geyer and Charles Bright, "World History in a Global Age," *American Historical Review* 100 (October 1995): 1034–1060; Sebastian Conrad and Dominic M. Sachsenmaier, eds., *Competing Visions of World Order: Global Moments and Movements, 1880–1935* (New York: Palgrave, 2007).

4. A. G. Hopkins, ed., *Global History: Interactions between the Universal and the Local* (New York: Palgrave Macmillan, 2006); Hopkins, ed., *Globalization in World History* (New York: W. W. Norton, 2002); Jerry H. Bentley, Renate Bridenthal, and Anand A. Yang, eds., *Interactions: Transregional Perspectives on World History* (Honolulu: University of Hawai'i Press, 2005).

5. Pierre-Yves Saunier and Shane Ewen, eds., *Another Global City: Historical Explorations into the Transnational Municipal Moment, 1850–2000* (New York: Palgrave, 2008).

6. James C. Scott, *The Art of Not Being Governed: An Anarchist History of Upland Southeast Asia* (New Haven: Yale University Press, 2009).

7. Sebastian Conrad, *Globalisation and the Nation in Imperial Germany,* trans. Sorcha O'Hagan (Cambridge: Cambridge University Press, 2010).

8. Eric Hobsbawm, *The Age of Extremes* (New York: Pantheon, 1995), 1–178.

9.   This estimate of deaths attributed to Stalin's policies in the 1930s is discussed in Norman M. Naimark, *Stalin's Genocides* (Princeton, NJ: Princeton University Press, 2010), 11.

10. Mark Mazower, *Dark Continent: Europe's Twentieth Century* (New York: Knopf, 1999), 1–249; Timothy Snyder, *Bloodlands: Europe between Hitler and Stalin* (New York: Basic Books, 2010); Shelley Baranowski, *Nazi Empire: German Colonialism and Imperialism from Bismarck to Hitler* (New York: Cambridge University Press, 2010); Louise Young, *Japan's Total Empire: Manchuria and the Culture of Wartime Imperialism* (Berkeley: University of California Press, 1999).

11. J. R. McNeill, *Something New under the Sun: An Environmental History of the Twentieth-Century World* (New York: W. W. Norton, 2001); David Blackbourn, *The Conquest of Nature: Water, Landscape, and the Making of Modern Germany* (New York: W. W. Norton, 2007).

1. Leviathan 2.0: Inventing Modern Statehood

The author wants to acknowledge the Woodrow Wilson International Center for Scholars in Washington, DC, which named him Distinguished Fellow and provided a stimulating milieu for writing the brunt of this history in the spring of 2011. He is grateful in particular to his former student, Vanessa Ogle, now teaching at the University of Pennsylvania, who commented on section drafts; to his American editors, Akira Iriye and Emily Rosenberg; his colleagues Niall Ferguson and Sven Beckert, who read the work and offered much-appreciated encouragement; and his wife, Pauline, who put up with his mental and physical absences after she completed her own splendid book, *Ratification*. This chapter is dedicated to the fellow faculty and student advisees of the past three decades in the Harvard History Department, who have collectively encouraged the most encompassing study of the past.

1.   See, most recently, Nathaniel Philbrick, *The Last Stand: Custer, Sitting Bull, and the Battle of the Little Bighorn* (New York: Viking, 2010).

2.   See Rudi Linder, "What Was a Nomadic Tribe?," *Comparative Studies in Society and History* 24 (1982): 689–711, at 691.

3.   Reşat Kasaba, *A Moveable Empire: Ottoman Nomads, Migrants, and Refugees* (Seattle: University of Washington Press, 2009), 116. For the long history of native American struggles, resistance, and removals, see Daniel Richter, *Facing East from Indian Country: A Native History of Early America* (Cambridge, MA: Harvard University Press, 2001); Pekka Hämäläinen, *The Comanche Empire* (New Haven, CT: Yale University Press, 2008); and Hämäläinen, "The Rise and Fall of Plains Indian Horse Cultures," *Journal of American History* 90 (2003): 833–862. For the Zulu and other peoples of southern Africa, I have relied on the contributions by Monica Wilson and Leonard Thompson, editors of *The Oxford History of South Africa,* vol. 1, *South Africa to 1870* (New York: Oxford University Press, 1969); also Andrew Roberts, *A History of Zambia* (New York: Holmes and Meier, Africana Publishing Co., 1976).

4.   James C. Scott, *The Art of Not Being Governed: An Anarchist History of Upland Southeast Asia* (New Haven, CT: Yale University Press, 2009). Scott writes, "The huge literature on state-making, contemporary and historic, pays virtually no attention to its obverse: the history of

deliberate and reactive statelessness" (p. x). But of course we have long celebrated "those who got away"—at least from Robin Hood on. For Scott's critique of state regulatory projects, see his *Seeing Like a State: How Certain Schemes to Improve the Human Condition Have Failed* (New Haven, CT: Yale University Press, 2008).

5. As Max Weber defined it, the state is the human community that claims a monopoly of legitimate power in a given territory. "Legitimate" is a crucial adjective—the mafia doesn't count—and "territory," he declared, was a critical attribute. See Weber, "Politics as a Vocation," in *From Max Weber: Essays in Sociology,* ed. H. H. Gerth and C. Wright Mills (New York: Oxford University Press, 1958), 78; also in Max Weber, *Gesamtausgabe,* Abt. 1, Bd. 17, ed. Wolfgang J. Mommsen, Wolfgang Schluchter and Birgitt Morgenbrod (Tübingen: Mohr, 1992).

6. Quentin Skinner, *The Foundations of Modern Political Thought,* 2 vols. (Cambridge: Cambridge University Press, 1978), 2:348–358. A useful discussion of the early development of the concept of the state in comparative contexts is provided by Oleg Kharkordin, "What Is the State? The Russian Concept of *Gosudarstvo* in European Context," *History and Theory* 40, no. 2 (May 2001): 206–240. See also Charles S. Maier, "Nation and State," in *Encyclopedia of Transnational History,* ed. Akira Iriye and Pierre-Yves Saunier (New York: Macmillan, 2009)—a summary I would now rewrite to allow for non-Western categories.

7. For an encyclopedic treatment of the development of the early modern state in particular, see Wolfgang Reinhard, *Geschichte der Staatsgewalt: Eine vergleichende Verfassungsgeschichte Europas von den Anfängen bis zur Gegenwart* (Munich: Beck, 1999). There are many treatments of sovereignty: among recent ones, see Robert Jackson: *Sovereignty: Evolution of an Idea* (Cambridge: Polity Press, 2007); Stephen D. Krasner, *Sovereignty: Organized Hypocrisy* (Princeton, NJ: Princeton University Press, 1999); Daniel Philpott, *Revolutions in Sovereignty: How Ideas Shaped Modern International Relations* (Princeton, NJ: Princeton University Press, 2001). Andreas Osiander has contested the importance of Westphalia—see Osiander, "Sovereignty, International Relations, and the Westphalian Myth," *International Organization* 55, no. 2 (2001): 251–287—but it has become the common designation for modern statehood.

8. David C. Kang, *East Asia before the West: Five Centuries of Trade and Tribute* (New York: Columbia University Press, 2010).

9. I am indebted to the ongoing dissertation research of Macabe Kelliher at Harvard on the Board of Rites in late imperial China. See too Joseph Peter McDermott, ed., *State and Court Ritual in China* (Cambridge: Cambridge University Press, 1999), in particular the summary essay by James Laidlaw, "On Theatre and Theory: Reflections on Ritual in Imperial Chinese Politics," 399–416, which stresses how ritual inserts state power into cosmological concepts. For a discussion of state power, see also Michael Mann, "The Autonomous Power of the State," in *States in History,* ed. John A. Hall (New York: Basil Blackwell, 1986).

10. There is a large literature, from the 1970s and 1980s in particular. See J. G. A. Pocock, *The Machiavellian Moment* (Princeton, NJ: Princeton University Press, 1975); Isaac Kramnick, *Bolingbroke and His Circle: The Politics of Nostalgia in the Age of Walpole* (Cambridge, MA: Harvard University Press, 1968); Charles S. Maier, " 'Fictitious Bonds of Wealth and Law,' " in *Organizing Interests in Western Europe,* ed. Suzanne Berger (Cambridge: Cambridge University Press, 1981); Pierre Rosanvallon, *Le moment Guizot* (Paris: Gallimard, 1985).

11. Two recent and important treatments of global history choose the entire nineteenth century as their temporal unit of analysis: C. A. Bayly, *The Birth of the Modern World, 1780–1914* (Malden, MA: Blackwell, 2004); and Jürgen Osterhammel, *Die Verwandlung der Welt* (Munich: Beck, 2009).

12. Eric J. Hobsbawm popularized the idea of the short twentieth century, 1914–1989, and then used it as the subtitle of the 1994 edition of his *The Age of Extremes: The Short Twentieth Century, 1914–1991* (London: Michael Joseph, 1994). Taking account of the transformative changes of the late eighteenth century and its impact, the German historian Reinhart Koselleck termed the era a *Sattelzeit* or "saddle time"—a metaphor he derived from the German expression for a "mountain saddle" or pass between two peaks—that is, the transition from one age to another. For the idea of moral narratives (as contrasted with analysis of long-term processes), see Charles S. Maier, "Consigning the Twentieth Century to History: Alternative Narratives for the Modern Era: Forum Essay," *American Historical Review* 105, no. 3 (June 2000): 807–831. The underlying idea of simultaneous scales—the history of events, of eras, and environmentally determined "longue durée"—was presented in Fernand Braudel, *The Mediterranean and the Mediterranean World in the Age of Philip II,* trans. Siân Reynolds (London: Collins, 1972–1973). For historians' theories of crisis, especially as applied to the late eighteenth century, see Reinhard Koselleck, "Crisis," *Journal of the History of Ideas* 67, no. 2 (2006): 357–400; and James R. Martin, "The Theory of Storms: Jacob Burckhardt and the Concept of 'Historical Crisis,'" in *Journal of European Studies* 40, no. 4 (2010): 307–327.

13. Shelley, *Prometheus Unbound,* act 4, lines 572, 576–578.

14. Karen Barkey, *An Empire of Difference: The Ottomans in Comparative Perspective* (Cambridge: Cambridge University Press, 2008); Halil Inalcik, *Essays in Ottoman History* (Istanbul: Erin, 1998); Cemal Cafadar, *Between Two Worlds: The Construction of the Ottoman State* (Berkeley: University of California Press, 1995); M. Sükrü Hanioğlu, *A Brief History of the Late Ottoman Empire* (Princeton, NJ: Princeton University Press, 2008); Donald Quataert, *The Ottoman Empire, 1700–1922* (New York: Cambridge University Press, 2000); *The Cambridge History of Turkey,* vol. 3, *The Later Ottoman Empire, 1603–1839,* ed. Suraiya N. Faroqhi (Cambridge: Cambridge University Press, 2008).

15. Karl Polanyi described this process for England in *The Great Transformation* (1944; Boston: Beacon Press, 1958) but paradoxically argued that the resulting unrest was responsible not for liberalism, but ultimately for fascism. E. P. Thompson emphasized the tenacious resistance to market trends in agriculture in "The Moral Economy of the English Crowd in the Eighteenth Century," *Past and Present,* no. 50 (February 1971): 76–131. For a discussion of peasant communalism in Southeast Asia, see James C. Scott, *Weapons of the Weak: Everyday Forms of Peasant Resistance* (New Haven, CT: Yale University Press, 1985).

16. Alfred W. Crosby Jr., *The Columbian Exchange: Biological and Cultural Consequences of 1492* (Westport, CT: Greenwood, 1972); for the impact of smallpox, measles and other diseases (comparable in the Americas to the Black Death in Europe two centuries earlier), see Sheldon Watts, *Epidemics and History: Disease, Power and Imperialism* (New Haven, CT: Yale University Press, 1997); and Suzanne Austin Alchon, *A Pest in the Land: New World Epidemics in a Global Perspective* (Albuquerque: University of New Mexico Press, 2003). For shadow acres, see Kenneth

Pomeranz, *The Great Divergence: China, Europe, and the Making of the Modern World Economy* (Princeton, NJ: Princeton University Press, 2000); and the classic text by Sidney Mintz, *Sweetness and Power: The Place of Sugar in Modern History* (New York: Viking, 1985).

17. Rhoda Murphey, "Deforestation in Modern China," in *Global Deforestation and the Nineteenth-Century World Economy,* ed. Richard P. Tucker and John F. Richards (Durham, NC: Duke University Press, 1983), 111–128, quotation at 111.

18. Cited in Mark Elvin, *The Retreat of the Elephants: An Environmental History of China* (New Haven, CT: Yale University Press, 2004), 57. The stele recorded the resolution to reserve all the land on Mount Houlong as communal land that could be neither bought nor sold, and to care for the trees.

19. Warren Dean, *With Broadax and Firebrand: The Destruction of the Brazilian Atlantic Forest* (Berkeley: University of California Press, 1995), 190.

20. Domingo F. Sarmiento, *Facundo: Or Civilization and Barbarism,* trans. Mary Mann (New York: Penguin, 1998). For a modern portrait, see John Lynch, *Argentine Dictator: Jan Manuel de Rosas, 1829–1852* (Oxford: Oxford University Press, 1981).

21. See Jan de Vries, *The Industrious Revolution: Consumer Behavior and the Household Economy, 1650 to the Present* (Cambridge: Cambridge University Press, 2008).

22. See John H. Elliott, *Empires of the Atlantic World: Britain and Spain in America, 1492–1830* (New Haven, CT: Yale University Press, 2006).

23. Jeremy Adelman, *Sovereignty and Revolution in the Iberian Atlantic* (Princeton, NJ: Princeton University Press, 2006); Fred Anderson and Andrew Cayton, *The Dominion of War: Empire and Liberty in North America, 1500–2000* (New York: Viking, 2005).

24. See Peter Perdue, *China Marches West: The Qing Conquest of Central Eurasia* (Cambridge, MA: Harvard University Press, 2005) for the campaign against the Zunghars; and for a summary of the new interpretations of the Qing empire as a dynamic, Manchu-run imperial structure, see William T. Rowe, *China's Last Empire: The Great Qing* (Cambridge, MA: Harvard University Press, 2009).

25. Phyllis Deane and W. A. Cole, *British Economic Growth, 1688–1959: Trends and Structure,* 2nd ed. (Cambridge: Cambridge University Press, 1969), 62 for the British estimate. Firm statistics were available only from the 1850s. As of midcentury the French share was about 53 percent, Russia about 63 percent, Spain 70 percent. See B. R. Mitchell, *European Historical Statistics, 1750–1950* (London: Macmillan, 1978), table B1, pp. 51–64.

26. E. P. Thompson, *The Making of the English Working Class* (New York: Vintage, 1963).

27. William B. Taylor, "Banditry and Insurrection: Rural Unrest in Central Jalisco, 1790–1816," and John M. Hart, "The 1840s Southwestern Mexico Peasants' War: Conflict in a Transitional Society," both in *Riot, Rebellion, and Revolution: Rural Social Conflict in Mexico,* ed. Friedrich Katz (Princeton, NJ: Princeton University Press, 1988), 205–268.

28. Jerome Blum, *The End of the Old Order in Rural Europe* (Princeton, NJ: Princeton University Press, 1978); Geroid T. Robinson, *Rural Russia under the Old Régime: A History of the Landlord-Peasant World and a Prologue to the Peasant Revolution of 1917* (1932; New York: Macmillan, 1967); Boris N. Mironov, *The Social History of Imperial Russia, 1700–1917* (Boulder CO: Westview Press, 2000), 1:286–370.

29. William W. Hagen, *Ordinary Prussians: Brandenburg Junkers and Villagers, 1500–1840* (Cambridge: Cambridge University Press, 2002).

30. John Locke, *The Second Treatise of Government,* para. 41, in Locke, *Two Treatises of Government,* ed. Peter Laslett (Cambridge: Cambridge University Press, 1966), 296–297. For an extensive discussion of the doctrine of *terra nullius,* see Stuart Banner, "Why Terra Nullius? Anthropology and Property Law in Early Australia," *Law and History Review* (Spring 2005), http://www.historycooperative.org/journals/lhr/23.1/banner.html (5 Sep. 2011). On Mexico, see Emilio Kouri, *A Pueblo Divided: Business, Property, and Community in Papantla, Mexico* (Stanford, CA: Stanford University Press, 2004); the studies *in Liberals, the Church, and Indian Peasants: Corporate Lands and the Challenge of Reform in Nineteenth-Century Spanish America,* ed. Robert H. Jackson (Albuquerque: University of New Mexico Press, 1997); Raymond B. Craib, *Cartographic Mexico: A History of State Fixations and Fugitive Landscapes* (Durham, NC: Duke University Press, 2004).

31. See the valuable case studies relating to the legal enforcement of land claims in *Contract and Property in Early Modern China,* ed. Madeleine Zelin, Jonathan K. Ocko, and Robert Cardella (Stanford, CA: Stanford University Press, 2004).

32. For insights into the reform program and its results, in addition to works cited in the notes above, see Richard Herr, *Rural Change and Royal Finances in Spain at the End of the Old Regime* (Berkeley: University of California Press, 1989); Franz A. J. Szabo, *Kaunitz and Enlightened Absolutism, 1753–1780* (Cambridge: Cambridge University Press, 1994); Emma Rothschild, *Economic Sentiments: Adam Smith, Condorcet, and the Enlightenment* (Cambridge, MA: Harvard University Press, 2001), 72–86; Luke S. Roberts, *Mercantilism in a Japanese Domain: The Merchant Origins of Economic Nationalism in 18th-Century Tosa* (Cambridge: Cambridge University Press, 1998); Ranajit Guha, *A Rule of Property for Bengal: An Essay on the Idea of Permanent Settlement* (Paris: Mouton, 1963); Sugata Bose, *Peasant Labour and Colonial Capital: Rural Bengal since 1770,* vol. 3, pt. 2, of *The Cambridge History of India* (Cambridge: Cambridge University Press, 1993).

33. For a good case study of the conquered Rhineland, annexed to France for twenty years, see Gabriele B. Clemens, *Immobilienhändler und Spekulanten: Die sozial- und wirtschaftsgeschichtliche Bedeutung der Grosskäufer bei den Nationalgüterversteigerungen in den rheinischen Departements (1803–1813)* (Boppard am Rhein: H. Boldt, 1995).

34. Jan Bazant, *Alienation of Church Lands in Mexico: Social and Economic Aspects of the Liberal Revolution, 1856–1875* (Cambridge: Cambridge University Press, 1971), chap. 1 for the years after 1821; case studies in Jackson, *Liberals, the Church, and Indian Peasants;* Ethelia Ruiz Medrano, *Mexico's Indigenous Communities: Their Lands and Histories, 1500–2010,* trans. Russ Davidson (Boulder CO: University Press of Colorado, 2010); Robert J. Knowlton, *Church Property and the Mexican Reform, 1856–1910* (DeKalb: Northern Illinois University Press, 1976).

35. It has remained a major challenge for historians and historical sociologists to determine which communities remained loyal to the Church and which ones joined the revolutionary coalitions, turned on local priests, and participated in the reshuffling of landed assets. Proximity to towns and markets has been suggested as one variable: For France see, among other studies,

Paul Bois, *Paysans de l'Ouest: Des structures économiques et sociales aux options politiques, depuis l'époque révolutionnaire, dans la Sarthe* (Paris: Flammarion, 1978); also Charles Tilly, *The Vendée* (Cambridge, MA: Harvard University Press, 1976).

36. Hagen, *Ordinary Prussians,* 652–653.

37. See Carlos Marichal, "Las finanzas y la construcción de las nuevas naciones latinoamericanas," in *Historia General de America Latina* (Paris: UNESCO, 2003), 6:399–420.

38. See James J. Reid, *Crisis of the Ottoman Empire: Prelude to Collapse, 1839–1878* (Stuttgart: Franz Steiner Verlag, 2000), and, for a comparison of Mount Lebanon and northern Albania, Maurus Reinkowski, *Die Dinge der Ordnung: Eine vergleichende Untersuchung über die osmanische Reformpolitik im 19 Jahrhundert* (Munich: R. Oldenbourg Verlag, 2000)—both of which stress the fragmentation, violence, and yet military incapacity of the Ottoman state despite the reforms of the Tanzimat.

39. On the social and political background of these conflicts, see Bruce McGowan, "The Age of the *Ayans,* 1699–1812," in *An Economic and Social History of the Ottoman Empire, 1300–1914,* ed. Halil Inalcik with Donald Quataert (Cambridge: Cambridge University Press, 1994), pt. 3, 637–758.

40. *The Cambridge History of Egypt,* vol. 2: *Modern Egypt from 1517 to the End of the Twentieth Century,* ed. M. W. Daly (Cambridge: Cambridge University Press, 1998). I have drawn on chapters 6, 7, and 8 (pp. 139–216), by Khaled Fahmy, F. Robert Hunter, and Hassan Ahmed Ibrahim, respectively.

41. Halil Inalcik, "The Nature of Traditional Society: Turkey" [1964], in *The Ottoman Empire: Conquest, Organization and Economy* (London: Variorum Reprints, 1978). For the balance between Istanbul and the elites and the efforts at tax reform and control of land, see Donald Quataert, "The Age of Reforms," in Inalcik and Quataert, *History of the Ottoman Empire,* pt. 4, esp. 854–861.

42. Dwight H. Perkins et al., *Agricultural Development in China, 1368–1968* (Chicago: Aldine, 1969), chaps. 2–4.

43. For the crisis of the late Qianlong reign, see Philip A. Kuhn, *Origins of the Modern Chinese State* (Stanford, CA: Stanford University Press, 2002).

44. Adam Smith, *An Inquiry into the Nature and Causes of the Wealth of Nations* (Oxford: Oxford University Press, 1976), 1:89.

45. Cited by Kuhn, *Origins,* 32.

46. See Jack Gray, *Rebellions and Revolutions: China from the 1800s to the 1980s* (Oxford: Oxford University Press, 1990), 8–15.

47. For a pro-British account, see ibid.; but cf. Fred Wakeman Jr., "The Canton Trade and the Opium War," in *The Cambridge History of China,* vol. 10, *Late Ch'ing, 1800–1911,* pt. 1, 163–212.

48. Stephen Vlastos, *Peasant Protests and Uprisings in Tokugawa Japan* (Berkeley: University of California Press, 1986), 75–79.

49. David Dean Commins, *Islamic Reform: Politics and Social Change in Late Ottoman Syria* (New York: Oxford University Press, 1990).

50. Bayly, *Birth of the Modern World,* 333–357.

51. For an analysis of goals, composition, ideas, and resources see Philip A. Kuhn, *Rebellion and Its Enemies in Late Imperial China* (Cambridge, MA: Harvard University Press, 1970); also Kuhn, "The Taiping Rebellion," in *The Cambridge History of China,* vol. 10, pt. 1, pp. 264–317.

52. C. A. Bayly, *Indian Society and the Making of the British Empire,* vol. 2, pt. 1, of *The New Cambridge History of India* (Cambridge: Cambridge University Press, 1988), 172.

53. For the looting and symbolism of the British conquest in 1860, see James L. Hevia, *English Lessons: The Pedagogy of Imperialism in Nineteenth-Century China* (Durham, NC: Duke University Press, 2003), 68–118.

54. Cited by Federico Chabod, *Italian Foreign Policy: The Statecraft of the Founders,* William Mc-Cuaig, trans. (Princeton, NJ: Princeton University Press, 1996), 552.

55. Bonnie Smith, *Ladies of the Leisure Class: The Bourgeoises of Northern France in the Nineteenth Century* (Princeton NJ: Princeton University Press, 1981); also Smith, *Changing Lives: Women in European History since 1700* (Lexington, MA: D. C. Heath, 1989); for British middle-class women's history: Leonore Davidoff and Catherine Hall, *Family Fortunes* (London: Routledge, 2002); *The Routledge History of Women in Europe since 1700,* Deborah Simonton, ed. (New York: Routledge, 2006).

56. Albert Hourani, *Arabic Thought in the Liberal Age, 1798–1939* (Cambridge: Cambridge University Press, 1983), 67–123.

57. Samuel Smiles, *Self-Help: With Illustrations of Conduct and Perseverance,* ed. Peter W. Sinnema (1859; Oxford: Oxford University Press, 2002); Bayly, *Birth of the Modern World,* 319.

58. Peter J. Hugill, *World Trade since 1431: Geography, Technology, and Capitalism* (Baltimore: Johns Hopkins University Press, 1993), 174.

59. From Charles Dickens, *Dombey and Son;* as quoted in Myron F. Brightfield, "The Coming of the Railroads to Victorian Britain as Viewed by Novels of the Period (1840–1870)," *Technology and Culture* 3, no. 1 (1962): 45–72, here 52. The second quote is from "Railroads in the United States," *Hunt's Merchant Magazine,* October 1840, 273–295, here 287.

60. Cavour's review of Pettiti in the *Revue Nouvelle* as cited in Harry Hearder, *Italy in the Age of the Risorgimento* (London: Longman, 1983), 212.

61. A. A. Den Otter, *The Philosophy of Railways: The Transcontinental Railway Idea in British North America* (Toronto: University of Toronto Press, 1997).

62. Cited in *China's Response to the West: A Documentary Survey, 1839–1923,* ed. Ssu-jü Teng and John K. Fairbank (Cambridge, MA: Harvard University Press, 1979), 117–119.

63. Clarence B. Davis, Kenneth E. Wilburn, with Ronald E. Robinson, *Railway Imperialism* (New York: Greenwood Press, 1991). On the cooperation of post–Civil War elites and the creation of a quasi-colonial economy in the South, see C. Vann Woodward, *Origins of the New South, 1877–1913* (Baton Rouge: Louisiana State University Press, 1951); and Robert L. Brandfon, *Cotton Kingdom of the New South: A History of the Yazoo Mississippi Delta from Reconstruction to the Twentieth Century* (Cambridge, MA: Harvard University Press, 1967). Where the older empires—Ottoman and Russian—retained railroad ownership, there was less opportunity for this coalition building, although private magnates emerged via contractual arrangements. The other investment opportunity that served as a sort of melting pot for old and new money was in urban real estate, as cities grew after 1870.

64. Cited by Chabod, *Italian Foreign Policy,* 53.

65. John Lynch, *Caudillos in Spanish America, 1800–1850* (New York: Oxford University Press, 1992); Tulio Halperín Donghi, *Guerra y finanzas en los orígenes del Estado Argentina, 1791–1850* (Buenos Aires: Belgrano, 1982); Halperín Donghi, ed., *Projecto y construcción de una nación: Argentina, 1846–1880* (Caracas: Biblioteca Ayacucho, 1980); Fernando López-Alves, *State Formation and Democracy in Latin America, 1810–1900* (Durham, NC: Duke University Press, 2000); Benedict Anderson, *Imagined Communities: Reflections on the Origin and Spread of Nationalism* (London: Verso, 1983).

66. For the Taiping, see Franz Michael and Chang Chung-li, *The Taiping Rebellion: History and Documents,* 3 vols. (Seattle: University of Washington Press, 1966–1971); Jonathan Spence, *God's Chinese Son: The Taiping Heavenly Kingdom of Hong Xiuquan* (New York: W. W. Norton, 1996); Jen Yu-wen (Chien Yu-wen), *The Taiping Revolutionary Movement* (New Haven, CT: Yale University Press, 1973); Vincent Shih, *The Taiping Ideology: Its Sources, Interpretations, and Influences* (Seattle: University of Washington Press, 1967); C. A. Curwen, *Taiping Rebel: The Deposition of Li Hsiu-ch'eng* (New York: Cambridge University Press, 1977).

67. Geoffrey Wawro, *The Austro-Prussian War* (Cambridge: Cambridge University Press, 1996), citation of the Albrecht memo, "Über die Verantwortlichkeit im Kriege," at 291. The Prussians also had much more rapidly reloadable breech-loading rifles (the so-called Needle Guns) vs. Austrian muzzle loaders.

68. George Frederickson, *The Inner Civil War: Northern Intellectuals and the Crisis of the Union* (New York: Harper and Row, 1965), 98–112, on the sanitary commission; for British wartime conditions, see Mark Bostridge, *Florence Nightingale: The Making of an Icon* (New York: Farrar, Straus and Giroux, 2008); also Hugh Small, *Florence Nightingale, Avenging Angel* (New York: St. Martin's, 1998).

69. David Blackbourn, *Marpingen: Apparitions of the Virgin in Nineteenth-Century Germany* (New York: Knopf, 1994); Emmet J. Larkin, *The Making of the Roman Catholic Church in Ireland, 1850–1860* (Chapel Hill: University of North Carolina Press, 1980), among his other works; E. E. Y. Hales, *Pio Nono: A Study in European Politics and Religion in the Nineteenth Century* (Garden City, NY: Doubleday, 1962); Frank Coppa, *Pope Pius IX: Crusader in a Secular Age* (Boston: Twayne, 1979).

70. For a selection of recent analyses of nineteenth-century nationalism, see Anderson, *Imagined Communities;* John Breuilly, *Nationalism and the State,* 2nd ed. (Chicago: University of Chicago Press, 1994); Rogers Brubaker, *Citizenship and Nationhood in France and Germany* (Cambridge, MA: Harvard University Press, 1993); Ernest Gellner, *Nations and Nationalism* (Ithaca, NY: Cornell University Press, 2002); Eric J. Hobsbawm, *Nations and Nationalism since 1780: Programme, Myth, Reality* (New York: Cambridge University Press, 1990); Miroslaw Hroch, *Social Preconditions of National Revolution in Europe: A Comparative Analysis of the Social Composition of Patriotic Groups among the Smaller European Nations* (New York: Columbia University Press, 2000). Works on Asian and African nationalism tend to focus on the twentieth century.

71. I am indebted to Marta Petrusevic for pointing to the role of agricultural improvement societies as proxies for nationalist organization.

72. Alexander Herzen, "From the Other Shore," trans. L. Navrozov, and "To an Old Comrade," both in *Selected Philosophical Works* (Moscow: Foreign Languages, 1956), 343, 577–578.

73. Ernest Satow, *A Diplomat in Japan: An Inner History of the Critical Years in the Evolution of Japan* (Rutland, VT: Charles E. Tuttle, 1983).

74. Carol Gluck, *Japan's Modern Myths: Ideologies in the Meiji Period* (Princeton, NJ: Princeton University Press, 1985).

75. Applied to Japan (as they had long been to European struggles from the seventeenth century), Marxist-derived analyses were represented by E. H. Norman, *Origins of the Modern Japanese State: Selected Writings of E. H. Norman,* ed. John W. Dower (New York: Pantheon, 1975).

76. Karl Marx, *The Eighteenth Brumaire of Louis Bonaparte* (New York: International, 1964); Karl Marx (and Friedrich Engels), *Revolution and Counter-Revolution: Or Germany in 1848,* ed. Eleanor Aveling Marx (New York: Scribner's, 1896).

77. For the major recent account, see James M. McPherson, *Ordeal by Fire: The Civil War and Reconstruction,* 3rd ed. (Boston: McGraw-Hill, 2001).

78. Still valuable, Albert D. Kirwan, *Revolt of the Rednecks: Mississippi Politics, 1865–1925* (Gloucester, MA: P. Smith, 1964).

79. Brian DeLay, *War of a Thousand Deserts: Indian Raids and the U.S.-Mexican War* (New Haven, CT: Yale University Press, 2008); Hämäläinan, *The Comanche Empire.* Both books have transformed our vision of the confrontation between Mexico and America.

80. Nelson Reed, *The Caste War of Yucatan* (Stanford, CA: Stanford University Press, 1964).

81. For fine comparative analysis, see López-Alves, *State Formation;* and J. G. Merquior, "Patterns of State-Building in Brazil and Argentina," in *States in History,* ed. John A. Hall (Oxford: Blackwell, 1987), 264–288; also thematic surveys in *Historia General de América Latina,* vol. 6, *La construcción de las naciones latinoamericanas, 1820–1870,* ed. Josefina Z. Vázquez and Manuel Miño Grijalva (Paris: UNESCO, 2003), esp. chaps. 1–6.

82. For Austria-Hungary, see Robert A. Kann, *A History of the Habsburg Empire, 1526–1918* (Berkeley: University of California Press, 1974); Arthur J. May, *The Hapsburg Monarchy, 1867–1914* (1951: New York: W. W. Norton, 1968); C. A. Macartney, *The Habsburg Empire, 1790–1918* (New York: Macmillan, 1969). For key internal developments: Louis Eisenmann, *Le compromis austro-hongrois de 1867* (Paris: G. Bellais, 1904); W. A. Jenks, *The Austrian Electoral Reform of 1907* (New York: Columbia University Press, 1960); and for constitutional issues, Josef Redlich, *Das Österreichische Staats- und Reichsproblem,* 2 vols. (Leipzig: P. Reinhold, 1921).

83. The growth of world's fairs or "Expositions Universelles" as registered with the Brussels-based Bureau International des Expositions, chartered in 1928—an NGO representative of the international organizational efforts of the 1920s—is a revealing development of global history. Cited here are Philadelphia 1876: 1.8 km^2 in area and over 10 million visitors; Paris 1878: 0.27 km^2 and over 13 million visitors; Paris 1889: 0.96 km^2 and 28 million visitors; Chicago ("Columbian Exposition") 1893: 2.4 km^2 and over 27 million visitors. The first major "expo" was the Crystal Palace Exhibit of 1851: 0.092 km^2 within one structure and over 6 million visitors; the largest would be the New York World's Fair of 1939–1940, covering almost 5 km^2 and attracting over 44 million visitors to view supposedly future-oriented exhibits based on "the world of tomorrow." "Tomorrow" turned out to be the Second World War.

84. See Alexander C. T. Geppert, *Fleeting Cities: Imperial Expositions in Fin-de-Siècle Europe* (Houdsmills, Basingstoke: Palgrave-Macmillan, 2010), 121–125.

85. Peter Sloterdijk, *Regeln für den Menschenpark: Ein Antwortschreiben zu Heideggers Brief über den Humanismus* (Frankfurt: Suhrkamp, 1999).

86. Suazanne Marchand, *German Orientalism in the Age of Empire: Religion, Race, and Scholarship* (Washington, DC: German Historical Institute; New York: Cambridge University Press, 2009); Yuri Slezkine, *Arctic Mirrors: Russia and the Small Peoples of the North* (Ithaca, NY: Cornell University Press, 1994); H. Glenn Penny and Matti Bunzl, eds., *Worldly Provincialism: German Anthropology in the Age of Empire* (Ann Arbor: University of Michigan Press, 2003).

87. Rudyard Kipling, "Recessional"; Henry Adams, "The Virgin and the Dynamo," in *Mont-Saint-Michel and Chartres* (1904; Princeton, NJ: Princeton University Press, 1981).

88. Patrice Higonnet has constructed his unsparing history of American interventions around this phrase used by Theodore Roosevelt. See his *Attendant Cruelties* (New York: New Press, 2008). For ecological transformations (and the labor patterns that attended them), see Scott, *Seeing Like a State;* and for a case study, Clifford Geertz, *Agricultural Involution: The Process of Ecological Change in Indonesia* (Berkeley: University of California Press, 1963).

89. 'Der Staat ist ein sittliches Wesen und er hat sittliche Lebensaufgaben." Johann Caspar Bluntschli, *Allgemeine Staatsrecht Geschichtlich Begründet,* 3rd rev. ed. (Munich: J. G. Cotta, 1863), 1:2.

90. Georg Jellinek, *Das Recht des modernen Staates,* vol. 1: *Allgemeine Staatslehre* (Berlin: O. Häring, 1900). "Durch Rechtssätze und Rechtszwang werden daher nationale Selbständigkeit und Macht, wirtschaftliches und geistiges Leben des Volkes auch gefördert, also sociale Resultate durch obrigkeitliche Macht bewirkt.... Briefe befördern, Eisenbahnen betreiben, Schulen gründen, Unterricht erteilen, Armenpflege üben, Strassen bauen sind an und für sich private Tätigkeiten, die im socialen, nicht im juristischen Sinne öffentlichen Charakter besitzen. Der Staat kann diese und ähnliche Tätigkeiten, wenn er sie ausübt oder durch Andere ausüben lässt, kraft seiner umfassenden Macht, mit der er Privat- in öffentliches Recht zu verwandeln vermag, zu öffentlichen im Rechtssinne erheben" (572).

91. Rudolph von Gneist, *The History of the English Constitution,* trans. Philip A. Ashworth, 2 vols. (London: William Clowes, 1886). Otto von Gierke, *Das deutsche Genossenschaftsrecht,* 4 vols. (Berlin: Weidman, 1868–1913), selections translated as *Community in Historical Perspective,* ed. Antony Black, trans. Mary Fischer (New York: Cambridge University Press, 1990). For French functionalists, see Léon Duguit, *Le droit social, le droit individuel et la transformation de l'état* (Paris: Felix Alcan, 1908), 37–38 and passim; Arthur Bentley, *The Process of Government: A Study of Social Pressure* (1908; Cambridge, MA: Harvard University Press, 1967). The groups that overthrew communist regimes in the 1990s claimed to be acting for "civil society"—a set of organizations, such as churches, unions, and voluntary associations, that exercised public functions but without relying on the coercive equipment of government in the 1990s—but this concept fell into increased disuse in the last decade as political parties slowly tightened their grip on postcommunist societies and did not relinquish it elsewhere.

92. Cf. Peter Baldwin, "Beyond Weak and Strong: Rethinking the State in Comparative Policy History," *Journal of Policy History* 17, no. 1 (2005): 12–33.

93. Jellinek, *Allgemeine Staatslehre,* 570–572. "Aus den früheren Untersuchungen bereits hat sich ergeben, dass nicht ausschliesslich auf sie beschränkt ist. Durch die Gemeinsamkeit der Herrschaft werden die ihr Unterworfenen Genossen. Die Förderung genossenschaftlicher Zwecke durch gesellschaftliche Mittel ist in stetig steigendem Masse Staatsaufgabe geworden" (570).

94. See James T. Kloppenburg, *Uncertain Victory: Social Democracy and Progressivism in European and American Thought, 1870–1920* (New York: Oxford University Press, 1986); and Daniel T. Rogers, *Atlantic Crossings: Social Politics in a Progressive Age* (Cambridge, MA: Harvard University Press, 1998). The American Economic Association divided between those who looked approvingly at the nascent German welfare state, such as Richard Ely, and those who condemned any infringement of laissez-faire principles. In Britain, social liberalism, which advocated state intervention, was represented preeminently by L. T. Hobhouse.

95. See Gluck, *Japan's Modern Myths.*

96. Michel Foucault, *Discipline and Punish: The Birth of the Prison* (New York: Pantheon, 1977), is a parable of state coerciveness and its change from physical punishment to the more universal concept of surveillance. See also Foucault, *The Archaeology of Knowledge,* trans. A. M. Sheridan Smith (New York: Harper and Row, 1972); James C. Scott, *Seeing Like a State.*

97. See James Joll, *The Anarchists* (London: Eyre and Spottiswoode, 1964); Temma Kaplan, *Anarchists of Andalusia, 1868–1903* (Princeton, NJ: Princeton University Press, 1977).

98. Michel Foucault, *Sécurité, territoire, population: Cours au Collège de France, 1977–1978* (Paris: Gallimard Seuil, 2004), esp. 111. See also Foucault's essay on governmentality in *The Foucault Effect,* ed. Graham Burchell, Colin Gordon, and Peter Miller (Chicago: University of Chicago Press, 1991); and cf. Mitchell Deane, *Governmentality: Power and Rule in Modern Society* (London: Sage, 1999). Foucault attributes this growing shift in agenda to the late medieval Catholic Church with its emphasis on pastoral care and administrative organization. Foucault suggests that the new efforts meant the advent of what he terms bio-politics: concern with bodies as the object of government and statecraft. Historians have also embraced this term, but I, for one, find it overinflated and generalized.

99. Jacques Donzelot, *L'invention du social: Essai sur le déclin des passions politiques* (Paris: Fayard, 1984).

100. For Britain, see Mary Poovey, *History of the Modern Fact: Problems of Knowledge in the Sciences of Wealth and Society* (Chicago: University of Chicago Press, 1998).

101. Matthew Edney, *Mapping an Empire: The Geographical Construction of British India* (Chicago: University of Chicago Press, 1997); Raymond B. Craig, *Cartographic Mexico: A History of State Fixations and Fugitive Landscapes* (Durham, NC: Duke University Press, 2004), 126–192.

102. Sabine Dabringhaus, *Territorialer Nationalismus in China: Historisch-geographisches Denken, 1900–1948* (Cologne: Böhlau, 2006).

103. Foucault, *Discipline and Punish.*

104. Scott, *Art of Not Being Governed.*

105. John Torpey, *The Invention of the Passport: Surveillance, Citizenship, and the State* (Cambridge: Cambridge University Press, 2000).

106. See John Wesley Powell, *Report on the Lands of the Arid Region of the United States* (Cambridge, MA: Harvard University Press, 1962).

107. Francis Amasa Walker, "The Eleventh Census of the United States," *Quarterly Journal of Economics* 2 (1848): 135–161, cited in Matthew O. Hannah, *Governmentality and the Mastery of Territory in Nineteenth-Century America* (New York: Cambridge University Press, 2000), 122. This material borrows from Hannah, who emphasizes Walker's efforts in his maps of climate, states, etc., to establish a sort of American exceptionalism.

108. Hannah, *Governmentality,* 139–140.

109. I borrow Vanessa Ogle's arguments about the so-called internationalism of the late nineteenth century; see Ogle, "Clocks, Calendars, and Conversion Charts: Reorganizing Time during the First Wave of Globalization, 1883–1930" (PhD diss., Harvard University, 2011).

110. Roberto Michels, *Political Parties: A Sociological Study of the Oligarchical Tendencies of Modern Democracy,* trans. Eden Paul and Cedar Paul (New York: Crowell-Collier, 1962); Moisei Ostrogorski, *Democracy and the Organisation of Political Parties* (New York: Macmillan, 1902), focusing on Britain, with an interesting preface by the observer of American politics Ambassador James Bryce; and Ostrogorski, *Democracy and the Party System in the United States: A Study in Extra-Constitutional Government* (New York: Macmillan, 1910).

111. On rightist political currents in late nineteenth- and early twentieth-century Europe, see, among a vast literature, Richard Drake, *Byzantium for Rome: The Politics of Nostalgia in Umbertian Italy, 1878–1900* (Chapel Hill: University of North Carolina Press, 1980); John W. Boyer, *Political Radicalism in Late Imperial Vienna: Origins of the Christian Social Movement, 1848–1897* (Chicago: University of Chicago Press, 1981); Eugene J. Weber, *Action Française: Royalism and Reaction in Twentieth-Century France* (Stanford, CA: Stanford University Press, 1962); Zeev Sternhell, *La Droite révolutionnaire: Les origines françaises du fascisme* (Paris: Fayard, 2000).

112. Cited by Wolfgang J. Mommsen, *Max Weber and German Politics, 1890–1920,* trans. Michael S. Steinberg (Chicago: University of Chicago Press, 1984), 69.

113. Carl Schmitt, *The Nomos of the Earth in the Jus Publicum Europeaum,* trans. G. L Ulmen (New York: Telos Press, 2003). For the Berlin conference and the process of partitioning Africa, see H. L. Wesseling, *Divide and Rule: The Partition of Africa, 1880–1914,* trans. Arnold J. Pomerans (Westport CT: Praeger, 1996). On the Congo, see Adam Hochschild, *King Leopold's Ghost: A Story of Greed, Terror and Heroism in Colonial Africa* (New York: Houghton Mifflin, 1998).

114. For the Marxist texts in recent versions, see Rosa Luxemburg, *The Accumulation of Capital,* trans. Agnes Schwarzschild (London: Routledge, 2003); Rudolf Hilferding, *Finance Capital: A Study of the Latest Phase of Capitalist Development,* ed. Tom Bottomore (London: Routledge and Kegan Paul, 1961); V. I. Lenin, *Imperialism: The Highest Stage of Capitalism,* ed. Norman Lewis and James Malone (London: Junius, 1996).

115. Hans Ulrich Wehler, *Bismarck und der Imperialismus,* 2nd ed. (1965; Frankfurt: Suhrkamp Verlag, 1984).

116. The Indian journal *Subaltern Studies,* founded by Ranajit Guha in 1982, served as the vehicle for this movement. See David Ludden, ed., *Reading Subaltern Studies: Critical History, Contested Meaning and the Globalization of South Asia* (London: Anthem, 2002); for the impact

of colonialism on metropole as well as colonial institutions, see Frederick Cooper and Ann Laura Stoler, *Tensions of Empire: Colonial Cultures in a Bourgeois World* (Berkeley: University of California Press, 1997); and for a less confrontational interpretation stressing the now-fashionable idea of hybridity, see Homi Bhabha, *The Location of Culture* (London: Routledge, 1994).

117. Frederic C. Cooper, *Colonialism in Question: Theory, Knowledge, History* (Berkeley: University of California Press, 2003).

118. Mahmood Mamdani, *Citizen and Subject: Contemporary Africa and the Legacy of Late Colonialism* (Princeton, NJ: Princeton University Press, 1996). For a concise description of the post-1918 colonial states that the French and British created out of the Ottoman provinces in the Middle East, see Roger Owen, *State, Power, and Politics in the Making of the Modern Middle East* (London: Routledge, 1992), 8–31. For a general description, see Jüergen Osterhammel, *Colonialism: A Theoretical Overview* (Princeton, NJ: Markus Wiener, 1997). For the British colonial administration's experience, see John W. Cell, "Colonial Rule," in *The Oxford History of the British Empire,* vol. 4: *The Twentieth Century,* ed. Judith M. Brown and Wm. Roger Louis (New York: Oxford University Press, 1998–1999), 232–254.

119. See Bayly, *Indian Society,* for the crises and transitions before the uprising of 1857. For a survey of the post-1857 organization of the Indian states (including their diverse origins), see Barbara M. Ramusack, *The Indian Princes and Their States,* vol. 3, pt. 6, of *The New Cambridge History of India* (Cambridge: Cambridge University Press, 2004), with a fine bibliography.

120. John R. McLane, *Indian Nationalism and the Early Congress* (Princeton, NJ: Princeton University Press, 1977), 22–26.

121. Michael O'Dwyer, *India as I Knew It, 1885–1925* (London: Constable and Co., 1925), 406; cf. Florence Deprest, *Géographes en Algérie (1880–1950): Savoirs universitaires en situation coloniale* (Paris: Bélin, 2009), for the tensions between colonialist hard-liners and those sympathetic to the Berber or Arab natives and their precapitalist economy.

122. See Alice Bullard, *Exile to Paradise: Savagery and Civilization in Paris and the South Pacific, 1790–1900* (Stanford, CA: Stanford University Press, 2000).

123. Stanislaw Lem, "Alfred Zellermann: 'Gruppenführer Louis XVI,'" in *A Perfect Vacuum,* trans. Michael Kandel (Evanston, IL: Northwestern University Press, 1999). The stories are cast in the form of book summaries that supposedly unite "elements that would appear to be totally irreconcilable . . . a thing that is at once the truth and a lie" (58). For a nonfictional and contested account of a state where ritual is claimed to be the whole purpose of rule, see Clifford Geertz, *Negara: The Theater State in Nineteenth-Century Bali* (Princeton, NJ: Princeton University Press, 1980). But state ritual certainly serves to codify stratification and domination.

124. Calculated from the figures provided (£360,000 costs, £75,000,000 revenues) in McLane, *Indian Nationalism,* 43.

125. See Margery Perham, *Lugard,* 2 vols. (London: Collins, 1960–1961); and Edmund Burke III, *Prelude to Protectorate in Morocco: Precolonial Protest and Resistance, 1860–1912* (Chicago: University of Chicago Press, 1976).

126. John William Burgess, *Political Science and Comparative Constitutional Law* (1890; Boston: Ginn and Co., 1900), 45–46.

127. George Steinmetz, *The Devil's Handwriting: Precoloniality and the German Colonial State in Qingdao, Samoa, and Southwest Africa* (Chicago: University of Chicago Press, 2007), 406–410; at the same time he recognized a value to Chinese civilization and saw himself as a type of super Mandarin.

128. Hevla, *English Lessons,* 223, 228. The looting of artifacts aroused criticism in the Western press. It had been outlawed by the Hague Conventions a couple of years earlier, and when the lapse had to be addressed, racial differences were cited as explanation.

129. See Yoshihisa Tak Matsusaka, *The Making of Japanese Manchuria, 1904–1932* (Cambridge, MA: Harvard University Press, 2001); also the introduction to Ronald Suleski, *The Modernization of Manchuria: An Annotated Bibliography* (Hong Kong: Chinese University Press, 1994). I owe bibliography to the Harvard dissertation research by Victor Seow on the coal-mining industry of Manchuria. See also Ramon Myers and Mark R. Peattie, eds., *The Japanese Colonial Empire* (Princeton, NJ: Princeton University Press, 1984).

130. Carl Schmitt, *Political Theology: Four Chapters on the Concept of Sovereignty* (Chicago: University of Chicago Press, 1985), 5. The German version, like the English, retains some ambiguity: did sovereignty imply the right to decide when an exceptional state existed and/or the right to decide when and to decree the measures needed? Did sovereignty mean more than just the de facto power to impose a state of emergency as in a coup d'état or was it sanctified with no more than force? From the context, he evidently believed that provision for determining and resolving the state of exception was implicitly a metaconstitutional measure. See also, for elaboration, Giorgio Agamben, *State of Exception* (Chicago: University of Chicago Press, 2005).

131. Again Foucault is the reference point for many contemporary historians, of Asia as well as Europe and the Americas. Whereas his earlier writing (e.g., *Discipline and Punish*) argued that the elaboration of a soft-power but carceral state represented only a modernization of concern with power, the late lectures separated the agenda of governmentality from sovereignty. See Eric Paras, *Foucault 2.0: Beyond Power and Knowledge* (New York: Other Press, 2006). Paras's valuable book originated as a Harvard doctoral dissertation, of which I was a second reader, and although I did not recall his work when I decided on the title of this work, his formulation of a second Foucault may well have stuck in my mind.

132. W. G. Beasley, *Japanese Imperialism, 1894–1945* (Oxford: Oxford University Press, 1987), 41–68.

133. A vast literature exists on this: see the relevant volumes of the monumental series by the Carnegie Endowment for International Peace, *Social and Economic History of the World War,* ed. James T. Shotwell (New Haven, CT: Yale University Press, 1928–); Gerald Feldman, *Army, Industry and Labor in Germany, 1914–1918* (Princeton, NJ: Princeton University Press, 1964); Keith Middlemas, *Politics in Industrial Society: The Experience of the British System since 1911* (London: A. Deutsch, 1979); Charles S. Maier, *Recasting Bourgeois Europe: Stabilization in France, Germany, and Italy in the Decade after World War I* (Princeton, NJ: Princeton University Press, 1975).

134. Niall Ferguson, *The War of the World: History's Age of Hatred* (London: Allen Lane, 2006). It is a view shared by scholars who generally take a political stance quite different from Ferguson's. See Robert Vitalis, "The Noble American Science of Imperial Relations and Its Laws of

Race Development," *Comparative Studies in Society and History* 52, no. 4 (2010): 909–938, esp. 911: "In the science of imperial relations, the world's biological boundaries mattered much more to theory building than did territorial boundaries." For the debate between "primordialists" and "constructivists," on the nature of ethnicity, see the recent discussion in Rogers Brubaker et al., *Nationalist Politics and Everyday Ethnicity in a Transylvanian Town* (Princeton, NJ: Princeton University Press, 2006); for a compromise stance I find congenial, see Anthony D. Smith, *The Antiquity of Nations* (Cambridge: Polity Press, 2004).

135. See Monica Wilson and Leonard Thompson, eds., *The Oxford History of South Africa,* 2 vols. (Oxford: Oxford University Press, 1971), 2:313–364, statistics on 338. For a comparison of South African and US racial practices, see John W. Cell, *The Highest Stage of White Supremacy: The Origins of Segregation in South Africa and the American South* (Cambridge: Cambridge University Press, 1982).

136. For the ambiguities of semicolonial status (as applied to China), see Tong Lam, "Policing the Imperial Nation: Sovereignty, International Law, and the Civilizing Mission in Late Qing China," *Comparative Studies in Society and History* 52, no. 4 (2010): 881–908.

137. Jack London, *The Iron Heel* (New York: Macmillan, 1907); Georges Sorel, *Réflexions sur la violence,* 4th ed. (1908; Paris: Marcel Rivière, 1919), which includes the preface saluting Lenin; "Agathon," pseudonym for Alfred deTarde and Henri Massis, *Les jeunes gens d'aujourd'hui: Le gout de l'action, la foi patriotique; Une renaissance catholique, le réalisme politique* (Paris: Plon-Nourrit, 1913); Robert Wohl, *The Generation of 1914* (Cambridge, MA: Harvard University Press, 1979).

138. Likhit Dhiravegin, *The Meiji Restoration, 1868–1912, and the Chakkri Reformation, 1865–1910: A Comparative Perspective* (Bangkok: Faulty of Political Science, Thammasat University, 1984); David K. Wyatt, *The Politics of Reform in Thailand: Education in the Reign of King Chulalongkorn* (New Haven, CT: Yale University Press, 1969); Walter E. J. Tips, *Gustave Rolin-Jaequemyns and the Making of Modern Siam: The Diaries and Letters of King Chulalongkorn's General Adviser* (Bangkok: Cheney, White Lotus, 1996); Bahru Zewde, *A History of Modern Ethiopia, 1855–1891,* rev. ed. (Columbus: Ohio University Press, 2001); Harold G. Marcus, *A History of Ethiopia* (Berkeley: University of California Press, 1994), 77–115; Marcus, *The Life and Times of Menelik II: Ethiopia, 1844–1913* (Oxford: Clarendon Press, 1975).

139. What they were *not* was a protest against economic stagnation. The years from 1896 to 1914 brought robust technological innovation and economic growth, certainly unevenly distributed but still vigorous and perhaps higher than any earlier period, and any era afterward until the 1950s and 1960s. Economics, however, did not assuage political discontent any more than the cross-border flows of capital, workers, and goods prevented war.

140. Cited from Nikki Keddi, "Iran under the Later Qajars, 1848–1922," in *The Cambridge History of Iran,* vol. 7: *From Nadir Shah to the Islamic Republic,* ed. Peter Avery, Gavin Hambly, Charles Melville (Cambridge: Cambridge University Press, 1991), 174–212, quotation at 196; see also Keddi, *Religion and Rebellion in Iran: The Tobacco Protest of 1891–1892* (London: Frank Cass, 1966).

141. Mangol Bayat, *Iran's First Revolution: Shi'is and the Constitutional Revolution of 1905–1909* (New York: Oxford University Press, 1991); Nikki Keddi, *Roots of Revolution: An Interpretive*

History of Modern Iran (New Haven, CT: Yale University Press, 1981); Firoozeh Kashani-Sabet, *Frontier Fictions: Shaping the Iranian Nation, 1804–1946* (Princeton, NJ: Princeton University Press, 1999); also Gavin R. G. Hambly, "The Pahlavi Autocracy: Riza Shah, 1921–1941," and P. Kazemzadeh, "Iranian Relations with Russia and the Soviet Union, to 1921," both in *The Cambridge History of Iran*, 213–225, 314–349.

142. Benjamin C. Fortna, "The Reign of Abdülhamid II," and M. Şükrü Hanioğlu, "The Second Constitutional Period, 1908–1918," both in *The Cambridge History of Turkey*, vol. 4, *Turkey in the Modern World*, ed. Reşat Kasaba (Cambridge: Cambridge University Press, 2008), 38–61, 62–101; also M. Şükrü Hanioğlu, *Preparation for a Revolution: The Young Turks, 1902–1908* (New York: Oxford University Press, 2001); Feroz Ahmad, *The Young Turks: The Committee of Union and Progress in Turkish Politics, 1908–1914* (Oxford: Clarendon Press, 1969); A. L. Macfie, *The End of the Ottoman Empire, 1908–1923* (New York: Addison Wesley Longman, 1998).

143. Hasan Kayali, "The Struggle for Independence," in *The Cambridge History of Turkey*, 4:112–146; Erik Jan Zürcher, *The Unionist Factor: The Role of the Committee of Union and Progress in the Turkish National Movement, 1905–1926* (Leiden: Brill, 1984); Andrew Mango, *Atatürk: The Biography of the Founder of Modern Turkey* (Woodstock NY: Overlook Press, 1999).

144. John Womack Jr., "The Mexican Revolution, 1910–1920," in *The Cambridge History of Latin America*, vol. 5: *c. 1870 to 1930*, ed. Leslie Bethell (Cambridge: Cambridge University Press, 1986), 79–152, quotation at 81; for the end of the Porfiriato, the presidential years of Porfirio Díaz, see also Friedrich Katz, "Mexico: Restored Republic and Porfiriato, 1867–1910," in Bethell, *The Cambridge History of Latin America*, esp. 62–78. On the role of foreign investment, see John Mason Hart, *Empire and Revolution: The Americans in Mexico since the Civil War* (Berkeley: University of California Press, 2002).

145. I draw on Friedrich Katz's monumental account, *The Life and Times of Pancho Villa* (Stanford, CA: Stanford University Press, 1998), esp. 354–487.

146. Jean Meyer, "Mexico: Revolution and Reconstruction in the 1920s," in Bethell, *The Cambridge History of Latin America*, 155–194.

147. Min Tu-Ki, *National Polity and Local Power: The Transformation of Late Imperial China* (Cambridge, MA: Harvard University Press and Harvard Yenching Institute, 1989), 89–179.

148. For a survey of Chinese development throughout the period covered in this chapter, see Jonathan D. Spence, *The Search for Modern China* (New York: W. W. Norton, 1990). Cf. Tong Lam, "Policing the Imperial Nation," esp. 907 for Lee Tinghou's lessons drawn from contemporary Japanese experience. On the reform movement of 1890–1898 and its aborting by the empress dowager's faction at the court, see Hao Chang, "Intellectual Change and the Reform Movement," in *The Cambridge History of China*, vol. 11, pt. 2, *Late Ch'ing, 1800–1911*, ed. John K. Fairbank and Kwang-ching Liu (Cambridge: Cambridge University Press, 1980), 274–338. See, in the same volume: on the Chinese military defeat by France in 1884 and by Japan in 1894, Kwang-ching Liu and Richard J. Smith, "The Military Challenge: the Northwest and the Coast," esp. 251–273; on the Boxers, Immanuel C. Y. Hsu, "Late Ch'ing Foreign Relations, 1866–1905," esp. 109–130; Michael Gasster, "The Republican Revolutionary Movement," 463–534.

149. On the hapless fate of the parliamentary experiments, see Andrew J. Nathan, "A Constitutional Republic: The Peking Government, 1916–28," and on warlordism, see James E. Sheridan, "The Warlord Era: Politics and Militarism under the Peking Government, 1916–28," both in *The Cambridge History of China,* vol. 12, pt. 1, *Republican China, 1912–1949,* ed. John K. Fairbank (Cambridge: Cambridge University Press, 1983), 256–283, 284–321. On Guomindang and Communist development and falling-out in the south, see, in the same volume: Jerome Ch'en, "The Chinese Communist Movement to 1927," 505–526, and C. Martin Wilbur, "The Nationalist Revolution: From Canton to Nanking, 1923–28," 527–721. See also William C. Kirby, *Germany and Republican China* (Stanford, CA: Stanford University Press, 1984).

150. On the interwar tensions faced by the colonial powers and the difficulty of reform, see Frederick C. Cooper, *Decolonization and African Society: The Labor Question in French and British Africa* (Cambridge: Cambridge University Press, 1996). For British difficulties in relinquishing control in Asia and the Middle East, see *The Oxford History of the British Empire,* vol. 4: *The Twentieth Century,* ed. Judith M. Brown and Wm. Roger Louis (New York: Oxford University Press, 1998–1999), 398–489.

151. V. I. Lenin, *What Is to Be Done? Burning Questions of Our Movement* (Moscow: Foreign Languages Publishing House, 1950).

152. Czesław Miłosz, *The Captive Mind,* trans. Jane Zielonka (New York: Vintage, 1955). Many similar critiques emerged by the 1940s and 1950s; among the fictional accounts, see Arthur Koestler's *Darkness at Noon,* trans. Dorothy Hardie (London: Jonathan Cape, 1940), and George Orwell's *Nineteen Eighty-Four: A Novel* (London: Secker and Warburg, 1949).

153. Georg Lukács, *History and Class Consciousness,* trans. Rodney Livingstone (Cambridge, MA: MIT Press, 1971), 319–320, 326–327.

154. On the purges, see Anne Applebaum, *Gulag: A History* (New York: Doubleday, 2003), esp. 584–585 for the effort to establish a tally of the victims; also Robert Conquest, *The Great Terror: A Reassessment* (New York: Oxford University Press, 2008). Of the works that sought to challenge the Stalin-centered narrative, see J. Arch Getty, *Origins of the Great Purges: The Soviet Communist Party Reconsidered, 1933–1938* (Cambridge: Cambridge University Press, 1985). For statistical analyses, see Paul R. Gregory, *Terror by Quota: State Security from Lenin to Stalin: An Archival Study* (New Haven, CT: Yale University Press, 2009). For insights into how ordinary Russians coped with this period, see Sheila Fitzpatrick, *Everyday Stalinism: Ordinary Life in Extraordinary Times: Soviet Russia in the 1930s* (New York: Oxford University Press, 1999). For the postwar purges in Communist Eastern Europe, see George H. Hodos, *Show Trials: Stalinist Purges in Eastern Europe, 1948–1954* (New York: Praeger, 1987).

155. On the sprawling organization of terror in Germany, see Helmut Krausnick et al., *Anatomie des SS-Staates* (Munich: Institut für Zeitgeschichte, 1968), translated as *Anatomy of the SS State* (London: Collins 1968). Timothy Snyder, *Bloodlands: Europe between Hitler and Stalin* (New York: Basic Books, 2010), for the toll in the vulnerable area of Poland and Ukraine; for the most recent detailed survey of the murder of the Jews by region, see David Cesarani, ed., *The Final Solution: Origins and Implementation* (London: Routledge, 1994).

156. Sorel, *Réflexions sur la violence*; and Sorel, *Les Illusions du Progrès* (Paris: Marcel Rivière, 1911). For Sorel's influence, see Steven Hirsch and Lucien van der Walt, eds., *Anarchism and Syndicalism in the Colonial and Postcolonial World, 1870–1940: The Praxis of National Liberation, Internationalism, and Social Revolution* (Leiden: Brill, 2010).

157. For the projects, see Steven Kotkin, *Magnetic Mountain: Stalinism as a Civilization* (Berkeley; University of California Press, 1995). The vast transformative projects not only characterized the totalitarian regimes but also were part of the vision of the 1930s—including the TVA and the New Deal. See Wolfgang Schivelbusch, *Three New Deals: Reflections on Roosevelt's America, Mussolini's Italy and Hitler's Germany, 1933–1939,* trans. Jefferson Chase (New York: Metropolitan Books, 2006).

158. Erez Manela, *The Wilsonian Moment: Self-Determination and the International Origins of Anticolonial Nationalism* (New York: Oxford University Press, 2007); Arno J. Mayer, *Wilson vs. Lenin: Political Origins of the New Diplomacy, 1917–1918* (Cleveland: World Publishers, 1964); Maier, *Recasting Bourgeois Europe.*

159. Rocco, "La Trasformazione dello Stato," in *Scritti e discorsi politici di Alfredo Rocco,* 3 vols. (Milano: A. Giuffrè, 1938), 3:775–778; Mussolini, "Fascismo," in *Enciclopedia italiana* (Roma: Istituto della Enciclopedia Italiana [Treccani], 1932), 14:848, 850; both cited in Sabino Cassese, *Lo Stato Fascista* (Bologna: Il Mulino, 2010), s.v. *Cassese,* 47, 37.

160. Notes on fascism and its institutions: For a narrative, see Adrian Lyttelton, *The Seizure of Power: Fascism in Italy, 1919–1929,* rev ed. (London: Routledge, 2004); and the multivolume biography of Mussolini by Renzo De Felice, *Mussolini il Fascista: L'organizzazione dello stato fascista, 1925–1929* (Turin: Einaudi, 1968); *Mussolini Il Duce: Lo stato totalitario, 1936–1940* (Turin: Einaudi, 1981); on institutions, see Alberto Aquarone, *L'organizzazione dello stato totalitario* (Turin: Einaudi, 1965); on parallel organizations, G. Melis, *Due modelli di amministrazione fra liberalismo e facissmo: Burocrazie tradizionali e nuovi apparati* (Roma: Ministero per I Beni culturali e ambientali, 1988); for comparative fascist movements, Michael Mann, *Fascists* (Cambridge: Cambridge University Press, 2004), a broad and sensible analysis.

161. Federico Finchelstein, *Los Origenes ideológicos de la dictadura* (Buenos Aires: Editorial Sudamericana, 2008); also Finchelstein, *Ideology, Violence and the Sacred in Argentina and Italy, 1919–1945* (Durham, NC: Duke University Press, 2010).

162. Of the numerous sources on the Nazi regime, see Richard Evans, *The Third Reich in Power, 1933–1939* (New York: Penguin, 2005); and Evans, *The Third Reich at War, 1939–1945* (London: Allen Lane, 2008); Ian Kershaw, *Hitler,* vol. 2, *1936–1945: Nemesis* (London: Penguin, 2000); Kershaw, *Hitler, 1889–1936: Hubris* (New York: W. W. Norton, 1999); Karl Dietrich Bracher; *Die deutsche Diktatur: Entstehung, Struktur, Folgen des Nationalsozialismus,* 6th ed. (Frankfurt am Main: Ulstein, 1979).

163. See Karen Painter, *Symphonic Ambitions* (Cambridge, MA: Harvard University Press, 2007); also Erik Levi, *Music in the Third Reich* (Basingstoke: Macmillan, 1994). On jazz, see Michael H. Kater, *Different Drummers: Jazz in the Culture of Nazi Germany* (New York: Oxford University Press, 1992).

164. Carl Schmitt, *The Crisis of Parliamentary Democracy,* ed. Ellen Kennedy (1923; Cambridge, MA: MIT Press, 1988); Schmitt, *The Concept of the Political,* trans. George Schwab (Chicago: University of Chicago Press, 1996), with a useful forward by Tracy Strong.

165. Carl Schmitt, *The Nomos of the Earth in the Jus Publicum Europeaum,* trans. G. L. Ulmen (New York: Telos Press, 2003).

166. István Bibó, *Misère des petits états d'Europe de l'est,* trans. György Kassai (Paris: Albin Michel, 1993).

167. For the narrative of expansion, see W. G. Beasley, *Japanese Imperialism, 1894–1945* (Oxford: Clarendon, 1987); and, among the many English-language contributions, Mark R. Peattie, *Ishiwara Kanji and Japan's Confrontation with the West* (Princeton, NJ: Princeton University Press, 1975); Hugh Borton, *Japan since 1931: Its Political and Social Development* (New York: Institute of Pacific Relations, 1940). For the debate on whether the regime was or was not fascist, see Marcus Willensky, "Japanese Fascism Revisited," *Stanford Journal of East Asian Affairs* 5, no. 1 (Winter 2005): 52–77. For ideological currents, see Maruyama Masao, *Thought and Behaviour in Modern in Japanese Politics* (London: Oxford University Press, 1963); on responsibilities, Herbert P. Bix, *Hirohito and the Making of Modern Japan* (New York: HarperCollins, 2000).

168. André Gide, *Retour de l'U.R.S.S.* (Paris: Gallimard, 1936); George Orwell, *Homage to Catalonia* (London: Secker and Warburg, 1938). The Auden line is from his poem "September 1, 1939."

169. On collectivization, see Moshe Lewin, *Russian Peasants and Soviet Power: A Study in Collectivization,* trans. Irene Nove (London: Allen and Unwin, 1968); Stephen F. Cohen, *Bukharin and the Bolshevik Revolution: A Political Biography, 1888–1938* (New York: Vintage, 1975); Alexander Erlich, *The Soviet Industrialization Debate, 1924–1928* (Cambridge, MA: Harvard University Press, 1960).

170. Renzo De Felice, ed., *Il Fascismo: Le interpretazioni dei contemporanei e degli historici* (Rome: Laterza, 1998).

171. Herbert Marcuse, *Reason and Revolution: Hegel and the Rise of Social Theory* (London: Oxford University Press, 1941); Franz Neumann, *Behemoth: The Structure and Practice of National Socialism, 1933–1944* (New York: Oxford University Press, 1944).

172. Snyder, *Bloodlands;* Andrea Graziosi, *Lettere da Kharkov: La carestia in Ucraina e nel Caucaso del Nord nei rapporti dei diplomatici italiani, 1923–33* (Torino: Einaudi, 1991). Also, Graziosi, *The Great Soviet Peasant War: Bolsheviks and Peasants, 1917–1933* (Cambridge, MA: Harvard University Press and Ukrainian Research Center, 1996).

173. Ian Kershaw has emphasized the Nazi concept of "working toward the Führer." See Kershaw, *Hitler,* vol. 2, *1936–1945: Nemesis,* 249–250.

174. David Rousset, *L'Univers concentrationnaire* (Paris: Éditions Du Pavois, 1946); Ernst Fraenkel, *The Dual State: A Contribution to the Theory of Dictatorship,* trans. E. A. Shils in collaboration with Edith Lowenstein and Klaus Knorr (New York: Oxford University Press, 1941). Fraenkel attributed "the prerogative state" (versus the constitutional state) to the emergency decrees issued at the outset of the regime, and he cited Schmitt: "The state continues to exist while the legal order is inoperative" (25).

175. Arendt, *The Origins of Totalitarianism* (New York: Harcourt, Brace, 1951); see also the more mechanistic account by Carl J. Friedrich and Zbigniew K. Brzezinski, *Totalitarian Dictatorship and Autocracy* (New York: Praeger, 1965); for a history of the concept, see Abbot Gleason, *Totalitarianism: The Inner History of the Cold War* (New York: Oxford University Press, 1995). There are many efforts to differentiate the different regimes and experiences. See the essays collected in Michael Geyer and Sheila Fitzpatrick, eds., *Beyond Totalitarianism: Stalinism and Nazism Compared* (Cambridge: Cambridge University Press, 2009), and the search for important qualifications of the model in the contributions to Paul Corner, ed., *Popular Opinion in Totalitarian Regimes: Fascism, Nazism, Communism* (Oxford: Oxford University Press, 2009). For a political-science approach, see Juan J. Linz, *Totalitarian and Authoritarian Regimes* (Boulder, CO: Lynne Rienner, 2000).

176. Among the helpful insights into such genocidal mentalities, see Jacques Semelin, *Purify and Destroy: The Political Uses of Massacre and Genocide,* ed. Cynthia Schoch (New York: Columbia University Press, 2007). For an approach that tends to dissolve genocidal violence into a broader process of stressful social change, see Christian Gerlach, *Extremely Violent Societies: Mass Violence in the Twentieth-Century World* (Cambridge: Cambridge University Press, 2010).

177. Peter Baldwin, *The Politics of Social Solidarity: Class Bases of the European Welfare State, 1875–1975* (Cambridge: Cambridge University Press, 1990); Susan Pedersen, *Family, Dependence, and the Origins of the Welfare State: Britain and France, 1914–1945* (Cambridge: Cambridge University Press, 1993); Gøsta Esping-Andersen, *The Three Worlds of Welfare Capitalism* (Princeton, NJ: Princeton University Press, 1990). The most interesting general coverage of Europe after 1945 is Tony Judt, *Postwar: A History of Europe since 1945* (New York: Penguin, 2005).

178. See Daniel Chirot, *Modern Tyrants: The Power and Prevalence of Evil in Our Age* (New York: Free Press, 1994).

179. Anne-Marie Slaughter, *A New World Order* (Princeton: Princeton University Press, 2004), 268–269. For a comprehensive discussion, see Jon Pierre and B. Guy Peters, *Governance, Politics and the State* (London: Macmillan, 2000).

2. Empires and the Reach of the Global

1. David Fieldhouse, *The Colonial Empires: A Comparative Survey from the Eighteenth Century,* 2nd ed. (London: Macmillan, 1982), 373.

2. Tony Ballantyne, "Empire, Knowledge, and Culture: From Proto-Globalization to Modern Globalization," in *Globalization in World History,* ed. A. G. Hopkins (New York: W. W. Norton, 2002), 122–123.

3. Manu Goswami, *Producing India: From Colonial Economy to National Space* (Chicago: University of Chicago Press, 2004).

4. Jan Nederveen Pieterse, *Empire and Emancipation: Power and Liberation on a World Scale* (New York: Praeger, 1989), 362–366.

5. See the special issue "Pairing Empires" edited by Paul Kramer and John Plotz: *Journal of Colonialism and Colonial History* 2, no. 1 (Spring 2001).

6. Karen Barkey and Mark Von Hagen, eds., *After Empire: Multi-Ethnic Societies and Nation-Building: The Soviet Union and the Russian Ottoman and Habsburg Empires* (Boulder, CO: Westview, 1997) is very much a counter to this approach. Quotation at 3.

7. For an attempt to think this through, see Antoinette Burton, "Getting Outside the Global: Re-Positioning British Imperialism in World History," in *Race, Nation and Empire: Making Histories, 1750 to the Present,* ed. Catherine Hall and Keith McLelland (Manchester: Manchester University Press, 2010), 199–216.

8. Robert J. Blyth, *The Empire of the Raj: India, Eastern Africa and the Middle East* (New York: Palgrave, 2003); Thomas R. Metcalf, *Imperial Connections: India in the Indian Ocean Arena, 1860–1920* (Berkeley: University of California, 2007); Pekka Hämäläinen, *The Comanche Empire* (New Haven, CT: Yale University Press, 2008).

9. Claude Markovits, *The Global World of Indian Merchants, 1750–1947: Traders of Sind from Bukhara to Panama* (Cambridge: Cambridge University Press, 2000); Tony Ballantyne, *Between Colonialism and Diaspora: Sikh Cultural Formations in an Imperial World* (Cambridge: Cambridge University Press, 2006); Sunil Amrith, "Tamil Diasporas across the Bay of Bengal," *American Historical Review* 114, no. 3 (2009): 547–572; Enseng Ho, *The Graves of Tarim: Genealogy and Mobility across the Indian Ocean* (Berkeley: University of California Press, 2006).

10. We gesture here to two important collections, published a decade apart: Catherine Hall and Sonya Rose, eds., *At Home with the Empire: Metropolitan Culture and the Imperial World* (Cambridge, 2007); Frederick Cooper and Ann Stoler, *Tensions of Empire: Colonial Cultures in a Bourgeois World* (Berkeley: University of California Press, 1997).

11. George Steinmetz, *The Devil's Handwriting: Precoloniality and the German Colonial State in Qingdao, Samoa and Southwest Africa* (Chicago: University of Chicago Press, 2007); Kenneth Pomeranz, *The Great Divergence: China, Europe and the Making of the Modern World Economy* (Princeton, NJ: Princeton University Press, 2000).

12. C. A. Bayly, "The First Age of Global Imperialism, c. 1760–1830," *Journal of Imperial & Commonwealth History* 26, no. 2 (1998): 28–47.

13. Richard Drayton, "The Collaboration of Labor: Slaves, Empires and Globalizations in the Atlantic World, c. 1600–1850," in *Globalization in World History,* ed. A. G. Hopkins (New York: Norton, 2002).

14. Christopher I. Beckwith, *Empires of the Silk Road: A History of Central Eurasia from the Bronze Age to the Present* (Princeton, NJ: Princeton University Press, 2009).

15. Donald Wright, *The World and a Very Small Place in Africa* (New York: M. E. Sharpe, 1997); Jean Allman and Victoria Tashjian, *I Will Not Eat Stone: A Women's History of Colonial Asante* (Portsmouth, NH: Heinemann, 2000).

16. Frederick Cooper, *Colonialism in Question: Theory, Knowledge, History* (Berkeley: University of California 2005); James Ferguson, *Global Shadows: Africa in the Neoliberal World Order* (Durham, NC: Duke University Press, 2006).

17. Epeli Hau'ofa, "Our Sea of Islands," in *We Are the Ocean: Selected Works* (Honolulu: University of Hawai'i Press, 2008), 27–40; T. Damon I. Salesa, "'Travel-Happy Samoa': Colonialism, Samoan Migration and a 'Brown Pacific'," *New Zealand Journal of History* 37, no. 2 (2003): 171–188.

18. See Jean Allman and Antoinette Burton, eds., special issue: "Destination Globalization? Women, Gender and Comparative Colonial Histories in the New Millennium," *Journal of Colonialism and Colonial History* 4 (April 2003), http://muse.jhu.edu/journals/cch.

19. Jan-Georg Deutsch, *Emancipation without Abolition in German East Africa, c. 1884–1914* (London: James Currey, 2006).

20. John Darwin, "Imperialism and the Victorians: The Dynamics of Historical Expansion," *English Historical Review* 112, no. 447 (1997): 614–642.

21. Sarah Ahmed, *Queer Phenomenology: Orientations, Objects, Others* (Durham, NC: Duke University Press, 2006); Sanjay Krishnan, *Reading the Global: Troubling Perspectives on Britain's Empire in Asia* (New York: Columbia University Press, 2007). This is something akin to seeing the global as a "heuristic device" in tandem with a "method of comparative connection." See Alys E. Weinbaum et al., eds., *The Modern Girl Around the World: Consumption, Modernity and Globalization* (Durham, NC: Duke University Press, 2009).

22. Ruth Rogaski, *Hygienic Modernity: Meanings of Health and Disease in Treaty-Port China* (Berkeley: University of California Press, 2004).

23. See Valerie Traub, "Mapping the Global Body," in *Early Modern Visual Culture: Representation, Race and Empire in Renaissance England,* ed. Peter C. Erickson and Clark Hulse (Philadelphia: University of Pennsylvania Press, 2000), 44–97; Irene Silverblatt, *Modern Inquisitions: Peru and the Colonial Origins of the Civilized World* (Durham, NC: Duke University Press, 2004); Herman Bennett, *Africans in Colonial Mexico: Absolutism, Christianity, and Afro-Creole Consciousness, 1570–1640* (Bloomington: Indiana University Press, 2003).

24. Explanations for this are wide-ranging; among the most succinct and compelling are those presented in Robert Young, *Colonial Desire: Hybridity in Theory, Culture, and Race* (London: Routledge, 1995); and Durba Ghosh, *Sex and the Family in Colonial India: The Making of Empire* (Cambridge: Cambridge University Press, 2006).

25. Tony Ballantyne, "Empire, Knowledge and Culture: From Proto-globalization to Modern Globalization," in *Globalization in World History,* ed. A. G. Hopkins (New York: W. W. Norton, 2002), 115–140.

26. Vinay Lal, "The Incident of the Crawling Lane: Women in the Punjab Disturbances of 1919," *Genders* 16 (1993): 35–60.

27. Mark Polelle, *Raising Cartographic Consciousness: The Social and Foreign Policy Vision of Geopolitics in the Twentieth Century* (Lanham, MD: Lexington Books, 1999), 97–98.

28. Jürgen Zimmerer, "The Birth of the Ostland out of the Spirit of Colonialism: A Postcolonial Perspective on the Nazi Policy of Conquest and Extermination," *Patterns of Prejudice* 39, no. 2 (2005), 197–219; Jürgen Zimmerer and Joachim Zeller, eds., *Genocide in Southwest Africa: The Colonial War of 1904–1908 and Its Aftermath,* trans. E. J. Neather (Monmouth, Wales: Merlin, 2006).

29. Cited in Jürgen Zimmerer, "Colonialism and the Holocaust: Towards an Archaeology of Genocide," in *Genocide and Settler Society: Frontier Violence and Stolen Indigenous Children in Australian History,* ed. A. Dirk Moses (New York: Berghahn Books, 2005), 49.

30. Madhu Kishwar, "Gandhi on Women," *Economic and Political Weekly,* October 5, 1985, p. 1696.

31. Henry Reynolds, *The Other Side of the Frontier: An Interpretation of the Aboriginal Response to the Invasion and Settlement of Australia* (Townsville, Queensland: Dept. of History, James Cook University, 1981).

32. See Samuel Truett, "Transnational Warrior: Emilio Kosterlitzky and the Transformation of the U.S.-Mexico Borderlands," in *Continental Crossroads: Remapping U.S.-Mexico Borderlands History,* ed. Samuel Truett and Elliott Young (Durham, NC: Duke University Press, 2004), 241–270.

33. Daniel Brower and Edward J. Lazzerini, eds., *Russia's Orient: Imperial Borderlands and Peoples, 1700–1917* (Bloomington: Indiana University Press, 1997).

34. Adeeb Khalid, *The Politics of Muslim Cultural Reform: Jadidism in Central Asia* (Berkeley: University of California Press, 1998), 14.

35. Thomas M. Barrett, *At the Edge of Empire: The Terek Cossacks and the North Caucasus Frontier, 1700–1860* (Boulder, CO: Westview, 1999); Adele Perry, *On the Edge of Empire: Gender, Race, and the Making of British Columbia, 1849–1871* (Toronto: University of Toronto Press, 2001); Sameetah Agha and Elizabeth Kolsky, eds., *Fringes of Empire: Peoples, Places, and Spaces in Colonial India* (Oxford: Oxford University Press, 2009).

36. Alfred Crosby, *Ecological Imperialism: The Biological Expansion of Europe, 900–1900* (Cambridge: Cambridge University Press, 1986); Ajay Skaria, *Hybrid Histories: Forests, Frontiers and Wildness in Western India* (Oxford: Oxford University Press, 1999).

37. For "meeting up spaces," see Doreen Massey, *For Space* (London: Sage, 2005), 63–64.

38. Robert A. Bickers and Jeffrey N. Wasserstrom, "Shanghai's 'Dogs and Chinese Not Admitted' Sign: Legend, History and Contemporary Symbol," *China Quarterly,* no. 142 (1995): 444–466.

39. Peter C. Perdue, "Erasing the Empire, Re-Racing the Nation: Racialism and Culturalism in Imperial China," in *Imperial Formations,* ed. Ann Laura Stoler, Carole McGranahan, and Peter C. Perdue (Santa Fe, NM: School for Advanced Research Press, 2007), 144.

40. A. G. Hopkins, "Globalization with and without Empires: From Bali to Labrador," in *Globalization and World History,* ed. A. G. Hopkins (London: Pimlico, 2002), 224.

41. Kirsten Zirkel, "Military Power in German Colonial Policy: The *Schutztruppen* and Their Leaders in East and South-West Africa, 1888–1918," in *Guardians of Empire: The Armed Forces of the Colonial Powers, c. 1700–1964,* ed. David Killingray and David Omissi (Manchester: Manchester University Press, 1999), 97.

42. Thaddeus Sunseri, "Reinterpreting a Colonial Rebellion: Forestry and Social Control in German East Africa, 1875–1945," *Environmental History* 8, no. 3 (July 2003): 430–451.

43. David Biggs, "Managing a Rebel Landscape: Conservation, Pioneers and the Revolutionary Past in the U Minh, Vietnam," *Environmental History* 10, no. 3 (2005): 448–476.

44. Heather Streets, *Martial Races: The Military, Race and Masculinity in British Imperial Culture, 1857–1914* (Manchester: Manchester University Press, 2004), 209.

45. Robert Bickers, "Shanghailanders: The Formation and Identity of the British Settler Community in Shanghai, 1843–1937," *Past and Present* 159, no. 1 (1998): 161–211.

46. Panivong Norindr, *Phantasmic Indochina: French Colonial Ideology in Architecture, Film and Literature* (Durham, NC: Duke University Press, 1996), 39ff.

47. Mire Koikari, "Gender, Power and US Imperialism: The Occupation of Japan, 1945–1952," in *Bodies in Contact: Rethinking Colonial Encounters in World History,* ed. Tony Ballantyne and Antoinette Burton (Durham, NC: Duke University Press, 2005), 349; Na Young Lee, "The Construction of Military Prostitution in South Korea for the U.S. Military Rule, 1945–48," *Feminist Studies* 33, no. 3 (2007): 453–481. See also Paul Kramer, "The Darkness That Enters the Home: The Politics of Prostitution during the Philippine American War," in *Haunted by Empire: Geographies of Intimacy in North American History,* ed. Ann L. Stoler (Durham, NC: Duke University Press, 2006), 366–404.

48. Yael Simpson Fletcher, "Unsettling Settlers: Colonial Migrants and Racialised Sexuality in Interwar Marseilles," in *Gender, Sexuality and Colonial Modernities,* ed. Antoinette Burton (London: Routledge, 1999), 85.

49. J. P. Daughton, *An Empire Divided: Religion, Republicanism, and the Making of French Colonialism, 1880–1914* (Oxford: Oxford University Press, 2006).

50. See Norman Etherington, ed., *Missions and Empire* (Oxford: Oxford University Press, 2005).

51. Susan Thorne, *Congregational Missions and the Making of an Imperial Culture in Nineteenth-century England* (Stanford, CA: Stanford University Press 1999); Susan Layton, "Nineteenth Century Russian Mythologies of Caucasian Savagery," in Brower and Lazzerini, *Russia's Orient,* 80–114.

52. The phrase is Michael Fisher's. See Fisher, *Counterflows to Colonialism: Indian Travellers and Settlers in Britain, 1600–1857* (Delhi: Permanent Black, 2004).

53. Elizabeth Schmidt, *Peasants, Traders, and Wives: Shona Women in the History of Zimbabwe, 1870–1939* (London: Heinemann, 1992), 123, 125.

54. Fadhma Amrouche, *My Life Story: The Autobiography of a Berber Woman* (New Brunswick, NJ: Rutgers University Press, 1988), 30–56; Tabitha Kanogo, *African Womanhood in Colonial Kenya, 1900–50* (Oxford: James Currey, 2005), 203, 204.

55. Frederick Cooper, *From Slaves to Squatters: Plantation Labor and Agriculture in Zanzibar and Coastal Kenya, 1890–1925* (New Haven, CT: Yale University Press, 1980).

56. Laurent Dubois, *A Colony of Citizens: Revolution and Slave Emancipation in the French Caribbean, 1787–1804* (Chapel Hill: University of North Carolina Press, 2004).

57. Diana Paton and Pamela Scully, "Introduction: Gendered and Slave Emancipation in Comparative Perspective," in *Gender and Slave Emancipation in the Atlantic World,* ed. Pamela Scully and Diana Paton (Durham, NC: Duke University Press, 2005), 1.

58. Donald Denoon, "New Economic Orders: Land, Labour and Dependency," in *The Cambridge History of the Pacific Islanders,* ed. Donald Denoon (Cambridge: Cambridge University Press, 1997), 225–226.

59. For "boy wives," see Marc Epprecht, *Hungochani: The History of a Dissident Sexuality in Southern Africa* (Montreal: McGill-Queen's University Press, 2004), 58, 63; for "gold-mine marriages," see T. Dunbar Moodie with Vivienne Ndatshe, *Going for Gold: Men, Mines and Migration* (Berkeley: University of California Press, 1994), 123.

60. Carolyn Brown, "Race and the Construction of Working-Class Masculinity in the Nigerian Coal Industry: The Initial Phase, 1914–1930," *International Labor and Working-Class History,* 69 (2006): 43, 45; John Chalcroft, "The Coal Heavers of Port Sa'id: State-Making and

Worker Protest, 1869–1914," *International Labor and Working-Class History* 60 (2001): 110–124.

61. Samita Sen, "'Without His Consent?'": Marriage and Women's Migration in Colonial India," *International Labor and Working-Class History,* 65 (2004): 79.

62. Philippa Levine, *Prostitution, Race and Politics: Policing Venereal Disease in the British Empire* (London: Routledge, 2003).

63. Antoinette Burton, *Dwelling in the Archive: Women Making House, Home and History in Late Colonial India* (Oxford: Oxford University Press, 2003).

64. Elisabeth Locher-Scholten, *Women and the Colonial State: Essays on Gender and Modernity in the Netherland Indies, 1900–1942* (Amsterdam: Amsterdam University Press, 2000), 89–91.

65. Jacklyn Cock, *Maids and Madams: A Study in the Politics of Exploitation* (Johannesburg: Ravan Press, 1980).

66. Anna Haebich, *Broken Circles: Fragmenting Indigenous Families, 1800–2000* (Fremantle, W.A.: Fremantle Arts Centre Press, 2000).

67. Jean Allman and Victoria B. Tashjian, *"I Will Not Eat Stone": A Woman's History of Colonial Asante* (London: Heinemann, 2000).

68. Felipe Fernandez-Arrnesto, *Millennium: A History of the Last Thousand Years* (New York: Touchstone, 1995), 311–313.

69. Joanna de Groot, "Metropolitan Desires and Colonial Connections: Reflections on Consumption and Empire," in *At Home with the Empire: Metropolitan Culture and the Imperial World,* ed. Catherine Hall and Sonya Rose (Cambridge: Cambridge University Press, 2006), 173.

70. James Belich, *Replenishing the Earth: The Settler Revolution and the Rise of the Anglo-World, 1783–1939* (Oxford: Oxford University Press, 2009), 365–368.

71. Dana S. Hale, "French Images of Race on Product Trademarks during the Third Republic (1871–1940)," in *The Color of Liberty: Histories of Race in France,* ed. Sue Peabody and Tyler Stovall (Durham, NC: Duke University Press, 2003), 131.

72. Kristin Hoganson, *Consumers' Imperium: The Global Production of American Domesticity, 1865–1920* (Chapel Hill: University of North Carolina Press, 2007); Christine Varga-Harris, "Constructing the Soviet Hearth: Home, Citizenship and Socialism in Russia, 1956—1964" (Ph.D. diss., University of Illinois, Urbana, 2005); Brian Moloughney and Tony Ballantyne, "Asia in Murihiku: Towards a Transnational History of a Colonial Culture," in *Disputed Histories: Imagining New Zealand's Pasts,* ed. Ballantyne and Moloughney (Dunedin: University of Otago Press, 2006), 65–92.

73. Carter Vaughn Findley, "An Ottoman Occidentalist in Europe: Ahmed Midhat Meets Madame Gülnar," in Ballantyne and Burton, *Bodies in Contact,* 277–292; Maria Grever and Berteke Waaldjik, *Transforming the Public Sphere: The Dutch National Exhibition of Women's Labor in 1898* (Durham, NC: Duke University Press, 2004), 158–161.

74. Brent Hayes Edwards, "The Shadow of Shadows," *positions: east asia cultures critique* 11, no. 1 (2003): 11–49.

75. Gary Wilder, *The French Imperial Nation-State: Negritude and Colonial Humanism between the Two World Wars* (Chicago: University of Chicago Press, 2005).

76. Richard Belsky, "Placing the Hundred Days: Native-Place Ties and Urban Space," in *Rethinking the 1898 Reform Period: Political and Cultural Change in Late Qing China,* ed. Rebecca Karl and Peter Zarrow (Cambridge, MA: Harvard University Press, 2002), 124–157; Todd Henry, "Respatializing Choson's Royal Capital: The Politics of Japanese Urban Reforms in Early Colonial Seoul, 1905–19," in *Sitings: Critical Approaches to Korean Geography,* ed. Timothy Tangherlini and Sallie Yea (Honolulu: University of Hawai'i Press, 2007), 33.

77. Jane Lydon, *Eye Contact: Photographing Indigenous Australians* (Durham, NC: Duke University Press, 2005), 11.

78. Gwendolyn Wright, *The Politics of Design: French Colonial Urbanism* (Chicago: University of Chicago Press, 1991), 235.

79. Lydon, *Eye Contact.*

80. Shula Marks, ed., *Not Either an Experimental Doll* (New York: Feminist Press, 1989).

81. Richard White, *The Middle Ground: Indians, Empires and Republics in the Great Lakes Region, 1650–1815* (Cambridge: Cambridge University Press, 1991), ix, x.

82. David Anderson, *Histories of the Hanged: Britain's Dirty War in Kenya and the End of Empire* (London: Weidenfeld, 2005); Caroline Elkins, *Britain's Gulag: The Brutal End of Empire in Kenya* (London: Jonathan Cape, 2005).

83. Judith Binney, "Maungapohatu Revisited: Or, How the Government Underdeveloped a Maori Community," *Journal of the Polynesian Society* 92, no. 3 (1983): 353–392.

84. Quoted in Charles-Robert Ageron, *L'Anticolonialisme en France de 1871 à 1914* (Paris: Presses Universitaires de France, 1973), 47.

85. Karl Marx, *Grundrisse: Foundations of the Critique of Political Economy,* trans. and ed. Martin Nicolaus (New York: Penguin, 1993), 706.

86. Laura Bear, *Lines of the Nation: Indian Railway Workers, Bureaucracy and the Intimate Historical Self* (New York: Columbia University Press, 2008).

87. Antoinette Burton, "Introduction: The Unfinished Business of Colonial Modernities," in Burton, *Gender, Sexuality and Colonial Modernities,* 1–16.

88. Alfred W. McCoy, *Policing America's Empire: The United States, the Philippines, and the Rise of the Surveillance State* (Madison: University of Wisconsin Press, 2009).

89. Erin O'Connor, *Raw Material: Producing Pathology in Victorian Culture* (Durham, NC: Duke University Press, 2000), 8.

90. "England and Diplomacy: Russia's Invasion of Manchuria and the Formosan Battle," *New York Times,* June 2, 1895.

91. D. A. Farnie, *East and West of Suez: The Suez Canal in History* (Oxford: Clarendon, 1969), 61–63.

92. Emily A. Haddad, "Digging to India: Modernity, Imperialism, and the Suez Canal," *Victorian Studies* 47, no. 3 (2005): 363–396; Farnie, *East and West of Suez,* 234–240.

93. Daniel R. Headrick, *Tentacles of Progress: Technology Transfer in the Age of Imperialism, 1850–1940* (Oxford: Oxford University Press, 1988), 26, table 2.3; Robert V. Kubicek, "British Expansion, Empire, and Technological Change," in *The Oxford History of the British Empire,* vol. 3: *The Nineteenth Century,* ed. Andrew Porter (Oxford: Oxford University Press, 1999), 254, table 12.1.

94. Richard Temple, *India in 1880* (London, 1880), 310.

95. Dwayne R. Winseck and Robert M. Pike, *Communication and Empire: Media, Markets, and Globalization, 1860–1930* (Durham, NC: Duke University Press, 2007), 70–71.

96. Headrick, *Tentacles of Progress,* 25–29; Max E. Fletcher, "The Suez Canal and World Shipping, 1869–1914," *Journal of Economic History* 18, no. 4 (1958): 558, 561.

97. Headrick, *Tentacles of Progress,* tables 2.1 and 2.2; Caroline Piquet, "The Suez Company's Concession in Egypt, 1854–1956: Modern Infrastructure and Local Economic Development," *Enterprise & Society* 5, no. 1 (2004): 107–127.

98. Joel Beinin and Zachary Lockman, *Workers on the Nile: Communism, Islam, and the Egyptian Working Class, 1882–1954* (Cairo: American University in Cairo Press, 1998), 106–110.

99. Headrick, *Tentacles of Progress,* 28.

100. Simon Potter, *News and the British World* (Oxford: Oxford University Press, 2003).

101. John M. MacKenzie, "'In Touch with the Infinite': The BBC and Empire, 1923–53," in *Imperialism and Popular Culture,* ed. John M. MacKenzie (Manchester: Manchester University Press, 1986), 165–191; Siân Nicholas, "'Brushing Up Your Empire': Dominion and Colonial Propaganda on the BBC's Home Services, 1939–1945," in *The British World: Diaspora, Culture, and Identity,* ed. Carl Bridge and Kent Fedorowich (London: Taylor and Francis, 2003), 207–230.

102. C. A. Bayly, *The Birth of the Modern World, 1780–1914: Global Connections and Comparisons* (Oxford: Blackwell, 2004), 432–450.

103. Michael S. Neiberg and Dennis E. Showalter, *Soldiers' Lives through History: The Nineteenth Century* (Westport, CT: Greenwood Press, 2006), 146–147.

104. Manu Goswami, *Producing India: From Colonial Economy to National Space* (Chicago: University of Chicago Press, 2004), 59–60.

105. Headrick, *Tentacles of Progress,* 269–276; A. J. Christopher, *Colonial Africa* (Beckenham, UK: Croom Helm, 1984), 78–79.

106. John Andrews, "The Emergence of the Wheat Belt in South Eastern Australia to 1930," in *Frontiers and Men,* ed. John Andrews (Melbourne: F. W. Cheshire, 1966), 5–65; S. Glynn, "The Transport Factor in Developmental Policy: Pioneer Agricultural Railways in the Western Australian Wheat Belt, 1900–1930," *Australian Journal of Politics & History* 15, no. 2 (1969): 60–78; Peter Griggs, "Sugar Plantations in Queensland, 1864–1912: Origins, Characteristics, Distribution, and Decline," *Agricultural History* 74, no. 3 (2000): 628–629.

107. Tony Ballantyne, "The State, Politics and Power, 1769–1893," in *Oxford History of New Zealand,* ed. Giselle Byrnes (Oxford: Oxford University Press, 2009), 99–124; K. T. Livingston, "Anticipating Federation: The Federalising of Telecommunications in Australia," *Australian Historical Studies* 26 (1994): 97–117.

108. Erik Olssen, "Working Gender, Gendering Work: Occupational Change and Continuity in Southern Dunedin," in *Sites of Gender: Women, Men and Modernity in Southern Dunedin, 1890–1939,* ed. Barbara Brookes, Annabel Cooper, and Robin Law (Auckland: Auckland University Press: 2003), 50–90.

109. Lucy Taska, "'About as Popular as a Dose of the Clap': Steam, Diesel and Masculinity at the New South Wales Eveleigh Railway Workshops," *Journal of Transport History* 26, no. 2 (2005): 82, 86–87.

110. Ian J. Kerr, *Building the Railways of the Raj, 1850–1900* (Delhi: Oxford University Press, 1995), 169–185.

111. Laura Tabili, "'A Maritime Race': Masculinity and the Racial Division of Labor in British Merchant Ships, 1900–1939," in *Iron Men, Wooden Women: Gender and Seafaring in the Atlantic World, 1700–1920,* ed. Margaret S. Creighton and Lisa Norling (Baltimore: Johns Hopkins University Press, 1996), 169–188; Frances Steel, "Oceania under Steam: Maritime Cultures, Colonial Histories, 1870s–1910s" (PhD diss., Australian National University, 2008).

112. John Robert Seeley, *The Expansion of England: Two Courses of Lectures* (1883; Boston: Little, Brown, 1909), 74.

113. Mary Kingsley, *Travels in West Africa* (London: Macmillan, 1895), chap. 4. For a completely different kind of ethnographic mission by boat, complete with depth gauge and bucket, see the journey of the telegraph from Khabarovsk into Manchuria, related at the start of David Wolff, *To the Harbin Station* (Stanford, CA: Stanford University Press, 1999), 14ff.

114. George Robb, "Women and White Collar Crime: Debates on Gender, Fraud and the Corporate Economy in England and America, 1850–1930," *British Journal of Criminology* 46, no. 6 (2006): 1058–1072; Nancy Henry, *George Eliot and the British Empire* (Cambridge: Cambridge University Press, 2002).

115. Laura Gbah Bear, "Miscegenations of Modernity: Constructing European Respectability and Race in the Indian Railway Colony, 1857–1931," *Women's History Review* 3, no. 4 (1994): 431–448; Barbara Welke, *Recasting American Liberty: Gender, Race, Law and the Railroad* (Cambridge: Cambridge University Press, 2001).

116. Quoted in W. G. Beasely, *Japanese Imperialism, 1894–1945* (Oxford: Oxford University Press, 1987), 74.

117. W. G. Beasley, *Japan Encounters the Barbarian: Japanese Travellers in America and Europe* (New Haven, CT: Yale University Press, 1995), 45.

118. Ibid., 45–48; Steven J. Ericson, "Importing Locomotives in Meiji Japan: International Business and Technology Transfer in the Railroad Industry," *Osiris,* ser. 2, 13 (1998): 129–153.

119. James A. Fujii, "Intimate Alienation: Japanese Urban Rail and the Commodification of Urban Subjects," *differences: A Journal of Feminist Cultural Studies* 11, no. 2 (1999): 106–133; Tessa Morris-Suzuki, *Re-Inventing Japan: Time, Space, Nation* (Armonk, NY: M. E. Sharpe, 1998), 23–28; Joshua B. Fogel, *The Literature of Travel in the Rediscovery of China, 1862–1945* (Stanford, CA: Stanford University Press, 1998), 129.

120. Akira Iriye, *China and Japan in the Global Setting* (Cambridge, MA: Harvard University Press, 1992), 20.

121. Jun Uchida, "'A Scramble for Freight': The Politics of Collaboration along and across the Railway Tracks of Korea under Japanese Rule," *Comparative Studies in Society and History* 51 (2009): 117–150.

122. Hyun Ok Park, "Korean Manchuria: The Racial Politics of Territorial Osmosis," *South Atlantic Quarterly* 99, no. 1 (2000): 198.

123. Ramon H. Myers, "Japanese Imperialism in Manchuria: The South Manchuria Railway Company, 1906–1933," in *The Japanese Informal Empire in China, 1895–1937,* ed. Peter Duus, Ramon H. Myers, and Mark Peattie (Princeton, NJ: Princeton University Press, 1989), 101–132;

Paul A. Cohen, *History in Three Keys: The Boxers as Event, Experience, and Myth* (New York: Columbia University Press, 1998), 47, 52.

124. Conrad Totman, *A History of Japan* (Malden, MA: Blackwell, 2000), 313, 387–389.

125. Ramon H. Myers and Thomas R. Ulie, "Foreign Influence and Agricultural Development in Northeast China: A Case Study of the Liaotung Peninsula, 1906–42," *Journal of Asian Studies* 31, no. 2 (1972): 329–350.

126. Kozo Yamamura, "Success Ill-Gotten? The Role of Meiji Militarism in Japan's Technological Progress," *Journal of Economic History* 37, no. 1 (1997): 114–115.

127. Shelley Baranowski, *Nazi Empire: German Colonialism and Imperialism from Bismarck to Hitler* (Cambridge: Cambridge University Press, 2010), 36–51.

128. Kozo Yamamura, "Success Ill-Gotten?," 113–135; J. Charles Schencking, *Making Waves: Politics, Propaganda, and the Emergence of the Imperial Japanese Navy, 1868–1922* (Stanford, CA: Stanford University Press, 2005), 85–87, 107–108.

129. J. Charles Schencking, "The Imperial Japanese Navy and the Constructed Consciousness of a South Seas Destiny, 1872–1921," *Modern Asian Studies* 33, no. 4 (1999): 769–796.

130. Ken'ichi Goto, *Tensions of Empire: Japan and Southeast in the Colonial and Postcolonial World,* trans. and ed. Paul H. Kratoska (Athens: Ohio University Press, 2003), 14–16.

131. Handan Nezir Akmese, "The Japanese Nation in Arms: A Role Model for Militarist Nationalism in the Ottoman Army, 1905–14," *Princeton Papers: Interdisciplinary Journal of Middle Eastern Studies* 14 (2007): 63–89.

132. Yakup Bektas, "The Sultan's Messenger: Cultural Constructions of Ottoman Telegraphy, 1847–1880," *Technology and Culture* 41, no. 4 (2000): 672–675; Eugene Rogan, "Instant Communication: The Impact of the Telegraph in Ottoman Syria," in *The Syrian Land: Processes of Integration and Fragmentation,* ed. Thomas Philipp and Birgit Schäbler (Stuttgart: Steiner, 1998), 115–118; Elizabeth B. Frierson, "Gender, Consumption and Patriotism: The Emergence of an Ottoman Public Sphere," in *Islam and the Common Good,* ed. Armando Salvatore and Dale Eickelman (London: Brill, 2006), 108.

133. Donald Quataert, *Miners and the State in the Ottoman Empire: The Zonguldak Coalfield, 1822–1920* (New York: Berghahn Books, 2006), 1; Quataert, *The Ottoman Empire, 1700–1922,* 2nd ed. (Cambridge: Cambridge University Press, 2005), 122; Walter Pinhas Pick, "Meissner Pasha and the Construction of Railways in Palestine and Neighboring Countries," in *Ottoman Palestine, 1800–1914: Studies in Economic and Social History,* ed. Gad G. Gilbar (London: Brill, 1990), 179–218; Margot Badran, ed., *Harem Years: The Memoirs of an Egyptian Feminist, 1879–1924* (New York: Feminist Press, 1986).

134. Quataert, *Ottoman Empire, 1700–1922,* 122–123; Palmira Brumett, *Image and Imperialism in the Revolutionary Ottoman Press, 1908–1911* (Albany, NY: SUNY Press, 2000), 301; Edward J. Erickson, *Ordered to Die: A History of the Ottoman Army in the First World War* (Westport, CT: Greenwood Press, 2000), 42, 63; Donald E. Miller and Lorna Touryan Miller, eds., *Survivors: An Oral History of the Armenian Genocide* (Berkeley: University of California Press, 1993), 19.

135. Ilhan Tekeli and Selim Ilkin, "The Public Works Program and the Development of Technology in the Ottoman Empire in the Second Half of the Nineteenth Century," *Turcica: Revue*

d'Études Turques 28 (1996): 195–234; Donald Quataert, "The Silk Industry of Bursa, 1880–1914," in *The Ottoman Empire and the World-Economy,* ed. Huri Islamoglu-Inan (Cambridge: Cambridge University Press, 1987), 284.

136. Abdul-Karim Rafeq, "Damascus and the Pilgrim Caravan," in *Modernity and Culture: From the Mediterranean to the Indian Ocean,* ed. Leila Tarazi Fawaz, C. A. Bayly, and Robert Ilbert (New York: Columbia University Press, 2002), 139; Quataert, "Silk Industry of Bursa," 284–286.

137. Quataert, "Silk Industry of Bursa," 284.

138. G. F. Deasy, "The Harbors of Africa," *Economic Geography* 18 (1942): 325–342.

139. Headrick, *Tools of Empire,* 193.

140. E.g., D. Lardner, *Railway Economy* (London, 1850), 35; Emily Clemens Pearson, *Gutenberg and the Art of Printing* (London: Noyes, Holmes and Co., 1871), 288.

141. Headrick, *Tentacles of Progress,* 51.

142. Christopher, *Colonial Africa,* 82; Lewis H. Gann and Peter Duignan, *The Rulers of British Africa, 1870–1914* (London: Routledge, 1978), 393n24.

143. Ruth took this business over from her mother, Maria. David Rooney, *Ruth Belville: The Greenwich Time Lady* (Greenwich: National Maritime Museum, 2008).

144. Tim Youngs, ed., *Travel Writing in the Nineteenth Century: Filling in the Blank Spaces* (London: Anthem, 2006), 42.

145. Headrick, *Tentacles of Progress,* 32–33.

146. Ian J. Kerr, ed., *Railways in Modern India* (Oxford: Oxford University Press, 2001), 15.

147. Laura Bear, "Miscegenations of Modernity: Constructing European Respectability and Race in the Indian Railway Colony, 1857–1931," *Women's History Review* 3 (1994): 531–548; Bear, *Lines of the Nation,* 80.

148. Jun Uchida, "'A Scramble for Freight,'" 117–150.

149. Quoted in Susan Tennant, *The 1918 Shikoku Pilgrimage of Takamure Itsue: An English Translation of Musume Junreiki* (Bowen Island, BC: Bowen Publishing, 2010), 66.

150. Peter Van der Veer, *Religious Nationalism: Hindus and Muslims in India* (Berkeley: University of California Press, 1994), 82; Ian J. Kerr, "Reworking a Popular Religious Practice: The Effects of Railways on Pilgrimage in 19th and 20th Century South Asia," in Kerr, *Railways in Modern India,* 304–327; F. E. Peters, *The Hajj: The Muslim Pilgrimage to Mecca and the Holy Places* (Princeton, NJ: Princeton University Press, 1994), 266–267, 282–289, 301–307; Siobhan Lambert-Hurley, ed., *A Princess's Pilgrimage* (Bloomington: Indiana University Press, 2008).

151. S. A. M. Adshead, *China in World History,* 3rd ed. (London: Palgrave, 2000), 299–300.

152. J. N. Hays, *Epidemics and Pandemics: Their Impacts on Human History* (Santa Barbara, CA: ABC-CLIO, 2005), 315–316, 385–391.

153. Ira Klein, "Plague, Policy and Popular Unrest in British India," *Modern Asian Studies* 22, no. 4 (1988): 737; William Beinart and Lotte Hughes, *Environment and Empire* (Oxford: Oxford University Press, 2007), 174; Lajpat Rai, *Young India: An Interpretation and a History of the Nationalist Movement* (New York: B. W. Huebsch, 1916), 249; M. K. Gandhi, *Hind Swaraj and Other Writings,* ed. Anthony J. Parel (1910; Cambridge: Cambridge University Press, 1997).

154. The expression "traveling incarceration" is Michel de Certeau's. See his *The Practice of Every-day Life,* trans. Steven Rendall (Berkeley: University of California, 1988), 111.

155. Parel, *Hind Swaraj,* 47.

156. Rudolph Peters, "Religious Attitudes towards Modernization in the Ottoman Empire: A Nineteenth Century Pious Text on Steamships, Factories and the Telegraph," *Die Welt des Islams,* n.s., 26, no. 1 (1986): 76–105.

157. Bektas, "The Sultan's Messenger," 669.

158. Ibid., 692–693; Abdul-Karim Rafeq, "Damascus and the Pilgrim Caravan," in Fawaz, Bayly, and Ilbert, *Modernity and Culture,* 141.

159. Benedict Anderson, *Imagined Communities: Reflections on the Origin and Spread of Nationalism,* 2nd rev. ed. rev. (London: Verso, 1991).

160. Manu Goswami, "From Swadeshi to Swaraj: Nation, Economy, Territory in Colonial South Asia, 1870 to 1907," *Comparative Studies in Society and History* 40, no. 4 (1998): 609–636.

161. Margaret McClure, *Wonder Country: Making New Zealand Tourism* (Auckland: Auckland University Press, 2004); Jeremy Foster, "'Land of Contrast' or 'Home We Have Always Known'? The SAR & H and the Imaginary Geography of White South African Nationhood, 1910–1930," *Journal of Southern African Studies* 29, no. 3 (2003): 657–680.

162. Jamie Mackie, *Bandung 1955: Non-Alignment and Afro-Asian Solidarity* (Paris: Éditions Didier Millet, 2005), 14; Christopher Lee, ed., *Making a World after Empire: The Bandung Moment and Its Political Afterlives* (Athens: University of Ohio Press, 2010).

163. Mackie, *Bandung 1955,* 78, 87. These tensions were also at the heart of conflicts in the Non-Aligned Movement of the 1960s and 1970s, which owed a significant debt to Nehru as well as to the Bandung Conference.

164. Mrinalini Sinha, *Specters of Mother India: The Global Restructuring of an Empire* (Durham, NC: Duke University Press, 2006), 18.

165. P. J. Cain and A. G. Hopkins, *British Imperialism, 1688–2000,* 2nd ed. (London: Longman, 2001). For similar arguments, see Antoinette Burton, *Empire in Question: Reading, Writing and Teaching British Imperialism* (Durham, NC: Duke University Press, 2011), esp. chap. 12.

166. Turkish historian Selim Deringil, cited in James Gelvin, "Developmentalism, Revolution, and Freedom in the Arab East: The Cases of Egypt, Syria and Iraq," in *The Idea of Freedom in Asia and Africa,* ed. Robert H. Taylor (Stanford, CA: Stanford University Press, 2002), 69.

167. Niall Ferguson, "The British Empire Revisited: The Costs and Benefits of 'Anglobalization,'" *Historically Speaking* 4, no. 4 (April 2003): 21–27.

168. Keith Wilson, ed., *The International Impact of the Boer War* (Chesham: Acumen, 2001); Burton, *Empire in Question,* chap. 12.

169. John Crawford and Ian McGibbon, eds., *One Flag, One Queen, One Tongue: New Zealand, the British Empire, and the South African War* (Auckland: Auckland University Press, 2003); Terence Denman, "'The Red Livery of Shame': The Campaign against Army Recruitment in Ireland, 1899–1914," *Irish Historical Studies* 29 (1994): 208–233; Donal P. McCracken, "'Fenians and Dutch Carpetbaggers': Irish and Afrikaner Nationalisms, 1877–1930," *Eire-Ireland* 29, no. 3 (1994): 109–125.

170. Simon Szreter, *Fertility, Class and Gender in Britain, 1860–1940* (Cambridge: Cambridge University Press, 1996), 183–186; Theodore M. Porter, *Karl Pearson: The Scientific Life in a Statistical Age* (Princeton, NJ: Princeton University Press, 2004), 282–284.

171. Elisa Camiscioli, "Reproducing the 'French Race': Immigration and Pronatalism in Early-Twentieth-Century France," in Ballantyne and Burton, *Bodies in Contact*, 219–233; Sabine Frühstück, *Colonizing Sex: Sexology and Social Control in Modern Japan* (Berkeley: University of California Press, 2003).

172. Apollon Davidson and Irina Filatova, "Seeking the Secrets of War: Russian Military Observers at the South African War (1899–1902)," *Kleio* 30 (1998): 45–63.

173. Rebecca Karl, *Staging the World: Chinese Nationalism at the Turn of the Twentieth Century* (Durham, NC: Duke University Press, 2002).

174. Jeff Sahadeo, *Russian Colonial Society in Tashkent, 1865–1923* (Ithaca, NY: Cornell University Press, 2007), 90, 170–173; Daniel Brower, *Turkestan and the Fate of the Russian Empire* (London: RoutledgeCurzon, 2003). See also Douglas Northrop, *Veiled Empire: Gender and Power in Stalinist Central Asia* (Ithaca, NY: Cornell University Press, 2004).

175. Lora Wildenthal, *German Women for Empire, 1884–1945* (Durham, NC: Duke University Press, 2001), esp. chaps. 2 and 4.

176. "Pan-German Creed of Lebensraum," in *The Imperialism Reader,* ed. Louis L. Snyder (New York: Van Nostrand, 1962), 89.

177. Frühstück, *Colonizing Sex,* 37, 22; Louise Young, *Japan's Total Empire: Manchuria and the Culture of Wartime Imperialism* (Berkeley: University of California Press, 1998), 248.

178. Adeeb Khalid, "'The World of Journalism, or the Reasons for the Establishment of the Newspaper *To'jorr,*' 1907," in *The Modern Middle East: A Sourcebook,* ed. Cameron Michael Amin, Benjamin C. Fortna, and Elizabeth Frierson (Oxford: Oxford University Press, 2006), 104–107; Tony Ballantyne, "Teaching Maori about Asia: Print Culture and Community Identity in Nineteenth-Century New Zealand," in *Asia in the Making of New Zealand,* ed. Brian Moloughney and Henry Johnson (Auckland: Auckland University Press, 2006), 13–25.

179. See Emma Jinhua Teng, *Taiwan's Imagined Geographies: Chinese Colonial Travel Writing and Pictures, 1683–1895* (Cambridge, MA: Harvard University Asia Center, 2004); Matt K. Matsuda, *Empire of Love: Histories of France and the Pacific* (Oxford: Oxford University Press, 2005).

180. Peter Duus, *The Abacus and the Sword: The Japanese Penetration of Korea, 1895–1910* (Berkeley: University of California Press, 1995), 398.

181. David Prochaska, "The Cagayous of Algiers," *American Historical Review* 101, no. 3 (1996): 695–696.

182. Patricia Lorcin, *Imperial Identities: Stereotyping, Prejudice and Race in Colonial Algeria* (New York: Tauris, 1995), 28–33, 260n70; Catherine Hall, "The Rule of Difference: Gender, Class and Empire in the Making of the 1832 Reform Act," in *Gendered Nations: Nationalisms and Gender Order in the Long Nineteenth Century,* ed. Ida Blom, Karen Hagemann, and Catherine Hall (New York: Oxford/Berg, 2000), 107–135; Antoinette Burton, "New Narratives of Imperial Politics in the 19th Century," in *At Home with the Empire: Metropolitan Culture and*

the Imperial World, ed. Catherine Hall and Sonya Rose (Cambridge: Cambridge University Press, 2006), 212–229.

183. Tony Ballantyne, "The State, Politics, and Power, 1769–1893," in *The New Oxford History of New Zealand,* ed. Giselle Byrnes (Oxford: Oxford University Press, 2009), 99–125; Carolyn Martin Shaw, *Colonial Inscriptions: Race, Sex and Class in Kenya* (Minneapolis: University of Minnesota Press, 1995), 36–59; Victoria B. Tashjian and Jean Allman, "Marrying and Marriage in a Shifting Terrain: Reconfigurations of Power and Authority in Early Colonial Asante," in *Women in African Colonial Histories,* ed. Jean Allman, Susan Geiger, and Nakanyike Musisi (Bloomington: Indiana University Press, 2002), 237; Belinda Bozzoli, *Women of Phokeng: Consciousness, Life Strategy and Migrancy in South Africa, 1900–1983* (London: Heinemann, 1991), 14.

184. Henry Reynolds, *The Other Side of the Frontier* (Townsville, Queensland: James Cook University, 1981; New York: Penguin, 1982); Reynolds, *Aboriginal Sovereignty: Reflections on Race, State and Nation* (London: Allen and Unwin, 1996), 1–15.

185. Raymond Evans, "'Plenty Shoot Em': The Destruction of Aboriginal Societies along the Queensland Frontier," in *Genocide and Settler Society: Frontier Violence and Stolen Indigenous Children in Australian History,* ed. A. Dirk Moses (New York: Berghahn, 2004), 150–173, quotation at 165.

186. See, for example, Fiona Paisley, *Loving Protection? Australian Feminism and Aboriginal Women's Rights, 1919–1939* (Melbourne: Melbourne University Press, 2000).

187. Clifton Crais, *The Politics of Evil: Politics, State Power and the Political Imagination in South Africa* (Cambridge: Cambridge University Press, 2002), 12.

188. Emilio Aguinaldo, *True Version of the Philippine Revolution* (Gloucestershire: Dodo, 2006); Benedict Anderson, *Under Three Flags: Anarchism and the Anti-Colonial Imagination* (New York: Verso, 2005).

189. See Madhavi Kale, *Fragments of Empire: Capital, Slavery, and Indian Indentured Labor Migration* (Philadelphia: University of Pennsylvania Press, 1998), 150ff.

190. Anthony De Verteuil, *Eight East Indian Immigrants: Gokool, Soodeen, Sookoo, Capildeo, Beccani, Ruknaddeen, Valiama, Bunsee* (Newtown, Trinidad: Paria, 1989).

191. Ian C. Fletcher, "Double Meanings: Nation and Empire in the Edwardian Era," in *After the Imperial Turn: Thinking with and through the Nation,* ed. Antoinette Burton (Durham, NC: Duke University Press, 2005), 251ff.

192. Nemata Blyden, "The Search for Anna Erskine: African American Women in Nineteenth Century Liberia," in *Stepping Forward: Black Women in Africa and the Americas,* ed. Catherine Higgs et al. (Athens: Ohio University Press, 2002), 31–43; Iris Berger, "An African American 'Mother of the Nation': Madie Hall Xuma in South Africa, 1940–1963," *Journal of Southern African Studies* 27, no. 1 (2001): 547–566; Rosalyn Terborg-Penn, "Enfranchising Women of Color: Woman Suffragists as Agents of Imperialism," in *Nation, Empire, Colony: Historicizing Gender and Race,* ed. Nupur Chaudhuri and Ruth Roach Pierson (Bloomington: Indiana University Press, 1998), 41–56.

193. Niam Lynch, "Defining Irish Nationalist Imperialism: Thomas Davis and John Mitchell," *Eire-Ireland* 42, nos. 1–2 (2007): 82–107; Jonathan Hyslop, "The World Voyage of James Keir

Hardie: Indian Nationalism, Zulu Insurgency and the British Labour Diaspora, 1907–1908," *Journal of Global History* 1 (2006): 359; My-Van Tran, "Testimony of a Twentieth Century Vietnamese Revolutionary: The Memoirs of Trăn Trong Khac," *Journal of Colonialism and Colonial History* 7, no. 3 (2007).

194. Christopher Abel, *José Martí: Revolutionary Democrat* (Dublin: Athlone, 1986).

195. See, for example, Rogaski, *Hygienic Modernity*.

196. Janet Afary, *The Iranian Constitutional Revolution, 1906–1911: Grassroots Democracy, Social Democracy and the Origins of Feminism* (New York: Columbia University Press, 1996), 179.

197. Susan Pennybacker, "The Universal Races Congress, London, Political Culture, and Imperial Dissent, 1900–1939," *Radical History Review* 92 (2005): 103–117; Mansour Bonakdarian, "Negotiating Universal Values and Cultural and National Parameters at the First Universal Races Congress," *Radical History Review* 92 (2005): 126n1.

198. Cameron Michael Amin, *The Making of the Modern Iranian Woman: Gender, State Policy and Popular Culture, 1865–1946* (Gainesville: University Press of Florida, 2002), 117–118.

199. Susan Zimmerman, "The Challenge of Multinational Empire for the International Women's Movement: The Habsburg Monarchy and the Development of Feminist International Politics," *Journal of Women's History* 17, no. 2 (2005): 87–117.

200. Meera Kosambi, ed., *Pandita Ramabai's American Encounter* (Bloomington: University of Indiana Press, 2003); Padma Anagol, *The Emergence of Feminism in India, 1850–1920* (London: Ashgate, 2005), esp. 37–46.

201. Bill V. Mullen, *Afro-Orientalism* (Minneapolis: University of Minnesota, 2004); Gerald Horne, *Race War: White Supremacy and the Japanese Attack on the British Empire* (New York: NYU Press, 2004); Erez Manela, *The Wilsonian Moment: Self-Determination and the International Origins of Anticolonial Nationalism* (Cambridge, MA: Harvard University Press, 2007). For a discussion of how this prismatic view of 1919 can be taught in world history courses, see Antoinette Burton, *A Primer for Teaching World History: Ten Design Principles* (Durham, NC: Duke University Press, 2011), chap. 5.

202. Though Koo was not an official delegate. Manela, *Wilsonian Moment*; Pat Walsh, *The Rise and Fall of Imperial Ireland: Redmondism in the Context of Britain's Conquest of South Africa and Its Great War on Germany, 1899–1916* (Dublin: Athol, 2003), 485–488.

203. Marilyn Lake and Henry Reynolds, *Drawing the Global Colour Line: White Men's Countries and the International Challenge of Racial Equality* (Cambridge: Cambridge University Press, 2008), chap. 7; Michael Adas, "Contested Hegemony: The Great War and the Afro-Asian Assault in the Civilizing Mission Ideology," *Journal of World History* 15, no. 1 (2004): 31–63; Leila Rupp, "Constructing Internationalism: The Case of Transnational Women's Organizations, 1885–1945," *American Historical Review* 99, no. 5 (1994): 1571–1600.

204. Lal, "Incident of the Crawling Lane," 36–37; Rana Mitter, *Bitter Revolution: China's Struggle with the Modern World* (Oxford: Oxford University Press, 2004), 162.

205. Anderson, *Under Three Flags*; Eiichiro Azuma, *Between Two Empires: Race, History and Transnationalism in Japanese America* (Oxford: Oxford University Press, 2005); Rashid Khalidi et al., *The Origins of Arab Nationalism* (New York: Columbia University Press, 1991); Stephen White, "Communism and the East: The Baku Congress, 1920," *Slavic Review* 33, no. 3

(1974): 492–514; John D. Hargreaves, "The Comintern and Anti-Colonialism: New Research Opportunities," *African Affairs* 92 (1993): 255–261; Michelle Stephens, *Black Empire: The Masculine Global Imaginary of Caribbean Intellectuals in the United States, 1914–1962* (Durham, NC: Duke University Press, 2005), 27; John Maynard, "Transcultural/Transnational Interaction and Influences on Aboriginal Australia," in *Connected Worlds: History in Transnational Perspective*, ed. Ann Curthoys and Marilyn Lake (Canberra: ANU E Press 2005), chap. 12.

206. Jason Knirk, "The Dominion of Ireland: The Anglo-Irish Treaty in an Imperial Context," *Eire-Ireland* 42, nos. 1–2 (2007): 241.

207. Prasenjit Duara, *Sovereignty and Authenticity: Manchuko and the East Asian Modern* (Lanham, MD: Rowman and Littlefield, 2004), 1–2; Manela, *Wilsonian Moment,* 195; Brent Hayes Edwards, "The Shadow of Shadows," *positions: east asia cultures critique* 11 (2003): 11–49.

208. Susan Pedersen, "Metaphors of the Schoolroom: Women Working the Mandates System of the League of Nations," *History Workshop* 66 (2008): 189–207.

209. Charlotte Weber, "Unveiling Scheherazade: Feminist Orientalism in the International Alliance of Women," *Feminist Studies* 27, no. 1 (2007); Sinha, *Specters of Mother India,* 8ff.

210. Tara Zahra, " 'Each Nation Only Cares for Its Own': Empire, Nation and Child Welfare Activism in the Bohemian Lands, 1900–1918," *American Historical Review* 111, no. 5 (2005); Elizabeth Thompson, *Colonial Citizens: Republican Rights, Paternal Privilege, and Gender in French Syria and Lebanon* (New York: Columbia University Press, 2000;) Lisa Pollard, *Nurturing the Nation: The Family Politics of Modernizing, Colonizing and Liberating Egypt, 1805–1923* (Berkeley: University of California Press, 2005).

211. Young, *Japan's Total Empire,* 283; John C. De Boer, "Circumventing the Evils of Colonialism: Yanaihara Tadao and Zionist Settler Colonialism in Palestine," *positions: east asia cultures critique* 14, no. 3 (2006): 567–595.

212. As Francine Hirsch has shown, Soviet ethnographers looked to Native American reservations as models for their own ethnic population "problem" in the context of a growing, systematized apparatus devoted to collecting knowledge about them. See Hirsch, *Empire of Nations: Ethnographic Knowledge and the Making of the Soviet Union* (Ithaca, NY: Cornell University Press, 2005), 87–88.

213. Vijay Prashad, *Everybody Was Kungfu Fighting: Afro-Asian Connections and the Myth of Cultural Purity* (Boston: Beacon Press, 2001), 79.

214. Goolam Vahed, "Constructions of Community and Identity among Indians in Natal, 1860–1910: The Role of the Muharram Festival," *Journal of African History* 43, no. 1 (2002): 77–94.

215. Eóin Flannery and Angus Mitchell, eds., *Enemies of Empire: New Perspectives on Imperialism, Literature and Historiography* (Dublin: Four Courts, 2007).

216. Mullen, *Afro-Orientalism,* chap. 1, "W. E. B. DuBois's Afro-Asian Fantasia."

217. Ibid., xxxvii. For Mississippi and Dubois seen in a different triangular matrix, see Marilyn Lake, "From Mississippi to Melbourne via Natal: The Invention of the Literacy Test as a Technology of Racial Exclusion," in Curthoys and Lake, *Connected Worlds,* chap. 13.

218. The phrase is Alys Eve Weinbaum's; see her *Wayward Reproductions: Genealogies of Race and Nation in Transatlantic Modern Thought* (Durham, NC: Duke University Press, 2004), esp.

chap. 5. See also Kate Baldwin, *Beyond the Color Line and the Iron Curtain: Reading Encounters between Black and Red* (Durham, NC: Duke University Press, 2002), esp. chap. 2.

219. William J. Duiker, *Ho Chi Minh* (New York: Hyperion, 2000), 79–85, 594.

220. Hue-Tam Ho Tai, *Radicalism and the Origins of the Vietnamese Revolution* (Cambridge, MA: Harvard University Press, 1992), 218; Phuong Bui-Tranh, "Femmes vietnammiennes pendant et après la colonisation française," in *Histoire des femmes en situation coloniale: Afrique et Asie, XXe siècle,* ed. Anne Hugon (Paris: Karthala, 2004), 77–78.

221. Rupp, "Constructing Internationalism," 1592.

222. Norman Smith, "The Difficulties of Despair: Dan Di and Chinese Literary Production in Manchukuo," *Journal of Women's History* 18, no. 1 (2006): 77–100.

223. Lake and Reynolds, *Drawing the Global Colour Line,* chap. 1; John McLeod, "A Night at the 'Cosmopolitan': Axes of Transnational Encounter in the 1930s and 1940s," *Interventions* 4, no. 1 (2002): 53–67.

224. Helen Hardacre, "Asano Wasaburô and Japanese Spiritualism in Early Twentieth-Century Japan," in *Japan's Competing Modernities: Issues in Culture and Democracy, 1900–1930,* ed. Sharon Minichiello (Honolulu: University of Hawai'i Press, 1998), 137.

225. Eric Hotta, "Rash Behari Bose and His Japanese Supporters: An Insight into Anti-Colonial Nationalism and Pan Asianism," *Interventions* 8, no. 1 (2006): 116–132.

226. Rustom Barucha, *Another Asia: Rabindranath Tagore and Okura Tenshin* (Oxford: Oxford University Press, 2006).

227. These are relationships with long histories, of course. See Surendra Bhana and Goolam Vahed, *The Making of a Political Reformer: Gandhi in South Africa, 1893–1914* (New Delhi: Manohar 2005); Goolam, "The Making of 'Indianness': Indian Politics in South Africa during the 1930s and 1940s," *Journal of Natal and Zulu History* 17 (1997): 1–36; E. C. Webster, "The 1949 Durban 'Riots': A Case-Study in Racism and Class," in *Working Papers in Southern African Studies,* ed. P. L. Bonner (Johannesburg: African Studies Institute, University of Witwatersrand, 1979), 21ff.

228. Hilda Bernstein, *For Their Triumphs and for Their Tears: Women in Apartheid South Africa,* rev. ed. (London: International Defence and Aid Fund for Southern Africa, 1985).

229. See his *The World and Africa* (New York: Viking, 1947), esp. chap. 9, "Asia in Africa."

230. Prasenjit Duara, *Sovereignty and Authenticity,* 4.

231. Here we are borrowing heavily from Elleke Boehmer, *Empire, the National and the Postcolonial, 1890–1920* (Oxford: Oxford University Press, 2002), 1–7.

232. Hee-Yeon Cho and Kuan-Hsing Chen, "Editorial Introduction: Bandung/Third Worldism," *Inter-Asia Cultural Studies* 6, no. 4 (2005): 473–475.

233. Lal, "Incident of the Crawling Lane."

3. Migrations and Belongings

1. This chapter is based on Dirk Hoerder, *Cultures in Contact: World Migrations in the Second Millennium* (Durham, NC: Duke University Press, 2002), chaps. 12–18. More extensive annotation can be found there.

2. Adam M. McKeown, "Global Migration, 1846–1940," *Journal of World History* 15, no. 2 (2005): 155–189.

3. Eric J. Hobsbawn and Terence Ranger, eds., *The Invention of Tradition* (Cambridge: Cambridge University Press, 1983); Benedict Anderson, *Imagined Communities: Reflections on the Origin and Spread of Nationalism* (London: Verso, 1983).

4. Adam McKeown, "Chinese Emigration in Global Context, 1850–1940," *Journal of Global History* 5 (2010): 1–30; José Moya and Adam McKeown, "World Migration in the Long Twentieth Century," in *Essays on Twentieth-Century History,* ed. Michael Adas (Philadelphia: Temple University Press, 2010), 9–52.

5. Marcus Rediker, *The Slave Ship: A Human History* (New York: Viking, 2007), 3, updating the statistics provided in Philip D. Curtin, *The Atlantic Slave Trade: A Census* (Madison: University of Wisconsin Press, 1969), and Paul E. Lovejoy, "The Volume of the Atlantic Slave Trade: A Synthesis," *Journal of African History* 23 (1982): 473–502.

6. David Northrup, *Indentured Labor in the Age of Imperialism, 1834–1922* (Cambridge: Cambridge University Press, 1995); Crispin Bates, ed., *Community, Empire and Migration: South Asian Diaspora* (Basingstoke: Palgrave, 2001).

7. Adam M. McKeown, "Conceptualizing Chinese Diasporas, 1842–1949," *Journal of Asian Studies* 58, no. 2 (1999): 306–337; Michael Mann, "Migration–Re-migration–Circulation: South Asian Kulis in the Indian Ocean and Beyond, 1840–1940," in *Connecting Seas and Connected Ocean Rims: Indian, Atlantic, and Pacific Oceans and China Seas Migrations from the 1830s to the 1930s,* ed. Donna Gabaccia and Dirk Hoerder (Leiden: Brill, 2011), 108–133.

8. Dirk Hoerder, ed., *Labor Migration in the Atlantic Economies: The European and North American Working Classes during the Period of Industrialization* (Westport, CT: Greenwood, 1985).

9. Hoerder, *Cultures in Contact,* chaps. 13–15.

10. John Torpey, *The Invention of the Passport: Surveillance, Citizenship and the State* (Cambridge: Cambridge University Press, 2000); Christiane Harzig and Dirk Hoerder, with Donna Gabaccia, *What Is Migration History?* (Cambridge: Polity, 2009), 72–85.

11. Harzig et al., *What Is Migration History?,* 1–7, 69–72.

12. José C. Curto and Renée Soulodre-La France, eds., *Africa and the Americas: Interconnections during the Slave Trade* (Trenton, NJ: Africa World Press, 2005).

13. Gerhard Jaritz and Albert Müller, eds., *Migration in der Feudalgesellschaft* (Frankfurt am Main: Campus, 1988); Rainer C. Schwinges, ed., *Neubürger im späten Mittelalter: Migration und Austausch in der Städtelandschaft des alten Reiches (1250–1550)* (Berlin: Duncker und Humblot, 2002).

14. David J. Robinson, ed., *Migration in Colonial Spanish America* (Cambridge: Cambridge University Press, 1990).

15. A particularly detailed study for one plantation regime is Ronald Takaki, *Pau Hana: Plantation Life and Labor in Hawaii, 1835–1920* (Honolulu: University of Hawai'i Press, 1983).

16. Paul Gilroy, *The Black Atlantic: Modernity and Double Consciousness* (Cambridge, MA: Harvard University Press, 1993), a book that is England-centered and somewhat male-biased. Two comprehensive studies are Vincent Bakpetu Thompson, *The Making of the African Diaspora in*

the Americas, 1441–1900 (Harlow, Essex: Longman, 1987); and John Thornton, *Africa and Africans in the Making of the Atlantic World, 1400–1800,* 2nd ed. (Cambridge: Cambridge University Press, 1998). David Patrick Geggus, *Haitian Revolutionary Studies* (Bloomington: Indiana University Press, 2002); Madison S. Bell, *Toussaint Louverture: A Biography* (New York: Pantheon Books, 2007); Emma Christopher, Cassandra Pybus, and Marcus Rediker, eds., *Many Middle Passages: Forced Migration and the Making of the Modern World* (Berkeley: University of California Press, 2007).

17. David Eltis and James Walvin, eds., *The Abolition of the Atlantic Slave Trade: Origins and Effects in Europe, Africa, and the Americas* (Madison: University of Wisconsin Press, 1981); Piet C. Emmer and Magnus Mörner, eds., *European Expansion and Migration: Essays on the Intercontinental Migration from Africa, Asia, and Europe* (New York: Berg, 1992); Seymour Drescher, *Abolition: A History of Slavery and Antislavery* (New York: Cambridge University Press, 2009); Katia M. de Queiros Mattoso, *To Be Slave in Brazil, 1550–1880,* 4th ed. (New Brunswick, NJ: Rutgers University Press, 1994).

18. Magnus Mörner, *Race Mixture in the History of Latin America* (Boston: Little, Brown, 1967); Bonham C. Richardson, "Caribbean Migrations, 1838–1985," in *The Modern Caribbean,* ed. Franklin W. Knight and Colin A. Palmer (Chapel Hill: University of North Carolina Press, 1989), 203–228.

19. Eugene D. Genovese, *Roll, Jordan, Roll: The World the Slaves Made* (New York: Pantheon Books, 1974); Lawrence W. Levine, *Black Culture and Black Consciousness: Afro-American Folk Thought from Slavery to Freedom* (New York: Oxford University Press, 1977); Robin D. G. Kelley and Earl Lewis, eds., *To Make Our World Anew: A History of African Americans* (New York: Oxford University Press, 2000); Stephan Palmié, ed., *Slave Culture and the Cultures of Slavery* (Knoxville: University of Tennessee Press, 1995); James N. Gregory, *The Southern Diaspora: How the Great Migrations of Black and White Southerners Transformed America* (Chapel Hill: University of North Carolina Press, 2005); Chad Berry, *Southern Migrants, Northern Exiles* (Urbana: University of Illinois Press, 2000).

20. Gabaccia and Hoerder, *Connecting Seas.*

21. John R. Willis, ed., *Slaves and Slavery in Muslim Africa,* 2 vols. (London: Cass, 1985); Patrick Manning, *Slavery and African Life: Occidental, Oriental, and African Slave Trades* (Cambridge: Cambridge University Press, 1990); Murray Gordon, *Slavery in the Arab World,* trans. from the French (orig. 1987; New York: New Amsterdam, 1989); W. Gervase Clarence-Smith, ed., *The Economics of the Indian Ocean Slave Trade in the Nineteenth Century* (London: Cass, 1989); Richard B. Allen, "Satisfying the Want for Labouring People: European Slave Trading in the Indian Ocean, 1500–1850," *Journal of World History* 21, no. 1 (2010): 45–73; Janet J. Ewald, "Slavery in Africa and the Slave Trades from Africa," *American Historical Review* 97 (1992): 465–485.

22. Kingsley Davis, *The Population of India and Pakistan* (Princeton, NJ: Princeton University Press, 1951); Jan C. Breman and E. Valentine Daniel, "The Making of a Coolie," *Journal of Peasant Studies* 19, nos. 3–4 (1992): 268–295; Jan Breman, *Labour Bondage in West India: From Past to Present* (New Delhi: Oxford University Press, 2007); Prasannan Parthasarathi, *The Transition to a Colonial Economy: Weavers, Merchants and Kings in South India, 1720–1800*

(Cambridge: Cambridge University Press, 2001); Morris D. Morris, *The Emergence of an Industrial Labour Force in India: A Study of the Bombay Cotton Mills, 1854–1947* (Bombay: Oxford University Press, 1965); Ranajit Das Gupta, "Factory Labour in Eastern India: Sources of Supply, 1855–1946," *Indian Economic and Social History Review* 13 (1976): 277–330; Dietmar Rothermund and D. C. Wadhwa, eds., *Zamindars, Mines, and Peasants: Studies in the History of an Indian Coalfield and Its Rural Hinterland* (New Delhi: Manohar, 1978).

23. Philip A. Kuhn, *Chinese among Others: Emigration in Modern Times* (Lanham: Rowman and Littlefield, 2008); Alfonso Felix Jr., ed., *The Chinese in the Philippines,* 2 vols. (Manila: Solidaridad, 1966–1969); Victor Purcell, *The Chinese in Southeast Asia,* 2nd rev. ed. (London: Oxford University Press, 1965); Wong Kwok-Chu, *The Chinese in the Philippine Economy, 1898–1941* (Quezon City: Ateneo de Manila University Press, 1999).

24. Harry G. Gelber, *Opium, Soldiers and Evangelicals: Britain's 1840–42 War with China and Its Aftermath* (New York: Palgrave Macmillan, 2004); Timothy Brook and Bob Tadashi Wakabayashi, eds., *Opium Regimes: China, Britain, and Japan, 1839–1952* (Berkeley: University of California Press, 2000).

25. Ping-ti Ho, *Studies on the Population of China, 1368–1953* (Cambridge, MA: Harvard University Press, 1959), 153–158; Jonathan D. Spence, *The Search for Modern China* (New York: Norton, 1990), 167–242.

26. Lynn Pan, gen. ed., *The Encyclopedia of the Chinese Overseas* (Richmond, UK: Curzon, 1999); Lynn Pan, *Sons of the Yellow Emperor: The Story of the Overseas Chinese* (London: Secker and Warburg, 1990), esp. 3–22; Wang Gungwu, *The Chinese Overseas: From Earthbound China to the Quest for Autonomy* (Cambridge, MA: Harvard University Press, 2000); Amarjit Kaur, *Wage Labour in Southeast Asia since 1840: Globalisation, the International Division of Labour and Labour Transformations* (Basingstoke: Palgrave Macmillan, 2004).

27. Irene B. Taeuber, *The Population of Japan* (Princeton, NJ: Princeton University Press, 1958), 173–190; Neville Bennett, "Japanese Emigration Policy, 1880–1941," in *Asians in Australia: The Dynamics of Migration and Settlement,* ed. Christine Inglis et al. (Singapore: Institute of Southeast Asian Studies, 1992), 23–43; Marius B. Jansen, "Japanese Imperialism: Late Meiji Perspectives," in *The Japanese Colonial Empire, 1895–1945,* ed. Ramon H. Myers and Mark R. Peattie (Princeton, NJ: Princeton University Press, 1984), 61–79; Douglas R. Howland, *Translating the West: Language and Political Reason in Nineteenth-Century Japan* (Honolulu: University of Hawai'i Press, 2002).

28. France had lost its first empire to Britain, resumed colonization in nearby Algeria in the 1830s, and began a new imperial expansion after its defeat by Prussia in 1871.

29. Hugh Tinker, *A New System of Slavery: The Export of Indian Labour Overseas, 1830–1920* (London: Oxford University Press, 1974); Northrup, *Indentured Labor;* Kay Saunders, ed., *Indentured Labour in the British Empire, 1834–1920* (London: Croom Helm, 1984).

30. Kenneth McPherson, Frank Broeze, Joan Wardrop, and Peter Reeves, "The Social Expansion of the Maritime World of the Indian Ocean: Passenger Traffic and Community Building, 1815–1939," in *Maritime Aspects of Migration,* ed. Klaus Friedland (Cologne: Böhlau, 1989), 427–440. The numerous studies on specific regions of destination include: Surendra Bhana, ed., *Essays on Indentured Indians in Natal* (Leeds: Peepal Tree Press, 1990); Uttama Bissoon-

doyal and S. B. C. Servansing, eds., *Indian Labour Immigration* (Moka, Mauritius: Mahatma Gandhi Institute, 1986); Marina Carter, *Voices from Indenture: Experiences of Indian Migrants in the British Empire* (Leicester: Leicester University Press, 1997); Adam McKeown, *Chinese Migrant Networks and Cultural Change: Peru, Chicago and Hawaii, 1900–1936* (Chicago: University of Chicago Press, 2001).

31. Hoerder, *Cultures in Contact,* 199–200, 211–215.

32. For a summary of the literature, see ibid., 191–199, 200–210, 216–227. For the postcolonial period, the best summary appears in José C. Moya, "A Continent of Immigrants: Postcolonial Shifts in the Western Hemisphere," *Hispanic American Historical Review* 86, no. 1 (2006): 1–28.

33. Mark Wyman, *Round-Trip to America: The Immigrants Return to Europe, 1880–1930* (Ithaca, NY: Cornell University Press, 1993).

34. Dirk Hoerder and Nora Faires, eds., *Migrants and Migration in Modern North America: Cross-Border Lives, Labor Markets, and Politics in Canada, the Caribbean, Mexico, and the United States* (Durham, NC: Duke University Press, 2011), esp. chaps. 2, 4, 6, 8, 10.

35. Case studies of migration internal to the United States include: Thomas Dublin, *Women at Work: The Transformation of Work and Community in Lowell, Mass., 1826–1860* (New York: Columbia University Press, 1979); Joe W. Trotter Jr., ed., *The Great Migration in Historical Perspective: New Dimensions of Race, Class, and Gender* (Bloomington: Indiana University Press, 1991). The flight of white sharecroppers from Depression and dustbowl conditions has been documented by the photographers of the US Farm Security Administration and is the theme of John Steinbeck's *Grapes of Wrath* (1939).

36. Hoerder, *Cultures in Contact,* 357–361.

37. Donald W. Treadgold, *The Great Siberian Migration: Government and Peasant in Resettlement from Emancipation to the First World War* (Princeton, NJ: Princeton University Press, 1957); Michael Khodarkovsky, *Russia's Steppe Frontier: The Making of a Colonial Empire, 1500–1800* (Bloomington: Indiana University Press, 2002); Andrew A. Gentes, *Exile to Siberia, 1590–1822* (New York: Palgrave Macmillan, 2008).

38. James H. Bater, *St. Petersburg: Industrialization and Change* (London: Arnold, 1976); Barbara A. Anderson, *Internal Migration during Modernization in Late Nineteenth-Century Russia* (Princeton, NJ: Princeton University Press, 1980); Inge Blank, "A Vast Migratory Experience: Eastern Europe in the Pre- and Post-Emancipation Era (1780–1914)," in *Roots of the Transplanted,* ed. Dirk Hoerder et al., 2 vols. (New York: Columbia University Press, 1994), 1:201–251.

39. Ben Eklof and Stephen P. Frank, eds., *The World of the Russian Peasant: Post-Emancipation Culture and Society* (Boston: Unwin Hyman, 1990).

40. The theoretical and methodological approaches to migration are summarized in Harzig et al., *What Is Migration History?* See also Caroline B. Brettell and James F. Hollifield, eds., *Migration Theory: Talking across Disciplines* (London: Routledge, 1999); Jan Lucassen and Leo Lucassen, eds., *Migration, Migration History, History: Old Paradigms and New Perspectives* (Frankfurt am Main: Lang, 1997; rev. ed. 2005). Migrant insertion and acculturation from a sociological perspective are best summarized in Wsevolod W. Isajiw, *Understanding Diversity:*

Ethnicity and Race in the Canadian Context (Toronto: Thompson, 1999). The Canadian case can be transposed to other societies.

41. Arjun Appadurai, "Global Ethnoscapes: Notes and Queries for a Transnational Anthropology," in *Recapturing Anthropology: Working in the Present,* ed. Richard Fox (Santa Fe, NM: School of American Research Press, 1991), 191–210; Allen F. Roberts, "La 'Géographie Processuelle': Un nouveau paradigme pour les aires culturelles," *Lendemains* 31, nos. 122–123 (2006): 41–61. See, in general, Henri Lefebvre, *The Production of Space,* trans. Donald Nicolson-Smith (French orig., 1974; Oxford: Blackwell, 1991).

42. McKeown, "Global Migration, 1846–1940"; and Moya and McKeown, "World Migration."

43. The regional approach is developed in Sylvia Hahn, *Migration–Arbeit–Geschlecht: Arbeitsmigration in Mitteleuropa vom 17. bis zum Beginn des 20. Jahrhunderts* (Göttingen: V&R Unipress, 2008), 18, 32–33, 157–244; and by Lynn Pan, *Sons of the Yellow Emperor,* esp. 3–22; as well as many others.

44. Dirk Hoerder, *"To Know Our Many Selves": From the Study of Canada to Canadian Studies* (Edmonton: Athabasca University Press, 2010), 260–390; and Hoerder, "Transnational–Transregional–Translocal: Transcultural," in *Handbook of Research Methods in Migration,* ed. Carlos Vargas-Silva (Cheltenham, UK: Edward Elgar, 2012), 69–91.

45. Harzig et al., *What Is Migration History?,* 66–69.

46. Dirk Hoerder, "From Migrants to Ethnics: Acculturation in a Societal Framework," in *European Migrants: Global and Local Perspectives,* ed. Dirk Hoerder and Leslie P. Moch (Boston: Northeastern University Press, 1996), 211–262.

47. Pierre Bourdieu, *Questions de sociologie* (Paris: Éditions de Minuit, 1980); Raymond Williams, *Culture and Society, 1780–1950* (London: Chatto and Windus, 1958).

48. James H. Jackson Jr. and Leslie Page Moch, "Migration and the Social History of Modern Europe," *Historical Methods* 22 (1989): 27–36, reprinted in Hoerder and Moch, *European Migrants,* 52–69; Harzig et al., *What Is Migration History?,* 87–114. See also Ewa Morawska and Michael Bommes, eds., *International Migration Research: Constructions, Omissions, and Promises of Interdisciplinarity* (Aldershot: Ashgate, 2005).

49. Raymond Breton, "Institutional Completeness of Ethnic Communities and Personal Relations of Immigrants," *American Journal of Sociology* 70 (September 1964): 193–205; John Goldlust and Anthony H. Richmond, "A Multivariate Model of Immigrant Adaptation," *International Migration Review* 8 (1974): 193–225.

50. Robin Cohen, *Global Diasporas: An Introduction* (Seattle: University of Washington Press, 1997); Khachig Tölölyan, "Rethinking *Diaspora(s):* Stateless Power in the Transnational Moment," *Diaspora* 5, no. 1 (1996): 9–36.

51. Michael R. Marrus, *The Unwanted: European Refugees in the Twentieth Century* (Oxford: Oxford University Press 1985), quotation at 51.

52. See, in general, Ernest Gellner, *Nations and Nationalism* (Oxford: Blackwell, 1983); Anthony D. Smith, *National Identity* (Reno: University of Nevada Press, 1991); and Smith, *Myths and Memories of the Nation* (Oxford: Oxford University Press, 1999).

53. Donna R. Gabaccia, "The 'Yellow Peril' and the 'Chinese of Europe': Global Perspectives on Race and Labor, 1815–1930," in Lucassen and Lucassen, *Migration, Migration History,* 177–196.

54. Ann L. Stoler, "Making Empire Respectable: The Politics of Race and Sexual Morality in 20th-Century Colonial Cultures," *American Ethnologist* 16 (1989): 634–660; Frederick Cooper and Ann L. Stoler, eds., *Tensions of Empire: Colonial Cultures in a Bourgeois World* (Berkeley: University of California Press, 1997); Anne McClintock, *Imperial Leather: Race, Gender and Sexuality in the Colonial Context* (New York: Routledge, 1995); Margaret Strobel, *Gender, Sex, and Empire* (Washington, DC: American Historical Association, 1993); Mary Louise Pratt, *Imperial Eyes: Travel Writing and Transculturation* (London: Routledge, 1992).

55. Mrinalini Sinha, *Colonial Masculinity: The "Manly Englishmen" and the "Effeminate Bengali" in the 19th Century* (Manchester: Manchester University Press, 1995).

56. See, for more detail, Hoerder, *Cultures in Contact,* chap. 16 and references.

57. Talal Asad, ed., *Anthropology and the Colonial Encounter* (New York: Humanities Press, 1973); Peter Pels, "The Anthropology of Colonialism: Culture, History, and the Emergence of Western Governmentality," *Annual Review of Anthropology* 26 (1997): 163–183; Sylvia Van Kirk, *"Many Tender Ties": Women in Fur Trade Society in Western Canada, 1670–1870* (Winnipeg: Watson, 1980).

58. Carey McWilliams, *Factories in the Field: The Story of Migratory Farm Labor in California* (Boston: Little, Brown, 1935); Eric R. Wolf, *Europe and the People without History* (Berkeley: University of California Press, 1982).

59. Isabelle Vagnoux, *Les États-Unis et le Mexique* (Paris: L'Harmattan, 2003); Steven C. Topik, "When Mexico Had the Blues: A Transatlantic Tale of Bonds, Bankers, and Nationalists, 1862–1910," *American Historical Review* 105 (2000): 714–738.

60. Moya, "A Continent of Immigrants"; Donald Denoon, *Settler Capitalism: The Dynamics of Dependent Development in the Southern Hemisphere* (Oxford: Oxford University Press, 1983). "Dependency theory" developed as analysis of Latin American economies in relation to more powerful economic actors in the Northern Hemisphere. André Gunder Frank, *Capitalism and Underdevelopment in Latin America* (New York: Monthly Review Press, 1969); Ian Roxborough, *Theories of Underdevelopment* (London: Macmillan, 1979); Ronald H. Chilcote, ed., *Dependency and Marxism: Toward a Resolution of the Debate* (Boulder, CO: Westview Press, 1982).

61. Thomas R. Gottschang and Diana Lary, *Swallows and Settlers: The Great Migration from North China to Manchuria* (Ann Arbor: University of Michigan Press, 2000); Isaiah Bowman, *The Pioneer Fringe* (New York: American Geographical Society, 1931); W. L. G. Joerg, ed., *Pioneer Settlement: Cooperative Studies by 26 Authors* (New York: American Geographical Society, 1932); David Wolff, *To the Harbin Station: The Liberal Alternative to Russian Manchuria, 1898–1914* (Stanford, CA: Stanford University Press, 1999); James H. Carter, *Creating a Chinese Harbin: Nationalism in an International City, 1916–1932* (Ithaca, NY: Cornell University Press, 2002).

62. Wilbur Zelinsky, "The Hypothesis of the Mobility Transition," *Geographical Review* 61 (1971): 219–249; Jan Lucassen and Leo Lucassen, "The Mobility Transition Revisited, 1500–1900: What the Case of Europe Can offer to Global History," *Journal of Global History* 4 (2009): 347–377; Moya and McKeown, "World Migration."

63. Brinley Thomas, *Migration and Economic Growth: A Study of Great Britain and the Atlantic Economy* (Cambridge: Cambridge University Press, 1954); Hoerder, *Labor Migration.*

64. *The Cambridge Economic History of Europe from the Decline of the Roman Empire,* ed. Michael M. Postan and John Habakkuk (Cambridge: Cambridge University Press, 1941–1969), and its second edition, edited by John H. Clapham and Eileen Power (from 1966), still emphasized the continuity from agriculture to textile and thus included family labor, in particular women's sphere. With the turn to industrialization, for which Eric J. Hobsbawm's classic *Industry and Empire* (London: Weidenfeld and Nicolson, 1968) stands as a core text, the steel industry came to be viewed as a lead industry and women's labor got lost. Hobsbawm, *Labouring Men: Studies in the History of Labour* (London: Weidenfeld and Nicolson, 1964). Parallel, Walt Rostow, *The Stages of Economic Growth: A Non-Communist Manifesto* (New York: Cambridge University Press, 1960), added another evolutionary approach. Throughout the period of industrialization and to the present, more men and women have been employed in textile and food production than in "heavy" industry. Sven Beckert, *The Empire of Cotton: A Global History* (New York: Knopf, forthcoming), chap. 9. See also "A Global History of Textile Workers, 1650–2000," International Institute of Social History, Amsterdam, November 2004, coordinators Lex Heerma van Voss, Els Hiemstra, and Elise van Nederveen Meerkerk, unpublished "Preliminary Papers."

65. Peter Kriedte, *Peasants, Landlords and Merchant Capitalists: Europe and the World Economy, 1500–1800,* trans. V. R. Berghahn (German orig. 1980; Cambridge: Cambridge University Press, 1983); Peter Kriedte, Hans Medick, and Jürgen Schlumbohm, *Industrialization before Industrialization: Rural Industry in the Genesis of Capitalism* (Cambridge: Cambridge University Press, 1981); Sheilagh C. Ogilvie and Markus Cerman, eds., *European Proto-Industrialization: An Introductory Handbook* (Cambridge: Cambridge University Press, 1996).

66. Gianfausto Rosoli, ed., *Un Secolo di Emigrazione Italiana, 1876–1976* (Rome: Centro studi emigrazione, 1980); and Rosoli, "Italian Migration to European Countries from Political Unification to World War I," in Hoerder, *Labor Migration,* 95–116; Donna R. Gabaccia and Fraser Ottanelli, eds., *Italian Workers of the World: Labor, Migration and the Making of Multi-Ethnic States* (Urbana: University of Illinois Press, 2001); Donna R. Gabaccia and Franca Iacovetta, eds., *Women, Gender, and Transnational Lives: Italian Workers of the World* (Toronto: University of Toronto Press, 2002).

67. Peter Doeringer and Michael J. Piore, *Internal Labor Markets and Manpower Analysis* (Lexington, MA: Heath, 1971); Edna Bonacich, "A Theory of Ethnic Antagonism: The Split Labor Market," *American Sociological Review* 37 (1972): 547–559; F. C. Valkenburg and A. M. C. Vissers, "Segmentation of the Labour Market: The Theory of the Dual Labour Market—The Case of the Netherlands," *Netherlands Journal of Sociology* 16 (1980): 155–170; Randy Hodson and Robert L. Kaufmann, "Economic Dualism: A Critical Review," *American Sociological Review* 47 (1982): 727–739.

68. Hoerder, *Labor Migration,* 3–31.

69. Hoerder, *Cultures in Contact,* 332–334.

70. Heinz Fassmann, "Emigration, Immigration and Internal Migration in the Austro-Hungarian Monarchy, 1910," in Hoerder et al., *Roots of the Transplanted,* 1:253–307; Hahn, *Migration–Arbeit–Geschlecht.*

71. Heinz Fassmann and Rainer Münz, *Einwanderungsland Österreich? Historische Migrations-muster, aktuelle Trends und politische Maßnahmen* (Wien: Wissenschaft, Jugend und Volk, 1995); Monika Glettler, *Die Wiener Tschechen um 1900: Strukturanalyse einer nationalen Min-derheit in der Großstadt* (Munich: Oldenbourg, 1972); Michael John and Albert Lichtblau, *Schmelztiegel Wien einst und jetzt: Zur Geschichte und Gegenwart von Zuwanderung und Minderheiten,* 2nd ed. (Vienna: Böhlau, 1993).

72. Matthew Frye Jacobson, *Whiteness of a Different Color: European Immigrants and the Alchemy of Race* (Cambridge, MA: Harvard University Press, 1998); Cheryl I. Harris, "Whiteness as Property," *Harvard Law Review* 106 (1993): 1707–1791; "Whiteness and the Historians' Imagi-nation," topical issue of *International Labor and Working-Class History* 60 (Fall 2001): 1–92. The imposition of whiteness was far more violent in other parts of the world. John W. Cell, *The Highest Stage of White Supremacy: The Origins of Segregation in South Africa and the American South* (Cambridge: Cambridge University Press, 1982); Ruth Frankenberg, *White Women, Race Matters: The Social Construction of Whiteness* (Minneapolis: University of Minnesota Press, 1993); George M. Fredrickson, *The Black Image in the White Mind: The Debate on Afro-American Character and Destiny, 1817–1914* (New York: Harper and Row, 1971). And in the US South: Johnpeter Horst Grill and Robert L. Jenkins, "The Nazis and the American South in the 1930s: A Mirror Image?," *Journal of Southern History* 58 (1992): 667–694; Grace E. Hale, *Making Whiteness: The Culture of Segregation in the South* (New York: Pantheon, 1998).

73. An overview is provided in Roger Daniels, *Coming to America: A History of Immigration and Ethnicity in American Life,* rev. ed. (New York: HarperCollins, 2002); and Ronald Takaki, *A Different Mirror: A History of Multicultural America* (Boston: Little, Brown, 1993). John Bod-nar, *The Transplanted: A History of Immigrants in Urban America* (Bloomington: Indiana University Press, 1985), deals with the proletarian mass migration and counters the term *up-rooted* migrants posited by Oscar Handlin in the early 1950s. James R. Barrett, "Americaniza-tion from the Bottom Up: Immigration and the Remaking of the Working Class in the United States, 1880–1930," *Journal of American History* 79 (1992): 997–1020.

74. Jean R. Burnet with Howard Palmer, *"Coming Canadians": An Introduction to a History of Canada's Peoples* (Toronto: McClelland and Stewart, 1988); Franca Iacovetta with Paula Draper and Robert Ventresca, eds., *A Nation of Immigrants: Women, Workers, and Communities in Canadian History, 1840s–1960s* (Toronto: University of Toronto Press, 1998); Bruno Ramirez, *On the Move: French-Canadian and Italian Migrants in the North Atlantic Economy, 1860–1914* (Toronto: McClelland and Stewart, 1991); John J. Bukowczyk, Nora Faires, David Smith, and Randy William Widdis, *Permeable Border: The Great Lakes Basin as Transnational Region, 1650–1990* (Pittsburgh: University of Pittsburgh Press; Calgary: University of Calgary Press, 2005).

75. Moisés Gonzáles Navarro, *Los extranjeros en México y los mexicanos en el extranjero, 1821–1970,* 3 vols. (Mexico City: Colegio de México, 1993–1994); Dolores Pla, Guadelupe Zárate, Mónica Palma, Jorge Gómez, Rosario Cardiel, and Delia Salazar, *Extranjeros en México (1821–1990): Bibliografía* (Mexico City: INAH, 1994); Jaime R. Aguila and Brian Gratton, "Mirando atrás: Mexican Immigration from 2008 to 1876," and Delia Gonzàles de Reufels and Dirk Hoerder, "Migration to Mexico, Migration in Mexico: A Special Case on the North Ameri-can Continent," both in Hoerder and Faires, *Migrants and Migration,* 188–209.

76. Richardson, "Caribbean Migrations, 1838–1985," 203–228; Howard Johnson, ed., *After the Crossing: Immigrants and Minorities in Caribbean Creole Society* (London: Cass, 1988); Elizabeth Maclean Petras, *Jamaican Labor Migration: White Capital and Black Labor, 1850–1930* (Boulder, CO: Westview Press, 1988); Lara Putnam, "Undone by Desire: Migration, Sex across Boundaries, and Collective Destinies in the Greater Caribbean, 1840–1940," in Hoerder and Faires, *Migrants and Migration,* 99–126.

77. A comparative perspective on South and North America is provided by Walter Nugent, *Crossings: The Great Transatlantic Migrations, 1870–1914* (Bloomington: Indiana University Press, 1992).

78. Nancy P. Naro, "The Transition from Slavery to Migrant Labour in Rural Brazil," in *Unfree Labour in the Development of the Atlantic World,* ed. Paul E. Lovejoy and Nicholas Rogers (Ilford, UK: Cass, 1994), 183–196; Magnus Mörner, "Immigration into Latin America, Especially Argentina and Chile," in Emmer and Mörner, *European Expansion and Migration,* 217–231; Mörner, *Adventurers and Proletarians: The Story of Migrants in Latin America* (Pittsburgh: University of Pittsburgh Press, 1985); Elizabeth Kuznesof, "A History of Domestic Service in Spanish America, 1492–1980," in *Muchachas No More: Household Workers in Latin America and the Caribbean,* ed. Elsa M. Chaney and Mary Garcia Castro (Philadelphia: Temple University Press, 1989), 17–35.

79. José C. Moya, *Cousins and Strangers: Spanish Immigrants in Buenos Aires, 1850–1930* (Berkeley: University of California Press, 1997); Samuel Baily, *Immigrants in the Land of Promise: Italians in Buenos Aires and New York City, 1870–1914* (Ithaca, NY: Cornell University Press, 1999); Fernando J. Devoto and Gianfausto Rosoli, eds., *L'Italia nella società argentina* (Rome: Centro Studi Emigrazione, 1988).

80. Pierre-Michel Fontaine, ed., *Race, Class and Power in Brazil* (Los Angeles: Center for African-American Studies, University of California, 1985); Thomas H. Holloway, *Immigrants on the Land: Coffee and Society in São Paulo, 1886–1934* (Chapel Hill: University of North Carolina Press, 1980).

81. The first conceptualization of transculturation was Fernando Ortiz, "Del fenómeno de la transculturación y su importancia en Cuba," *Revista Bimestre Cubana* 27 (1940): 273–278 (numerous reprints and translations); of the reaction to Yankee self-elevation, José Vasconcelos, *Raza cósmica* (1925), bilingual edition *The Cosmic Race: La raza cósmica* (Baltimore: Johns Hopkins University Press, 1997). For one of many late twentieth-century contributions, see Néstor Garcia Canclini, *Culturas híbridas: Estrategias para entrar y salir de la modernidad* (Mexico, D.F.: Grijalbo, 1989); English translation: *Hybrid Cultures: Strategies for Entering and Leaving Modernity,* trans. Christopher L. Chiappari and Silvia L. López (Minneapolis: University of Minnesota Press, 1995).

82. Mann, "Migration–Re-Migration–Circulation," 108–133; Moya and McKeown, "World Migration."

83. Samuel Truett and Elliott Young, eds., *Continental Crossroads: Remapping U.S.-Mexican Borderlands History* (Durham, NC: Duke University Press, 2003); Carlos G. Vélez-Ibáñez, *Border Visions: Mexican Cultures of the Southwest United States* (Tucson: University of Arizona Press, 1996); Daniel D. Arreola, ed., *Hispanic Spaces, Latino Places: Community and*

Cultural Diversity in Contemporary America (Austin: University of Texas Press, 2004); Evelyn Hu-DeHart, "Racism and Anti-Chinese Persecution in Mexico," *Amerasia Journal* 9, no. 2 (1982): 1–27.

84. Rita J. Simon and Caroline B. Brettell, *International Migration: The Female Experience* (Totowa, NJ: Rowman, 1986); M. D. North-Coombes, "Indentured Labour in the Sugar Industries of Natal and Mauritius, 1834–1910," in Bhana, *Indentured Indians in Natal,* 12–88; Christiane Harzig, ed., *Peasant Maids, City Women: From the European Countryside to Urban America* (Ithaca, NY: Cornell University Press, 1997).

85. Tinker, *New System of Slavery;* David Northrup, *Indentured Labor in the Age of Imperialism, 1834–1922* (Cambridge: Cambridge University Press, 1995); Moya and McKeown, "World Migration."

86. Brij V. Lal, Peter Reeves, and Rajesh Rai, eds., *The Encyclopedia of the Indian Diaspora* (Singapore: Millet, 2006); Crispin Bates, ed., *Community, Empire and Migration: South Asian Diaspora* (Basingstoke: Palgrave, 2001).

87. K. Hazareesingh, *History of Indians in Mauritius* (London: Macmillan, 1975); Bissoondoyal and Servansing, *Indian Labour Immigration;* Marina Carter, "Strategies of Labour Mobilisation in Colonial India: The Recruitment of Indentured Workers for Mauritius," *Journal of Peasant Studies* 19, nos. 3–4 (1992): 229–245; Carter, *Voices from Indenture;* Tinker, *New System of Slavery.*

88. Hilda Kuper, *Indian People in Natal* (Pietermaritzburg: University of Natal Press, 1960; repr. Westport, 1974); Bhana, *Indentured Indians in Natal.*

89. Bridglal Pachai, *The International Aspects of the South African Indian Question, 1860–1971* (Cape Town: Struik, 1971); Surendra Bhana and Joy B. Brain, *Setting Down Roots: Indian Migrants in South Africa, 1860–1911* (Johannesburg: Witwatersrand University Press, 1990); Patrick Harries, *Work, Culture, and Identity: Migrant Laborers in Mozambique and South Africa, c. 1860–1910* (Portsmouth, NH: Heinemann, 1994); Martin Legassick and Francine de Clerq, "Capitalism and Migrant Labour in Southern Africa: The Origins and Nature of the System," and Peter Richardson, "Coolies, Peasants, and Proletarians: The Origins of Chinese Indentured Labour in South Africa, 1904–1907," both in Shula Marks and Peter Richardson, eds., *International Labour Migration: Historical Perspectives* (Hounslow, UK: Temple Smith, 1984), 140–166, 167–185; Melanie Yap and Dianne L. Man, *Colour, Confusion and Concessions: The History of the Chinese in South Africa* (Hong Kong: Hong Kong University Press, 1996).

90. Usha Mahajani, *The Role of Indian Minorities in Burma and Malaya* (Bombay: Vora, 1960; repr. Westport, CT: Greenwood Press, 1973); Michael Adas, *The Burma Delta: Economic Development and Social Change on an Asian Rice Frontier, 1852–1941* (Madison: University of Wisconsin Press, 1974); Kaur, *Wage Labour.*

91. Gabaccia and Hoerder, *Connecting Seas,* esp. essays in sections 1 and 2.

92. Kirti N. Chaudhuri, *Asia before Europe: Economy and Civilization of the Indian Ocean from the Rise of Islam to 1750* (Cambridge: Cambridge University Press, 1990); Milo Kearney, *The Indian Ocean in World History* (London: Routledge, 2003); G. Balachandran, "Circulation through Seafaring: Indian Seamen, 1890–1945," in *Society and Circulation: Mobile People and Itinerant Cultures in South Asia, 1750–1950,* ed. Claude Markovits, Jacques Pouchepadass, and

Sanjay Subrahmanyam (Delhi: Permanent Black, 2003), 89–130; Sugata Bose, *A Hundred Horizons: The Indian Ocean in the Age of Global Empire* (Cambridge, MA: Harvard University Press, 2006); Thomas R. Metcalf, *Imperial Connections: India in the Indian Ocean Arena, 1860–1920* (Berkeley: University of California Press, 2007).

93. Jagdish S. Gundara, "Fragments of Indian Society in Zanzibar: Conflict and Change in the 19th Century," *Africa Quarterly* 21, nos. 2–4 (1981): 23–40; Michael Twaddle, "East African Asians through a Hundred Years," in *South Asians Overseas: Migration and Ethnicity,* ed. Colin Clarke, Ceri Peach, and Steven Vertovec (Cambridge: Cambridge University Press, 1990), 149–163.

94. Ranajit Das Gupta, "Plantation Labour in Colonial India," *Journal of Peasant Studies* 19, nos. 3–4 (1992): 173–198.

95. Hoerder, *Cultures in Contact,* 380–383.

96. Kaur, *Wage Labour,* 3–58.

97. Ramon H. Myers and Mark R. Peattie, eds., *The Japanese Colonial Empire, 1895–1945* (Princeton, NJ: Princeton University Press, 1984); Edward R. Beauchamp and Akira Iriye, eds., *Foreign Employees in Nineteenth-Century Japan* (Boulder, CO: Westview Press, 1990); Taeuber, *The Population of Japan,* 173–190; Keizo Yamawaki, "Foreign Workers in Japan: A Historical Perspective," in *Japan and Global Migration: Foreign Workers and the Advent of a Multicultural Society,* ed. Michael Douglass and Glenda S. Roberts (New York: Routledge, 2000), 38–51.

98. Clarence E. Glick, *Sojourners and Settlers: Chinese Migrants in Hawaii* (Honolulu: University of Hawai'i Press, 1980); John M. Liu, "Race, Ethnicity, and the Sugar Plantation System: Asian Labor in Hawaii, 1850 to 1900," in *Labor Migration under Capitalism: Asian Workers in the United States before World War II,* ed. Lucie Cheng and Edna Bonacich (Berkeley: University of California Press, 1984), 186–209; Takaki, *Pau Hana.*

99. Walton L. Lai, *Indentured Labor, Caribbean Sugar: Chinese and Indian Migrants to the British West Indies* (Baltimore: Johns Hopkins University Press, 1993), 1–18; Keith O. Laurence, *Immigration into the West Indies in the 19th Century* (Barbados: Caribbean Universities Press, 1971).

100. Evelyn Hu-DeHart, "Latin America in Asia-Pacific Perspective," in *What Is in a Rim? Critical Perspectives on the Pacific Region Idea,* 2nd ed., ed. Arif Dirlik (Lanham, MD: Rowman and Littlefield, 1998), 251–282; Hu-DeHart, "Coolies, Shopkeepers, Pioneers: The Chinese of Mexico and Peru, 1849–1930," *Amerasia Journal* 15, no. 2 (1989): 91–116; McKeown, *Chinese Migrant Networks.*

101. Cheng and Bonacich, *Labor Migration under Capitalism;* Erika Lee, *At America's Gates: Chinese Immigration during the Exclusion Era, 1882–1943* (Chapel Hill: University of North Carolina Press, 2003); Peter S. Li, *The Chinese in Canada,* 2nd ed. (Toronto: Oxford University Press, 1998).

102. Ping-ti Ho, *Population of China,* 153–158; Gottschang and Lary, *Swallows and Settlers.*

103. Hoerder, *Cultures in Contact,* 369–373; Spence, *Search for Modern China,* 117–268; Michael R. Godley, "China's Policy towards Migrants, 1842–1949," in Inglis et al., *Asians in Australia,* 1–21; Ching-huang Yen, *Coolies and Mandarins: China's Protection of Overseas Chinese during the Late Ch'ing Period (1851–1911)* (Singapore: Singapore University Press, 1985), 32–36; Yen, "Ch'ing Changing Images of Overseas Chinese," *Modern Asian Studies* 15 (1981): 261–285.

104. Andreas Kappeler, *The Russian Empire: A Multiethnic History* (London: Longman Pearson, 2001); Treadgold, *Great Siberian Migration;* Daniel R. Brower and Edward J. Lazzerini, eds., *Russia's Orient: Imperial Borderlands and Peoples, 1700–1917* (Bloomington: Indiana University Press, 1997); Blank, "A Vast Migratory Experience."

105. Anderson, *Internal Migration;* Eklof and Frank, *World of the Russian Peasant;* Robert E. Johnson, *Peasant and Proletarian: The Working Class of Moscow in the Late Nineteenth Century* (New Brunswick, NJ: Rutgers University Press, 1979); Jeffrey Burds, *Peasant Dreams and Market Politics: Labor Migration and the Russian Village* (Pittsburgh: University of Pittsburgh Press, 1998); Lewis H. Siegelbaum, "The Odessa Grain Trade: A Case Study in Urban Growth and Development in Tsarist Russia," *Journal of European Economic History* 9, no. 1 (Spring 1980): 113–151.

106. Nancy L. Green, ed., *Jewish Workers in the Modern Diaspora* (Berkeley: University of California Press, 1998); Jack Wertheimer, *Unwelcome Strangers: European Jews in Imperial Germany* (Oxford: Oxford University Press, 1987); Irving Howe, *The World of Our Fathers* (New York: Simon and Schuster, 1976); Susan A. Glenn, *Daughters of the Shtetl: Life and Labor in the Immigrant Generation* (Ithaca, NY: Cornell University Press, 1990); Hasia R. Diner, *The Jews of the United States, 1654–2000* (Berkeley: University of California Press, 2004); Elena Shulman, *Stalinism on the Frontier of the Empire: Women and State Formation in the Soviet Far East* (Cambridge: Cambridge University Press, 2008).

107. Ahmet İçduygu and Kemal Kirişçi, eds., *Land of Diverse Migrations: Challenges of Emigration and Immigrations in Turkey* (Istanbul: MiReKoc, 2008); Reşat Kasaba, *A Moveable Empire: Ottoman Nomads, Migrants, and Refugees* (Seattle: University of Washington Press, 2009).

108. John D. Ruedy, *Modern Algeria: The Origins and Development of a Nation* (Bloomington: Indiana University Press, 1992), 22–29; Neil MacMaster, "Labour Migration in French North Africa," in *The Cambridge Survey of World Migration,* ed. Robin Cohen (Cambridge: Cambridge University Press, 1995), 190–195; Michael J. Heffernan, "The Parisian Poor and the Colonization of Algeria during the Second Empire," *French History* 3 (1989): 377–403; Michael J. Heffernan and Keith Sutton, "The Landscape of Colonialism: The Impact of French Colonial Rule in the Algerian Rural Settlement Pattern, 1830–1987," in *Colonialism and Development in the Contemporary World,* ed. Chris Dixon and Michael J. Heffernan (London: Mansell, 1991), 121–152.

109. Alan Jeeves, *Migrant Labour in South Africa's Mining Economy: The Struggle for the Gold Mines' Labor Supply, 1890–1920* (Montreal: McGill-Queen's University Press, 1985); Jonathan Crush, Alan Jeeves, and David Yudelman, *South Africa's Labor Empire: A History of Black Migrancy to the Gold Mines* (Boulder, CO: Westview Press, 1991); Patrick Harries, *Work, Culture, and Identity: Migrant Laborers in Mozambique and South Africa, c. 1860–1910* (Portsmouth, NH: Heinemann, 1994).

110. Babacar Fall, *Le travail forcé en Afrique Occidentale française (1900–1945)* (Paris: Karthala, 1993); Sheldon Gellar, *Structural Changes and Colonial Dependence: Senegal, 1885–1945* (Beverly Hills: Sage, 1976), 36–48; Martin A. Klein, *Slavery and Colonial Rule in French West Africa* (Cambridge: Cambridge University Press, 1998); Sharon B. Stichter, *Migrant Labour in Kenya: Capitalism and African Response, 1895–1975* (Harlow, UK: Longman, 1982); François

Manchuelle, *Willing Migrants: Soninke Labor Diasporas, 1848–1960* (Athens: Ohio University Press, 1997).

111. Edward W. Saïd, *Orientalism* (London: Henley, Routledge, and Kegan Paul, 1978).

112. Hoerder, *Cultures in Contact,* 419–442; Sinha, *Colonial Masculinity;* Waltraud Ernst, *Mad Tales from the Raj: The European Insane in British India, 1800–1858* (London: Routledge, 1991); Catherine Hall, *White, Male, and Middle Class: Explorations in Feminism and History* (London: Routledge, 1991); Dirk Hoerder, *Creating Societies: Immigrant Lives in Canada* (Montreal: McGill-Queen's University Press, 1999), chap. 16; Antoinette Burton, *At the Heart of the Empire: Indians and the Colonial Encounter in Late Victorian Britain* (Berkeley: University of California Press, 1998); Frederick Cooper and Ann Laura Stoler, eds., *Tensions of Empire: Colonial Cultures in a Bourgeois World* (Berkeley: University of California Press, 1997); Ann L. Stoler, "Making Empire Respectable: The Politics of Race and Sexual Morality in 20th-Century Colonial Cultures," *American Ethnologist* 16 (1989): 634–660; Strobel, *Gender, Sex, and Empire* (Washington, DC: American Historical Association, 1993); Nupur Chaudhuri and Margaret Strobel, eds., *Western Women and Imperialism: Complicity and Resistance* (Bloomington: Indiana University Press, 1992); Linda Bryder, "Sex, Race, and Colonialism: An Historiographic Review," *International History Review* 20 (1998): 806–822.

113. The League of Nations, under Fridtjof Nansen, established the International Office for Refugees.

114. Bowman, *The Pioneer Fringe,* v–vii, quotation at 200; Joerg, *Pioneer Settlement,* quotation at 362–363. These studies had a French equivalent in the proceedings of the *Congrès de la Colonisation Rurale, Alger, 26–29 mai 1930,* 4 vols. (Algiers: V. Heintz, 1931). Vol. 4, *La colonisation rurale dans les principaux pays de peuplement,* provided a comparative perspective.

115. Sean Callahan, ed., *The Photographs of Margaret Bourke-White* (New York: Bonanza, 1972), 69–89; Christine Hoffmeister, *Heinrich Vogeler: Die Komplexbilder* (Worpswede: Worpsweder Verlag, 1980); Otto Heller, *Sibirien: Ein anderes Amerika* (Berlin: Neuer Deutscher Verlag, 1930); Fridtjof Nansen, *Sibirien, ein Zukunftsland* (Leipzig: Brockhaus, 1914).

116. A concise discussion of the nation-to-refugee-generation continuum is provided by Marrus, *The Unwanted,* 9–60; Robin Cohen, "Shaping the Nation, Excluding the Other: The Deportation of Migrants from Britain," in Lucassen and Lucassen, *Migration, Migration History,* 351–373; Andrew Bell-Fialkoff, *Ethnic Cleansing* (New York: St. Martin's Press, 1996), 7–49.

117. Klaus J. Bade, Pieter C. Emmer, Leo Lucassen, and Jochen Oltmer, eds., *Encyclopedia of Migration and Minorities in Europe: From the Seventeenth Century to the Present* (Cambridge: Cambridge University Press, 2011), xxv–xxxix.

118. William Cunningham, *Alien Immigrants to England* (London: Swann Sonnenschein, 1897), provided a solitary call to appreciate the economic contributions of migrants. A thoughtful discussion of alienation is Georg Simmel, "The Stranger," in *The Sociology of Georg Simmel,* trans. Kurt Wolff (New York: Macmillan, 1950), 402–408. Other renowned scholars joined the anti-immigrant campaigns: Max Weber considered Poles inferior, demographer Friedrich Burgdörfer advocated deportation of non-German peoples, George Mauco in *Les étrangers en France* (1932) equated Frenchness with natural superiority and was a population planner both under the Fascist Vichy regime and in the French Republic of the 1950s. Ber-

nard Gainer, *The Alien Invasion: The Origins of the Alien Act of 1905* (London: Heinemann, 1972).

119. Gérard Chaliand and Yves Ternon, *Le Génocide des Arméniens* (Brussels: Éditions Complexe, 1980).

120. Fikret Adanir and Hilmar Kaiser, "Migration, Deportation, and Nation-Building: The Case of the Ottoman Empire," in *Migrations and Migrants in Historical Perspective: Permanencies and Innovations,* ed. René Leboutte (Brussels: Centre for Migration Law of the University of Nijmegen, 2000), 373–393; Daniela Bobeva, "Emigration from and Immigration to Bulgaria," in *European Migration in the Late Twentieth Century: Historical Patterns, Actual Trends, and Social Implications,* ed. Heinz Fassmann and Rainer Münz (Aldershot, UK: Elgar, 1994), 221–237; Joseph B. Schechtman, *The Refugee in the World: Displacement and Integration* (New York: Barnes, 1963), 54–67; André Wurfbain, *L'Échange greco-bulgare des minorités ethniques* (Lausanne: Payot, 1930); Stephen P. Ladas, *The Exchange of Minorities: Bulgaria, Greece and Turkey* (New York: Macmillan, 1932); Charles B. Eddy, *Greece and the Greek Refugees* (London: Allen and Unwin, 1931); Ludger Kühnhardt, *Die Flüchtlingsfrage als Weltordnungsproblem: Massenzwangswanderungen in Geschichte und Politik* (Vienna: Braumüller, 1984).

121. Ramon H. Myers and Mark R. Peattie, eds., *The Japanese Colonial Empire, 1895–1945* (Princeton, NJ: Princeton University Press, 1984); Chih-ming Ka, *Japanese Colonialism in Taiwan: Land Tenure, Development, and Dependency, 1895–1945* (Boulder, CO: Westview Press, 1995); Andrew C. Nahm, ed., *Korea under Japanese Colonial Rule: Studies of the Policy and Techniques of Japanese Colonialism* (Kalamazoo, MI: Center for Korean Studies, Western Michigan University, 1973), 261–269; Taeuber, *The Population of Japan,* 123–170, 198–203; International Labour Office, *Industrial Labour in Japan* (Geneva: ILO, 1933).

122. Fritz Fischer, *Griff nach der Weltmacht: Die Kriegszielpolitik des kaiserlichen Deutschland 1914/18* (Düsseldorf: Droste, 1961), 128–133, 310–321, 601; David Stevenson, *1914–1918: The History of the First World War* (London: Allen Lane, 2004), 3–43; Fall, *Le travail forcé,* 126–145.

123. Peter Gatrell, *A Whole Empire Walking: Refugees in Russia during World War I* (Bloomington: Indiana University Press, 1999).

124. See Hoerder, *Cultures in Contact,* chap. 17, sec. 1; Eugene M. Kulischer, *Europe on the Move: War and Population Changes, 1917–1947* (New York: Columbia University Press, 1948), 64–128.

125. *Statistik des Deutschen Reichs,* vol. 401 (Berlin, 1930), 412–423, 491–492, 623–640; Marrus, *The Unwanted,* 52–61.

126. Kulischer, *Europe on the Move,* 64–88, 99–128.

127. Frank Caestaecker and Bob Moore, eds., *Refugees from Nazi Germany and the Liberal European States* (New York: Berghahn, 2010); Dariusz Stola, "Forced Migrations in Central European History," *International Migration Review* 26 (1992): 324–341.

128. Kulischer, *Europe on the Move,* 206–225 (Italy), 227–239 (Spain); Walter Wilson, *Forced Labor in the United States* (New York: International, 1933), 28–83, passim; Pete Daniel, *The Shadow of Slavery: Peonage in the South, 1901–1969* (Urbana: University of Illinois Press, 1972), 21, passim; Donald H. Avery, *Reluctant Host: Canada's Response to Immigrant Workers, 1896–1994* (Toronto: McClelland and Stewart, 1995), chaps. 4–5.

129. Marcel van der Linden, "Forced Labour and Non-Capitalist Industrialization: The Case of Stalinism (ca. 1929–ca.1956)," in *Free and Unfree Labour,* ed. Tom Brass et al. (Amsterdam: IISG, 1993), 19–30; Brass and van der Linden, eds., *Free and Unfree Labour: The Debate Continues* (Bern: Lang, 1997); Lewis H. Siegelbaum and Ronald G. Suny, eds., *Making Workers Soviet: Power, Class, and Identity* (Ithaca, NY: Cornell University Press, 1994), 1–26; Kulischer, *Europe on the Move,* 88–93; Robert A. Lewis and Richard H. Rowland, *Population Redistribution in the USSR: Its Impact on Society, 1897–1977* (New York: Praeger, 1979), 158–198; Andrea Graziosi, "Foreign Workers in Soviet Russia, 1920–1940: Their Experience and Their Legacy," *International Labor and Working-Class History* 33 (1988): 38–59; Edwin Bacon, "'Glasnost' and the Gulag: New Information on Soviet Forced Labour around World War II," *Soviet Studies* 44 (1992): 1069–1086. Numerous memoirs of internees and forced laborers have been published.

130. Ulrich Herbert, *A History of Foreign Labor in Germany, 1880–1980* (German orig., 1986; Ann Arbor: University of Michigan Press, 1990), 9–119; Lothar Elsner and Joachim Lehmann, *Ausländische Arbeiter unter dem deutschen Imperialismus, 1900–1985* (Berlin: Dietz, 1988).

131. Louise Young, *Japan's Total Empire: Manchuria and the Culture of Wartime Imperialism* (Berkeley: University of California Press, 1998), 307–411; Joseph B. Schechtman, *Population Transfers in Asia* (New York: Hallsby Press, 1949); Taeuber, *The Population of Japan,* 173–190; Narihiko Ito, "Eine Skizze über Kolonialherrschaft, Invasionskrieg und Arbeiterbewegung unter dem japanischen Imperialismus," in *Internationale Tagung der Historiker der Arbeiterbewegung,* ed. Hans Hautmann (Vienna: ITH, 1989), 436–441; Ehud Harari, *The Politics of Labor Legislation in Japan: National-International Interaction* (Berkeley: University of California Press, 1973), 10–50; Andrew Gordon, *Labor and Imperial Democracy in Prewar Japan* (Berkeley: University of California Press, 1991), 302–342; Ramon H. Myers, *The Japanese Economic Development of Manchuria, 1932 to 1945* (New York: Garland, 1982), 158–200; George Hicks, *The Comfort Women: Sex Slaves of the Japanese Imperial Forces* (Sydney: Allen and Unwin, 1995); Ustinia Dolgopol and Snehal Paranjape, *Comfort Women: An Unfinished Ordeal—Report of a Mission* (Geneva: International Commission of Jurists, 1994).

132. Bill Freund, *The African Worker* (Cambridge: Cambridge University Press, 1988), 40; Freund, *Capital and Labour in the Nigerian Tin Mines* (London: Longman, 1981), 82–84; Kaur, *Wage Labour,* 68, 106, passim.

133. Diana Lary and Stephen R. MacKinnon, *Scars of War: The Impact of Warfare on Modern China* (Vancouver: University of British Columbia Press, 2001); MacKinnon, *Wuhan, 1938: War, Refugees, and the Making of Modern China* (Berkeley: University of California Press, 2008).

134. Joseph Schechtman, *European Population Transfers, 1939–1945* (New York: Oxford University Press, 1946); Grzegorz [Gregory] Frumkin, *Population Changes in Europe since 1939* (New York: Allen and Unwin, 1951); Malcolm J. Proudfoot, *European Refugees, 1939–52: A Study of Forced Population Movement* (London: Faber and Faber, 1956); Marrus, *The Unwanted,* 174–204; Norman Davis, *Heart of Europe: A Short History of Poland* (Oxford: Oxford University Press, 1986), 63–83.

135. Jarrell C. Jackman and Carla M. Borden, eds., *The Muses Flee Hitler: Cultural Transfer and Adaptation, 1930–1945* (Washington, DC: Smithsonian Institution Press, 1983); Claus-Dieter Krohn, *Intellectuals in Exile: Refugee Scholars and the New School for Social Research* (Am-

herst: University of Massachusetts Press, 1993); Aristide R. Zolberg, "The École Libre at the New School, 1941–1946," *Social Research* 65, no. 4 (Winter 1998): 921–951.

136. Bernd-Peter Lange and Mala Pandurang, "Dialectics of Empire and Complexities of Culture: British Men in India, Indian Experiences of Britain," in *The Historical Practice of Diversity: Transcultural Interactions from the Early Modern Mediterranean to the Postcolonial World,* ed. Dirk Hoerder with Christiane Harzig and Adrian Shubert (New York: Berghahn, 2003), 177–200; Karen J. Leong, *The China Mystique: Pearl S. Buck, Anna May Wong, Mayling Soong, and the Transformation of American Orientalism* (Berkeley: University of California Press, 2005).

137. Bruno Lasker, *Asia on the Move: Population Pressure, Migration and Resettlement in Eastern Asia under the Influence of Want and War* (New York: Holt, 1945).

138. Wolfgang Jacobmeyer, *Vom Zwangsarbeiter zum Heimatlosen Ausländer: Die Displaced Persons in Westdeutschland, 1945–1951* (Göttingen: Vandenhoeck und Ruprecht, 1985); Göran Rystad, ed., *The Uprooted: Forced Migration as an International Problem in the Post-War Era* (Lund: Lund University Press, 1990); Mark Wyman, *DP: Europe's Displaced Persons, 1945–1951* (Philadelphia: Balch, 1988).

139. Keith Sword, "The Repatriation of Soviet Citizens at the End of the Second World War," in Cohen, *Cambridge Survey,* 323–325.

140. Elfrieda B. Shukert and Barbara S. Scibetta, *War Brides of World War Two* (New York: Presidio, 1988).

141. Hoerder, *Cultures in Contact,* chaps. 17.3, 19.2, 19.3.

142. Raul Hilberg, *The Destruction of the European Jews* (Chicago: Quadrangle, 1961); Eliezer Ben-Rafael, *The Emergence of Ethnicity: Cultural Groups and Social Conflict in Israel* (New York: Greenwood, 1982); Benny Morris, *Righteous Victims: A History of the Zionist-Arab Conflict, 1881–1999* (New York: Knopf, 1999).

143. Hoerder, *Cultures in Contact,* chap. 18.4.

144. Ibid., chap. 18.3.

4. Commodity Chains in a Global Economy

The authors thank Jürgen Osterhammel, Kenneth Pomeranz, Erika Rappaport, Emily Rosenberg, William Gervase Clarence-Smith, Jennifer Scanlon, and Matthew Klingle for their helpful comments. They would also like to thank Natalia Topik for her help.

1. Lance Davis and Robert Huttenback, *Mammon and the Pursuit of Empire: The Political Economy of British Imperialism, 1860–1912* (New York: Cambridge University Press, 1987); C. A. Bayly, *The Birth of the Modern World, 1780–1914: Global Connections and Comparisons* (Malden, MA: Blackwell, 2004), 472; Karl Polanyi, *The Great Transformation: The Political and Economic Origins of Our Time* (1944; Boston: Beacon Press, 2001).

2. Kevin H. O'Rourke and Jeffrey G. Williamson, *Globalization and History: The Evolution of a Nineteenth-Century Atlantic Economy* (Cambridge, MA: MIT Press, 1999), 2. The word *globalization* entered into use in the 1960s and became popular in the 1970s and 1980s. Nayan

Chanda, *Bound Together: How Traders, Preachers, Adventurers, and Warriors Shaped Globalization* (New Haven, CT: Yale University Press, 2007), 245–251; Jürgen Osterhammel and Niels P. Peterson, *Globalization: A Short History,* trans. Dona Geyer (Princeton, NJ: Princeton University Press, 2005).

3. Jürgen Osterhammel, *Die Verwandlung der Welt: Eine Geschichte des 19. Jahrhunderts* (Munich: C. H. Beck, 2009), 1029–1030.

4. Frank Trentmann, "Before Free Trade: Empire, Free Trade and the Moral Economies of Food in the Modern World," in *Food and Globalization: Consumption, Markets and Politics in the Modern World,* ed. Alexander Nützenadl and Frank Trentmann (Oxford: Berg, 2008), 254.

5. Michael Adas, *Machines as the Measure of Men* (Ithaca, NY: Cornell University Press, 1989). For first-rate works of economic history that accentuate the Eurocentric stress on technology, see David Landes, *The Unbound Prometheus: Technological Change and Industrial Development in Western Europe from 1750 to the Present* (Cambridge: Cambridge University Press, 1969); Landes, *The Wealth and Poverty of Nations* (New York: Norton, 1999); and Joel Mokyr, *The Lever of Riches* (New York: Oxford University Press, 1990).

6. Eric Hobsbawm, *The Age of Extremes: The Short Twentieth Century, 1914–1991* (London: Abacus, 1995), 112–141; José Ortega y Gasset, *La rebelión de las masas* (Madrid: Revista de Occidente, 1930); Jackson Lears, *Rebirth of a Nation: The Making of Modern America, 1877–1920* (New York: HarperCollins, 2009), 92–132.

7. Eric Hobsbawm, *The Age of Empire, 1875–1914* (New York: Pantheon, 1987); Rudolf Hilferding, *Das Finanzkapital: Eine Studie über die jüngste Entwicklung des Kapitalismus* (1910; Berlin: Dietz, 1955).

8. Kaoru Sugihara, "An Introduction," Man-houng Lin, "China's 'Dual Economy' in International Trade Relations, 1842–1949," and Hajime Kose, "Foreign Trade, International Trade, and Industrialization: A Statistical Analysis of Regional Commodity Flows in China, 1914–1931," all in *Japan, China, and the Growth of the Asian International Economy, 1850–1949,* vol. 1, ed. Kaoru Sugihara (Oxford: Oxford University Press, 2005), 5, 179–197, 198–213; John Gallagher and Ronald Robinson, "The Imperialism of Free Trade," *Economic History Review* 6, no. 1 (1953): 1–15. For a perceptive overview of colonialism that emphasizes the role of "indirect rule," see Jürgen Osterhammel, *Colonialism: A Theoretical Overview,* trans. Shelley Fritsch (Princeton, NJ: Marcus Wiener, 2005). See also James Belich, *Replenishing the Earth: The Settler Revolution and the Rise of the Anglo-World, 1783–1939* (Oxford: Oxford University Press, 2009), 554–559. For examples of neo-imperialist approaches, see Andre Gunder Frank, *Capitalism and Underdevelopment in Latin America: Historical Studies of Chile and Brazil* (New York: Monthly Review Press, 1967); Fernando Henrique Cardoso and Enzo Faletto, *Dependency and Development in Latin America,* trans. Marjorie Mattingly Urquidi (Berkeley: University of California Press, 1979); and Immanuel Wallerstein, *The Modern World-System,* 3 vols. (New York: Academic Press, 1974, 1980, 1989).

9. Osterhammel, *Die Verwandlung der Welt,* 20. Thanks to Bob Moeller for help with the translation.

10. J. F. de Barros Pimental, *A política do café* (São Paulo: Empreza Graphica da Revista dos Tribunais, 1930), 4.

11. Victoria de Grazia, *Irresistible Empire: America's Advance through Twentieth-Century Europe* (Cambridge, MA: Belknap Press of Harvard University Press, 2005), 75–129; Kristin L. Hoganson, *Consumers' Imperium: The Global Production of American Domesticity, 1865–1920* (Chapel Hill: University of North Carolina Press, 2007).

12. Gary Gereffi, G. J. Humphrey, and T. Sturgeon, "The Governance of Global Value Chains," *Review of International Political Economy* 12, no. 1 (2005): 78–104. Also see Jennifer Bair, ed., *Frontiers of Commodity Chain Research* (Stanford, CA: Stanford University Press, 2009); Arjun Appadurai, *The Social Life of Things: Commodities in Cultural Perspective* (New York: Cambridge University Press, 1986); Victoria de Grazia and Ellen Furlough, eds., *The Sex of Things: Gender and Consumption in Historical Perspective* (Berkeley: University of California Press, 1996); Jan de Vries, *The Industrious Revolution: Consumer Behavior and the Household Economy, 1650 to the Present* (Cambridge: Cambridge University Press, 2008), 270.

13. Walt W. Rostow, *The British Economy of the Nineteenth Century* (Oxford: Clarendon Press, 1948); Rostow, *The World Economy: History and Prospect* (Austin: University of Texas Press, 1978), 81–88; Giovanni Arrighi, *The Long Twentieth Century* (London: Verso, 1994), 85–238; Eric Hobsbawm, *Industry and Empire: An Economic History of Britain since 1750* (London: Weidenfeld and Nicolson, 1968), 101; Landes, *The Unbound Prometheus*, 231; W. Arthur Lewis, *Growth and Fluctuations, 1870–1913* (London: George Allen and Unwin, 1978), 15–32.

14. Hobsbawm, *The Age of Empire*, 44. One could argue that the neoliberalism of our day surpasses the pre-1945 period in its worship of free markets and capital efficiency. But the era after 1870 was nonetheless a striking departure. Before 1870 the world had never experienced such international flows of goods, people, and capital. See Hilferding, *Das Finanzkapital*.

15. Alfred D. Chandler Jr., *Scale and Scope: The Dynamics of Industrial Capitalism* (Cambridge, MA: Belknap Press of Harvard University Press, 1990).

16. Paul Boyer, ed., *The Oxford Companion to United States History* (New York: Oxford University Press, 2001); James C. Riley, *Rising Life Expectancy: A Global History* (New York: Cambridge University Press, 2001). Nonwhites experienced markedly lower life expectancies in the United States, graphic evidence of racism and inequality. For a visual graphing of changing world life expectancies and per capita incomes, see www.gapminder.org.

17. Joseph Schumpeter, *Capitalism, Socialism and Democracy* (New York: Harper, 1947), which borrowed the concept from Werner Sombart, *Krieg und Kapitalismus* (Leipzig: Duncker und Humblot, 1913), 207.

18. Diarmuid Jeffreys, *Hell's Cartel: IG Farben and the Making of Hitler's War Machine* (New York: Metropolitan Books, 2008).

19. Chandler, *Scale and Scope*. Liebig's was a molasses-like black spread of reduced meat stock used as a supplement for the malnourished, and in cooking, more generally.

20. Daniel Yergin, *The Prize: The Epic Quest for Oil, Money, and Power* (New York: Free Press, 1991), 59, 63; Chandler, *Scale and Scope*, 270–273; Kenne Fant, *Alfred Nobel: A Biography* (New York: Arcade, 2006).

21. Kenneth Pomeranz, *The Great Divergence: China, Europe and the Making of the Modern World Economy* (Princeton, NJ: Princeton University Press, 2000); Jeffrey Williamson, "Globalization

and the Great Divergence: Terms of Trade Booms, Volatility and the Poor Periphery, 1782–1913," *European Review of Economic History* 12 (2008): 355–391.

22. Hobsbawm, *The Age of Empire,* 15. See also François Bourguignon and Christian Morrisson, "Inequality among World Citizens: 1820–1992," *American Economic Review* 92, no. 4 (September 2002): 728, 737, 739. For a thoughtful discussion of studies on the Great Divergence after 1800, see M. Shahid Alam, "Global Disparities since 1800: Trends and Regional Patterns," *Journal of World-Systems Research* 12, no. 2 (July 2006): 37–59.

23. Alam, in "Global Disparities since 1800," 52, defines "periphery" as East Asia minus Japan, West Asia, Africa, and Latin America.

24. Bourguignon and Morrisson, "Inequality among World Citizens," 734. Mark Twain meant "the Gilded Age" ironically in his 1873 novel to underline corruption rather than plenty. Twain, *The Gilded Age* (Hartford: Hartford American, 1874).

25. Landes, in his *Wealth and Power of Nations,* 32, awards the West the prize of having invented the notion of development, whereas Frank, in *Capitalism and Underdevelopment,* contends that it had fostered underdevelopment. Even though O'Rourke and Williamson, in *Globalization and History,* find *convergence* in our period, they concentrate on the Northern Atlantic. They note that "true, much of the unconditional convergence since 1870 disappears when the net is widened to include Eastern Europe and . . . if it were widened still further to the Third World, unconditional convergence would totally evaporate" (9). Our chapter considers the entire world.

26. Warren Dean, *With Broadsword and Firebrand: The Destruction of the Brazilian Atlantic Forest* (Berkeley: University of California Press, 1995); Gary Okihiro, *Pineapple Culture: A History of the Tropical and Temperate Zones* (Berkeley: University of California Press, 2009); Alfred Crosby, *Ecological Imperialism: The Biological Expansion of Europe, 900–1900* (New York: Cambridge University Press, 1986).

27. See, for example, Patricia Seed, *Ceremonies of Possession in Europe's Conquest of the New World, 1492–1640* (New York: Cambridge University Press, 1995); and Seed, *American Pentimento: The Invention of Indians and the Pursuit of Riches* (Minneapolis: University of Minnesota Press, 2001).

28. Stephen Yaffa, *Cotton: The Biography of a Revolutionary Fiber* (New York: Penguin Books, 2005), 130; Sven Beckert, "Emancipation and Empire: Reconstructing the Worldwide Web of Cotton Production in the Age of the American Civil War," *American Historical Review* 109, no. 5 (December 2004): 1405–1438.

29. Michael Mulhall, *The Dictionary of Statistics* (London: G. Routledge, 1899), 130; Susan B. Carter et al., eds., *Historical Statistics of the United States, from Colonial Times to the Present* (New York: Cambridge University Press), 546, online at http://www.cambridge.org; A. G. Kenwood and A. L. Lougheed, *The Growth of the International Economy, 1820–1990: An Introductory Text* (London: Routledge, 1999), 215–219.

30. Vernon, *Storm over the Multinationals: The Real Issues* (Cambridge, MA: Harvard University Press, 1977).

31. Jean-Yves Grenier, *L'économie d'Ancien Régime: Un monde de l'échange et de l'incertitude* (Paris: Albin Michel, 1996); Edmund Whittaker, *Schools and Streams of Economic Thought*

(Chicago: Rand McNally, 1960); Frank Trentmann, *Free Trade Nation: Commerce, Consumption and Civil Society in Modern Britain* (Oxford: Oxford University Press, 2008).

32. Paul Gootenberg, *Between Silver and Guano: Commercial Policy and the State in Postindependence Peru* (Princeton, NJ: Princeton University Press, 1989); Gootenberg, *Imagining Development: Economic Ideas in Peru's Fictitious Prosperity of Guano, 1840–1880* (Berkeley: University of California Press, 1993). On the relative advantages of backwardness, see Alexander Gerschenkron, *Economic Backwardness in Historical Perspective: A Book of Essays* (Cambridge, MA: Belknap Press of Harvard University Press, 1962). See also Thomas Smith, *Native Sources of Japanese Industrialization, 1750–1920* (Berkeley: University of California Press, 1988).

33. John Coatsworth and Jeffrey G. Williamson, "Always Protectionist? Latin American Tariffs from Independence to the Great Depression," *Journal of Latin American Studies* 36, no. 2 (2004): 205–232; Carlos Marichal and Steven Topik, "The State and Economic Growth in Latin America: Brazil and Mexico, Nineteenth and Early Twentieth Centuries," in *Nation, State, and the Economy in History,* ed. Alice Teichova and Herbert Matis (Cambridge: Cambridge University Press, 2003).

34. See, for example, E. Bradford Burns, *The Poverty of Progress: Latin America in the Nineteenth Century* (Berkeley: University of California Press, 1980); Nícea Vilela Luz, *A luta pela industrialização do Brasil* (1967; São Paulo: Alfa-Omega, 1975); and Domingo Sarmiento, *Life in the Argentine Republic in the Days of the Tyrant,* trans. Mrs. Horace Mann (1868; New York: Collier Books, 1961).

35. For a discussion of these debates, see Steven C. Topik, *Trade and Gunboats: The United States and Brazil in the Age of Empire* (Stanford, CA: Stanford University Press, 1996); Edward Stanwood, *American Tariff Controversies in the Nineteenth* Century (Boston: Houghton and Mifflin, 1903); Frank Taussig, *The Tariff History of the United States,* 8th ed. (New York: G. P. Putnam's Sons, 1931); Edward Crapol, *America for Americans: Anglophobia in the Late Nineteenth Century* (Westport, CT: Greenwood, 1973).

36. Donald Denoon, *Settler Capitalism: The Dynamics of Dependent Development in the Southern Hemisphere* (New York: Oxford University Press, 1983), 50; Belich, *Replenishing the Earth,* 456–501; P. J. Cain and A. G. Hopkins, *British Imperialism: Innovation and Expansion, 1688–1914* (London: Longmans, 1993), 272.

37. Steven C. Topik, *The Political Economy of the Brazilian State, 1889–1930* (Austin: University of Texas Press, 1987); Gunnar Myrdal, *Development and Underdevelopment: A Note on the Mechanism of National and International Economic Inequality* (Cairo: National Bank of Egypt, 1956).

38. Charles Bergquist, *Labor in Latin America: Comparative Essays on Chile, Argentina, Venezuela, and Colombia* (Stanford, CA: Stanford University Press, 1986); Thomas O'Brien, *The Revolutionary Mission: American Enterprise in Latin America, 1900–1945* (New York: Cambridge University Press, 1996); John Hart, *Empire and Revolution: The Americans in Mexico since the Civil War* (Berkeley: University of California Press, 2002).

39. De Grazia, *Irresistible Empire.*

40. Kenwood and Lougheed, *Growth,* 10, 83, 86. Peter Stearns, *The Industrial Revolution in World History,* 3rd ed. (Boulder, CO: Westview Press, 2007), 1, 2; Landes, *The Unbound Prometheus;* Cain and Hopkins, *British Imperialism: Innovation and Expansion,* 44.

41. Niall Ferguson, *Empire: How Britain Made the Modern World* (London: Penguin Books, 2004), xxii; Cain and Hopkins, *British Imperialism: Innovation and Expansion,* 170.

42. For useful case studies of states' roles in Latin American export economies, see Joseph Love and Nils Jacobsen, *Guiding the Invisible Hand: Economic Liberalism and the State in Latin America* (New York: Praeger, 1988); and Steven C. Topik and Allen Wells, eds., *The Second Conquest of Latin America: Coffee, Henequen and Oil during the Export Boom, 1850–1930* (Austin: University of Texas Press, 1998).

43. Thanks to William Clarence-Smith for reminding us of these crucial actors. See Philip D. Curtin, *Cross-Cultural Trade in World History* (Cambridge: Cambridge University Press, 1984), for an overview of trade diasporas before the Age of Empire.

44. Hobsbawm, *The Age of Empire,* 43, 44; Frank B. Tipton, "Government and the Economy in the Nineteenth Century," and Volker Wellhöner and Harald Wixforth, "Finance and Industry," both in *Germany since 1800: A New Social and Economic History,* ed. Sheilagh Ogilvie and Richard Overy (London: Arnold, 2003), 118, 122, 161–164.

45. Chandler, *The Visible Hand: The Managerial Revolution in American Business* (Cambridge, MA: Harvard University Press, 1977), 311–312.

46. Ibid., 89.

47. Allison Frank, "The Petroleum War of 1910: Standard Oil, Austria, and the Limits of the Multinational Corporation," *American Historical Review* 114, no. 1 (February 2009): 16–41, esp. 17; Rondo Cameron and V. I. Bovykin, eds., *International Banking, 1870–1914* (New York: Oxford University Press, 1991); Niall Ferguson, *The House of Rothschild,* vol. 2, *The World's Banker, 1849–1999* (New York: Penguin, 1999); and Barbara Stallings, *Banker to the World: U.S. Portfolio Investment in Latin America, 1900–1986* (Berkeley: University of California Press, 1987).

48. Akira Iriye, *Global Community: The Role of International Organizations in the Making of the Contemporary World* (Berkeley: University of California Press, 2002), 9–36.

49. Jon Savage, *Teenage: The Prehistory of Youth Culture, 1875–1945* (New York: Viking Penguin, 2007), 38.

50. Landes, *Wealth and Poverty of Nations,* 274.

51. Leon Trotsky, *The History of the Russian Revolution,* trans. Max Eastman (1932; London: Pluto Press, 1977), 26–27; Stephen Haber, *Industry and Underdevelopment: The Industrialization of Mexico, 1890–1940* (Stanford, CA: Stanford University Press, 1989); Steven C. Topik, "The Emergence of Finance Capital in Mexico," in *Five Centuries of Mexican History/Mexico en el medio milenio,* ed. Virginia Guedea and Jaime Rodríguez (Mexico City: Instituto de Investigaciones Doctor José Maria Mora, 1992), 227–242; Mario Cerutti and Carlos Marichal, eds., *La banca regional en México, 1870–1930* (Mexico City: El Colegio de México, Fondo de Cultura Económica, 2003); Jeffrey Bortz and Stephen Haber, *The Mexican Economy, 1870–1910: Essays on the Economic History of Institutions, Revolution and Growth* (Stanford, CA: Stanford University Press, 2002); Vladimir Lenin, *Imperialism, the Highest Stage of Capitalism: A Popular Outline* (New York: International, 1939); and William E. Lockwood, *The Economic Development of Japan,* 2nd ed. (Princeton, NJ: Princeton University Press, 1968).

52. Jang-Sup Shin, *The Economics of the Latecomers: Catching-up, Technology Transfer and Institutions in Germany, Japan and South Korea* (London: Routledge, 1996); Hidemasa Morikawa, "Japan's Unstable Course during Its Remarkable Economic Development," in Teichova and Matis, *Nation, State, and the Economy*, 332–345; Lockwood, *Economic Development of Japan*, 214–232; Carl Mosk, "Japanese Industrialization and Economic Growth," EH.Net, http://eh.net/encyclopedia/article/mosk.japan.final.

53. The Chinese Empire, of course, had preceded the imperialist era by millennia.

54. D. C. M. Platt, *Britain's Investment Overseas on the Eve of the First World War: The Use and Abuse of Numbers* (Basingstoke, UK: Macmillan, 1986). We include some estimates on capital flows, but these numbers are only approximations. Students of foreign investment acknowledge that the nationality of investment and the amount repatriated cannot always be identified, because global investors put capital into markets and corporations in many areas.

55. Kenwood and Lougheed, *Growth*, 86, 215; P. J. Cain and A. G. Hopkins, *British Imperialism: Crisis and Deconstruction, 1914–1990* (London: Longman, 1993), 37, 123.

56. Cain and Hopkins, *British Imperialism: Crisis and Deconstruction*, 45, 231.

57. League of Nations, *Statistical Year-Book of the League of Nations, 1926* (Geneva: League of Nations, Economic and Financial Section, 1927–1945), 77, 78, http://digital.library.northwestern.edu/league/stat.html.

58. We thank Ken Pomeranz for this observation.

59. "Vacant areas" is a term used by Oswaldo Sunkel, *Development from Within: Toward a Neostructuralist Approach for Latin America* (Boulder, CO: L. Rienner, 1993); "Neo-Europe" is taken from Crosby's *Ecological Imperialism;* "settler colonies" is adopted from Denoon, *Settler Capitalism;* and "Western offshoot" is preferred by Angus Maddison, *The World Economy* (Paris: Development Centre of the Organization for Economic Cooperation and Development, 2006).

60. Stephen Haber, *How Latin America Fell Behind: Essays on the Economic History of Brazil and Mexico, 1800–1914* (Stanford, CA: Stanford University Press, 1997).

61. Emily Rosenberg, *Financial Missionaries to the World: The Politics and Culture of Dollar Diplomacy* (Durham, NC: Duke University Press, 2003); Paul Drake, *Money Doctors: Foreign Debts and Economic Reforms in Latin America from the 1890s to the Present* (Wilmington, DE: Scholarly Resources, 1994); J. P. Wileman, *Brazilian Exchange: The Study of an Inconvertible Currency* (1896; New York: Greenwood, 1969); Marichal and Topik, "The State and Economic Growth"; Thomas G. Rawski, *Economic Growth in Prewar China* (Berkeley: University of California Press, 1989), 155–164.

62. For a trenchant contemporary discussion of the gold standard and the ideology behind it, see Polanyi, *The Great Transformation*. For the most recent overview of the international debate and system, see Barry Eichengreen, *Globalizing Capital: A History of the International Monetary System* (Princeton, NJ: Princeton University Press, 2008).

63. Niall Ferguson, *Paper and Iron: Hamburg Business and German Politics in the Era of Inflation, 1897–1927* (Cambridge: Cambridge University Press, 1995).

64. There was an interruption in the decline between 1852 and 1873. Douglass North, "Ocean Freight Rates and Economic Development, 1750–1913," *Journal of Economic History* 18, no. 4 (December 1958): 537–555, esp. 542.

65. Hobsbawm, *The Age of Empire,* 28, 350; Daniel Headrick, *The Tentacles of Progress: Technology Transfer in the Age of Imperialism, 1850–1940* (New York: Oxford University Press, 1988), 23–25; Peter J. Hugill, *World Trade since 1431: Geography, Technology, and Capitalism* (Baltimore: Johns Hopkins University Press, 1993), 125–158.

66. There was a reciprocal relationship between the rapid expansion of faster, cheaper freight carriers and the growth of world commerce. Ship technology continued to improve with the invention of the steam turbine in 1894 and the introduction of the diesel engine in the 1920s. The fourfold growth in ship size brought with it further economies because fuel consumed per pound of freight declined proportionately, as did the size of the crew. Headrick, *The Tentacles of Progress,* 27–31; Rostow, *The World Economy,* 669. The change in fuel would have enormous consequences after World War I, though in 1914 only 2 percent of world shipping was fueled by oil. Kenwood and Lougheed, *Growth,* 15.

67. John Soluri, *Banana Cultures: Agriculture, Consumption, and Environmental Change in Honduras and the United States* (Austin: University of Texas Press, 2005). The world would have to wait until 1956 for the next giant step in the shipping revolution, the shipping container. Marc Levinson, *The Box: How the Shipping Container Made the World Smaller and the World Economy Bigger* (Princeton, NJ: Princeton University Press, 2006).

68. North, "Ocean Freight Rates," 543.

69. Okihiro, *Pineapple Culture;* and Lawrence Clayton, *Grace: W. R. Grace and Company, the Formative Years, 1850–1930* (Ottawa, IL: Jameson Books, 1985).

70. Robert Greenhill, "Shipping," in *Business Imperialism,* ed. D. C. M. Platt (Oxford: Clarendon Press, 1977).

71. Jeffrey G. Williamson, "Winners and Losers over Two Centuries of Globalization," National Bureau of Economic Research Working Paper Series, Working Paper No. 9161, September 2002.

72. Mulhall, *The Dictionary of Statistics,* 520.

73. Hobsbawm, *The Age of Empire,* 51.

74. US Bureau of the Census, *Historical Statistics of the United States from Colonial Times to 1957* (Washington, DC: US Government Printing Office, 1960), 450.

75. Quoted in Yergin, *The Prize,* 12, 154. Alfred Thayer Mahan, *The Influence of Sea Power upon History, 1660–1783* (1892; New York: Hill and Wang, 1957); Harold Sprout and Margaret Sprout, *The Rise of American Naval Power, 1776–1918* (Princeton, NJ: Princeton University Press, 1939).

76. Charles Flint, *Memories of an Active Life* (New York: G. P. Putnam's Sons, 1923); Topik, *Trade and Gunboats;* V. G. Kiernan, *Marxism and Imperialism* (London: Edward Arnold, 1974), 105.

77. Greenhill, "Shipping," 141.

78. E. Sydney Crawcour, "Industrialization and Technological Change, 1885–1920," in *The Economic Emergence of Modern Japan,* ed. Kozo Yamamura (Cambridge: Cambridge University Press, 1997), 97–99; Lockwood, *Economic Development of Japan,* 348–351, 544–549; Peter N. Davies, "Japanese Shipping and Shipbuilding: An Introduction to the Motives behind Its Early Expansion," and Kunio Katayama, "Japanese Economic Development Strategy and the

Shipping Industries, 1881–1894," both in Discussion Paper No. JS/99/376, November 1999, The Suntory Centre, Suntory and Toyota International Centres for Economic and Related Disciplines, London School of Economics and Political Science.

79. Headrick, *The Tentacles of Progress,* 20.

80. Mira Wilkins, *The Emergence of Multinational Enterprise* (Cambridge, MA: Harvard University Press, 1970), 35.

81. Hugill, *World Trade since 1431,* 159–166; Landes, *Wealth and Poverty of Nations,* 215–216; Pomeranz, *The Great Divergence,* 183–185.

82. Kenneth Pomeranz, *The Making of a Hinterland: State, Society, and Economy in Inland North China, 1853–1937* (Berkeley: University of California Press, 1993), 153–211.

83. Headrick, *The Tentacles of Progress,* 28. In the days of the pharaohs, the canal linked the Red Sea to the Nile and from there to the Mediterranean.

84. Had Senator John McCain won the US presidential election in 2008, he could have taken office because the Panama Canal Zone, where he was born, was considered US soil.

85. Julie Greene, *The Canal Builders: Making America's Empire at the Panama Canal* (New York: Penguin, 2009), 367, 2, 132, 133, 396–399, quotation at 367; Michael Conniff, *Black Labor on the White Canal: Panama, 1904–1908* (Pittsburgh: University of Pittsburgh Press, 1985), 30–31.

86. Quoted in Greene, *The Canal Builders,* 351.

87. Headrick, *Power over Peoples: Technology, Environments, and Western Imperialism, 1400 to the Present* (Princeton, NJ: Princeton University Press, 2010), 226–251; Paul Janosz, "Dr. Gorgas and Yellow Fever: Destiny through Disease" (unpublished manuscript, University of California, Irvine, February 2011).

88. Paul Cottrell, *Industrial Finance, 1830–1914: The Finance and Organization of English Manufacturing Industry* (London: Methuen, 1983), 40–55; Geoffrey Jones, *British Multinational Banking, 1830–1990* (New York: Oxford University Press, 1993).

89. Headrick, *The Tentacles of Progress,* 36–38.

90. Hobsbawm, *The Age of Empire,* 27, 52.

91. Robert Fogel, *Railroads and American Economic Growth: Essays in Econometric History* (Baltimore: Johns Hopkins University Press, 1964); Chandler, *The Visible Hand;* Michael J. Twomey, *A Century of Foreign Investment in the Third World* (London: Routledge, 2000), 44.

92. Kenwood and Lougheed, *Growth,* 36. Admittedly, miles of track do not necessarily reflect the intensity of use, because the smaller lines tended to pass through more heavily used areas. For example, in 1887–1888 the United States had 20 percent more track than all of Europe but carried only one-fourth the number of passengers and 80 percent as much freight. Mulhall, *The Dictionary of Statistics,* 496.

93. Headrick, *The Tentacles of Progress,* 55.

94. Kenwood and Lougheed, *Growth,* 13.

95. Pomeranz, *Making of a Hinterland,* 146–152; B. R. Mitchell, *International Historical Statistics: Africa, Asia and Oceania, 1750–2005,* 5th ed. (London: Palgrave, 2007), 723, 724.

96. Mulhall, *The Dictionary of Statistics,* 523 for world port capacities.

97. John H. Coatsworth, *Growth against Development: The Economic Impact of Railroads in Porfirian Mexico* (De Kalb: Northern Illinois University, 1981).

98. Sandra Kuntz Ficker, *Empresa extranjera y mercado interno: El Ferrocarril Central Mexicano, 1850–1950* (Mexico City: El Colegio de México, 1995); Kuntz Ficker and Paolo Riguzzi, eds., *Ferrocarriles y vida económica en México, 1850–1950* (Mexico City: El Colegio Mexiquense-Universidad Autónomo Metropolitana, Xochimilco, 1996); Mario Cerruti and José Reséndiz Balderas, eds., *Monterrey, Nuevo León, el Noreste: Siete estudios históricos* (Monterrey: Universidad Autónoma de Nueva León, 1987).

99. James Scobie, *Argentina: A City and a Nation* (New York: Oxford University Press, 1964); Carlos Díaz Alejandro, *Essays on the Economic History of the Argentine Republic* (New Haven, CT: Yale University Press, 1970); Roberto Cortés Conde, *Argentina since Independence* (New York: Cambridge University Press, 1993).

100. Topik, *The Political Economy*, 93–128; and Julian Duncan, *Public and Private Ownership of Railroads in Brazil* (New York: Faculty of Political Science, Columbia University, 1932).

101. Quoted in H. A. Mwanzi, "African Initiatives and Resistance in East Africa, 1880–1914," in *General History of Africa,* vol. 7: *Africa under Colonial Domination, 1880–1935,* ed. A. Adu Boahen (Berkeley: University of California Press, 1985), 163.

102. Colin Leys, *The Political Economy of Neo-Colonialism, 1964–1971* (Berkeley: University of California Press, 1975), 28–35,

103. Mwanzi, "African Initiatives," 164, 165; Brad Weiss, *Sacred Trees, Bitter Harvests: Globalizing Coffee in Northwest Tanzania* (Portsmouth, NH: Heinemann, 2003), 14–21.

104. Calculated from Mitchell, *International Historical Statistics: Africa, Asia and Oceania, 1750–2005,* 715–718.

105. Ibid.; Denoon, *Settler Capitalism,* 51.

106. Headrick, *The Tentacles of Progress,* 55–91.

107. Quoted in ibid., 73.

108. Ibid., 87.

109. Rawski, *Economic Growth in Prewar China,* 181–189.

110. Wolfgang Schivelbusch, *Geschichte der Eisenbahnreise,* translated as *The Railway Journey: The Industrialization of Time and Space in the Nineteenth Century* (Berkeley: University of California Press, 1986).

111. Headrick, *The Tentacles of Progress,* 277.

112. Rostow, *The World Economy,* 199; calculated from the *Statistical Year-Book of the League of Nations, 1926,* 87; calculated from the *Statistical Year-Book of the League of Nations, 1942–44,* 159; Lockwood, *Economic Development of Japan,* 106.

113. Headrick, *The Tentacles of Progress,* 293–295.

114. *Statistical Year-Book of the League of Nations, 1942–44,* 85.

115. Brasil, Presidente, *Mensagem dirigida ao Congresso Nacional, 1926* (Rio de Janeiro: Imprensa Nacional, 1926), 152.

116. On early Mexico estimate, see Coatsworth, *Growth against Development.* For revised estimates, see Kuntz Ficker, *Empresa extranjera;* and Kuntz Ficker and Riguzzi, eds., *Ferrocarriles y vida económica.* For Brazil, see Topik, *The Political Economy.* On different periods showing the domestic multiplier effects of railroads, see William Summerhill, *Order against Progress: Government, Foreign Investment and Railroads in Brazil* (Stanford, CA: Stanford University Press, 2003).

117. Coatsworth and Williamson, "Always Protectionist?"

118. Topik, *The Political Economy,* 93–129.

119. See Greg Grandin, *Fordlandia: The Rise and Fall of Henry Ford's Forgotten Jungle City* (New York: Metropolitan Books, 2009), for the positive and repressive sides of Fordism in the United States.

120. Ibid., 80, 194, 208; and US Bureau of the Census, *Historical Statistics of the United States,* 462; Hugill, *World Trade since 1431,* 218; and Lockwood, *Economic Development of Japan,* 107.

121. US Bureau of the Census, *Historical Statistics of the United States,* 546.

122. James M. Laux, *The European Automobile Industry* (New York: Twayne, 1992), 104, 115; Joel Wolff, *Autos and Progress: The Brazilian Search for Modernity* (New York: Oxford University Press, 2010), 38.

123. Calculated from Laux, *The European Automobile Industry,* 74; Rostow, *The World Economy,* 196–197; Hugill, *World Trade since 1431,* 238, 241–244; Osterhammel, *Die Verwandlung der Welt,* 318.

124. James E. Vance Jr., *Capturing the Horizon: The Historical Geography of Transportation since the Transportation Revolution of the Sixteenth Century* (New York: Harper and Row, 1986), 530–539; Yergin, *The Prize,* 172.

125. Charles Quilter, "In Any Weather" (PhD diss., University of California, Irvine, 2010).

126. R. E. G. Davies, *Airlines of Latin America since 1919* (Washington, DC: Smithsonian Institution Press, 1984).

127. Ibid., 2; Hugill, *World Trade since 1431,* 249–283; R. E. G. Davies, *Airlines of Asia since 1920* (McLean, VA.: Paladwr Press, 1997), 340–349; Vance, *Capturing the Horizon,* 545–576.

128. Vance, *Capturing the Horizon;* Davies, *Airlines of Latin America,* 336–344.

129. Davies, *Airlines of Asia,* 1, 231–233.

130. Ibid., 6–14.

131. Headrick, *Power over Peoples,* 306–328.

132. Tom Standage, *The Victorian Internet: The Remarkable Story of the Telegraph and the Nineteenth Century's On-line Pioneers* (New York: Walker and Co., 1998).

133. Dwayne R. Winseck and Robert M. Pike, *Communication and Empire: Media, Markets, and Globalization, 1860–1939* (Durham, NC: Duke University Press, 2007), 90.

134. This is a controversial point. Some scholars, like Rondo Cameron (in Cameron and Bovykin, *International Banking, 1870–1914,* 4), argue that banks were the first multinational companies, dating back to medieval Italy. Others point to the Dutch East India Company's charter in 1602. Wilkins, in *The Emergence of Multinational Enterprise,* 35, puts it around 1865 for the United States.

135. Standage, *The Victorian Internet;* Rudolf Stöber, *Deutsche Pressgeschichte: Von den Anfängen bis zum Gegenwart* (Constance: UVK Verlagsgesellschaft, 2005), 131–136; and Winseck and Pike, *Communication and Empire,* 5, 149, 203, 258.

136. B. R. Mitchell, *International Historical Statistics: Europe, 1750–2000,* 6th ed. (Basingstoke, UK: Palgrave Macmillan, 2007), 52–760; and US Bureau of the Census, *Historical Statistics of the United States,* 485.

137. Rawski, *Economic Growth,* 217; Henry Brunton, *Building Japan, 1868–1876* (1877; London: Routledge, 1991), 27–29.

138. Quoted in Headrick, *The Tentacles of Progress,* 121.

139. Mitchell, *International Historical Statistics: Africa, Asia and Oceania, 1750–2005,* 830–835.

140. Winseck and Pike, *Communication and Empire,* 105, 147.

141. Brunton, *Building Japan,* 28.

142. Quoted in Winseck and Pike, *Communication and Empire,* 36.

143. F. Leslie Smith, John Wright II, and David H. Ostroff, *Perspectives on Radio and Television: Telecommunication in the United States,* 4th ed. (Mahwah, NJ: Erlbaum, 1998), 37.

144. Carole E. Scott, "The Technological Development of Radio: From Thales to Marconi," http://eh.net/encyclopedia/article/scott.radio.industry.history.

145. Calculated from Mitchell, *International Historical Statistics: Africa, Asia and Oceania, 1750–2005,* and Mitchell, *International Historical Statistics: Europe, 1750–2005;* US Bureau of the Census, *Historical Statistics of the United States;* Winseck and Pike, *Communication and Empire,* 315; Hugill, *World Trade since 1431,* 321–322.

146. Hans-Ulrich Wehler, *Deutsche Gesellschaftsgeschichte: Von der "Deutschen Doppelrevolution" bis zum Beginn des Ersten Weltkrieges, 1849–1914* (Munich: C. H. Beck, 1995), 612, 613.

147. Wellhöner and Wixforth, "Finance and Industry," 161–164; William J. Hausman, Peter Hertner, and Mira Wilkins, *Global Electrification: Multinational Enterprise and International Finance in the History of Light and Power, 1878–2007* (New York: Cambridge University Press, 2008), 75–124.

148. Steven C. Topik, "Economic Nationalism and the State in an Underdeveloped Country: Brazil, 1889–1930" (PhD diss., University of Texas, Austin, 1978); Hausman et al., *Global Electrification,* 75–124.

149. Hausman et al., 102–103.

150. Lockwood, *Economic Development of Japan,* 49, 224–225.

151. Hausman et al., 94, 95, 253, 254.

152. Ibid., 201, 234.

153. Wolfgang Schivelbusch, *Lichtblicke: Zur Geschichte der Kunstlichen Helligkeiten im 19 Jahrhundert* (Munich: C. Hauser, 1983).

154. Calculated from Mulhall, *The Dictionary of Statistics,* 156; *Statistical Year-Book of the League of Nations, 1939–40,* 146; *Statistical Year-Book of the League of Nations, 1926,* 88.

155. *Statistical Year-Book of the League of Nations, 1939–40,* 146.

156. Chandler, *Scale and Scope,* 125; Wilkins, *Emergence of Multinational Enterprise,* 80–82, 116–118, 178–184.

157. Robert Franz, "The Statistical History of the German Banking System," *Miscellaneous Articles on German Banking,* US Senate Document 508 (Washington, DC: US Government Printing Office, 1910), 29–33; Albert Broder, "Banking and the Electrotechnical Industry in Western Europe," in Cameron and Bovykin, *International Banking, 1870–1914,* 474–480; and Hans-Ulrich Wehler, *Von der "Deutschen Doppelrevolution" bis zum Beginn des Ersten Weltkrieges, 1849–1914,* vol. 3 of *Deutsche Gesellschaftsgeschichte* (Munich: C. H. Beck, 1995).

158. Rosemary Thorpe and Geoffrey Bertram, *Peru, 1890–1977: Growth and Policy in an Open Economy* (New York: Columbia University Press, 1978), 72–95; Wilkins, *Emergence of Multinational Enterprise,* 80–82, 116–118, 178–184.

159. Bergquist, *Labor in Latin America;* O'Brien, *The Revolutionary Mission;* Thomas Klubock, *Contested Communities: Class, Gender, and Politics in Chile's El Teniente Copper Mine, 1904–1951* (Durham, NC: Duke University Press, 1998); John Hart, *Revolutionary Mexico: The Coming and Process of the Mexican Revolution* (Berkeley: University of California Press, 1987); Alan Knight, *The Mexican Revolution,* 2 vols. (New York: Cambridge University Press, 1986).

160. Dennis Kortheuer, "Santa Rosalía and Compagnie du Boleó: The Making of a Town and Company in the Porfirian Frontier, 1885–1900" (PhD diss., University of California, Irvine, 2001).

161. Chandler, *Scale and Scope,* 70, 122–124.

162. Yergin, *The Prize,* 55.

163. Ibid., 100, 113; Naomi Lamoreaux, *The Great Merger Movement in American Business, 1895–1904* (New York: Cambridge University Press, 1985).

164. Quoted in Yergin, *The Prize,* 14–56, 110.

165. Ibid., 79, 80, 112.

166. Quoted in ibid., 154.

167. Nuno Luís Madureira, "Oil in the Age of Steam," *Journal of Global History* 5, no. 1 (2010): 75–94.

168. Jonathan Brown, *Oil and Revolution* (Berkeley: University of California Press, 1992); Sandra Kuntz Ficker, *Las exportaciones mexicanas durante la primera globalizacion, 1870–1929* (Mexico City: El Colegio de México, 2010); Miguel Tinker Salas, *The Enduring Legacy: Oil, Culture, and Society in Venezuela* (Durham, NC: Duke University Press, 2009).

169. Calculated from Susan B. Carter et al., *Historical Statistics of the United States: Millennial Edition Online* (Cambridge: Cambridge University Press, 2006–), tables 184–186, 208–217, online at http://www.cambridge.org; Grandin, *Fordlandia,* 22–23; Hugill, *World Trade since 1431,* 208–212.

170. US Bureau of the Census, *Historical Statistics of the U.S. 1960,* 548; Brasil, Diretoria Geral da Estatística (DGE), *Anuário Estatístico, 1930/1940* (Rio de Janeiro: Imprensa Nacional, 1940), 1380; Zephyr Frank and Aldo Mussachio, "Brazil in the International Rubber Trade, 1870–1930," in Steven C. Topik, Carlos Marichal, and Zephyr Frank, eds., *From Silver to Cocaine: Latin American Commodity Chains and the Building of the World Economy, 1500–2000* (Durham, NC: Duke University Press, 2006), 275.

171. Michael Stanfield, *Red Rubber, Bleeding Trees: Violence, Slavery and Empire in Northwest Amazonia, 1850–1933* (Albuquerque: University of New Mexico Press, 1998); Barbara Weinstein, *The Amazon Rubber Boom, 1850–1920* (Stanford, CA: Stanford University Press, 1983); Burns, *The Unwritten Alliance: Rio Branco and Brazilian-American Relations* (New York: Columbia University Press, 1966).

172. Mark Finlay, *Growing American Rubber: Strategic Plants and the Politics of National Security* (New Brunswick, NJ: Rutgers University Press, 2009).

173. Joe Jackson, *The Thief at the End of the World: Rubber, Power and the Seeds of Empire* (New York: Penguin, 2009).

174. Ann Stoler, *Capitalism and Confrontation in Sumatra's Plantation Belt, 1870–1979* (New Haven, CT: Yale University Press, 1985), 209; T. A. Tengwall, "History of Rubber Cultivation and Research in the Netherlands Indies," in *Science and Scientists in the Netherlands Indies,* ed.

Pieter Honig and Frans Verdoom (New York: Board for the Netherlands Indies, Surinam and Curação, 1945); and *Statistical Year-Book of the League of Nations, 1926,* 80.

175. Adam Hochschild, *King Leopold's Ghost: A Story of Greed, Terror, and Heroism in Colonial Africa* (Boston: Houghton Mifflin, 1998).

176. Finlay, *Growing American Rubber,* 152–157; Kuntz Ficker, *Las exportaciones mexicanas,* 394–405.

177. Victor Bulmer-Thomas, *The Economic History of Latin America since Independence* (Cambridge: Cambridge University Press, 1994), 15.

178. For a discussion of international regimes, see Stephen Krasner, *The Structural Conflict: The Third World against Global Liberalism* (Berkeley: University of California Press, 1985); and David Smith, Dorothy Solinger, and Steven C. Topik, eds., *States and Sovereignty in the Global Economy* (London: Routledge, 1999).

179. For cocaine chains, see Gootenberg, *Andean Cocaine: The Making of a Global Drug* (Chapel Hill: University of North Carolina Press, 2008); Gootenberg, "Cocaine in Chains: The Rise and Demise of a Global Commodity, 1860–1950," in Topik et al., *From Silver to Cocaine,* 321–351.

180. This is less true in studies of US agriculture in our period because of the early rise of agro-industry, but that is an exceptional case.

181. This is in response to Landes's concentration on the industrial side of the story in *The Unbound Prometheus.*

182. Sidney Mintz, *Sweetness and Power: The Place of Sugar in Modern History* (New York: Penguin, 1986); Hobsbawm, *The Age of Empire,* 50.

183. According to Mulhall's 1889 estimate, already in that year Australia had the highest per capita income in the world, with Canada not far behind France and the Low Countries. *The Dictionary of Statistics,* 589.

184. David S. Jacks, "Intra- and International Commodity Market Integration in the Atlantic Economy, 1800–1913," *Explorations in Economic History* 42 (2005): 381–413, esp. 399.

185. C. Knick Harley, "Transportation, the World Wheat Trade and the Kuznets Cycle, 1850–1913," *Explorations in Economic History* 17 (1980): 218–250, esp. 218; Patricia Herlihy, *Odessa: A History, 1794–1914* (Cambridge, MA: Harvard University Press, 1986).

186. *World Agriculture: An International Survey* (London: Oxford University Press, 1932), 138.

187. Quoted in Edgars Dunsdorfs, *The Australian Wheat-Growing Industry, 1788–1948* (Melbourne: University Press, 1956), 167.

188. Quoted in Dan Morgan, *Merchants of Grain* (New York: Viking, 1979), 36–37.

189. Harley, "Transportation, the World Wheat Trade," 218, 233; Carl Solberg, *The Prairies and the Pampas: Agrarian Policy in Canada and Argentina, 1880–1930* (Stanford, CA: Stanford University Press, 1987), 39; Peter Dondlinger, *The Book of Wheat: An Economic History and Practical Manual of the Wheat Industry* (New York: Orange, Judd Co., 1912), 238.

190. Alan Olmstead and Paul Rhode, "Biological Globalization: The Other Grain Invasion," in *The New Comparative Economic History: Essays in Honor of Jeffrey G. Williamson,* ed. Timothy Hatton, Kevin H. O'Rourke, and Alan Taylor (Cambridge, MA: MIT Press, 2007): 115–140, quotation at 122; Dunsdorfs, *Australian Wheat-Growing Industry,* 190.

191. William P. Rutter, *Wheat-Growing in Canada, the United States and the Argentine: Including Comparisons with Other Areas* (London: Adam and Charles Black, 1911), 118.

192. Dondlinger, *The Book of Wheat,* 106.

193. *World Agriculture,* 38ff.

194. Dondlinger, *The Book of Wheat,* 237.

195. O'Rourke and Williamson, *Globalization and History,* 220.

196. Dondlinger, *The Book of Wheat,* 241.

197. *World Agriculture,* 209.

198. Kevin H. O'Rourke, "The European Grain Invasion," *Journal of Economic History* 57, no. 4 (December 1977): 775–781, esp. 781. Compare a recent econometric analysis of the wheat market that questions price convergence: Giovanni Federico and Karl Gunnar Perrson, "Market Integration and Convergence in the World Wheat Market," in Hatton et al., *New Comparative Economic History,* 87–113. Rory Miller and Robert Greenhill, "The Fertilizer Commodity Chains: Guano and Nitrate, 1840–1930," in Topik et al., *From Silver to Cocaine,* 228–270.

199. Gootenberg, *Between Silver and Guano;* Thorp and Bertram, *Peru, 1890–1977;* Heraclio Bonilla, *Guano y burguesia* (Lima: Instituto de Estudios Peruanos, 1973); Shane A. Hunt, "Distribution, Growth, and Government Economic Behavior in Peru," in *Government and Economic Development,* ed. G. Ranis (New Haven, CT: Yale University Press, 1971); Jonathan Levin, *The Export Economies: Their Patterns of Development in Historical Perspective* (Cambridge, MA: Harvard University Press, 1960); Thomas F. O'Brien, *The Nitrate Industry and Chile's Crucial Transition, 1870–1891* (New York: New York University Press, 1982); Michael Monteon, *Chile in the Nitrate Era: The Evolution of Economic Dependence, 1880–1930* (Madison: University of Wisconsin Press, 1982).

200. A. J. H. Latham and Larry Neal, "The International Market in Rice and Wheat, 1868–1914," *Economic History Review* 36, no. 2 (May 1983): 260–280, esp. 270–272; Frank Surface, *The Grain Trade during the World War: Being a History of the Food Administration and the United States Grain Corporation* (New York: Macmillan, 1928), 212.

201. Mintz, *Tasting Food, Tasting Freedom: Excursions into Eating, Culture and the Past* (Boston: Beacon Press, 1996), 24.

202. *World Agriculture,* 31; Morgan, *Merchants of Grain,* 77.

203. Rutter, *Wheat-Growing,* 7; Vernon Wickizer and M. K. Bennett, *The Rice Economy of Monsoon Asia* (Palo Alto, CA: Stanford University Food Research Institute, 1941), 2.

204. N. Jasny, *Competition among Grains* (Palo Alto, CA: Stanford University Food Research Institute, 1940), 7.

205. William Cronon, *Nature's Metropolis: Chicago and the Great West* (New York: Norton, 1991), 99–100; Denoon, *Settler Capitalism,* 46; Jasny, *Competition among Grains,* 24–25, 84.

206. Wheat is or has been grown in highland areas on or near the equator, in such disparate climatic zones as Ecuador, Colombia, Nigeria, Saudi Arabia, and Brazil. Wilfred Malenbaum, *The World Wheat Economy, 1885–1939* (Cambridge, MA: Harvard University Press, 1953), 52, 62–63.

207. M. K. Bennett, "World Wheat Crops, 1885–1932: New Series, with Areas and Yields by Countries," *Wheat Studies* 9 (1933): 239–266, esp. 241.

208. Ibid., 258.

209. C. Knick Harley, "Western Settlement and the Price of Wheat, 1872–1913," *Journal of Economic History* 38, no. 4 (December 1978): 865–878, esp. 878; Wickizer and Bennett, *Rice Economy of Monsoon Asia,* 2; Morgan, *Merchants of Grain,* 78–80.

210. Sally Clarke, *Regulation and the Revolution in United States Farm Productivity* (New York: Cambridge University Press, 1994), 249.

211. Ibid., 47.

212. George Pavlovsky, *Agricultural Russia on the Eve of the Revolution* (London: Routledge, 1930), quotation at 254; Alexis Antsiferov et al., *Russian Agriculture during the War* (New Haven, CT: Yale University Press, 1930), chaps. 1–2.

213. Cronon, *Nature's Metropolis,* chap. 3; Jonathan Dekel-Chan, *Farming the Red Land: Jewish Agricultural Colonization and Local Soviet Power, 1924–1941* (New Haven, CT: Yale University Press, 2005).

214. *World Agriculture,* 152–154.

215. Solberg, *Prairies and the Pampas,* 35; *World Agriculture,* 78ff.

216. US Bureau of the Census, *Historical Statistics of the United States,* 14; Solberg, *Prairies and the Pampas,* 35.

217. Surface, *The Grain Trade,* 273, 289; Morgan, *Merchants of Grain,* 45; Dunsdorfs, *Australian Wheat-Growing Industry,* 169–170.

218. *World Agriculture,* 81.

219. Rutter, *Wheat-Growing,* 134–135.

220. Ibid., 188; Dondlinger, *The Book of Wheat,* 191.

221. Cronon, *Nature's Metropolis,* 83–84, quotation at 80.

222. Ibid., 109; and Solberg, *Prairies and the Pampas,* 114. Although Argentine governments were laissez-faire prior to the Great Depression, populist governments during the 1930s and 1940s would become more protective of their farmers after grain prices collapsed.

223. Cronon, *Nature's Metropolis,* 111–112. Elsewhere, the transition to bulk storage and transport of grain was more gradual. Australia, for instance, did not make the change from sacks to bulk shipments until the 1920s. Dunsdorfs, *Australian Wheat-Growing Industry,* 260.

224. Dondlinger, *The Book of Wheat,* 203–208, quotation at 207.

225. Harley, "Transportation, the World Wheat Trade," 227–233.

226. The classic formulation of the US frontier is Frederick Jackson Turner, "The Significance of the Frontier in American History," in *The Frontier in American History* (New York: H. H. Holt, 1920). For a critique, see Paul Gates, *Landlords and Tenants on the Prairie Frontier: Studies in American Land Policy* (Ithaca, NY: Cornell University Press, 1973); and Allan Bogue, *From Prairie to Corn Belt: Farming on the Illinois and Iowa Prairies in the Nineteenth Century* (Chicago: University of Chicago Press, 1963). On Canada, see Harold Innis, *Problems of Staple Production in Canada* (Toronto: Ryerson Press, 1933); Melville Watkins, "A Staple Theory of Economic Growth," *Canadian Journal of Economics and Political Science* 29 (May 1963): 141–158; and John Richards, "The Staples Debates," in *Explorations in Canadian Economic History: Essays in Honor of Irene Spry,* ed. Cameron Duncan (Ottawa: University of Ottawa Press, 1985). On Argentina, see James Scobie, *Revolution on the Pampas: A Social His-*

tory of Argentine Wheat (Austin: University of Texas Press, 1964); Jonathan Brown, *A Socio-Economic History of Argentina, 1776–1860* (New York: Cambridge University Press, 1979); David Rock, *Argentina, 1516–1982: From Spanish Colonization to Alfonsín* (Berkeley: University of California Press, 1987); and Aldo Ferrer, *La economía argentina: Las etapas de su desarrollo y problemas actuales* (Mexico City: Fondo de Cultura Económica, 1963). On Chile, see Carl Solberg, *Immigration and Nationalism, Argentina and Chile, 1890–1914* (Austin: University of Texas Press, 1970); and Arnold Bauer, *Chilean Rural Society from the Spanish Conquest to 1930* (New York: Cambridge University Press, 1975).

227. Peter Smith, *Politics and Beef in Argentina: Patterns of Conflict and Change* (New York: Columbia University Press, 1969); Bergquist, *Labor in Latin America;* Hilda Sabato, *Agrarian Capitalism and the World Market: Buenos Aires in the Pastoral Age, 1840–1890* (Albuquerque: University of New Mexico Press, 1990), 29–52.

228. Jeremy Adelman, *Frontier Development: Land, Labour and Capital in the Wheatlands of Argentina and Canada, 1890–1914* (Oxford: Clarendon Press, 1994), 80; Solberg, *Prairies and the Pampas,* 63.

229. Adelman, *Frontier Development,* 94.

230. Solberg, *Prairies and the Pampas,* 28; Malenbaum, *The World Wheat Economy,* 138–139.

231. Denoon, *Settler Capitalism,* 100.

232. Adelman, *Frontier Development,* 117–118.

233. Malenbaum, *The World Wheat Economy,* 139–140.

234. Solberg, *Prairies and the Pampas,* 106–108; Malenbaum, *The World Wheat Economy,* 139–140.

235. Quoted in Solberg, *Prairies and the Pampas,* 107.

236. Dondlinger, *The Book of Wheat,* 231–232.

237. Solberg, *Prairies and the Pampas,* 3–4.

238. Ibid., 40. Only Canada, Australia, and Argentina exported more than half of their wheat crop. The same held true for the rice market. Siam and Indochina, where rice constituted 60 to 70 percent of exports during this period, exported only a quarter of all the rice they produced. *World Agriculture,* 7.

239. The following discussion of Canadian wheat farming draws largely on Adelman, *Frontier Development,* and Solberg, *Prairies and the Pampas.*

240. Adelman, *Frontier Development,* 53.

241. Ibid., 61.

242. Quoted in ibid., 61.

243. Dondlinger, *The Book of Wheat,* 228–231, quotation at 230.

244. Morgan, *Merchants of Grain,* 36.

245. Rutter, *Wheat-Growing,* 187–188.

246. The ensuing discussion on futures markets draws on Cronon, *Nature's Metropolis;* Lapham and Neal, "The International Market"; Rutter, *Wheat-Growing;* Paul Allen, "The Past and Future of the Commodity Exchanges," *Agricultural History* 56, no. 1 (January 1982): 287–305; Jeffrey Williams, "The Origin of Futures Markets," *Agricultural History* 56, no. 1 (January 1982): 306–316; Williams, *The Economic Function of Futures Markets* (New York: Cambridge

University Press, 1986); and Owen Gregory, "Futures Markets: Comment," *Agricultural History* 56, no. 1 (January 1982): 317–325.

247. Rutter, *Wheat-Growing,* 210; Cronon, *Nature's Metropolis,* 115–116.

248. Cronon, *Nature's Metropolis,* 116, quotation at 126.

249. Quoted in ibid., 210–211.

250. Morgan, *Merchants of Grain,* 59; Cronon, *Nature's Metropolis,* 127.

251. Rutter, *Wheat-Growing,* 194–198.

252. Ibid., 199–200; Dondlinger, *The Book of Wheat,* 219–222.

253. Rutter, *Wheat-Growing,* 203.

254. Arturo Warman, *Corn and Capitalism: How a Botanical Bastard Grew to Global Dominance,* trans. Nancy Westrate (Chapel Hill: University of North Carolina Press, 2003).

255. Ibid., 223.

256. Hungarian millers were the first to adopt iron and porcelain rollers to process local hard-wheat varieties. In 1839 the Budapest Walzmuhle flour mill opened and soon gained a well-deserved reputation for producing "flours of such fineness" by employing rollers and sifters in addition to the traditional millstones. French innovation focused on the purifier, which helped recoup the middlings. G. R. Stevens, *Ogilvie in Canada: Pioneer Millers, 1801–1951* (Toronto: Ashton-Potter, 1951), 23–24, 28.

257. Charles Kuhlmann, *The Development of the Flour-Milling Industry in the United States with Special Reference to the Industry in Minneapolis* (Boston: Houghton Mifflin, 1929), 113–115.

258. John Storck and Walter D. Teague, *Flour for Man's Bread: A History of Milling* (Minneapolis: University of Minnesota Press, 1952), 241.

259. Stephen George, *Enterprising Minnesotans: 150 Years of Business Pioneers* (Minneapolis: University of Minnesota Press, 2003), 23–24.

260. Harry Bullis, *Buffalo: Its Flour Milling Heritage* (New York: Newcomen Society of England, 1948), 10.

261. Hungarian exports to England were hard hit by this surge in US exports. Storck and Teague, *Flour for Man's Bread,* 269; Kuhlmann, *Flour-Milling Industry,* 295–296.

262. George, *Enterprising Minnesotans,* 23–30.

263. Storck and Teague, *Flour for Man's Bread,* 128, 240.

264. Kuhlmann, *Flour-Milling Industry,* 134, 240; Storck and Teague, *Flour for Man's Bread,* 308–309.

265. General Mills, "History of Innovation: Our Milling Roots and Beyond," http://www.generalmills.com/Company/History.aspx.

266. Chandler, *The Visible Hand;* Chandler, *Scale and Scope.*

267. The farm implement industry went through a similar trajectory. See Allen Wells and Gilbert M. Joseph, *Summer of Discontent, Seasons of Upheaval: Elite Politics and Rural Insurgency in Yucatán, 1876–1915* (Stanford, CA: Stanford University Press, 1996), chap. 4.

268. Storck and Teague, *Flour for Man's Bread,* 269.

269. Ibid., 272; Kuhlmann, *Flour-Milling Industry,* 295–296.

270. Kuhlmann, *Flour-Milling Industry,* 274–275, 295–296, 310; Stevens, *Ogilvie in Canada,* 50–51; George, *Enterprising Minnesotans,* 29.

271. Kuhlmann, *Flour-Milling Industry,* 232.

272. Stevens, *Ogilvie in Canada,* 50.

273. A number of states went farther, passing laws to ban artificially bleached flour, but the US Supreme Court, siding with the flour companies, ruled the statutes unconstitutional. Ibid., 232–239.

274. Storck and Teague, *Flour for Man's Bread,* 327.

275. Ibid., 231.

276. *Washington Post,* September 4, 2005, http://www.washingtonpost.com/wp-dyn/content/article/2005/09/02/AR2005090200846.html.

277. Storck and Teague, *Flour for Man's Bread,* 219–220.

278. Ibid; George, *Enterprising Minnesotans,* 25–26.

279. Bullis, *Buffalo,* 12–15; Kuhlmann, *Flour-Milling Industry,* 176–177, 218, 221.

280. This discussion of consumption relies principally on Harvey Levenstein, *Revolution at the Table: The Transformation of the American Diet* (New York: Oxford University Press, 1988), esp. chap. 3.

281. Quoted in Jackson Lears, *Fables of Abundance: A Cultural History of Advertising in America* (New York: Basic Books, 1994), 225.

282. Ibid., 139.

283. Quoted in ibid., 158.

284. Levenstein, *Revolution at the Table,* 33.

285. Quoted in ibid., 153. For a comic view of the Kellogg sanitarium, read T. Coraghessan Boyle, *The Road to Wellville* (New York: Viking, 1993), or see the movie.

286. Thomas Hine, *The Total Package: The Evolution of and Secret Meanings of Boxes, Bottles, Cans and Tubes* (Boston: Little, Brown, 1995), 61–62.

287. Storck and Teague, *Flour for Man's Bread,* 275.

288. Quoted in Levenstein, *Revolution at the Table,* 155.

289. Stevens, *Ogilvie in Canada,* 54.

290. James Gray, *Business without Boundary: The Story of General Mills* (Minneapolis: University of Minnesota Press, 1954), 60.

291. Lears, *Fables of Abundance,* 138.

292. Scanlon, *Inarticulate Longings,* 172, 197–198.

293. Lears, *Fables of Abundance,* 384.

294. Roland Marchand, *Advertising the American Dream: Making Way for Modernity, 1920–1940* (Berkeley: University of California Press, 1985), 353–354.

295. Gray, *Business without Boundary,* 173, quotation at 182; General Mills, "History of Innovation."

296. Gray, *Business without Boundary,* chap. 11.

297. Ibid.

298. Levenstein, *Revolution at the Table,* 35; William G. Panschar, *Baking in America,* 2 vols. (Evanston, IL: Northwestern University Press, 1956), 1:83. British bakers had been putting crackers in tins for quite some time. What was different was Nabisco's massive advertising, which was so ubiquitous that "Uneeda is widely thought to be the first packaged product." Hine, *The Total Package,* 82.

299. Gray, *Business without Boundary,* 88.

300. Ibid., 102.

301. This section on rice relies on Randolph Barker and Robert Herdt with Beth Rose, *The Rice Economy of Asia* (Washington, DC: Resources for the Future, 1985); Francesca Bray, *The Rice Economies: Technology and Development in Asian Societies* (Oxford: Basil Blackwell, 1986); Lapham and Neal, "The International Market in Rice"; Wickizer and Bennett, *Rice Economy of Monsoon Asia;* Michael Adas, *The Burma Rice Delta: Economic Development and Social Change on an Asian Rice Frontier, 1852–1941* (Madison: University of Wisconsin Press, 1974); and Cheng Siok-Hwa, *The Rice Industry of Burma, 1852–1940* (Kuala Lumpur: University of Malaya Press, 1968).

302. Rice can grow in temperate or more arid zones as well, but only with the aid of irrigation.

303. Adas suggests that disease was a formidable obstacle in the Lower Burma rice delta, however. Adas, *The Burma Rice Delta,* 62.

304. Bray, *The Rice Economies,* 15.

305. Ibid., 26.

306. Wickizer and Bennett, *Rice Economy of Monsoon Asia,* 56–57.

307. Ibid., 70.

308. Ibid., 74, 79.

309. Ibid., 100.

310. Adas, *The Burma Rice Delta,* 33.

311. Ibid., 141.

312. This section draws on Allen Wells, "Reports of Its Demise Are Not Exaggerated: The Life and Times of Yucatecan Henequen," in Topik et al., *From Silver to Cocaine,* 300–320; Sterling Evans, *Bound in Twine: The History and Ecology of the Henequen-Wheat Complex for Mexico and the American and Canadian Plains, 1880–1950* (College Station: Texas A&M Press, 2007); Rakibuddin Ahmed, *The Progress of the Jute Industry and Trade, 1855–1966* (Dacca: Pakistan Central Jute Committee, 1966); Samita Sen, *Women and Labour in Late Colonial India: The Bengal Jute Industry* (New York: Cambridge University Press, 1999); Dipesh Chakrabarty, *Rethinking Working-Class History: Bengal, 1890–1940* (Princeton, NJ: Princeton University Press, 1999); Gordon Stewart, *Jute and Empire: The Calcutta Jute Wallahs and the Landscapes of Empire* (Manchester: Manchester University Press, 1998); Omkar Goswami, *Industry, Trade and Peasant Society: The Jute Economy of Eastern India, 1900–1947* (New York: Oxford University Press, 1991); Norman Owen, *Prosperity without Progress: Manila Hemp and Material Life in the Colonial Philippines* (Berkeley: University of California Press, 1984).

313. Quoted in Stewart, *Jute and Empire,* 44.

314. Ibid., quotation at 2.

315. Ibid., 3.

316. Goswami, *Industry, Trade,* 4–5, 54.

317. Ibid., 240.

318. Warman, *Corn and Capitalism.*

319. Landes, "The 'Great Drain' and Industrialisation: Commodity Flows from Periphery to Centre in Historical Perspective," in *Economic Growth and Resources,* vol. 2: *Trends and Factors,* ed. R. C. O. Matthews (London: Macmillan, 1980), 294, 297, 303.

320. Useful overviews of stimulants include: David R. Courtwright, *Forces of Habit: Drugs and the Making of the Modern World* (Cambridge, MA: Harvard University Press, 2001); Jordan Goodman, Paul Lovejoy, and Andrew Sherratt, eds., *Consuming Habits: Drugs in History and Anthropology* (London: Routledge, 1995); R. Rudgley, *Essential Substances: A Cultural History of Intoxicants in Society* (New York: Kodassha International, 1993); Wolfgang Schivelbusch, *Tastes of Paradise: A Social History of Spices, Stimulants, and Intoxicants,* trans. David Jacobsen (New York: Vintage Books, 1993).

321. W. Arthur Lewis, ed., *Tropical Development, 1880–1913* (Evanston, IL: Northwestern University Press, 1970).

322. J. H. Galloway, "Sugar," in *The Cambridge History of Food,* vol. 1, ed. K. F. Kiple and K. C. Ornelas (Cambridge: Cambridge University Press, 2000), 437–449.

323. For an overview of sugar's journey to the modern world, see Stuart Schwartz, *Sugar Plantations in the Formation of Brazilian Society: Bahia, 1550–1835* (New York: Cambridge University Press, 1985).

324. Courtwright, *Forces of Habit,* 28.

325. Noël Deerr, *The History of Sugar,* 2 vols. (London: Chapman and Hall, 1950), 2:467.

326. Ibid., 490–491; Mintz, *Sweetness and Power,* 197.

327. Manuel Moreno Fraginals, *The Sugarmill: The Socio-Economic Complex of Sugar in Cuba,* trans. Cedric Belfrage (New York: Monthly Review Press, 1976). Also see Rebecca Scott, *Slave Emancipation in Cuba: The Transition to Free Labor, 1860–1899* (Princeton, NJ: Princeton University Press, 1985).

328. For nineteenth- and twentieth-century technical advances, see Alan Dye, *Cuban Sugar in the Age of Mass Production: Technology and the Economics of the Sugar Central, 1899–1929* (Stanford, CA: Stanford University Press, 1998).

329. William Albert and Adrian Graves, eds., *Crisis and Change in the International Sugar Economy, 1860–1914* (Norwich, England: ISC Press, 1984), 3.

330. Dye, *Cuban Sugar,* 1.

331. Mintz, *Sweetness and Power,* 143.

332. Scott, *Slave Emancipation.*

333. Fernando Ortiz, *Cuban Counterpoint: Tobacco and Sugar,* trans. Harriett de Onís (New York: Knopf, 1947), 53–54.

334. Rebecca J. Scott, "The Transformation of Sugar Production in Cuba after Emancipation," in Albert and Graves, *Crisis and Change,* 112–117; Mulhall, *The Dictionary of Statistics,* 633; Victor Bulmer-Thomas, *The Economic History of Latin America since Independence* (New York: Cambridge University Press, 1994), 74; Ramiro Guerra y Sánchez, *Sugar and Society in the Caribbean: An Economic History of Cuban Agriculture,* trans. Marjory M. Urquidi (1927; New Haven, CT: Yale University Press, 1964), 77–79.

335. Deerr, *The History of Sugar,* 2:530–531.

336. Guerra y Sánchez's *Sugar and Society in the Caribbean* was published in 1927. Other, later good examples of this literature are Ortiz, *Cuban Counterpoint* (1947); Eric Williams, *Capitalism and Slavery* (New York: Capricorn Books, 1944); and Frank, *Capitalism and Underdevelopment* (1967).

337. Deerr, *The History of Sugar,* 1:131; Christian Schnakenbourg, "From the Sugar Estate to the Central Factory," in Albert and Graves, *Crisis and Change,* 93.

338. Geertz, *Agricultural Involution: The Processes of Ecological Change in Indonesia* (Berkeley: University of California Press, 1971), 69–79; Horacio Crespo, "Trade Regimes and the International Sugar Market, 1850–1980: Protectionism, Subsidies, and Regulation," in Topik et al., *From Silver to Cocaine,* 150.

339. Geertz, *Agricultural Involution,* 61–62.

340. Denoon, *Settler Capitalism,* 102, 103; Robert F. McKillop, "Australia's Sugar Industry," Light Railway Research Society of Australia, http://www.lrrsa.org.au/LRR_SGRa.htm#Early History.

341. Waden Narsey, "Fiji's Economic History, 1874–1939," *The Contemporary Pacific* (Spring 1990): 208–213.

342. One could say "British," but D. C. M. Platt has shown, in *Britain's Investment Overseas on the Eve of the First World War: The Use and Abuse of Numbers* (Basingstoke, UK: Macmillan 1986), that a considerable amount of the funds invested in London actually derived from small-scale continental investors, mostly from northwest Europe. Also, Denoon, *Settler Capitalism,* 121.

343. Kelly Olds, "The Economic History of Taiwan," EH Network, http://eh.net/encyclopedia/article/olds.taiwan.economic.history.

344. University of Hawai'i–West O'ahu, Center for Labor Education and Research, "Hawai'i Labor History: A Brief Overview," http://homepages.uhwo.hawaii.edu/clear/Lhistory.html.

345. Okihiro, *Pineapple Culture.*

346. Deerr, *The History of Sugar,* 1:113; and Peter Eisenberg, *The Sugar Industry in Pernambuco: Modernization without Change, 1840–1910* (Berkeley: University of California Press, 1974).

347. Michael Gonzales, "Economic Crisis: Chinese Workers and Peruvian Sugar Planters, 1875–1900," and William Albert, "The Labour Force on Peru's Sugar Plantations 1820–1930," both in Albert and Graves, *Crisis and Change,* 181–195, 198–215.

348. Scobie, *Argentina,* 144; Denoon, *Settler Capitalism,* 99; Donna Guy, *Argentine Sugar Politics: Tucumán and the Generation of 80* (Tempe: Arizona State University, 1980).

349. Deerr, *The History of Sugar,* 1:248–249; Rebecca Scott, *Degrees of Freedom: Louisiana and Cuba after Slavery* (Cambridge MA: Belknap Press of Harvard University Press, 2005), 72, 73, 258; Gail M. Hollander, *Raising Cane in the 'Glades: The Global Sugar Trade and the Transformation of Florida* (Chicago: University of Chicago Press, 2008).

350. Karl Hufbauer, *The Formation of the German Chemical Community (1720–1795)* (Berkeley: University of California Press, 1982), 145; Martin Kitchen, *The Political Economy of Germany, 1815–1914* (London: Croom Helm, 1978), 200–206; Cornelius Torp, *Die Herausforderung der Globalisierung: Wirtschaft und Politik in Deutschland, 1860–1914* (Göttingen: Vandenhoeck und Ruprecht, 2005), 77, 81.

351. Mulhall, *The Dictionary of Statistics,* 550.

352. John Perkins, "The Political Economy of Sugar Beet in Imperial Germany," in Albert and Graves, *Crisis and Change,* 39; Galloway, "Sugar."

353. Perkins, "Political Economy of Sugar Beet," 31–46.

354. Ibid., 41. Perkins points out that the inventor Constantin Fahlberg was working in the United States at the time. One should add that although saccharin was cheaper than sugar, it did not provide calories so it was an empty sweetener.

355. Galloway, "Sugar."

356. Nikolai Bukharin, *Imperialism and World Economy* (Moscow: International, 1929), chap. 8; Mulhall, *The Dictionary of Statistics,* 809.

357. Calculated from Deerr, *The History of Sugar,* 2:490–498; Mulhall, *The Dictionary of Statistics,* 626.

358. Ph. G. Chalmin, "The Important Trends in Sugary Diplomacy before 1914," in Albert and Graves, *Crisis and Change,* 17.

359. Horacio Crespo, "Trade Regimes and the International Sugar Market," in Topik et al., *From Silver to Cocaine,* 148.

360. Calculated from Deerr, vols. 1 and 2.

361. Mintz, *Sweetness and Power,* 125–150.

362. The numbers may be skewed toward the more affluent countries, where it was sold in markets. In the lands where it was grown, probably a good deal of sugar was consumed as cane or juice and not tabulated.

363. Michel Tuchscherer, "Coffee in the Red Sea Areas from the Sixteenth Century to the Nineteenth Century," in *The Global Coffee Economy in Africa, Asia and Latin America, 1500–1989,* ed. William G. Clarence-Smith and Steven C. Topik (New York: Cambridge University Press, 2003).

364. Kristof Glamann, *Dutch-Asiatic Trade, 1620–1740* (Copenhagen: Danish Science Press, 1958); Brian Cowan, *The Social Life of Coffee: The Emergence of the British Coffeehouse* (New Haven, CT: Yale University Press, 2005).

365. William Clarence-Smith, "The Coffee Crisis in Asia, Africa, and the Pacific, 1870–1914," in Clarence-Smith and Topik, *Global Coffee Economy,* 100.

366. Steven C. Topik and Michelle Craig McDonald, "Culture and Consumption: National Drinks and National Identity in the Atlantic World," in *Food and Globalization: Consumption, Markets and Politics in the Modern World,* ed. Alexander Nützenadel and Frank Trentmann (Oxford: Berg, 2008); N. Posthumus, *Inquiry into the History of Prices in Holland,* vol. 1 (Amsterdam: Brill, 1946), 75–79.

367. M. R. Fernando, "Coffee Cultivation in Java, 1830–1917," in Clarence-Smith and Topik, *Global Coffee Economy,* 161, 162.

368. Cain and Hopkins, *British Imperialism: Innovation and Expansion,* 298–306; Richard Graham, *Britain and the Onset of Modernization in Brazil* (Cambridge: Cambridge University Press, 1968); Platt, *Business Imperialism;* and Rory Miller, *Britain and Latin America in the Nineteenth and Twentieth Centuries* (London: Longman, 1993).

369. Anne Hanley, *Native Capital: Financial Institutions and Economic Development in São Paulo, Brazil, 1850–1920* (Stanford, CA: Stanford University Press, 2005); Gail Triner, *Banking and Economic Development: Brazil, 1889–1930* (New York: Palgrave, 2000); Miller, *Britain and Latin America;* and Topik, *Political Economy.* On the history of milk consumption in the United States, see E. Melanie DuPuis, *Nature's Perfect Food: How Milk Became America's Drink* (New York: New York University Press, 2002); and Chandler, *Scale and Scope,* 156.

370. Calculated from Robert Greenhill, "E. Johnston: 150 Anos em Café," in *150 Anos de Café,* ed. Marcellino Martins and E. Johnston (Rio: Marcellino Martins, 1993), 307; José Antonio Ocampo, *Colombia y la economía mundial, 1830–1910* (Bogotá: Siglo Veintiuno Ocampo, 1984), 303; and Brazil, IGBE *Séries Estatísticas Retrospectivas,* vol. 1 (Rio: IBGE, 1986), 84; Mulhall, *The Dictionary of Statistics,* 130. Admittedly, this datum privileges coffee, because other important internationally traded goods such as sugar and grains often traveled more by land than by sea.

371. Vernon Wickizer, *Coffee, Tea, and Cocoa* (Palo Alto, CA: Stanford University Food Research Institute, 1951), 36.

372. Frederick Stirton Weaver, *Latin America in the World Economy: Mercantile Colonialism to Global Capitalism* (Boulder, CO: Westview Press, 2000), 69; Summerhill, *Order against Progress,* 54.

373. Franz Daffert, *Über die gegenwärtige Lage des Kaffeebaus in Brasilien* (Amsterdam: J. H. de Bussy, 1898).

374. Almir Chaiban El-Kareh, *Filha branca de mae preta: A Companhia de Estrade de Ferro Dom Pedro II* (Petrópolis, R.J. Brazil: Editora Vozes, 1980); Steven Topik, "Coffee," in Topik and Wells, *Second Conquest of Latin America.*

375. Topik, "La hacienda brasilena: Fabrica en el campo o pueblo campesino?" *Revista de Historia* (San José, Costa Rica), no. 36 (July–December 1997); Cary McWilliams, *Factories in the Field: The Story of Migratory Farm Labor in California* (Boston: Little, Brown, 1939).

376. We are referring to the predominant scale of production in different countries. There were some very large, medium, and small coffee fields in every country. For excellent studies of the Nicaraguan system, see Elizabeth Dore, *Myths of Modernity: Peonage and Patriarchy in Nicaragua* (Durham, NC: Duke University Press, 2006), and Julie Charlip, *Cultivating Coffee: The Farmers of Carazo, Nicaragua, 1880–1930* (Athens: Ohio University Press, 2003); for Guatemala, see David McCreery, *Rural Guatemala, 1760–1940* (Stanford, CA: Stanford University Press, 1994); for El Salvador, see Jeffrey L. Gould and Aldo A. Lauria-Santiago, *To Rise in Darkness: Revolution, Repression, and Memory in El Salvador, 1920–1932* (Durham N.C.: Duke University Press, 2008); and for Costa Rica, see Mario Samper, *Generations of Settlers: Rural Households and Markets on the Costa Rican Frontier, 1850–1935* (Boulder, CO: Westview Press, 1990).

377. It is worth noting that "quality" was in the palate of the drinker. There was no chemical scale, such as those used to determine purity or sucrose content in sugar. Probably most of the difference between Central American/Colombian coffee and its Brazilian competitor stemmed from the greater care the former took during harvest.

378. Greenhill, "Shipping," 119–155; Paul Bairoch, "Geographical Structure and Trade from 1800 to 1970," *Journal of European Economic History* 3, no. 3 (Winter 1974): 606; North, "Ocean Freight Rates."

379. Marcelo de P. Abreu and Afonso S. Bevilaqua, "Brazil as an Export Economy, 1880–1930," in *An Economic History of Twentieth-Century Latin America,* 2 vols., ed. Enrique Cárdenas, José Antonio Ocampo, and Rosemary Thorp (New York: Palgrave, 2000), 1:32–54.

380. Topik, *Trade and Gunboats.*

381. Calculated from Greenhill, "Shipping," 119–155, and Greenhill, "E. Johnston," 330–331; A. Wakeman, "Reminiscences of Lower Wall Street," *Spice Mill,* March 1911, 193; Joseph Walsh, *Coffee: Its History, Classification and Description* (Philadelphia: Henry T. Coates and Co., 1902); Mario Samper and Radin Fernando, "Historical Statistics of Coffee Production and Trade from 1700 to 1960," in Clarence-Smith and Topik, *Global Coffee Economy,* 443, 446–447.

382. The US Federal Trade Commission estimated income elasticity in 1954 at only 0.2 percent. US Federal Trade Commission, *Investigation of Coffee Prices* (Washington, DC: US Government Printing Office, 1954), 39–40. Edmar Bacha, "Política brasileira de café," in Martins and Johnston, *150 Anos de Café,* 20; José Antonio Ocampo, *Colombia y la economia mundial, 1830–1910* (Bogotá: Siglo Veintiuno, 1984), 302–303; Mintz, *Sweetness and Power.*

383. Greenhill, "E. Johnston"; Greenhill, "Investment Group, Free-Standing Company or Multinational: Brazilian Warrant 1909–1952," *Business History* 37 (1995): 86–111; Siegfried Zimmerman, *Theodor Wille* (Hamburg: n.p., 1969). Also see Steven C. Topik and Mario Samper, "The Latin American Coffee Commodity Chain: Brazil and Costa Rica," in Topik et al., *From Silver to Cocaine.*

384. John Talbot, "The Struggle for the Control of a Commodity Chain: Instant Coffee from Latin America," *Latin American Research Review* 32 (1997); Talbot, *Grounds for Agreement: The Political Economy of the Coffee Commodity Chain* (Lanham, MD: Rowman and Littlefield, 2004), 140–156.

385. Martins and Johnston, *150 Anos de Café,* 371.

386. Richard Tucker, *Insatiable Appetite: The United States and the Ecological Degradation of the Tropical World* (Berkeley: University of California Press, 2000), 190–191.

387. Francis L. Fugate, *Arbuckles: The Coffee That Won the West* (El Paso: Texas Western Press, 1994).

388. Julia Laura Rieschbieter, "Kaffee im Kaiserreich: Eine Geschichte der Globalisierung" (PhD diss., Europea-Universität Viadrina Frankfurt, Oder, 2009).

389. *Spice Mill,* January 1912, 28. Little has been done on the history of consumption outside of North America and Western Europe, but one breakthrough study on Costa Rica is Patricia Vega Jiménez's *Con sabor a tertulia: Historia del consume del café en Costa Rica (1840–1940)* (San José: Editorial de la Universidad de Costa Rica, 2004). For a collection on European coffee drinking, see Daniela U. Ball, ed., *Kaffee im Speigel euopäischer Trinksitten* (Zurich: Johann Jacobs Museum, 1991).

390. M. E. Goetzinger, *History of the House of Arbuckle* (n.p.: The Percolator, 1921), 3; Zimmerman, *Theodor Wille,* 123; Morris Adelman, *A&P: A Study in Price-Cost Behavior and Public Policy* (Cambridge, MA: Harvard University Press, 1959). Richard S. Tedlow, *New and Improved: The Story of Mass Marketing in America* (New York: Basic Books, 1990); Levenstein, *Revolution at the Table.*

391. Quoted in William Ukers, *All about Coffee* (New York: Tea and Coffee Trade Journal, 1935), 466.

392. Stuart McCook, "Global Rust Belt: *Hemileia vastatrix* and the Ecological Integration of World Coffee Production since 1850," *Journal of Global History* 1, no. 2 (2006): 177–195.

393. Paul C. Daniels, "The Inter-American Coffee Agreement," *Law and Contemporary Problems* 8, no. 4 (Autumn, 1941): 708.

394. A new account of the British planting of tea in India by Sarah Rose has that name: *For All the Tea in China: How England Stole the World's Favorite Drink and Changed History* (New York: Viking, 2010).

395. William Ukers, *All about Tea* (New York: Tea and Coffee Trade Journal Co., 1935), 2:333.

396. *Statistical Year-Book of the League of Nations, 1925,* 58.

397. Ranajit das Gupta, "Plantation Labor in Colonial India," *Journal of Peasant Studies* 19, nos. 3–4 (1992): 173–198; Kavita Philip, *Civilizing Nature: Race, Resources, and Modernity in Colonial India* (New Brunswick, NJ: Rutgers University Press, 2004); Erika Rappaport, "Tea Parties: Britain, Empire and the Making of a Global Consumer Culture" (unpublished manuscript), chaps. 4 and 5; Mintz, *Sweetness and Power.*

398. Alan Macfarlane and Iris Macfarlane, *The Empire of Tea: The Remarkable History of the Plant That Took Over the World* (Woodstock, NY: Overlook, 2004), 195–197.

399. Ibid., quotation at 206. Also see Roy Moxham, *Tea: Addiction, Exploitation and Empire* (New York: Carroll and Graf, 2003), 127–155.

400. MacFarlane and MacFarlane, *The Empire of Tea,* 214.

401. Ibid., 199; Ukers, *All about Tea,* 2:334.

402. Ukers, *All about Tea,* 1:407.

403. Roland Wenzlhuemer, *From Coffee to Tea Cultivation in Ceylon, 1880–1900: An Economic and Social History* (Leiden: Brill, 2008), 316–317.

404. Erica Rappaport, "Packaging China: Foreign Articles and Dangerous Tastes in the Mid-Victorian Tea Party," in *The Making of the Consumer: Knowledge, Power and Identity in the Modern World,* ed. Frank Trentmann (London: Berg, 2006), 125–146; Ukers, *All about Tea,* 2:334, 345.

405. Fernando Rocchi, "From Consumption to Consumer Society: The Evolution of Demand in Argentina, 1920s–1940s" (paper presented at Institute of Latin American Studies, University of London, workshop, November 14–15, 2002); Rocchi, *Chimneys in the Desert: Industrialization in Argentina during the Export Boom Years, 1870–1930* (Stanford, CA: Stanford University Press, 2006).

406. Calculated from Ukers, *All about Tea,* 2:349, 350.

407. Robert Gardella, *Harvesting Mountains: Fujian and the China Tea Trade, 1757–1937* (Berkeley: University of California Press, 1994), 171, emphasis in the original.

408. Ukers, *All about Tea,* 2:334; Macfarlane and Macfarlane, *The Empire of Tea,* 99–165.

409. Lockwood, *Economic Development of Japan,* 357–358; Ukers, *All about Tea,* 2:328, 334.

410. Moxham, *Tea,* 202.

411. Ibid.

412. Sophie D. Coe, *America's First Cuisines* (Austin: University of Texas Press, 1994), 101–104; Murdo Macleod, "Cacao," in *Cambridge World History of Food,* vol. 1, ed. K. Kipler (Cambridge: Cambridge University Press, 2000), 635–640.

413. Mary Ann Mahoney, "The Local and the Global: Internal and External Factors in the Development of Bahia's Cacao Sector," in Topik et al., *From Silver to Cocaine,* 184–190; Courtwright, *Forces of Habit,* 23–25; Schivelbusch, *Tastes of Paradise.*

414. DuPuis, *Nature's Perfect Food;* Andrew F. Smith, *Eating History: Turning Points in the Making of American Cuisine* (New York: Columbia University Press, 2009), 127, 128.

415. *Cambridge World History of Food,* vol. 2, ed. Kiple and Ornelas, 1874–1875; Kuntz Ficker, *Las exportaciones mexicanas,* 350–357.

416. William Clarence-Smith, *Cocoa and Chocolate, 1765–1914* (London: Routledge, 2000), 238–239; Robin Dand, *The International Cocoa Trade* (New York: Wiley, for Woodhead Publishing, 1997), 15, 54; calculated from Dand, *International Cocoa Trade;* Mario Samper and Radin Fernando, "Appendix: Historical Statistics of Coffee Production and Trade from 1700 to 1960," in Clarence-Smith and Topik, *Global Coffee Economy,* 418; Ukers, *All about Tea,* 2:234.

417. Clarence-Smith, *Cocoa and Chocolate,* 7.

418. Ibid.

419. Ibid., 195–225.

420. Martin Booth, *Opium: A History* (New York: St. Martin's Griffin, 1996), 175–190; Gootenberg, *Andean Cocaine.*

421. O'Rourke and Williamson, *Globalization and History,* 3.

422. Ibid., 2.

5. Transnational Currents in a Shrinking World

1. Quoted in Nayan Chanda, *Bound Together: How Traders, Preachers, Adventurers, and Warriors Shaped Globalization* (New Haven, CT: Yale University Press, 2007), 127.

2. C. A. Bayly, *The Birth of the Modern World, 1780–1914: Global Connections and Comparisons* (Oxford: Blackwell, 2004), quotations at 476.

3. For a discussion of the emergence of the concept of "transnational" history, see Kiran Klaus Patel, "Überlegungen zu einer transnationalen Geschichte," in *Weltgeschichte,* ed. Jürgen Osterhammel (Stuttgart: Franz Steiner, 2008), 67–90; and Pierre-Yves Saunier, "Transnational," in *The Palgrave Dictionary of Transnational History from the Mid-nineteenth Century to the Present Day,* ed. Akira Iriye and Pierre-Yves Saunier (New York: Palgrave Macmillan, 2009), 1047–1055. Two examples are Sebastian Conrad and Jürgen Osterhammel, eds., *Das Kaiserreich transnational: Deutschland in der Welt, 1871–1914* (Göttingen: Vandenhoeck und Ruprecht, 2004); and Akira Iriye, *Global Community: The Role of International Organizations in the Making of the Contemporary World* (Berkeley: University of California Press, 2002).

4. Aihwa Ong, *Flexible Citizenship: The Cultural Logics of Transnationality* (Durham, NC: Duke University Press, 1999), is suggestive on this point.

5. Mary Louise Pratt, *Imperial Eyes: Travel Writing and Transculturation,* 2nd ed. (New York: Routledge, 2008); Anna Lowenhaupt Tsing, *Friction: An Ethnography of Global Connection* (Princeton, NJ: Princeton University Press, 2004).

6. The term *differentiated commonalities* is indebted to the idea of "structures of common difference," explored in Alys Eve Weinbaum et al., eds., *The Modern Girl Around the World: Consumption, Modernity, and Globalization* (Durham, NC: Duke University Press, 2008). On global/local, see essays in A. G. Hopkins, ed., *Global History: Interactions between the Universal and the Local* (New York: Palgrave, 2006).

7. Beyond conveying this broad sense of disjuncture, I am not using the word *modernity* as an analytical category with precise meaning. Rather I see the word *modernity* as the representation of

a claim that appeared frequently and transnationally over this period and helped animate a wide range of views and disputes over possible futures.

8. James C. Scott, *The Art of Not Being Governed: An Anarchist History of Upland Southeast Asia* (New Haven, CT: Yale University Press, 2009); Frederick Cooper, "What Is the Concept of Globalization Good For? An African Historian's Perspective," *African Affairs* 100 (2001): 189–213.

9. John Tomlinson, *Globalization and Culture* (Chicago: University of Chicago Press, 1999).

10. Albert Marrin, *Sir Norman Angell* (Boston: Twayne, 1979), quotation at 28.

11. *Independent,* February 27, 1913, quoted in J. D. B. Miller, *Norman Angell and the Futility of War: Peace and the Public Mind* (Houndmills, UK: Macmillan, 1986), 9.

12. K. C. Hsiao, *A Modern China and a New World: K'ang Yu-wei, Reformer and Utopian, 1858–1927* (Seattle: University of Washington Press, 1975), 456–460.

13. Helga Haftendorn, Robert O. Keohane, and Celeste A. Wallander, eds., *Imperfect Unions: Security Institutions over Time and Space* (New York: Oxford University Press, 1999), 1–2; Iriye, *Global Community.*

14. As communications networks expanded globally, struggles arose among communications companies, national policies, and advocates of international agreements: Daniel R. Headrick, *The Invisible Weapon: Telecommunications and International Politics, 1851–1945* (New York: Oxford University Press, 1991); Jill Hills, *The Struggle for Control of Global Communication: The Formative Century* (Champaign: University of Illinois Press, 2002); Dwayne R. Winseck and Robert M. Pike, *Communication and Empire: Media, Markets, and Globalization, 1860–1930* (Durham, NC: Duke University Press, 2007); and Jonathan Winkler, *Nexus: Strategic Communications and American Security in World War I* (Cambridge, MA: Harvard University Press, 2008). John Darwin, *The Empire Project: The Rise and Fall of the British World-System, 1830–1870* (Cambridge: Cambridge University Press, 2009), 25, stresses the importance of new communications in propelling Britain's global "empire project" in the late nineteenth century.

15. George A. Codding Jr. and Anthony M. Rutkowski, *The International Telecommunication Union in a Changing World* (Dedham, MA: Artech House, 1982), 3.

16. George A. Codding Jr., *The Universal Postal Union: Coordinator of the International Mails* (New York: NYU Press, 1964); *The Universal Postal Union: Its Creation and Development* (Berne: Universal Postal Union, 1974).

17. David M. Henkin, *The Postal Age: The Emergence of Modern Communications in Nineteenth-Century America* (Chicago: University of Chicago Press, 2006), charts postal connections across the United States.

18. On the standardization of time zones, see Clark Blaise, *Time Lord: Sir Sandford Fleming and the Creation of Standard Time* (New York: Pantheon Books, 2000).

19. Stephen Kern, *The Culture of Time and Space, 1880–1918* (Cambridge, MA: Harvard University Press, 1983).

20. Nils Brunsson and Bengt Jacobsson, *A World of Standards* (Oxford: Oxford University Press, 2000); Miloš Vec, *Recht und Normierung in der industriellen Revolution: Neue Strukturen der Normsetzung in Völkerrecht, staatlicher Gesetzgebung und gesellschaftlicher Selbstnormierung*

(Frankfurt am Main: Klostermann, 2006); the first half of James W. Nixon, *A History of the International Statistical Institute, 1885–1960* (The Hague: International Statistical Institute, 1960); J. Adam Tooze, *Statistics and the German State, 1900–1945: The Making of Modern Economic Knowledge* (Cambridge: Cambridge University Press, 2001).

21. Martin H. Geyer and Johannes Paulmann, eds., *The Mechanics of Internationalism: Culture, Society, and Politics from the 1840s to the First World War* (Oxford: Oxford University Press, 2001).

22. John E. Findling and Kimberly D. Pelle, eds., *Historical Dictionary of the Modern Olympic Movement* (Westport CT: Greenwood Press, 1996); Allen Guttmann, *The Olympics: A History of the Modern Games,* 2nd ed. (Champaign: University of Illinois Press, 2002), 7–84.

23. Maurice Roche, *Mega-events and Modernity: Olympics and Expos in the Growth of Global Culture* (London: Routledge, 2000), 108.

24. Barbara J. Keys, *Globalizing Sport: National Rivalry and International Community in the 1930s* (Cambridge, MA: Harvard University Press, 2006); David Clay Large, *Nazi Games: The Olympics of 1936* (New York: W. W. Norton, 2007).

25. Martti Koskenniemi, *The Gentle Civilizer of Nations: The Rise and Fall of International Law, 1870–1960* (Cambridge: Cambridge University Press, 2002), 11–97.

26. Jürgen Osterhammel, *Europe, the "West" and the Civilizing Mission* (London: German Historical Institute, 2006). On the intersection between colonialism and international law, see Wilhelm G. Grewe, *The Epochs of International Law,* trans. Michael Byers (Berlin: Walter de Gruyter, 2000), 445–524; Antony Anghie, *Imperialism, Sovereignty, and the Making of International Law* (Cambridge: Cambridge University Press, 2005).

27. Arthur Eyffinger, *The 1899 Hague Peace Conference: "The Parliament of Man, the Federation of the World"* (The Hague: Kluwer Academic, 1999), 365.

28. Quoted in Merze Tate, *The Disarmament Illusion: The Movement for a Limitation of Armaments to 1907* (New York: Russell and Russell, 1942), 55.

29. Multilateral conventions signed between 1890 and 1940 are in "Miscellaneous Historical Documents," http://fletcher.tufts.edu/multi/chrono.html#99.

30. Jost Dülffer, *Regeln gegen den Krieg? Die Haager Friedenskonferenzen von 1899 und 1907 in der internationalen Politik* (Frankfurt am Main: Ullstein, 1981).

31. Raymond L. Bridgman, *The First Book of World Law* (Boston: Ginn and Co., 1911).

32. Gary B. Ostrower, *The League of Nations from 1919 to 1929* (Garden City Park, NY: Avery, 1996); Thomas W. Burkman, *Japan and the League of Nations: Empire and World Order, 1914–1938* (Honolulu: University of Hawai'i Press, 2008).

33. Thomas J. Knock, *To End All Wars: Woodrow Wilson and the Quest for a New World Order* (New York: Oxford University Press, 1992).

34. John Milton Cooper Jr., *Woodrow Wilson: A Biography* (New York: Knopf, 2009), 362–534; Derek B. Heater, *National Self-Determination: Woodrow Wilson and His Legacy* (Basingstoke, UK: Macmillan, 1994).

35. JoAnne Pemberton, "New Worlds for Old: The League of Nations in the Age of Electricity," *Review of International Studies* 28 (2002): 311.

36. Several essays in Paul Weindling, ed., *International Health Organisations and Movements, 1918–1939* (Cambridge: Cambridge University Press, 1995).

37. Jasmien Van Daele, "Engineering Social Peace: Networks, Ideas, and the Founding of the International Labour Organization," *International Review of Social History* 50 (2005): 435–466.

38. Susan Pedersen, "The Meaning of the Mandates System: An Argument," *Geschichte und Gesellschaft* 32 (2006): 560–582; Erez Manela, *The Wilsonian Moment: Self-Determination and the International Origins of Anticolonial Nationalism* (Oxford: Oxford University Press, 2007).

39. Norman Angell, *Peace and the Public Mind: Nobel Peace Lecture Delivered at Oslo, June 12, 1935* (Stockholm: P. A. Norstedt, 1935).

40. Mark Mazower, *Hitler's Empire: How the Nazis Ruled Europe* (New York: Penguin Press, 2008); Louise Young, *Japan's Total Empire: Manchuria and the Culture of Wartime Imperialism* (Berkeley: University of California Press, 1998); Prasenjit Duara, *Sovereignty and Authenticity: Manchukuo and the East Asian Modern* (Lanham, MD: Rowman and Littlefield, 2003), 70–71.

41. Akira Iriye, *The Globalizing of America, 1913–1945,* vol. 3 of *The Cambridge History of American Foreign Relations,* ed. Warren I. Cohen (New York: Cambridge University Press, 1995), 116–215.

42. Elizabeth Borgwardt, *A New Deal for the World: America's Vision for Human Rights* (Cambridge, MA: Harvard University Press, 2005); more critical perspectives are reviewed in Sunil S. Amrith and Glenda Sluga, "New Histories of the United Nations," *Journal of World History* 19 (2008): 251–274; and Mark Mazower, *No Enchanted Palace: The End of Empire and the Ideological Origins of the United Nations* (Princeton, NJ: Princeton University Press, 2009), 28–31.

43. On "cultural internationalism," see Akira Iriye, *Cultural Internationalism and World Order* (Baltimore: Johns Hopkins University Press, 1997).

44. Pierre Janton, *Esperanto: Language, Literature, and Community,* ed. Humphrey Tonkin, trans. Humphrey Tonkin, Jane Edwards, and Karen Johnson-Weiner (Albany: SUNY Press, 1993), xii.

45. Young S. Kim, "Constructing a Global Identity: The Role of Esperanto," in *Constructing World Culture: International Nongovernmental Organizations since 1875,* ed. John Boli and George M. Thomas (Stanford, CA: Stanford University Press, 1999), 127–148, quotation at 147.

46. "The Photographs of John Thompson," at http://www.nls.uk/thomson/index.html.

47. David Okuefuna, *The Dawn of the Color Photograph: Albert Kahn's Archives of the Planet* (Princeton, NJ: Princeton University Press, 2008); Jay M. Winter, *Dreams of Peace and Freedom: Utopian Moments in the Twentieth Century* (New Haven, CT: Yale University Press, 2006), 11–28.

48. Barbara D. Metcalf and Thomas R. Metcalf, *A Concise History of Modern India,* 2nd ed. (Cambridge: Cambridge University Press, 2006), 112–113. See also James R. Ryan, *Picturing Empire: Photography and the Visualization of the British Empire* (Chicago: University of Chicago Press, 1997), 155–175; Christopher Pinney, *Camera Indica: The Social Life of Indian Photographs* (Chicago: University of Chicago Press, 1997), 34–60; John Falconer, "'A Pure Labor of Love': A Publishing History of *The People of India,*" in *Colonialist Photography: Imag(in)ing Race and Place,* ed. Eleanor M. Hight and Gary D. Sampson (London: Routledge, 2002), 51–83.

49. Jürgen Osterhammel, *Die Verwandlung der Welt: Eine Geschichte des 19. Jahrhunderts* (Munich: C. H. Beck, 2009), 79.

50. Many of the essays in Hight and Sampson, *Colonialist Photography,* develop these themes; Rosalind C. Morris, ed., *Photographies East: The Camera and Its Histories in East and Southeast Asia* (Durham, NC: Duke University Press, 2009).

51. Laura Wexler, *Tender Violence: Domestic Visions in an Age of U.S. Imperialism* (Chapel Hill: University of North Carolina Press, 2000); Alexander Missal, *Seaway to the Future: American Social Visions and the Construction of the Panama Canal* (Madison: University of Wisconsin Press, 2008), 95–108.

52. Vicente Rafael, *White Love and Other Events in Filipino History* (Durham, NC: Duke University Press, 2000), quotation at 86; Leonard Bell, "Eyeing Samoa: People, Places, and Spaces in Photographs of the Late Nineteenth and Early Twentieth Centuries," in *Tropical Visions in an Age of Empire,* ed. Felix Driver and Luciana Martins (Chicago: University of Chicago Press, 2005), 156–174; Esther Gabara, *Errant Modernism: The Ethos of Photography in Mexico and Brazil* (Durham, NC: Duke University Press, 2008).

53. David Welch, *The Third Reich: Politics and Propaganda,* 2nd ed. (London: Routledge, 2002).

54. David Brion Davis, *Inhuman Bondage: The Rise and Fall of Slavery in the New World* (Oxford: Oxford University Press, 2006), 323–331; Suzanne Miers, *Slavery in the Twentieth Century: The Evolution of a Global Problem* (Lanham, MD: Rowman and Littlefield, 2003); Adam Hochschild, *Bury the Chains: Prophets and Rebels in the Fight to Free an Empire's Slaves* (Boston: Houghton Mifflin, 2005); Patrick Manning, *The African Diaspora: A History through Culture* (New York: Columbia University Press, 2009), 209–282. William Gervase Clarence-Smith, *Islam and the Abolition of Slavery* (New York: Oxford University Press, 2006), examines the uneven pace of abolition in the Islamic world and how its continued practice in some places was used to help justify colonialism.

55. Harvey Goldberg, *The Life of Jean Jaurés* (Madison: University of Wisconsin Press, 2003).

56. Marcel van der Linden, *Transnational Labour History: Explorations* (Aldershot, UK: Ashgate, 2003), 75–76; Francis Shor, "Masculine Power and Virile Syndicalism: A Gendered Analysis of the IWW in Australia," *Labour History* 63 (1992): 83–99.

57. John Riddell, ed., *To See the Dawn: Baku, 1920—First Congress of the Peoples of the East* (New York: Pathfinder Press, 1993).

58. Robert Service, *Comrades! A History of World Communism* (Cambridge, MA: Harvard University Press, 2007).

59. Patricia Ward D'Itri, *Cross Currents in the International Women's Movement, 1848–1948* (Bowling Green, OH: Bowling Green State University Popular Press, 1999), 101.

60. Rajmohan Gandhi, *Gandhi: The Man, His People, and the Empire* (Berkeley: University of California Press, 2008).

61. Sugata Bose, *A Hundred Horizons: The Indian Ocean in the Age of Global Empire* (Cambridge, MA: Harvard University Press, 2006), 31.

62. Tony Ballantyne and Antoinette Burton, "Empires and the Reach of the Global," in this volume; Josephine Fowler, *Japanese and Chinese Immigrant Activists: Organizing in American and International Communist Movements, 1919–1933* (New Brunswick, NJ: Rutgers University Press, 2007); Jonathan Derrick, *Africa's 'Agitators': Militant Anti-colonialism in Africa and the West, 1918–1939* (London: Hurst, 2008).

63. Marilyn Lake and Henry Reynolds, *Drawing the Global Colour Line: White Men's Countries and the International Challenge of Racial Equality* (Cambridge: Cambridge University Press, 2008), 246. On Du Bois, see David Levering Lewis, *W. E. B. DuBois: Biography of a Race, 1868–1919* (New York: Henry Holt, 1993); and Lewis, *W. E. B. DuBois: The Fight for Equality and the American Century, 1919–1963* (New York: Henry Holt, 2000).

64. Saheed A. Adejumobi, "The Pan-African Congress," in *Organizing Black America: An Encyclopedia of African American Associations,* ed. Nina Mjagkij (New York: Garland, 2001); Derrick, *Africa's 'Agitators.'*

65. Colin Grant, *Negro with a Hat: The Rise and Fall of Marcus Garvey* (New York: Oxford University Press, 2008).

66. Gary Wilder, *The French Imperial Nation-State: Negritude and Colonial Humanism between the Two World Wars* (Chicago: University of Chicago Press 2005), 252.

67. Paul Gilroy, *The Black Atlantic: Modernity and Double Consciousness* (Cambridge, MA: Harvard University Press, 1993).

68. James T. Campbell, *Middle Passages: African American Journeys to Africa, 1787–2005* (New York: Penguin Press, 2006); Kevin Kelly Gaines, *American Africans in Ghana: Black Expatriates and the Civil Rights Era* (Chapel Hill: University of North Carolina Press, 2006); Winston James, *Holding Aloft the Banner of Ethiopia: Caribbean Radicalism in Early Twentieth-Century America* (New York: Verso, 1998).

69. Duara, *Sovereignty and Authenticity.*

70. The expression "international nationalism" is used by Michael Brenner in *Zionism: A Brief History,* trans. Shelley Frisch (Princeton, NJ: Markus Wiener, 2003), 255–318. A more controversial history of the Jews is Shlomo Sand, *The Invention of the Jewish People,* trans. Yael Lotan (New York: Verso, 2009).

71. Bayly, *Birth of the Modern World,* quotation at 362.

72. Diarmaid MacCulloch, *Christianity: The First Three Thousand Years* (New York: Viking, 2010), 915.

73. Harold Fischer-Tiné, "Global Civil Society and the Forces of Empire: The Salvation Army, British Imperialism, and the 'Prehistory' of NGOs," in *Competing Visions of World Order: Global Moments and Movements, 1880s–1930s,* ed. Sebastian Conrad and Dominic Sachsenmaier (London: Palgrave Macmillan, 2007), 30–31.

74. Sherwood Eddy, *A Pilgrimage of Ideas; or, the Reeducation of Sherwood Eddy* (New York: Farrar and Rinehart, 1934), quotation at 59; Ian R. Tyrrell, *Reforming the World: The Creation of America's Moral Empire* (Princeton, NJ: Princeton University Press, 2010), 49–89.

75. Merle Curti, *American Philanthropy Abroad: A History* (New Brunswick, NJ: Rutgers University Press, 1963), 134–174.

76. Dana L. Robert, *Christian Mission: How Christianity Became a World Religion* (Malden, MA: Wiley-Blackwell, 2009), 62–63; MacCulloch, *Christianity,* 879–882.

77. Adam Mohr, "Capitalism, Chaos, and Christian Healing: Faith Tabernacle Congregation in Southern Colonial Ghana, 1918–26," *Journal of African History* 52 (2011): 63–83.

78. Robert, *Christian Mission,* 56–64; J. P. Daughton, *An Empire Divided: Religion, Republicanism, and the Making of French Colonialism, 1880–1914* (New York: Oxford University Press, 2006).

79. Robert Bickers, *Britain in China: Community, Culture, and Colonialism, 1900–1949* (Manchester: Manchester University Press, 1999), 92–94.

80. For the complicated relationship between British missionary activity and empire, see Andrew N. Porter, *Religion versus Empire? British Protestant Missionaries and Overseas Expansion, 1700–1914* (Manchester: Manchester University Press, 2004); and Richard Price, *Making Empire: Colonial Encounters and the Creation of Imperial Rule in Nineteenth-Century Africa* (New York: Cambridge University Press, 2008).

81. Robert, *Christian Mission*, 159–171.

82. Sean Hanretta, *Islam and Social Change in French West Africa: History of an Emancipatory Community* (New York: Cambridge University Press, 2009); Donald R. Wright, *The World and a Very Small Place in Africa* (Armonk, NY: M. E. Sharpe, 1997), 197–200.

83. Ira M. Lapidus, *A History of Islamic Societies,* rev. ed. (New York: Cambridge University Press 2002); see also David Gilmartin, "A Networked Civilization?" in *Muslim Networks from Hajj to Hip Hop,* ed. Miriam Cooke and Bruce B. Lawrence (Chapel Hill: University of North Carolina Press, 2005), 51–68.

84. Quotation from Bose, *A Hundred Horizons,* 195.

85. Ghislaine Lydon, *On Trans-Saharan Trails: Islamic Law, Trade Networks, and Cross-Cultural Exchange in Nineteenth-Century Western Africa* (Cambridge: Cambridge University Press, 2009). The interface between Islam and Christianity is illuminated in Benjamin F. Soares, ed., *Muslim-Christian Encounters in Africa* (Leiden: Brill, 2006); and Roman Loimeier and Rüdiger Seesemann, *The Global Worlds of the Swahili: Interfaces of Islam, Identity and Space in 19th- and 20th-Century East Africa* (Berlin: LIT, 2006).

86. Robert R. Bianchi, *Guests of God: Pilgrimage and Politics in the Islamic World* (New York: Oxford University Press, 2004), 42–46.

87. Bose, *A Hundred Horizons,* 232; Ayesha Jalal, *Self and Sovereignty: Individual and Community in South Asian Islam since 1850* (London: Routledge, 2000), 188–189.

88. P. R. Bhuyan, *Swami Vivekananda: Messiah of Resurgent India* (New Delhi: Atlantic, 2003), 22; Dorothea Lüddeckens, *Das Weltparlament der Religionen von 1893: Strukturen interreligiöser Begegnung im 19. Jahrhundert* (Berlin: Walter de Gruyter, 2002).

89. Gauri Viswanathan, *Outside the Fold: Conversion, Modernity, and Belief* (Princeton, NJ: Princeton University Press, 1998), 177–209.

90. Jacob K. Olupona and Terry Rey, eds., *Òrìṣà Devotion as World Religion: The Globalization of Yorùbá Religious Culture* (Madison: University of Wisconsin Press, 2008).

91. Richard J. Evans, *The Feminists: Women's Emancipation Movements in Europe, America and Australasia, 1840–1920* (London: Croom Helm, 1977); Leila Rupp, *Worlds of Women: The Making of an International Women's Movement* (Princeton, NJ: Princeton University Press, 1997); and Karen M. Offen, *European Feminisms, 1700–1950: A Political History* (Stanford, CA: Stanford University Press, 2000), suggest the diversity of goals.

92. Nitza Berkovitch, *From Motherhood to Citizenship: Women's Rights and International Organizations* (Baltimore: Johns Hopkins University Press, 1999), surveys major issues for advocacy.

93. Albert Hourani, *A History of the Arab Peoples* (Cambridge, MA: Harvard University Press, 1991), 345.

94. Ian R. Tyrrell, *Woman's World / Woman's Empire: The Woman's Christian Temperance Union in International Perspective, 1880–1930* (Chapel Hill: University of North Carolina Press, 1991).

95. D'Itri, *Cross Currents,* 163.

96. Padma Anagol, *Emergence of Feminism in India, 1850–1920* (Aldershot, UK: Ashgate, 2005); Gauri Viswanathan, *Outside the Fold: Conversion, Modernity, and Belief* (Princeton, NJ: Princeton University Press, 1998), 118–152.

97. Quoted from Catt's journal in D'Itri, *Cross Currents,* 104.

98. Rupp, *Worlds of Women,* 60–62.

99. Provocative works include Ann Laura Stoler, *Carnal Knowledge and Imperial Power: Race and the Intimate in Colonial Rule,* 2nd ed. (Berkeley: University of California Press, 2 ed., 2010); Ulrike Strasser and Heidi Tinsman, "It's a Man's World? World History Meets the History of Masculinity, in Latin American Studies, for Instance," *Journal of World History* 21 (2010): 75–96; and Leela Gandhi, *Affective Communities: Anticolonial Thought, Fin-de-Siècle Radicalism, and the Politics of Friendship* (Durham, NC: Duke University Press, 2006).

100. For example, the first attempt to sketch the outlines of a global history of scouting organizations may be found in Nelson R. Block and Tammy R. Proctor, eds., *Scouting Frontiers: Youth and the Scout Movement's First Century* (Newcastle upon Tyne, UK: Cambridge Scholars, 2009).

101. Thomas Richards, *The Imperial Archive: Knowledge and the Fantasy of Empire* (London: Verso, 1993), 1–9, quotation at 4. See also Tony Bennett, *The Birth of the Museum: History, Theory, Politics* (London: Routledge, 1995).

102. See John E. Findling and Kimberly D. Pelle, eds., *Encyclopedia of World's Fairs and Expositions,* rev. 2nd ed. (Jefferson, NC: McFarland, 2008).

103. Hermione Hobhouse, *Crystal Palace and the Great Exhibition: Art, Science, Productive Industry* (London: Athlone Press, 2004); Peter Henry Hoffenberg, *An Empire on Display: English, Indian and Australian Exhibitions from the Crystal Palace to the Great War* (Berkeley: University of California Press, 2001).

104. Lara Kriegel, *Grand Designs: Labor, Empire, and the Museum in Victorian Culture* (Durham, NC: Duke University Press, 2007), 16.

105. Paul Young, "Mission Impossible: Globalization and the Great Exhibition," in *Britain, the Empire, and the World at the Great Exhibition of 1851,* ed. Jeffrey A. Auerbach and Peter H. Hoffenberg (Aldershot, UK: Ashgate, 2008), quotation at 11.

106. Jeffrey A. Auerbach, *The Great Exhibition of 1851: A Nation on Display* (New Haven, CT: Yale University Press, 1999).

107. Zeynep Çelik, *Displaying the Orient: Architecture and Islam at Nineteenth-Century World's Fairs* (Berkeley: University of California Press, 1992), quotation at 152.

108. Quoted in Paul Greenhalgh, *Ephemeral Vistas: The Expositions Universelles, Great Exhibitions, and World's Fairs, 1851–1939* (Manchester: Manchester University Press, 1988), 88.

109. Annegret Fauser, *Musical Encounters at the 1889 Paris World's Fair* (Rochester, NY: University of Rochester Press, 2005), 183–206.

110. Quoted in Charles Desnoyers, "'Toward One Enlightened and Progressive Civilization': Discourses of Expansion and Nineteenth Century Chinese Missions Abroad," *Journal of World History* 8 (1997): 135–156, quotation at 152.

111. Quotations from http://libwww.library.phila.gov/CenCol/exh-testimony.htm.

112. Camilla Fojas, "American Cosmopolis: The World's Columbian Exposition and Chicago across the Americas," *Comparative Literature Studies* 42 (2005): 264–287.

113. John E. Findling, *Chicago's Great World's Fairs* (Manchester: Manchester University Press, 1994), 27.

114. Christopher Robert Reed, *All the World Is Here! The Black Presence at White City* (Bloomington: Indiana University Press, 2000).

115. Lee D. Baker, *From Savage to Negro: Anthropology and the Construction of Race, 1896–1954* (Berkeley: University of California Press, 1998), 26.

116. Daniel T. Rodgers, *Atlantic Crossings: Social Politics in a Progressive Age* (Cambridge, MA: Harvard University Press, 1998), 20.

117. Richard D. Mandell, *Paris 1900: The Great World's Fair* (Toronto: University of Toronto Press, 1967); Diana P. Fischer, et al., eds., *Paris 1900: The "American School" at the Universal Exposition* (New Brunswick, NJ: Rutgers University Press, 1999); Patricia Morton, *Hybrid Modernities: Architecture and Representation at the 1931 Colonial Exposition, Paris* (Cambridge, MA: MIT Press, 2000).

118. Çelik, *Displaying the Orient,* 49.

119. Quoted in Greenhalgh, *Ephemeral Vistas,* 83.

120. Robert W. Rydell, *All the World's a Fair: Visions of Empire at American International Expositions, 1876–1916* (Chicago: University of Chicago Press, 1984).

121. Morton, *Hybrid Modernities.*

122. David Levering Lewis and Deborah Willis, *A Small Nation of People: W. E. B. DuBois and African-American Portraits of Progress* (New York: Amistad, 2003).

123. Findling, *Chicago's Great World's Fairs,* 124–126; Robert W. Rydell, *World of Fairs: The Century-of-Progress Expositions* (Chicago: University of Chicago Press, 1993); Cheryl R. Ganz, *The 1933 Chicago World's Fair: A Century of Progress* (Champaign: University of Illinois Press, 2008).

124. Winter, *Dreams of Peace and Freedom,* 86.

125. Bennett, *Birth of the Museum.*

126. H. Glenn Penny, *Objects of Culture: Ethnology and Ethnographic Museums in Imperial Germany* (Chapel Hill: University of North Carolina Press, 2002); Rainer F. Buschmann, *Anthropology's Global Histories: The Ethnographic Frontier in German New Guinea, 1870–1935* (Honolulu: University of Hawai'i Press, 2009).

127. Carla Yanni, *Nature's Museums: Victorian Science and the Architecture of Display* (London: Athlone Press, 1999), 144–146.

128. Maria Margaret Lopes and Irina Podgorny, "The Shaping of Latin American Museums of Natural History, 1850–1990," in *Nature and Empire: Science and the Colonial Enterprise,* ed. Roy MacLeod (Chicago: University of Chicago Press, 2000), 108–118.

129. Robert E. Kohler, *All Creatures: Naturalists, Collectors, and Biodiversity, 1850–1950* (Princeton, NJ: Princeton University Press, 2006), 111, 117; Lopes and Podgorny, "Latin American Museums," 116.

130. Bennett, *Birth of the Museum.*

131. Kenn Harper, *Give Me My Father's Body: The Life of Minik, the New York Eskimo* (New York: Washington Square Press, 2001). For background, see Michael F. Robinson, *The Coldest Crucible: Arctic Exploration and American Culture* (Chicago: University of Chicago Press, 2006).

132. Young-tsu Wong, *A Paradise Lost: The Imperial Garden Yuanming Yuan* (Honolulu: University of Hawai'i Press, 2001), quotation at 160; James L. Hevia, *English Lessons: The Pedagogy of Imperialism in Nineteenth-Century China* (Durham, NC: Duke University Press, 2003).

133. Michael A. Osborne, "Acclimatizing the World," in MacLeod, *Nature and Empire,* 135–151.

134. Darin Kinsey, " 'Seeding the Water as the Earth': The Epicenter and Peripheries of a Western Aquacultural Revolution," *Environmental History* 11 (July 2006): 527–566, quotation at 550.

135. C. Wayne Smith and J. Tom Cothren, eds., *Cotton: Origin, History, Technology, and Production* (New York: John Wiley, 1999), 159; Thomas Kearney, "Louis Trabut: Botanist and Plant Breeder," *Journal of Heredity* 13 (1922): 153–160.

136. Richard H. Drayton, *Nature's Government: Science, Imperial Britain, and the "Improvement" of the World* (New Haven, CT: Yale University Press, 2000); Ray Desmond, *The History of the Royal Botanic Gardens Kew* (London: Royal Botanic Gardens, Kew, 2007).

137. Lucile H. Brockway, *Science and Colonial Expansion: The Role of the British Royal Botanic Gardens* (New York: Academic Press, 1979), 101.

138. Christophe Bonneuil, "The Manufacture of Species: Kew Gardens, The Empire, and the Standardisation of Taxonomic Practices in Late Nineteenth-Century Botany," in *Instruments, Travel, and Science: Itineraries of Precision from the Seventeenth to the Twentieth Century,* ed. Marie-Noëlle Bourguet, Christian Licoppe, and H. Otto Sibum (London: Routledge, 2002), 189–215.

139. Brockway, *Science and Colonial Expansion,* 102, 124.

140. Fa-ti Fan, *British Naturalists in Qing China: Science, Empire, and Cultural Encounter* (Cambridge, MA: Harvard University Press, 2004), 110–154, examines the textual and interpersonal practices involved in the cross-cultural exchange of information about plants and animals.

141. Ernst Mayr, "In Memorium: Jean (Theodore) Delacour," *The Auk* 103 (1986): 603–605.

142. Elizabeth Hanson, *Animal Attractions: Nature on Display in American Zoos* (Princeton, NJ: Princeton University Press, 2002), 14; Eric Baratay and Elisabeth Hardouin-Fugier, *Zoo: A History of Zoological Gardens in the West,* trans. Oliver Welsh (London: Reaktion Books, 2002); Vernon N. Kisling Jr., ed., *Zoo and Aquarium History: Ancient Animal Collections to Zoological Gardens* (Boca Raton, FL: CRC Press, 2001).

143. Baratay and Hardouin-Fugier, *Zoo,* 135–136.

144. Hanson, *Animal Attractions,* 1–40. Quote from Robert J. Hoage and William A. Deiss, eds., *New Worlds, New Animals: From Menagerie to Zoological Park in the Nineteenth Century* (Baltimore: Johns Hopkins University Press, 1996), x; see Michael A. Osborne, "Zoos in the Family: The Geoffroy Saint-Hilaire Clan and the Three Zoos of Paris," in Hoage and Deiss, *New Worlds, New Animals,* 33–42.

145. Nigel Rothfels, *Savages and Beasts: The Birth of the Modern Zoo* (Baltimore: Johns Hopkins University Press, 2002).

146. Hanson, *Animal Attractions,* 79.

147. Quotation in ibid., 112.

148. Ibid., 117–118.

149. Oliver H. Orr Jr., *Saving American Birds: T. Gilbert Pearson and the Founding of the Audubon Movement* (Gainesville: University of Florida Press, 1992); Hilda Kean, *Animal Rights: Political and Social Change in Britain since 1800* (London: Reaktion, 1998); Mark Cioc, *The Game of Conservation: International Treaties to Protect the World's Migratory Animals* (Athens: Ohio University Press, 2009), 14–57.

150. John M. MacKenzie, *The Empire of Nature: Hunting, Conservation, and British Imperialism* (Manchester: Manchester University Press, 1988); Alexandra Minna Stern, *Eugenic Nation: Faults and Frontiers of Better Breeding in Modern America* (Berkeley: University of California Press, 2005); Thomas Lekan, *Imagining the Nation: Landscape Preservation and German Identity, 1885–1945* (Cambridge, MA: Harvard University Press, 2004), 262; Jane Carruthers, "Creating a National Park, 1910–1925," *Journal of Southern Africa Studies* 15 (January 1989): 188–216.

151. On Japan, see William G. Beasley, *Japan Encounters the Barbarian: Japanese Travellers in America and Europe* (New Haven, CT: Yale University Press, 1995), 157–177; on China, Benjamin A. Elman, *A Cultural History of Modern Science in China* (Cambridge, MA: Harvard University Press, 2006), 132–157. Elman points out, however, that many of these missionary-inspired works hardly mentioned Darwin or evolutionary thought, so the Western science they brought to China had distinctive omissions.

152. The phrase "shared developmentalist project" comes from Kenneth Pomeranz, introduction to *The Environment and World History,* ed. Edmund Burke III and Kenneth Pomeranz (Berkeley: University of California Press, 2009).

153. Peter Wagner, "Introduction to Part I," in *Transnational Intellectual Networks: Forms of Academic Knowledge and the Search for Cultural Identities,* ed. Christophe Charle, Jürgen Schriewer, and Peter Wagner (Frankfurt: Campus, 2004), quotation at 17.

154. Michael Adas, *Machines as the Measure of Men: Science, Technology, and Ideologies of Western Dominance* (Ithaca, NY: Cornell University Press, 1989), 156–162, 339, makes the point that the use of technology, even more than racial ideology, constructed the social categories that encompassed "advanced" and "backward" peoples. See also Daniel R. Headrick, *The Tools of Empire: Technology and European Imperialism in the Nineteenth Century* (New York: Oxford University Press, 1981); Headrick, *The Tentacles of Progress: Technology Transfer in the Age of Imperialism, 1850–1940* (New York: Oxford University Press, 1988); and Headrick, *Power over Peoples: Technology, Environments, and Western Imperialism, 1400 to the Present* (Princeton, NJ: Princeton University Press, 2010).

155. S. Irfan Habib and Dhruv Raina, eds., *Social History of Science in Colonial India* (New Delhi: Oxford University Press, 2007), introduction.

156. For the emphasis on circulation and coproduction, see Kapil Raj, *Relocating Modern Science: Circulation and the Construction of Knowledge in South Asia and Europe, 1650–1900* (New York: Palgrave, 2007); and see David Turnbull, "Travelling Knowledge: Narratives, Assemblage and Encounters," in Bourguet, Licoppe, and Sibum, *Instruments, Travel, and Science,* 273–294, along with other essays in that volume.

157. Michael Shermer, *In Darwin's Shadow: The Life and Science of Alfred Russel Wallace* (New York: Oxford University Press, 2002), 258–261.

158. John Noble Wilford, *The Mapmakers: The Story of the Great Pioneers in Cartography from Antiquity to the Space Age* (New York: Knopf, 1981), pt. 2; Raj, *Relocating Modern Science*, 181–222; John Keay, *The Great Arc: The Dramatic Tale of How India Was Mapped and Everest Was Named* (London: HarperCollins, 2000).

159. Donald Worster, *A River Running West: The Life of John Wesley Powell* (New York: Oxford University Press, 2001); Paul N. Edison, "Conquest Unrequited: French Expeditionary Science in Mexico, 1864–1867," *French Historical Studies* 26 (2003): 459–495; Francis Sejersted, *The Age of Social Democracy: Norway and Sweden in the Twentieth Century,* trans. Richard Daly (Princeton, NJ: Princeton University Press, 2011), quotation at 17.

160. Ian J. Barrow, *Making History, Drawing Territory: British Mapping in India, c. 1765–1905* (New Delhi: Oxford University Press, 2003). For background, see Matthew H. Edney, *Mapping an Empire: The Geographical Construction of British India, 1765–1843* (Chicago: University of Chicago Press, 1997).

161. Rafael, *White Love.*

162. Suzanne L. Marchand, *Down from Olympus: Archaeology and Philhellenism in Germany, 1750–1970* (Princeton, NJ: Princeton University Press, 1996); Stephen L. Dyson, *In Pursuit of Ancient Pasts: A History of Classical Archaeology in the Nineteenth and Twentieth Centuries* (New Haven, CT: Yale University Press, 2006), which stresses the role in nationalism and museum building in Europe; Michael D. Coe, *Breaking the Maya Code* (London: Thames and Hudson, 1992); Neil Asher Silberman, *Digging for God and Country: Exploration, Archeology, and the Secret Struggle for the Holy Land, 1799–1917* (New York: Alfred A. Knopf, 1982), 147–170; and David A. Traill, *Schliemann of Troy: Treasure and Deceit* (New York: St. Martin's Press, 1995).

163. Blaise, *Time Lord,* 67.

164. Julie Greene, *The Canal Builders: Making America's Empire at the Panama Canal* (New York: Penguin Press, 2009).

165. Zaheer Baber, "Science, Technology, and Colonial Power," and Russell Dionne and Roy Mac-Leod, "Science and Policy in British India, 1858–1914: Perspectives on a Persisting Belief," both in Habib and Raina, *Science in Colonial India,* 102–158, 159–195. On British colonialism, expertise, and agrarian development in Africa, see Joseph Morgan Hodge, *Triumph of the Expert: Agrarian Doctrines of Development and the Legacies of British Colonialism* (Athens: Ohio University Press, 2007).

166. Edmund Burke III, "The Transformation of the Middle Eastern Environment, 1500 B.C.E.–2000 C.E.," in Burke and Pomeranz, *Environment and World History,* 99.

167. Elman, *Modern Science in China,* 158–181; William C. Kirby, *Germany and Republican China* (Stanford, CA: Stanford University Press, 1984).

168. Essays in Ardath W. Burks, ed., *The Modernizers: Overseas Students, Foreign Employees and Meiji Japan* (Boulder, CO: Westview Press, 1985).

169. Quoted in Beasley, *Japan Encounters the Barbarian,* 223.

170. Mark Cioc, *The Rhine: An Eco-Biography, 1815–2000* (Seattle: University of Washington Press, 2002); David Blackbourn, *The Conquest of Nature: Water, Landscape, and the Making of Mod-

ern Germany (New York: Norton, 2006), 189–303; Kenneth Pomeranz, "China's Environment, 1500–2000," in Burke and Pomeranz, *Environment and World History,* 135; William Kirby, "Engineering China: Birth of the Developmental States, 1928–1937," in *Becoming Chinese: Passages to Modernity and Beyond,* ed. Wen-hsin Yeh (Berkeley: University of California Press, 2000).

171. David Ekbladh, "'Mr. TVA': Grass-Roots Development, David Lilienthal, and the Rise and Fall of the Tennessee Valley Authority as a Symbol for U.S. Overseas Development, 1933–1973," *Diplomatic History* 26 (2007): 335–374.

172. Quoted in S. Irfan Habib and Dhruv Raina, "Copernicus, Columbus, Colonialism, and the Role of Science in Nineteenth-Century India," in Habib and Raina, *Science in Colonial India,* 246. See also Gyan Prakash, *Another Reason: Science and the Imagination of Modern India* (Princeton, NJ: Princeton University Press, 1999).

173. Quoted in Shiv Visvanathan, *Organizing for Science: The Making of an Industrial Research Laboratory* (New Delhi: Oxford University Press, 1985), 108; Zaheer Baber, *The Science of Empire: Scientific Knowledge, Civilization, and Colonial Rule in India* (Albany: SUNY Press, 1996), 184–245.

174. Ashis Nandy, *Alternative Sciences: Creativity and Authenticity in Two Indian Scientists* (New Delhi: Oxford University Press, 1980).

175. Baber, *The Science of Empire,* 129; Randall E. Stross, *The Stubborn Earth: American Agriculturalists on Chinese Soil, 1898–1937* (Berkeley: University of California Press, 1986).

176. Grace Carswell, *Cultivating Success in Uganda: Kigezi Farmers and Colonial Policies* (Athens: Ohio University Press, 2007).

177. Leslie Potter, "Forests versus Agriculture: Colonial Forest Services, Colonial Ideas, and Regulation of Land-Use Change in Southeast Asia," in *The Political Ecology of Tropical Forests in Southeast Asia: Historical Perspectives,* ed. Ken-ichi Abe, Wil de Jong, and Tuck-Po Lye (Melbourne: Trans Pacific Press, 2003); Richard P. Tucker and J. F. Richards, eds., *Global Deforestation and the Nineteenth-Century World Economy* (Durham, NC: Duke University Press, 1983); Richard P. Tucker, *Insatiable Appetite: The United States and the Ecological Degradation of the Tropical World* (Berkeley: University of California Press, 2000); Michael Williams, *Deforesting the Earth: From Prehistory to Global Crisis: An Abridgement* (Chicago: University of Chicago Press, 2006), 242–419; Thaddeus R. Sunseri, *Wielding the Ax: State Forestry and Social Conflict in Tanzania, 1820–2000* (Athens: Ohio University Press, 2009).

178. Ian R. Tyrrell, *True Gardens of the Gods: Californian-Australian Environmental Reform, 1860–1930* (Berkeley: University of California Press, 1999), 17–35.

179. Shermer, *In Darwin's Shadow.*

180. Daniel T. Rodgers, *Atlantic Crossings* (Cambridge, MA: Harvard University Press, 1998). See also Theodore M. Porter and Dorothy Ross, eds., *The Modern Social Sciences,* vol. 7 of *The Cambridge History of Science* (Cambridge: Cambridge University Press, 2003); Charle, Schriewer, and Wagner, *Transnational Intellectual Networks.*

181. James B. Gilbert, *Designing the Industrial State: The Intellectual Pursuit of Collectivism in America, 1880–1940* (New York: Quadrangle, 1972), 45.

182. Frank Andre Guridy, *Forging Diaspora: Afro-Cubans and African Americans in a World of Empire and Jim Crow* (Chapel Hill, NC: University of North Carolina Press, 2010), 17–60; Andrew Zimmerman, *Alabama in Africa: Booker T. Washington, the German Empire, and the Globalization of the New South* (Princeton, NJ: Princeton University Press, 2010); Sebastian Conrad, *Globalisation and the Nation in Imperial Germany,* trans. Sorcha O'Hagan (Cambridge: Cambridge University Press, 2010), 101.

183. Price, *Making Empire,* 179, on Holden; Joel Pfister, *Individuality Incorporated: Indians and the Multicultural Modern* (Durham, NC: Duke University Press, 2004), 31–97, on Pratt.

184. *New York Times,* June 24, 1910.

185. Warwick P. Anderson, *The Cultivation of Whiteness: Science, Health and Racial Destiny in Australia* (New York: Basic Books, 2003); Radhika Mohanram, *Imperial White: Race, Diaspora, and the British Empire* (Minneapolis: University of Minnesota Press, 2007).

186. Thomas E. Skidmore, *Black into White: Race and Nationality in Brazilian Thought* (Oxford: Oxford University Press, 1974), provides an extensive interpretation of this theme.

187. Stern, *Eugenic Nation,* and Edwin Black, *War against the Weak: Eugenics and America's Campaign to Create a Master Race* (New York: Four Walls Eight Windows Press, 2003), on the United States; Sejersted, *The Age of Social Democracy,* on Sweden; Chloe Campbell, *Race and Empire: Eugenics in Colonial Kenya* (Manchester: Manchester University Press, 2007), on Kenya.

188. George W. Stocking, *Victorian Anthropology* (New York: Free Press, 1987); Baker, *From Savage to Negro;* and H. Glenn Penny and Matti Bunzl, eds., *Worldly Provincialism: German Anthropology in the Age of Empire* (Ann Arbor: University of Michigan Press, 2003).

189. The large and varied scholarship may be sampled in Andrew D. Evans, *Anthropology at War: World War I and the Science of Race in Germany* (Chicago: University of Chicago Press, 2010); Paul Weindling, *Epidemics and Genocide in Eastern Europe, 1890–1945* (New York: Oxford University Press, 2000); Jürgen Zimmerer and Joachim Zeller, eds., *Genocide in German South-West Africa: The Colonial War of 1904–1908 and Its Aftermath,* trans. E. J. Neather (Monmouth, Wales: Merlin Press, 2007); Sandra Mass, *Weisse Helden, schwarza Krieger: Zur Geschichte kolonialer Männlichkeit in Deutschland, 1918–1964* (Cologne: Böhlau Verlag, 2006); essays in Conrad and Osterhammel, *Das Kaiserreich Transnational;* Robert Proctor, *Racial Hygiene: Medicine under the Nazis* (Cambridge, MA: Harvard University Press, 1988); Götz Aly, Peter Chroust, and Christian Pross, eds., *Cleansing the Fatherland: Nazi Medicine and Racial Hygiene,* trans. Belinda Cooper (Baltimore: Johns Hopkins University Press, 1994).

190. Mark B. Adams, ed., *The Wellborn Science: Eugenics in Germany, France, Brazil, and Russia* (New York: Oxford University Press, 1990); Daniel J. Kevles, *In the Name of Eugenics: Genetics and the Uses of Human Heredity* (New York: Knopf, 1985); Matthew J. Connelly, *Fatal Misconception: The Struggle to Control World Population* (Cambridge, MA: Harvard University Press, 2008).

191. Lake and Reynolds, *Drawing the Global Colour Line,* 251–261.

192. Alfred L. Kroeber, "Eighteen Professions," *American Anthropologist* 17 (1915): 285.

193. Jeffrey D. Needell, "Identity, Race, Gender, and Modernity in the Origins of Gilberto Freyre's Oeuvre," *American Historical Review* 100 (1995): 51–77.

194. J. R. McNeill, *Something New under the Sun: An Environmental History of the Twentieth-Century World* (New York: Norton, 2000), 58.

195. Thomas G. Andrews, *Killing for Coal: America's Deadliest Labor War* (Cambridge, MA: Harvard University Press, 2008), 70.

196. Thomas Parke Hughes, *Networks of Power: Electrification in Western Society, 1880–1930* (Baltimore: Johns Hopkins University Press, 1983), 1; William J. Hausman, Peter Hertner, and Mira Wilkins, eds., *Global Electrification: Multinational Enterprise and International Finance in the History of Light and Power, 1878–2007* (New York: Cambridge University Press, 2008).

197. Hausman, Hertner, and Wilkins, *Global Electrification*.

198. Pierre-Yves Saunier and Shane Ewen, eds., *Another Global City: Historical Explorations into the Transnational Municipal Moments, 1850–2000* (New York: Palgrave Macmillan, 2008), 8.

199. Catherine Coquery-Vidrovitch, *The History of African Cities South of the Sahara: From Origins to Colonization,* trans. Mary Baker (Princeton, NJ: Markus Wiener, 2005), 209–318; Patrick Manning, *Migration in World History* (New York: Routledge, 2005), 157–180; Bill Freund, *The African City: A History* (New York: Cambridge University Press, 2007); Dianne Scott, "Creative Destruction: Early Modernist Planning in the South Durban Industrial Zone, South Africa," *Journal of Southern African Studies* 29 (2003): 235–259.

200. Renaud Payre and Pierre-Yves Saunier, "A City in the World of Cities: Lyon, France; Municipal Associations as Political Resources in the Twentieth Century," Andrew Brown-May, "In the Precincts of the Global City: The Transnational Network of Municipal Affairs in Melbourne, Australia, at the End of the Nineteenth Century," and Jeffrey Hanes, "Pacific Crossings? Urban Progressivism in Modern Japan," all in Saunier and Ewen, *Another Global City,* 69–84, 19–34, 51–68 ; Stephen V. Ward, *Planning the Twentieth Century City: The Advanced Capitalist World* (Chichester, UK: Wiley, 2002).

201. Michael P. Smith, *Transnational Urbanism: Locating Globalization* (London: Blackwell, 2001).

202. Myron Echenberg, *Plague Ports: The Global Urban Impact of Bubonic Plague, 1894–1901* (New York: NYU Press, 2007).

203. Context is provided by Mark Harrison, *Disease and the Modern World: 1500 to the Present Day* (Cambridge: Polity Press, 2004), 93–96; Sheldon J. Watts, *Epidemics and History: Disease, Power, and Imperialism* (New Haven, CT: Yale University Press, 1999); and Nancy Tomes, *The Gospel of Germs: Men, Women, and Microbe in American Life* (Cambridge, MA: Harvard University Press, 1998). On Gambia, see Wright, *Very Small Place in Africa,* 194–195.

204. Mariola Espinosa, *Epidemic Invasions: Yellow Fever and the Limits of Cuban Independence, 1878–1930* (Chicago: University of Chicago Press, 2009); Sherman Cochrane, *Chinese Medicine Men: Consumer Culture in China and Southeast Asia* (Cambridge, MA: Harvard University Press, 2006); Ruth Rogaski, *Hygienic Modernity: Meanings of Health and Disease in Treaty-Port China* (Berkeley: University of California Press, 2004); Anne Digby, *Diversity and Division in Medicine: Health Care in South Africa from the 1800s* (Oxford: Peter Lang, 2006).

205. William Gallois, *The Administration of Sickness: Medicine and Ethics in Nineteenth-Century Algeria* (Basingstoke, UK: Palgrave Macmillan, 2008), 4–6.

206. Janice Boddy, *Civilizing Women: British Crusades in Colonial Sudan* (Princeton, NJ: Princeton University Press, 2007).

207. Rod Edmond, "Returning Fears: Tropical Disease and the Metropolis," and other essays in Driver and Martins, *Tropical Visions.*

208. David Arnold, *Colonizing the Body: State Medicine and Epidemic Disease in Nineteenth-Century India* (Berkeley: University of California Press, 1993), suggests the complicated interactions.

209. David P. Forsythe, *The Humanitarians: The International Committee of the Red Cross* (New York: Cambridge University Press, 2005); Caroline Moorehead, *Dunant's Dream: War, Switzerland and the History of the Red Cross* (London: HarperCollins, 1998).

210. Curti, *American Philanthropy Abroad,* 339–360.

211. Steven P. Palmer, *Launching Global Health: The Caribbean Odyssey of the Rockefeller Foundation* (Ann Arbor: University of Michigan Press, 2010); Steven C. Williams, "Nationalism and Public Health: The Convergence of Rockefeller Foundation Technique and Brazilian Federal Authority during the Time of Yellow Fever, 1925–1930," in *Missionaries of Science: The Rockefeller Foundation and Latin America,* ed. Marcos Cueto (Bloomington: Indiana University Press, 1994), 23–51; Ann Zulawski, *Unequal Cures: Public Health and Political Change in Bolivia, 1900–1950* (Durham, NC: Duke University Press, 2007), 86–117.

212. Elman, *Modern Science in China,* 225; Adam K. Webb, "The Countermodern Moment: A World-Historical Perspective on the Thought of Rabindranath Tagore, Muhammad Iqbal, and Liang Shuming," *Journal of World History* 19 (2008): 189–212. On the World War I break, see Michael Adas, "Contested Hegemony: The Great War and the Afro-Asian Assault on the Civilizing Mission Ideology," *Journal of World History* 15 (2004): 31–63.

213. Mary Parker Follett, *The New State* (1918), 196, http://sunsite.utk.edu/FINS/Mary_Parker_Follett/Fins-MPF-01.html. Thanks to Daniel Immerwahr for calling this quotation to my attention.

214. On Burnham, see Gilbert, *Designing the Industrial State;* and Daniel Kelly, *James Burnham and the Struggle for the World: A Life* (Wilmington, DE: Isi Books, 2002).

215. Bayly, *Birth of the Modern World,* 1–2; Arjun Appadurai, *Modernity at Large: Cultural Dimensions of Globalization* (Minneapolis: University of Minnesota Press, 1996); Weinbaum et al., *Modern Girl.*

216. Felipe Fernández-Armesto, *Pathfinders: A Global History of Exploration* (New York: W. W. Norton, 2006), 385.

217. Kenneth Mason, *Abode of Snow: A History of Himalayan Exploration and Mountaineering from Earliest Times to the Ascent of Everest* (1955; repr., London: Diadem Books, 1987), xvi.

218. Maurice Isserman and Stewart Weaver, *Fallen Giants: A History of Himalayan Mountaineering from the Age of Empire to the Age of Extremes* (New Haven, CT: Yale, 2008), xi.

219. Beau Riffenburgh, *The Myth of the Explorer: The Press, Sensationalism, and Geographical Discovery* (New York: Oxford University Press, 1994); Winseck and Pike, *Communication and Empire,* 294.

220. James L. Newman, *Imperial Footprints: Henry Morton Stanley's African Journeys* (Dulles, VA: Potomac, 2006). Tim Jeal, *Stanley: The Impossible Life of Africa's Greatest Explorer* (New Ha-

ven, CT: Yale University Press, 2007), claims that Stanley greatly exaggerated his accounts of brutality and killing.

221. Claire Pettitt, *Dr. Livingstone, I Presume? Missionaries, Journalists, Explorers and Empire* (London: Profile Books, 2007).

222. *National Geographic Magazine,* 13 (1903): 405–406.

223. Fanny Bullock Workman and William Hunter Workman, *Ice-Bound Heights of the Mustagh: An Account of Two Seasons of Pioneer Exploration in the Baltistan Himalaya* (New York: Scribner's, 1908).

224. Fernández-Armesto, *Pathfinders,* 362.

225. Beau Riffenburgh, *The Myth of the Explorer,* 196. Osterhammel, *Die Verwandlung der Welt,* 63–76, surveys the worldwide spread of newspapers, popular journalism, and international news services before World War I.

226. Isserman and Weaver, *Fallen Giants,* 83–222.

227. Quoted from Stefan Zweig, *The World of Yesterday,* 196, in Kern, *Culture of Time and Space,* 244.

228. Rosalie Schwartz, *Flying Down to Rio: Hollywood, Tourists, and Yankee Clippers* (College Station: Texas A&M University Press, 2004); Jennifer Van Vleck, *No Distant Places* (Cambridge, MA: Harvard University Press, forthcoming).

229. Daniel Boorstin, *The Discoverers: A History of Man's Search to Know His World and Himself* (New York: Random House, 1983); Traill, *Schliemann of Troy.*

230. Charles Gallenkamp, *Dragon Hunter: Roy Chapman Andrews and the Central Asiatic Expeditions* (New York: Viking, 2001).

231. Hanson, *Animal Attractions,* 36.

232. John S. Clarke, *Circus Parade* (1936; Yorkshire, UK: Jeremy Mills, 2008), 1–30.

233. Janet Davis, *The Circus Age: Culture and Society under the American Big Top* (Chapel Hill: University of North Carolina Press, 2002), 34; Richard W. Flint, "American Showmen and European Dealers: Commerce in Wild Animals in Nineteenth-Century America," in Hoage and Deiss, *New Worlds, New Animals,* 97–108.

234. Davis, *The Circus Age,* 218.

235. Greenhalgh, *Ephemeral Vistas.*

236. Robert W. Rydell and Rob Kroes, *Buffalo Bill in Bologna: The Americanization of the World, 1869–1922* (Chicago: University of Chicago Press, 2005).

237. Osterhammel, *Die Verwandlung der Welt,* 80–81.

238. Emily S. Rosenberg, *Spreading the American Dream: Economic and Cultural Expansion, 1890–1945* (New York: Hill and Wang, 1982); Kristin Thompson, *Exporting Entertainment: America in the World Film Market, 1907–1934* (London: BFI, 1985).

239. Rachel Dwyer and Divia Patel, *Cinema India: The Visual Culture of Hindi Film* (New Brunswick, NJ: Rutgers University Press, 2002); Zhang Zhen, *An Amorous History of the Silver Screen: Shanghai Cinema, 1896–1937* (Chicago: University of Chicago Press, 2005), 296; Priti Ramamurthy, "All-Consuming Nationalism: The Indian Modern Girl in the 1920s and 1930s," in Weinbaum et al., *Modern Girl,* 147–173.

240. The author thanks Shanon Fitzpatrick for sharing her ongoing research on this topic.

241. Catherine Russell, "New Women of the Silent Screen: China, Japan, Hollywood," in *Camera Obscura: Feminism, Culture, and Media Studies Special Issue* (Durham, NC: Duke University Press, 2005), 4.

242. Eric Ames, *Carl Hagenbeck's Empire of Entertainments* (Seattle: University of Washington Press, 2008), 198–229.

243. Melanie McGrath, *The Long Exile: A Tale of Inuit Betrayal and Survival in the High Arctic* (New York: Knopf, 2007).

244. Pascal James Imperato and Eleanor M. Imperato, *They Married Adventure: The Wandering Lives of Martin and Osa Johnson* (New Brunswick, NJ: Rutgers University Press, 1992).

245. Ruth Vasey, *The World according to Hollywood* (Madison: University of Wisconsin Press, 1997).

246. Richard Mullen and James Munson, *"The Smell of the Continent": The British Discover Europe* (London: Macmillan, 2009); Frank Costigliola, *Awkward Dominion: American Political, Economic and Cultural Relations with Europe, 1919–1933* (Ithaca, NY: Cornell University Press, 1984).

247. Kristin Hoganson, *Consumers' Imperium: The Global Production of American Domesticity, 1865–1920* (Chapel Hill: University of North Carolina Press, 2007), 171.

248. Ian R. Tyrrell, *Transnational Nation: United States History in Global Perspective since 1789* (New York: Palgrave, 2007), 97.

249. Shelley Baronowski and Ellen Furlough, eds., *Being Elsewhere: Tourism, Consumer Culture, and Identity in Modern Europe and North America* (Ann Arbor: University of Michigan Press, 2001).

250. Hoganson, *Consumers' Imperium,* 153–196.

251. Emily S. Rosenberg, *Financial Missionaries to the World: The Politics and Culture of Dollar Diplomacy* (Durham, NC: Duke University Press, 2000).

252. Miriam Silverberg, *Erotic Grotesque Nonsense: The Mass Culture of Japanese Modern Times* (Berkeley: University of California Press, 2006), employs this concept.

253. Joanne Hershfield, *Imagining la Chica Moderna: Women, Nation, and Visual Culture in Mexico, 1917–1936* (Durham, NC: Duke University Press, 2008), 126–155; and many essays in Weinbaum et al., *Modern Girl.*

254. On consumption communities, see Daniel Boorstin, *The Americans: The Democratic Experience* (New York: Random House, 1973).

255. Victoria de Grazia, *Irresistible Empire: America's Advance through Twentieth-Century Europe* (Cambridge, MA: Harvard University Press, 2005).

256. Georgine Clarsen, *Eat My Dust: Early Women Motorists* (Baltimore: Johns Hopkins University Press, 2008).

257. For international automobile ads, see N. W. Ayer Collection No. 59, Ford Motor Company, series 3, boxes 220–225, National Museum of American History Archives, Washington, DC.

258. Weinbaum et al., *Modern Girl;* Francesca Orsini, ed., *Love in South Asia: A Cultural History* (Cambridge: Cambridge University Press, 2006); Rachel Dwyer and Christopher Pinney, eds., *Pleasure and the Nation: The History, Politics and Consumption of Public Culture in India* (New Delhi: Oxford University Press, 2001); Michel Gobat, *Confronting the American Dream: Nicaragua under U.S. Imperial Rule* (Durham, NC: Duke University Press, 2005), 175–202; Julio

Moreno, *Yankee Don't Go Home: Mexican Nationalism, American Business Culture, and the Shaping of Modern Mexico, 1920–1950* (Chapel Hill: University of North Carolina Press, 2003), 137–151; Jeffrey H. Jackson, *Making Jazz French: Music and Modern Life in Interwar Paris* (Durham, NC: Duke University Press, 2003); Mary Nolan, *Visions of Modernity: American Business and the Modernization of Germany* (New York: Oxford University Press, 1994); Michael H. Kater, *Different Drummers: Jazz in the Culture of Nazi Germany* (New York: Oxford University Press, 1992).

259. Jonathan D. Spence, *The Search for Modern China* (New York: W. W. Norton, 1990), 311–333, for context.

260. Jian Wang, *Foreign Advertising in China: Becoming Global, Becoming Local* (Ames: Iowa State University Press, 2000), 25–32; Beverley Jackson, *Shanghai Girl Gets All Dressed Up* (Berkeley: Ten Speed Press, 2005), 38, 104–105; Lynn Pan, *Shanghai Style: Art and Design between the Wars* (San Francisco: Long River Press, 2008), explores the diverse sources of Shanghai modernist style.

261. Antonia Finnane, *Changing Clothes in China: Fashion, History, Nation* (New York: Columbia University Press, 2008), 101–175; Jackson, *Shanghai Girl,* 45–67, 81–90; Sherman Cochrane, ed., *Inventing Nanjing Road: Commercial Culture in Shanghai, 1900–1945* (Ithaca, NY: Cornell University Press, 1999).

262. Karl Gerth, *China Made: Consumer Culture and the Creation of the Nation* (Cambridge, MA: Harvard University Press, 2003).

263. Leo Ou-fan Lee, *Shanghai Modern: The Flowering of a New Urban Culture in China, 1930–1945* (Cambridge, MA: Harvard University Press, 1999), 64–74, quotation at 74; Finnane, *Changing Clothes in China,* 125–137.

264. Jackson, *Shanghai Girl,* 111–112. Ou-fan Lee, *Shanghai Modern,* 82–119, 199–231, explains the interpretive controversies over the influence of Hollywood cinema on Chinese film and portrayals of "modern girls." See also Yingjin Zhang, ed., *Cinema and Urban Culture in Shanghai, 1922–1943* (Palo Alto, CA: Stanford University Press, 1999). On the *qipao,* see Finnane, *Changing Clothes in China,* 139–175.

265. Wen-hsin Yeh, *Shanghai Splendor: Economic Sentiments and the Making of Modern China, 1843–1949* (Berkeley: University of California Press, 2007), 101.

266. Weinbaum et al., *Modern Girl;* Silverberg, *Erotic Grotesque Nonsense;* Finnane, *Changing Clothes in China,* 167; Hershfield, *Imagining la Chica Moderna.*

267. Helena Michie and Ronald R. Thomas, "Introduction," and Jon Hegglund, "Empire's Second Take: Projecting America in Stanley and Livingstone," both in *Nineteenth-Century Geographies: The Transformation of Space from the Victorian Age to the American Century,* ed. Helena Michie and Ronald R. Thomas (New Brunswick, NJ: Rutgers University Press, 2003), 17, 265–278.

268. John Tully, "A Victorian Ecological Disaster: Imperialism, the Telegraph, and Gutta-Percha," *Journal of World History* 20 (2009): 559–579.

Selected Bibliography

Leviathan 2.0: Inventing Modern Statehood

Adelman, Jeremy. *Sovereignty and Revolution in the Iberian Atlantic.* Princeton, NJ: Princeton University Press, 2006.

Ahmad, Feroz. *The Young Turks: The Committee of Union and Progress in Turkish Politics, 1908–1914.* Oxford: Clarendon Press, 1969.

Anderson, Benedict. *Imagined Communities: Reflections on the Origin and Spread of Nationalism.* London: Verso, 1983.

Anderson, Fred, and Andrew Cayton. *The Dominion of War: Empire and Liberty in North America, 1500–2000.* New York: Viking, 2005.

Applebaum, Anne. *Gulag: A History.* New York: Doubleday, 2003.

Aquarone, Alberto. *L'organizzazione dello stato totalitario.* Turin: Einaudi, 1965.

Arendt, Hannah. *The Origins of Totalitarianism.* New York: Harcourt, Brace, 1951.

Baldwin, Peter. "Beyond Weak and Strong: Rethinking the State in Comparative Policy History." *Journal of Policy History* 17, no. 1 (2005): 12–33.

———. *The Politics of Social Solidarity: Class Bases of the European Welfare State, 1875–1975.* Cambridge: Cambridge University Press, 1990.

Banner, Stuart. "Why *Terra Nullius?* Anthropology and Property Law in Early Australia." *Law and History Review* 23, no. 1 (2005): 95–132.

Barkey, Karen. *An Empire of Difference: The Ottomans in Comparative Perspective.* Cambridge: Cambridge University Press, 2008.

Bayat, Mangol. *Iran's First Revolution: Shi'ism and the Constitutional Revolution of 1905–1909.* New York: Oxford University Press, 1991.

Bayly, C. A. *The Birth of the Modern World, 1780–1914: Global Connections and Comparisons.* Malden, MA: Blackwell, 2004.

———. *Indian Society and the Making of the British Empire.* Vol. 2, part 1, of *The New Cambridge History of India,* edited by Gordon Johnson. Cambridge: Cambridge University Press, 1988.

Bazant, Jan. *Alienation of Church Lands in Mexico: Social and Economic Aspects of the Liberal Revolution, 1856–1875.* Edited and translated by Michel P. Costeloe. Cambridge: Cambridge University Press, 1971.

Beasley, W. G. *Japanese Imperialism, 1894–1945.* Oxford: Clarendon Press, 1987.

Bentley, Arthur F. *The Process of Government: A Study of Social Pressure.* Edited by Peter H. Odegard. Cambridge, MA: Belknap Press of Harvard University Press, 1967.

Bibó, István. *Misère des petits états d'Europe de l'est.* Translated by György Kassai. Paris: Albin Michel, 1993.

Bix, Herbert P. *Hirohito and the Making of Modern Japan.* New York: HarperCollins, 2000.

Blum, Jerome. *The End of the Old Order in Rural Europe.* Princeton, NJ: Princeton University Press, 1978.

Bluntschli, Johann Caspar. *Allgemeine Staatsrecht.* 3rd ed. Munich: J. G. Cotta, 1863.

Bose, Sugata. *Peasant Labour and Colonial Capital: Rural Bengal since 1770.* Vol. 3, part 2, of *The Cambridge History of India,* edited by Gordon Johnson. Cambridge: Cambridge University Press, 1993.

Boyer, John W. *Political Radicalism in Late Imperial Vienna: Origins of the Christian Social Movement, 1848–1897.* Chicago: University of Chicago Press, 1981.

Bracher, Karl Dietrich. *Die deutsche Diktatur: Entstehung, Struktur, Folgen des Nationalsozialismus.* 6th ed. Frankfurt: Ulstein, 1979.

Brandfon, Robert L. *Cotton Kingdom of the New South: A History of the Yazoo Mississippi Delta from Reconstruction to the Twentieth Century.* Cambridge, MA: Harvard University Press, 1967.

Brubaker, Rogers. *Citizenship and Nationhood in France and Germany.* Cambridge, MA: Harvard University Press, 1992.

Buchheim, Hans, et al. *Anatomie des SS-Staates.* Munich: Institut für Zeitgeschichte, 1968.

Bullard, Alice. *Exile to Paradise: Savagery and Civilization in Paris and the South Pacific, 1790–1900.* Stanford, CA: Stanford University Press, 2000.

Burchell, Graham, Colin Gordon, and Peter Miller, eds. *The Foucault Effect: Studies in Governmentality.* Chicago: University of Chicago Press, 1991.

Burke, Edmund, III. *Prelude to Protectorate in Morocco: Precolonial Protest and Resistance, 1860–1912.* Chicago: University of Chicago Press, 1976.

The Cambridge History of China, vols. 10 and 11: *Late Ch'ing, 1800–1911,* edited by John K. Fairbank and Kwang-ching Liu. Cambridge: Cambridge University Press, 1980.

The Cambridge History of China, vol. 12: *Republican China, 1912–1949,* part 1, edited by John K. Fairbank. Cambridge: Cambridge University Press, 1983.

The Cambridge History of Egypt, vol. 2: *Modern Egypt from 1517 to the End of the Twentieth Century,* edited by M. W. Daly. Cambridge: Cambridge University Press, 1998.

The Cambridge History of Iran, vol. 7: *From Nadir Shah to the Islamic Republic,* edited by Peter Avery, Gavin Hambly, and Charles Melville. Cambridge: Cambridge University Press, 1991.

The Cambridge History of Latin America, vols. 4 and 5: *c. 1870 to 1930,* edited by Leslie Bethell. Cambridge: Cambridge University Press, 1986.

The Cambridge History of Turkey, vol. 3: *The Later Ottoman Empire, 1603–1839,* edited by Suraiya N. Faroqhi. Cambridge: Cambridge University Press, 2008.

The Cambridge History of Turkey, vol. 4: *Turkey in the Modern World,* edited by Reşat Kasaba. Cambridge: Cambridge University Press, 2009.

Cassese, Sabino. *Lo stato fascista.* Bologna: Mulino, 2010.

Cell, John W. *The Highest Stage of White Supremacy: The Origins of Segregation in South Africa and the American South.* Cambridge: Cambridge University Press, 1982.

Cesarani, David, ed. *The Final Solution: Origins and Implementation.* London: Routledge, 1994.

Chabod, Federico. *Italian Foreign Policy: The Statecraft of the Founders.* Translated by William McCuaig. Princeton, NJ: Princeton University Press, 1996.

Cohen, Stephen F. *Bukharin and the Bolshevik Revolution: A Political Biography, 1888–1938.* New York: Vintage, 1975.

Commins, David Dean. *Islamic Reform: Politics and Social Change in Late Ottoman Syria.* New York: Oxford University Press, 1990.

Cooper, Frederick. *Colonialism in Question: Theory, Knowledge, History.* Berkeley: University of California Press, 2005.

———. *Decolonization and African Society: The Labor Question in French and British Africa.* Cambridge: Cambridge University Press, 1996.

Cooper, Frederick, and Ann Laura Stoler, eds. *Tensions of Empire: Colonial Cultures in a Bourgeois World.* Berkeley: University of California Press, 1997.

Corner, Paul, ed. *Popular Opinion in Totalitarian Regimes: Fascism, Nazism, Communism.* Oxford: Oxford University Press, 2009.

Craib, Raymond B. *Cartographic Mexico: A History of State Fixations and Fugitive Landscapes.* Durham, NC: Duke University Press, 2004.

Crosby, Alfred W., Jr. *The Columbian Exchange: Biological and Cultural Consequences of 1492.* Westport, CT: Greenwood, 1972.

Dabringhaus, Sabine. *Territorialer Nationalismus in China: Historisch-geographisches Denken, 1900–1948.* Cologne: Böhlau, 2006.

Davis, Clarence B., and Kenneth E. Wilburn Jr., with Ronald E. Robinson, eds. *Railway Imperialism.* New York: Greenwood, 1991.

Dean, Mitchell. *Governmentality: Power and Rule in Modern Society.* London: Sage, 1999.

Dean, Warren. *With Broadax and Firebrand: The Destruction of the Brazilian Atlantic Forest.* Berkeley: University of California Press, 1995.

Deane, Phyllis, and W. A. Cole. *British Economic Growth, 1688–1959: Trends and Structure.* 2nd ed. London: Cambridge University Press, 1967.

De Felice, Renzo, ed. *Il fascismo: Le interpretazioni dei contemporanei e degli historici.* Rev. ed. Rome: Laterza, 1998.

———. *Mussolini il duce: Lo stato totalitario, 1936–1940.* Turin: Einaudi, 1981.

———. *Mussolini il fascista: L'organizzazione dello stato fascista, 1925–1929.* Turin: Einaudi, 1968.

DeLay, Brian. *War of a Thousand Deserts: Indian Raids and the U.S.-Mexican War.* New Haven, CT: Yale University Press, 2008.

Den Otter, A. A. *The Philosophy of Railways: The Transcontinental Railway Idea in British North America.* Toronto: University of Toronto Press, 1997.

Deprest, Florence. *Géographes en Algérie, 1880–1950: Savoirs universitaires en situation coloniale.* Paris: Belin, 2009.

De Vries, Jan. *The Industrious Revolution: Consumer Behavior and the Household Economy, 1650 to the Present.* Cambridge: Cambridge University Press, 2008.

Donzelot, Jacques. *L'invention du social: Essai sur le déclin des passions politiques.* Paris: Fayard, 1984.

Drake, Richard. *Byzantium for Rome: The Politics of Nostalgia in Umbertian Italy, 1878–1900.* Chapel Hill: University of North Carolina Press, 1980.

Duguit, Léon. *Le droit social, le droit individuel et la transformation de l'état.* Paris: Félix Alcan, 1908.

Edney, Matthew H. *Mapping an Empire: The Geographical Construction of British India, 1765–1843.* Chicago: University of Chicago Press, 1997.

Elliott, John H. *Empires of the Atlantic World: Britain and Spain in America, 1492–1830.* New Haven, CT: Yale University Press, 2006.

Elvin, Mark. *The Retreat of the Elephants: An Environmental History of China.* New Haven, CT: Yale University Press, 2004.

Evans, Richard J. *The Third Reich at War, 1939–1945.* London: Allen Lane, 2008.

———. *The Third Reich in Power, 1933–1939.* New York: Penguin, 2005.

Feldman, Gerald. *Army, Industry and Labor in Germany, 1914–1918.* Princeton, NJ: Princeton University Press, 1966.

Ferguson, Niall. *The War of the World: History's Age of Hatred.* London: Allen Lane, 2006.

Finchelstein, Federico. *Transatlantic Fascism: Ideology, Violence, and the Sacred in Argentina and Italy, 1919–1945.* Durham, NC: Duke University Press, 2010.

Foucault, Michel. *Discipline and Punish: The Birth of the Prison.* Translated by Alan Sheridan. New York: Pantheon, 1977.

———. *Sécurité, Territoire, Population: Cours au Collège de France, 1977–1978.* Paris: Gallimard, 2004.

Fraenkel, Ernst. *The Dual State: A Contribution to the Theory of Dictatorship.* Translated by E. A. Shils in collaboration with Edith Lowenstein and Klaus Knorr. New York: Oxford University Press, 1941.

Friedrich, Carl J., and Zbigniew K. Brzezinski. *Totalitarian Dictatorship and Autocracy.* 2nd rev. ed. New York: Praeger, 1965.

Gall, Lothar. *Bismarck: Der weisse Revolutionär.* Frankfurt: Propyläen, 1980.

Geertz, Clifford. *Agricultural Involution: The Process of Ecological Change in Indonesia.* Berkeley: Association of Asian Studies/University of California Press, 1963.

———. *Negara: The Theater State in Nineteenth-Century Bali.* Princeton, NJ: Princeton University Press, 1980.

Gellner, Ernest. *Nations and Nationalism.* 2nd ed. Ithaca, NY: Cornell University Press, 2008.

Geppert, Alexander C. T. *Fleeting Cities: Imperial Expositions in Fin-de-Siècle Europe.* New York: Palgrave-Macmillan, 2010.

Gerth, H. H., and C. Wright Mills, eds. *From Max Weber: Essays in Sociology.* Translated by H. H. Gerth and C. Wright Mills. New York: Oxford University Press, 1958.

Geyer, Michael, and Sheila Fitzpatrick, eds. *Beyond Totalitarianism: Stalinism and Nazism Compared.* Cambridge: Cambridge University Press, 2009.

Gleason, Abbot. *Totalitarianism: The Inner History of the Cold War.* New York: Oxford University Press, 1995.

Gluck, Carol. *Japan's Modern Myths: Ideologies in the Late Meiji Period.* Princeton, NJ: Princeton University Press, 1985.

Gneist, Rudolph. *The History of the English Constitution.* Translated by Philip A. Ashworth. 2 vols. London: W. Clowes, 1886.

Gray, Jack. *Rebellions and Revolutions: China from the 1800s to the 1980s.* New York: Oxford University Press, 1990.

Graziosi, Andrea. *The Great Soviet Peasant War: Bolsheviks and Peasants, 1917–1933.* Cambridge, MA: Ukrainian Research Center, Harvard University/Harvard University Press, 1996.

Hagen, William W. *Ordinary Prussians: Brandenburg Junkers and Villagers, 1500–1840.* Cambridge: Cambridge University Press, 2002.

Hall, John A., ed. *States in History.* New York: Basil Blackwell, 1987.

Halperín Donghi, Tulio. *Guerra y finanzas en los orígines del estado argentina, 1791–1850.* Buenos Aires: Belgrano, 1982.

Hämäläinen, Pekka. *The Comanche Empire.* New Haven, CT: Yale University Press, 2008.

Hanioğlu, M. Şükrü *Preparation for a Revolution: The Young Turks, 1902–1908.* New York: Oxford University Press, 2001.

Hannah, Matthew G. *Governmentality and the Mastery of Territory in Nineteenth-Century America.* New York: Cambridge University Press, 2000.

Hart, John Mason. *Empire and Revolution: The Americans in Mexico since the Civil War.* Berkeley: University of California Press, 2002.

Hearder, Harry. *Italy in the Age of the Risorgimento, 1790–1870.* London: Longman, 1983.

Hevia, James L. *English Lessons: The Pedagogy of Imperialism in Nineteenth-Century China.* Durham, NC: Duke University Press, 2003.

Hobsbawm, Eric. *The Age of Extremes: The Short Twentieth Century, 1914–1991.* London: Michael Joseph, 1994.

———. *Nations and Nationalism since 1780: Programme, Myth, Reality.* Cambridge: Cambridge University Press, 1990.

Hochschild, Adam. *King Leopold's Ghost: A Story of Greed, Terror and Heroism in Colonial Africa.* Boston: Houghton Mifflin, 1998.

Hugill, Peter J. *World Trade since 1431: Geography, Technology, and Capitalism.* Baltimore: Johns Hopkins University Press, 1993.

Inalcik, Halil. *The Ottoman Empire: Conquest, Organization and Economy.* London: Variorum, 1978.

Jackson, Robert. *Sovereignty: Evolution of an Idea.* Cambridge: Polity, 2007.

Jellinek, Georg. *Das Recht des modernen Staates.* Vol. 1, *Allgemeine Staatslehre.* Berlin: O. Häring, 1900.

Jen Yu-wen. *The Taiping Revolutionary Movement.* Edited by Adrienne Suddard. New Haven, CT: Yale University Press, 1973.

Joll, James. *The Anarchists.* London: Eyre and Spottiswoode, 1964.

Jonas, Raymond. *The Battle of Adwa: African Victory in the Age of Empire.* Cambridge, MA: Harvard University Press, 2011.

Kang, David C. *East Asia before the West: Five Centuries of Trade and Tribute.* New York: Columbia University Press, 2010.

Kaplan, Temma. *Anarchists of Andalusia, 1868–1903.* Princeton, NJ: Princeton University Press, 1977.

Kasaba, Reşat. *A Moveable Empire: Ottoman Nomads, Migrants, and Refugees.* Seattle: University of Washington Press, 2009.

Kashani-Sabet, Firoozeh. *Frontier Fictions: Shaping the Iranian Nation, 1804–1946.* Princeton, NJ: Princeton University Press, 1999.

Katz, Friedrich. *The Life and Times of Pancho Villa.* Stanford, CA: Stanford University Press, 1998.

———, ed. *Riot, Rebellion, and Revolution: Rural Social Conflict in Mexico.* Princeton, NJ: Princeton University Press, 1988.

Keddie, Nikki R., with Yann Richard. *Roots of Revolution: An Interpretive History of Modern Iran.* New Haven, CT: Yale University Press, 1981.

Kershaw, Ian. *Hitler, 1889–1936: Hubris.* New York: W. W. Norton, 1999.

———. *Hitler, 1936–1945: Nemesis.* New York: W. W. Norton, 2000.

Kirby, William C. *Germany and Republican China.* Stanford, CA: Stanford University Press, 1984.

Kirwan, Albert D. *Revolt of the Rednecks: Mississippi Politics, 1865–1925.* Gloucester, MA: P. Smith, 1964.

Kloppenberg, James T. *Uncertain Victory: Social Democracy and Progressivism in European and American Thought, 1870–1920.* New York: Oxford University Press, 1986.

Knowlton, Robert J. *Church Property and the Mexican Reform, 1856–1910.* DeKalb: Northern Illinois University Press, 1976.

Koselleck, Reinhard. "Crisis," translated by Michaela W. Richter. *Journal of the History of Ideas* 67, no. 2 (2006): 357–400.

Kotkin, Stephen. *Magnetic Mountain: Stalinism as a Civilization.* Berkeley: University of California Press, 1995.

Kourí, Emilio. *A Pueblo Divided: Business, Property, and Community in Papantla, Mexico.* Stanford, CA: Stanford University Press, 2004.

Krasner, Stephen D. *Sovereignty: Organized Hypocrisy.* Princeton, NJ: Princeton University Press, 1999.

Kuhn, Philip A. *Origins of the Modern Chinese State.* Stanford, CA: Stanford University Press, 2002.

———. *Rebellion and Its Enemies in Late Imperial China.* Cambridge, MA: Harvard University Press, 1970.

Larkin, Emmet. *The Making of the Roman Catholic Church in Ireland, 1850–1860.* Chapel Hill: University of North Carolina Press, 1980.

Lenin, V. I. *Imperialism: The Highest Stage of Capitalism.* London: Junius, 1996.

———. *What Is to Be Done? Burning Questions of Our Movement.* Moscow: Foreign Languages, 1950.

Lewin, Moshe. *Russian Peasants and Soviet Power: A Study in Collectivization.* Translated by Irene Nove with John Biggart. London: Allen and Unwin, 1968.

Linz, Juan J. *Totalitarian and Authoritarian Regimes.* Boulder, CO: Lynne Rienner, 2000.

López-Alves, Fernando. *State Formation and Democracy in Latin America, 1810–1900.* Durham, NC: Duke University Press, 2000.

Lukács, Georg. *History and Class Consciousness.* Translated by Rodney Livingstone. Cambridge, MA: MIT Press, 1971.

Lynch, John. *Argentine Dictator: Juan Manuel de Rosas, 1829–1852.* Oxford: Clarendon Press, 1981.

Lyttelton, Adrian. *The Seizure of Power: Fascism in Italy, 1919–1929.* Rev. ed. London: Routledge, 2004.

Macartney, C. A. *The Habsburg Empire, 1790–1918.* New York: Macmillan, 1969.

Macfie, A. L. *The End of the Ottoman Empire, 1908–1923.* New York: Longman, 1998.

Maier, Charles S. "Consigning the Twentieth Century to History: Alternative Narratives for the Modern Era." *American Historical Review* 105, no. 3 (2000): 807–831.

———. "'Fictitious Bonds . . . of Wealth and Law': On the Theory and Practice of Interest Representation." In *Organizing Interests in Western Europe: Pluralism, Corporatism, and the Transformation of Politics,* edited by Suzanne Berger. Cambridge: Cambridge University Press, 1981.

———. "Nation and State." In *The Palgrave Dictionary of Transnational History,* edited by Akira Iriye and Pierre-Yves Saunier. Basingstoke, UK: Palgrave Macmillan, 2009.

———. *Recasting Bourgeois Europe: Stabilization in France, Germany, and Italy in the Decade after World War I.* Princeton, NJ: Princeton University Press, 1975.

Mamdani, Mahmoud. *Citizen and Subject: Contemporary Africa and the Legacy of Late Colonialism.* Princeton, NJ: Princeton University Press, 1996.

Manela, Erez. *The Wilsonian Moment: Self-Determination and the International Origins of Anticolonial Nationalism.* New York: Oxford University Press, 2007.

Mann, Michael. *Fascists.* Cambridge: Cambridge University Press, 2004.

Marcus, Harold G. *A History of Ethiopia.* Berkeley: University of California Press, 1994.

———. *The Life and Times of Menelik II: Ethiopia, 1844–1913.* Oxford: Clarendon Press, 1975.

Marichal, Carlos. "Las finanzas y la construcción de las nuevas naciones latinoamericanas." In *Historia general de América Latina,* vol. 6, edited by Josefina Z. Vázquez and Manuel Miño Grijalva. Paris: UNESCO, 2003.

Martin, James R. "The Theory of Storms: Jacob Burckhardt and the Concept of 'Historical Crisis.'" *Journal of European Studies* 40, no. 4 (2010): 307–327.

Marx, Karl. *The Eighteenth Brumaire of Louis Bonaparte.* New York: International, 1964.

———. *Revolution and Counter-revolution, or, Germany in 1848.* Edited by Eleanor Marx Aveling. New York: C. Scribner's Sons, 1896.

Matsusaka, Yoshihisa Tak. *The Making of Japanese Manchuria, 1904–1932.* Cambridge, MA: Harvard University Asia Center/Harvard University Press, 2001.

May, Arthur J. *The Hapsburg Monarchy, 1867–1914.* New York: W. W. Norton, 1968.

Mayer, Arno J. *Wilson vs. Lenin: Political Origins of the New Diplomacy, 1917–1918.* Cleveland: World, 1964.

McLane, John R. *Indian Nationalism and the Early Congress.* Princeton, NJ: Princeton University Press, 1977.

McPherson, James M. *Ordeal by Fire: The Civil War and Reconstruction.* 3rd ed. Boston: McGraw-Hill, 2001.

Medrano, Ethelia Ruiz. *Mexico's Indigenous Communities: Their Lands and Histories, 1500–2010.* Translated by Russ Davidson. Boulder: University Press of Colorado, 2010.

Michael, Franz, with Chung-li Chang. *The Taiping Rebellion: History and Documents.* 3 vols. Seattle: University of Washington Press, 1966–1971.

Michels, Robert. *Political Parties: A Sociological Study of the Oligarchical Tendencies of Modern Democracy.* Translated by Eden Paul and Cedar Paul. New York: Collier, 1962.

Middlemas, Keith. *Politics in Industrial Society: The Experience of the British System since 1911.* London: A. Deutsch, 1979.

Miłosz, Cseław. *The Captive Mind.* Translated by Jane Zielonko. New York: Vintage, 1955.

Min, Tu-Ki. *National Polity and Local Power: The Transformation of Late Imperial China.* Edited by Philip A. Kuhn and Timothy Brook. Cambridge, MA: Harvard Yenching Institute/Harvard University Press, 1989.

Mintz, Sidney W. *Sweetness and Power: The Place of Sugar in Modern History.* New York: Viking, 1985.

Mironov, Boris N. *The Social History of Imperial Russia, 1700–1917.* 2 vols. Boulder, CO: Westview Press, 2000.

Mommsen, Wolfgang J. *Max Weber and German Politics, 1890–1920.* Translated by Michael S. Steinberg. Chicago: University of Chicago Press, 1984.

Myers, Ramon H., and Mark R. Peattie, eds. *The Japanese Colonial Empire, 1895–1945.* Princeton, NJ: Princeton University Press, 1984.

Neumann, Franz. *Behemoth: The Structure and Practice of National Socialism, 1933–1944.* Rev ed. New York: Oxford University Press, 1944.

Norman, E. H. *Origins of the Modern Japanese State: Selected Writings of E. H. Norman.* Edited by John W. Dower. New York: Pantheon, 1975.

Osterhammel, Jürgen. *Colonialism: A Theoretical Overview.* Translated by Shelley L. Frisch. Princeton, NJ: M. Wiener, 1997.

———. *Die Verwandlung der Welt: Eine Geschichte des 19. Jahrhunderts.* Munich: C. H. Beck, 2009.

Ostrogorski, Moisei. *Democracy and the Organization of Political Parties.* Translated by Frederick Clarke. New York: Macmillan, 1902.

———. *Democracy and the Party System in the United States: A Study in Extra-Constitutional Government.* New York: Macmillan, 1910.

Owen, Roger. *State, Power, and Politics in the Making of the Modern Middle East.* London: Routledge, 1992.

The Oxford History of the British Empire, vol. 4: *The Twentieth Century,* edited by Judith M. Brown and Wm. Roger Louis. New York: Oxford University Press, 1999.

The Oxford History of South Africa. 2 vols. Edited by Monica Wilson and Leonard Thompson. Oxford: Oxford University Press, 1969–1971.

Perdue, Peter C. *China Marches West: The Qing Conquest of Central Eurasia.* Cambridge, MA: Harvard University Press, 2005.

Perham, Margery. *Lugard.* 2 vols. London: Collins, 1960–1961.

Perkins, Dwight H., with Yeh-chien Wang, Kuo-ying Wang Hsiao, and Fung-ming Su. *Agricultural Development in China, 1368–1968.* Chicago: Aldine, 1969.

Pflanze, Otto. *Bismarck and the Development of Germany.* 3 vols. 2nd ed. Princeton, NJ: Princeton University Press, 1990.

Philbrick, Nathaniel. *The Last Stand: Custer, Sitting Bull, and the Battle of the Little Bighorn.* New York: Viking, 2010.

Pocock, J. G. A. *The Machiavellian Moment: Florentine Political Thought and the Atlantic Republican Tradition.* Princeton, NJ: Princeton University Press, 1975.

Polanyi, Karl. *The Great Transformation.* Boston: Beacon Press, 1957.

Pomeranz, Kenneth. *The Great Divergence: China, Europe, and the Making of the Modern World Economy.* Princeton, NJ: Princeton University Press, 2000.

Quataert, Donald. *The Ottoman Empire, 1700–1922.* New York: Cambridge University Press, 2000.

Ramusack, Barbara M. *The Indian Princes and Their States.* Vol. 3, part 6, of *The New Cambridge History of India,* edited by Gordon Johnson. Cambridge: Cambridge University Press, 2004.

Redlich, Josef. *Das Österreichische Staats- und Reichsproblem: Geschichtliche Darstellung der inneren Politik der habsburgischen Monarchie von 1848 bis zum Untergang des Reiches.* 2 vols. Leipzig: P. Reinhold, 1920–1921.

Reed, Nelson. *The Caste War of Yucatan.* Stanford, CA: Stanford University Press, 1964.

Reid, Brian Holden. *The Civil War and the Wars of the Nineteenth Century*. New York: HarperCollins/Smithsonian Books, 2006.

Reid, James J. *Crisis of the Ottoman Empire: Prelude to Collapse, 1839–1878*. Stuttgart: F. Steiner, 2000.

Reinhard, Wolfgang. *Geschichte der Staatsgewalt: Eine vergleichende Verfassungsgeschichte Europas von den Anfängen bis zur Gegenwart*. Munich: C. H. Beck, 1999.

Richter, Daniel K. *Facing East from Indian Country: A Native History of Early America*. Cambridge, MA: Harvard University Press, 2001.

Roberts, Andrew. *A History of Zambia*. New York: Africana, 1976.

Robinson, Geroid Tanquary. *Rural Russia under the Old Régime: A History of the Landlord-Peasant World and a Prologue to the Peasant Revolution of 1917*. New York: Macmillan, 1967.

Rodgers, Daniel T. *Atlantic Crossings: Social Politics in a Progressive Age*. Cambridge, MA: Harvard University Press, 1998.

Rosanvallon, Pierre. *Le moment Guizot*. Paris: Gallimard, 1985.

Rowe, William T. *China's Last Empire: The Great Qing*. Cambridge, MA: Harvard University Press, 2009.

Sarmiento, Domingo. *Facundo, or, Civilization and Barbarism*. Translated by Mary Mann. New York: Penguin, 1998.

Schivelbusch, Wolfgang. *Three New Deals: Reflections on Roosevelt's America, Mussolini's Italy and Hitler's Germany, 1933–1939*. Translated by Jefferson Chase. New York: Metropolitan, 2006.

Schmitt, Carl. *Der Begriff des Politischen*. Berlin: Duncker und Humblot, 1932.

———. *The Crisis of Parliamentary Democracy*. Translated by Ellen Kennedy. Cambridge, MA: MIT Press, 1985.

———. *The Nomos of the Earth in the Jus Publicum Europaeum*. Translated by G. L. Ulmen. New York: Telos, 2003.

———. *Political Theology: Four Chapters on the Concept of Sovereignty*. Translated by George Schwab. Chicago: University of Chicago Press, 2005.

Scott, James C. *The Art of Not Being Governed: An Anarchist History of Upland Southeast Asia*. New Haven, CT: Yale University Press, 2009.

———. *Seeing Like a State: How Certain Schemes to Improve the Human Condition Have Failed*. New Haven, CT: Yale University Press, 2008.

———. *Weapons of the Weak: Everyday Forms of Peasant Resistance*. New Haven, CT: Yale University Press, 1985.

Skinner, Quentin. *The Foundations of Modern Political Thought*. 2 vols. Cambridge: Cambridge University Press, 1978.

Smith, Anthony D. *The Antiquity of Nations*. Cambridge: Polity, 2004.

Smith, Denis Mack. *Cavour and Garibaldi, 1860: A Study in Political Conflict*. Cambridge: Cambridge University Press, 1954.

Snyder, Timothy. *Bloodland: Europe between Hitler and Stalin.* New York: Basic Books, 2010.

Sorel, Georges. *Réflexions sur la violence.* 4th ed. Paris: M. Rivière, 1919.

Spence, Jonathan D. *God's Chinese Son: The Taiping Heavenly Kingdom of Hong Xiuquan.* New York: W. W. Norton, 1996.

———. *The Search for Modern China.* Rev ed. New York: W. W. Norton, 1999.

Steinmetz, George. *The Devil's Handwriting: Precoloniality and the German Colonial State in Qingdao, Samoa, and Southwest Africa.* Chicago: University of Chicago Press, 2007.

Sternhell, Zeev. *La droite révolutionnaire: Les origines françaises du fascisme.* Rev. ed. Paris: Fayard, 2000.

Szabo, Franz A. J. *Kaunitz and Enlightened Absolutism, 1753–1780.* Cambridge: Cambridge University Press, 1994.

Teng, Ssu-yü, and John K. Fairbank, eds. *China's Response to the West: A Documentary Survey, 1839–1923.* Cambridge, MA: Harvard University Press, 1979.

Thompson, E. P. *The Making of the English Working Class.* New York: Vintage, 1963.

———. "The Moral Economy of the English Crowd in the Eighteenth Century." *Past and Present,* no. 50 (1971): 76–136.

Tips, Walter E. J. *Gustave Rolin-Jaequemyns and the Making of Modern Siam: The Diaries and Letters of King Chulalongkorn's General Adviser.* Bangkok: White Lotus, 1996.

Tucker, Richard P., and J. F. Richards, eds. *Global Deforestation and the Nineteenth-Century World Economy.* Durham, NC: Duke University Press, 1983.

Vázquez, Josefina Z., and Manuel Miño Grijalva, eds. *La construcción de las naciones latinoamericanas, 1820–1870.* Vol. 6 of *Historia general de América Latina.* Paris: UNESCO, 2003.

Vlastos, Stephen. *Peasant Protests and Uprisings in Tokugawa Japan.* Berkeley: University of California Press, 1986.

Watts, Sheldon. *Epidemics and History: Disease, Power, and Imperialism.* New Haven, CT: Yale University Press, 1997.

Wawro, Geoffrey. *The Austro-Prussian War: Austria's War with Prussia and Italy in 1866.* Cambridge: Cambridge University Press, 1996.

Weber, Eugen. *Action Française: Royalism and Reaction in Twentieth-Century France.* Stanford, CA: Stanford University Press, 1962.

Weber, Max. *Gesamtausgabe.* Part 1, vol. 17: *Wissenschaft als Beruf: Politik als Beruf.* Edited by Wolfgang J. Mommsen, Wolfgang Schluchter, and Birgitt Morgenbrod. Tübingen: Mohr, 1992.

Wehler, Hans-Ulrich. *Bismarck und der Imperialismus.* Rev. ed. Frankfurt: Suhrkamp, 1984.

Wesseling, H. L. *Divide and Rule: The Partition of Africa, 1880–1914.* Translated by Arnold J. Pomerans. Westport, CT: Praeger, 1996.

Wohl, Robert. *The Generation of 1914.* Cambridge, MA: Harvard University Press, 1979.

Woodward, C. Vann. *Origins of the New South, 1877–1913.* Baton Rouge: Louisiana State University Press, 1951.

Wyatt, David K. *The Politics of Reform in Thailand: Education in the Reign of King Chulalong-korn*. New Haven, CT: Yale University Press, 1969.

Zewde, Bahru. *A History of Modern Ethiopia, 1855–1891*. Rev. ed. Athens: Ohio University Press, 2001.

Empires and the Reach of the Global

Adas, Michael. *Machines as the Measure of Men: Science, Technology, and Ideologies of Western Dominance*. Ithaca, NY: Cornell University Press, 1989.

Ahmed, Sara. *Queer Phenomenology: Orientations, Objects, Others*. Durham, NC: Duke University Press, 2006.

Akita, Shigeru, ed. *Gentlemanly Capitalism, Imperialism, and Global History*. Basingstoke, UK: Palgrave Macmillan, 2002.

Aldrich, Robert. *Vestiges of the Colonial Empire in France: Monuments, Museums and Colonial Memories*. Basingstoke, UK: Palgrave Macmillan, 2005.

Allman, Jean, Susan Geiger, and Nakanyike Musisi, eds. *Women in African Colonial Histories*. Bloomington: Indiana University Press, 2002.

Allman, Jean, and Victoria Tashjian. *I Will Not Eat Stone: A Women's History of Colonial Asante*. Portsmouth, NH: Heinemann, 2000.

Andall, Jacqueline, and Derek Duncan, eds. *Italian Colonialism: Legacy and Memory*. Oxford: Peter Lang, 2005.

Anderson, Benedict. *Imagined Communities: Reflections on the Origin and Spread of Nationalism*. London: Verso, 1983.

———. *Under Three Flags: Anarchism and the Anti-Colonial Imagination*. London: Verso, 2005.

Arnold, David. *Science, Technology, and Medicine in Colonial India*. Cambridge: Cambridge University Press, 2000.

Baber, Zaheer. *The Science of Empire: Scientific Knowledge, Civilization, and Colonial Rule in India*. Albany: State University of New York Press, 1996.

Balce, Nerissa S. "The Filipina's Breast: Savagery, Docility, and the Erotics of the American Empire." *Social Text* 24, no. 2 (2006): 89–110.

Baldwin, Kate. *Beyond the Color Line and the Iron Curtain: Reading Encounters between Black and Red*. Durham, NC: Duke University Press, 2002.

Ballantyne, Tony. *Orientalism and Race: Aryanism in the British Empire*. Basingstoke, UK: Palgrave, 2002.

Ballantyne, Tony, and Antoinette Burton, eds. *Bodies in Contact: Rethinking Colonial Encounters in World History*. Durham, NC: Duke University Press, 2005.

———, eds. *Moving Subjects: Gender, Mobility, and Intimacy in an Age of Global Empire*. Urbana: University of Illinois Press, 2009.

Barkey, Karen. *Empire of Difference: The Ottomans in Comparative Perspective*. Cambridge: Cambridge University Press, 2008.

Barkey, Karen, and Mark von Hagen, eds. *After Empire: Multiethnic Societies and Nation-Building: The Soviet Union and Russian, Ottoman, and Habsburg Empires.* Boulder, CO: Westview Press, 1997.

Barlow, Tani E. *Formations of Colonial Modernity in East Asia.* Durham, NC: Duke University Press, 1997.

Bayly, C. A. *Imperial Meridian: The British Empire and the World, 1780–1830.* London: Longman, 1989.

Beasley, W. G. *Japan Encounters the Barbarian: Japanese Travellers in America and Europe.* New Haven, CT: Yale University Press, 1995.

———. *Japanese Imperialism, 1894–1945.* Oxford: Clarendon Press, 1987.

Bell, Duncan, ed. *Victorian Visions of Global Order: Empire and International Relations in Nineteenth-Century Political Thought.* Cambridge: Cambridge University Press, 2007.

Ben-Ghiat, Ruth, and Mia Fuller, eds. *Italian Colonialism.* Basingstoke, UK: Palgrave Macmillan, 2005.

Bose, Sugata. *A Hundred Horizons: The Indian Ocean in the Age of Global Empire.* Cambridge, MA: Harvard University Press, 2006.

Brower, Daniel R., and Edward J. Lazzerini, eds. *Russia's Orient: Imperial Borderlands and Peoples, 1700–1917.* Bloomington: Indiana University Press, 1997.

Burbank, Jane, Mark von Hagen, and Anatolyi Remnev, eds. *Russian Empire: Space, People, Power, 1700–1930.* Bloomington: Indiana University Press, 2007.

Burton, Antoinette. *Burdens of History: British Feminists, Indian Women, and Imperial Culture, 1865–1915.* Chapel Hill: University of North Carolina Press, 1994.

———, ed. *Gender, Sexuality, and Colonial Modernities.* London: Routledge, 1999.

———. "Getting Outside of the Global: Re-Positioning British Imperialism in World History." In *Race, Nation and Empire: Making Histories, 1750 to the Present,* edited by Catherine Hall and Keith McClelland. Manchester: Manchester University Press, 2010.

Bush, Barbara. *Imperialism and Postcolonialism.* Harlow, UK: Longman, 2006.

Cain, P. J., and A. G. Hopkins. *British Imperialism, 1688–2000.* 2nd ed. Harlow, UK: Longman, 2002.

Chakrabarty, Dipesh. *Provincializing Europe: Postcolonial Thought and Historical Difference.* Princeton, NJ: Princeton University Press, 2000.

Clancy-Smith, Julia, and Frances Gouda, eds. *Domesticating the Empire: Race, Gender, and Family Life in French and Dutch Colonialism.* Charlottesville: University Press of Virginia, 1998.

Cohn, Bernard S. *Colonialism and Its Forms of Knowledge: The British in India.* Princeton, NJ: Princeton University Press, 1996.

Conrad, Sebastian, and Dominic Sachsenmaier, eds. *Competing Visions of World Order: Global Moments and Movements, 1880s–1930s.* London: Palgrave Macmillan, 2007.

Cooper, Frederick. *Colonialism in Question: Theory, Knowledge, History.* Berkeley: University of California Press, 2005.

———. *From Slaves to Squatters: Plantation Labor and Agriculture in Zanzibar and Coastal Kenya, 1890–1925.* New Haven, CT: Yale University Press, 1980.

Dickinson, Edward Ross. "The German Empire: An Empire?" *History Workshop Journal* 66 (2008): 129–162.

Duara, Prasenjit. *Sovereignty and Authenticity: Manchukuo and the East Asian Modern.* Lanham, MD: Rowman and Littlefield, 2003.

Duus, Peter. *The Abacus and the Sword: The Japanese Penetration of Korea, 1859–1910.* Berkeley: University of California Press, 1995.

Duus, Peter, Ramon H. Myers, and Mark R. Peattie, eds. *The Japanese Informal Empire in China, 1895–1937.* Princeton, NJ: Princeton University Press, 1989.

Epprecht, Marc. *Hungochani: The History of a Dissident Sexuality in Southern Africa.* Montreal: McGill-Queen's University Press, 2004.

Esselstrom, Erik. *Crossing Empire's Edge: Foreign Ministry Police and Japanese Expansionism in Northeast Asia.* Honolulu: University of Hawai'i Press, 2009.

Farnie, D. A. *East and West of Suez: The Suez Canal in History, 1854–1956.* Oxford: Clarendon Press, 1969.

Fawaz, Leila Tarazi, and C. A. Bayly, with Robert Ilbert, eds. *Modernity and Culture: From the Mediterranean to the Indian Ocean.* New York: Columbia University Press, 2002.

Fay, Mary Ann, ed. "Early Twentieth-Century Middle Eastern Feminisms, Nationalism, and Transnationalism." *Journal of Middle East Women's Studies* 4, no. 1 (2008).

Ferguson, James. *Global Shadows: Africa in the Neoliberal World Order.* Durham, NC: Duke University Press, 2006.

Fletcher, Ian Christopher, Laura E. Nym Mayhall, and Philippa Levine, eds. *Women's Suffrage in the British Empire: Citizenship, Nation, and Race.* London: Routledge, 2000.

Frank, Andre Gunder. *ReOrient: Global Economy in the Asian Age.* Berkeley: University of California Press, 1998.

Frühstück, Sabine. *Colonizing Sex: Sexology and Social Control in Modern Japan.* Berkeley: University of California Press, 2003.

Geraci, Robert P., and Michael Khodarkovsky, eds. *Of Religion and Empire: Missions, Conversion, and Tolerance in Tsarist Russia.* Ithaca, NY: Cornell University Press, 2001.

Ghosh, Durba, and Dane Kennedy, eds. *Decentring Empire: Britain, India, and the Transcolonial World.* Hyderabad: Orient Longman, 2006.

Gilbar, Gad G., ed. *Ottoman Palestine, 1800–1914: Studies in Economic and Social History.* Leiden: E. J. Brill, 1990.

Gilroy, Paul. *The Black Atlantic: Modernity and Double Consciousness.* Cambridge, MA: Harvard University Press, 1993.

———. *"There Ain't No Black in the Union Jack": The Cultural Politics of Race and Nation.* London: Hutchinson, 1987.

Go, Julian. *American Empire and the Politics of Meaning: Elite Political Cultures in the Philippines and Puerto Rico during U.S. Colonialism.* Durham, NC: Duke University Press.

Go, Julian, and Anne L. Foster, eds. *The American Colonial State in the Philippines: Global Perspectives.* Durham, NC: Duke University Press, 2003.

Goswami, Manu. *Producing India: From Colonial Economy to National Space.* Chicago: University of Chicago Press, 2004.

Goto, Ken'ichi. *Tensions of Empire: Japan and Southeast Asia in the Colonial and Postcolonial World.* Edited by Paul H. Kratoska. Athens: Ohio University Press, 2003.

Grewal, Inderpal. *Transnational America: Feminisms, Diasporas, Neoliberalisms.* Durham, NC: Duke University Press, 2005.

Hall, Catherine. *Civilising Subjects: Colony and Metropole in the English Imagination, 1830–1867.* Chicago: University of Chicago Press, 2002.

Hall, Catherine, and Sonya O. Rose, eds. *At Home with the Empire: Metropolitan Culture and the Imperial World.* Cambridge: Cambridge University Press, 2006.

Hall, Stuart. "Cultural Studies: Two Paradigms." *Media, Culture & Society* 2, no. 1 (1980): 57–72.

———. *The Hard Road to Renewal: Thatcherism and the Crisis of the Left.* London: Verso, 1988.

Hall, Stuart, et al. *Policing the Crisis: Mugging, the State, and Law and Order.* London: Macmillan, 1978.

Headrick, Daniel R. *The Invisible Weapon: Telecommunications and International Politics, 1851–1945.* Oxford: Oxford University Press, 1991.

———. *The Tentacles of Progress: Technology Transfer in the Age of Imperialism, 1850–1940.* Oxford: Oxford University Press, 1988.

———. *The Tools of Empire: Technology and European Imperialism in the Nineteenth Century.* Oxford: Oxford University Press, 1981.

Hirsch, Francine. *Empire of Nations: Ethnographic Knowledge and the Making of the Soviet Union.* Ithaca, NY: Cornell University Press, 2005.

Ho, Engseng. *The Graves of Tarim: Genealogy and Mobility across the Indian Ocean.* Berkeley: University of California Press, 2006.

Hoganson, Kristin L. *Consumers' Imperium: The Global Production of American Domesticity, 1865–1920.* Chapel Hill: University of North Carolina Press, 2007.

———. *Fighting for American Manhood: How Gender Politics Provoked the Spanish-American and Philippine-American Wars.* New Haven, CT: Yale University Press, 1998.

İhsanoğlu, Ekmeleddin. *Science, Technology, and Learning in the Ottoman Empire: Western Influence, Local Institutions, and the Transfer of Knowledge.* Aldershot, UK: Ashgate, 2004.

Innis, H. A. *Empire and Communications.* Oxford: Clarendon Press, 1950.

Iriye, Akira. *China and Japan in the Global Setting.* Cambridge, MA: Harvard University Press, 1992.

İslamoğlu-İnan, Huri, ed. *The Ottoman Empire and the World-Economy*. Cambridge: Cambridge University Press, 1987.

Joseph, Gilbert M., Catherine C. LeGrand, and Ricardo D. Salvatore, eds. *Close Encounters of Empire: Writing the Cultural History of U.S.–Latin American Relations*. Durham, NC: Duke University Press, 1998.

Kale, Madhavi. *Fragments of Empire: Capital, Slavery, and Indian Indentured Labor Migration in the British Caribbean*. Philadelphia: University of Pennsylvania Press, 1998.

Kaplan, Amy. *The Anarchy of Empire in the Making of U.S. Culture*. Cambridge, MA: Harvard University Press, 2002.

Kaplan, Amy, and Donald E. Pease, eds. *Cultures of United States Imperialism*. Durham, NC: Duke University Press, 1993.

Karl, Rebecca E. *Staging the World: Chinese Nationalism at the Turn of the Twentieth Century*. Durham, NC: Duke University Press, 2002.

Kern, Stephen. *The Culture of Time and Space, 1880–1918*. Cambridge, MA: Harvard University Press, 1983.

Kerr, Ian J. *Building the Railways of the Raj, 1850–1900*. Delhi: Oxford University Press, 1995.
———, ed. *Railways in Modern India*. Oxford: Oxford University Press, 2001.

Khoury, Dina Rizk, and Dane Kennedy, eds. "Comparing Empires: The Ottoman Domains and the British Raj in the Long Nineteenth Century." *Comparative Studies of South Asia, Africa and the Middle East* 27, no. 2 (2007): 233–244.

Klein, Christina. *Cold War Orientalism: Asia in the Middlebrow Imagination, 1945–1961*. Berkeley: University of California Press, 2003.

Kramer, Paul A. *The Blood of Government: Race, Empire, the United States, and the Philippines*. Chapel Hill: University of North Carolina Press, 2006.

Kramer, Paul, and John Plotz, eds. "Pairing Empires: Britain and the United States, 1857–1947." *Journal of Colonialism and Colonial History* 2, no. 1 (2001).

Lake, Marilyn, and Henry Reynolds, eds. *Drawing the Global Colour Line: White Men's Countries and the International Challenge of Racial Equality*. Cambridge: Cambridge University Press, 2008.

Lambert, David, and Alan Lester, eds. *Colonial Lives across the British Empire: Imperial Careering in the Long Nineteenth Century*. Cambridge: Cambridge University Press, 2006.

Lebovics, Herman. *Bringing the Empire Back Home: France in the Global Age*. Durham, NC: Duke University Press, 2004.

Lee, Christopher J., ed. *Making a World after Empire: The Bandung Moment and Its Political Afterlives*. Athens: Ohio University Press, 2010.

Lester, Alan. *Imperial Networks: Creating Identities in Nineteenth-Century South Africa and Britain*. London: Routledge, 2001.

Levine, Philippa, ed. *Gender and Empire*. Oxford: Oxford University Press, 2004.

———. *Prostitution, Race, and Politics: Policing Venereal Disease in the British Empire.* London: Routledge, 2003.

Loomba, Ania. *Colonialism/Postcolonialism.* London: Routledge, 1998.

Lorcin, Patricia M. E. *Imperial Identities: Stereotyping, Prejudice and Race in Colonial Algeria.* New York: St. Martin's Press, 1995.

MacKenzie, John M. *Propaganda and Empire: The Manipulation of British Public Opinion, 1880–1960.* Manchester: Manchester University Press, 1984.

Mackie, Jamie. *Bandung, 1955: Non-Alignment and Afro-Asian Solidarity.* Paris: Didier Miller, 2005.

Manela, Erez. *The Wilsonian Moment: Self-Determination and the International Origins of Anticolonial Nationalism.* Oxford: Oxford University Press, 2007.

Matsuda, Matt K. *Empire of Love: Histories of France and the Pacific.* Oxford: Oxford University Press, 2005.

Metcalf, Thomas R. *Imperial Connections: India in the Indian Ocean Arena, 1860–1920.* Berkeley: University of California Press, 2007.

Millward, James A. *Beyond the Pass: Economy, Ethnicity, and Empire in Qing Central Asia, 1759–1864.* Stanford, CA: Stanford University Press, 1998.

Morris-Suzuki, Tessa. *Re-inventing Japan: Time, Space, Nation.* Armonk, NY: M. E. Sharpe, 1998.

———. *The Technological Transformation of Japan: From the Seventeenth to the Twenty-First Century.* Cambridge: Cambridge University Press, 1994.

Ngai, Mae M. *Impossible Subjects: Illegal Aliens and the Making of Modern America.* Princeton, NJ: Princeton University Press, 2004.

Northrop, Douglas. *Veiled Empire: Gender and Power in Stalinist Central Asia.* Ithaca, NY: Cornell University Press, 2004.

Osterhammel, Jürgen. *Colonialism: A Theoretical Overview.* Translated by Shelley L. Frish. Princeton, NJ: M. Wiener, 1997.

Peabody, Sue, and Tyler Stovall, eds. *The Color of Liberty: Histories of Race in France.* Durham, NC: Duke University Press, 2003.

Pennybacker, Susan D. "The Universal Races Congress, London Political Culture, and Imperial Dissent, 1900–1939." *Radical History Review* 92 (2005): 103–117.

Perdue, Peter C. *China Marches West: The Qing Conquest of Central Eurasia.* Cambridge, MA: Belknap Press of Harvard University Press, 2005.

Perry, Adele. *On the Edge of Empire: Gender, Race, and the Making of British Columbia, 1849–1871.* Toronto: University of Toronto Press, 2001.

Pollard, Lisa. *Nurturing the Nation: The Family Politics of Modernizing, Colonizing and Liberating Egypt, 1805–1923.* Berkeley: University of California Press, 2005.

Pomeranz, Kenneth. *The Great Divergence: China, Europe, and the Making of the Modern World Economy.* Princeton, NJ: Princeton University Press, 2000.

Porter, Bernard. *The Absent-Minded Imperialists: Empire, Society, and Culture in Britain.* Oxford: Oxford University Press, 2004.

Porter, Simon J. "Webs, Networks, and Systems: Globalization and the Mass Media in the Nineteenth- and Twentieth-Century British Empire." *Journal of British Studies* 46 (2007): 621–646.

Prashad, Vijay. *The Darker Nations: A People's History of the Third World.* New York: New Press, 2007.

———. *Everybody Was Kung Fu Fighting: Afro-Asian Connections and the Myth of Cultural Purity.* Boston: Beacon Press, 2001.

Rupp, Leila J. "Constructing Internationalism: The Case of Transnational Women's Organizations, 1885–1945." *American Historical Review* 99 (1994): 1571–1600.

Sachsenmaier, Dominic. "Alternative Visions of World Order in the Aftermath of World War I: Global Perspectives on Chinese Approaches." In *Competing Visions of World Order: Global Moments and Movements, 1880s–1930s,* edited by Sebastian Conrad and Dominic Sachsenmaier. London: Palgrave Macmillan, 2007.

Sahadeo, Jeff. *Russian Colonial Society in Tashkent, 1865–1923.* Bloomington: Indiana University Press, 2007.

Said, Edward W. *Orientalism.* New York: Vintage, 1978.

Schivelbusch, Wolfgang. *The Railway Journey: The Industrialization of Time and Space in the 19th Century.* Berkeley: University of California Press, 1986.

Shaw, Carolyn Martin. *Colonial Inscriptions: Race, Sex, and Class in Kenya.* Minneapolis: University of Minnesota Press, 1995.

Silva, Noenoe K. *Aloha Betrayed: Native Hawaiian Resistance to American Colonialism.* Durham, NC: Duke University Press, 2004.

Sinha, Mrinalini. *Colonial Masculinity: The 'Manly Englishman' and the 'Effeminate Bengali' in the Late Nineteenth Century.* Manchester: Manchester University Press, 1995.

———. *Specters of Mother India: The Global Restructuring of an Empire.* Durham, NC: Duke University Press, 2006.

Smith, Bonnie G., ed. *Women's History in Global Perspective.* 3 vols. Urbana: University of Illinois Press, 2004–2005.

Smith, Neil. *American Empire: Roosevelt's Geographer and the Prelude to Globalization.* Berkeley: University of California Press, 2003.

Spivak, Gayatri Chakravorty. "The Rani of Simur: An Essay in Reading the Archives." *History and Theory* 24 (1985): 247–272.

Stephens, Michelle Ann. *Black Empire: The Masculine Global Imaginary of Caribbean Intellectuals in the United States, 1914–1962.* Durham, NC: Duke University Press.

Stoler, Ann Laura, ed. *Haunted by Empire: Geographies of Intimacy in North American History.* Durham, NC: Duke University Press, 2006.

Sunderland, Willard. *Taming the Wild Field: Colonization and Empire on the Russian Steppe.* Ithaca, NY: Cornell University Press, 2004.

Thomas, Martin. *The French Empire between the Wars: Imperialism, Politics and Society*. Manchester: Manchester University Press, 2005.

Thompson, Andrew. *The Empire Strikes Back? The Impact of Imperialism on Britain from the Mid-Nineteenth Century*. Harlow, UK: Pearson Longman, 2005.

Todd, Jan. *Colonial Technology: Science and the Transfer of Innovation to Australia*. Cambridge: Cambridge University Press, 1995.

Townsend, Susan C. *Yanaihara Tadao and Japanese Colonial Policy: Redeeming Empire*. Richmond, UK: Curzon, 2000.

Truett, Samuel, and Elliott Young, eds. *Continental Crossroads: Remapping U.S.-Mexico Borderlands History*. Durham, NC: Duke University Press, 2004.

Visram, Rozina. *Ayahs, Lascars, and Princes: Indians in Britain, 1700–1947*. London: Pluto, 1986.

Von Eschen, Penny M. *Race against Empire: Black Americans and Anticolonialism, 1937–1957*. Ithaca, NY: Cornell University Press, 1997.

Weinbaum, Alys Eve, et al., eds. *The Modern Girl Around the World: Consumption, Modernity, and Globalization*. Durham, NC: Duke University Press, 2008.

West, Michael O., William G. Martin, and Fanon Che Wilkins, eds. *From Toussaint to Tupac: The Black International since the Age of Revolution*. Chapel Hill: University of North Carolina Press, 2009.

Winseck, Dwayne R., and Robert M. Pike. *Communication and Empire: Media, Markets, and Globalization, 1860–1930*. Durham, NC: Duke University Press, 2007.

Wong, Aliza S. *Race and the Nation in Liberal Italy, 1861–1911: Meridionalism, Empire, and Diaspora*. Basingstoke, UK: Palgrave Macmillan, 2006.

Woollacott, Angela. *To Try Her Fortune in London: Australian Women, Colonialism, and Modernity*. New York: Oxford University Press, 2001.

Young, Louise. *Japan's Total Empire: Manchuria and the Culture of Wartime Imperialism*. Berkeley: University of California Press, 1998.

Migrations and Belongings

Appadurai, Arjun. "Global Ethnoscapes: Notes and Queries for a Transnational Anthropology." In *Recapturing Anthropology: Working in the Present,* edited by Richard G. Fox. Santa Fe, NM: School of American Research Press, 1991.

Bade, Klaus J. *Europa in Bewegung: Migration vom späten 18. Jahrhundert bis zur Gegenwart*. Munich: C. H. Beck, 2000.

Bade, Klaus J., Pieter C. Emmer, Leo Lucassen, and Jochen Oltmer, eds. *The Encyclopedia of European Migration and Minorities: From the Seventeenth Century to the Present*. Cambridge: Cambridge University Press, 2011.

Balachandran, G. "Circulation through Seafaring: Indian Seamen, 1890–1945." In *Society and Circulation: Mobile People and Itinerant Cultures in South Asia, 1750–1950,* edited by

Claude Markovits, Jacques Pouchepadass, and Sanjay Subrahmanyam. Delhi: Permanent Black, 2003.

Belich, James. *Replenishing the Earth: The Settler Revolution and the Rise of the Anglo-World, 1783–1939.* Oxford: Oxford University Press, 2009.

Bell-Fialkoff, Andrew. *Ethnic Cleansing.* New York: St. Martin's Press, 1996.

Bose, Sugata. *A Hundred Horizons: The Indian Ocean in the Age of Global Empire.* Cambridge, MA: Harvard University Press, 2006.

Bremen, Jan. *Labour Bondage in West India: From Past to Present.* New Delhi: Oxford University Press, 2007.

———. *Taming the Coolie Beast: Plantation Society and the Colonial Order in Southeast Asia.* Delhi: Oxford University Press, 1989.

Bremen, Jan, and E. Valentine Daniel. "Conclusion: The Making of a Coolie." *Journal of Peasant Studies* 19, nos. 3–4 (1992): 268–295.

Brettell, Caroline B., and James F. Hollifield, eds. *Migration Theory: Talking Across Disciplines.* Rev. ed. London: Routledge, 2008.

Chaudhuri, Nupur, and Margaret Strobel, eds. *Western Women and Imperialism: Complicity and Resistance.* Bloomington: Indiana University Press, 1992.

Cheng, Lucie, and Edna Bonacich, eds. *Labor Immigration under Capitalism: Asian Workers in the United States before World War II.* Berkeley: University of California Press, 1984.

Christopher, Emma, Cassandra Pybus, and Marcus Rediker, eds. *Many Middle Passages: Forced Migration and the Making of the Modern World.* Berkeley: University of California Press, 2007.

Cohen, Robin, ed. *The Cambridge Survey of World Migration.* Cambridge: Cambridge University Press, 1995.

Coniff, Michael L., and Thomas J. Davis. *Africans in the Americas: A History of the Black Diaspora.* New York: St. Martin's Press, 1994.

Cooper, Frederick, and Ann Laura Stoler, eds. *Tensions of Empire: Colonial Cultures in a Bourgeois World.* Berkeley: University of California Press, 1997.

Curto, José C., and Renée Soulodre-LaFrance. "Introduction: Interconnections between Africa and the Americas during the Era of the Slave Trade." In *Africa and the Americas: Interconnections during the Slave Trade,* edited by José C. Curto and Renée Soulodre-LaFrance. Trenton, NJ: Africa World Press, 2005.

Daniels, Roger. "No Lamps Were Lit for Them: Angel Island and the Historiography of Asian American Immigration." *Journal of American Ethnic History* 17 (1997): 3–18.

Drescher, Seymour. *Abolition: A History of Slavery and Antislavery.* New York: Cambridge University Press, 2009.

Dupeux, Georges, ed. *Les Migrations internationale de la fin du XVIIIe siècle à nos jours.* Paris: Centre National de la Recherche Scientifique, 1980.

Eltis, David, ed. *Coerced and Free Migration: Global Perspectives*. Stanford, CA: Stanford University Press, 2002.

Fahrmeir, Andreas, Olivier Faron, and Patrick Weil, eds. *Migration Control in the North Atlantic World: The Evolution of State Practices in Europe and the United States from the French Revolution to the Inter-War Period*. New York: Berghahn, 2003.

Feys, Torsten, Lewis R. Fischer, Stéphane Hoste, and S. en Vanfraechem, eds. *Maritime Transport and Migration: The Connections between Maritime and Migration Networks*. St. John's, NL: International Maritime Economic History Association, 2007.

Gabaccia, Donna R. *Italy's Many Diasporas*. Seattle: University of Washington Press, 2000.

Gabaccia, Donna R., and Dirk Hoerder, eds. *Connecting Seas and Connected Ocean Rims: Indian, Atlantic, and Pacific Oceans and China Seas Migrations from the 1830s to the 1920s*. Leiden: Brill, 2011.

Gatrell, Peter. *A Whole Empire Walking: Refugees in Russia during World War I*. Bloomington: Indiana University Press, 1999.

Gilroy, Paul. *The Black Atlantic: Modernity and Double Consciousness*. Cambridge, MA: Harvard University Press, 1993.

Gottschang, Thomas R., and Diana Lary. *Swallows and Settlers: The Great Migration from North China to Manchuria*. Ann Arbor: Center for Chinese Studies, University of Michigan, 2000.

Green, Nancy L., and François Weil, eds. *Citizenship and Those Who Leave: The Politics of Emigration and Expatriation*. Urbana: University of Illinois Press, 2007.

Harzig, Christiane, and Dirk Hoerder, with Donna Gabaccia. *What Is Migration History?* Cambridge: Polity, 2009.

Harzig, Christiane, and Danielle Juteau, with Irina Schmitt, eds. *The Social Construction of Diversity: Recasting the Master Narrative of Industrial Nations*. New York: Berghahn, 2003.

Ho, Engseng. *The Graves of Tarim: Genealogy and Mobility across the Indian Ocean*. Berkeley: University of California Press, 2006.

Hoerder, Dirk. *Cultures in Contact: World Migrations in the Second Millennium*. Durham, NC: Duke University Press, 2002.

———, ed. *Labor Migration in the Atlantic Economies: The European and North American Working Classes during the Period of Industrialization*. Westport, CT: Greenwood Press, 1985.

Hoerder, Dirk, with Christiane Harzig and Adrian Shubert, eds. *The Historical Practice of Diversity: Transcultural Interactions from the Early Modern Mediterranean to the Postcolonial World*. New York: Berghahn, 2003.

Jackson, James H., Jr. and Leslie Page Moch. "Migration and the Social History of Modern Europe." *Historical Methods* 22 (1989): 27–36.

Karras, Alan L., and J. R. McNeill, eds. *Atlantic American Societies: From Columbus through Abolition, 1492 to 1888*. London: Routledge, 1992.

Lal, Brij V., Peter Reeves, and Rajesh Rai, eds. *The Encyclopedia of the Indian Diaspora*. Singapore: Didier Millet/National University of Singapore, 2006.

Lary, Diana, and Stephen MacKinnon, eds. *The Scars of War: The Impact of Warfare on Modern China*. Vancouver: UBC Press, 2001.

Lucassen, Jan, and Leo Lucassen, eds. *Migration, Migration History, History: Old Paradigms and New Perspectives*. Bern: Peter Lang, 1997.

Markovits, Claude. *The Global World of Indian Merchants, 1750–1947: Traders of Sind from Bukhara to Panama*. Cambridge: Cambridge University Press, 2000.

Marrus, Michael R. *The Unwanted: European Refugees in the Twentieth Century*. Oxford: Oxford University Press, 1985.

McClintock, Anne. *Imperial Leather: Race, Gender, and Sexuality in the Colonial Contest*. New York: Routledge, 1995.

McKeown, Adam. "Chinese Emigration in Global Context." *Journal of Global History* 5 (2010): 95–124.

———. *Chinese Migrant Networks and Cultural Change: Peru, Chicago, Hawaii, 1900–1936*. Chicago: University of Chicago Press, 2001.

———. "Global Migration, 1846–1940." *Journal of World History* 15, no. 2 (2004): 155–189.

———. *Melancholy Order: Asian Migration and the Globalization of Borders*. New York: Columbia University Press, 2008.

McPherson, Kenneth. "Processes of Cultural Interaction in the Indian Ocean: An Historical Perspective." *Great Circle* 6, no. 2 (1984): 78–92.

Metcalf, Thomas R. *Imperial Connections: India in the Indian Ocean Arena, 1860–1920*. Berkeley: University of California Press, 2007.

Midgley, Clare, ed. *Gender and Imperialism*. Manchester: Manchester University Press, 1998.

Moch, Leslie Page. *Moving Europeans: Migration in Western Europe since 1650*. 2nd ed. Bloomington: Indiana University Press, 2003.

Moya, José C. "A Continent of Immigrants: Postcolonial Shifts in the Western Hemisphere." *Hispanic American Historical Review* 86, no. 1 (2006): 1–28.

Moya, José C., and Adam McKeown. "World Migration in the Long Twentieth Century." In *Essays on Twentieth-Century History,* edited by Michael Adas. Philadelphia: Temple University Press, 2010.

Ness, Immanuel, ed. *The Encyclopedia of Global Human Migration*. Oxford: Wiley-Blackwell, forthcoming.

Northrup, David. *Indentured Labor in the Age of Imperialism, 1834–1922*. Cambridge: Cambridge University Press, 1995.

Nugent, Walter. *Crossings: The Great Transatlantic Migrations, 1870–1914*. Bloomington: Indiana University Press, 1992.

Pan, Lynn, ed. *The Encyclopedia of the Chinese Overseas*. Cambridge, MA: Harvard University Press, 1999.

Pearson, Michael. *The Indian Ocean*. London: Routledge, 2003.

Pierson, Ruth Roach, and Nupur Chaudhuri, with Beth McAuley, eds. *Nation, Empire, Colony: Historicizing Gender and Race*. Bloomington: Indiana University Press, 1998.

Rediker, Marcus. *The Slave Ship: A Human History.* New York: Viking, 2007.

Roberts, Allen F. "La 'Géographie Processuelle': Un nouveau paradigme pour les aires culturelles." *Lendemains* 31, nos. 122–123 (2006): 41–61.

Said, Edward W. *Orientalism.* New York: Vintage, 1994.

Sharpe, Pamela, ed. *Women, Gender, and Labour Migration: Historical and Global Perspectives.* London: Routledge, 2001.

Sinha, Mrinalini. *Colonial Masculinity: The 'Manly Englishman' and the 'Effeminate Bengali' in the Late Nineteenth Century.* Manchester: Manchester University Press, 1995.

Skeldon, Ronald. "International Migration within and from the East and Southeast Asian Region: A Review Essay." *Asian and Pacific Migration Journal* 1 (1992): 19–63.

Smith, Alan K. *Creating a World Economy: Merchant Capital, Colonialism, and World Trade, 1400–1825.* Boulder, CO: Westview Press, 1991.

Stola, Dariusz. "Forced Migrations in Central European History." *International Migration Review* 26 (1992): 324–341.

Stoler, Ann Laura. *Capitalism and Confrontation in Sumatra's Plantation Belt, 1870–1979.* New Haven, CT: Yale University Press, 1985.

———. "Making Empire Respectable: The Politics of Race and Sexual Morality in 20th-Century Colonial Cultures." *American Ethnologist* 16 (1989): 634–660.

———. *Race and the Education of Desire: Foucault's* History of Sexuality *and the Colonial Order of Things.* Durham, NC: Duke University Press, 1995.

Strobel, Margaret. *Gender, Sex, and Empire.* Washington, DC: American Historical Association, 1993.

Thornton, John. *Africa and Africans in the Making of the Atlantic World, 1400–1800.* Rev ed. New York: Cambridge University Press, 1998.

Tinker, Hugh. *A New System of Slavery: The Export of Indian Labour Overseas, 1830–1920.* London: Institute of Race Relations/Oxford University Press, 1974.

Torpey, John. *The Invention of the Passport: Surveillance, Citizenship, and the State.* Cambridge: Cambridge University Press, 2000.

Van Kirk, Sylvia. *"Many Tender Ties": Women in Fur-Trade Society in Western Canada, 1670–1870.* Winnipeg: Watson and Dwyer, 1980.

Vargas-Silva, Carlos, ed. *Handbook of Research Methods in Migration.* Cheltenham, UK: Edward Elgar, 2012.

Vecoli, Rudolph J., and Suzanne M. Sinke, eds. *A Century of European Migrations, 1830–1930.* Urbana: University of Illinois Press, 1991.

Vidal, Cécile. "La Nouvelle histoire atlantique: Nouvelle perspectives sur les relations entre l'Europe, l'Afrique et les Amériques du XVe au XIXe siècle." *Revue internationale des livres et des idées* 4 (2008): 23–28.

Wang Gungwu, ed. *Global History and Migrations.* Boulder, CO: Westview Press, 1997.

Willcox, Walter F., ed. *International Migrations.* 2 vols. New York: National Bureau of Economic Research, 1929–1931.

Williams, Raymond. *Culture and Society, 1780–1950.* New York: Columbia University Press, 1958.

Wolf, Eric R. *Europe and the People without History.* Berkeley: University of California Press, 1982.

Yu, Henry. *Thinking Orientals: Migration, Contact, and Exoticism in Modern America.* Oxford: Oxford University Press, 2001.

Zolberg, Aristide R. *A Nation by Design: Immigration Policy in the Fashioning of America.* New York: Russell Sage Foundation/Harvard University Press, 2006.

Commodity Chains in a Global Economy

Adas, Michael. *The Burma Delta: Economic Development and Social Change on an Asian Rice Frontier, 1852–1941.* Madison: University of Wisconsin Press, 1974.

Adelman, Jeremy. *Frontier Development: Land, Labour, and Capital on the Wheatlands of Argentina and Canada, 1890–1914.* Oxford: Clarendon Press, 1994.

Albert, Bill, and Adrian Graves, eds. *Crisis and Change in the International Sugar Economy, 1860–1914.* Norwich, UK: ISC Press, 1984.

Appadurai, Arjun, ed. *The Social Life of Things: Commodities in Cultural Perspective.* New York: Cambridge University Press, 1986.

Arrighi, Giovanni. *The Long Twentieth Century: Money, Power, and the Origins of Our Times.* London: Verso, 1994.

Bair, Jennifer, ed. *Frontiers of Commodity Chain Research.* Stanford, CA: Stanford University Press, 2009.

Bairoch, Paul, and Bouda Etemad. *Structure par produits des exportations du Tiers-monde.* Geneva: Droz, 1985.

Ball, Daniel U., ed. *Kaffee im Spiegel europäischer Trinksitten.* Zurich: Johann Jacobs Museum, 1991.

Barker, Randolph, and Robert W. Herdt, with Beth Rose. *The Rice Economy of Asia.* Washington, DC: Resources for the Future, 1985.

Bayly, C. A. *The Birth of the Modern World, 1780–1914: Global Connections and Comparisons.* Malden, MA: Blackwell, 2004.

Boahen, A. Adu, ed. *Africa under Colonial Domination, 1880–1935,* vol. 7 of *General History of Africa.* Berkeley: University of California Press, 1985.

Brasil, Diretoria Geral da Estatística (DGE). *Anuário Estatístico, 1930/1940.* Rio de Janeiro: Imprensa Nacional, 1940.

Bray, Francesca. *The Rice Economies: Technology and Development in Asian Societies.* Oxford: Blackwell, 1986.

Brown, Jonathan C. *Oil and Revolution in Mexico.* Berkeley: University of California Press, 1992.

Bulmer-Thomas, Victor. *The Economic History of Latin America since Independence.* New York: Cambridge University Press, 1994.

Burke, Edmund, III, and Kenneth Pomeranz, eds. *The Environment and World History.* Berkeley: University of California Press, 2009.

Cain, P. J., and A. G. Hopkins. *British Imperialism: Innovation and Expansion, 1688–1914.* London: Longman, 1993.

Cameron, Rondo, and V. I. Bovykin, eds. *International Banking, 1870–1914.* New York: Oxford University Press, 1991.

Cárdenas, Enrique, José Antonio Ocampo, and Rosemary Thorp, eds. *An Economic History of Twentieth-Century Latin America.* 3 vols. New York: Palgrave, 2000.

Carter, Susan B., et al., eds. *Historical Statistics of the United States: Millennial Edition Online.* Cambridge: Cambridge University Press, 2006–. http://www.cambridge.org.

Chakrabarty, Dipesh. *Rethinking Working-Class History: Bengal, 1890–1940.* Princeton, NJ: Princeton University Press, 1989.

Chandler, Alfred D., Jr. *The Visible Hand: The Managerial Revolution in American Business.* Cambridge, MA: Belknap Press of Harvard University Press, 1977.

Chandler, Alfred D., Jr., with Takashi Hikino. *Scale and Scope: The Dynamics of Industrial Capitalism.* Cambridge, MA: Belknap Press of Harvard University Press, 1990.

Cheng, Siok-Hwa. *The Rice Industry of Burma, 1852–1940.* Kuala Lumpur: University of Malaya Press, 1968.

Clarence-Smith, William Gervase. *Cocoa and Chocolate, 1765–1914.* London: Routledge, 2000.

Clarence-Smith, William Gervase, and Steven Topik, eds. *The Global Coffee Economy in Africa, Asia and Latin America, 1500–1989.* New York: Cambridge University Press, 2003.

Coatsworth, John H., and Alan M. Taylor, eds. *Latin America and the World Economy since 1800.* Cambridge, MA: Harvard University Press/David Rockefeller Center for Latin American Studies, 1998.

Cronon, William. *Nature's Metropolis: Chicago and the Great West.* New York: W. W. Norton, 1991.

Crosby, Alfred W. *Ecological Imperialism: The Biological Expansion of Europe, 900–1200.* New York: Cambridge University Press, 1986.

Davis, Lance E., and Robert A. Huttenback, with Susan Gray Davis. *Mammon and the Pursuit of Empire: The Political Economy of British Imperialism, 1860–1912.* New York: Cambridge University Press, 1986.

Davis, Lance E., Robert A. Huttenback, and Douglass North. *Institutional Change and American Economic Growth.* Cambridge: Cambridge University Press, 1971.

Dand, Robin. *The International Cocoa Trade.* New York: J. Wiley, 1997.

Dean, Warren. *With Broadax and Firebrand: The Destruction of the Brazilian Atlantic Forest.* Berkeley: University of California Press, 1995.

Deerr, Noël. *The History of Sugar.* 2 vols. London: Chapman and Hall, 1949–1950.

De Grazia, Victoria. *Irresistible Empire: America's Advance through Twentieth-Century Europe.* Cambridge, MA: Belknap Press of Harvard University Press, 2005.

De Vries, Jan. *The Industrious Revolution: Consumer Behavior and the Household Economy, 1650 to the Present.* Cambridge: Cambridge University Press, 2008.

Dore, Elizabeth. *Myths of Modernity: Peonage and Patriarchy in Nicaragua.* Durham, NC: Duke University Press, 2006.

Dunsdorfs, Egards. *The Australian Wheat-Growing Industry, 1788–1948.* Melbourne: University Press, 1956.

Dye, Alan. *Cuban Sugar in the Age of Mass Production: Technology and the Economics of the Sugar Central, 1899–1929.* Stanford, CA: Stanford University Press, 1998.

Eichengreen, Barry J. *Globalizing Capital: A History of the International Monetary System.* 2nd ed. Princeton, NJ: Princeton University Press, 2008.

Evans, Sterling. *Bound in Twine: The History and Ecology of the Henequen-Wheat Complex for Mexico and the American and Canadian Plains, 1880–1950.* College Station: Texas A&M University Press, 2007.

Ferguson, Niall. *Empire: How Britain Made the Modern World.* London: Allen Lane, 2003.

Finlay, Mark R. *Growing American Rubber: Strategic Plants and the Politics of National Security.* New Brunswick, NJ: Rutgers University Press, 2009.

Fishlow, Albert. *American Railroads and the Transformation of the Antebellum Economy.* Cambridge, MA: Harvard University Press, 1965.

Fogel, Robert William. *Railroads and American Economic Growth: Essays in Econometric History.* Baltimore: Johns Hopkins University Press, 1964.

Gallagher, John, and Ronald Robinson. "The Imperialism of Free Trade." *Economic History Review* 6 (1953): 1–15.

Gardella, Robert. *Harvesting Mountains: Fujian and the China Tea Trade, 1757–1937.* Berkeley: University of California Press, 1994.

Gereffi, Gary, John Humphrey, and Timothy Sturgeon. "The Governance of Global Value Chains." *Review of International Political Economy* 12 (2005): 78–104.

Gootenberg, Paul. *Andean Cocaine: The Making of a Global Drug.* Chapel Hill: University of North Carolina Press, 2008.

Goswami, Omkar. *Industry, Trade, and Peasant Society: The Jute Economy of Eastern India, 1900–1947.* New York: Oxford University Press, 1991.

Gould, Jeffrey L., and Aldo A. Lauria-Santiago. *To Rise in Darkness: Revolution, Repression, and Memory in El Salvador, 1920–1932.* Durham, NC: Duke University Press, 2008.

Haber, Stephen, ed. *How Latin America Fell Behind: Essays on the Economic Histories of Brazil and Mexico, 1800–1914.* Stanford, CA: Stanford University Press, 1997.

Headrick, Daniel R. *Power over Peoples: Technology, Environments, and Western Imperialism, 1400 to the Present.* Princeton, NJ: Princeton University Press, 2010.

———. *The Tentacles of Progress: Technology Transfer in the Age of Imperialism, 1850–1940.* New York: Oxford University Press, 1988.

Hine, Thomas. *The Total Package: The Evolution and Secret Meanings of Boxes, Bottles, Cans, and Tubes.* Boston: Little, Brown, 1995.

Hobsbawm, Eric. *The Age of Empire, 1875–1914*. New York: Pantheon, 1987.

———. *The Age of Extremes: The Short Twentieth Century, 1914–1991*. London: Michael Joseph, 1994.

Hochschild, Adam. *King Leopold's Ghost: A Story of Greed, Terror, and Heroism in Colonial Africa*. Boston: Houghton Mifflin, 1998.

Hoganson, Kristin L. *Consumers' Imperium: The Global Production of American Domesticity, 1865–1920*. Chapel Hill: University of North Carolina Press, 2007.

Hugill, Peter J. *World Trade since 1431: Geography, Technology, and Capitalism*. Baltimore: Johns Hopkins University Press, 1993.

Innis, Harold A. *Problems of Staple Production in Canada*. Toronto: Ryerson, 1933.

Jackson, Joe. *The Thief at the End of the World: Rubber, Power, and the Seeds of Empire*. New York: Viking, 2008.

Jones, Geoffrey. *British Multinational Banking, 1830–1930*. Oxford: Clarendon Press, 1993.

Kenwood, A. G., and A. L. Lougheed. *The Growth of the International Economy, 1820–2000: An Introductory Text*. 4th ed. London: Routledge, 1999.

Kuntz Ficker, Sandra. *Las exportaciones mexicanas durante la primera globalización, 1870–1929*. Mexico City: El Colegio de México, Centro de Estudios Históricos, 2010.

Landes, David S. *The Wealth and Poverty of Nations: Why Some Are So Rich and Some So Poor*. New York: W. W. Norton, 1998.

———. "The 'Great Drain' and Industrialisation: Commodity Flows from Periphery to Centre in Historical Perspective." In *Economic Growth and Resources*, vol. 2: *Trends and Factors,* ed. R. C. O. Matthews. London: Macmillan, 1980.

Laux, James M. *The European Automobile Industry*. New York: Twayne, 1992.

League of Nations. *Statistical Year-Book of the League of Nations*. Geneva: League of Nations, Economic and Financial Section, 1927–1945. http://digital.library.northwestern.edu /league/stat.html.

Lears, T. J. Jackson. *Fables of Abundance: A Cultural History of Advertising in America*. New York: Basic Books, 1994.

Levenstein, Harvey A. *Revolution at the Table: The Transformation of the American Diet*. New York: Oxford University Press, 1988.

Levin, Jonathan V. *The Export Economies: Their Pattern of Development in Historical Perspective*. Cambridge, MA: Harvard University Press, 1960.

Lewis, W. Arthur. *Growth and Fluctuations, 1870–1913*. London: Allen and Unwin, 1978.

Macfarlane, Alan, and Iris Macfarlane. *The Empire of Tea: The Remarkable History of the Plant That Took Over the World*. Woodstock, NY: Overlook, 2004.

Maddison, Angus. *The World Economy*. Paris: Development Centre of the Organisation for Economic Co-operation and Development, 2006.

McCreery, David. *Rural Guatemala, 1760–1940*. Stanford, CA: Stanford University Press, 1994.

Miller, Rory. *Britain and Latin America in the Nineteenth and Twentieth Centuries*. London: Longman, 1993.

Mintz, Sidney W. *Sweetness and Power: The Place of Sugar in Modern History*. New York: Penguin, 1986.

Mitchell, B. R. *International Historical Statistics: Africa, Asia and Oceania, 1750–2005*. 5th ed. Basingstoke, UK: Palgrave Macmillan, 2007.

———. *International Historical Statistics: The Americas, 1750–2005*. 6th ed. Basingstoke, UK: Palgrave Macmillan, 2007.

———. *International Historical Statistics: Europe, 1750–2005*. 6th ed. Basingstoke, UK: Palgrave Macmillan, 2007.

Mokyr, Joel. *The Lever of Riches: Technological Creativity and Economic Progress*. New York: Oxford University Press, 1990.

Moreno Fraginals, Manuel. *The Sugarmill: The Socioeconomic Complex of Sugar in Cuba, 1760–1860*. Translated by Cedric Belfrage. New York: Monthly Review Press, 1976.

Morgan, Dan. *Merchants of Grain*. New York: Viking, 1979.

Moxham, Roy. *Tea: Addiction, Exploitation and Empire*. New York: Carroll and Graf, 2003.

Mulhall, Michael G. *The Dictionary of Statistics*. 4th ed. London: G. Routledge and Sons, 1899.

Nützenadel, Alexander, and Frank Trentmann, eds. *Food and Globalization: Consumption, Markets and Politics in the Modern World*. Oxford: Berg, 2008.

O'Brien, Patrick. *The New Economic History of the Railways*. New York: St. Martin's Press, 1977.

O'Brien, Thomas F. *The Revolutionary Mission: American Enterprise in Latin America, 1900–1945*. New York: Cambridge University Press, 1996.

Ocampo, José Antonio. *Colombia y la economía mundial, 1830–1910*. Mexico City: Siglo Veintiuno, 1984.

Ogilvie, Sheilagh, and Richard Overy, eds. *Germany since 1800*. Vol. 3 of *Germany: A New Social and Economic History*. London: Arnold, 2003.

Okihiro, Gary Y. *Pineapple Culture: A History of the Tropical and Temperate Zones*. Berkeley: University of California Press, 2009.

O'Rouke, Kevin H., and Jeffrey G. Williamson. *Globalization and History: The Evolution of a Nineteenth-Century Atlantic Economy*. Cambridge, MA: MIT Press, 1999.

Osterhammel, Jürgen. *Die Verwandlung der Welt: Eine Geschichte des 19. Jahrhunderts*. Munich: C. H. Beck, 2009.

Owen, Norman G. *Prosperity without Progress: Manila Hemp and Material Life in the Colonial Philippines*. Berkeley: University of California Press, 1984.

Platt, D. C. M., ed. *Business Imperialism, 1840–1930: An Inquiry Based on British Experience in Latin America*. Oxford: Clarendon Press, 1977.

Polanyi, Karl. *The Great Transformation: The Political and Economic Origins of Our Time*. 2nd paperback ed. Boston: Beacon Press, 2001.

Pomeranz, Kenneth. *The Great Divergence: China, Europe, and the Making of the Modern World Economy*. Princeton, NJ: Princeton University Press, 2000.

Rappaport, Erika. "Packaging China: Foreign Articles and Dangerous Tastes in the Mid-Victorian Tea Party." In *The Making of the Consumer: Knowledge, Power and Identity in the Modern World,* edited by Frank Trentmann. Oxford: Berg, 2006.

Rawski, Thomas G. *Economic Growth in Prewar China.* Berkeley: University of California Press, 1989.

Richards, John. "The Staples Debates." In *Explorations in Canadian Economic History: Essays in Honour of Irene M. Spry,* edited by Duncan Cameron. Ottawa: University of Ottawa Press, 1985.

Rieschbieter, Julia Laura. "Kaffee im Kaiserreich: Eine Geschichte der Globalisierung." PhD diss., Europa-Universität Viadrina Frankfurt, 2009.

Rosenberg, Emily S. *Financial Missionaries to the World: The Politics and Culture of Dollar Diplomacy, 1900–1930.* Durham, NC: Duke University Press, 2003.

Rostow, W. W. *The World Economy: History and Prospect.* Austin: University of Texas Press, 1978.

Sen, Samita. *Women and Labour in Late Colonial India: The Bengal Jute Industry.* New York: Cambridge University Press, 1999.

Shin, Jang-Sup. *The Economics of the Latecomers: Catching-Up, Technology Transfer, and Institutions in Germany, Japan, and South Korea.* London: Routledge, 1996.

Smith, Andrew F. *Eating History: Thirty Turning Points in the Making of American Cuisine.* New York: Columbia University Press, 2009.

Smith, F. Leslie, John W. Wright II, and David H. Ostroff, eds. *Perspectives on Radio and Television: Telecommunication in the United States.* 4th ed. Mahwah, NJ: Erlbaum, 1998.

Soluri, John. *Banana Cultures: Agriculture, Consumption, and Environmental Change in Honduras and the United States.* Austin: University of Texas Press, 2005.

Stanfield, Michael Edward. *Red Rubber, Bleeding Trees: Violence, Slavery, and Empire in Northwest Amazonia, 1850–1933.* Albuquerque: University of New Mexico Press, 1998.

Stewart, Gordon T. *Jute and Empire: The Calcutta Jute Wallahs and the Landscapes of Empire.* Manchester: Manchester University Press, 1998.

Stoler, Ann Laura. *Capitalism and Confrontation in Sumatra's Plantation Belt, 1870–1979.* New Haven, CT: Yale University Press, 1985.

Sugihara, Kaoru, ed. *Japan, China, and the Growth of the Asian International Economy, 1850–1949.* Oxford: Oxford University Press, 2005.

Tedlow, Richard S. *New and Improved: The Story of Mass Marketing in America.* New York: Basic Books, 1990.

Tinker Salas, Miguel. *The Enduring Legacy: Oil, Culture, and Society in Venezuela.* Durham, NC: Duke University Press, 2009.

Topik, Steven, Carlos Marichal, and Zephyr Frank, eds. *From Silver to Cocaine: Latin American Commodity Chains and the Building of the World Economy, 1500–2000.* Durham, NC: Duke University Press, 2006.

Topik, Steven, and Allen Wells, eds. *The Second Conquest of Latin America: Coffee, Henequen, and Oil during the Export Boom, 1850–1930.* Austin: University of Texas Press, 1998.

Torp, Cornelius. *Die Herausforderung der Globalisierung: Wirtschaft und Politik in Deutschland, 1860–1914.* Göttingen: Vandenhoeck und Ruprecht, 2005.

Trentmann, Frank. *Free Trade Nation: Commerce, Consumption, and Civil Society in Modern Britain.* Oxford: Oxford University Press, 2008.

Tucker, Richard P. *Insatiable Appetite: The United States and the Ecological Degradation of the Tropical World.* Berkeley: University of California Press, 2000.

Twomey, Michael J. *A Century of Foreign Investment in the Third World.* London: Routledge, 2000.

Ukers, William H. *All about Coffee.* 2nd ed. New York: The Tea and Coffee Trade Journal Co., 1935.

———. *All about Tea.* 2 vols. New York: The Tea and Coffee Trade Journal Co., 1935.

Vance, James E., Jr. *Capturing the Horizon: The Historical Geography of Transportation since the Transportation Revolution of the Sixteenth Century.* New York: Harper and Row, 1986.

Wallerstein, Immanuel. *The Modern World-System.* 3 vols. to date. New York: Academic Press, 1974–.

Weaver, Frederick Stirton. *Latin America in the World Economy: Mercantile Colonialism to Global Capitalism.* Boulder, CO: Westview Press, 2000.

Wehler, Hans-Ulrich. *Von der "Deutschen Doppelrevolution" bis zum Beginn des Ersten Weltkrieges, 1849–1914.* Vol. 3 of *Deutsche Gesellschaftsgeschichte.* Munich: C. H. Beck, 1995.

Wells, Allen. "Reports of Its Demise Are Not Exaggerated: The Life and Times of Yucatecan Henequen." In *From Silver to Cocaine: Latin American Commodity Chains and the Building of the World Economy, 1500–200,* edited by Steven Topik, Carlos Marichal, and Zephyr Frank. Durham, NC: Duke University Press, 2006.

Wells, Allen, and Gilbert M. Joseph. *Summer of Discontent, Seasons of Upheaval: Elite Politics and Rural Insurgency in Yucatán, 1876–1915.* Stanford, CA: Stanford University Press, 1996.

Wenzlhuemer, Roland. *From Coffee to Tea Cultivation in Ceylon, 1880–1900: An Economic and Social History.* Leiden: Brill, 2008.

Wickizer, V. D., and M. K. Bennett. *The Rice Economy of Monsoon Asia.* Palo Alto, CA: Stanford University Food Research Institute, 1941.

Wilkins, Mira. *The Maturing of Multinational Enterprise: American Business Abroad from 1914 to 1970.* Cambridge, MA: Harvard University Press, 1974.

Wilkins, Mira, and Harm Schröter, eds. *The Free-Standing Company in the World Economy, 1830–1996.* Oxford: Oxford University Press, 1998.

Wright, Donald R. *The World and a Very Small Place in Africa.* Armonk, NY: M. E. Sharpe, 1997.

Yafa, Stephen. *Big Cotton: How a Humble Fiber Created Fortunes, Wrecked Civilizations, and Put America on the Map*. New York: Viking, 2005.

Yamamura, Kozo, ed. *The Economic Emergence of Modern Japan*. Cambridge: Cambridge University Press, 1997.

Yergin, Daniel. *The Prize: The Epic Quest for Oil, Money, and Power*. New York: Simon and Schuster, 1991.

Transnational Currents in a Shrinking World

Abu-Lughod, Lila, ed. *Remaking Women: Feminism and Modernity in the Middle East*. Princeton, NJ: Princeton University Press, 1998.

Adams, Mark B., ed. *The Wellborn Science: Eugenics in Germany, France, Brazil, and Russia*. New York: Oxford University Press, 1990.

Adas, Michael. *Machines as the Measure of Men: Science, Technology, and Ideologies of Western Dominance*. Ithaca, NY: Cornell University Press, 1989.

Adi, Hakim, and Marika Sherwood. *Pan-African History: Political Figures from Africa and the Diaspora since 1787*. London: Routledge, 2003.

Anagol, Padma. *The Emergence of Feminism in India, 1850–1920*. Aldershot, UK: Ashgate, 2005.

Anderson, Warwick. *The Cultivation of Whiteness: Science, Health and Racial Destiny in Australia*. New York: Basic Books, 2003.

Anghie, Antony. *Imperialism, Sovereignty, and the Making of International Law*. Cambridge: Cambridge University Press, 2005.

Appadurai, Arjun. *Modernity at Large: Cultural Dimensions of Globalization*. Minneapolis: University of Minnesota Press, 1996.

Arnold, David. *Colonizing the Body: State Medicine and Epidemic Disease in Nineteenth-Century India*. Berkeley: University of California Press, 1993.

Auerbach, Jeffrey A. *The Great Exhibition of 1851: A Nation on Display*. New Haven, CT: Yale University Press, 1999.

Baber, Zaheer. *The Science of Empire: Scientific Knowledge, Civilization, and Colonial Rule in India*. Albany: State University of New York Press, 1996.

Baratay, Éric, and Élisabeth Hardouin-Fugier. *Zoo: A History of Zoological Gardens in the West*. Translated by Oliver Welch. London: Reaktion Books, 2002.

Barrow, Ian J. *Making History, Drawing Territory: British Mapping in India, c. 1756–1905*. New Delhi: Oxford University Press, 2003.

Bayly, C. A. *The Birth of the Modern World, 1780–1914: Global Connections and Comparisons*. Oxford: Blackwell, 2004.

Beasley, William G. *Japan Encounters the Barbarian: Japanese Travellers in America and Europe*. New Haven, CT: Yale University Press, 1995.

Beinart, William, and Lotte Hughes. *Environment and Empire.* New York: Oxford University Press, 2007.

Bennett, Tony. *The Birth of the Museum: History, Theory, Politics.* London: Routledge, 1995.

Berkovitch, Nitza. *From Motherhood to Citizenship: Women's Rights and International Organizations.* Baltimore: Johns Hopkins University Press, 1999.

Blackbourn, David. *The Conquest of Nature: Water, Landscape, and the Making of Modern Germany.* New York: Norton, 2006.

Blaise, Clark. *Time Lord: Sir Sandford Fleming and the Creation of Standard Time.* New York: Pantheon, 2000.

Block, Nelson R., and Tammy R. Proctor, eds. *Scouting Frontiers: Youth and the Scout Movement's First Century.* Newcastle upon Tyne: Cambridge Scholars, 2009.

Boli, John, and George M. Thomas, eds. *Constructing World Culture: International Nongovernmental Organizations since 1875.* Stanford, CA: Stanford University Press, 1999.

Bose, Sugata. *A Hundred Horizons: The Indian Ocean in the Age of Global Empire.* Cambridge, MA: Harvard University Press, 2006.

Bottenburg, Maarten van. *Global Games.* Translated by Beverley Jackson. Urbana: University of Illinois Press, 2001.

Brunsson, Nils, and Bengt Jacobsson. *A World of Standards.* Oxford: Oxford University Press, 2000.

Burke, Edmund, III, and Kenneth Pomeranz, eds. *The Environment and World History.* Berkeley: University of California Press, 2009.

Camiscioli, Elisa. *Reproducing the French Race: Immigration, Intimacy, and Embodiment in the Early Twentieth Century.* Durham, NC: Duke University Press, 2009.

Campbell, James T. *Middle Passages: African American Journeys to Africa, 1787–2005.* New York: Penguin, 2006.

Çelik, Zeynep. *Displaying the Orient: Architecture of Islam at Nineteenth-Century World's Fairs.* Berkeley: University of California Press, 1992.

Charle, Christophe, Jürgen Schriewer, and Peter Wagner, eds. *Transnational Intellectual Networks: Forms of Academic Knowledge and the Search for Cultural Identities.* Frankfurt: Campus, 2004.

Clarsen, Georgine. *Eat My Dust: Early Women Motorists.* Baltimore: Johns Hopkins University Press, 2008.

Cioc, Mark. *The Game of Conservation: International Treaties to Protect the World's Migratory Animals.* Athens: Ohio University Press, 2009.

Cochran, Sherman. *Chinese Medicine Men: Consumer Culture in China and Southeast Asia.* Cambridge, MA: Harvard University Press, 2006.

Codding, George A., Jr. *The International Telecommunication Union: An Experiment in International Cooperation.* Leiden: E. J. Brill, 1952.

———. *The Universal Postal Union: Coordinator of the International Mails.* New York: New York University Press, 1964.

Connelly, Matthew J. *Fatal Misconception: The Struggle to Control World Population.* Cambridge, MA: Belknap Press of Harvard University Press, 2008.

Conrad, Sebastian. *Globalisation and the Nation in Imperial Germany.* Translated by Sorcha O'Hagan. Cambridge: Cambridge University Press, 2010.

Conrad, Sebastian, and Jürgen Osterhammel, eds. *Das Kaiserreich transnational: Deutschland in der Welt, 1871–1914.* Göttingen: Vandenhoeck und Ruprecht, 2004.

Conrad, Sebastian, and Dominic Sachsenmaier, eds. *Competing Visions of World Order: Global Moments and Movements, 1880s–1930s.* London: Palgrave Macmillan, 2007.

Cooper, Frederick. "What Is the Concept of Globalization Good For? An African Historian's Perspective." *African Affairs* 100 (2001): 189–213.

Cooper, John Milton, Jr. *Woodrow Wilson: A Biography.* New York: Alfred A. Knopf, 2009.

Crosby, Alfred W. *Ecological Imperialism: The Biological Expansion of Europe, 900–1900.* Cambridge: Cambridge University Press, 1986.

Curti, Merle. *American Philanthropy Abroad: A History.* New Brunswick, NJ: Rutgers University Press, 1963.

Darby, Paul. *Africa, Football, and FIFA: Politics, Colonialism, and Resistance.* London: Routledge, 2002.

Darwin, John. *The Empire Project: The Rise and Fall of the British World-System, 1830–1870.* Cambridge: Cambridge University Press, 2009.

Daughton, J. P. *An Empire Divided: Religion, Republicanism, and the Making of French Colonialism, 1880–1914.* New York: Oxford University Press, 2006.

Davis, Mike. *Late Victorian Holocausts: El Niño Famines and the Making of the Third World.* New York: Verso, 2001.

De Grazia, Victoria. *Irresistible Empire: America's Advance through Twentieth-Century Europe.* Cambridge, MA: Belknap Press of Harvard University Press, 2005.

Dennis, Richard. *Cities in Modernity: Representations and Productions of Metropolitan Space, 1840–1930.* New York: Cambridge University Press, 2008.

Desmond, Ray. *The History of the Royal Botanic Gardens Kew.* London: Harvill Press, 1995.

Digby, Anne. *Diversity and Division in Medicine: Health Care in South Africa from the 1800s.* Oxford: Lang, 2006.

Drayton, Richard H. *Nature's Government: Science, Imperial Britain, and the "Improvement" of the World.* New Haven, CT: Yale University Press, 2000.

Duara, Prasenjit. *Sovereignty and Authenticity: Manchukuo and the East Asian Modern.* Lanham, MD: Rowman and Littlefield, 2003.

Dülffer, Jost. *Regeln gegen den Krieg? Die Haager Friedenskonferenzen von 1899 und 1907 in der internationalen Politik.* Frankfurt: Ullstein, 1981.

Ďurovičová, Nataša, and Kathleen Newman, eds. *World Cinemas, Transnational Perspectives.* New York: Routledge, 2010.

Dyson, Stephen L. *In Pursuit of Ancient Pasts: A History of Classical Archaeology in the Nineteenth and Twentieth Centuries.* New Haven, CT: Yale University Press, 2006.

Echenberg, Myron. *Plague Ports: The Global Urban Impact of Bubonic Plague, 1894–1901.* New York: New York University Press, 2007.

Ekbladh, David. *The Great American Mission: Modernization and the Construction of an American World Order.* Princeton, NJ: Princeton University Press, 2010.

Elman, Benjamin A. *A Cultural History of Modern Science in China.* Cambridge, MA: Harvard University Press, 2006.

Evans, Andrew D. *Anthropology at War: World War I and the Science of Race in Germany.* Chicago: University of Chicago Press, 2010.

Eyffinger, Arthur. *The 1899 Hague Peace Conference: "The Parliament of Man, the Federation of the World."* The Hague: Kluwer Academic, 1999.

Fan, Fa-ti. *British Naturalists in Qing China: Science, Empire, and Cultural Encounter.* Cambridge, MA: Harvard University Press, 2004.

Férnandez-Armesto, Felipe. *Pathfinders: A Global History of Exploration.* Oxford: Oxford University Press, 2006.

Findling, John E., and Kimberly D. Pelle, eds. *Historical Dictionary of the Modern Olympic Movement.* Westport, CT: Greenwood Press, 1996.

Finnane, Antonia. *Changing Clothes in China: Fashion, History, Nation.* New York: Columbia University Press, 2008.

Forster, John, and Nigel K. Ll. Pope. *The Political Economy of Global Sporting Organisations.* London: Routledge, 2004.

Forsythe, David P. *The Humanitarians: The International Committee of the Red Cross.* New York: Cambridge University Press, 2005.

Foucault, Michel. *The Order of Things: An Archaeology of the Human Sciences.* New York: Pantheon, 1971.

Gandhi, Leela. *Affective Communities: Anticolonial Thought, Fin-de-Siècle Radicalism, and the Politics of Friendship.* Durham, NC: Duke University Press, 2006.

Geyer, Martin H., and Johannes Paulmann, eds. *The Mechanics of Internationalism: Culture, Society, and Politics from the 1840s to the First World War.* Oxford: Oxford University Press, 2001.

Geyer, Michael, and Charles Bright. "World History in a Global Age." *American Historical Review* 100 (1995): 1034–1060.

Gilroy, Paul. *The Black Atlantic: Modernity and Double Consciousness.* Cambridge, MA: Harvard University Press, 1993.

Grant, Colin. *Negro with a Hat: The Rise and Fall of Marcus Garvey.* New York: Oxford University Press, 2008.

Greene, Julie. *The Canal Builders: Making America's Empire at the Panama Canal.* New York: Penguin, 2009.

Greenhalgh, Paul. *Ephemeral Vistas: The Expositions Universelles, Great Exhibitions, and World's Fairs, 1851–1939*. Manchester: Manchester University Press, 1988.

Grewe, Wilhelm G. *The Epochs of International Law*. Translated by Michael Byers. Berlin: Walter de Gruyter, 2000.

Guttmann, Allen. *The Olympics: A History of the Modern Games*. 2nd ed. Urbana: University of Illinois Press, 2002.

Habib, S. Irfan, and Dhruv Raina, eds. *Social History of Science in Colonial India*. New Delhi: Oxford University Press, 2007.

Hanson, Elizabeth. *Animal Attractions: Nature on Display in American Zoos*. Princeton, NJ: Princeton University Press, 2002.

Harrison, Mark. *Disease and the Modern World, 1500 to the Present Day*. Cambridge: Polity, 2004.

Headrick, Daniel R. *The Invisible Weapon: Telecommunications and International Politics, 1851–1945*. New York: Oxford University Press, 1991.

———. *Power over Peoples: Technology, Environments, and Western Imperialism, 1400 to the Present*. Princeton, NJ: Princeton University Press, 2010.

———. *The Tentacles of Progress: Technology Transfer in the Age of Imperialism, 1850–1940*. New York: Oxford University Press, 1988.

———. *The Tools of Empire: Technology and European Imperialism in the Nineteenth Century*. New York: Oxford University Press, 1981.

Heptulla, Najma. *Indo-West Asian Relations: The Nehru Era*. Bombay: Allied, 1991.

Hight, Eleanor M., and Gary D. Sampson, eds. *Colonialist Photography: Imag(in)ing Race and Place*. London: Routledge, 2002.

Hills, Jill. *The Struggle for Control of Global Communication: The Formative Century*. Urbana: University of Illinois Press, 2002.

Hoage, R. J., and William A. Deiss, eds. *New Worlds, New Animals: From Menagerie to Zoological Park in the Nineteenth Century*. Baltimore: Johns Hopkins University Press, 1996.

Hoffenberg, Peter H. *An Empire on Display: English, Indian, and Australian Exhibitions from the Crystal Palace to the Great War*. Berkeley: University of California Press, 2001.

Hopkins, A. G., ed. *Global History: Interactions between the Universal and the Local*. New York: Palgrave Macmillan, 2006.

———, ed. *Globalization in World History*. New York: W. W. Norton, 2002.

Iriye, Akira. *Cultural Internationalism and World Order*. Baltimore: Johns Hopkins University Press, 1997.

———. *Global Community: The Role of International Organizations in the Making of the Contemporary World*. Berkeley: University of California Press, 2002.

———. *The Globalizing of America, 1913–1945*. Vol. 3 of *The Cambridge History of American Foreign Relations*. Edited by Warren I. Cohen. New York: Cambridge University Press, 1993.

Isserman, Maurice, and Stewart Weaver. *Fallen Giants: A History of Himalayan Mountaineering from the Age of Empire to the Age of Extremes*. New Haven, CT: Yale University Press, 2008.

Jackson, Jeffrey H. *Making Jazz French: Music and Modern Life in Interwar Paris*. Durham, NC: Duke University Press, 2003.

James, Winston. *Holding Aloft the Banner of Ethiopia: Caribbean Radicalism in Early Twentieth-Century America*. New York: Verso, 1998.

Janton, Pierre. *Esperanto: Language, Literature, and Community*. Edited by Humphrey Tonkin. Translated by Humphrey Tonkin, Jane Edwards, and Karen Johnson-Weiner. Albany: State University of New York Press, 1993.

Jensen, Kimberly, and Erika Kuhlman, eds. *Women and Transnational Activism in Historical Perspective*. Dordrecht: Republic of Letters, 2010.

Kern, Stephen. *The Culture of Time and Space, 1880–1918*. Cambridge, MA: Harvard University Press, 1983.

Kevles, Daniel J. *In the Name of Eugenics: Genetics and the Uses of Human Heredity*. New York: Knopf, 1985.

Keys, Barbara J. *Globalizing Sport: National Rivalry and International Community in the 1930s*. Cambridge, MA: Harvard University Press, 2006.

Knock, Thomas J. *To End All Wars: Woodrow Wilson and the Quest for a New World Order*. New York: Oxford University Press, 1992.

Kohler, Robert E. *All Creatures: Naturalists, Collectors, and Biodiversity, 1850–1950*. Princeton, NJ: Princeton University Press, 2006.

Koskenniemi, Martti. *The Gentle Civilizer of Nations: The Rise and Fall of International Law, 1870–1960*. Cambridge: Cambridge University Press, 2002.

Lake, Marilyn, and Henry Reynolds. *Drawing the Global Colour Line: White Men's Countries and the International Challenge of Racial Equality*. Cambridge: Cambridge University Press, 2008.

Lapidus, Ira M. *A History of Islamic Societies*. Rev. ed. New York: Cambridge University Press, 2002.

Large, David Clay. *Nazi Games: The Olympics of 1936*. New York: W. W. Norton, 2007.

Lewis, David Levering. *W. E. B. DuBois: Biography of a Race, 1868–1919*. New York: Henry Holt, 1993.

Linden, Marcel van der. *Transnational Labour History: Explorations*. Aldershot, UK: Ashgate, 2003.

Lydon, Ghislaine. *On Trans-Saharan Trails: Islamic Law, Trade Networks, and Cross-Cultural Exchange in Nineteenth-Century Western Africa*. Cambridge: Cambridge University Press, 2009.

MacLeod, Roy, ed. *Nature and Empire: Science and the Colonial Enterprise*. Chicago: University of Chicago Press, 2000.

MacCulloch, Diarmaid. *Christianity: The First Three Thousand Years*. New York: Viking, 2010.

MacKenzie, John M. *The Empire of Nature: Hunting, Conservation, and British Imperialism.* Manchester: Manchester University Press, 1988.

Manela, Erez. *The Wilsonian Moment: Self-Determination and the International Origins of Anticolonial Nationalism.* New York: Oxford University Press, 2007.

Manning, Patrick. *The African Diaspora: A History through Culture.* New York: Columbia University Press, 2009.

———. *Migration in World History.* New York: Routledge, 2005.

Marchand, Suzanne L. *Down from Olympus: Archaeology and Philhellenism in Germany, 1750–1970.* Princeton, NJ: Princeton University Press, 1996.

Mazower, Mark. *No Enchanted Palace: The End of Empire and the Ideological Origins of the United Nations.* Princeton, NJ: Princeton University Press, 2009.

McNeill, J. R. *Mosquito Empires: Ecology and War in the Greater Caribbean, 1620–1914.* New York: Cambridge University Press, 2010.

———. *Something New under the Sun: An Environmental History of the Twentieth-Century World.* New York: W. W. Norton, 2000.

Morris, Rosalind C. *Photographies East: The Camera and Its Histories in East and Southeast Asia.* Durham, NC: Duke University Press, 2009.

Murray, Bill. *The World's Game: A History of Soccer.* Urbana: University of Illinois Press, 1996.

Nandy, Ashis. *Alternative Sciences: Creativity and Authenticity in Two Indian Scientists.* New Delhi: Allied, 1980.

Nixon, James W. *A History of the International Statistical Institute, 1885–1960.* The Hague: International Statistical Institute, 1960.

Nowell-Smith, Geoffrey, ed. *The Oxford History of World Cinema.* New York: Oxford University Press, 1996.

Okuefuna, David. *The Dawn of the Color Photograph: Albert Kahn's Archives of the Planet.* Princeton, NJ: Princeton University Press, 2008.

Olupona, Jacob K., and Terry Rey, eds. *Òrìṣà Devotion as World Religion: The Globalization of Yorùbá Religious Culture.* Madison: University of Wisconsin Press, 2008.

Osterhammel, Jürgen. *Die Verwandlung der Welt: Eine Geschichte des 19. Jahrhunderts.* Munich: C. H. Beck, 2009.

Palmer, Steven P. *Launching Global Health: The Caribbean Odyssey of the Rockefeller Foundation.* Ann Arbor: University of Michigan Press, 2010.

Patel, Kiran Klaus. "Überlegungen zu einer Transnationalen Geschichte." In *Weltgeschichte,* edited by Jürgen Osterhammel. Stuttgart: Franz Steiner, 2008.

Pedersen, Susan. "The Meaning of the Mandates System: An Argument." *Geschichte und Gesellschaft* 32 (2006): 560–582.

Penny, H. Glenn. *Objects of Culture: Ethnology and Ethnographic Museums in Imperial Germany.* Chapel Hill: University of North Carolina Press, 2002.

Penny, H. Glenn, and Matti Bunzl, eds. *World Provincialism: German Anthropology in the Age of Empire.* Ann Arbor: University of Michigan Press, 2003.

Pinney, Christopher. *Camera Indica: The Social Life of Indian Photographs.* Chicago: University of Chicago Press, 1997.

Porter, Andrew. *Religion versus Empire? British Protestant Missionaries and Overseas Expansion, 1700–1914.* Manchester: Manchester University Press, 2004.

Prakash, Gyan. *Another Reason: Science and the Imagination of Modern India.* Princeton, NJ: Princeton University Press, 1999.

Pratt, Mary Louise. *Imperial Eyes: Travel Writing and Transculturation.* 2nd ed. New York: Routledge, 2008.

Raj, Kapil. *Relocating Modern Science: Circulation and the Construction of Knowledge in South Asia and Europe, 1650–1900.* New York: Palgrave, 2007.

Rajan, S. Ravi. *Modernizing Nature: Forestry and Imperial Eco-Development, 1800–1950.* Oxford: Clarendon Press, 2006.

Richards, Thomas. *The Imperial Archive: Knowledge and the Fantasy of Empire.* London: Verso, 1993.

Riddell, John, ed. *To See the Dawn: Baku, 1920; First Congress of the Peoples of the East.* New York: Pathfinder, 1993.

Riffenburgh, Beau. *The Myth of the Explorer: The Press, Sensationalism, and Geographical Discovery.* New York: Oxford University Press, 1994.

Robert, Dana L. *Christian Mission: How Christianity Became a World Religion.* Malden, MA: Wiley-Blackwell, 2009.

Rodgers, Daniel T. *Atlantic Crossings: Social Politics in a Progressive Age.* Cambridge, MA: Belknap Press of Harvard University Press, 1998.

Rogaski, Ruth. *Hygienic Modernity: Meanings of Health and Disease in Treaty-Port China.* Berkeley: University of California Press, 2004.

Rothfels, Nigel. *Savages and Beasts: The Birth of the Modern Zoo.* Baltimore: Johns Hopkins University Press, 2002.

Rupp, Leila J. *Worlds of Women: The Making of an International Women's Movement.* Princeton, NJ: Princeton University Press, 1997.

Ryan, James R. *Picturing Empire: Photography and the Visualization of the British Empire.* Chicago: University of Chicago Press, 1997.

Rydell, Robert W. *All the World's a Fair: Visions of Empire at American International Expositions, 1876–1916.* Chicago: University of Chicago Press, 1984.

Rydell, Robert W., and Rob Kroes. *Buffalo Bill in Bologna: The Americanization of the World, 1869–1922.* Chicago: University of Chicago Press, 2005.

Salvatore, Ricardo D., ed. *Culturas imperiales: Experiencia y representación en América, Asia y Africa.* Rosario: Beatriz Viterbo, 2005.

———. *Imágenes de un imperio: Estados Unidos y las formas de representación de América Latina.* Buenos Aires: Sudamericana, 2006.

Saunier, Pierre-Yves. "Transnational." In *The Palgrave Dictionary of Transnational History, from the Mid-19th Century to the Present Day,* edited by Akira Iriye and Pierre-Yves Saunier. New York: Palgrave Macmillan, 2009.

Saunier, Pierre-Yves, and Shane Ewen, eds. *Another Global City: Historical Explorations into the Transnational Municipal Moment, 1850–2000*. New York: Palgrave Macmillan, 2008.

Scott, James C. *Seeing like a State: How Certain Schemes to Improve the Human Condition Have Failed*. New Haven, CT: Yale University Press, 1998.

Service, Robert. *Comrades! A History of World Communism*. Cambridge, MA: Harvard University Press, 2007.

Silverberg, Miriam. *Erotic Grotesque Nonsense: The Mass Culture of Japanese Modern Times*. Berkeley: University of California Press, 2006.

Stocking, George W. *Victorian Anthropology*. New York: Free Press, 1987.

Strasser, Ulrike, and Heidi Tinsman. "It's a Man's World? World History Meets the History of Masculinity, in Latin American Studies, for Instance." *Journal of World History* (2010): 75–96.

Sufian, Sandra M. *Healing the Land and the Nation: Malaria and the Zionist Project in Palestine, 1920–1947*. Chicago: University of Chicago Press, 2007.

Thompson, Kristin. *Exporting Entertainment: America in the World Film Market, 1907–34*. London: BFI, 1985.

Tomlinson, John. *Globalization and Culture*. Chicago: University of Chicago Press, 1999.

Tooze, J. Adam. *Statistics and the German State, 1900–1945: The Making of Modern Economic Knowledge*. Cambridge: Cambridge University Press, 2001.

Tsing, Anna Lowenhaupt. *Friction: An Ethnography of Global Connection*. Princeton, NJ: Princeton University Press, 2005.

Tucker, Richard P. *Insatiable Appetite: The United States and the Ecological Degradation of the Tropical World*. Berkeley: University of California Press, 2000.

Tucker, Richard P., and J. F. Richards, eds. *Global Deforestation and the Nineteenth-Century World Economy*. Durham, NC: Duke University Press, 1983.

Tyrrell, Ian R. *Reforming the World: The Creation of America's Moral Empire*. Princeton, NJ: Princeton University Press, 2010.

———. *Transnational Nation: United States History in Global Perspective since 1789*. New York: Palgrave, 2007.

———. *Woman's World/Woman's Empire: The Woman's Christian Temperance Union in International Perspective, 1880–1930*. Chapel Hill: University of North Carolina Press, 1991.

Vec, Miloš. *Recht und Normierung in der industriellen Revolution: Neue Strukturen der Normsetzung in Völkerrecht, staatlicher Gesetzgebung und gesellschaftlicher Selbstnormierung*. Frankfurt am Main: V. Klostermann, 2006.

Walters, F. P. *A History of the League of Nations*. 2 vols. London: Oxford University Press, 1952.

Watts, Sheldon J. *Epidemics and History: Disease, Power, and Imperialism*. New Haven, CT: Yale University Press, 1999.

Weinbaum, Alys Eve, et al., eds. *The Modern Girl Around the World: Consumption, Modernity, and Globalization*. Durham, NC: Duke University Press, 2008.

Weindling, Paul. *Epidemics and Genocide in Eastern Europe, 1890–1945*. New York: Oxford University Press, 2000.

———, ed. *International Health Organisations and Movements, 1918–1939*. Cambridge: Cambridge University Press, 1995.

Weston, Timothy B. *The Power of Position: Beijing University, Intellectuals, and Chinese Political Culture, 1898–1929*. Berkeley: University of California Press, 2004.

Wexler, Laura. *Tender Violence: Domestic Visions in an Age of U.S. Imperialism*. Chapel Hill: University of North Carolina Press, 2000.

Wilder, Gary. *The French Imperial Nation-State: Negritude and Colonial Humanism between the Two World Wars*. Chicago: University of Chicago Press, 2005.

Williams, Michael. *Deforesting the Earth: From Prehistory to Global Crisis*. Chicago: University of Chicago Press, 2003.

Winseck, Dwayne R., and Robert M. Pike. *Communication and Empire: Media, Markets, and Globalization, 1860–1930*. Durham, NC: Duke University Press, 2007.

Winter, Jay M. *Dreams of Peace and Freedom: Utopian Moments in the Twentieth Century*. New Haven, CT: Yale University Press, 2006.

Wong, Young-tsu. *A Paradise Lost: The Imperial Garden Yuanming Yuan*. Honolulu: University of Hawai'i Press, 2001.

Worboys, Michael. *Spreading Germs: Disease Theories and Medical Practice in Britain, 1865–1900*. New York: Cambridge University Press, 2000.

Wright, Donald R. *The World and a Very Small Place in Africa*. Armonk, NY: M. E. Sharpe, 1997.

Yanni, Carla. *Nature's Museums: Victorian Science and the Architecture of Display*. London: Athlone Press, 1999.

Yeh, Wen-hsin. *Shanghai Splendor: Economic Sentiments and the Making of Modern China, 1843–1949*. Berkeley: University of California Press, 2007.

Contributors

Tony Ballantyne is Professor of History at the University of Otago. He has published widely on the cultural history of the British Empire and on transnational approaches to imperial and colonial history. He is the author of *Orientalism and Race* (2002) and *Between Colonialism and Diaspora* (2006). Together with Antoinette Burton, he co-edited *Bodies in Contact* (2005) and *Moving Subjects* (2009).

Antoinette Burton is Catherine C. and Bruce A. Bastian Professor of Global and Transnational Studies and Professor of History at the University of Illinois, Urbana. A scholar of nineteenth- and twentieth-century Britain and its empire, she specializes in the history of colonial India and in issues of gender. She is the author of *Burdens of History* (1994), *At the Heart of the Empire* (1998), *Dwelling in the Archive* (2003), *The Postcolonial Careers of Santha Rama Rau* (2007), and *Empire in Question* (2011).

Dirk Hoerder taught North American social history and the history of migrations at Arizona State University and, previously, at the University of Bremen. His areas of expertise include European labor migration in the Atlantic economies and the history of worldwide migration systems. His publications include *Labor Migration in the Atlantic Economies* (1985), *Creating Societies* (1999), *Cultures in Contact* (2002), and *Geschichte der deutschen Migration* (2010).

Charles S. Maier is the Leverett Saltonstall Professor of History at Harvard University. His major publications include *Recasting Bourgeois Europe* (1975), *In Search of Stability* (1988), *The Unmasterable Past* (1988), *Dissolution* (1997), and *Among Empires* (2006). He is currently writing a history of territory and its transformations in the modern era.

Emily S. Rosenberg is Professor of History at the University of California, Irvine. Her areas of specialization include the transnational history of the United States, especially in its economic and cultural connections, and issues related to historical memory. Her books include *Spreading the American Dream* (1982), *Financial Missionaries to the World* (1999), and *A Date Which Will Live* (2003).

Steven C. Topik is Professor of History at the University of California, Irvine. His research focuses on political economy and international trade in Latin America and the world. Among his works are *Trade and Gunboats* (1996), *From Silver to Cocaine* (co-edited, 2006), and *The World That Trade Created* (2006). He is completing a world history of coffee.

Allen Wells is Roger Howell, Jr. Professor of History at Bowdoin College. His publications include *The Second Conquest of Latin America: Coffee, Henequen, and Oil during the Export Boom, 1850–1930* (co-edited with Steven Topik, 1998), *Tropical Zion* (2009), and, with Gilbert M. Joseph, *Summer of Discontent, Seasons of Upheaval* (1996).

Index

Abdülhamid II (Sultan), 103, 170, 214, 219, 375, 853, 875, 896
Abdülmecid I (Sultan), 374
Aborigines, 313–315, 329, 337, 343, 365, 405, 406, 420, 549
Acadians, 541
Achebe, Chinua, 194
Action Française, 178, 241
Adams, Henry, 155, 895
Adas, Michael, 8, 737, 922
Adelman, Jeremy, 705
Adenauer, Konrad, 272
Adorno, Theodor, 578
Adwa, 31
AEG. *See* Allgemeine Elektricitäts-Gesellschaft
Aeneid (Virgil), 969
Afghanistan, 218, 806, 859
Africa, 20, 39, 180, 189, 288–290, 298–301, 310, 331, 358, 361, 364, 378–380, 393, 396, 400, 405, 407, 410, 420, 423, 429, 445, 467, 493, 512, 516, 541, 543–544, 550, 576, 585, 603, 605–607, 609, 611, 614, 622, 645, 665–666, 672, 683, 695, 735, 752, 761, 776, 791, 796, 803, 804, 810, 816, 821, 863, 870–871, 873, 925, 946, 948, 963–964
African-Americans, 410–411, 425, 446, 501, 897, 937
African-Brazilians, 507
African-Caribbeans, 447, 448, 504
African Direct Telegraph Company, 666
African National Congress, 409, 411, 429, 430, 937
African Times and Orient Review, 412
Afrikaners, 394–395, 398, 411, 541, 917
Age of Empire, 596, 618, 622, 776
Age of Enlightenment, 577
Aggrey, James, 937
Aguinaldo, Emilio, 407

AIC. *See* Association Internationale Africaine
Air France, 660
Alabama Treaty of 1873, 835
Alberdi, Juan Bautista, 939–940
Albert (King), 916
Albert (Prince), 888
Albert, Bill, 756
Albert, Charles, 117
Alberto, Carlo (King), 86
Albrech (Archduke), 111
Alcoa. *See* Aluminum Company of America
Alexander II (Tsar), 162, 920
Algeria, 180, 181, 308, 378, 403, 404, 540, 541, 586, 588, 863, 893, 953
Ali, Dusé Mohamed, 412
Ali, Mehmet, 96
Aliens Expulsion Act, 541
Aliens Immigration Restriction Act, 541
Allenby, Edmund, 357
Allende, Salvador, 278
Allgemeine Elektricitäts-Gesellschaft (AEG), 669, 670
Allmänna Svenska Elektriska AB (ASEA), 670
Alsace, 551, 561
Aluminum Company of America (Alcoa), 674
Ambedkar, Bhimrao, 575
American Anthropologist (journal), 943
American Century, 994
American Civil War, 44, 99, 102, 103, 105, 108, 110, 111, 125–127, 179, 273, 441, 449, 461, 491, 607, 634, 635, 640, 662, 740, 764, 835, 856, 955
American Economic Association, 167, 1010n94
American Historical Association, 312
American Indians, 39, 108, 937. *See also specific tribes*
Americanization, 976

American Jewish Joint Distribution Committee, 698
American Metal, 672, 673
American Museum of Natural History, 906, 969
American Red Cross (ARC), 955
American Smelting and Refining, 673
American Sugar Refining Company, 771
American System, 612
American Telegraph and Telephone (AT&T), 662, 667
Amin, Idi, 268
Amritsar massacre, 192, 309, 418
Amundsen, Roald, 966
Amur River, 535
Anaconda Copper, 673
Anarchists, 161, 601, 858
Anarcho-syndicalists, 161, 858
Anasazi, 969
Anatolia, 32, 47
Andalusia, 150
Anderson, Benedict, 387
Anderson, Warwick, 939
Andes Mountains, 47, 646
Andrews, Roy Chapman, 969
Angel Island, 837
Angell, Norman, 211, 823, 844, 845
Anglican Church, 873
Anglo-Afghan Treaty of 1875, 926
Anglo-Afghan wars, 314
Anglo-Chinese Labour Convention of 1904, 516
Anglo-Irish Treaty, 420
Anglo-Persian Oil Company, 677
Anglo-Russian Convention, 218–219
Anglo-Zulu War of 1879, 11, 358
Angola, 517, 544, 588, 804
Anschluss, 254
Anticolonial movements, 8, 20, 238, 303, 318, 319, 414–416, 418, 420, 422–424, 427, 825, 840, 848, 855–863, 866, 873, 878, 945, 946

Anti-imperialism, 5–6, 19–20, 155, 391, 406, 407, 409, 414, 420, 423, 430, 840, 860, 991
Anti-Semitism, 169, 176–178, 243, 264, 266, 269, 563, 581, 584, 867, 868
Anti-Sinicism, 521
Anti-Slavery Act of 1890, 835
Antwerp Fair of 1930, 904
A&P. See Great Atlantic and Pacific Tea Company
Apache, 31, 809
Apartheid, 429
Apostolic Church, 871
Appadurai, Arjun, 9, 470, 820, 961
Arabia, 859
Arabs, 584–585, 875, 925
Arakawa, Goro, 403
Arapaho, 29
Arbuckle, 787
ARC. See American Red Cross
Archeology, 926–927
"The Archives of the Planet" (Kahn), 852
Arendt, Hannah, 269, 281, 578
Argentina, 12, 16, 105, 108, 130–131, 149, 175, 179, 241, 242, 268, 277, 492, 496, 498, 506, 595, 602, 605, 617, 624, 627, 634, 637, 645–647, 650, 653–665, 698, 700, 702, 704–709, 711, 712, 764, 797, 798, 810, 939, 977, 1066n222, 1067n228
Arid Regions, 167
Aristotle, 282
Armenia, 561, 859
Armenians, 377, 552
Armour meat-processing plant, 604, 705
Around the World in Eighty Days. See Le tour du monde en quatre-vingts jours
Arrow War. See Second Opium War
Arteli, 536–537
ASEA. See Allmänna Svenska Elektriska AB
Ashkenazi Jews, 464–465, 484, 614, 867
Asia, 8, 18, 39, 180, 298, 449–452, 475, 521, 596, 605, 608, 611, 614, 623, 645, 810
Aspirin, 603, 805
Assam, 523, 524, 623, 795

Associated Press, 662
Association des Étudiants Martiniquais en France, 576
Association Internationale Africaine (AIC), 182
Atlantic Charter, 272, 846
Atlantic Crossings (Rodgers), 936
AT&T. See American Telegraph and Telephone
Auden, W. H., 258
Auerbach, Jeffrey, 890
Ausgleich, 147, 175
Australia, 11, 12, 286, 290, 300, 337, 339, 340, 343, 361, 362, 395, 401, 405, 427, 457, 485, 486, 488, 493, 496, 513, 515, 541, 549, 595, 596, 602, 605, 610, 617, 618, 624, 627, 634, 639, 645, 650, 664, 697, 698, 700, 702, 757, 760, 761, 810, 879, 901, 907, 935, 939, 1064n183, 1067n228
Austria, 111, 114, 135, 136, 143–144, 148, 253, 296, 491, 500, 554, 555, 616, 778, 828, 901, 927
Austria-Hungary, 16, 94, 147–148, 150, 178, 204, 472, 635, 765, 767, 768, 974
Austrian Empire, 85–86, 147–148
Austro-Hungarian Empire, 151, 178, 556, 838, 840, 859, 869, 879
Authoritarianism, 837, 841, 845, 848
Avellaneda, Nicolás, 131
Axis, 253, 257, 357, 442, 550
Azerbaijan, 217, 859
Aztecs, 800

Back to Africa movement, 503
Bacon, Francis, 161
Baedeker, 597, 983
Baja California, 674
Baker, Josephine, 944
Baker, Lee, 898
Bakhtin, Mikhail, 578
Baku Congress, 420
Bakunin, Mikhail, 118
Balboa Park, 909
Balfour Declaration, 552, 868
Bali, 183
Balkan League, 221
Balkans, 552, 867
Balkan War of 1912, 221
Ballantyne, Tony, 5, 18, 19

Bandung Conference, 5, 390–392, 415, 419, 421, 429–431, 589
Bank of England, 69
Bansho Shirabesho (Office for the Investigation of Barbarian Books), 367
Baratay, Eric, 912
Barbados, 640
Barnum, Phineas Taylor, 972, 974
Barrés, Maurice, 178
Barrose Pimental, J. F. de, 597
Barthes, Roland, 578
Barua, Pramathesh, 977
Battle of Isandlwana, 31
Battle of Magenta, 140
Battle of Solferino, 140
Bayer Chemical Company, 805
Bayly, C. A., 9, 11, 90, 359, 815, 868, 961, 985
BBC. See British Broadcasting Corporation
Bear, Laura, 382
Beard, Charles, 949
Bedford Level Experiment, 923
Bedouins, 30, 39, 387
Beer Hall Putsch, 243
Bektas, Yakup, 386
Belgian Congo, 568, 672
Belgium, 12, 187, 288, 406, 407, 493, 555, 556, 583, 649, 670, 683, 768, 852, 916
Bell, Alexander, 153
Bell, Alexander Graham, 666, 669
Belle époque, 600
Belloc, Hilaire, 359, 603
Bell Telephone, 669
Belville, Ruth, 380
Benga, Ota, 913
Bennet, James Gordon, Jr., 963, 965–966
Bennett, Tony, 904
Bergman, Ingrid, 977
Berlin, 947
Berlin-Baghdad Railroad, 646
Berlin Conference, 181, 182, 285, 399, 401, 683, 788
Berlin Declaration of 1885, 856
Berlin Exchange, 716
Bernardes, Artur, 653
Berne Convention, 828
Berry, Chuck, 741
Besant, Annie, 877
Bessemer process, 652

Betty Crocker, 727–728

Betty Crocker School of the Air (radio show), 728

Beveridge, William, 273

Bey, Osman Hamdi, 927

Bhattacharya, Narendra Nath (M. N. Roy), 860, 861

Bihar, 451, 457, 522–524

Bingham, Hiram, 969

Birmingham Caucus, 173

Birobidzhan, 581

The Birth of the Modern World (Bayly), 9

Bismarck, Otto von, 96, 97, 110, 114, 115, 122, 140, 143–147, 159, 167, 174, 176, 179, 186, 207, 399, 595, 827

Black and Tan war, 208

Black Atlantic, 865

Black Atlantic (Gilroy), 446

Black Star shipping line, 864

Blériot, Louis, 967

Blondin, Charles, 889

Bloody Sunday, 216

Bluntschli, Johann Caspar, 157

Bly, Fred, 319

Board of Scientific Advice, 929

Boas, Franz, 941, 943

Bodin, Jean, 35, 55

Boer Republics, 188, 206, 649

Boer War, 206, 289, 381

Bogart, Humphrey, 977

Bohemian revolts, 64

Bohemians, 85

Bolívar, Simón, 96, 108

Bolivia, 624, 678, 680, 686, 806

Bolshevik Party, 230, 232, 234, 238, 260, 261, 262

Bolshevik Revolution, 419, 698, 840, 858

Bolshevism, 17, 177, 186, 207, 216, 219, 227, 235, 415, 420, 562

Bonald, Louis de, 252

Bonaparte, Napoleon, 41, 51, 66, 107, 111, 135, 446

Bonnerjee, Hemangini, 335

Bonnerjee, W. C., 335

Book of Odes, 75

Boorstin, Daniel, 987

Bose, J. C., 923

Bose, Rash Behari, 427, 428

Bose, Subhas Chandra, 303, 575

Bose, Sugata, 861, 874

Bose, Toshiko, 427

Bostock, Frank, 972

Boswell Brothers Circus and Menagerie, 973

Botanical Garden of St. Petersburg, 909

Boulanger, Georges, 178

Bourbon dynasty, 51–52, 66–68, 70, 113, 116, 141

Bourdieu, Pierre, 312, 578

Bow, Clara, 979

Boxer Rebellion, 184, 194, 212, 226, 287, 370

Boy Scouts, 812

BP. *See* British Petroleum

Bracero Program, 584, 707

Brahmaputra River, 925

Braille, Louis, 851

Brasileiro, Lloyd, 636

Brazil, 48–49, 131, 132, 149, 207, 242, 277, 291, 446, 448, 463, 492, 505–507, 526, 528, 577, 608, 609, 624, 634–637, 640, 646–648, 650, 653–655, 658–660, 664, 665, 668, 679–683, 736, 755, 762, 763, 773, 776–783, 786, 788, 791–793, 797, 804, 810, 811, 827, 852, 855, 877, 920, 939, 940, 944, 956

Brazilian Light and Power, 670

Brecht, Bertolt, 577

Bretton Woods agreements, 846–847

Bridgman, Raymond Landon, 837

Bring 'em Back Alive (film), 982

British American Tobacco Company, 533, 991

British Broadcasting Corporation (BBC), 359, 668

British Commonwealth, 610, 654, 691, 770, 796

British Empire, 180, 208–209, 296–297, 338, 339, 352, 354, 357–359, 361, 366, 372, 374–375, 393–401, 409, 411–414, 430–431, 441, 446, 447, 451, 455, 457, 467, 472, 487, 488, 493, 511–513, 517–519, 521–523, 527, 539, 541–543, 548, 549, 581, 614, 622, 624, 631, 634–638, 641, 650, 660, 663, 676–677, 736, 762, 774, 795–798, 804, 808, 810, 828, 847, 869, 875, 880, 901, 907–909, 924, 928, 929, 935, 953–954, 960

British Guiana, 527

British Museum, 546, 886, 915

British North America Act, 132

British Petroleum (BP), 677, 678

British Tobacco, 616

Bronx Zoo, 911, 913

Bronze Age, 672

Brookings Institution, 937

Brown, Boveri & Co., 670

Brown, John, 125

Bruce, Frederick, 89

Brussels Act of 1890, 856

Brussels Sugar Conference, 768

Buck, Frank, 915, 969, 970, 982

Buddhism, 56, 74, 868

Budge, Don, 728

Buenos Aires, 647, 705, 764, 808, 905, 949

Buffalo Bill's Wild West and Congress of Rough Riders of the World, 975

Buganda Kingdom, 188

Bukharin, Nikolai, 262, 596, 601

Bulgaria, 556

La bureaucratisation du monde (Rizzi), 958

Bureau International des Expositions, 1008n83

Burgdörger, Friedrich, 1048n118

Burke, Edmund, 64

Burma, 183, 210, 390, 457, 487, 513, 515, 518, 519, 580, 586, 587, 623, 732, 733, 735, 736, 737, 741, 876, 879, 883

Burmeister, Hermann Konrad, 905

Burnham, Daniel, 949

Burnham, James, 958

Burroughs, Edward Rice, 970

Burton, Antoinette, 5, 18, 19

Burton, Richard Francis, 925

Burton Holmes' Head Hunters (film), 984

Burundi, 649

Bush, George W., 196

Butler, Josephine, 880

Byzantine Empire, 46

Cadbury, John, 801

Cairo, 891

Calcutta, 451, 456, 517, 523, 524, 741, 742, 795, 876, 928, 932

Calcutta Botanic Gardens, 908

Calcutta Zoological Gardens, 912

Caledonia, 544

Calhoun, John, 124
California, 119, 419, 458, 503, 526, 528, 529, 927, 935
Caliphate movement, 303
Calles, Plutarco Elías, 225
Calvinism, 81
Cambodia, 183, 268, 289
Cameron, Rondo, 1061n134
Cameroon, 181, 804
Canada, 16, 94, 101–102, 127, 131–132, 132, 179, 339, 362, 395, 396, 462, 472, 491, 501–503, 525, 529, 535, 539, 549, 563, 580, 581, 583, 584, 596, 605, 610, 617, 624, 634, 645, 647, 650, 664, 665, 672, 698, 700, 702, 704, 707–712, 810, 861, 877, 879, 901, 926, 935, 976, 980, 1064n183, 1067n228
Canadian Pacific Railroad, 102, 132, 646, 709
Candomblé, 877
Cánovas, Antonio, 175
Cape Colony, 180, 206, 411, 906
Cape Horn, 639, 700
Cape Verde, 448, 665, 804
Capitalism, 66, 265, 594, 601, 603, 609, 611, 616, 617, 659, 675, 724, 749, 756, 857, 890, 957
Capone, Al, 603
The Capture of Rome (film), 975
Carbonari, 84
Cárdenas, Lázaro, 678
Carducci, Giosuè, 177
Caribbean, 408, 447, 448, 455–456, 471, 475, 491–493, 495, 504, 513, 516, 525–527, 575–576, 634, 665, 753, 756, 759, 760, 762, 778, 801, 803, 864, 897
Caritas Internationalis, 954
Carlist War, 106, 113
Carlsbad Decrees, 117
Carnegie, Andrew, 652
Carnival Scenes at Nice and Cannes (film), 975
Carranza, Venustiano, 224–225
Caruso, Enrico, 680
Casablanca (film), 977
Casely-Hayford, J. E., 410
Casement, Roger, 683
Caspian Railway, 360
Castillo de González, Aurelia, 896
Castro, Fidel, 763

Catholic Action, 242
Catt, Carrie Chapman, 883
Caudillos, 609
Cavour, Camillo Benso di (Count), 101, 137, 138, 140, 141
CBS. See Columbia Broadcasting Corporation
CBT. See Chicago Board of Trade
CCP. See Chinese Communist Party
Centennial International Exhibition, 893–894
Center Party, 174
Central America, 181, 492, 624, 665, 803
Central Asiatic Expedition, 969
Central Powers, 286
Césaire, Aimé, 576, 589, 865
Cetewayo, 359
Ceylon, 390, 392, 513, 523, 623, 650, 682, 707, 733, 735, 774, 777, 791, 796–799, 935, 956
Cézanne, Paul, 904
CGT, 858
Chamberlain, Joseph, 173
Chamberlain, Neville, 246
Chandler, Alfred, 615, 644
Chao Phraya Delta, 736
Charles III (King), 64
Château Clères, 911
Chechens, 582
Cheka, 268
Cherokee, 31
Cherry-Garrard, Apsley, 966
Cheyenne, 29
Chiang Kai-shek, 227, 256, 574
Chicago, 483, 603–604, 702, 705, 895–898, 946, 949, 974
Chicago Board of Trade (CBT), 714–715, 738
Chicago Fair of 1933–1934, 902
Chicago River, 638
Chile, 175, 241, 278, 617, 624, 627, 635–636, 646, 672, 673, 693, 939, 977
China, 16, 17, 34, 36–37, 41, 43–44, 48, 52–54, 61, 70, 73–77, 87–89, 91, 94, 96, 102, 105, 110, 123, 149–150, 159, 166, 171, 183, 194, 198, 200, 210, 214, 226–228, 256, 258, 268, 289, 296, 302, 316, 320, 338, 343, 353, 370–373, 392, 397, 398, 411, 416, 419, 421, 423, 426, 427, 441, 448, 452–457,

468, 472, 475, 477, 484–486, 493–494, 512–515, 518–519, 525–534, 549, 553, 563, 564, 568, 569, 573–574, 580, 587, 608, 609, 612, 618, 623, 629, 636, 645, 650, 651, 660, 664, 665, 682, 683, 688, 699, 718, 731–738, 752, 754, 770, 775, 793–796, 798, 799, 808, 836, 859, 863, 871, 873, 876, 877, 879, 894, 906–908, 910, 920, 929–931, 933, 936, 952, 956, 960, 963, 969, 973, 977, 990–992, 1015n148
China Made (Gerth), 991
China Medical Board, 956
China Today (magazine), 574
Chinese Communist Party (CCP), 227
Chinese Revolution, 287, 840
Chishawasha Mission, 326
Christian Democrats, 272, 274
Christian Herald, 870
Christianity, 322–327, 410, 488, 868, 870–874, 883, 938
Christian-Social Party, 253
Christian Socials, 176
Christina (Queen), 113
C&H Sugar, 771
Chulalongkorn (King Rama V), 210
Churchill, Winston, 272, 676, 846
Cisleithania, 148
City Beautiful movement, 948
Cixi (Empress Dowager), 184, 287
Clarence-Smith, William, 804
Clarke, Sally, 696
Clay, Henry, 124
Clemenceau, Georges, 416
Cleveland, Grover, 183
Clifford, James, 9
CNT. See National Confederation of Labor
Coal, 48, 607, 669
Cobbett, William, 45
Coca-Cola, 616, 686
Cochin China, 733, 737, 738
Cody, Buffalo Bill, 974–975
Cold War, 198–199, 228, 269, 278, 390, 391, 848
Colgate, 991
Colombia, 131, 175, 624, 639–640, 659, 660, 680, 782, 806
Colonial Exhibition, 893, 903

Colonial Goods stores, 788
Colonial Office, 395, 400, 546
Colonial Sugar Refining
    Company (CSR), 760–761
Colonos, 758
Colorado River, 925
Colt, 603
Columbia Broadcasting
    Corporation (CBS), 667
Columbian Exposition, 877, 895,
    897, 904, 974. *See also* White
    City
Columbus, Christopher, 307,
    308, 923
Comanche, 31, 128
Comanche Empire, 296
Cominform, 264
Comintern, 419, 420, 858–860,
    864
Comisión Interamericana de
    Mujeres. *See* Inter American
    Commission of Women
Committee for Union and
    Progress (CUP), 177, 219,
    220–221
Communards, 191, 544
Communism, 13, 227–228,
    230–232, 238, 243, 244, 266,
    269, 271, 272, 278, 279, 565,
    580, 583, 618, 623, 653, 678,
    837, 845, 858–859, 863, 945
Communist International,
    260
Communist International of
    Labour Union, 576
Communist Party, 232, 262, 263,
    864
Communist Party of India, 860
Communist Party of the Soviet
    Union (CPSU), 264
Community Strength Through
    Joy agency, 983
Compagnie Belge des Chemins
    de Fer Réunis, 670
Compañia Sud-America de
    Vapores, 636
Comte, Auguste, 164, 936
Condor Syndicate, 660
Coney Island, 914
Confederate States of America,
    91, 103, 111, 112, 125, 127, 132,
    610, 640
Conference of Non-Aligned
    Countries, 589
Confucianism, 44, 74, 75, 88,
    94, 151, 160, 210, 226

Congo, 406, 517, 527, 568, 804,
    916
Congo Act of 1885, 835
Congo Free State, 182, 683
Congorilla (film), 980
Congress of Berlin, 182
Congress of Paris, 140
Congress of Peoples of the East,
    859
Congress of the Young Turkish
    Party, 413
Congress of Vienna, 68, 180,
    441
Congress System, 68
Conquest of the Desert, 627
Conrad, Joseph, 194, 595, 683,
    848
Conrad, Sebastian, 11
Conservative Party, 179, 208
Contagious Diseases Acts, 321,
    401
Convention Relative to the
    Preservation of Fauna and
    Flora in Their Natural State,
    916
Conze, Alexander, 926
Cook, Frederick, 965
Cooke, William Fothergill,
    661–662
Coolidge, Calvin, 955
Coolie Commission, 517
Cooper, Frederick, 299
Cooperative movement, 711–712,
    716
Corliss Steam Engine, 153,
    894
Corn Laws, 70, 689
The Coronation of Edward VII
    (film), 975
Corradini, Enrico, 186
Costa Rica, 504, 781, 782, 804,
    910, 956
Côte d'Ivoire, 776, 803, 871
Cotton, 496, 607–608, 613, 623,
    740, 908, 937
Cotton, Henry, 795
Coubertin, Pierre, 168, 831
CPSU. *See* Communist Party of
    the Soviet Union
Creative destruction, 603
Creek, 31
Cremer, William Randal,
    835
Creole cultures, 446, 447, 448,
    462, 507
Crespo, Horatio, 768–769

Crimean War, 44, 99, 106, 111,
    138, 216, 374, 740
The Crisis (newspaper), 866
Crispi, Francesco, 105, 142
Cronon, William, 701
Crosby, Alfred, 47, 314
Crystal Palace Exhibition, 887,
    889, 890, 891, 983
CSR. *See* Colonial Sugar
    Refining Company
Cuba, 116, 129, 162, 212, 291, 293,
    411, 412, 447, 448, 454, 455,
    488, 492, 503, 504, 528, 624,
    641, 650, 707, 753, 755–759,
    762, 763, 767, 770, 772, 877,
    879, 897, 899, 937, 952
Cuban-Spanish-American war,
    771
CUP. *See* Committee for Union
    and Progress
Curaçao, 801
Curtiz, Michael, 977
Curzon, George Nathaniel
    (Lord), 317, 929, 933
Custer, George, 29, 153
Customs Union Parliament
    (Zollparlament), 174
Czechoslovakia, 246, 254,
    879

Dadoo, Yusuf M., 429
Daffert, Franz, 781
Daily Mail (newspaper), 823
Daily Telegraph (newspaper),
    964
Dalí, Salvador, 830
Dalmatia, 582
Damas, Léon-Gontran, 576
Dan Di, 426
Danesh (Knowledge), 413
D'Annunzio, Gabriele, 238
Danse du ventre, 900
Daoguang emperor, 76
Darjeeling, 524, 795
Darwin, Charles, 42, 935,
    940
Darwin, John, 301
Darwinism, 164, 169, 396,
    823
Das, Sarat Chandra, 925
Davies, R. E. G., 660
Davis, Janet, 972
Davis, Kingsley, 450
Davis, Lance, 628
Davis, Mike, 933
Davis, Thomas, 411

Dawes Act of 1887 (US), 166
Dawes Plan of 1924, 243
Dawlatabadi, Yahya, 413
Deák, Ferenc, 147
Debussy, Claude, 893
Decisionism, 270
Declaration of Independence, 893
Deere, John, 692
Deering Company, 693, 744
Deerr, Noël, 754
Defense of the Realm Act (DORA) (Great Britain), 199
De Forest, Lee, 669
De Gasperi, Alcide, 272
de Gaulle, Charles, 272
Delacour, Jean, 911
Democratic Party, 132, 172, 173, 176, 183, 205, 206, 610, 839
Democratic Republic of Congo, 672
Dempsey, Jack, 728
Deng Xiaoping, 226
Denmark, 762, 879
Denver, 947
Derrida, Jacques, 578
Desert Garden, 910
Deutsche Bank, 673
Deutsche Russische Luftverkeh-rsgesellschaft, 660
de Vries, Jan, 807
Dharasana Salt Works, 311
Díaz, Porfirio, 103, 129, 165, 214, 223–224, 509, 617, 893
Dickens, Charles, 625, 722
Didrikson, Mildred "Babe," 833
Dietrich, Marlene, 979
di Lampedusa, Giuseppe, 142
al-Din, Muzaffar, 217
Diop, Alioune, 576
Diop, Cheikh Anta, 576
Dirpsose, Harry, 320
Disarmament Conference, 255
"Discours sur le colonialisme" (Césaire), 589
Diver, Maud, 334
Division of Military Information, 350
Doctor Zhivago (Pasternak), 263
Dogali, 31
Doheny, Edward, 678
Dole Pineapple, 762
Domesday Book, 165
Dominican Republic, 759, 762, 804, 839

Domino Sugar, 771
Dom Pedro (Emperor), 153
Donoso Cortés, Juan, 252
DORA. See Defense of the Realm Act
Douglas, Stephen, 103, 124
Dower, John, 855
Drake, Edwin, 675
Drayton, Richard, 298
Dred Scott decision, 124
Dreyfus affair, 174, 178, 544
Drumont, Edmond, 178, 403
Dube, John, 937
Du Bois, W. E. B., 316, 415, 425, 430, 863–866, 902
Duguit, Léon, 158
Dumont, Alberto Santos, 658
Dunant, Henri, 835, 955
Dundee, 741, 742
Dunlop, James, 679
Dunlop, Marion Wallace, 425
DuPont, 603, 682, 743
Durban riots, 429
The Durbar at Delhi (film), 975
Durham (Lord), 132
Durkheim, Émile, 164
Dutch East India Company, 760, 1061n134
Dutch East Indies, 189, 258, 293, 457, 660, 735, 798, 899, 915
Dutch Guiana, 781
Dutch National Exhibition of Women's Labor, 341
Dye, Alan, 756
Dyer, Reginald, 192, 309

Eagle Company, 678
Eakins, Thomas, 168
Earhart, Amelia, 967
The Earth as Modified by Human Action (Marsh), 934–935
East Africa, 527, 542, 543, 649, 735, 750, 934, 942
Eastern Telegraph, 665
East India Company (EIC), 63, 76, 90, 451, 459, 641, 794, 928
East Indies, 587–588, 682
East Pakistan, 587
École Libre des Hautes Études, 578
École Polytechnique, 929
Economic and Financial Organization (EFO), 842
Economic liberalism, 609, 611, 810
The Economist, 690

Ecuador, 528, 803, 804, 879
Edeson, Arthur, 977
Edison, Thomas, 666, 667, 669, 676, 893
Edison Tower of Light, 895
Edkins, Joseph, 920
Edo shogunate, 367
Edward VII (King), 191
EFO. See Economic and Financial Organization
Egypt, 41, 47, 181, 286, 354, 357, 376, 378, 416, 421, 493, 540, 553, 607, 638, 700, 736, 827, 852, 859, 860, 875, 879, 891, 900, 929
Egyptian Feminist Union, 879
Ehlers, Otto von, 965
EIC. See East India Company
Eiffel Tower, 891, 893, 897, 898
Eight-Nation Alliance, 287
Eight O'Clock coffee, 790
Einstein, Albert, 808
Eisenhower, Dwight, 278
Elgin (Lord), 91
Eliot, Charles, 648
Eliot, George. See Evans, Mary Anne
Ellis Island, 468
El Salvador, 782
Elvin, Mark, 48
Ely, Richard, 167, 1010n94
Emancipation Proclamation, 126, 607, 764
Empire of India, 151
The End of the Trail (painting), 168
Engels, Friedrich, 122, 234, 700
England, 12, 638, 642, 649, 664, 665, 682, 759, 793–795, 799, 827, 880, 883
English Channel, 604, 664, 826, 967
The Enlightenment, 38, 40, 79, 113, 237, 269, 444, 545
Enola Gay (aircraft), 14
Enugu Government Colliery, 331
Epstein, Israel, 574
Epstein, Julius, 977
Epstein, Philip, 977
Era of High Imperialism, 593
Erie Canal, 638
Erskine, Anna, 410
Esperanto, 812, 850–851
Essay on the Inequality of Human Races (Gobineau), 900

Estados Unidos Mexicanos, 492. *See also* United States of Mexico

Ethiopia, 17, 31, 210, 291, 401, 406, 540, 582, 648, 649, 660, 773, 780, 845

Ethiopia Unbound (Casely-Hayford), 410

Étoile Nord-Africaine, 863

L'Étudiant martiniquais, 576

L'Étudiant noir, 576

Eugenics, 596, 940–943

Eugenic Society, 903

Europe, 7–8, 12–14, 20, 33, 39, 41, 43, 439, 445, 459, 468, 471, 485, 492, 493, 499–501, 579, 581, 596–597, 608, 623, 666, 676–677, 778, 783–786, 792, 826, 863, 867. *See also specific countries*

European Right, 177, 178

Evangelism, 871

Evans, Mary Anne (George Eliot), 365

The Expansion of England (Seeley), 180, 363

Exposition Internationale des Arts Décoratifs et Industriels Modernes, 904, 944

Expositions Universelles, 1008n83

Fahlberg, Constantin, 1073n354

Faisal I (King), 419

Faith Tabernacle Congregation, 871

Falange, 255

Famine Commission, 929

Fanon, Frantz, 578

Farrer, William, 691

Fascio di Combattimento, 235

Fascism, 13, 17, 234, 235, 240–244, 255–256, 264–266, 270, 544, 550, 562, 565, 577, 578, 837, 841, 845, 859, 1048n118

Fascist Confederation of Industry, 240

Fascist Party, 251

Faulkner, William, 812

Federalists, 130

Federal Radio Commission, 667

Federal Security Main Office, 246

Federal Trade Commission, 791

Fédération Internationale de Football Association (FIFA), 833

Feminism, 365, 422, 576, 840, 883, 884

Fenollosa, Ernest, 894

Ferdinand, Francis, 869

Ferdinand VII (King), 113

Ferguson, Adam, 157

Ferguson, James, 299

Ferguson, Niall, 203, 614

Fernández-Armesto, Felipe, 962

Ferris, George Washington Gale, Jr., 897

Fichte, Johann Gottlieb, 116

FIFA. *See* Fédération Internationale de Football Association

Fiji, 329, 456, 512, 513, 757, 761

Finland, 571, 582, 879

Finlay, Carlos, 952

Firestone, Harvey, 683, 684

First Indian War for Independence, 488

First Industrial Revolution, 5, 594, 607, 612, 613, 631, 642, 652

First International Women's Day Celebration Conference, 879

First International Workingman's Association, 207

First Spanish Republic, 162

First Universal Races Congress, 864

Fish and Wildlife Service Bureau (US), 925

Fitzpatrick, James, 984, 985

Flaherty, Robert, 980

Fleming, Sandford, 927

Flint, Charles, 635

Flower, William Henry, 905

Fogel, Robert, 644

Folgers, 790

Follett, Mary Parker, 958

Following the Equator (Twain), 960

Food Research Institute, 733

FOR. *See* International Fellowship of Reconciliation

Ford, Henry, 656, 666, 683

Fordlandia, 641, 683

Ford Motors, 656, 658

Formosa, 612, 636, 732, 733, 736, 762, 798, 799

Forster, E. M., 194

Foucault, Michel, 161, 163, 197, 312, 578, 1010n98, 1013n131

Four Freedoms, 272

Fourier, Charles, 83

Fourteen Points speech, 416, 838

Fourth International, 859

Fox, 979

Fraenkel, Ernst, 269

Fraginals, Manuel Moreno, 755

France, 12, 16, 41, 51–52, 58, 65, 70, 84, 89, 93, 102, 105, 112, 128–129, 137, 149, 154, 156, 173, 180–183, 207, 210, 246, 254, 258, 272, 275–276, 286, 289, 308, 319–321, 340, 341, 353, 357, 396, 403, 404, 421, 426, 445–447, 493, 494, 498, 503, 511, 539, 540, 542, 544, 556, 564, 573–576, 583, 586–588, 628, 638–640, 644, 645, 648, 650, 653, 656, 664, 668, 669, 671, 677, 680, 690, 735, 737, 738, 762, 765, 767, 768, 774–776, 803, 810, 828, 851, 852, 855, 857, 858, 861, 863, 865, 871, 873, 879, 880, 890–893, 900, 903, 904, 907, 922, 925, 929, 935, 941, 944, 948, 949, 953, 975–977, 983, 1064n183, 1068n256

Franco, Francisco, 241, 255, 277

Franco-Prussian War of 1870–1871, 11, 106, 828

Franz Joseph (Emperor), 85, 115, 117

Fraser, James Earle, 168

Frederick the Great, 63

Frederick William IV (King), 137

Free-Soulers, 124

Free trade, 594, 608–612, 654, 655, 768, 809

French Empire, 548–549, 764

French Foreign Legion, 181

French Guiana, 527, 576

French Guinea, 543

French Polynesia, 289

French Republic, 136, 1048n118

French Revolution, 41, 64, 69, 71, 106, 107, 112, 116, 173, 271, 404, 459

French Section of the Workers' International party (SFIO), 174

French Socialist Party, 857

French Somaliland, 648

Freyre, Gilberto, 943, 944

Friends (Quakers), 954

Fromm, Erich, 578

Frontier, 49, 312–313, 316, 1066n226
The Frontier in American History (Turner), 312
Frost, Robert, 132
Fukui Makoto, 895
Fundidora de Hierro, 653
Futures markets, 688, 693, 714–716, 786–787
Fuzhou Naval Yard, 929

Gabara, Esther, 855
Gadr movement, 866
Gallagher, John, 596
Galton, Francis, 940
Gambia, 359, 951
Gamio, Manuel, 943
Gandhi, Mohandas, 311, 341, 344, 385–386, 388, 410, 423, 424, 427, 575, 860, 861
Gardella, Robert, 798
Garden City Association, 948
Garibaldi, Giuseppe, 96, 141, 142
Garvey, Marcus, 420, 864–866
Gauguin, Paul, 893, 904
Gauss, Carl Friedrich, 165
GE. *See* General Electric
Geertz, Clifford, 760
Geheime Staatspolizei (Gestapo), 246
General Electric (GE), 616, 667, 669, 670, 720, 895, 930
General Exposition of 1863, 891
General Foods, 720
General Mills, 720, 721, 728
General Motors (GM), 656, 658, 720
General Postal Union, 826. *See also* Universal Postal Union
Geneva Convention, 841
Geneva Protocol, 844
Genghis Khan, 307
George III (King), 64
George Washington's Instant Coffee, 790
Georgia, 859
German Labor Front, 245
German Progressive Party, 186
Germany, 12, 13, 16, 44, 53, 84, 85, 89, 93–95, 99, 110, 116, 122, 133–137, 143–147, 160, 161, 174, 207, 235, 237, 243–246,

251–254, 260, 265, 266, 269–271, 274, 275, 286, 290, 294, 296, 297, 300, 306, 309, 310, 317–318, 372, 399–401, 411, 419, 460–461, 472, 477, 488, 491, 493, 496, 498, 500, 511, 542, 554, 555, 561–569, 571, 572, 577, 579, 581–583, 586, 596, 597, 602, 609, 612, 617, 622, 638, 644, 649, 650, 653, 656, 658–660, 668, 669, 677, 682, 694, 765–768, 778, 787, 788, 804, 810, 827, 828, 840, 843–845, 851, 852, 857, 861, 879, 882, 901, 902, 908, 915, 926, 927, 929–931, 934, 936, 940–942, 948, 949, 958, 983, 1010n94
Gershenkron, Alexander, 617
Gerth, Karl, 991
Gestapo. *See* Geheime Staatspolizei
Ghadar Conspiracy, 427
Ghana, 803, 866, 871
Ghose, Aurobindo, 575
Ghosh, Rabindra Narayan, 932
Giap, Vo Nguyen, 234
Gide, André, 258
Gierke, Otto von, 157, 158
Gilded Age, 720, 721
Gilroy, Paul, 446, 865
Gish, Lillian, 979
GM. *See* General Motors
GMD. *See* Guomindang
Gneist, Rudolph, 158
Gobi Desert, 969
Gobineau, Joseph-Arthur de, 900
God Worshipping Society, 88
Goebbels, Joseph, 248, 250, 668
Goering, Hermann, 246, 248
Gold Coast, 289, 293, 803, 804, 937
Gold Medal, 720, 727, 728
Golondrinas, 706
Gompers, Samuel, 843
Goodrich, 683
"Good Words to Exhort the Age" (Hong), 87
Goodyear, 683
Goodyear, Charles, 678, 679
Gorbachev, Mikhail, 260
Gordon, Arthur, 329
Gosney, Eugene, 941

Goswami, Manu, 361
Goto Shimpei, 401
Governments Medical Stores, 909
Goya, Francisco, 66
Grace Line, 632
Grains, 688–704, 706, 708, 712, 729, 1065n198, 1066n223
Gramsci, Antonio, 104, 578
Grand Canal, 638
Grand Canyon, 925
Grand Council of Fascism, 239
Grand Trunk railway, 132
Grant, Ulysses, 126, 153
Graves, Adrian, 756
Great American Desert, 534
Great Atlantic and Pacific Tea Company (A&P), 790, 799
Great Awakenings, 80
Great Britain, 47, 48, 58, 67, 69–71, 76–77, 84, 91, 97, 112, 149, 150, 158, 173, 179, 180, 181, 183, 188, 207, 217–219, 246, 272, 286, 287, 289–290, 296, 301, 308, 309, 311, 314–318, 321, 329, 330–331, 345, 363, 365, 380, 381, 385, 395, 447, 492, 494, 556, 564, 573, 581, 608, 609, 617, 637, 644, 645, 655, 656, 660, 668, 669, 690, 691, 704, 720, 721, 754–755, 760, 767, 768, 796, 846, 861, 878, 879, 886, 940, 948, 963, 976, 983
Great Circle Route, 700
Great Depression, 6, 8, 13, 199, 251, 253, 262, 273, 275, 442, 494, 503, 528, 562, 564, 567, 568, 600, 605, 611, 629, 635, 642, 655, 696, 700, 721, 734, 737, 742, 750, 759, 760, 783, 792, 845, 846, 852, 864, 902, 1066n222
Great Divergence, 604–606, 807
Greater East Asia Co-prosperity Sphere, 373, 611
Great Exhibition of 1851, 887, 888, 889
Great Illusion, 846
The Great Illusion (Angell), 211, 823, 837
Great Indian Peninsular Railway, 365
Great Lakes, 30, 51, 542, 634, 638, 701, 723
Great Migration, 448, 501

Great Plains, 704
Great Royal Circus of India, 973
Great Terror, 845
Great Transformation, 593
Great Trigonometrical Survey of India, 924
Great Turning Point, 565
Great War. *See* World War I
Great Western Railway, 662
Great White Fleet, 632
Greece, 136, 254, 483, 552
Greene, Julie, 640
Greenstreet, Sydney, 977
Greenwich Mean Time, 170, 380, 381
Greenwich Observatory, 380, 829
Gropius, Walter, 949
Gross National Monetized Transactions, 625
Grotius, Hugo, 834
Guadeloupe, 527
Guatemala, 782, 788, 804
Gujarat, 516, 521–522
Gulbenkian, Calouste, 677
Gulf of Cambay, 543
Gulf of Kutch, 522
Gunning, J. W. B., 906
Guomindang (GMD/National People's Party), 227, 580, 623
Gurwitsch, Aron, 578
Guyana, 528, 680, 781
Guyot, Yves, 348

Habsburg Empire, 12, 65, 85, 105, 117, 129, 133–137, 143, 147, 204, 229, 393, 414, 472, 484, 491, 548, 554, 555, 859
Hagenbeck, Carl, 912, 914, 915, 972, 973, 979, 980
The Hague, 835, 836, 837, 881
Hague Codification Conference, 844
Hague Convention, 844, 849
The Hague Peace Conferences of 1899 and 1907, 835–836, 841, 967
Haiti, 51, 64, 445, 446, 448, 576, 707, 753, 775, 781, 839, 865, 937
Hajj, 383–384, 479, 874–876, 950
Hall, Catherine, 578
Hall, Stuart, 578

Hallen, Ernest, 854
Hampton Institute, 937
Han dynasty, 46, 73–74
Han people, 316
Hanson, Miriam, 976
Harari people, 648
Hardie, Keir, 411
Hardouin-Fugier, Elisabeth, 912
Hard Times (Dickens), 625, 722
Harlem, 865
Harlem Renaissance, 576
Harmonization Society, 567
Harris, William Wadé, 870
Harrods, 613
Havas, 662
Havemeyer, H. O., 771
Hawai'i, 156, 181, 293, 455, 458, 513, 525–528, 574, 580, 762, 767, 770, 771, 897, 960
Hay, John, 897
Hayek, Friedrich, 197
Haymarket bombing, 207
Hayworth, Rita, 979
Headrick, Daniel, 651, 660
Heart of Darkness (Conrad), 194, 595, 683
Heavenly Kingdom of Great Peace, 88
Hegel, Georg Friedrich Wilhelm, 157, 160
Hejaz Railway, 387
"Hellas" (Shelley), 40
Henreid, Paul, 977
Hereditary Health Courts, 941
Herero people, 12, 152, 192, 271, 310, 942
Hershey, Milton, 801
Herzen, Alexander, 42, 118
Heydrich, Reinhard, 246
Hilferding, Rudolf, 186, 596, 601
Hill, Rowland, 827
Hills Brothers, 790
Hilton, James, 970
Himmler, Heinrich, 246
Hind Swaraj (Gandhi), 385
Hinduism, 868, 877
Hirobumi, Ito, 96
Hirohito (Emperor), 256
Hirschman, Albert, 672
History and Class Consciousness (Lukács), 232
A History of Hindu Chemistry (Ray), 932

Hitler, Adolf, 14, 235, 240, 242–246, 248, 251, 253, 254, 257, 258, 260, 261, 263, 269, 270, 309, 310, 845, 851, 903, 941, 942
Hobbes, Thomas, 35, 40, 197, 281, 282
Hobhouse, L. T., 1010n94
Hobsbawm, Eric, 13, 596, 601, 642, 841
Ho Chi Minh, 234, 303, 341, 421, 425, 426, 574
Hoerder, Dirk, 5, 20, 21
Hohenzollern dynasty, 472, 491, 548, 554
Hokkaido, 525
Holden, William, 938
Hollywood, 976, 977, 979, 982
Holmes, Burton, 984
Holmes, Oliver Wendell, 715
Holocaust, 134, 581, 584, 585, 596, 868
Holtby, Winifred, 421
Holy Alliance, 80, 108, 135
Holy Roman Empire, 36, 65, 134
Homer, 969
Home Rule (Autonomista) Party, 411
Hong Kong, 77, 91, 353, 368, 453–454, 457, 529, 580, 639, 908
Hong Ren'gan, 89
Hong Xiuquan, 87–88, 89
Hooghly River, 741
Hope, Hamilton, 407
Hopkins, A. G., 9, 850
Hora do Brasil, 668
Horkheimer, Max, 578
Horticultural Society of London, 908
Hosay, 408–409
House Un-American Activities Committee, 577
Howqua, 338
Hu Die, 979
Hudson's Bay Company, 459, 709
Huerta, Victoriano, 224
Hughes, Langston, 425, 576
Hughes, T. P., 947
Hugo, Victor, 625
Huguenots, 486
Human Betterment Foundation, 941

Humann, Carl, 927
Humboldt, Alexander von, 934
Hungary, 85–86, 133, 134, 147, 148, 171, 175, 254, 556, 561, 563, 569, 582, 879, 1068n256
Huntington, Henry, 910
Huntington Library and Gardens, 910
Hunton, Addie, 864
Hurgronje, Snouck, 876
Hurston, Zora Neale, 943
Husayn ibn Ali, 408

IACS. *See* Indian Association for the Cultivation of Science
IALL. *See* International Association for Labour Legislation
Ibn Saud dynasty, 72
Ice-Bound Heights of the Mustagh (Workman and Workman), 965
ICRC. *See* International Committee of the Red Cross
ICSU. *See* International Council of Scientific Unions
IEC. *See* International Electrotechnical Commission
IG Farben, 603
IHB. *See* International Health Board
Ihering, Hermann von, 906
Iliad (Homer), 969
Illinois Central Railroad, 103
Illustrations of China and Its People (Thompson), 852
ILO. *See* International Labour Organization
Imperial Rescript of 1893 (Japan), 160
Imperial Rescript on education of 1890 (Japan), 121
Imperial Rule Assistance Association, 256
Imperial Trans-Antarctic Expedition, 966
In Darkest Africa (Stanley), 970
Indentured labor, 447, 471, 472, 493, 512–515, 526, 527, 528, 564, 761, 796
India, 22, 70, 105, 151, 182, 183, 188, 189, 192, 201, 208–209, 218, 238, 289, 308, 309, 311, 317, 318, 329, 333, 334, 344–345,

352, 360, 361, 374, 385, 390, 392, 399, 401, 411, 412, 416, 421, 424, 427, 429, 441, 449, 450–452, 456–457, 471, 472, 475, 512–519, 521, 526, 527, 542, 543, 545, 574–575, 586, 587, 596, 607, 608, 611, 612, 618, 623, 634, 645, 648–653, 660, 663–665, 682, 683, 712, 718, 732, 733, 735, 736, 739, 741, 742, 754, 757, 770, 794, 796, 797, 852, 859–863, 866, 879, 883, 889, 890, 901, 909, 920, 924, 925, 928, 929, 932, 933, 935, 948, 956, 976, 977
India House, 575
Indiana Jones (movies), 969
Indian Association for the Cultivation of Science (IACS), 932
Indian-Caribbeans, 527–528
Indian Civil Service, 189
Indian Forestry Service, 319
Indian Jute Mills Association, 741
Indian Mutiny of 1856–1857, 84, 90, 91
Indian National Congress, 208, 303–304, 335, 344, 409, 412, 415, 418, 427, 860
India Survey, 886
Indigenismo, 944
Individualism, 594, 601, 809
Indochina, 210, 319, 426, 455, 457, 519, 544, 574, 587, 660, 665, 733, 871, 1067n228
Indonesia, 278, 336, 390, 513, 519, 523, 588, 589, 623, 660, 665, 683, 754, 791, 798, 874, 876, 935
Indonesian People's Army, 588
Industrial Revolution, 5, 44, 54, 110, 594, 607, 612–614, 625, 631, 634, 642, 685, 756, 796, 888
Industrious Revolution, 807
The Influence of Sea Power upon History (Mahan), 635
Ingush, 582
Inquisition, 308
Institute for Industrial Reconstruction (IRI), 274
Institute of Social Research, 577
Inter American Commission of Women (Comisión

Interamericana de Mujeres), 879
Inter-American Price Coffee Board, 792
Interdepartmental Committee on Physical Deterioration, 396
Intergovernmental Committee on Refugees, 563
International African Association, 288
International Air Traffic Association, 844
International Alliance of Women, 422, 426
International Association for Labour Legislation (IALL), 842
International Brigades, 254
International Broadcasting Union, 844
International Bureau of Weights and Measures, 830
International Coffee Agreement, 792
International Commission for Air Navigation, 844
International Committee of the Red Cross (ICRC), 955
International Congress against Colonialism and Imperialism, 860
International Convention on Safety of Life at Sea, 834
International Council for Bird Preservation, 916
International Council of Scientific Unions (ICSU), 932
International Council of Women, 413, 879
International Court of Justice, 812, 836
International date line, 829
International Electrotechnical Commission (IEC), 830
International Electrotechnical Vocabulary, 830
International Exhibition of Arts, Manufactures, and Products of the Soil and Mine, 893
International Fellowship of Reconciliation (FOR), 861
International Harvester Company, 745, 746
International Health Board (IHB), 955, 956–957

International Labor Day, 857
International Labour Organization (ILO), 842–843, 858
International Meridian Conference, 380, 829–830
International Olympic Committee (IOC), 831
International Peace Crusade, 836
International Photographic Exhibition, 852
International Refugee Organization (IRO), 569, 582
International Research Council, 932
International Settlement, 990, 991
International Socialist Bureau, 857
International Statistical Institute (ISI), 830–831
International Suffrage Alliance, 879
International Telecommunication Union (ITU), 826, 828, 834
International Telegraph Union, 666, 826
International Trade Union Committee of Negro Workers, 577, 864
International Union of Local Authorities, 949
International Wheat Agreement, 696
International Woman Suffrage Alliance, 413
International Women's Day, 858, 879
Inter-Parliamentary Union (IPU), 835, 841
Inuit, 980
Investiture Conflict, 36
IOC. See International Olympic Committee
IPU. See Inter-Parliamentary Union
Iqbal, Muhammad, 957
Iran, 17, 171, 212, 216–219, 412, 677, 678
Iraq, 14, 32, 419, 860
Ireland, 208, 290, 395, 404, 411, 412, 420, 463, 613, 770, 866
IRI. See Institute for Industrial Reconstruction
Irish Republic, 420

IRO. See International Refugee Organization
Iron Curtain, 584
The Iron Heel (London), 207
Iroquois, 31
Irrawaddy Delta, 623
Irrawaddy-Sittaung Delta, 736, 737
Ishimoto Shizue Katō (Baroness), 881–882
Ishiwara Kanji, 256
Islam, 43, 46, 56–57, 72, 81, 302, 383–384, 386–387, 407, 868, 874–876, 879, 883
Ismail (Pasha), 354
Israel, 585
Isserman, Maurice, 962
Istanbul Archeological Museum, 927
Italian Confederation of Industry, 240
Italian National Movement, 137
Italo-Turkish War, 286
Italy, 16, 84, 86, 94, 96, 101, 104, 115, 140–143, 237, 238, 239, 240, 251, 253, 260, 267, 274, 291, 294, 306, 495, 498, 582, 623, 638, 656, 660, 669, 736, 768, 841, 844, 845, 858, 975
ITU. See International Telecommunication Union
Iturbide, Augustín de, 128
IU. See Union Intercoloniale
Iwakura Tomomi, 920
IWW, 858

J. Walter Thompson (JWT), 988
Jack Armstrong, All-American Boy (radio show), 728
Jackson, Andrew, 96, 108, 131
Jackson, William, 795
Jacobins, 66, 69, 230
Jakarta, 183, 915
Jallianwalla Bagh massacre, 309, 310
Jalpaiguri, 524
Jamaica, 446, 448, 492, 527, 528, 640, 775, 865
James, C. L. R., 577, 866
Japan, 12–14, 16, 36, 43–44, 52, 77–78, 94, 104, 118–121, 149, 176, 183, 184, 198, 200, 210, 216, 255, 257, 258, 293–294, 296, 305, 306, 315, 316, 325, 352, 366–373, 381, 383, 401, 415, 416, 419, 423, 426–429, 442,

452, 453, 455, 477, 488, 513, 525–527, 532, 533, 550, 553–554, 567–569, 568, 569, 573, 579, 580, 582, 586, 587, 608, 609, 611, 612, 615, 617, 618, 623, 635–637, 645, 651, 653, 656, 663–665, 668, 677, 682, 683, 686, 688, 730, 732–734, 737, 738, 752, 762, 764, 793, 794, 798, 799, 810, 816, 827, 828, 836, 844, 845, 859, 863, 866, 871, 873, 877, 879, 882, 894, 920, 930, 936, 956, 970, 976, 987, 992
Jardín Botánico Lankester, 910
Jardin d'Acclimatation, 913
Jardin d'Essai, 907
Jaurès, Jean, 857
Java, 183, 336, 455, 509, 525, 527, 623, 686, 731, 735, 759, 763, 770, 771, 774, 775, 777, 781, 791, 794, 798, 909
Jazz, 990
Jazz Age, 789
Jefferson, Thomas, 130
Jellinek, Georg, 157, 159
Jesuits, 326, 573
Jews, 464–465, 483–484, 539–541, 544, 563, 581, 584–585, 698, 845, 850, 851, 858, 867–868, 903, 942
Jiangnan Arsenal, 929
Jim Crow laws, 191, 205, 316, 365, 898
"Johnny B. Goode" (Berry), 741
Johnson, Martin, 980, 981
Johnson, Osa, 980, 981
Johnston, Edward, 785
Johnston, Francis Benjamin, 854
Jonas, Hans, 578
Jordan, David Starr, 823
Journal of Home Economics, 727
Juárez, Benito, 96, 128, 129, 462, 492
Judaism, 868
June Days of 1848, 117–118
JWT. See J. Walter Thompson

Kabaka, 588
Kabikolan Peninsula, 743
Kabyles, 403–404, 540
Kahn, Albert, 852, 855
Kalakaua (King), 3, 960
Kalmyk, 582
Kangra, 795

Kangxi emperor, 74
Kang Youwei, 823, 824
Kansas-Nebraska Act of 1854, 103, 124
Karen people, 587
Kartini, Raden Ayu, 341
Katayama, Sen, 863
Kato Satori, 790
Kaufman, K. P., 398–399
Kautsky, Karl, 186, 396
Kazakhstan, 550, 561
KDKA radio station, 667
Kellogg-Briand Pact, 844
Kellogg's, 725
Kelly Foreign Air Mail Act, 659
Kemal, Mustafa (Atatürk), 222–223, 277, 936
Kenana, Rua, 346
Kennecott, 673
Kenya, 327, 345, 405, 493, 543, 545, 549, 586, 649, 750, 775, 780, 796, 935, 941, 953
Kew Gardens, 908–909
Keynesian Revolution, 612
Khama III (King), 423
Khan, Reza, 219
Khrushchev, Nikita, 264
Kikuyu, 542–543, 588
Kim (Kipling), 314, 925
Kingdom of the Two Sicilies, 84
Kingdon-Ward, Frank, 910
King Kong (film), 970, 982
Kingsley, Mary, 364, 365
Kino, 980
Kinthup, 925
Kipling, Rudyard, 155, 314, 925
Kiralfy, Imre, 974
Kishwar, Madhu, 311
Kita Ikki, 256
Kitasato Institute, 950
Kitchener, Herbert, 359
KLM, 660
Knights of Labor, 207
Kodak, 983
Kokand, 39
Kokka eisei genri (The Principles of State Hygiene) (Goto), 401
Konoe Fumimaro (Prince), 256
Koo, Wellington, 416
Kooti, Te, 404
Korea, 181, 183, 184, 198, 294, 321, 369, 370, 373, 401, 416, 453, 488, 525, 532, 553, 554, 567, 579, 580, 588, 612, 635, 732, 733, 859, 873, 920
Korean War, 278

Kortheuer, Dennis, 674
Kosovo, 555
Kossuth, Lajos, 117, 136
Kotelawala, John, 392
Kroeber, Alfred, 943
Kruger National Park, 917
Krupp, 603
Kurds, 852
Kuwait, 678
Kyrgyzstan, 561

Labor and Socialist International, 857
Labor Importation Ordinance of 1903, 516
Labour Party, 274, 411
Ladies Home Journal, 721, 984
LaFarge, John, 894
Laila. See Zaynab (Laila) bint Shaykh Muhammad
Laissez-faire, 96, 167, 596, 609, 929, 1010n94
Lakota, 29
Lamennais, Félicité, 114
Landes, David, 617
Lang, Fritz, 577
Laos, 183, 580
Lapidus, Ira, 874
Lasalle, Ferdinand, 174
Lateran Pact, 240
Latin America, 18, 20, 51, 70, 96, 150, 175, 448, 457, 485, 486, 488, 498, 505–506, 526, 602, 608–611, 614, 624, 628, 629, 645, 695, 752, 783, 788–791, 838, 858, 879, 896, 905, 906, 936, 940, 977
Latin Monetary Union, 628, 629
Latter-day Saints, 55
Lawrence, John, 663
League Against Imperialism, 420, 552
League of Nations, 303, 421, 548, 551, 770, 805, 812, 826, 836, 837–847, 849, 851, 858, 868, 880, 903, 937. See also International Statistical Institute
League of Nations Health Organization (LNHO), 842, 952
Lears, Jackson, 724
Leaving Jerusalem by Railway (film), 975
Lebeau, Madeleine, 977
Le Bon Marché, 613

Le Corbusier, 949
Lee, Leo Ou-fan, 992
Lee, Robert, 111, 132
Le Havre, 783, 786
Lem, Stanislaw, 191
Lenin, Vladimir I., 186, 212, 230, 237, 596, 601, 616, 858, 859
The Leopard (di Lampedusa), 142
Leopold (King), 12, 63
Leopold (Prince), 915
Leopold II (King), 182, 288, 406, 683
Leo XIII (Pope), 871
Lerdo Law, 86, 128
Lesseps, Ferdinand de, 354, 355, 638, 639
Lettow-Vorbeck, Paul von, 942
Leviathan (Hobbes), 35
Lewis, W. Arthur, 753
Liang Gaddi, Sang, 915
Liang Qichao, 824, 957
Liang Shuming, 957
Liaodong Peninsula, 184
Liberalism, 69–71, 114, 137, 228, 273, 593, 596, 609–611, 810, 860, 1010n94
Liberal Party, 175, 770
Liberia, 641, 648, 684, 865, 915
Libya, 660
Li Gui, 894, 960
Lilienthal, David, 931
Liliuokalani (Queen), 293
Lincoln, Abraham, 96, 124, 125, 126, 204, 607
Lindbergh, Charles, 967
Lindt, 801
Lin Zexu, 76
Lipton, 799
Lister Institute, 950
Little Bighorn River, 29, 31, 38, 153, 280
Livingstone, David, 321, 815, 817, 963, 964
Lloyd George, David, 416
LNHO. See League of Nations Health Organization
Locke, John, 60
Lombroso, Cesare, 169
London, Jack, 207
"The Lone Ranger" (radio program), 667
Longfellow, Henry Wadsworth, 96
Lorre, Peter, 977
Lost Horizon (Hilton), 970
Louisiana, 764

Louis XIV (King), 191
Lowe Kong Meng, 427
Luce, Henry, 994
Lueger, Karl, 176
Lufthansa, 660
Lugard, Frederick, 191
Luhan, Mabel Dodge, 944
Lukács, Georg, 232, 233
Lutheran Church Diet, 96
Luxemburg, Rosa, 184, 601
Luyten, Edwin, 307
Luzon, 743
Lyautey, Hubert, 191
Lynch violence, 501

Macao, 580
Macaroni Journal, 729
MacArthur, Douglas, 278
MacCulloch, Diarmaid, 869
Macfadden, Bernarr, 977, 978
Machu Picchu, 852, 969
MacKay, Claude, 425, 576
Macy's, 613
Madagascar, 803, 804, 871
Madeira-Mamoré Railway, 646
Madero, Francisco, 224
Madison, James, 130
Madras, 457, 517, 522, 523, 909, 928
Mafia, 617
Magellan, Ferdinand, 639
Magyar, 133, 147
Mahan, Alfred Thayer, 635
Mahdist regime, 12, 31
Mahmud II (Sultan), 72
Maier, Charles, 5, 11, 12, 16–18, 994
Maistre, Joseph de, 252
Maji-Maji Rebellion, 318
Malabar Coast, 516, 521
Malacca, 513
Malaria, 640, 953, 955
Malawi, 796
Malaya, 455, 457, 475, 493, 513, 515, 519, 587, 588, 733, 735
Malay Peninsula, 516, 518, 519, 521, 735
Malaysia, 587, 623, 682, 683, 935
Maler, Teobert, 927
Mallory, George, 966, 967
Malta, 553
The Managerial Revolution (Burnham), 958
Man and Nature (Marsh), 934
Manchester School, 610
Manchukuo, 677, 867

Manchu people, 74, 316, 398
Manchuria, 14, 53, 181, 303, 315, 353, 369–370, 385, 441, 493, 530–534, 549, 845
Manchurian incident, 255
Manchu state, 151
Mandela, Nelson, 279
Mandinka, 542
Mann, Thomas, 577
Mann, William, 915
Manzanar concentration camp, 683
Maori, 302, 329, 346, 362, 395, 404
Mao Zedong, 226, 227, 234, 268, 421
Mapuche, 627
Marconi, Guglielmo, 666, 923
Marcuse, Herbert, 265, 578
Marggraf, Andreas, 765
Margoliouth, D. S., 413
Maria Theresa (Queen), 63
Marks, Owen, 977
Marks, Shula, 344
Mars Company, 801
Marsh, George Perkins, 934
Marshall, George, 278
Marshall Field's, 613
Martí, José, 411, 412
Martin, Kingsley, 273
Martinique, 527, 576, 781
Marx, Karl, 94, 122, 184, 230, 234, 348, 499, 601, 868, 890
Marxism, 121–122, 162, 184, 186, 264–266, 396, 859, 868, 936, 991
Masaryk, Tomáš, 254
Mason, Kenneth, 962
Mata Atlântica, 607
Matteotti, Giacomo, 239
Mauco, George, 1048n118
Mau Mau Rebellion, 345
Mauritius, 509, 516
Maurras, Charles, 178
Max Factor, 991
Maximilian (Emperor), 129, 639, 926, 927
Maximowicz, Carl, 909
Maxwell, James Clerk, 167
Maxwell House, 790
May, Karl, 970
Mayans, 108, 129, 151, 804, 809, 927, 969
May Fourth era, 990
May Fourth Movement, 419
May Laws of 1882, 465

Mazower, Mark, 847
Mazzini, Giuseppe, 105, 114, 136, 272
McCain, John, 1059n84
McClelland, George, 125
McCormick, Cyrus, 692, 693
McCormick Harvesting Machine Company, 744
McKay, Claude, 866
McKeown, Adam, 435, 471, 514
McKinley, William, 183, 897
McNeill, William, 7
McWilliams, Carey, 491
Mead, Margaret, 943
Meah, Haji Gokool, 409
Mecca, 874, 876, 950
Medina, 875
Meiji era, 96, 104, 168, 176, 181, 198, 306, 366–368, 371, 372, 393, 401, 455, 513, 548–549, 553, 573, 617, 920, 936, 949, 987
Meiji Restoration, 120–121, 160
Mekong Delta, 736
Mekong River, 183, 319, 519
Melilla, 31, 39
Menelik II (Emperor), 210, 406, 648
Mennonites, 485, 535, 537
Mensheviks, 216
Messageries Impériales, 353
"Message to the Free Nations of the World," 420
Metallgesellschaft, 672
Metaxas, Ioannis, 254
Metternich, Klemens von (Prince), 117, 134–135
Mexico, 16, 17, 31, 52, 57, 86, 94, 105, 108, 115, 122, 124, 127–130, 132, 175, 180, 214, 215, 223–226, 261, 448, 462, 478, 492, 501, 503, 509–510, 577, 584, 608, 609, 612, 617, 618, 624, 627, 628, 639, 646, 647, 650, 653–655, 659, 660, 665, 670, 673, 677, 678, 683, 707, 739, 743–746, 753, 757, 763, 781, 782, 788, 794, 800, 803, 804, 810, 836, 841, 855, 859, 893, 920, 925–927, 939, 944, 977
Mexican Communist Party, 860
Mexican Eagle Oil Company, 677
Mexican National Railroad, 647
Mexican Revolution, 673, 678, 747, 840, 944
Mexican War, 124

Makonnen, Ras, 427
Mhlontlo (Chief), 407
Michelin, 983
Michels, Roberto, 173
Middle East, 18, 41, 46, 426, 603, 677, 678, 688, 874, 927
Middle Passage, 435
Midhat, Ahmed, 341
Mies van der Rohe, Ludwig, 949
Mill, James, 545
Mill, John Stuart, 878
Milner, Alfred, 186
Milosz, Czeslaw, 231
Mindanao, 12
The Mind of Primitive Man (Boas), 943
Ming dynasty, 74, 165, 307
Ministry of Public Enlightenment, 248
Minneapolis, 701, 718–720, 722, 723, 733
Mintz, Sidney, 694
Miranda, Carmen, 979
Mir system, 537
Les Misérables (Hugo), 625
Misr al-Qahira, 403
Missionaries, 870–874, 938
The Missionary Voice, 420
Mississippi River, 448, 634, 638, 718
Mississippi Valley, 51, 103, 124
Missouri Valley, 108, 124
Mitchel, John, 411
Mitre, Bartolomé, 131
Mizeki, Bernard, 873
"Modern Girl Around the World" project, 992
Modern Girl collective, 961
Moivre, Abraham de, 165
Molina Y Compañía, 746
Mongolia, 30, 47, 54, 74, 532, 533, 852
Mongols, 49, 307
Monnet, Jean, 274
Mon people, 587
Monroe Doctrine, 52
Montgomery Ward, 613
Moravia, 133
Morgan, J. P., 616, 652, 673
Mori Yoshichika, 120
Mormonism, 80
Morocco, 31, 39, 188, 540, 562, 948
Moro War, 12
Morris, William, 890

Morse, Edward, 894
Morse, Samuel, 662, 826
Mosca, Gaetano, 177, 200
Movietone News (film series), 979
Moxham, Roy, 799
Moya, Lily, 343–344
Mozambique, 330, 518, 541, 544, 588, 804, 873
Mughal Empire, 35, 36, 43, 81, 90, 151, 183, 308, 317
Muhammad Ali (Pasha), 72, 138
Muhammad Ali (Shah), 218
Muhurram, 424
Muir, John, 606
Mukabi, Serah, 326, 333
Mukti Mission, 415, 883
Müller, Ferdinand von, 935
Mumbai, 449, 522, 523, 524, 928
Murray, John, 983
Musée de la France d'outre-mer, 546
Musée des Arts Africains et Océaniens, 546
Musée d'Histoire Naturelle, 906
Musée Permanent des Colonies, 546
Musée Social, 898
Museo Público, 905
Museum of African and Oceanic Art, 904
Museum of Natural History, 168, 980
Museums, 904–907
Museu Nacional do Rio de Janeiro, 906, 940
Museu Paulista, 906
Mussolini, Benito, 177, 192, 208, 235, 238–245, 251, 253, 260, 261, 291
Mutiny of 1857, 488
Mycenaean civilization, 969

NABISCO. *See* National Biscuit Company
Nader. *See* Tournachon, Gaspard-Félix
Naicker, G. M., 429
Nama people, 12, 310
Namibia, 181
Nandy, Ashis, 933
Nanook of the North: A Story of Life and Love in the Actual Arctic (film), 980
Nansen, Fridtjof, 551
Nansen Passport, 551

Naoroji, Dadabhai, 575
Naples, 84, 140
Napoleon, Louis, 85, 86, 123, 136
Napoleon I (Emperor), 116
Napoleonic wars, 65, 67–68, 69, 70, 106, 110, 293, 441
Napoleon III (Emperor), 91, 112, 123, 129, 138, 140, 142, 144–145, 180, 182, 343, 628, 639, 925
Nardal, Andrée, 576
Nardal, Jeanne, 576
Nardale, Paulette, 576
Natal, 475, 515, 516, 517, 761
Natal Indian Congress, 429
National Audubon Society, 916
National Biscuit Company (NABISCO), 728, 1069n298
National Broadcasting Corporation (NBC), 667
National Bureau of Economic Research, 937
National Confederation of Labor (CNT), 162, 858
National Essence Society, 567
National Fascist Party, 239
National Geographic, 852, 963
National Health Service, 274
National identities, 480–486
National Industrial Conference Board, 937
Nationalist China, 574, 580, 930, 931
National Liberals, 179
National Park Albert, 916
National Party, 429
National People's Party. *See* Guomindang
National Recovery Administration (NRA), 250
National Socialism, 157, 182, 191, 235, 274, 941. *See also* Nazis
National Socialist Party, 233, 243, 244
National Zoological Garden, 912
National Zoo of the United States, 914, 915
Native Code, 540
Native Registration Amendment Ordinance of 1920, 345
Natural History Museum, 905
Naumann, Friedrich, 186
Nazis, 14, 17, 196, 235, 241–244, 251–253, 256, 258, 263, 265, 266, 269, 271, 290, 310, 563, 566, 571, 586, 596, 660, 668,

810, 845, 855, 868, 903, 931, 941, 942, 958, 983, 990
NBC. *See* National Broadcasting Corporation
Negrelli, Alois, 354
Négritude, 865
Negro Bureau, 577
The Negro Worker, 420, 860, 864
The Negro World (newspaper), 866
Nehru, Jawarharlal, 392, 575, 860, 861
"Nellie Bly." *See* Seaman, Elizabeth Cochrane ("Nellie Bly")
Neo-Confucianism, 80, 82, 160, 210
Neo-corporatism, 280
Neo-Europes, 634, 695, 807
Neoliberalism, 1053n14
Neo-Nazis, 270
NEP. *See* New Economic Policy
Nescafé, 791
Nestlé, 791
Nestlé, Henri, 801
The Netherlands, 291, 293, 317, 447, 452, 455, 541, 545, 556, 583, 586–588, 602, 638, 683, 760, 762, 774, 775, 778, 787, 793, 794, 798, 801, 879, 909
Netto, Landislau, 906
Neumann, Franz, 265
Neurath, Konstantin von, 248
New Caledonia, 289
New Citizen (journal), 824
New Deal, 237, 250, 265, 273, 696, 931, 958
New Economic Policy (NEP), 261, 561
New Era, 138
New Guinea, 754, 965
New Humanism, 860
New Order for Labor, 567
New Poor Law of 1834 (Great Britain), 166
New Process, 719–720, 721, 723
New School for Social Research, 577–578
New Spain, 452, 458, 526
New State, 242
The New State (Follett), 958
New World, 8, 46–47, 51, 298, 344, 610
New York City, 947
New York Coffee Exchange, 786
New York World's Fair of 1930, 902
New York World's Fair of 1939, 902, 970
New York Herald (newspaper), 963, 964, 965
New York Times (newspaper), 353, 965
New York World (newspaper), 960
New Zealand, 12, 286, 290, 300, 305, 339, 340, 346, 361, 362, 395, 513, 515, 549, 602, 605, 610, 611, 624, 627, 634, 650, 700, 761, 879, 901, 907, 935
Ngonde, 542
Ngoni, 542
NGOs. *See* Nongovernmental organizations
Ngoyi, Lilian, 430
Nguyen Ai Quoc. *See* Ho Chi Minh
Nguyen Sinh Cung, 574
Nguyen Thai Hoc, 426
Nguyen Thi Giang, 426
NHK, 668
Niagara Falls, 674, 723
Niass, Ibrahim (Sheikh), 874
Nicaragua, 14, 504, 528, 660, 782, 839
Nicholas II (Tsar), 835, 854
Nietzsche, Friedrich, 868
Nigeria, 331, 803, 804, 935
Nightingale, Florence, 111
Nihon (newspaper), 930
Nil (newspaper), 891
Nile River, 925, 963
Nippon Yusen Kabushiki Kaisha (NYK), 636
Nkrumah, Kwame, 866
NKVD, 565
Nobel, Alfred, 604, 666, 835
Nobel Peace Prize, 604, 844, 955
Noncooperation movement, 575
Nongovernmental organizations (NGOs), 280, 616, 812
Nordisk, 979
North, Douglass, 628
North Africa, 493, 494, 540, 650, 695, 860, 863
North America, 47, 312–313, 457, 462, 486, 494, 496, 501–504, 526, 529, 541, 549, 584, 595–597, 602, 605, 611, 771, 807, 808, 811
Northern Elevator Company, 720
North German Confederation, 146, 174
North German Federation, 144
North Pole, 852, 965, 966
Northwest Passage, 926, 966
Norway, 926
NRA. *See* National Recovery Administration
Nyasaland, 796
Nyerere, Julius, 866
NYK. *See* Nippon Yusen Kabushiki Kaisha
Nylon, 682, 743

OAU. *See* Organization of African Unity
Obregón, Álvaro, 225–226
Office International d'Hygiène Publique, 952
Ogilvie Flour Mills, 721
Ogoshi Heiriku, 369
Okakura Tenshin, 429
Okinawa, 525
Old Imperial Garden and Palace (Yuanming Yuan), 906–907
Olmecs, 800
Olympic games, 812, 831–833, 974
Oman, 522, 540
Omdurman, 39, 359
Opel, 658
Open Door doctrine, 52
Opium War of 1839–1842, 41, 73, 106, 338, 441, 636, 929
Oregon, 119
Organization of African Unity (OAU), 866
Organization Todt, 248
Oriental Railway, 375
Orient Express, 646
Oromo people, 648
Orthodox church, 56, 868
Ortiz, Fernando, 757
Orwell, George, 258
Osaka Shosen Kaisha (OSK), 636
Oshikawa Shunro, 970
OSK. *See* Osaka Shosen Kaisha
Osterhammel, Jürgen, 8, 596
Ostrogorski, Moisei, 173

Ottoman Empire, 12, 16, 17, 30, 31, 32, 34, 36, 43, 47, 63, 70, 71–73, 80, 95, 103, 105, 106, 122, 138, 151, 160, 171, 177, 182, 208, 210, 213, 214, 219, 220, 222, 229, 286, 287, 289, 296, 302, 308, 330, 332, 341, 352, 366, 373–378, 384, 386–387, 412, 413, 461, 464, 484, 493, 539, 548, 550–554, 562, 655, 665, 677, 840, 843, 853, 869, 875, 879, 891, 896, 927, 936, 955
Outback, 627, 810
Owen, Robert, 82, 83

Pacific Settlement of International Disputes, 836
Pact of Steel, 257
Padmore, George, 576, 860, 864
Pahlavi, Reza Shah, 268
Pakistan, 277, 390
Pale of Settlement, 539, 698
Palestine, 423, 552, 563, 581, 584–585, 859, 860, 867, 868
Palmerston (Lord), 69, 91
Palm oil, 803
Palmolive, 991
Pan-African Conference of 1945, 577
Pan-African Congress, 863, 864
Pan-Africanism, 412, 420, 427, 863–866, 867, 937
Panama, 503, 639, 640, 952
Panama Canal, 172, 355, 504, 639, 640, 854, 897, 928
Panama Canal Zone, 640, 1059n84
Panama-Pacific International Exposition of 1915, 640
Panama Scandal, 178
Pan American Airlines, 659
Pan-Americanism, 609, 866
Pan American Pact, 838
Pan-American Railroad, 647
Pan American Union, 866, 879
Pan-Asianism, 427, 428, 866
Pan Islamic Congress, 413
Pan-Islamism, 220, 875–876
A Paradise Lost (Young-tsu), 907
Paraguay, 108, 110, 271
Paraguayan Republic, 149
Paramount News, 979
Paramount Pictures, 984
Pareto, Vilfredo, 177, 208
La Paria (newspaper), 341, 426

Paris Colonial Exposition of 1931, 899, 904
Paris Commune, 145, 154, 161, 164, 191, 207, 208, 403
Paris Exhibition of 1900, 857, 898–899, 902, 904
Paris Exposition Universelle, 891, 897
Paris Fair of 1937, 902
Paris Peace Conference, 419
Partido Nacional Revolucionario (PNR), 225
Partido Revolucionario Institucional (PRI), 225
A Passage to India (Forster), 194
Passy, Frédéric, 835
Pasternak, Boris, 263
Pasteur, Louis, 922
Pasteur Institute, 950
Patagonia, 150
Paxton, Joseph, 888
Pearl Harbor, 294, 580
Pearl River, 638
Pearson, Karl, 396
Pearson, T. Gilbert, 916
Peary, Robert, 906, 965
Penang, 513
Peninsular and Oriental Steam Navigation Company (P&O), 353
Pentecostals, 81, 869
The People of India, 853
People's Charter, 84, 87
People's Commissariat for Foreign Affairs, 260
People's Liberation Army, 228
People's Party. See Republican People's Party
People's Republic of China, 584, 587
Permanent Court of Arbitration, 836
Permanent Court of International Justice, 841
Permanent Mandates Commission, 421
Permanent Museum of the Colonies, 904
Perón, Juan, 277
Perry, Matthew, 78, 118–119, 367, 636, 894
Persia, 754, 827, 836, 859
Persian Empire, 36, 287, 665, 677
Persian Gulf, 539
The Persistence of Memory (Dalí), 830

Peru, 31, 448, 454, 505, 513, 525, 528, 609, 624, 646, 665, 673, 680, 685, 693, 763, 764, 768, 770, 794, 909
Pescadores Islands, 532
Peter, Daniel, 801
Peterloo massacre, 69
Pettitt, Clare, 964
Petty, William, 165
Phelps Dodge, 673
Phelps-Stokes Fund, 937
Philippine-American War of 1899–1903, 12
Philippine Reservation, 900
Philippines, 22, 192, 291, 293, 350–351, 397, 407, 452, 453, 457, 513, 519, 526, 529, 586, 684, 735, 744, 746, 750, 767, 770, 897, 926, 934, 937
Physical Culture (magazine), 978
Physiocracy, 61–63, 65, 69, 164, 609
Picasso, Pablo, 902
Pietism, 641
Pike, Robert, 661
Pillsbury, 720, 721, 727, 733
Pillsbury, Charles, 718, 720
Pinchot, Gifford, 935
Pine Ridge Reservation, 974
Pinochet, Augusto, 241
Piscator, Erwin, 577
Pius IX (Pope), 114, 137
Pius XI (Pope), 871
Pi y Margall, Francisco, 162
Plan of Ayala, 225
Plantation Belts, 435, 438, 442, 467, 469, 472, 491, 493, 494, 508, 509
Plant Hunting on the Edge of the World (Kingdon-Ward), 910
PNR. See Partido Nacional Revolucionario
P&O. See Peninsular and Oriental Steam Navigation Company
Pogroms, 464, 465, 809, 868
Poland, 134, 246, 254, 266, 464, 465, 488, 496, 537, 539, 555, 557, 561, 563, 566, 569, 571, 581, 766, 845, 850, 879
Polanyi, Karl, 601
Polish Corridor, 243
Polish-Lithuanian Commonwealth, 539
Polk, James, 128
Pol Pot, 268

Polynesia, 871
Pomeranz, Kenneth, 8, 47, 604, 605
Pontifical States, 903
Pony Express, 662
Poona, 928
Popenoe, Paul, 941
Popular Front, 254, 274
Populists, 601, 610
Port Arthur, 184, 198, 532
Portugal, 12, 63, 183, 242, 291, 446, 544, 645, 665, 775, 793, 803, 804, 841
Post, Charles W., 725
Post Ministry (Germany), 668
Powell, John Wesley, 925
Prain, David, 908
Pratt, Mary Louise, 819
Pratt, Richard, 938
Présense africaine, 576, 589
PRI. *See* Partido Revolucionario Institucional
Prime Meridian reform movement, 927
Primers for Science Studies (Edkins), 920
Primers of Western Learning (Edkins), 920
Primitivism, 944
Primo de Rivera, Miguel, 242
Proclamation of 1763, 461
Progressive era, 722
Progressive Republicans, 610
Progressives, 676
Prokudin-Gorskii, Sergei Mikhailovich, 853–854
Protectionism, 609, 689–690, 734, 768
Protestantism, 82, 113, 114, 115, 174, 208, 395, 641, 673, 869, 870
Proudhon, Pierre-Joseph, 83
Prussia, 59, 65, 84, 85, 86, 97, 101, 111, 112, 114, 116, 134, 135, 137, 140, 142, 143, 145, 146, 158, 204, 400, 403, 544, 765, 766, 941
Public Debt Administration, 220
Public Works Administration (PWA), 250
Publishers' International Congress, 828
Puerto Rico, 291, 293, 759, 762, 767, 770, 897
Pugachev rebellion, 64

Pulitzer, Joseph, 960
Pullman, 830
Pure Food and Drug Act of 1906, 722, 789
Pu Yi, "Henry," 228, 255
PWA. *See* Public Works Administration

Qadir, Abdul, 404
Qajar dynasty, 216, 286, 287
Qing dynasty, 30, 31, 47, 54, 73, 74, 156, 160, 166, 194, 213, 226, 228, 286, 287, 294, 298, 307, 316, 366, 370, 419, 438, 441, 472, 482, 907, 920, 929
Quaker Oats, 616
Quaker Oats Company, 724, 725
Quanlong emperor, 74
Quesnay, François, 62
Quinine, 603, 640, 909, 953

Racism, 442, 485, 503, 529, 535, 549, 550, 563, 585, 593, 760, 809, 863, 865, 881, 943
Radama II (King), 343
Radical Socialist Party, 174
Radio, 666–671, 728
Radio Corporation of America (RCA), 667, 991
Rafael, Vicente, 854
Rai, Lala Lajpat, 416, 418
Railroads, 99–103, 131–132, 209, 214, 348, 360, 362, 375–380, 383–388, 496, 503, 534, 642–652, 654, 655, 670, 701–702, 709, 717–718, 733, 780, 782, 829, 830, 1058n66, 1059n92
Railway Bureau, 369
Rains, Claude, 977
Raj, 35, 151, 152, 156, 189, 277, 296, 320, 335, 344, 413, 431, 742, 909
Ramabai, Pandita, 414, 883
Ramahyuck, 343
Ramakrishna, 876
Raman, C. V., 932
Ramanujan, Srinivasa Aiyangar, 933
Rama V (King), 210
Ranavalona III (Queen), 343
Rangoon, 733
Ratzel, Friedrich, 309
Ray, P. C., 932

RCA. *See* Radio Corporation of America
Reagan, Ronald, 280
Realpolitik, 641
Reconstruction, 103, 462, 596
Red Crescent, 108, 954, 955
Red Cross, 108, 571, 572, 812, 835, 954, 955
Red Fife wheat, 709
Red Scare, 499
Red Sea, 354, 355, 637, 773
Reform Act of 1832 (Great Britain), 69
Reiche, Charles, 915
Reichsrat, 148
Renz, Herman, 972
Republicanism, 411, 420, 903
Republican Party, 123–125, 127, 149, 179, 205, 206
Republican People's Party (RPP), 223
Republic of China, 226, 256, 287
Rerum Novarum (Leo XIII), 871
Restoration, 66
Réunion, 509, 803
Reuters, 662
Revolution of Ayutla, 128
Revolutions of 1848–1849, 84–87, 104, 136, 164
Revue du Monde Noir, 576
Reynolds, Henry, 313
Rhee, Syngman, 416
Rhine Commission, 931
Rhine River, 49, 931
Rhine-Westphalian Coal Syndicate, 615
Rhodes, Cecil, 316, 326, 363, 423, 650, 666
Rhodesia, 544, 568, 611, 650, 672, 873
Ricardo, David, 609
Ribbentrop, Joachim von, 248
Richards, Thomas, 886
Richartz, Francis, 326
Richtofen, Ferdinand von (Baron), 194
Rif, 31
Riffenburgh, Beau, 965
Riot Act, 409
Rise of the West (McNeill), 7
Risorgimento, 136
Rivera, Diego, 215, 944
Rizal, José, 407, 423
Rizzi, Bruno, 958

Robert Koch Institute, 950
Robeson, Paul, 425, 866
Robinet, Auguste, 403
Robinson, Ronald, 596
Rocco, Alfredo, 240, 241
Rockefeller, John D., 641, 675, 955
Rockefeller Foundation, 578, 842, 954, 956
Rodgers, Daniel, 899, 936
Rogaski, Ruth, 952
Roma, 845
Roman Catholic Church, 36, 52, 56, 60, 63, 66, 113–114, 115, 138, 150, 160, 163, 174, 240, 242, 463, 871, 954, 1010n98
Roman Empire, 46, 49, 319
Romania, 152, 563, 569, 582, 676, 677
Romanov dynasty, 30, 466, 472, 548, 551, 553
Roman revolution, 137
Romantic era, 84, 136
Roorkee, 928
Roosevelt, Eleanor, 728
Roosevelt, Franklin, 250, 251, 265, 271, 846, 931
Roosevelt, Theodore, 155, 167, 168, 169, 198, 488, 595, 939
Rosas, Juan Manuel de, 49, 130–131
Rothschilds, 673, 674, 677
Roundtable Conferences, 423
Rouvroy, Claude Henri, de. See Saint-Simon (Count)
Rowland, John, 963
Roy, M. N. See Bhattacharya, Narendra Nath
Royal Dutch Company, 677
Royal Dutch Shell, 677
Royal Geographical Society, 886, 925, 964
Royal Navy, 358
RPP. See Republican People's Party
Ruan Lingyu, 979
Ruhr Valley, 942
Russell Sage Foundation, 937
Russia, 32, 41, 53–54, 59, 67, 86, 105, 138, 150, 156, 159, 177, 183, 198, 200, 204, 207, 209, 214, 216–219, 229, 230, 237, 260, 266, 287, 293, 294, 296, 305, 308, 314, 318, 325, 353, 360, 372, 381, 396–399, 411, 415, 464–467, 493–494, 496, 534,

537, 553, 555, 557, 562, 565, 572, 579, 582, 609, 617, 618, 637, 645, 672, 677, 689, 694, 695, 697, 698, 765, 767, 768, 798, 809, 810, 827, 835, 853–854, 858, 868, 879, 899, 901, 909, 920, 925
Russian Empire, 12, 17, 94, 102, 122, 151, 160, 287, 366, 370, 385, 393, 472, 531–532, 840, 850, 879
Russian Orthodox Church, 56, 138, 869
Russian Revolution, 539, 557, 812, 840, 869
Russo-Japanese War of 1904–1905, 6, 11, 198, 203, 369, 415, 429, 637, 920
Russo-Siberian migration system, 464–467, 534–535, 547
Russo-Turkish War of 1877–1878, 286
Rwanda, 189, 649
Ryukyu Islands, 525

S. Pearson company, 670
SA. See Sturmabteilung
Saga Plain, 730
Saha, Meghnad, 932
Sahay, Ananda Mohan, 427
Said (Pasha), 354
Saïd, Edward, 546, 575
Saigo Takimori, 120, 168
Sailing Alone around the World (Slocum), 965
Sainte-Croix, Ghenia Avril de, 880
Saint-Hilaire, Albert Geoffroy, 913
Saint-Simon (Count), 83
St. Louis World's Fair, 900
St. Vincent de Paul societies, 96
Sajour, Leo, 576
Salafism, 81, 875
Salafiyya, 875
Salazar, António de Oliveira, 242
Salamonsky, Albert, 972
Salt Act of 1882, 311
Salt March, 311, 861
Salvation Army, 869, 872
Samoa, 855
Samuel, Marcus, 677
Samuel, Samuel, 677
San Francisco Conference, 847
Sanger, George, 972

Sanger, Margaret, 881–882
Sanitary Commission, 955
Santa Anna, Antonio López de, 96, 128
Santería, 877
Sanyal, Ram Bramha, 911–912
Sardinia, 114
Sarmiento, Domingo Faustino, 49, 131
Sartre, Jean-Paul, 258
Satow, Ernest, 120
Saudi Arabia, 678, 875, 876
Saunier, Pierre-Yves, 949
Savarkar, Vinayak Damodar, 575
Save the Children International, 954
Say's Law, 597
SCADTA, 660
Schacht, Hjalmar, 248
Schliemann, Heinrich, 927, 969
Schmitt, Carl, 182, 196–197, 200, 201, 252, 260–261, 270, 280
Schumpeter, Joseph, 603
Schuster, William Morgan, 219
Schwarzenberg, Felix zu, 85, 136
Scientific Commission of Mexico, 925
Scientific management, 612
Scientific method, 868, 924
Scott, James, 10, 32, 161, 166, 197
Scott, Robert Falcon, 966
Scramble for Africa, 290, 391, 400, 622
Seaman, Elizabeth Cochrane ("Nellie Bly"), 3, 960
Sears, Roebuck & Co., 613
Second Boer War, 649. See also South African War
Second Industrial Revolution, 5, 593, 594, 612–614, 671, 685, 695
Second International, 207, 857
Second Opium War, 91
Second Sino-Japanese War, 568
"Secret Speech" (Khrushchev), 264
Security Services (SS), 246
Seddon, John, 395
Seeley, John Robert, 180, 363, 364, 365
Seki Hajime, 949
Self-Help (Smiles), 96
Selfridges, 613
Selim III (Sultan), 71
Seme, Pixley ka Isaka, 410

Seminole, 31
Semper, Gottfried, 86
Seneca Falls Declaration, 879
Senegal, 542, 576, 665
Senghor, Lamine, 341, 420, 421
Senghor, Léopold Sédar, 576, 865
Sephardic Jews, 484, 867
September 20, 1870 (film), 975
Serbia, 554, 899
Sertão, 151
Sessions, Kate, 909–910
Sétif uprising, 404
SFIO. *See* French Section of the Workers' International Party
Shaarawi, Huda, 376, 879
Shackleton, Ernest, 966
Shaka, 32, 188
Shandong Peninsula, 184
Shelley, Percy Bysshe, 40, 42
Sherman, William Tecumseh, 112, 126
Sherman Silver Purchase Act of 1890, 628
Shi'ism, 876
Shimazu Nariakira, 120
Shinto, 82
Shofu no Tomo (magazine), 992
Showa restoration, 256
Siam, 515, 516, 518, 521, 525, 587, 732, 733, 836, 1067n228
Siberia, 534, 535, 550, 926
Sicily, 84, 96, 140–142
Siemens, 603, 616, 670
Siemens, Werner von, 666
Siemens-Martin process, 652
Sierra Leone, 410, 447, 736
Sikhs, 511, 866
Silverberg, Miriam, 992
Simba (film), 980
Singapore, 183, 513, 519
Singer sewing machines, 895, 991
Singh, Nain, 925
Sinha, Mrinalini, 487
Sinn Fein, 208
Sino-Japanese War of 1894–1895, 11, 287, 294, 369, 636
Sioux, 31
Siqueiros, David Alfaro, 944
Sircar, Mahendra Lal, 932
Sitting Bull (Chief), 29, 162
Skinner, Quentin, 35
Slavery, 58, 64, 69, 123–124, 327–329, 446–450, 467, 492, 507, 517, 522, 527, 542, 546,

596, 683, 755–757, 777, 795, 804, 809, 841, 856, 863
Sloan, Alfred, 656
Slocum, Joshua, 965
Smiles, Samuel, 44, 96
Smith, Adam, 74, 157, 447, 609, 756
Smith, Michael, 949
Smithsonian Institution, 896
Smuts, Jan, 206, 847
Snyder, Timothy, 14
Social Darwinism, 169, 595, 935, 939, 940, 944
Social Democracy movement, 146, 186, 230, 235
Social Democratic parties, 154, 262
Social Democratic Party (SPD), 148, 174, 207, 245
Socialism, 238, 240, 241, 254, 276, 396, 400, 562, 594, 601, 655, 840, 851, 858, 859, 866, 878, 879, 936
Socialist International, 163
Socialist parties, 154, 253
Socialist Systems (Pareto), 177
Social Revolutionaries, 216
Society for the Preservation of the Wild Fauna of the Empire, 915
Society of Oppressed Peoples of Asia, 426
Soma Aizo, 427
Soma Kokko, 427
Sonderbund, 113
Soong Ch'ing-ling, 574
Soong May-ling, 574
Sorel, Georges, 208, 237
Soulié de Morant, George, 952
The Souls of Black Folk (Du Bois), 316–317
South (Shackleton), 966
South Africa, 188, 300, 336, 343, 378, 386, 394, 395, 397, 406, 407, 410, 411, 419, 421, 429, 455, 493, 515, 516, 541, 544, 545, 550, 567, 585, 596, 608, 610, 611, 622, 649, 650, 664, 665, 700, 770, 796, 847, 861, 901, 906, 917, 935, 939, 948
South African Native National Congress, 937
South African War (Second Boer War), 11, 206, 289, 319, 394, 395, 396, 398, 411, 649
South Asia, 874

South China Sea, 637
South Manchurian Railway, 255, 369–370, 533
South Pole, 966, 967
South Seas Association, 373
Sovereignty, 34, 35, 60, 1013n130
Soviet Party, 233, 237
Soviet Union, 13, 17, 41, 233, 246, 257, 258, 261, 263, 264, 268, 269, 279, 287, 310, 314, 392, 419, 550, 552, 561, 563, 569, 571, 572, 581, 582, 584, 588, 611, 652, 653, 655, 660, 668, 671, 672, 678, 698, 770, 810, 811, 843, 845, 851, 858–859, 860, 861, 873, 879, 902, 930, 936, 958
Spain, 16, 31, 36, 47, 51–52, 63, 66, 94, 106, 113, 161, 183, 242, 254, 258, 277, 291, 401, 407, 412, 446, 447, 452, 503, 528, 553, 562–563, 565, 645, 672, 736, 757, 758, 760, 762, 764, 768, 775, 841, 858, 901
Spanish-American War, 293, 639, 641, 897
Spanish Civil War, 258, 903
Spanish Guinea, 804
Spanish Republic, 254, 562, 903
SPD. *See* Social Democratic Party
Speer, Albert, 248, 903
Speke, John Hanning, 925
Spencer, Herbert, 164
Spice Islands, 509
Spreckels Sugar, 762, 771
Sri Lanka, 623
SS. *See* Security Services
Staatsmuseum, 906
Stahl, Friedrich Julius, 157
Stalin, Joseph, 14, 227, 230, 233, 260–264, 266, 269, 565, 678, 698, 845, 847, 851, 859, 860
Stalinism, 547, 571, 578, 579
Standage, Tom, 661, 676
Standard Oil, 615, 616, 675, 678
Standard Time Act, 380
Stangen, 983
Stanley, Henry Morton, 392, 595, 925, 963, 964, 970
Statistical Analysis of the United States (Walker), 166
Statutes (Definition of Time) Act, 380
Stead, William Thomas, 836
Stein, Lorenz von, 45
Steiner, Max, 977

Stephan, Heinrich von, 827
Sterilization for Human Betterment (Gosney and Popenoe), 941
Stevenson Plan, 683
Stoddard, John, 984
Stolen Generations, 337
Stoler, Ann, 487, 682, 936
Stolypin, Pyotr, 534
Strait of Malacca, 449
Straits Settlements, 513, 515
Strauss, Leo, 578
Strength Through Joy, 983, 985
Student Volunteer Movement for Foreign Missions (SVM), 870
Sturmabteilung (SA), 234, 245
Sub-Saharan Africa, 665
Suchard, Philippe, 801
Sudan, 12, 31, 39, 180, 286, 540, 953
Suez Canal, 180, 353–358, 377, 381, 382, 449, 511, 540, 638–641, 700, 712, 760, 875, 891, 914, 928
Suffrage, 156, 171–172, 204, 413–415, 425, 879
Sufis, 874, 876
Suleiman, 307
Sullivan, Thomas, 799
Sumatra, 183, 509, 525, 623, 682
Sumner, William Graham, 164
Sunnis, 875
Sun Yat-sen, 226, 227, 574, 823
Sun Yu, 977
Surinam, 527, 804
Suttner, Bertha von, 835
SVM. *See* Student Volunteer Movement for Foreign Missions
Swahili war, 407
Sweden, 879, 926
Swift meat-processing plant, 604, 705
Switzerland, 84, 113, 156, 801
Sylla, Yacouba, 874
"Syllabus of Errors," 114
Sylvester-Williams, Henry, 863
Syndicalists, 237, 858
Syria, 47, 419, 859, 860

Taft, William Howard, 676
Tagore, Rabindranath, 3, 429, 575, 957, 960
Taiaroa, H. K., 404
Taine, Hippolyte, 164

Taiping rebellion, 87–89, 91, 96, 110, 271, 454, 623, 920
Taishō Democracy, 256
Taishō era, 372
Taiwan, 325, 373, 532, 553, 554, 579, 580. *See also* Formosa
Taj Mahal, 852
Takamure Itsue, 383
Tamils, 796, 809
Tammany Hall, 172, 173
Tanganyika, 649, 750, 780, 915, 963
Tanzania, 181, 649, 866
Tanzimat, 73, 81, 138, 920
Tarbell, Ida, 675
Tatars, 582
Tarzan (Burroughs), 970
Tashkent, 398–399
Tasmania, 549
Tata, J. R. D., 660
Tata, Jamshedji Nusserwanji, 653
Tata Iron and Steel Company (TISCO), 653
Taylor, Frederick, 612, 830
Taylor, William, 57
Temple, Henry John. *See* Palmerston (Lord)
Temple, Richard, 355
Tennessee Valley Authority (TVA), 671, 931
Ten Years War, 757
Terra nullius, 405, 1004n30
Tesla, Nikola, 923
Tetley, 799
Tevfik, Riza, 413
Texas, 128, 665
Thailand, 17, 122, 277, 587
Thatcher, Margaret, 280
Théâtre Annamite, 893
Theory of the Governed (Mosca), 177
Theosophical Society, 877
Theosophy, 877
Things Fall Apart (Achebe), 194
Third International, 264, 419, 843, 858
Third World, 390, 431, 605
Thirty Years War, 35
Thomas Cook Company, 597, 983
Thompson, Alex, 900
Thompson, Dorothy, 722
Thompson, E. P., 55, 625
Thompson, J. Walter, 988
Thompson, John, 852

Thomson-Houston Electric Company, 667, 669
The Three Clerks (Trollope), 365
Three doctors pact, 429
Tibet, 852
Tierpark, 912, 915, 973–974, 980
Tijani Sufis, 874
Times (newspaper), 983
Timur, 307
Timurids, 46, 49
Tinker, Hugh, 516
Tinkler, Maurice, 320
Tip, Tippu, 406
TISCO. *See* Tata Iron and Steel Company
Tobler, 801
Tocqueville, Alexis de, 104
Todt, Fritz, 248
Togo, 181, 804, 871, 937
Tojo Hideki, 256
Tokugawa Ieyasu, 119
Tokugawa rebellion, 91
Tokugawa shogunate, 43–44, 77–78, 119, 210, 636
Tomlinson, John, 822
Tongs, 617, 866
Tonkin Delta, 731
Topik, Gertrude, 660
Topik, Steven, 5–6, 14, 21–23
Torrid Tampico (film), 984
Totalitarianism, 196, 223, 232, 241–242, 261, 268–270, 596
Totonac Indians, 800
Le tour du monde en quatre-vingts jours (Around the World in Eighty Days) (Verne), 3, 960, 974
Tournachon, Gaspard-Félix ("Nadar"), 851
Trabut, Louis, 908
Trans-Caspian Railway, 360
Transkei Territories, 330
Trans-Siberian Railroad, 209, 535, 646
Transvaal Indian Congress, 429
Transvaal Museum, 906
Transylvania, 582
Tran Trong Khac, 411
Travels in West Africa (Kingsley), 364
Traveltalks (film series), 984
Treaties of Westphalia, 35, 133
Treaty of Bardo, 181
Treaty of Sèvres, 222
Treaty of Shimonoseki, 532
Treaty of the Meter, 830

Treaty of Utrecht, 51
Treaty of Versailles, 245, 253, 266, 290, 303, 415, 416, 418–422, 424, 429, 840, 842, 942
Treccani Encyclopedia, 241
Trent, Evelyn, 860
Triads, 89
Trinidad, 409, 446, 455, 458, 504, 527, 528, 576, 577, 803, 804, 860
Tripartite Pact, 294
Triple Entente, 218
Triple Intervention, 184
Trollope, Anthony, 365
Trotsky, Leon, 261, 264, 859, 860
Trotha, Lothar von, 192, 271
True Romances (magazine), 978
True Story (magazine), 978
Truman, Harry, 278
Tsing, Anna, 820
Tucumán, 764
Tunisia, 378, 540, 582, 893
Túpac Amaru II, 64
Turkestan, 39, 318, 561, 859
Turkey, 36, 177, 223, 277, 287, 374–375, 376, 403, 412, 413, 477, 552, 553, 563, 645, 655, 671, 806, 809, 827, 836, 859, 869, 879
Turner, Frederick Jackson, 312, 704
Tuskegee Institute, 937
TVA. *See* Tennessee Valley Authority
Twain, Mark, 848, 960
Twentieth Century Fund, 937
Twinings, 799
Tyrrell, Ian, 881

Uganda, 268, 608, 648, 649, 775, 780, 796, 925, 933
Uganda Railroad, 648
Ukraine, 262, 267, 287, 539, 561, 579, 582, 698, 845, 930
Ultramontanists, 114
Unequal Treaties, 512
UNIA. *See* Universal Negro Improvement Association
Union Intercoloniale (IU), 341, 421, 425, 426
Union International des Villes, 948–949

Union of South Africa, 188, 343, 412, 541
Union Pacific Railroad, 646
Unit 731, 845
United Fruit Company, 616, 632, 673
United Kingdom, 412, 492, 597, 602, 607, 610, 611, 613, 622, 644, 653, 690–691, 712, 742, 767, 770, 771, 797
United Landtag, 84
United Nations, 584–585, 805, 846–847, 848
United Nations Organization, 846
United Provinces, 523
United States, 16, 31, 41, 51, 52, 58, 87, 89, 94, 101–102, 105, 118–120, 123–127, 131, 149, 166, 167, 171–173, 179, 183, 184, 191, 204, 205, 209, 225, 250, 258, 273, 275–276, 278, 286, 293, 296, 301, 305, 316, 321, 340, 350–351, 365, 401, 407, 411, 412, 418, 420, 429, 446, 447, 455, 458–463, 468, 472, 475, 478, 487, 488, 492, 496, 498, 501–504, 525, 527, 529–530, 535, 550, 553, 563, 568, 575, 577, 580–582, 584, 586, 588, 596, 597, 602, 605, 607–610, 612, 616, 622, 624, 627–629, 634–636, 638–640, 644, 647, 650, 652, 653, 655, 656, 658, 659, 662–665, 668, 671, 672, 674, 676, 686, 694, 696–702, 707, 709, 717, 724, 736, 740, 756–759, 762, 764, 767, 768, 770, 771, 775, 778, 783–788, 796, 798, 799, 805, 806, 810, 823, 826–829, 831, 836, 847, 856, 858, 860, 861, 863, 866, 867, 869, 877–879, 881, 883, 895, 897, 900, 902, 908, 912, 925, 929, 930, 933, 934, 936, 937, 939, 940, 948, 955, 963, 974–976, 983
United States of Mexico, 503
United States Steel Corporation, 652
Universal Negro Improvement Association (UNIA), 864–865
Universal Peace Congress, 836
Universal Postal Union (UPU), 824, 826, 827, 828

Universal Race Congress, 412, 413, 943
UN Relief and Works Agency, 585
The Uprooted (Barrés), 178
UPU. *See* Universal Postal Union
Uriburu, José Félix, 242, 277
Uruguay, 105, 277, 602, 624, 646, 650, 810, 977
al-Urwa al-Wuthqa, 403
US Forest Service, 935
US Geological Survey, 925
US Rubber, 683
US Sanitary Commission, 111
USSR. *See* Soviet Union
US Sugar Company, 771

Valentino, Rudolph, 979
Vancouver Island, 458
Van Houten, C. J., 801
Van Kirk, Sylvia, 488
Vargas, Getúlio, 242, 654
VARIG, 660
Vasconcelos Calderón, José, 225, 944
Vatican, 240
Veblen, Thorstein, 597
Vedanta, 877
Veidt, Conrad, 977
Venezuela, 624, 678, 680, 782, 801, 803, 804
Verne, Jules, 3, 595, 658, 664, 851, 960, 970, 974
Vernon, Raymond, 608
Versailles Peace Conference, 840, 864, 926. *See also* Treaty of Versailles
Vesey, Ruth, 982
Veuillot, Louis, 114
Vichy regime, 1048n118
Victor Emmanuel (King), 140
Victoria (Empress), 151
Victoria (Queen), 32, 888
Vietnam, 180, 182, 258, 289, 320, 411, 421, 426, 564, 574, 587, 588, 731, 732, 791, 852
Viet Nam Quoc Dan Dang (Vietnamese Nationalist Party), 426
Villa, Pancho, 224–225
Vinck, Emile, 948–949
Virgil, 969
Virgin Islands, 762

Visual Instruction Committee, 546

Vivekananda (Swami), 876–877

Volksempfänger, 668

Volstead Act, 806

Volta Redonda, 654

Die Waffen Nieder! (Lay Down Your Arms!) (Suttner), 835

Wagner, Peter, 922

Wagner, Richard, 42, 86

Wagons-Lits, 830

Wahhabism, 72, 81, 876

Wainwright, Jacob, 964

Waldersee, Alfred von, 194

Walker, Francis Amasa, 166, 167

Wallace, Alfred Russel, 923, 924, 935

Wallerstein, Immanuel, 7

Wallis, Hal, 977

Walpole, Robert, 51

Wanamaker's, 613

War against War (journal), 836

War of the Reform, 129

War of the Spanish Succession, 51

War of the Triple Alliance, 108

War Resisters' International (WRI), 861

Washburn, Cadwallader, 718, 719, 720, 723

Washburn-Crosby, 720, 721, 727

Washington, Booker T., 937

Washington Treaty of 1922, 844

Watt, James, 97–98

WCTU. *See* Woman's Christian Temperance Union

Wealth of Nations (Smith), 74, 447

Weaver, Stewart, 962

Webb, Sidney, 396

Weber, Max, 173, 174, 179, 1048n118

Webster, Daniel, 124

Weekly Sun (newspaper), 395

Wehler, Hans Ulrich, 186

Weimar Republic, 156, 174, 243, 831

Weissmuller, Johnny, 728

Wei Yan, 75

Wells, Alan, 5–6, 14, 21–23

Wenzlhuemer, Roland, 796

Wertheimer, Max, 578

West Africa, 493, 542, 586

Western Electric, 667

Western Europe, 602, 605, 618, 624, 634, 786, 807, 808

Western Telegraph Union, 662

Western Union, 662, 826

West Germany, 584

West Indies, 339, 577, 735, 863

Westinghouse Electric, 667, 670, 895

Westphalian paradigm, 35–37

Wexler, Laura, 854

Weyl, Carl Jules, 977

WGY radio station, 667

What Is to Be Done? (Lenin), 230

Whig party (Great Britain), 37, 51, 69–70, 73, 91, 595

Whig party (US), 105, 124

White, Arnold, 395

White Australia Policy, 401

White City, 895, 896, 897, 949, 974. *See also* Columbian Exposition

White House, 788

White Lotus Buddhism, 74, 89

White Lotus rebellion, 64, 87, 88

Whiti, Te, 404

Whitney, Eli, 607

Wickham, Henry, 682

Wild West, 974–975

Wilhelm (Kaiser), 399

Wille, Theodor, 785

William I (King), 138

William II (King), 174, 221

Williams, Eric Eustace, 577

William the Conqueror, 165

WILPF. *See* Women's International League for Peace and Freedom

Wilson, Dooley, 977

Wilson, Woodrow, 68, 225, 416, 418, 837–840, 843

Windsor dynasty, 472

Winseck, Dwayne, 661

Winter, Jay, 903

Witte, Sergei (Count), 102, 209

Wolf, Eric, 491

Wolff, 662

Wollstonecraft, Mary, 878

Womack, John, 224

Woman's Christian Temperance Union (WCTU), 881

Women's International League for Peace and Freedom (WILPF), 418, 864, 881

Women's World Games, 832

Wong, Anna May, 979

Woolson Spice Company, 787

Workers' Communist Party, 859

Workman, Fanny Bullock, 965

Workman, William Hunter, 965

Works Progress Administration (WPA), 250

World Bank, 931

World Congress (at Columbian Exposition), 895

World Court, 836

World Economic Conferences, 842

World Esperanto Association, 850

World Missionary Conference, 870

World Parliament of Religions, 877

World's Columbian Exposition, 312

World's Work, 640

World War I, 6, 12–14, 17, 20, 41, 110, 125, 134, 154, 168–169, 186, 196, 199, 201, 204, 208, 234, 237, 273, 275, 286, 289, 300, 319, 346, 353, 359, 368, 373, 376, 381, 385, 392, 404, 415, 423, 448, 485, 494, 495, 503, 511, 539, 543, 552, 554–562, 564, 576, 600, 603, 611, 624, 630, 637, 642, 649, 653, 655, 657, 659, 669, 672, 674, 676, 677, 687, 690, 691, 693, 697, 698, 750, 752, 755, 756, 758, 770, 780, 816, 825, 826, 833, 836, 837, 843–845, 848, 852, 857–860, 869, 872, 875, 879, 903, 931, 940, 942, 955, 980

World War II, 5, 8, 14, 18, 134, 156, 199, 233, 246, 260, 271, 273, 274, 278, 291, 294, 319, 354, 357, 390, 391, 435, 441, 442, 530, 534, 550, 568–572, 579, 600, 602, 603, 605, 635, 642, 648, 654, 656, 667, 671, 677, 682, 695, 707, 725, 736, 792, 826, 837, 842, 844, 846, 848, 855, 911, 990

The Worst Journey in the World (Cherry-Garrard), 966

WPA. *See* Works Progress Administration

WRI. *See* War Resisters' International

Wright, Frank Lloyd, 894

Wright Brothers, 658

Wrigley, 616

Xhosa, 343–344, 938
Xinjiang, 30, 47, 54, 152
Xue Fucheng, 102
Xuma, A. B., 429
Xuma, Madie Hall, 411
xxxx (Pillsbury flour brand), 721

Yacoubist movement, 874
Yang Xiuqing, 88
Yangzi River, 638, 931
Yemen, 773, 774, 781
Yen Bai uprising, 426
Yen-bay mutiny, 320
YMCA. *See* Young Men's Christian Association
Yoruba, 868, 877
Young America, 116
Young Companion (Liangyu huabao) (magazine), 992
Young Ireland, 411
Young Italy, 116

Young Men's Buddhist Association, 876
Young Men's Christian Association (YMCA), 870, 872, 873, 876
Young Plan of 1930, 243
Young-tsu Wong, 907
Young Turks, 177, 212, 218, 220, 412, 413, 550, 552. *See also* Committee for Union and Progress
Yuanming Yuan, 906–907
Yuan Shikai, 226
Yubin Kisen Mitsubishi Kaisha, 636
Yucatán, 22, 129
Yucatán Peninsula, 739, 743–745, 750
Yugoslavia, 263, 582

Zaghloul, Saad, 416
Zaibatsus, 617

Zamenhof, Ludwik Lazar, 850
Zamindary system, 451, 524
Zanzibar, 327, 406, 517, 522, 542
Zapata, Emiliano, 225, 763
Zaynab (Laila) bint Shaykh Muhammad, 407
Zeng Guofan, 88, 89, 96
Zeng Guoquan, 89
Zeppelin Company, 659
Zetkin, Clara, 858
Zhang Zuolin, 227
Zhou Enlai, 392
Zimbabwe, 672, 922, 963
Zimmerer, Jürgen, 310
Zionism, 412, 423, 867, 903
Zollparlament. *See* Customs Union Parliament
Zou Rong, 316
Zulu, 31, 32, 108, 188, 359, 649, 809
Zunghar, 54
Zweig, Stefan, 967